CONSUMER TRANSACTIONS

FIFTH EDITION

by

MICHAEL M. GREENFIELD
George Alexander Madill Professor of Contracts and Commercial Law
Washington University in St. Louis

FOUNDATION PRESS

2009

Mat #40590283

© 1983, 1991, 1999, 2003 FOUNDATION PRESS
© 2009 By THOMSON REUTERS/FOUNDATION PRESS

     195 Broadway, 9th Floor
     New York, NY 10007
     Phone Toll Free 1–877–888–1330
     Fax (212) 367–6799
     foundation–press.com
Printed in the United States of America

ISBN 978–1–59941–334–1

 TEXT IS PRINTED ON 10% POST CONSUMER RECYCLED PAPER

TO THE MEMORY OF MY PARENTS
ROSE WALNER GREENFIELD
SIDNEY IRVING GREENFIELD

*

PREFACE

This book is designed for use in a two-, three-, or four-hour course or seminar on the law of consumer transactions. Consumer law has grown dramatically in the last four decades, and this growth, along with the conceptual challenge of the subject matter and students' interest in it, has led to the establishment of separate courses on consumer law. The principal pedagogic justification for this separate treatment, however, may be that the study of consumer transactions requires the student to grasp and bring to bear on any given problem the substantive law of several traditionally discrete subjects. While the law of contracts is the backbone of consumer law, the law of torts also plays an important role. Indeed, the first topic in this book is misrepresentation, and tort law also is central to products liability (Chapter 7) and debt collection (Chapter 11). In addition, the book also presents materials on agency, administrative law, civil procedure, constitutional law, insurance, dispute resolution, and remedies. It thus aims to counteract the tendency to pigeonhole the law into discrete substantive categories. And since much of the law of consumer transactions is statutory, it also aims to encourage development of the skills of statutory analysis.

The organization of the book is transactional. It first examines problems in the formation of consumer transactions, then moves to the substance of the deal, and concludes with remedies. At each stage of the transaction, the first inquiry is whether any intervention on behalf of consumers is warranted. To determine if intervention is warranted, one must identify both the benefits and costs of any contemplated reform, especially whether the contemplated reform will remedy the problem and whether it will have unintended consequences. If intervention is warranted, one must determine whether it should consist of regulating parties, regulating the subject matter of the transaction, or regulating the transaction itself, i.e. the bargaining process and substantive terms of the resulting bargain.

The development of a body of consumer law distinct from commercial law embodies a belief that intervention is warranted. This development has been in the direction of "protecting" the consumer, i.e. conferring on consumers assorted rights and remedies that are not conferred on commercial entities. I believe that the general thrust of this development is desirable, but I am not so sure about many of the specifics. This belief and this uncertainty pervade the book.

In the course of editing judicial opinions and other materials, I have omitted numerous citations and footnotes without any notation of the omissions. The footnotes that remain bear their original numbers, and superimposed letters indicate footnotes that I have added to the opinions. I have corrected obvious typographical errors in reprinted materials without using the conventional "sic." Unless otherwise indicated, all references to Article 1 of the Uniform Commercial Code are to the 2003 revised version, and all references to Article 2 are to the 1978 version. Finally, because the law of consumer transactions is so largely statutory, a supplement containing various federal and state statutes accompanies the book. When the book refers to a statute that does not appear in the book, it is in the supplement.

MICHAEL M. GREENFIELD

St. Louis, Missouri
December, 2008

ACKNOWLEDGMENTS

Many people have helped me during the preparation of the five editions of this book over the last thirty years. I thank you all, but I would like to single out Dean Edward T. Foote for providing important personal and institutional support during my work on the first edition. Special thanks also to Dean Dorsey D. Ellis, Jr., who was a mainstay during my work on the next two editions. His successors, Joel Seligman and Kent Syverud, provided helpful research support in connection with the latest editions. Biggest thanks of all, however, go to my wife, Claire, for her enduring and unwavering support in so many ways.

*

SUMMARY OF CONTENTS

P A R T II Regulation of the Bargain

TABLE OF CONTENTS

TABLE OF CASES

Principal cases are in bold type. Non-principal cases are in roman type. References are to Pages.

*

TABLE OF STATUTES

TABLE OF FEDERAL RULES AND REGULATIONS

*

CONSUMER TRANSACTIONS

*

INTRODUCTION

A. FREEDOM OF CONTRACT AND GOVERNMENT INTERVENTION

One of the foundations of the law of contracts is the freedom of parties to make a deal on whatever terms they choose. While never without limitations (e.g., contracts to commit crimes), this doctrine of freedom of contract has come to be widely accepted as central to the American commercial system. The doctrine and its corollary, caveat emptor, developed in the simpler times of the eighteenth and nineteenth centuries. The classical economic theory justifying the doctrine makes several assumptions: the existence of perfect information known to all buyers and sellers, the existence of a large number of parties willing to do business with each other, and the absence of government controls on transactions.

Whatever the accuracy of this model in the eighteenth and nineteenth centuries, it is not an accurate description today. As producers and sellers have expanded their operations, standardization has become essential. This means not only mass production of goods, but also mass production of contracts. Sellers now offer their goods pursuant to contractual obligations that contain many seller-oriented provisions drafted by seller-oriented attorneys. Buyers do not always read these documents, and, even when they do, they do not always understand the significance of these provisions. The relatively small amount of money involved and the relatively infrequent purchase of any given item make it infeasible for a consumer buyer to seek the aid of an attorney before entering the transaction. The result is that competition does not operate as it does in the model: the knowledge of consumers is inferior to the knowledge of sellers, and there is no real bargaining. Further, behavioral economics teaches that consumers are not necessarily rational actors and that sellers may structure transactions in such a way as to take advantage of this lack of rationality. The result is the formation of contracts on an adhesion or take-it-or-leave-it basis that gives sellers the power to overreach consumers. If overreaching is not to occur, the consumer must look to either the seller's conscience, the development of a more competitive market, or assistance from a governmental or nongovernmental institution.

Early efforts at consumer protection focused on protecting businesses from the anticompetitive behavior of other businesses. Examples are the Sherman Act (1890), the Clayton Act (1914), and the original Federal Trade Commission Act (1914). These efforts continue, of course, but now there is also a more direct intervention on behalf of consumers. Sometimes this intervention seeks to prevent overreaching by sellers and creditors. But frequently, as with disclosure regulation such as the Truth-in-Lending Act, the objective is to make the market more competitive.

Governmental entities are not the only sources of consumer protection. On the contrary, numerous nongovernmental entities attempt to enhance

1

and protect the position of consumers in the marketplace. They include labor unions, advertising media, co-ops and buying clubs, public interest research groups (PIRGs), general purpose national consumer organizations such as the Consumer Federation of America, narrowly focused local groups such as state-wide organizations of utility consumers, and industry-sponsored consumer action panels and Better Business Bureaus. Through the exercise of their economic and political power, these nongovernmental entities have become an important source of consumer protections. The role of these and other nongovernmental entities, however, is largely beyond the scope of this book, which concentrates on governmental intervention.

Governmental sources of assistance may exist at all three levels of government—federal, state, and local—and in all three branches of government. For example, at the federal level, legislative assistance includes the Consumer Credit Protection Act and the Consumer Product Safety Act; administrative assistance comes from the Federal Trade Commission (FTC), the Federal Reserve Board (FRB), and several other agencies. At the state and local level, legislative assistance ranges from comprehensive statutory regulation of credit transactions to statutes aimed at a single narrow abuse such as door-to-door sales; administrative or executive assistance may come from the state's attorney general and the city's or county's administrator for consumer affairs.

Until the late 1960s most regulation of consumer affairs occurred at the state level. This regulation consisted primarily of statutes governing the sales and financing of goods (now covered by the Uniform Commercial Code), usury statutes, and statutes authorizing the making of small loans at rates in excess of the rate permitted by the usury statute. In the 1950s most states enacted retail installment sales acts (RISAs) as comprehensive regulation of credit sales. Another round of legislation started in the late 1960s with the promulgation in 1968 of the Uniform Consumer Credit Code (UCCC) by the National Conference of Commissioners on Uniform State Laws (NCCUSL). This comprehensive code deals with both loans and credit sales. Several states enacted it, but consumer advocates criticized it as being too business oriented. The National Consumer Law Center produced a more consumer-oriented proposal, the National Consumer Act, which it later refined and promulgated as the Model Consumer Credit Act of 1973 (MCCA). Meanwhile, NCCUSL reconsidered the UCCC and promulgated a revised, more consumer-oriented version in 1974. The MCCA and the revised UCCC have served as guides in several other states that have adopted comprehensive consumer credit statutes. In addition, states adopting consumer legislation on a piecemeal basis frequently have based their provisions on corresponding parts of these model acts.

Since the late 1960s the role of the federal government in the regulation of consumer transactions has expanded dramatically. In 1968 Congress enacted the Consumer Credit Protection Act (CCPA), whose main part was the Truth-in-Lending Act. Congress has repeatedly amended the CCPA, adding the Fair Credit Reporting Act (1970), the Fair Credit Billing Act

(1974), the Equal Credit Opportunity Act (1974), the Consumer Leasing Act (1976), the Fair Debt Collection Practices Act (1977), the Electronic Funds Transfer Act (1978), the Fair Credit and Charge Card Disclosure Act (1988), the Home Equity Loan Consumer Protection Act (1988), the Home Ownership and Equity Protection Act (1994), the Credit Repair Organizations Act (1996), and the Fair and Accurate Credit Transactions Act (2003). In addition, Congress enacted the Consumer Product Safety Act (1972), the Magnuson–Moss FTC Improvement—Consumer Warranty Act (1975), a new Bankruptcy Code (1978), the Expedited Funds Availability Act (1987), the Telephone Consumer Protection Act (1991), the Telephone Disclosure and Dispute Resolution Act (1992), and the Telemarketing and Consumer Fraud and Abuse Prevention Act (1994). As a result of these waves of legislation, a substantial portion of the law of consumer transactions is now a federal matter.

B. TYPES OF CONSUMER CREDIT TRANSACTIONS

This book explores some non-credit aspects of consumer transactions, e.g., misrepresentation and products liability, but concentrates primarily on credit aspects of consumer transactions. Hence, a description of the types of credit transactions is in order. There are two elementary forms of credit transactions. In one, the consumer borrows money from a lender and uses the proceeds to buy goods or services from a seller. Common examples include loans by a bank or other financial institution in connection with the purchase of an automobile, a house, a vacation, etc. Another common example is the use of a bank credit card (Visa, MasterCard, Discover, American Express, Diners Club), in which by using the credit card the consumer borrows from the bank at the time of each purchase.

In the second elementary form of credit transaction, the credit is extended by a seller rather than by a lender. This form of credit typically entails the use of a credit card issued by the seller, and common examples of these sellers include the oil companies, nationwide chains of department stores, and local department and clothing stores. Many retailers, however, are unable or unwilling to wait many months to receive the contract price of their goods and services. Consequently, there is a variation of this form of transaction, in which the seller sells goods or services to the consumer on credit, using an installment sales contract and perhaps also a promissory note. The contract price of course includes interest or finance charges. The seller assigns (i.e., sells) the contract and/or note to a financial institution, and the consumer thereafter makes payments to the financer. The financer pays the seller less than the face amount of the consumer's obligation and then receives the face amount of the obligation from the consumer over a period of time. The difference between the amount the financer pays the seller and the amount the consumer pays the financer is the financer's compensation, known as the "discount." In this way, the seller receives the price of the goods or services without having to wait the twelve to sixty months covered by the typical installment sales contract. This third form of credit transaction is common in connection with the purchase of automobiles, televisions, major appliances, and home improvements.

Each of these forms of credit may be either secured or unsecured. If the credit is unsecured, the creditor trusts the consumer to repay in accordance with the contract. If the consumer fails to do so, the creditor may enforce the obligation by suing, obtaining judgment, and enforcing the judgment (by garnishment of the consumer's cash assets or by seizure and sale of the consumer's non-exempt physical assets). If the credit is secured, however, the creditor has an additional right. The consumer gives a property interest in specifically identified real or personal property. This property is known as "collateral," and the creditor's interest is known as a "security interest" or, if the collateral is real property, a "mortgage" or "deed of trust." If the consumer fails to perform in accordance with the contract, the creditor may repossess or foreclose on the collateral, have it sold, and apply the proceeds of that sale toward satisfying the consumer's obligation. If the proceeds are not sufficient to satisfy the obligation, the creditor typically may sue, obtain judgment against the consumer, and then proceed to enforce that judgment (again, by garnishment of cash assets or by seizure and sale of physical assets). The use of collateral varies widely with the type of transaction: it is nearly universal in some kinds of credit transactions, e.g., loans to finance the purchase of motor vehicles and real estate, but it rarely appears in some other kinds of transactions, e.g., gasoline credit cards.

PART I

PROBLEMS IN FORMATION

CHAPTER 1

DECEPTION—THE RESPONSE OF THE COMMON LAW

Advertising and salesmanship are the primary devices for inducing consumers to enter exchange transactions. When the seller engages in false or misleading statements or practices, the consumer may enter a transaction very different from the one he or she contemplated. The common law deals with problems of deception in the formation of agreements under both tort and contract theories. In tort there are several closely related theories, each of which is subsumed under the broad category of fraud. They include deceit, concealment, innocent misrepresentation, and nondisclosure. Since tort law seeks to redress injury by placing the injured party back where he or she was before the injury, the measure of damages is the price paid by the consumer less the actual value of what the consumer received. The contract theories for dealing with deception are misrepresentation and breach of warranty. Since contract law seeks to redress injury by placing the injured party where he or she would have been had there been no deception, the measure of damages is the value that the product would have had if it had been as represented less the value that the product actually had.[1]

The tort and contract theories for dealing with deception have a common origin. Deceit first became available in the thirteenth century, when the distinctions between tort and contract had not yet developed. Until late in the eighteenth century, deceit was available only if there was a contractual relationship (known as "privity") between the plaintiff and the defendant. When in 1789 courts began to recognize deceit even in the absence of privity of contract, they continued to require privity as an element of breach of warranty. Tort liability thus existed whether or not there was privity of contract, but warranty liability existed only when privity was present. Another major difference between tort and contract liability was the necessity, for tort liability, of an intent to deceive. Recent decades have seen the erosion of both the requirement of privity (for warranty liability) and the requirement of intent to deceive (for tort liability). The result is that, while they still are not identical, tort and contract theories overlap to an ever-increasing extent.

---

1. Uniform Commercial Code (UCC) § 2–714(2). Alternatively, misrepresentation enables the consumer to rescind the contract and return the parties to their pre-contract positions. Id. § 2–711(1).

Under the law of contracts, an express warranty exists when a seller of goods makes an affirmation of fact or a promise relating to the goods if that affirmation or promise becomes part of the basis of the bargain.[2] Under the law of torts, on the other hand, a seller of goods is liable for deceit only if he or she 1) makes a representation 2) of present fact that is 3) material and 4) false, 5) if the seller knew it was false or made the representation in reckless disregard of the facts, 6) if the seller made it for the purpose of inducing the buyer, and the buyer 7) relied on the representation, 8) was justified in relying on it, and 9) sustained injury as a result of the misrepresentation. The tort theories of misrepresentation, concealment, and nondisclosure evolved from the remedy of deceit, primarily by virtue of a relaxation of one or another of the elements of deceit.

Jones v. West Side Buick Auto Co.

Court of Appeals of Missouri, 1936.
231 Mo.App. 187, 93 S.W.2d 1083.

BENNICK, COMMISSIONER.

[Plaintiff purchased a three-year-old car from defendant dealer. When defendant acquired the car from its previous owner, the odometer registered 48,800 miles. Defendant reconditioned the car, turned the odometer back to read 22,400 miles, and sold the car to plaintiff for $825. Defendant's service manager testified that rolling back the odometer "was not an unusual practice on defendant's part, and that in some cases he turned the speedometer back on his own accord, while in other cases he would be ordered to do so either by one of the salesmen or else by the sales manager." When plaintiff discovered the true mileage of the car, he sued and recovered actual damages of $150 and punitive damages of $2000. Defendant appealed.]

Plaintiff had evidence to show that the resale value of a used automobile is materially affected in the eyes of the general public by the number of miles the automobile has been driven; that the greater the mileage of a car may be, the greater has been the wear and tear upon it; that a car which has been driven 48,000 miles, even after being reconditioned, is not as valuable as a car that has been driven only 22,000 miles; and that the difference in value of the particular car in question, if driven only 22,000 miles, or if driven 48,000 miles, was approximately $300.*

Other evidence tended to show, though not very conclusively, that it is a sort of general practice among dealers of used automobiles to turn the speedometers back for purposes of resale, the theory apparently being that the dealer, after the reconditioning process is completed, is entitled to set the speedometer back to such a figure as the general condition of the repaired car might warrant.

---

2. UCC § 2–313(1)(a).

* Or approximately 35% of the purchase price.—Ed.

Defendant argues as a matter of first insistence that no case was made by plaintiff for submission to the jury.

The case concededly turns upon the question of the legal consequences to be ascribed to defendant's admitted act in turning back the speedometer before offering the car for sale to plaintiff. In other words, the decisive issue in the case is that of whether such act may be said to have constituted a representation on defendant's part, and, if so, of whether such act was fraudulent and malicious.

Defendant first argues that the mere turning back of the speedometer could not have constituted a representation; that in the first instance it was but a compliance on defendant's part with a custom of the trade; and that in any event speedometer readings in their very nature are or may be so inaccurate that they are not to be taken as a guide in buying a used car.

We cannot agree with any of such suggestions. That defendant may have been following a trade custom in turning back the speedometer could not have served to make its act any the less a representation. The sole purpose of manufacturers in equipping automobiles with speedometers which register total mileage is to show at all times the total number of miles that the particular car has gone. In fact, speedometers are so built and constructed that the average person would not know how or have the power to change the mileage reading upon them if he wished. In ordinary usage, when one looks at a speedometer reading, he feels that he is rightfully entitled to rely upon that reading and to believe that the car has gone the number of miles shown by the speedometer and no more. Of course, we appreciate the fact that speedometers, being mere mechanical devices, are not infallible, and that there are instances where a speedometer breaks and is out of operation until such time as it may be repaired, but these instances are the exception and not the rule. It is significant, however, that in this instance the speedometer was shown by defendant's own shop foreman to have been a "good, reliable" type, and there is not the least claim by any one that it had ever been out of operation or that its reading was inaccurate at the time Smith traded the car in to defendant.

The only possible reason defendant could have had in turning the speedometer back was to make it appear that the car had been run only the number of miles which the speedometer was made to indicate. We grant that the record discloses no statement by defendant either oral or written regarding the mileage of the car. However, a representation is not confined to words or positive assertions; it may consist as well of deeds, acts, or artifices of a nature calculated to mislead another and thereby to allow the fraudfeasor to obtain an undue advantage over him. Both reason and precedent tell us, and we so rule, that a representation with reference to the mileage of an automobile is a representation with reference to a material fact, and that it is none the less a representation of such a material character if made through the medium of turning back the speedometer than if made by word of mouth or written guarantee.

But defendant says that even though the mere turning back of the speedometer is to be regarded as a representation, it was nevertheless not a fraudulent representation, but was to be justified on the ground of the trade custom heretofore referred to permitting a dealer in used cars, having reconditioned a particular car, to set the speedometer back to such a figure as would reflect and give credit to the dealer for the value of the repairs and improvements made upon the car.

There are two prime reasons which at once suggest themselves why defendant may not justify its act upon the ground of a custom of the trade to turn speedometers back before offering used cars for sale to the unsuspecting public. In the first place, there is no showing or contention that plaintiff was himself in anywise engaged in the used car business or familiar with the custom in question if such custom exists, and consequently he could not be bound by it, absent any proof either of his actual knowledge of it or that the custom was itself so widespread and well-known as to require that knowledge of it be imputed to him.

Furthermore, regardless of any lack of notoriety of the custom in question, it is one designed only to deceive and allow the sellers of used cars to obtain an unfair and undue advantage over their customers, and for such reason would in no event be recognized or countenanced by the law. The reasonableness of a particular custom for which legal effect is sought is always a subject of inquiry by the court, and when it is ascertained that the custom is contrary to the public good and is prejudicial to the many and beneficial only to the favored few, it will find itself repugnant to the principles of fair dealing which otherwise entitle a custom to be recognized in a court of justice.

It could hardly be questioned but that the custom of setting back speedometers on used cars to some odd number of miles before offering the cars for sale to the public is patently designed to serve the interests of the few at the expense of the many. If the customer were told that the speedometer upon the car he was about to purchase had been set back so as to reflect the value of the car after being repaired, by which we mean that if he were frankly advised that the reconditioned car had been put in a state of mechanical perfection the equivalent of a car which had been run the approximate number of miles shown by the speedometer but without repairs upon it, our conclusion would be entirely different. However, the only legitimate inference from the evidence is, not that the customer is induced to buy a car upon which the speedometer reading has been admittedly lowered so as to represent the value of the improvements put upon the car, but instead that he is given or left to believe that he is buying a car which has been repaired and reconditioned after having been run only the number of miles shown on the speedometer. The evidence shows, and defendant unquestionably knew, not only that the mileage shown upon a car is a very material factor affecting its resale for the simple reason that the greater is the mileage, the greater has been the corresponding wear and tear upon the car, but also that no amount of reconditioning save a complete replacement of parts can compensate for the wear and tear to which a car has been subjected over a long period of use. The act of defendant complained of was therefore a fraud upon plaintiff, and the evidence in the case would fairly warrant no other conclusion.

As a further reason why in its opinion the evidence was insufficient to have warranted the submission of the case to the jury, defendant makes the point that plaintiff wholly failed to prove one of the essential elements of his cause of action, which was that he had relied upon defendant's representation regarding the mileage of the car and would have acted differently if he had known the truth.

It is a fact, just as defendant suggests, that plaintiff did not testify directly to any such reliance on his part. This, however, does not necessarily militate against the sufficiency of the evidence to have made the case one for the jury to determine.

The rule is that while the plaintiff who complains of the defendant's fraud must show that the false representations made to him by the defendant induced him to act to his prejudice, the fact of his reliance upon such false representations need not invariably be established by direct evidence to that effect, but may be inferred from all the facts and circumstances in the case.

. . .

In this case the evidence shows that before going through with the bargain plaintiff looked at the speedometer reading and observed the odd number of miles it showed. He must have done this to obtain the information which the speedometer was designed to disclose. He had a right to rely upon that reading, and he had no reason to suspect and no means of knowing that the speedometer had been deliberately set back by defendant. It is useless to say, as defendant does, that plaintiff made his purchase primarily upon the strength of the car's apparently good condition, for this is to disregard his positive testimony that he did take occasion to notice the speedometer reading. With plaintiff ignorant of the true facts and without ready means of information concerning them other than from what was represented to him by defendant, and with the fact of the car's mileage being a highly material factor upon the question of its desirability as we have already pointed out, we would be in accord with authority if we held as a matter of law that plaintiff relied upon what the speedometer showed. To say the least the question was one for the jury upon the inferences fairly deducible from all the facts and circumstances in the case, and the demurrer to all the evidence was therefore properly overruled.

. . .

Regardless of what the rule may be in other jurisdictions or of the refinements and limitations with which textwriters may see fit to state it, the courts of this state seem now to be committed to the proposition that in cases of fraud and deceit punitive damages may be awarded where legal malice is present. Moreover, by legal malice the courts have in mind simply the accepted theory of the intentional doing of a wrongful act without just cause or excuse, and not the necessity for the showing of any spite or ill will, or that the particular act was willfully or wantonly done.

We have already determined upon both reason and precedent that defendant's act in setting back the speedometer so as to deceive plaintiff in regard to the mileage of the car was wrongful, and there is no claim that it was not intentionally done. The only excuse claimed is the alleged custom of the trade, and, of course, that custom, being itself wrongful, could furnish no just cause or excuse for any one to follow it. Moreover, defendant must have known its act was wrongful since it was careful not to inform plaintiff of what had been done. The issue of punitive damages was therefore one for the jury along with the other issues in the case, and the court's refusal of the instruction designed to withdraw that issue from the consideration of the jury was entirely proper.

For its final point, defendant insists that the jury's allowance of punitive damages in the sum of $2,000 was not only excessive but so grossly so as to indicate that the allowance was the result of sympathy on the part of the jury for plaintiff and passion and prejudice against the defendant.

The ground upon which defendant puts its point evinces its appreciation of the true measure of our responsibility in such matters, which is to interfere with the jury's verdict upon the issue of punitive damages only where it plainly appears that the verdict was so out of all proper proportions as to reveal improper motives and an absence of honest exercise of judgment by the jury in its rendition. . . .

Punitive damages are, of course, allowed not only to punish the defendant for the particular offense he has committed against the plaintiff, but also to serve as a warning and example to deter the defendant and others from committing like wrongs in the future. It obviously follows, therefore, that while the punitive damages allowed in a given case should bear some reasonable proportion to the actual damages sustained by the plaintiff, it is not so much a mathematical proportion which the jury are to have in mind as it is a due regard for the character of the injury which has been inflicted.

The case at hand is unique in that it does not present an isolated wrong on the part of some person, attributable perhaps to passing anger or passion and unlikely to occur again, but instead it discloses the perpetration of a fraud purposely and deliberately done and sought to be justified on the ground of conformity by defendant with what is said to be a common trade practice followed by dealers in used automobiles at the expense of the general buying public. Undoubtedly the jury had all this in mind, and properly so, in fixing the amount of its allowance, and the refusal of the lower court to interfere on motion for new trial evinces its belief that the jury were actuated by no improper motives.

Under such circumstances, we think there is no warrant for our interference with the amount of the verdict, and all of defendant's insistence to the contrary stands for disapproval.

The judgment rendered by the circuit court should, therefore, be affirmed. . . .

QUESTIONS AND NOTES

1. What elements of the cause of action are in issue?

2. In *Jones* the court holds that a misrepresentation may be actionable even though it is nonverbal. In King v. Towns, 118 S.E.2d 121 (Ga.App. 1960), defendant made an unsolicited appearance at plaintiff's home for the purpose of demonstrating (and selling) a set of stainless steel cookware, to replace plaintiff's aluminum cookware. Plaintiff testified,

> And so he said, "Give me one of your boilers, and I'm going to take one of mine." That's what he said. I said, "Yes, sir." And so he put the water in his and then he put some in mine. He said, "I'm just going to show you how this material you've got here is going to cause you to have cancer, you and your children, before the year's out." I said, "Mister, you don't mean it." He said, "It really is. You and your children probably will come down with cancer before the year's out." He said, "All that material you've got there is no good to you." And he opened up a big book had a whole lot of pictures of aluminum ware he said was what they collected from homes and it wasn't no good. I said, "What you going to do with it?" He said, "Might as well take it and throw it away; it's no good. I'm telling you what's the truth, you better throw this away; it's no good to you." I said, "Mister, you don't mean to tell me that's what's causing people to have cancer." He said, "That's what's causing it." So he had this big book about this thick, looked like. He said, "If you don't believe it, call these doctors here"— and he was going through that book—"and they can tell you." I said, "Lord have mercy, I don't want my children to have cancer, and I don't want to have it, either." So he [took] my boiler and his boiler and put water in both of them. He said, "I'm going to show you what come out of your boiler and goes in your system." I said, "Lord have mercy." So he put the water in his boiler and put the water in my boiler, and he put them on the stove, and all the while he was talking. He said, "Look. This is your boiler, and this is my boiler." I said, "Yes, sir, surely is." He said, "Look what's going on in your system." I said, "Lord have mercy." That what was in my boiler was thick as starch. I said, "You don't mean to tell me that stuff come out of my boiler." He said, "Yes, it really does, and," he said, "it's going to cause you and your children to have cancer before the year's out." I got so scared I didn't know what to do. He said, "I'll just take your aluminum ware and throw it away." He said, "I'll take it with me." I said, "If it's no good to me, if it's going to cause me and my children to have cancer," I said, "it's no good to me."

Id. at 124.

How does the misrepresentation in King v. Towns differ from the misrepresentation in Jones v. West Side?

In *Saylor v. Handley Motor Co.*, 169 A.2d 683 (D.C.Mun.App.1961), plaintiffs informed defendant's salesman that they could afford monthly payments of no more than $80. The parties reached agreement on the terms of the sale, including monthly payments of $80. Plaintiffs signed a blank conditional sales contract, which the salesman later filled in, requiring monthly payments of $88.15. The court wrote,

> appellee contends that the Saylors were bound to know the contents of the contract before they signed. Appellee argues that the couple must assume responsibility for having entrusted its salesman with the transcription of the prior oral understanding of the parties on a form bearing their signature.
>
> The proposition that one is obligated by his contract, though signed without knowledge of its terms, does not extend to situations where assent to such terms is procured by the proponent's fraud. . . .
>
>   . . .
>
> Not only will relief be afforded where a party's signature is procured upon the misrepresentation that the writing before him faithfully reflects a prior oral agreement; it will also be granted to the person who delivers a signed form under the false promise that it will contain certain terms.
>
> Accordingly, where a party is induced to sign a paper as a result of a false representation that it will be filled in or prepared as orally agreed, the intentional omission of terms required by the authorization to be included, or the inclusion of terms not so authorized, constitutes fraud invalidating the instrument as between the parties thereto, notwithstanding that the party signing was negligent in relying on the misrepresentation. The rule is that where one party to an oral agreement entrusts the other with the obligation of reducing it to writing, he has a right to rely upon the representation that it will be drawn accurately and in accordance with the oral understanding between them. The presentation of the paper for signature is in itself a representation that the terms of such oral agreement have been or will be embodied in the writing.

Id. at 684–685.

How does the misrepresentation in *Saylor v. Handley* differ from the misrepresentations in *Jones v. West Side* and in *King v. Towns*?

3. In *Jones*, exactly how was defendant trying to use the (alleged) fact of trade custom? To which element(s) is it relevant? Why does the court reject defendant's argument?

4. What standard does the court use to determine whether plaintiff relied on the misrepresentation?

5. According to the court, punitive damages may be awarded when there is legal malice. What does the adjective "legal" add to the word "malice"?

Is the alleged trade custom (any more) relevant to the propriety of punitive damages than it is to the right of plaintiff to recover actual damages?

In King v. Towns, described in Note 2 supra, the court wrote,

> It is pleaded and shown by the evidence that the plaintiff is an illiterate person. The jury may well observe and weigh the divergence of intelligence between the parties as a circumstance in a case of this nature when such is shown by the evidence, and the method or scheme to weave a web of fright whereby the plaintiff was overreached and induced to purchase the goods and depart with her own property, as well as money. The court is not unmindful of those who prey upon the ignorant. The illiterate are entitled to the protection of the law as well as the educated. The jurors, who are the arbiters of fact, may weigh all the facts and circumstances in determining whether to award punitive damages. The application of the law to the facts rested upon the 12 jurors. Judge Lumpkin observed: "It has been truly said, that more instructive lessons are taught in Courts of Justice, than the Church is able to inculcate. Morals come in the cold abstract from the pulpit; but men smart under them practically, when Juries are the preachers."

> . . . The question of punitive damages is one for the jury. Code § 105–2002 provides that additional damages may be allowed for a tort where there are aggravating circumstances for two purposes: (1) to deter the wrongdoer, or (2) as compensation for the wounded feelings of the plaintiff. It should be observed that the rule which requires that the amount of punitive damages have some reasonable proportion to the extent of injury refers to those cases where exemplary damages are awarded for wounded feelings. In the instant case the pleadings and the evidence show that additional damages were sought to deter the defendants from repeating acts such as alleged in the instant case. The facts and circumstances as shown by the several witnesses testifying as to their similar experiences with the defendant corporation and its agents, together with the documentary evidence, are sufficient to show an over-all scheme to mislead potential purchasers. This court cannot say that the jury's verdict reflects bias and prejudice, or that the amount is so excessive as to demand a reversal. Under such circumstances, the measure of damages is within the enlightened conscience of the jury.

118 S.E.2d at 127, 128.

6. Compare the elements of deceit (page 7 supra) with the elements of express warranty. Which elements of deceit are also elements of express warranty? Which elements of express warranty are not also elements of deceit? In each of the three cases described above (*Jones, King, Saylor*), the court upheld the plaintiff's claim of fraud. In which of the cases would there be an express warranty? *All 3.*

In view of the differences you have identified between deceit and express warranty, which of them is more advantageous to the consumer?

Can you think of any other factors, procedural or otherwise, that might affect this assessment?

7. Examine the elements of deceit. What is the justification for requiring each of them before a plaintiff may recover? In particular, why require reliance by the plaintiff? Why require that the reliance relate to a material fact? Why require that the reliance be justifiable? Why require that the defendant know of the falsity of the representation?

8. The defendant in *Jones* undoubtedly was correct in asserting that it was a common practice for sellers of used cars to turn back odometers. There were even people, known as "speedo men," who would travel from dealer to dealer with a special machine to reset odometers. To deal specifically with deception in rolling back odometers, Congress and many state legislatures have created special rules for used car dealers. See 49 U.S.C. §§ 32701–32711, and the accompanying regulations, reproduced in the Statutory Supplement. These statutes and regulations prohibit tampering with odometers and require sellers of automobiles to disclose certain information about the vehicles. See section 580.5 of the regulations.

Have you ever sold a used car? If so, did you supply the buyer with the statement required by the federal regulation? Note that the statute and regulation apply to consumer sellers as well as to dealers, and see section 32710 (civil liability for treble damages or $1,500, whichever is more, and two-year statute of limitations).

Chapter 2, Section E contains additional material on the statutory regulation of odometer fraud.

9. Enactment of the odometer statutes is an example of a common phenomenon in the regulation of consumer transactions. Although common law deceit provides a remedy for those injured by odometer rollbacks, the availability of that remedy has not eradicated the objectionable behavior. Therefore, the legislatures—at both the federal and state levels—responded by enacting statutes to deal with the problem. And since the common law rules were not effective to prevent odometer rollbacks, it is not surprising that these statutes go further than the common law rules. The federal statute, for example, not only prohibits changing an odometer reading, it also prohibits operating a motor vehicle with the odometer disconnected and prohibits the sale of any device that changes odometer readings. In addition to these prohibitions, the statute (and regulations) impose an affirmative requirement that the seller make a written disclosure of the odometer reading and affirm its accuracy. The statute authorizes a federal agency to promulgate regulations and provides for enforcement by both federal and state officials. These additional prohibitions, the affirmative disclosure requirement, and the enforcement mechanism all go well beyond the requirements of the common law. Hence, the case of odometer fraud provides a good example of what may happen when the conduct of actors in the market place does not conform to the requirements of the common law.

Enactment of legislation is also a common response when the common law rules do not regulate particular conduct at all. This is true with respect to deceptive conduct that does not rise to the level of deceit (e.g., see the New York false advertising statute on page 79), and it is true with respect to conduct that is not deceptive but nevertheless injures consumers (e.g., see the Equal Credit Opportunity Act, which is the subject of Chapter 6). Consequently, much of the law of consumer transactions is statutory law that legislatures have enacted because the common law does not address some of the problems in consumer transactions, either adequately or at all. The common law remains relevant, however, and the remaining materials in this chapter reveal ways in which the common law of deceit has evolved to recognize, and reflect, changes in the standard of conduct appropriate for bargain transactions.

Vokes v. Arthur Murray, Inc.

Court of Appeals of Florida, 1968.
212 So.2d 906.

PIERCE, JUDGE.

This is an appeal by Audrey E. Vokes, plaintiff below, from a final order dismissing with prejudice, for failure to state a cause of action, her fourth amended complaint, hereinafter referred to as plaintiff's complaint.

Defendant Arthur Murray, Inc., a corporation, authorizes the operation throughout the nation of dancing schools under the name of "Arthur Murray School of Dancing" through local franchised operators, one of whom was defendant J. P. Davenport whose dancing establishment was in Clearwater.

Plaintiff Mrs. Audrey E. Vokes, a widow of 51 years and without family, had a yen to be "an accomplished dancer" with the hopes of finding "new interest in life." So, on February 10, 1961, a dubious fate, with the assist of a motivated acquaintance, procured her to attend a "dance party" at Davenport's "School of Dancing" where she whiled away the pleasant hours, sometimes in a private room, absorbing his accomplished sales technique, during which her grace and poise were elaborated upon and her rosy future as "an excellent dancer" was painted for her in vivid and glowing colors. As an incident to this interlude, he sold her eight ½–hour dance lessons to be utilized within one calendar month therefrom, for the sum of $14.50 cash in hand paid, obviously a baited "come-on."

Thus she embarked upon an almost endless pursuit of the terpsichorean art during which, over a period of less than sixteen months, she was sold fourteen "dance courses" totalling in the aggregate 2302 hours of dancing lessons for a total cash outlay of $31,090.45, all at Davenport's dance emporium. All of these fourteen courses were evidenced by execution of a written "Enrollment Agreement—Arthur Murray's School of Dancing" with the addendum in heavy black print, "No one will be informed that you are taking dancing lessons. Your relations with us are held in strict confidence," setting forth the number of "dancing lessons" and the "lessons in rhythm sessions" currently sold to her from time to time, and always of course accompanied by payment of cash of the realm.

These dance lesson contracts and the monetary consideration therefor of over $31,000 were procured from her by means and methods of Davenport and his associates which went beyond the unsavory, yet legally permissible, perimeter of "sales puffing" and intruded well into the forbidden area of undue influence, the suggestion of falsehood, the suppression of truth, and the free exercise of rational judgment, if what plaintiff alleged in her complaint was true. From the time of her first contact with the dancing school in February 1961, she was influenced unwittingly by a constant and continuous barrage of flattery, false praise, excessive compliments, and panegyric encomiums, to such extent that it would be not only inequitable, but unconscionable, for a Court exercising inherent chancery power to allow such contracts to stand.

Sales Puffing → Undue Influence

She was incessantly subjected to overreaching blandishment and cajolery. She was assured she had "grace and poise"; that she was "rapidly improving and developing in her dancing skill"; that the additional lessons would "make her a beautiful dancer, capable of dancing with the most accomplished dancers"; that she was "rapidly progressing in the development of her dancing skill and gracefulness," etc., etc. She was given "dance aptitude tests" for the ostensible purpose of "determining" the number of remaining hours instructions needed by her from time to time.

At one point she was sold 545 additional hours of dancing lessons to be entitled to award of the "Bronze Medal" signifying that she had reached "the Bronze Standard," a supposed designation of dance achievement by students of Arthur Murray, Inc.

Later she was sold an additional 926 hours in order to gain the "Silver Medal," indicating she had reached "the Silver Standard," at a cost of $12,501.35.

At one point, while she still had to her credit about 900 unused hours of instructions, she was induced to purchase an additional 24 hours of lessons to participate in a trip to Miami at her own expense, where she would be "given the opportunity to dance with members of the Miami Studio."

She was induced at another point to purchase an additional 126 hours of lessons in order to be not only eligible for the Miami trip but also to become "a life member of the Arthur Murray Studio," carrying with it certain dubious emoluments, at a further cost of $1,752.30.

At another point, while she still had over 1,000 unused hours of instruction she was induced to buy 151 additional hours at a cost of $2,049.00 to be eligible for a "Student Trip to Trinidad," at her own expense as she later learned.

Also, when she still had 1100 unused hours to her credit, she was prevailed upon to purchase an additional 347 hours at a cost of $4,235.74, to qualify her to receive a "Gold Medal" for achievement, indicating she had advanced to "the Gold Standard."

On another occasion, while she still had over 1200 unused hours, she was induced to buy an additional 175 hours of instruction at a cost of $2,472.75 to be eligible "to take a trip to Mexico."

Finally, sandwiched in between other lesser sales promotions, she was influenced to buy an additional 481 hours of instruction at a cost of $6,523.81 in order to "be classified as a Gold Bar Member, the ultimate achievement of the dancing studio."

All the foregoing sales promotions, illustrative of the entire fourteen separate contracts, were procured by defendant Davenport and Arthur Murray, Inc., by false representations to her that she was improving in her dancing ability, that she had excellent potential, that she was responding to instructions in dancing grace, and that they were developing her into a beautiful dancer, whereas in truth and in fact she did not develop in her dancing ability, she had no "dance aptitude," and in fact had difficulty in "hearing the musical beat." The complaint alleged that such representations to her "were in fact false and known by the defendant to be false and contrary to the plaintiff's true ability, the truth of plaintiff's ability being fully known to the defendants, but withheld from the plaintiff for the sole and specific intent to deceive and defraud the plaintiff and to induce her in the purchasing of additional hours of dance lessons." It was averred that the lessons were sold to her "in total disregard to the true physical, rhythm, and mental ability of the plaintiff." In other words, while she first exulted that she was entering the "spring of her life," she finally was awakened to the fact there was "spring" neither in her life nor in her feet.

The complaint prayed that the Court decree the dance contracts to be null and void and to be cancelled, that an accounting be had, and judgment entered against the defendants "for that portion of the $31,090.45 not charged against specific hours of instruction given to the plaintiff." The Court held the complaint not to state a cause of action and dismissed it with prejudice. We disagree and reverse.

The material allegations of the complaint must, of course, be accepted as true for the purpose of testing its legal sufficiency. Defendants contend that contracts can only be rescinded for fraud or misrepresentation when the alleged misrepresentation is as to a material fact, rather than an opinion, prediction or expectation, and that the statements and representations set forth at length in the complaint were in the category of "trade puffing," within its legal orbit.

It is true that "generally a misrepresentation, to be actionable, must be one of fact rather than of opinion." But this rule has significant qualifications, applicable here. It does not apply where there is a fiduciary relationship between the parties, or where there has been some artifice or trick employed by the representor, or where the parties do not in general deal at "arm's length" as we understand the phrase, or where the representee does not have equal opportunity to become apprised of the truth or falsity of the fact represented. As stated by Judge Allen of this Court in Ramel v. Chasebrook Construction Company, Fla.App.1961, 135 So.2d 876:

* * * A statement of a party having * * * superior knowledge may be regarded as a statement of fact although it would be considered as opinion if the parties were dealing on equal terms.

It could be reasonably supposed here that defendants had "superior knowledge" as to whether plaintiff had "dance potential" and as to whether she was noticeably improving in the art of terpsichore. And it would be a reasonable inference from the undenied averments of the complaint that the flowery eulogiums heaped upon her by defendants as a prelude to her contracting for 1944 additional hours of instruction in order to attain the rank of the Bronze Standard, thence to the bracket of the Silver Standard, thence to the class of the Gold Bar Standard, and finally to the crowning plateau of a Life Member of the Studio, proceeded as much or more from the urge to "ring the cash register" as from any honest or realistic appraisal of her dancing prowess or a factual representation of her progress.

Even in contractual situations where a party to a transaction owes no duty to disclose facts within his knowledge or to answer inquiries respecting such facts, the law is if he undertakes to do so he must disclose the *whole truth*. From the face of the complaint, it should have been reasonably apparent to defendants that her vast outlay of cash for the many hundreds of additional hours of instruction was not justified by her slow and awkward progress, which she would have been made well aware of if they had spoken the "whole truth."

        . . .

We repeat that where parties are dealing on a contractual basis at arm's length with no inequities or inherently unfair practices employed, the Courts will in general "leave the parties where they find themselves." But in the case sub judice, from the allegations of the unanswered complaint, we cannot say that enough of the accompanying ingredients, as mentioned in the foregoing authorities, were not present which otherwise would have barred the equitable arm of the Court to her. In our view, from the showing made in her complaint, plaintiff is entitled to her day in Court.

It accordingly follows that the order dismissing plaintiff's last amended complaint with prejudice should be and is reversed.

Reversed.

QUESTIONS AND NOTES

1. Does the court hold that plaintiff's complaint stated that defendant made actionable misrepresentations of fact? If so, what were they? If not, how does the complaint state a cause of action for deceit? A case similar to *Vokes* is Parker v. Arthur Murray, Inc., 295 N.E.2d 487 (Ill.App.1973). Excerpts from the court's opinion follow:

> The operative facts are not in dispute. In November, 1959 plaintiff went to the Arthur Murray Studio in Oak Park to redeem a certificate

entitling him to three free dancing lessons. At that time he was a 37–year-old college-educated bachelor who lived alone in a one-room attic apartment in Berwyn, Illinois. During the free lessons the instructor told plaintiff he had "exceptional potential to be a fine and accomplished dancer" and generally encouraged further participation. Plaintiff thereupon signed a contract for 75 hours of lessons at a cost of $1000. At the bottom of the contract were the bold-type words, "NON–CANCELLABLE NEGOTIABLE CONTRACT." This initial encounter set the pattern for the future relationship between the parties. Plaintiff attended lessons regularly. He was praised and encouraged regularly by the instructors, despite his lack of progress. Contract extensions and new contracts for additional instructional hours were executed. . . .

On September 24, 1961 plaintiff was severely injured in an automobile collision, rendering him incapable of continuing his dancing lessons. At that time he had contracted for a total of 2734 hours of lessons, for which he had paid $24,812.80. Despite written demand defendants refused to return any of the money, and this suit in equity ensued. At the close of plaintiff's case the trial judge dismissed the fraud count (Count II), describing the instructors' sales techniques as merely "a matter of pumping salesmanship." . . . It is contended on appeal that representations to plaintiff that he had "exceptional potential to be a fine and accomplished dancer," that he had "exceptional potential" and that he was a "natural born dancer" and a "terrific dancer" fraudulently induced plaintiff to enter into the contracts for dance lessons.

Generally, a mere expression of opinion will not support an action for fraud. In addition, misrepresentations, in order to constitute actionable fraud, must pertain to present or pre-existing facts, rather than to future or contingent events, expectations or probabilities. Whether particular language constitutes speculation, opinion or averment of fact depends upon all the attending facts and circumstances of the case. Mindful of these rules, and after carefully considering the representations made to plaintiff, and taking into account the business relationship of the parties as well as the educational background of plaintiff, we conclude that the instructors' representations did not constitute fraud. The trial court correctly dismissed Count II. We affirm.

Does the court conclude that defendant made no misrepresentations of fact? Are the sales practices or specific statements in the two cases materially different? How can the difference in results be justified?

Plaintiff in *Vokes* sought rescission and return of the money she had paid. Plaintiff in *Parker* sought not only rescission but also punitive damages. Does this difference justify or explain the difference in results?

2. It may be difficult to determine whether a statement amounts to a representation of fact or an expression of opinion. In Morehouse v. Behlmann, 31 S.W.3d 55, 59–60 (Mo.App.2000), defendant sold plaintiff a minivan, describing it as " 'in good condition,' 'in tip-top shape' and 'reliable.' '' In fact, the minivan tended to overheat and eventually became inoperable. The court stated:

> A given representation can be an expression of opinion or a statement of fact depending upon the circumstances surrounding the representation. . . . [T]he evidence established that [the salesman] assured [plaintiff] that the vehicle was in excellent condition when he, at best, had no knowledge as to whether his statements were true or false. . . . [A case cited by defendant is distinguishable because an] integral part of that holding . . . was that the buyer and the seller were on equal footing in terms of knowledge of car mechanics and the seller gave no impression of knowledge about cars. In the present case, [plaintiff] told [the salesman] several times that she was an inexperienced car buyer and that she had no idea what to look for in a car. [He] responded that he had years of experience selling cars and knew what was good. Given [the salesman's] advantage in experience and his representation thereof, his statements to [plaintiff] about the condition of the car conveyed sufficient information to be representations of fact, and not merely statements of opinion.

3. A similar problem of differentiating representations of fact from statements of opinion exists under the law of warranties. Thus UCC section 2–313(2) states that "an affirmation merely of the value of the goods or a statement purporting to be merely the seller's opinion or commendation of the goods does not create a warranty." (See also Official Comment 8 to that section.) It is not always easy, however, to draw the line between an affirmation of fact that creates a warranty under subsection (1) and a statement of opinion under subsection (2). Thus, courts have differed on whether a seller's statement that a motor vehicle is in "mint" or "excellent" condition creates a warranty. Grabinski v. Blue Springs Ford Sales, Inc., 136 F.3d 565 (8th Cir.1998) ("very nice," warranty); Taylor v. Alfama, 481 A.2d 1059 (Vt.1984) ("mint condition," warranty); Valley Datsun v. Martinez, 578 S.W.2d 485 (Tex.Civ.App.1979) ("excellent condition," warranty); Web Press Servs. Corp. v. New London Motors, Inc., 525 A.2d 57 (Conn.1987) ("mint condition" and "excellent condition," no warranty). What criteria should a court use to determine whether a statement is a warranty or merely puffing?

A seller of copying machines made the following statements: the copier and its component parts are of high quality; experience and testing have shown that frequency of repairs is very low; replacement parts are readily available; the cost of maintenance is less than ½ cent per copy; the copier is safe and cannot cause fires; and service calls will be required on the average of once every 8,000 copies. Which, if any, of these statements could give rise to liability for deceit? Which, if any, could give rise to liability for breach of express warranty? See Royal Business Machines, Inc. v. Lorraine Corp., 633 F.2d 34 (7th Cir.1980).

4. In Sunderhaus v. Perel & Lowenstein, 388 S.W.2d 140 (Tenn.1965), plaintiff purchased a diamond ring from defendant jeweler for $699.25. When plaintiff later sought to trade the ring in on another ring, two other jewelers appraised its value as $300 and $350. Plaintiff sued, seeking either rescission or damages, alleging that defendant represented to her at the time of sale that the ring was worth what she was paying for it. The trial court sustained defendant's demurrer to plaintiff's complaint. The Supreme Court of Tennessee stated:

> The alleged false representations of the appellee's agent relate to the value of the diamond purchased by appellant. We find the general rule to be that ordinarily representations of value made by one seeking to dispose of property commercially are to be regarded as expressions of opinion or commendatory trade statements not constituting a basis of fraud. There are, however, a number of exceptions to this general rule. In 23 Am.Jur., Fraud and Deceit, § 59, at Page 830, it is stated:
>
> > "* * * Likewise, a statement of value may be of such a character, so made and intended, and so received, as to constitute fundamental misrepresentation; and if it is made as an assertion of fact, and with the purpose that it shall be so received, and it is so received, it may amount to a fraud. Moreover, a statement of value involving and coupled with a statement of a material fact is fraud.
> >
> > "Value is frequently made by the parties themselves the principal element in a contract; and there are many cases where articles possess a standard commercial value, in which it is a chief criterion of quality among those who are not experts. . . .
>
> The rule is stated as follows in 3 Pomeroy, Equity Jurisprudence, § 878b (5th ed. 1941):
>
> > "There is still another and perhaps more common form of such misrepresentation. Wherever a party states a matter, which might otherwise be only an opinion, and does not state it *as the mere expression of his own opinion*, but affirms it *as an existing fact* material to the transaction, so that the other party may reasonably treat it as a fact, and rely and act upon it as such, then the statement clearly becomes an affirmation of fact within the meaning of the general rule, and may be a fraudulent misrepresentation.
> >
> > "Value.—The statements which most frequently come within this branch of the rule are those concerning value.". . .
>
> Of necessity, in the purchase of a diamond or other precious stone, the purchaser must rely upon the integrity of the jeweler from whom he purchases. The layman is in no position to weigh the stone and make his own determination as to its true value, but must rely upon statements of value made to him by the jeweler. Here, the bill charges the agent of the appellee falsely represented the value of the diamond to the complainant, knowing the falsity of the representation, that the appellant was not familiar with the value of the diamond and relied upon the false representation of the appellee's agent. These averments contain all of the elements necessary to state a cause of action for fraud and deceit. . . .

In our judgment it cannot be said that the bill as amended fails to state a cause of action for fraud and deceit. Therefore, the decree of the Chancery Court is reversed and the cause is remanded. . . .

Id. at 142–44.

If there is to be a requirement that the misrepresentation be a misrepresentation of fact, what reason is there for excusing that requirement in cases like *Vokes* and *Sunderhaus*?

5. Under certain circumstances even an expression of opinion may be actionable as fraud. In Rodi v. Southern New England School of Law, 389 F.3d 5 (1st Cir.2004), the dean of defendant law school wrote plaintiff a letter stating that he was "highly confident" that the school would gain accreditation before plaintiff graduated. A year later the dean's successor wrote plaintiff that there should be "no cause for pessimism" concerning accreditation in time for plaintiff to sit for the bar exam. During plaintiff's third year, the ABA denied the school's application for accreditation, and he was unable to take the bar exam. When he sued, the trial court dismissed the complaint for failing to state a claim. The appellate court reversed, responding to defendants' argument that the deans merely expressed their opinions:

> That is true, in a sense, but it does not get the defendants very far.
>
> A statement, though couched in terms of opinion, may constitute a statement of fact if it may reasonably be understood by the reader or listener as implying the existence of facts that justify the statement (or, at least, the non-existence of any facts incompatible with it). See . . . Restatement (Second) of Torts § 539 (1977) (explaining that "[a] statement of opinion as to facts not disclosed [may] be interpreted . . . as an implied statement that the facts known to the maker are not incompatible with his opinion"). Thus, . . . it is an actionable misrepresentation for a car dealer to tell a buyer that he "believes" a vehicle is in "good" condition when he knows that it has significant mechanical defects. Briggs v. Carol Cars, Inc., 407 Mass. 391, 553 N.E.2d 930, 933 (Mass. 1990).
>
> . . . The plaintiff's complaint alleges that the ABA has formulated certain objective criteria that inform its decisions about whether and when to accredit law schools. It also alleges that [the dean], knowing of these criteria, wrote a letter to the plaintiff implying that the school was reasonably capable of satisfying them. If [the dean] did know of disqualifying and probably irremediable deficiencies (as the plaintiff has alleged), his statement that [the school] was "highly confident" of accreditation was actionably misleading. [The] statement that there was "no cause for pessimism" about the fate of the school's renewed accreditation application is subject to much the same analysis.

6. Consider also Williams v. Rank & Son Buick, Inc., 170 N.W.2d 807 (Wis.1969):

> On March 19, 1968, respondent and his brother went to appellant's used car lot where they examined a 1964 Chrysler Imperial

automobile. While doing so, they were approached by a salesman who permitted them to take the car for a test run. They drove the car for approximately one and one-half hours before returning the car to the appellant's lot. During that time they tested the car's general handling as well as its radio and power windows. According to the respondent, however, it was not until several days after he had purchased the car that he discovered that the knobs marked "AIR" were for ventilation and that the car was not air-conditioned.

At the trial the respondent testified that while examining the car he discussed its equipment with the salesman and was told that it was air-conditioned. . . .

Upon these facts the trial court found that the respondent had proven fraud on the part of the appellant and awarded him $150 in damages. . . .

This court has consistently held that the party alleging fraud has the burden of proving it by clear and convincing evidence and that factual findings of the trial court will not be upset unless contrary to the great weight and clear preponderance of the evidence. Based upon these principles it is this court's duty on this appeal to determine if all the elements of fraud have been properly established.

. . .

In regard to the alleged oral misrepresentations of the appellant's salesman, there is, of course, conflict in testimony. Despite denial by the salesman, however, there is sufficient evidence upon which the trial court could find that such statements were made and that they were made with intent to defraud the respondent.

Appellant's counsel argues that there was no reliance by the respondent and that therefore there was no fraud. . . .

In response to his attorney's question as to whether the car was represented as having certain features, the respondent answered, "Oh, yes, that it was full power and air conditioning and everything, and that Chrysler was a nice car, it was, and all that kind of jazz." He then added that he had purchased the car "Mainly because it was a Chrysler Imperial and that it had air-conditioning."

Despite denials by the salesman, the trial court, having had an opportunity to view the witnesses, apparently determined that the respondent's testimony was more credible than that of the salesman.

The question of reliance is another matter. Many previous decisions of this court have held that one cannot justifiably rely upon obviously false statements. In Jacobsen v. Whitely (1909), 138 Wis. 434, 436, 437, 120 N.W. 285, 286, the court said:

> * * * It is an unsavory defense for a man who by false statements, induces another to act to assert that if the latter had disbelieved him he would not have been injured. * * * Neverthe-less courts will refuse to act for the relief of one claiming to have

been misled by another's statements who blindly acts in disregard of knowledge of their falsity or with such opportunity that by the exercise of ordinary observation, not necessarily by search, he would have known. He may not close his eyes to what is obviously discoverable by him. * * *

It is apparent that the obviousness of a statement's falsity vitiates reliance since no one can rely upon a known falsity. Were the rule otherwise a person would be free to enter into a contract with no intent to perform under the contract unless it ultimately proved profitable. On the other hand, a party who makes an inadvertent slip of the tongue or pencil would continually lose the benefit of the contract.

The question is thus whether the statement's falsity could have been detected by ordinary observation. Whether the falsity of a statement could have been discovered through ordinary care is to be determined in light of the intelligence and experience of the misled individual. Also to be considered is the relationship between the parties.

. . . The respondent specifically testified that, being a high school graduate, he was capable of both reading and writing. It is also fair to assume that he possessed a degree of business acumen in that he and his brother operated their own business. No fiduciary relationship existed between the parties. They dealt with each other at arms' length. The appellant made no effort to interfere with the respondent's examination of the car, but, on the contrary, allowed him to take the car from the premises for a period of one and one-half hours.

Although the obviousness of a statement's falsity is a question of fact, this court has decided some such questions as a matter of law. . . .

In the instant case the respondent had ample opportunity to determine whether the car was air-conditioned. He had examined the car on the lot and had been allowed to remove the car from the lot unaccompanied by a salesman for a period of approximately one and one-half hours. This customers were normally not allowed to do.

No great search was required to disclose the absence of the air conditioning unit since a mere flip of a knob was all that was necessary. If air conditioning was, as stated by the respondent, the main reason he purchased the car, it is doubtful that he would not try the air conditioner.

"It seems plain that, whether the representation in question was made, the [respondent] failed to exercise that care for [his] own protection which was easily within [his] power to exercise, and, under all the circumstances, [he] was not justified in relying upon such a representation, if made." Acme Chair & M. C. Co. v. Northern C. Co., supra, at page 17, 243 N.W. at p. 418.

We conclude that as a matter of law the respondent under the facts and circumstances was not justified in relying upon the oral representation of the salesman. This is an action brought in fraud and not an action for a breach of warranty.

No— he was not justified in relying on misrep.

Does the court hold that, as a matter of law, plaintiff did not rely on the misrepresentation? What is the relevance of the observation by three dissenting justices that cars with factory-installed air conditioning have no visible sign of that feature in the passenger compartment?

Reconsider *Parker v. Arthur Murray*. Does *Williams* provide any additional support for the court's decision in *Parker*? Does *Williams* support the court's opposite decision in *Sunderhaus*? in King v. Towns (the cancer-causing cookware case)?

In some jurisdictions the standard of proof for establishing fraud is not "clear and convincing," but rather is "preponderance of the evidence." In some states the lowering of the standard resulted from judicial decision (e.g., see the next case); in others, it resulted from legislation.

Halpert v. Rosenthal

Supreme Court of Rhode Island, 1970
107 R.I. 406, 267 A.2d 730.

KELLEHER, JUSTICE.

[Defendant contracted to buy plaintiff's house for $54,000, making a down payment of $2,000. During the negotiations plaintiff and her real estate agent each stated that there was no termite infestation in the house. When an inspection revealed the presence of termites, defendant refused to proceed. Plaintiff sold the house to another person for $35,000 and brought this action against defendant to recover the $19,000 difference. Defendant counterclaimed for return of his $2,000 deposit. Plaintiff moved for a directed verdict on the counterclaim. The trial court denied the motion and rendered judgment for defendant on both the claim and the counterclaim. Plaintiff appealed.]

In contending that she was entitled to a directed verdict, plaintiff contends that to sustain the charge of fraudulent misrepresentation, some evidence had to be produced showing that either she or her agent knew at the time they said there were no termites in the house, that such a statement was untrue. Since the representations made to defendant were made in good faith, she argues that, as a matter of law, defendant could not prevail on his counterclaim.

The defendant concedes that there was no evidence which shows that plaintiff or her agent knowingly made false statements as to the existence of the termites but he maintains that an innocent misrepresentation of a material fact is grounds for rescission of a contract where, as here, a party relies to his detriment on the misrepresentation.

We affirm the denial of the motion for a directed verdict.

The plaintiff, when she made her motion for a directed verdict, stated that her motion was restricted to the issue of "fraud." The word "fraud" is a generic term which embraces a great variety of actionable wrongs. It is a word of many meanings and defies any one all-inclusive definition. Fraud may become important either for the purpose of giving the defrauded person the right to sue for damages in an action for deceit or to enable him to rescind the contract. 12 Williston, Contracts § 1487 at 322 (Jaeger 3d ed. 1970). In this jurisdiction a party who has been induced by fraud to enter into a contract may pursue either one of two remedies. He may elect to rescind the contract to recover what he has paid under it, or he may affirm the contract and sue for damages in an action for deceit.

The distinction between a claim for damages for intentional deceit and a claim for rescission is well defined. Deceit is a tort action, and it requires some degree of culpability on the misrepresenter's part. Prosser, Law of Torts (3d ed.) § 100. An individual who sues in an action of deceit based on fraud has the burden of proving that the defendant in making the statements knew they were false and intended to deceive him. On the other hand, a suit to rescind an agreement induced by fraud sounds in contract. It is this latter aspect of fraud that we are concerned with in this case, and the pivotal issue before us is whether an innocent misrepresentation of a material fact warrants the granting of a claim for rescission. We believe that it does.

When he denied plaintiff's motion, the trial justice indicated that a false, though innocent, misrepresentation of a fact made as though of one's knowledge may be the basis for the rescission of a contract. While this issue is one of first impression in this state, it is clear that the trial judge's action finds support in the overwhelming weight of decision and textual authority which has established the rule that where one induces another to enter into a contract by means of a material misrepresentation, the latter may rescind the contract. It does not matter if the representation was "innocent" or fraudulent.

. . . .

This statement of law is in accord with Restatement of Contracts, § 476 at 908 which states:

> Where a party is induced to enter into a transaction with another party that he was under no duty to enter into by means of the latter's fraud or material misrepresentation, the transaction is voidable as against the latter * * *

Misrepresentation is defined as

> " * * * any manifestation by words or other conduct by one person to another that, under the circumstances, amounts to an assertion not in accordance with the facts." Restatement of Contracts, § 470 at 890–91.

The comment following this section explains that a misrepresentation may be innocent, negligent or known to be false. A misrepresentation becomes material when it becomes likely to affect the conduct of a reasonable man with reference to a transaction with another person. Restatement of Contracts, § 470(2) at 891. Section 28 of Restatement of Restitution is also in accord with this proposition of law that a transaction can be rescinded for innocent misrepresentation of a material fact. In addition, many courts have also adopted this rule including the following: [citations of fourteen cases omitted].

It is true that some courts require proof of knowledge of the falsity of the misrepresentation before a contract may be invalidated. However, the weight of authority follows the view that the misrepresenter's good faith is immaterial. We believe this view the better one.

A misrepresentation, even though innocently made, may be actionable, if made and relied on as a positive statement of fact. The question to be resolved in determining whether a wrong committed as the result of an innocent misrepresentation may be rectified is succinctly stated in 12 Williston, supra, § 1510 at 462 as follows:

> When a defendant has induced another to act by representations false in fact although not dishonestly made, and damage has directly resulted from the action taken, who should bear the loss?

The question we submit is rhetorical. The answer is obvious. Simple justice demands that the speaker be held responsible. Accordingly, we hold that here defendant vendee could maintain his counterclaim.

The plaintiff's second contention is to the effect that even if an innocent misrepresentation without knowledge of its falsity may under certain circumstances entitle the misrepresentee to relief by way of rescission, defendant cannot maintain his action because the sales agreement contains a merger clause. This provision immediately precedes the testimonium clause and provides that the contract " * * * contains the entire agreement between the parties, and that it is subject to no understandings, conditions or representations other than those expressly stated herein." The plaintiff argues that in order to enable a purchaser to rescind a contract containing a merger clause because of a misrepresentation, proof of a fraudulent misrepresentation must be shown. We find no merit in this argument.

If, as plaintiff concedes, a merger clause, such as is found within the sales contract now before us, will not prevent a rescission based on a fraudulent misrepresentation,[1] there is no valid reason to say that it will prevent a rescission of an agreement which is the result of a false though innocent misrepresentation where both innocent and fraudulent misrepresentations render a contract voidable. See Restatement of Contracts, § 476. As we observed before, the availability of the remedy of rescission is motivated by the obvious inequity of allowing a person who has made the

---

1. In Bloomberg v. Pugh Bros. Co., 45 R.I. 360, 121 A. 430, the contract contained a merger clause similar to the one before us. Such a provision, this court said, would not bar the introduction of evidence designed to show that the contract had been procured by fraud.

innocent misrepresentation to retain the fruits of the bargain induced thereby. If we are to permit a party to rescind a contract which is the result of an innocent misrepresentation, the "boiler plate" found in the merger clause shall not bar the use of this remedy.

. . .

Before leaving this phase of plaintiff's appeal, we think it appropriate that we allude to the tendency of many courts to equate an innocent misrepresentation with some species of fraud. Usually the word "fraud" connotes a conscious dishonest conduct on the part of the misrepresenter. Fraud, however, is not present if the speaker actually believes that what he states as the truth is the truth. We believe that it would be better if an innocent misrepresentation was not described as some specie of fraud. Unqualified statements imply certainty. Reliance is more likely to be placed on a positive statement of fact than a mere expression of opinion or a qualified statement. The speaker who uses the unqualified statement does so at his peril. The risk of falsity is his. If he is to be liable for what he states, the liability is imposed because he is to be held strictly accountable for his words. Responsibility for an innocent misrepresentation should be recognized for what it is—an example of absolute liability rather than as many courts have said, an example of constructive fraud.

. . .

The plaintiff states that the trial judge should have instructed the jury that misrepresentations had to be proved by "clear and convincing evidence" and not by a "preponderance of the evidence" as they were charged. We disagree. Long ago in Smith v. Rhode Island Co., 39 R.I. 146, 98 A. 1, we stated in clear and express language that fraud must be proved by a preponderance of the evidence, and there is no reason why we should require a higher degree of proof when the good faith of the misrepresenter is unquestioned.

The plaintiff complains that the trial justice erred when he told the jury that defendant could recover even though he might have been "negligent" in signing the sales agreement.[2] The thrust of this objection is plaintiff's contention that either defendant's neglect to include in the contract a clause which would have protected his interest in the event termites were found on the property or his failure to have the premises inspected for termites prevent his recovery of the deposit. Such an argument is really aimed at the question of whether or not defendant was justified in relying on the representations made by plaintiff and her agent. We can see nothing patently absurd or ridiculous in the statements attributed to them which would warrant us in saying that defendant should be denied relief because of his failure to do what plaintiff now says he

2. The plaintiff concedes that this court has permitted the victim of an intentional misrepresentation to recover even though he had failed to make any investigation into the truth or falsity of the statements made to him.

should have done. On the record before us, defendant was amply justified in believing that the home he was purchasing was free of termites.

. . .

The appeal of the plaintiff is denied.

QUESTIONS AND NOTES

1. Assume that defendant paid the full purchase price and moved into the house before discovering the presence of termites. At this point it would have been quite burdensome for defendant to rescind the contract and give up the house. Could defendant elect to keep the house and recover damages representing the out-of-pocket loss caused by the misrepresentation: the contract price ($54,000) less the actual value of the house ($35,000)?

2. The requirement that the defendant make a statement of fact either with knowledge that it is false or without any basis for believing it to be true is frequently referred to as a requirement of scienter. The availability of relief for misrepresentation originated in courts of equity, which were willing to grant rescission and restitution without proof of scienter. Courts of law have generally followed the equity courts in granting rescission in the absence of scienter.

3. The opinion in *Halpert* suggests one answer to Question 1 supra. Pumphrey v. Quillen, 135 N.E.2d 328 (Ohio 1956), suggests another. Plaintiffs purchased a house after their broker told them the walls were constructed of tile. In fact, the walls were constructed of earth, clay, and straw, with a thin veneer of ersatz tile. Plaintiffs sought damages from the sellers and the broker, among others. The trial court gave judgment for plaintiffs against the broker but not against the sellers. The broker appealed. The intermediate court of appeals affirmed, stating:

> While the law in this state, governing actions in deceit, is by no means clearly settled, yet, there may be found, in the Supreme Court decisions, a tendency to treat the necessary element of intent, or, in other language, *scienter*, as an intent to deceive, to mislead, to convey a false impression. Obviously, this must be a matter of belief or of absence of belief that the representation is true. The state of the speaker's mind must be inquired into in determining whether an action of deceit can be maintained. The required intent is indeed present in cases where the speaker believed his statement to be false, as also in cases where the representation is made without any belief whatsoever of its truth or falsity.

> Most courts in this country have gone further and held that, where representations are made by a person who is conscious that he has no sufficient basis of information to justify them, he may be culpably liable in an action in deceit. When one asserts a fact as of his own knowledge, or so positively as to imply that he has knowledge, when he knows that he has not sufficient information to justify it, he may be found to have the intent to deceive.

141 N.E.2d 675 (Ohio App.1955).

The Supreme Court of Ohio also affirmed, but not without dissent:

TAFT, JUDGE (dissenting).

In my opinion, this decision . . . represents a radical departure from previous pronouncements of this court with respect to the necessity of scienter in an action for deceit.

As appears from plaintiffs' petition, the alleged representation of defendant Taylor relied upon by plaintiffs was "that the outside walls of said house were of tile construction." That they were not of such construction appears from the allegations of the petition as to the manner of their construction which allegations are quoted in the majority opinion.

As indicated by the syllabus in the instant case, defendant Taylor did not know that his representation as to "tile construction" was false. On the evidence in the record, reasonable minds could reach no other conclusion.

This house had been built by a man named Rogers in 1939. In 1946, it was purchased by a man named Mack who thought its walls were constructed of tile and who did not learn of its peculiar type of construction until he had lived in it for several months and then not from any examination or discovery but only by being informed by neighbors who had seen it built. In 1950, Mack applied Perma–Stone to the exterior walls below the roof line. In 1952, the Quillens, who are codefendants with Taylor, acquired the house from Mack, who did not tell them about its peculiar type of construction. The Quillens, as well as the real estate man who represented Mack in selling the house to them and who was a builder, believed that the house was of masonry construction. The Quillens listed the house for sale with a real estate man named Force who is also a codefendant. Defendant Taylor learned of the availability of the Quillen property through the Akron Real Estate Board multiple listing arrangement. Defendant Taylor obtained permission from Force to show the property to the plaintiffs. An appraiser examined the property for his bank and reported it as a masonry building; and a loan in a substantial amount was granted to plaintiffs on the basis of that appraisal. There is no evidence that anyone who had any contact with the house after Mack had disposed of it, either as an owner, a real estate salesman, an appraiser or in any other capacity, even suspected the true nature of its construction until February 1953 when plaintiffs removed the wall boards in the attic and drilled one-inch holes through the exterior walls. This was after plaintiffs had lived in the house for over six months. Even plaintiffs' building expert admitted on cross-examination that, if he had examined the property before those wall boards had been pulled down, he would have assumed the building to be of masonry construction.

The "rule" quoted in the majority opinion from American Jurisprudence is by its words to apply only "when in fact he [the maker of a false statement] has no knowledge as to whether his assertion is true or false," a situation wholly different from that in the instant case where defendant Taylor believed as everyone else did that this building was of masonry construction.

. . . In 23 American Jurisprudence 910, Section 122, it is said:

> The rule is well settled * * * in a majority of American jurisdictions and in the English courts, that in a law action of deceit in tort scienter must be established. Scienter, a term usually employed in legal issues involving fraud, means knowledge on the part of a person making representations, at the time when they are made, that they are false.

Ohio has always followed the majority rule. See 19 Ohio Jurisprudence 368, Section 67. . . .

If, in the instant case, plaintiffs had sought to rescind the transaction of sale and give back title to the purchased property in exchange for what they had paid the Quillens for it, then they might be entitled to such relief against the Quillens even though the Quillens did not know about the alleged untrue representation by Taylor. If it was only because of that representation that the Quillens received the substantial price paid them by plaintiffs for this property, equity might well prevent such enrichment of them at plaintiffs' expense by decreeing rescission of the transaction of sale.

Also, if this were an action merely to "recover back * * * the price paid for" this house from the Quillens to whom it was paid, perhaps the same reasons which justify having no requirement of proof of *scienter* in rescission actions (i.e., prevention of unjust enrichment) might support such relief at law against the Quillens. However, defendant Taylor never received any such purchase price from plaintiffs. He only received, as his commission one-half of the five per cent real estate commission paid. In the absence of proof of *scienter*, it is difficult to justify any relief against him by way of recovery from him of more than he received out of the transaction. Bohlen, Misrepresentation as Deceit, Negligence, or Warranty, 42 Harvard Law Review, 733, 746.

In the instant case, the majority opinion apparently recognizes the following anomalous situation as being reasonable and in accordance with the law of this state:

Q owns a house having no value. He employs T to sell it for him. T represents to P that the house is of masonry construction. If it were, it would be worth $8,000. In reliance on that representation, P pays Q $8,000 for the house and Q pays T a commission of $200. Thus Q gets $7,800 for nothing. Under the decision of this court, Q is allowed to keep the $7,800 and P gets his $8,000 back from T who had received only $200 out of the transaction and did not know that his representation was not true.

135 N.E.2d at 332–35.

a.   In many jurisdictions the plaintiff must prove scienter before he or she can recover damages. In a substantial number of states, however, scienter is not necessary. The Restatement (Second) of Torts section 552C adopts the latter position:

552C.   Misrepresentation in Sale, Rental or Exchange Transaction

(1) One who, in a sale, rental or exchange transaction with another, makes a misrepresentation of a material fact for the purpose of inducing the other to act or to refrain from action in reliance upon it, is subject to liability to the other for the harm caused by his justifiable reliance upon the misrepresentation, even though it is made without knowledge of its falsity or negligence.

(2) Damages recoverable . . . are limited to the difference between the value of what the other has parted with and the value of what he has received in the transaction.

b.   Is the position taken by section 552C desirable: why should a person who innocently and even non-negligently makes a false statement have to pay substantial damages?

c.   Under the dissent's view, that scienter is necessary unless the plaintiff merely seeks to rescind the contract, should plaintiff in *Pumphrey* be able to rescind?

d.   Under the hypothetical at the very end of the dissenting opinion, is it reasonable and fair for T, a real estate agent, to be liable for $8,000? Is it more or less reasonable and fair to hold T liable if T is the agent of Q rather than P? What if P sought rescission of the contract instead of damages?

4.   The parol evidence rule bars enforcement of prior or contemporaneous agreements that add to, vary, or contradict the terms of a writing that the parties intend to embody their entire agreement. The rule does not, however, prevent rescission of agreements procured by fraud. Why not? And why does the court in *Halpert* extend the fraud exception to this case of innocent misrepresentation? Should it matter whether the consumer seeks damages rather than rescission?

In Eicher v. Mid America Financial Investment Corp., 702 N.W.2d 792 (Neb.2005), defendants told plaintiffs, whose homes were in foreclosure, that they would loan plaintiffs the funds necessary to enable them to keep their homes. The documents presented for signature, however, provided for conveyance of title to the homes. When plaintiffs sought to rescind, defendants asserted the rule that one is bound by what he signs, whether or not he has read it. The court held that this rule "applies only in the absence of fraud" and affirmed the trial court's judgment granting rescission of the sales.

For extensive discussion of the parol evidence rule in the context of consumer transactions, see Broude, The Consumer and the Parol Evidence Rule: Section 2–202 of the Uniform Commercial Code, 1970 Duke L.J. 881;

see also Sweet, Promissory Fraud and the Parol Evidence Rule, 49 Cal. L.Rev. 877 (1960).

5. In each of the preceding cases, one of the parties made a false representation. What if the seller of a house with a leaky basement says nothing about the leakage or the watertightness of the basement but paints the basement walls, thereby eliminating the tell-tale lines? See Russow v. Bobola, 277 N.E.2d 769 (Ill.App.1972); Allred v. Demuth, 890 S.W.2d 578 (Ark.1994). See also Campbell v. Booth, 526 S.W.2d 167 (Tex.Civ.App.1975) (seller of house used deodorizers and scented candles to conceal odor of dog urine that permeated the carpeting throughout the house); VanBooven v. Smull, 938 S.W.2d 324 (Mo.App.1997) (similar).

6. What if the seller does nothing whatsoever to conceal any facts, but simply remains silent about a material fact? A frequently litigated example of this is termite infestation: should the seller of a house be obliged to inform a prospective buyer that the house is infested? Cf. Swinton v. Whitinsville Savings Bank, 42 N.E.2d 808 (Mass.1942) (no) with Obde v. Schlemeyer, 353 P.2d 672 (Wash.1960) (yes).

Ollerman v. O'Rourke Co., Inc.

Supreme Court of Wisconsin, 1980
94 Wis.2d 17, 288 N.W.2d 95.

ABRAHAMSON, JUSTICE.

[Plaintiff's complaint alleged that, for $12,600, defendant developer sold him a vacant lot for the purpose of building a home. Beneath the surface of the land was a well, the existence of which was not apparent on the surface. Plaintiff alleged that defendant knew of the well but failed to disclose its existence to plaintiff. Excavation for plaintiff's house uncapped the well and released a large quantity of water. After spending $2,700 to recap the well and $10,500 for increased construction expenses, plaintiff sued for damages for defendant's failure to disclose the presence of the well. Defendant moved to dismiss the complaint for failure to state a claim. The trial court overruled the motion, and defendant appealed.]

. . . [T]he complaint recites that the seller failed to disclose a fact, the existence of the well. The general rule is that silence, a failure to disclose a fact, is not an intentional misrepresentation unless the seller has a duty to disclose. If there is a duty to disclose a fact, failure to disclose that fact is treated in the law as equivalent to a representation of the non-existence of the fact. . . .

The question thus presented in the case at bar is whether the seller had a duty to disclose to the buyer the existence of the well. If there is a duty to disclose, the seller incurs tort liability for intentional misrepresentation (i.e. the representation of the non-existence of the fact), if the elements of the tort of intentional misrepresentation are proved. . . .

We recognize that the traditional rule in Wisconsin is that in an action for intentional misrepresentation the seller of real estate, dealing at arm's length with the buyer, has no duty to disclose information to the buyer and therefore has no liability in an action for intentional misrepresentation for failure to disclose.

The traditional legal rule that there is no duty to disclose in an arm's-length transaction is part of the common law doctrine of caveat emptor which is traced to the attitude of rugged individualism reflected in the business economy and the law of the 19th century. The law of misrepresentation has traditionally been closely aligned with mores of the commercial world because the type of interest protected by the law of misrepresentation in business transactions is the interest in formulating business judgments without being misled by others—that is, an interest in not being cheated.

Under the doctrine of caveat emptor no person was required to tell all that he or she knew in a business transaction, for in a free market the diligent should not be deprived of the fruits of superior skill and knowledge lawfully acquired. The business world, and the law reflecting business mores and morals, required the parties to a transaction to use their faculties and exercise ordinary business sense, and not to call on the law to stand *in loco parentis* to protect them in their ordinary dealings with other business people.

"The picture in sales and in land deals is, in the beginning, that of a community whose trade is simple and face to face and whose traders are neighbors. The goods and the land were there to be seen during the negotiation and particularly in the case of land, everybody knew everybody's land; if not, trade was an arm's length proposition with wits matched against skill. Of course caveat emptor would be the rule in such a society. But caveat emptor was more than a rule of no liability; it was a philosophy that left each individual to his own devices with a minimum of public imposition of standards of fair practice. In the beginning the common law did grant relief from fraud and did recognize that if the seller made an express promise as to his product at the time of the sale he remained liable after the sale on this 'collateral' promise. Indeed covenants for title in the deed were such collateral promises which survived the sale." Dunham, Vendor's Obligation as to Fitness of Land for a Particular Purpose, 37 Minn.L.R. 108, 110 (1953).

Over the years society's attitudes toward good faith and fair dealing in business transactions have undergone significant change, and this change has been reflected in the law. Courts have departed from or relaxed the "no duty to disclose" rule by carving out exceptions to the rule and by refusing to adhere to the rule when it works an injustice. Thus courts have held that the rule does not apply where the seller actively conceals a defect or where he prevents investigation; where the seller has told a half-truth or has made an ambiguous statement if the seller's intent is to create a false impression and he does so; where there is a fiduciary relationship between the parties; or where the facts are peculiarly and exclusively within the knowledge of one party to the transaction and the other party is not in a position to discover the facts for himself.

On the basis of the complaint, the case at bar does not appear to fall into one of these well-recognized exceptions to the "no duty to disclose" rule. However, Dean Prosser has found a "rather amorphous tendency on the part of most courts toward finding a duty of disclosure in cases where the defendant has special knowledge or means of knowledge not open to the plaintiff and is aware that the plaintiff is acting under a misapprehension as to facts which could be of importance to him, and would probably affect his decision."[15]

Dean Keeton described these cases abandoning the "no duty to disclose" rule as follows:

"In the present stage of the law, the decisions show a drawing away from this idea [that nondisclosure is not actionable], and there can be seen an attempt by many courts to reach a just result in so far as possible, but yet maintaining the degree of certainty which the law must have. The statement may often be found that if either party to a contract of sale conceals or suppresses a material fact which he is in good faith bound to disclose then his silence is fraudulent.

"The attitude of the courts toward nondisclosure is undergoing a change and . . . it would seem that the object of the law in these cases should be to impose on parties to the transaction a duty to speak whenever justice, equity, and fair dealing demand it. This statement is made only with reference to instances where the party to be charged is an actor in the transaction. This duty to speak does not result from an implied representation by silence, but exists because a refusal to speak constitutes unfair conduct." Fraud—Concealment and Nondisclosure, 15 Tex.L.Rev. 1, 31 (1936).

The test Dean Keeton derives from the cases to determine when the rule of nondisclosure should be abandoned—that is, "whenever justice, equity and fair dealing demand it"—presents, as one writer states, "a somewhat nebulous standard, praiseworthy as looking toward more stringent business ethics, but possibly difficult of practical application." Case Note, Silence as Fraudulent Concealment—Vendor & Purchaser—Duty to Disclose, 36 Wash.L.Rev. 202, 204 (1961).

. . .

An analysis of the cases of this jurisdiction and others indicates that the presence of the following elements is significant to persuade a court of the fairness and equity of imposing a duty on a vendor of real estate to disclose known facts: the condition is "latent" and not readily observable by the purchaser; the purchaser acts upon the reasonable assumption that the condition does (or does not) exist; the vendor has special knowledge or means of knowledge not available to the purchaser; and the existence of the

---

15. Prosser, Law of Torts 697 (1971).

condition is material to the transaction, that is, it influences whether the transaction is concluded at all or at the same price.

The seller argues that public policy demands that we not abandon the traditional rule that no action lies against the seller of real estate for failure to disclose in an arm's-length transaction. The seller contends, in its brief, that if this court affirms the circuit court's order overruling the motion to dismiss and allows the buyer to proceed to trial, the court is adopting "what really amounts to a strict policy of 'let the seller beware.' " The seller goes on to state, "Woe indeed to anyone who sells a home, a vacant lot or other piece of real estate and fails to itemize with particularity or give written notice to each prospective buyer of every conceivable condition in and around the property, regardless of whether such a condition is dangerous, defective or could become so by the negligence or recklessness of others. A seller of real estate is not and should not be made an insurer or guarantor of the competence of those with whom the purchaser may later contract."

The seller's position is that imposing a duty to disclose on a vendor of real estate dealing at arm's length with a purchaser would result in an element of uncertainty pervading real estate transactions; that there would be chaos if a vendor were subject to liability after parting with ownership and control of the property; that a rash of litigation would ensue; and that a purchaser could protect himself or herself by inspection and inquiry and by demanding warranties.

The seller's arguments are not persuasive in light of the facts alleged in the complaint and our narrow holding in this case.

Where the vendor is in the real estate business and is skilled and knowledgeable and the purchaser is not, the purchaser is in a poor position to discover a condition which is not readily discernible, and the purchaser may justifiably rely on the knowledge and skill of the vendor. Thus, in this instant case a strong argument for imposing a duty on the seller to disclose material facts is this "reliance factor." The buyer portrayed in this complaint had a reasonable expectation of honesty in the marketplace, that is, that the vendor would disclose material facts which it knew and which were not readily discernible. Under these circumstances the law should impose a duty of honesty on the seller.

In order to determine whether the complaint in the case at bar states a claim for intentional misrepresentation, we hold that a subdivider-vendor of a residential lot has a duty to a "non-commercial" purchaser to disclose facts which are known to the vendor, which are material to the transaction, and which are not readily discernible to the purchaser. A fact is known to the vendor if the vendor has actual knowledge of the fact or if the vendor acted in reckless disregard as to the existence of the fact. This usage of the word "know" is the same as in an action for intentional misrepresentation based on a false statement. A fact is material if a reasonable purchaser would attach importance to its existence or nonexistence in determining the choice of action in the transaction in question; or if the vendor knows or has reason to know that the purchaser regards or is likely to regard the matter as important in determining the choice of action, although a reasonable purchaser would not so regard it. See 3 Restatement (Second) of Torts, sec. 538 (1977). Whether the fact is or is not readily discernible will depend on the nature of the fact, the relation of the vendor and purchaser and the nature of the transaction.

The seller's brief asserts that the well is not a material fact because it does not constitute a defective condition; that the existence of the well was well known in the community; and that the buyer should have made inquiry about the lot. These are matters to be raised at trial, not on a motion to dismiss. The buyer must prove at trial that the existence of the well was a material fact and that his reliance was justifiable.

. . .

QUESTIONS AND NOTES

1. Three months after deciding *Ollerman*, the Supreme Court of Wisconsin decided a case in which the purchasers of a house sued the sellers to recover damages for the sellers' failure to disclose what the purchasers described in their complaint as a "serious water leakage problem." The trial court granted the sellers' motion for summary judgment and dismissed the buyers' complaint. The buyers appealed. The Supreme Court cited *Ollerman* but affirmed the trial court. Is this decision consistent with *Ollerman*?

2. In Blaine v. J.E. Jones Construction Co., 841 S.W.2d 703 (Mo.Ct.App. 1992), the Jones Company developed a residential subdivision and sold single-family homes in it without disclosing that it intended to build a 150–unit apartment complex and six acres of commercial buildings at the entrance to the subdivision. Plaintiffs, who purchased the homes, sued the developer and the real estate company that acted as its sales agent. The trial court dismissed the claims against the real estate company and entered judgment on a verdict against the developer. The appellate court held that neither the real estate company nor the developer was liable:

> The formula developed by our courts to determine when to impose a duty to disclose on the seller in the marketplace is a not surprising formula that weighs significant factors. The formula is designed to set an operable standard of fair conduct in the marketplace. The list of factors is open-ended. Our courts, however, emphasize the relative intelligence of the parties to the transaction, the relation the parties bear to each other, the nature of the fact not disclosed, the nature of the contract, whether the concealer is a buyer or seller, the importance of the fact not disclosed and the respective knowledge and means of acquiring knowledge of the parties. These factors are articulated as separate factors for analytical purposes; in fact, they are interrelated and overlap.
>
> For the purpose of our discussion, we have assumed, without deciding, that the Jones Company did intend to build apartments when

plaintiffs purchased their homes; therefore, it did have superior knowledge of this fact. Nonetheless, we still find it had no duty to disclose that fact.

First, there is no indication that any party's intelligence was superior to another. Plaintiffs were college educated. Second, the parties did not bear any special relation to each other beyond their status as buyer and seller. There was no evidence that a confidential relationship of any sort developed between the parties or that the parties were in a fiduciary relationship, such as executor and beneficiary of an estate, or attorney and client. The existence of such a relationship makes it more likely that a duty to disclose would be found. However, here the transactions at issue were the normal arm's length sales of homes.

Third, the nature of the fact not disclosed is an extrinsic fact, not an intrinsic defect. In sales contracts, if the vendor conceals an intrinsic defect not discoverable by reasonable care, there is a greater likelihood that a duty to disclose will be found than if the fact is something extrinsic to the property likely to affect market value. The intent to build apartments in the future is not a defect in plaintiffs' houses which is not discoverable by reasonable care, rather, the intent is a fact that normally can be ascertained by reasonable inquiry. And, as will be explained in detail under the sixth factor, "materiality," the alleged false representations allegedly made by the Jones Company or its agent Gundaker [are] not relevant to the Jones Company's passive nondisclosure.

Fourth, the contract is an arm's length sales contract for property, it is not a release or contract of insurance where arguably, all material facts must be disclosed. Fifth, the concealer in this case is a seller. A seller is more likely to have a duty to disclose than a buyer.

The sixth factor is the importance or materiality of the fact not disclosed. Admittedly, a developer's intent to build apartments on nearby property could have an effect on a reasonable buyer's decision to buy a house, and, thus, intent is an important fact. However, the significance of this fact is lessened by its extrinsic nature. The fact may affect the market value of the house, but is not a defect in the house itself. Moreover, the Jones Company's intent to build apartments was a decision about the use of land zoned multi-family which could have changed at any time. . . . Furthermore, a developer could reasonably expect that a potential buyer would inquire about the zoning of his and nearby undeveloped property, as well as potential uses for the undeveloped property.

. . .

Finally, the seventh factor is the respective knowledge of the parties of the fact and their means of acquiring this knowledge. There is no question in this case that the existence of multi-family zoning and a proposed layout of the multi-family buildings were a part of the public record. . . .

. . . [T]he public disclosure of zoning for multi-family units puts a reasonable purchaser of a house in close proximity on notice to inquire about the type of multi-family units to be built.

The fact the Jones Company or its agent allegedly responded with false representations may be the factual basis for fraud based upon false representation. It is not, however, a factual basis for nor relevant to the imposition of a naked duty to disclose on the Jones Company. Plaintiffs abandoned the former theory and chose to proceed on the latter theory. The irrelevancy of the testified to false representations is exemplified in and demonstrated by plaintiffs' respective verdict directing instruction. Under those instructions, the jury could have disbelieved that any false representations were made and still found for plaintiffs merely by finding the Jones Company or its agent, Gundaker, failed to disclose the intent to build an apartment complex.

It is clear then that the respective knowledge of each party and the means of acquiring of this knowledge was not unbalanced or unfair. The zoning information was available and within the reasonable reach of the plaintiffs. It is true that public record of an undisclosed fact may not necessarily negate a party's duty to disclose, however, reasonable availability of the fact to the party claiming fraudulent disclosure still remains a factor in the analysis.

Quite simply, the undisclosed fact in this case, the Jones Company's intent, should not trigger a duty to disclose. The undisclosed fact was not an intrinsic defect not discoverable by reasonable care; rather, it was, under plaintiffs' chosen theory, an extrinsic fact which was discoverable by reasonable inquiry.

A developer in the marketplace should not be saddled with the duty to disclose that, as one of the available options under multi-family zoning, he intends to build apartments. The Jones Company, as any other developer, could assume, quite sensibly and rationally, that a buyer would check the public record or ask the developer or its agent to acquire information about the zoning of his and nearby property. It is not unreasonable for an innocent developer with no intent to deceive to believe that the disclosure of multi-family zoning is sufficient notice to a rational buyer of a house near a then undeveloped multi-family zone.

In addition, a developer's decision about developing is not absolute but can and probably will change depending on the marketplace. To saddle a developer with an affirmative duty to disclose these decisions as they vary would act as a straight jacket that the marketplace does not need.

Compare Strawn v. Canuso, 657 A.2d 420 (N.J.1995), in which the New Jersey Supreme Court held that a developer may have a duty to disclose that its homes have been constructed near an abandoned hazardous waste dump. The court wrote:

> In the absence of such legislation or other regulatory requirements affecting real estate brokers, the question is whether our common-law precedent would require disclosure of off-site conditions that materially affect the value of property. [Precedent] establishes that a seller of real estate or a broker representing the seller would be liable for nondisclosure of on-site defective conditions if those conditions were known to them and unknown and not readily observable by the buyer. Such conditions, for example, would include radon contamination and a polluted water supply. Whether and to what extent we should extend this duty to off-site conditions depends on an assessment of the various policies that have shaped the development of our law in this area.

> As noted, the principal factors shaping the duty to disclose have been the difference in bargaining power between the professional seller of residential real estate and the purchaser of such housing, and the difference in access to information between the seller and the buyer. Those principles guide our decision in this case.

> The first factor causes us to limit our holding to professional sellers of residential housing (persons engaged in the business of building or developing residential housing) and the brokers representing them. Neither the reseller of residential real estate nor the seller of commercial property has that same advantage in the bargaining process. Regarding the second factor, professional sellers of residential housing and their brokers enjoy markedly superior access to information. Hence, we believe that it is reasonable to extend to such professionals a similar duty to disclose off-site conditions that materially affect the value or desirability of the property.

>   . . .

> The duty that we recognize is not unlimited. We do not hold that sellers and brokers have a duty to investigate or disclose transient social conditions in the community that arguably affect the value of property. In the absence of a purchaser communicating specific needs, builders and brokers should not be held to decide whether the changing nature of a neighborhood, the presence of a group home, or the existence of a school in decline are facts material to the transaction. Rather, we root in the land the duty to disclose off-site conditions that are material to the transaction. That duty is consistent with the development of our law and supported by statutory policy.

> We hold that a builder-developer of residential real estate or a broker representing it is not only liable to a purchaser for affirmative and intentional misrepresentation, but is also liable for nondisclosure of off-site physical conditions known to it and unknown and not readily observable by the buyer if the existence of those conditions is of sufficient materiality to affect the habitability, use, or enjoyment of the property and, therefore, render the property substantially less desir-

able or valuable to the objectively reasonable buyer. Whether a matter not disclosed by such a builder or broker is of such materiality, and unknown and unobservable by the buyer, will depend on the facts of each case.

. . .

Ultimately, a jury will decide whether the presence of a landfill is a factor that materially affects the value of property; whether the presence of a landfill was known by defendants and not known or readily observable by plaintiffs; and whether the presence of a landfill has indeed affected the value of plaintiffs' property. Location is the universal benchmark of the value and desirability of property. Over time the market value of the property will reflect the presence of the landfill. Professional builders and their brokers have a level of sophistication that most home buyers lack. That sophistication enables them better to assess the marketability of properties near conditions such as a landfill, a planned superhighway, or an office complex approved for construction. With that superior knowledge, such sellers have a duty to disclose to home buyers the location of off-site physical conditions that an objectively reasonable and informed buyer would deem material to the transaction, in the sense that the conditions substantially affect the value or desirability of the property.

Should it be actionable for a seller to fail to disclose that her house is located in a flood plain? If she does disclose this fact, should it be actionable for her to fail to disclose that the municipal code prohibits expanding the house?

3. Problem. *Consumer* purchases a house from *Seller*. Neither *Seller* nor *Seller's* real estate agent informs *Consumer* that ten years earlier the owner of the house and her four children were murdered there. After *Consumer* moves in, one of her new neighbors tells her of the grisly event. *Consumer* comes to you for advice. Under the standard of *Ollerman*, if she can prove that the market value of the property is 10% less than it would have been if it had not been the site of a mass murder, should she be entitled to rescission? to damages?

If you believe that *Consumer* should be entitled to relief, is it essential that she establish an adverse impact on the market value of the house: should it suffice if she is emotionally distraught and completely unable to continue living there?

What if *Seller* has left the state and cannot be located: is *Seller's* real estate agent liable?

4. In Bramlett v. Adamson Ford, 717 So.2d 772 (Ala.Civ.App.1996), plaintiff sued Adamson Ford and Ford Motor Credit Company for failing to disclose that when FMCC purchased Bramlett's contract from Adamson, it allowed Adamson to receive a portion of the 15.49% interest rate. The court wrote:

Viewed most favorably to Bramlett, the evidence shows that Bramlett negotiated the purchase of an automobile at Adamson. FMCC and Adamson had a mutual agreement whereby Adamson received a 3% commission on all financing contracts it obtained for FMCC. Bramlett was experienced in the purchase and financing of automobiles. After Bramlett made his selection, an agent of Adamson told Bramlett that Adamson would get the best financing available. The agent disclosed the financing rate and cost of financing the purchase to Bramlett; however, the agent did not disclose Adamson's agreement with FMCC or the amount of the 3% commission.

When Bramlett asked why the cost of financing was so high, the agent informed him that the high cost was because Bramlett was a poor credit risk. At the time the agent made this representation to Bramlett, Adamson intended to finance Bramlett's purchase through FMCC under its agreement with FMCC. The financing contract was prepared by FMCC and executed on FMCC forms. Although the 3% commission was disclosed in the financing documentation between Adamson and FMCC, it was not disclosed in the financing documentation provided to Bramlett.

Bramlett argues that Adamson and FMCC fraudulently suppressed the 3% commission agreement between them because, he says, the commission resulted in a higher interest rate to Bramlett. Bramlett testified that had he known of the commission, he would have obtained financing elsewhere. Bramlett further argues that he was defrauded because he justifiably relied on Adamson's agent's representation that he would obtain the best financing available. Bramlett argues that Adamson and FMCC conspired to defraud him, and he asserts that the contract he signed was unconscionable.

. . .

A. Suppression

. . .

Under the facts of the present case, we do not address whether Adamson had a duty to disclose the commission in the absence of any inquiry. We hold that Bramlett's inquiry as to why the finance charge was so high is substantial evidence from which the trier of fact could infer that Adamson had a duty to disclose the full nature of Adamson's commission agreement with FMCC. A duty to disclose can arise from a request for information. One who responds to an inquiry has the duty to speak the entire truth.

Bramlett's request why the financing rate was so high is substantial evidence from which a reasonable person could infer that Adamson had a duty to disclose its commission arrangement with FMCC. Moreover, FMCC's preparation of the loan documentation to prevent disclosure of the 3% commission to Bramlett raises a question of fact as to whether FMCC was a participant in the alleged suppression. Accordingly, the trial court's entry of summary judgment with respect to Bramlett's claim of fraudulent suppression is due to be reversed as to both Adamson and FMCC.

B.   Misrepresentation

As distinct from fraudulent suppression, fraud by misrepresentation requires that the plaintiff prove a false statement of a material fact that the plaintiff relied on to his detriment.

The evidence raises a question of fact about two representations: (1) after Bramlett agreed to purchase the automobile, Adamson Ford told him that they would obtain the best financing available, and (2) the reason Bramlett's financing rate was high was because of his credit history. These representations, taken together, support the inference that Adamson falsely assured Bramlett that he was getting the best financing contract available. Bramlett argues that he justifiably relied on these statements and obtained financing with Adamson Ford and FMCC, and as a result, Bramlett was damaged by paying a higher interest rate than he could have obtained elsewhere.

In light of the evidence of the agreement between FMCC and Adamson as to the 3% commission, reasonable persons could disagree as to whether Adamson obtained the best financing or simply acted to obtain the 3% commission by delivering the financing contract to FMCC. We conclude that there is a question of fact for the jury whether these representations by Adamson were false.

5.   Restatement (Second) of Torts section 551(1)* provides that nondisclosure in the context of a business transaction is actionable only if the silent party owes a duty to the other to use reasonable care to disclose the matter. In defining when a person has a duty to disclose, subsection (2) provides

(2) One party to a business transaction is under a duty to exercise reasonable care to disclose to the other before the transaction is consummated

. . .

(e) facts basic to the transaction, if he knows that the other is about to enter into it under a mistake as to them, and that the other, because of the relationship between them, the customs of the trade or other objective circumstances, would reasonably expect a disclosure of those facts.

The comments elaborate:

k.   Nondisclosure of basic facts. The rule stated in Subsection (1) reflects the traditional ethics of bargaining between adversaries, in the absence of any special reason for the application of a different rule. When the facts are patent, or when the plaintiff has equal opportunity for obtaining information that he may be expected to utilize if he cares to do so, or when the defendant has no reason to think that the plaintiff is acting under a misapprehension, there is no obligation to give aid to a bargaining antagonist by disclosing what the defendant has himself discovered. To a considerable extent, sanctioned by the customs and mores of the community, superior information and better business acumen are legitimate advantages, which lead to no liability. The defendant may reasonably expect the plaintiff to make his own investigation, draw his own conclusions and protect himself; and if the plaintiff is indolent, inexperienced or ignorant, or his judgment is bad, or he does not have access to adequate information, the defendant is under no obligation to make good his deficiencies. This is true, in general, when it is the buyer of land or chattels who has the better information and fails to disclose it. Somewhat less frequently, it may be true of the seller.

l.   The continuing development of modern business ethics has, however, limited to some extent this privilege to take advantage of ignorance. There are situations in which the defendant not only knows that his bargaining adversary is acting under a mistake basic to the transaction, but also knows that the adversary, by reason of the relation between them, the customs of the trade or other objective circumstances, is reasonably relying upon a disclosure of the unrevealed fact if it exists. In this type of case good faith and fair dealing may require a disclosure.

It is extremely difficult to be specific as to the factors that give rise to this known, and reasonable, expectation of disclosure. In general, the cases in which the rule stated in Clause (e) has been applied have been those in which the advantage taken of the plaintiff's ignorance is so shocking to the ethical sense of the community, and is so extreme and unfair, as to amount to a form of swindling, in which the plaintiff is led by appearances into a bargain that is a trap, of whose essence and substance he is unaware. In such a case, even in a tort action for deceit, the plaintiff is entitled to be compensated for the loss that he has sustained. Thus a seller who knows that his cattle are infected with tick fever or contagious abortion is not free to unload them on the buyer and take his money, when he knows that the buyer is unaware of the fact, could not easily discover it, would not dream of entering into the bargain if he knew and is relying upon the seller's good faith and common honesty to disclose any such fact if it is true.

There are indications, also, that with changing ethical attitudes in many fields of modern business, the concept of facts basic to the transaction may be expanding and the duty to use reasonable care to disclose the facts may be increasing somewhat. This Subsection is not intended to impede that development.

6.   For a misrepresentation to be actionable, the misrepresented fact must be material and the aggrieved party must reasonably rely on the misrepresentation. Should those elements be required also for actionable nondisclosure? Should they suffice, i.e. should there perhaps be a higher standard than materiality? In Williams v. Benson, 141 N.W.2d 650 (Mich.App.1966), one of the leading cases imposing liability for the failure of a home seller to disclose termite infestation, the court stated,

> . . . . we do not intend to impose liability where no knowledge has ever existed. Nor do we intend to make everyone an insurer of everything that is sold.
>
> Rather, we hold that where a vendor has knowledge of the past or present existence of an instrumentality of progressive destruction or substantial impairment, notwithstanding reason to believe that the progression has been halted, a duty to disclose the circumstances arises. . . . Silence as to the existence or pre-existence of . . . known instrumentalities of progressive destruction or substantial impairment, even absent specific inquiry, can create liability.

What is the court's standard for determining materiality? Restatement (Second) of Torts section 551 (note 5 supra) imposes liability for the failure to disclose "basic" facts. Comment *j* elaborates:

> Comment *j* provides:
>
> *j.* *"Facts basic to the transaction."* . . . . A basic fact is a fact that is assumed by the parties as a basis for the transaction itself. It is a fact that goes to the basis, or essence, of the transaction, and is an important part of the substance of what is bargained for or dealt with. Other facts may serve as important and persuasive inducements to enter into the transaction, but not go to its essence. These facts may be material, but they are not basic. If the parties expressly or impliedly place the risk as to the existence of a fact on one party or if the law places it there by custom or otherwise the other party has no duty of disclosure. (Compare Restatement, Second, Contracts [§§ 153–54].)

But see the last paragraph of comment *l* (Note 5 supra).

Under the standard of the Restatement (or of Williams v. Benson), how should the hypotheticals in Question 3 be resolved?

In an omitted passage, the court in *Ollerman* quoted extensively from Restatement section 551 and comments *j* and *l*, reproduced above. Is the decision in *Ollerman* consistent with comment *j*?

7. In all the materials thus far in this chapter, a seller made a misrepresentation directly to a consumer. But in the context of sales of used goods or houses, often the knowing misrepresentation is made to a prior owner of the property. For example, a car dealer may roll back an odometer and then sell the car to another dealer, which sells the car to a consumer. The second dealer who is ignorant of the rollback does not make a knowing misrepresentation to the consumer, nor does it knowingly fail to disclose a material fact. In these circumstances, can the consumer look to the first dealer? In Clark v. McDaniel, 546 N.W.2d 590 (Iowa 1996), a dealer welded the front of a 1989 Ford Taurus to the back of a 1986 Taurus and sold the vehicle as a 1989 Taurus without disclosing this fact. Sometime thereafter, the purchaser, still ignorant of the facts, sold the vehicle to the plaintiffs. When the purchasers discovered the true nature of the vehicle, they sued the dealer, which defended on the ground that they could not have relied on any misrepresentation or omission because he dealt only with the first purchaser. The court rejected the argument, citing section 533 of the Restatement (Second) of Torts (1977), which provides:

> The maker of a fraudulent misrepresentation is subject to liability for pecuniary loss to another who acts in justifiable reliance upon it if the misrepresentation, although not made directly to the other, is made to a third person and the maker intends or has reason to expect that its terms will be repeated or its substance communicated to the other, and that it will influence his conduct in the transaction or type of transaction involved.

The court stated,

> It is difficult to conceive of a commodity that is any more likely to involve knowledge by a seller that there is an especial likelihood that a misrepresentation will reach third persons and will influence their conduct than in the case of a motor vehicle. It is reasonable to charge a seller, especially a dealer in vehicles, with knowledge that his buyer will pass along information to a second buyer that has been provided by the original seller concerning such significant matters as [welding halves of two cars together] and as to the model year of the vehicle.

546 N.W.2d at 593–94.

8. Not all concur with the direction in which the foregoing materials point. In addition to *Blaine* (Question 2 supra), consider Johnson v. Davis, 480 So.2d 625 (Fla.1985). Prior to the closing of a transaction for the purchase of a house, the purchasers discovered that the roof leaked. Alleging that the sellers knew of the leak but failed to disclose it, they sought to rescind the contract and recover back their downpayment. The Supreme Court of Florida granted rescission, but not without dissent:

> I do not agree with the Court's belief that the distinction between nondisclosure and affirmative statement is weak or nonexistent. It is a distinction that we should take special care to emphasize and preserve. Imposition of liability for seller's nondisclosure of the condition of improvements to real property is the first step toward making the seller a guarantor of the good condition of the property. Ultimately this trend will significantly burden the alienability of property because sellers will have to worry about the possibility of catastrophic post-sale judgments for damages sought to pay for repairs. The trend will proceed somewhat as follows. At first, the cause of action will require proof of actual knowledge of the undisclosed defect on the part of the seller. But in many cases the courts will allow it to be shown by circumstantial evidence. Then a rule of constructive knowledge will develop, based on the reasoning that if the seller did not know of the defect, he should have known about it before attempting to sell the property. Thus the burden of inspection will shift from the buyer to

the seller. Ultimately the courts will be in the position of imposing implied warranties and guaranties on all sellers of real property.

Although as described in the majority opinion this change in the law sounds progressive, high-minded, and idealistic, it is in reality completely unnecessary. Prudent purchasers inspect property, with expert advice if necessary, before they agree to buy. Prudent lenders require inspections before agreeing to provide purchase money. Initial deposits of earnest money can be made with the agreement to purchase being conditional upon the favorable results of expert inspections. It is significant that in the present case the major portion of the purchase price was to be financed by the [sellers] who were to hold a mortgage on the property. If they had been knowingly trying to get rid of what they knew to be a defectively constructed house, it is unlikely that they would have been willing to lend $200,000 with the house in question as their only security.

In light of these views, you may not find it surprising that the Supreme Court of Alabama reversed the decision of court in Bramlett v. Adamson Ford (Question 4 supra), 717 So.2d 781 (Ala.1997) ("We decline to recognize a common law duty that would require the seller of a good or service, absent special circumstances, to reveal to its purchaser a detailed breakdown of how the seller derived the sales price of the good or service, including the amount of profit to be earned on the sale.")

9. As you might imagine, real estate agents were quite alarmed at the prospect of liability for failing to disclose facts concerning the property they were helping to sell. Under the rule of Easton v. Strassburger, 199 Cal.Rptr. 383 (Cal.App.1984), this alarm was quite real: the court in effect imposed on real estate agents a duty to inspect the property they were handling and disclose any material problems with it. Their response was to persuade the legislature to enact a statute requiring sellers to complete a detailed disclosure form. Cal.Civ. Code §§ 1102–1102.15. Another statute codifies the real estate agent's common law duty to inspect ("to conduct a reasonably competent and diligent visual inspection"), but it declares that the duty does not encompass "areas that are reasonably and normally inaccessible to such an inspection, nor an affirmative inspection of areas off the site of the subject property or public records or permits concerning the title or use of the property" (§§ 2079(a), 2079.3). Many states have followed California's lead and have enacted statutes mandating disclosure in real estate transactions. And in states in which there is no such statute, real estate agents often insist that sellers make similar disclosures anyway. In addition to mandating disclosure concerning numerous aspects of the property, the statutes also often foreclose liability for failing to disclose that the property was the site of a homicide, suicide, or other stigma. E.g., Mich. Comp. Laws § 339.2518.

10. Reconsider the traditional elements of deceit listed on page 7 supra. In light of the materials you have been reading, which of these elements does a plaintiff today have to establish to recover damages for misrepresentation?

Under the rules established by these cases for misrepresentation, what differences are there between the elements of misrepresentation and the elements of breach of express warranty? Have you changed your assessment of the comparative desirability of the two theories (Question 6, page 14 supra)?

Reconsider Question 1, page 30 supra: if the buyer in *Halpert* had already paid the $54,000 purchase price, could he recover the $19,000 loss on the theory of breach of express warranty? Although section 2–313 of the UCC applies only to transactions in goods, express warranties may arise in other kinds of transactions. For example, in Johnson v. Healy, 405 A.2d 54 (Conn.1978), the court held that the builder of a house expressly warranted the soundness of its construction. The builder therefore was liable for loss caused by unstable subsoil conditions.

Reconsider also Question 3(b), page 33 supra: if an innocent misrepresentation serves as the basis for express warranty, and therefore expectancy-based damages, why shouldn't it also serve as the basis for damages for the tort of misrepresentation?

11.   The Restatement (Second) of Torts section 525 provides:

> One who fraudulently makes a misrepresentation of fact, opinion, intention or law for the purpose of inducing another to act or to refrain from action in reliance upon it, is subject to liability to the other in deceit for pecuniary loss caused to him by his justifiable reliance upon the misrepresentation.

Which of the traditional elements of deceit are eliminated by this formulation? See also sections 537–38, 540–42. In addition to these sections dealing with deceit, the Restatement also contains provisions on concealment, nondisclosure, and innocent misrepresentation (sections 550, 551, 552C).

12.   For the position of the American Law Institute when the consumer seeks only rescission of the contract and restoration of the status quo ante, see Restatement (Second) of Contracts sections 160 (concealment), 161 (nondisclosure), and 164(1) (misrepresentation) ("If a party's manifestation of assent is induced by *either* a fraudulent *or* a material misrepresentation by the other party upon which the recipient is justified in relying, the contract is voidable by the recipient") (emphasis added).

Davey v. Brownson

Court of Appeals of Washington, 1970.
3 Wn.App. 820, 478 P.2d 258.

GREEN, J.

[Plaintiff purchased a motel from defendant, making a down payment of $13,000. After paying installments totaling $3500, plaintiff discovered termites. Plaintiff sued for rescission on grounds of fraud, later amending her complaint to allege mutual mistake. The trial court granted rescission and ordered defendant to return the down payment, but allowed defendant to retain the installment payments. Defendant appealed].

. . .

The trial court, in essence, found the parties contracted for the purchase and sale of a motel in sound condition, free of latent defects such as termite infestation; the defendant would not have sold nor plaintiff purchased the motel if the true condition had been known; all parties were operating under a mutual mistake and without full knowledge of the actual condition of the property; plaintiff was not negligent in failing to discover the true condition since only an expert could have done so; defendant was not guilty of any fraud or intentional misleading of plaintiff, although defendant had implied notice of dry rot; the latent defect of termite infestation requiring structural repairs went to the essence of the contract—a motel in a basically sound condition; and the contract should be canceled and the loss apportioned between the parties. The first thirteen errors assigned by defendant are directed to these findings and conclusions, contending they are not in accordance with the evidence or the law.

. . .

. . . It seems evident, as the trial court concluded, the parties both bargained for a motel in fair-to-good condition and structurally sound. The contemplated upgrading was in terms of cleaning, painting and minor repairs. It is clear the parties were mistaken when it was discovered the motel was extensively infested with termites. Senske, the expert, testified termite infestation would not be discovered by a layman on reasonable inspection because of its concealment. Since this condition went to the very heart of the subject matter of the transaction, we believe the trial court properly granted rescission.

In Lindeberg v. Murray, 117 Wash. 483, at 495, 201 P. 759, at 763 (1921), the court said:

> We think it is elementary that, where there is a clear *bona fide* mistake regarding material facts, without culpable negligence on the part of the person complaining, the contract may be avoided, and equity will decree a rescission. We take it that the true test in cases involving mutual mistake of fact is whether the contract would have been entered into had there been no mistake. Stahl v. Schwartz, 67 Wash. 25, 120 P. 856; 10 R.C.L. 296–299. We are clear that there was such a mistake here. . . . The evidence leaves no doubt plaintiff would not have purchased the motel had she known of the termite condition.

Because neither plaintiff nor defendant had knowledge of the termite condition when the sale agreements were executed, it is defendant's position the doctrine of caveat emptor applies to bar rescission. Defendant relies upon Hughes v. Stusser, 68 Wash.2d 707, at 712, 415 P.2d 89, at 92 (1966), wherein the court said:

[C]aveat emptor, means nothing more than saying that the risks of latent defects in residences ought to fall on the purchaser rather than the vendor *where those defects are unknown to the vendor*.

In *Hughes*, a residence was sold for cash. Shortly thereafter, the purchaser discovered termites and brought an action for damages. The theory was fraudulent misrepresentation and concealment. The trial court ruled on a challenge to the sufficiency of the evidence that fraud and concealment had not been proved by clear, cogent and convincing evidence and dismissed the complaint. This was affirmed on appeal. The language cited by defendants from *Hughes* is dictum since the purchaser in *Hughes* failed in its burden to prove fraud and concealment.

The instant case is distinguishable from *Hughes* because here the plaintiff seeks rescission based on mutual mistake. The elements of mutual mistake are different than the elements of fraud. As in *Hughes*, plaintiff in this case was unable to prove the elements of fraud; rescission for this reason was denied. However, the trial court properly concluded both plaintiff and defendant dealt under a mutual mistake as to the actual condition of the property since both considered it to be in fair-to-good condition, free of a need for structural repair. Since the termite infestation went to the very heart, the sine qua non or the essence of the transaction, it was proper to grant rescission for mutual mistake.

Defendant contends if the instant agreement can be rescinded, then any contract can be set aside under a set of circumstances rendering a building no longer attractive to a purchaser. To the contrary, we hold a purchaser is bound by facts a reasonable investigation would normally disclose. However, in the instant case it is clear a reasonable investigation by a layman would not have disclosed termite infestation, nor does the record show that a purchaser making a reasonable investigation should employ an expert to investigate the premises for termites. Consequently, the contention of defendant is without merit.

. . .

Judgment is affirmed.

QUESTIONS AND NOTES

1. In 1960, or more than ten years before the decision in *Davey*, the Supreme Court of Washington held a vendor of realty liable for failing to disclose the existence of termite infestation that the vendor had attempted to remedy. Obde v. Schlemeyer, 353 P.2d 672 (Wash.1960). Why didn't the appellate court in *Davey* rely on *Obde* in granting relief to the plaintiff? Why didn't the court even cite *Obde*?

2. When is mutual mistake a ground for relief? What elements of deceit need not be proved if the plaintiff's theory of relief is mutual mistake? Does the plaintiff have to prove any elements for mistake that are not necessary for misrepresentation? See Restatement (Second) of Contracts section 152.

REVIEW QUESTION

Consumer goes to *Dealer* to purchase a new car. After selecting the model, *Consumer* and *Dealer's* salesperson sit down to prepare the purchase order. The salesperson writes down the make and model of the car and then lists the factory-installed options and accessories on the car. She then makes a sales pitch for several dealer-installed options, one of which is undercoating. *Consumer* asks why, in view of the manufacturer's highly advertised five-year warranty against rust, undercoating is necessary. The salesperson replies, "Well, you may have the car for more than five years. In any event, the road salt they use around here in the winter is hard on cars. It's a lot easier to have the undercoating now than it is to patch the body later on, when rust will be a progressive, continuing problem." *Consumer* is still hesitant, so the salesperson continues, "Let me show you how harmful chemicals like the ones in road salt can be." She pulls out a vial of clear liquid and pours some of it on a concrete block she has on the floor near her desk. When the liquid contacts the concrete block, smoke starts rising from it. *Consumer* promptly agrees to buy the undercoating. A week after taking delivery of the car, *Consumer* reads in the newspaper an exposé of this sales practice. The article discloses that if the liquid were to be poured on an untreated auto body, it would run off without any effect on the metal.

Is the salesperson's conduct actionable? Is *Consumer* entitled to rescission? to damages?

DECEPTION—LEGISLATIVE SOLUTIONS AT THE FEDERAL LEVEL: THE FEDERAL TRADE COMMISSION ACT

A. INTRODUCTION

In 1914 Congress enacted the Federal Trade Commission Act, which created the FTC. Designed to promote competition and protect competitors, the Act provided, "Unfair methods of competition in commerce are hereby declared unlawful." The focus on "unfair methods of competition" led the Supreme Court to hold that the statute applied only if the respondent's conduct injured competitors; injury just to consumers did not suffice. FTC v. Raladam Co., 283 U.S. 643 (1931). Consequently, to afford greater protection to consumers, Congress amended section 5 in 1938 to prohibit not only unfair methods of competition, but also "unfair or deceptive acts or practices."

A second limitation under the original statute concerned the requirement that the unfair method occur "in commerce." The Supreme Court interpreted this to mean that wholly intrastate activity was not within the scope of the Act. FTC v. Bunte Brothers, Inc., 312 U.S. 349 (1941). Congress eliminated this limitation in 1975, by amending section 5 to apply to practices "in *or affecting* commerce." Section 5(a)(1) now provides, "Unfair methods of competition in or affecting commerce, and unfair or deceptive acts or practices in or affecting commerce, are hereby declared unlawful." 15 U.S.C. § 45(a)(1).

The FTC may proceed either by rule making or by adjudication. The Commission has promulgated trade practice rules (also called industry guides) to explain the Commission's interpretation of the Act as applied in various contexts. For example, the Commission has issued guides dealing with conduct known as bait and switch and with the permissible use of the word "free." 16 C.F.R. §§ 238, 251. Violation of trade practice rules, however, does not amount to a violation of the statute. The FTC still has to establish the ultimate fact—an unfair or deceptive act or practice. More recently, since the early 1970s, the FTC has promulgated trade *regulation* rules. These rules are substantive provisions that have the force of law. Violations of trade regulation rules are violations of the Act itself. The business community objected to the FTC's authority to issue substantive rules, but the Court of Appeals upheld the Commission in National Petroleum Refiners Association v. FTC, 482 F.2d 672 (D.C.Cir.1973), and two years later Congress codified the FTC's authority. FTC Act § 18(a)(1)(B), (d)(3). As the FTC became more active in the late 1970s, the objections of sellers and creditors became louder. Congress responded in 1980 by amending the Act to place certain businesses beyond the FTC's rulemaking authority. Congress also mandated procedures to give the business community ample opportunity for participation in rulemaking proceedings and to require the FTC to base its rules on sound economic analysis. The amendments also gave Congress the power to veto any rule adopted by the Commission (§§ 18(a)(1)(B), (b), (d)(1), (i), 21(a)). The Supreme Court held the veto provision to be unconstitutional. Consumers Union of United States, Inc. v. Federal Trade Commission, 691 F.2d 575 (D.C.Cir.1982), affirmed 463 U.S. 1216 (1983).

Chapter 9 pursues rulemaking in the context of the FTC's unfairness jurisdiction. The materials in this chapter are concerned with the adjudicative context and explore the kinds of conduct that are within the scope of "*deceptive* acts or practices."

B. THE MEANING OF "DECEPTIVE ACTS OR PRACTICES"

Charles of the Ritz Distributors Corp. v. FTC

United States Court of Appeals, Second Circuit, 1944.
143 F.2d 676.

CLARK, CIRCUIT JUDGE.

This is a petition to review and set aside a cease and desist order issued by the Federal Trade Commission, pursuant to a complaint charging petitioner with having violated the Federal Trade Commission Act, by falsely advertising its cosmetic preparation "Charles of the Ritz Rejuvenescence Cream." Petitioner is a New York corporation engaged in the sale and distribution in interstate commerce of various cosmetics, one of which is the cream in issue. This is a preparation of the type commonly known to the trade as a powder base or foundation cream for make-up. During the years from 1934 until December 1939, when sales were "temporarily discontinued" because of the issuance of the present complaint, petitioner's Rejuvenescence Cream enjoyed a vast popularity, with total sales amounting to approximately $1,000,000. The extensive advertising campaign which accompanied this business placed emphasis upon the rejuvenating proclivities of the product. The advertisements typically referred to "a vital organic ingredient" and certain "essences and compounds" which Rejuvenescence Cream allegedly contained, and stated that the preparation brings to the user's "skin quickly the clear radiance . . . the petal-like quality and texture of youth," that it "*restores natural moisture* necessary for a live, healthy skin," with the result that "Your face need know no *drought years*," and that it gives to the skin "a bloom which is wonderfully rejuvenating," and is "constantly active in keeping your skin clear, radiant, and young looking." (Emphasis as in the original.)

After a hearing, the Commission found that such advertising falsely represented that Rejuvenescence Cream will rejuvenate and restore youth or the appearance of youth to the skin, regardless of the condition of the skin or the age of the user, since external applications of cosmetics cannot overcome skin conditions which result from systemic causes or from physiological changes occurring with the passage of time and since there is no treatment known to medical science by which changes in the condition of the skin of an individual can be prevented or by which an aged skin can be rejuvenated or restored to a youthful condition. It, therefore, ordered petitioner to cease and desist disseminating in commerce any advertisement of Charles of the Ritz Rejuvenescence Cream: "(a) In which the word 'Rejuvenescence,' or any other word or term of similar import or meaning, is used to designate, describe, or refer to [petitioner's] said cosmetic preparation; or (b) which represents, directly or by inference, that [petitioner's] said cosmetic preparation will rejuvenate the skin of the user thereof or restore youth or the appearance of youth to the skin of the user."

. . .

On the merits, petitioner first attacks the finding of fact that its preparation does not act as a rejuvenating agent and preserve or restore the youthful appearance of the skin. Two medical experts, one a leading dermatologist, testified for the Commission; and both affirmatively stated that there was nothing known to medical science which could bring about such results. There was no testimony to the contrary; but petitioner asserts that, since neither expert had ever used Rejuvenescence Cream or knew what it contained—petitioner being unwilling to reveal its secret formula—their testimony was not the substantial evidence necessary to support the final findings and order below. Despite their lack of familiarity with petitioner's product, however, the general medical and pharmacological knowledge of the doctors qualified them to testify as to the lack of therapeutic value of the cream. Further, petitioner was not privileged, under the circumstances, to stand upon its refusal to disclose the true formula of its preparation as a trade secret, and its failure to introduce evidence thus within its immediate knowledge and control, if existing anywhere, of the rejuvenating constituents and therapeutic effect of its preparation is strong confirmation of the Commission's charges.

Next, and as the crux of its appeal, petitioner attacks the propriety of the finding that by use of the trade-mark "Rejuvenescence" it has represented that its preparation will rejuvenate and restore the appearance of youth to the skin. In view of the finding which we have just held supported on the evidence, that in fact there are no rejuvenating qualities in petitioner's cream, the question is then simply whether or not the trade-mark is deceptive and misleading within the meaning of the Federal Trade Commission Act. But the dictionaries treat "rejuvenescence" as a common word with a plain meaning of "a renewing of youth" or the perhaps more usual "rejuvenation"; cf. Webster's New International Dictionary, 2d Ed., Unabridged, 1939. Nor does the record show any other special meaning to have developed in the trade. On the contrary, the Commission's expert and practicing dermatologist testified directly that rejuvenescence still meant not only to him, but also, as far as he knew, to his female patients, the restoration of youth. In the light of this plain meaning, petitioner's contention can hardly be sustained that "rejuvenescence" is a nondeceptive "boastful and fanciful word," utilized solely for its attractiveness as a trade-mark. That the Patent Office has registered "Rejuvenescence" as a trade-mark is not controlling. Even conceding its nondescriptive quality and hence its validity as a trademark—a concession sufficiently doubtful in itself to be made only arguendo—the fact of registration does not prevent its use from falling within the prohibition of the Federal Trade Commission Act.

There is no merit to petitioner's argument that, since no straight-thinking person could believe that its cream would actually rejuvenate, there could be no deception. Such a view results from a grave misconception of the purposes of the Federal Trade Commission Act. That law was not "made for the protection of experts, but for the public—that vast multitude which includes the ignorant, the unthinking and the credulous," Florence Mfg. Co. v. J. C. Dowd & Co., 2 Cir., 178 F. 73, 75; and the "fact that a false statement may be obviously false to those who are trained and experienced does not change its character, nor take away its power to deceive others less experienced." Federal Trade Commission v. Standard Education Soc., 302 U.S. 112, 116, 58 S.Ct. 113, 115, 82 L.Ed. 141. The important criterion is the net impression which the advertisement is likely to make upon the general populace. And, while the wise and the worldly may well realize the falsity of any representations that the present product can roll back the years, there remains "that vast multitude" of others who, like Ponce de Leon, still seek a perpetual fountain of youth. As the Commission's expert further testified, the average woman, conditioned by talk in magazines and over the radio of "vitamins, hormones, and God knows what," might take "rejuvenescence" to mean that this "is one of the modern miracles" and is "something which would actually cause her youth to be restored." It is for this reason that the Commission may "insist upon the most literal truthfulness" in advertisements, Moretrench Corp. v. Federal Trade Commission, 2 Cir., 127 F.2d 792, 795, and should have the discretion, undisturbed by the courts, to insist if it chooses "upon a form of advertising clear enough so that, in the words of the prophet Isaiah, 'wayfaring men, though fools, shall not err therein.'" General Motors Corp. v. Federal Trade Commission, 2 Cir., 114 F.2d 33, 36, certiorari denied 312 U.S. 682, 61 S.Ct. 550, 85 L.Ed. 1120.

That the Commission did not produce consumers to testify to their deception does not make the order improper, since actual deception of the public need not be shown in Federal Trade Commission proceedings. Representations merely having a "capacity to deceive" are unlawful, Federal Trade Commission v. Algoma Lumber Co., 291 U.S. 67, 81, 54 S.Ct. 315, 78 L.Ed. 655; Herzfeld v. Federal Trade Commission, supra; General Motors Corp. v. Federal Trade Commission, supra; and, as we have seen, the facts here more than warrant a conclusion of such capacity. Likewise it is not material that there was no consumer testimony as to the meaning of petitioner's representations. The testimony of the dermatologist, a person whose occupation took him among the buyers of Rejuvenescence Cream, is a qualified source of information "as to the buyers' understanding of the words they hear and use." Benton Announcements v. Federal Trade Commission, 2 Cir., 130 F.2d 254, 255.

. . .

The order is affirmed and an enforcement decree will be entered.

QUESTIONS AND NOTES

1.   What representation did Charles of the Ritz make?

Would any reasonable person believe that Rejuvenescence would make her skin young? Did the FTC establish that anyone actually did believe that the product would rejuvenate her skin?

Under *Charles of the Ritz,* may a cosmetic company market a facial cream under the name "Angelskin"? "Babyskin"? Is it a deceptive practice for a toilet paper manufacturer to call its product "Cottonelle"?

May the seller of an arthritis product market the product under the name "Aspercreme" if it does not contain aspirin? In addition to selecting that suggestive name, the manufacturer of Aspercreme ran television ads that promoted the perception that the product contained aspirin. The FTC brought an action against the manufacturer, Thompson Medical Co., seeking, among other things, that it be prohibited from using the name "Aspercreme." The administrative law judge held that the manufacturer had engaged in deceptive conduct but refused to prohibit use of the name. On appeal to the Commission, the FTC concurred:

[Complaint counsel have urged that we adopt a cease and desist order] that would require Thompson to excise the "Aspercreme" brand name. Complaint counsel have asserted that brand name excision is a remedy the Commission has employed in the past when a brand name was deceptive and when no less restrictive alternative would suffice to eliminate deception. Complaint counsel further argue that such is the case here.

We agree with complaint counsel that brand name excision is a remedy available to us for use in extreme circumstances.[88] We do not find, however, that complaint counsel have made a sufficient case to warrant employing the remedy here. To order brand name excision, we would have to be persuaded that a less severe remedy, such as

88.   See, e.g., FTC v. Algoma Lumber Co., 291 U.S. 67, 54 S.Ct. 315, 78 L.Ed. 655 (1934); Resort Car Rental System, Inc. v. FTC, 518 F.2d 962 (9th Cir.), cert. denied, 423 U.S. 827, 96 S.Ct. 41, 46 L.Ed.2d 42 (1975); Continental Wax Corp. v. FTC, 330 F.2d 475 (2d Cir.1964); Bakers Franchise Corp. v. FTC, 302 F.2d 258 (3d Cir.1962); El Moro Cigar Co. v. FTC, 107 F.2d 429 (4th Cir.1939).

affirmative disclosures, could not correct the misimpression that Aspercreme contains aspirin. Complaint counsel have argued that the evidence in this case leads to such a conclusion. However, we do not find that this evidence justifies brand name excision. The evidence consists in part of the testimony by complaint counsel's marketing expert. He stated that the brand name is the most salient part of a commercial to consumers and that, therefore, the misperceptions generated by the brand name "Aspercreme" cannot be overcome by any disclaimers included in ads. This line of reasoning appears to prove too much. It leads to the conclusion that the Commission must ban any brand name suggesting an ingredient not contained in the product. As Thompson has pointed out, however, there are numerous products on the market whose names suggest an ingredient they do not contain.[89] While no evidence is before us showing whether or not consumers are confused by those names, we think it probable that a properly designed ad campaign for such products, or for Aspercreme, could convey to consumers the message that the product is similar to but not identical with the ingredient suggested by the brand name. In any event, we are not willing to discount this possibility based upon one expert's opinion.

In re Thompson Medical Co., 104 F.T.C. 648 (1984), affirmed 791 F.2d 189 (D.C.Cir.1986). The Commission's order enjoined the manufacturer from:

A. Employing the brand name "Aspercreme" for such products or otherwise representing directly or by implication that an active ingredient of such product is aspirin, unless such product contains aspirin in therapeutically significant quantities; *provided, however,* that the brand name "Aspercreme" may be used for such product if its advertising and labeling clearly and prominently disclose that the product does not contain aspirin.

(1) In television advertisements, an explicit and simple aspirin disclaimer statement (such as "ASPIRIN–FREE") shall be superimposed on the television screen simultaneously with a vocal aspirin disclaimer statement (such as "Aspercreme does not contain aspirin") at the end of each advertisement.

(2) In radio advertisements, an explicit aspirin disclaimer statement (such as "Aspercreme does not contain aspirin") shall be made at the end of each advertisement.

(3) In print advertisements, an explicit aspirin disclaimer statement (such as "ASPERCREME DOES NOT CONTAIN ASPIRIN") shall be displayed prominently and conspicuously in relation to each such advertisement as a whole.

89. See Respondent's Appeal Brief 41:

The marketplace abounds with products whose marks suggest but do not describe a character or quality of the goods, as for example Bacos (no bacon), Sugar Twin (no sugar), Egg Beater (no egg), Cremora (no cream), Silkience (no silk), Cottonelle (no cotton), Tuna Twist (no tuna), Chock Full O'Nuts (no nuts), Chicken of the Sea (no chicken), Apple Beer (no beer), and Rubbermaid (no rubber). The common sense "message" inherent in these names is "similar to," i.e., similar to bacon, similar to sugar, etc.

(4) In labeling, an explicit aspirin disclaimer statement (such as "DOES NOT CONTAIN ASPIRIN") shall be prominently and conspicuously printed in the front package panel (or in the front of the container if no package is used).

2. In In re Kirchner, 63 F.T.C. 1282 (1963), affirmed 337 F.2d 751 (9th Cir.1964), respondent manufactured and sold "Swim–Ezy," a swimming aid consisting of an inflatable rubber bladder to be worn under a swim suit. Respondent's advertisements stated "New, unique 4 oz. device, 1/25″ thin, worn INVISIBLE under bathing suit or swim trunks, floats you at ease, without effort, is comfortable all day" and "it's invisible." The hearing officer held these and other statements were deceptive. The FTC agreed that the other, safety-related statements were deceptive, but rejected that conclusion with respect to the invisibility claims:

> To be sure, "Swim–Ezy" is not invisible or impalpable or dimensionless, and to anyone who so understood the representation, it would be false. It is not likely, however, that many prospective purchasers would take the representation thus in its literal sense. True, as has been reiterated many times, the Commission's responsibility is to prevent deception of the gullible and credulous, as well as the cautious and knowledgeable (see e.g., Charles of the Ritz Dist. Corp. v. F.T.C., 143 F.2d 676 (2d Cir.1944)). This principle loses its validity, however, if it is applied uncritically or pushed to an absurd extreme. An advertiser cannot be charged with liability in respect of every conceivable misconception, however outlandish, to which his representations might be subject among the foolish or feebleminded. Some people, because of ignorance or incomprehension, may be misled by even a scrupulously honest claim. Perhaps a few misguided souls believe, for example, that all "Danish pastry" is made in Denmark. Is it, therefore, an actionable deception to advertise "Danish pastry" when it is made in this country? Of course not. A representation does not become "false and deceptive" merely because it will be unreasonably misunderstood by an insignificant and unrepresentative segment of the class of persons to whom the representation is addressed. If, however, advertising is aimed at a specially susceptible group of people (e.g., children), its truthfulness must be measured by the impact it will make on them, not others to whom it is not primarily directed.

> The essence of the representation of "invisibility" is, simply, that "Swim–Ezy" may be worn without other swimmers or bystanders realizing that the wearer is using a swimming aid. In advertising an "invisible" swimming aid, respondent is obviously catering to the feeling of embarrassment which many people feel in publicly revealing that they cannot swim. All the representation was intended to convey, and all that it would be understood by most prospective purchasers to mean, is that "Swim–Ezy" may be worn inconspicuously. The possibility that some persons might believe that "Swim–Ezy" is, not merely inconspicuous, but wholly invisible or bodiless, seems to us too far-fetched to warrant this Commission's intervention in the public inter-

est. And, there is a dearth of substantial, probative evidence to demonstrate the falsity of the claim that "Swim–Ezy" can be worn in an inconspicuous manner.

Id. at 1289–90.

3. To be actionable as deceit, a representation must concern a material fact and there must be reasonable reliance resulting in injury. To what extent are these elements present in the language of section 5? To what extent are these elements present in *Charles of the Ritz?* Exactly what must the FTC establish before finding a violation of section 5?

4. Another element of deceit is scienter or intent to deceive. A seller may violate section 5(a) even in the absence of this intent. But section 5(b) provides

> Whenever the Commission shall have reason to believe that any such person, partnership, or corporation has been or is using any unfair method of competition or unfair or deceptive act or practice in or affecting commerce, and if it shall appear to the Commission that a proceeding by it in respect thereof would be *to the interest of the public,* it shall issue and serve upon such person, partnership, or corporation a complaint stating its charges in that respect and containing a notice of a hearing upon a day and at a place therein fixed at least thirty days after the service of said complaint. . . . (emphasis added)

If the deception is unintentional, does the public interest justify FTC intervention? The FTC believes it may. In re Chrysler Corp., 87 F.T.C. 743 (1976).

It is not clear how much the language "to the interest of the public" limits the FTC. Over seventy years ago, in FTC v. Klesner, 280 U.S. 19 (1929), the Supreme Court interpreted the limitation this way:

> Section 5 of the Federal Trade Commission Act does not provide private persons with an administrative remedy for private wrongs. The formal complaint is brought in the Commission's name; the prosecution is wholly that of the Government; and it bears the entire expense of the prosecution. A person who deems himself aggrieved by the use of an unfair method of competition is not given the right to institute before the Commission a complaint against the alleged wrongdoer. Nor may the Commission authorize him to do so. He may of course bring the matter to the Commission's attention and request it to file a complaint. But a denial of his request is final. And if the request is granted and a proceeding is instituted, he does not become a party to it or have any control over it. . . .
>
> While the Federal Trade Commission exercises under § 5 the functions of both prosecutor and judge, the scope of its authority is strictly limited. A complaint may be filed only "if it shall appear to the Commission that a proceeding by it in respect thereof would be to the interest of the public." . . .

In determining whether a proposed proceeding will be in the public interest the Commission exercises a broad discretion. But the mere fact that it is to the interest of the community that private rights shall be respected is not enough to support a finding of public interest. To justify filing a complaint the public interest must be specific and substantial. Often it is so, because the unfair method employed threatens the existence of present or potential competition. Sometimes, because the unfair method is being employed under circumstances which involve flagrant oppression of the weak by the strong. Sometimes, because, although the aggregate of the loss entailed may be so serious and widespread as to make the matter one of public consequence, no private suit would be brought to stop the unfair conduct, since the loss to each of the individuals affected is too small to warrant it.

The order here sought to be enforced was entered upon a complaint which had in terms been authorized by a resolution of the Commission. The resolution declared, in an appropriate form, both that the Commission had reason to believe that Klesner was violating § 5, and that it appeared to the Commission that a proceeding by it in respect thereof would be to the interest of the public. Thus, the resolution was sufficient to confer upon the Commission jurisdiction of the complaint. Section 5 makes the Commission's finding of facts conclusive, if supported by evidence. Its preliminary determination that institution of a proceeding will be in the public interest, while not strictly within the scope of that provision, will ordinarily be accepted by the courts. But the Commission's action in authorizing the filing of a complaint, like its action in making an order thereon, is subject to judicial review. The specific facts established may show, as a matter of law, that the proceeding which it authorized is not in the public interest, within the meaning of the Act. If this appears at any time during the course of the proceeding before it, the Commission should dismiss the complaint. If, instead, the Commission enters an order, and later brings suit to enforce it, the court should, without enquiry into the merits, dismiss the suit.

The undisputed facts, established before the Commission, at the hearings on the complaint, showed affirmatively the private character of the controversy. It then became clear (if it was not so earlier) that the proceeding was not one in the interest of the public; and that the resolution authorizing the complaint had been improvidently entered. . . .

Id. at 25–30.

On the other hand, no case since 1929 has reversed a Commission conclusion that a given proceeding was in the public interest. The following excerpt from an opinion by the Second Circuit is a more accurate statement of the modern view:

Although the Federal Trade Commission can act against a deceptive advertiser only if it finds such action to be "to the interest of the public," Federal Trade Commission Act § 5(b), and although its finding of public interest is subject to our review, F.T.C. v. Klesner, we think there is sufficient public interest in preventing Exposition's deceptive advertising to justify our enforcement of the Commission's order. This is not, like the Klesner case, an instance of Federal Trade Commission intervention in a private dispute. Nor was the deception only as to trivial matters. That the deception may be remedied before the customer has suffered any more pecuniary loss than the price of a postage stamp does not foreclose the Commission from acting to proscribe it in the first instance.

Judge Friendly argues with great force that this violation was trivial and that it is not in the public interest to kill this gnat with Commission dynamite. But it seems to us that once we say that the courts should exercise their judgment as to whether an alleged deception is of sufficient importance to warrant Commission action, we get into matters which are not entrusted to us and as to which we have little qualification and even less necessary information. For example, we cannot know but what a proceeding such as this might be the means whereby in the long run the Commission may use its influence to prevent continuance of many similar deceptions. It is by such means that laws are enforced and the government is able to bring about a better moral climate in the field of advertising. From the many hundreds of complaints it has before it, surely the Commission is better able to judge whether this proceeding is a step forward in the attainment of a higher morality in the great mass of information and propaganda designed to influence the public.

Exposition Press, Inc. v. FTC, 295 F.2d 869, 873–74 (2d Cir.1961). See FTC v. Standard Oil Co. of California, 449 U.S. 232 (1980).

5. If taken literally, the test for deception articulated by the court in *Charles of the Ritz* is quite extreme, because almost every statement has the capacity to deceive at least some unsophisticated, gullible consumers. The FTC never pushed the test to its limits, but in the late 1970s many in the business community believed that the Commission was going too far. Political pressure, coupled with a change in the composition of the FTC, led to a proposal to amend section 5 to add a definition of "deceptive" and to include in the definition several of the elements of common law deceit. Congress did not enact this amendment, but it stimulated further discussion. Ultimately, the House committee that oversees the activities of the FTC asked the Commission for its analysis of the law of deception under section 5. The Commission's response was a policy statement that is described and applied in the next case.

In re International Harvester Co.

Federal Trade Commission, 1984.
104 F.T.C. 949.

By DOUGLAS, COMMISSIONER:

This matter presents the issue of when and under what circumstances a manufacturer has a duty to notify customers about hidden hazards in his product. . . .

. . .

1.   THE FACTS

The facts in this matter are not seriously in dispute. The evidence
shows that Harvester tractors were subject to fuel geysering under certain
conditions, and that the company knew of this for seventeen years before
directly notifying its customers. The evidence also shows that such accidents were relatively rare and could be avoided entirely by following certain
safety rules.

. . . "Fuel geysering" is a phenomenon in which hot liquid fuel is
forcibly ejected upward through the filler cap on a tractor gas tank. It can
occur because gasoline is a volatile fuel with a boiling point that begins at
about 95–97° Fahrenheit. This temperature is easily reached in ordinary
use, since a Harvester fuel tank is located immediately above and behind
the engine, where it is subject to both direct engine heat and the current of
hot air from the radiator. Fuel at this temperature can begin to boil. If the
fuel vaporizes more rapidly than it can be vented, pressure will begin to
build up in the tank. This vapor pressure can suppress further boiling, and
energy will then continue to build up in the tank in the form of still higher
temperatures in the liquid mass of fuel. If the pressure is suddenly
released, as through the sudden removal of the fuel cap, the accumulated
heat energy can cause a quantity of gasoline to suddenly boil, sending both
fuel and vapors up through the filler neck.

A fuel geyser can reach to a height well above the tractor and its
operator. In one test that Harvester conducted the geyser shot twenty feet
high and the tank lost seven gallons of fuel. . . .

The gasoline sent up from the tank may fall back on the operator,
soaking him with raw flammable fuel. This hot fuel can itself cause severe
burns. But the great hazard of fuel geysering is, of course, fire. . . .

Serious injury and death have resulted from such fires. The record
contains evidence of more than 90 fuel geysering incidents involving
Harvester tractors. Testimony at trial identified twelve incidents in which
there were significant burn injuries. . . .

These dangers and injuries could have been avoided, however, if the
tractor operators had observed a few relatively simple precautions. The
most basic precaution was to keep the fuel cap securely fastened, and not to
remove it while the tractor engine was running or hot. As a result,
operators could remain safe simply by leaving their caps secured. For many
years the operating manuals had warned tractor owners to do just that.

There are, on the other hand, a number of factors which incline
operators toward opening the caps. Some of the older models of Harvester
tractors had no fuel gauge, so it was common to open the cap to check on
fuel level. More importantly, the symptoms of excessive tank pressure tend

to resemble the symptoms of fuel exhaustion. These include "vapor lock" caused by fuel vaporizing in the fuel line or carburetor, which can cause the engine to sputter or stop; surging of the engine as pressure forces extra fuel into the carburetor; and stalling of the engine due to flooding when this extra fuel flow becomes excessive. Any of these symptoms might lead the operator of even a modern, gas-gauge-equipped tractor to stop and visually check his fuel level. In doing so he is encouraged by the sense that this action entails little risk. The operator knows enough to ensure that open flame does not come near the gas tank, and being unaware of the potential for a fuel geyser he took no particular steps to avoid it.

By 1955 Harvester was aware of the pattern of accidents that had begun to develop. . . . In 1963 Harvester revised its operator's manuals to include a warning against removal of the gas cap from a hot or running tractor. This warning was incomplete in a number of respects, however. It was included only in the manuals for new tractors, leaving the manuals for the more numerous older models unrevised, and it did not specifically mention fuel geysering as a possible consequence of cap removal, thus leading readers to attach less significance to the warning than they would otherwise have done. In 1976 Harvester produced a new fuel tank decal which repeated the warning against removing the cap from a hot tractor, and added an injunction to tighten the cap securely. This was perhaps the most effective warning yet, but it had a very limited distribution. Only 980 gasoline-powered tractors were produced after 1975—because the industry was switching to diesel fuel—and the decals reached the older tractors only on an irregular basis. Moreover, this decal again failed to spell out the exact nature of the hazard at a level of detail that would effectively motivate compliance.

In 1979 Harvester began work on the warning program that all parties agree was finally effective. This was the Fuel Fire Prevention Program. It was an initiative of the Product Integrity Group, an organization within the company that had responsibility for studying safety problems. The centerpiece of the program was a direct mailing made to some 630,000 Harvester customers in August 1980. This mailing explicitly warned about the existence of fuel geysering: "[The] sudden eruption of gasoline exposes the operator to, and may cover him with, liquid fuel and vapors and is a clear fire hazard if a source of ignition is present. . . . ." Coupled with this warning was an announcement that Harvester was providing, free of charge, a new gas cap that would prevent geysering. The ALJ found that the 1980 warning was complete and was effectively distributed to the people in need of the information. He therefore concluded that Harvester's duties to its customers were discharged as of that date.

II.   APPLICABLE LEGAL STANDARDS

The above facts are, as we have said, not seriously in dispute. The principal issues in this case instead revolve around the proper legal construction that should be placed on the facts. In this section of the opinion we will review, in general terms, the legal standards applicable to the case.

In the following section we will bring the facts and the law together in an analysis of the ultimate issues of liability.

The basic law of this case is Section 5 of the FTC Act. That section states that "unfair or deceptive acts or practices . . . are declared unlawful." The Administrative Law Judge found violations of both parts of the statute. He concluded that Harvester's failure to warn about the hazards of fuel geysering was a form of deception, a failure to dispel an incorrect belief among consumers that the tractors would be fit for their ordinary use. He also found that the failure to warn was unfair, since it subjected consumers to a risk of harm that they could not reasonably have avoided, but that Harvester could have prevented at relatively small cost. We will discuss these two charges in sequence.

Deception

The first charge considered in this case was deception. "Deception" is specifically prohibited by the FTC Act, and the Commission has had particular experience over the years in applying this concept. In most deception cases injury comes about when consumers are led to purchase a product that they would not otherwise have selected. In such cases the Commission's deception jurisdiction acts to safeguard the exercise of consumer sovereignty.[16] Consumers may also incur injury through choices relating to their post-purchase conduct, however, such as decisions on the care and use of the product. These decisions may likewise be protected by the Commission's deception jurisdiction.[17]

Our approach to deception cases was described in a policy statement that the Commission issued in 1983.[18] That document explains how the Commission reads its precedents and thus how it will apply that body of law. In brief, a deception case requires a showing of three elements: (1) there must be a representation, practice, or omission likely to mislead consumers; (2) the consumers must be interpreting the message reasonably under the circumstances; and (3) the misleading effects must be "material," that is, likely to affect consumers' conduct or decision with regard to a product. Our deception analysis thus focuses on risk of consumer harm, and actual injury need not be shown.

Deception is a particularly troublesome form of conduct. It is harmful to consumers, undermines the rational functioning of the marketplace, and, unlike some other practices we are called upon to review, never offers increased efficiency or other countervailing benefits that must be considered. In view of deception's unalloyed negative qualities, the three elements

---

16. The touchstone here is free consumer choice. We do not look for evidence that the product selected is actually inferior to its alternatives.

17. The underlying theory is that the care-and-use requirement of a product, if known by consumers, will affect their initial purchase decisions.

18. Letter from Federal Trade Commission to Congressman Dingell (Oct. 14, 1983) (hereinafter cited as Deception Statement). This letter is reproduced as an Appendix to our opinion in Cliffdale Associates, Inc., [103 F.T.C. 110 (1984)].

of the deception analysis represent streamlined procedures adopted by the Commission to deal most effectively with such practices.

The first element in the analysis states that there must be a representation, practice, or omission that is likely to mislead the consumer. The essence of deception is its misleading effects, and we therefore require some evidence that this undesirable consequence is indeed likely to come about. However, as one instance of streamlining, we do not go beyond likelihood to require evidence on the incidence of actual false belief.

The second element states that consumers must be interpreting the advertisement reasonably under the circumstances. A company cannot be liable for every possible reading of its claims, no matter how farfetched. We therefore require that the consumer interpretation in any particular case be reasonable. The Commission, however, will not require evidence that a claim has been interpreted in a certain way by some threshold number of consumers. Consumers acting reasonably under the circumstances are those who have acted in a way consistent with the broad range of ordinary or average people.[22]

Finally, the third element in a deception case states that the misleading effects must be material. A material effect is one which is likely to influence a consumer's conduct or purchase decision. We therefore require that the seller's conduct be likely to distort the ultimate exercise of consumer choice. The Commission, however, presumes that all express claims are material, and that implied claims are material if they pertain to the central characteristics of the product, such as its safety, cost, or fitness for the purpose sold. Our reasoning here is that the seller is in the best position to assess the effects of his ads, and if he finds it beneficial to make such claims it must be because they are likely to have an influence on consumers. We therefore conclude that claims on these particular topics are likely to affect consumer choice. If the claims are also false, moreover, we can make the further presumption that prohibiting them will cause a net increase in consumer welfare, without the need for us to engage in our own detailed inquiry into the costs and benefits of various courses.

In short, the deception case addresses an especially harmful form of behavior, and so it embodies a number of expediting and simplifying elements in order to do so most effectively.

Actionable deception theory is not limited to false or misleading statements. Under two general circumstances it can also reach omissions. First, it can be deceptive to tell only half the truth, and to omit the rest. This may occur where a seller fails to disclose qualifying information necessary to prevent one of his affirmative statements from creating a misleading impression. The Commission has brought a number of cases on this theory. It has challenged "Geritol" advertising for claiming that the product can reduce tiredness while failing to disclose that in most cases

---

22. This range applies to any relevant quality, such as intelligence, experience, or credulity. If the representations or sales practices are targeted to a specific audience, then reasonable consumers are representative members of that group.

those symptoms are caused by factors other than a lack of the vitamins and iron that the medicine contains; it has challenged the advertising of baldness cures for failing to disclose that most baldness results from male heredity and cannot be treated, and it has challenged claims that a product can produce weight losses of a certain amount while failing to disclose that losses of this magnitude, rather than being typical, are extremely rare.

It can also be deceptive for a seller to simply remain silent, if he does so under circumstances that constitute an implied but false representation. Such implied representations may take any of several forms. They may arise from the physical appearance of the product, or from the circumstances of a specific transaction, or they may be based on ordinary consumer expectations as to the irreducible minimum performance standards of a particular class of good. The Commission has brought several cases on this theory. It has upheld charges against sellers who failed to disclose that an apparently new product was actually used,[30] that a simulated-wood product was actually made of paper,[31] that a sales contract would be sold to a holder in due course,[32] that land sold for investment purposes was poorly suited to that use due to its remote location,[33] and that a book was an abridged rather than a complete edition.[34] One generalization that emerges from these cases is that by the very act of offering goods for sale the seller impliedly represents that they are reasonably fit for their intended uses.[35] The concept of reasonable fitness includes a further implied representation that the products are free of gross safety hazards, although not necessarily of all or relatively improbable dangers.

Not all omissions are unlawfully deceptive under Section 5. Such is the case with what is sometimes characterized as a "pure omission." This is a subject upon which the seller has simply said nothing, in circumstances that do not give any particular meaning to his silence. Like any other form of omission, pure omissions may lead to erroneous consumer beliefs if consumers had a false, pre-existing conception which the seller failed to correct.

The Commission does not treat pure omissions as deceptive, however. There are two reasons for this. First, we could not declare pure omissions to be deceptive without expanding that concept virtually beyond limits. Individual consumers may have erroneous preconceptions about issues as diverse as the entire range of human error, and it would be both impractical and very costly to require corrective information on all such points.

30. Olson Radio Corp., 60 F.T.C. 1758 (1962). . . .

31. Haskelite Mfg. Corp., 33 F.T.C. 1212, 1216 (1941), aff'd, 127 F.2d 765 (7th Cir.1942).

32. All–State Industries of North Carolina, 75 F.T.C. 465, aff'd, 423 F.2d 423 (4th Cir.), cert. denied, 400 U.S. 828 (1970). . . .

33. Horizon Corp., 97 F.T.C. 464 (1981).

34. Bantam Books, Inc., 55 F.T.C. 779 (1958). . . .

35. . . . This point is also similar to the implied warranty of merchantability in the Uniform Commercial Code. See U.C.C. Section 2–314(2). For a general discussion see III R. Anderson, The Uniform Commercial Code Sections 314:29–:30 (1983).

Second, pure omissions do not presumptively or generally reflect a deliberate act on the part of the seller, and so we have no basis for concluding, without further analysis, that an order requiring corrective disclosure would necessarily engender positive net benefits for consumers or be in the public interest.

If we were to ignore this last consideration, and were to proceed under a deception theory without a cost-benefit analysis, it would surely lead to perverse outcomes. The number of facts that may be material to consumers—and on which they may have prior misconceptions—is literally infinite. Consumers may wish to know about the life expectancy of clothes, or the sodium content of canned beans, or the canner's policy on trade with Chile. Since the seller will have no way of knowing in advance which disclosure is important to any particular consumer, he will have to make complete disclosures to all. A television ad would be completely buried under such disclaimers, and even a full-page newspaper ad would hardly be sufficient for the purpose. For example, there are literally dozens of ways in which one can be injured while riding a tractor, not all of them obvious before the fact, and under a simple deception analysis these would presumably all require affirmative disclosure. The resulting costs and burden on advertising communication would very possibly represent a net harm for consumers.

Although pure omissions are not appropriately characterized as deceptive or reached through deception analysis, however, they may nonetheless cause significant consumer injury. In that event they might still be reached as unfair. It is to that part of our jurisdiction that we now turn. [This portion of the opinion is omitted.—Ed.]

III.   Analysis of the Case

In this section we will apply our general legal theory to the specific facts of the case. Since the analytical elements of deception and unfairness differ in so many particulars, we will again consider those two approaches separately.

Deception

As discussed above, the omission of information about a product may be deceptive under certain circumstances. In the present case the seller's silence is said to have led to an implied warranty that the tractor was fit for its intended use, when it in fact was not.

We believe that this charge cannot be sustained, however. The implied warranty of fitness is not violated by all undisclosed safety problems. The critical issue is the degree of risk involved.[50] Where the risk of mishap is very small it cannot be said that the product is unfit for normal use. Such a case could therefore not satisfy the first element of the deception test,

---

50. To put this point another way, a seller impliedly warrants only that a product is *reasonably* safe, not that it is free of all hazards. We recognize that there is no such thing as a totally safe product, and especially not when dealing with relatively complex machinery.

which requires the showing of a misleading representation. It would therefore not be appropriately analyzed under the law against deception.

Harvester manufactured approximately 1.3 million gasoline-powered tractors in the period after 1939. Of this number, twelve are known to have been involved in geysering accidents involving bodily injury. This is an accident rate of less than .001 percent, over a period of more than 40 years. Since the state of maintenance was shown to have some effect on a tractor's susceptibility to fuel geysering, moreover, the rate for tractors in a good state of repair is likely to have been even less than this. Reflecting the low accident rate, one government study of tractor accidents did not even list fuel geysering as one of the tabulated kinds of mishaps, but simply lumped it into the residual category of "all other causes."[51]

This relatively low level of danger does not mean that the use of Harvester tractors is inherently unreasonable or imprudent. This case therefore does not involve a breach of the implied warranty of fitness, and so does not involve the element of deception.[52]

We do not mean to imply by this that the accident rate for Harvester tractors was inconsequential, or that persons who are injured in relatively rare kinds of mishaps do not deserve legal protection. Quite the contrary, such persons may well be entitled to a remedy under other portions of the FTC Act. We merely hold here that such close cases should not be pursued without undertaking a cost-benefit analysis, and that they therefore do not qualify for the streamlined legal procedures of a deception action.

. . .

51. See DOT Report, RX 32; I.D. 105. Also reflecting the improbability of a fuel geyser, Harvester's own engineers and testers, who might be expected to be most sensitive to such dangers, *themselves* commonly removed the gas caps during the course of tests. I.D. 99; I.D.F. 151.

52. The dissenting opinion takes issue with our use of accident rates in this analysis, claiming that such an approach implies a tacit requirement that the staff show actual injury rather than merely risk of harm, and further suggesting that the approach amounts to an *ex post* review of events rather than being, as it should be, a before-the-fact assessment of the risks to which consumers may be subjected. These objections misinterpret the role of statistical evidence in cases such as this. The ultimate question at issue is, indeed, risk. What is the risk of consumer harm? If we have no actual experience with a

particular problem we will endeavor to assess this risk from the most probative indirect evidence that is available. Where we have a statistically significant body of experience to draw upon, however, as we surely do here with 40 years' experience and hundreds of thousands of tractors, then the empirical incidence of harm, in the form of accident rates, is the best available measure of risk. To suggest, as the dissent does, that there is also some other kind of risk which is separate from this statistical risk, amounts really to no more than a conversational use of the term in the sense of "at risk." In this sense everyone is "at risk" at every moment, with respect to every danger which may possibly occur. When divorced from any measure of the probability of occurrence, however, such a concept cannot lead to useable rules of liability.

COMMISSIONER PATRICIA P. BAILEY CONCURRING IN PART AND DISSENTING IN PART

. . .

I dissent because the Commission has concluded that Harvester's conduct . . . was not deceptive. In order to reach that conclusion, the Commission has adopted an entirely novel and nearly incomprehensible theory of the law of deception. This is not a complicated case. It is a straightforward example of a manufacturer's duty to warn customers of a latent safety hazard in its product. But the Commission today decides that that failure was not deceptive because it involved a "pure omission" of material fact, which according to this opinion, is not a deceptive act or practice.

. . . [T]he Commission reverses the ALJ's conclusion that Harvester's conduct constitutes a deceptive practice under Section 5. In order to reach this conclusion, the Commission rejects the ALJ's finding that Harvester's sale of its gasoline-powered tractors without an adequate warning constituted an implied, but false, representation that the product is safe for its intended use. The Commission resolves this threshold obstacle by asserting that no implied warranty of fitness for normal use attaches where the statistical risk of incident from an undisclosed hazard is too remote to find that the use of a product is inherently unwise. Because the rate of actual injury from fuel geysering in Harvester tractors was small in relation to the number of tractors sold, the Commission concludes that the respondent made no misrepresentation of safety concerning what it believes was a relatively improbable phenomenon and, therefore, that the first element of the Commission's deception standard, the existence of a representation which is likely to mislead, is not present.

Having found no implied misrepresentation of safety, the Commission concludes that Harvester is guilty of complete silence only. The Commission further concludes that the seller's mere failure to dispel incorrect operator notions about the possible but unlikely consequences of removing or failing to secure the gas cap does not, without more, lead to an assessment of liability under a deception theory. Rather, according to this opinion, if Harvester is to be found liable at all for its silence, then it must be because the injury which ensued outweighed the costs to the company of providing an adequate warning, since only an unfairness theory affords the proper formula for determining whether the benefits to the public of mandating disclosure under such circumstances are greater than the costs of providing it.

I believe the Commission's conclusions are wrong, both as to the existence of an implied representation of safety in this case and as to the broader determination that certain "pure omissions," such as Harvester's, are not deceptive practices. The failure to disclose material facts, whether in the context of a truthful representation that, without more, has the capacity to mislead, an implied misrepresentation, or a completely omitted fact, has long been acknowledged by the Commission and the courts to be an integral part of the law of deception. Specifically, deception may occur when important information is omitted from the sales presentation or from other aspects of a commercial transaction. While in order to be material a misleading omission must generally pertain to a consumer's purchasing decision, it may also concern the use or care of a product.

Significantly, because deception will be found only if consumers could actually be misled by a seller's silence, it is axiomatic that not every material fact about a product must be revealed. Rather, in order to be considered deceptive, the undisclosed facts must be both material and necessary to correct a reasonable false expectation held by a substantial body of consumers, whether that incorrect belief is created by the seller's representations or results from consumers' own expectations in the circumstances of the transaction.[13] Thus, the Commission must first find that consumers have beliefs that are contrary to an undisclosed material fact.

In accordance with these principles, the Commission has found in the past that the nondisclosure of safety risks is deceptive because such warnings are necessary to controvert the consumer's justifiably held assumption of product safety.[15] In addition to what may be generally termed "hazardous commodities" cases, several other categories of FTC matters have at times acquired a "pure omissions" label. These include the failure to disclose the true properties of a product where the appearance of the product, absent disclosure, would mislead the public[16] and silence concerning the foreign origin of a product.[17]

In a number of matters involving seller omissions, the Commission has found that the deception actually derives from or is promoted by implied representations or other actions by the seller.[18] Thus, the Commission has determined that the sale of a product carries with it the implication that the product is safe for the use for which it is sold.[19] As is true under a pure

---

13. The Commission has stated that "[t]he principle crystallized in [the caselaw] is that Section 5 forbids sellers to exploit the normal expectations of consumers in order to deceive just as it forbids sellers to create false expectations by affirmative acts." Statement of Basis and Purpose for the Cigarette Rule, 29 FR 8324, 8352 (July 2, 1964).

Also, in promulgating the Home Insulation Rule the Commission asserted, "[i]t is an established principle of Section 5 that when a consumer's normal expectations concerning a product are at odds with actual information about the product, this disparity must be corrected through disclosure." Statement of Basis and Purpose for the Labeling and Advertising of Home Insulation Rule, 44 FR 50218, 50223 (Aug. 27, 1979).

15. See Stupell Enterprises, Inc., 67 F.T.C. 173 (1965); Fisher & Deritis, 49 F.T.C. 77 (1952); Seymour Dress & Blouse Co., 49 F.T.C. 1278 (1953); Academy Knitted Fabrics Corp., 49 F.T.C. 697 (1952).

16. E.g., Haskelite Mfg. Corp., 33 F.T.C. 1212 (1941), aff'd 127 F.2d 765 (7th Cir.1942).

17. E.g., Manco Strap Co., Inc., 60 F.T.C. 495 (1962).

18. For instance, in some cases it has been determined that the normal appearance of a product impliedly represents that it is new or that it is made from a certain material. See e.g., Peacock Buick, Inc., 86 F.T.C. 1532, 1557–58 (1975), aff'd 553 F.2d 97 (4th Cir.1977) (opinion unpublished); Haskelite Mfg. Corp., 33 F.T.C. 1212 (1941), aff'd 127 F.2d 765 (7th Cir.1942).

19. See, e.g., Stupell Enterprises, Inc., 67 F.T.C. 173, 194 (1965) (offering a product for sale may impliedly represent that it will perform its intended function and do so without posing an unusual risk of harm).

From my review of Commission caselaw, it appears that most if not all of the hazardous commodities cases brought by the FTC under what has been called a "pure omission" theory were also found to involve an

omission analysis, in such instances it is deceptive to market the product absent adequate disclosure of latent safety hazards.[20]

In my judgment, the facts of this matter place it squarely within the ambit of prior Commission decisions involving the deceptive nondisclosure of safety hazards, whether the case is analyzed from an implied representation or pure omission perspective. . . .

Commission law holds that a manufacturer impliedly warrants the safety of its product in normal use and that the manufacturer must disclose specific safety hazards which are not obvious to the users of its products. Given Harvester's own in-plant characterization of fuel geysering as a safety hazard, as well as other information in this record documenting the company's burgeoning awareness over the course of many years of the risks and possibly injurious results of geysering, I do not see how it is possible to conclude, as the Commission does here, that Harvester's overall implied representation of product safety did not encompass this particular safety hazard.

Putting aside for the moment Harvester's implied representation of safety, I believe that these same facts define a basis for finding that the company's silence about geysering in the face of reasonable consumer beliefs about the safety of its product was a deceptive practice under Section 5. Since consumers' normal expectations are that, in the absence of a warning to the contrary, products can be used safely, they are likely to be deceived if a product is dangerous and the warning is omitted.[23]

Here, the ALJ properly concluded that farmers and farm experts alike reasonably believed that removing or improperly fastening the fuel cap on a gasoline-powered tractor was not an especially dangerous practice, even though it was unadvised, and that Harvester was aware of this common procedure. (Indeed, some of Harvester's own employees removed gas caps during tests at company facilities while tractors were still hot or running.) In view of the cumulative knowledge Harvester possessed concerning the circumstances which could lead to geysering and the substantial risk of injury if it occurred, as well as the almost complete lack of information available to tractor operators about this possibility, I believe it is patent that Harvester's unwillingness or delay in disclosing this potential hazard had the tendency to deceive numerous tractor operators in a highly material respect. Such conduct is, by definition, deceptive under Section 5.

My strong disagreement in the instant matter does not end with the Commission's rejection of FTC precedent to find that there was no element of deceit in Harvester's conduct. Rather, I find it necessary to address several aspects of the Commission's underlying reasoning and policy assumptions as well.

implied representation of safety. See Fisher & Deritis, 49 F.T.C. 77 (1952); Seymour Dress & Blouse Co., 49 F.T.C. 1278 (1953); Academy Knitted Fabrics Corp., 49 F.T.C. 697 (1952).

20. Stupell Enterprises, Inc., 67 F.T.C. 173 (1965).

23. See Cigarette Statement, supra note 13, 29 FR at 8352; see also Stupell Enterprises, Inc., 67 F.T.C. 173 (1965).

First, I am frankly dismayed by the Commission's reliance on the statistical probability of physical harm to find that Harvester's general implied representation of safety did not extend to fuel geysering. There is simply no basis in Commission law for requiring that the rate of injury from a latent hazard reach some threshold level before the Commission will infer a misrepresentation of an implied warranty of safety from a seller's silence. To the contrary, an implied representation of safety, like any representation the Commission might consider, conveys a message that can be ascertained when it is made; the message does not change its meaning under varying circumstances nor depend for its interpretation on *ex post facto* analyses of later developments. The Commission's suggestion that an implied representation of safety, made at the time a product is sold, is somehow limited after the fact when the product proves to be unsafe (but not so unsafe as to kill more than a few people) cannot be sustained legally or logically.

If the Commission does not contend—as it cannot possibly—that no representation of safety from fuel geysering was made, then the opinion must mean that the representation was made but, because of the low incidence of injury, was not likely to mislead. Rather than focusing on a product's actual accident rate to determine whether an implied representation of safety is misleading, however, I believe the Commission should instead determine whether the existence of factors giving rise to a particular type of incident can reasonably be expected to occur, thereby placing substantial numbers of consumers at risk. The frequency of accidents merely helps to substantiate the presence of a substantial risk, the existence of which may already be known or foreseeable to the seller.

Here, the ALJ concluded that there was the potential for heat and pressure build-up in all Harvester tractors of a particular type. As I have noted, he also found that it was reasonably likely that tractor operators would remove or fail adequately to secure the gas cap during the normal operation of their vehicles. The combination of these factors introduced a substantial risk of an accident which could lead to injury or death, the existence of which was further confirmed by numerous reports to Harvester of geysering incidents. Thus, while the *rate* of actual physical injury from geysering may have been only .001 percent, the *risk* of a fuel geysering incident, and the accompanying possibility of harm, was present each and every time the operator used his Harvester machinery in the field. It is the foreseeability of this substantial risk of injury, coupled here with Harvester's actual notice of the problem—and not some arbitrary number of injuries or deaths which gives rise to a duty to warn consumers about the hazards of fuel geysering and leads to a finding of deception in the absence of such a disclosure.

Second, I cannot accept the Commission's conclusory finding that only a cost-benefit analysis can prevent a conceptually open-ended category of "pure omissions" from requiring the correction of literally all product-related misconceptions consumers may have. While the FTC's deception authority clearly encompasses deception by silence, the Commission has actually exercised its powers judiciously against such conduct. In large measure, this reflects the Commission's understanding that sellers are held legally accountable for correcting a disparity between normal consumer expectations that the sellers may have had little direct role in creating and truthful information about a product. In recognition of this additional responsibility, the Commission has held, for example, that silence can be deceptive only where erroneous consumer expectations about a product are normal and reasonable and where danger is not readily observable to the user of a product.

There is an even more fundamental safeguard against unwarranted results, however, and that is the deception standard itself, evolved by the Commission and the courts over a fifty year period to analyze potentially misleading conduct. Contrary to the Commission's implication that there is a virtual "per se" standard for deceptive conduct, a finding of deception actually requires specific and well-developed findings by the Commission, based on the facts of each case, as to each of the three principal components of deception. Thus, the Commission must determine in all cases that there is (1) a representation or omission capable of misleading (2) a substantial number of consumers (3) as to a material product purchasing or use decision before liability may be found. Most "omissions" of product or use information could not be ruled deceptive under this standard.

QUESTIONS AND NOTES

1. Only three of the five Commissioners concurred in the 1983 Policy Statement, which they described merely as an articulation of the standard of deception that the Commission had developed over the years. The other two Commissioners vehemently disagreed, asserting that the standard articulated in the Policy Statement is much more restrictive than the *Charles of the Ritz* standard. Do you agree? If so, in precisely what way(s) is it more restrictive?

2. On pages 67–68 the Commission addresses what it calls "pure" omissions. What is a pure omission? Why are pure omissions not deceptive? Do the cases cited on page 67 concern pure omission? Is *International Harvester* a case of pure omission? See the dissenting opinion at pages 71–72.

3. Is Ollerman v. O'Rourke Co. (page 34 supra) a case of pure omission? Would the majority in *International Harvester* hold the seller's conduct to be deceptive within the meaning of section 5? Should it? With respect to the hypothetical in Question 3, page 42 supra, would the *International Harvester* Commission hold the seller's conduct to be deceptive?

4. In Part III of its opinion, the majority concludes that there is no misleading representation in *International Harvester*. What is its reasoning for this conclusion? In footnote 35 the majority cites section 2–314 of the Uniform Commercial Code. What is the relevance of that section? Note that the majority does not mention section 2–314 in its analysis in Part III. Should it have done so? If it had, would that have changed the outcome?

C. Bait and Switch

The first step in a merchant's making a sale is inducing the consumer into considering a transaction with the merchant. Advertising immediately comes to mind as a principal way to do this. Difficulties arise when the advertising is not entirely truthful, that is, when the advertising is deceptive. One form of deceptive advertising is known as bait and switch, which is defined as an attractive but insincere offer (the bait) that is designed to initiate contact with the consumer, followed by an attempt to persuade the consumer to purchase something other than the advertised product or service (the switch). In the classic form of bait and switch, the seller induces the consumer to form a contract for the advertised product. After the consumer has become obligated to purchase the bait, the seller proceeds to disparage it, while simultaneously praising the virtues of a similar (but inevitably more expensive) product. E.g., All–State Industries of North Carolina, Inc. v. FTC, 423 F.2d 423 (4th Cir.1970). In another form of bait and switch, the seller uses the bait to make contact with the consumer but disparages the bait during the course of showing it to the consumer, even before the consumer has entered a contract. E.g., In re Household Sewing Machine Co., 76 F.T.C. 207 (1969), modified in 77 F.T.C. 1186 (1970). But the tactic may be more subtle than this.

In re Leon A. Tashof

Federal Trade Commission, 1968.
74 F.T.C. 1361, affirmed 437 F.2d 707 (D.C.Cir.1970).

By Jones, Commissioner:

Complaint in this matter was filed on September 29, 1966, charging the respondent Leon A. Tashof, trading as New York Jewelry Company, with violations of Section 5 of the Federal Trade Commission Act.

. . .

The hearing examiner[a] dismissed the complaint because in his view counsel supporting the complaint failed to carry the burden of proof on any of the complaint allegations. . . . Counsel supporting the complaint has appealed. . . .

Respondent's store is located in one of the low-income market areas in the District of Columbia. Many of respondent's customers hold extremely low-paying jobs, have no bank accounts or charge accounts, and do not own their own home. . . .

---

a. At the time of these proceedings, the title of the hearing officer was "Hearing Examiner." In 1973 the title was changed to "Administrative Law Judge."—Ed.

The complaint alleges that respondent advertised eyeglasses at a price which was not a bona fide offer ($7.50). . . .

The hearing examiner concluded that the bait and switch allegation was not sustained because counsel supporting the complaint failed to prove that respondent had ever refused to honor the terms of its alleged "bait" advertisement or that respondent had ever disparaged the quality of these advertised eyeglasses or discouraged a customer from purchasing a pair, which practices were included in the complaint as part of the bait and switch allegation. . . .

We believe that the . . . hearing examiner applied an erroneous standard of law to the record facts bearing on the bait and switch charge. . . .

Respondent advertised both in the newspaper and on radio that it was offering discount eyeglasses at $7.50 and up. One of its newspaper advertisements for discount eyeglasses which ran once a week for a year and a half . . . contains a headline "CREDIT in a FLASH says MR. TASH, The Manager," which is then followed by bold faced legends "DISCOUNT EYE-GLASSES," "Made While You Wait," "Price Includes lenses, frame and case," "From $7.50 complete." These are followed by the words in somewhat less prominent type:

Glasses attractively Styled

Made Individually to Your Prescription.

Immediately following this legend is an additional statement in smaller type which is the least prominent of any in the advertisement:

Oculists' prescription filled—or

have your eyes examined by our

registered optometrist.

Moderate Examining Fee.

. . .

Respondent regularly maintained a sign in its store, and apparently also in the window for a period of time, which states "Free eye examination, our doctor is in the store." Respondent also had mailed out cards offering "Free eye examinations" and one of its employees stationed in front of the store offered "free eye examinations" to attract people into the store.

Respondent urges that the $7.50 discount price was not false or deceptive and that the advertising only represented the price of respondent's eyeglasses if its customers brought an optical prescription already made out for New York Jewelry to fill. Moreover, respondent's counsel argues that respondent honored the terms of these advertisements, according to its interpretation of them, that there is no direct evidence that it disparaged the quality of such glasses or otherwise discouraged their sale, and that, therefore, the bait and switch allegation must fail as a matter of fact and of law.

There is no doubt that respondent's newspaper advertisement highlighted the availability of DISCOUNT eyeglasses complete from $7.50 while at the same time—albeit in less prominent type—referring to a "Moderate examining fee." But reference to moderate examining fee was in direct conflict with respondent's direct mail solicitations, its signs in its store and the oral representations of its salesmen that eye examinations would be given free. Moreover, its radio commercial was consistent with its mail solicitations and point of sale representations. This commercial made no mention of examination fees and indeed represented that respondent was offering "eyeglass service" at economy prices and later on spoke of "complete" eyeglasses for as low as $7.50. We do not believe that any listener would be aware from this commercial that eyeglass service did not include an examination or that they would be charged an extra examination fee in addition to the quoted price of $7.50. . . .

Consequently, we hold that the fair interpretation of respondent's advertisements, when viewed in their entirety in the context of respondent's overall promotion and its sales practices involving eyeglasses, is that customers would expect to get new eyeglasses at respondent's store for as low as $7.50 whether they brought an oculist's prescription or had their eyes examined on the premises.

The evidence in the record demonstrates clearly that respondent did not sell eyeglasses for $7.50 with or without an eye examination. . . . Indeed, there is no affirmative evidence in the record that a single sale was made by respondent at the advertised price of $7.50. Moreover, a tabulation prepared by complaint counsel of respondent's eyeglass prices for a six month period in 1966, projectible for that year as well as 1964 and 1965, shows no eyeglasses sold by respondent even at $12.50, respondent's advertised price plus its cost for an eye examination. Quite to the contrary, the tabulation shows that 90% of respondent's eyeglasses were sold for more than $23 and only 1 pair was sold for less than $17. This tabulation shows 17% of respondent's eyeglass sales were at $79.50 and 72% at prices in excess of $39. It is obvious that respondent's eyeglass prices are drastically higher than $7.50. . . .

Respondent argued that the evidence fails to support the complaint allegations that it engaged in bait and switch advertising because no evidence was offered that respondent had disparaged the bait product. We disagree.

The essence of the deception involved in an alleged bait and switch practice is that an offer is made which is not bona fide in that the seller has no intention to sell the advertised product at the advertised price but is using the advertisement as a "come-on" in order to sell a higher priced or different product. Disparagement is frequently the technique used by sellers to "switch" the customer. A failure to prove affirmatively that this technique was used in no sense constitutes a failure of proof of the basic illegal practice. Such factors as whether it would have been economically feasible for respondents to make many sales at the advertised price, whether there were in fact a substantial number of sales of the advertised product, or whether the salesman received commissions on the advertised product have been relied upon by the Commission in finding illegal bait and switch practices in addition to evidence of disparagement. . . .

It is inconceivable to us that a retailer would expend the monies necessary to advertise $7.50 eyeglasses over a year and a half period and make virtually no sales of the advertised product if he had any bona fide intention at all to sell glasses at this price. Under such circumstances, the seller must come forward with some evidence to show at a minimum that the advertised product was in its store, freely available to consumers and that they purchased the substantially higher priced goods on the basis of having knowingly made a free choice between the two priced categories of goods. Absent any such evidence we certainly cannot assume that respondent's customers responding to this advertisement, typically people of very limited financial means, were honestly confronted with the choice of $7.50 glasses or glasses costing many times more and freely and consistently purchased the higher priced glasses and in no single instance that we know of purchased the advertised glasses.

We are of the opinion that respondent's advertisement was not a bona fide offer, that respondent had no intention of selling glasses at this price and took whatever steps were necessary to persuade its customers to fill their eyeglass needs with glasses which cost substantially more than the advertised price and that complaint counsel's failure to show direct affirmative evidence of disparagement in the instant case is in no sense fatal to the allegation.

We conclude, therefore, that respondent has engaged in bait and switch advertising with respect to its eyeglasses in violation of Section 5 of the Federal Trade Commission Act.

. . .

QUESTIONS AND NOTES

1. In view of the absence of evidence that Tashof disparaged the inexpensive eyeglasses either before or after his customers contracted to purchase them, what evidence is there that the offer of cheap eyeglasses was insincere?

2. Problem. *Seller* advertises in a newspaper, "Hair Blower $9.95." *Consumer* goes to the store to purchase the advertised hair blower. The salesperson shows it to *Consumer*, saying, "I'll be happy to sell this to you, but there's one little thing I think you should know. It only blows cold air and therefore will take a very long time to dry your hair." *Consumer* immediately decides to buy another model (that just happens to be available) for $19.95. Is there a violation of section 5? What additional facts would be relevant?

Is *Seller's* conduct actionable under the common law principles studied in Chapter 1?

3.   Problem. *Seller* advertises hair blowers, regularly $26.88, on sale for $18.88. Between 9:30, when the store opens, and noon, three hundred consumers stream into the store to buy the hair blower. All but the first twenty are told, "Sorry, but we have sold out of the advertised blower. We do have other models, however. May I show you one?" Does this violate section 5?

Is *Seller's* conduct actionable under the common law principles of Chapter 1?

4.   The New York legislature responded to the phenomenon of bait and switch with the following statute:

> No person, firm, partnership, association, or corporation, or agent or employee thereof, shall, in any manner, or by any means of advertisement, or other means of communication, offer for sale any merchandise, commodity, or service, as part of a plan or scheme with the intent, design, or purpose not to sell the merchandise, commodity, or service so advertised at the price stated therein, or with the intent, design or purpose not to sell the merchandise, commodity, or service so advertised. Nothing in this section shall apply to any television or sound radio broadcasting station or to any publisher or printer of a newspaper, magazine, or other form of printed advertising, who broadcasts, publishes, or prints such advertisement.

McKinney's N.Y.Gen.Bus.Law § 396(1). Would the sellers in the preceding two problems violate this statute? Would they violate section 3(b)(6) of the Uniform Consumer Sales Practices Act (which is reproduced in the Statutory Supplement)?

5.   Would the practices that the FTC held to be deceptive in *Tashof* be deceptive under the standard articulated in *International Harvester*?

6.   The prohibition of deception has an economic, as well as a moral, basis. The existence of deception negates the assumption of classical economic theory that all persons have perfect information.[1] But while all commentators agree that deception is undesirable, not all agree on the extent to which the government should intervene to prevent it. Some believe intervention is largely unnecessary because market forces and common law remedies will operate to eliminate deception or at least reduce it to a tolerable level. Representative of that view is R. Posner, Regulation of Advertising by the FTC (1973). Other persons doubt the sufficiency of market forces and common law remedies. E.g., Pitofsky, Beyond Nader: Consumer Protection and the Regulation of Advertising, 90 Harv.L.Rev. 661, 666–67 (1977) ("The inability of the free market to generate sufficient incentives for sellers to expose deceptive claims by competitors is indicated

---

1.   Recall *International Harvester*, where the FTC referred to the "unalloyed negative qualities" of deception: "It is harmful to consumers, undermines the rational functioning of the marketplace, and . . . never offers increased efficiency or other benefits. . . ."

by the fact that in the scores of proceedings in which the FTC successfully challenged the truth of major advertising themes, there was not a single instance in which rivals used their own access to channels of consumer information to expose deceptions.'')

7.   Since the early 1970s, the Federal Trade Commission has taken the position that it violates section 5 for a seller to make a claim for its product if the seller, at the time of making the claim, does not have proof that the claim is true. See In re Pfizer, Inc., 81 F.T.C. 23 (1972). In 1983 the Commission issued a Policy Statement Regarding Advertising Substantiation, published as an Appendix to In re Thompson Medical Co., 104 F.T.C. 648, at 839 (1984) (reproduced in the Statutory Supplement). In subsequent cases the Commission has concluded that, at least in the context of advertisements for over-the-counter drugs, if the seller claims, expressly or impliedly, that the effectiveness or superiority of its product has been proven or established, the seller must have two or more ''adequate and well-controlled clinical investigations, conducted by independent experts.'' E.g., In re Bristol–Myers Co., 102 F.T.C. 21, 390 (1983), affirmed 738 F.2d 554 (2d Cir.1984), cert. denied 469 U.S. 1189 (1985). The Commission also ordered Bristol–Myers not to make any therapeutic performance claim for a product unless it possesses a ''reasonable basis,'' consisting of ''competent and reliable scientific evidence,'' for the claim. It addressed the meaning of ''reasonable basis'' in this way:

> In general, the amount of substantiation necessary to constitute a reasonable basis must be determined case-by-case. In part for that reason, . . . the order does not describe in detail the amount and kinds of evidence necessary to constitute a reasonable basis for Bristol–Myers' future claims. It is clear, however, that two well-controlled clinical tests, the amount of evidence necessary to establish a claim, would constitute a reasonable basis for any therapeutic performance or side effects claim. Thus, Paragraph II states that that amount of evidence will be deemed to provide a reasonable basis for such claims.

> Whether any lesser amount of evidence could also constitute a reasonable basis is more difficult to determine. The experts who testified in this case indicated that the scientific community requires two well-controlled clinical tests to evaluate therapeutic claims. Thus, even if some lesser amount of evidence were appropriate for nonestablishment claims, it is difficult to see where that level could possibly be set. Nonetheless, we cannot rule out the possibility that other types of evidence might be adequate on the record before us in this case. Accordingly, order Paragraph II does permit respondent to substantiate its claims with evidence other than two clinical tests if it can show that such evidence is sufficiently reliable to support a good faith belief in the truth of the claim. Such a showing must be based on the factors set forth in the *Pfizer* line of cases—the nature of the claim, the degree of consumer reliance on the claim, the consequence to consumers if the claim is, in fact, false, and the accessibility of various types of evidence.

Concededly, permitting such a showing creates some ambiguity regarding the absolute minimum amount of evidence necessary to provide a reasonable basis for respondent's future claims. But this is inherent in any reasonable basis order by virtue of the factors set forth in *Pfizer*. . . .

102 F.T.C. at 376–77. See In re Removatron International Corp., 111 F.T.C. 206, 296–312 (1988), affirmed 884 F.2d 1489, 1498–1500 (1st Cir.1989).

8. The FTC's authority does not extend to federally insured financial institutions (and other entities specified in section 5(a)(2)). Nevertheless, the prohibition in section 5(a)(1) extends to those entities. The Act is silent as to how it is to be enforced against them, and until very recently the federal agencies that regulate them have not attempted to exercise their authority in an adjudicative (as opposed to rule-making) context. In 2001, however, the Office of the Comptroller of the Currency began asserting its power to enforce section 5 with respect to institutions within its jurisdiction.

D. REMEDIES UNDER THE FTC ACT

The primary remedy under the FTC Act has been the issuance of a cease and desist order. FTCA § 5(a)(2), (b). A person who violates a cease and desist order is subject to a civil penalty of up to $10,000 for each violation. FTCA § 5(*l*). The same sanction is available for violation of a trade regulation rule. FTCA § 5(m). Furthermore, once the FTC issues a cease and desist order in a proceeding against one person, if another person has actual knowledge of the order and engages in the conduct found to be unfair or deceptive, that other person is subject to a civil penalty even though he or she was not a party to the original proceeding. FTCA § 5(m). Consequently, the FTC may send copies of cease and desist orders to persons in the industries of, or engaging in similar practices as, persons against whom orders have been issued. Use of this procedure gives adjudication some of the effects of rulemaking. Is the procedure constitutional? Is it fair?

On its face, the remedy embodied by the phrase "cease and desist" may appear to be a fairly coarse tool, more an axe than a scalpel. But in the hands of the FTC, the cease and desist remedy has become finely honed. For example, to prevent deceptive practices, the Commission ordered one seller to cease and desist entering contracts for more than $1,500 (on the rationale that the seller would not find it worthwhile to use the particular practices for contracts smaller than this amount). Arthur Murray Studio of Washington, Inc. v. FTC, 458 F.2d 622 (5th Cir.1972). It ordered another seller to cease and desist transferring consumer contracts to finance companies unless the seller so informs the consumer at the time the contract is formed. All–State Industries of North Carolina, Inc. v. FTC, 423 F.2d 423 (4th Cir.1970). And it has ordered sellers to cease and desist entering contracts without giving consumers a short cooling-off period in which to rescind the contracts. E.g., In re Household Sewing Machine, 76 F.T.C. 207 (1969), modified in 77 F.T.C. 1186 (1970).[2] Thus under the rubric of "cease and desist," the FTC has been able to compel an alteration of the terms on which sellers do business. The following case examines another creative use of the cease and desist remedy.

Warner–Lambert Co. v. FTC

United States Court of Appeals, District of Columbia Circuit, 1977.
562 F.2d 749, cert. denied 435 U.S. 950, 98 S.Ct. 1576, 55 L.Ed.2d 800 (1978).

J.   SKELLY WRIGHT, CIRCUIT JUDGE:

The Warner–Lambert Company petitions for review of an order of the Federal Trade Commission requiring it to cease and desist from advertising that its product, Listerine Antiseptic mouthwash, prevents, cures, or alleviates the common cold. The FTC order further requires Warner–Lambert to disclose in future Listerine advertisements that: "Contrary to prior advertising, Listerine will not help prevent colds or sore throats or lessen their severity." We affirm but modify the order to delete from the required disclosure the phrase "Contrary to prior advertising."

I.   BACKGROUND

. . .

Listerine has been on the market since 1879. Its formula has never changed. Ever since its introduction it has been represented as being beneficial in certain respects for colds, cold symptoms, and sore throats. Direct advertising to the consumer, including the cold claims as well as others, began in 1921.

. . .

II.   SUBSTANTIAL EVIDENCE

The first issue on appeal is whether the Commission's conclusion that Listerine is not beneficial for colds or sore throats is supported by the evidence. The Commission's findings must be sustained if they are supported by substantial evidence on the record viewed as a whole. We conclude that they are. . . .

III.   THE COMMISSION'S POWER

Petitioner contends that even if its advertising claims in the past were false, the portion of the Commission's order requiring "corrective advertising" exceeds the Commission's statutory power. The argument is based upon a literal reading of Section 5 of the Federal Trade Commission Act, which authorizes the Commission to issue "cease and desist" orders

---

2. The Commission has since promulgated trade regulation rules addressing two of these practices. Cooling-Off Period for Door-to-Door Sales, 16 C.F.R. Part 429 (considered in Chapter 9); Preservation of Consumers' Claims and Defenses, 16 C.F.R. Part 433 (considered in Chapter 15).

against violators and does not expressly mention any other remedies. The Commission's position, on the other hand, is that the affirmative disclosure that Listerine will not prevent colds or lessen their severity is absolutely necessary to give effect to the prospective cease and desist order; a hundred years of false cold claims have built up a large reservoir of erroneous consumer belief which would persist, unless corrected, long after petitioner ceased making the claims.

The need for the corrective advertising remedy and its appropriateness in this case are important issues which we will explore infra. But the threshold question is whether the Commission has the authority to issue such an order. We hold that it does.

Petitioner's narrow reading of Section 5 was at one time shared by the Supreme Court. In FTC v. Eastman Kodak Co. the Court held that the Commission's authority did not exceed that expressly conferred by statute. The Commission has not, the Court said, "been delegated the authority of a court of equity."

But the modern view is very different. In 1963 the Court ruled that the Civil Aeronautics Board has authority to order divestiture in addition to ordering cessation of unfair methods of competition by air carriers. The CAB statute, like Section 5, spoke only of the authority to issue cease and desist orders, but the Court said, "We do not read the Act so restrictively. * * * [W]here the problem lies within the purview of the Board, * * * Congress must have intended to give it authority that was ample to deal with the evil at hand." The Court continued, "Authority to mold administrative decrees is indeed like the authority of courts to frame injunctive decrees * * *. [The] power to order divestiture need not be explicitly included in the powers of an administrative agency to be part of its arsenal of authority * * *."[28]

Later, in FTC v. Dean Foods Co., the Court applied *Pan American* to the Federal Trade Commission. In upholding the Commission's power to seek a preliminary injunction against a proposed merger, the Court held that it was not necessary to find express statutory authority for the power. Rather, the Court concluded, "It would stultify congressional purpose to say that the Commission did not have the * * * power * * *. * * * Such ancillary powers have always been treated as essential to the effective discharge of the Commission's responsibilities."

Thus it is clear that the Commission has the power to shape remedies which go beyond the simple cease and desist order. Our next inquiry must be whether a corrective advertising order is for any reason outside the range of permissible remedies. Petitioner and amici *curiae*[a] argue that it is because (1) legislative history precludes it, (2) it impinges on the First Amendment, and (3) it has never been approved by any court.

---

28.   [Pan American World Airways, Inc. v. United States, 371 U.S. 296, 311–312, 83 S.Ct. 476, 9 L.Ed.2d 325 (1963).]

a.   Two trade associations of the advertising industry filed briefs as *amici curiae.*— Ed.

A. *Legislative History*

Petitioner relies on the legislative history of the 1914 Federal Trade Commission Act and the Wheeler–Lea amendments to it in 1938 for the proposition that corrective advertising was not contemplated. In 1914 and in 1938 Congress chose not to authorize such remedies as criminal penalties, treble damages, or civil penalties, but that fact does not dispose of the question of corrective advertising.[33]

Petitioner's reliance on the legislative history of the 1975 amendments to the Act is also misplaced. The amendments added a new Section 19 to the Act authorizing the Commission to bring suits in federal District Courts to redress injury to consumers resulting from a deceptive practice. The section authorizes the court to grant such relief as it "finds necessary to redress injury to consumers or other persons, partnerships, and corporations resulting from the rule violation or the unfair or deceptive act or practice," including, but not limited to,

> rescission or reformation of contracts, the refund of money or return of property, the payment of damages, and public notification respecting the rule violation or the unfair or deceptive act or practice * * *.

Petitioner and *amici* contend that this congressional grant *to a court* of power to order public notification of a violation establishes that the Commission by itself does not have that power.

We note first that "public notification" is not synonymous with corrective advertising; public notification is a much broader term and may take any one of many forms.[36] Second, the "public notification" contemplated by the amendment is directed at *past* consumers of the product ("to redress injury"), whereas the type of corrective advertising currently before us is directed at *future* consumers. Third, petitioner's construction of the section runs directly contrary to the congressional intent as expressed in a later subsection: "Nothing in this section shall be construed to affect any authority of the Commission under any other provision of law." Moreover, this intent is amplified by the conference committee's report:

> The section * * * is not intended to modify or limit any existing power the Commission may have to itself issue orders designed to [remedy] violations of the law. That issue is now before the courts. It is not the intent of the Conferees to influence the outcome in any way.

33. It is true that one Court of Appeals has relied on this history in concluding that the Commission does not have power to order restitution of ill-gotten monies to the injured consumers. Heater v. FTC, 503 F.2d 321 (9th Cir.1974). But restitution is not corrective advertising. Ordering refunds to *past* consumers is very different from ordering affirmative disclosure to correct misconceptions which *future* consumers may hold. Moreover, the *Heater* court itself recognized this distinc- tion and expressly distinguished corrective advertising, which it said the Commission is authorized to order, from restitution. 503 F.2d at 323 n. 7 and 325 n. 13.

36. For example, it might encompass requiring the defendant to run special advertisements reporting the FTC finding, advertisements advising consumers of the availability of a refund, or the posting of notices in the defendant's place of business.

In re Int'l Harvester (1984)

3 elements of deception

1) Rep likely to _mislead_ consumer
2) Comm must be interp. messg REASONABLy
3) mislead'g effects must be MATERIAL

Focus is on RISK OF HARM not
actual injury

Pure:
A subject
upon which
seller has
said nothing,
in cir. that
do not
give
any
part.
meg to
his silent

Rep = • Omissions (Half-Truth)
      • Kemainsient (Implied but
                     false Rep)

{
UCC
2-314(2)
Implied
Warty of
Merchantability
}

We conclude that this legislative history cannot be said to remove corrective advertising from the class of permissible remedies.

. . .

C. *Precedents*

According to petitioner, "The first reference to corrective advertising in Commission decisions occurred in 1970, nearly fifty years and untold numbers of false advertising cases after passage of the Act." In petitioner's view, the late emergence of this "newly discovered" remedy is itself evidence that it is beyond the Commission's authority. This argument fails on two counts. First the fact that an agency has not asserted a power over a period of years is not proof that the agency lacks such power. Second, and more importantly, we are not convinced that the corrective advertising remedy is really such an innovation. The label may be newly coined, but the concept is well established. It is simply that under certain circumstances an advertiser may be required to make affirmative disclosure of unfavorable facts.

One such circumstance is when an advertisement that did not contain the disclosure would be misleading. For example, the Commission has ordered the sellers of treatments for baldness to disclose that the vast majority of cases of thinning hair and baldness are attributable to heredity, age, and endocrine balance (so-called "male pattern baldness") and that their treatment would have no effect whatever on this type of baldness.[49] It has ordered the promoters of a device for stopping bedwetting to disclose that the device would not be of value in cases caused by organic defects or diseases.[50] And it has ordered the makers of Geritol, an iron supplement, to disclose that Geritol will relieve symptoms of tiredness only in persons who suffer from iron deficiency anemia, and that the vast majority of people who experience such symptoms do not have such a deficiency.[51]

Each of these orders was approved on appeal over objections that it exceeded the Commission's statutory authority. The decisions reflect a recognition that, as the Supreme Court has stated,

> If the Commission is to attain the objectives Congress envisioned, it cannot be required to confine its road block to the narrow lane the transgressor has traveled; it must be allowed effectively to close all roads to the prohibited goal, so that its order may not be by-passed with impunity.[53]

Affirmative disclosure has also been required when an advertisement, although not misleading if taken alone, becomes misleading considered in light of past advertisements. For example, for 60 years Royal Baking

---

49. Ward Laboratories, Inc. v. FTC, 276 F.2d 952 (2d Cir.), cert. denied, 364 U.S. 827, 81 S.Ct. 65, 5 L.Ed.2d 55 (1960); Keele Hair & Scalp Specialists, Inc. v. FTC, 275 F.2d 18 (5th Cir.1960).

50. Feil v. FTC, 285 F.2d 879 (9th Cir. 1960).

51. J. B. Williams Co. v. FTC, 381 F.2d 884 (6th Cir.1967).

53. FTC v. Ruberoid Co., 343 U.S. 470, 473, 72 S.Ct. 800, 803, 96 L.Ed. 1081 (1952). . . .

Powder Company had stressed in its advertising that its product was superior because it was made with cream of tartar, not phosphate. But, faced with rising costs of cream of tartar, the time came when it changed its ingredients and became a phosphate baking powder. It carefully removed from all labels and advertisements any reference to cream of tartar and corrected the list of ingredients. But the new labels used the familiar arrangement of lettering, coloration, and design, so that they looked exactly like the old ones. A new advertising campaign stressed the new low cost of the product and dropped all reference to cream of tartar. But the advertisements were also silent on the subject of phosphate and did not disclose the change in the product.

The Commission held, and the Second Circuit agreed, that the new advertisements were deceptive, since they did not advise consumers that their reasons for buying the powder in the past no longer applied.

The court held that it was proper to require the company to take affirmative steps to advise the public. To continue to sell the new powder

> on the strength of the reputation attained through 60 years of its manufacture and sale and wide advertising of its superior powder, under an impression induced by its advertisements that the product purchased was the same in kind and as superior as that which had been so long manufactured by it, was unfair alike to the public and to the competitors in the baking powder business.[55]

In another case[56] the Waltham Watch Company of Massachusetts had become renowned for the manufacture of fine clocks since 1849. Soon after it stopped manufacturing clocks in the 1950's, it transferred its trademarks, good will, and the trade name "Waltham" to a successor corporation, which began importing clocks from Europe for resale in the United States. The imported clocks were advertised as "product of Waltham Watch Company since 1850," "a famous 150–year-old company."

The Commission found that the advertisements caused consumers to believe they were buying the same fine Massachusetts clocks of which they had heard for many years. To correct this impression the Commission ordered the company to disclose in all advertisements and on the product that the clock was not made by the old Waltham company and that it was imported. The Seventh Circuit affirmed, relying on "the well-established general principle that the Commission may require affirmative disclosure for the purpose of preventing future deception."

It appears to us that the orders in *Royal* and *Waltham* were the same kind of remedy the Commission has ordered here. Like *Royal* and *Waltham*, Listerine has built up over a period of many years a widespread reputation. When it was ascertained that that reputation no longer applied to the

---

55. Royal Baking Powder Co. v. FTC, 281 F. 744, 753 (2d Cir.1922).

56. Waltham Watch Co. v. FTC, 318 F.2d 28 (7th Cir.), cert. denied, 375 U.S. 944, 84 S.Ct. 349, 11 L.Ed.2d 274 (1963).

product, it was necessary to take action to correct it.[58] Here, as in *Royal* and *Waltham*, it is the accumulated impact of *past* advertising that necessitates disclosure in *future* advertising. To allow consumers to continue to buy the product on the strength of the impression built up by prior advertising—an impression which is now known to be false—would be unfair and deceptive.[60]

IV.   THE REMEDY

Having established that the Commission does have the power to order corrective advertising in appropriate cases, it remains to consider whether use of the remedy against Listerine is warranted and equitable. We have concluded that part 3 of the order should be modified to delete the phrase "Contrary to prior advertising." With that modification, we approve the order.

Our role in reviewing the remedy is limited. The Supreme Court has set forth the standard:

> The Commission is the expert body to determine what remedy is necessary to eliminate the unfair or deceptive trade practices which have been disclosed. It has wide latitude for judgment and the courts will not interfere except where the remedy selected has no reasonable relation to the unlawful practices found to exist.[62]

The Commission has adopted the following standard for the imposition of corrective advertising:

> [I]f a deceptive advertisement has played a substantial role in creating or reinforcing in the public's mind a false and material belief which lives on after the false advertising ceases, there is clear and continuing

---

58. In *Royal* and *Waltham* the advertising claims that had given rise to the products' reputations were concededly true when made, but because the products themselves had changed that reputation was no longer deserved. Consumers would have been deceived, in the future, if they had continued to make purchases in reliance upon this reputation. Here, of course, the Commission has determined that Listerine's cold claims were *never* true, and that its reputation as a cold remedy was thus never deserved. What has changed in this case is not the product itself, but the extent of our knowledge of the evidence underlying the advertising claims. But the result here is the same as in the earlier cases—like Royal baking powder or Waltham watches, Listerine continues to enjoy a reputation it does not deserve, and consumers would therefore be deceived if they were to make purchases in reliance upon that reputation.

60. . . .

While we do not know and do not decide whether our petitioner made its false cold

claims in good faith or bad, we do observe that for an advertiser who knowingly advertises falsely a simple cease and desist order provides no real deterrent. He has nothing to lose but attorneys' fees. He gets to use the deceptive advertisements until he is caught—more precisely, until Commission proceedings, which usually drag on for years, are completed against him. By the time the order has become final, the particular campaign has probably been squeezed dry, if not already discarded. In the meantime the seller has increased his market share and reaped handsome profits. The order to cease making the false claims takes none of this away from him. In short, "[a] cease and desist order which commands the respondent only to 'go, and sin no more' simply allows every violator a free bite at the apple." Note, "Corrective Advertising" Orders of the Federal Trade Commission, 85 Harv.L.Rev. 477, 482–483 (1971).

62. Jacob Siegel Co. v. FTC, 327 U.S. 608, 612–613, 66 S.Ct. 758, 760, 90 L.Ed. 888 (1946). . . .

injury to competition and to the consuming public as consumers continue to make purchasing decisions based on the false belief. Since this injury cannot be averted by merely requiring respondent to cease disseminating the advertisement, we may appropriately order respondent to take affirmative action designed to terminate the otherwise continuing ill effects of the advertisement.

We think this standard is entirely reasonable. It dictates two factual inquiries: (1) did Listerine's advertisements play a substantial role in creating or reinforcing in the public's mind a false belief about the product? and (2) would this belief linger on after the false advertising ceases? It strikes us that if the answer to both questions is not yes, companies everywhere may be wasting their massive advertising budgets. Indeed, it is more than a little peculiar to hear petitioner assert that its commercials really have no effect on consumer belief.

For these reasons it might be appropriate in some cases to presume the existence of the two factual predicates for corrective advertising. But we need not decide that question, or rely on presumptions here, because the Commission adduced survey evidence to support both propositions. We find that the "Product Q" survey data and the expert testimony interpreting them[65] constitute substantial evidence in support of the need for corrective advertising in this case.

We turn next to the specific disclosure required: "Contrary to prior advertising, Listerine will not help prevent colds or sore throats or lessen their severity." Petitioner is ordered to include this statement in every future advertisement for Listerine for a defined period. In printed advertisements it must be displayed in type size at least as large as that in which the principal portion of the text of the advertisement appears and it must be separated from the text so that it can be readily noticed. In television commercials the disclosure must be presented simultaneously in both audio and visual portions. During the audio portion of the disclosure in television and radio advertisements, no other sounds, including music, may occur.

These specifications are well calculated to assure that the disclosure will reach the public. It will necessarily attract the notice of readers, viewers, and listeners, and be plainly conveyed. Given these safeguards, we believe the preamble "Contrary to prior advertising" is not necessary. It can serve only two purposes: either to attract attention that a correction

---

65. The Commission used the results of a series of market surveys known as "Product Q" reports on the "Mouthwash Market." The surveys were conducted by petitioner for its own purposes from 1963 to 1971. . . . The surveys showed that about 70% of the consumers questioned recalled "effective for colds and sore throats" as a main theme of Listerine advertising. During the summer, when no cold claims had been broadcast for about six months, the percentage fell to only 64%; i.e., the recall of cold claims after six months of silence was very substantial. . . .

The Commission also relied on the testimony of two experts in the field of consumer marketing surveys. Dr. Bass testified that cold efficacy belief levels would continue at about 60% for two years after colds advertising ceased and would remain high after five years. Dr. Rossi testified that cold efficacy beliefs would decline at no greater a rate than 5% per year.

follows or to humiliate the advertiser. The Commission claims only the first purpose for it, and this we think is obviated by the other terms of the order. The second purpose, if it were intended, might be called for in an egregious case of deliberate deception,[69] but this is not one. While we do not decide whether petitioner proffered its cold claims in good faith or bad, the record compiled could support a finding of good faith.[70] On these facts, the confessional preamble to the disclosure is not warranted.

Finally, petitioner challenges the duration of the disclosure requirement. By its terms it continues until respondent has expended on Listerine advertising a sum equal to the average annual Listerine advertising budget for the period April 1962 to March 1972. That is approximately ten million dollars. Thus if petitioner continues to advertise normally the corrective advertising will be required for about one year. We cannot say that is an unreasonably long time in which to correct a hundred years of cold claims. But, to petitioner's distress, the requirement will not expire by mere passage of time. If petitioner cuts back its Listerine advertising, or ceases it altogether, it can only postpone the duty to disclose. The Commission concluded that correction was required and that a duration of a fixed period of time might not accomplish that task, since petitioner could evade the order by choosing not to advertise at all. The formula settled upon by the Commission is reasonably related to the violation it found.

Accordingly, the order, as modified, is Affirmed.

ROBB, CIRCUIT JUDGE, dissenting in part:

I agree with the majority that there is substantial evidence in the record to support an order requiring Warner–Lambert to cease and desist from advertising Listerine as a remedy for colds and sore throats. . . .

I dissent from the [portion of the order concerning corrective advertising]. In my judgment this requirement of corrective advertising is beyond the statutory authority of the Federal Trade Commission. The Commission's authority to enter cease and desist orders is prospective in nature; the purpose of cease and desist orders is "to prevent illegal practices in the future," FTC v. Ruberoid Co., 343 U.S. 470, 473, 72 S.Ct. 800, 803, 96 L.Ed. 1081 (1952), not "to punish or to fasten liability on respondents for past conduct." FTC v. Cement Institute, 333 U.S. 683, 706, 68 S.Ct. 793, 806, 92 L.Ed. 1010 (1948). The cases that have construed the Commission's remedial power stand only for the proposition that the Commission has broad discretion in determining what conduct of a respondent shall be forbidden prospectively. I think this authority does not encompass the

---

69. We express no view on the question whether an order intended to humiliate the wrongdoer would be so punitive as to be outside the Commission's proper authority.

70. . . .

While good faith may be relevant to the fairness of a confessional preamble, it is irrelevant to the need for corrective advertising in general. Innocence of motive is not a defense if an advertisement is prejudicial to the public interest.

power to employ the retrospective remedy of corrective advertising; and I find no other basis for that asserted power.

.   .   .

The majority comments briefly that the 1975 Amendment "cannot be said to remove corrective advertising from the class of permissible remedies"; the expressed "congressional intent," says the majority, is to the contrary. I think the 1975 legislation cannot be so lightly dismissed. The amendment indicates to me that at least in the judgment of the Congress the Commission does not have, and is not intended to have, the power to order "public notification" by way of corrective advertising. If the Commission already had that power, why was the amendment necessary? Moreover, the majority fails to note that under the amendment a district court can order public notification only on a showing that the respondent acted in bad faith. Yet the theory of the Commission, accepted by the majority, is that the Commission may enter a corrective advertising order even though a false advertisement was published in good faith. To me it is strange that the Congress would require a court to find bad faith, while authorizing the Commission to act in the absence of bad faith.

.   .   .

I find nothing in the cases that justifies the Commission's corrective advertising order.   .   .   .   In those cases an affirmative disclosure was required because failure to reveal material facts, in the light of the representations made in advertisements, made them misleading.   .   .   .

The majority finds "that the orders in *Royal* and *Waltham* were the same kind of remedy the Commission has ordered here." I cannot agree. In those cases advertisements falsely represented that the products offered for sale were the same as the products, well-known to the public, which had been offered in the past. The Commission's orders simply required these false representations to be corrected in future advertisements using the same or similar format or copy. In the present case, however, when Warner–Lambert has ceased and desisted from advertising Listerine as a remedy for colds and sore throats there will be nothing to correct in the text of the Listerine advertisements. Any "corrective statement" will relate solely to past advertising.

.   .   .

The theory of the majority is that whenever "advertisements play a substantial role in creating or reinforcing in the public's mind a false belief about [a] product" and "this belief [may] linger on after the false advertising ceases", corrective advertising may be ordered. As the majority apparently concedes, this test would apply to almost any advertisement which is the subject of a cease and desist order. I cannot accept this concept. I reject the proposition that the after-effects of advertising which has been discontinued pursuant to a cease and desist order can thus expand the Commission's statutory power to prevent future illegal practices. See Heater v.

FTC, 503 F.2d 321, 323–25 (9th Cir.1974). In my opinion such an expansion must be made by the Congress, not by this court.

SUPPLEMENTAL OPINION ON PETITION FOR REHEARING

. . . The primary argument raised in the petition for rehearing is that the Commission is barred by the First Amendment from imposing a corrective advertising order in this case. Having considered this claim carefully, it is our conclusion that it must be rejected. Because of the importance of the issues raised, however, we think it desirable to set forth in some detail our reasons for so concluding.

I

In Virginia State Board of Pharmacy v. Virginia Citizens Consumer Council, Inc., 425 U.S. 748 (1976), the Supreme Court rejected prior precedents holding that commercial speech is "wholly outside the protection of the First Amendment." In reaching this conclusion the Court emphasized the interest of consumers in the free flow of truthful information necessary for formulation of intelligent opinions and proper resource allocation. Consistent with this concern, the Court was careful to distinguish truthful commercial speech from that which is false, misleading, or deceptive: "Untruthful speech, commercial or otherwise, has never been protected for its own sake. * * * Obviously, much commercial speech is not probably false, or even wholly false, but only deceptive or misleading. We foresee no obstacle to a State's dealing effectively with this problem." Furthermore, the Court went on to suggest that, because of the "common-sense differences" between commercial speech and other varieties, even commercial speech subject to First Amendment protections may nonetheless enjoy a "different degree of protection" than that normally accorded under the First Amendment.

Applying these principles to the case at bar, there can be no question of the legitimacy of the FTC's role in regulating and preventing false and deceptive advertising. In this case it has been found that Warner–Lambert has, over a long period of time, worked a substantial deception upon the public; it has advertised Listerine as a cure for colds, and consumers have purchased its product with that in mind. That the Commission has authority to prohibit Warner–Lambert from continuing to make such false and deceptive claims in its advertisements is not disputed, for it is only truthful claims which are protected under the First Amendment. Here, however, the FTC has determined on substantial evidence that the deception of the public occasioned by Warner–Lambert's past advertisements will not be halted by merely requiring Warner–Lambert to cease making such claims in the future. To be sure, current and future advertising of Listerine, when viewed in isolation, may not contain any statements which are themselves false or deceptive. But reality counsels that such advertisements cannot be viewed in isolation; they must be seen against the background of over 50 years in which Listerine has been proclaimed—and purchased—as a remedy for colds. When viewed from this perspective, advertising which fails to rebut the prior claims as to Listerine's efficacy inevitably builds upon those claims; continued advertising continues the deception, albeit implicitly rather than explicitly. It will induce people to continue to buy Listerine thinking it will cure colds. Thus the Commission found on substantial evidence that the corrective order was necessary to "dissipate the effects of respondent's deceptive representations."

Under this reasoning the First Amendment presents no direct obstacle. The Commission is not regulating truthful speech protected by the First Amendment, but is merely requiring certain statements which, if not present in current and future advertisements, would render those advertisements themselves part of a continuing deception of the public. As the Supreme Court recognized in *Virginia State Board,* in some cases it may be "appropriate to require that a commercial message appear in such a form, or include such additional information, warnings, and disclaimers, as are necessary to prevent its being deceptive." We must conclude—as did the Commission—that this is such a case.

II

Admittedly, corrective advertising orders such as that imposed here may give rise to concern as to their chilling effect on protected truthful speech. The potential advertiser must consider not only the possibility that he will be forced, at some future date, to abandon his advertising campaign, but also that he may be required to include specific disclaimers in future advertisements. But this danger seems more theoretical than real. As the Supreme Court pointed out in *Virginia State Board,* not only is the truth of commercial speech "more easily verifiable by its disseminator" than other forms of speech, but "[s]ince advertising is the *sine qua non* of commercial profits, there is little likelihood of its being chilled by proper regulation and forgone entirely."

Moreover, whatever incremental chill is caused by a corrective advertising order beyond that which would result from a cease and desist order may well be necessary if the interest of consumers in truthful information is to be served at all. Otherwise, advertisers remain free to misrepresent their products to the public through false and deceptive claims, knowing full well that even if the FTC chooses to prosecute they will be required only to cease an advertising campaign which by that point will, in all likelihood, have served its purpose by deceiving the public and already been replaced.

III

A more serious First Amendment problem which may be raised by corrective advertising orders involves the burden thereby imposed upon the constitutional right recognized in *Virginia State Board* to advertise truthfully: the party subject to a corrective advertising order may be precluded from exercising his right to advertise unless he also includes specified statements undermining his prior deceptive claims. On the facts of this case, no burden is imposed upon truthful, protected advertising since, as the Commission makes clear, Listerine's current advertising, if not accompanied by a corrective message, would itself continue to mislead the public. Even if, in the circumstances of this case, the current and future advertising of Listerine is considered constitutionally protected speech, however, we think the corrective advertising order in this case remains appropriate.

The Supreme Court, in invalidating the state ban on advertising of prescription drug prices in *Virginia State Board,* considered the scope of the restriction on First Amendment rights, the governmental purposes and public interests affected by the ban, and the availability of alternative means to accomplish the legitimate governmental objectives. As we have indicated, it is not at all clear, even after *Virginia State Board,* that commercial speech protected by the First Amendment is, apart from "commonsense differences," entitled to the same degree of protection as other forms. Indeed, the opposite conclusion seems the more appropriate one. But in any event, it does seem clear that the corrective advertising order in this case is the least restrictive means of achieving a substantial and important governmental objective and that, on balance, it must be upheld. The governmental interest here, of course, is in protecting citizens against deception—with its attendant waste and misallocation by consumers to the benefit of the wrongdoers—by ensuring that advertising conveys truthful information to the public. As we noted earlier, it is this very interest which was invoked by the *Virginia State Board* Court as support for its conclusion that commercial speech is protected by the First Amendment.

And the facts of this case make it eminently clear that this interest will not be substantially served by the less restrictive remedy—a cease and desist order. . . .

Finally, the corrective advertising order in this case, by tying the quantity of correction required to the investment in deception, is tailored to serve the legitimate governmental interest in correcting public misimpressions as to the value of Listerine—and no more. Taking all these factors into account, we think it beyond doubt that the FTC order is a valid one.

Petition for rehearing denied.

ROBB, CIRCUIT JUDGE, dissenting [dissenting opinion omitted]

QUESTIONS AND NOTES

1. Examine the FTC's standard for determining when a corrective advertising order is appropriate. Under this standard when would a corrective advertising order not be an appropriate remedy for deceptive advertising? Can the standard be improved? See In re Standard Oil Co., 84 F.T.C. 1401, 1476 (1974); In re Sun Oil Co., 84 F.T.C. 247, 277–80 (1974); In re Firestone Tire & Rubber Co., 81 F.T.C. 441, 467–73 (1972), affirmed 481 F.2d 246 (6th Cir.), cert. denied 414 U.S. 1112 (1973).

2. The dissent cites several Supreme Court cases for the proposition that the FTC does not have the power to punish for past misdeeds. Its remedy is prospective. Is a corrective advertising order retrospective in focus and therefore in excess of the Commission's power?

Exactly how does the dissent attempt to distinguish *Warner-Lambert* from *Ward Laboratories* and the other cases on which the majority relies as precedent for ordering corrective ads? Or, to turn the question around, is there an essential similarity between representing "that the products offered for sale were the same as the products . . . which had been offered in the past" (dissent at page 90, supra) and representing that the mouthwash sold by Warner–Lambert is "Listerine"?

In AMREP Corporation v. FTC, 768 F.2d 1171 (10th Cir.1985), cert. denied 475 U.S. 1034 (1986), a real estate developer formed contracts for the sale of vacant lots that contained a forfeiture clause empowering it, in the event of default by the purchaser, to retain all amounts previously paid. The FTC determined this clause to be unlawful and ordered AMREP not to enforce it in any way. AMREP appealed, contending that the Commission lacked authority to order this retrospective relief. The Court of Appeals responded:

> [The rule prohibiting retroactive relief] does not impede the Commission from forbidding the enforcement of illegal contracts. If it did the Commission would be stripped of power. The Supreme Court has upheld the Commission's power to order respondents in proceedings before it not to enforce illegal contracts. See, e.g., Atlantic Refining Company v. Federal Trade Commission, 381 U.S. 357, 372, 375–77, 85 S.Ct. 1498, 1507, 1509–10, 14 L.Ed.2d 443 (1965). The Commission's order in this case falls squarely within the ambit of the *Atlantic Refining* holding. The Commission's order does not order AMREP to repay monies to past lot purchasers; it operates only prospectively, and merely prevents AMREP from continuing to profit from its inclusion of an illegal forfeiture clause in its past contracts. Accordingly, we find this portion of the Commission's order to be a proper exercise of its broad remedial discretion and affirm it.

Id. at 1180.

3. The dissent in *Warner-Lambert* points to the 1975 amendment conferring on the FTC the power to seek a court order requiring "public notification" by a seller who has violated section 5. What answer is there to the dissent's rhetorical question, if the FTC already had the power to order corrective advertising, why did Congress amend the Act to say so?

The majority says that the remedy of public notification is directed at past consumers, while corrective advertising is directed at future consumers. What purpose would public notification of past customers serve? And exactly what is the rationale for requiring corrective ads?

In *AMREP Corporation* (Question 2 supra) the Court of Appeals affirmed the FTC's order requiring AMREP to notify past customers that they did not have to continue making payments, that they would not be liable if they stopped making payments, and that they might be able to sue AMREP for individual relief. The court stated:

. . . . FTC orders requiring affirmative disclosures and corrective advertising have often been sustained by the courts. See, e.g., Warner–Lambert Co. v. Federal Trade Commission, 562 F.2d 749, 756 (D.C.Cir. 1977) (corrective advertising designed to correct misinformation given to past buyers), cert. denied, 435 U.S. 950, 98 S.Ct. 1575, 55 L.Ed.2d 800 (1978). Here, the FTC has merely ordered AMREP to make affirmative disclosures designed to dissipate any misimpressions that purchasers might have as a result of AMREP's promotional tactics. We find this portion of the order to be reasonably related to AMREP's past violations and practices and affirm it.

768 F.2d at 1180.

Is the court's characterization of the order correct? Justice White dissented from the denial of certiorari on the grounds that the lower court's affirmance of the notification requirement conflicts with the conclusion reached by two other courts of appeal. 475 U.S. at 1035. See Barrett Carpet Mills, Inc. v. Consumer Product Safety Commission, 635 F.2d 299 (4th Cir.1980); Congoleum Industries, Inc. v. Consumer Product Safety Commission, 602 F.2d 220 (9th Cir.1979).

4.   What limits are there on cease and desist orders? For example, as a result of prior advertising—over a period of at least fifty years—the public believed Listerine would cure colds. And the "Product Q" surveys revealed that consumers continued to believe this even six months after Warner–Lambert stopped advertising. To remedy the false impression, the FTC ordered Warner–Lambert to include a corrective statement in any future advertising. But it did not compel Warner–Lambert to advertise. Conceivably, Warner–Lambert could have suspended all advertising for Listerine until public recall of the cold-curing properties of Listerine had faded. In the interim Warner–Lambert would have reaped the benefit of the false impression its earlier advertising had created. Then when it resumed advertising, inclusion of the corrective statement would be relatively harmless because few persons would associate the curing of colds with Listerine. Could the FTC require Warner–Lambert to spend ten million dollars in the next year on advertising that includes the corrective statement, whether or not Warner–Lambert wants to advertise at all?

5.   As the court in *Warner-Lambert* indicates, the Supreme Court has held that even commercial speech is protected by the First Amendment. In Virginia State Board of Pharmacy v. Virginia Citizens Consumer Council, Inc., 425 U.S. 748 (1976), the Court held that a state may not prohibit pharmacists from advertising their prescription drug prices. The Court also stated, however, that the Constitution protects only truthful speech. Therefore, the FTC may prohibit speech that is false and even speech that is not false but only misleading or deceptive. "The First Amendment . . . does not prohibit the State from insuring that the stream of commercial information flows cleanly as well as freely." 425 U.S. at 771–72. See also Bates v. State Bar of Arizona, 433 U.S. 350, 383 (1977) ("[T]he public and private benefits from commercial speech derive from confidence in its accuracy and reliability. Thus, the leeway for untruthful or misleading expression that has been allowed in other contexts has little force in the commercial arena.")

Does the Constitution pose any limits on what the FTC may do? This breaks down into at least two questions: does the First Amendment affect the standard of deception? does the First Amendment affect the remedies available to the FTC?

a. Recall the standard articulated by the court in *Charles of the Ritz* for determining whether a seller has violated section 5. Does the First Amendment require a modification of this standard? Does it require a modification of the standard articulated in *International Harvester?*

b. The question of constitutional limits on the FTC has not been before the Supreme Court, but it has been before the courts of appeals on several occasions. On these occasions, including in *Warner-Lambert*, the courts have held that the First Amendment prohibits the FTC from going any further than necessary to eliminate deception. This contrasts with the general standard for reviewing the FTC's selection of remedy, which is whether the remedy is reasonably related to the violation. Jacob Siegel Co. v. FTC, 327 U.S. 608, 612–13 (1946).

In National Commission on Egg Nutrition v. FTC, 570 F.2d 157 (7th Cir.1977), a trade association of the egg industry placed advertisements that contained statements concerning cholesterol and the consumption of eggs, including among others "there is no scientific evidence that eating eggs increases the risk of heart disease." The FTC found these claims to be deceptive: while it had not been conclusively established that eating eggs increases the risk of heart disease, there were respectable studies reaching that conclusion. May the FTC require that in any future ad concerning the relationship between eating eggs and heart disease the advertiser also state "many medical experts believe that existing evidence indicates that increased consumption of dietary cholesterol, including that in eggs, may increase the risk of heart disease"?

In Beneficial Corp. v. FTC, 542 F.2d 611 (3d Cir.1976), Beneficial advertised an income tax preparation service and a consumer loan program in this way: Beneficial would prepare a consumer's federal income tax return. If the consumer were entitled to a refund, and if the consumer so desired, Beneficial would make the amount of the refund available immediately as part of its so-called "Instant Tax Refund" plan. In fact, Beneficial would make the loan only if the consumer met the usual requirements for a loan, and the amount of the loan was not limited to the amount of the tax refund. In other words, neither the availability nor the amount of the loan had anything to do with any income tax refund. The FTC ordered Beneficial to cease and desist using the phrase "Instant Tax Refund." Has the FTC gone too far, i.e. further than necessary to eliminate deception?

In Zauderer v. Office of Disciplinary Counsel, 471 U.S. 626 (1985), the Supreme Court upheld a state's disciplinary action against an attorney who advertised, "If there is no recovery, no legal fees are owed by our clients." The state had concluded that the statement was deceptive because it failed to disclose that even if unsuccessful, litigants would still have to pay court costs. The defendant argued that it violates the First Amendment for the state to compel him to disclose information that he would rather not disclose. The Court responded:

> We have, to be sure, held that in some instances, compulsion to speak may be as violative of the First Amendment as prohibitions on speech. . . .

> . . . We recognize that unjustified or unduly burdensome disclosure requirements might offend the First Amendment by chilling protected commercial speech. But we hold that an advertiser's rights are adequately protected as long as disclosure requirements are reasonably related to the State's interest in preventing deception of consumers.

Id. at 650–51.

In a footnote to this passage, the Court added:

> We reject appellant's contention that we should subject disclosure requirements to a strict "least restrictive means" analysis under which they must be struck down if there are other means by which the State's purposes may be served. Although we have subjected outright prohibitions on speech to such analysis, all our discussions of restraints on commercial speech have recommended disclosure requirements as one of the acceptable less restrictive alternatives to actual suppression of speech. Because the First Amendment interests implicated by disclosure requirements are substantially weaker than those at stake when speech is actually suppressed, we do not think it appropriate to strike down such requirements merely because other possible means by which the State might achieve its purposes can be hypothesized.

The Court also rejected the proposition that the First Amendment requires the state to prove the existence of actual deception before it may compel affirmative disclosure:

> The advertisement makes no mention of the distinction between "legal fees" and "costs," and to a layman not aware of the meaning of these terms of art, the advertisement would suggest that employing appellant would be a no-lose proposition in that his representation in a losing cause would come entirely free of charge. The assumption that substantial numbers of potential clients would be so misled is hardly a speculative one: it is a commonplace that members of the public are often unaware of the technical meanings of such terms as "fees" and "costs"—terms that, in ordinary usage, might well be virtually interchangeable. When the possibility of deception is as self-evident as it is in this case, we need not require the State to "conduct a survey of the . . . public before it [may] determine that the [advertisement] had a tendency to mislead." FTC v. Colgate–Palmolive Co., [380 U.S. 374, 391–392, 85 S.Ct. 1035, 1046, 13 L.Ed.2d 904].

Id. at 652.

c.   Reconsider Question 4, supra: does the First Amendment have any implications for the power of the FTC to require a seller to place corrective ads even if the seller does not want to advertise at all?

d.   Note 7, page 80 supra, describes the prior substantiation doctrine, under which an advertiser must have proof of the accuracy of a claim before making it. Is the requirement of prior substantiation constitutional? Or does the First Amendment require that a seller be free to make a claim without prior substantiation, so long as he or she is able to establish the truthfulness of the claim in an FTC enforcement action? If not, does the First Amendment at least invalidate the requirement that the prior substantiation consist of "competent and reliable scientific evidence"?

6.   Assume that by using practices that the FTC determines to have been deceptive, a seller induces consumers to enter contracts to purchase major appliances. Can the FTC order the seller to cease and desist selling appliances unless he offers each prior customer an opportunity to rescind the contract and obtain a refund of money paid? The FTC thinks it can. In re Universal Credit Acceptance Corp., 85 F.T.C. 524 (1975). The Ninth Circuit disagrees. Heater v. FTC, 503 F.2d 321 (9th Cir.1974). How is this different from ordering a seller to cease and desist enforcing its existing contracts?

In 1975 Congress added section 19 to the FTC Act, 15 U.S.C. § 57b. That section authorizes the FTC to seek restitution on behalf of persons injured either by a violation of a trade regulation rule (§ 19(a)(1)) or by conduct with respect to which the FTC has issued a cease and desist order (§ 19(a)(2)).

With respect to a violation of the latter section, the court may grant redress only if a reasonable person would have known that the conduct prohibited by the cease and desist order was dishonest or fraudulent. Presumably, many cease and desist orders relate to acts or practices that are deceptive but not "dishonest or fraudulent." What justification is there for this requirement of a bad faith violation of section 5? Does this justification apply also to conduct that violates the terms of a cease and desist order and that occurs after the cease and desist order is issued?

Pursuant to section 19 the FTC obtained an order compelling restitution of up to $49,950,000 by a manufacturer of fire alarm detection devices. FTC v. Figgie International, Inc., 994 F.2d 595 (9th Cir.1993), cert. denied 510 U.S. 1110.

In 1975 Congress also revised the Act to permit the FTC to seek a preliminary injunction or temporary restraining order to stop alleged violations of section 5 pending initiation and completion of the administrative proceedings. FTC Act § 13(b), 15 U.S.C. § 53(b). The Commission often uses this procedure rather than administrative cease-and-desist proceedings. The courts have held that the grant of injunctive powers means that they may grant ancillary relief to accomplish complete justice. E.g., FTC v. Southwest Sunsites, Inc., 665 F.2d 711 (5th Cir.1982). In furtherance of the objective of complete justice, the courts have even granted restitution of moneys paid by consumers, e.g., FTC v. Amy Travel Service, Inc., 875 F.2d 564 (7th Cir.1989), and have upheld decrees that call for any unclaimed funds to be paid into the U.S. Treasury. FTC v. Gem Merchandising Corp., 87 F.3d 466 (11th Cir.1996).

7. Noticeably absent from the FTC Act is authorization for a suit by an injured consumer. At least three federal circuit courts have rejected the existence of a private remedy for consumers who have been injured by acts or practices alleged to be unfair or deceptive. Summey v. Ford Motor Credit Co., 573 F.2d 1306 (4th Cir.1978); Carlson v. Coca–Cola Co., 483 F.2d 279 (9th Cir.1973); Holloway v. Bristol–Myers Corp., 485 F.2d 986 (D.C.Cir. 1973). On the other hand, a district court in another circuit upheld the existence of a private remedy for violation of a cease and desist order. Guernsey v. Rich Plan, 408 F.Supp. 582 (N.D.Ind.1976). But another district court disagreed. Bott v. Holiday Universal, Inc., CCH 1976–2 Trade Reg. Cases ¶ 60,973 (D.D.C.1976).

E.   TOPICAL STATUTES

(1)   ODOMETER FRAUD

The Federal Trade Commission Act, which broadly prohibits any form of deception in or affecting interstate commerce, represents one approach to dealing with deception. Other approaches exist as well. Thus, some statutes address a particular form of deception, and others address deception in a particular trade or industry. Examples of the former include the statutes dealing with mail fraud, 18 U.S.C. § 1341 (making it a crime), and telemarketing (discussed in the next subsection of this chapter). An example of the statutes that address a particular trade or industry is the federal odometer statute, 49 U.S.C. §§ 32701–32711, referred to in Question 8 after *Jones v. West Side Buick*, page 7 supra. This statute imposes criminal and civil liability for resetting an odometer or operating a motor vehicle with the odometer disconnected. See sections 32703, 32709, 32710. In addition, section 32705 requires sellers to affirm the accuracy of the vehicle's odometer reading. The National Highway Traffic Safety Administration has promulgated regulations to implement these requirements. 49 C.F.R. Part 580. These statutes and regulations appear in the Statutory Supplement. Unfortunately, they have not ended the problem of odometer rollbacks.

Double Dealers*

State Plans to Brake Fraud in Auto Sales

"Let's take 'em to Missouri, Sam."

John Wayne was talking about cows when he uttered that line (or something close to it) in the closing scene of "Red River." Today it's automobiles, and some of the folks down there along the Red River would

---

* St. Louis Post-Dispatch, August 27, 1982, at A1.

like to see it stopped. So would [Missouri] Revenue Director Richard A. King.

King says about 1,000 motor vehicles a day are brought in from neighboring states to be bought and sold on paper by unscrupulous dealers to make the cars' histories and past ownerships difficult to trace before they are finally sold to unwary purchasers.

Some of the cars are "hot," some just a bit "warm," but all are questionable.

Why Missouri? Part of the reason, King says, is that his department has not enforced a 5–year-old state law requiring a certified odometer reading on a vehicle title document every time the vehicle changes hands. He estimates that 40 percent of the vehicle titles on file in Jefferson City lack the required mileage readings. . . .

The absence of a mileage reading on a title has made Missouri a haven for shady transactions, King says. The system works like this:

An unscrupulous dealer in Oklahoma acquires a 3–year-old car that has had two owners. Say the first owner put 35,000 miles on the car, and the second an additional 25,000, so the clock reads 60,000.

The dealer turns the clock back to 25,000. But because Oklahoma requires title transfers to bear a certified odometer reading as of the time of sale, the prospective purchaser could call the state vehicle registry and learn that the car already had more than 25,000 miles when ownership passed from owner one to owner two.

So the dealer takes the car to Missouri and wholesales it to an equally shady dealer here. The Missouri dealer then sells it to another dealer, who sells it to another and so forth. In none of the transactions is the mileage recorded on the title.

In fact, transactions may take place without the car leaving the dealer's lot, King said. He said one dealer in western Missouri, whom he refused to identify, operates more than 20 different dealerships out of a Quonset hut next to a lot that holds about 20 cars. Records show the dealer sometimes has as many as 5,000 cars in his possession at one time, at least on paper, King says.

The dealer can, in effect, buy and sell the same car a dozen times, take the title documents to Jefferson City and have them recorded, and then move the car to another state. King says he has seen dealers come into the Revenue Department office with satchels full of title documents to be processed and recorded.

If the prospective buyer tries to follow the ownership trail backward, he will run into an impenetrable thicket of paper work, none of which shows how far the car has been driven.

The problem is not confined to Missouri. Not only may automobiles whose odometers have been rolled back be sold across state lines, but the practice of rolling back odometers occurs in many or all parts of the country. For detailed judicial descriptions of how rollbacks occur, see Pelster v. Ray, 987 F.2d 514 (8th Cir.1993); United States v. Henson, 848 F.2d 1374 (6th Cir.1988). In 2002 the United States Department of Transportation estimated that every year more than 450,000 used-car sales involve odometer rollbacks, causing consumers to overpay an average of $2,336 per vehicle. In the aggregate, consumers pay more than one billion dollars per year in excess of the value of the vehicles.[1] In 2005 the Department reported that the problem had gotten worse.

Consumers face several difficulties in trying to enforce the federal statute. One, implicit in the newspaper excerpt above, is tracing ownership back through numerous transfers to ascertain whether the odometer has actually been rolled back. Another is establishing a violation by the seller if the seller has delivered a disclosure statement that discloses the odometer reading of the car at the time of the sale. The problem lies in the fact that the rollback may have occurred before the seller has received the car. Can a seller who has not participated in the rollback scheme nevertheless violate the statute? If the seller knows that a prior owner of the car has rolled back the odometer, surely the seller violates the statute by certifying that "to the best of my knowledge [the odometer reading] reflects the actual mileage of the vehicle." But what if the seller does not actually know that a prior owner has rolled back the odometer: does it suffice if the seller suspects a rollback? Does it suffice if the seller should suspect the rollback?

Tusa v. Omaha Auto Auction, Inc.

United States Court of Appeals, Eighth Circuit, 1983.
712 F.2d 1248.

FLOYD R. GIBSON, SENIOR CIRCUIT JUDGE:

. . .

I. Facts

OAA runs an automobile auction which sells primarily to registered dealers. The Tusas are not dealers, but a friend of Teresa Tusa who was a registered dealer agreed to make a bid on her behalf. On July 12, 1979, Teresa and her brother Gary looked over the cars on the OAA lot. They picked out a car they liked, a 1974 Chevrolet Nova, and Gary made a successful bid of $1,800. Gary presented OAA with a money order for $1,820 (the purchase price plus a buyer's fee) and then signed documents on behalf of T & M Auto, the name of the friend's dealership. The Tusas

---

1. National Highway Traffic Safety Administration, Preliminary Report: The Incidence of Odometer Fraud (April 2002), available at www.nhtsa.dot.gov/cars/rules/regrev/ evaluate/pdf/809441.pdf. The actual cost is even higher, once sales taxes, finance charges, and other expenses are considered.

drove off in the car that day. They started having problems with the car shortly thereafter.

The transfer of title to Teresa Tusa and her mother Jean followed an indirect path. Title went from Allan Studna (a dealer who delivered the car to the OAA premises) to OAA to T & M to Teresa and Jean Tusa. Studna, d/b/a Way Low Auto Sales, had acquired title on July 6, 1979, from Tracy Waton, d/b/a Way Low Auto Sales. The car had a Kansas title at that time. According to the odometer disclosure statement which Waton had received when he acquired title three weeks before selling it to Studna, the car had an odometer reading of 80,720 miles. When Studna delivered the car to OAA on July 12, the odometer read 60,239 miles. OAA employees recorded this mileage figure on an odometer mileage disclosure statement which had been previously signed in blank by Studna as the transferor. Apparently due to a clerical error, OAA was listed as the transferor on this form which Studna had signed and T & M was listed as the transferee. Perhaps to correct the mistake, OAA employees prepared another odometer statement on July 30 which correctly stated that Studna transferred title to OAA. Also, on July 30, OAA acquired the Kansas title from Studna, took it to the Douglas County Clerk in Nebraska, and acquired a Nebraska title. The clerk at the Douglas County office took the 60,239 mileage figure from the OAA mileage statement and put it on the Nebraska title. The acquisition of this new title was significant because, according to the district court, the mileage figure on the Kansas title had been intentionally altered by someone before OAA received it. Because of the acquisition of the new title, T & M and the Tusas did not have a chance to see that the mileage figure on the Kansas title had been changed. OAA transferred title to T & M on July 30 and T & M transferred to the Tusas on the next day. A few days later the Tusas acquired their own Nebraska title.

Waton, who had received a mileage statement with an 80,720 reading, and Studna, who delivered the car with the 60,239 odometer reading, were both named as defendants in the Tusas' complaint along with OAA. Waton could not be located and was never served. Studna failed to appear or defend and a default judgment was entered against him. The district court found OAA liable under the Disclosure Act and awarded the Tusas damages of $1,500, the minimum allowed under the Act. The court acknowledged there was no allegation that OAA itself had tampered with the odometer. . . . OAA contests its liability on the basis that it was neither a transferor nor a transferee and that it lacked the requisite intent to defraud. . . .

II. Liability of OAA

Section [32705] requires a transferor of a car to disclose mileage information to a transferee. It also authorizes the Secretary of Transportation to issue regulations imposing specific disclosure requirements. . . .

Section [32705] imposes certain requirements, but it does not provide a remedy. One of the remedies provided by the Disclosure Act is contained in

§ [32710]. This section allows for private civil actions to enforce liability for violations of odometer requirements. . . .

. . . OAA argues that its liability under § [32710] is limited to situations where the violation is committed with an "intent to defraud," and it had no such intent.[2]

. . .

Congress clearly wanted each transferor to prepare as accurate a disclosure statement as possible, even if the person had no role in odometer tampering. If OAA's argument that it cannot be liable under the Act were adopted, OAA could routinely process cars and give out mileage disclosure statements which, in the exercise of reasonable care, OAA knew were false. Such a practice would be at odds with the Act's purpose of getting as much information to the consumer as possible about a vehicle's mileage. Congress did not limit liability to the odometer tamperers and their cohorts.

. . .

Section [32710] allows a civil action against "[a]ny person who, *with intent to defraud,* violates any requirement imposed under this subchapter. . . ." OAA argues that it did not give the inaccurate mileage information with an intent to defraud.

OAA concedes that it violated § [32705]. . . . The legislative history to that section makes it clear that a party must use "reasonable care" to assure the accuracy of odometer disclosure statements. The Senate Report states: "[T]he auto dealer with expertise now would have an affirmative duty to mark 'true mileage unknown' if, in the exercise of reasonable care, he would have reason to know that the mileage was more than that which the odometer had recorded or which the previous owner had certified." S.Rep. No. 413, 92d Cong., 2d Sess., reprinted in 1972 U.S.Code Cong. & Ad.News 3960, 3971–72. Nevertheless, OAA can be civilly liable only if its violation of § [32705] was done with the intent to defraud. Ryan v. Edwards, 592 F.2d 756, 761 (4th Cir.1979); Nieto v. Pence, 578 F.2d 640, 642 (5th Cir.1978). The district court concluded that OAA did have an intent to defraud. This factual finding may be rejected by us only if it is clearly erroneous.

The wrongdoer's intent to defraud is ordinarily proved by circumstantial evidence. All the cases we can find dealing with the Disclosure Act have been willing to infer an intent to defraud where the seller had actual knowledge that an odometer disclosure statement was false. See, e.g., cases cited in *Nieto,* 578 F.2d at 642. Both federal appeals courts which have considered the issue of intent to defraud and most district courts which have considered the issue have been willing to infer an intent to defraud

---

2. OAA does not attempt to defend itself on the basis that there is no privity between it and the Tusas. Such an argument would be unavailing. We agree with the Fourth Circuit that privity is unnecessary between the defrauded party and the party that violated the Disclosure Act with an intent to defraud. Ryan v. Edwards, 592 F.2d 756, 761–62 (4th Cir.1979). . . .

where the seller exhibited gross negligence or a reckless disregard for the truth in preparing odometer disclosure statements. *Ryan,* 592 F.2d at 762; *Nieto,* 578 F.2d at 642 and district court cases cited therein.

The approach taken by the great majority of courts is sensible. If a person violates an odometer disclosure requirement with actual knowledge that he is committing a violation, a fact finder can reasonably infer that the violation was committed with an intent to defraud a purchaser. Likewise, if a person lacks knowledge that an odometer disclosure statement is false only because he displays a reckless disregard for the truth, a fact finder can reasonably infer that the violation was committed with an intent to defraud a purchaser. The inference of an intent to defraud is no less compelling when a person lacks actual knowledge of a false odometer statement only by "clos[ing] his eyes to the truth." *Nieto,* 578 F.2d at 642.

The district court inferred an intent to defraud on OAA's part because it evidenced a reckless disregard for preparing an accurate odometer statement. The court acknowledged that there was no evidence that OAA had actual knowledge the odometer reading on the Nova was wrong. However, the court found two items which led it to conclude that OAA was acting with a reckless disregard for the truth. First, OAA ignored the alteration of the mileage figure on the Kansas title. The district court said the erasure was clear and apparent. Our own examination of the title leads us to the same conclusion. The district court reasonably inferred that the failure to investigate in the face of an obvious change on the title was due to an intent on OAA's part to defraud the purchaser.

The district court's inference of a fraudulent intent is buttressed by the second item which the district court believed showed a reckless disregard for the truth—the method by which OAA prepared the odometer disclosure statements. OAA filled in Studna's disclosure statement to OAA. Studna had signed the statement in blank and OAA filled in the mileage simply by looking at the odometer. OAA made no effort to obtain any previous disclosure statements and it did not even try to find out if the car had already been driven over 100,000 miles. Also, the second disclosure statement filled out by OAA relied on nothing but the odometer reading. Because a car buyer can read an odometer the way OAA did, a disclosure form based solely on reading the odometer does nothing to give the car buyer additional information. OAA's method of compiling the disclosure statements shows a total disregard for the purposes of the Act. The district court could reasonably infer that OAA's disregard for making accurate disclosure statements stemmed from an intent to defraud purchasers.

When OAA's procedure for filling out the odometer disclosure statements is combined with its ignoring an altered title, the district court could reasonably find that OAA showed a reckless disregard for the truth. Therefore, we cannot call the district court's finding of an intent to defraud on OAA's part clearly erroneous.[5]

5. The district court and some other courts have said that "constructive knowl- edge" of the inaccuracy of a mileage statement is grounds for inferring an intent to

[The court affirmed the trial court's judgment of liability, but reversed and remanded the trial court's judgment awarding plaintiffs attorney's fees.]

Levine v. Parks Chevrolet, Inc.

Court of Appeals of North Carolina, 1985.
76 N.C.App. 44, 331 S.E.2d 747.

JOHNSON, JUDGE:

[Defendant dealer acquired a 2½–year-old pickup truck from a consumer. The odometer reading was 14,485. Unknown to defendant, however, a prior owner had used the truck in its business, and the truck actually had been driven 100,000 miles more than the amount registered on the odometer. Defendant sold the truck to plaintiff, giving a disclosure form certifying that the mileage on the odometer was 14,563 and that figure represented the actual mileage of the vehicle. Shortly after the purchase, plaintiff "noticed the front and rear tires were of different brands, neither of which was the original brand. He examined the spare tire, which was of the original brand, and saw that it was worn. He also noticed that the place 'where your feet skid' as you get in and out of the truck was also worn. He subsequently discovered that the battery was not an original battery, but a NAPA brand battery, and that the shock absorbers were also NAPA brand. Plaintiff contacted a mechanic, Larry Melvin, who examined the vehicle and observed a large amount of grease and grime underneath the vehicle. Melvin indicated at trial that this grease and grime buildup was an indicator of high mileage."

[Plaintiff sued for violation of the federal statute and an analogous state statute. The trial court gave judgment for plaintiff, and defendant appealed. After reviewing *Tusa* and two other cases, the Court of Appeals continued:]

Based upon the foregoing authorities, we hold the evidence in the present case was sufficient to permit a jury to find that defendant Parks Chevrolet, in the exercise of reasonable care, should have known that the mileage was other than that recorded by the odometer and that defendant Parks Chevrolet acted with the intent to defraud. The evidence showed that defendant Parks Chevrolet had some question as to the verity of the odometer mileage, yet all it did to confirm the mileage was to drive the vehicle, examine the interior and compare the mileage on the inspection sticker with the mileage on the odometer. The evidence also showed, however, that any mechanic could ascertain from the grease buildup on the

defraud. We have avoided use of that phrase because constructive knowledge can be defined as knowledge which one would acquire in the exercise of reasonable care. Black's Law Dictionary 284 (rev. 5th ed. 1979). The failure to exercise reasonable care might not alone allow a fact finder to infer an intent to defraud. However, the district court's use of the phrase "constructive knowledge" in this case does not undermine our decision because the district court found that OAA's conduct evidenced a "reckless disregard for the purposes of the Act."

chassis that the vehicle had been driven more than 14,000 or 15,000 miles, that several pieces of equipment, most noticeably the tires, were not of the original brand, and that the truck showed other signs of wear. As the legislative history to § [32705] indicates, to allow a dealer with expertise to ignore such indicators of wear would be to eviscerate the purpose of the statute.

.   .   .

For the foregoing reasons, we find

No error.

QUESTIONS

1. Under these decisions, what is expected of used car dealers? How would you advise a dealer to complete the disclosure form in Appendix B of the regulations? Should the dealer routinely check the entry that the odometer reading is not accurate?

2. Compare the elements necessary for civil liability under the odometer statute to the elements of common law deceit and the elements of deception under section 5 of the FTC Act. To recover under the odometer statute, must the consumer establish any of the elements of deceit? Must the consumer establish anything in addition to the elements of deceit? Is the standard of proof the same? Consider the same questions with respect to the FTC's burden under section 5.

3. Would the result in *Tusa* have been different if OAA's standard form contract had contained the following paragraphs:

> The selling dealer received this vehicle with approximately the mileage shown on the odometer (less miles driven for testing and demonstration). However, selling dealer makes no warranty or representation as to the accuracy of said odometer reading, either express or implied, except that said odometer reading has not been altered by selling dealer, and that dealer has no knowledge that it was altered or disconnected prior to the time this vehicle came into dealer's possession.

> Purchaser understands that dealer has no control over what may have been done to the odometer by previous owners, and that dealer has no way to ascertain the correctness of the odometer reading. Dealer has offered to give to buyer the name of the individual or entity from whom dealer purchased the vehicle and to provide purchaser with information as to how he may contact the previous owners, and to ascertain from the department of Revenue the mileage shown on the odometer on any previous transactions concerning this vehicle.

Would the presence of this language affect the outcome in *Levine v. Parks*? See Fields v. Mitch Crawford's Holiday Motors, 908 S.W.2d 877 (Mo.App. 1995).

4. Car titles may contain information in addition to the identity of the car, the identity of the owner, and the odometer reading. They may, for example, indicate that the vehicle has been declared a total loss by its insurer, in which event the title is a "salvage" title. A vehicle with a salvage title is supposed to be sold only for scrap or for the salvage of its parts.

Until 1985 the Odometer Act required disclosure of the odometer reading but it did not require that disclosure to be on the title certificate. By giving the disclosure on a separate piece of paper, a seller could avoid disclosing that the vehicle was a salvage, or that the prior owner was the owner of a fleet of vehicles (e.g., a car rental company). Consequently, in 1985 Congress amended the Act to require the odometer disclosure on the title certificate itself. NHTSA amended the regulation accordingly, but it permitted sellers to continue to disclose on a separate document if the seller does not have possession of the title certificate (which might be the case if it is still in the possession of a lien holder). A car dealer that is selling a car formerly owned by a rental company or a car with a salvage title has a powerful temptation to make the odometer disclosure in a separate document even if the dealer is in possession of the title certificate. If the dealer gives in to this temptation, does the consumer have a claim under the Odometer Act?

The answer turns on the nature of the requisite "intent to defraud," and the question is whether the seller's intent to defraud must relate to the disclosure of the odometer reading or, alternatively, whether it may relate to the seller's failure to comply with the other requirements of the Act. Addressing this question, the Seventh Circuit stated:

> . . . Based upon this delegation of authority, the National Highway Traffic Safety Administration ("NHTSA") promulgated the following regulation: "In connection with the transfer of ownership of a motor vehicle, each transferor shall disclose the mileage to the transferee in writing on the title or . . . on the document being used to reassign the title." 49 C.F.R. § 580.5(c). . . . [T]he section of the Odometer Act which creates a private right of action provides in relevant part:

>> (a) Violation and amount of damages.—A person that violates this chapter or a regulation prescribed or order issued under this chapter, with intent to defraud, is liable for 3 times the actual damages or $1,500, whichever is greater.

>> (b) Civil actions.—A person may bring a civil action to enforce a claim under this section in an appropriate United States district court or in another court of competent jurisdiction.

> 49 U.S.C. § 32710.

> Based on these provisions, Ioffe presents the following syllogism: a plaintiff has a private right of action under § 32710 if there has been a violation of the Odometer Act or any of its implementing regulations and the violator intended to defraud the plaintiff; Sherman Dodge violated 49 C.F.R. § 580.5(c), promulgated pursuant to 49 U.S.C.

§ 32705(a)(1), by disclosing the Tercel's mileage on a document other than its title, and Sherman Dodge intended to defraud Ioffe by hiding the title's "rebuilt" designation; therefore, Ioffe has a claim against Sherman Dodge under the Act. Upon consideration of the language of the statute and the regulation, the specific context in which that language is used, and the broader context of the statute and its implementing regulations, *see Robinson*, 519 U.S. at 341, we conclude that Ioffe's first premise misstates the law. Section 32710 does not create a private right of action for all violations of the Act and regulations that are accompanied by any "intent to defraud." Rather, where a plaintiff alleges a violation of 49 C.F.R. § 580.5(c), he must prove intent to defraud as to a vehicle's mileage. With a correct statement of the law, Ioffe's syllogism, and his claim, fall apart.

The provision of the Odometer Act that provides a private right of action states: "A person that violates this chapter or a regulation prescribed . . . under this chapter, with intent to defraud, is liable." 49 U.S.C. § 32710(a). The verb "to violate" and its object "this chapter or a regulation" state the prohibited conduct, while the adverbial phrase "with intent to defraud" modifies the prohibited conduct and defines the way in which it must be committed for a private claim to arise. Ioffe first tries to get to his desired interpretation by separating these two aspects of the provision. He contends that we first should ask if there was any violation, and then if there was any contemporaneous intend to defraud. This is not a proper way to read the statute.

When analyzing a prohibited act, we must construe general statements of prohibited conduct (such as "[violation of] this chapter or a regulation") as "shorthand designations for specific acts or omissions which violate the Act [or a regulation]." *United States v. International Minerals & Chem. Corp.*, 402 U.S. 558, 562 (1971). Because intent requirements modify specific alleged violations, we must replace any shorthand designation for prohibited conduct with a specific violation before interpreting the intent element. *Cf. Int'l Minerals*, 402 U.S. at 561–62. Here, Ioffe alleges a violation of 49 C.F.R. § 580.5(c), which provides in relevant part that each transferor of a motor vehicle "shall disclose the mileage to the transferee in writing on the title." Replacing § 32710(a)'s shorthand designation with the specific conduct prohibited by § 580.5(c), we find that the Act creates the following private right of action: "A person that [does not disclose the mileage to the transferee in writing on the title], with intent to defraud, is liable."

Word choice and sentence structure help clarify how the "intent to defraud" element operates in this context. The use of "with" in "with intent to defraud" indicates a link between the violative conduct and the intent requirement. The conduct and the fraudulent intent are not two independent elements such that any contemporaneous fraud will do. Rather, there is a prohibited act—not disclosing the mileage to the transferee in writing on the title—which is modified by the adverbial phrase "with intent to defraud." Thus, the private right of action covers prohibited acts that are committed with fraudulent intent and excludes cases where some fraudulent act happens to coincide with a violation of a regulation but the violative act is done for reasons other than to perpetrate a fraud.

Next, Ioffe essentially argues that even if the "intent to defraud" element must be read in connection with the specific violation, the intent requirement does not necessarily apply to the prohibited conduct as a whole. He divides the prohibited act into two parts—"does not disclose the mileage to the transferee" and "in writing on the title"—and argues that § 32710 is satisfied if there is fraudulent intent as to either the transferor's decision not to disclose the mileage or its decision not to provide the title. There is no logical or grammatical reason for this division. The more natural reading is to understand the prohibited conduct as a whole—does not disclose the mileage to the transferee in writing on the title—and to require that the intent to defraud apply to the violation in its entirety. This reading suggests that there must be fraudulent intent as to the decision not to disclose the mileage on the title, not merely as to the decision to withhold the certificate of title for reasons unrelated to the mileage disclosure.

The specific context in which the statutory language appears also supports this reading. Section 32705, the source of NHTSA's authority to promulgate 49 C.F.R. § 580.5(c), requires only that a transferor of a motor vehicle provide written disclosure of "the cumulative mileage registered on the odometer." 49 U.S.C. § 32705(a)(1). In granting authority to issue implementing regulations, Congress directed the Secretary of Transportation to prescribe "the way in which [the cumulative mileage] information is disclosed and retained." *Id.* We have understood this language as "limiting the NHTSA's regulatory authority to the promulgation of mere procedural or logistical rules." *Diersen v. Chicago Car Exch.*, 110 F.3d 481, 485–86 (7th Cir. 1997).

In *Diersen*, a purchaser of a used car brought suit against a dealership, alleging violation of the disclosure requirements of the Odometer Act. The district court granted the dealership's motion for summary judgment based on a regulation which purported to exempt cars ten years old or older from the disclosure requirements of the Act. In reviewing the decision, we observed that the regulation "effectively removed a cause of action that Congress has unambiguously provided to *all* victims of odometer fraud," and we held that to do so was beyond NHTSA's delegated authority to promulgate "mere procedural or logistical rules."

In enacting the Odometer Act, Congress created a private right to sue a transferor for failure to disclose "the cumulative mileage registered on the odometer," "with intent to defraud." *See* 49 U.S.C. §§ 32705(a)(1)(A); 32710(a). In other words, it created a private claim for odometer or mileage fraud. If Ioffe is correct about the interaction between § 32710 and 49 C.F.R. § 580.5(c), NHTSA substantively and dramatically changed the law by creating a broad new right of action for all fraud that involves the withholding of a certificate of title. The regulation would do much more than prescribe "the way in which [the cumulative mileage] information is disclosed and retained" by dramatically increasing the number and types of private claims available under the Act and expanding the private right of action far beyond its scope under the statute. There is no indication that Congress intended to authorize NHTSA to effect such a dramatic change in the law or that NHTSA intended to do so.

Finally, looking to the broader context of the statute and its implementing regulations, we see that a requirement that a transferor's fraudulent intent relate to the vehicle's mileage comports with the expressed purposes of the Act and regulations. The only stated purposes of the Act are "(1) to prohibit tampering with motor vehicle odometers; and (2) to provide safeguards to protect purchasers in the sale of motor vehicles with altered or reset odometers." 49 U.S.C. § 32701(b). Section 580.5(c) appears in Part 580 of Title 49 of the Code of Federal Regulations, entitled "Odometer Disclosure Requirements," which has the following stated "scope": "This part prescribes rules requiring transferors . . . of motor vehicles to make written disclosure to transferees . . . concerning the odometer mileage and its accuracy as directed by sections [32705(a) and (c)]." 49 C.F.R. § 580.1. The stated purpose of Part 580, in relevant part, is "to provide purchasers of motor vehicles with odometer information to assist them in determining a vehicle's condition and value by making the disclosure of a vehicle's mileage a condition of title." 49 C.F.R. § 580.2. These statements of purpose and scope indicate that the legislation is concerned specifically with fraud related to a vehicle's mileage rather than with all types of fraud that might involve the withholding of a vehicle's title.

Ioffie v. Skokie Motor Sales, Inc., 414 F.3d 708 (7th Cir.2005).

Compare the response of the Eleventh Circuit:

The Odometer Act allows private parties to recover money damages from those that violate its provisions with the intent to defraud: "A person that violates this chapter or a regulation prescribed or order issued under this chapter, with intent to defraud, is liable for 3 times the actual damages or $1,500, whichever is greater." 49 U.S.C. § 32710(a) (2005). There is no dispute that Owens has properly alleged violations of the Odometer Act. The complaint alleges that Marlin Mazda, with the intent to defraud Owens, violated a "regulation prescribed . . . under" the Odometer Act. Specifically, Owens alleged the violation of 49 C.F.R. § 580.5(c), which provides that "in connection with the transfer of ownership of a motor vehicle, each transferor shall disclose the mileage to the transferee in writing on the title. . . ." (emphasis added). The Act defines "title" as "the certificate of title or other document issued by the State indicating ownership." 49 U.S.C. § 32702(7). Thus, the complaint alleged all of the necessary elements required for a private cause of action pursuant to this statute: (1) that the defendant violated the Act or its regulations, (2) with intent to defraud.

. . .

On its face, this statute's meaning is direct, clear and unambiguous. No language limits the meaning of the clause "with intent to defraud." Absent any such limitation, the statute's meaning is clear—if you violate the Odometer Act, and you do so with the intent to defraud your victim in any respect relating to the Odometer Act or the regulations passed pursuant to it, you are liable. . . . To augment the statutory language with an additional element, never mentioned by Congress, that the fraud must be "with respect to the vehicle's mileage" violates the cardinal rule of statutory construction.[4]

We do note, however, that a plain-language reading is also consistent with the general principle that the Odometer Act is remedial legislation that should be "broadly construed to effectuate its purpose," Ryan v. Edwards, 592 F.2d 756, 760 (4th Cir. 1979) . . . , and a plain reading is not inconsistent with the Act's stated purposes.

. . . Congress established a remedial scheme that not only punished violators, but deterred would-be violators through a complex regulatory system that made even sophisticated odometer fraud difficult to attempt unnoticed. The regulations include, as one would expect, a flat prohibition on odometer tampering. 49 U.S.C. § 32703 (2000). However, Congress also mandated standardized disclosure requirements and record-keeping procedures formulated to provide consumers with transparent information about a vehicle's background, to ease investigation and prosecution of violators, and to prevent would-be violators from taking advantage of titling and registration loopholes to perpetrate odometer fraud. See, e.g., 49 U.S.C. § 32705 (2000) (setting forth disclosure requirements for transferring ownership of a motor vehicle); 49 C.F.R. § 580.1 et seq. (2004) (specifying, among other things, the content of odometer information disclosures and record keeping procedures, and requiring titles and power of attorney forms to be printed using a secure printing process); see also 49 U.S.C. § 32706 (2000) (conferring investigatory authority and the power to require car dealers or distributors to keep records of motor vehicle sales available for inspection by the Secretary of Transportation).

---

4. For this reason, we disagree with the court in *Ioffe v. Skokie Motor Sales,* 414 F.3d 708 (7th Cir. 2005) ("An Odometer Act claim that is brought by a private party and is based on a violation of § 580.5(c) requires proof that the vehicle's transferor intended to defraud a transferee with respect to mileage"). We believe the Seventh Circuit failed to apply the statute's plain language, which unambiguously requires that a transferor of a motor vehicle disclose the actual mileage to the transferee *on the title.*

Nor do we agree with *Ioffe*'s construction of the "intent to defraud" language of § 32710(a) as a "shorthand designation for specific acts or omissions which violate [the regulation]." *Id.* In this case, "intent to defraud" is not an element of the prohibited conduct, but an independent requirement for a private claim arising out of the violation.

In particular, the disclosure and title regulations that Samkle allegedly violated aim in part to thwart "title laundering," a practice unscrupulous sellers employ to falsify the mileage listed on a car's title to conform with an altered odometer reading:

> Title laundering is a scheme commonly used by dealers involved in odometer fraud. The main purpose of title laundering is to get a low mileage title from a State motor vehicle titling office in exchange for a high mileage title. The most basic form of title laundering is to simply alter the high odometer reading on the title to a low odometer reading and apply for and receive a title containing the lower reading. A more sophisticated scheme involves sending the high mileage title to a State not requiring odometer readings on title documents and obtaining a new title which does not contain an odometer reading.

Odometer Disclosure Requirements, 52 Fed. Reg. 27022, 27023 (proposed July 17, 1987) (later codified with modifications at 49 C.F.R. § 580.1 et seq. (2004)).

Requiring mileage disclosures to be made on a securely printed title proved critical to fighting title laundering. Prior to the 1988 revisions establishing the present-day regulations, . . . federal law required mileage disclosure only on a "federal odometer statement." Odometer Disclosure Requirements, 52 Fed. Reg. at 27023. A piece of paper separate from the title, the odometer statement could be easily altered or discarded and did not travel with the title. Consequently, it did not warn subsequent purchasers about the vehicle's mileage and ownership history, and did little to curb title laundering. On the other hand, when the title itself must contain the mileage disclosure and be shown to the buyer, a seller will find it difficult to conceal the vehicle's history and true mileage. Id. Also, to require the mileage disclosure directly on the title establishes a "paper trail" for consumers and law enforcement to deter potential violators and help apprehend sellers that break the law. Similarly, the rule that requires sellers to print titles and power of attorney forms using a secure process, and states to issue power of attorney forms by the state, see 49 C.F.R. § 580.4 (2004), makes alteration or forgery of titles more difficult and creates an official paper record tracing the vehicle's ownership.

In other words, the regulations at issue in this case are the "safeguards" designed "to protect purchasers in the sale of motor vehicles with altered or reset odometers" that are contemplated by the Act's purposes. See 49 U.S.C. § 32701(b)(2) (2000). They prevent unscrupulous dealers from using their own procedures to mislead a purchaser about a vehicle's mileage—not only with respect to the actual number of miles driven, but where those miles were driven and by whom. . . . The identity of former owners, of critical import to the consumer, is also critical to law enforcement, who rely on the chain of title to ascertain the true ownership and mileage of a vehicle. See Odometer Disclosure Requirements, 53 Fed. Reg. at 29468–69 ("Congress noted that 'one of the major barriers to decreasing odometer fraud is the lack of evidence or "paper trail" showing incidence of rollbacks[.]' . . . Under [the title disclosure requirements], the integrity of the paper trail has been maintained since the disclosure will be on the title and consumers will be able to see the disclosures and examine the titles for alterations, erasures, or other marks. Furthermore, consumers will learn the names of previous owners that appear on the title.") (quoting H.R. Rep. No. 99–833, at 18 (1986) (committee report for the Truth in Mileage Act of 1986, Pub. L. No. 99–579, 100 Stat. 3309 (1986), which modified the original federal odometer laws in the Motor Vehicle Information and Cost Savings Act of 1972, Pub. L. No. 92–513, §§ 401–13, 86 Stat. 947, 961–63)).[7] Thus, the success of the complex remedial scheme Congress has created depends on compliance with a multitude of interdependent and seemingly "technical" provisions, such as those Samkle allegedly violated. Violations of these "technical" regulations can defeat the entire remedial scheme—even if they are not committed with the intent to defraud with respect to the vehicle's mileage—by creating gaps in the vehicle's "paper trail" that: (1) thwart investigation of future violations; and (2) make it difficult for future purchasers of a vehicle to spot odometer fraud by preventing them from accurately assessing the vehicle's ownership history.

Owens v. Samkle Automotive, Inc., 425 F.3d 1318 (11th Cir.2005).

Which court is correct? Is it relevant that in *Owens* the title certificate would have revealed that the vehicle in question had been owned by Hertz whereas in *Ioffe* the title certificate would have revealed that the vehicle had been "rebuilt"?

5. As Levine v. Parks Chevrolet reveals, statutes prohibiting odometer fraud also exist at the state level. Almost every state has enacted a criminal statute, and more than a third also provide for civil liability.

(2) TELEMARKETING

Odometer regulation is an example of a topical statute that focuses on the subject matter of a consumer transaction. Another kind of topical statute focuses on the medium of the transaction. An example is telemarketing, which has become an increasingly large form of commerce and charitable solicitations. Among its unwelcome attributes are fraud and intrusion into the consumer's home. Congress has enacted several pieces of legislation to regulate telemarketing. In 1991 it enacted the Telephone Consumer Protection Act, codified at 47 U.S.C. § 227 (and reproduced in the Statutory Supplement). The focus of this statute is protection of the

---

7. Accordingly, the Secretary of Transportation rejected suggestions that a dealer be allowed to substitute a "special power of attorney" form on secure paper for the title in all cases. Odometer Disclosure Requirements, 53 Fed. Reg. at 29468–69. This procedure, the Secretary stated, "would not allow transferees to see the actual title document, including the disclosures, and could easily be discarded. A forged substitute could then be submitted to the titling office" in order to retitle the car with the false odometer reading. *Id.* at 29469.

consumer's interest in being left alone. It bans the use of unsolicited prerecorded telephone calls, and it bans the sending of unsolicited advertisements to facsimile machines. The Federal Communications Commission has promulgated implementing regulations at 47 C.F.R. § 64.1200 (also reproduced in the Supplement). These regulations require telemarketers to create and maintain lists of consumers who ask not to be called and to refrain from calling those consumers. 47 C.F.R. § 64.1200(e)(2).

Szefczek v. Hillsborough Beacon, 668 A.2d 1099 (N.J.Super.1995), illustrates the operation of these rules. After receiving several marketing calls from defendant newspaper, plaintiff phoned defendant's general sales manager, informed him that she was tending her terminally ill husband, and requested that she not receive any more calls. He assured her he would take care of the matter. Nevertheless, over the next ten months plaintiff received five more telemarketing calls from defendant. Plaintiff sued under section 227(c)(5), and the court awarded her $2,000.

Unlike almost all other federal consumer protection legislation, there is no federal-question jurisdiction over private actions to enforce this statute. The aggrieved consumer must sue in state court. E.g., Chair King, Inc. v. Houston Cellular Corp., 131 F.3d 507 (5th Cir.1997); International Science & Technology Institute, Inc. v. Inacom Communications, Inc., 106 F.3d 1146 (4th Cir.1997). If, however, the plaintiff's claim exceeds $75,000, a court may exercise diversity jurisdiction. Gottlieb v. Carnival Corp., 436 F.3d 335 (2d Cir.2006). Since statutory damages under the Act are limited to $1,500 per unsolicited fax, this ruling is likely to be of benefit only to business plaintiffs, like the travel agent in *Gottlieb*.

In 1992 Congress followed up with the Telephone Disclosure and Dispute Resolution Act, codified at 47 U.S.C. § 228 and 15 U.S.C. § 5711, with implementing regulations by the FCC at 47 C.F.R. § 64.1500 and by the FTC at 16 C.F.R. § 308 (all reproduced in the Statutory Supplement). This statute shifts the focus from the consumer's right of privacy to the right to be free from deception and abuse. It regulates various aspects of pay-per-call services, more popularly known as 900–numbers. It attempts to ensure that consumers are aware of the fact and amount of charges they will incur by using the pay-per-call service.

Finally, in 1994 Congress enacted the Telemarketing and Consumer Fraud and Abuse Prevention Act, codified at 15 U.S.C. §§ 6101–6108. Incorporating the finding that "Interstate telemarketing fraud has become a problem of such magnitude [$40 billion per year] that the resources of the Federal Trade Commission are not sufficient to ensure adequate consumer protection," this legislation directs the FTC to promulgate a regulation that prohibits deceptive and abusive telemarketing practices, ensures the consumer's privacy, and requires a telemarketer to disclose the purpose of the call and "such other [information] as the Commission deems appropriate." 15 U.S.C. § 6102(a). The FTC promptly adopted the Telemarketing Sales Rule, 16 C.F.R. § 310. (The statute and the regulation are reproduced in the Supplement.)

In addition to generally prohibiting false or misleading statements, the Telemarketing Sales Rule

- requires disclosure of specified information (§ 310.3(a)(1))

- prohibits misrepresentation of specified information (§ 310.3(a)(2))

- prohibits direct access to a consumer's checking account without one of several specified forms of authorization by the consumer (§ 310.3(a)(3))

- limits telemarketing calls to the period from 8 a.m. to 9 p.m. (§ 310.4(c))

- prohibits calling a consumer who previously has stated that he or she does not wish to receive calls from that entity

- requires the telemarketer promptly to disclose his or her identity and the purpose of the call (§ 310.4(d)).

The Rule also prohibits several other defined forms of abusive telemarketing conduct, including requesting or receiving payment for certain specified services before those services are provided. The specified services are cleaning up a consumer's credit record (to be considered in detail in Chapter 5), assisting the consumer in recovering money or property lost in a prior telemarketing transaction, and obtaining a loan or other extension of credit for the consumer (§ 310.4(a)(2)-(4)).

Enforcement of the Act is in the hands of the public authorities. The statute expressly confers a private right of action on consumers only if the amount in controversy exceeds $50,000 actual damages for each consumer. 15 U.S.C. § 6104(a). Section 6105 gives the FTC enforcement authority and confers all the enforcement powers that the Commission has under the FTC Act. In addition, and most significantly, section 6103 empowers the attorneys general of all the states to bring actions in federal court to enforce the FTC's rule. Whatever powers a state has under its own laws regulating telemarketing, those powers are limited by the geographic boundaries of the state. Section 6013 changes this: it enables the attorney general of every state to attack telemarketing abuses that originate outside that state's borders and to obtain injunctive relief that cannot be evaded by moving the telemarketer's boiler room to still another state. The case that follows is an example of enforcement by state officials.

New York v. Financial Services Network, USA

United States District Court, Western District of New York, 1996.
930 F.Supp. 865.

TELESCA, D.J.

.   .   .

The states of New York and North Carolina commenced this action pursuant to 15 U.S.C. § 1601 et seq. Seeking both restitution and a preliminary injunction claiming that defendants engage in deceptive, fraudulent and illegal practices by their promotion of advance fee credit services and debt consolidation services in violation of the Federal Trade Commission's Telemarketing Sales Rule. . . .

Plaintiffs allege that since 1988, defendants [Financial Services Network (FSN) and its principal officers] have engaged in the business of telemarketing advance fee credit services to consumers throughout the United States. Specifically, they claim that defendants mailed advertisements to consumers representing that they can provide a pre-approved $30,000 line of credit and debt consolidation services for an advance fee, when, in fact, consumers receive nothing more than a packet of information consisting of consumer forms, booklets and pamphlets on business financing, obtaining credit and earning investment income.

Defendants' direct mailings to consumers which advertise FSN's services consists of the following:

IMMEDIATE ACTION REQUIRED

CONGRATULATIONS! YOU ARE APPROVED FOR

FINANCIAL SERVICES NETWORK'S

RESOURCE CARD

PRE–APPROVED

$30,000 CREDIT LINE

(Complaint Ex. B)

CONGRATULATIONS! YOU ARE APPROVED FOR FINANCIAL

SERVICES NETWORK'S RESOURCE CARD

PRE–APPROVED

$30,000.00 CREDIT LINE

ANNUAL FEE: $48.00

(Complaint Ex. C)

URGENT

Card Provider: Financial Services Network   Annual Fee: $48

Telephone Number: 1–800–210–4323

Account Type: Resource Card

Member Status: Pending

Account Status: Pre–Approved

Credit Line Amount: $30,000.00   Approval Expires: 03/21/96

(Plaintiffs' Supplemental Authority in Further Support of Motion for Preliminary Injunction, Exhibit D)

Defendants' mailings encourage consumers to call a toll-free "800" number for further information. Plaintiffs allege that when a consumer calls, they hear a pre-recorded message which represents that defendants can provide various benefits including a line of credit, debt consolidation, business financing and collateralized credit cards. An investigator for plaintiffs called the telephone number and recorded the message, portions of which states as follows:

> The Resource Card features a $30,000 line of credit for investments. You can use your resource card to make big money by making investments that you find with our money.

> As a Resource Card Member, you can take advantage of our debt consolidation service. By next week, all your bills can be combined into one convenient monthly payment.

(Transcript of Recorded Message attached as Exhibit A to O'Mara Affidavit)

Before providing any services to consumers, defendants collect payment of an amount varying from $48 to $78, which is paid for either by credit card, check or money order. Although the prerecorded message is not programmed to allow consumers to contact a live representative from FSN, it is programmed to allow the consumer to accept the Resource Card at any time during the message by pressing "1" for c.o.d. or "2" for activation by credit card.

Plaintiffs allege that defendants' mailings and telephone recordings are misleading by representing that all consumers are guaranteed to receive the offered line of credit, debt consolidation or credit card for an upfront fee and that in the event consumers do not receive the promised extension of credit, they will receive a refund of the fee paid to defendants. Finally, plaintiffs allege that defendants fail to disclose that the $30,000 line of credit is limited to mortgage investments made by defendants based on information supplied by the consumer. In support of their allegations, plaintiffs submit more than 27 affidavits from consumers who responded to defendants' solicitations hoping to obtain an extension of credit as advertised but instead were denied credit and/or denied refunds.

Defendants contend that the business they conduct is not in violation of any state licensing laws and that the advertisements and telephone messages fairly and adequately represent the services offered by FSN. Defendants claim that FSN is a "membership organization" which provides consumers with various services, including investment opportunity information, debt consolidation information, applications for secured credit cards and business planning advice. FSN claims that it has not issued any loans or credit cards to consumers and denies that it has provided budget planning or debt adjustment services to the public.

Defendants explain that the "$30,000 credit" offered in the FSN promotions is a sum offered to members who find mortgages to be purchased by FSN which meet certain investment criteria. In order to obtain this line of credit, a member must contact FSN with an opportunity to buy a mortgage note and if FSN deems the investment favorable, it will supply the capital to purchase the mortgage note, sell the note to an institutional investor for a higher amount and share the profit (finders fee) equally with the member. Defendants claim that this investment program was submitted to both the New York and North Carolina banking departments for review and both found that a license is not required by the Banking Departments nor would FSN be required to register as a mortgage banker or broker.

Defendants also explain that FSN does not itself provide any services to directly adjust members debts or to make payments on behalf of members to their creditors. Rather, FSN directs consumers to companies and attorneys who accept applications for that service. Similarly, FSN does not issue MasterCards, Visas or any other credit card. Rather, FSN has agreements with two banking institutions which are willing to offer collateralized credit cards to persons with poor credit histories. FSN provides its members with applications for credit cards which consumers send directly to the issuing financial institution. FSN also provides information and applications for consumers to obtain loans but does not itself issue direct loans.

Plaintiffs allege that defendants have violated both the Telemarketing Sales Rule ("FTC Telemarketing Rule"), 16 C.F.R. Part 310 which was promulgated pursuant to the Telemarketing and Consumer Fraud and Abuse Prevention Act ("Telemarketing Act", 15 U.S.C. §§ 6101 et seq.) as well as numerous New York and North Carolina state statutes.

DISCUSSION

. . .

Preliminary injunctions are authorized under the Telemarketing Act "upon a proper showing that, weighing the equities and considering the Commission's likelihood of ultimate success, such action would be in the public interest." 15 U.S.C. § 53(b). I find that plaintiffs have met their burden of showing a likelihood of success on the merits on the claims that defendants have violated the FTC Telemarketing Rule.

A. False and Misleading Advertisement

The complaint alleges that defendants violated Section 310.3(a)(1)(ii) and 310.3(a)(2) of the FTC Telemarketing Rule by failing to disclose in a clear and conspicuous manner prior to a consumer paying money, that there are material limitations on the consumer's use of the Resource Card to obtain a loan or credit and Section 310.3(a)(4) of the FTC Telemarketing Rule, by not providing the offered loan and debt consolidation services, business financing and credit card to consumers as advertised. The relevant provisions of the FTC Telemarketing Rule provide in pertinent part:

> (a) Prohibited deceptive telemarketing acts or practices. It is a deceptive telemarketing act or practice and a violation of this Rule for any seller or telemarketer to engage in the following conduct:

(1) Before a customer pays for goods or services offered, failing to disclose in a clear and conspicuous manner, the following material information:

. . .

(ii) All material restrictions, limitations, or conditions to purchase, receive or use the goods or services that are the subject of the sales offer. . . .

(2) Misrepresenting, directly or by implication, any of the following material information:

. . .

(ii) Any material restriction, limitation, or condition to purchase, receive, or use goods or services that are the subject of a sales offer;

(iii) Any material aspect of the performance, efficacy, nature or central characteristics of goods or services that are the subject of a sales offer;

. . .

(4) Making a false or misleading statement to induce any person to pay for goods or services.

Id. (footnote omitted).

Defendants contend that their written advertisements sent as direct mailings to consumers accurately and fairly depicts its services. For example, they emphasize that the advertisements contain the explanatory language "THE RESOURCE CARD FEATURES A $30,000 LINE OF CREDIT FOR INVESTMENTS . . ." or

"Imagine this—Next week you can start your own business. We have approved you for a credit line to purchase investments that you find in your neighborhood. You don't need to use any of your own funds because we give you 100% of the funds necessary to make the investments . . ."

Defendants argue that this language fairly and adequately informs the consumer that the line of credit is not a guaranteed loan without limitation but is an amount of money that FSN will make available to the member for the purchase of a specific type of investment, i.e., private mortgage purchases, described in the membership information.

Defendants further rely on the explanatory information contained in the membership materials which is provided to consumers only upon enrollment as members of FSN and after payment of the annual fee. Defendants readily admit that the only type of transaction for which the $30,000 line of credit is available is the investment arrangement whereby the Resource Card member finds a mortgage for FSN to purchase at a discount rate for which the Card member shares in any profit in resale.

Defendants claim that the only debt consolidation service they offer to consumers is providing an application for debt consolidation with one of several debt consolidation companies or attorneys. Yet the advertisement clearly states that "as a Resource Card member you can take advantage of our debt consolidation service. By next week all your bills can be combined into one convenient monthly payment."

Defendants also view the language of their advertisements which states " . . . you can get your own collateralized MasterCard or Visa even if you have poor credit" as a fair portrayal of their service since members are furnished applications to apply for a credit with certain banking institutions.

B.   Advance Payment for Arranging Credit or Loan

Section 310.4(a)(4) of the FTC Telemarketing Rule, provides in pertinent part:

(a) Abusive conduct generally. It is an abusive telemarketing act or practice and a violation of this Rule for any seller or telemarketer to engage in the following conduct:

. . .

(4) Requesting or receiving payment of any fee or consideration in advance of obtaining a loan or other extension of credit when the seller or telemarketer has guaranteed or represented a high likelihood of success in obtaining or arranging a loan or other extension of credit for a person.

Defendants argue that they have not violated this provision because they do not obtain loans or issue credit directly to its customers. However, defendants admit that FSN accepts a fee from its customers to become "members." They also admit that FSN arranges for its members to obtain a loan or extension of credit. Further, FSN's advertisements clearly represent a high likelihood of success in obtaining or arranging for credit by stating that a consumer is "pre-approved" for an extension of credit and that by "next week" they can have all their debts consolidated into one payment. By defendants' own admissions together with evidence presented, the plaintiffs have demonstrated a likelihood of success of this claim on the merits.

FINDINGS AND CONCLUSIONS

I find that defendants' advertising practice is patently misleading and deceptive. Defendants not only make representations that they offer "a line of credit" and "debt consolidation" services but they pitch their services in the form of the "Resource Card" which is "pre-approved" and has a "line of credit." The advertisements are clearly designed to foster the appearance that FSN is offering a credit card with related services commonly offered by credit card companies to consumers with questionable credit rating. Only after paying the up-front fee will consumers learn that the Resource Card is not a credit card and that the line of credit they thought they would obtain is actually an investment offer of a finders fee for locating prospective mortgage holders interested in selling a mortgage debt to FSN at a discount. In fact, consumers paying FSN the fee to obtain the Resource

Card will only receive applications for a credit card and for debt consolidation services with other institutions. The reality of what a consumer receives as a Resource Card member is a far cry from the benefits offered in defendants' advertising.

This Court finds that defendants' have violated the Telemarketing Act (1) by failing to disclose in a clear and conspicuous manner prior to a consumer paying money, that there are material limitations on the consumer's use of the Resource Card to obtain a loan or credit; (2) by requesting and receiving payment of a fee in advance of arranging a loan or credit when they have guaranteed a likelihood of success in obtaining the loan or other extension or credit for a consumer; and (3) by not providing the offered loan and debt consolidation services, business financing and credit card to consumers as advertised.

I find that the plaintiffs have demonstrated that they are likely to succeed on the merits of their claim. I also find that the plaintiffs have made a proper showing that, after weighing the equities and considering the plaintiffs' likelihood of ultimate success, the issuance of a preliminary injunction is in the public interest. Accordingly, plaintiffs' motion for a preliminary injunction is granted.

QUESTIONS AND NOTES

1. Problem. At 6:15 p.m. an employee of *Home Improvement Co.* telephones *Consumer* to interest her in thermal windows and aluminum siding. "We can cut your utility bills in half, guaranteed." *Consumer* says that she and her family "just sat down to dinner, don't bother us, and in any event we're not interested." At 8:30 the *Home Improvement Co.* representative calls again and starts his sales pitch. *Consumer* interrupts, "I told you we're not interested" and hangs up. At 9:45 another employee phones and asks to speak to *Consumer's* husband. *Consumer* asks for the identity of the caller and when she hears *Home Improvement Co.*, she says, "I already told you not to call. We are not interested in home improvements. Please do not call us again." *Consumer* and her family retire for the night. A few days later she receives another call from *Home Improvement Co.* She again explains that she does not want to be bothered by *Home Improvement Co.*, she's not interested in their products or services. After hanging up, she phones the Attorney General's Hotline, where you are working. She wants to know what can be done to stop the calls. What would you advise:

(a) What are her rights under the Telemarketing and Consumer Fraud and Abuse Prevention Act (and the FTC's Telemarketing Sales Rule)? See 15 U.S.C. § 6104(a).

(b) What can the Attorney General do? See section 310.4(b), (c) of the FTC Rule.

(c) What is the relevance of section 310.6(b)(3)?

2. To protect consumers from undesired intrusions by telemarketers, many states have enacted statutes that establish do-not-call lists. Once a consumer registers his or her phone number, it is a violation of state law for a merchant to place a telephone call to that consumer. The statutes often create exemptions for various classes of callers, e.g., persons soliciting for charities, telephone companies, and merchants that have an existing business relationship with the consumer. Under the authority of the Telemarketing and Consumer Fraud and Abuse Prevention Act of 1994, the FTC has established a national do-not-call list. 16 C.F.R. § 310.4(b)(1)(iii)(B). In Mainstream Marketing Services, Inc. v. FTC, 358 F.3d 1228 (10th Cir.2004), the court upheld the constitutionality of the rule creating the list, and in United States v. DirectTV, Civil Action No. SACV05 1211 (C.D.Cal., Dec. 12, 2005), DirectTV and its telemarketers agreed to pay a civil penalty of $5.3 million to settle charges that they violated the rule.

3. To evade the proscriptions on making prerecorded telephone calls, merchants have attempted to take advantage of exemptions for those conducting surveys or seeking charitable contributions. The Telephone Consumer Protection Act contains a private right of action, and courts have been attentive to these evasionary tactics. E.g., see Margulis v. P & M Consulting, Inc., 121 S.W.3d 246 (Mo.App.2003) (survey to identify targets for subsequent telephone solicitation); Irvine v. Akron Beacon Journal, 770 N.E.2d 1105 (Ohio App.2002) (prerecorded calls to determine whether the telephone number was a working number, in which even a subsequent call would be made).

4. European Union. Regulation of telemarketing is common in other countries, too. For example, the EU adopted a Directive requiring its members to enact rules that permit consumers to opt out of telephone solicitations. Directive 97/7/EC of May 20, 1997, on the protection of consumers in respect of distance contracts, 1997 O.J. L44/19, art. 10(2) ("Member States shall ensure that means of distance communication . . . which allow individual communications may be used only where there is no clear objection from the consumer"). Germany has gone further, requiring the telemarketer to obtain the consumer's consent before it makes calls to the consumer's home.

CHAPTER 3

DECEPTION—LEGISLATIVE SOLUTIONS AT THE STATE LEVEL

A. COMPREHENSIVE STATUTES

Almost every state has enacted legislation proscribing deception. These statutes are similar in scope to the FTC Act and appear to duplicate it. Nevertheless, their existence is important to consumers for at least two reasons: 1) the FTC has limited resources and cannot possibly deal with all deception, and 2) the FTC Act confers no private remedy, whereas nearly all the state statutes do.

The various state deceptive practices statutes are of three basic types:

1) FTC-type statutes, broadly prohibiting unfair or deceptive acts or practices (in effect in about a dozen states, including Illinois, Massachusetts, and Washington);

2) deceptive practices statutes, broadly prohibiting deception and numerous specific practices (in effect in about twenty states, including Texas, Michigan, and Ohio); and

3) consumer fraud acts, broadly prohibiting the use of deception, fraud, misrepresentation, concealment, etc. (in effect in more than a dozen states, including California, New York, and New Jersey).

All three types of statutes frequently are referred to as "little-FTC acts" or "UDAPs" (for Unfair or Deceptive Acts or Practices). The Statutory Supplement contains an example of each of the three types. It also contains the Uniform Consumer Sales Practices Act, promulgated by the National Conference of Commissioners on Uniform State Laws.

To what extent does each of the three types differ from the FTC Act? from each other? from deceit? Indeed, in view of the existence of common law remedies for misrepresentation, what justification is there for these state statutes? Do they help consumers in any way other than empowering a state official to pursue persons engaging in deceitful conduct?

Searle v. Exley Express, Inc.

Supreme Court of Oregon, 1977.
278 Or. 535, 564 P.2d 1054.

O'CONNELL, JUSTICE PRO TEM.

This is an action brought by the purchaser of a White Freightliner truck-tractor to recover damages for the alleged misrepresentation of the condition of the truck. The action was brought under the Unlawful Trade Practices Act, ORS 646.605, et seq. Defendant appeals from a judgment on a verdict of $2,950 in favor of plaintiff.

Defendant, which is engaged in the business of interstate trucking, advertised for sale some of its used trucks on a lease-back arrangement. Under this arrangement defendant was obliged to supply the lessor with a refrigeration trailer unit and also to provide hauling jobs from which the purchaser-operator would receive a portion of the operating revenue from the use of the truck.

Plaintiff's son, Wayne Searle, saw the advertisement in the newspaper and called it to plaintiff's attention. At that time plaintiff and his wife were looking for something in which to invest, and since plaintiff's son, who was a truck driver, was out of work, plaintiff decided to purchase the truck and operate it under the lease-back arrangement. Plaintiff alleges that defendant's agent misrepresented the condition of the truck.

Defendant contends on appeal that there was no evidence to establish a false or misleading representation of the condition of the truck, but that in any event the Unlawful Trade Practices Act has no application to the facts of this case.

It is not necessary for us to discuss defendant's first contention because we hold that the sale in this case is not within the Unlawful Trade Practices Act. The pertinent sections of the Act are as follows:

"(1) A person engages in a practice hereby declared to be unlawful when in the course of his business, vocation or occupation he:

" * * *

"(g) Represents that real estate, goods or services are of a particular standard, quality, or grade, or that real estate or goods are of a particular style or model, if they are of another;

" * * *." ORS 646.608(1).

ORS 646.605(7) provides:

"Real estate, goods or services" means those which are or may be used or bought primarily for personal, family or household purposes, and includes franchises, distributorships and other similar business opportunities, but does not include insurance.[1]

The construction of ORS 646.605(7) as it relates to the transaction in the case at bar presents some difficulties. It is clear enough that if the

---

1. ORS 646.638(1):

Any person who suffers any ascertainable loss of money or property, real or personal, as a result of the wilful use or employment by another person of a method, act or practice declared unlawful by ORS 646.608, may bring an individual action in an appropriate court to recover actual damages or $200, whichever is greater. The court or the jury, as the case may be, may award punitive damages and the court may provide such equitable relief as it deems necessary or proper.

subject matter of the sale is "real estate, goods or services," the Act purports to cover only those transactions in which the real estate, goods or services "are or may be used or bought primarily for personal, family or household purposes."[2]

The constructional problem is to determine what meaning is to be given to the latter phrase. Certainly it was not intended that the statute was to be applied solely on a subjective basis by inquiring in each case as to whether the purchaser was motivated in making the purchase by a desire to satisfy some personal, family or household objective. Rather, the statute purports to describe transactions involving the purchase of goods and services which customarily are entered into with the objective of satisfying some personal, family or household purpose. Obviously included would be the purchase of a sack of potatoes, furniture for a home, a wedding gown, an engagement ring or a set of golf clubs. In all of these the purpose of the purchase is to serve some personal, family or household need. Obviously excluded would be the purchase of a carload of potatoes, a Xerox machine, or a gross of women's stockings.

But as is always true when it is important to make a differentiation between two categories, there will be factual situations which will be difficult, and sometimes impossible, to classify on a definitional basis. Because this is so, we can expect to encounter difficult constructional problems in applying the statute with which we are now concerned. The difficulty will arise because some human activities are ambivalent, having some characteristics which would prompt us to describe them as personal and other characteristics prompting us to describe them as commercial or business in nature. For instance, the purchase of an automobile by an architect for use in carrying on his profession could be viewed as also serving a personal purpose in the sense that the pursuit of a person's profession is usually regarded as something more than the carrying on of a business. Neither the language of the statute nor its legislative history gives us any clue as to how we should approach these problems of construction.

It would not be irrational to treat the statute as having been designed to cover the situation posed above and any other cases where we are able to discern that the activity is commonly understood to have in it a personal ingredient.

But even if we were to give the statute this broad treatment, the transaction in the present case does not fall within the statute.

We will assume, as plaintiff asserts, that the truck was purchased as a family investment and to provide employment for plaintiff's son. In this sense the purchase could be deemed to have been made for "personal, family or household purposes." But this looks solely at the subjective

---

2. Plaintiff does not assert that defendant made any misrepresentations with respect to any matter other than the condition of the truck. Therefore, we are not called upon to interpret that part of ORS 646.605(7) which reads "and includes franchises, distributorships and other similar business opportunities."

motivation of the purchaser, and as we have already stated, we do not regard the statute as having this broad sweep. If goods are customarily bought by a substantial number of purchasers for personal, family or household uses and were, in fact, bought by the plaintiff for his or someone else's use and not for resale, the statute applies. Certainly a truck designed for the business of hauling freight does not fall within that classification. The purchase of a truck to carry on a freight business may fulfill personal and family needs in a particular case but generally it would be purchased to carry on a business, and it is this customary or predominant purpose which is to be used in characterizing the transaction. Therefore, we hold that the purchase in the present case did not come within the statute.

Judgment reversed.

QUESTIONS AND NOTES

1. Most little-FTC and consumer fraud acts apply to the sale of land as well as to the sale of goods (e.g., see the statute in *Searle)*. Some of them, however, apply only if the land is located in another state. E.g., 815 Ill. Consol. Stat. § 505/1(b). In some states the statutes have been revised expressly to cover land transactions. E.g., New Jersey Stat.Ann. § 56:8–2. And if the statute is silent on the question, the court may hold land transactions to be included. See Commonwealth v. Monumental Properties, Inc., 329 A.2d 812 (Pa.1974) (FTC-type act, drawing extensively on judicial interpretation of the FTC Act); contra, Neveroski v. Blair, 358 A.2d 473 (N.J.Super.1976) (consumer fraud act).

2. FTC-type acts and consumer fraud acts uniformly apply to the sale of services. But courts do not necessarily interpret the statutes literally. Consider, for example, Neveroski v. Blair, 358 A.2d 473, 481 (N.J.Super.1976), where the court stated,

> Certainly no one would argue that a member of any of the learned professions is subject to the provisions of the Consumer Fraud Act despite the fact that he renders "services" to the public. . . . [I]t would be ludicrous to construe the legislation with that broad a sweep. . . .

The court went on to hold that the practices of a real estate broker were not covered by the statute, even though it acknowledged that a broker is not a member of a learned profession. Some states expressly exempt professional services. E.g., Md. Com. Law Code Ann. § 13–104; Tex.Bus. & Com. Code Ann. § 17.49(c). See Head v. U.S. Inspect DFW, Inc., 159 S.W.3d 731 (Tex.App.2005) (exemption applies to home inspection service).

3. In addition to prohibiting false representations concerning "standard, quality, or grade," the Oregon statute also prohibits representations that real estate, goods, or services have "characteristics, . . . uses, benefits, . . . or qualities that they do not have" (subsection 1(e)). Does it violate this statute for the seller of a mobile home to fail to disclose that the mobile home park in which it is located has been sold and will be converted to other uses?

Would this nondisclosure be actionable at common law?

4. *Searle* illustrates that not all sales of goods are within the scope of anti-deception legislation. What additional requirement is there? What justification is there for having this requirement? Why does the court hold that the requirement is not satisfied?

5. Problem. *Consumer* takes her 1948 Jaguar to *Merchant*, which is in the business of restoring classic autos in Portland, Oregon. *Merchant* estimates that it will cost approximately $25,000 to restore *Consumer's* car. *Consumer* agrees, and *Merchant* commences work, billing *Consumer* on a time and materials basis. When the work is completed, the bills total $68,000. *Consumer* sues *Merchant* for making representations that violate the Unlawful Trade Practices Act. Should the Oregon court permit *Consumer* to maintain the action: are the services "used or bought primarily for personal, family or household purposes"?

In *Feldman v. Al Prueitt & Sons, Inc.*, 1986 WL 55324, 1986–2 CCH Trade Cases ¶ 67,269 (Pa.Ct.C.P.1986), the basis for this problem, the court wrote:

> We shall . . . accept the view taken by the Oregon Court in *Searle v. Exley Express*, which dealt with . . . a statute similar to the one before us. . . . The services purchased were not to fix the family car, but to restore a valuable antique. While the plaintiff will likely gain personal satisfaction from such a vehicle, and the value will appreciate from automobile show recognition, but such a vehicle is not for usual personal, family or household purposes—nor are the services restoring such a vehicle.

Is the Pennsylvania court correct: under the test of the court in *Searle*, are the services for personal, family, or household purposes? Should the result be different if defendant provides services to restore an antique bugle that *Consumer* uses in Civil War reenactments?

6. Some statutes define "consumer" as "any person who purchases or contracts for the purchase of merchandise not for resale in the ordinary course of his trade or business but for his use or that of a member of his household or in connection with the operation of his household." Would *Searle* be decided the same way under this language? Cf. People v. Cardet International, Inc., 321 N.E.2d 386 (Ill.App.1974); State v. Koscot Interplanetary, Inc., 512 P.2d 416 (Kan.1973).

7. The court in *Searle* considers the nature of the goods and the nature of the purchaser. Problems of scope may also arise with respect to the nature of the seller. In Young v. Joyce, 351 A.2d 857, 860 (Del.1975), plaintiff purchased a house and subsequently sued the seller to recover for flooding in the basement of the house. The court held that the seller

> is not covered by the Consumer Fraud Act, cannot be held liable under 6 Del.C. § 2513, and that judgment as to her must be reversed.

> Although § 2513 applies to "any person," which includes an "individual" under § 2511, that statute must be read in light of the stated purpose of the Consumer Fraud Act: ". . . to protect consumers and legitimate business enterprises from unfair or deceptive merchandising practices *in the conduct of any trade or commerce*. . . ." While the [italicized] terms are not statutorily defined, we do not believe that the isolated sale of real estate by its owner, in this case, constitutes the conduct of trade or commerce. . . .

Accord, Allen v. Anderson, 557 P.2d 24 (Wash.App.1976) (consumer seller not subject to the statute); contra, Chong v. Parker, 361 F.3d 455 (8th Cir.2004) (Missouri law); Pennington v. Singleton, 606 S.W.2d 682 (Tex. 1980).

Would it have been relevant for the court in *Searle* to have considered the nature of the seller?

8.   Would a seller of goods be covered with respect to a sale of something other than the goods he normally sells? For example, if the owner of an appliance store sells the van he uses to make deliveries and service calls, is the transaction within the scope of anti-deception legislation? See Wolverton v. Stanwood, 563 P.2d 1203 (Ore.), rehearing denied 565 P.2d 755 (Ore.1977), where the statute applied to practices occurring "in the course of his business, vocation, or occupation" (see *Searle* at page 123 supra). The court stated,

> It could be argued that the phrase "in the course of his business, vocation or occupation" should be construed so as to apply to all unlawful practices except those which arise out of strictly private transactions and which are totally unconnected with the business or employment of the defendant. On the other hand, the statute could be interpreted so as to apply only to those unlawful practices which arise out of the ordinary, everyday activities of the defendant's business or occupation. The former construction could be justified on the basis of a broad reading of the general policy of the statute to discourage deceptive trade practices and to provide a viable remedy for consumers who are damaged by such conduct. The latter construction could be supported by a broad reading of the limitation which restricts the application of the statute to those unlawful practices that arise out of the course of the defendant's business. Such an interpretation would reflect a presumption that this restriction was intended to limit the application of the statute to those situations which tend to present a continuing, and therefore more serious, threat to the general public.
>
> In the absence of any guidance as to which of these policies the legislature would have intended to prevail, we have determined to seek a middle ground. We believe that the statute should be applied only to those unlawful practices which arise out of transactions which are at least indirectly connected with the ordinary and usual course of defendant's business, vocation or occupation.

Id. at 1204–05.

9. Activities subject to regulation in certain other specified ways may be exempt from the requirements of deceptive practices legislation. For example, until 1974 the Washington statute provided:

> Nothing in this chapter shall apply to actions or transactions otherwise permitted, prohibited or regulated under laws administered by the insurance commissioner of this state, the Washington [utilities and transportation] commission, the federal power commission or any other regulatory body or officer acting under statutory authority of this state or the United States: *Provided, however,* . . .

Since literally hundreds of activities are regulated by federal, state, and local governments (see M. Carrow, The Licensing Power in New York City 3–4 (1968)), the scope of this exemption is critical. In Dick v. Attorney General, 521 P.2d 702 (Wash.1974), the attorney general commenced an investigation of respondent, a drugless healer. Respondent sought to cut off the investigation on the grounds, inter alia, that he was subject to a licensing statute and was therefore exempt from the Consumer Protection Act. The court stated:

> The petitioner first maintains that the director of licenses is not a "regulatory body or officer" within the meaning of RCW 19.86.170, because his regulatory powers are not as comprehensive as those of the Insurance Commissioner, the Washington Utilities and Transportation Commission, or the Federal Power Commission. The meaning of the language "other regulatory body or officer" is not before this court for the first time in this action. In State v. Reader's Digest Ass'n, 81 Wash.2d 259, 279, 501 P.2d 290, 303 (1972), the Attorney General successfully argued that the defendant in that action was not exempt under RCW 19.86.170, even though it was regulated by the Federal Trade Commission. Agreeing with the petitioner's interpretation of the provision in question, we said:
>
> > The FTC, however, is not a regulatory body within the meaning of RCW 19.86.170. The term "other regulatory body" must be construed in light of the preceding terms and the intent of the entire act. The *ejusdem generis* rule is that specific words or terms modify and restrict the interpretation of general words or terms where both are used in sequence. [Citing cases.] The specific agencies or bodies mentioned in the statute all regulate areas where permission or registration is necessary to engage in an activity. Once the requisite permission is obtained, the activity is subject to monitoring and regulation. The FTC, however, is not such an agency. It has no control over entry into its area of concern. It merely monitors the business practices of those who freely enter its domain. In this respect its position is analogous to that of the United States Attorney General in his capacity of enforcing the anti-trust laws. In State v. Sterling Theatres Co., 64 Wash.2d 761, 394 P.2d 226 (1964), we concluded that he was not a "regulatory officer" within the meaning of RCW 19.86.170. We held that "surveillance and enforcement activities undertaken by

the federal authorities pursuant to consent decrees" do not make a business "a regulated industry within the meaning of the state Act."

Thus it will be seen that we have, applying the rule of *ejusdem generis*, held that where an activity is licensed and subject to regulation, that is, where an officer or agency has control over entry into an area of concern, the exemption section applies.

The Court of Appeals correctly held that the respondent's practice is regulated generally within the meaning of RCW 19.86.170. However, we do not read the statute to exempt a transaction or action merely because the business or trade is regulated generally.

We have stated that the Consumer Protection Act should be liberally construed to effect its purpose, in accordance with the direction contained in RCW 19.86.920. If a particular practice found to be unfair or deceptive is not regulated, even though the business is regulated generally, it would appear to be the legislative intent that the provisions of the act should apply. The use of the word "actions or transactions" rather than "business or trade" makes it clear, we think, that this was the legislative intent.

The Court of Appeals held that because the respondent's practice was regulated generally under the provisions of RCW 18.36, it was exempt from the provisions of the Consumer Protection Act. We think this holding is broader than the statute justifies. However, dismissal of the action was not improper, in view of the posture of the case as it reached the Court of Appeals. The petitioner had not at that time and has not yet specified what actions or transactions he believes are violative of the act. The only evidence that we can find in the record which throws any light on this question is a statement made to the superior court in answer to its question directed to a member of the Attorney General's staff who appeared there. This attorney stated:

> [W]e have reason to believe that there is an unauthorized practice in medicine, and that he is prescribing medication without authorization, and that, there are other unfair and unaccepted practicing by the individual concerned.

The unauthorized practice of medicine is prohibited under RCW 18.71.020. RCW 18.36.010 declares that the term "drugless therapeutics" as used therein shall in no way include the giving, prescribing or recommending of pharmaceutic drugs and poisons for internal use. It appears therefore that the actions or transactions under investigation are otherwise regulated within the meaning of RCW 19.86.170. If there were other actions or transactions under investigation which were not otherwise prohibited or regulated, that fact has not been brought to our attention nor was it brought to the attention of the lower courts, insofar as the record reveals.

When the respondent showed that his practice was regulated generally under a statute administered by a regulatory officer within the meaning of the act, it became incumbent upon the petitioner to show that the actions or transactions under investigation were not covered by those regulations. Since he did not provide the information necessary to make a determination upon the point, he cannot claim that the Court of Appeals was in error in dismissing the action.

The judgment of the Court of Appeals is affirmed.

Id. at 704–05.

The court cites earlier holdings that the United States Attorney General and the FTC are not within the meaning of the phrase "regulatory body or officer." Does the court hold in *Dick* that the state director of licenses is not within the meaning of that phrase?

In the last paragraph of the excerpt, the court states a two-step test to determine whether the Act applies. What basis in the statute is there for this test?

In 1974 the Washington legislature amended the statute to read:

Nothing in this chapter shall apply to actions or transactions otherwise permitted, prohibited or regulated under laws administered by the insurance commissioner of this state, the Washington utilities and transportation commission, the federal power commission or actions or transactions permitted by any other regulatory body or officer acting under statutory authority of this state or the United States: *Provided, however,* . . .

Rev.Code Wash.Ann. § 19.86.170. What effect does the amendment have on the result in *Dick*?

The Virginia Consumer Protection Act states that the Act does not apply to "any aspect of a consumer transaction which aspect is authorized under laws or regulations of this Commonwealth." An auto dealer argued that because another Virginia statute regulates deceptive advertising, the dealer's ad was not subject to challenge under the Consumer Protection Act. The court noted that "authorized" is not synonymous with "regulated" and held that the exemption in the Consumer Protection Act does not apply unless the specific aspect of the consumer transaction is authorized. Manassas Autocars, Inc. v. Couth, 645 S.E.2d 443 (Va.2007).

In New Jersey the Consumer Fraud Act (CFA) is silent on the question whether it applies to activities or entities regulated by state agencies. In Lemelledo v. Beneficial Management Corp., 696 A.2d 546 (N.J.1997), the court held that the Act applies to the sale of credit insurance by a small loan company even though there were four other distinct statutes specifically governing small loans and the sale of credit insurance. The court emphasized a provision in the CFA that states the Act's rights, remedies, and prohibitions are cumulative to those created by other laws (N.J.Stat. Ann. § 56:8–2.13, reproduced in the Statutory Supplement). The court also emphasized that the existence of a private cause of action fostered the creation of a cadre of private attorneys general to aid in the enforcement of the Act. The court stated:

Both of those aspects of the CFA—its recognition of cumulative remedies and its empowerment of citizens as private attorneys general—reflect an apparent legislative intent to enlarge fraud-fighting authority and to delegate that authority among various governmental and nongovernmental entities, each exercising different forms of remedial power. That legislative intent is readily inferable from the ongoing need for consumer protection and the salutary benefits to be achieved by expanding enforcement authority and enhancing remedial redress. When remedial power is concentrated in one agency, underenforcement may result because of lack of resources, concentration on other agency responsibilities, lack of expertise, agency capture by regulated parties, or a particular ideological bent by agency decisionmakers. Underenforcement by an administrative agency may be even more likely where, as in this case, the regulated party is a relatively powerful business entity while the class protected by the regulation tends to consist of low-income persons with scant resources, lack of knowledge about their rights, inexperience in the regulated area, and insufficient understanding of the prohibited practice. The primary risk of underenforcement— the victimization of a protected class—can be greatly reduced by allocating enforcement responsibilities among various agencies and among members of the consuming public in the forms of judicial and administrative proceedings and private causes of action.

.   .   .

In order to overcome the presumption that the CFA applies to a covered activity, a court must be satisfied . . . that a direct and unavoidable conflict exists between application of the CFA and application of the other regulatory scheme or schemes. It must be convinced that the other source or sources of regulation deal specifically, concretely, and pervasively with the particular activity, implying a legislative intent not to subject parties to multiple regulation that, as applied, will work at cross-purposes. We stress that the conflict must be patent and sharp, and must not simply constitute a mere possibility of incompatibility. If the hurdle for rebutting the basic assumption of applicability of the CFA to covered conduct is too easily overcome, the statute's remedial measures may be rendered impotent as primary weapons in combatting clear forms of fraud simply because those fraudulent practices happen also to be covered by some other statute or regulation.

In the modern administrative state, regulation is frequently complementary, overlapping, and comprehensive. Absent a nearly irreconcilable conflict, to allow one remedial statute to preempt another or to co-opt a broad field of regulatory concern, simply because the two statutes regulate the same activity, would defeat the purposes giving rise to the need for regulation. It is not readily to be inferred that the Legislature, by enacting multiple remedial statutes designed to augment protection, actually intended that parties be subject only to one source of regulation.

Id. at 553–54. For a distinctly contrasting view, see Liss v. Lewiston–Richards, Inc., 732 N.W.2d 514 (Mich.2007), holding that conduct is exempt if the general transaction is authorized by another statute even if the challenged conduct is not specifically authorized.

Weigel v. Ron Tonkin Chevrolet Co.

Supreme Court of Oregon, 1984.
298 Or. 127, 690 P.2d 488.

LINDE, JUSTICE.

[Defendant automobile dealer told the plaintiff that a car was "new" and that it had 260 miles on the odometer because it was driven from another dealership as part of a dealer-to-dealer trade. In fact, the dealer had sold the car to another consumer, who took delivery of it but returned it five days later when her financing fell through. Plaintiff sued, alleging a violation of the Oregon Unlawful Trade Practices Act, section 646.608 of which provides

(1) A person engages in an unlawful practice when in the course of the person's business, vocation or occupation the person does any of the following:

. . .

(f) Represents that real estate or goods are original or new if they are deteriorated, altered, reconditioned, reclaimed, used or secondhand.

The trial court held that the dealer violated this statute, and the Court of Appeals affirmed.]

I.

What ORS 646.608(1)(f) forbids is the representation that goods are "original or new" if they are, among other things, "used or secondhand."

What is meant by the words "new" and "used" is a question of statutory interpretation. It is not a question for a factfinder to decide case by case, with the possibility that different results might be reached on identical facts.[1] . . .

The answer turns on at least two elements. One is the significance of actual, physical "use" of the automobile. The other element is the significance of prior transactions involving the same vehicle. Both are important.

Doubtless the legislature did not intend an automobile to become "used" goods as soon as it is driven. Legislatures must be assumed to know that many new automobiles are driven some distance to the showroom or sales lot of the retail dealer, and that sales personnel and potential

---

1. Whether a representation that an item is "new" is a misrepresentation may be a jury question in a common law fraud action, see Krause v. Eugene Dodge, Inc., 265 Or. 486, 504–505, 509 P.2d 1199 (1973), but here we are interpreting the legislature's use of the terms.

customers drive new automobiles in the course of considering a purchase. An automobile does not become a "used" car because several potential buyers have driven it solely for that purpose any more than a coat becomes used clothing because several customers have tried it on in the clothing store. Misrepresentation of the mileage accumulated during such trial drives is a separate matter, but in this case the mileage was accurately stated to plaintiff.

It is equally improbable that the legislature intended an automobile to become "used" goods by a mere paper transaction, later revoked, without being driven at all. This might happen whenever a customer orders a particular model and completes all steps in the sale (or lease), including payment, but the parties rescind the sale, perhaps in order to substitute a different model, by the time the ordered vehicle is delivered or even reaches the dealer. The prior sales contract alone cannot satisfy the statutory concept of "used" goods; actual use at least to the extent of taking possession is required.

We therefore do not accept the emphasis that defendant would place on the question whether a sale had been completed in this case. Nor does the result depend on the kind of warranty given with the vehicle or how the prior transaction was treated for purposes of the dealer's inventory and financing practices. Merchandise other than automobiles sometimes is sold, examined or tried out at home, and returned to the seller. Whether such merchandise is "new" or "used" does not depend on the fact of an earlier sale; it depends on whether the article was used. In the case of automobiles, moreover, the test cannot be confined to prior sales; doubtless the statute encompasses prior use under a lease, a loan, or by the dealer himself as a personal or business vehicle beyond the narrow uses involved in moving the merchandise to the dealer's place of business, testing or servicing it, and demonstrating it in the sales process. If an automobile has been physically used by anyone for purposes beyond the uses incidental to the sales process, that fact must be disclosed. If the nature of the prior use is fully disclosed to a buyer, there is no actionable misrepresentation regardless whether the automobile is sold on terms otherwise employed for "new" cars.

. . .

III.

Civil recovery under ORS 646.638[a] requires that the defendant's commission of an unlawful trade practice must be "wilful" and result in an "ascertainable loss of money or property" to plaintiff. Defendant contends that plaintiff's evidence does not satisfy the second requirement.

---

a. Section 646.638 provides, in part: " . . . any person who suffers any ascertainable loss of money or property . . . as a result of wilful use or employment by another person of a method, act or practice declared unlawful by ORS 646.608, may bring an individual action in an appropriate court to recover actual damages or $200, whichever is greater. . . ."—Ed.

What the legislature meant by an "ascertainable loss of money or property" is not free from doubt. The case was tried on the theory that a plaintiff must show an economic loss in the sense of a difference between the price paid and some objective measure of market value. This is one plausible reading of the statute, but it is not the only one. Another possible reading is that the legislature meant to exclude a civil action by a customer who was attracted by a forbidden misrepresentation but in fact did not act upon it, or who received immediate satisfaction at no expense when bringing the matter to the seller's attention, yet that a "loss of money or property" includes the expenditure of funds for goods that are not as desired by the customer and represented by the seller irrespective of their market value to others. We therefore invited the parties to submit additional memoranda on this question.[3]

The overall structure of the Unlawful Trade Practices Act lends some support to the second view of the legislative policy. The act provides for both public and private enforcement. It authorizes district attorneys to seek injunctions against an unlawful trade practice, ORS 646.632, which are enforceable by statutory penalties, ORS 646.642, and possible loss of licenses and franchises, ORS 646.646.

The civil action authorized by ORS 646.638 is designed to encourage private enforcement of the prescribed standards of trade and commerce in aid of the act's public policies as much as to provide relief to the injured party. This is apparent from the section itself. It allows recovery of actual damages or $200, whichever is greater, plus punitive damages, costs, and attorney fees. It requires a plaintiff to notify the Attorney General when filing a complaint, or plaintiff cannot obtain entry of judgment. The action must be commenced within one year rather than the longer periods ordinarily allowed for civil actions, and it is expressly made additional to other common law or statutory remedies. The evident purpose is to encourage private actions when the financial injury is too small to justify the expense of an ordinary lawsuit, provided that the action is timely initiated while the unlawful practice may be continuing and that the state is given an opportunity to investigate the practice for possible wider enforcement action.

All of this suggests that in enacting ORS 646.638, the legislature was concerned as much with devising sanctions for the prescribed standards of

---

3. Our question included two illustrations:

"To illustrate the first possibility, assume that a person orders and pays for merchandise on the representation that it is unique (e.g., a buyer who wants assurance that the dealer has not sold the same model of car—or jewelry or other merchandise—in the identical color), or orders and pays for golf clubs represented to be lefthanded but righthanded clubs are delivered and not ex-

changed. Has such a buyer suffered a loss of money regardless of whether the property may be worth the price or more than the price to another buyer? In other words, was the purpose of the statutory requirement to allow a civil action only if a person bought merchandise or otherwise entered into a transaction on the strength of the unlawful trade practice, but not to allow an action by a person who did not act upon the misrepresentation or other unlawful practice?"

trade and commerce as with remedying private losses, and that such losses therefore should be viewed broadly. The private loss indeed may be so small that the common law likely would reject it as grounds for relief, yet it will support an action under the statute. In Crooks v. Pay Less Drug Stores, 285 Or. 481, 592 P.2d 196 (1979), plaintiff recovered the statutory $200 because he had been charged $2.89 for a razor which by an error had been advertised at 89 cents.

Other courts have taken divergent views of the requirement of ascertainable loss. Defendant cites Bartner v. Carter, 405 A.2d 194 (Me.1979), which denied recovery under Maine's Unfair Trade Practices Act to purchasers of land who found that they received less land than the sellers had represented. The Supreme Judicial Court concluded that the Maine statute provided an action "for restitution" only in the "technical sense" of recovering benefits gained by the seller, not in the sense of making the plaintiff whole, but the court reached this conclusion because the Maine legislature had substituted the word "restitution" for the word "damages" in adopting the Massachusetts act. 405 A.2d at 202–203.[6] That change does not appear in the Oregon law. The Supreme Court of Connecticut, on the other hand, allowed recovery of damages to buyers of an automobile that did not meet advertised specifications without requiring plaintiffs to prove a specific amount of actual damages. Hinchliffe v. American Motors Corporation, 184 Conn. 607, 440 A.2d 810 (1981). The Court concluded that ascertainable "loss" encompassed a broader meaning than the term "damage." It wrote:

"Whenever a consumer has received something other than what he bargained for, he has suffered a loss of money or property. That loss is ascertainable if it is measurable even though the precise amount of the loss is not known. [The Unfair Trade Practices Act] is not designed to afford a remedy for trifles. In one sense the buyer has lost the purchase price of the item because he parted with his money reasonably expecting to receive a particular item or service. When the product fails to measure up, the consumer has been injured; he has suffered a loss. In another sense he has lost the benefits of the product which he was led to believe he had purchased. That the loss does not consist of a diminution in value is immaterial although obviously such diminution would satisfy the statute. To the consumer who wishes to purchase an energy saving subcompact, for example, it is no answer to say that he should be satisfied with a more valuable gas guzzler." 440 A.2d at 814.

Scrutiny of the record reveals that the present case also does not turn on the question whether any objective loss in market value is required.

---

6. "According to the principal draftsman of G.L. c. 93A, § 9, the 'sole purpose' of the requirement that the plaintiff suffer loss of money or property 'is to guard against vicarious suits by self-constituted private attorneys general when they spot an apparently deceiving advertisement in the newspaper, on television or in a store window.' Rice, New Private Remedies for Consumers: The Amendment of Chapter 93A, 54 Mass.L.Q. 307, 314 (1969)." Baldassari v. Public Finance Trust, 369 Mass. 33, 46, 337 N.E.2d 701 (1975), quoted in 405 A.2d at 202.

There is evidence besides plaintiff's own testimony that the automobile would have suffered a reduction in value if its prior "use" by a hopeful but unsuccessful customer had been disclosed. Defendant's salesman was asked: "If the vehicle was found to be a used vehicle, would it still be your testimony that it would have depreciated in value to some extent?", and he answered the question in the affirmative. Defendant, of course, denied that the car was a "used vehicle," but since under Parts I and II of this opinion it was "used" as a matter of law, the salesman's testimony was additional evidence that the required disclosure of the prior use would have depreciated its value to some extent. Even if the difference in value fell far short of the $1000 asserted by plaintiff, it would suffice for some ascertainable loss of money or property, and allow a court or jury to award the statutory $200 in general damages.

. . .

QUESTIONS AND NOTES

1.   The court states that there are two elements to consider in determining whether an automobile is new, and it states that both are important. Are they both necessary: can you think of a situation in which a court should conclude that a car is not new even though there was no prior transaction? even though there was no prior use?

2.   Is intent to deceive an element of section 646.608(1)(f)? section 646.638? Is knowledge of falsity an element? Is reliance an element? Exactly what are the elements?

3.   Problem. *Consumer* purchases a used car that *Dealer* received as a trade-in on a new-car purchase by another customer. Unknown to *Dealer*, the prior customer had rolled back the odometer from 64,348 to 34,596. In connection with *Consumer's* purchase, *Dealer* gave her an odometer statement that listed the car's mileage as 34,596. Six months later *Consumer* obtains the car's title history from the department of motor vehicles and learns that at some time prior to her purchase the car's title showed mileage in excess of 50,000. Is *Dealer* liable for this innocent misrepresentation under a deceptive practices statute that broadly makes unlawful any unfair or deceptive conduct?

4.   Automobile contracts typically have boxes for the seller to use to indicate the nature of the vehicle: new, used, or demo. Assume that the seller in *Weigel* checked the box labeled "used." Assume further that when plaintiff asked why he had not checked the "new" box, defendant told him, "The Department of Motor Vehicles requires us to check the 'used' or 'demo' box any time the odometer reads more than 250, and we didn't use this one as a demo." Plaintiff thereupon signed the contract. The parol evidence rule provides that when the parties to a contract have reduced their agreement to a writing that they intend as the final embodiment of their entire agreement, that agreement may not be varied by a prior or contemporaneous agreement. When plaintiff discovers the truth about the car and sues, can defendant invoke the parol evidence rule to defeat his claim?

5. In Weitzel v. Barnes, 691 S.W.2d 598 (Tex.1985), a developer sold a house, representing that it complied with the local housing code and used a sales contract in which the buyers agreed to accept the property "in its present condition." The house failed to comply with the code, and the buyers sued, asserting a violation of the Texas Deceptive Trade Practices Act, a statute similar to the Oregon statute in *Weigel*. Defendant argued that in view of the "in its present condition" language, the court ought not consider plaintiffs' allegations that defendant represented that the house complied with the housing code. The court rejected this argument:

> . . . [T]he parol evidence rule [is] not applicable because purchasers [are] not seeking to change or contradict the terms of the contract but [are] relying upon deceptive oral representations as the basis of their suit. [The DTPA] provides that the remedies under [it] are cumulative and in addition to other remedies; [it also] provides that [it] shall be liberally construed to protect consumers from deceptive business practices. Following such broad guidelines, we conclude that oral representations are not only admissible but can serve as the basis of a DTPA action. There was no effort on the part of the [plaintiffs] to show a breach of contract by [defendant]. The oral misrepresentations, which were made both before and after the execution of the agreement, constitute the basis of this cause of action, so traditional contractual notions do not apply.

Accord, Wang v. Massey Chevrolet, 118 Cal.Rptr.2d 770 (Cal.App.2002) (misrepresentation that the consumers could pay off an automobile lease without penalty but the contract committed them to 60 monthly payments).

The excerpt from *Weitzel* reveals a second reason why the parol evidence rule did not preclude recovery in that case. Can you identify it?

6. States typically have several statutes regulating various aspects of automobile sales. Among other things, these statutes may establish licensing requirements and may limit the amount of interest a lender may charge in connection with financing the purchase of a car. Often they distinguish between new and used motor vehicles and therefore need to define "new" or "used" for purposes of characterizing automobiles. The Illinois Vehicle Code, for example, defines "used motor vehicle" as

> Every motor vehicle which has been sold . . . or had title transferred from the person who first acquired it from the manufacturer . . . and so used as to have become what is commonly known as "second hand" within the ordinary meaning thereof: Provided, that a new motor vehicle shall not be considered as a "used motor vehicle" until it has been placed in a bona fide consumer use, notwithstanding the number of transfers of such motor vehicle. The term "bona fide consumer use" means actual operation by an owner who acquired the vehicle for use

in business or for pleasure purposes and who has been granted a Certificate of Title. . . .

625 Ill. Consol. Stat. § 5/1–216.

7. Why did the court conclude that plaintiff suffered "an ascertainable loss of money"? Did plaintiff suffer this loss "as a result of" defendant's representation that the car was new?

8. The courts have uniformly concluded that a plaintiff need not prove reliance in order to establish a violation of an Oregon-type anti-deception statute. E.g., State v. Master Distributors, Inc., 615 P.2d 116 (Idaho 1980); Sanders v. Francis, 561 P.2d 1003 (Ore.1977). But might not reliance by the consumer be necessary in order to establish the causal connection between the defendant's conduct and the plaintiff's injury? Compare Bartlett v. Schmidt, 33 S.W.3d 35 (Tex.App.2000) with Fernandez v. Schultz, 15 S.W.3d 648 (Tex.App.2000). In *Bartlett*, a seller of land misrepresented that the land could be used for plaintiff's intended purpose. As contemplated by the contract, plaintiff thereafter received a report from a title insurance company that was sufficiently complicated that neither plaintiff nor his attorney discovered that the seller's representation was false. The court held that because plaintiff had received this report, defendant's misrepresentation was not the cause of plaintiff's injury. In *Fernandez* the seller of a house knowingly misrepresented that the house was free of termites. As contemplated by the contract, plaintiffs thereafter obtained a report from a termite inspector who failed to discover the existence of termite infestation inside the house. The court held that, notwithstanding that plaintiffs obtained a termite inspection, defendant's misrepresentation was a cause of plaintiffs' injury. Can these cases be reconciled?

9. In Wiegand v. Walser Automotive Groups, Inc., 683 N.W.2d 807 (Minn. 2004), plaintiff purchased a car from defendant. During the negotiations defendant's sales rep told plaintiff that in order to obtain financing he was required to purchase credit insurance ($340) and a service contract ($1,500). In fact, these representations were false, and the credit contract document expressly stated that the purchase of those items was not required (though plaintiff evidently was unaware that the contract so stated). A year after the purchase plaintiff brought a class action on behalf of customers to whom defendant made these misrepresentations. Plaintiff sought recovery for violation of the Consumer Fraud Act, which permits recovery by "any person injured by a violation." The trial court granted defendant's motion to dismiss, holding that reliance on an oral representation is unjustified when a written, signed contract specifically negates the representation. On appeal, the intermediate appellate court affirmed. On further appeal, the Supreme Court stated:

> In Group Health Plan, Inc. v. Philip Morris, Inc., 621 N.W.2d 2 (Minn. 2001), . . . we were asked to answer the following certified question: must private plaintiffs "plead and prove reliance on the defendant's statements or conduct in order to be eligible for relief in the form of damages under the [Consumer Fraud Act]?" We held that a plaintiff "need only plead that the defendant engaged in conduct prohibited by

the statutes and that the plaintiff was damaged thereby." (emphasis added). In other words, "allegations of reliance are * * * not necessary to state a claim under section 8.31, subdivision 3a, for damages resulting from a violation." . . .

We recognized . . . , however, that in order to ultimately prove allegations of consumer fraud, the "injured" element of [the statute] requires that a private plaintiff prove a "causal nexus" between the plaintiff's injuries and the defendant's wrongful conduct. We explained that in a case such as Group Health, in which the plaintiffs' damages were "alleged to be caused by a lengthy course of prohibited conduct that affected a large number of consumers," direct evidence of reliance by individual consumers was not required. Rather, in a case such as Group Health, "the causal nexus and its reliance component may be established by other direct or circumstantial evidence that the district court determines is relevant and probative as to the relationship between the claimed damages and the alleged prohibited conduct."

In the case before us, Wiegand alleges in his complaint that a Walser representative falsely told him and potentially at least 100 other consumers that he was required to purchase a $1,500 service contract in order to obtain financing, and that he did so. Wiegand also alleges that a Walser representative falsely told him and potentially others that they had to purchase a credit insurance policy in order to obtain financing, and that he did so. Wiegand alleges that he agreed to purchase the service contract and credit insurance based on the misrepresentations of Walser's representative. In sum, the complaint alleges that misrepresentations were made and consumers were damaged thereby. Wiegand's complaint, therefore, meets the requirements we set forth in *Group Health* to establish a legally sufficient claim for relief.

This conclusion, however, does not end our analysis. Dismissal . . . is still appropriate if the moving party can demonstrate that it is not possible to grant relief on any evidence that might be produced consistent with the complaint. Walser asserts . . . that the existence of a written contract that contradicts the alleged oral misrepresentations of Walser's representative means that Wiegand cannot prove a causal nexus between the alleged misrepresentations and his injuries as a matter of law. . . . According to Walser, because the alleged violations took place through one-on-one transactions, Minnesota law requires proof of individual reliance as a causal link to damages, rather than the causal nexus requirement that we adopted in *Group Health*.[1]

The policy and purpose underlying the Consumer Fraud Act, however, suggest that Walser's assertion that Wiegand and potentially others cannot prove a causal nexus as a matter of law is wrong. We

---

1. Neither party has argued that the issues before us implicate the parol evidence rule. The touchstone of the parol evidence rule is that evidence that contradicts the terms of a written contract may not be admitted to alter the terms of a contract. We do not address the applicability of the parol evidence rule to the issues before us.

have recognized that the Consumer Fraud Act . . . eliminates elements of common law fraud, such as reliance on misrepresentations. . . . This is so because the Consumer Fraud Act reflects the legislature's intent "to make it easier to sue for consumer fraud than it had been to sue for fraud at common law." Furthermore, one of the central purposes of the Consumer Fraud Act is to address the unequal bargaining power that is often found in consumer transactions.

We held in *Group Health* that reliance is a component of the causal nexus requirement for a private consumer fraud class action under [the Consumer Fraud Act. But the causal nexus requirement is not the same as] the justifiable reliance standard of common law fraud. We conclude that the existence of a written contract that contradicts Walser's alleged oral misrepresentations does not, as a matter of law, negate any possibility of Wiegand and potentially others proving a causal nexus between oral representations and consumer injuries.

At this point in the proceedings, it is unclear what evidence might be produced consistent with the complaint. . . . The district court erred when it dismissed Wiegand's complaint.

What evidence would suffice to establish a causal connection between the dealer's misrepresentations and the consumers' injuries?

In footnote 1 the court sidesteps the question of applicability of the parol evidence rule. How would the parol evidence rule affect the ability of plaintiffs to recover?

10. Problem. *Consumer* collects Corvettes. He asks *Dealer* if he can purchase a limited-production Corvette "Indy Pace Car," of which only six thousand are produced. *Dealer* tells him, "If I can get one, you can have it for the manufacturer's suggested retail price." When the car arrives *Dealer* sells it to someone else for $5,000 over the $28,000 sticker price. After conducting an extensive search, *Consumer* is able to purchase a Corvette Indy Pace Car for $31,000. Can *Consumer* recover under a statute that declares unlawful the "use of any deception, fraud, false pretense, false promise, or misrepresentation" and provides a right of action for "any person who purchases or leases goods or services primarily for personal, family, or household purposes and thereby suffers an ascertainable loss of money or property"?

11. Problem. On March 1 *Consumer* and *Dealer* discuss the purchase of a car. They agree on a price of $12,600 and *Consumer* tells *Dealer* that she intends to obtain financing through her credit union, but that the money will not be available for three weeks. *Dealer* tells *Consumer* that he will hold the car for her. She pays $250 and gets a receipt. On March 21 *Consumer* returns, only to learn that defendant sold the car to someone else on March 4. *Dealer* returns the $250. *Consumer* ultimately purchases an identical car from another dealer for $12,750. Has she suffered an ascertainable loss of money or property? Can she recover under the statute in Problem 9? What if the purchase price from the other dealer is $12,600?

12. In determining that plaintiff suffered an ascertainable loss, the court quotes *Hinchliffe v. American Motors* ("To the consumer who wishes to purchase an energy saving subcompact, for example, it is no answer to say that he should be satisfied with a more valuable gas guzzler.") Compare Fields v. Yarborough Ford, Inc., 414 S.E.2d 164 (S.C.1992). Plaintiffs told defendant they wanted to buy a new pickup truck of particular specifications, including a 351 cubic-inch engine. A few days later defendant's salesman told plaintiffs he had found a truck meeting their specifications, and they formed a contract. Approximately a month after taking delivery, plaintiffs discovered that the truck had a 460 cubic-inch engine. Plaintiffs continued to drive it for another three months, then returned it to defendant, stating that they could no longer afford it "because it got such atrocious gas mileage." Plaintiffs sued, alleging that they suffered an ascertainable loss of money as a result of defendant's deceptive act of misrepresenting the 460 cubic-inch engine as a 351 cubic-inch engine. The court rejected the claim. It stated that plaintiffs had elected to affirm the contract and that the proper measure of damages is the "difference between the value the plaintiff would have received if the facts had been as represented and the value he actually received." Since the truck with the larger engine was more valuable than the truck defendants had misrepresented it to be, the court held that plaintiffs had not suffered any ascertainable loss. Is this consistent with the quote from *Hinchliffe*? If not, which is the preferable view?

Golt v. Phillips

Court of Appeals of Maryland, 1986.
308 Md. 1, 517 A.2d 328.

COLE, JUDGE.

. . .

In August 1983, Appellant, John Golt, an elderly, disabled retiree, with the aid of his daughter-in-law, responded to an advertisement placed in the East Baltimore Guide by Phillips Brothers and Associates (Phillips Brothers), a partnership owned by Appellees. The advertisement offered to rent a furnished apartment for $135.00 per month plus utilities. . . .

Upon inspection of the apartment, Golt and his daughter-in-law discovered that it was in need of cleaning and repairing. After receiving assurances that the necessary work would be done, Golt and his daughter-in-law signed a month-to-month lease, paid the rent for August, and also paid a $200.00 security deposit. When Golt moved into the apartment, he learned that the toilet facilities were located outside of his apartment and that he would have to share them with another tenant. Some of the repairs . . . were not completed. After repeating his requests and getting no response, Golt called the Baltimore City Department of Housing and Community Development, which in response to Golt's complaint, inspected the premises on October 19, 1983. The housing inspector discovered that Phillips

Brothers did not have the necessary license or inspection to operate the building as a multiple dwelling. Additional Baltimore City housing code violations, including the lack of toilet facilities in Golt's apartment, defective door locks, and the lack of fire exits and fire doors, were found by the inspector. The Department issued violation notices ordering Phillips Brothers to correct the enumerated violations and to either obtain a proper license or discontinue the use of the building as a multiple family dwelling. The housing inspector stated that simply removing one tenant would not abate the multiple family dwelling violation; the cooking unit in one of the three apartments would have to be removed.

Phillips Brothers sent an eviction notice to Golt on October 24, 1983. The notice informed Golt that his apartment was not properly licensed and was being illegally rented. Golt was therefore ordered to vacate the premises by January 1, 1984. No other tenant was ordered to vacate.

Golt moved to another apartment in early November and returned his keys to Phillips Brothers approximately ten days after moving. . . . [He sued.] The District Court denied any relief under the [Maryland Consumer Protection Act (CPA)] because Golt inspected the dwelling unit before entering the lease agreement and thus "knew what the premises looked like." . . .

Golt appealed to the Circuit Court for Baltimore City, and, following argument, that court dismissed the appeal. We then granted Golt's petition for a writ of certiorari.

. . .

I

We will begin our analysis by examining the CPA. . . .

The CPA specifically prohibits any person from engaging in unfair and deceptive procedures in the rental or offer for rental of consumer realty. [Maryland Code Commercial Law Article (1983 Repl.Vol.) I § 13–303(1) and (2).] The mandates of this law therefore squarely apply to the rental agreement between Golt and Phillips Brothers. It is with this backdrop in place that we examine Appellant's allegations of CPA violations.

The CPA provides a nonexclusive list of unfair and deceptive trade practices. Section 13–301, in pertinent part, states:

Unfair or deceptive trade practices include any:

(1) False, falsely disparaging, or misleading oral or written statement, visual description, or other representation of any kind which has the capacity, tendency, or effect of deceiving or misleading consumers;

(2) Representation that: (i) Consumer . . . realty . . . [has] a sponsorship, approval, accessory, characteristic . . . which [it does] not have;

. . .

(3) Failure to state a material fact if the failure deceives or tends to deceive.

In our view, advertising and renting an unlicensed dwelling violates §§ 13–301(1), (2), and (3).

Implicit in any advertisement and rental of an apartment is the representation that the leasing of the apartment is lawful. Baltimore City Code, Art. 13, § 1101 (1983 Repl.Vol.), expressly prohibits the operation of any multiple family dwelling without a license or temporary certificate. As Phillips Brothers had neither a license nor a temporary certificate, it violated the City Code. Phillips Brothers could not provide Golt with the unimpeded right to possession during the lease term. Consequently, Phillips Brothers advertisement and rental of the apartment was a "misleading . . . statement . . . or other representation of any kind which has the capacity, tendency, or effect of deceiving or misleading consumers." § 13–301(1).

Furthermore, such a representation is in essence a representation that the "realty . . . [has] a sponsorship, approval . . . [or] characteristic . . . which [it does] not have," id. § 13–301(2)—namely, licensing for operation as a multiple family dwelling. It makes no difference that Appellees did not expressly state that the premises were properly licensed; such a basic prerequisite to any lease agreement is implied. For consumer protection purposes, the meaning of any statement or representation is determined not only by what is explicitly stated, but also by what is reasonably implied. Spiegel, Inc. v. Federal Trade Commission, 411 F.2d 481, 483 (7th Cir.1969).[3]

Finally, Phillips Brothers also violated § 13–301(3) of the CPA, which states that the failure to disclose a material fact, which deceives or tends to deceive, is an unfair or deceptive trade practice. The lack of proper licensing is a material fact that Phillips Brothers failed to state. In addition, failure to disclose this fact deceived Golt or at least had the tendency to deceive consumers. An omission is considered material if a significant number of unsophisticated consumers would attach importance to the information in determining a choice of action. See, e.g., Charles of the Ritz Distributors Corp. v. Federal Trade Commission, 143 F.2d 676, 679–80 (2d Cir.1944). . . . In our view, the lack of proper licensing for an apartment under most circumstances is a material fact that any tenant would find important in his determination of whether to sign a lease agreement and move into the premises.

Phillips Brothers asserts in defense that it was unaware that its building was unlicensed for multiple family use. Ignorance of the law, however, is no defense. A landlord must be held to be aware of all laws concerning the validity of leasing its premises. Furthermore, none of the

---

3. The CPA states that in construing the term "unfair or deceptive trade practices," due consideration and weight should be given to the interpretations of the Federal Trade Commission Act by the Federal Trade Commission and the federal courts. Maryland Code (1983 Repl.Vol.), § 13–105 of the Commercial Law Article.

applicable CPA sections requires the landlord to have knowledge of the falsity or intent to deceive. Section 13–301(1) requires only a "[f]alse, falsely disparaging or misleading statement"; § 13–301(2) requires only a "representation"; and § 13–301(3) prohibits a "failure to state a material fact." Cf. § 13–301(9) (which requires "[d]eception, fraud, false pretense, false premise, misrepresentation, or knowing concealment . . . with the intent that a consumer rely on the same . . ."). In other words, § 13–301(1), (2), and (3) does not require scienter on the part of the landlord; the subsections require only a false or deceptive statement that has the capacity to mislead the consumer tenant.

Appellees also contend that because Appellant viewed the apartment before agreeing to lease the premises, Appellees made no misrepresentation in violation of the CPA. This defense, however, is ineffective. Simply viewing an apartment cannot inform a prospective tenant that the premises are unlicensed. Therefore, at the time Golt signed the lease, he cannot be said to have had knowledge that the premises was not licensed.

. . .

It is fully apparent, then, that Phillips Brothers's actions in renting the unlicensed dwelling constitutes an unfair and deceptive trade practice under the CPA. The next question is to determine the amount of damages that may be received under the CPA. Appellant argues that he should recover (1) restitutionary damages—the rent paid for August, September, and October, and (2) consequential damages—the cost of moving and the difference between the rental cost of the apartment and the higher rental cost of substitute housing maintained for three months. Appellees urge the court to deny Appellant any relief. We agree with Appellant and explain.

Section 13–408 of the CPA sets forth the private remedy created by the act: "any person may bring an action to recover for injury or loss sustained by him as the result of a practice prohibited by this title." This private remedy is purely compensatory; it contains no punitive component. Indeed, any punitive assessment under the CPA is accomplished by an imposition of a civil penalty recoverable by the State under § 13–410, as well as by criminal penalties imposed under § 13–411. Thus, in determining the damages due the consumer, we must look only to his actual loss or injury caused by the unfair or deceptive trade practices.

It is well settled in this State that if a statute requires a license for conducting a trade or business, and the statute is regulatory in the sense that it is for the protection of the public, an unlicensed person will not be able to enforce a contract within the provisions of that regulatory statute. Moreover, it is also well established that the unlicensed person will not be able to recover under quantum meruit, regardless of any unjust enrichment to the other party; to permit a recovery under quantum meruit would defeat the efficacy of the regulatory statute.

The Baltimore City Code, Art. 13, § 1101 (1983 Repl.Vol.), states: "No person shall conduct or operate . . . any . . . multiple family dwelling . . . without having first obtained a license or a temporary certificate to do so." It is undisputed that Appellees operated the building as a multiple family dwelling without procuring a license. As such, if the license is designed to protect the public, Appellees are prohibited from benefiting from the illegal lease of the apartment.

We find that the Baltimore City licensing requirement for multiple family dwellings is a model example of a public health and safety regulation. . . . Therefore, Phillips Brothers may not retain any benefits from the unlicensed lease, and Golt may recover his full damages.

Golt's actual loss is comprised of restitutionary and consequential damages. He is entitled to restitution for the three months of rent paid for the unlicensed apartment, $405.00. He is also entitled to recover consequential damages, such as the cost of moving from the premises to substitute housing, and the difference in cost between reasonable substitute housing and the rental charged for the remainder of the legal term of his lease with Phillips Brothers. After vacating the premises, Golt incurred three months of substitute housing. Golt's lease with Phillips Brothers was a month-to-month lease with a sixty day notice to vacate requirement. As such, Golt is entitled to the difference in the cost of sixty days rent in his substitute housing and sixty days rent at Appellees' apartment. This amount is limited, however, to the extent that the substitute housing was reasonable and of similar quality to the vacated premises.

. . .

JUDGMENT OF THE CIRCUIT COURT FOR BALTIMORE CITY VACATED; CASE REMANDED TO THAT COURT WITH INSTRUCTIONS TO . . . REMAND TO DISTRICT COURT FOR FURTHER PROCEEDINGS NOT INCONSISTENT WITH THIS OPINION. APPELLEES TO PAY THE COSTS.

QUESTIONS AND NOTES

1. The court holds that defendants violated section 13–301(1), which declares unlawful the making of a misleading oral or written statement that has the capacity, tendency, or effect of deceiving or misleading consumers. What misleading oral or written statement did defendants make?

2. The court also holds that defendants violated section 13–301(3), by failing to state a material fact if the failure deceives or tends to deceive. What elements must a consumer prove to establish a violation of this section? Does this section make "pure omissions" actionable? (Recall *International Harvester,* page 62 supra.)

3. Problem. *Consumer* subscribes to *Webco,* an internet service provider. For this service *Webco* charges $10 per month for 2 hours of access and 104/minute for any excess. To calculate *Consumer's* bill each month, *Webco* adds 15 seconds "connect time" to the actual number of seconds on each call that *Consumer* is connected to the internet. Further, *Webco* calculates its bills in full-minute increments, so that, for example, a 2 minute–40 second connection is calculated as 3 minutes. Does *Webco* violate section 13–301(3)?

4. The landlords in *Golt* claimed that they did not know that their building was not licensed for multi-family use. Why did the court hold that this did not matter? Would it matter if the tenant's complaint related not to the existence of a license, but rather related to the quality of the premises, e.g., the presence of lead-based paint on the walls? (Assume the landlord is not aware of this fact.)

5. Note the consumer's remedy in *Golt*: restitution of all rent paid plus consequential damages. What is the court's reason for permitting restitution of all rent paid? What if the building and the apartment complied in all respects with the housing code but the landlord failed to obtain a license: should the tenant be entitled to restitution of all rent paid?

6. Problem. Since 1997 *Consumer* has had a MasterCard issued by *Bank*. On June 5, 2002, *Bank* sends a three-page billing statement and includes with it a one-page promotional flyer for its "newly developed customer benefit package." According to the flyer, the consumer will receive a credit card protection service, pursuant to which the consumer may register all her various credit card accounts with *Bank*, which in turn will notify all those creditors in the event *Consumer* notifies *Bank* that her credit cards have been lost or stolen. In addition, *Consumer* will receive a "Dining Discount Card," which will entitle her to a 25% reduction on all her purchases at a large number of local restaurants. On the bottom of the last page of the billing statement is an entry:

> *Customer Benefit Package* *$5.95*
> *(If for any reason you choose not to take the Customer Benefit Package, check here ☐ and deduct $5.95 from your bill. If you do not check here, the amount of $5.95 will be assessed for a period of 12 months.)*

Consumer does not notice this entry on the billing statement and does not check in the indicated space. Is *Consumer* contractually obligated to pay $5.95 per month for 12 months for the "Customer Benefit Package"? Has *Bank* violated the state's little-FTC act?

Fenwick v. Kay American Jeep, Inc.

Superior Court of New Jersey, Appellate Division, 1975.
136 N.J.Super. 114, 344 A.2d 785.

ALLCORN, J. A. D.

In July 1973, under the authority delegated to him to "promulgate such rules and regulations * * * as may be necessary" to "accomplish the objectives and to carry out the duties prescribed" by the Consumer Fraud Act, N.J.S.A. 56:8–1 et seq., the Attorney General adopted a set of rules "concerning motor vehicle advertising practices." Among the motor vehicle advertising practices declared to be "unlawful" by those rules was the following (N.J.A.C. 13:45A–2.2(a)(2)):

    ii.   The failure in any price advertisement to disclose * * *:

* * *

        (4) The bona fide odometer reading of any specifically adver-
    tised * * * used car. * * *

So far as here pertinent, a "price advertisement" is defined as "any
advertisement [of a motor vehicle] in which a specified price is stated."
N.J.A.C. 13:45A–2.1.

    Appellant Joseph Friedman owns and operates an advertising agency
under the firm name Friedman Associates. Among his clientele during the
period critical to this proceeding were some 30 to 35 separate retail
automobile dealers, for whom he prepared and delivered to local newspapers for publication advertisements numbering an estimated "100 individual ads per day." The essential factual details to be included in the
advertisements were supplied to Friedman Associates by the respective
automobile dealers, from which the advertisements would be prepared by a
member of the Friedman staff and then delivered by the latter to the
newspaper for publication.

    On December 14, 1973, there was published in the *Newark Star
Ledger,* under the name of Kay American Jeep, an advertisement offering
for sale a used motor vehicle for a stated price. The advertisement,
concededly prepared by Friedman Associates on behalf of Kay, did not set
forth the odometer reading of the advertised vehicle. As a result the
Division of Consumer Affairs issued its complaint and notice of hearing to
Kay American Jeep, charging a violation [for] failing "to disclose the BONA
FIDE Odometer reading of any specifically advertised * * * used motor
vehicle" in "a price advertisement."

    At the hearing held March 13, 1974, Mr. Friedman appeared in
company with a representative of Kay American Jeep, both without counsel. After consenting to the joinder of himself as a party respondent to the
proceedings, Friedman admitted to the hearing officer that the offending
advertisement had been prepared by Friedman Associates; that the odometer reading of the advertised vehicle had in fact been furnished to Friedman
Associates by Kay, and that the omission of the odometer reading from the
advertisement was due entirely to the oversight of Friedman Associates.
The representative of Kay corroborated Friedman. No other witnesses were
called by either side.

    At the conclusion of the hearing the hearing officer found both Kay
American Jeep and Mr. Friedman "guilty of violating the rule [regula-
tion]," and by order of March 15, 1974, assessed a fine of $150 and $50
costs against them jointly and severally, and directed that each "thereafter
cease and desist from failing to disclose in any price advertisement for a
used motor vehicle * * * the bona fide odometer reading of said motor
vehicle." The present appeal from that order has been taken by respondent
Joseph Friedman.

    It is the contention of the respondent Friedman that there can be no
violation of the act or the implementing regulations in the absence of

intent, and inasmuch as it is uncontroverted that the omission of the odometer reading was inadvertent, the finding and order of the Division must be reversed. The Division takes the position that the language of the act, as well as the policy underlying it, make manifest a legislative purpose to prohibit the proscribed conduct and impose liability without regard to intent.

Manifestly, the design of the Consumer Fraud Act is to protect the consumer against imposition and loss as a result of fraud and fraudulent practices by persons engaged in the sale of goods and services. Kugler v. Romain, 58 N.J. 522, 279 A.2d 640 (1971). The pertinent portion of the controlling section of that act is found in N.J.S.A. 56:8–2, and provides:

> The act, use or employment by any person of any unconscionable commercial practice, deception, fraud, false pretense, false promise, misrepresentation, or the knowing concealment, suppression, or omission of any material fact with intent that others rely upon such concealment, suppression or omission, in connection with the sale or advertisement of any merchandise or with the subsequent performance of such person as aforesaid, whether or not any person has in fact been misled, deceived or damaged thereby, is declared to be an unlawful practice; * * *

In the context of this language it is plain that, however the fraud or fraudulent conduct may be designated or characterized, if it consists of or rests upon "concealment, suppression, or omission of any material fact," the nondisclosure must be "knowing * * * [and] with intent that others rely" thereon. Ibid. As a consequence, the nondisclosure of a material fact unknowingly and by reason of inadvertence does not constitute an unlawful practice under the Act.

Notwithstanding this clear expression of legislative intent the dissent suggests that, by virtue of the authority delegated to the Attorney General to promulgate regulations, he may declare the unknowing and inadvertent nondisclosure of a material fact to constitute an "unconscionable commercial practice." The argument overlooks (and does not touch upon) the fact that such an interpretation would nullify absolutely and render completely meaningless the clause of the statute relating to fraud and fraudulent conduct arising out of the "knowing concealment, suppression, or omission of any material fact." The phrase "unconscionable commercial practice" has no special properties. In consumer goods transactions, "unconscionability must be equated with the concepts of deception, fraud, false pretense, misrepresentation, concealment and the like * * * stamped unlawful under N.J.S.A. 56:8–2." Kugler v. Romain, supra at 544, 279 A.2d at 652.

The legislative history of the Consumer Fraud Act supplies further evidence of the intent of the Legislature. As originally introduced, the portion of the section with which we are here concerned provided (Senate Bill No. 199, § 2):

> The act, use or employment of any deception, fraud, false pretense, misrepresentation, concealment, suppression, or omission of any mate-

rial fact by any person in connection with the sale or advertisement of any merchandise, whether or not any person has in fact been misled, deceived or damaged thereby, is declared to be an unlawful practice; * * *.

Significantly, the concealment, suppression or omission of any material fact was constituted an unlawful practice without regard to knowledge or intent.

On passage in the Senate, however, the bill was amended in several respects, including the qualifications that the concealment, suppression or omission of any material fact had to be knowing and with intent that others rely thereon, in order to constitute an unlawful practice. . . . The critical significance of the amendments needs no elaboration; it is manifestly self-evident.

However broad the authority of the Attorney General to "promulgate such rules and regulations * * * as may be necessary" to effectuate the purpose and policy of the act, it does not extend to or authorize the promulgation of any regulation that would nullify and run counter to the express language and specific limitations of the statute from which that authority stems.

Accordingly, . . . the cause is remanded to the Division of Consumer Affairs with directions to dismiss the complaint as against respondent Joseph Friedman.

KOLOVSKY, P. J. A. D., dissenting.

. . .

"The subject of consumer fraud has emerged as a major problem of our commercial scene. Being unequal to the vendor, the consumer is easily overreached." Riley v. New Rapids Carpet Center, 61 N.J. 218, 224, 294 A.2d 7, 10 (1972). To remedy and alleviate that problem, our Legislature adopted statutes whose purpose is to protect the consumer against deceptive and improper practices.

Among them was [the Consumer Fraud Act.] The act has been amended over the years to expand the protection afforded the consumer. Concomitantly, the governmental machinery provided for enforcement and regulation has been upgraded and expanded.

Power to promulgate rules and regulations "to accomplish the objectives and to carry out the duties prescribed by [the Consumer Fraud Act]," regulations "which shall have the force of law," was granted to the Attorney General by N.J.S.A. 56:8–4. There can be no question but that "the Legislature intended to confer on the Attorney General the broadest kind of power to act in the interest of the consumer public * * * ." Kugler v. Romain, 58 N.J. 522, 537, 279 A.2d 640, 648 (1971).

Acting pursuant to the power thus granted, regulations have been adopted outlawing specific practices in various types of business, thus delineating specific standards of conduct with which persons engaged in those businesses must comply.

Among the practices so regulated are those involved in the advertising of motor vehicles for sale. . . .

The reasonableness of the requirement that the bona fide odometer reading be set forth is beyond dispute. The number of miles an automobile has been driven is of critical importance in evaluating the worth of the automobile. . . .

The regulation here involved—mandating the inclusion in the advertisement of the odometer reading of the vehicle—establishes a standard of conduct with which advertisers must comply, under pain of penal sanctions, regardless of intent or moral culpability. The regulation falls within the class of "strict liability" penal statutes and regulations which a legislature or an authorized administrative agency may adopt to eliminate the social or economic problems with which they are concerned.

. . .

[According to the majority,] N.J.S.A. 56:8–2 mandates that before one may be found guilty of violating the regulation in question, it must be shown that he did so knowingly and intentionally.

I find no such mandate in N.J.S.A. 56:8–2 nor do I find therein any legislative intent to limit the broad powers granted the Division to delineate standards of conduct or permissible commercial practices to which those who advertise used automobiles for sale must adhere.

. . .

The majority's interpretation ignores that the word "knowing" appears only after the word *or* . . . and applies only to the conduct thereinafter referred to. The word "knowing" does not appear in, nor does it have any application to, the preceding provision of the section proscribing "the act, use or employment by any person of any unconscionable commercial practice, deception" etc.

The omission of the word "knowing" from the provision just quoted is cogent evidence that the Legislature intended that, irrespective of the offender's intent, it is unlawful to use or employ an "unconscionable commercial practice."

Were there no prior enunciated governing and controlling standard of conduct, the issue of whether particular conduct constitutes an unconscionable commercial practice might present a factual issue. Here, however, there is no room for debate; a preexisting regulation seeking to compel truth in advertising has declared that the failure to include the odometer reading, as well as the other required information, in the advertisement is an unlawful "motor vehicle advertising practice."

I find no justification in the statute or elsewhere for the interpretation adopted by the majority which would impose on the Division, in its efforts to protect the consumer, the almost impossible task of showing an intentional failure to comply with one or more of the myriad regulations it has adopted to eliminate improper commercial practices, regulations of which all in the regulated business have been forewarned.

. . .

I would affirm. . . . .

QUESTIONS AND NOTES

1. The preceding principal cases were all decided under deceptive practices acts. *Fenwick,* on the other hand, concerns a consumer fraud act. What elements of common law misrepresentation must be proved to establish a violation of the New Jersey Consumer Fraud Act?

2. What is the precise holding of *Fenwick?*

3. According to the majority, intent to defraud is necessary for a violation of the New Jersey statute. Is it always necessary? According to the dissent, intent to defraud is not necessary for a violation of the statute. Is it always unnecessary?

4. The Division of Consumer Affairs appealed to the Supreme Court of New Jersey, which stated, in part:

> We think the dissent is correct. The Consumer Fraud Act was passed in response to widespread complaints about selling practices which victimized consumers. The purpose of the Act was to prevent deception, fraud or falsity, whether by acts of commission or omission, in connection with the sale and advertisement of merchandise and real estate. To accomplish the objectives of the Act, the Attorney General is empowered to promulgate such rules and regulations as might be necessary.
>
> . . .
>
> Significantly, the [statutory] requirement that knowledge and intent be shown is limited to the concealment, suppression or omission of any material fact. Respondent argues that his failure to include the mileage in each sales ad was at most the omission of a material fact and would not be an unlawful practice unless knowledge and intent were shown.
>
> However, this argument overlooks the power of the Attorney General to adopt rules to further the purpose of the act to prevent fraud and other deceptive practices. When a used car is advertised for sale without indicating its mileage there is a substantial possibility that a prospective purchaser would be misled by assuming the vehicle has been driven an average number of miles for its model year whereas in fact the car may have been driven a far greater number of miles. The regulation here adopted by the Attorney General has the effect of preventing the possibility of such deception if strictly enforced without regard to the intent of the advertiser. It therefore is within the broad rule-making power conferred by the statute on the Attorney General.

Moreover, we are satisfied that failure to disclose the mileage in the present cases was more than the mere omission of a material fact. As noted above, such disclosure was specifically required by the administrative regulation as a preventive measure against deception or an unconscionable commercial practice. The capacity to mislead is the prime ingredient of deception or an unconscionable commercial practice. Intent is not an essential element. Since consumer protection is the ultimate goal, the standards of conduct established by the Act and implementing regulations must be met regardless of intent except when the Act specifically provides otherwise. We therefore hold that the charges herein, in order to be sustained did not require a showing of intent. . . .

The judgments of the Appellate Division are reversed and the Final Orders of the Division of Consumer Affairs reinstated.

371 A.2d 13, 15–17 (N.J.1977).

5. In enacting a consumer fraud act, some states have omitted the requirement that "concealment, suppression, or omission of any material fact" be "knowing." E.g., 6 Del.Code § 2513(a); Iowa Code Ann. § 714.16(2)(a).

6. Does it violate the Maryland statute in *Golt* (§ 13–301(3), pages 143–44) for a dealer to advertise a used car without disclosing the odometer reading?

7. Recall Bramlett v. Adamson Ford, page 42 supra, in which plaintiff sought to recover in fraud for a car dealer's failure to disclose that it was receiving a portion of the finance charge that plaintiff believed was going to the entity that was financing the transaction. Although the intermediate court held that plaintiff stated a good claim, the Alabama Supreme Court held (see page 48 supra) that the seller had no duty to disclose this information. Would plaintiff fare better under one of the statutes in this chapter?

8. Statutes modeled after the FTC Act frequently direct the courts to be guided by the interpretation given to the federal Act. E.g., 815 Ill.Consol.Stat. § 505/2; West's Rev.Code Wash.Ann. § 19.86.920. So do deceptive practices statutes. E.g., *Golt* at n. 3. Moreover, even when the statute is silent, the courts may find interpretations of the FTC Act persuasive. E.g., *Fenwick*.

Pursuant to a direction to be guided by interpretations of the FTC Act, a Washington court held it unnecessary to show that a consumer had actually been deceived. Rather, it held that, as under the federal Act, the test is whether the defendant's act or omission had the capacity to deceive. Testo v. Russ Dunmire Oldsmobile, Inc., 554 P.2d 349 (Wash.App.1976). Accord, Guggenheimer v. Ginzburg, 372 N.E.2d 17 (N.Y.1977). Even assuming that "capacity to deceive" is an appropriate standard under the FTC Act, is it an appropriate standard under a state statute?

9. Would the conduct of the defendant in Parker v. Arthur Murray, Inc., page 19 supra, violate a consumer fraud act? the Maryland statute? a statute that tracks the language of the FTC Act? Would the conduct of the defendant in Williams v. Rank & Son Buick, page 23 supra, violate either type of statute?

10.   Consider whether *Seller* in the following hypotheticals would violate the New Jersey *(Fenwick)* or Maryland *(Golt)* statutes:

a.   *Seller* places the following advertisement in college newspapers:

> Want to go to law school? With our assistance you can. We will help you gain admission to the school of your choice. We are so confident of our ability to help you that we are willing to give you a guarantee: if you are not admitted to at least one accredited school of law, we will gladly refund our $200 fee.

b.   *Seller* is a car dealer whose advertisement in the Yellow Pages includes a coupon worth $100 off the price of any new car. *Consumer* negotiates with *Seller* for the purchase of a car, and they agree on a price, after deducting the trade-in value of *Consumer's* jalopy, of $9000. *Seller* writes up the purchase order, and *Consumer* whips out a stack of ninety coupons. *Seller* refuses to accept them in payment, asserting "one to a customer." Nothing in the ad or the coupons expresses this limitation.

11.   Problem. *Consumer* purchases a used car from *Dealer*. After experiencing severe problems with it, she obtains a history of the car from the Department of Motor Vehicles. This history reveals that the car had been in an accident and was declared a total loss by its owner's insurance company, which paid the owner and thereupon acquired title to the car. The title then passed from the insurance company to *Auto Salvage Company,* to *Used Cars,* and finally to *Dealer*. Further investigation reveals that *Used Cars* had completely rebuilt the car. *Consumer* sues *Dealer*. Does *Dealer's* failure to disclose this history violate the Maryland or New Jersey statutes?

Would it matter if *Dealer* did not know of this history? What if *Dealer* did not actually know of it but could have obtained it from the Department of Motor Vehicles? from a private information provider, such as Carfax?

12.   As *Fenwick* reveals, the New Jersey statute empowers the attorney general to promulgate rules to further the purpose of the act. Statutes in approximately thirty other states grant similar authority. Even if the statute does not expressly confer the authority to promulgate rules that have the force of law, the enforcement agency nevertheless may have that power. Purity Supreme, Inc. v. Attorney General, 407 N.E.2d 297 (Mass. 1980).

In exercise of this power, the Massachusetts Attorney General adopted a regulation defining deception to include the failure "to disclose to a buyer or prospective buyer any fact, the disclosure of which may have influenced the buyer or prospective buyer not to enter into the transaction." 940 Code Mass.Reg. § 3.16(2).

Would the sellers in Question 10 and 11 violate the Massachusetts statute?

13. The New Jersey and Maryland statutes both stipulate that conduct is unlawful "whether or not any person has in fact been misled, deceived or damaged." This language enables the attorney general or other public official to enforce the statute without the need to show any injury to consumers. To bring a private action, however, a consumer must establish a loss or injury as a result of the unlawful conduct. E.g., Knapp v. Potamkin Motors Corp., 602 A.2d 302 (N.J.Super.1991).

14. Some statutes expressly apply only when the aggrieved party is a consumer. And some expressly apply only when the alleged violator is a commercial entity. E.g., Or.Rev.Stat. §§ 646.605(7), 646.608(1) (pages 124– 125 supra). Not all statutes, however, contain these limitations. On their face, therefore, they apply also when the aggrieved party is a business or when the alleged violator is a consumer. (See note 7, page 127 supra.) Should broad anti-deception statutes protect business plaintiffs? Should they apply to consumer defendants?

Every consumer who enters a contract reasonably believes that the other party will perform as promised. Therefore, if the other party fails to perform, the consumer has been misled. The making of the promise and the subsequent failure to perform are acts or practices that have the capacity (and the likelihood) of deceiving a (reasonable) consumer. Since the courts uniformly reject any requirement of intent to deceive as an element of deception under little-FTC acts, does this mean that every breach of contract is also a violation of the statute? In addition to permitting recovery of actual damages, many of the statutes provide for minimum damages, multiple damages, or punitive damages, and most provide for the recovery of attorney's fees. Are these remedies now available for every breach of contract?

To deal with these problems of scope and remedy, several courts have construed their statutes not to apply to some situations that a literal reading would suggest are covered. One approach has been to hold that a private remedy is available only if the defendant's conduct impacts the public interest. Indeed, the Washington statute expressly says, "It is, however, the intent of the legislature that this act shall not be construed to prohibit acts or practices which are reasonable in relation to the development and preservation of business or which are not injurious to the public interest. . . ." West's Rev.Code Wash.Ann. § 19.86.920. In the other states in which the courts have imposed a public interest requirement, the statutes do not expressly refer to the public interest. Courts in these states typically justify the limitation by pointing to a provision in the statute directing the courts to be guided by federal interpretations of section 5(a) of the FTC Act. The courts then reason that since the federal statute empowers the FTC to proceed against an unfair or deceptive act or practice only when it is "to the interest of the public" to do so (see page 60 supra), the state statute should be construed similarly. This reasoning contains a fatal flaw. Can you identify it? (Hints: what is the rationale for the state statute's reference to the FTC Act, and to precisely what section is the reference?)

Another rationale for a public interest requirement is the belief that the focus of the statute is the protection of the public, i.e. consumers generally. Thus, a Georgia court held that there was no private remedy for a seller's misrepresentation of the size of a residential tract of land:

> [The statute] does not create an additional remedy for redress of private wrongs occurring outside the context of the public consumer marketplace. . . . [It is not] the basis for a new private remedy for individuals who are damaged by acts or practices which have no potential for impact on the general consuming public.

Zeeman v. Black, 273 S.E.2d 910, 914 (Ga.App.1980).

The most extensive development of the public interest requirement has been in Washington. In Hangman Ridge Training Stables, Inc. v. Safeco Title Insurance Company, 719 P.2d 531, 537–38 (Wash.1986), the court identified several factors relevant to the existence of a public interest in providing a private remedy:

- whether the alleged acts were committed in the course of the defendant's business;

- whether the acts were part of a pattern or generalized course of conduct;

- whether there were repeated acts committed prior to the act of which the plaintiff complains;

- whether there is a real and substantial potential for repetition after the act of which the plaintiff complains;

- whether, if the act involved a single instance, it affected or was likely to affect numerous consumers.

Only a handful of states impose any requirement that the plaintiff's action be in the public interest or that the defendant's violation impact the public interest. And in at least two states in which the courts construed the statute to contain a public interest requirement, the legislature amended the statute specifically to negate any such requirement. Conn.Gen.Stat. Ann. § 42–110g(a); 815 Ill. Consol. Stat. § 505/10a (subsequently amended to impose a public interest requirement when the alleged violator is a car dealer). Thus, in the vast majority of states, there is no public interest requirement.

Another approach to the problem of excessive scope has been to conclude that the legislature did not intend for the statute to apply to every breach of contract. If "mere breach of contract" is not deceptive, what more should be necessary for deception?

15.   Since deceptive practices statutes were patterned after the FTC Act, it is not surprising to see that they typically provide for a system of administrative enforcement. The attorney general or other enforcement official may obtain an injunction against conduct that violates the statute, and in almost every state, may seek restitution on behalf of injured consumers. In addition, in more than half the states, the court may impose a civil penalty for engaging in conduct that violates the statute.

Unlike the FTC Act, state statutes typically provide a private right of action for injured consumers. Even when the statute does not expressly provide it, the court may hold that a private right of action is implied. Sellinger v. Freeway Mobile Home Sales, Inc., 521 P.2d 1119 (Ariz.1974). Usually the statutes provide that a successful consumer may recover costs and attorney's fees. About a third of the statutes authorize class actions. Private enforcement of deceptive practices statutes is considered further in Chapter 15 infra.

16. The preceding materials have examined regulation at the state level. Counties and municipalities may also intervene to protect consumers against deception. New York City, for example, has enacted a comprehensive deceptive practices ordinance, "No person shall engage in any deceptive or unconscionable trade practice in the sale . . . of any consumer goods or services. . . ." N.Y.City Admin. Code § 20–700.

B. Topical Statutes

In addition to statutes that prohibit deception in broad terms, virtually every state has statutes designed to deal with specific deceptive practices. In some states these topical statutes are part of the state's comprehensive deceptive practices act, so all the remedies of the comprehensive statute are available for violations of the topical statute. (For example, see the table of contents of the New Jersey Consumer Fraud Act and section 646.608(v)-(ii) of the Oregon Unlawful Trade Practices Act, both reproduced in the Statutory Supplement.) In others, the topical statutes are scattered more or less throughout the compilation of the state's laws. Some kinds of deceptive practices have been so widespread that most states have enacted specialized statutes to deal with them. Other practices, however, have not been so widespread or at least have not given rise to the level of outrage necessary to induce most legislatures to act.

The preceding chapters have examined two widespread forms of deception that have prompted state legislatures to enact special statutes. Many states, for example, have enacted odometer statutes similar to the federal statute on page 99 supra; statutes to regulate dance studios that engage in the tactics seen in *Vokes* (page 16 supra); and statutes to deal specifically with bait and switch tactics (e.g., the New York statute, page 79 supra). The following materials illustrate some other statutes dealing with specific forms of deception.

(1) Referral Sales

A common reaction to a seller's sales presentation is, "I can't afford to spend that much." The referral sales plan is designed to permit the seller to convince the buyer that he or she can indeed afford the purchase. The seller's script might read as follows:

TV and radio advertising are very expensive. I could advertise anyway, of course, but I don't. I'd rather rely on you and my other customers to get the good word around. And I'll pay you for it. For every person whose name you give me and who subsequently buys one of these freezers, I'll give you $25. Surely you have at least a dozen friends. That's $300 right there.

The deception present in this referral sale scheme is similar to that of a chain letter. It is unlikely that the seller will make a sale to every person whose name the consumer supplies. But even assuming that the seller does make a sale to each of them, they each will receive the same referral fee offer. To benefit fully, they would each submit twelve names, or a total of 144. The 144 would submit the names of 1,728 persons, who in turn would submit the names of 20,736. By the eighth round, the number of names would be more than the entire population of the United States! Thus a person participating at the inception of the scheme *might* receive the contemplated benefit, but disappointment necessarily awaits the later participants.

The FTC, under the all-encompassing language of FTC Act section 5, has successfully interceded to prevent referral sales plans. E.g., All–State Industries of North Carolina, Inc. v. FTC, 423 F.2d 423 (4th Cir.1970). State officials and injured consumers have successfully invoked little-FTC acts with similarly broad language. E.g., Pliss v. Peppertree Resort Villas, 663 N.W.2d 851 (Wis.App.2003); State by Lefkowitz v. ITM, Inc., 275 N.Y.S.2d 303 (N.Y.Sup.1966). But several states have enacted statutes singling out this specific deceptive practice for separate treatment. One example is 815 Ill. Consol. Stat. § 505/2A(1):

> The use or employment of any chain referral sales technique, plan, arrangement or agreement whereby the buyer is induced to purchase merchandise upon the seller's promise or representation that if buyer will furnish seller names of other prospective buyers of like or identical merchandise that seller will contact the named prospective buyers and buyer will receive a reduction in the purchase price by means of a cash rebate, commission, credit toward balance due or any other consideration, which rebate, commission, credit or other consideration is contingent upon seller's ability to sell like or identical merchandise to the named prospective buyers, is declared to be an unlawful practice within the meaning of this Act.

Another is the Uniform Consumer Sales Practices Act § 3(b)(11):

> (b) Without limiting the scope of subsection (a) the act or practice of a supplier in indicating any of the following is deceptive:
>
> . . .
>
> (11) that the consumer will receive a rebate, discount, or other benefit as an inducement for entering into a consumer transaction in return for giving the supplier the names of prospective consumers or otherwise helping the supplier to enter into other consumer transac-

tions, if receipt of the benefit is contingent on an event occurring after the consumer enters into the transaction.

Would each of these statutes make unlawful the specific referral sales scheme described above?

PROBLEMS

1. When *Consumer* balks at the price *Seller* quotes for a color TV, *Seller* says that she will credit against the price five dollars each for names of prospective customers, up to a total of ten names. Further, she will credit an additional $25 for every one of those persons who actually buys a TV from her.

Does *Seller* violate the Illinois statute? the UCSPA?

2. Desiring to acquire a cellular telephone and service, *Consumer* goes to *Wonderful Wireless*, where she discusses the various plans and examines a variety of cell phones manufactured by several different companies. She likes the features of a model made by *Fabulous Fone Co.*, and she especially likes the rebate that *Fabulous* is offering. It promises to send purchasers of the phone a rebate check of $100 if the purchaser activates a phone plan with *Wonderful Wireless*, completes and mails a rebate application within 30 days of the purchase, and is still a customer of *Wonderful Wireless* when *Fabulous Fone* processes the rebate application. In addition, it states that the rebate check must be cashed within 30 days of when it is received. *Consumer* agrees to the wireless service plan, purchases the phone, and mails in the rebate application. Has *Fabulous Fone* violated the UCSPA?

(2) REGULATION OF A TRADE OR INDUSTRY

Sometimes rules dealing with deception are found in legislation that deals comprehensively with an entire trade or industry. Indeed, widespread deception in a trade may induce comprehensive regulation of the trade. An example of comprehensive regulation is California's Automotive Repair Act, West's Ann.Cal.Bus. & Prof.Code, § 9880 et seq. This Act provides for registration of auto repair dealers and imposes constraints on the way they do business. Some excerpts:

§ 9884.7   Grounds for refusal to validate or to invalidate registration

(1) The director, where the automotive repair dealer cannot show there was a bona fide error, may refuse to validate, or may invalidate temporarily or permanently, the registration of an automotive repair dealer for any of the following acts or omissions related to the conduct of the business of the automotive repair dealer, which are done by the automotive repair dealer or any mechanic, employee, partner, officer, or member of the automotive repair dealer:

(a) Making or authorizing in any manner or by any means whatever any statement written or oral which is untrue or misleading, and which is known, or which by the exercise of reasonable care should be known, to be untrue or misleading.

(b) Causing or allowing a customer to sign any work order which does not state the repairs requested by the customer or the automobile's odometer reading at the time of repair.

(c) Failing or refusing to give to a customer a copy of any document requiring his signature, as soon as the customer signs such document.

(d) Any other conduct which constitutes fraud.

(e) Conduct constituting gross negligence.

(f) Failure in any material respect to comply with the provisions of this chapter or regulations adopted pursuant to it.

(g) Any willful departure from or disregard of accepted trade standards for good and workmanlike repair in any material respect, which is prejudicial to another without consent of the owner or his duly authorized representative.

(h) Making false promises of a character likely to influence, persuade, or induce a customer to authorize the repair, service or maintenance of automobiles.

(i) Having repair work done by someone other than the dealer or his employees without the knowledge or consent of the customer unless the dealer can demonstrate that the customer could not reasonably have been notified.

. . .

Upon refusal to validate a registration, the director shall notify the applicant thereof, in writing, by personal service or mail addressed to the address of the applicant set forth in the application, and the applicant shall be given a hearing under Section 9884.12 if, within 30 days thereafter, he files with the bureau a written request for hearing, otherwise the refusal is deemed affirmed.

. . .

§ 9884.8   Invoice

All work done by an automotive repair dealer, including all warranty work, shall be recorded on an invoice and shall describe all service work done and parts supplied. Service work and parts shall be listed separately on the invoice, which shall also state separately the subtotal prices for service work and for parts, not including sales tax, and shall state separately the sales tax, if any, applicable to each. If any used, rebuilt, or reconditioned parts are supplied, the invoice shall clearly state that fact. If a part of a component system is composed of new and used, rebuilt or reconditioned parts, such invoice shall clearly state that fact. One copy shall be given to the customer and one copy shall be retained by the automotive repair dealer.

§ 9884.9   Written estimates; consent of customer; notation and acknowledgment

(a) The automotive repair dealer shall give to the customer a written estimated price for labor and parts necessary for a specific job. No work shall be done and no charges shall accrue before authorization to proceed is obtained from the customer. No charge shall be made for work done or parts supplied in excess of the estimated price without the oral or written consent of the customer which shall be obtained at some time after it is determined that the estimated price is insufficient and before the work not estimated is done or the parts not estimated are supplied. If such consent is oral, the dealer shall make a notation on the work order of the date, time, name of person authorizing the additional repairs and telephone number called, if any, together with a specification of the additional parts and labor and the total additional cost, and shall either:

(1) Make a notation on the invoice of the same facts set forth in the notation on the work order; or

(2) Upon completion of repairs shall obtain the customer's signature or initials to an acknowledgment of notice and consent, where there is an oral consent of the customer to additional repairs, in the following language:

"I acknowledge notice and oral approval of an increase in the original estimated price.

_____

(Signature or initials)"

Nothing in this section shall be construed as requiring an automotive repair dealer to give a written estimated price if the dealer does not agree to perform the requested repair.

(b) The automotive repair dealer shall include with the written estimated price a statement of any automotive repair service which, if required to be done, will be done by someone other than the dealer or his employees. No service shall be done by other than the dealer or his employees without the consent of the customer, unless the customer cannot reasonably be notified. The dealer shall be responsible, in any case, for any such service in the same manner as if he or his employees had done the service.

§ 9884.10   Return of parts to customer; exceptions

Upon request of the customer at the time the work order is taken, the automotive repair dealer shall return replaced parts to the customer at the time of the completion of the work excepting such parts as may be exempt because of size, weight, or other similar factors from this requirement by regulations of the department and excepting such parts as the automotive repair dealer is required to return to the manufacturer or distributor under a warranty arrangement. If such parts must be returned to the manufacturer or distributor, the dealer at the time the work order is taken shall offer to show, and upon acceptance of such offer or request shall show, such parts to the customer upon completion of the work, except that the dealer shall not be required to show a replaced part when no charge is being made for the replacement part.

· · ·

§ 9884.14 Injunction

The superior court in and for the county wherein any person carries on, or attempts to carry on, business as an automotive repair dealer or as a mechanic in violation of the provisions of this chapter, or any regulation made pursuant to this chapter, shall, on application of the director or the chief, issue an injunction or other appropriate order restraining such conduct. This section shall be cumulative to and shall not prohibit the enforcement of any other law.

· · ·

§ 9884.18 Civil actions against dealer

Nothing in the provisions of this chapter shall prohibit the bringing of a civil action against an automotive repair dealer by an individual.

PROBLEM

One morning while *Consumer* is driving to work, a truck crashes into the rear of her car. She calls *Dealer,* who tows the car to his place of business. *Dealer* looks over the car and tells *Consumer* he will have to examine it in some detail to determine exactly what needs to be done. *Consumer* leaves the car there and takes a taxi to work. Several hours later *Dealer* telephones *Consumer* and tells her the car needs a new radiator, fan blade, wheel, tire, and brake. The cost for all of this will be $985. In addition, the car needs a new fender, hood, grill, and bumper, but *Dealer* tells her that he does not do any body work. He tells her, however, that *Body Shop,* located across the street from him, does good work and she could have the body work done there. "Do you want me to take the car over there when I'm finished with it?" *Consumer* tells him to do the repairs and take the car to *Body Shop* when he's done.

The next day *Dealer* calls *Consumer* to tell her that he just discovered that the engine block is cracked, and it will cost another $670 to replace. *Consumer* tells him to go ahead.

Four days later *Consumer* goes to pick up the car. *Dealer* hands her a "Work Order and Invoice" itemizing charges that total $1,748. This document also states the date, time, and telephone number of the two calls that *Dealer* made to *Consumer*. He also hands her a bill from *Body Shop* for $812 for the body work. She is surprised at the unexpected expense, and she also suspects that perhaps all that repair work was not really necessary, so she asks *Dealer* to give her the parts of her car that he has replaced. *Dealer* responds that he removed and discarded them the previous day.

     a) Has *Dealer* violated the Act?

     b) Has *Body Shop* violated the Act?

     c) If the answer to either question is yes, what can *Consumer* do about it?

     d) What can *Dealer* and/or *Body Shop* do about *Consumer's* refusal to pay the bills?

C.   PREEMPTION

The Tenth Amendment of the United States Constitution reserves to the states the power to legislate with respect to all matters that are neither prohibited by other parts of the Constitution nor delegated to the federal government. On the other hand, Article I, section 8 confers on Congress the power to regulate interstate commerce, and Article VI provides that "the Laws of the United States . . . shall be the supreme Law of the Land. . . ." Under these constitutional provisions, then, states may legislate consumer protection, but this legislation may be preempted under the Supremacy Clause if Congress also enacts consumer protection legislation. Sometimes it is relatively easy to determine whether state law is preempted; sometimes it is not easy. The next case illustrates both halves of this statement.

Jones v. Rath Packing Co.

Supreme Court of the United States, 1977.
430 U.S. 519, 97 S.Ct. 1305, 51 L.Ed.2d 604.

MR. JUSTICE MARSHALL delivered the opinion of the Court.

Petitioner Jones is Director of the Department of Weights and Measures in Riverside County, Cal. In that capacity he ordered removed from sale bacon packaged by respondent Rath Packing Co. and flour packaged by three millers, respondents, General Mills, Inc., Pillsbury Co., and Seaboard Allied Milling Corp. (hereafter millers). Jones acted after determining, by means of procedures set forth in 4 Cal. Admin.Code c. 8, Art. 5, that the packages were contained in lots whose average net weight was less than the net weight stated on the packages. The removal orders were authorized by Cal.Bus. & Prof.Code § 12211.

Rath and the millers responded by filing suits in the District Court for the Central District of California. They sought both declarations that § 12211 and Art. 5 are preempted by federal laws regulating net-weight labeling and injunctions prohibiting Jones from enforcing those provisions. The District Court granted the requested relief and, insofar as is relevant here, the Court of Appeals affirmed. We granted Jones' petition for certiorari, 425 U.S. 933 (1976), and now affirm the judgments of the Court of Appeals.

I

In its present posture, this litigation contains no claim that the Constitution alone denies California power to enact the challenged provisions. We are required to decide only whether the federal laws which govern respondents' packing operations preclude California from enforcing § 12211, as implemented by Art. 5.

Our prior decisions have clearly laid out the path we must follow to answer this question. The first inquiry is whether Congress, pursuant to its power to regulate commerce, U.S.Const., Art. 1, § 8, has prohibited state regulation of the particular aspects of commerce involved in this case. Where, as here, the field which Congress is said to have preempted has been traditionally occupied by the States, "we start with the assumption that the historic police powers of the States were not to be superseded by the Federal Act unless that was the clear and manifest purpose of Congress." Rice v. Santa Fe Elevator Corp., 331 U.S. 218, 230 (1947). This assumption provides assurance that "the federal-state balance" will not be disturbed unintentionally by Congress or unnecessarily by the courts. But when Congress has "unmistakably . . . ordained" that its enactments alone are to regulate a part of commerce, state laws regulating that aspect of commerce must fall. This result is compelled whether Congress' command is explicitly stated in the statute's language or implicitly contained in its structure and purpose.

Congressional enactments that do not exclude all state legislation in the same field nevertheless override state laws with which they conflict. U.S.Const., Art. VI. The criterion for determining whether state and federal laws are so inconsistent that the state law must give way is firmly established in our decisions. Our task is "to determine whether, under the circumstances of this particular case, [the State's] law stands as an obstacle to the accomplishment and execution of the full purposes and objectives of Congress." Hines v. Davidowitz, 312 U.S. 52, 67 (1941). This inquiry requires us to consider the relationship between state and federal laws as they are interpreted and applied, not merely as they are written.

II

Section 12211 of the Cal.Bus. & Prof.Code (West Supp.1977) applies to both Rath's bacon and the millers' flour. The standard it establishes is straightforward: "[T]he average weight or measure of the packages or containers in a lot of any . . . commodity sampled shall not be less, at the time of sale or offer for sale, than the net weight or measure stated upon the package."

In order to determine whether that standard has been violated, local officials such as Jones follow the statistical sampling procedure set forth in Art. 5.[9] . . .

III

A. Rath's bacon is produced at plants subject to federal inspection under the Federal Meat Inspection Act (FMIA or Act), as amended by the Wholesome Meat Act, 81 Stat. 584, 21 U.S.C. § 601 et seq. Among the requirements imposed on federally inspected plants, and enforced by Department of Agriculture inspectors, are standards of accuracy in labeling. On the record before us, we may assume that Rath's bacon complies with these standards. . . .

Section 1(n) of the FMIA, 21 U.S.C. § 601(n), defines the term "misbranded." As relevant here, it provides that meat or a meat product is misbranded

"(5) if in a package or other container unless it bears a label showing . . . (B) an accurate statement of the quantity of the contents in terms of weight, measure, or numerical count: *Provided*, That . . . reasonable variations may be permitted, and exemptions as to small packages may be established, by regulations prescribed by the Secretary." 81 Stat. 586.

Other sections of the FMIA prohibit dealing in misbranded products, as defined by § 1(n).

The Secretary of Agriculture has used his discretionary authority to permit "reasonable variations" in the accuracy of the required statement of quantity:

"The statement [of net quantity of contents] as it is shown on a label shall not be false or misleading and shall express an accurate statement of the quantity of contents of the container exclusive of wrappers and packing substances. Reasonable variations caused by loss or gain of moisture during the course of good distribution practices or by unavoidable deviations in good manufacturing practice will be recognized. Variations from stated quantity of contents shall not be unreasonably large." 9 CFR § 317.2(h)(2) (1976).

Thus, the FMIA, as implemented by statutorily authorized regulations, requires the label of a meat product accurately to indicate the net weight of the contents unless the difference between stated and actual weights is reasonable and results from the specified causes.

B. Section 408 of the FMIA, 21 U.S.C. § 678, prohibits the imposition of "[m]arking, labeling, packaging, or ingredient requirements in addition to, or different than, those made under" the Act. This explicit pre-emption provision dictates the result in the controversy between Jones and Rath. California's use of a statistical sampling process to determine the average net weight of a lot implicitly allows for variations from stated weight

---

9. The District Court concluded that the Art. 5 "procedure is a statistical determination based upon normal and proven statistical standards." 357 F.Supp., at 533. The statistical validity of the procedure has not been challenged.

caused by unavoidable deviations in the manufacturing process. But California makes no allowance for loss of weight resulting from moisture loss during the course of good distribution practice. Thus, the state law's requirement—that the label accurately state the net weight, with implicit allowance only for reasonable manufacturing variations—is "different than" the federal requirement, which permits manufacturing deviations *and* variations caused by moisture loss during good distribution practice.

. . .

We therefore conclude that with respect to Rath's packaged bacon, § 12211 and Art. 5 are pre-empted by federal law.

IV

A. The federal law governing net-weight labeling of the millers' flour is contained in two statutes, the Federal Food, Drug, and Cosmetic Act (FDCA), 21 U.S.C. § 301 et seq., and the Fair Packaging and Labeling Act (FPLA), 15 U.S.C. §§ 1451–1461. For the reasons stated below, we conclude that the federal weight-labeling standard for flour is the same as that for meat.

The FDCA prohibits the introduction or delivery for introduction into interstate commerce of any food that is misbranded. 21 U.S.C. § 331. A food is misbranded under the FDCA,

> "[i]f in package form unless it bears a label containing . . . an accurate statement of the quantity of the contents in terms of weight, measure, or numerical count: *Provided*, That . . . reasonable variations shall be permitted, and exemptions as to small packages shall be established, by regulations prescribed by the Secretary." § 343(e).

This provision is identical to the parallel provision in the FMIA, see supra, at 529, except that the FDCA mandates rather than allows the promulgation of implementing regulations. The regulation issued in response to this statutory mandate is also substantially identical to its counterpart under the FMIA:

> "The declaration of net quantity of contents shall express an accurate statement of the quantity of contents of the package. Reasonable variations caused by loss or gain of moisture during the course of good distribution practice or by unavoidable deviations in good manufacturing practice will be recognized. Variations from stated quantity of contents shall not be unreasonably large." 21 CFR § 1.8b(q) (1976).

Since flour is a food under the FDCA, its manufacture is also subject to the provisions of the FPLA. See 15 U.S.C. §§ 1452, 1459(a). That statute states a congressional policy that "[p]ackages and their labels should enable consumers to obtain accurate information as to the quantity of the contents and should facilitate value comparisons." § 1451. To accomplish those goals, insofar as is relevant here, the FPLA bans the distribution in commerce of any packaged commodity unless it complies with regulations which shall provide that—

 . . .

 (2) The net quantity of contents (in terms of weight, measure, or numerical count) shall be separately and accurately stated in a uniform location upon the principal display panel of [the required] label. § 1453(a).

The FPLA also contains a saving clause which specifies that nothing in the FPLA "shall be construed to repeal, invalidate, or supersede" the FDCA. § 1460. Nothing in the FPLA explicitly permits any variation between stated weight and actual weight.

[But the saving clause in FPLA preserves the regulation under FDCA permitting reasonable variations.]

 B. The FDCA contains no pre-emptive language. The FPLA, on the other hand, declares that

> "it is the express intent of Congress to supersede any and all laws of the States or political subdivisions thereof insofar as they may now or hereafter provide for the labeling of the net quantity of contents of the package of any consumer commodity covered by this chapter which are less stringent than or require information different from the requirements of section 1453 of this title or regulations promulgated pursuant thereto." 15 U.S.C. § 1461.

The Court of Appeals, although recognizing that this section leaves more scope for state law than does the FMIA, concluded that § 12211, as implemented by Art. 5, is pre-empted because it is less stringent than the Federal Acts, 530 F.2d, at 1324–1327.

 The basis for the Court of Appeals' holding is unclear. Its opinion may be read as based on the conclusion that the state law is inadequate because its enforcement relies on a statistical averaging procedure. We have rejected that conclusion. See supra, at 531, and n. 18. Alternatively, the Court of Appeals may have found California's approach less stringent because the State takes no enforcement action against lots whose average net weight *exceeds* the weight stated on the label, even if that excess is not a reasonable variation attributable to a federally allowed cause.

 We have some doubt that by pre-empting less stringent state laws, Congress intended to compel the States to expend scarce enforcement resources to prevent the sale of packages which contain more than the stated net weight. We do not have to reach that question, however, because in this respect California law apparently differs not at all from federal law, as applied. . . . Since neither jurisdiction is concerned with overweighting in the administration of its weights and measures laws, we cannot say that California's statutory lack of concern for that "problem" makes its laws less stringent than the federal.

 Respondents argue that California's law is pre-empted because it requires information different from that required by federal law. The meaning of the statutory pre-emption of laws that require "information different from" the federal net-weight labeling provisions, like the meaning of the phrase "less stringent," is unclear. Respondents attribute to the ban on requiring different information a broad meaning, similar in scope to the pre-emption provision of the FMIA. They contend that since California law requires the label to state the minimum net weight, it requires "information different from" the federal laws, which demand an accurate statement with allowance for the specified reasonable variations. Brief for Respondents 31–32. The legislative history, however, suggests that the statute expressly pre-empts as requiring "different information" only state laws governing net quantity labeling which impose requirements inconsistent with those imposed by federal law.[34] Since it would be possible to comply with the state law without triggering federal enforcement action we conclude that the state requirement is not inconsistent with federal law. We therefore hold that 15 U.S.C. § 1461 does not pre-empt California's § 12211 as implemented by Art. 5.

That holding does not, however, resolve this case, for we still must determine whether the state law "stands as an obstacle to the accomplishment and execution of the full purposes and objectives of Congress." As Congress clearly stated, a major purpose of the FPLA is to facilitate value comparisons among similar products. Obviously, this goal cannot be accomplished unless packages that bear the same indicated weight in fact contain the same quantity of the product for which the consumer is paying. The significance of this requirement for our purposes results from the physical attributes of flour. . . .

The moisture content of flour does not remain constant after milling is completed. If the relative humidity of the atmosphere in which it is stored is greater than 60%, flour will gain moisture, and if the humidity is less than 60%, it will lose moisture. The federal net-weight labeling standard permits variations from stated weight caused by this gain or loss of moisture.

Packages that meet the federal labeling requirements and that have the same stated quantity of contents can be expected to contain the same amount of flour solids. Manufacturers will produce flour with a moisture content fixed by the requirements of the milling process. Since manufacturers have reason not to pack significantly more than is required and federal law prohibits underpacking, they will pack the same amount of this similarly composed flour into packages of any given size. Despite any changes in weight resulting from changes in moisture content during distribution, the packages will contain the same amount of flour solids when they reach the consumer. This identity of contents facilitates consumer value comparisons.

---

34. The language of 15 U.S.C. § 1461 was contained in the House bill. The Senate bill, by contrast, provided for pre-emption of state requirements which "differ from" those in the FPLA. S.Rep. No. 1186, 89th Cong., 2d Sess., 38 (1966). The language accepted by the House was adopted by the conference committee, along with the House committee's explanation that "preemption would take place to the extent that 'State laws or State regulations with respect to the labeling of net quantity of contents of packages impose inconsistent or less stringent requirements than are imposed under section 4 of this legislation.'" H.R.Rep. No. 2286, 89th Cong., 2d Sess., 11 (1966).

The State's refusal to permit reasonable weight variations resulting from loss of moisture during distribution produces a different effect. In order to be certain of meeting the California standard, a miller must ensure that loss of moisture during distribution will not bring the weight of the contents below the stated weight. Local millers, which serve a limited area, could do so by adjusting their packing practices to the specific humidity conditions of their region. For example, a miller in an area where the humidity is typically higher than 60% would not need to overpack at all. By contrast, a miller with a national marketing area would not know the destination of its flour when it was packaged and would therefore have to assume that the flour would lose weight during distribution. The national manufacturer, therefore, would have to overpack.

Similarly, manufacturers who distribute only in States that followed the federal standard would not be concerned with compensating for possible moisture loss during distribution. National manufacturers who did not exclude the nonconforming States from their marketing area, on the other hand, would have to overpack. Thus, as a result of the application of the California standard, consumers throughout the country who attempted to compare the value of identically labeled packages of flour would not be comparing packages which contained identical amounts of flour solids. Value comparisons which did not account for this difference—and there would be no way for the consumer to make the necessary calculations— would be misleading.

We therefore conclude that with respect to the millers' flour, enforcement of § 12211, as implemented by Art. 5, would prevent "the accomplishment and execution of the full purposes and objectives of Congress" in passing the FPLA. Under the Constitution, that result is impermissible, and the state law must yield to the federal.

The judgments are affirmed.

It is so ordered.

QUESTIONS AND NOTES

1. With respect to flour, exactly why is the California statute not preempted by the preemption clause of the FPLA? Again with respect to flour, what federal law preempts the California statute?

2. The Court concludes that the state requirement is not "less stringent than" the federal requirement and that the state requirement is not inconsistent with the federal requirement. (See text at footnote 34). The Court also states that neither the federal nor the state government is concerned about overweighting. How then can the Court possibly conclude that the state statute so frustrates the purposes and objectives of the federal statute that it is preempted?

3. Compare the preemption clause of the FMIA, section 408 (page 165 supra), with the preemption clause of the FPLA (page 167 supra). Why does the Court say that the FPLA clause "leaves more scope for state law than does the FMIA" clause?

Rath Packing teaches us that preemption clauses (in those federal statutes that have them) are not always identical and even when they are identical, are not always construed identically. A 1992 Supreme Court decision, however, seems to teach just the opposite. Congress enacted the Airline Deregulation Act (ADA) in 1978 to minimize federal regulation of the business practices of the airline industry and to rely on market forces to enhance competition among carriers. The ADA contains a preemption provision, which states that states "may not enact or enforce any law, rule, regulation, standard, or other provision . . . relating to rates, routes, or services of any air carrier" (now codified at 49 U.S.C. § 41713(b)(1)). Notwithstanding this Act, the National Association of Attorneys General developed guidelines for airlines to follow in advertising their services. Among other things, these guidelines called for airlines to include in their ads all unavoidable charges in addition to the basic fare, any limitations on the availability of seats at the advertised prices, and any other restrictions or limitations on the advertised tickets. When several attorneys general threatened to enforce these guidelines under their respective little-FTC acts, several airlines sued to obtain a declaratory judgment that the ADA preempted the state laws underlying the guidelines. The Supreme Court agreed with the airlines:

> . . . As we have often observed, "[p]re-emption may be either express or implied, and is compelled whether Congress' command is explicitly stated in the statute's language or implicitly contained in its structure and purpose." The question, at bottom, is one of statutory intent, and we accordingly "begin with the language employed by Congress and the assumption that the ordinary meaning of that language accurately expresses the legislative purpose."

> [Section 41713(b)(1)] expressly pre-empts the States from "enact[ing] or enforc[ing] any law, rule, regulation, standard, or other provision having the force and effect of law relating to rates, routes, or services of any air carrier. . . ." For purposes of the present case, the key phrase, obviously, is "relating to." The ordinary meaning of these words is a broad one—"to stand in some relation; to have bearing or concern; to pertain; refer; to bring into association with or connection with," Black's Law Dictionary 1158 (5th ed. 1979)—and the words thus express a broad pre-emptive purpose. We have repeatedly recognized that in addressing the similarly worded pre-emption provision of the Employee Retirement Income Security Act of 1974 (ERISA), which pre-empts all state laws "insofar as they . . . relate to any employee benefit plan." We have said, for example, that the "breadth of [that provision's] pre-emptive reach is apparent from [its] language"; that it has a "broad scope" and an "expansive sweep"; and that it is "broadly worded," "deliberately expansive," and "conspicuous for its breadth." True to our word, we have held that a state law "relates to" an employee benefit plan, and is pre-empted by ERISA, "if

it has a connection with or reference to such a plan." Since the relevant language of the ADA is identical, we think it appropriate to adopt the same standard here: State enforcement actions having a connection with or reference to airline "rates, routes, or services" are pre-empted under [section 41713(b)(1)].

Petitioner raises a number of objections to this reading, none of which we think is well taken. First, he claims that we may not use our interpretation of identical language in ERISA as a guide, because the sweeping nature of ERISA pre-emption derives not from the "relates to" language, but from "the wide and inclusive sweep of the comprehensive ERISA scheme," which he asserts the ADA does not have. This argument is flatly contradicted by our ERISA cases, which clearly and unmistakably rely on express pre-emption principles and a construction of the phrase "relates to."

Morales v. Trans World Airlines, Inc., 504 U.S. 374 (1992).

Three years later, in American Airlines, Inc. v. Wolens, 513 U.S. 219 (1995), the Court held that the ADA also preempts the states' little-FTC acts insofar as they might provide a remedy for an airline's retroactive modification of its frequent flyer program (by increasing the number of miles required to claim an award). "In light of the full text of the preemption clause, and of the ADA's purpose to leave largely to the airlines themselves, and not at all to States, the selection and design of marketing mechanisms appropriate to the furnishing of air transportation services, we conclude that [the ADA] preempts plaintiffs' claims under the Illinois Consumer Fraud Act."

4. Does section 5 of the FTC Act preempt state legislation dealing with deceptive practices?

Some federal statutes do not contain any express preemption provision. The Supremacy Clause still operates to preempt some state law. The next case is an example of this. It concerns the interplay between a federal statute regulating interstate telephone service and a state statute prohibiting unfair or deceptive acts or practices. The Communications Act of 1934, 47 U.S.C. § 151 et seq., contains the following provisions:

§ 201(b). All charges, practices, classifications, and regulations for and in connection with such communication service, shall be just and reasonable, and any such charge, practice, classification, or regulation that is unjust or unreasonable is declared to be unlawful. . . . The [Federal Communications] Commission may prescribe such rules and regulations as may be necessary in the public interest to carry out the provisions of this chapter.

§ 205(a). . . . [T]he Commission is authorized and empowered to determine and prescribe what will be the just and reasonable charge

. . . and what . . . practice is or will be just, fair, and reasonable. . . .

§ 206.   In case any common carrier shall do . . . any act, matter, or thing in this chapter prohibited or declared to be unlawful, . . . such common carrier shall be liable to the person or persons injured thereby for the full amount of damages sustained. . . .

§ 207.   Any person claiming to be damaged by any common carrier subject to the provisions of this chapter may either make complaint to the Commission as hereinafter provided for, or may bring suit for the recovery of the damages for which such common carrier may be liable under the provisions of this chapter. . . .

§ 414.   Nothing in this chapter contained shall in any way abridge or alter the remedies now existing at common law or by statute, but the provisions of this chapter are in addition to such remedies.

Kellerman v. MCI Telecommunications Corporation

Supreme Court of Illinois, 1986.
112 Ill.2d 428, 98 Ill.Dec. 24, 493 N.E.2d 1045.

JUSTICE THOMAS J. MORAN delivered the opinion of the court:

Plaintiffs, subscribers of defendant MCI's long-distance telephone service, brought these class action suits in the circuit court of Cook County alleging that certain advertisements, which described defendant's service charges, violate the Consumer Fraud and Deceptive Business Practices Act [815 Ill. Consol. Stat. § 505/1 et seq.] and the Uniform Deceptive Trade Practices Act [815 Ill. Consol. Stat. § 510/1 et seq.]. Plaintiffs also allege that defendant's advertising practices constitute a breach of contract and common law fraud. They seek damages and an accounting for themselves and other persons similarly situated.

. . .

The advertisements and promotional material in question compare the cost of defendant's long-distance telephone service with the cost of a service provided by a competitor, American Telephone & Telegraph Company (AT&T). Plaintiffs allege that in order to induce them to purchase its service, defendant disseminated certain advertisements and promotional materials through various media which claimed that "although its rates are substantially lower" than AT&T's, "its billing practices and procedures were identical to those of" AT&T. They allege that AT&T charges its customers only for completed calls and no charge is made to customers for calls which are initiated but not completed, i.e. where the recipient does not answer or the caller terminates the call before it is answered. In contrast, plaintiffs allege that defendant has billed its customers for uncompleted calls.

Plaintiffs further allege that it was defendant's practice to impose a surcharge in situations where the telephone rang six or more times before it was answered—a charge not customarily imposed in the industry. It also is alleged that every time customers used defendant's service they paid a local telephone charge which AT&T customers did not have to pay. Plaintiffs do not challenge the reasonableness of the additional charges imposed by defendant, but only the fact that its advertising did not disclose that the additional charges would be made. It is alleged that through these advertisements and promotions, defendant "engaged in a course of conduct to falsely represent to the plaintiff[s] and the general public that its practice and policy [were] . . . to bill its customers only for the actual time of communication during completed long distance calls" when in fact its practice was to bill its customers for uncompleted calls and to impose a surcharge when a telephone rang six or more times before it was answered. Plaintiffs allege that defendant's conduct constitutes common law fraud, a breach of contract, and that it violates the Uniform Deceptive Trade Practices Act and the Consumer Fraud and Deceptive Business Practices Act.

[The trial court denied defendant's motion to dismiss or stay the proceeding, and the intermediate appellate court affirmed. Defendant appealed, claiming first that the Federal Communications Commission Act preempts the state Consumer Fraud and Deceptive Business Practices Act and the State Uniform Deceptive Trade Practices Act.]

The preemption doctrine, which has its origin in the supremacy clause of the Federal Constitution (U.S. Const., art. VI, cl. 2), provides that Federal law will in some instances override or preempt State laws on the same subject. The key inquiry in all preemption cases is the objective or purpose of Congress in enacting the particular statute. The doctrine requires courts to examine the Federal statute in question to determine whether Congress intended it to supplant State laws on the same subject. Generally this is no easy task because rarely does Congress, in enacting legislation, expressly provide that concurrent State laws will be preempted. Rather, a court must usually divine for itself whether the statute evidences an intent by Congress to preempt State law.

Although there is no "rigid formula or rule which can be used" to determine if Congress intended Federal law to preempt plaintiffs' actions for fraud, deceptive advertising and breach of contract (Hines v. Davidowitz (1941), 312 U.S. 52, 67, 61 S.Ct. 399, 404, 85 L.Ed. 581, 587), our "consideration of that question is guided by familiar and well-established principles" (Capital Cities Cable, Inc. v. Crisp (1984), 467 U.S. 691, 698, 104 S.Ct. 2694, 2700, 81 L.Ed.2d 580, 588), which the Supreme Court has enumerated as follows:

> "Absent explicit pre-emptive language, Congress' intent to supersede state law altogether may be inferred because '[t]he scheme of federal regulation may be so pervasive as to make reasonable the inference that Congress left no room for the States to supplement it,' because 'the Act of Congress may touch a field in which the federal

interest is so dominant that the federal system will be assumed to preclude enforcement of state laws on the same subject,' or because 'the object sought to be obtained by federal law and the character of obligations imposed by it may reveal the same purpose.' [Citation.]

"Even where Congress has not completely displaced state regulation in a specific area, State law is nullified to the extent that it actually conflicts with federal law. Such a conflict arises when 'compliance with both federal and state regulations is a physical impossibility,' [citation] or when state law 'stands as an obstacle to the accomplishment and execution of the full purposes and objectives of Congress' . . . ." Fidelity Federal Savings & Loan Association v. de la Cuesta (1982), 458 U.S. 141, 153, 102 S.Ct. 3014, 3022, 73 L.Ed.2d 664, 675.

The express purpose of the Communications Act is to "make available, so far as possible, to all the people of the United States a rapid, efficient . . . communication service with adequate facilities at reasonable charges." To that end, the Act applies "to all interstate and foreign communication by wire or radio . . . and to all persons engaged within the United States in such communication," and provides that an interstate telephone carrier's "charges, practices, classifications, and regulations for and in connection with [its] communication service, shall be just and reasonable." Under section 206, any carrier which violates a provision of the Act is liable "to the person or persons injured thereby for the full amount of damages sustained in consequence of any such violation." An injured party may file a complaint against the carrier with the FCC, which has the power "to investigate the matters complained of," and to award damages when appropriate. Alternatively, an aggrieved party can file an action against the carrier in Federal district court.

Defendant essentially makes two arguments as to why plaintiffs' actions are preempted by the Communications Act. First, it argues that the "comprehensive nature" of the Act, as briefly outlined above, demonstrates that Congress "intended to occupy the entire field of long distance telephone service" to the exclusion of State law. It asserts that the conduct challenged here falls within the broad field of interstate long-distance telephone service, and, hence, is preempted. Defendant's second argument is much narrower. While conceding for purposes of argument that the Act may not preempt all State regulation of long-distance telephone carriers, it contends that the Act specifically governs a carrier's "charges, practices and tariffs." Defendant maintains that plaintiffs, although "artfully emphasizing advertising and state law theories of liability," in reality are challenging "FCC-regulated charges, practices and tariffs." It argues that since plaintiffs are attacking "charges, practices and tariffs" regulated by Federal law, the State-law actions are preempted by the Act.

While we agree with defendant that the Communications Act represents a "broad scheme for the regulation of interstate service by communications carriers" (Ivy Broadcasting Co. v. American Telephone & Telegraph Co. (2d Cir.1968), 391 F.2d 486, 490), we cannot agree that Congress intended to supplant all State regulation of interstate telephone carriers, no matter how unrelated the State regulation is from Congress' objective of creating an interstate telephone network that is rapid, efficient and reasonably priced. The Act contains a saving clause which provides that "[n]othing in this chapter contained shall in any way abridge or alter the remedies now existing at common law or by statute, but the provisions of this chapter are in addition to such remedies." (47 U.S.C. sec. 414 (1982).) Thus, to argue, as defendant has, that Congress has "occupied the field of interstate long distance telephone service" does not answer the question of whether these particular State-law actions are preempted by the Act. Rather, as the appellate court in this case keenly observed, the relevant inquiry is what are the "precise contours" of the field that Congress has chosen to occupy. 134 Ill.App.3d 71, 74, 89 Ill.Dec. 51, 479 N.E.2d 1057.

Little guidance can be gleaned from the Communications Act itself, and few cases have discussed Federal preemption with respect to the Act. In Ivy Broadcasting Co. v. American Telephone & Telegraph Co., the court concluded that an action against two telephone companies for the negligent "installation and testing" of telephone lines was governed exclusively by Federal common law. The court, reasoning that the "congressional purpose of uniformity and equality of rates should be taken to imply uniformity and equality of service," stated that "questions concerning the duties, charges and liabilities of telegraph or telephone companies with respect to interstate communications service are to be governed solely by federal law." (391 F.2d 486, 491.) The *Ivy* court, however, did not discuss the scope of the saving clause of the Act, section 414. Subsequent cases have viewed section 414 as "preserving causes of action for breaches of duties distinguishable from those created under the Act." Comtronics, Inc. v. Puerto Rico Telephone Co. (1st Cir.1977), 553 F.2d 701, 707–08 n. 6.

In Ashley v. Southwestern Bell Telephone Co. (W.D.Tex.1976), 410 F.Supp. 1389, the court, relying on section 414 of the Act, held that a State-law action brought against an FCC-regulated carrier for invasion of privacy was not preempted by the Act. Similarly, in Bruss Co. v. Allnet Communication Services, Inc. (N.D.Ill.1985), 606 F.Supp. 401, a case closely analogous to the case at bar, the court held that State-law claims alleging common law fraud and violations of Illinois' deceptive trade and consumer fraud acts were not preempted by the Act. In that case, it was alleged that the defendants had charged plaintiffs and other long-distance customers rates in excess of the tariffs filed with the FCC. The court, reasoning that the State claims "challenged conduct that is not contemplated by the Communications Act," held that the actions were preserved under section 414.

In interpreting a statutory provision, courts " 'will not look merely to a particular clause in which general words may be used, but will take in connection with it the whole statute . . . and the objects and policy of the law.' " (Stafford v. Briggs (1980), 444 U.S. 527, 535, 100 S.Ct. 774, 780, 63 L.Ed.2d 1, 9.) Therefore, it is implausible to think that section 414 of the Act preserved all State-law remedies affecting interstate telephone carriers no matter how repugnant those State laws are to the purposes and objectives of Congress. It is reasonable to presume that State laws which interfere with Congress' objective of creating "a rapid, efficient, Nationwide, . . . communication service with adequate facilities at reasonable charges" (47 U.S.C. sec. 151), such as State attempts to regulate interstate carriers' charges or services, would be preempted by the Act. (See, e.g., Komatz Construction, Inc. v. Western Union Telegraph Co. (1971), 290 Minn. 129, 186 N.W.2d 691 (action against telegraph company for damages caused by delay in transmission of telegram is governed by Federal law).) However, we believe that section 414, when considered in the context of the entire act, should be construed as preserving State-law "causes of action for breaches of duties distinguishable from those created under the Act." (Comtronics, Inc. v. Puerto Rico Telephone Co. (1st Cir.1977), 553 F.2d 701, 708.) State-law remedies which do not interfere with the Federal government's authority over interstate telephone charges or services, and which do not otherwise conflict with an express provision of the Act, are preserved by section 414.

Defendant argues that plaintiffs, while "artfully" pleading fraud and deceptive-advertising claims, in reality "seek recovery for federally regulated charges." As such, it asserts that plaintiffs' actions are preempted by the Act. Although a similar argument has prevailed in at least one Federal district court (see In re Long Distance Telecommunications Litigation (E.D.Mich.1984), 598 F.Supp. 951), we think the better view is that plaintiffs' actions are not preempted by the Act. (See Bruss Co. v. Allnet Communication Services, Inc. (N.D.Ill.1985), 606 F.Supp. 401.) The subject matter of plaintiffs' complaints involves neither the quality of defendant's service nor the reasonableness and lawfulness of its rates. Plaintiffs only allege that defendant disseminated fraudulent and deceptive advertisements concerning the cost of its long-distance telephone service. As such, plaintiffs seek to hold defendant to the same standards as they would any other business which advertises on a nationwide basis and which, in the course of its business, is subject to regulation from a number of Federal and State agencies. Moreover, these actions do not present "an obstacle to the accomplishment" of the Federal policy of promoting a "rapid, efficient . . . communication service with adequate facilities at reasonable charges." The prosecution of these claims will in no way interfere with the delivery of long-distance telephone service to defendant's customers, and any possible effect the litigation could have on defendant's telephone rates is speculative at best. Finally, no Federal statute or regulation has been brought to our attention which would expressly prohibit these actions. Therefore, we find that Congress did not intend to occupy the field of interstate telephone service to the extent of barring these State-law claims for fraud, breach of contract and deceptive practices, and hold that plaintiffs' actions are not preempted.

. . .

Judgment affirmed.

QUESTIONS AND NOTES

1. In view of the existence of Communications Act section 414, expressly preserving state common law and statutory remedies, how can MCI possibly argue that the Communications Act preempts the Illinois statute?

2. If, as the court acknowledges, the FCC has the *exclusive* power to regulate "all charges, practices, classifications and regulations . . . in connection with a carrier's communications services," how can the Illinois statute apply to the facts of *Kellerman*: are not the plaintiffs challenging the reasonableness of one of MCI's practices, viz., its practice of not disclosing that it bills for uncompleted calls?

3. The Seventh Circuit has interpreted the reach of section 201(a) ("all charges, practices, classifications, and regulations . . . shall be just and reasonable") quite differently. It has held that section 201 preempts the Illinois law of deceptive practices and the Illinois law of contracts with respect to certain terms in AT&T's contract for telephone service. These contractual terms prohibit class actions and require that disputes under the contract be resolved by arbitration. In holding that Illinois law is preempted, the court stated

> [It] is clear from Section 201(b) that Congress intended federal law to govern the validity of the rates, terms and conditions of long-distance service contracts. . . . [The] language demonstrates Congress's intent that federal law determine the reasonableness of the terms and conditions of long-distance contracts. . . . While [plaintiff] challenges the arbitration clause under the state law doctrine of unconscionability and various state consumer protection statutes, in essence the question is the same—whether the term is fair and reasonable. Permitting such state law challenges would open the door for direct conflicts between federal and state law on the validity of terms and conditions contained in a long-distance service contract. For example, . . . in the past, tariffs filed by other carriers have included arbitration clauses and those clauses have been enforced. . . . Yet, if [plaintiff] would have his way, arbitration provisions and clauses prohibiting class actions would be illegal under state law, even if they were considered "just and reasonable" under federal law. The Supremacy Clause prohibits such an outcome.

Boomer v. AT&T Corp., 309 F.3d 404 (7th Cir.2002).

4. A major segment of consumer transactions is increasingly subject to only federal regulation. Starting with a Supreme Court decision in 1978, the courts and federal administrative agencies have held that federal statutes governing financial institutions displace the states' ability to regulate financial services. The initial focus was regulation of interest rates, but the preemption now extends to regulation of deception as well. The subject is addressed further in Chapter 8.

5. Preemption of state law is not confined to federal statutes. Federal *regulations* also may preempt state law. In Katharine Gibbs School, Inc. v. FTC, 612 F.2d 658 (2d Cir.1979), petitioners challenged an FTC regulation concerning vocational schools. The regulation provided, in part, "This trade regulation rule preempts any provision of any state law, rule, or regulation which is inconsistent with or otherwise frustrates the purpose of the provisions of this trade regulation rule, except where the Commission has exempted such a state or local law, rule or regulation." The court responded:

> It has long since been firmly established that state statutes and regulations may be superseded by validly enacted regulations of federal agencies such as the FTC. However, before preemption shall be deemed to have occurred, there must be either a clear manifestation of such congressional intent or a conflicting inconsistency between state and federal regulations. This is particularly true where the field of regulation is one that has been traditionally occupied by the states. Jones v. Rath Packing Co., 430 U.S. 519, 525, 97 S.Ct. 1305, 51 L.Ed.2d 604 (1977).

> [In authorizing the FTC to promulgate regulations], Congress did not intend that the Commission's regulations should "occupy the field" so as to preclude any state regulation whatever. The [enabling legislation] contains no preemption provisions. Such indications of congressional intent as may be gleaned from the legislative history of the 1975 enactment and the predecessor bills considered by Congress show that the Commission's regulations were to have no more preemptive effect than that which flows inevitably from a repugnancy between the Commission's valid enactments and state regulations. If the Commission had defined with specificity the acts or practices it deemed unfair or deceptive, questions of preemption could be answered with relatively little difficulty. An entirely different picture is presented when the Commission assumes the authority to decree preemption of any state law or regulation which "frustrates the purpose" of its Rule's inadequately spelled out provisions. One may well wonder, for example, what state regulations might be said to frustrate the purpose of the refund provisions, designed as they are to create structural disincentives to indiscriminate enrollment. The fact that the Rule permits state governmental agencies to come before the Commission seeking grace from preemption does not solve the problem of overbreadth.

> Where an explicitly formulated federal statute or regulation is in conflict with state law, preemption of state law follows inevitably from the supremacy clause of the Constitution. . . . There is no need for the Commission to so state. The preemption provisions of the Commission's Rule go beyond this. They are overbroad, and their enactment was beyond the Commission's power.

Id. at 667. This position drew a dissent:

> I agree with the majority that Congress did not intend the Commission's rules to have any greater preemptive effect than that which results from a conflict between these rules and state enactments. The Commission also agrees and has explicitly disclaimed any greater power. The language of the provision states that the Rule "preempts

any provision of any state law, rule, or regulation which is inconsistent with or otherwise frustrates the purpose of the provisions of this trade regulation rule." This simply paraphrases the test for preemption that has been established by the Supreme Court. . . .

The majority seizes upon the word "purpose" in the preemption provision of the Rule to inflate the scope of the provision beyond what the Commission intends. In the majority's view, the provision would preempt any state law that conflicts not only with the Rule and its operation but also with the reasons for adopting the Rule. . . . The Rule is properly understood to mean that a state law would frustrate the purpose of the Rule if it provided for [less protection], not if it attempted to regulate vocational school abuses in some unrelated way. As the Court has said, "The test of whether both federal and state regulations may operate, or the state regulation must give way, is whether both regulations can be enforced without impairing the federal superintendence of the field, not whether they are aimed at similar or different objectives." Florida Lime & Avocado Growers, Inc. v. Paul, 373 U.S. 132, 142, 83 S.Ct. 1210, 1217, 10 L.Ed.2d 248 (1963). This was the test that was clearly intended by the Rule, and it does not exceed the Commission's power.

Contrary to the majority's suggestion, a preemption provision limited as this one is to displacement of conflicting state laws is not rendered unnecessary by the existence of the Supremacy Clause. To begin with, the provision makes clear that this preemptive effect is intended, rather than leaving the question of Commission intent open for subsequent litigation. More importantly, the preemption provision adopted by the Commission actually reduces the natural scope of preemption in certain circumstances, such as those where the Commission determines that the state regulation offers consumers more protection than the Rule does. Invalidating the entire provision risks increasing the impact of the federal rule on state legislation, since even state laws that are stronger than the federal requirements might be preempted under the Supremacy Clause in the absence of the Commission's modest provision.

Id. at 682–83. For additional materials on preemption, see Pierce, Regulation, Deregulation, Federalism, and Administrative Law: Agency Power to Preempt State Regulation, 46 U.Pitt.L.Rev. 607 (1985); Miller, The Problem of Preemption in Consumer Credit Regulation, 3 Okla.City L.Rev. 529 (1979); Verkuil, Preemption of State Law by the Federal Trade Commission, 1976 Duke L.J. 225.

6. Preemption may also occur at the state level, i.e. one state statute may preempt another state statute. Reconsider Problem 3, page 137 supra: does either the federal odometer statute or the state odometer statute foreclose recovery under the deceptive trade practices act for *Dealer's* innocent misrepresentation? Compare Dover v. Stanley, 652 S.W.2d 258 (Mo.App. 1983) (state odometer statute preempts consumer fraud act), with Washburn v. Vandiver, 379 S.E.2d 65 (N.C.App.1989) (contra).

Similarly, a state statute may preempt legislation enacted by a city or a county. For example, in American Financial Services Association v. City of Oakland, 104 P.3d 813 (Cal.2005), a state statute regulating sub-prime loans did not contain an express preemption of municipal ordinances, but the court held that the state legislation was so extensive that it manifested a legislative intent to occupy the entire field. Consequently, a city within the state was not permitted to adopt additional, more stringent standards. Accord, American Financial Services Association v. City of Cleveland, 859 N.E.2d 923 (Ohio 2006).

7. It is common for little-FTC acts to contain provisions stating that they do not apply to transactions regulated by certain state agencies. See Note 9, page 129 supra.

D. CRIMINAL SANCTIONS

The preceding materials have examined civil sanctions for deception by sellers. Criminal sanctions may be available as well. Indeed, the first major legislative thrust against deception consisted of making it a crime to engage in deceptive advertising. In 1911 an advertising industry trade journal, *Printer's Ink,* published a model statute. This law, which came to be known as the Printer's Ink statute, provides:

Any person, firm, corporation or association who, with intent to sell, or in any wise dispose of, merchandise, service, or anything offered by such person, firm, corporation or association, directly or indirectly, to the public for sale, distribution, or with intent to increase the consumption of or to induce the public in any manner to enter into any obligation relating thereto, or to acquire title thereto, or makes, publishes, disseminates, circulates, or places before the public, or causes, directly or indirectly, to be made, published, disseminated, circulated, or placed before the public, in this state, in a newspaper, or other publication, or in the form of a book, notice, circular, pamphlet, letter, handbill, poster, bill, or in any other way an advertisement, of any sort regarding merchandise, securities, service, or anything so offered to the public, which advertisement contains any assertion, representation or statement of fact which is untrue, deceptive, or misleading, shall be guilty of a misdemeanor.

This statute was adopted, sometimes with modifications, in more than forty states.

Criminal legislation against deception exists also at the federal level. Examples of conduct that Congress has made criminal include using the mail to defraud, 18 U.S.C. § 1341; making false or misleading statements or omissions in registration statements required by the Securities Act of 1933, 15 U.S.C. § 77x; and making inaccurate disclosures under the Truth-in-Lending Act, 15 U.S.C. § 1611. In 1996 the federal government successfully prosecuted a con artist who telephoned elderly people who earlier had been victimized by telemarketers. He informed them that he worked for a company that the government had hired to return the money that they had lost. To get the money, however, the victims needed to send ten percent of the refund to be held in escrow for taxes. The court sent him to prison. Bryant, "Double Whammy" Scam Artist Handed 2½ Years Behind Bars, St. Louis Post–Dispatch, May 3, 1996, p. A5.

QUESTIONS AND NOTES

1. With respect to the Printer's Ink statute, what are the elements of the crime? How do they differ from the elements necessary to permit a consumer to recover damages for a seller's misrepresentation?

2. Printer's Ink statutes were never very rigorously enforced, and there are few appellate reports of prosecutions. Green v. United States, 312 A.2d 788 (D.C.App.1973); People v. Glubo, 158 N.E.2d 699 (N.Y.1959); People v. Minjac Corp., 151 N.E.2d 180 (N.Y.1958). Other than improved behavior by sellers, what might explain the paucity of prosecutions under Printer's Ink statutes?

3. Even if the false advertising statute expressly provides only criminal and injunctive remedies, the courts may recognize a private right of action for damages. E.g., Fargo Women's Health Organization, Inc. v. FM Women's Help & Caring Connection, 444 N.W.2d 683 (N.D.1989) (pregnancy services clinic that provided abortions recovered damages from a pregnancy services clinic that opposed abortion, for using deception to divert consumers who sought abortion counseling and services).

4. Topical statutes frequently provide that failure to comply with their requirements is a crime. E.g., criminal sanctions are common in statutes regulating home improvement contracts. In Stepniewski v. Gagnon, 732 F.2d 567 (7th Cir.1984), the Seventh Circuit rejected a constitutional attack on a statute regulating home improvement contractors that provided criminal sanctions even for a negligent or inadvertent failure to comply with administrative regulations promulgated pursuant to the statute.

In a few states the legislature has made it a crime for a person to violate a little-FTC act. Although intent to deceive is not an element of those statutes, the deceptive conduct is a *crime* only if the defendant engaged in it wilfully, knowingly, and with intent to defraud. As so limited, the Missouri Supreme Court rejected a claim that the statute was unconstitutionally vague. State v. Shaw, 847 S.W.2d 768 (Mo.1993).

5. The existence of the criminal mail fraud statute, 18 U.S.C. § 1341, opens up another avenue of civil relief. The Racketeer Influenced and Corrupt Organizations Act (RICO), 18 U.S.C. §§ 1961–68, provides a civil remedy for persons injured by mail fraud. E.g., Morosani v. First National Bank of Atlanta, 703 F.2d 1220 (11th Cir.1983). The mail fraud statute prohibits "any scheme or artifice to defraud, or for obtaining money or property by means of false or fraudulent pretenses, representations, or promises . . .," and the courts have construed this language broadly. See United States v. Mandel, 591 F.2d 1347, 1360–61 (4th Cir.1979); Note,

Survey of the Law of Mail Fraud, 1975 U.Ill.L.F. 237. Civil liability under RICO does not depend upon a prior criminal conviction of the defendant. For a discussion of the elements of a RICO claim, see J. Sheldon & C. Carter, Unfair and Deceptive Acts and Practices § 9.2.3 (6th ed.2004) (NCLC Series). Under RICO a successful plaintiff recovers treble damages and attorney's fees. 18 U.S.C. § 1964(c).

In Emery v. American General Finance, Inc., 71 F.3d 1343 (7th Cir.1995), defendant loaned money to plaintiff and then later solicited her to refinance the loan and obtain additional cash. Defendant failed to tell plaintiff that, because of the expense entailed by rewriting the original loan, it would have been less expensive for plaintiff to have obtained an entirely new, separate loan than to refinance the original one. The court held that plaintiff's claim of a RICO violation based on allegations of mail fraud was sufficient to withstand defendant's motion to dismiss. See Fairman v. Schaumberg Toyota, Inc., 1996 WL 392224 (N.D.Ill.1996) (allegations that auto dealer represented it would obtain best financing for consumer but actually obtained financing at a higher cost than necessary from a lender that was willing to share the finance charge with the dealer states a RICO claim).

In Kenty v. Bank One, Columbus, N.A., 92 F.3d 384 (6th Cir.1996), on the other hand, the loan contract required plaintiffs to maintain casualty insurance on the collateral and provided that if they failed to do so, defendant could purchase the insurance on plaintiff's behalf and add the premium to their loan. Plaintiffs brought a RICO action, alleging that defendant failed to disclose that it had obtained insurance that covered more risks than the contract authorized. The court affirmed the trial court's summary judgment for the defendant.

The substance of the practices in *Emery*, *Fairman*, and *Kenty* are considered in greater detail in chapters 8 and 10 (on interest rate regulation and credit insurance).

Many state legislatures also have enacted RICO statutes. E.g., see Combs v. Bakker, 886 F.2d 673 (4th Cir.1989) (North Carolina statute applied to fraudulent televangelist).

CHAPTER 4

THE NEED FOR INFORMATION

A. INTRODUCTION TO THE TRUTH-IN-LENDING ACT

In considering the problem of deception, the preceding chapters have focused on representations made by sellers or creditors. At the risk of oversimplification, if a seller or creditor imparts information to a consumer, that information must be accurate. As a general rule, however, the seller or creditor is under no obligation to disclose any particular information in the first place. To be sure, there are exceptions, e.g., Ollerman v. O'Rourke Co., page 34 supra. But they are exceptions. For example, assume that a consumer borrows $1,200 and gives the lender a note calling for repayment in twelve monthly installments of $110, for a total of $1,320. Does *Ollerman* impose liability on the lender who fails to disclose the rate of interest? Do the FTC or little-FTC acts impose liability for that omission?

If businesses fail to disclose important information voluntarily, and if that failure is not an actionable tort, then enactment of a statute requiring disclosure may be in order. On the other hand, if particular information is important to consumers, one would expect them to seek it out. The failure of businesses to provide the particular information therefore may suggest that it is not really all that important to consumers. Nevertheless, Congress and state legislatures have enacted numerous statutes that require disclosure to consumers. These disclosures range from the information required by the securities laws to the health warning on cigarette packages; from labeling the contents of food packages to itemizing the elements of the price of automobiles. They all are designed to protect consumers and therefore might properly be the subject of this chapter. This chapter, however, has a narrower focus. It is limited to statutes that require disclosure of the terms of consumer contracts, specifically the terms relating to credit and to warranties.

For most of the twentieth century, state laws have required disclosure of specified terms in some contracts. Early in the century, the legislation focused on small loans. Then the enactment of retail installment sales acts extended disclosure requirements to credit sales of consumer goods. By the early 1960s, however, not all states had enacted disclosure statutes, and the statutes that had been enacted were not uniform in substance or terminology and did not apply to all forms of consumer credit. Hence Congress began considering the need for legislation at the federal level. The following problem illustrates the situation that consumers faced.

PROBLEM

Consumer needs a new refrigerator and shops around for the best deal. He ultimately selects one that costs $600, but he cannot pay for it in cash. He checks with several sources of credit and learns the following:

1) The seller of the refrigerator will allow him to pay in installments, charging him $8.50 per $100 per year. The seller explains that this means the credit will cost $8.50 x 6 (because there are 6 100's in 600), or $51. *Consumer* would repay $651 in 12 monthly installments of $54.25.

2) *BestLoan* will loan *Consumer* $600 at a cost of $8 per $100 per year discounted. *BestLoan* explains that this means the cost is $8 x 6 (100's) or $48, which it will discount (i.e. deduct) from the amount of the loan. So *Consumer* would receive $552 ($600 − $48) and repay $600 in 12 monthly installments of $50.

3) *FirstBank* will loan *Consumer* $600 at a cost of 14.25%, computed on the declining balance. The bank explains this means he would pay 12 monthly installments in the amount of $50 plus one-twelfth of 14.25% times the amount remaining unpaid during the preceding month or

$$(\$50 \ + \ \frac{14.25\%}{12} \ (\$600)) \ + \ (\$50 \ + \ \frac{14.25\%}{12} \ (\$550)) \ +$$

$$(\$50 \ + \ \frac{14.25\%}{12} \ (\$500)) \ + \ . \ . \ . \ (\$50 \ + \ \frac{14.25\%}{12} \ (\$50)).$$

The total amount repaid would be $646.32.

4) *Consumer's* sister-in-law will loan him $600 at a cost of 12%, to be repaid in one lump sum payment of $672 one year later.

Should *Consumer* take the 8%, 8.5%, 12%, or 14.25% credit? (Before reading any further, write down your answer.)

One way to approach the preceding problem is to compare the dollar cost of each alternative. This approach suggests that *FirstBank* is offering the best deal, then *BestLoan,* then the seller, and finally the sister-in-law. But the four possibilities have differing amounts of credit and differing periods of time in which *Consumer* will have those amounts of credit. Therefore, it is misleading to compare them only in terms of the total dollar cost. What is needed is some uniform way of stating the cost that takes account of these differences. This can be done by means of the following formula, which produces the cost in terms of an annual rate of charge:

$$R \ = \ \frac{2(n)(C)}{P(N+1)}, \text{ where}$$

R   is the rate

n   is the number of installments per year

C   is the dollar amount of the finance charge

P   is the principal amount of the credit

N   is the total number of installments during the entire transaction.

Which offer of credit is the best deal? Which should *Consumer* accept? Are these two questions the same?

Credit costs were quoted, computed, and disclosed in each of the ways described above. Indeed, these examples are not exhaustive. A variation of alternative 3 is to total the amounts of the monthly finance charges, add that to the principal amount of the loan, and divide by 12. This variation, known as a precomputed loan, permits the lender to receive the same dollar finance charge as in alternative 3, but has the added convenience of repayment in equal monthly installments.

Only the most sophisticated and diligent of consumers could hope to be able to compare precisely the real costs of alternative offers of credit. So in 1968 Congress enacted the Truth-in-Lending Act, as Title I of the Consumer Credit Protection Act (CCPA). Since then Congress has enacted additional titles, making the CCPA the main repository of federal consumer credit regulation. (Subsequent chapters of this book explore other titles of the CCPA.) The stated objective of the Truth-in-Lending Act is "to assure a meaningful disclosure of credit terms so that the consumer will be able to compare more readily the various credit terms available to him and avoid the uninformed use of credit" (§ 102(a)). The principal reform of the Act is to make uniform the method of determining the rate of charge for consumer credit. That method is known as the actuarial method and is considerably more complex than the above formula. For practical reasons creditors originally used electronic calculators or rate tables derived from the actuarial formula. Today they use computers. (The formula itself appears at 12 C.F.R. Part 226, Appendix J, which is included in the Statutory Supplement. Rate tables are available from the Federal Reserve Board.)

In addition to specifying the disclosures that creditors must make, Congress also provided for administration of the Act. It directed the Federal Reserve Board (FRB) to promulgate regulations to carry out the purposes of the Act (§ 105). The regulations, known collectively as Regulation Z, appear at 12 C.F.R. Part 226. In Mourning v. Family Publications Service, Inc., 411 U.S. 356 (1973), the Supreme Court held that the enforceability of the FRB's regulations is to be tested by the relatively low standard of whether they are reasonably related to the objectives of the statute. See also Consumers Union, Inc. v. Federal Reserve Board, 938 F.2d 266 (D.C.Cir.1991). For a decision holding that the regulation fails to meet this standard, see Pfennig v. Household Credit Services, Inc., 286 F.3d 340 (6th Cir.2002).

The original statute and regulations were quite complex. Compliance was exceptionally difficult, perhaps even impossible, and trivial violations resulted in substantial losses for creditors. So in 1980 Congress enacted the Truth-in-Lending Simplification and Improvement Act. The main reforms of this legislation were a reduction in the amount of information creditors must disclose, a contraction of civil liability for failure to disclose the required information, and a command to the FRB to promulgate model disclosure forms for creditors to use.

Under the statute as originally enacted, the FRB promulgated not only Regulation Z but also Interpretations of the regulation. These Interpretations stated the Board's application of Regulation Z to selected situations. In addition, the staff of the FRB, as opposed to the Board itself, also issued interpretations. The staff interpretations were of two types, official and unofficial. Unofficial staff interpretations, called "Public Information Letters," were issued at the discretion of the staff. Official staff interpretations, on the other hand, were issued only pursuant to specified procedures, which included an opportunity for public comment on the proposed interpretation. These FRB, official staff, and unofficial staff interpretations constituted a formidable body of material: between 1968 and 1980, the Board and its staff issued more than 60 Board Interpretations, 160 official staff interpretations, and 1300 unofficial staff interpretations. To what extent are these agency interpretations binding? The Supreme Court had this to say:

> Notwithstanding the absence of an express statutory mandate that [the contractual provision in question] be invariably disclosed, the Court of Appeals has held that the "creditor must [always] disclose [it]." * * * In so deciding, the Court of Appeals in *St. Germain* explicitly rejected the view of the Federal Reserve Board staff that [it] need not be disclosed * * * . FRB Official Staff Interpretation No. FC–0054, supra; see FRB Public Information Letter No. 851, [1974–1977 Transfer Binder] CCH Consumer Credit Guide & 31,173; FRB Public Information Letter No. 1208, id., & 31,647; FRB Public Information Letter No. 1324, 5 CCH Consumer Credit Guide & 31,827 (1979). Rather, *St. Germain* declared that it would "choose the direction that makes more sense to us in trying to achieve the congressional purpose of providing meaningful disclosure to the debtor about the costs of his borrowing."

It is a commonplace that courts will further legislative goals by filling the interstitial silences within a statute or a regulation. Because legislators cannot foresee all eventualities, judges must decide unanticipated cases by extrapolating from related statutes or administrative provisions. But legislative silence is not always the result of a lack of prescience; it may instead betoken permission or, perhaps, considered abstention from regulation. In that event, judges are not accredited to supersede Congress or the appropriate agency by embellishing upon the regulatory scheme. Accordingly, caution must temper judicial creativity in the face of legislative or regulatory silence.

At the very least, that caution requires attentiveness to the views of the administrative entity appointed to apply and enforce a statute. And deference is especially appropriate in the process of interpreting the Truth in Lending Act and Regulation Z. Unless demonstrably irrational, Federal Reserve Board staff opinions construing the Act or Regulation should be dispositive for several reasons.

The Court has often repeated the general proposition that considerable respect is due "the interpretation given [a] statute by the officers or agency charged with its administration." An agency's construction of its own regulations has been regarded as especially due that respect. This traditional acquiescence in administrative expertise is particularly apt under TILA, because the Federal Reserve Board has played a pivotal role in "setting [the statutory] machinery in motion. . . . ." As we emphasized in Mourning v. Family Publications Service, 411 U.S. 356, 93 S.Ct. 1652, 36 L.Ed.2d 318 (1973), Congress delegated broad administrative lawmaking power to the Federal Reserve Board when it framed TILA. The Act is best construed by those who gave it substance in promulgating regulations thereunder.[9]

Furthermore, Congress has specifically designated the Federal Reserve Board and staff as the primary source for interpretation and application of truth-in-lending law. Because creditors need sure guidance through the "highly technical" Truth in Lending Act, S.Rep. No. 93–278, p. 13 (1973), legislators have twice acted to promote reliance upon Federal Reserve pronouncements. In 1974, TILA was amended to provide creditors with a defense from liability based upon good-faith compliance with a "rule, regulation, or interpretation" of the Federal Reserve Board itself. § 130(f). The explicit purpose of the amendment was to relieve the creditor of the burden of choosing "between the Board's construction of the Act and the creditor's own assessment of how a court may interpret the Act." S.Rep. No. 93–278, supra, at 13. The same rationale prompted a further change in the statute in 1976, authorizing a liability defense for "conformity with any interpretation or approval by an official or employee of the Federal Reserve System duly authorized by the Board to issue such interpretations or approvals. . . . ." § 130(f).[a]

The enactment and expansion of § 130(f) has significance beyond the express creation of a good-faith immunity. That statutory provision signals an unmistakable congressional decision to treat administrative rulemaking and interpretation under TILA as authoritative. Moreover, language in the legislative history evinces a decided preference for resolving interpretive issues by uniform administrative decision, rather than piecemeal through litigation. Courts should honor that congressional choice. Thus, while not abdicating their ultimate judicial respon-

---

9. To be sure, the administrative interpretations proffered in this case were issued by the Federal Reserve staff rather than the Board. But to the extent that deference to administrative views is bottomed on respect for agency expertise, it is unrealistic to draw a radical distinction between opinions issued under the imprimatur of the Board and those submitted as official staff memoranda. At any rate, it is unnecessary to explore the Board/staff difference at length, because Congress has conferred special status upon official staff interpretations. See § 130(f); see 12 CFR § 226.1(d) (1979).

a. This reference is to the statute authorizing official staff interpretations.—Ed.

sibility to determine the law, judges ought to refrain from substituting their own interstitial lawmaking for that of the Federal Reserve, so long as the latter's lawmaking is not irrational.

Finally, wholly apart from jurisprudential considerations or congressional intent, deference to the Federal Reserve is compelled by necessity; a court that tries to chart a true course to the Act's purpose embarks upon a voyage without a compass when it disregards the agency's views. The concept of "meaningful disclosure" that animates TILA cannot be applied in the abstract. *Meaningful* disclosure does not mean more disclosure. Rather, it describes a balance between "competing considerations of complete disclosure . . . and the need to avoid . . . [informational overload]." And striking the appropriate balance is an empirical process that entails investigation into consumer psychology and that presupposes broad experience with credit practices. Administrative agencies are simply better suited than courts to engage in such a process.

The Federal Reserve Board staff treatment of [the problem at hand] rationally accommodates the conflicting demands for completeness and for simplicity. [It would have been reasonable for the FRB to have decided that the term in question here must be disclosed. But it was also reasonable for the Board to conclude that disclosure is not necessary.] Faced with an apparent lacuna in the express prescriptions of TILA and Regulation Z, the Court of Appeals had no ground for displacing the Federal Reserve staff's expert judgment.

Accordingly, we decide that the Court of Appeals erred in rejecting the views of the Federal Reserve Board and staff. . . .

Ford Motor Credit Co. v. Milhollin, 444 U.S. 555, 562–70 (1980).

Pursuant to the 1980 amendments, the FRB comprehensively revised Regulation Z. In connection with this revision the staff adopted a lengthy "Official Staff Commentary" to replace the official Board Interpretations, the official staff interpretations, and the unofficial staff interpretations issued under the original Regulation Z. This Commentary appears as Supplement I to Regulation Z. The staff periodically revises the Commentary, but no longer issues formal or informal interpretations. The courts continue to defer to it. E.g., Cowen v. Bank United, 70 F.3d 937, 943 (7th Cir.1995).

B. SCOPE OF THE TRUTH-IN-LENDING ACT

Despite its title the Truth-in-Lending Act applies to sales as well as loans. With respect to both sales and loans, however, the Act is limited to credit transactions between "consumers" and "creditors." These terms are common enough, but understanding their precise *statutory* meaning is critical to the application of the Act.

PROBLEMS

1. *Seller* agrees to sell her house to *Buyer* for $60,000. *Buyer* can pay $10,000 down, but needs to borrow the rest. A bank is willing to loan him $42,000, but not the other $8,000. So *Seller* agrees to finance the $8,000 herself, i.e. she will let *Buyer* pay it in monthly installments. They agree on 14% interest. Does *Seller* have to give the disclosures required by section 128? See section 103.

[handwritten: No, not a creditor]

What if the $8,000 loan is made by the real estate agency that *Buyer* employed to help him find the house?

[handwritten: It depends]

What if instead the real estate agent refers *Buyer* to a lender who specializes in second mortgage loans: does the real estate agent have to comply with the Act?

[handwritten: No.]

2. *Attorney* agrees to represent *Consumer*, who is being prosecuted for robbery. *Consumer* cannot pay the entire $3,000 fee at once, so *Attorney* says he may pay it in installments. To ensure payment, however, *Attorney* requires him to give a security interest in his house. Must *Attorney* comply with the Truth-in-Lending Act? If the purpose of disclosure is to facilitate comparative shopping, *should* she be required to make disclosures?

If you conclude that *Attorney* need not comply, assume that *Attorney's* fee agreement provides that if *Consumer* does not pay an installment within 30 days of receiving a bill, he will have to pay a service charge of 1½% per month. Does this additional fact affect your conclusion? What other facts would be helpful in answering this question?

3. *Appliance Co.* borrows $12,000 from *Bank* to buy a new delivery truck. Must *Bank* make the disclosures?

Would it matter if the loan were made to Bill Adams, the sole owner of the appliance company?

4. *Consumer,* an insurance broker, agrees to buy a Chagall painting for $60,000. To pay for it, she borrows $30,000 from *Bank*. Must *Bank* make the disclosures?

What if she borrows the $30,000 in connection with her purchase of an eight-unit apartment building, and she intends to occupy one unit and rent the other seven?

Would it matter if the property were a duplex instead of an apartment building? If she were a real estate agent instead of an insurance broker?

*[handwritten: * yes % c they are a bank]*

5. *Consumer* bought a house in 1995, in connection with which she borrowed $100,000 from *FirstBank* at 8.5%. *FirstBank* gave the disclosures required by the Truth-in-Lending Act. The balance on the loan is now $85,000.

a. *Consumer* refinances this loan by borrowing $85,000 from *Second-Bank* at 7%. Must *SecondBank* give the Truth-in-Lending disclosures?

[handwritten: Yes]

b. Assume instead that in 1999 *Consumer* moved into a condominium and since then has rented the house to a series of tenants. If she now refinances (still with a balance of $85,000), does the answer change:

[handwritten: Not for P, F, H] For Bus so NO]

[handwritten: always look to purpose of loan.]

must *SecondBank* give the disclosures in connection with the refinancing?

c. Now assume that *Consumer*, who is still living in the house, needs to borrow $40,000 for her business, a greeting card store. Since the house is now worth $200,000 and the balance of the loan is $85,000, she has more than $100,000 equity in the house, and *SecondBank* is willing to loan the money to *Consumer*, at 9.5%. But *SecondBank* does not make second-mortgage loans. Therefore, *Consumer* borrows $125,000 from *SecondBank*, pays off the $85,000 debt to *FirstBank*, and uses $40,000 in her business. Must *SecondBank* give the disclosures?

[handwritten margin notes: You could argue either way / 226.1(c) / Hybrid / but "primarily for" / But Exemption: 226.3(b) No disclosure]

C. TIMING OF THE DISCLOSURE

To effectuate the shopping function of the Truth-in-Lending Act, it would seem that the disclosures should be made while the consumer is still shopping. Yet the statute and regulations only require that the disclosures in closed-end transactions be made "before consummation of the transaction." Regulation Z § 226.17(b). This means that the disclosures may be made contemporaneously with the execution of the contract documents. In most cases, however, by the time the parties sit down to sign the documents, the consumer is done shopping and is psychologically so committed to the deal that he or she will sign no matter what the Truth-in-Lending Act disclosure statement reveals. What rationale is there for permitting the creditor to delay making disclosures until so late in the transaction? Does this delay undermine the whole purpose of the Act? Please draft a regulation that would make the disclosures available at a more useful time. See Landers & Rohner, A Functional Analysis of Truth In Lending, 26 U.C.L.A.L.Rev. 711, 734–37 (1977); Whitford, The Functions of Disclosure Regulation in Consumer Transactions, 1973 Wis.L.Rev. 400, 442–44, 448–52.

Consumer acceptance of automated teller machines (ATMs) has spawned the development of automated loan machines (ALMs), located in supermarkets, shopping malls, and elsewhere. By entering specified information into the machine, the consumer triggers a lender's (automated) evaluation of his or her creditworthiness and the loan is approved or denied. According to a newspaper article, "If your application is approved, you 'sign' for the loan with an inkless pen on an electronic pad. The machine takes your photograph and issues a note, disclosure statement and check for the approved amount. . . ." Jeffrey, Attention Shoppers: Get a Loan While Picking Up Groceries, Wall St. J., Dec. 20, 1995, p. C1. Does this comply with section 128(b)(1) and Regulation Z section 226.17(b)?

Regulation Z also requires that the disclosures be made "in a form that the consumer may keep." Regulation Z § 226.17(a)(1). Reading this requirement together with the requirement that disclosures be made "before consummation," courts hold that the creditor must give the disclosures in such a way that the consumer has them even if he or she decides not to consummate the transaction. E.g., Polk v. Crown Auto, Inc., 221 F.3d 691 (4th Cir.2000). This certainly facilitates the shopping function, but it is troublesome to sellers that do not have fixed prices, e.g., most automobile dealers. They are most reluctant to let a customer leave the showroom with a document showing the negotiated price of the car and the terms of the financing, because they fear the customer will show this information to a competitor and invite the competitor to offer a better deal. Is there any way for a seller to comply with the Act without also placing itself at a competitive disadvantage?

In a large percentage of automobile purchases, the consumer obtains financing from the dealer. This is convenient, but often it is unwise because the consumer could obtain better terms from a bank or other financial institution. In most of these transactions the dealer does not intend to keep the contract and receive monthly payments from the consumer. Rather, the dealer intends to sell the contract to a financial institution so that the dealer receives the full purchase price at the outset and the consumer makes monthly payments to the financial institution. Sometimes the dealer will have a commitment from a financial institution by the time the consumer has contracted to purchase the car. Sometimes, however, this commitment only comes later. When this is the case, the dealer uses forms in the contract with the consumer which provide that the deal is contingent on the approval of a financial institution and which obligate the consumer to return the car if there is no approval. At what point must the dealer give the Truth-in-Lending disclosures: when the consumer signs the contract or when the financial institution approves it? To meet the objectives of the Act, when *should* the disclosures be made?

D. CONTENT OF THE DISCLOSURE

The specific disclosures to be made depend on the nature of the credit. Thus the statute and regulations have separate sections governing open-end credit (§ 127, Regulation Z §§ 226.5–226.16), closed-end credit (§ 128, Regulation Z §§ 226.17–226.24), and leases (§ 182, Regulation M, 12 C.F.R. §§ 213.1–213.9). Since the requirements of these sections are not identical, it is essential to determine the nature of the transaction.

Credit may be either closed end or open end. Closed-end credit typically contemplates a single extension of credit in which the consumer's payments cause a steady decline in the amount of the debt. Open-end credit, on the other hand, contemplates a series of transactions in which the total amount of indebtedness may not exceed a limit established by the creditor. The consumer may repay the debt either in full or in installments, and as the consumer reduces the debt, additional credit is available. For this reason, open-end credit is also known as revolving credit. The Truth-in-Lending Act defines open-end credit in section 103(i) and in Regulation Z section 226.2(a)(20).

Sections 127–28 and Regulation Z sections 226.6–226.9 and 226.18 state the specific disclosures required for open-end credit and for closed-end credit, respectively. In what ways do the required disclosures differ? Is there any justification for the differences in requirements? As a creditor, which set of disclosures would you prefer to make?

(1) CLOSED-END CREDIT

The Truth-in-Lending Act requires the seller to make specified disclosures when the consumer either is obligated to pay a finance charge or has the privilege of paying for a purchase in more than four installments (Regulation Z §§ 226.2(a)(17)(i), 226.18)). (And one of the terms that the seller must disclose is the finance charge (§ 226.18(d)). Hence, it is essential to determine the amount of the finance charge.

PROBLEMS AND NOTES

1.   Problem. *Health Spa* sells one-year memberships for $30 per month. Purchasers may make monthly payments for a year or they may pay $360 in a lump sum in advance. How must *Health Spa* disclose the finance charge? See section 226.4. Would it be relevant to know what percentage of *Spa's* customers pay in a lump sum?

Would it matter if *Spa* routinely assigns its contracts to *Financer* for $330? Compare Yazzie v. Reynolds, 623 F.2d 638 (10th Cir.1980); Glaire v. LaLanne–Paris Health Spa, Inc., 528 P.2d 357 (Cal.1974).

Would it matter if *Spa* offers a $10 discount to those customers who pay in a lump sum?

2.   Problem. *Bank* finances *Consumer's* purchase of a used car by loaning her $6,000. In connection with this loan, *Bank* requires *Consumer* to hire one of seven specified attorneys to prepare a document that gives *Bank* a security interest in the car. *Consumer* selects one of the seven, who charges $50. *Bank* increases the loan to $6,050 and pays the attorney out of the proceeds of the loan. Is the $50 within the definition of "finance charge"?

3.   Problem. *Manufacturer* promotes its automobiles by advertising that the consumer may choose either a $1,000 rebate or 2% financing. *Consumer* purchases a car and finances it through *Manufacturer Credit Corporation*, which discloses the annual percentage rate as 2.0%. Has *MCC* violated the Act by failing to include the $1,000 rebate in the finance charge?

4.   In addition to disclosing "finance charge," the creditor must disclose the "annual percentage rate." For any given amount of finance charge, the annual percentage rate varies with the duration of the extension of credit. Usually it is easy to determine the duration of the debt. But "usually" is not "always."

Problem. *TaxPrep Services* prepares tax returns and offers to make a loan to any of its customers who are entitled to an income tax refund from the IRS. Under this program, for a flat fee of $89 *TaxPrep's* customers receive an amount equal to their refunds within two days after signing their tax returns instead of having to wait the 2–3 weeks it would take to receive the refund from the IRS. The customer completes an IRS form directing the IRS to deposit the refund by electronic transfer to an account in the customer's name at a bank designated by *TaxPrep,* and *TaxPrep* is repaid by the funds in that account.

On February 1 *Consumer* signs her tax return and completes an application for a loan in the amount of the refund that the IRS will be sending. *TaxPrep* approves the loan and tells *Consumer* to come in for her check. In addition to the check, she receives the Truth-in-Lending disclosure statement and signs the loan agreement, which obligates her to repay the loan on demand. The disclosure statement lists the annual percentage rate as 2.4%, which is accurate if the duration of the loan is one year, but is inaccurate if the duration is 2–3 weeks. Has *TaxPrep* accurately disclosed the annual percentage rate? See Reg. Z § 226.17(c)(5).

5. The Truth-in-Lending Act and Regulation Z require numerous other disclosures in addition to finance charge and annual percentage rate.

Problem. *Consumer* contracts to buy a duplex from *Seller* for $50,000, contingent on her being able to obtain suitable financing. *Consumer* talks to *Lender* and, after *Lender* investigates the proposed transaction, obtains a commitment from *Lender* to loan her $40,000 at 9.1% interest, to be secured by a mortgage. At the closing *Seller* gives *Consumer* the deed; *Lender* and *Consumer* sign the loan documents; *Lender* gives *Consumer* a check for $38,615; and *Consumer* gives *Seller* the check for $38,615 and also her own check for $11,385. The loan documents between *Consumer* and *Lender* obligate *Consumer* to repay $40,000 plus interest, to give *Lender* a mortgage on the property, and to maintain insurance on the property. Included among the documents is the following:

TRUTH IN LENDING DISCLOSURE STATEMENT

Amount of credit		40,000
Less: loan fee	1200	
title exam	75	
credit report	30	
termite report	20	
appraisal fee	50	
photo of prop.	10	
		1,385
Cash received		38,615
Amount repayable		40,000

Plus 9% annual interest on the declining balance, repayable in 240 monthly installments of $364.00, due on the first day of each month.

Bank has a security interest in the property being purchased with the proceeds of this loan.

In the event of default in any payment, Bank may impose a delinquency fee and and may declare the entire balance immediately due. Borrower is liable for Bank's reasonable attorney's fees of 15% of the amount in default. Borrower may prepay the loan at any time. If Borrower prepays during the first five years, there is a prepayment penalty of 3% of the principal amount of the loan at the time of prepayment. If Borrower prepays after the first five years, there is no prepayment penalty.

In what respects, if any, has *Bank* violated the Truth-in-Lending Act? (You may assume that $364 represents the monthly payment required to pay off a 20–year loan of $40,000 at 9.1%.)

Other federal statutes also require disclosure in connection with housing. Real Estate Settlement Procedures Act, 12 U.S.C. §§ 2601 et seq.; Interstate Land Sales Full Disclosure Act, 15 U.S.C. §§ 1701 et seq. The Real Estate Settlement Procedures Act (RESPA) requires the lender to disclose the cost of certain settlement services, such as title examinations, property surveys, and credit reports. The lender must make a good faith estimate of these costs and deliver that estimate, along with other specified information, within three days after the borrower applies for a loan. 12 U.S.C. § 2604(c)-(d); Regulation X, 24 C.F.R. § 3500.6(a). On the day of closing, the lender must provide a final statement of these costs.

The Truth-in-Lending Act applies to many more kinds of lenders and transactions than RESPA does, but the two statutes do overlap. For transactions within the scope of both acts, the Truth-in-Lending Act defers to RESPA (§ 128(b)(2), Regulation Z § 226.19).

6. Problem. *Consumer* purchases a satellite TV system from *Seller* for $1,150, pursuant to a contract whose front side appears below. Has *Seller* violated the Truth-in-Lending Act? (You may assume that 17.25% accurately represents the annual percentage rate.)

Seller

444 Mainline Dr.

Seller hereby agrees to sell the following items to __*Consumer*__ (hereinafter referred to as Customer):

Qty	Description	Unit Price	Price
1	Satellite System Avanti XL	1150	1150.00
	Extended Protection Plan		300.00
	Subtotal		$1450.00
	Tax		58.00
	Total		$1508.00
	Downpayment		$158.00
	Balance		$1350.00
	Finance Charge		$134.29

Federal Truth-in-Lending Act Disclosure Statement

ANNUAL PERCENTAGE RATE The cost of your credit as a yearly rate.	FINANCE CHARGE The dollar amount the credit will cost you.
17.25%	$134.29

Amount Financed The amount of credit provided to you or on your behalf.	Total of Payments The amount you will have paid after you have made all payments as scheduled.	Total Sale Price The total cost of your purchase on credit, including your downpayment of $158
$1350.00	$1484.29	$1642.29

Seller affirms that the above items are free of defects. *Seller* will repair or replace defective parts in accordance with the terms of the Warranty delivered at the time of purchase.

Customer agrees to pay a total of __$1484.29__ in __12__ monthly installments of __$123.70__ and 1 installment of _____. In the event of default by Customer, Seller shall be entitled to repossess the above-described items, wheresoever located.

This agreement is subject to the terms and conditions on the reverse, which are incorporated and made part of this agreement.

Read this agreement before you sign it, and do not sign if it contains any blank spaces.

Payment Schedule: __12__ payments of __$123.70__ due on __the 1st of each month commencing 3/1/03__

Default: If payment is late, there will be a charge of $5 or 5% of the payment, whichever is less.

Prepayment: If the obligation is paid off early, you will be entitled to a rebate calculated according to the Rule of 78's.

Refer to the reverse side of this contract for additional information about your rights and obligations.

Itemization of Amount Financed:

Unpaid balance of Avanti System	$1050.00
Amounts paid others: Extended Protection Plan	300.00
Prepaid finance charge:	
Total:	$1350.00

Signed this __1st__ day of __February__, __2009.__

__*Seller*__
Seller

__*Consumer*__
Customer

7. Some additional facts for Problem 6: the Extended Protection Plan (EPP) is a product of *Universal Service Co.*, an entity with no ownership connection to *Seller*. In the event that the satellite system needs repairs during the first three years of *Consumer's* ownership, *Universal* will repair it at no additional cost. *Universal* authorizes *Seller* to sell the EPP, at a recommended price of $300, and pays *Seller* a commission for doing so. The commission for each sale is $120, which *Seller* collects simply by sending Universal $180. Should these facts affect the answer to Problem 6?

8. In Problem 6, assume that after making seven payments of $123.70, *Consumer* is short of cash and sends in a check for $50. *Seller* sends *Consumer* a letter informing her of the default and assessing a delinquency charge of $3.69 (5% of $73.70). Has *Seller* violated the Truth-in-Lending Act?

If the answer is no, would it change if the state retail installment sales act limits default or delinquency charges to the lesser of $3 or 3% of the delinquency?

9. *Consumer* contracts to purchase a two-year old Mercedes from *Dealer*, trading in his six-year-old Acura. The guidebook value of the Acura is $8,000, but *Consumer* still owes $10,000 to the bank that six years earlier had loaned him the money to buy it. The price of the Mercedes is $28,000, and *Consumer* needs to finance the purchase. If *Dealer* were to take the trade-in and sell it for $8,000, *Consumer* would have to come up with $2,000 to pay off the balance of the bank loan. One way to generate this $2,000 is to roll the $2,000 debt into the financing of the Mercedes. To do this, *Dealer* adds $2,000 to the price of the Mercedes, so that when a financial institution buys the contract from *Dealer*, *Dealer* receives $2,000 more than the amount for which she agreed to sell the car to *Consumer*. *Dealer* can use the extra $2,000 (along with the proceeds from the sale of the trade-in) to pay off the bank. So *Dealer* tells *Consumer* she will allow him $10,000 on the trade-in and add $2,000 to the price of the Mercedes. *Dealer* gives a disclosure statement that states the amount financed as $30,450 and lists the Itemization of Amount Financed as:

I.	Total Cash Price		
	A.	Cash price	$30,000
	B.	Doc prep	200
	C.	Sales tax on (A + B)	2,340
	D.	Luxury tax	N/A
	E.	Service contract	N/A
	F.	Prior balance paid by seller	N/A
Total Cash Price			$32,540
II.	Total Down Payment		
	A.	Gross trade-in	$10,000
		Less balance due	10,000
		Net trade-in	$ 0
	B.	Manufacturer rebate	N/A
	C.	Cash	3,000
Total Down Payment			$3,000
III.	Amount Financed (I–II)		$29,540

Has *Dealer* complied with the Act?

(2) OPEN-END CREDIT

The preceding problems concern closed-end credit. Other sections of the Act govern disclosures in connection with open-end credit. These sections establish a multi-tiered system of disclosure. In recognition of the ineffectiveness of disclosures that occur only after a consumer has become committed to a transaction, Congress amended the Act in 1988 to require an initial set of disclosures when the creditor first solicits the consumer to apply for open-end credit. Among the required first-tier disclosures are the annual percentage rate; any annual fee; any grace period between the time of purchase and the time the finance charge begins to accrue; and the method of computing the balance on which the finance charge is assessed. See Regulation Z section 226.5a(b) and Appendix G, Forms G–10(A),–10(B). If the credit is secured by the consumer's residence, the requirements appear in section 226.5b. See Appendix G, Forms G–14(A),–14(B).

The second-tier disclosures must occur before the consumer's first loan or purchase under the plan. Many of them are the same as the first-tier disclosures. See Regulation Z section 226.6(a)-(d). If the credit is secured by the consumer's home, the creditor also must disclose the information specified in section 226.6(e).

The third-tier disclosures must occur at the end of each billing cycle. Section 226.7 governs their content. Still additional disclosures are required annually and whenever the creditor renews the consumer's account or makes certain changes in the terms of the plan. See section 226.9.

The disclosures for open-end credit differ from the disclosures for closed-end credit. They differ in number, with many more items of information required for closed-end credit. And they differ in nature, with more specific information concerning the cost of credit required for closed-end credit. For example, in a closed-end credit transaction, the creditor must disclose the dollar amount of the finance charge. In an open-end transaction, however, since the consumer may defer payment or may pay the entire balance at any time, the creditor does not know at the time of formation of the contract the total amount of finance charge the consumer will pay. Accordingly, the Act does not require the creditor to disclose it then. Rather, the creditor must disclose it when it is imposed, at the end of the billing cycle. See section 226.7(f).

The differences between the disclosures required for open- and closed-end credit provide an incentive for creditors to structure their transactions as open end. To qualify as open-end credit—and the relaxed disclosure requirements—however, the transaction must satisfy the definition of "open-end credit" in the statute and regulation.

Problem. *Consumer* purchases a new car from *Dealer*. The price of the car is $19,500, and *Consumer* makes a downpayment of $4,000. The contract provides that *Consumer* is to make monthly payments of at least

$310, but may make larger payments if she wishes, even to the extent of paying the entire balance. The finance charge is 1½% per month, computed on the unpaid balance at the end of each month. The contract also provides that from time to time *Consumer* may make additional credit purchases of accessories, repairs, or routine servicing from *Dealer*, in which event the amount of the new credit will be added to the existing unpaid balance.

Is this open-end or closed-end credit?

If you believe this transaction is closed-end credit, what does it take to be open-end credit? If you believe the transaction is open-end credit, why don't all retailers adopt this form? (Compare section 226.6(a)(2) with section 226.18(d), (e), (h), (j).)

Benion v. Bank One

United States District Court, Northern District of Illinois, 1997.
967 F.Supp. 1031, aff'd 144 F.3d 1056 (7th Cir.), cert. denied, 525 U.S. 963 (1998).

CASTILLO, DISTRICT JUDGE.

Plaintiffs Harry and Patricia Benion have brought this class action suit against Bank One, Dayton, N.A., Echo Acceptance Corporation, and Superior Satellite, Inc., alleging violations of the Truth In Lending Act ("TILA"). . . . Bank One and Echo have moved for summary judgment pursuant to Fed. R. Civ. P. 56. Superior has filed a piggyback motion for summary judgment, arguing that if summary judgment is granted in favor of Bank One and Echo, it cannot be liable either. . . .

RELEVANT FACTS

In February 1995, the Benions visited a Sam's Club store in which a salesman for Superior Satellite, a local consumer electronics retailer, was demonstrating and selling satellite television systems. Patricia Benion—like many Chicagoans, an avid sports fan—was entranced by the astounding number of sports games available with a satellite television system. On the spot, the Benions agreed to purchase a satellite television system for $4,297.52. In addition to a satellite dish, roof mount, and various free accessories, the sale included one year's worth of programming (the most expensive programming package available, so that Patricia Benion could be sure to get all her games) which cost $996.00 by itself. When Patricia Benion expressed doubt that her credit rating was good enough to enable her to make this purchase, the salesman suggested that she apply for an EchoStar Revolving Charge Plan. The Benions signed the application for the charge plan without reading it. The parties disagree about what information the Benions were given about the charge plan before they signed the application. A charge account was opened for the Benions with a credit limit of $4,500.00, a few hundred dollars above the amount of their first purchases. There is no evidence of whether it is typical that the credit limits on EchoStar accounts are set just above the amount of the first purchases.

The application completed by the Benions was for the EchoStar Revolving Charge Plan ("Plan"), a private label credit card offered by Bank One, a national bank with its principal place of business in Dayton, Ohio. Bank One began issuing this credit card in 1994 through an agreement with Echo Acceptance Corporation, a consumer finance company specializing in arranging credit for the sales of equipment and programming related to satellite television systems. Once an account under the Plan is opened for a consumer, the consumer is issued a plastic credit card that may be used to make purchases at any Echo authorized dealer, of which there are several hundred throughout the country, or to order products or television programming directly from Echo or programming packagers. Authorized dealers sell satellite dishes, receivers, accessories, and programming distributed by EchoStar Communications Corporation, and also typically stock other consumer electronics products including televisions, VCRs, and stereo equipment. Superior Satellite is one such authorized dealer. According to instructions issued to Echo dealers, a satellite receiver must be included in the first purchase a consumer makes using the new credit card. The initial purchase of a satellite receiver, related equipment, and installation generally totals between $2,000 and $4,000, although a low-cost satellite dish standing alone can cost as little as $199.

The EchoStar Revolving Charge Plan is set up much as any other credit card account. A consumer may make purchases using the card up to the credit limit set for the account. Paying part or all of the outstanding balance on the account replenishes the available credit to the extent of the payment. Bank One periodically imposes a finance charge on outstanding balances. Consumers receive monthly statements listing the outstanding balance, the minimum payment due on that balance, and the amount of remaining available credit. When enrolling in the Plan, consumers are supposed to receive all disclosures required by TILA for open-end credit plans, although the plaintiffs state that they did not receive such disclosures when they signed up for the EchoStar plan.

The central issue in all of the pending motions for summary judgment is whether, in deciding to structure the EchoStar plan as a credit card plan, Bank One reasonably expected that consumers would continue to make purchases using the EchoStar card over time. Many of the parties' factual submissions relate to this issue. Fairly summarized, the submissions show that Bank One viewed repeat sales as a goal of the Plan, and genuinely believed that the credit card would encourage repeat sales to a relatively captive consumer base. Bank One planned to encourage such sales through advertising enclosed with the monthly account statements, as well as through other promotions.

Before entering into the agreement with Echo to create the Plan, Bank One reviewed sales data from a similar private label credit card plan that another company, Household Retail Services, had operated in conjunction with Echo. In 1993, there were 30,420 first-time purchases made under the Household plan, and 4,260 repeat purchases through the plan. Thus, 12.3% of all purchases made using the Household plan in 1993 were repeat purchases. The plaintiffs point out that these repeat sales only amounted to 2.3% of the income from purchases under the plan. For the first five months of 1994, repeat purchases were 17% of all Household plan purchases; these repeat purchases accounted for 3.8% of the dollar amount produced by sales under the plan. The above figures do not reflect accounts opened under the plan that were never used for any purchases.

After the inception of the Bank One/EchoStar Revolving Charge Account plan in November 1994, Bank One included advertisements for Echo products and programming packages in its monthly statements to consumers. In its instructions to Echo dealers, Bank One also encouraged the dealers to promote the availability of the credit card for future purchases. Whether as a result of these promotions or for some other reason, consumers have made some additional purchases using their EchoStar credit cards. In April 1995, repeat sales were 6.97% of all sales under the Plan. One year later, repeat sales accounted for 11.40% of the sales under the Plan. . . . By August 1996, 51,476 accounts had been opened under the Plan. Just under 60% of the accounts had been used to finance a purchase; a little over 40% had never been used. Of the 30,673 accounts that had been used for at least one purchase, 6,356 had also been used for an additional purchase. Thus, 12.3% of all accounts (active and inactive), or 20.7% of the active accounts, had been used for repeat purchases. A random sample of 75 repeat purchases made between March 1995 and May 1996 shows that 29% of the repeat purchases were for programming packages. Repairs or parts accounted for almost one quarter of the "add-on" sales. Another 25% was for satellite-related equipment such as additional receivers, remote controls, or surge protectors. The remaining purchases were stereo or sound equipment, televisions, VCRs, extended warranties, and programming guides.

LEGAL STANDARDS

Summary judgment is proper only if the record shows that there is no genuine issue as to any material fact and that the moving party is entitled to judgment as a matter of law. Fed. R. Civ. P. 56(c). A genuine issue for trial exists only when "the evidence is such that a reasonable jury could return a verdict for the nonmoving party." The court must view all evidence in the light most favorable to the nonmoving party and draw all inferences in the nonmovant's favor. In making its decision, the court's sole function is to determine whether sufficient evidence exists to support a verdict in the nonmovant's favor. Credibility determinations, weighing evidence, and drawing reasonable inferences are jury functions, not those of a judge when deciding a motion for summary judgment.

. . .

ANALYSIS

TILA sets out two different types of credit that may be extended to consumers: open-end credit (the prototypical example is a credit card account), and closed-end credit, such as a car loan or other retail installment contract. Those who extend credit to consumers are responsible under TILA for knowing the difference between the two and making the appropriate mandatory disclosures to consumers. The regulation applicable to TILA (known as Regulation Z) requires that closed-end disclosures be made unless the credit at issue qualifies as an open-end plan. Among other things, closed-end disclosures must include the total amount financed, including both the sale price and the total amount of interest that will be paid, the length of time over which payments may be made, the amount of each installment payment and the intervals between payments, and the amount of any finance charges. These disclosures must be made at the point of sale.

The disclosures required for open-end accounts are somewhat less onerous. They may be contained in a pre-printed form given to consumers before the account is opened, telling them (among other things) the annual percentage rate of interest charged on the account, and the nature and amount of any finance charges. Creditors have considerable incentive to structure credit in an open-end form if they can, both because the disclosures are less burdensome to provide, and because "they fear that certain closed-end credit disclosures, such as the total dollar amount of finance charge, the total of payments, and 'total sale price' might engender consumer resistance to the sale." However, creditors may only treat a credit plan as open-end if it qualifies as such under TILA regulations. The plaintiffs contend that TILA required that the EchoStar Plan be structured as a closed-end credit plan, and that Bank One and Echo violated TILA by failing to provide them with closed-end disclosures.

The regulations define "open-end credit" as having the following three characteristics:

(i) The creditor reasonably contemplates repeated transactions;

(ii) The creditor may impose a finance charge from time to time on an outstanding unpaid balance; and

(iii) The amount of credit that may be extended to the consumer during the term of the plan (up to any limit set by the creditor) is generally made available to the extent that any outstanding balance is repaid.

12 C.F.R. § 226.2(a)(20). Closed-end credit is defined as any consumer credit other than open-end credit. Id., § 226.2(a)(10). The parties agree that the EchoStar Plan had the latter two characteristics of open-end credit. The dispute is over the first requirement—whether Bank One and Echo "reasonably contemplated" that consumers would make repeated purchases under the Plan.

The only guidance to the intended meaning of "reasonably contemplate" is contained in the Official Staff Commentary to Regulation Z, located at 12 C.F.R. Part 226, Supplement I:

. . . . Reasonably contemplate repeated transactions . . . means that the credit plan must be usable from time to time and the creditor must legitimately expect that there will be repeat business rather than a one-time credit extension. The creditor must expect repeated dealings with the consumer under the credit plan as a whole, and need not believe the consumer will reuse a particular feature of the plan. A standard based on reasonable belief by a creditor necessarily includes some margin for judgmental error. The fact that a particular consumer does not return for further credit extensions does not prevent a plan from having been properly characterized as open-end.

Id., § 2(a)(20)–3. The Commentary goes on to provide the following examples: (1) a thrift institution chartered for the benefit of its members could more reasonably expect repeat credit extensions than a seller of aluminum siding; and (2) a bank could reasonably make a loan for a consumer to purchase a car under a line of credit, whereas a car dealer could not reasonably sell a car under an open-end plan (because it is much less likely that the car dealer will have frequent regular repeat business from the same car buyer). Id.

Although the Commentary uses big-ticket items such as a home improvement or a car as examples of appropriate subjects for closed-end credit, the overall focus of the regulations is clearly on the likelihood of repeated purchases, not on the amount financed. Aluminum siding, which often carries a "lifetime guarantee," is unlikely to be purchased again and again by the same consumer. Likewise, the average American often goes years between purchasing cars. It is not merely that these items are expensive, but that they usually involve a "one-time credit extension" that makes them appropriate for closed-end financing.

In considering whether repeated transactions are likely, we are to consider the nature of the creditor's business and the relationship between the creditor and the consumer. Id. Here, the relevant "business" is that of the Echo-approved retailers, which provide the only places that an Echo-Star credit card may be used. These retailers sell a variety of consumer electronics; although the product line that is most important for the Plan's purposes is satellite-related products and programming, the retailers generally sell other popular audio/video equipment including televisions, VCRs, and stereo equipment. Echo and its dealers also sell satellite television programming, another product that must be bought or renewed at regular intervals. Because these dealers carry a wide array of products that are appealing to consumers, as well as television programming that regularly expires and must be renewed, we find that the nature of the business supports the hypothesis that repeat sales are likely. The relationship between the creditor/retailers and the consumer also makes repeat sales likely: although it is certainly possible that a consumer who buys something at an Echo-approved dealer will never enter those doors again, it is not unreasonable to suppose that a consumer visits a particular retailer because it is conveniently located, has good products or prices, or for some other reason that would remain equally valid over time. The number and accessibility of Echo-approved dealers—over 750 dealers across the country—also affects the likelihood of future purchases under the Plan, since consumers who relocate may still be able to use the Plan credit card to make purchases.

The Household Retail sales data also support Bank One's judgment that repeat credit sales were sufficiently likely to warrant adopting an open-end plan. The data showed repeat sales of between 12 and 17 percent of total sales.[2] While these figures are not overwhelming evidence that repeat sales were likely under Bank One's similar Plan, they do not make it unreasonable as a matter of law to structure the Plan as open-end rather than closed-end credit. This conclusion is buttressed by Regulation Z's requirement that creditors be given some leeway for judgmental error in predicting the likelihood of repeated transactions.

Finally, although this factor standing alone would not be persuasive, Bank One was not unreasonable in taking its own plans to aggressively encourage repeat purchases into account in deciding whether repeat sales were likely. Bank One set up marketing plans, including the use of inserts in its monthly statements to EchoStar credit card holders, that appear to have been genuinely calculated to produce future purchases. The results since the EchoStar Plan was initiated demonstrate that repeat sales in fact occur: over 20% of the Plan's active accounts have been used for repeat purchases.

The plaintiffs do not argue with these facts, although they do dispute the weight to be assigned them. The plaintiffs' central contention is that the Plan is falsely set up as an open-end plan when it should really be a closed-end plan because it involves the purchase of big-ticket goods. Indeed, the instructions to retailers require that a satellite television system—an item that typically costs between $2,000 and $4,000—be among the first purchases made upon opening an EchoStar credit account. The plaintiffs are correct in suggesting that frequent repeat sales of satellite television systems themselves are unlikely, as consumers are not likely to want more than one of these. And, in many ways the use of a credit card to purchase items costing several thousand dollars undermines the goals of TILA because it makes it easier for consumers to finance large purchases on credit without truly realizing the costs associated with that credit.

Nevertheless, it is clear that under the law as it is presently written, the legitimate expectation of repeat sales, and not the probability that consumers may plunge deeply into debt without realizing the finance charges they will pay, is the test for whether credit should be considered open-end or closed-end. Although the requirement that the EchoStar credit card must be first used to make a large, one-time purchase is an unusual feature for a credit card account, we cannot see that it removes the account from the category of open-end credit plans or otherwise violates TILA.

---

2. It is true that these repeat sales accounted for less than 5% of the total revenue from sales under the Household plan. However, there is no requirement in TILA or Regu- lation Z that the repeat sales amount to a certain threshold percentage of the creditor's/retailer's income.

: . . . We therefore grant summary judgment in the defendants' favor on the plaintiffs' TILA claim.

. . .

QUESTIONS AND NOTES

1.   Open-end credit plans typically require the consumer to make a payment each month in an amount equal to a stated percentage of the current outstanding balance. A common figure is 2%. Assume that the initial balance in *Benion* were $4,000 and that the Plan called for an annual percentage rate of 18%. If the Benions were to make the minimum monthly payment, how long do you suppose it would take them to pay off the entire amount? How much finance charge would they pay?

2.   In the second paragraph of its opinion, the court says there is no evidence whether it was typical for the creditor to set the credit limit at an amount barely large enough to accommodate the purchase of the satellite system. What would be the relevance of this evidence?

3.   In the fifth paragraph the court states that "Bank One viewed repeat sales as a goal of the Plan, and genuinely believed that the credit card sales would encourage repeat sales. . . ." What is the relevance of this belief?

4.   The court observes that Bank One required that the account be opened only in connection with the purchase of the big-ticket satellite system and not in connection with just other lower-priced items that the retailer might sell. What is the relevance of this practice?

5.   What is the critical fact on which the definition of "open-end credit" depends? Please reconsider the passage "Legal Standards" concerning the requirements for granting a motion for summary judgment. Why did the court grant defendants' motion?

Would plaintiffs' case have been stronger if they had filed an affidavit in opposition to defendant's motion, affirming that they thought the transaction was closed end and they had no intention of buying anything else from any EchoStar dealer?

6.   Should it matter, when a consumer seeks to buy a VCR from Superior Satellite and charge it on the EchoStar credit card, that EchoStar requires the consumer to provide information such as place of employment, salary, and amount of indebtedness to other creditors? Should it matter if EchoStar obtains a report from a credit bureau?

7.   Plaintiffs responded to the trial court's decision by appealing to the Seventh Circuit Court of Appeals. At the oral argument plaintiffs' attorney informed the court that plaintiffs were not seeking a trial of the issue whether defendant reasonably contemplated repeat transactions. Rather, they had filed a motion for summary judgment with the trial court, and on appeal they wanted the court to reverse the trial court's denial of that motion. The Court of Appeals declined to grant this relief and affirmed the trial court's grant of summary judgment for defendant. The court stated:

> It is beyond contestation that the bank . . . hoped and expected, and *reasonably* expected, to have at least some repeat transactions with the holders of the EchoStar card. The card was usable at any dealer in a nationwide chain of dealers. Bank One had an aggressive marketing strategy designed to promote repeat purchases, which was very much in its financial self-interest. The bank had studied the performance of EchoStar's financing plan in an earlier incarnation and had obtained statistics which showed that repeat purchases had been an increasing fraction of total purchases under the plan. And, although we must not confuse hindsight with foresight, what actually happens is some evidence of what was reasonably expected to happen, and so it is relevant though not determinative to note that 20 percent of all holders of the EchoStar card issued by Bank One who used the card at least once (some never used it) made one or more additional purchases with the card after the initial purchase. The Benions bought only one year's worth of programming; it was likely that they would use the card to buy programming for the next year.

144 F.3d 1056, 1058 (7th Cir.1998).

Other courts continue to grapple with this definitional problem. For example, in Long v. Fidelity Water Systems, Inc., 2000 WL 760328 (N.D.Cal.2000), the evidence showed that only one percent of the accounts generated a repeat transaction in any given month. Further, the dollar volume of repeat transactions was less than three percent of the total volume of the customer accounts. The court denied a creditor's motion for summary judgment. On the other hand, in Speakman v. Household Retail Services, Inc., 1999 WL 515500 (N.D.Ill.1999), the court granted summary judgment when the evidence showed that defendant anticipated and enjoyed a repeat purchase rate of five percent. Which of these is more consistent with the guidance provided in the Official Staff Commentary excerpt quoted by the District Court in Benion?

8. In the preceding problems, the contracts all had fixed annual percentage rates. Many extensions of credit, however, have adjustable rates, tied to some index that varies with the general cost of obtaining funds. The Truth-in-Lending Act has specific disclosure requirements for these transactions. See Regulation Z sections 226.5b(d)(12)(f), 226.18(f). If the variable-rate credit is secured by the consumer's residence, there are additional requirements. See sections 226.19(b), 226.30.

9. The problems on pages 192–96 concern determination of the finance charge in closed-end transactions. Similar problems may arise in the context of open-end credit, too.

Problem. *Consumer* has a credit card issued by *Bank*. The credit limit on her account is $3,000. *Consumer* knows that the outstanding balance on the account is $2,880, but she wants to purchase a piece of furniture that costs $400. When she attempts to charge the purchase, the merchant's authorization device displays a message, "Verbal authorization required. Please call (800) 123–4567." The merchant calls, and a representative of *Bank* reviews *Consumer's* account and approves the transaction. *Consum-*

er's next billing statement contains an entry, "Over limit fee $39." So does each subsequent billing statement until the balance falls below $3,000. Must *Bank* include the over-the-limit fee in the amount it discloses as "finance charge"? Compare section 106(a) of the Act and section 226.4(a) of Regulation Z with section 226.4(c)(2) of Regulation Z.

10. As described in the introduction to this section, the Truth-in-Lending Act requires disclosures when a card issuer first solicits a consumer. One of the required disclosures is the fee, if any, "for the issuance or availability" of the card. Regulation Z § 226.5a(b)(2).

Problem. *Bank* sends a solicitation to a large number of consumers. "You have been pre-approved for a credit card. All you need to do is verify the information on the attached form, supply your annual income, and sign the form." The solicitation describes the terms of the account, including the interest rate, the minimum monthly payment, the grace period, the method of computing the monthly balance, and the absence of any annual fee. *Consumer* completes the form, returns it, and receives a credit card. He uses it for two months and then receives an enclosure with a monthly billing statement, informing him that because of rising interest rates the bank is going to impose an annual fee of $35, effective with the next billing statement. He comes to you for advice. What additional information, if any, would you like to have? What advice will you give? Would your advice be any different if *Bank* imposed the $35 fee after nine months rather than after three months?

(3) LEASES

As an alternative to acquiring goods for cash or on credit, consumers may acquire goods by lease. As originally enacted, the Truth-in-Lending Act did not require any disclosures in connection with consumer leases. The definition of "credit sale," however, included leases in which the lessee contracts to pay a sum substantially equal to the value of the leased property and will become owner of the property with no additional substantial payment. See section 103(g). Why should the definition of credit sale extend to this kind of lease?

In 1976 Congress amended the Act to require disclosures in connection with consumer leases. See sections 181–86. Although the courts typically refer to these sections as the "Consumer Leasing Act," they actually are part of the Truth-in-Lending Act. Note that the definition of credit sale in section 103 continues to include some leases. Should it? Why not apply the lease requirements to the kind of lease contemplated by section 103(g)? (Compare the requirements of section 128(a) and Regulation Z section 226.18 with those of section 182 and Regulation M section 213.4.)

Like credit, leases may be either closed end or open end. The closed-end lease is similar to the typical lease of real property: the consumer agrees to pay a fixed rent for a fixed period of time, at the end of which the consumer surrenders possession of the property. Under this kind of lease, the risk of unexpected depreciation (or appreciation) of the property during the term of the lease is on the lessor. If the property depreciates more than expected, the lessor bears the loss. The open-end lease transfers this risk to the consumer. In addition to providing a fixed rental for a fixed term, an open-end lease agreement stipulates the value the lessor expects the property to have at the end of the term of the lease. If the actual value is less than this stipulated value, the consumer must pay the difference. The lease may also provide that if the actual value exceeds the stipulated amount, the lessor will pay the excess to the consumer.[1]

Aside from the risk of greater than expected depreciation, what risk does an open-end lease pose for the consumer? Does section 182(4)-(5) adequately deal with this problem?

Perhaps because of these provisions, open-end leases are not common in consumer transactions.[2] Hence, for most consumer leases the consumer returns the item to the lessor and has no further liability.

The extension of credit is implicit in both open-end and closed-end leases. From the lessor's perspective, the lessor invests in the goods and allows the consumer to use them for a fixed period of time. At the end of this period, the lessor regains possession of the goods and sells them. To the extent the goods are worth less than the amount the lessor paid for them, the lessor wants to be compensated. In addition the lessor has committed its capital to this asset for the period of the lease, thereby costing it the amount it could have earned by using its capital in some other way. The lessor wants compensation for this, too. From the consumer's perspective, the consumer wants the use of the goods over the period of the lease, with no burden with respect to disposition of the goods at the end of the lease. The consumer also wants the convenience of periodic payments during the term of the lease. These periodic payments thus reflect the diminution in the value of the goods (i.e. depreciation) and the lessor's other costs of doing business (including profit).

Leases are used by consumers to acquire many kinds of goods, from appliances to computers to musical instruments. The most prevalent use of leases, however, is in connection with motor vehicles. The reason is plain: in a credit purchase the monthly payment reflects the full purchase price (less any downpayment). In a lease, however, the payment encompasses the depreciation of the vehicle, not its entire value, so the monthly payment on a lease is considerably less than the monthly payment on a credit purchase. Especially for expensive items, this difference enables consumers to acquire new goods rather than used goods. It also enables consumers to acquire more expensive versions of those goods. Thus it has been true for years that a majority of luxury cars are acquired by lease rather than purchase.

The terminology of the leasing industry differs from the terminology of the sales industry. For example, price becomes "capitalized cost"; downpay-

---

1. Under both forms of lease, the consumer is responsible for diminution in value resulting from improper use or care of the product.

2. They are, however, common in commercial transactions.

ment becomes "capitalized cost reduction"; interest rate becomes "money factor"; and interest becomes "rent charge." The estimated value of the goods at the end of the lease term is the "residual value." The depreciation for which the consumer pays is represented by the capitalized cost less the residual value. In promulgating the regulation governing disclosures in consumer lease transactions, the Federal Reserve Board has adopted many of the industry terms.[3]

QUESTIONS AND NOTES

1. Problem. *Consumer* decides to acquire a new car by means of a lease. After shopping around, he decides to buy a Mercury, with a manufacturer's suggested retail price of $21,500. To promote the vehicle, the manufacturer is offering a $1,000 rebate to any consumer who purchases or leases one. The dealer says that if *Consumer* assigns his rebate and makes a refundable security deposit, *Consumer* can lease the car for three years for $290 per month, with the option of buying it at the end of the lease for $11,500. For $300 *Dealer* will throw in a service contract that will pay for any repairs not covered by the manufacturer's warranty. *Consumer* and *Dealer* sign a lease, obligating *Consumer* to make the payments to *Leaseco. Dealer* gives *Consumer* the following disclosure statement.

3. When Congress amended the Truth-in-Lending Act in 1980, it did not amend the provisions governing leases. In revising Regulation Z to reflect the 1980 amendments, the Federal Reserve Board did not make any substantive changes in the leasing regulations, but it moved them out of Regulation Z and into newly created Regulation M. Congress still has not amended the sections that govern leases, but the Federal Reserve Board has extensively revised the regulations. The revised Regulation M appears in the Statutory Supplement.

Federal Consumer Lending Act Disclosures

Date Jan. 2, 2009

Amount Due at Lease Signing:	Monthly Payments	Other Charges (not part of your monthly payment)	Total Payments (The amount you will have paid by the end of the lease)
(Itemized below)*	Your first monthly payment of $310 is due on Jan. 2, 2009, followed by 35 payments of $310 due on the 1st of each month. The total of your monthly payments is $11,160.	Disposition fee (if you do not purchase the vehicle) $250 [Annual tax] — Total $250	$13,030
$1,655			

---

* Itemization of Amount Due at Lease Signing:

Amount Due At Lease Signing		How the Amount Due at Lease Signing will be paid:	
Capitalized cost reduction	$1,000	Net trade-in allowance	$ ——
First monthly payment	310	Amount to be paid in cash	1,655
Refundable security deposit	310		
Title fees	—		
Registration fees	35		
Total	$1,655	Total	$1,655

Your monthly payment is determined as shown below:

Gross capitalized cost. The agreed upon value of the vehicle ($21,500) and any items you pay over the lease term (such as service contracts, insurance, and any outstanding prior loan or lease balance)......$ 21,800

If you want an itemization of this amount, please check this box. ☒

Capitalized cost reduction. The amount of any net trade-in allowance, rebate, noncash credit, or cash you pay that reduces the gross capitalized cost .... − 1,000
Adjusted capitalized cost. The amount used in calculating your base monthly payment .... = 20,800
Residual value. The value of the vehicle at the end of the lease used in calculating your base monthly payment .... − 11,500
Depreciation and any amortized amounts. The amount charged for the vehicle's decline in value through normal use and for other items paid over the lease term .... = 9,300
Rent charge. The amount charged in addition to the depreciation and any amortized amounts .... + 1,284
Total of base monthly payments. The depreciation and any amortized amounts plus the rent charge ..... = 10,584
Lease term. The number of months in your lease .... ÷ 36
Base monthly payment .... = 294
Monthly sales/use tax .... + 16
.... +
Total monthly payment .... =$ 310

Early Termination. You may have to pay a substantial charge if you end this lease early. The charge may be up to several thousand dollars. The actual charge will depend on when the lease is terminated. The earlier you end the lease, the greater this charge is likely to be.

Excessive Wear and Use. You may be charged for excessive wear based on our standards for normal use and for mileage in excess of 12,000 miles per year at the rate of 9¢ per mile.

Purchase Option at End of Lease Term. You have an option to purchase the vehicle at the end of the lease term for $11,500 and a purchase option fee of $350.

Other Important Terms. See your lease documents for additional information on early termination, purchase options and maintenance responsibilities, warranties, late charges, and default charges.

Does this disclosure comply with Regulation M?

2. If the disclosure statement in Question 1 does not comply with Regulation M, who is in violation, *Dealer* or *Leaseco*? See section 213.2(h) and compare Regulation Z section 226.2(a)(17).

3. According to section 102 of the Act,

> (b) It is the purpose of this title to assure a meaningful disclosure of the terms of leases of personal property for personal, family, or household purposes so as to enable the lessee to compare more readily

. . . [and] enable comparison of lease terms with credit terms where appropriate.

Consumer in the preceding problem could have purchased the Mercury for $20,000, with a downpayment of $3,000 and 36 monthly installments of $503. Did he make the right choice?

Consumer had still another alternative: another dealer would have sold him the same car for $268/month for 36 months (with a downpayment of $1,000), at the end of which time *Consumer* would have an obligation to pay the sum of $11,500. He could satisfy this obligation either by paying the full sum or by returning the car. Would the dealer have been obligated by the Truth-in-Lending Act to disclose the finance charge and the annual percentage rate? If instead of structuring the transaction this way, the dealer structures it as in Question 1 above, must the dealer disclose the finance charge and the annual percentage rate?

4. What if the following appears on the reverse side of the document:

> DISCLAIMER: This vehicle is leased AS IS and Lessor DISCLAIMS ALL IMPLIED WARRANTIES OF MERCHANTABILITY AND FITNESS FOR PURPOSE. The vehicle may be subject to a separate written warranty of the manufacturer of the vehicle, and your rights under any manufacturer warranty shall not be impaired by this lease.

Has *Dealer* or *Leaseco* violated the Act?

5. One of the major areas of concern in motor vehicle leases is the consumer's liability in the event of early termination. A lease may terminate early for any of several reasons: the consumer may wish to have a different vehicle; the vehicle may be stolen or destroyed in an accident; or the consumer may default in the payment obligation, causing the lessor to terminate the lease. When any of these events occurs, the lessor stands to wind up with less than it would have received had the consumer fully performed. To the extent the termination of the lease entails a breach by the lessee, the law of contracts provides that the lessor is entitled to damages to place it in its expectancy position.[4] Compensation for the lessor's lost expectancy includes an amount representing that portion of the depreciation that has not yet been paid. This amount is likely to be surprisingly large: a major portion of the total depreciation of a car occurs within the first few months, but the consumer's payments in those months are not large enough to cover that depreciation. The problem is exacerbated because, as with any extension of credit, the lessor allocates each payment first to the financing costs, then to the depreciation. The portion of the payment allocable to the financing costs is larger in the early months of the lease than it is in the later months. The net result is that the earlier in the lease that termination occurs, the larger the amount of damages. This liability usually amounts to thousands of dollars.

---

4. So does UCC section 2A–528(2) (lessor is entitled to the present value of the profit it would have made from full performance).

Rather than rely on remedies developed under the law of contracts, the lessor typically includes a provision in the lease to determine the amount of the consumer's liability in the event of early termination. Section 183 of the Act imposes a limit on this liability. It is one of the very few provisions in the Act that imposes any substantive limit on creditors or lessors. Please read section 183. Section 213.4(g) of the Regulation requires disclosure of the amount or method for determining the amount of any charge for early termination. Do the following disclosures comply:

a) In the event of default or early termination, Lessor will sell the vehicle and Lessee shall pay Lessor an amount equal to (*i*) the total of the unpaid monthly payments; plus (*ii*) the estimated residual value at scheduled termination; plus (*iii*) all reasonable charges that Lessor pays to repossess and dispose of the vehicle; plus (*iv*) all other amounts due but unpaid under this agreement; less (*v*) the amount received from the sale of the vehicle; less (*vi*) eighty percent of the unearned lease charges, based upon the constant yield method rules for leases in the current Statement of Financial Accounting Standards No. 13 as published by the American Institute of Certified Public Accountants, or its equivalent; less (*vii*) any insurance proceeds Lessor has received.

b) In the event of default or early termination, Lessee will pay the following: (*i*) any lease payments or other amounts due and owing under the lease at the time of default; plus (*ii*) the balance of the lease payments that would have been made had the lease gone to term, less a deduction for the time-value of such payments computed in accordance with the Rule of 78's; plus (*iii*) the estimated residual value; plus (*iv*) an amount equal to one monthly lease payment; plus (*v*) any and all commissions, fees, or other amounts paid by Lessor as consideration for the assignment of the lease.

6. Another area of concern is the extent of the consumer's liability for excess wear and tear. Over the course of a lease, the lessor will receive a stream of payments, and at the end of the lease the lessor will get the car back. The payment stream is based on several factors, one of which is the anticipated depreciation of the car. If the vehicle depreciates more than predicted, the transaction may not be profitable, or not as profitable as the lessor anticipated at the outset. That is the lessor's risk in a closed-end lease. But the lessor need not bear the risk that the consumer will return a severely damaged car. And typically the lessor does not bear that risk, because the lease provides that the lessee must return the vehicle in good working condition except for reasonable wear and use. Further, it typically imposes liability on the lessee for excess wear and tear. See Regulation M § 213.4(h), which requires disclosure of this fact. Does the following comply:

You will maintain the vehicle and, except for reasonable wear and use, will return it in good working condition, including (*i*) the odometer must reflect the actual mileage; (*ii*) the vehicle will have a matching set of tires with at least 25% of tread remaining; (*iii*) the engine, drive train, and other mechanical and electrical parts shall operate properly and not be damaged; (*iv*) there will be no scratches, dents, pits, rust areas; (*v*) there will be no cracks in the windshield or window and the interior will not be damaged.

(4) RENT-TO-OWN

The introduction to the preceding section notes that the Truth-in-Lending Act defines certain leases as credit sales. When a consumer leases goods for a fixed term and acquires ownership simply by completing the monthly lease payments, the transaction is functionally equivalent to a sale. At one time merchants constructed transactions this way to evade laws governing secured credit or usury. For more than 40 years the Uniform Commercial Code has defined these evasionary leases as security interests, thereby subjecting them to the UCC rules governing secured credit. Congress borrowed this approach when it enacted Truth-in-Lending. The principle is that substance, not form, is to determine how a transaction is treated. How, then, are rent-to-own transactions to be treated?

In a rent-to-own transaction, the consumer acquires the use of some item of personal property for a very short time, typically a week or a month, with a right to renew the lease for successive periods of equal length. At the end of any period, the consumer may return the item and end the relationship, with no further obligation. If, however, the consumer keeps the item and makes the rental payments for a specified time, typically 18 months, the consumer acquires ownership of the item. Hence, the transaction resembles the spurious lease that is within the definition of "credit sale" in section 103(g), but it differs from that kind of lease because the nominal duration is one rental period and the consumer may terminate the lease at the end of any rental period. Under the Truth-in-Lending Act, is this transaction to be treated as a lease or as a credit sale?

The answer, it turns out, is neither. Section 103(g) defines a lease as a credit sale only if the lessee "contracts to pay . . . a sum substantially equivalent to . . . the aggregate value of the property . . . and it is agreed that the . . . lessee will become . . . the owner of the property upon full compliance with his obligations under the contract." Arguably the lessee "contracts to pay" only one installment, a sum far less than the value of the property. To that extent, then, the rent-to-own transaction is not a "credit sale."[5] Similarly, it is not a "consumer lease." Section 181

---

5. "Arguably" because often the lease renews automatically for another period if the consumer does not affirmatively terminate it. If the lease automatically renews, then the transaction is no different from a credit sale in which the consumer promises to make all scheduled payments but has a right to terminate the contract any time after the first installment. Notwithstanding the right of termination, this transaction is within the definition of credit sale.

defines "consumer lease" as "a contract in the form of a lease . . . for the use of personal property . . . for a period of time exceeding four months." Since the rent-to-own contract is for a period of one week or one month, it is not within this definition either. Hence, the Truth-in-Lending Act does not apply, and the merchant need give no disclosures whatever.

This is remarkable, because of the economics of rent-to-own transactions. In one case, for example, a consumer acquired a 19-inch television in a transaction that called for weekly rent of $21 and provided that if he rented it for 78 weeks he would acquire ownership.[6] A little arithmetic reveals that he would pay $1,638 over a period of one and a half years, for a TV that retailed for less than a fourth of that sum. This example is typical. Yet, because the Truth-in-Lending Act does not apply, the merchant need not disclose any finance charge or annual percentage rate (typically 250–400%, if all amounts in excess of the retail value are viewed as finance charge).[7]

Although rent-to-own transactions are not within the relevant definitions of the federal law, courts in several states have concluded that the transactions are within the definition of sales for purposes of their retail installment sales acts. This conclusion means that rent-to-own merchants must comply with the disclosure requirements of those statutes. It also means that they must comply with the substantive requirements of those laws, a topic beyond the scope of this chapter. In addition, approximately half the states have enacted special statutes to apply to rent-to-own transactions. These statutes require disclosure of specified information and prohibit the use of specified terms and practices.

To the extent the disclosures occur immediately before the consummation of the transaction, they are not likely to have any impact on whether the consumer goes through with the deal. Consequently, a few states require that certain information be posted on the products themselves. The New York statute, for example, requires the product to display the cash price, the amount of the periodic payment, the total number of payments required for ownership, and the total amount the consumer must pay to acquire ownership. McKinney's N.Y. Pers.Prop.Law § 505(3).

In most states the rent-to-own statutes do not impose any limit on the price that the merchant may charge. Some, however, require that at least a

---

6. Stewart v. Remco Enterprises, Inc., 487 F.Supp. 361 (D.Neb.1980).

7. Assuming an amount financed of $400, the $21 weekly payments in *Stewart* would produce an annual percentage rate of approximately 360%.

specified percentage of each periodic payment apply toward the purchase price. Thus, the New York statute provides

> No merchant shall offer a rental-purchase agreement requiring periodic payments totalling more than an amount, fifty percent of which equals the cash price of merchandise. When periodic payments made by a consumer total an amount, fifty percent of which equals the cash price of the merchandise, the consumer shall acquire ownership of the merchandise and the rental-purchase agreement shall terminate.

Id. § 503. If a department store regularly sells a particular model of refrigerator for $800, what is the maximum monthly payment that a rent-to-own merchant may charge for that refrigerator in a transaction in which the consumer may acquire ownership by making 24 consecutive monthly payments?

For extensive legal analysis of rent-to-own transactions, see Nehf, Effective Regulation of Rent-to-Own Contracts, 52 Ohio St. L.J. 751 (1991); Ramp, Renting to Own in the United States, 24 Clearinghouse Rev. 797 (1990). For an economic analysis suggesting that the pricing in rent-to-own transactions is appropriate, see Anderson & Jackson, A Reconsideration of Rent-to-Own, 35 J. Consumer Affairs 295 (2001).

(5) CLARITY

Section 102(a) declares, "It is the purpose of this title to assure a meaningful disclosure of credit terms so that the consumer will be able to compare more readily the various credit terms available to him and avoid the uninformed use of credit. . . ." To implement this purpose, the statute and regulations require the use of specific terminology. Some courts have construed this requirement very strictly: any departure from the stipulated language is a violation. Thus, a creditor who disclosed "total finance charges" instead of "finance charge" was held to have violated the Act. Powers v. Sims & Levin Realtors, 396 F.Supp. 12 (E.D.Va.1975), affirmed on other grounds, 542 F.2d 1216 (4th Cir.1976). Although this approach is hypertechnical, its justification is twofold: the use of uniform terminology will enhance consumers' understanding, and it is a simple matter for creditors to use the precise terms specifically required by the regulations. Thus "the applicable standard is strict compliance with the technical requirements of the Act. Only adherence to a strict compliance standard will promote the standardization of terms which will permit consumers readily to make meaningful comparisons of available credit alternatives." Smith v. Chapman, 614 F.2d 968, 971 (5th Cir.1980). Section 122 authorizes the FRB to permit the use of varying terminology, so long as the meaning of the terminology is not changed.

Lack of clarity may result not only from confusing terminology, but also from the manner in which the material is presented. Regulation Z requires that the disclosures be made "clearly and conspicuously."

(§ 226.17(a)). The Official Staff Commentary states that the "clear and conspicuous" standard "requires that disclosures be in a reasonably understandable form. For example, while the regulation requires no mathematical progression or format, the disclosures must be presented in a way that does not obscure the relationship of the terms to each other." FRB Official Staff Commentary § 17(a)(1)–1.

The clear and conspicuous standard applies not only to the sequence of disclosures but also to the terms that are disclosed. Hence it prohibits the use of confusing terminology even when Regulation Z does not prescribe the specific terminology that the creditor must use. For example, in Burton v. Public Finance Corp., 657 F.2d 842 (6th Cir.1981), the creditor disclosed its default or delinquency charge in this way:

> A deferment charge may be made for deferred payments equal to the portion of the regular finance charge applicable by the sum-of-the-digits method to the installment period immediately following the due date of the first deferred installment times the number of months of deferment.

The Court of Appeals stated:

> This clause is not "clear," it borders on the incomprehensible. Complex accounting terms and confusing syntax are used to obscure the meaning of this clause, not to explain its terms.
>
> . . .
>
> Finance companies can write simple sentences and use simple words to inform consumers of the terms of loan agreements. However, when a loan agreement is drafted to obscure the relevant terms of the agreement, rather than to explain the terms in clear and meaningful language, the agreement violates [the Act].
>
> Id. at 843.

Lack of clarity may result not only from confusing presentation or confusing terminology, but also from the inclusion of information extraneous to the required disclosures. For example, even before enactment of the Truth-in-Lending Act, the retail installment sales acts and small loan acts of most states required disclosure of certain credit terms. Most states did not repeal these laws upon enactment of the federal law. Since the federal act preempts state laws only to the extent that those laws are inconsistent with the federal act, creditors must comply with both federal and state disclosure laws. But state statutes typically require different terminology than the federal statute. If a creditor were to intermix the two sets of disclosures, confusion would be inevitable. So the FRB requires that the disclosures required by state law be segregated from and subordinated to the federal disclosures.

The Act authorizes the Federal Reserve Board to determine whether particular state laws are inconsistent. If the Board determines that a particular disclosure required by state law is inconsistent with the federal requirement, creditors may no longer make that disclosure (§ 111(a)(1)). Regulation Z addresses preemption in sections 226.28–226.29. The Board elaborated further in the course of responding to a request for a determination that the laws of several states are preempted:

> In the Board's view, the congressional scheme contemplates that a state law is contradictory, and therefore preempted, if it interferes with the intent of the federal scheme. Those state laws that do not interfere with the federal scheme would be left in place. Moreover, the fact that a state law requires information beyond the disclosure called for by Truth in Lending or imposes procedural requirements beyond those imposed by Truth in Lending will not, in and of itself, trigger federal preemption of that state law. However, a state disclosure or procedural requirement would be preempted if it significantly impeded the operation of the federal law or interfered with the purposes of the federal statute. Applying this principle, state provisions on disclosure of the cost of credit, analogous to the finance charge or annual percentage rate disclosures under Regulation Z, will be reviewed more strictly; since these disclosures are particularly significant, any contradiction of the corresponding federal disclosure would interfere with the intent of the federal scheme.

47 Fed.Reg. 16,201–16,202.

Regulation Z section 226.28(a) defines inconsistency to include (1) using a Truth-in-Lending Act label to describe something other than what that label describes in the federal act, and (2) giving a federally defined item some label other than the one required by the federal act. Would it be inconsistent with the Truth-in-Lending Act for a state to require disclosure of the cost of credit as "time charge" if it defined that term differently from the federal definition of "finance charge"?

To facilitate compliance with the Act, section 105(b) requires the FRB to promulgate model forms and clauses for common transactions, and the Board has done so. See Regulation Z Apps. G, H. The Act does not require creditors to use these forms, but proper use of them constitutes compliance with the Act.

For a discussion of preemption, see Miller, The Problem of Preemption in Consumer Credit Regulation, 3 Okla. City U.L.Rev. 529 (1979).

E. ADVERTISING CREDIT TERMS

One of the most difficult tasks of a seller or lender is to attract customers. An important means of doing this, of course, is advertising, and among the facts that may be advertised are the terms on which credit is available. The shopping rationale of required disclosures is perhaps stronger at the advertising stage of a transaction than it is at the consummation stage. And the Truth-in-Lending Act, in sections 141–146 and Regulation Z (sections 226.16, 226.24), regulates credit advertising.

QUESTIONS

1. The Act requires disclosure of credit terms only when a specified "trigger" is advertised. What is the rationale for this approach? In other words, why not require that all ads contain disclosures concerning credit?

2. In what respects, if any, do the following ads violate the Act?

(a)

[C6032]

(b)

Save 40.00
ON
SELF–PROPELLED

MULCHING
MOWER

POWERFUL 4 H.P. ELIMINATES
CLIPPINGS AND THE RAKING,
BAGGING AND HAULING THAT
GOES WITH THEM.

274⁹⁹

6 MONTHS FREE FINANCING

MULCHING MOWER

MOWER PRICE	**274.99**
SALES TAX	**12.72**
	287.71
FINANCE CHARGE	**0.00**
TOTAL	**287.71**

6 MONTHLY PAYMENTS
OF **47.95**

* TO QUALIFIED
HOME OWNERS

[C6101]

(c)

(d)

(e)

(f)

3. In addition to the requirements of Regulation Z sections 226.16 and 226.24, dealing expressly with advertising, ads must comply also with the general requirements of sections 226.5 and 226.17. This means, among other things, that the required information must be clear and conspicuous (§§ 226.5(a)(1), 226.17(a)(1)). For print advertising this requirement may not be troublesome. But the Act applies to radio and television advertising, too. What standard determines whether a radio ad is clear and conspicuous? How large must the required disclosures be in a TV ad? How long must they appear on the screen? Regulation M section 213.7 contains the advertising rules for leases. See section 213.7(f).

F.   ENFORCEMENT OF THE TRUTH-IN-LENDING ACT

The Truth-in-Lending Act has a triple system of enforcement: it provides a remedy to consumers who do not receive proper disclosures; it empowers federal administrative agencies to enforce compliance; and it establishes criminal liability for willful and knowing violations (§§ 108, 112, 130).

Although the Federal Reserve Board has the authority to promulgate regulations (§ 105), primary administrative enforcement rests with the Federal Trade Commission. As to certain financial and other institutions already regulated by federal agencies (e.g., banks, credit unions, and airlines), enforcement authority belongs to the federal agency already supervising their activities (§ 108(a)). As to other creditors, the FTC enforces the Act (§ 108(c)). Remedies include not only cease and desist orders, but also restitution to consumers (§ 108(e)).

The private remedy appears in section 130, which provides for recovery of the consumer's actual loss, twice the finance charge (with a minimum recovery of $100 and a maximum recovery of $1,000),[8] costs of the action, and attorney's fees. In addition, section 125 entitles the consumer to rescind the contract in certain situations, and section 130 authorizes class actions. These remedies, however, are limited to violations of sections 121–135. They do not apply to violations of the provisions regarding credit advertising (§§ 141–146). Enforcement of the advertising provisions is by administrative action only. Smeyres v. General Motors Corp., 820 F.2d 782 (6th Cir.), affirming 660 F.Supp. 31 (N.D.Ohio 1986).

Before the 1980 amendments the Truth-in-Lending Act was perhaps the most important tool of the consumer in resolving all kinds of disputes with a creditor. Even if the original cause of the dispute was the poor quality of the goods or the creditor's use of deception, once the consumer consulted an attorney, the dispute typically centered around the Truth-in-Lending Act. There were several reasons for this. First, because of the complexity of the Act and Regulation Z, violations were almost inevitable. In other words, the Truth-in-Lending Act remedies were always available. Secondly, while it typically is difficult to prove fraud or breach of warranty, proving a violation of the Truth-in-Lending Act does not require resolution of difficult questions of fact. Thirdly, the attorney's fees and other litigation expenses of establishing fraud or breach of warranty may leave no net recovery for the consumer. The Truth-in-Lending Act, on the other hand, permits recovery of costs and attorney's fees, in addition to the damages specified in section 130. See Landers, Some Reflections on Truth-in-Lending, 1977 U.Ill.L.F. 669, 672–80.

The 1980 amendments made three major changes in the Act. They reduced the amount of information that creditors must disclose; they directed the Federal Reserve Board to promulgate model forms and insulated from liability creditors who properly use those forms; and they reduced the kinds of violations for which consumers have a private civil remedy. In a closed-end transaction, for example, a consumer may recover the section 130(a)(2) damages only if the creditor has failed to properly disclose the amount financed, the finance charge, the annual percentage rate, the total of payments, the terms of repayment, the existence of a security interest, or the existence of the right to rescind under section 125.[9] Enforcement of other requirements is left to administrative action. For the effects of the changes, see Pettit, Representing Consumer Defendants in Debt Collection Actions: The Disclosure Defense Game, 59 Tex.L.Rev. 255 (1981). The 1980 reduction in violations that give rise to a private remedy does not extend to violations of the provisions that govern leases. The remedy under section 130 continues to exist for any violation of the provisions requiring disclosure in consumer leases.

---

8. In a closed-end real estate transaction, the figures are $200 and $2,000.

9. The consumer still may recover actual damages for the creditor's failure to disclose other required information, but claims under the Truth-in-Lending Act invariably have been for twice the finance charge pursuant to section 130(a)(2).

QUESTIONS

1. Problem. If *Seller* in Question 7, page 195 supra, violates section 128(a)(2)(B) by failing to disclose the amount paid to *Universal Service Co.*, what is *Consumer's* remedy?

2. Problem. *Consumer* negotiates the price of a new car with *Creditor*, who prepares the paperwork and presents it to *Consumer* for review and signature. *Consumer* has second thoughts and decides to think about the transaction overnight. She asks for a copy of the contract and disclosure statement to take home to review. *Creditor* refuses to let her have it. See section 128(b)(1), Regulation Z section 226.17(a)(1), (b). Can *Consumer* recover statutory damages?

3. Problem. *Consumer* borrows money from a *Lender*, a consumer finance company. *Lender's* disclosure lists the finance charge and annual percentage rate in the same size and color type as the other required disclosures. See section 122(a), Regulation Z section 226.17(a)(2). Can *Consumer* recover statutory damages?

The private remedial provisions of the Truth-in-Lending Act are considered further in Chapter 15.

G.   MAGNUSON–MOSS WARRANTY ACT

The sale of consumer (and other) goods carries with it an implied warranty that the goods are of a certain quality. Historically, however, the parties to a contract have had the power to modify this quality standard. In commercial transactions this modification of the standard may occur after both parties expressly consider whether or not to adopt it. But in consumer transactions, there is no negotiation concerning the warranty terms. Similarly, the buyer and seller have the power to specify the remedies available in the event the goods fail to meet the applicable quality standard, but in consumer transactions the seller exercises that power unilaterally. The superior position of the seller, perhaps coupled with a desire to make an express warranty appear attractive to consumers, has resulted in warranties that state high standards of quality but also contain hard-to-understand boilerplate that qualifies and limits the standard and especially the remedy. Thus, at one time piano manufacturers warranted that for twenty years their product would be free of defects. But a provision limiting the consumer's remedy to repair of the piano made damages unavailable; and even this limited remedy was undermined by a provision that required the consumer who sought repairs to return the piano to the manufacturer. Manufacturers of some other products have conspicuously warranted their products to be free of defects, but in the fine print have limited the remedy to replacement of any defective parts and excluded the labor to install the new parts. Hence, the consumer might wind up with a bill for labor that far exceeds the value of the product.

These and other practices raise two questions: should sellers be able to disclaim warranties and stipulate remedies? If so, should they be required to disclose them in a manner likely to be understood by consumers before they buy? In 1975 Congress enacted the Magnuson–Moss Warranty Act, which is reproduced in the Statutory Supplement. In this Act Congress answered the second question "yes." Under section 102 the FTC may prescribe rules requiring sellers to "fully and conspicuously disclose in simple and readily understood language the terms and conditions" of their warranties. (The FTC's rules, 16 C.F.R. Parts 700–703, also appear in the Supplement).

Warranty documents typically are located with the product inside a package. The package may be sealed, so that the consumer has no access to the warranty document until after making the purchase. Hence, the regulations require the retailer to make readily available to consumers the manufacturers' warranties on all the products in the store (§ 702.3(a)). This enables the consumer to ascertain the terms of the warranty during the shopping stage of the transaction and to use that information in the course of deciding whether to purchase the product. The FTC has enforced these requirements against several retailers, but compliance remains spotty. E.g., In re Montgomery Ward & Co., 97 F.T.C. 363 (1981).

As to the question whether sellers should continue to be able to disclaim warranties and stipulate remedies, Congress answered "yes, but. . . ." As part of the disclosure process, warrantors must label their warranties as either "Full" or "Limited." To be labeled "Full" the warranty must meet the standards of section 104, which prohibits several practices and provisions that undercut the apparent value of the warranty (e.g., section 104(a)(1) (cannot charge for labor in connection with repair of the product), section 104(b)(1) (cannot require the consumer to pay the expenses of returning a piano to the factory for repairs)). Congress did not prohibit these practices altogether for all products. Rather, the objectionable practices are prohibited only if the warrantor gives a Full Warranty. The rationale is that competitive pressures and the manufacturers' pride in their products will induce them to provide Full Warranties. Reliance on competition and pride in the product has proven be to be misplaced: very few manufacturers of consumer goods give a Full Warranty.

H. PLAIN-LANGUAGE LAWS

Another problem for the consumer is the creditor's use of language that the consumer cannot readily understand. Many contract documents contain language that may be understood by lawyers but not by most consumers. Insurance and real estate contracts are renowned for this, but at least until recently most consumer credit contracts probably fell into this category, too. For example, one credit card contract contained this statement of how the issuer would determine the amount on which a finance charge would be assessed:

The average daily balance will equal the sum of the principal amounts of purchases included in the previous balance shown on your statement that are unpaid each day of such statement's billing period, divided by the number of days in such period. Such daily unpaid principal amounts will be determined by deducting from the principal amount of such purchases unpaid as of the beginning of a day all payments and other credits made or received as of that day which were applied to reduce such unpaid principal amount; however, if a previous balance is shown on your statement and the amount of payments and credits shown on such statement does not equal or exceed such previous balance, there will be added to such unpaid principal amount for each day all purchases or debits posted to your account as of that day.

Several states have responded to the prevalence of legalese by enacting so-called plain-language laws. A New York statute, for example, requires each consumer contract to be "[w]ritten in a clear and coherent manner using words with common and every day meanings" and to be "[a]ppropriately divided and captioned by its various sections." McKinney's N.Y.Gen. Ob.Law § 5–702(a). For additional materials on plain-language laws, see Davis, Protecting Consumers from Overdisclosure and Gobbledygook: An Empirical Look at the Simplification of Consumer Credit Contracts, 63 Va.L.Rev. 841 (1977); Landers & Rohner, A Functional Analysis of Truth in Lending, 26 U.C.L.A.L.Rev. 711, 721–24 (1979); Note, A Model Plain Language Law, 33 Stan.L.Rev. 255 (1981). See also R. Flesch, How To Write Plain English (1979); R. Wydick, Plain English for Lawyers (5th ed.2005).

I.   Perspectives

The foregoing materials have explored some of the intricacies of the Truth-in-Lending Act and the Magnuson–Moss Warranty Act, but have not directly addressed the larger question: should there be a truth-in-lending act or a truth-in-warranty act at all?

The purpose of truth-in-lending legislation is to facilitate the informed use of credit. The underlying premise is either that consumers *will* use the additional information or that consumers *ought* to use the additional information. Is either premise sound? Consider the question in light of the following facts:

(1) Many consumers have relatively little income that is not already committed and therefore do not really have a choice. If they want to purchase goods or services, the transaction must be on a credit basis. For these consumers the most important term may be the amount of the monthly payment. This amount is in part a function of the duration of the transaction. So long as the creditor may make the monthly payment attractive, by extending the duration of the transaction, disclosure of the finance charge or annual percentage rate may have no effect on the consumer's decision.

(2) Some consumers have no real choice in selecting their creditors. In other words, a Mr. Tash with "Credit in a Flash" (page 75

supra) may be the only available source of credit. For these consumers, disclosure of the cost of credit is of no use.

(3) For some consumers the credit terms are not the most important factors in making the decision to purchase (or borrow). They may be more influenced by convenience, loyalty to the creditor because of past experiences, and psychological or social factors (e.g., sex appeal and peer pressure). Is it appropriate to make the normative judgment that decisions of consumers ought to be governed by relative costs rather than these non-cost factors?

In light of these facts, should the Truth-in-Lending Act perhaps be repealed altogether? If not, should we nevertheless modify the statute still further? For example, should we merge the separate disclosure requirements for closed-end credit and open-end credit into a single, unified set of common disclosures? If so, what should they be? If any one term is to be disclosed, surely the annual percentage rate ought to be. But beyond the annual percentage rate, what terms should the statute require to be disclosed? What reason is there, for example, for requiring disclosure of the finance charge? And why require disclosure of the non-cost terms of the agreement, such as the existence of a security interest, default charges, and whether the creditor will rebate unearned finance charges if the consumer prepays? The following excerpt, from Whitford, The Functions of Disclosure Regulation in Consumer Transactions, 1973 Wis.L.Rev. 400,* suggests reasons for requiring at least some kinds of non-cost disclosure.

In commentaries on compulsory disclosure as a technique of consumer protection regulation, little is ever said about the utility of disclosure in aiding the consumer in his postcontract activities. After the contract is concluded, there is little, of course, that the consumer can do to insure that he gets the "best buy." But often there are actions he needs to take if he is to maximize his economic gain from the contract he entered. For example, frequently the contract requires the consumer to take certain actions in order to preserve his contract rights—a product warranty may require the consumer to procure maintenance regularly for the product and keep receipts as evidence thereof.

If the consumer is to structure his postcontract activities so as to maximize his gain from the contract, he will need information that is not always easily available. To take actions required by the contract to preserve contractual rights, for example, the consumer needs to be aware of the contents of the contract. . . .

A second purpose of postcontract disclosure regulation can be to provide information that can assist a consumer when a seller breaches a contract. A consumer usually needs to take a number of actions in this situation in order to maximize his contractual gain. But unless he takes some initiative, he almost certainly will not receive his due under the contract. Studies have demonstrated that many consumers, and especially low-income consumers, will not undertake any effective action in such circumstances to protect their rights. The reasons for this lack of initiative vary, but in many instances an important contributor is lack of knowledge, either about effective courses of action or that a breach has occurred.

Some consumers may believe that their only recourse upon breach is in court, but feel that without a lawyer, who cannot feasibly be retained in view of the amount in dispute, they would not stand a chance there. Today, however, consumers very commonly have effective avenues of redress other than a *pro se* appearance in court. There are now many statutes providing a victorious consumer litigant with punitive damages and attorney's fees, and if one of these statutes is applicable, it may be much more feasible for the consumer to retain an attorney. Informal consumer complaint mediation services of various kinds may also be available.

Commentators have rarely indicated that this type of information is an appropriate subject for disclosure regulation, yet it is the type of information that will not usually be provided by the seller absent compulsion.

Id. at 463–465. See also Peterson, Truth, Understanding, and High–Cost Consumer Credit: The Historical Context of the Truth in Lending Act, 55 Fla. L.Rev. 807 (2003); Landers & Rohner, A Functional Analysis of Truth In Lending, 26 U.C.L.A.L.Rev. 711, 737–52 (1979); Schwartz & Wilde, Intervening in Markets on the Basis of Imperfect Information: A Legal and Economic Analysis, 127 U.Pa.L.Rev. 630 (1979) (relying heavily on economic analysis); Willis, Decisionmaking and the Limits of Disclosure: The Problem of Predatory Lending, 65 Md. L.Rev. 707 (2006) (relying on behavioral economics); Kofele–Kale, The Impact of Truth-in-Lending Disclosures on Consumer Market Behavior: A Critique of the Critics of Truth-in-Lending Law, 9 Okla.City U.L.Rev. 117 (1984). For a suggestion that the separate disclosure rules for open-end and closed-end credit be merged into a single set of disclosures for all transactions, see Rohner, Whither Truth in Lending? 50 Consumer Fin.L.Q.Rep. 114 (1996).

J.   FOREIGN PERSPECTIVES

Notwithstanding critiques of the implementation of truth-in-lending law, the rationale for it has been embraced in other countries. For more than 20 years, the European Union has required disclosure of the terms of consumer credit. In 2008 the EU replaced its existing law by adopting the Directive on Consumer Credit Loans, which requires creditors in all EU countries to use a single method for calculating annual percentage rates and a uniform disclosure form for other important terms. Directive 08/____. Before adoption of the Directive, cross-border transactions within the EU represented only one percent of all consumer credit transactions. The objective is to produce a single market for consumer credit throughout the European Union.

CHAPTER 5

QUALIFYING FOR CREDIT

A. INTRODUCTION TO THE FAIR CREDIT REPORTING ACT

When a consumer seeks credit, the creditor needs information in order to determine whether the consumer presents an acceptable risk. Typically, the creditor's first source of information is the application form the consumer completes. Since the applicant is likely to present the most favorable picture possible, the creditor probably will investigate further. This investigation may consist simply of verifying the accuracy of the application by contacting the employer and the persons whom the consumer lists as creditors. Or it may consist of contacting a credit reporting agency, or credit bureau, to verify the information supplied by the consumer and to obtain additional information that the consumer may not have supplied and may not have wished to supply. At one time the decision to grant credit was made largely on the basis of the credit grantor's face-to-face evaluation of the consumer. Today it is common for the decision to be made on the basis of the cold data obtained by the creditor, with little or no personal contact between creditor and consumer. Thus the credit reporting agency plays a critical role in the determination whether a consumer will obtain credit.

Credit grantors traditionally have cooperated with each other, so that when one creditor wants information concerning a customer of another creditor, the latter readily supplies it. Creditors also cooperate with credit bureaus, whose role is to collect and transmit information. The following passage from the report of the Privacy Protection Study Commission[1] describes this process.

---

1. In 1974 Congress enacted the Privacy Act of 1974, 5 U.S.C. § 552(a). Section 5 of that Act created the Privacy Protection Study Commission (hereinafter referred to as "Privacy Commission") to consider the extent to which the principles and requirements of that Act, which applies to agencies of the federal executive branch, should be extended to other entities that collect information on individuals. The Privacy Commission submitted its report, Personal Privacy in an Information Society, in 1977. Chapters 2–8 deal with consumer reporting agencies. This report is the source of most of the information in this introductory passage.

Privacy Protection Study Commission, Personal Privacy in an Information Society (1977)

pp. 47–51.

DISCLOSURES TO CREDIT BUREAUS AND TO OTHER CREDIT GRANTORS

Cooperation among credit grantors is a basic tenet of the credit-granting business. Its most visible manifestation is the way credit grantors have traditionally used credit bureaus to exchange information about their customers.

. . .

What information is disclosed to credit bureaus? Most of the credit grantors with computer-based record-keeping systems provide the following information to one or more credit bureaus every 30 days: customer account number, customer name, spouse's name (if account is a joint account), street address, city, State, ZIP code, account type, date of last activity, scheduled payment date (if an installment plan account), date account opened (month and year), highest credit accumulated, amount owing, amount past due, the credit grantor's rating of the account, which is typically reported under the heading "usual manner of payment," and an indicator as to any outstanding billing dispute (as required by the Fair Credit Billing Act). . . .

Of these items regularly disclosed to credit bureaus, "usual manner of payment" and "amount owing," deserve particular attention. As to the former, credit grantors rate an individual (or individuals in a joint account) as illustrated below.

0   Too new to rate; approved but not used

1   Pays (or paid) within 30 days of billing; pays accounts as agreed

2   Pays (or paid) in more than 30 days, but not more than 60 days, or not more than one payment past due

3   Pays (or paid) in more than 60 days, but not more than 90 days, or two payments past due

4   Pays (or paid) in more than 90 days, but not more than 120 days, or three or more payments past due

5   Account is at least 120 days overdue but is not yet rated "9"

7   Making regular payments under Wage Earner Plan or similar arrangement

8   Repossession. (Indicate if it is a voluntary return of merchandise by the customer.)

9   Bad debt; place for collection; skip

. . . [T]he codes shown above are standard throughout the credit-reporting industry . . . , although the significance of these ratings for credit decisions still varies with different credit grantors. This is but one example of industry efforts to standardize credit-related information.

The second item regularly disclosed to credit bureaus—amount owing—is significant because it enables credit grantors to avoid consumers who are already or may become overextended. . . .

One result of this routine reporting is to make the credit evaluation process more efficient. Another is to concentrate information that historically was scattered among credit grantors until needed for a specific purpose. Still another result is to facilitate or improve processes such as "prescreening" mailing lists[18] and continuous monitoring of accounts for signs of overextension.

In addition to the regular reports, most credit grantors also notify credit bureaus of other events bearing on the credit relationship. For example, when an account limit is changed, when an account becomes delinquent or a delinquency is paid, when an inactive account is purged from the credit grantor's files, or when a customer dies, credit bureaus will normally be notified.

Not all credit grantors with open-end accounts routinely disclose all of the above customer information to credit bureaus. . . .

Reports to credit bureaus on closed-end accounts are less frequent than those on open-end accounts. The monthly account balance for a closed-end account is predetermined by the credit agreement. Once a credit bureau records the terms of a new closed-end account, the credit grantor need only report on changes in the account's status, such as delinquencies, repossessions, charge offs, and final completion of the contract.

———

Credit reporting agencies also obtain information from newspapers, public records (arrests, judicial proceedings, and property transactions), and debt collectors. See generally FTC, Report to Congress Under Section 318 and 319 of the Fair and Accurate Credit Transactions Act of 2003 6–16 (2004), available at www.ftc.gov.

Historically, most credit bureaus have been small operations confined to a relatively small geographic area, each usually having a monopoly in its area. The advent of computers and the mobility of modern consumers have produced a drastic change. Several agencies now operate nationwide, and the three largest agencies[2] together have files on more than 200 million consumers.

In addition to these three, there are a number of entities known as resellers, information brokers, or "superbureaus." These entities act as intermediaries between the big three and the end users of credit reports.

---

18. According to the Federal Trade Commission, "Prescreening is the process by which a list of potential customers is submitted to a credit bureau which then audits the list by deletion of those names that have an adverse credit record. Normally, such lists would be used for mail order solicitation or credit card solicitation." 16 C.F.R. 600.5. [The FTC's current description of prescreening appears at FCRA Commentary, Comment 604(3)(A)–6, 16 C.F.R. Part 600, App.—Ed.]

2. Equifax, Experian, and TransUnion.

Rather than collecting data from creditors, they purchase the data from one or more of the big three credit bureaus and resell it to users who may not need a quantity of reports large enough to justify establishing a relationship with the big three. They also may purchase reports from all of the major bureaus and combine the information into one comprehensive report. This enables creditors to get information from all three major bureaus without contracting with any of them. This has become the standard practice in connection with home mortgage loans.

Whether a creditor receives a report from one of the big three credit bureaus or from an intermediary, the information in the report ultimately comes from the files of one of the big three. The Privacy Commission described the contents of these files:

> Except for [Experian's] limitations on the types of public-record information it reports, there is consensus within the industry as to the categories of information on an individual a bureau should maintain and report. These include: *identifying information*, usually the individual's full name, Social Security number, address, telephone number, and spouse's name; *financial status and employment information*, including income, spouse's income, place, position, and tenure of employment, other sources of income, duration, and income in former employment; *credit history*, including types of credit previously obtained, names of previous credit grantors, extent of previous credit, and complete payment history; *existing lines of credit*, including payment habits and all outstanding obligations; *public-record information*, including pertinent newspaper clippings, arrest and conviction records, bankruptcies, tax liens, and law suits; and finally a *listing of bureau subscribers that have previously asked for a credit report on the individual*.

Id. at 56.

In addition to the main credit bureaus described above, there are others that collect only some of the kinds of information gathered by the big three or that collect a different kind of information altogether:

> There are also a number of smaller, less well-known credit bureaus that serve particular niche markets. Many personal finance companies participate in associations (called lenders' exchanges) that maintain records of credit extended to an individual from members in the association. There is a medical credit bureau that primarily serves doctors and dentists. Another bureau (the Medical Information Bureau) pools certain health information of applicants for life insurance. There are a number of highly automated credit bureaus that serve retailers that accept personal checks and banks that seek information on customers opening checking accounts (Telecredit, SCAN, and Chexsystems). There are a variety of bureaus that serve landlords evaluating prospective tenants (Landlord Connections, for example), and there is even a bureau that serves telephone companies (the National Consumer Telecommunications Exchange.)

Hunt, The Development and Regulation of Consumer Credit Reporting in America 12, Working Paper No. 02–21, Federal Reserve Bank of Philadelphia (2002).

Credit bureaus supply information in their files not only to creditors, but also to employers and insurance companies who are contemplating transactions with consumers. Indeed, there are special reporting agencies who compile information specifically for these other purposes. The information in these files goes beyond facts bearing on creditworthiness, extending to matters of personal characteristics, morals, and reputation. Reporting agencies gather this information by contacting persons who know or know of the consumer, including family, neighbors, and co-workers. In the words of a federal statute, these are known as investigative consumer reports.[3]

An additional form of credit reporting exists in the context of credit cards. When a consumer presents a credit card to a merchant, the merchant may check with the card issuer for authorization of the transaction. This permits the card issuer to enforce the credit limit on the accounts of cardholders who are overextended. It also provides a method for the issuer to gain possession of stolen or lost credit cards. Banks that issue Master-Card or Visa cards belong to organizations that provide this authorization service. Some large creditors operate their own authorization services. Others, such as oil companies, subscribe to independent authorization services. Before processing a credit card transaction, the merchant must obtain separate electronic or telephonic authorization.

Since all these forms of credit reporting facilitate the extension of credit, they are obviously of benefit to the consumer. But they also pose several risks, the most significant of which are inaccuracy of the information and invasion of the consumer's privacy. According to one study, 25% of credit reports contained errors that were serious enough to result in the denial of credit, and another 54% contained less serious errors. Altogether, then, 79% of all credit reports contain erroneous information. Cassady & Mierzwinski, Mistakes Do Happen: A Look at Errors in Consumer Credit Reports 11–13 (2004).

As for privacy, the agency may collect and disseminate information that the consumer does not wish to circulate, even if the absence of that information means a denial of credit. Indeed, the consumer may not even know that a consumer report is being or has been prepared and may not know its scope or content. The ignorance of the existence and content of a report also exacerbates the problem of inaccuracy. The presence of inaccurate information may cause a creditor to deny credit to a consumer who actually qualifies for credit under the creditor's standards. But the consumer who does not know why credit was denied cannot do anything to correct the inaccuracy. And that inaccuracy may continue indefinitely to cause other potential creditors to deny credit, too.

The common law remedies for these problems—defamation and invasion of the right of privacy—are wholly inadequate to protect the consumer

---

3. Fair Credit Reporting Act § 603(e), 15 U.S.C. § 1681a(e).

against these risks. For an invasion of privacy to be actionable, in the context of consumer reports, the agency must make a public disclosure of private facts or must place the consumer in a false light in the public eye. Dissemination of information by a credit bureau to a creditor or to several creditors is not sufficiently public to be an invasion of the right of privacy.[4]

For a false statement to be actionable defamation, it must be made by a person who has no "privilege" to make honest but false statements. And courts hold that credit bureaus have that privilege.[5] Hence, a statutory remedy is necessary, and statutory remedies exist at both the state and federal levels.

In 1970 Congress added the Fair Credit Reporting Act (FCRA)[6] as Title VI of the Consumer Credit Protection Act. Many states (as well as some local governments) also have enacted legislation to regulate the relationship among consumers, reporting agencies, and creditors. In 1996 and again in 2003 Congress extensively revised the FCRA. This chapter focuses on the federal act, which is reproduced in the Statutory Supplement.

The FCRA applies to "consumer reporting agencies" that issue "consumer reports" to "users." It limits the kind of information that agencies may report (§ 605) and the uses for which they may provide that information (§ 604); mandates procedures to assure the accuracy of reports (§§ 607, 614, 623); empowers consumers to learn the contents of their files and correct inaccuracies (§§ 609, 611); and requires users to inform consumers when adverse action results from information in a consumer report (§ 615). This chapter examines each of these protections, but starts with the critical question, what kinds of communications are within the definition of "consumer report" and therefore are subject to the provisions of the Act?

B. SCOPE OF THE ACT

The key definition for determining the scope of the Act appears in section 603(d)(1) ("consumer report"). The Act defines "consumer report" as a communication of certain kinds of information for certain kinds of purposes. Please read that section and consider the following questions and problems.

1. Problem. *GoodChex* has a system for helping merchants determine whether to accept a personal check in payment for their goods and services. The merchants report to *GoodChex* whenever a customer's check is returned unpaid, and *GoodChex* compiles this information. When a customer offers to pay by check, the merchant submits an electronic request to *GoodChex* asking, in effect, whether that individual has ever bounced a

---

4. E.g., Tureen v. Equifax, Inc., 571 F.2d 411 (8th Cir.1978).

5. E.g., Barker v. Retail Credit Co., 100 N.W.2d 391 (Wis.1960).

Privilege may also apply with respect to invasion of the right of privacy.

6. 15 U.S.C. § 1681 et seq.

check. Is *GoodChex's* response to one of these inquiries a "consumer report": is it a communication of the type of information specified in section 603(d)(1)? Is it used, expected to be used, or collected for one of the specified purposes?

2. Problem. *SafeChex* has a different business model than *GoodChex*. Instead of simply providing information about a consumer's bounced-check history, *SafeChex* offers to guarantee payment: if an approved check is returned, the merchant forwards the check to *SafeChex*, which pays the merchant the amount of the check and attempts to collect that amount (plus fees) from the consumer. *Consumer* presents a check to *Merchant*, which submits an electronic request to *SafeChex*. When *SafeChex* responds that it will not guarantee payment, is this response a "consumer report"?

3. In order to market their products and financial services to consumers who meet specific standards of creditworthiness, merchants may seek the assistance of consumer reporting agencies. For example, a credit card issuer may say to an agency, "Give us the name of everyone in the state of Michigan who has mortgage debt, a car loan, and no more than two bank credit cards." In response, the agency supplies a list of names and addresses, to each of whom the merchant mails a credit card solicitation. Does the consumer reporting agency have to comply with the FCRA, i.e. is it supplying "consumer reports"?

4. Problem. Andrews owns a furniture store and is also the mayor of Littletown. Her opponent in an upcoming election is Barker. Andrews asks *Credit Bureau* for a report on Barker. *Credit Bureau* responds with the information. If a "consumer report" is a communication of specified kinds of information for specified kinds of purposes, is *Credit Bureau's* response a "consumer report": was the communication for one of the specified purposes?

5. If the owner of an apartment building asks an information service for information concerning a prospective tenant, do the requirements of the FCRA apply?

6. Problem. *Consumer* wants to buy a refrigerator. *Seller* asks whether he wants to use cash, credit card, or installment sales contract. *Consumer* says he wants to use his Visa card and swipes it through the terminal at *Seller's* cash register, which sends an electronic request to *Authorization Service* for authorization. A few seconds later the screen on the cash register (though not the screen on the terminal) contains *Authorization Service's* response: "Cardholder is delinquent and over the credit limit. Seize the card." *Seller* asks to see the card and then informs *Consumer* that he is overextended and that she has been directed to return the card to *Bank*. She also tells him that she is no longer willing to sell him the refrigerator under an installment contract.

In fact, *Authorization Service* has made a mistake, as *Consumer's* Visa balance is well within the limit of his account and he has made satisfactory payments every month.

Is the conduct of *Bank* and *Seller* within the purview of the FCRA: is there a "consumer report" here? Cf. Wood v. Holiday Inns, Inc., 508 F.2d 167 (5th Cir.1975). See section 603(d)(2)(B).

7. Problem. The three largest retail stores in a small city have an arrangement under which every month each of them sends the other two a list of consumers who have defaulted on their payment obligations. Is the list a "consumer report," so that a store sending one of these lists must comply with the FCRA standards for "consumer reporting agencies" and a store receiving one of these lists must perform the FCRA duties imposed on users? See section 603(f).

C.   OBLIGATIONS OF CONSUMER REPORTING AGENCIES

The primary focus of the Act is on the consumer reporting agency. For example, the Act restricts the agency's freedom to disseminate a report (§§ 604, 607(a)). It requires the agency to "follow reasonable procedures to assure maximum possible accuracy" of its reports (§ 607(b)), and it prohibits the agency from reporting information that Congress determined was too stale to be reported (§ 605(a)). Upon request by the consumer, the agency must disclose the contents of its file on him or her (§ 609(a)(1)); the sources of the information in the report (§ 609(a)(2)); the names of recent recipients of the report (§ 609(a)(3)); and a summary of all the consumer's rights under the FCRA (§ 609(c)). If the consumer asserts that information in the report is inaccurate, the agency must reinvestigate and make any necessary corrections (§ 611(a)). If the consumer still believes the report is inaccurate, he or she may file a brief statement to that effect (§ 611(b)). Thereafter, when the agency issues a report on the consumer, it must include this statement or a summary of it (§ 611(c)). The following materials explore some of these obligations of consumer reporting agencies.

(1)   COLLECTION OF INFORMATION

The two primary concerns of the Fair Credit Reporting Act are privacy and accuracy. To ensure privacy of the information in a consumer reporting agency's possession, the Act provides that persons may request consumer reports, and consumer reporting agencies may furnish them, only for limited, specified purposes. This matter is addressed later in the chapter. The current section addresses accuracy.

> The credit bureau's job is to make sure they do not miss anything in your credit history, because if they disclose a credit report, and they miss something bad, the credit granter will blame them. So, they have to maximize the amount of information they possibly disclose about a consumer, and to do that, they use what is known as partial matches— partial matches of names, partial matches of Social Security numbers. This can work, and it can also be a major cause of inaccuracy.

[For example,] Judy Thomas of Klamath Falls, Oregon was mixed with Judith Upton of Stevens, Washington, because their Social Security numbers were one digit different, and the algorithm just assumed it was a mistake and they were the same person.

Myra Coleman of Itta Bena, Mississippi was mixed with Maria Gaytan of Madera, California. The person had used Ms. Coleman's Social Security number, so it was an exact match on that, and that wiped out all the differences in their names and locations and allowed Ms. Gaytan to basically have a joyride in an identity theft situation.

Testimony of Evan Hendricks, Sen. Hearing 108–579 on the Fair Credit Reporting Act and Issues Presented by Reauthorization of the Expiring Preemption Provisions, Before the Committee on Banking, Housing, and Urban Affairs of the United States Senate 391 (2003).

Mr. Hendricks' testimony identifies two of the principal reasons for inaccuracy in consumer reports:

- mixed files because of similarity in the names or social security numbers of two consumers
- identity theft

There is a third principal reason as well: creditor error. A creditor may make a mistake and communicate information about a consumer that is not accurate, e.g., as a result of failing to credit a consumer's account for one or more payments. The creditor may report the consumer as delinquent when the consumer actually has paid the debt in full.

Regardless of the reason for an alleged inaccuracy, if a consumer complains that a report contains erroneous information, the first step in determining whether a consumer reporting agency has discharged its obligations is determining whether the information is inaccurate. Usually it is easy to make this determination. But "usually" is not "always," as the next two cases reveal.

Austin v. BankAmerica Service Corp.

United States District Court, Northern District of Georgia, 1974.
419 F.Supp. 730.

Moye, District Judge.

.   .   .

The uncontested facts of this action are that plaintiff applied for credit at the First National Bank of Atlanta in 1972 which the bank refused to extend as explained by its letter of May 15, 1972. The bank's letter advised the plaintiff that its refusal to extend credit was based on information obtained from a consumer credit reporting agency, Credit Bureau of Atlanta. Over one year later, in October 1973, plaintiff again applied to the First National Bank of Atlanta for credit. In response, the bank wrote plaintiff that it was unable to approve plaintiff's application immediately but requested him to visit a bank office to discuss the type of credit account which would best suit his needs. The bank's action in both of these instances was based on a consumer credit report which had been issued by Credit Bureau of Atlanta containing a reference to a lawsuit in which Mr. Austin was named as a defendant. . . . But his involvement in that suit was in his official capacity as Deputy Marshal for DeKalb County. Austin contends that there is a great distinction between his personal involvement as a defendant in a lawsuit and his official involvement as a defendant in a lawsuit because a lawsuit against Austin in his official capacity would ordinarily have no bearing on his credit rating whereas his personal involvement in a lawsuit could be relevant to his credit rating. Austin contends that this inaccuracy in the Credit Bureau's records entitles him to a recovery under the Fair Credit Reporting Act.

Defendant Credit Bureau of Atlanta's motion for summary judgment is predicated on the theory that the fact contained in the credit report was true; Mr. Austin was named as a defendant in a lawsuit. Credit Bureau argues that its failure to distinguish whether Mr. Austin was named as a defendant individually or in his official capacity does not constitute a violation of the Fair Credit Reporting Act. Relying on Judge O'Kelley's opinion in Peller v. Retail Credit Company (C.A. 17900, December 6, 1973), Atlanta Credit Bureau contends that the truth of the matter contained in the credit report constitutes an absolute defense to an action based on the Fair Credit Reporting Act. In *Peller,* the plaintiff took a polygraph examination in connection with an application for a job. Plaintiff was not hired and subsequently obtained a position with another company which shortly thereafter discharged him because a check with defendant Retail Credit Company showed that the results of plaintiff's polygraph examination administered in connection with his application for the first job indicated that plaintiff had used marijuana in the past. The Court found that information was true and therefore granted summary judgment in favor of Retail Credit Company stating that "in order to pursue a cause of action based on a willful or negligent violation of § 607(b), the report sought to be attacked must be inaccurate."

The Court is of the opinion that the *Peller* holding is equally applicable to the instant action. In the instant action Mr. Austin was in fact named as a defendant in a lawsuit. The fact that he was being sued in his official capacity rather than his individual capacity is an additional fact, which, if known, would enhance a credit report user's ability to evaluate Mr. Austin's credit standing, but did not make the credit report inaccurate. If this Court were to require Credit Bureau of Atlanta to ascertain the nature of a defendant's capacity in a lawsuit it would be tantamount to requiring consumer credit reporting agencies to evaluate the litigation; whether it is merely for injunctive relief or for damages, the amount of damages recoverable against any particular defendant, or the probability of success in a lawsuit against a particular defendant. Requiring such an evaluation would, in this Court's opinion, force compliance beyond the intended scope of the Act. Although the Fair Credit Reporting Act clearly requires consumer reporting agencies to "follow reasonable procedures to assure maximum possible accuracy of the information," the Act does not impose a strict civil liability for an agency's inaccuracy or incompleteness in a report. The consumer credit reporting agency is liable for civil damages only if it has not followed reasonable procedures to assure the maximum possible accuracy of the information upon which the credit report is based. The Fair Credit Reporting Act does not set forth any guidelines for what constitutes reasonable procedures and this Court also declines to do so for in the instant action the Court need not reach this question since it has held that the information contained in Mr. Austin's credit report was accurate. The failure to include the capacity in which Mr. Austin was being sued as the defendant does not impugn the accuracy of the report but instead would merely be helpful in making a complete evaluation of Mr. Austin's credit worthiness, as would an evaluation of any notation of a lawsuit in light of the considerations mentioned above. Therefore, relying on *Peller,* supra, this Court finds that plaintiff has failed to state a cause of action based upon an either willful or negligent violation of § 607(b) because the credit report sought to be attacked is accurate.

    . . .

Based on the reasoning presented above, the Court hereby GRANTS full summary judgment to all defendants with respect to plaintiff's claims based on the Fair Credit Reporting Act and . . . they are accordingly DISMISSED.

QUESTIONS AND NOTES

1.   The court cites Peller v. Retail Credit Co., 359 F.Supp. 1235 (N.D.Ga. 1973), for the proposition that accuracy of the report is an absolute defense to an action based section 607(b) of the FCRA. On appeal, the Fifth Circuit affirmed. Peller v. Retail Credit Co., 505 F.2d 733 (5th Cir.1974). Other courts agree, e.g. Fite v. Retail Credit Co., 386 F.Supp. 1045 (D.Mont.1975), affirmed per curiam 537 F.2d 384 (9th Cir.1976). What is the rationale for this position? Is it compelled by section 607(b)? Is it consistent with section 607(b)?

2.   Why does the court in *Austin* conclude that the report was accurate? Could the court have decided this question the other way? If so, how? And why do you suppose the court decided it the way it did? Is the court's parade of horribles realistic?

3.   If a consumer disputes the "completeness or accuracy" of the information in a consumer report, section 611 requires the consumer reporting agency to reinvestigate and amend the report. Does the use of the phrase "completeness or accuracy" in section 611 have any implications for the interpretation of section 607(b), which refers to "accuracy" but does not mention "completeness"?

4.   Under the approach of *Austin*, would the following statements in consumer reports be sufficiently inaccurate to raise a section 607(b) issue:

a) "had two vehicles repossessed," if the consumer had guaranteed a debt owed by another person and that other person had defaulted, leading to repossession of the vehicles?

b) "litigation pending," if the litigation consists of a lawsuit by the consumer against a creditor?

c) "suffered judgment in favor of *FirstBank*, judgment satisfied," if, with *FirstBank's* consent, the judgment had been set aside and the action dismissed?

d) "*FirstBank* installment loan, I–9," if (1) "I–9" indicates either that the debtor cannot be located; or that the creditor has written off a debt as uncollectible, has placed a debt for collection, or has sued to collect a debt, and (2) *FirstBank* referred the debt to a collection agency, the consumer paid the entire amount due, and the collection agency forwarded that payment (less its fee) to *FirstBank?*

5. *Austin* and the cases cited in Question 1 supra stand for the proposition that if a consumer report is accurate, the consumer has no right of action against the reporting agency. How about the converse of this proposition: may the consumer recover simply upon a showing that a report was inaccurate and that the inaccuracy caused damages? See sections 616–17; 607(b).

Koropoulos v. Credit Bureau, Inc.

United States Court of Appeals, District of Columbia Circuit, 1984.
734 F.2d 37.

WALD, CIRCUIT JUDGE: . . .

I. BACKGROUND

On June 7, 1976, Mr. Koropoulos borrowed $2,034.92 from Virginia National Bank (VNB), to be paid off in twelve monthly installments beginning in July, 1976. Mr. Koropoulos subsequently defaulted on the loan; VNB charged the loan off as a bad debt and referred it to Nationwide Credit Corporation (NCC) for collection. Mr. Koropoulos paid the loan in full to NCC, the final payment occurring in November, 1977. NCC kept a 40% collection fee on the payments by Mr. Koropoulos, and sent the remaining 60% of his payments to VNB.

In 1981, the Bank of Virginia denied Mr. Koropoulos' application for a credit card, allegedly on the basis of a credit report from CBI. At about the same time, Lord & Taylor turned down Mrs. Koropoulos' application for a credit card, also allegedly because of a credit report from CBI. Over the next few months Mr. Koropoulos was denied credit on a number of occasions; each time he claims that the lending institution mentioned a CBI credit report as the reason for denial.

In January, 1982, after plaintiffs' attorney contacted CBI, it disclosed Mr. Koropoulos' file to the plaintiffs. The file reported the VNB loan as having a current status of "I9" with a "0" balance. According to CBI's own definition, the "I9" status indicates that VNB either wrote the loan off as a bad debt, placed it for collection, instituted a civil suit against the debtor to collect it, or determined that the debtor "skipped" (i.e. could not be located). The "0" balance indicates that the balance, as it appears on VNB's books, is zero.

On June 1, 1982, plaintiffs filed suit alleging that this characterization of the VNB loan was misleading because it indicated to potential creditors that VNB wrote the loan off as a total loss, and that Mr. Koropoulos never paid the debt. In fact, CBI knew in November 1977 that Mr. Koropoulos had paid off the loan in full. Less than a month later, CBI moved for summary judgment on the grounds that the information it reported on Mr. Koropoulos was entirely accurate and that it never issued a credit report on Mrs. Koropoulos. . . .

The district court granted CBI's motion for summary judgment. It dismissed plaintiffs' claim based on the inaccuracy of the report on Mr. Koropoulos, stating that "Mr. Koropoulos fundamentally misunderstands the institutional arrangements underlying his 1976 VNB loan and the impact on his credit record of VNB's extraordinary measures in securing collection of the defaulted loan." The district court held that the rating was accurate because VNB lost 40% of the money owed it due to its need to take collection measures. Thus, it concluded that the "9" rating—indicating a bad debt—was appropriate, and the "0" balance accurately reflected the balance on VNB's books. It also dismissed Mrs. Koropoulos' claim based on the report issued to Lord & Taylor because "[a]t most, defendant provided the department store with accurate credit information regarding Mr. Koropoulos that caused the department store to deny a credit card for his wife." This appeal from dismissal of plaintiffs' FCRA claims followed.

II. THE VNB LOAN

A. The Accuracy Defense

The FCRA requires that

> [w]henever a consumer reporting agency prepares a consumer report it shall follow reasonable procedures to assure maximum possible accuracy of the information concerning the individual about whom the report relates.

Section 607(b). The Act further provides a cause of action by a consumer against

> [a]ny consumer reporting agency or user of information which is negligent in failing to comply with any requirement imposed by this subchapter [the FCRA] with respect to any consumer . . . [for] an amount equal to . . . any actual damages sustained by the consumer as a result of the failure.

Section 617(1). Read together, these provisions allow a consumer to bring suit for a violation of section 607(b) only if a credit reporting agency issues an inaccurate report on the consumer, since only then does harm flow from the agency's violation.

Many cases construing section 607(b) have limited liability of credit reporting agencies to technically inaccurate reports—reports which include false information—and have dismissed actions where reports were factually correct but nonetheless misleading or materially incomplete. . . . The district court here followed this line of cases in dismissing plaintiffs' claims. It noted that CBI clearly states, in explanations provided to its customers, that a classification of "9" applies to any debt charged off as a loss, referred for collection, requiring a civil action, or uncollectible because the debtor "skipped." Mr. Koropoulos' loan was charged off as a bad debt by VNB, and therefore, the district court reasoned, came within CBI's classification of "9". The district court also found that CBI "adjusted Mr. Koropoulos' credit report to reflect a '0' balance for the VNB loan," upon notification by VNB that the loan had been paid. It considered the affidavit of plaintiffs' expert, attesting that the "9–0" designation would be read as indicating a total default on the loan, to be irrelevant because it found the report itself "totally accurate."

First of all, we do not agree with the district court that section 607(b) makes a credit reporting agency liable for damages only if the report contains statements that are technically untrue. Congress did not limit the Act's mandate to reasonable procedures to assure only technical accuracy; to the contrary, the Act requires reasonable procedures to assure "maximum accuracy." The Act's self-stated purpose is "to require that consumer reporting agencies adopt reasonable procedures for meeting the needs of commerce for consumer credit . . . in a manner which is fair and equitable to the consumer, with regard to the confidentiality, accuracy, relevancy, and proper utilization of such information."[4] Section 602(b). Certainly reports containing factually correct information that nonetheless mislead their readers are neither maximally accurate nor fair to the consumer who is the subject of the reports.

The several district court cases adopting the technical accuracy defense to a section 607(b) claim fail to convince us that such a defense, applied to these facts, is in accord with congressional intent. These cases, which purport to follow Peller v. Retail Credit Co., misread its rationale. . . . We have no difficulty with the result in *Peller* because, in fact, the report was neither misleading nor materially incomplete.

Several subsequent cases, however, have invoked the language of *Peller* to justify an absolute accuracy defense that precludes section 607(b) actions

---

4. The purpose of the FCRA, as further elaborated in its legislative history, is "to protect consumers from being unjustly damaged because of inaccurate *or arbitrary* information in a credit report." S.Rep. No. 517, 91st Cong., lst Sess. 1 (1969) (emphasis supplied). And, in introducing the fair credit reporting bill, Senator Proxmire said: "[p]er- haps the most serious problem in the credit reporting industry is the problem of inaccu- rate *or misleading* information." 115 Cong. Rec. 2411 (1969) (emphasis supplied). We think it clear that Congress meant the Act to address more than technically inaccurate re- ports.

even where, unlike in *Peller,* the reports at issue are misleading. To the extent these cases cite *Peller* and give no further rationale for invoking the defense, they are unpersuasive because *Peller* involved no claim that the information in the report, though technically true, was misleading or incomplete. We note as well that in some cases, the additional information necessary for clarification would have required the agencies to conduct further investigations, a burden that the courts may have considered unreasonable. See Alexander v. Moore & Associates, Inc., 553 F.Supp. 948, 951–52 (D.Haw.1982) [hereinafter cited as *Moore*]. In this case plaintiffs do not complain about any failure on CBI's part to reinvestigate the VNB loan, or to update a file. They claim rather that the manner in which CBI reported the information already in its possession was misleading. Thus, to the extent cases following *Peller* reflect a determination that Congress did not mean to impose any burden of reinvestigation on credit agencies, they have no bearing on this case.

In any event, we do not subscribe to the restrictive interpretation of ''maximum accuracy'' in the *Peller* line of cases; we find more in line with congressional intent and purpose the position taken in *Moore*.

[S]ection 607(b) of the Act, fairly read, would apply to consumer reports even though they may be technically accurate, if it is shown that such reports are not accurate to the maximum possible extent. The inquiry however would not end there. The statute does not flatly require maximum possible accuracy, only that the consumer reporting agency must follow *reasonable procedures* to assure such accuracy. Thus, the determination of this issue would seem to involve a balancing test.

Under this approach, the court, in determining whether a violation of 607(b) has occurred, would weigh the potential that the information will create a misleading impression against the availability of more accurate [or complete] information and the burden of providing such information. Clearly the more misleading the information [i.e., the greater the harm it can cause the consumer] and the more easily available the clarifying information, the greater the burden upon the consumer reporting agency to provide this clarification. Conversely, if the misleading information is of relatively insignificant value, a consumer reporting agency should not be required to take on a burdensome task in order to discover or provide additional or clarifying data, and it should not be penalized under this section if the procedures used are otherwise reasonable.

553 F.Supp. at 952 (emphasis in original).

Applying that interpretation in this case, we find that the district court's dismissal of the Koropoulos' claims by summary judgment on the grounds that the information in the report was technically accurate, regardless of any confusion generated in the recipients' minds as to what it meant, was improper. We find there is a genuine issue of fact as to whether the report was sufficiently misleading so as to raise the issue of whether CBI's procedures for assuring ''maximum possible accuracy'' were reasonable. The affidavit of plaintiffs' expert stated that "the only reasonable interpretation of the Code [CBI's classification of the VNB loan] is that . . . the creditor took a loss of $2182 on the account after the account was placed for collection." It also impugned the affidavit of Janice Cummings, a CBI manager, as "not accurate in that it states that the Code signifies that plaintiff [Mr. Koropoulos] had fully paid off his account." Were the plaintiffs' expert to be credited, the report could be found to be misleading, since in fact VNB did not take a total loss, and Mr. Koropoulos did repay the debt. Summary judgment on the issue of whether the report was misleading is thus not appropriate at this juncture in the case. Indeed, it was granted by the district court on an altogether different theory which we reject—that the report was technically accurate.

B.   Incomplete Credit Reports

Plaintiffs also argue that even if the report on the VNB loan is not misleading, CBI's classification system is so imprecise that, as a matter of law, it fails to constitute a reasonable procedure to assure maximum possible accuracy. Specifically, they object to "CBI . . . classif[ying] all adverse information into a single '9' category." CBI relies on the explanation it gives its customers, which clearly states that a "9" rating means the "debtor failed to pay back a loan in a timely fashion and the creditor had to take extraordinary measures to collect the debt." The issue we must decide is whether using the classification "9" for all bad debts, whether ultimately paid or not, renders the report of the VNB loan sufficiently incomplete that plaintiffs may invoke the protection of section 607(b).

We must first determine whether section 607(b) requires credit reporting agencies to adopt procedures to reasonably assure that reports which are neither factually untrue nor misleading are also not incomplete. Essentially, plaintiffs contend that even where the reader of a report would be unlikely to infer an untruth, the Act mandates that the report must not omit any relevant information which it is reasonable to include, i.e. the report must be reasonably complete.

In introducing the bill which ultimately became the FCRA, Senator Proxmire reviewed the types of inaccuracy that can harm credit consumers. He explicitly addressed "[i]ncomplete information" as a type of inaccuracy distinct from misleading information, stating that "[b]ecause of the increased computerization and standardization of credit bureau files, all of the relevant information is not always reflected in a person's files." 115 Cong.Rec. 2411 (1969). The conference report's explanation of section 607(b) is also a significant indicator that that section covers incomplete, as well as false and misleading reports.[10] That report states:

> The House conferees intend that this requirement [to follow reasonable procedures to assure maximum possible accuracy] shall include

---

10. "Perhaps the most useful document illuminating Congressional purpose is a Conference Report which bears on the final draft that is used by the conferees in explaining to the entire Congress why the bill should pass." *Vitrano v. Marshall,* 504 F.Supp. 1381, 1383 (D.D.C.1981).

the duty to differentiate between types of individual bankruptcies (e.g., between straight bankruptcies and chapter XIII wage earner plans), and that the disposition of a wage earner plan where the consumer conscientiously carries out his responsibilities under it should be duly noted.

H.R.Rep. No. 1587, 91st Cong., 2d Sess. 29 (1970) (conference report), U.S.Code Cong. & Admin.News 1970, pp. 4394, 4415. Thus, if a credit reporting agency were to report all bankruptcies under a single classification, it would violate section 607(b), even if it clearly stated that it so classified bankruptcies and thereby ensured that its credit reports were neither erroneous nor misleading.[a] The situation with respect to defaulted loans is not qualitatively different. For this reason, we are inclined to believe that section 607(b) covers at least some types of incomplete information.

We are aware that a separate section in the Act explicitly deals with incomplete information. It provides that "[i]f the completeness or accuracy of any item of information . . . is disputed by a consumer . . . the consumer reporting agency shall reinvestigate and record the current status of that information." Section 611. This section might suggest that Congress did not mean to include "incomplete information" within its definition of "inaccurate information" in section 607(b); it demonstrates that Congress recognized the differences between the two kinds of error. Nonetheless, we believe that Congress did not, in fact, intend to exclude altogether incomplete reports from section 607(b)'s requirement of reasonable procedures, as shown by the conference report.[12] The failure of section 607(b)'s language itself to specifically mention completeness in addition to accuracy may well be attributable to the fact that it was added so late in the legislative process that there was not time for careful semantic accommodation with earlier adopted provisions.[13]

---

a. When the court wrote this paragraph, the Act was silent on the agency's obligation to differentiate between types of bankruptcy proceedings. The 1996 amendments added subsection 605(d), which requires the agency to identify the type.—Ed.

12. Congressmen often used the words "accuracy" and "completeness" interchangeably during the congressional debates and hearings. See e.g., 115 Cong. Rec. 2411 (1969) (remarks of Sen. Proxmire); 116 Cong.Rec. 36569–73 (1970) (remarks of Rep. Sullivan); Fair Credit Reporting, Hearings on S. 823 Before the Subcomm. on Financial Institutions of the Senate Comm. on Banking and Currency, 91st Cong., 1st Sess. 33 ("I don't think that a report that is incomplete can be said to be accurate") (remarks of Sen. Bennett).

13. The fair credit reporting bill did not follow the usual route of full consideration by

both Houses; the previously passed Senate version was attached on the Senate floor as a rider to a House-passed bill on bank records and foreign transactions. Section 607(b) was later added in conference at the insistence of House conferees, who favored greater consumer protections than those the Senate bill provided. See 116 Cong.Rec. 38570 (1970) (statement of Rep. Sullivan reporting conference committee bill). In reporting the bill out of conference committee, Representative Sullivan stated:

> because in the final days of a Congress some legislative shortcuts sometimes have to be taken—a majority of the House conferees voted to offer amendments . . . to bring the . . . credit reporting bill . . . into such form as we could in good conscience recommend them to the House as part of a conference report on H.R. 15073.

Having thus concluded that the FCRA imposes some duty on credit reporting agencies to assure their reports are not overly imprecise, we do not suggest that the Act requires all relevant credit information be included in agencies' reports: The Act only requires that agencies adopt reasonable procedures to ensure complete and precise reporting. Cf. *Moore*, 553 F.Supp. at 952 (discussing reasonable procedures to assure reports are not misleading). Imprecise or incomplete reports that are not misleading, although undesirable, are not as noxious as erroneous and misleading ones. The potential creditor is not misled; he is merely missing information which might be relevant to his decision whether to grant credit. Unlike the case of erroneous or misleading reports, the potential creditor can often correct inaccuracies himself by asking the credit applicants or the source to supply the missing information. Thus the likelihood that consumers will be harmed by incomplete reports that are neither misleading nor erroneous is less, and in many cases it may well be a "reasonable procedure" to let the potential creditor supplement the missing information himself.

The reasonableness requirement thus severely limits an agency's duty to maximally assure precise and complete reporting. Nevertheless, Congress apparently felt that, at some point, certain distinctions, such as those between bankruptcy and wage earner plans, may be so fundamental to the message credit report conveys that it is reasonable to place a burden on the credit reporting agency to report them. See H.R.Rep. No. 1587, 91st Cong., 2d Sess. 29 (1970).

Plaintiffs argue that lumping together all bad debts, ranging from loans totally paid off after referral for collection to flagrant defaults where the debtor has "skipped" town, is unreasonable, and that it is fundamental to the accuracy of a credit report under section 607(b) that such disparate circumstances be distinguished. CBI's explanation of its Code, which it gives to its customers, itself states that the "9" classification even includes debts that were not repaid because the debtor declared bankruptcy; that would seem very much at odds with the section's purpose. In this case, the record is too sparse for us to conclude at this early stage in the proceeding either that CBI's "9" classification is so broad that it unreasonably fails to distinguish between fundamentally different credit histories, or that it is sufficiently narrow to be reasonable. The parties did not address the reasonableness of the "9" classification in the district court, and the record is therefore devoid of such evidence as: (1) the likelihood that a potential creditor would deny credit to an individual who has failed to pay back a loan, but would grant it to one who repaid the loan after the loan was

116 Cong.Rec. 36570 (1970).

There is an additional explanation why section 611 might explicitly mention "incomplete information" while other sections of the Act do not. Section 611 allows a consumer to dispute information in his file. It also explicitly provides, as a remedy, deletion of information "found to be inaccurate or [which] can no longer be verified." Section 611(a). Without more, this remedy might suggest that a consumer could dispute only "inaccurate" information capable of being deleted. Obviously, where a report is inaccurate due to omission of information (i.e. is incomplete), deletion is of no use. In order to make clear that a consumer could correct a record on the grounds of incompleteness, the section explicitly mentioned incomplete reports.

referred for collection; and (2) the burden imposed on agencies by requiring a distinction between "skips," loans never repaid, loans repaid after referral for collection, and loans repaid only after civil suit is instituted. We therefore leave to the district court the determination whether the "9" classification is unreasonable *per se.*

III. THE LORD & TAYLOR CREDIT CARD

Plaintiff, Mrs. Koropoulos, also claims damages from Lord & Taylor's denial of her application for a credit card. The complaint alleges that this denial resulted from "adverse information contained in a consumer credit report supplied to Lord & Taylor, Inc. by CBI." The district court found that this assertion did not put into contest CBI's counter-assertion that it had no credit file on Mrs. Koropoulos, and that CBI at most provided Lord & Taylor with a report on Mr. Koropoulos, which the court found to be accurate.

We cannot sustain the dismissal of this claim either, because, even under the district court's assumption that CBI may have sent Lord & Taylor a report on Mr. Koropoulos, CBI may be liable to plaintiffs for violation of the FCRA. The Act addresses the confidentiality of credit information as well as the accuracy of credit reports. To protect confidentiality it provides that:

> [a] consumer reporting agency may furnish a consumer report [only] . . . [t]o a person which it has reason to believe—intends to use the information in connection with a credit transaction *involving the consumer on whom the information is to be furnished* and involving the extension of credit to, or review or collection of an account of, the consumer.

[Section 604(a)(3)(A)] (emphasis supplied). The plain language of this provision seems to prohibit CBI from sending a report on Mr. Koropoulos in response to a request for a report on Mrs. Koropoulos. The issue is somewhat complicated, however, by the Act's definition of a consumer report as,

> any . . . communication bearing on a consumer's credit worthiness, credit standing, credit capacity, character, general reputation, personal characteristics, or mode of living which is used or expected to be used for . . . purpose authorized under section 604.

Thus, the Act seems to allow CBI to communicate information about Mr. Koropoulos as long as it has a bearing on Mrs. Koropoulos' credit worthiness; such a communication would not violate the Act because it would constitute a consumer report on Mrs. Koropoulos. In this case, however, CBI itself maintains that it issued a report on Mr. Koropoulos, *and not Mrs. Koropoulos*. And, as the record now stands, there is no indication that CBI reported only information that had a bearing on Mrs. Koropoulos' credit worthiness,[17] or that it had reason to believe that Mrs. Koropoulos'

---

17. As both the Federal Trade Commission and we read section [604(a)(3)(A)] "a consumer reporting agency may not report information from spouse A's file which re-

application for a credit card in any way "involv[ed]" Mr. Koropoulos.[18] Given the silence of the record on whether Lord & Taylor requested a report on Mr. Koropoulos, on what information CBI actually furnished Lord & Taylor, and on whether CBI otherwise had reason to believe that Lord & Taylor contemplated a credit transaction with Mr. (as opposed to Mrs.) Koropoulos, summary judgment on this claim is inappropriate.

In addition to a possible claim under section [604(a)(3)(A)], our conclusion that CBI's credit reports on Mr. Koropoulos may have been inaccurate under the Act also requires remand of Mrs. Koropoulos' Lord & Taylor credit card claim. If Lord & Taylor denied Mrs. Koropoulos a credit card because of inaccuracy in Mr. Koropoulos' report, that inaccuracy harmed her. We can see no logical reason why the mere fact that the harmful inaccuracy appeared in another individual's credit report should shield a credit reporting agency for harm to an individual flowing from a negligent violation of the Act.

IV. CONCLUSION

We find that genuine issues of material fact exist with respect to whether (1) CBI negligently issued a misleading or incomplete report, in violation of section 607(b), and (2) CBI negligently or willfully issued a report for an impermissible purpose, a violation of section [604(a)(3)(A)]. For the foregoing reasons we vacate the district court's grant of summary judgment for CBI, and remand for further proceedings consistent with this opinion.

QUESTIONS AND NOTES

1. The court in *Koropoulos* agrees with the court in *Austin* that before a consumer may challenge a consumer reporting agency's procedures under section 607(b), he or she must prove that the report was not accurate. But *Koropoulos* rejects the standard of accuracy adopted in *Austin*. What standard does *Koropoulos* adopt? How misleading or incomplete must a report be before the consumer may challenge the agency's procedures? In a companion case to *Koropoulos*, the court cited *Koropoulos* for the proposi-

lates only to his or her individual credit history when spouse B applies for credit." Division of Credit Practices, Bureau of Consumer Protection, Federal Trade Comm., Compliance With the Fair Credit Reporting Act 20.1 (2d ed. revised 1979). The problem arises, however, where information is "undesignated . . . [i.e. the] information [is] in a married consumer's file . . . [and] was not reported to the consumer reporting agency with a designation indicating that the information relates to either the consumer's joint or individual credit experience." Id. We do not suggest that a consumer reporting agency is automatically

liable if it supplies undesignated information on a consumer in response to a request for information about his or her spouse. Taking the ease or difficulty of verification into account, the agency need only act on a reasonable belief that the information bears on the credit worthiness of the spouse to be free from liability for a willful or negligent violation. See sections 616–17.

18. This would be a different case if the record showed that CBI had knowledge that Mr. Koropoulos agreed or was legally obligated to satisfy Mrs. Koropoulos' unpaid debts.

tion that the "lack of completeness must be of a fundamental nature." Stewart v. Credit Bureau, Inc., 734 F.2d 47, 55 (D.C.Cir.1984).

2. How is a consumer reporting agency to know when and whether to obtain more information? Does the court's interpretation place an intolerable burden on consumer reporting agencies, which must process large quantities of information very quickly and inexpensively? In *Stewart* (Question 1 supra), the court held that a consumer reporting agency was not liable for failing to note that a tax lien against a consumer's property was in connection with his unincorporated business, not his personal life. Nor was it liable for having failed to include the fact that the consumer disputed liability for the tax. Are these conclusions consistent with the court's decision in *Koropoulos* concerning the degree of inaccuracy necessary to enable a consumer to assert that a consumer reporting agency has violated section 607(b)?

3. Assuming that a consumer can establish that a report is inaccurate, what is necessary to establish that the agency failed to follow reasonable procedures? Does *Koropoulos* suggest any way to give content to the standard "reasonable procedures"?

4. Plaintiff in *Koropoulos* challenged the use of the rating category I–9 as per se a violation of section 607(b). In Pinner v. Schmidt, 805 F.2d 1258 (5th Cir.1986), a consumer sued Chilton, a consumer reporting agency, for reporting "litigation pending" when the litigation consisted of a lawsuit by the consumer against a creditor. The court stated

> [A]ny person could easily have construed the notation "Litigation Pending" as an indication that the plaintiff was being sued by Sherwin–Williams, while the actual situation was the reverse. It would have been a simple matter to prevent this ambiguity, particularly in light of Chilton's knowledge of Pinner's dispute with Sherwin–Williams. As the court noted in the well-reasoned opinion of *Alexander v. Moore & Associates, Inc.*, 553 F.Supp. 948, 952 (D.Hawai'i 1982):
>
>> Section 607(b) does not require that a consumer reporting agency follow reasonable procedures to assure simply that the consumer report be "accurate," but to assure "maximum possible accuracy." Otherwise it would seem that a consumer reporting agency could report that a person was "involved" in a credit card scam, and without regard to this section fail to report that he was in fact one of the victims of the scam. This result cannot have been contemplated under the Act.
>
> In determining liability under the FCRA, "[T]he standard of conduct by which the trier of fact must judge the adequacy of agency procedures is what a reasonably prudent person would do under the circumstances." [Thompson v. San Antonio Retail Merchants Ass'n, 682 F.2d 509, 513 (5th Cir.1982).] The evidence suffices to show that Chilton's procedures did not meet this requirement.

5. To what extent does the standard "reasonable procedures to assure maximum possible accuracy" contemplate verification of adverse information before including it in a report? In *Stewart* (Question 1 supra), the companion case to *Koropoulos,* the consumer reporting agency erroneously reported that the consumer had filed a wage-earner plan. According to the court:

> Judging the reasonableness of an agency's procedures involves weighing the potential harm from inaccuracy against the burden of safeguarding against such inaccuracy. *See Koropoulos.* Under this standard a plaintiff need not introduce direct evidence of unreasonableness of procedures: In certain instances, inaccurate credit reports by themselves can fairly be read as evidencing unreasonable procedures, and we hold that in such instances plaintiff's failure to present direct evidence will not be fatal to his claim.

> . . . [The plaintiff] contends that the wage earner plan entry was facially inconsistent with the rest of his file, which he claims showed "minimal debt obligations and . . . [no] substantial delinquency." Reply Brief for Appellant at 3. He notes that, in adding section 607(b) to the FCRA, Congress was particularly concerned with the potentially devastating effects that reports of bankruptcies and wage earner plans can have on a consumer's ability to get credit. Certainly, inconsistencies within a single file or report involving an inaccuracy as fundamental as a falsely reported wage earner plan, as well as inconsistencies between two files or reports involving less fundamental inaccuracies, can provide sufficient grounds for inferring that an agency acted negligently in failing to verify information. And, at least as the record now stands, CBI has not impugned such an inference either by asserting that, in fact, it does verify information where a file shows internal inconsistencies, or that the rest of Stewart's file was sufficiently consistent with a wage earner plan so as not to give rise reasonably to any such inference.

6. Problem. In January *Consumer* files a petition seeking relief under the Bankruptcy Act. In March *Consumer* asks the bankruptcy court to dismiss the petition, and the court does so. *Consumer* thereafter fully pays all the persons who were creditors in January. Two years later *Consumer* applies for a loan, and *Lender* asks *Agency* for a consumer report. *Agency* prepares a report that includes the fact that two years earlier *Consumer* filed a bankruptcy petition but fails to mention the dismissal of the proceedings. *Lender* denies *Consumer*'s loan application. Does *Consumer* have a claim against *Agency* for violation of the FCRA? Is this case distinguishable from *Austin*?

In McPhee v. Chilton Corp., 468 F.Supp. 494 (D.Conn.1978), whose facts are the basis of this hypothetical, the court held that the agency was not liable for failing to include the subsequent dismissal of the bankruptcy proceedings in its report. "To require an agency independently to update information after receipt and verification would burden commercial dealings beyond any currently required legislative mandate." Id. at 498. Do you agree?

Compare Miller v. Credit Bureau, Inc., [1969–1973 Transfer Binder] Consumer Credit Guide (CCH) ¶ 99,173 (D.C.Super.1972), in which Humble Oil Co. denied plaintiff's application for a credit card based on a consumer report that reflected plaintiff's failure to pay a bill. The report failed to include the fact that it was a bill for only $12 and that plaintiff disputed liability. The court stated:

The Fair Credit Reporting Act itself does not attempt to set forth any specific elements of a reasonable procedure. If the Act is to have any meaning at all, however, it must be read to require credit agencies to do more than merely collect and distribute credit information. The agencies must be required to ask basic questions about the adverse information they receive—i.e., to exercise reasonable care to verify that the individual about whom derogatory information is received is in fact the Consumer they are investigating and that, if such derogatory information does relate to such individual, that there are no extenuating circumstances (e.g., disputed obligation, no attempt at collection, etc.) that are unreported.

This requirement is . . . necessary to give the Act any meaningful purpose at all. . . .

There is no indication in the record that the procedures employed by the defendant Credit Bureau, Inc. include such basic verification and safeguard procedures. The operation outlined in the testimony of the defendant's manager can be characterized almost exclusively as intake. The defendant's evidence shows that the defendant deals daily with numerous reports and requests regarding credit information about residents of the Washington Metropolitan Area. Some are written and some are verbal, and such information comes in and goes out to numerous and varied sources. Although the witness's description of the defendant's operations was admittedly a brief one, it appears that no check is made as to the accuracy of the information received until a consumer appears to question the information which has, as here, already served as the basis of an adverse report. Surely an Act so heralded as a reform measure was meant to impose upon credit reporting agencies more of a responsibility for the accuracy of the information reported than a post hoc correction of erroneously reported information.

. . .

The defendant was . . . negligent in not adopting any procedures to evaluate adverse credit information. The defendant argues here that its function in this case was to merely collect information and apply to that information the standards that Humble had instructed be used. . . .

. . . The defendant is a consumer reporting agency under the Act, and the information which it furnished was a consumer report, so that its obligations under the Act cannot be voided by Humble's or anyone else's instructions. Under the Act, when any consumer report is prepared reasonable care must be followed so as to assure the maximum possible accuracy of the report.

In this case, the defendant should have adopted such reasonable procedures as to include in its consumer report the information in its file that the plaintiff was an employee of the U.S. House of Representatives in what appeared to be a responsible position and that the adverse item was a relatively old item from a hospital in the amount of about $12.00. Failure to adopt such procedure was negligent and therefore in non-compliance with the Act.

In Stevenson v. Employers Mutual Associates, 960 F.Supp. 141 (N.D.Ill.1997), a consumer reporting agency reported that a consumer was a convicted felon, prompting his employer to fire him. The report was erroneous, and the consumer sued the agency. Denying defendant's motion to dismiss the complaint, the court pointed to the following facts: defendant failed to check the court files for a physical description of the felon; failed to check with the consumer's former employer to determine if he was absent from work during the years that the felon was in prison; failed to investigate a discrepancy between the birth date of the felon and the birth date of the consumer; and failed to reconcile how the consumer could be working at the time of the report when its sources indicated that he was in prison. According to the court, these failures amount to a willful noncompliance with the Act.

Consider also the following excerpt from the FTC Commentary on the FCRA, Comment 607–3(D), 16 C.F.R. Part 600 (App.):

> D. *Reliability of sources.* Whether a consumer reporting agency may rely on the accuracy of information from a source depends on the circumstances. This section does not hold a consumer reporting agency responsible where an item of information that it receives from a source that it reasonably believes to be reputable appears credible on its face, and is transcribed, stored and communicated as provided by that source. Requirements are more stringent where the information furnished appears implausible or inconsistent, or where procedures for furnishing it seem likely to result in inaccuracies, or where the consumer reporting agency has had numerous problems regarding information from a particular source.

7. The observation of the court in *Miller* that the consumer reporting agency's operation "can be characterized almost exclusively as intake" remains true, and agencies deal with very high volumes of information:

> Experian has provided an account of its procedures. The affidavit of David Browne, Experian's compliance manager, explains that the company gathers credit information originated by approximately 40,-000 sources. The information is stored in a complex system of national databases, containing approximately 200 million names and addresses and some 2.6 billion trade lines, which include information about consumer accounts, judgments, etc. The company processes over 50 million updates to trade information each day. Lenders report millions

of accounts to Experian daily; they provide identifying information, including address, social security number, and date of birth. The identifying information is used to link the credit items to the appropriate consumer. Mr. Browne also notes that Experian's computer system does not store complete credit reports, but rather stores the individual items of credit information linked to identifying information. The credit report is generated at the time an inquiry for it is received.

One can easily see how, even with safeguards in place, mistakes can happen. But given the complexity of the system and the volume of information involved, a mistake does not render the procedures unreasonable. In his attempt to show that Experian's procedures are unreasonable, Sarver [the plaintiff] argues that someone should have noticed that only the Cross Country accounts were shown to have been involved in bankruptcy. That anomaly should have alerted Experian, Sarver says, to the fact that the report was inaccurate. What Sarver is asking, then, is that each computer-generated report be examined for anomalous information and, if it is found, an investigation be launched. In the absence of notice of prevalent unreliable information from a reporting lender, which would put Experian on notice that problems exist, we cannot find that such a requirement to investigate would be reasonable given the enormous volume of information Experian processes daily.

. . .

Sarver's report, dated August 26, 2002, contains entries from six different lenders. The increased cost to Experian to examine each of these entries individually would be enormous. We find that as a matter of law there is nothing in this record to show that Experian's procedures are unreasonable.

Sarver v. Experian Information Solutions, 390 F.3d 969, 972–73 (7th Cir.2004).

In contrast, another court, without citing *Sarver*, held that a jury could find a failure to use reasonable procedures when one—and only one—of several creditors erroneously reported that a consumer was deceased:

Plaintiff has also raised a disputed issue as to whether Equifax unreasonably failed to detect and inquire after a "gross inconsistency" in her credit file. Plaintiff points to the fact that only her Wells Fargo account contained the deceased notation, while numerous other accounts were opened or remained active. She alleges that despite such inconsistencies, Equifax prepared at least five consumer reports with the inaccurate deceased notation. . . . [P]laintiff's deceased status was caused by a standard notation that was plainly inconsistent with other information in her file. Such inconsistencies could lead a jury to infer that Equifax's failure to detect them was unreasonable.

Gohman v. Equifax Information Services, LLC, 395 F.Supp.2d 822, 827 (D.Minn.2005).

What does section 607(b) require of a consumer reporting agency: most requests for reports are communicated electronically, and most reports similarly are communicated electronically without any personal review by anyone at the consumer reporting agency. Given the volume of reports transmitted every day, it would not be feasible for an agency assign an employee to review every report before it is communicated to a user. Does this mean that consumer reporting agencies are immune to a claim of failure to follow reasonable procedures when the reports contain inconsistencies?

8. Consumers are not likely to complain about erroneous information in their files if the erroneous information favors them. That erroneous information may cause creditors to extend credit to consumers who they otherwise would not consider creditworthy.

Problem. *Agency* prepares reports for use by mortgage lenders. In addition to requesting consumer reports from the big three, it obtains information from the applicants for these loans. *Agency* inquires about such things as the consumer's history of payments to landlords, utility companies, rent-to-own businesses, and other entities that do not regularly report information to the big three. *Agency* then includes this information in the report it sends to a lender who requests a report on a particular consumer. *Consumer* applies to *Lender* for a loan and, in accordance with *Lender's* established procedures, *Lender* asks *Agency* for a report. *Agency* calls *Consumer* for information pertaining to her credit history. *Consumer* lies about her history of payments to her landlords and her utility companies. *Agency* assembles a report and transmits it to *Lender*, who makes the loan. When *Consumer* defaults, *Lender* discovers the inaccuracy of the consumer report supplied by *Agency*. Can *Lender* recover from *Agency* for its failure to verify the accuracy of the information it included in the report on *Consumer*? See sections 616–17.

9. Problem. *Employer* is considering *Consumer* for a job. *Employer* asks *Agency* for a report on *Consumer*, including whether *Consumer* has ever been convicted of a felony. *Agency* consults an electronic database, which reveals that *Consumer* was convicted in another state of third-degree assault. *Agency* telephones the clerk of the appropriate court in that other state and inquires about this information. The clerk confirms that *Consumer* was indeed convicted of third-degree assault. *Agency* asks whether this is a felony or a misdemeanor. The clerk responds, "It's a felony." *Agency* reports to *Employer* that *Consumer* was convicted of a felony, and *Employer* refuses to employ *Consumer*. In fact, in the state of the conviction, third-degree assault is a misdemeanor. Has *Agency* violated the Act?

10. In Millstone v. O'Hanlon Reports, Inc., 383 F.Supp. 269 (E.D.Mo. 1974), affirmed 528 F.2d 829 (8th Cir.1976), the reporting agency's employee devoted only thirty minutes to the preparation of an investigative report. (Recall that investigative reports entail interviews with persons who know, or know of, the subject of the report.) In another case the nation's largest investigative reporting agency, Equifax Services, was found to have imposed production requirements that a substantial number of its employees could not meet, at least without taking shortcuts, such as making up information to put in the files. In re Equifax, Inc., 96 F.T.C. 844, 1004–11 (A.L.J.), affirmed 96 F.T.C. 1045 (F.T.C.1980), reversed in part 678 F.2d 1047 (11th Cir.1982). See also Privacy Protection Study Commission, Personal Privacy in an Information Society 326–27 (1977) (agency expected its employees to produce four reports per hour).

Can a reporting agency that expects its investigators to prepare an investigative report in a half hour or less possibly have "reasonable procedures to assure maximum possible accuracy"? See In re Equifax, Inc., 96 F.T.C. at 1059–62.

11. Even if a consumer may not assert an agency's violation of section 607(b) unless its report is inaccurate, should the rule be the same when the action is brought by the FTC, rather than by a consumer? To what extent must the FTC establish inaccuracy before it can conclude that a reporting agency failed to maintain reasonable procedures to assure maximum possible accuracy? Should the FTC have to show that some of the agency's files are inaccurate; that a particular procedure has the capacity to produce inaccurate reports; or that a particular procedure systematically does produce inaccurate reports? See In re Equifax, 96 F.T.C. 1045, 1055–57 (1980).

(2) Reinvestigation of Disputed Information

When a creditor terminates a consumer's account or denies an application for credit because of information in a consumer report, the creditor must inform the consumer of that fact and the name of the consumer reporting agency that provided the information. In addition, it must disclose that the consumer has a right to obtain a copy of the report (§ 615(a)). Upon obtaining the report, the consumer may discover for the first time that information in the report is inaccurate, whether it be that a creditor has made an error, the agency has mixed someone else's information in with the consumer's, or someone has stolen the consumer's identity. This last phenomenon, identity theft, can be a traumatic experience, as can the process of trying to deal with its consequences. The following excerpt describes the experience of one victim of identity theft:

> On June 25, 2003, Suzanne Sloane entered Prince William Hospital to deliver a baby. She left the hospital not only a new mother, but also the victim of identity theft. A recently hired hospital employee named Shovana Sloan noticed similarity in the women's names and birth dates and, in November and December 2003, began using Suzanne's social security number to obtain credit cards, loans, cash advances, and other goods and services totaling more than $30,000. At the end of January 2004, Suzanne discovered these fraudulent transactions when Citibank notified her that it had cancelled her credit card and told her to contact Equifax if she had any concerns.
>
> Unable to reach Equifax by telephone on a Friday evening, Suzanne went instead to the Equifax website, where she was able to

access her credit report and discovered Shovana Sloan's name and evidence of the financial crimes Shovana had committed. Suzanne promptly notified the police[1] and contacted Equifax, which assertedly placed a fraud alert on her credit file. Equifax told Suzanne to "roll up her sleeves" and start calling all of her "20–some" creditors to notify them of the identity theft. Suzanne took the next two days off from work to contact each of her creditors, and, at their direction, she submitted numerous notarized forms to correct her credit history.

Suzanne, however, continued to experience problems with Equifax. On March 31, 2004, almost two months after reporting the identity theft to Equifax and despite her efforts to work with individual creditors as Equifax had advised, Suzanne and her husband, Tracey, tried to secure a pre-qualification letter to buy a vacation home, but were turned down. The loan officer told them that Suzanne's credit score was "terrible"—in fact, the "worst" the loan officer had ever seen—and that no loan would be possible until the numerous problems in Suzanne's Equifax credit report had been corrected. The loan officer also told Suzanne not to apply for additional credit in the meantime, because each credit inquiry would appear on her credit report and further lower her score.

Chagrined that Equifax had not yet corrected these errors in her credit report, Suzanne refrained from applying for any type of consumer credit for seven months. But, in October 2004, after the repeated breakdown of their family car, Suzanne and Tracey attempted to rely on Suzanne's credit to purchase a used car at a local dealership. Following a credit check, the car salesman pulled Tracey aside and informed him that it would be impossible to approve the financing so long as Suzanne's name appeared on the loan. Similarly, when the Sloanes returned to the mortgage company to obtain a home loan in January 2005, eight months after their initial visit, they were offered only an adjustable rate loan instead of a less expensive 30–year fixed rate loan in part because of Equifax's still inaccurate credit report.

In frustration, on March 9, 2005, more than thirteen months after first reporting the identity theft to Equifax, Suzanne sent a formal letter to the credit reporting agency, disputing twenty-four specific items in her credit report and requesting their deletion. Equifax agreed to delete the majority of these items, but after assertedly verifying two accounts with Citifinancial, Inc., Equifax notified Suzanne that it would not remove these two items. . . .

Two months later, on May 9, 2005, Suzanne again wrote to Equifax, still disputing the two Citifinancial accounts, and now also contesting two Washington Mutual accounts that Equifax had previously deleted but had mistakenly restored to Suzanne's report. When Equifax attempted to correct these mistakes, it exacerbated matters

---

1. The police subsequently apprehended Shovana Sloan, and she was then convicted of and imprisoned for the identity theft.

further by generating a second credit file bearing Shovana Sloan's name but containing Suzanne's social security number. Compounding this mistake, on May 23, 2005, Equifax sent a letter to Suzanne's house addressed to Shovana Sloan, warning Shovana that she was possibly the victim of identity theft and offering to sell her a service to monitor her credit file. Then, on June 7, 2005, Equifax sent copies of both credit reports to Suzanne; notably, both credit reports still contained the disputed Citifinancial accounts.

The stress of these problems weighed on Suzanne and significantly contributed to the deterioration of her marriage to Tracey. As a result of the constant denials of credit, she refused to seek routine credit from local stores, which, in turn, sparked angry recriminations from Tracey. In May 2005, the credit situation forced Tracey, a high school teacher, to abandon his plans to take a sabbatical during which he had hoped to develop land for modular homes with his father. The Sloanes frequently fought during the day and slept in separate rooms at night. In desperation, Suzanne sought the name of a marriage counselor, but her husband refused to go. For his part, Tracey researched how the couple could secure a divorce and left the information for Suzanne to find when she arrived at home from work one day. Also, during this period, Suzanne was frequently unable to sleep at night, and as her insomnia worsened, she found herself nodding off while driving home from work in the evening. Even after the couple took a vacation to reconcile in August 2005, when they returned home, they were greeted with the denial of a line of credit from Wachovia Bank. Two months later, in November 2005, Suzanne again applied to Wachovia for a line of credit, and again the bank turned her down.

On November 4, 2005—following twenty-one months of struggle to correct her credit report—Suzanne filed this action. . . . The jury returned a verdict against Equifax, awarding Suzanne $106,000 for economic loss and $245,000 for mental anguish, humiliation, and emotional distress.

Sloane v. Equifax Information Services, LLC, 510 F.3d 495, 498–99 (4th Cir.2007).

Identity theft has become the leading cause of complaint for consumers who complain to the FTC about fraud. *Sloane* exemplifies some of the consequences of identity theft. It often takes many hours and thousands of dollars of expense and lost wages to deal with the problem. The victim's frustration and sense of powerlessness can be palpable. Emotional injury is common. The 2003 amendments to the FCRA attempt to address the issue. Section 605A empowers the consumer to place a fraud alert in his or her file, after which the consumer reporting agency must include that alert in any consumer report it transmits. If the consumer identifies any information in the file as the product of identity theft, section 605B requires the agency to block that information and thereafter not include it in any consumer report. State legislatures have taken the approach of empowering consumers to place freezes on their reports, after which a consumer reporting agency may furnish a report only if the consumer lifts the freeze. See, e.g., Md. Com. Law Code Ann. § 14–1212.1. These laws are in effect in almost every state.

An important protection for consumers against the risk of inaccuracy is the right to review the contents of his or her file. A consumer is entitled to obtain a free copy of his or her report annually from each nationwide consumer reporting agency (§ 612(a)(1)(A); 16 C.F.R. § 610). Upon request, the agency must "clearly and accurately" disclose all the information in the consumer's file and the sources of that information (§ 609(a)(1)-(2)). In Gillespie v. Equifax Information Services, LLC, 484 F.3d 938, 941 (7th Cir.2007), the court elaborated:

> Webster's Third New International Dictionary (3d ed. 1986), defines "clearly" as: "(1) in a clear manner (that which is and distinctly conceived as the truth); (2) of something asserted or observed: without doubt or question." "Accurately" is defined "in an accurate manner." A primary purpose of the statutory scheme provided by the disclosure in [§ 611(a)(1)] is to allow consumers to identify inaccurate information in their credit files and correct this information via the grievance procedure established under [§ 611]. We conclude that the consumer reporting agency must do more than simply make an accurate disclosure of the information in the consumer's credit file. The disclosure must be made in a manner sufficient to allow the consumer to compare the disclosed information from the credit file against the consumer's personal information in order to allow the consumer to determine the accuracy of the information set forth in her credit file. In writing [§ 611(a)(1)], Congress requires disclosure that is both "clearly and accurately" made. An accurate disclosure of unclear information defeats the consumer's ability to review the credit file, eliminating a consumer protection procedure established by Congress under the FCRA.

If the consumer believes the information is inaccurate or incomplete, section 611 requires the agency to reinvestigate the matter in dispute. Under procedures revised by the 1996 amendments, section 611(a)(2) gives the consumer reporting agency five days to notify the person that provided the disputed information that the consumer disputes it. Another section, to be examined later in this chapter, requires the person that supplied the information to investigate and report back to the consumer reporting agency. Meanwhile the agency must consider any relevant information submitted by the consumer. If any item of information "is found to be inaccurate or incomplete or cannot be verified, the consumer reporting agency shall promptly delete . . . or modify that item" (§ 611(a)(5)(A)). The agency also must send the consumer a written notice of the results of the investigation, a copy of his or her consumer report, and a notice that the consumer has a right to add to the file a statement disputing the accuracy or completeness of the information in it (§ 611(a)(5)(B)). The agency may limit this statement to 100 words (§ 611(b)), but it must include this consumer statement in any report it subsequently distributes.

Historically, one of the more serious problems that consumers have encountered is a result of the way creditors transmit data to reporting agencies. Every month the creditor transmits to the agency information containing data on all its accounts. Even if the creditor has notified the agency that a particular item of information is erroneous, the creditor may not get around to removing it from its own data base. When the creditor next transmits its monthly data, the inaccurate information then reappears in the consumer's file. To prevent this from happening, section 611(a)(5)(C) requires agencies to maintain reasonable procedures to prevent the reappearance of deleted information. (Similarly, the 2003 amendments require creditors to "permanently block the reporting" of such information (§ 623(b)(1)(E))).

If the information in a file is inaccurate, the agency must delete it. Therefore, section 611 can give rise to a question similar to one that arises under section 607(b), viz., whether a report is "accurate." In Swoager v. Credit Bureau of Greater St. Petersburg, 608 F.Supp. 972 (M.D.Fla.1985), plaintiff disputed the accuracy of a report stating that a creditor had repossessed two vehicles from him. Upon inquiry to the creditor, defendant consumer reporting agency learned that plaintiff had guaranteed payment by the purchaser of the vehicles and that when the purchaser defaulted, the creditor had repossessed those vehicles. The court held that it violated section 611(a) for the agency to continue reporting that two vehicles had been repossessed from plaintiff.

Questions may arise also concerning the adequacy of the reporting agency's investigation. An example of this is Pinner v. Schmidt, 805 F.2d 1258 (5th Cir.1986). Pinner worked for Sherwin–Williams and also had a credit account there. Because of a personality conflict with Schmidt, his supervisor, plaintiff quit his job. He also disputed the balance due on his account. Sherwin–Williams reported him as delinquent but did not report the dispute. When plaintiff later was denied credit, he learned of the contents of his file. His attorney wrote Chilton, the consumer reporting agency, notifying it that plaintiff disputed the accuracy of the amount reported as delinquent and requesting a reinvestigation. The consumer reporting agency contacted plaintiff's former supervisor, who verified that plaintiff's account was delinquent. When the agency continued to report simply that he was delinquent, plaintiff sued. The trial court gave judgment for plaintiff, and the Court of Appeals affirmed:

> The record reveals evidence from which a jury could find a negligent violation of § 611. Once Chilton received notice of the dispute over the Sherwin–Williams account from Pinner's attorney, it was obligated to re-verify the accuracy of the delinquent entry. The letter informed Chilton of the Pinner–Schmidt dispute. It was unreasonable for Chilton to contact only Schmidt in its reinvestigation.

> The Sixth Circuit has held that where a credit agency knew of a dispute between the consumer and creditors and where the consumer had complained about his consumer report, merely making two telephone calls to the creditors was insufficient to re-verify the informa-

tion contained in the report. Bryant v. TRW, Inc., 689 F.2d 72, 79 (6th Cir.1982). Here, Chilton not only called the creditor to re-verify the report but consulted the man they knew to have had disagreements with Pinner in the past. Because of Schmidt's involvement, contacting only him was insufficient to reverify the entry as Chilton was required to do under § 611(a). If, as Chilton argues, there was no other authority to turn to to verify Pinner's account, Chilton should have deleted the information altogether, as is required by § 611(a)[(5)(A)].

Dennis v. BEH–1, LLC

United States Court of Appeals, Ninth Circuit, 2008.
520 F.3d 1066.

KOZINSKI, CIRCUIT JUDGE. . . .

In October 2002, Jason Dennis was sued for unlawful detainer. Eventually, his landlord agreed to drop the suit, in exchange for $2,938.50, payable in installments. The parties agreed that no judgment would be entered against Dennis, and filed a written stipulation to that effect. The court's Register of Civil Actions inaccurately reports this event as "11/25/2002 Court Trial Concluded—Judgment Entered." Two months later, after Dennis paid the promised sums, the parties presented a "Request for Dismissal," which the court clerk endorsed and filed. The corresponding Register entry accurately reports how this action resolved the dispute "01/28/2003 Dismissal Without Prejudice—Entire Action, Filed & Entered."

Defendant Experian Information Solutions, Inc. subsequently prepared a credit report on Dennis, which indicated that a "Civil Claim judgment" had been entered against him in the amount of $1,959. Dennis called Experian and informed it that the report was wrong, as he had settled the dispute and no judgment was ever entered against him.

Experian commissioned Hogan Information Services, a third-party public records vendor, to verify the disputed information. Hogan reported that the information Experian had was accurate and sent Experian a copy of the written stipulation between Dennis and his landlord, presumably as support for this conclusion. Experian thereupon advised Dennis that it would not amend the report.

Dennis sued Experian, alleging violations of . . . the FCRA. The district court granted summary judgment for Experian. . . .

After Dennis notified Experian of the error, Experian had a duty to "conduct a reasonable reinvestigation to determine whether the disputed information [was] inaccurate." [§ 611(a)(1)(A)]. By granting summary judgment to Experian, the district court held that the company complied with its reinvestigation obligations. . . . [T]he district court erred.

Experian asked Hogan Information Services to review Dennis's court file. That file contained exactly what Dennis and the court Register said that it contained: the "Request for Dismissal," which resulted in the dismissal of the entire action. Hogan's investigator seems to have overlooked this document, or failed to understand its legal significance, because he reported back that judgment *had* been entered against Dennis.

Experian could have caught Hogan's error if it had consulted the Civil Register in Dennis's case, which can be viewed free of charge on the Los Angeles Superior Court's excellent website.[3] As described above, the Register clearly indicates that the case against Dennis was dismissed. Experian apparently never looked at the Register.

Experian also could have detected Hogan's mistake by examining the document Hogan retrieved from Dennis's court file. Hogan mistakenly believed that this document proved that judgment had been entered against Dennis; in fact, the document confirms Dennis's account of what happened. The document is a written stipulation between Dennis and his landlord that no judgment would be entered against Dennis so long as Dennis complied with the payment schedule. The parties couldn't have been clearer on this point: "If paid, case dismissed. If not paid, judgment to enter upon [landlord's] declaration of non-payment. . . ." The parties altered the preprinted form accordingly. They crossed out part of the document's title ("STIPULATION FOR JUDGMENT"); wrote "NO JUDGMENT SO LONG AS PAYMENTS MADE" over "Judgment shall be entered in favor of plaintiff"; and struck the final line, "Judgment is hereby ordered," replacing it with "Stipulation Approved." Experian incorrectly interpreted this document as an entry of judgment against Dennis.

Ordinarily we would remand Dennis's claim for trial so that a jury could determine whether Experian's failure to reinvestigate was negligent. Here, however, a remand would be pointless. Even accepting as true everything Experian has claimed, no rational jury could find that the company wasn't negligent. The stipulation Hogan retrieved from Dennis's court file may be unusual, but it's also unambiguous, and Experian was negligent in misinterpreting it as an entry of judgment. Experian is also responsible for the negligence of Hogan, the investigation service it hired to review Dennis's court file. Hogan appears to have overlooked the legal significance of the Request for Dismissal and the Register entry showing that the case against Dennis was dismissed. *See* [Gagnon Co. v. Nevada Desert Inn, 289 P.2d 466, 472 (Cal.1955)] ("A dismissal without prejudice . . . has the effect of a final judgment in favor of the defendant. . . .").

When conducting a reinvestigation pursuant to [§ 611], a credit reporting agency must exercise reasonable diligence in examining the court file to determine whether an adverse judgment has, in fact, been entered against the consumer. A reinvestigation that overlooks documents in the court file expressly stating that *no* adverse judgment was entered falls far short of this standard [and is negligent as a matter of law]. On our own motion, therefore, we grant summary judgment to Dennis on his claim that Experi-

3. Superior Court of California—County of Los Angeles, http: //www.lasuperior court.org. To view the Register of Actions in Dennis's case, one would click on the "Case Summaries" link beneath the "Civil" heading, and enter the case number, 02U17296.

an negligently failed to conduct a reasonable reinvestigation in violation of [section 611]. . . .

* * *

This case illustrates how important it is for Experian, a company that traffics in the reputations of ordinary people, to train its employees to understand the legal significance of the documents they rely on. *See generally* Rudy Kleysteuber, Note, Tenant Screening Thirty Years Later: A Statutory Proposal To Protect Public Records, 116 Yale L.J. 1344, 1356–64 (2007). Because Experian negligently failed to conduct a reasonable reinvestigation, we grant summary judgment to Dennis on this claim. We remand only so that the district court may calculate damages and award attorney's fees. . . .

QUESTIONS AND NOTES

1. In Henson v. CSC Credit Services, 29 F.3d 280 (7th Cir.1994), the consumer notified the reporting agency that its report inaccurately stated that a money judgment had been entered against him. The court held that because the judgment docket in fact, albeit erroneously, listed the consumer, the agency was not in violation of section 607(b) for failing to maintain reasonable procedures to assure maximum possible accuracy. The court also held, however, that the agency may have breached its obligations under section 611(a) to reinvestigate:

> A credit reporting agency that has been notified of potentially inaccurate information in a consumer's credit report is in a very different position than one who has no such notice. . . . [A] credit reporting agency may initially rely on public court documents, because to require otherwise would be burdensome and inefficient. However, such exclusive reliance may not be justified once the credit reporting agency receives notice that the consumer disputes information contained in his credit report. When a credit reporting agency receives such notice, it can target its resources in a more efficient manner and conduct a more thorough investigation.

> Accordingly, a credit reporting agency may be required, in certain circumstances, to verify the accuracy of its initial source of information, in this case the Judgment Docket. . . . Whether the credit reporting agency has a duty to go beyond the original source will depend, in part, on whether the consumer has alerted the reporting agency to the possibility that the source may be unreliable or the reporting agency itself knows or should know that the source is unreliable. The credit reporting agency's duty will also depend on the cost of verifying the accuracy of the source versus the possible harm inaccurately reported information may cause the consumer.

2. *Dennis* and *Henson* concern the accuracy of public-record information. When a consumer challenges the accuracy of public-record information, the logical step for the consumer reporting agency to take is to consult the public record. But most disputes over information in a consumer's file pertain to the accuracy of information reported by a creditor. In these cases the agency's typical response is to convey the fact that the consumer disputes the report by sending the creditor a form called Consumer Dispute Verification, or CDV. Typically this is done electronically, and the form is known as ACDV (Automated Consumer Dispute Verification). These forms were developed by a trade association of consumer reporting agencies for all member agencies (and creditors) to use. The agency typically examines the consumer's complaint to determine how to code it and then transmits a 2–letter or 2–digit code to the creditor. The creditor decodes the message and conducts its investigation, then reports back, again typically by transmitting a 2–digit code. When a consumer complains to a consumer reporting agency of inaccuracy in a report, the consumer may submit documentation supporting his or her position. When the agency transmits the information to the creditor in the form of a 2–digit code, however, it does not also transmit this documentation. Does the agency meet its obligations under section 611(a)(2)?

3. As does any employer, consumer reporting agencies set performance standards for their employees. These standards may be relevant to the reasonableness of a reinvestigation. See Cushman v. Trans Union Corp., 115 F.3d 220, 226 (3d Cir.1997), in which the court indicates that it is relevant to the reasonableness of the reporting agency's reinvestigation procedures that its investigators are paid $7.50 per hour and are expected to conduct ten investigations per hour ("the jury could have concluded that seventy-five cents per investigation was too little to spend when weighed against [plaintiff's] damages"). Compare Note 10, page 252 supra.

(3) DISSEMINATION OF CONSUMER REPORTS

Section 604 provides that a consumer reporting agency may furnish a consumer report only for one of several specified reasons. Foremost among these reasons is that the consumer has authorized it (§ 604(a)(2)). Credit applications typically contain a statement authorizing the creditor to obtain a consumer report. Even in the absence of this authorization, however, a creditor to whom the consumer has submitted an application may obtain a consumer report: section 604(a)(3)(A) provides that a consumer reporting agency may furnish a consumer report to a person whom the agency has reason to believe intends to use the information in connection with the extension of credit to a consumer who has applied for the credit. Other paragraphs of section 604(a)(3) authorize issuance of reports for certain other purposes, including for use in connection with employment, insurance, other business transactions initiated by the consumer, and debt collection. See also section 604(f)(1). In addition to specifying the purposes for which a consumer reporting agency may furnish a consumer report, the Act also imposes an affirmative obligation to "maintain reasonable procedures designed to . . . limit the furnishing of consumer reports to the purposes listed under section 604" (§ 607(a)). These procedures must require that prospective users certify the purposes for which they are or will be seeking consumer reports, and the agency must investigate to verify the accuracy of this certification. See *Pintos v. Pacific Creditors Ass'n*, 504 F.3d 792 (9th Cir.2007).

In Problem 4, page 233, does *Credit Bureau* violate the Act by furnishing the report to Andrews?

D.   OBLIGATIONS OF USERS OF CONSUMER REPORTS

If an entity is a "consumer reporting agency," the FCRA imposes certain obligations on it and also on the recipients (known as "users") of its reports. The Act singles out "investigative consumer reports" for special treatment, so the definition of that term is important. According to section 603(e), an investigative consumer report is a consumer report in which the agency obtains information on a consumer's character or reputation by interviewing persons other than the consumer. Reports bearing only on creditworthiness, credit standing, or credit capacity are not investigative consumer reports.

If the user asks an agency for an investigative report, the user must promptly inform the consumer of the request and of the consumer's right to request disclosure of the "nature and scope" of the investigation (§ 606). Reports prepared in connection with an extension of credit ordinarily do not contain information concerning the consumer's character, general reputation, personal characteristics, or mode of living. Nor do they ordinarily entail interviews with persons other than the consumer. Hence, they are not investigative consumer reports, and the user need not inform the consumer that a report will be or has been requested.

With respect to either kind of report, the Act prohibits persons from requesting a report unless the person intends to use it for a permissible purpose (§§ 604(a), 604(f), 616(a)(1)(B), 619). The primary purposes for which a person may seek a consumer report are the extension of credit, review of a credit account, employment, and sale of insurance. But section 604 also permits access to a consumer report by one who has a "legitimate business need for the information . . . in connection with a business transaction that is initiated by the consumer. . . ."

PROBLEMS

1. In Problem 4, page 233, does Andrews violate the Act by asking for the report on Baker?

2. On behalf of *Patient*, *Attorney* files a lawsuit against *Dentist*, alleging that *Dentist* improperly touched her during the course of dental treatment. To determine whether *Dentist* will be able to satisfy the judgment he hopes to obtain, *Attorney* obtains a consumer report on *Dentist*. In addition, to determine if *Dentist* has been shielding his assets by making fraudulent transfers to his children, *Attorney* obtains consumer reports on them, too. Has *Attorney* violated the Act?

3.   *Consumer* is the chief collections officer at *FirstBank*. Without any advance warning, one day she resigns, causing her superiors to wonder if perhaps she has been embezzling bank funds. To obtain information concerning Consumer's recent spending habits, they obtain a report from the agency that regularly supplies reports on *FirstBank's* loan applicants.

a) Is the information a "consumer report"?

b) Does *FirstBank* violate the Act by asking for the report? See sections 603(d)(1), 604(a)(3)(B), (F).

4.   The police found *Owner's* car with expired license plates and impounded it. Under the municipal code a company that tows and stores a car acquires a claim against the owner for the cost of towing and storage. When *Owner* failed to claim the car, *TowCo*, the towing company, sold the car for an amount less than it was owed for towing and storage. In connection with its attempt to enforce *Owner's* obligation to pay the balance of the claim for towing and storage, *TowCo* obtained a consumer report on him. Has *TowCo* violated the Act?

5.   *Consumer* decides to acquire a new car, though she has not decided whether to purchase or lease. Since she also is not sure which brand she wants, she goes to several dealers to look at and test drive different models. At *Dealer Dodge* the salesperson asks whether she is planning to lease or purchase, to which *Consumer* replies that she is not sure. While she is taking the car for a test drive, the salesperson calls *Credit Bureau* and obtains her consumer report. Has *Dealer Dodge* violated the Act?

6.   At the time of completing an application to rent a house, *Consumer* informs *Rental Agent* that she does not want anyone to obtain her credit report. The agent agrees. *Owner*, however, insists to *Rental Agent* that she must see a consumer report on any prospective tenant. *Rental Agent* obtains a report on *Consumer*. Has *Owner* or *Rental Agent* violated the Act?

7.   In the context of consumer credit, an important obligation of the user arises when it either denies credit or increases the cost of credit because of information contained in a consumer report. Please read section 615(a). Even if the information in the report is only partly responsible for the user's adverse action, the user must inform the consumer of this fact and of the name and address of the agency that prepared the report.[8]

Consumer goes to *Money Company* seeking to borrow $500. She completes the application, listing her prior and current creditors, one of which is *Cashco*. *Money Company* calls *Cashco* and asks about *Consumer*. *Cashco* responds that she had borrowed $350, was consistently three-to-four days late in her payments, but now owes only $68. As a result of the information concerning *Consumer's* late payments, *Money Company* denies her application. What, if anything, must *Money Company* do to comply with section 615?

---

8.   Under another federal statute, the Equal Credit Opportunity Act, 15 U.S.C. § 1691 et seq., the user must inform the consumer also of the reasons for a denial of credit.   ECOA § 701(d)(2), 15 U.S.C. § 1691(d)(2). Chapter 6 examines the Equal Credit Opportunity Act.

8. "Adverse action" is defined in section 603(k). With respect to credit transactions, the term has the same meaning that it does in the Equal Credit Opportunity Act. With respect to insurance and employment, however, the definition appears in section 603(k)(1)(B) and, with respect to insurance, includes an increase in the charge for insurance. The courts have held that if an insurer sets the premium at an amount higher than it would have been in the absence of information from a third party, the insurer has taken adverse action. If that action was the result, in full or in part, of information obtained from a third party, the obligation of disclosure under section 615 is triggered. Safeco Insurance Company of America v. Burr, ___ U.S. ___, 127 S.Ct. 2201 (2007) (auto insurance); Whitfield v. Radian Guaranty, Inc., 501 F.3d 262 (3d Cir.2007) (mortgage insurance).

E.   OBLIGATIONS OF CREDITORS

Creditors occupy two roles in the credit information process: they use the information, and they supply the information. The preceding section addressed the role of creditors (and others) as users. This section concentrates on the role of creditors as suppliers. Sometimes the two roles clash. For example, in the 1990s some lenders that used consumer reports withheld information from the consumer reporting agencies. Some of them refused to report at all. Others refused to report the consumer's credit limit or highest balances. Their fear was that their competitors would use this information to decide which of their customers to try to steal away. Banking regulators object to this practice because it means that lenders must make credit decisions with less than full information. Consumers object because the creditor's failure to report account experience impairs the consumer's creditworthiness. In response, consumer reporting agencies threatened to deprive creditors of access to the system if they failed to report their experience with their customers. Fickenscher, Credit Bureaus Move Against Lenders That Withhold Info, Am. Banker, Dec. 30, 1999, at 1.

Until 1997 creditors—as suppliers of information—had no obligations under the FCRA. Now, however, section 623 prohibits a creditor from reporting information that it knows to be inaccurate (§ 623(a)(1)(A)). It also prohibits a creditor from reporting inaccurate information after a consumer has notified it of the inaccuracy (§ 623(a)(1)(B)) and obligates the creditor to notify the consumer reporting agency of the correct information (§ 623(a)(2)).

As described earlier, one of the more serious problems that consumers have encountered is a result of the way creditors transmit data to reporting agencies. Every month the creditor sends the agency information about all its accounts. Even if the creditor has notified the agency that a particular item of information is erroneous, the creditor may not remove the item from its data base. Similarly, if the creditor cannot verify the information, the consumer reporting agency may delete the information (as required by section 611(a)(5)(A)) but the creditor may not. When the creditor next transmits its monthly data, the inaccurate information reappears in the consumer's file. As a result of the 2003 amendments, section 623 now provides that, after correcting inaccurate information, the creditor "shall not thereafter furnish to the agency any of the information that remains incomplete or inaccurate" (§ 623(a)(2)). This obligation, along with all the other obligations newly imposed by section 623(a), may be enforced only by federal and state officials, not by consumers (§ 623(c)-(d)).

A separate set of obligations for creditors comes into play if the creditor is notified by a consumer reporting agency (as opposed to notification by a consumer) that the consumer disputes the accuracy or completeness of information in a consumer report. Section 623(b) requires the creditor to investigate the dispute. If the creditor determines that the information is inaccurate, incomplete, or cannot be verified, it must modify or delete the information, notify the consumer reporting agency, and permanently block the reporting of all information that its reinvestigation does not verify (§ 632(b)(1)(E)). In addition to reporting the correction to the agency that notified it of the consumer's dispute, the creditor must report the correction to every other consumer reporting agency to which it had reported the disputed information. Thus by complaining to one agency, the consumer may have the corrected information sent to all agencies that received the inaccurate or incomplete information. If a creditor fails to comply with its obligations under section 623(b), the private enforcement remedies of the Act (§§ 616–17) are available. Nelson v. Chase Manhattan Mortgage Corp., 282 F.3d 1057 (9th Cir.2002).

Johnson v. MBNA America Bank, NA

United States Court of Appeals, Fourth Circuit, 2004.
357 F.3d 426.

WILKINS, CHIEF JUDGE.

MBNA America Bank, N.A. (MBNA) appeals a judgment entered against it following a jury verdict in favor of Linda Johnson in her action alleging that MBNA violated [§ 623(b)(1)] of the Fair Credit Reporting Act (FCRA) by failing to conduct a reasonable investigation of Johnson's dispute concerning an MBNA account appearing on her credit report. Finding no reversible error, we affirm.

I.

The account at issue, an MBNA MasterCard account, was opened in November 1987. The parties disagree regarding who applied for this account and therefore who was legally obligated to pay amounts owed on it. It is undisputed that one of the applicants was Edward N. Slater, whom Johnson married in March 1991. MBNA contends that Johnson was a co-applicant with Slater, and thus a co-obligor on the account. Johnson claims, however, that she was merely an authorized user and not a co-applicant.

In December 2000, Slater filed for bankruptcy, and MBNA promptly removed his name from the account. That same month, MBNA contacted Johnson and informed her that she was responsible for the approximately

$17,000 balance on the account. After obtaining copies of her credit report from the three major credit reporting agencies—Experian, Equifax, and Trans Union—Johnson disputed the MBNA account with each of the credit reporting agencies. In response, each credit reporting agency sent to MBNA an automated consumer dispute verification (ACDV). The ACDVs that Experian and Trans Union sent to MBNA specifically indicated that Johnson was disputing that she was a co-obligor on the account. See J.A. 278 (Experian) ("CONSUMER STATES BELONGS TO HUSBAND ONLY"); id. at 283 (Trans Union) ("WAS NEVER A SIGNER ON ACCOUNT. WAS AN AUTHORIZED USER"). The ACDV that Equifax sent to MBNA stated that Johnson disputed the account balance.

In response to each of these ACDVs, MBNA agents reviewed the account information contained in MBNA's computerized Customer Information System (CIS) and, based on the results of that review, notified the credit reporting agencies that MBNA had verified that the disputed information was correct. Based on MBNA's responses to the ACDVs, the credit reporting agencies continued reporting the MBNA account on Johnson's credit report.

Johnson subsequently sued MBNA, claiming, inter alia, that it had violated the FCRA by failing to conduct a proper investigation of her dispute. See [§ 623(b)(1)]. A jury trial was held, and, following the presentation of Johnson's case, MBNA moved for judgment as a matter of law. That motion was denied. After the close of the evidence, the jury found that MBNA had negligently failed to comply with the FCRA, and it awarded Johnson $90,300 in actual damages. MBNA renewed its motion for judgment as a matter of law, asserting that [§ 623(b)(1)] only required MBNA to conduct a cursory review of its records to verify the disputed information. Alternatively, MBNA argued that even if it were required to conduct a reasonable investigation of Johnson's dispute, the evidence showed that MBNA had met that obligation. The district court again denied MBNA's motion, concluding that [§ 623(b)(1)] required MBNA to conduct a reasonable investigation and that there was sufficient evidence from which the jury could conclude that MBNA had failed to do so.

II.

MBNA first maintains that the district court erred in ruling that [§ 623(b)(1)]requires furnishers of credit information to conduct a reasonable investigation of consumer disputes. Section [623(b)(1)] imposes certain duties on a creditor who has been notified by a credit reporting agency that a consumer has disputed information furnished by that creditor:

> After receiving notice pursuant to section [623(a)(2)] of this title of a dispute with regard to the completeness or accuracy of any information provided by a person to a consumer reporting agency, the person shall—
>
> > (A) conduct an investigation with respect to the disputed information;

(B) review all relevant information provided by the consumer reporting agency . . . ;

(C) report the results of the investigation to the consumer reporting agency; and

(D) if the investigation finds that the information is incomplete or inaccurate, report those results to all other consumer reporting agencies to which the person furnished the information and that compile and maintain files on consumers on a nationwide basis.

MBNA argues that the language of [§ 623(b)(1)(A)], requiring furnishers of credit information to "conduct an investigation" regarding disputed information, imposes only a minimal duty on creditors to briefly review their records to determine whether the disputed information is correct. Stated differently, MBNA contends that this provision does not contain any qualitative component that would allow courts or juries to assess whether the creditor's investigation was reasonable. By contrast, Johnson asserts that [§ 623(b)(1)(A)] requires creditors to conduct a reasonable investigation. We review this question of statutory interpretation de novo.

In interpreting a statute, we must first "determine whether the language at issue has a plain and unambiguous meaning with regard to the particular dispute in the case. Our inquiry must cease if the statutory language is unambiguous and the statutory scheme is coherent and consistent. . . . The plainness or ambiguity of statutory language is determined by reference to the language itself, the specific context in which that language is used, and the broader context of the statute as a whole." *Robinson v. Shell Oil Co.*, 519 U.S. 337, 340, 341 (1997).

The key term at issue here, "investigation," is defined as "[a] detailed inquiry or systematic examination." *Am. Heritage Dictionary* 920 (4th ed. 2000); see *Webster's Third New Int'l Dictionary* 1189 (1981) (defining "investigation" as "a searching inquiry"). Thus, the plain meaning of "investigation" clearly requires some degree of careful inquiry by creditors. Further, [§ 623(b)(1)(A)] uses the term "investigation" in the context of articulating a creditor's duties in the consumer dispute process outlined by the FCRA. It would make little sense to conclude that, in creating a system intended to give consumers a means to dispute—and, ultimately, correct—inaccurate information on their credit reports, Congress used the term "investigation" to include superficial, unreasonable inquiries by creditors. Cf. *Cahlin v. General Motors Acceptance Corp.*, 936 F.2d 1151, 1160 (11th Cir. 1991) (interpreting analogous statute governing reinvestigations of consumer disputes by credit reporting agencies to require reasonable investigations); *Pinner v. Schmidt*, 805 F.2d 1258, 1262 (5th Cir. 1986) (same). We therefore hold that [§ 623(b)(1)] requires creditors, after receiving notice of a consumer dispute from a credit reporting agency, to conduct a reasonable investigation of their records to determine whether the disputed information can be verified.

III.

MBNA next contends that even if [§ 623(b)(1)] requires creditors to conduct reasonable investigations of consumer disputes, no evidence here supports a determination by the jury that MBNA's investigation of Johnson's dispute was unreasonable. . . .

As explained above, MBNA was notified of the specific nature of Johnson's dispute—namely, her assertion that she was not a co-obligor on the account. Yet MBNA's agents testified that their investigation was primarily limited to (1) confirming that the name and address listed on the ACDVs were the same as the name and address contained in the CIS [Customer Information System],[3] and (2) noting that the CIS contained a code indicating that Johnson was the sole responsible party on the account. The MBNA agents also testified that, in investigating consumer disputes generally, they do not look beyond the information contained in the CIS and never consult underlying documents such as account applications. Based on this evidence, a jury could reasonably conclude that MBNA acted unreasonably in failing to verify the accuracy of the information contained in the CIS.

MBNA argues that other information contained in the CIS compels the conclusion that its investigation was reasonable. For example, in support of its alleged belief that Johnson was a co-applicant, MBNA presented evidence that Johnson's last name had been changed on the account following her marriage to Slater and that Johnson's name was listed on the billing statements. But this evidence is equally consistent with Johnson's contention that she was only an authorized user on Slater's account and that, to the extent MBNA's records listed her as a co-obligor, those records were incorrect. MBNA also points to evidence indicating that, during her conversations with MBNA following Slater's bankruptcy filing, Johnson attempted to set up a reduced payment plan and changed the address on the account to her business address. However, a jury could reasonably conclude that this evidence showed only that Johnson had tried to make payment arrangements even though she had no legal obligation to do so. Indeed, Johnson testified that, during her conversations with MBNA, she had consistently maintained that she was not responsible for paying the account.

Additionally, MBNA argues that Johnson failed to establish that MBNA's allegedly inadequate investigation was the proximate cause of her damages because there were no other records MBNA could have examined that would have changed the results of its investigation. In particular, MBNA relies on testimony that, pursuant to its five-year document retention policy, the original account application was no longer in MBNA's possession. Even accepting this testimony, however, a jury could reasonably conclude that if the MBNA agents had investigated the matter further and

---

3. Under MBNA's procedures, agents are only required to confirm two out of four pieces of information contained in the CIS— name, address, social security number, and date of birth—in order to verify an account holder's identity. Johnson's social security number and date of birth were not listed on the CIS summary screen.

determined that MBNA no longer had the application, they could have at least informed the credit reporting agencies that MBNA could not conclusively verify that Johnson was a co-obligor.[4] *See* [§ 611(a)(5)(A)] (providing that if disputed information "cannot be verified, the consumer reporting agency shall promptly delete that item of information from the consumer's file or modify that item of information, as appropriate, based on the results of the reinvestigation").

IV.

MBNA next asserts that the district court improperly instructed the jury regarding the standards for determining liability. We review challenges to jury instructions for abuse of discretion. . . .

MBNA . . . argues that the district court erred in instructing the jury that, in determining whether MBNA's investigation was reasonable, it should consider "the cost of verifying the accuracy of the information versus the possible harm of reporting inaccurate information." MBNA apparently contends that the balancing test described in this instruction is inapplicable here because it is derived from cases involving the reasonableness of a *credit reporting agency's* reinvestigation, *see, e.g., Cushman v. Trans Union Corp.*, 115 F.3d 220, 225 (3d Cir. 1997); *Henson v. CSC Credit Servs.*, 29 F.3d 280, 287 (7th Cir. 1994). We recognize that creditors and credit reporting agencies have different roles and duties in investigating consumer disputes under the FCRA. Nevertheless, we believe that the general balancing test articulated by the district court—weighing the cost of verifying disputed information against the possible harm to the consumer—logically applies in determining whether the steps taken (and not taken) by a creditor in investigating a dispute constitute a reasonable investigation. The district court therefore did not abuse its discretion in giving this instruction.

. . . For the reasons set forth above, we affirm the judgment of the district court.

QUESTIONS AND NOTES

1. MBNA's argument that the statute only requires it to conduct a less-than-reasonable investigation seems on its face to be frivolous. What possible basis could its lawyers have had in mind?

2. What more could MBNA have done to verify the accuracy of its report that Johnson was obligated on the account? It is not clear when Johnson became associated with the MBNA account. The account was opened in 1987, and Johnson married Slater in 1991. If she was not originally on the

---

4. Because we conclude there is sufficient evidence to support a jury finding that MBNA failed to conduct a reasonable investigation of Johnson's dispute, we do not consider Johnson's argument that the judgment should be affirmed on the alternative ground that MBNA failed to "report the results of the investigation to the consumer reporting agencies," [§ 623(b)(1)(C)].

account, the application for the account would not have been helpful. So, to repeat, what more could MBNA have done?

3.   If MBNA had no original documentation that Johnson was a co-obligor, how should it have responded to the ACDVs?

4.   As described in Note 2, page 260 supra, consumers who identify inaccuracies in their consumer reports and complain to the consumer reporting agencies often accompany those complaints with documentation of why they think the reports are wrong. The reporting agency often informs the creditor of the dispute by transmitting merely an ACDV that captures the consumer's dispute in the form of a code or a short phrase (e.g., "consumer disputes balance" or "consumer states belongs to husband only.") What, if any, is the relevance of this practice to the creditor's liability under section 623(b)?

5.   Problem. *Consumer* borrows money from Bank to purchase a car. *Consumer* makes regular payments as agreed, but *Bank* fails to apply all the payments properly to satisfaction of *Consumer's* debt. After making all the scheduled payments, *Consumer* refuses to pay more, and ultimately *Bank* assigns what it believes to be a bad debt to *Collector* for collection. In due course, after receiving no payment from *Consumer*, *Collector* reports the delinquency to *CRA Credit Bureau*. *Consumer* informs *CRA* that she has fully paid the debt and owes nothing. *CRA* informs *Collector* that *Consumer* disputes liability and claims that she has paid the debt in full. Does section 623 require anything of *Collector*?

   Collector asks *Bank* to verify that *Consumer* still owes on the debt, and *Bank* reports back that she does. *Collector* in turn reports to *CRA* that the debt has been verified. Has *Collector* discharged its obligations under section 623?

6.   Notable for its absence from the FCRA is any requirement that consumer reports contain only information that is relevant to the purpose for which the report is issued. Why should Congress sanction the collection and circulation of data that has nothing to do with eligibility for credit, insurance, or employment? Cf. former 10 Me.Rev.Stat.Ann. § 1321(2) ("A consumer reporting agency shall not prepare, use or report information which it has reason to believe is inaccurate or not relevant to the purpose for which it is sought"); McKinney's N.Y.Gen.Bus.Law § 380–j(a)(1) (agency may not report that individual was arrested unless conviction followed).

7.   Sections 616–17 contain the remedies for violation of the FCRA. For negligent noncompliance with any requirement of the Act, the user or reporting agency is liable for the consumer's actual damages, as well as costs and attorney's fees. For willful noncompliance, the consumer is also entitled to "such amount of punitive damages as the court may allow."

   Actual damages, of course, include pecuniary losses, but they also include such nonpecuniary losses as mental anguish, injury to reputation, embarrassment, and humiliation. E.g., Sloane v. Equifax Information Services, LLC, 510 F.3d 495 (4th Cir.2007). They may even include the lost opportunity when a consumer is deterred from applying for credit because he or she knows that an inaccurate report will cause creditors to deny the application. Guimond v. Trans Union Credit Information, 45 F.3d 1329 (9th Cir.1995). Contra, Casella v. Equifax Credit Information Services, 56 F.3d 469 (2d Cir.1995). Punitive damages are available even in the absence of any actual damages. Saunders v. Branch Banking & Trust Co., 526 F.3d 142 (4th Cir.2008).

F.   CREDIT REPAIR ORGANIZATIONS

Many consumers are not aware of their rights to gain access to their reports, to have the agencies and creditors reinvestigate adverse information, and to append their own explanatory statements. Hence, several kinds of businesses have arisen. To protect against identity theft and other causes of inaccuracies in consumer reports, consumer reporting agencies and others have developed credit-monitoring services. For a fee, these entities send a consumer his or her consumer report on a monthly or other periodic basis and inform the consumer as soon as adverse information is added to the file.

Other entities, often called credit-service clinics, also have sprung into being. These businesses explain the availability of correction procedures and may handle or direct the consumer's interaction with the consumer reporting agencies (including identifying the agencies that have files on the consumer, writing letters to creditors or the agencies, and advising the consumer what to do). Unfortunately, their advertisements often claim or suggest that they can deliver more than they actually can. Thus, some clinics have advertised that they can "fix" a consumer's credit, "correct" a poor credit record, "correct" a bad credit rating, or enable the consumer to obtain credit. One advertised on the internet, "FOR JUST $99.00 WE WILL SHOW YOU HOW TO CREATE A BRAND NEW CREDIT FILE AT ALL 3 OF THE MAJOR CREDIT BUREAUS . . . 100% LEGAL AND 200% GUARANTEED." Many states have enacted statutes to regulate these businesses. E.g., West's Ann.Cal.Civil Code § 1789.10 et seq. So has Congress. Credit Repair Organizations Act, 15 U.S.C. §§ 1679–1679j. And both the Federal Trade Commission and state officials have proceeded against persons making deceptive claims on behalf of credit clinics.

The federal legislation (reproduced in the Statutory Supplement as Subchapter IV of the Consumer Credit Protection Act) addresses several common practices of these businesses. According to the Director of the FTC's Bureau of Consumer Protection:

> Although there are legitimate, not-for-profit *counseling* services, the FTC has never seen a legitimate credit *repair* company. . . . This fraud is particularly appalling because it preys on consumers who already find themselves in financial difficulty as a result of layoffs, divorce, or heavy medical expenses.[9]

9. Credit Repair? Buyer Beware! FTC Press Release, March 5, 1998.

Credit-repair promoters . . . don't deliver on their claims. The fact is, they can't. No one can legally remove accurate and timely information from your credit report.[10]

In addition to misrepresenting what they can accomplish for the consumer with a bad credit record, these businesses have advised consumers to apply for an Employer Identification Number (EIN) from the Internal Revenue Service. They then advise the consumer to use this 9–digit number in lieu of a social security number when applying for credit, thereby creating a new identity. Alas, they fail to disclose that by doing this the consumer commits fraud and violates federal statutes by representing on a credit application that the EIN is his or her social security number.

The Credit Repair Organizations Act requires pre-contract disclosure (§ 405) and prohibits anyone in the "credit repair" business from making false or misleading statements or encouraging the consumer to do so (§ 404(a)). It also gives the consumer a three-day cooling off period in which to cancel any contract formed with a credit repair organization (§ 407) and prohibits the organization from receiving any compensation before it has performed the services for which it is being paid (§ 404(b)). Contracts that do not comply with the Act are void (§ 408(c)), and the consumer is entitled to recover actual damages, such punitive damages as the court may allow, and attorney's fees (§ 409(a)). In addition, the Act may be enforced by both the FTC and the attorney general of every state. (§ 410). For an example of enforcement of the Act, see FTC v. Gill, 265 F.3d 944 (9th Cir.2001), in which the court awarded $1.3 million in civil redress for representations by a credit repair organization that it could remove adverse information from consumers' credit reports.

The definition of "credit repair organization" is capable of very expansive interpretation. For example, courts have held that lenders and retailers that assist consumers in dealing with their indebtedness or in obtaining financing may be within the definition. Parker v. 1–800 Bar None, 2002 WL 215530 (N.D.Ill.2002) (lender advertised that it could help consumers purchase a car on credit); Cortese v. Edge Solutions, Inc., 2007 WL 2782750 (E.D.N.Y.2007) (debt-settlement company); Zimmerman v. Cambridge Credit Counseling Corp., 529 F.Supp.2d 254 (D.Mass.2008) (credit-counseling company); Helms v. Consumerinfo.com, 436 F.Supp.2d 1220 (N.D. Ala.2005) (credit-monitoring service); Premium Air, Inc. v. Luchinski, 735 N.W.2d 194 (Wis.App.2007) (unpublished) (state statute); Midstate Siding & Window Co. v. Rogers, 722 N.E.2d 1156 (Ill.App.1999) (state statute). Contra, Sannes v. Jeff Wyler Chevrolet, Inc., 1999 WL 33313134 (S.D.Ohio 1999) (auto dealer and financer); Plattner v. Edge Solutions, Inc., 422 F.Supp.2d 969 (N.D.Ill.2006) (debt-settlement company) It is noteworthy that the operator of the organization in *Gill* was an attorney. Could an attorney in ordinary practice helping consumers with problems under the FCRA be classified as a credit repair organization under section 403?

---

10. 'Project Credit Despair' Snares 20 'Credit Repair' Scammers, FTC Press Release, Feb. 2, 2006.

G. PREEMPTION

As an incentive for agencies to comply with section 609 of the FCRA (requiring disclosure to consumers), Congress provided in section 610(e) that information provided pursuant to section 609 could not serve as the basis for a common law action for defamation or invasion of the right of privacy. See Rodrigues v. R. H. Macy & Co., 391 N.Y.S.2d 44 (N.Y. City Civ.Ct.1977). Nevertheless, in Collins v. Retail Credit Co., 410 F.Supp. 924 (E.D.Mich.1976), the court gave judgment for $21,750 actual damages and $50,000 punitive damages for defendant's violation of the FCRA and also defamation. In view of section 610(e), how could the court permit recovery for defamation?

Section 625 is the Act's preemption provision. State laws governing credit reporting remain valid "except to the extent that those laws are inconsistent with any provision of [the FCRA], and then only to the extent of the inconsistency." In 1996 and 2003 Congress amended the Act to broaden the preemptive effect of the federal statute.

H. CREDIT REPORTING ABROAD

Credit reporting is more highly developed in the United States that elsewhere. According to one authority, however,

> Outside the U.S., consumer credit bureaus are on the rise. A recent World Bank survey found at least 25 new private bureaus were created in Europe, Asia, and Latin America during the 1990s. Quite a few public credit registries were also created, especially in Latin America. The big American bureaus have begun to expand abroad. Experian, now owned by a British firm, has concentrated on Europe, while Equifax has acquired a number of bureaus in Latin America.

Hunt, The Development and Regulation of Consumer Credit Reporting in America 12, Working Paper No. 02–21, Federal Reserve Bank of Philadelphia (2002).

In many countries development of the industry is constrained by the local laws and customs governing privacy of information about individuals. E.g., see Waters, Implementing Privacy Principles in Credit Reporting (2007) (prepared for the Australian Law Reform Commission). The barriers may be formidable: in Argentina the highest court upheld a statute requiring creditors to report delinquencies to the country's central bank but also upheld a provision in that statute that prohibits credit card issuers from reporting delinquencies to privately owned credit bureaus. Organizacion Veraz S.A. c/E.N.-P.E.N.-MEE. y O.S.P. s, CSJN, No. ampero ley 16.986 (La Corte Suprema de Justicia de la Nación 2007).

CHAPTER 6

Discrimination in Granting Credit

A. Introduction to the Equal Credit Opportunity Act

Upon receiving the consumer's application, and perhaps also a report from a consumer reporting agency, the creditor is in a position to determine whether to extend credit to the consumer. This determination depends in part on the creditor's assessment of the risk of default by the consumer. The level of risk acceptable to the creditor varies from creditor to creditor and for any given creditor may vary from time to time. It depends upon several factors, including the supply of money to the creditor, the cost of that money, the rate of finance charge that the law and the market allow the creditor to charge, and the remedies available to the creditor in the event the consumer defaults.

The creditor's evaluation of the information concerning a proposed extension of credit typically takes one of two forms. Under the traditional approach, a loan officer examines the application and the consumer report to evaluate the consumer's character, capacity (to carry the proposed debt), and capital (resources available for satisfaction of the obligation). More specifically, the loan officer considers such factors as income, length of employment, whether and for how long the consumer has owned a house, and the consumer's experiences with other creditors. The factors to be considered depend on the creditor's determination or hunch as to what factors bear most directly on creditworthiness. This is known as the judgmental method.

With the advent of computers, a second, purportedly more objective, method has emerged. It is known as credit scoring. The creditor selects several factors as most relevant and assigns differing numbers of points to each of the factors. The creditor awards points to each applicant depending on the extent to which each of the factors is present. For example, employment for more than ten years might be worth 15 points; employment for 6–10 years, 10 points; employment for 2–5 years, 8 points; employment for less than 2 years, 6 points; and unemployed, 0 points. After assigning points in this way for each factor, the points are totaled. If the total exceeds the number the creditor has fixed as the minimum score, the consumer gets the credit. If the total is below the minimum score, either the application is rejected or the creditor procures a consumer report and evaluates all the available information using the judgmental method.

274

The critical steps in the development of a scoring system are the selection of the relevant factors and the determination of the number of points to allocate to each factor. The existence of computers has made these steps possible. By subjecting the payment records of the creditor's prior customers to complex statistical analysis, it is possible to determine the one characteristic that, for that creditor, is the best predictor of satisfactory performance by the consumer. It is also possible to determine which other characteristic, when considered in conjunction with the first characteristic, will most increase the predictiveness of that first factor. The analyst then determines which characteristic, when considered in conjunction with the first two characteristics, most increases the predictiveness of those two. The process continues until the marginal increase in predictiveness is negligible. Ordinarily, a scoring system will contain fewer than a dozen factors (but one reported case states that the creditor's system considered 38 factors, Cherry v. Amoco Oil Co., page 297 infra). The computer analysis also determines the number of points that should be awarded to each characteristic, as well as the probability of default associated with each total score.

Since the factors are selected purely on the basis of statistical correlation, the factors (or some of them) may not appear very directly related to creditworthiness. An example might be "the existence of a telephone in the applicant's home." Another example might be distinctions based on whether the prior credit extended to the applicant was by banks, finance companies, or department stores. For a description of the scoring method and how a system is constructed, see Hsia, Credit Scoring and the Equal Credit Opportunity Act, 30 Hastings L.J. 371 (1978). Development of a scoring system is expensive and requires a large data base, so use of the scoring method is most feasible for very large creditors. Therefore, several entities (including the major consumer reporting agencies) have developed scoring systems that they make available to creditors.[1] The use of credit scores has become so widespread that it has been estimated that 75–90% of all credit decisions are determined by the applicant's score.

In theory at least, the objective of both the judgmental system and the scoring system is to assess the creditworthiness of each applicant. Historically, however, some creditors have had another objective as well—to avoid doing business with persons who possess certain characteristics, such as sex, race, or ethnic background, that are unrelated to creditworthiness. And some creditors who did not intend to discriminate on these grounds actually did so, because they associated these factors with characteristics that are related to creditworthiness. For example, denying credit to persons who do not have steady income is rational, but denying credit to all women because of an assumption that they are going to be leaving the work force to care for husbands and children is not. Yet, despite this irrationality, the National Commission on Consumer Finance[2] concluded that sex discrimina-

1. The most widely known score is known as FICO, created by Fair, Isaac & Co.

2. The Consumer Credit Protection Act in 1968 established the National Commission

tion was widespread: not only did single women have more difficulty than single men in obtaining credit, but many creditors required women who got married to reapply for credit in their husbands' names, refused to extend credit to married women in their own names, ignored or discounted the income of married women who applied for credit jointly with their husbands, or were reluctant to extend credit to women who were recently widowed or divorced. NCCF, Consumer Credit in the United States 152–53 (1972). The irony is that some studies showed women to be better credit risks than men.

Since long-held customs and stereotypes are slow to die, Congress accelerated their demise in 1974 by adding the Equal Credit Opportunity Act (ECOA) as Title VII of the Consumer Credit Protection Act (CCPA). 15 U.S.C. § 1691 et seq.[3] As enacted, the ECOA prohibited discrimination because of sex or marital status in the granting of credit. In 1976 Congress amended the Act to prohibit discrimination on several other grounds as well—race, color, religion, national origin, age, receipt of funds from public assistance programs, and exercise of rights under the CCPA (ECOA § 701).

Unlike most of the rest of the CCPA, the ECOA is not limited to consumers. Rather, it applies to "any creditor" and "any applicant." Thus the Act falls into the larger category of civil rights legislation.[4] And despite the fact that the statute uses the term "applicant" to refer to the person protected by the Act, the Act is not limited to discrimination in the granting of credit. Section 701 expressly covers discrimination in "any aspect of a credit transaction."

The statute on its face is relatively simple. Section 701, the heart of the Act, proscribes discrimination in credit transactions and, when the creditor takes adverse action against the applicant, requires the creditor to inform the applicant of the reasons for that adverse action (§ 701(a), (d)). Section 705 elaborates on the concept of discrimination, providing that certain conduct by the creditor to take advantage of state contract and property law is not prohibited by section 701. The rest of the Act is procedural—directing the Federal Reserve Board to promulgate regulations and providing for administrative and private enforcement. This simplicity is deceptive,

on Consumer Finance (NCCF) to study the consumer finance industry and consumer credit transactions. The Commission submitted its report, Consumer Credit in the United States, in 1972. Its recommendations encompassed unfair contractual provisions, interest rate regulation, and mandatory disclosure of credit terms, as well as discrimination in the granting of credit.

3. The CCPA also contains the Truth-in-Lending Act, the Fair Credit Reporting Act, the Fair Debt Collection Practices Act, and others.

4. As civil rights legislation, the ECOA overlaps other federal statutes that prohibit

discrimination. E.g., see the Fair Housing Act, 42 U.S.C. § 3605, which applies to residential housing loans. As amended in 1988, section 3605 prohibits discrimination on the basis of race, color, religion, sex, national origin, handicap, and family status. See also the Americans with Disabilities Act of 1990, 42 U.S.C. § 12182, which prohibits discrimination against persons with disabilities and requires those who provide public accommodations to modify their policies, practices, procedures, and physical facilities so as to make their services available to persons with disabilities.

however, as the statute and the regulations—known as Regulation B—have given rise to numerous and sometimes very difficult questions. The staff of the Federal Reserve Board has issued an Official Staff Interpretation that addresses some of them.

In section 202.4, Regulation B repeats the broad prohibition of section 701(a). The Regulation then translates this broad injunction into a prohibition against using information concerning the sex, race, etc., of applicants (§ 202.6(b)(1)) and a prohibition against even asking for that information (§ 202.5(d)). Each of these prohibitions, however, applies only connection with credit transactions, and each has exceptions and qualifications. The following questions explore these matters.

QUESTIONS AND NOTES

1. The ECOA (and Regulation B) prohibit discrimination on a prohibited basis regarding any aspect of a credit transaction. One of the prohibited bases is receipt of public assistance. May a cellular phone service provider refuse to provide service to a person because he receives public assistance? May the owner of an apartment building refuse to rent to a person because she receives public assistance? Is this discrimination in a credit transaction? Regulation B section 202.2(j) defines "credit" as "the right granted by a creditor to an applicant to defer payment of a debt, incur debt and defer its payment, or purchase property or services and defer payment therefor." The Seventh Circuit wrote:

> We hold that typical residential lease does not involve a credit transaction. The typical residential lease involves a contemporaneous exchange of consideration—the tenant pays rent to the landlord on the first of each month for the right to continue to occupy the premises for the coming month. A tenant's responsibility to pay the total amount of rent due does not arise at the moment the lease is signed; instead a tenant has the responsibility to pay rent over roughly equal periods of the term of the lease. The rent paid each period is credited towards occupancy of the property for that period (i.e., rent paid November 1 is credited towards the right of a tenant to occupy the premises in November). As such, there is no deferral of a debt, the requirement for a transaction to be a credit transaction under the Act.

Laramore v. Ritchie Realty Management Co., 397 F.3d 544, 547 (7th Cir.2005).

Is the court right? Another prohibited basis is the exercise of any right under the Truth-in-Lending Act. If a consumer sues a car dealer for failing to make disclosures required by that Act, may the dealer later refuse to do business with the consumer when she wants to lease a new car, i.e. is an auto lease a credit transaction? According to the Ninth Circuit:

. . . [T]he lease obligation that [plaintiff] would have incurred under the automobile lease falls within the ECOA's definition of "credit."*
. . .

Although "credit transactions" might in some contexts lend itself to a narrow interpretation, we cannot give it such a construction in the ECOA in view of the overriding national policy against discrimination that underlies the Act and in view of the current structure of the Consumer Credit Protection Act, the umbrella statute. We must construe the literal language of the ECOA in light of the clear, strong purpose evidenced by the Act and adopt an interpretation that will serve to effectuate that purpose. . . .

In enacting and amending the ECOA, Congress recognized that a prohibition against discrimination in credit provides a much-needed addition to the previously existing strict prohibitions against discrimination in employment, housing, voting, education, and numerous other areas. The ECOA is simply one more tool to be used in our vigorous national effort to eradicate invidious discrimination "root and branch" from our society.

. . .

In enacting the Consumer Leasing Act [to amend the Truth in Lending Act], Congress explicitly recognized the "recent trend toward leasing automobiles and other durable goods for consumer use as an alternative to installment credit sales," *see* 15 U.S.C. § 1601(b). Prospective lessors run extensive credit checks on consumer lease applicants just as they do in the case of credit sales applicants. The problems of persons discriminated against with respect to credit under the Truth in Lending Act and the [Consumer Leasing Act] are for the most part identical. Therefore, interpreting "credit transactions" so that the ECOA applies to lease transactions as well as to credit sales and loans, is essential to the accomplishment of the Act's antidiscriminatory goal.

Brothers v. First Leasing, 724 F.2d 789, 790–794 (9th Cir.1984).

2. Regulation B section 202.6(a) permits the creditor to consider any available information. But section 202.6(b)(1)–(2) prohibits the creditor from considering the fact that the applicant's income derives from welfare payments. Then section 202.6(b)(2)(iii) turns right around and permits the creditor who uses a judgmental system (but not the creditor who uses a scoring system) to consider the fact that the applicant's income derives from welfare payments. What policies underlie each of these provisions? Compare section 202.6(a) with section 202.6(b)(3).

What is the rationale for permitting creditors to consider the source of income in judgmental systems but not in scoring systems?

---

* The ECOA defines credit as "the right granted by a creditor to a debtor to defer payment of debt. . . ." Under the terms of the lease that [plaintiff] applied for, she would have been obligated to pay a total amount of $16,280.16. Payment of that debt would have been deferred, and [plaintiff] would have been required to make 48 monthly installment payments of $339.17.

3. What are the justifications for the prohibition in section 202.5(d) against seeking information concerning sex, race, etc.?

To facilitate compliance with section 202.5, the FRB has promulgated model application forms. Regulation B, 12 C.F.R. Part 202, Appendix B. A creditor who uses the model forms is deemed to be in compliance with section 202.5.

4. Regulation B section 202.5(d)(5) prohibits the creditor from asking for the applicant's race, color, or national origin. But would it violate Regulation B for the creditor to assign positive value to an applicant whenever it appeared from the application or from the creditor's personal knowledge that the applicant was Spanish-surnamed or Spanish-speaking? See section 202.4.

5. Problem. *Seller* sells china, cookware, and tableware on credit. Its customer base is persons between the ages of 18 and 21. Does it violate the ECOA for *Seller* to extend credit on more advantageous terms to single women who are enrolled in any four-year college than to other 18–21 year olds? See ECOA section 701(c)(3), Regulation B section 202.8(a)(3), (b).

6. To what extent does the ECOA interfere with the creditor's discretion in deciding whether (and to whom) to extend credit? One person has written:

> Simply stated, ECOA has as its purpose to put all borrowers on a parity—man or woman, married or single, white or black, young or old and, according to 701(a)(2), rich or poor, because being on public assistance is not a permissible reason for rejecting credit.

Schiller, The Equal Credit Opportunity Act: A Wellspring of Litigation? 32 J.Mo.Bar 407, 408 (1976).

Does the ECOA deprive the creditor of discretion to discriminate between rich and poor? May a creditor deny credit to all persons who have annual incomes under $20,000? who have more than $8,000 in non-mortgage debt? whose net worth is less than $30,000? May a creditor who uses a scoring system and whose minimum score for granting credit has been 610 raise the minimum score to 625?

7. To develop a scoring system, the analyst examines the records of previous customers to determine which personal characteristics best correlate with satisfactory payment. If the large majority of a creditor's past customers have been men, the characteristics selected as predictors will be heavily influenced by the characteristics of satisfactory male customers. Yet for any given creditor, the characteristics that best predict satisfactory performance by men may not be the same as the characteristics that best predict satisfactory performance by women. Granted that it is unlawful discrimination for a creditor to assign more points because an applicant is male than it assigns because an applicant is female, is it also unlawful for a creditor to have entirely separate scoring systems for men and women?

8. Problem. *Creditor* has a furniture and appliance store in the center of a city of 400,000 persons. The city's racial composition is 40% black, 60%

white. The eastern part of the city is predominantly white, the western part is predominantly black, and the small central part is about evenly mixed. *Creditor* advertises heavily in the East Ender, a community paper distributed on the east side. *Creditor* does not advertise in the West Sider (the other community paper), in the city's general circulation newspaper, or on radio or TV. Is *Creditor* in violation of the Act? Are there other facts you would like to know?

B.   PROHIBITED BASES

Section 701(a) and Regulation B sections 202.2(z) and 202.4 prohibit discrimination on the basis of sex or marital status. The following materials examine this prohibition.

Markham v. Colonial Mortgage Service Co., Associates, Inc.

United States Court of Appeals, District of Columbia Circuit, 1979.
605 F.2d 566.

SWYGERT, CIRCUIT JUDGE.

The Equal Credit Opportunity Act, 15 U.S.C. §§ 1691 et seq., prohibits creditors from discriminating against applicants on the basis of sex or marital status. We are asked to decide whether this prohibition prevents creditors from refusing to aggregate the incomes of two unmarried joint mortgage applicants when determining their creditworthiness in a situation where the incomes of two similarly situated married joint applicants would have been aggregated. The plaintiffs in this action, Jerry and Marcia Markham, appeal the judgment of the district court granting defendant Illinois Federal Service Savings and Loan Association's motion for summary judgment. We reverse. The plaintiffs also appeal the judgment of the district court granting a motion for summary judgment on behalf of defendants Colonial Mortgage Service Co. Associates, Inc., Al Shoemaker, and B.W. Real Estate, Inc. As to this matter, we affirm.

I

In November 1976 plaintiffs Marcia J. Harris[2] and Jerry Markham announced their engagement and began looking for a residence in the Capitol Hill section of Washington, D.C. One of the real estate firms which they contacted, defendant B.W. Real Estate, Inc., found suitable property for them, and in December 1976 Markham and Harris signed a contract of sale for the property.

2. Plaintiffs were married on April 9, 1977, and the complaint was amended to   reflect the name change of Marcia Harris.

Upon the recommendation of B.W. Real Estate, plaintiffs agreed to have defendant Colonial Mortgage Service Co. Associates, Inc. (Colonial Mortgage) conduct a credit check. Plaintiffs subsequently submitted a joint mortgage application to Colonial Mortgage, who in turn submitted it to Colonial Mortgage Service Company (Colonial–Philadelphia), a business entity located in Philadelphia and not a party to this action.

In March 1976 Colonial–Philadelphia had entered into an agreement with defendant Illinois Federal Service Savings and Loan Association (Illinois Federal), whereby Illinois Federal agreed to purchase certain mortgages and trust deeds offered it by Colonial–Philadelphia. Pursuant to this agreement, Colonial–Philadelphia offered plaintiffs' mortgage application to Illinois Federal.

Plaintiffs and B.W. Real Estate had decided that February 4, 1977, would be an appropriate closing date for the purchase of the Capitol Hill residence. Accordingly, plaintiffs arranged to terminate their current leases, change mailing addresses, and begin utility service at the new property. On February 1 the loan committee of Illinois Federal rejected the plaintiffs' application. On February 3, the eve of the settlement date, plaintiffs were informed through a B.W. Real Estate agent that their loan application had been denied because they were not married. They were advised that their application would be resubmitted to the "investor"—who was not identified—on February 8, but that approval would be contingent upon the submission of a marriage certificate.

On February 8 the Illinois Federal loan committee reconsidered the plaintiffs' application, but again denied it. A letter was sent that date from Illinois Federal to Colonial–Philadelphia, which letter stated that the application had been rejected with the statement: "Separate income not sufficient for loan and job tenure."

On February 9, 1977, plaintiffs filed this suit, alleging violation of the Equal Credit Opportunity Act. After the district court separately granted the motions of Illinois Federal and the other defendants for summary judgment on May 25, 1978, plaintiffs brought this appeal.

II

A.

We address first the appeal from the district court's summary judgment entered in favor of Illinois Federal. The district court concluded as a matter of law that plaintiffs could not state a claim under the Equal Credit Opportunity Act even if they showed that Illinois Federal's refusal to aggregate their incomes resulted, in whole or in part, in the denial of their loan application. This conclusion was based on the premise that creditors need not ignore the "special legal ties created between two people by the marital bond." It was the court's conclusion that under Illinois law the mere fact of marriage provides creditors with greater rights and remedies against married applicants than are available against unmarried applicants. Presumably the district court believed that this excused Illinois Federal under § 705(b), which allows a creditor to take "[s]tate property laws directly or indirectly affecting creditworthiness" into consideration in making credit decisions.

We fail to see the relevance of any special legal ties created by marriage with respect to the legal obligations of joint debtors. This was not an instance where a single person is applying for credit individually and claiming income from a third party for purposes of determining creditworthiness. In such an instance, the absence of a legal obligation requiring continuance of the income claimed by the applicant from the third party would reflect on the credit applicant's creditworthiness. Inasmuch as the Markhams applied for their mortgage jointly, they would have been jointly and severally liable on the debt. Each joint debtor would be bound to pay the full amount of the debt; he would then have a right to contribution from his joint debtor. . . . While it may be true that judicially-enforceable rights such as support and maintenance are legal consequences of married status, they are irrelevancies as far as the creditworthiness of joint applicants is concerned. Illinois Federal would have had no greater rights against the Markhams had they been married, nor would the Markhams have had greater rights against each other on this particular obligation. Thus, inasmuch as the state laws attaching in the event of marriage would not affect the creditworthiness of these joint applicants, section 705(b) may not be used to justify the refusal to aggregate the plaintiffs' incomes on the basis of marital status.

B.

We turn to a consideration of whether the Equal Credit Opportunity Act's prohibition of discrimination on the basis of sex or marital status makes illegal Illinois Federal's refusal to aggregate plaintiffs' income when determining their creditworthiness. Illinois Federal contends that neither the purpose nor the language of the Act requires it to combine the incomes of unmarried joint applicants when making that determination.

We start, as we must, with the language of the statute itself. March v. United States, 506 F.2d 1306, 1313 (1974). Section 701(a) provides:

> It shall be unlawful for any creditor to discriminate against any applicant, with respect to any aspect of a credit transaction—
>
> (1) on the basis of . . . sex or marital status
>
> . . .

This language is simple, and its meaning is not difficult to comprehend. Illinois Federal itself has correctly phrased the standard in its brief: The Act forbids discrimination "on the basis of a person's marital status, that is, to treat persons differently, all other facts being the same, because of their marital status. . . ." Brief for Defendant Illinois Federal at 18. Illinois Federal does not contend that they would not have aggregated plaintiffs' income had they been married at the time. Indeed, Illinois

Federal concedes that the law would have required it to do so.[4] Thus, it is plain that Illinois Federal treated plaintiffs differently—that is, refused to aggregate their incomes solely because of their marital status, which is precisely the sort of discrimination prohibited by section 701(a)(1) on its face.

Despite the section's clarity of language, Illinois Federal seeks to avoid a finding of prohibited discrimination by arguing that it was not the Congressional purpose to require such an aggregation of the incomes of non-married applicants. It can be assumed, *arguendo*, that one, perhaps even the main, purpose of the act was to eradicate credit discrimination waged against women, especially married women whom creditors traditionally refused to consider apart from their husbands as individually worthy of credit. But granting such an assumption does not negate the clear language of the Act itself that discrimination against *any* applicant, with respect to *any* aspect of a credit transaction, which is based on marital status is outlawed. When the plain meaning of a statute appears on its face, we need not concern ourselves with legislative history, especially when evidence of the legislation's history as has been presented to us does not argue persuasively for a narrower meaning than that which is apparent from the statutory language. We believe that the meaning of the words chosen by Congress is readily apparent.

Illinois Federal expresses the fear that a holding such as we reach today will require it to aggregate the incomes of all persons who apply for credit as a group. Lest it be misinterpreted, we note that our holding is not itself that far-reaching. It does no more than require Illinois Federal to treat plaintiffs—a couple jointly applying for credit—the same as they would be treated if married. We have not been asked to decide what the effect of the Act would have been had plaintiffs not applied for credit jointly. Nor do we have before us a question of whether the Act's marital status provision in any way applies to a situation where more than two people jointly request credit. We hold only that, under the Act Illinois Federal should have treated plaintiffs—an unmarried couple applying for credit jointly—the same as it would have treated them had they been married at the time.

C.

Illinois Federal also contends that, regardless of this court's decision on the issue of income aggregation, the judgment of the district court should be affirmed. The premise of this contention is that, even had the incomes of plaintiffs' been combined, Illinois Federal would still not have extended the loan because of lack of sufficient job tenure or credit history.

---

4. 12 U.S.C. § 1735f–5 requires that "every person engaged in making mortgage loans secured by residential real property consider without prejudice the combined income of both husband and wife for the purpose of extending mortgage credit . . . to a married couple or either member thereof." See also Brief for Defendant Illinois Federal at 14.

Due to the district court's basis for decision and the state of the record, we are not in position to pass on the validity of this separate issue.

The district court entered summary judgment for Illinois Federal on the ground that the failure to aggregate incomes was not a violation of the Act. Thus, having no need to do so, it never reached the question of whether plaintiffs were otherwise eligible for the loan. Whether Illinois Federal would have otherwise extended the loan is a question of fact that is material, given our disposition of the aggregation issue. Accordingly, if there is a genuine dispute over that issue, summary judgment is inappropriate. On the record, there appears to be such a dispute. Although Illinois Federal contends that plaintiffs would remain ineligible regardless of aggregation, plaintiffs assert that they were told the loan would be forthcoming if they produced a marriage certificate. Because we remand the case to the district court, we deem it sufficient to note the appearance of a genuine issue of material fact on this state of the record. Following remand, further discovery and additional affidavits may either confirm or dispel this appearance.[6]

. . .

In sum, the order of the district court granting summary judgment to defendant Illinois Federal is reversed, and the cause is remanded. . . .

QUESTIONS AND NOTES

1. At the time of the facts in *Markham,* the ECOA prohibited only discrimination on the basis of sex or marital status. The court says that the statutory language "is simple, and its meaning is not difficult to comprehend." The critical phrase, of course, is "marital status." According to the court, what is the plain meaning of this phrase?

Under the court's definition, what would be the result in the following hypothetical: Aaron and Claire are amateur pilots and decide to buy a small plane together. Aaron is married to Alice, and Claire is married to Carl. Neither Aaron nor Claire alone has sufficient income to obtain the necessary financing. So they apply jointly to *FirstBank* for a loan. *FirstBank's* policy is to aggregate the income of joint applicants who are married to each other. Must *FirstBank* aggregate Aaron's and Claire's incomes for purposes of determining whether they are creditworthy?

2. What if eight unmarried persons jointly apply for a loan to enable them to purchase recreational property at a nearby lake? The court in *Markham* expressly refrains from deciding this question. By what reasoning could the court, if later confronted with this question, decide that the creditor need not aggregate the incomes of the joint applicants?

3. In McFadden v. Elma Country Club, 613 P.2d 146 (Wash.App.1980), plaintiff contracted to purchase a share of stock in the Elma Country Club.

---

6. For example, it may be determined how the marital status of applicants affects Illinois Federal's "judgmental evaluation" of their job tenure and credit history.

Ownership of the share carried with it the right to occupy a house owned by the Club, and transfer of the share required approval of the Club's board of directors. The board of directors refused to approve the sale to plaintiff when it learned that she planned to live there with a man whom she had no immediate plans to marry. A state statute made it unlawful to refuse to engage in a real estate transaction because of sex or marital status. West's Ann.Rev.Wash. Code § 49.60.222. The court concluded that even though there was no sale or exchange of real estate here, this was a "real estate transaction." Hence, the statute applied. But the court held that the Club had not violated the statute:

> [I]nclusion of "unmarried *couples* of the opposite sex" within the protection of RCW 49.60.222 is inconsistent with the statutory language, which repeatedly prohibits discrimination against "a person." (Italics ours.) We do not dispute that discrimination against a person on the basis of sex, marital status, race, creed, color, national origin, or a handicap could be practiced against more than one person in violation of the statute. This does not mean, however, that the Commission was correct when it purported to find discrimination against unmarried couples where there was no claim of discrimination against either person individually because of his or her marital status.

Id. at 151.

The ECOA (§ 701) and Regulation B (§ 202.4) both speak of discrimination against any "applicant," which is defined, in part, as "any person" (Regulation B § 202.2(e)). Under the approach of the court in *McFadden*, how would the hypotheticals in Questions 1–2 be decided?

In County of Dane v. Norman, 497 N.W.2d 714 (Wis.1993), an ordinance prohibited discrimination in housing on the basis of marital status. Prospective tenants challenged a landlord's policy of refusing to rent to persons who were not related to each other. The court wrote:

> [The landlord's] motivation for denying rental to the individuals in this case was triggered by their "conduct," not their "marital status." . . . "[M]arital status" refers to the state or condition of being married, the state or condition of being single, and the like. . . . It is undisputed that [the landlord] would have rented to any of the prospective tenants, regardless of their individual "marital status," if they had not intended to live together. Their living together is "conduct," not "status."

Under this approach how would the hypotheticals in Questions 1–2 be decided?

4. *Should* a creditor be able to treat joint applicants who are married differently from joint applicants who are not married?

5. May a bank that issues Visa cards send letters to each cardholder offering to issue cards to members of the cardholder's family?

6. Problem. Pat, who is attired in a dress and high heels, asks *Loan Officer* at *Bank* for a loan application. *Loan Officer* asks Pat for identification, and Pat produces a driver's license bearing the name Patrick and a photo in which Pat is dressed in male attire. *Loan Officer* tells Pat she will not provide a loan application form "until you go home and change clothes." Has *Bank* violated the Act?

7. Regulation B is more detailed in its treatment of permissible inquiries and use of information in the context of sex and marital status than it is in its treatment of the other prohibited bases. See sections 202.5(c), (d); 202.6(b)(3)–(6), (c); 202.7.

     a) Problem. *W* applies for an individual credit card at *Bank*. *W* and her husband, *H*, have a joint checking account at *Bank*, and *H* regularly deposits his paycheck into this account. *W* deposits her paycheck at another bank. The average balance in the account has been $2,000. In a routine check of its records in connection with *W's* application, *Bank* discovers the existence of the joint checking account. *Bank's* standard credit card agreement states, "In the event of default by Cardholder, Bank may set off against Cardholder's liability any then-existing liability of Bank to Cardholder." May *Bank* request credit information concerning *H*? See section 202.5(c)(2)(iii).

     b) Problem. *W* applies for a loan from *Bank*. *Bank* insists on collateral, and *W* proposes to give *Bank* a security interest in her car. May *Bank* ask if *W* is married? Should *Bank* be permitted to ask? If title to the car is held jointly by *H* and *W*, may *Bank* require *H* to sign the note and security agreement?

8. Regulation B contains some special rules for consumers who live in community property states. See sections 202.5(d)(2)(iv), 202.7(d) (3). These special rules recognize the creditor's greater rights in these states to reach the income and assets generated by an applicant's spouse. See ECOA section 705(b), Regulation B section 202.6(c). Under what circumstances, if any, may a lender in a community property state require that a consumer's spouse sign the loan contract?

9. One of the phenomena documented by the National Commission on Consumer Finance was the disappearance, upon their marriage, of any separate identity for women. Women could no longer obtain individual credit in their own names, frequently lost any existing credit, and had no existence in the eyes of credit bureaus. The ECOA has changed all that: Regulation B requires creditors to consider women for individual accounts (§ 202.7(a)), prohibits creditors from automatically terminating accounts when women marry (§ 202.7(c)(1)), and requires creditors to report information to consumer reporting agencies in the names of each spouse (§ 202.10(a)).

     a) May a creditor require that *H* and *W* select only one of their names to place on the account even though both are contractually liable for paying the joint account? May a creditor, such as a bank, require that all accounts of *H* and *W* at the bank (e. g., Visa, checking, savings, auto loan) be in one name?

b) When *H* and *W*, who have a joint Visa account at *Bank*, obtain a divorce, may *Bank* terminate *W's* credit and require her to reapply for an account?

c) If Claire Halpern applies for individual, unsecured credit, using the name Mrs. Michael Halpern, does the creditor violate the Act by opening the account in the name of Michael Halpern? See Regulation B section 202.5(d)(3).

10.   Under the Fair Credit Reporting Act, a consumer reporting agency may issue a consumer report on a person only if the person requesting the report has a permissible use for it (FCRA § 604). If an applicant seeks individual, unsecured credit, may the creditor obtain a credit report on the applicant? the applicant's spouse as well? See Regulation B section 202.6(b)(6).

In *Koropoulos v. Credit Bureau* (page 238 supra), did Lord & Taylor violate the Equal Credit Opportunity Act?

11.   In section 202.6(b)(2), Regulation B deals with age as a criterion of creditworthiness. Subsection (i) contains a general prohibition against taking age into account. Subsections (ii)–(iv) then provide that the creditor may take age into account. What is left of the general prohibition? To what extent may a creditor consider the age of an applicant? What is the underlying rationale of section 202.6(b)(2)?

Problem. *Mother*, age 84, and *Daughter*, age 59, live together in *Daughter's* house. Their income consists entirely of pension benefits, Social Security retirement benefits, and Social Security disability benefits. In the aggregate, these benefits provide just enough income for them to qualify for a 30–year mortgage loan from *Bank*. Their credit records also meet *Bank's* standards for this type of loan. If *Bank* rejects the application primarily because of *Mother's* age, has *Bank* violated the Act?

12.   Problem. *Consumer* applies for a three-year loan, relying in part on his social security retirement benefits as the source of funds for repayment. In evaluating the application, *Creditor* excludes this income from its determination of *Consumer's* assets. Has *Creditor* violated the Act? See ECOA section 701(a)(2) and Regulation B sections 202.2(z), 202.6(b)(5).

What is the relevance of 42 U.S.C. § 407, which provides that "none of the moneys paid . . . under [this portion of the Social Security Act] shall be subject to execution, levy, attachment, garnishment, or other legal process"?

What if, instead of social security benefits, *Consumer* were relying on unemployment compensation benefits that are not beyond the reach of creditors? Does *Creditor* violate the Act when it excludes those benefits from consideration in determining *Consumer's* creditworthiness? What if *Consumer* were relying on his union's unemployment benefits?

13.   *Clinic* operates a full-service primary care medical facility. *Clinic* refuses to accept patients whose treatment is covered by Medicaid. Does this violate the Act? See ECOA section 701(a)(2). The Federal Reserve

Board's Official Staff Interpretation states that with respect to income deriving from a "public assistance program": "Only physicians, hospitals, and others to whom the benefits are payable need consider Medicare and Medicaid as public assistance." Official Staff Interpretation 2(z)–3, 12 C.F.R. Part 202, Supp. I.

14. In determining the creditworthiness of a consumer, most creditors consider the amount of the consumer's existing debt. Unfortunately, a report from a consumer reporting agency may not reveal the outstanding balances on all the existing accounts. It does, however, reveal the existence of the accounts and the identity of creditors who previously have requested the report.

Problem. *Consumer* applies to *Card Issuer* for a credit card. *Card Issuer* obtains a consumer report, which reveals that in the last sixty days the report has been sent to American Express, Carte Blanche, Diners Club, and six banks that issue credit cards. Because of these numerous requests for a report on *Consumer*, *Card Issuer* rejects the application. Has *Card Issuer* violated the Act? See section 701(a)(3), Regulation B section 202.2(z).

C. REASONS FOR ADVERSE ACTION

The ECOA has two major thrusts. The preceding section considered one, viz., the prohibition of discrimination on the specified bases. This section examines the other, viz., the requirement that the creditor inform the applicant of the reasons for a denial of credit. ECOA section 701(d) requires the creditor to act promptly on a consumer's application for credit. If the creditor's action is adverse, the creditor must either inform the applicant of the reasons for the adverse action or inform the applicant of his or her right to request a statement of the reasons from the creditor. Please read section 701(d) and Regulation B section 202.9(a)(1)–(2), (b)(2).

The requirement of prompt action on an application is intended to prevent a creditor from effectively rejecting the application, perhaps because of a prohibited basis, by delaying tactics. The requirement of notification of reasons is intended to deter discrimination on account of prohibited bases because Congress believed that a creditor is less likely to discriminate if it must disclose the reasons for adverse action. In addition, if the consumer knows the characteristics that led to the adverse action, he or she may correct any possible errors and alter those characteristics so as to be creditworthy in the future. According to one study, of those customers of a particular creditor who were given reasons for the rejection of their applications, fifty percent supplied corrective or additional information and received credit. FRB, Exercise of Consumer Rights Under the Equal Credit Opportunity and Fair Credit Billing Acts, 64 Fed.Res.Bull. 363, 365–66 (1978) (for one of seven creditors studied; for the other six, the percentages ranged from two to eighteen).

The following questions explore the creditor's obligation to supply the reasons for adverse action.

QUESTIONS

1. The obligation to give reasons is triggered by "adverse action." What is "adverse action"? Obviously, it includes rejection of an application. What else does it include? See Regulation B section 202.2(c).

a) Problem. *Consumer* signs a contract to purchase a house. As part of his attempt to obtain financing, *Consumer* telephones *Bank* and asks about the terms and availability of home loans. *Bank's* employee says *Bank* is not making home loans at the present time. Is this "adverse action"?

b) Problem. Same as (a), except *Bank's* employee asks how much *Consumer* is paying for the house, how much he wants to borrow and for how long, and what his income is. Upon hearing *Consumer's* answers, the employee says *Bank* would not be willing to make the loan. Is this "adverse action"?

c) Problem. *Consumer* wants to buy a car on credit. Pursuant to an existing arrangement, *Seller* telephones *FirstBank*, supplies information concerning *Consumer's* income, assets, and debts, and asks whether it will loan *Consumer* the necessary money. *FirstBank* says no. *Seller* in turn calls *SecondBank* and *ThirdBank*, with similar results. Must any of the banks send notice to *Consumer*? *Seller* calls *FourthBank*, which says that upon formal, written application, it will make the loan. Does this affect the obligations of the first three banks?

d) Problem. *H* and *W*, who are married to each other, submit a written, joint application for credit. *Bank* approves the loan, but before the transaction is consummated, *H* changes his mind and tells *Bank* that he wants the credit individually rather than jointly with *W*. *Bank's* employee says that *H* will have to submit a written application. Must *Bank* give notice to *H*? See sections 202.9(a)(1) (introductory clause), 202.2(e), and Cragin v. First Federal Savings and Loan Association, 498 F.Supp. 379 (D.Nev.1980).

e) Problem. To pay for a sofa, *Consumer* presents her MasterCard. The seller telephones *Bank*, which issued the card, for authorization of this $500 transaction. *Bank* tells *Seller* the transaction is not authorized. Is this "adverse action"? What if *Bank's* reason is that the credit limit on *Consumer's* account is $1,000 and the sofa purchase would make her balance more than $1,000?

f) Problem. *W* has a credit card account with *Bank*. The outstanding unpaid balance is $430. *H*, her husband, files a petition commencing a case under the Bankruptcy Code. *Bank* thereupon treats *W's* account as in default and offsets against her liability of $430 its liability on *W* and *H's* joint checking account, which has a balance of $800, leaving the account with a balance of $370. Must *Bank* notify *W* pursuant to section 202.9?

2. Sections 202.9(a)(2) and (b) govern the content of the creditor's notice of reasons for adverse action. The notice must indicate the principal reasons and must be specific. The creditor may use the sample forms in Appendix C, thereby insulating itself from a claim that its notice was not sufficient. Most creditors use these forms.

Creditors who use a judgmental system for evaluating applications should have little difficulty complying with section 202.9(b)(2). The main problem is being truthful. E.g., Carroll v. Exxon Co., 434 F.Supp. 557 (E.D.La.1977) (notice stated "credit report did not supply enough information," but the court found that the real reasons for adverse action were the consumer's employment history and her failure to have a major credit card, a savings account, or any dependents).

3. In Fischl v. General Motors Acceptance Corp., 708 F.2d 143 (5th Cir.1983), a creditor using a judgmental system of evaluating applications denied an application for credit to finance $12,000 of the purchase price of an automobile. Its reason for the denial was that other than a home mortgage loan, the consumer had had no prior extension of credit in an amount or for a duration comparable to that for which he was applying. The letter informing him of this adverse action stated that the reason for the denial was, "credit references are insufficient." Does this meet the requirement of ECOA section 701(d)(3) that the statement of reasons contain the "specific reasons" for the adverse action? The court thought not:

> After considering the notice transmitted in light of the congressional language and purpose of § 701(d), together with the Board's rational interpretation thereof, see Ford Motor Credit Co. v. Milhollin, 444 U.S. 555, 100 S.Ct. 790, 63 L.Ed.2d 22 (1980), we find that GMAC's perfunctory reliance on the Board's sample checklist was manifestly inappropriate. While it resembles the category of "insufficient credit references" deemed acceptable by the Board, § 202.9(b)(2), the reason for refusal of credit noted by GMAC, "credit references are insufficient," arguably communicates a different meaning. The Board's statement connotes quantitative inadequacy; that of GMAC implies some qualitative deficiency in Fischl's credit status. GMAC's statement does not signal the nature of that deficiency and, since the name and address of the credit bureau was not supplied, did not provide the mandated opportunity for the applicant to correct erroneous information.

> Assuming, *arguendo,* that GMAC's phrase "credit references are insufficient" conveys substantially the same message as its regulatory counterpart, the notice provided in this case fails to satisfy the informative purposes of the ECOA. . . .

> The Federal Trade Commission (FTC) and the Justice Department, both charged with administrative enforcement responsibilities under the ECOA, §§ 704 and 706(h), have strictly construed § 701(d)(3)'s command in relation to several of the suggested reasons propounded in the Board's sample checklist. Use of such generic descriptive terms as "insufficient credit references" or "insufficient credit file" is not sanctioned by these governmental entities absent an

explanation by the creditor of the manner in which the credit reference or file was insufficient. See, e.g., United States of America v. Montgomery Ward & Co., [1980 Transfer Binder] Consumer Credit Guide (CCH) ¶ 97,732 (D.D.C. May 29, 1979) (consent judgment obtained by Justice Department, enjoining Wards from using as the reason for adverse action such terms as "insufficient credit references" without stating specifically in what respect the credit references were insufficient).

Given that a combination of factors contributed to GMAC's adverse credit determination, the reason articulated was misleading, or at best excessively vague. A GMAC employee acknowledged at trial that "many things can come under the definition of 'credit references are insufficient.' " Being unaware of the creditor's minimum standards of creditworthiness, Fischl was unable to translate this reason into concrete criteria. He could neither improve his credit application, correct any misinformation in his credit record, or guard against discrimination, thus thwarting both the educational and protective objectives of the ECOA.

Compare Higgins v. J.C. Penney, Inc., 630 F.Supp. 722 (E.D.Mo.1986). A creditor using a scoring system denied an application because the applicant did not have a checking account, a bank credit card, or an oil company credit card. The letter informing the consumer of this adverse action stated as the reasons, "type of bank accounts" and "type of credit references." Is this statement of reasons sufficiently specific? The court thought so:

> Plaintiff contends that Penney could not reasonably expect her to know that the company's credit rating system considers applicants with checking accounts better credit risks than applicants with just savings accounts. . . .

> Similarly, the plaintiff contends that the reason "type of credit reference" did not adequately inform her that her credit application score was low because she did not have a major bank card or gas card. The decision of the Fifth Circuit in Fischl v. General Motors Acceptance Corp., 708 F.2d 143 (5th Cir.1983), supports plaintiff's contentions. The Court in *Fischl* found that the reason actually given there, "credit references are insufficient," differed from one of the reasons included in the Federal Reserve's list of approved reasons "insufficient credit references." As a consequence, the Court in *Fischl* held that the creditor there could not escape liability by pointing to the similarity between the reason it gave and that authorized in the operative regulations. The Court will not follow the Fifth Circuit's approach since it requires rigid, exact quotation of the reasons listed in the regulation.

> The Court will decline to follow *Fischl* for another reason. The Fifth Circuit in that case found not only that the reason proffered by the potential creditor differed from an item on the regulation's list of acceptable reasons, but also that

> Use of such generic descriptive terms as "insufficient credit refer-
> ences" or "insufficient credit file" are not sanctioned by these
> governmental entities absent an explanation by the creditor of the
> manner in which the credit reference or file was insufficient.

Id. at 148. Here, the Fifth Circuit's opinion directly contradicts the
Federal Reserve regulations, which state, in part

> In providing reasons for adverse action, creditors need not describe
> how or why a factor adversely affected an applicant. For example,
> the notice may say "length of residence" rather than "too short a
> period of residence."

12 C.F.R. § 202.1101.[a] The Court cannot follow the Fifth Circuit's
approach in *Fischl* since it does not evidence sufficient deference to
agency regulatory expertise required in this Circuit.

The second and third reasons provided to plaintiff by Penney
resemble, in their degree of specificity, those included in the exemplary
list of reasons in the Federal Reserve regulations. While Penney's
response required some degree of deductive reasoning by plaintiff, the
Board's interpretive regulation states that this is not impermissible.
These regulations represent the Federal Reserve Board's view as to the
amount of specificity necessary to comply with the statute. While the
reasons given by plaintiff might have required her to exert more
investigative effort than some might think is appropriate, the Court
cannot say that application of the regulations here frustrates the
policies underlying the ECOA.

Plaintiff obviously knew she had only a savings account. The
reason given by Penney, "type of bank account," when considered
within the context of this knowledge, directed plaintiff to the appropriate area of inquiry. Further, plaintiff knew she did not have the type of
credit experience other applicants might have. She should have reasonably suspected, after receiving Penney's second letter, that a creditor
would look with disfavor on her relatively unsophisticated financial
background.

This was not a frivolous lawsuit. Penney could have easily provided plaintiff with more detailed and explanatory information, and
should consider varying its practices. The Court finds, though, on a
close question, that the reasons given by Penney for denying plaintiffs
credit card application did not violate the specificity requirement of
§ 701(d).

a.   The court states that it declines to follow *Fischl*. Are the decisions
really inconsistent?

b.   In *Higgins* the court quotes part of an Official Board Interpretation, 12 C.F.R. § 202.1101, which now appears as part of Appendix C to
Regulation B. The court omitted another portion of that same interpreta-

---

a. This official interpretation of section
202.9 now appears as Official Staff Interpretation 9(b)(2)–3, 12 C.F.R. Part 202, Supp.
I.—Ed.

tion: "The sample form is illustrative and may not be appropriate for all creditors. It was designed to disclose those factors which creditors most commonly consider. Some of the reasons listed on the form could be misleading when compared to the factors actually scored. In such cases, it is improper to complete the form by simply checking the closest identifiable factor listed."[5] Does this affect the soundness of the holding?

4. Achieving the requisite specificity is one of the creditor's tasks. Another, at least for creditors using a scoring system, is determining which factors led to the adverse action.

Problem. *Creditor* sends a rejection letter that states, "The principal reason for our denial of your application is insufficient credit references." Does this comply?

> Consumers have complained that the reasons for denial given by credit scoring creditors violate the ECOA specificity requirement. One rejected applicant complained to the F.T.C. that the credit scoring system itself was not adequately explained to her. The applicant, rejected under a creditor's scoring system, received a statement of reasons which related the denial to the creditor's point formula. The statement showed the applicant scored lowest in the "time on the job" and "credit references" categories. Dissatisfied with this response, the rejected applicant wrote for further clarification of the reasons for denial, and for the creditor's minimum requirement for time on the job and the number and type of credit references required. The creditor responded that the information requested could not be given because there were no minimum standards, and apologetically explained that because different point values are assigned to each factor considered, concrete standards for any one factor could not be established. The creditor further explained that the most information it could provide would be to list the five categories in which the applicant failed to score the maximum number of points. Still frustrated, the applicant again corresponded with the creditor and voiced her dissatisfaction, stating that she still could not understand why she was denied credit.

Taylor, Meeting the Equal Credit Opportunity Act's Specificity Requirement: Judgmental and Statistical Scoring Systems, 29 Buff. L.Rev. 73, 107–08 (1980).

> Scoring systems consist of anywhere from four to forty (or more) characteristics on which each applicant is rated. The determination to grant or deny credit depends upon the applicant's total score, which will be an individualized combination of the scores for each characteristic. Even if a rejected applicant's score on one or two characteristics is very low, the adverse decision is not necessarily attributable just to those characteristics, since higher scores on several other characteristics might have produced a sufficiently higher overall score. What, then, is the creditor to disclose?

---

5. The current version appears as Official Staff Interpretation 9(b)(2)–4, 12 C.F.R. Part 202, Supp. I.—Ed.

a) Problem. *Creditor* denies *Consumer's* application and sends a letter saying "we use a scoring system that assigns a numerical value to various items of information on your application. Unfortunately, your score was below the minimum score necessary for opening an account. No single item of information, by itself, is determinative; rather, our decision is based on your total score." Has *Creditor* complied with section 701(d) of the Act?

b) Should the creditor disclose all the characteristics on which the applicant failed to score the maximum number of points? the characteristics on which the applicant's score deviated most from the average scores?

c) In United States v. Montgomery Ward & Co., [1974–1980 Transfer Binder] Consumer Credit Guide (CCH) ¶ 97,732 (D.D.C.1979), a consent judgment required the creditor to provide the four or more characteristics that produced the greatest point differential between the rejected applicant's score on each characteristic and the maximum number of points obtainable for that characteristic. The FTC adopted a similar standard in In re Alden's, 92 F.T.C. 901 (1978). In a letter to the FRB, however, the FTC suggested using the difference between the applicant's score and the median score of marginally approved applicants. [1974–1980 Transfer Binder] Consumer Credit Guide (CCH) ¶ 97,663 at p. 87,118 (1979). And the Official Staff Interpretations suggest, as still another possibility, the difference between the applicant's score and the average score of all applicants. Official Staff Interpretation 9(b)(2)–5, 12 C.F.R. Part 202, Supp. I. Are these satisfactory? Are there any other alternatives? One commentator has concluded:

> Thus, the inherent conflict between the scoring system and the specificity requirement is apparent. Credit scoring creditors are incapable of giving precise, specific reasons for denial, even though Congress has mandated that precision and simplicity are of paramount importance in the statement of reasons. From all indications, scoring systems and the specificity requirement, as presently formulated, cannot coexist. In light of this realization, the practicality of prohibiting the use of scoring systems should be carefully examined.

Taylor, Meeting the ECOA's Specificity Requirement, supra, at 116. Banning scoring systems is only one possible response. What are the others?

5. The Fair Credit Reporting Act also requires the creditor to notify the consumer when the creditor has taken adverse action (FCRA § 615). "Adverse action" has the same meaning under both statutes (FCRA § 603(k)(1)(A)).

The two notices may be combined. See Regulation B, Appendix C.

D.   ENFORCEMENT

The ECOA provides for both administrative and private enforcement. Federal agencies that already supervise certain classes of creditors (e.g., banks, savings and loans, credit unions, and airlines) enforce the Act with respect to those creditors. As to the rest, the FTC enforces the Act (§ 704). If an agency believes litigation is necessary, it refers the matter to the Department of Justice (§ 706(g)). The Justice Department has brought several cases, some of which have resulted in consent decrees providing for compensation for victims of discrimination, e.g., United States v. Fleet Mortgage Corp., C.A. No. 96CV2279 (ERK) (E.D.N.Y. May 7, 1996) ($4 million); United States v. Northern Trust Co., No. 95–C–3239 (N.D.Ill. June 1, 1995) ($700,000); or for substantial civil penalties, e.g., United States v. General Electric Credit Corp., 57 Antitrust & Trade Reg.Rep. (BNA) 465 (D.Conn.1989) ($275,000). State officials may proceed under state statutes analogous to the ECOA. E.g., see Traiger, New York Seizes Fair Lending Initiative, N.Y.L.J. p. 1, March 16, 1998 (describing $3 million settlement by Roslyn Savings Bank).

In addition to administrative enforcement, the Act provides that a consumer injured by a creditor's failure to comply with the Act may recover actual and punitive damages (§ 706(a), (b)). Actual damages may include inconvenience, embarrassment, humiliation, mental distress, and injury to credit reputation. Shuman v. Standard Oil Co., 453 F.Supp. 1150 (N.D.Cal. 1978). Punitive damages are recoverable even if there are no actual damages. Anderson v. United Finance Co., 666 F.2d 1274 (9th Cir.1982); Cherry v. Amoco Oil Co., page 297 infra.

Section 706(b) lists several factors for the court to consider in determining the amount of punitive damages. One of those factors is "the extent to which the creditor's failure of compliance was intentional." Does the inclusion of this as one of many factors rather than as a prerequisite mean that punitive damages are available even for an unintentional violation? See *Anderson v. United Finance*, supra, 666 F.2d at 1278; *Shuman v. Standard Oil*, supra, 453 F.Supp. at 1154–56.

The successful plaintiff is entitled to costs and attorney's fees (§ 706(d)). This is true even if the court does not award any damages. O'Quinn v. Diners Club, Inc., No. 77C 3491 (N.D.Ill.1978) (defendant ordered to inform plaintiff of specific reasons for adverse action).

Section 202.2(e) defines "applicant" to include "any person who is or may become contractually liable regarding an extension of credit." Further, for purposes of section 202.7, the definition specifically includes "guarantors, sureties, endorsers and similar parties." Consequently, if a creditor requires a spouse to sign a debt instrument in violation of section 202.7(d)(4)–(5), the spouse has a claim against the creditor under ECOA section 706(a)–(b). But the spouse has signed the debt instrument and may be liable on that instrument for an amount far in excess of the amount of statutory damages for which the creditor is liable. This is especially true if, as typically is the case, the spouse is unaware of the ECOA claim until long after the statute of limitations has expired. (Section 706(f) creates a 2–year limitations period, and the spouse usually first learns of the ECOA rights when the loan is in default and the creditor sues.) Hence, the question arises whether the spouse can assert the creditor's violation as a defense to the enforcement of the debt. The federal court for the Eastern District of Michigan has held "no." Stringing together quotations from other cases, it wrote:

> "ECOA cannot be asserted as an affirmative defense. There is not express or implicit language in the ECOA that grants this Court the 'sweeping power' to invalidate the underlying guaranty in this case." "[N]owhere does [the ECOA] afford relief by way of affirmative defense. A counterclaim certainly can be premised upon a violation of the ECOA, but such a violation cannot be alleged to avoid basic liability on the underlying debt. . . . Invalidation of the debt is a remedy too drastic for the Court to implement simply by reading between the lines of the ECOA."

McPherson v. Commerce Bank, 1993 WL 939366 (E.D.Mich.1993).

Other courts have not found it necessary to read between the lines:

> Congress—in enacting the ECOA—intended that creditors not affirmatively benefit from proscribed acts of credit discrimination. To permit creditors—especially sophisticated credit institutions—to affirmatively benefit by disregarding the requirements of the ECOA would seriously undermine the Congressional intent to eradicate gender and marital status based credit discrimination. I conclude, therefore, that while an ECOA violation should not void the underlying credit transaction, an offending creditor should not be permitted to look for payment to parties who, but for the ECOA violation, would not have incurred personal liability on the underlying debt in the first instance. This rule places a creditor in no worse position than if it had adhered to the law when the credit transaction occurred. A creditor may not claim to have relied factually upon a guarantor's assets if it has never requested nor received financial information regarding them. Further, a creditor may not claim legal reliance on a signature that was illegally required in the first instance.

Integra Bank v. Freeman, 839 F.Supp. 326, 329 (E.D.Pa.1993). The Third Circuit endorsed this view. Silverman v. Eastrich Multiple Investor Fund, L.P., 51 F.3d 28 (3d Cir.1995). Hence, a spouse whom the creditor wrongfully requires to sign a debt instrument may assert that violation by way of recoupment as a defense to liability on the instrument even after expiration of the statute of limitations for asserting violations of the ECOA. In Eure v. Jefferson National Bank, 448 S.E.2d 417 (Va.1994), the court rested its similar conclusion on the ground that a contract formed in violation of the law cannot be enforced. Since the contract with the spouse was formed in violation of federal law, it was unenforceable against her. These courts differentiate between the spouse who was wrongfully required to sign the instrument and the primary obligor, whose signature was not procured in violation of the Act. Only the spouse is released from liability.

To obtain relief, of course, the enforcing party must establish that the creditor has violated the Act. If the violation consists of asking a prohibited question (see Regulation B section 202.5(b)–(d)), proving the violation poses no unusual difficulties. But how would you prove that the creditor discriminates on the basis of race or sex? Since it is unlikely that the creditor will admit discrimination on a prohibited basis, it may be very difficult to prove the violation.

In addition to direct proof of a violation of the Act, there is an indirect way to prove a violation. By way of illustration, assume that a creditor includes in the application form the question "When was the last time you wore a dress?" The creditor is not explicitly asking for the sex of the applicant, but the answer to the question ordinarily reveals that information. The question asked is a proxy for the question the creditor really wants to ask. The link between the proxy and the prohibited basis may be fairly clear, as where the creditor automatically rejects every applicant who receives child support payments or who works as a waitress.[6] A scoring system may assign more points to employment in industries or jobs that are traditionally heavily male (e.g., electrician, brick mason) than it assigns to industries or jobs that are traditionally heavily female (e.g., nurse, secretary).[7] Or it may assign negative value to the fact that an applicant's employment is part time.[8]

Regulation B recognizes the phenomenon of proxy information, expressly prohibiting some and permitting others. For example, section 202.6(b)(4) permits the creditor to consider whether there is a telephone in the applicant's home but prohibits consideration of whether the phone is listed in the applicant's name. (Do you see why that information is a proxy?) On the other hand, section 202.5(d)(5) permits the creditor to inquire about the applicant's permanent residence and immigration status, even though that information facilitates discrimination on account of race, color, and national origin.

The link between the alleged proxy and a prohibited basis may not be as clear as it is in some of the preceding examples. How does a rejected applicant establish that link? See section 202.6(a) n. 2 and the following case.

Cherry v. Amoco Oil Co.

United States District Court, Northern District of Georgia, 1980.
490 F.Supp. 1026.

ORINDA DALE EVANS, DISTRICT JUDGE.

. . .

I. SUMMARY OF CASE

Plaintiff is a white woman who resides in a predominately nonwhite residential area in Atlanta, Georgia. She applied for but was denied a

---

6. In re Alden's, 92 F.T.C. 901 (1978).

7. Shuman v. Standard Oil Co., 453 F.Supp. 1150 (N.D.Cal.1978).

8. Women are five times as likely as men to have part-time employment. Letter from FTC to FRB, [1974–1980 Transfer Binder] Consumer Credit Guide (CCH) ¶ 97,663 (1979).

gasoline credit card by Defendant Amoco Oil Company. She seeks damages under the Equal Credit Opportunity Act, which provides in part that it is unlawful for a creditor to discriminate against a credit applicant on the basis of race. She contends the reason for rejection of her application was race-related and that as such, said denial is proscribed by the Act.

Defendant Amoco Oil utilizes a complex computerized system to evaluate credit card applications. The system takes into account 38 objective factors in scoring each application, including level of income, occupation, and Amoco's prior credit experience in the U.S. Postal Service zip code area where the applicant resides. The information provided with respect to each of the 38 factors is scored by the computer. Credit is granted to those who receive a passing aggregate score; it is automatically denied to others.

Amoco's testimony indicated that its scoring system assigns a low rating to those zip code areas in which it has had unfavorable delinquency experience. Of those Atlanta zip code areas bearing the prefix 303–,[4] low ratings were assigned to all predominantly non-white zip code areas[5] as well as to many predominantly white areas. Plaintiff zip code area, 30310, was assigned a rating of 1, the least desirable rating on a scale of 1 to 5.[6] The evidence showed without dispute that if Plaintiff lived in a zip code area rated 3 or above, and all other information including level of income shown on her application had remained constant, she would have been granted a credit card by Amoco.

Plaintiff asserts that Amoco's utilization of zip code ratings is racially discriminatory. She contends she has standing to complain of such discrimination because she was adversely affected by it; to wit, she lives in a predominantly non-white zip code area which has been low-rated by Amoco's system.

Plaintiff produced two witnesses, herself and a sociologist. Plaintiffs testimony established that she received a letter from Amoco indicating her application had been turned down; the letter specified that one of the reasons was "our previous credit experience in your immediate geographical area."[8] Plaintiff testified she was humiliated and embarrassed by

---

4. The 303– zip code areas appear to encompass all of Fulton County except the northernmost part (Alpharetta and Roswell); north DeKalb County is included. Downtown Atlanta lies in the central part of Fulton County. The low-rated areas basically include the central urban area, plus all of south Fulton County below the downtown area. The north Fulton County and north DeKalb areas tend not to lie in the low-rated category, although certain zip codes in those areas (30305, 30324, 30341, 30340) are low-rated.

5. . . . The percentage of Atlanta's black population living in these zip code areas is close to 70%.

6. In fact, no Atlanta zip code areas are rated 5; only one is rated 4. All the rest are rated 1, 2, or 3. A rating of 1 or 2 has a negative impact on an application. 3 is a neutral rating which has no effect on acceptance or rejection of the application.

8. Amoco admits this is a reference to zip code area.

rejection of her credit card application. She further testified she subsequently has had to reveal this denial on other credit applications, but there was no testimony that she has been denied other credit. In short, Plaintiff presented no testimony of actual damages, unless the statutory term "actual damages" is to be interpreted by the Court as permitting an award of damages for mental anguish.

Plaintiff's other witness testified he had received from Plaintiff's counsel a list of those Atlanta zip code areas bearing a 303 prefix which were rated 1 or 2 by Amoco, along with information as to credit application acceptance rate in each area. He then compiled, based on estimates derived from 1970 census data, percentage estimates of nonwhite population in each of these areas. These two sets of percentages were then correlated on a scattergram he prepared (Plaintiff's Exhibit 5, Figure 4). As may be seen from an examination of the scattergram, it shows a significant correlation between acceptance rate/percentage of white population or conversely, rejection rate/percentage of nonwhite population.

Defendant Amoco produced witnesses who opined that the methodology used by Plaintiff was faulty for various reasons. Amoco claimed the scattergram was based on incorrect demographic data and that even assuming the correctness of the data reflected in the scattergram, it did not prove anything about relationship between use of zip code ratings and rejection of black credit applicants, because (1) it made the unsupported assumption that the reason for rejection was the applicant's residence in his particular zip code area and (2) it made the unsupported assumption that Amoco's applicant pool for each zip code area reflected the racial composition of the population as a whole.

II.   LAW APPLICABLE

. . . There has been relatively little judicial interpretation of the Act, thus leaving unresolved many provocative issues, including some presented in this case. In the first place, must a plaintiff show actual damages in order to be entitled to any relief under the Act? Secondly, what must a plaintiff show in order to make out a prima facie case? Can discrimination be inferred by using an "effects test" concept, per Griggs v. Duke Power Company, 401 U.S. 424, 91 S.Ct. 849, 28 L.Ed.2d 158 (1971)? If so, what is the proper methodology to be utilized?

Dealing with the damages question first, the Court holds that it is not necessary for plaintiff to prove actual damages to be entitled to relief. In this case, Plaintiff did state she was humiliated by Amoco's failure to grant her credit and that she felt she had been damaged by having to reveal the refusal of credit on future credit applications. This does not constitute proof of actual damage. However, it is clear to the Court that the Act did not envision the necessity of proof of actual damages as a prerequisite to entitlement to punitive damages, equitable or declaratory relief, or attorney's fees. Section 706(d) provides that "in the case of any successful action under subsection (a), (b), or (c) of this section, the cost of the action, together with a reasonable attorney's fee as determined by the Court, shall be added to any damages awarded by the court under such subsection." Subsection (a) is the subsection dealing with actual damages; subsection (b) pertains to punitive damages; and subsection (c) relates to equitable and declaratory relief. Obviously, § 706(d) envisions that there could be a recovery of punitive damages or equitable or declaratory relief in a situation where no actual damages are found. Therefore, the Court determines that should a violation be found, it has the power to award Mrs. Cherry punitive damages, even where no actual damages have been shown.

The question of what a plaintiff must show under the Equal Credit Opportunity Act to make out a prima facie case is a more subtle one. The Court notes that the drafters of the regulations accompanying the Act, see 12 C.F.R. § 202.6, footnote [2] as well as the legislative history of the Act, assume that the "effects test" will be utilized in cases under the Equal Credit Opportunity Act. See also Hsia, Credit Scoring and the Equal Credit Opportunity Act, 30 Hastings L.J. 371 (1978).

The so-called "effects test" is derived from a decision of the U.S. Supreme Court, Griggs v. Duke Power Company, a Title VII case under 42 U.S.C. § 2000e, et seq. There, the employer required persons hired in the labor department of its power generating facility to have a high school diploma. The effect of this requirement was to exclude a significantly higher percentage of black applicants from qualifying for employment than white applicants. In reversing the Fourth Circuit Court of Appeals' determination that Title VII required proof of intent to discriminate, and that such intent could not be inferred from mere disparate impact of the diploma requirement on black persons, the Supreme Court held that Title VII not only proscribes intentionally discriminatory conduct but also looks to the consequences of conduct, whether intent to discriminate is present or not. It held that plaintiff's evidence of disparate impact on a protected class was sufficient to make out a prima facie case. At that point, it became the employer's burden to show that the job requirement was related to job performance.

Although there are significant differences between the scope and purpose of Title VII and the Equal Credit Opportunity Act, and between the employment and credit settings, the court nonetheless concludes that use of an effects test concept is an available method for a plaintiff to make out a prima facie case. This conclusion is based upon the Court's assumption that otherwise, the Act will provide a remedy only in those rare cases where a company deciding on credit expressly states it is denied for a prohibited reason. Also, the Court is cognizant of the fact that discrimination in credit transactions is more likely to be of the unintentional, rather than the intentional, variety. The employment setting necessarily involves day-to-day dealings and contact between employer and employees; the relationship between a creditor and its customers tends to be more attenuated. Presumably, the creditor will act in whatever manner it deems best calculated to assure the creditworthiness of its customers and the maximum sales of its products. More personal considerations are not likely to be a factor. However, a given creditor could operate under the notion that a particular class of persons protected under the Act, are, for whatever reason, less reliable or creditworthy than others and may consciously or subconsciously select criteria which will have a tendency to "screen out" applicants in that class. If so, such criteria should be subjected to scrutiny to see if they are really necessary to meet legitimate business objectives, namely, accurately predicting creditworthiness.

The Court notes, however, that utilization of the effects test based on statistical methodology is apt to be quite difficult for a plaintiff. In the first place, the Act specifically proscribes inquiry by the creditor into the race, sex or marital status of a credit applicant, except in loans secured by residential real estate. See 12 C.F.R. § 202.5(d)(5); 12 C.F.R. § 202.13. Therefore, a creditor will not have direct information indicating the racial or other profile of its applicants or of the class of persons whose credit applications were granted. The conventional statistical methodology for showing disparate effect of a facially neutral test or practice is to compare representation of the protected class in the applicant pool with representation in the group actually accepted from the pool. If the statistical disparity is significant, then plaintiff is deemed to have made out a prima facie case.

III.   FINDINGS AND CONCLUSIONS

Here, Plaintiff did not seek to make a statistical comparison based on the actual applicant pool. Presumably this was not done because it could not be, based on the specific proscription in the Act. Instead, she attempted to show that the zip code criterion has a disparate impact on black people by showing that the percentage of applicants rejected in various low-rated zip code areas correlated to the percentage of black population in each of said zip code areas. This evidence does not make out a prima facie case.

The Court agrees with Amoco's contention that Plaintiff's proof fails to show that the zip code ratings tend to adversely affect black applicants disproportionately. Rather, it shows only that the computerized grading system taken as a whole tends to reject a disproportionate number of persons living in predominantly black areas. In other words, it is deficient for two reasons: (1) It does not test the effect of zip code as a criterion involved but rather tests the effect of the overall 38–criteria grading scheme and (2) it does not deal with either an actual applicant pool or with one which could reasonably be assumed to possess the approximate characteristics of the applicant pool.[9]

Having rejected the only theory advanced by Plaintiff herein, the Court nonetheless looks to see if other theories exist by which Plaintiff might prevail, based on the evidence introduced at the trial.

The Court does not think that proof of disparate impact need be shown by statistics in every case nor need it be shown by proof of actual

---

9. The Court recognizes that some Title VII cases have permitted reference to the general population on the assumption that the applicant pool would possess approximately the same characteristics. But this assumption is not valid in every case, and Plaintiff did not show the Court why it would be valid here.

disproportionate exclusion from the applicant pool. Because of the particular nature of the criterion complained of here, it may be possible to gain some enlightenment as to its effect from examination of the zip code map and the demographic data before the Court.

If the housing pattern in Atlanta is such that virtually all white persons live in neutrally-rated or high-rated zip code areas, but virtually all black persons live in low-rated areas, then the zip code criterion becomes suspect. Indeed, if the zip code/race correlation is high enough, the criterion itself takes on racial aspects so that it may be considered as a mere substitute for consideration of the applicant's race. The Court's examination of the evidence here indicates that no distinct racial pattern is evident, however. The low-rated zip code areas bearing prefix 303—on which Plaintiff's proof is based are not all predominantly black. In fact, the majority of them are predominantly white. Further, looking at the aggregate population of all such low-rated areas, one finds that 60% of such population is white and 40% is black.

A possible problem with zip code ratings in an area with a segregated housing pattern, such as Atlanta, is that as a result of actual or perceived lack of housing opportunities, black persons of all economic strata may tend to be grouped in certain zip code areas. If so, and if the economic housing pattern for white persons differs, it could mean there is a greater likelihood that an otherwise qualified black applicant would live in a low-rated zip code area than a similarly qualified white credit applicant. In order to test this hypothesis, it would be necessary to construct a hypothetical applicant pool on some basis reasonably gauged to approximate the actual applicant pool—for example, an income qualified group.[10] By looking at both the economic and racial composition of various areas of the city, one might determine whether the zip code ratings adversely affect income-qualified black persons more than income-qualified whites. Thus, if the segregated housing pattern in Atlanta means that the zip code ratings penalize[11] a high percentage of income-qualified black persons but only a low percentage of income-qualified white persons, then Plaintiff will have made out a prima facie case. At that point, it becomes Defendant's burden to show that the zip code ratings make Amoco's credit evaluation system more predictive than it would be otherwise.

The problem here, however, is that the Court does not have before it the data necessary to make such an analysis. Although the Court has some personal familiarity with the racial and economic makeup of various areas of the city, this general knowledge is an insufficient basis for such an analysis. Further, the Court notes that certain facts run counter to a theory that zip code ratings penalize income-qualified blacks but not income-qualified whites in Atlanta. For example, zip code areas 30305 (Buckhead) and 30309 (Ansley Park, Brookwood Hills) both of which are rated 2 by

10. I.e., a group meeting the median income standard of the applicant pool. Presumably, this information is available from Amoco's computer.

11. By "penalize" the Court means the negative weight or impact assigned to low-rated zip code areas. See footnote 6, supra.

Amoco, are well-known as predominantly moderate to high income white areas. Therefore, even if the Court were to take liberal judicial notice of facts not presented to it by counsel, there would nonetheless be insufficient evidence from which to draw a conclusion as to whether Amoco's use of zip code ratings treats otherwise qualified white applicants and otherwise qualified black applicants in a significantly different manner.

For the foregoing reasons, the Clerk is DIRECTED to enter judgment in favor of Defendant Amoco Oil Company, with costs cast upon Plaintiff.

QUESTIONS AND NOTES

1. Under the "effects test" the consumer establishes a prima facie case by showing that the creditor's standard or criterion has a disproportionate impact on a class of persons protected by the Act. It then is incumbent on the creditor to justify the standard or criterion by establishing that the standard or criterion is predictive of creditworthiness. Even if the creditor establishes this, the consumer may still prevail if he or she can supply an alternative standard or criterion that is equally predictive without having as disparate an impact on the protected class.

This three-part approach originated in the Supreme Court cases cited in Regulation B footnote 2. In the context of discrimination in employment, the test has received considerable judicial attention. For a description of the test and consideration of this line of cases in the credit discrimination context, see Hsia, Credit Scoring and the Equal Credit Opportunity Act, 30 Hastings L.J. 371, 417–28 (1978); Maltz and Miller, The Equal Credit Opportunity Act and Regulation B, 31 Okla.L. Rev. 1, 36–46 (1978); Blakely, Credit Opportunity for Women: The ECOA and Its Effects, 1981 Wis.L.Rev. 655, 679–89; Note, Credit Scoring and the ECOA: Applying the Effects Test, 88 Yale L.J. 1450, 1474–86 (1979). In 1991 Congress amended the Civil Rights Act of 1964 to clarify the allocation of the burden of proof in disparate impact cases. 42 U.S.C. § 2000e–2(k).

2. The court in *Cherry* recognizes a major difficulty in using the effects test. In the context of discrimination against blacks, establishing the existence of a disparate impact requires a comparison between the percentage of blacks in the applicant pool and the percentage of blacks among those who receive credit from the defendant. But Regulation B section 202.5(d)(5) prohibits the creditor from requesting applicants to indicate their race. Consequently, the creditor will not have the data necessary to make this comparison. How did plaintiff in *Cherry* attempt to establish disparate impact? Why was it inadequate? How does the court suggest a consumer might establish disparate impact? Why not presume that the racial composition of defendant's applicant pool is the same as the racial composition of the general population?

3. If the consumer succeeds in establishing disparate impact on a protected class, what will the creditor have to do to rebut the prima facie case? Will it matter whether the creditor uses a judgmental or a scoring system?

4. Consider also the consumer's burden at the third stage: proving the existence of a less discriminatory alternative. What would be necessary to establish that a proposed alternative is less discriminatory than the one being challenged? Reread page 275 supra.

5. The FTC and the Department of Justice have taken the position that use of ZIP codes in a scoring system is racially discriminatory. They have obtained consent judgments ending the practice. United States v. Amoco Oil Co., FTC News Summary, May 2,1980 (D.D.C.1980); United States v. Montgomery Ward & Co., [1974–1980 Transfer Binder] Consumer Credit Guide (CCH) ¶ 97,732 (D.D.C.1979).

6. In Williams v. First Federal Savings & Loan Association of Rochester, 554 F.Supp. 447 (N.D.N.Y.1981), the court recognized another method of establishing discrimination under the Equal Credit Opportunity Act. Pointing to an employment discrimination case, McDonnell Douglas Corp. v. Green, 411 U.S. 792 (1973), the court applied the "disparate treatment" test. In *Green* the Supreme Court stated that a person alleging racial discrimination could make a prima facie case by showing 1) he or she (a) belongs to a racial minority, (b) applied for and was qualified for an available job, and (c) was rejected; and 2) the position remained open and the employer continued to seek applications from persons of similar qualifications.

In *Williams* plaintiff alleged she applied for and was denied a mortgage loan by defendant but subsequently received a mortgage loan from another creditor. The court held that while she may have established the first three requirements above, she failed to prove the last one. Asserting that "[borrower]-lender transactions do not conveniently fit the scenario adopted in *McDonnell* to evaluate employment discrimination cases," the court held that since the loan extended by the second creditor was on different terms (a higher interest rate) and was based on more complete information than plaintiff had supplied defendant, plaintiff failed to make out a prima facie case. It granted summary judgment for defendant, and the Second Circuit affirmed without opinion. 697 F.2d 302 (2d Cir.1982). Note that plaintiff might have fared better had she proved that defendant solicited or acted favorably on applications from others with her financial qualifications, but note also that that information was much less accessible to her than was the information concerning her experience with the second lender.

A comparison between the treatment of the plaintiff and the treatment of other comparable applicants may be essential: the Court of Appeals for the Seventh Circuit has rejected the *McDonnell-Douglas* test when the plaintiff fails to establish the appropriate comparison. In Latimore v. Citibank Federal Savings Bank, 151 F.3d 712, 714, 715 (7th Cir.1998), the court stated

> The fact that a qualified black is passed over for promotion in favor of a white has been thought sufficiently suspicious to place on the defendant the minimum burden of presenting a noninvidious reason why the black lost out. But it is the competitive situation—the black facing off as it were against the white—that creates the (minimal)

suspicion, and there is no comparable competitive situation in the usual allegation of credit discrimination. Latimore was not competing with a white person for a $51,000 loan. A bank does not announce, "We are making a $51,000 real estate loan today; please submit your applications, and we'll choose the application that we like best and give that applicant the loan." If a bank did that, and a black and a white each submitted an application, and the black's application satisfied the bank's criteria of creditworthiness and value-to-loan ratio yet the white received the loan, we would have a situation roughly parallel to that of a *McDonnell Douglas* case. And when we have an approximation to such a situation, a variant of the *McDonnell Douglas* standard may apply, as we shall see. But such cases are rare, and this is not one of them.

. . .

At the heart of *McDonnell Douglas* is the idea that if the black is treated worse than the white in a situation in which there is no obvious reason for the difference in treatment (such as that the black lacks an essential qualification for the promotion), there is something for the employer to explain; and although the competitive situation which invites and facilitates comparison is usually missing from credit discrimination cases, sometimes there will be another basis for comparison. Suppose, for example, that Latimore and Eromital (who is white), apply at roughly the same time for roughly the same-sized loan from the same Citibank office. The two prospective borrowers are equally creditworthy and the collateral they offer to put up is appraised at the same amount. Both applications are forwarded to Ms. Lundberg and she turns down Latimore's application and approves Eromital's. The similarity in the situations of the white and the black would be sufficient to impose on Citibank a duty of explaining why the white was treated better. No effort at making such a comparison was attempted here.

7. In 1998 plaintiffs in separate cases filed class actions against the credit company subsidiaries of Nissan Motors and General Motors. Other plaintiffs later sued subsidiaries of other automobile manufacturers and banks. In each of these suits, plaintiffs challenged an aspect of the practice exposed in Bramlett v. Adamson Ford (page 42 supra): the dealer that arranges for financing increases the finance charge above the amount for which the finance company is willing to extend the credit. Specifically, plaintiffs in these suits alleged that the upcharge is greater for African–Americans and Latinos than for whites. To support this claim, they undertook complex statistical analysis of the amount of the upcharges. Their statistical analysis was facilitated by the fact that in many states the department of motor vehicles records the race of licensed drivers. The cases ultimately settled, with the defendants agreeing to permit the dealers to increase the interest rate by no more than two-and-a-half percent. In 2005 California enacted legislation limiting upcharges to two-and-a-half percent. Cal.Civ.Code § 2982.10.

8. Using geographic location as a factor in the extension of credit has drawn much attention in recent years. Creditors making home mortgage loans have been alleged to refuse loans to persons wanting to buy houses in certain areas. In effect, they have drawn lines around various neighborhoods in a city, making them off-limits. These so-called redlined areas typically contain older, sometimes deteriorating housing and are disproportionately populated by classes of persons protected by the ECOA. Hence, violation of the ECOA may also be a violation of the Fair Housing Act of 1968, 42 U.S.C. § 3601 et seq., which prohibits discrimination (on the basis of race, color, religion, sex, national origin, handicap, or family status) in the sale or rental of housing. (But see ECOA section 707(i)).

To obtain more information about redlining, Congress enacted the Home Mortgage Disclosure Act of 1975, 12 U.S.C. § 2801 et seq., which requires mortgage lenders to compile and disclose data concerning the number and amount of loans they have made in each geographic area. Two years later Congress enacted the Community Reinvestment Act, 12 U.S.C. § 2901 et seq., which requires the appropriate federal supervisory agencies to assess each mortgage lender's record of meeting the credit needs of its community.

A related problem is the use of geographic location by creditors or real estate agents as a factor in determining which lender a consumer should approach for a home mortgage loan. See Dennis & Field, Racial Credit Steering As a Discriminatory Credit Practice Under the Equal Credit Opportunity Act, 13 Akron L.Rev. 483 (1980).

E. PREEMPTION

The main preemption provision of the ECOA is section 705(f), which provides that the Act displaces state law only to the extent it is inconsistent with the Act. In addition, sections 705(c)–(d) specifically preempt certain state laws. In regulating small loan companies, it is common for states to have graduated limits on finance charges (e.g., 30% on the first $300, 18% on the balance) and to have limits on the maximum amount that may be loaned at these high rates. Lenders might try to evade these limits by splitting one loan into two smaller ones or by making separate loans to each member of a married couple seeking to borrow money. To prevent these evasionary tactics, state laws either may prohibit lenders from making separate loans to spouses or may require lenders to aggregate the credit extended to spouses. These laws are intended to and have the effect of treating the couple as a unit. This is directly contrary to one of the goals of the ECOA—ending discrimination against women—and sections 705(c)–(d) leave no doubt that these state laws are preempted.

QUESTIONS

1. Problem. *H* and *W*, who are married to each other, have an outstanding joint loan of $200 from *Lender*. Their state limits the finance charge to 30% on the first $300 and 18% on the balance, up to a total maximum loan of

$1,000. State law also requires that loans to spouses and multiple loans to individuals be aggregated for purposes of applying these limits. *H* and *W* each wants to borrow an additional $500. May they borrow it from *Lender*? What is the maximum rate *Lender* may charge?

2. If a state statute prohibits a creditor from refusing credit because of the applicant's "exercise of legal rights," must a creditor extend credit to persons who have declared bankruptcy? Is this state law preempted by section 701(a)(3)? See Regulation B section 202.11(a).

3. May a state anti-discrimination statute prohibit the creditor from asking the age of an applicant? marital status?

4. May a state provide a younger age of majority for married persons than for unmarried persons?

5. May a state require creditors to provide a copy of the credit contract to each person who signs it, except when the person is a spouse of an obligor?

F.   IS IT WORKING?

From 1975 through 1980 consumers filed fewer than thirty cases to enforce their rights under the ECOA. With respect to the requirement of prompt notification of the reasons for adverse action, the FRB's annual reports to Congress consistently revealed that 20–40% of financial institutions still failed to comply. To determine the early effect of the ECOA, the FRB (and two other federal agencies) commissioned an empirical study in 1977. Note, An Empirical Analysis of the Equal Credit Opportunity Act, 13 U.Mich.J.L.Ref. 102 (1979). As a result of a survey of consumers in August–September 1977, this study found that while 20% of all persons surveyed had recently been denied credit, only 18% of women had been denied credit. Similarly, fewer than 10% of the elderly had been rejected. On the other hand, for persons who were divorced or separated, rejections amounted to 25%, and for blacks, rejections amounted to 26%. The study also found, however, that marital status and race were not as accurate for predicting whether a person would be denied credit as were a half dozen other, lawful characteristics: age, time at present address, total debt, family size, income, and home ownership. Still, a disproportionate number of blacks and divorced or separated persons reported being denied credit. Thus the study suggests that while the ECOA, within three years of its enactment, was effective in eliminating discrimination on account of sex and old age, it was not so effective in eliminating discrimination on account of race and marital status. More recent studies focusing on racial discrimination indicate that discrimination on the basis of race continues to be a problem, especially in connection with housing loans, but also in connection with auto loans (see Note 7, page 305) and credit cards (see Cohen–Cole, Credit Card Redlining, QAU Working Paper No. QAU08–1 (Boston Federal Reserve Bank 2008) (available at www.bos.frb.org/bankinfo/qau/wp/2008/qau0801.htm)). Since the early 1990s the federal agencies charged with enforcement of the ECOA and other anti-discrimination states have been active in addressing racial discrimination.

*

PART II

REGULATION OF THE BARGAIN

The first Part of this book addresses problems in the formation of consumer contracts. Part II focuses on the substantive aspects of the transaction. This focus includes (1) the quality of the goods or services that constitute the subject matter of the transaction and (2) the terms under which sellers and lenders may extend credit or provide goods or services. Accordingly, Chapter 7 considers limits on the seller's ability to dictate the quality of the goods or services being provided. Chapters 8 and 9 consider limits on the creditor's ability to determine unilaterally the price and other terms of the deal. And Chapter 10 addresses problems regarding insurance sold in connection with the extension of credit.

CHAPTER 7

QUALITY STANDARDS

A. INTRODUCTION

A sense of history is necessary for a real understanding of any given area of the law. This is especially true of products liability. At the very beginning, "warranty" actually existed as a part of what is now the law of torts. But at a still early stage it became identified with what is now known as contract. The law of products liability has developed along both lines: one who produces and sells a product has a duty not only to use reasonable care in the production of the product but also to deliver what has been promised. The tort inquiries include the meaning of reasonable care and the persons to whom the duty of reasonable care is owed. The contract inquiries include the content of the performance and the persons to whom the duty of performance is owed. The second questions in each context are similar, and historically the answers have been similar: the duty is owed to the person with whom the producer has dealt. In the early years of the common law, this answer posed few problems. But over the centuries, commerce has become more complex, moving from a system of artisans selling their work directly to consumers, to a system of mass production and distribution through intermediaries before the product reaches the consumer. Limiting the producer's duty to persons with whom the producer has dealt means that the remote manufacturer is not liable to the consumer for injuries caused by the manufacturer's negligent production of a defective product. One of the stories of products liability in the twentieth century is how this doctrine of privity has broken down.

The breakdown occurred first in connection with the production and sale of food and other products (such as drugs and cosmetics) intended for intimate bodily use. Then in a landmark torts case in 1916, the New York Court of Appeals scrapped the requirement of privity for any product that, if negligently made, was dangerous and caused personal injuries. MacPherson v. Buick Motor Co., 111 N.E. 1050 (N.Y.1916). As for warranty law, it was not until decades later that two other landmark decisions eliminated the requirement of privity for products not intended for intimate bodily use. Baxter v. Ford Motor Co., 12 P.2d 409 (Wash.1932) (express warranty); Henningsen v. Bloomfield Motors, 161 A.2d 69 (N.J.1960) (implied warranty). Today the role of the privity doctrine is pretty much confined to cases in which the consumer's loss is something other than personal injuries. For a fuller discussion of the abandonment of privity, see Prosser, The Assault Upon the Citadel, 69 Yale L.J. 1099 (1960); Prosser, The Assault Upon the Citadel (Strict Liability to the Consumer), 60 Minn.L.Rev. 791 (1966).

The breakdown of the privity requirement is only part of the tale. The content of the manufacturer's duty has also changed. In tort, for several centuries, the content has been reasonable care. In contracts, the duty has been defined in two ways: first, by express warranty, under which the seller is obligated to produce whatever quality the parties agree upon; second, by the implied warranty of merchantability, under which the seller is obligated to produce a product that is reasonably fit for its intended purposes. For example, a chain saw must cut wood, and it must not fly into pieces the first time it is used. This implied warranty exists even if the agreement of the parties is silent on the matter. But historically it has been possible for the parties, by agreement, to modify this warranty, even to the point of negating it altogether. Another part of the story of products liability in the twentieth century is the movement in tort law away from negligence as the standard of conduct and the erosion in contract law of the seller's power to disclaim implied warranties.

The materials in the next section of this chapter show something of how the courts have developed tort doctrines to deal with defective products. The third section shows something of how the courts have developed contract doctrines under the Uniform Commercial Code to deal with defective products. The fourth section shows some legislative responses to the problems. And the final section shifts the entire inquiry from defective products to defective services.

B. STRICT LIABILITY IN TORT

Greenman v. Yuba Power Products, Inc.

Supreme Court of California, 1963.
59 Cal.2d 57, 27 Cal.Rptr. 697, 377 P.2d 897.

TRAYNOR, JUSTICE.

Plaintiff brought this action for damages against the retailer and the manufacturer of a Shopsmith, a combination power tool that could be used as a saw, drill, and wood lathe. He saw a Shopsmith demonstrated by the retailer and studied a brochure prepared by the manufacturer. He decided he wanted a Shopsmith for his home workshop, and his wife bought and gave him one for Christmas in 1955. In 1957 he bought the necessary attachments to use the Shopsmith as a lathe for turning a large piece of wood he wished to make into a chalice. After he had worked on the piece of wood several times without difficulty, it suddenly flew out of the machine and struck him on the forehead, inflicting serious injuries. About ten and a half months later, he gave the retailer and the manufacturer written notice of claimed breaches of warranties and filed a complaint against them alleging such breaches and negligence.

After a trial before a jury, the court ruled that there was no evidence that the retailer was negligent or had breached any express warranty and that the manufacturer was not liable for the breach of any implied warranty. Accordingly, it submitted to the jury only the cause of action alleging breach of implied warranties against the retailer and the causes of action alleging negligence and breach of express warranties against the manufacturer. The jury returned a verdict for the retailer against plaintiff and for plaintiff against the manufacturer in the amount of $65,000. The trial court denied the manufacturer's motion for a new trial and entered judgment on the verdict. The manufacturer and plaintiff appeal. Plaintiff seeks a reversal of the part of the judgment in favor of the retailer, however, only in the event that the part of the judgment against the manufacturer is reversed.

Plaintiff introduced substantial evidence that his injuries were caused by defective design and construction of the Shopsmith. His expert witnesses testified that inadequate set screws were used to hold parts of the machine together so that normal vibration caused the tailstock of the lathe to move away from the piece of wood being turned permitting it to fly out of the lathe. They also testified that there were other more positive ways of fastening the parts of the machine together, the use of which would have prevented the accident. The jury could therefore reasonably have concluded that the manufacturer negligently constructed the Shopsmith. The jury could also reasonably have concluded that statements in the manufacturer's brochure were untrue, that they constituted express warranties,[1] and that plaintiffs injuries were caused by their breach.

The manufacturer contends, however, that plaintiff did not give it notice of breach of warranty within a reasonable time and that therefore his cause of action for breach of warranty is barred by section 1769 of the Civil Code. Since it cannot be determined whether the verdict against it was based on the negligence or warranty cause of action or both, the manufacturer concludes that the error in presenting the warranty cause of action to the jury was prejudicial.

Section 1769 of the Civil Code provides: "In the absence of express or implied agreement of the parties, acceptance of the goods by the buyer shall not discharge the seller from liability in damages or other legal remedy for breach of any promise or warranty in the contract to sell or the sale. But, if, after acceptance of the goods, the buyer fails to give notice to the seller of the breach of any promise or warranty within a reasonable time after the buyer knows, or ought to know of such breach, the seller shall not be liable therefor."[a]

---

1. In this respect the trial court limited the jury to a consideration of two statements in the manufacturer's brochure. (1) "WHEN SHOPSMITH IS IN HORIZONTAL POSITION—Rugged construction of frame provides rigid support from end to end. Heavy centerless-ground steel tubing insures perfect alignment of components." (2) "SHOPSMITH maintains its accuracy because every component has positive locks that hold adjustments through rough or precision work."

a. This California statute is section 49 of the Uniform Sales Act. The UCC has superseded the USA but retains the requirement that the buyer give notice within a reasonable time after learning of the breach (§ 2–607).—Ed.

Like other provisions of the uniform sales act, section 1769 deals with the rights of the parties to a contract of sale or a sale. It does not provide that notice must be given of the breach of a warranty that arises independently of a contract of sale between the parties. Such warranties are not imposed by the sales act, but are the product of common-law decisions that have recognized them in a variety of situations. (See Gagne v. Bertran, 43 Cal.2d 481, 486–487, 275 P.2d 15, and authorities cited.) It is true that in many of these situations the court has invoked the sales act definitions of warranties in defining the defendant's liability, but it has done so, not because the statutes so required, but because they provided appropriate standards for the court to adopt under the circumstances presented.

The notice requirement of section 1769, however, is not an appropriate one for the court to adopt in actions by injured consumers against manufacturers with whom they have not dealt. (La Hue v. Coca–Cola Bottling, 50 Wash.2d 645, 314 P.2d 421, 422.) "As between the immediate parties to the sale [the notice requirement] is a sound commercial rule, designed to protect the seller against unduly delayed claims for damages. As applied to personal injuries, and notice to a remote seller, it becomes a booby-trap for the unwary. The injured consumer is seldom 'steeped in the business practice which justifies the rule,' [James, Product Liability, 34 Texas L.Rev. 44, 192, 197] and at least until he has had legal advice it will not occur to him to give notice to one with whom he has had no dealings." (Prosser, Strict Liability to the Consumer, 69 Yale L.J. 1099, 1130, footnotes omitted.) It is true that in [several cases] the court assumed that notice of breach of warranty must be given in an action by a consumer against a manufacturer. Since in those cases, however, the court did not consider the question whether a distinction exists between a warranty based on a contract between the parties and one imposed on a manufacturer not in privity with the consumer, the decisions are not authority for rejecting the rule of the La Hue case, supra. We conclude, therefore, that even if plaintiff did not give timely notice of breach of warranty to the manufacturer, his cause of action based on the representations contained in the brochure was not barred.

Moreover, to impose strict liability on the manufacturer under the circumstances of this case, it was not necessary for plaintiff to establish an express warranty as defined in section 1732 of the Civil Code.[2] A manufacturer is strictly liable in tort when an article he places on the market, knowing that it is to be used without inspection for defects, proves to have a defect that causes injury to a human being. Recognized first in the case of unwholesome food products, such liability has now been extended to a variety of other products that create as great or greater hazards if defective.

---

2. "Any affirmation of fact or any promise by the seller relating to the goods is an express warranty if the natural tendency of such affirmation or promise is to induce the buyer to purchase the goods, and if the buyer purchases the goods relying thereon. No affirmation of the value of the goods, nor any statement purporting to be a statement of the seller's opinion only shall be construed as a warranty." [This is section 12 of the Uniform Sales Act. The UCC counterpart is section 2–313.—Ed.]

Although in these cases strict liability has usually been based on the theory of an express or implied warranty running from the manufacturer to the plaintiff, the abandonment of the requirement of a contract between them, the recognition that the liability is not assumed by agreement but imposed by law, and the refusal to permit the manufacturer to define the scope of its own responsibility for defective products make clear that the liability is not one governed by the law of contract warranties but by the law of strict liability in tort. Accordingly, rules defining and governing warranties that were developed to meet the needs of commercial transactions cannot properly be invoked to govern the manufacturer's liability to those injured by their defective products unless those rules also serve the purposes for which such liability is imposed.

We need not recanvass the reasons for imposing strict liability on the manufacturer. They have been fully articulated in the cases cited above.[b] The purpose of such liability is to insure that the costs of injuries resulting from defective products are borne by the manufacturers that put such products on the market rather than by the injured persons who are powerless to protect themselves. Sales warranties serve this purpose fitfully at best. (See Prosser, Strict Liability to the Consumer, 69 Yale L.J. 1099, 1124–1134.) In the present case, for example, plaintiff was able to plead and prove an express warranty only because he read and relied on the representations of the Shopsmith's ruggedness contained in the manufacturer's brochure. Implicit in the machine's presence on the market, however, was a representation that it would safely do the jobs for which it was built. Under these circumstances, it should not be controlling whether plaintiff selected the machine because of the statements in the brochure, or because of the machine's own appearance of excellence that belied the defect lurking beneath the surface, or because he merely assumed that it would safely do the jobs it was built to do. It should not be controlling whether the details of the sales from manufacturer to retailer and from retailer to plaintiff's wife were such that one or more of the implied warranties of the sales act arose. "The remedies of injured consumers ought not to be made to depend upon the intricacies of the law of sales." (Ketterer v. Armour & Co., D.C., 200 F. 322, 323; Klein v. Duchess Sandwich Co., 14 Cal.2d 272, 282, 93 P.2d 799.) To establish the manufacturer's liability it was sufficient that plaintiff proved that he was injured while using the Shopsmith in a way it was intended to be used as a result of a defect in design and manufacture of which plaintiff was not aware that made the Shopsmith unsafe for its intended use.

. . .

The judgment is affirmed.

b. The court's citation of twenty cases, a treatise, and a law review article has been omitted.—Ed.

QUESTIONS

1. In the first part of its opinion, is the court deciding this case on the basis of express warranty or implied warranty?

2. Section 1769 of the Civil Code required the buyer to give the seller notice within a reasonable time. Why does the court conclude that this requirement is inapplicable to this case?

Why do you suppose the statute required notice to the seller? Are these purposes or reasons applicable to disputes between consumers and retailers, or are they limited to disputes between merchants? If they are applicable when the consumer asserts the liability of the retailer, are they also applicable when the consumer asserts the liability of the manufacturer?

3. UCC section 2–607(3) continues the requirement that the buyer reasonably notify the seller of any breach. Is *Greenman* authority for concluding that this requirement does not apply to a dispute between the consumer and the manufacturer? Of what relevance is comment 2 to section 2–313, ". . . the warranty sections of this Article are not designed in any way to disturb those lines of case law growth which have recognized that warranties need not be confined . . . to the direct parties to [a sales] contract"?

4. What justification is there for strict liability in tort for defective products? You may wish to consider comment *c* to Restatement (Second) of Torts section 402A, page 316 infra.

  a) Why is negligence less adequate than strict liability for providing compensation for injuries caused by defective products?

  b) If a manufacturer may be liable, as in *Greenman*, for breach of warranty, what need is there for strict liability in tort?

5. In what ways is *Greenman* related to the materials in Chapter 1 on deception? Consider especially Halpert v. Rosenthal, page 26, Pumphrey v. Quillen, page 30, and Ollerman v. O'Rourke, page 34. See Shapo, A Representational Theory of Consumer Protection: Doctrine, Function and Legal Liability for Product Disappointment, 60 Va.L.Rev. 1109 (1974).

A year and a half after the California Supreme Court decided *Greenman*, the American Law Institute approved the following provision for inclusion in the Restatement (Second) of Torts.*

§ 402A. Special Liability of Seller of Product for Physical Harm to User or Consumer

(1) One who sells any product in a defective condition unreasonably dangerous to the user or consumer or to his property is subject to liability for physical harm thereby caused to the ultimate user or consumer, or to his property, if

(a) the seller has engaged in the business of selling such a product, and

(b) it is expected to and does reach the user or consumer without substantial change in the condition in which it is sold.

(2) The rule stated in Subsection (1) applies although

(a) the seller has exercised all possible care in the preparation and sale of his product, and

(b) the user or consumer has not bought the product from or entered into any contractual relation with the seller.

Comment:

a. This Section states a special rule applicable to sellers of products. The rule is one of strict liability, making the seller subject to liability to the user or consumer even though he has exercised all possible care in the preparation and sale of the product. . . .

c. On whatever theory, the justification for the strict liability has been said to be that the seller, by marketing his product for use and consumption, has undertaken and assumed a special responsibility toward any member of the consuming public who may be injured by it; that the public has the right to and does expect, in the case of products which it needs and for which it is forced to rely upon the seller, that reputable sellers will stand behind their goods; that public policy demands that the burden of accidental injuries caused by products intended for consumption be placed upon those who market them, and be treated as a cost of production against which liability insurance can be obtained; and that the consumer of such products is entitled to the maximum of protection at the hands of someone, and the proper persons to afford it are those who market the products. . . .

g. Defective condition. The rule stated in this Section applies only where the product is, at the time it leaves the seller's hands, in a condition not contemplated by the ultimate consumer, which will be unreasonably dangerous to him. The seller is not liable when he delivers the product in a safe condition, and subsequent mishandling or other causes make it harmful by the time it is consumed. The burden of proof that the product was in a defective condition at the time that it left the hands of the particular seller is upon the injured plaintiff; and unless evidence can be produced which will support the conclusion that it was then defective, the burden is not sustained.

. . .

h. A product is not in a defective condition when it is safe for normal handling and consumption. . . .

i. Unreasonably dangerous. The rule stated in this Section applies only where the defective condition of the product makes it unreasonably dangerous to the user or consumer. Many products cannot possibly be made entirely safe for all consumption, and any food or drug necessarily involves some risk of harm, if only from over-consumption. Ordinary sugar is a deadly poison to diabetics, and castor oil found use under Mussolini as an instrument of torture. That is not what is meant by "unreasonably dangerous" in this Section. The article sold must be dangerous to an extent beyond that which would be contemplated by the ordinary consumer who purchases it, with the ordinary knowledge common to the community as to its characteristics. Good whiskey is not unreasonably dangerous merely because it will make some people drunk, and is especially dangerous to alcoholics; but bad whiskey, containing a dangerous amount of fusel oil, is unreasonably dangerous. Good tobacco is not unreasonably dangerous merely because the effects of smoking may be harmful; but tobacco containing something like marijuana may be unreasonably dangerous. Good butter is not unreasonably dangerous merely because, if such be the case, it deposits cholesterol in the arteries and leads to heart attacks; but bad butter, contaminated with poisonous fish oil, is unreasonably dangerous.

j. Directions or warning. In order to prevent the product from being unreasonably dangerous, the seller may be required to give directions or warning, on the container, as to its use. The seller may reasonably assume that those with common allergies, as for example to eggs or strawberries, will be aware of them, and he is not required to warn against them. Where, however, the product contains an ingredient to which a substantial number of the population are allergic, and the ingredient is one whose danger is not generally known, or if known is one which the consumer would reasonably not expect to find in the product, the seller is required to give warning against it, if he has knowledge, or by the application of reasonable, developed human skill and foresight should have knowledge, of the presence of the ingredient and the danger. Likewise in the case of poisonous drugs, or those unduly dangerous for other reasons, warning as to use may be required.

. . .

k. Unavoidably unsafe products. There are some products which, in the present state of human knowledge, are quite incapable of being made safe for their intended and ordinary use. These are especially common in the field of drugs. . . . Such a product, properly prepared, and accompanied by proper directions and warning, is not defective, nor is it unreasonably dangerous.

. . .

l. User or consumer. In order for the rule stated in this Section to apply, it is not necessary that the ultimate user or consumer have acquired the product directly from the seller, although the rule applies equally if he does so. He may have acquired it through one or more intermediate dealers. It is not even necessary that the consumer have purchased the product at all. He may be a member of the family of the final purchaser, or his employee, or a guest at his table, or a mere donee from the purchaser. The liability stated is one in tort, and does not require any contractual relation, or privity of contract, between the plaintiff and the defendant.

. . .

. . . Consumption includes all ultimate uses for which the product is intended, and the customer in a beauty shop to whose hair a permanent wave solution is applied by the shop is a consumer. . . .

m. "Warranty." The liability stated in this Section does not rest upon negligence. It is strict liability, similar in its nature to that covered by Chapters 20 and 21. The basis of liability is purely one of tort.

A number of courts, seeking a theoretical basis for the liability, have resorted to a "warranty," either running with the goods sold, by analogy to covenants running with the land, or made directly to the consumer without contract. In some instances this theory has proved to be an unfortunate one. Although warranty was in its origin a matter of tort liability, and it is generally agreed that a tort action will still lie for its breach, it has become so identified in practice with a contract of sale between the plaintiff and the defendant that the warranty theory has become something of an obstacle to the recognition of the strict liability where there is no such contract. There is nothing in this Section which would prevent any court from treating the rule stated as a matter of "warranty" to the user or consumer. But if this is done, it should be recognized and understood that the "warranty" is a very different kind of warranty from those usually found in the sale of goods, and that it is not subject to the various contract rules which have grown up to surround such sales.

The rule stated in this Section does not require any reliance on the part of the consumer upon the reputation, skill, or judgment of the seller who is to be held liable, nor any representation or undertaking on the part of that seller. The seller is strictly liable although, as is frequently the case, the consumer does not even know who he is at the time of consumption. The rule stated in this Section is not governed by the provisions of the Uniform Sales Act, or those of the Uniform Commercial Code, as to warranties; and it is not affected by limitations on the scope and content of warranties, or by limitation to "buyer" and "seller" in those statutes. Nor is the consumer required to give notice to the seller of his injury within a reasonable time after it occurs, as is provided by the Uniform Act. The consumer's cause of action does not depend upon the validity of his contract with the person from whom he acquires the product, and it is not affected by any disclaimer or other agreement, whether it be between the seller and his immediate buyer, or attached to and accompanying the product into the consumer's hands. In short, "warranty" must be given a new and different meaning if it is used in connection with this Section. It is much simpler to regard the liability here stated as merely one of strict liability in tort.

   n. Contributory negligence. Since the liability with which this Section deals is not based upon negligence of the seller, but is strict liability, the rule applied to strict liability cases (see § 524) applies. Contributory negligence of the plaintiff is not a defense when such negligence consists merely in a failure to discover the defect in the product, or to guard against the possibility of its existence. On the other hand the form of contributory negligence which consists in voluntarily and unreasonably proceeding to encounter a known danger, and commonly passes under the name of assumption of risk, is a defense under this Section as in other cases of strict liability. If the user or consumer discovers the defect and is aware of the danger, and nevertheless proceeds unreasonably to make use of the product and is injured by it, he is barred from recovery.

.   .   .

QUESTIONS AND NOTES

1. For liability to exist, the product must be defective. With respect to defects in production, what should be the test for determining whether the product is defective? With respect to defects in design, what should the test be? Do you suppose that it would be difficult to locate an expert witness to testify, after the fact, that the plaintiff's injury could have been prevented by a hypothetical change in design?

   What definition of defective does section 402A contemplate? See comments *g, h, i.* Compare Barker v. Lull Engineering Co., 573 P.2d 443 (Cal.1978). For contrasting views, see Keeton, Products Liability—Design Hazards and the Meaning of Defect, 10 Cum.L.Rev. 293 (1979); Epstein, Products Liability: The Search for a Middle Ground, 56 N.C.L.Rev. 643 (1978); G. Schwartz, Foreword: Understanding Products Liability, 67 Cal. L.Rev. 435 (1979).

2. For liability to exist under section 402A, a defect must render the product unreasonably dangerous. Why? The California Supreme Court has rejected this additional requirement. Cronin v. J.B.E. Olson Corp., 501 P.2d 1153 (Cal.1972). A few other courts have done likewise, but most require the product to be unreasonably dangerous.

3. As part of its formulation of the Restatement (Third) of Torts, in 1997 the American Law Institute approved a new version of the part entitled "Products Liability."* It retains the general principle of section 402A, but appears to drop the requirement of "unreasonably dangerous."

   § 1. Liability of Commercial Seller or Distributor for Harm Caused by Defective Products

   One engaged in the business of selling or otherwise distributing products who sells or distributes a defective product is subject to liability for harm to persons or property caused by the defect.

The next section of the new Restatement distinguishes manufacturing defects from design defects and defects consisting of the failure to warn. Note that the definitions of the latter two kinds of defects incorporate a version of the "unreasonably dangerous" requirement.

§ 2.   Categories of Product Defect

A product is defective when, at the time of sale or distribution, it contains a manufacturing defect, is defective in design, or is defective because of inadequate instructions or warnings. A product:

(a) contains a manufacturing defect when the product departs from its intended design even though all possible care was exercised in the preparation and marketing of the product;

(b) is defective in design when the foreseeable risks of harm posed by the product could have been reduced or avoided by the adoption of a reasonable alternative design by the seller or other distributor, or a predecessor in the commercial chain of distribution, and the omission of the alternative design renders the product not reasonably safe;

(c) is defective because of inadequate instructions or warnings when the foreseeable risks of harm posed by the product could have been reduced or avoided by the provision of reasonable instructions or warnings by the seller or other distributor, or a predecessor in the commercial chain of distribution, and the omission of the instructions or warnings renders the product not reasonably safe.

Comment:

d.   Design defects: general considerations. Whereas a manufacturing defect consists of a product unit's failure to meet the manufacturer's design specifications, a product asserted to have a defective design meets the manufacturer's design specifications but raises the question whether the specifications themselves create unreasonable risks. Answering that question requires reference to a standard outside the specifications. Subsection (b) adopts a reasonableness ("risk-utility" balancing) test as the standard for judging the defectiveness of product designs. More specifically, the test is whether a reasonable alternative design would, at reasonable cost, have reduced the foreseeable risks of harm posed by the product and, if so, whether the omission of the alternative design by the seller . . . rendered the product not reasonably safe. Under prevailing rules concerning allocation of burden of proof, the plaintiff must prove that such a reasonable alternative was, or reasonably could have been, available at the time of sale or distribution. . . .

Assessment of a product design in most instances requires a comparison between an alternative design and the product design that caused the injury, undertaken from the viewpoint of a reasonable person. That standard is also used in administering the traditional reasonableness standard in negligence. . . . The policy reasons that support use of a reasonable person perspective in connection with the general negligence standard also support its use in the products liability context.

How the defendant's design compares with other, competing designs in actual use is relevant to the issue of whether the defendant's design is defective. . . . This Section states that a design is defective if the product could have been made safer by the adoption of a reasonable alternative design. If such a design could have been practically adopted, the plaintiff establishes defect under subsection (b). When a defendant demonstrates that its product design was the safest in use at the time of sale, it may be difficult for plaintiff to prove that an alternative design could have been practically adopted. . . .

4. According to comment *n* to Restatement (Second) section 402A, the contributory negligence of the consumer is not a defense. This may not be an accurate reflection of the present status of the law. Most states have now adopted the doctrine of comparative negligence, which changes the traditional common law rule that the plaintiff's contributory negligence is a complete bar to recovery for the defendant's negligence. Instead, under the doctrine of comparative negligence, the plaintiff's recovery is reduced to the extent the injury is attributable to the plaintiff's own conduct. In many states, the courts have extended the doctrine of comparative negligence to cases predicated on strict liability. So, contrary to comment *n*, the negligence of the plaintiff may indeed be a defense.

At first glance, it seems anomalous to compare the negligence of the parties in a strict liability action since the defendant is liable even in the absence of negligence. The anomaly fades, however, if the focus is on the cause of the injury, rather than on the characterization of the parties' conduct. There is a parallel defense to breach of warranty:

> In an action based on breach of warranty, it is of course necessary to show not only the existence of the warranty but the fact that the warranty was broken and that the breach of the warranty was the proximate cause of the loss sustained. In such an action an affirmative showing by the seller that the loss resulted from some action or event following his own delivery of the goods can operate as a defense.

UCC § 2–314, Official Comment 13. Cf. Kennedy v. City of Sawyer, 618 P.2d 788 (Kan.1980).

The Restatement (Third) concurs:

§ 17. Apportionment of Responsibility Between or Among Plaintiff, Sellers and Distributors of Defective Products, and Others

(a) A plaintiff's recovery of damages for harm caused by a product defect may be reduced if the conduct of the plaintiff combines with the product defect to cause the harm and plaintiff's conduct fails to conform to generally applicable rules establishing appropriate standards of care.

(b) The manner and extent of the reduction under subsection (a) . . . are governed by generally applicable rules apportioning responsibility.

5. *Greenman* and the Restatement provisions are merely an introduction to the law of products liability. Since its birth in *Greenman*, the growth of strict liability in tort has been phenomenal and controversial. The preceding questions and notes indicate several of the difficult legal issues. For treatment of these and other aspects of strict liability, see L. Frumer & M. Friedman, Products Liability (2007); D. Owen, M. Madden & M. Davis, Products Liability (3rd ed.2000); Owen, The Moral Foundations of Products Liability Law: Toward First Principles, 68 Notre Dame L.Rev. 427 (1993). For a focus on the Restatement (Third), see Henderson & Twerski, The Products Liability Restatement in the Courts: An Initial Assessment, 27 Wm. Mitchell L.Rev. 7 (2000); Symposium, The Restatement (Third) of Torts and the Future of Tort Law, 10 Kan.J.L. & Pub.Policy 1 (2000).

6. Two years after the Supreme Court of California adopted strict liability in *Greenman*, the Supreme Court of New Jersey adopted strict liability and extended it to economic loss. In Santor v. A & M Karagheusian, Inc., 207 A.2d 305 (N.J.1965), a consumer purchased carpeting that, upon installation, had an unusual line in it. Contrary to the seller's repeated assurances that the line would disappear after the carpet was broken in, the condition worsened. When the consumer again tried to contact the seller, he discovered that the seller had gone out of business. Unlike *Greenman*, in which the consumer suffered personal injuries, the consumer's injury in *Santor* was purely economic: the carpet was not worth what he had paid for it. Nevertheless, the New Jersey Supreme Court applied strict liability and held the manufacturer liable.

Several months later the California court had the opportunity to address this question of strict liability for economic loss. In Seely v. White Motor Co., 403 P.2d 145 (Cal.1965), the Supreme Court of California specifically rejected the reasoning of *Santor* and held that the purchaser of a dangerously defective truck could not use strict tort liability to recover lost profits. The court confined strict liability to defects that cause personal injury to the consumer or physical injury to the consumer's property. Almost every case since 1965 has agreed with *Seely*. For example, consider Morrow v. New Moon Homes, Inc., 548 P.2d 279, 285–86 (Alaska 1976), in which plaintiffs sued for diminution in value of a defective mobile home:

> *Seely* appears to enjoy the support of the vast majority of the other courts which have considered the question whether strict liability in tort should extend to instances of economic loss. We also prefer the result in *Seely* although our reasoning differs slightly in emphasis from that of the *Seely* court. Under the Uniform Commercial Code the manufacturer is given the right to avail himself of certain affirmative defenses which can minimize his liability for a purely economic loss. Specifically, the manufacturer has the opportunity, pursuant to [§ 2–316] to disclaim liability and under [§ 2–719] to limit the consumer's remedies, although the Code further provides that such disclaimers

and limitations cannot be so oppressive as to be unconscionable and thus violate [§ 2–302]. In addition, the manufacturer is entitled to reasonably prompt notice from the consumer of the claimed breach of warranties, pursuant to [§ 2–607].

In our view, recognition of a doctrine of strict liability in tort for economic loss would seriously jeopardize the continued viability of these rights. The economically injured consumer would have a theory of redress not envisioned by our legislature when it enacted the U.C.C., since this strict liability remedy would be completely unrestrained by disclaimer, liability limitation and notice provisions. Further, manufacturers could no longer look to the Uniform Commercial Code provisions to provide a predictable definition of potential liability for direct economic loss. In short, adoption of the doctrine of strict liability for economic loss would be contrary to the legislature's intent when it authorized the aforementioned remedy limitations and risk allocation provisions of Article [2] of the Code. To extend strict tort liability to reach the Morrows' case would in effect be an assumption of legislative prerogative on our part and would vitiate clearly articulated statutory rights. This we decline to do. Thus, we hold that the theory of strict liability in tort . . . does not extend to the consumer who suffers only economic loss because of defective goods.

Is the court saying that it would be bad policy to extend strict liability to economic loss or that the court does not have the power to do it? The Supreme Court of Maryland rejected the latter view:

General Motors argues that we should not adopt the doctrine of strict liability for several reasons. It contends . . . even if we were to conclude that the differences between the two theories of liability were significant enough to adopt § 402A of the Restatement, the Legislature in enacting the warranty provisions of the Uniform Commercial Code has "preempted the field of products liability law." . . .

[W]e cannot agree with General Motors that the Legislature has preempted the field of product liability law, precluding our adoption of Restatement § 402A. . . . [T]here is no indication that the Legislature, in enacting the Uniform Commercial Code, intended to prevent the further development of product liability law by the courts. In the absence of any expression of intent by the Legislature to limit the remedies available to those injured by defective goods exclusively to those provided by the Maryland Uniform Commercial Code, we believe that General Motors' preemption contention is without merit.

Phipps v. General Motors Corp., 363 A.2d 955, 961–62 (Md.1976). Contra, Cline v. Prowler Industries of Maryland, Inc., 418 A.2d 968 (Del.1980). Cf. Superwood Corp. v. Siempelkamp, 311 N.W.2d 159 (Minn.1981). Does the argument of preemption have more force if it is confined to economic loss? Of what effect is UCC section 2–719(3)?

C. THE UNIFORM COMMERCIAL CODE AND CONTRACTUAL MODIFICATION OF QUALITY STANDARDS

Although strict liability in tort does not exist in most jurisdictions for loss other than physical injury to person or property, warranty liability does. Liability for breach of warranty is governed primarily by Articles 1 and 2 of the Uniform Commercial Code. In 2002 and 2003 the American Law Institute and the National Conference of Commissioners on Uniform State Laws approved a revision of those Articles. More than half the states have enacted the revision of Article 1, but as of late 2008 no state had enacted the amendments to Article 2. Hence, the materials in this section focus on the revised version of Article 1 and the pre-amendment version of Article 2.* Both versions of each Article are in the Statutory Supplement.

The law expects sellers to provide goods that are reasonably fit for the ordinary purposes the goods are designed to serve (UCC § 2–314(1), (2)(c)). In certain instances the goods must be of even higher quality, as where the seller expressly states that they will be (§ 2–313), or where the seller has reason to know that the buyer is relying on the seller to furnish goods that will meet the buyer's special purpose (§ 2–315).

The question arises, however, whether privity of contract is an element of warranty liability for economic loss. If the consumer seeks to recover for breach of the implied warranty of fitness, the answer usually is, yes. That warranty arises only if the seller has the requisite reason to know, and the manufacturer is unlikely to know the consumer's particular purpose for the goods. If the consumer seeks to recover for breach of an express warranty, the answer to the privity question usually is, no. E.g., Randy Knitwear, Inc. v. American Cyanamid Co., 181 N.E.2d 399 (N.Y.1962). If the consumer seeks to recover for breach of the implied warranty of merchantability, the answer is less clear. Courts in many states have held that if the consumer seeks to recover economic loss caused by a breach of the implied warranty of merchantability, privity is necessary.

The trend, however, seems to be the other way. E.g., Nobility Homes of Texas, Inc. v. Shivers, 557 S.W.2d 77 (Tex.1977). In Morrow v. New Moon Homes, Inc., 548 P.2d 279, 290–92 (Alaska 1976), the court stated:

> A number of courts recently confronting this issue have declined to overturn the privity requirement in warranty actions for economic loss. One principal factor seems to be that these courts simply do not find the social and economic reasons which justify extending enterprise liability to the victims of personal injury or property damage equally compelling in the case of a disappointed buyer suffering "only" economic loss. There is an apparent fear that economic losses may be of a far greater magnitude in value than personal injuries, and being

---

* Unless otherwise specifically indicated, all references are to the 2002 revised version of Article 1 and the current, 1978 version of Article 2.

somehow less foreseeable these losses would be less insurable, undermining the risk spreading theory of enterprise liability.

Several of the courts which have recently considered this aspect of the privity issue have found those arguments unpersuasive. We are in agreement and hold that there is no satisfactory justification for a remedial scheme which extends the warranty action to a consumer suffering personal injury or property damage but denies similar relief to the consumer "fortunate" enough to suffer only direct economic loss. Justice Peter's separate opinion in Seely v. White Motor Co. persuasively establishes that the cleavage between economic loss and other types of harm is a false one, that each species of harm can constitute the "overwhelming misfortune" in one's life which warrants judicial redress. The Supreme Court of New Jersey is also in complete agreement with this view:

> From the standpoint of principle, we perceive no sound reason why the implication of reasonable fitness should be attached to the transaction and be actionable against the manufacturer where the defectively made product has caused personal injury and not actionable when inadequate manufacture has put a worthless article in the hands of an innocent purchaser who has paid the required price for it. In such situations considerations of justice require a court to interest itself in originating causes and to apply the principle of implied warranty on that basis, rather than to test its application by whether personal injury or simply loss of bargain resulted in the breach of the warranty. True, the rule of implied warranty had its gestative stirrings because of the greater appeal of the personal injury claim. But, once in existence, the field of operation of the remedy should not be fenced in by such a factor. [Santor v. A & M Karagheusian, Inc., 207 A.2d 305, 309 (N.J. 1965).]

The fear that if the implied warranty action is extended to direct economic loss, manufacturers will be subjected to liability for damages of unknown and unlimited scope would seem unfounded. The manufacturer may possibly delimit the scope of his potential liability by use of a disclaimer in compliance with [§ 2–316] or by resort to the limitations authorized in [§ 2–719]. These statutory rights not only preclude extending the theory of strict liability in tort, but also make highly appropriate this extension of the theory of implied warranties. Further, by expanding warranty rights to redress this form of harm, we preserve ". . . the well developed notion that the law of contract should control actions for purely economic losses and that the law of tort should control actions for personal injuries." We therefore hold that a manufacturer can be held liable for direct economic loss attributable to a breach of his implied warranties, without regard to privity of contract between the manufacturer and the ultimate purchaser.

In some states the abandonment of the requirement of privity is a result of legislative action:

> Lack of privity between plaintiff and defendant shall be no defense in any action brought against the manufacturer, seller, lessor or supplier of goods to recover damages for breach of warranty, express or implied, or for negligence, although the plaintiff did not purchase the goods from the defendant if the plaintiff was a person whom the manufacturer, seller, lessor or supplier might reasonably have expected to use, consume or be affected by the goods. A manufacturer, seller, lessor or supplier may not exclude or limit the operation of this section. Failure to give notice shall not bar recovery under this section unless the defendant proves that he was prejudiced thereby. All actions under this section shall be commenced within three years next after the date the injury and damage occurs.

Mass.Gen.Laws Ann. ch. 106, § 2–318. Compare UCC section 2–318 (Alts. A, B, C). Which alternative has the Massachusetts legislature adopted?

In addition to lack of privity, there are several other obstacles to a consumer's recovery for breach of warranty. One is the need to notify the seller of the breach within a reasonable time. UCC § 2–607(3)(a). E.g., Hebron v. American Isuzu Motors, Inc., 60 F.3d 1095 (4th Cir.1995) (failure to give notice until two years after discovering defect bars recovery). Even if the buyer gives notice, section 2–607(3)(a) still may be an obstacle if, for example, a consumer notifies his or her immediate seller but fails to notify the manufacturer. For contrasting views on the resolution of this problem, see Prince, Overprotecting the Consumer? § 2–607(3)(a) Notice of Breach in Nonprivity Contexts, 66 N.C.L.Rev. 107 (1987); Reitz, Against Notice: A Proposal To Restrict the Notice of Claims Rule in UCC § 2–607(3)(a), 73 Cornell L.Rev. 534 (1988).

Two other obstacles to recovery are disclaimers of warranties (permitted by UCC section 2–316) and limitations of remedies (permitted by UCC sections 2–718 and 2–719). The following materials explore these two matters.

Many sellers include in their sales contracts a provision that there are "no warranties, express or implied." Under section 2–313, however, an express warranty is created by an affirmation of fact concerning the goods or by a description of the goods. On its face, then, this disclaimer conflicts with the other terms of the contract (e.g., a contract providing for the sale of a new Chevrolet with factory-installed air conditioning). Section 2–316(1) resolves this conflict: the express warranty prevails. An express warranty may also be created by the seller's use of a sample or model (§ 2–313(1)(c)). In Mobile Housing, Inc. v. Stone, 490 S.W.2d 611 (Tex.Civ.App.1973), appellees contracted to purchase a mobile home from appellant. When appellees saw that the home delivered to them was very different from the model home they had seen at appellant's place of business, they refused to accept it. Appellees sued for return of their down payment.

> The conclusion is inescapable, it seems to us, that appellees' agreement to buy the mobile home was induced by and based upon their numerous inspections of Unit No. 103 on appellant's sales lot and the representations of appellant's salesman that the home he was

trying to sell them would be precisely like it. There is no evidence that they had ever seen the home they were buying, or even a picture of it, or that the salesman described it in any other manner than by referring to Unit No. 103. The salesman testified that in drawing the contract they took the description from this Unit 103.

We hold that appellant made express warranties, within the meaning of § [2–313(1)(b), (c)], that the mobile home would conform to the description given by the salesman and the model called Unit No. 103. It is true, the written contract provides that the article is sold "as is" and disclaims all warranties, either express or implied, and the use of descriptions, samples or models as a part of the contract. However, we hold that these express warranties rest on "dickered" aspects of the individual bargain, and go so clearly to the essence of that bargain that words of disclaimer in the purchase agreement are repugnant to the basic dickered terms. See Comment 1 under § 2–313.

The Code according to Comment 4 under § 2–313 seems to take the view that the whole purpose of the law of warranty is to determine what it is that the seller has in essence agreed to sell, and refuses except in unusual circumstances to recognize a material deletion of the seller's obligation. Thus, a contract is normally one for a sale of something describable and described. A clause generally disclaiming "all warranties, express or implied," cannot reduce the seller's obligation with respect to such description and therefore cannot be given literal effect under § 2–316.

Id. at 614–15. Since the seller breached an express warranty, the buyers were able to reject the mobile home, cancel the contract, and recover their down payment (§ 2–711(1)).

Mobile Housing v. Stone concerns disclaimers and express warranties. Disputes concerning disclaimers, however, arise most frequently in connection with the seller's attempt to disclaim implied warranties, specifically the implied warranty of merchantability created by section 2–314.

Berg v. Stromme

Supreme Court of Washington, 1971.
79 Wn.2d 184, 484 P.2d 380.

HALE, J.

Plaintiff bought a new Pontiac station wagon automobile but claimed that it had so many things wrong with it he felt justified in rescinding the deal. When he tried to return the car and get a refund, the dealer refused, saying not only that the sale carried no warranty of quality but that plaintiff had in writing waived all warranties of fitness, express or implied, and had acknowledged that he was buying without any guarantee whatever.

Seeking damages for depreciated value, costs of repairs and time loss, plaintiff brought this action against the dealer who had sold him the automobile. At the close of plaintiff's case, the superior court on defendant's motion ordered a dismissal with prejudice. The order of dismissal specified two grounds: (1) . . . (2) that plaintiff had signed a disclaimer of warranty. The Court of Appeals affirmed, with one judge dissenting. We granted review and reverse the Court of Appeals and the superior court.

. . . The issue, as we see it, is whether the buyer, despite the printed disclaimer of warranty, was entitled under the circumstances and conditions of the purchase, to receive delivery from the dealer of a new automobile that would operate with reasonable efficiency, safety and comfort. . . .

The printed documents constituting the written agreement between the parties and the execution of them in writing will show, we think, why printed disclaimers of warranty in the purchase of new automobiles are now regarded with increasing disfavor by the courts. Although competent parties may make any lawful contract they choose, there exists a strong presumption that the buyer, in negotiating the purchase of a brand new car from a dealer, after discussing and agreeing upon all of the details as to its style, type, price, equipment, accessories and condition of delivery, would not in the same agreement negate and undo his bargain by disclaiming the right to a car of merchantable quality.[3] Merchantable quality in a new car means a car that is reasonably safe, trouble free and dependable (Appleman v. Fabert Motors, Inc., 30 Ill.App.2d 424, 174 N.E.2d 892 (1961); Fillet v. Curry, 12 App.Div.2d 519, 207 N.Y.S.2d 522 (1960)); and that it is reasonably suited for the purpose for which it was manufactured.

Nothing in the purchase order form other than the printed disclaimer indicates that the purchaser here intended to bargain away or waive his right to a serviceable automobile. The price of the car, without optional equipment, as written in ink on the purchase order form, was $3,632. Nearly 40 separately listed items—handwritten in pen and ink on the same order form—described and priced the items of extra optional equipment to be added to the car, these running from a vanity mirror at $1.45 to air conditioning at $430.40, with such in between devices as power brakes, $43; wind deflector, $26.90; power seat, $96.84; tilt steering, $43.04. Optional items brought the total cash price to $6,048.14. Thus, the extra equipment, specifically ordered, item by item, with the price of each set opposite each, all in handwriting, nearly equaled the cost of the vehicle alone. . . .

The order of dismissal was entered after the court had received substantial proof that this brand new car was not reasonably fit for the purpose for which it was sold—i.e. a serviceable automobile capable of transporting a driver and passengers with reasonable efficiency, comfort and security upon the roads and highways of the state. There was proof of

---

3. At the time of this purchase, RCW 63.04.160 of the Uniform Sales Act was in effect:

(2) Where the goods are bought by description from a seller who deals in goods of that description (whether he be the grower or manufacturer or not), there is an implied warranty that the goods shall be of merchantable quality.

serious trouble in the car shortly after its delivery in February, 1965. The motor ran roughly and unevenly, and it clattered; the car steered inaccurately and would veer at times; it overheated under normal driving conditions; the turn signals were defective; and the car accelerated unevenly and did what is called "surging." Its air shock absorbers were defective, and the brakes failed after only 4 months' normal use. The shift lever did not work properly, and for no apparent reason the car stalled several times in traffic. The shift indicator showed the car at times to be in neutral when it was actually in drive. The windows needed fixing, and the heater did not work properly.

A safety engineer testified that the car was dangerous to drive either during daylight or darkness. Additionally, there were minor defects such as scratches on the paint and loosely secured chrome and molding. Plaintiff returned the car to defendant periodically for repairs, and it spent 20 days during the first 4 months after delivery—a total of 45 days before the first year of ownership had expired—in defendant's repair shop.

The trial court and the Court of Appeals based their decisions on the written statement above the plaintiffs signature on the purchase order and conditional sale contract that no warranties, express or implied, had been made by the seller, or as stated in the judgment of dismissal, "That the plaintiff signed a disclaimer of warranty and therefore under the law is not entitled to rely on implied warranty of fitness."

The defense of written waiver of warranty invites a detailed examination of the order form signed by the plaintiff February 8, 1965. The purported printed waiver appears in the automobile sales order which the plaintiff, after discussion and negotiation with defendant, had signed at the bottom of the first or major page. On its major side, the order form consisted almost entirely of blank lines and spaces containing printed notations—designed to be and which were filled in in handwritten words and numbers, presumably by one of the defendant's salesmen or by the prospective buyer. All items of contract sufficient to identify the car by name, kind, style, size, power and all optional extra equipment on it were handwritten or hand printed in the blank spaces of the order form, including the name and address of the purchaser, the make, type and engine number of the car, along with descriptive names of 40 separate items of equipment and attachments with a price set opposite each in handwriting. Also set forth in handwriting were four itemized labor services each separately priced, with the costs of these services totaled in handwriting. Right below a merger clause[4] on the major side of the form, Dr. Berg and defendant's agent had signed the contract for the purchase and sale of the automobile.

---

4. "I have read the matter printed on the back hereof and agree to it as a part of this order the same as if it were printed above my signature. The front and back of this order comprise the entire agreement pertaining to this purchase, and no other agreement of any kind, verbal understanding or promise whatsoever, will be recognized. Receipt of a copy of this order is hereby acknowledged."

The reverse side (or "back hereof") of the sales order form referred to in the merger clause was a solid mass of even sized and style of printing from top to bottom divided in two columns by a center space a little larger than the side margins. Without indentation for paragraphing, it set forth in block form 15 numbered and itemized terms of contract, the last of which contained subordinate unindented paragraphs running from 15(a) to 15(f), inclusive. This reverse side contained no spaces whatever for signatures, filling in, interlining, or references to other documents. It had no blank spaces, signature lines or other devices by which one would indicate assent, concurrence or agreement.

The printed material on the reverse side of the order, among other things, said that the agreement was not valid unless signed by an executive of the company; that verbal promises or representations of the salesman were not binding; that the dealer did not warrant the correctness of either the speedometer reading, mileage, year of manufacture or model of automobile; that if the buyer failed to complete the purchase, he forfeited his trade-in or down payment to the extent that they equaled one-third of the purchase price—in this case over $2,000—as liquidated damages; that the dealer was not responsible for delay caused by strikes, riot, war, shutdowns at factory, or other delays caused by conditions beyond his control; and that price increases during the interim caused by changes in taxes or imposed in the meanwhile by the manufacturer would be absorbed by the purchaser, and that the dealer was not to be held liable for changes in design or models during the delay even if the buyer disapproved of them. Also in the first column, reverse side, the purchaser purported to agree that he "hereby certifies that he (or she) is twenty-one years of age or over, and is fully competent to make this agreement," and that the purchaser authorized the dealer to place insurance on the car with a loss payable clause for the benefit of the mortgagee only and "affords no protection whatever for the purchaser's interest." This last provision did not specify who should pay the premium other than that it be "included" in the contract. Item 11 ended the first column by stating that purchaser did not then and would not need any extension of credit other than what was shown on the reverse side. So much for the first column.

The second column of the reverse side began with a provision that if the dealer should teach the purchaser to drive, the former would be held harmless for any of the instructor's negligence, and that the instructor was the servant of the purchaser. Then followed a provision that the purchaser guaranteed all credit statements made by him to be true, and promised to pay all attorney's fees and costs in connection with any legal action brought by dealer to enforce the purchase order agreement. Items 15(a) through 15(f) consisted of a solid mass of printing concerning the trade-in vehicle, including the purchaser's acknowledgment that in many instances the market value of the trade-in was considerably different from the allowance shown on the order.

There, among the 11 items of these printed conditions on the reverse side in the first column, lay the principal basis for the defense of written waiver of warranty. Item 3 of the 11 stated:

There is no guarantee on the automobile in connection with this agreement. The purchaser has no guarantee whatsoever unless a separate written agreement is obtained at the time of sale. This applies to new cars as well as used cars. The purchaser must have a written guarantee in his possession to secure an adjustment.

Defendant dealer also relied on a printed disclaimer of warranty provision in the conditional sale contract signed by the plaintiff as purchaser. There, taking up but 1 of 26 lines of mass-printed material in the printed conditional sale contract form, among 5 printed paragraphs which occupied nearly one-half the entire page, was the second paragraph, reading:

No warranties, express or implied, have been made by the Seller unless endorsed hereon in writing.

The purported disclaimers of warranty in the conditional sale contract form and the waiver of warranty in the purchase order form highlight the absurdity of a rule of law which elevates these bland and substantially meaningless terms and conditions above the individually and expressly negotiated terms and conditions, and gives them controlling effect over specifically agreed upon items and conditions of the contract. To adhere to such a rule means that the law presumes that the buyer of a brand new automobile intends to nullify in general all of the things for which he has specifically bargained and will pay. We would presume the buyer does just the opposite.

The record shows that the parties reached an agreement as to the size, style, color, power and model of the automobile; they agreed, item by item, on the kinds of extra equipment to be added to and made a part of the new car and the price the buyer would pay for each one. The record does not show that they ever discussed, contemplated or agreed that the buyer intended to waive his right to delivery of a new car of merchantable quality, nor that the seller, aside from the printed statements, intended to exact such a waiver.

It is error, we think, to hold the buyer in the purchase of a brand new automobile to such a printed waiver of quality or capability where neither party is shown to have referred to it in the contract and where the waiver has not been included among all of the specific terms and conditions particularly written by the parties into the contract. Such waiver, even though printed, should not be allowed to arise from the fine print to haunt the buyer of a new car unless he has agreed to be bound by it with the same degree of explicitness that he bound himself to the other vital conditions of the contract of purchase.

This court has held that a merger clause will not be enforced where it does not in fact express the true intentions of the parties. Black v. Evergreen Land Developers, Inc., 75 Wn.2d 241, 450 P.2d 470 (1969). There we said that "the recent trend of the courts has been to discredit fine print clauses when to enforce them would be against public policy." We think it a sound rule, therefore, that, when a purchaser discusses with the seller of a new article and makes a definite part of the contract many variable items such as size, shape, power, color and items of extra equipment or adornment not ordinarily a part of the article but attached to it at the purchaser's option and only upon his explicit assent and agreement and thereby includes them specifically in the contract of purchase, it is presumed that the purchaser does not intend to waive any warranties, implied or express, that the article and the equipment will perform or will reasonably accomplish the function for which it was sold and purchased. In this instance, while the new Pontiac Safari station wagon had the general lines, appearance and attributes of a station wagon automobile and seemingly would operate as a new automobile, it did not do so with reasonable safety, efficiency and comfort. Plaintiff bought but, therefore, did not receive a brand new automobile.

Parties to an agreement may make any contract that comports with general law, and if a "seller positively and expressly refuses to give any warranty, and the contract is not induced by fraud, no warranty of any kind can be implied by law." Jones v. Mallon, 3 Wn. 2d 382, 101 P.2d 332 (1940). But to come within these principles, the burden is upon the dealer to show with particularity just what the buyer is waiving, that is, which particular defects or conditions the purchaser of a brand new automobile explicitly waives.

Thus, in the sale of a brand new automobile, there does exist an implied warranty of fitness. The seller impliedly warrants that the automobile is reasonably fit for and adapted to the purposes for which it is purchased, i.e., a vehicle that will carry a driver and passengers with reasonable safety and efficiency and comfort. The parties may agree to do more or to do less, but unless there is proof of explicit departure from this norm, the presumption is that the dealer intended to deliver and the buyer intended to receive a reasonably safe, efficient and comfortable brand new car.

These principles do not, we think, represent a drastic departure from but rather an adaptation of the prevailing trends in the law of torts to the law of contracts. In Ulmer v. Ford Motor Co., 75 Wn.2d 522, 452 P.2d 729 (1969), this court adopted the rule of strict liability against the manufacturer—not the dealer—in accordance with the modern views declared in Restatement (Second) of Torts § 402A. Strict liability—liability without proof of negligence—in torts has been applied to the retail dealer despite disclaimers of warranty with greater and impressive frequency.

. . .

That the rule of strict liability of the manufacturer for reasonable fitness of a brand new article originating as it did in torts should be adapted in contract law to the retail dealer is evident in House v. Thornton, 76 Wn.2d 428, 457 P.2d 199 (1969), a case involving the sale of a new house to its first purchaser-occupant. In holding that the house was presumed by both seller and buyer to be reasonably fit for occupancy as a dwelling house by the buyer and his family, this court, we think, did no more than apply a rule of common sense to the kind of transaction that recurs perhaps more than a million times annually in the country—the purchase of a brand new house. Accordingly, when the foundation and substructure of the house proved to be so defective and inadequate that it could not be occupied by its first purchaser with reasonable safety and comfort, we imposed a rule of strict liability holding the builder-seller to the principle that he was under a duty to supply a structure adequate in foundation and supporting terrain to be used by the buyer for the purposes for which the house and lot had been sold.

This same rationale should be applied to the purchase of a brand new automobile. We are, therefore, of the opinion that, in the sale by a dealer or retailer of a brand new automobile, the dealer impliedly warrants that the automobile is of merchantable quality and that the new car is fit to transport the driver and his passengers with reasonable safety, efficiency and comfort—according to the size, model and power of the vehicle. Waivers of such warranties, being disfavored in law, are ineffectual unless explicitly negotiated between buyer and seller and set forth with particularity showing the particular qualities and characteristics of fitness which are being waived.

Reversed and remanded to the trial court to try the issue of damages, i.e., to ascertain and grant the plaintiff judgment for the difference between the price paid and its fair market value in its delivered condition.

HAMILTON, C.J., FINLEY, ROSELLINI, and HUNTER, JJ., concur.

NEILL, J. (concurring).

I concur in the result but have not signed the majority opinion as I believe it is inappropriate to commingle considerations regarding the application of the parol evidence rule to implied warranties of contract with considerations pertaining to the strict tort liability of a manufacturer. Further, the conclusion that waivers are ineffectual "unless explicitly negotiated between buyer and seller and set forth with particularity showing the particular qualities and characteristics of fitness which are being waived" is too restrictive. A rule which requires proof by a preponderance of the evidence that the purchaser was specifically made aware that he was waiving warranties is sufficient to protect the buyer from surprise without unduly restricting freedom of contract. This also comports with the current statutory law of sales. RCW 62A.2–202; RCW 62A.2–316. See Broude, The Consumer and the Parol Evidence Rule: Section 2–202 of the Uniform Commercial Code, 5 Duke L.J. 881 (1970).

STAFFORD and McGOVERN, JJ., concur with NEILL, J.

QUESTIONS

1. In the last four paragraphs of its opinion, the court refers to the doctrine of strict liability. Is the court adopting that doctrine and thereby imposing strict liability in Berg for purely economic loss? In answering this question, consider especially the next to last paragraph in the court's opinion and comments *m* and *n* to Restatement (Second) of Torts section 402A (pages 318–19 supra).

2.   What happened to the principle of contract law that a person is bound by what he or she signs? In addition to Berg, see Parton v. Mark Pirtle Oldsmobile–Cadillac–Isuzu, Inc., 730 S.W.2d 634 (Tenn.App.1987).

3.   The sale in Berg occurred before the effective date of the UCC. Consider section 2–316(2). Could the court have decided Berg the same way if the UCC had been in effect?

4.   Before going any further, draft a clause that would be effective under the UCC to disclaim the implied warranty of merchantability and the implied warranty of fitness for a particular purpose.

5.   What should the result be if the disclaimer reads:

> THIS VEHICLE IS SOLD WITHOUT ANY GUARANTEE OR WARRANTY, EXPRESS OR IMPLIED, INCLUDING BUT NOT LIMITED TO, ANY IMPLIED WARRANTY OF MER-CHANTABILITY.

Is it relevant that the language of disclaimer appears in a warranty booklet placed in the glove compartment of the automobile?

6.   Section 2–316(2) provides that "to exclude or modify the implied warranty of merchantability . . . the language . . . must be conspicuous. . . ." "Conspicuous" is defined in section 1–201(b)(10). If the language does not meet the test of section 1–201(b)(10) but the consumer actually reads it, should the disclaimer be effective?

Knipp v. Weinbaum

Court of Appeals of Florida, 1977.
351 So.2d 1081.

NATHAN, JUDGE.

Plaintiff appeals from a summary final judgment for defendants in a personal injury action against the seller of a used motorcycle, and from the trial court's denial of plaintiff's motion to amend his complaint, which originally charged breach of warranties and negligence, to include a count in strict liability.

In 1973, plaintiff purchased a three-wheeled motorcycle ("trike") from defendant, Allan Weinbaum, doing business as Homestead Cycle Shop. The trike had been constructed at home approximately two years earlier by a young motorcycle enthusiast for his own use, and had been privately traded to three other individuals before it reached defendant's shop. Plaintiff signed a bill of sale which included the prominent statement: CYCLE SOLD AS IS—ONE CUSTOM TRIKE HONDA THREE WHEELER. Several hours later, on the date of purchase, plaintiff was severely injured, allegedly because a defective weld on the rear axle gave way, causing plaintiff to lose control of the trike while on a major highway.

Suit was filed in August of 1974, recovery initially being sought on grounds of breach of express and implied warranties, and negligence. Summary final judgment was rendered in favor of defendants. . . .

Appellant contends: (1) The trial court erred in granting summary judgment on the count of implied warranty because the testimony of both parties shows that neither intended the "as is" provision to operate as a disclaimer of the implied warranties of merchantability and fitness for a particular purpose. . . .

Plaintiff avers that the parties had differing understandings of the intended meaning of the phrase "as is" on the bill of sale. If the law implies no warranties at all on the facts of this case, the intent of the parties would be immaterial to the first assignment of error. Therefore we must decide initially whether the implied warranties of merchantability, Section 672.2–314, Florida Statutes (1973), and fitness for a particular purpose, Section 672.2–315, have viability in this action. This in turn will depend on whether these warranties are applicable to the sale of used goods; the effect of the words "as is" in a personal injury action based on an alleged defect in used goods sold; and the intent of the parties in the circumstances surrounding the transaction at issue.

On the question of whether implied warranties are applicable to the sale of used goods, we find the rationale of Brown v. Hall, 221 So.2d 454 (Fla.2d D.C.A. 1969) compelling. This case imposed an implied warranty as to fitness, condition, and quality on the sale of used goods when the seller knew the purpose for which the buyer purchased the goods, a used truck, and that he had relied on the seller's skill and judgment in making the purchase. Though decided on the basis of pre-Code law, the applicability of this case is both pertinent and continuous. We find that implied warranties may be imposed on the sale of used goods in limited circumstances, despite ostensible disclaimers.

The plaintiff in this case alleged that his injuries resulted from a defect in the goods sold. To foreclose consideration of his claim by permitting an "as is" disclaimer to operate as an automatic absolution from responsibility through the mechanism of summary judgment would belie the policy behind Section 672.2–719(3), which states that "limitation of consequential damages for injury to the person in the case of consumer goods is prima facie unconscionable."

Moreover, Section 672.2–316(3) provides:

(a) *Unless the circumstances indicate otherwise,* all implied warranties are excluded by expressions like "as is", "with all faults" or other language which in common understanding calls the buyer's attention to the exclusion of warranties and makes plain that there is no implied warranty. . . . (emphasis supplied).

It is the clause "unless the circumstances indicate otherwise" which precludes a finding that automatic absolution can be achieved in the sale of used consumer goods merely by the inclusion in a bill of sale of the magic words "as is."

This is not to say that a seller of used goods may not absolve himself from responsibility for defects in the goods sold when both he and the buyer understand this to be the intended meaning of the phrase "as is." See Comment 3 to Section 672.2–719. The Uniform Commercial Code contemplates that a seller may disclaim warranties as long as the buyer reasonably understands this is being done. But a disclaimer, to be effective, must be a part of the basis of the bargain between the parties.

The record reveals conflicting statements in the depositions of the parties regarding the intended meaning of the disclaimer in this case. Indeed, there are statements which indicate that the seller himself may have intended the term "as is" to apply only to minor defects which would have rendered the trike incapable of passing the inspection required in order to get a motor vehicle sticker. Since the law does imply warranties in this sale of used merchandise, and since there is conflicting evidence as to the parties' understanding of the purpose of the "as is" disclaimer, there remain disputed questions of material fact in this case. Therefore summary judgment was improper.

. . .

Reversed and remanded for further proceedings consistent with the views expressed herein.

QUESTIONS

1. The court cites Brown v. Hall to support its conclusion that an implied warranty of merchantability "may be imposed on the sale of used goods." Is that case controlling? What does the UCC provide? Should there be an implied warranty of merchantability in connection with the sale of a used car?

2. What level of quality must a used car meet in order to be merchantable? In Overland Bond & Investment Corp. v. Howard, 292 N.E.2d 168, 172–73 (Ill.App.1972), the court stated:

> Defects which have been held to make operation of a new automobile unfit and thereby cause a breach of implied warranties may result in the breach of the same warranties on a used automobile. See Appleman v. Fabert Motors, Inc., 30 Ill.App.2d 424, 174 N.E.2d 892, a case arising under the Uniform Sales Act where the court held that a buyer had the right to expect reasonably trouble-free transportation from his recently purchased car. (See also Berg v. Stromme, 79 Wash.2d 184, 484 P.2d 380.) Fitness for the ordinary purpose of driving implies that the vehicle should be in a safe condition and substantially free of defects. It should be obvious that any car without an adequate transmission and proper brakes is not fit for the ordinary purpose of driving. Any other conclusion would entitle unscrupulous sellers to foist inherently dangerous and potentially worthless vehicles on unwary consumers and thereby avoid the obvious intent of the statute.

Does this mean that a used car must meet the same standard as a new car?

3. What level of quality must a *new* car meet in order to be merchantable? In Isip v. Mercedes–Benz USA, LLC, 65 Cal.Rptr.3d 695 (Cal.App.2007), plaintiff purchased a new Mercedes–Benz for $46,000. Shortly after the purchase, she began experiencing problems, which included the following:

> The air-conditioning emitted an offensive smell every time it was turned on, giving [plaintiff] a headache and making her sister sneeze. The car made a loud tugging noise when she engaged the gear, and it made a clanking noise when [she] released the brake in reverse. When the car automatically shifted gears to pick up speed, the car pulled back, hesitated, and then took off like a slingshot. It also hesitated and pulled back before slowing down. The engine made a loud knocking sound and there were fluid leaks. White smoke came out of the exhaust system.

Id. at 696. Does this amount to a breach of the implied warranty of merchantability? Defendant asked the trial court to instruct the jury:

> In the case of automobiles, the implied warranty of merchantability can be breached only if the vehicle manifests a defect that is so basic that it renders the vehicle unfit for its ordinary purpose of providing transportation.

Id. at 697. Is that the correct standard? The court thought not:

> . . . [Defendant's] attempt to define a vehicle as unfit only if it does not provide transportation is an unjustified dilution of the implied warranty of merchantability. We reject the notion that merely because a vehicle provides transportation from point A to point B, it necessarily does not violate the implied warranty of merchantability. A vehicle that smells, lurches, clanks, and emits smoke over an extended period of time is not fit for its intended purpose.

Id. at 700.

Problem. Consumer purchases a new boat. Immediately after purchase, cracks begin emerging in the finish of the boat. Consumer has them repaired. New cracks emerge, requiring repairs on three occasions over the next year. New cracks continue to emerge. Has there been a breach of the implied warranty? In Carey v. Chaparral Boats, Inc., 514 F.Supp.2d 1152, 1156 (D.Minn.2007), the court held not, granting the seller's motion for summary judgment:

> Under Minnesota law, an implied warranty of merchantability requires that goods be "fit for the ordinary purposes for which such goods are used." . . . In this case, the overwhelming evidence demonstrates that the cracks in the boat's finish are a cosmetic problem and in no way impact the boat's ordinary use. [A fiberglass specialist] testified that the cracks are a "cosmetic issue," as did [another witness] who stated that the cracks could be characterized as a cosmetic problem that does not impact the structural integrity of the boat. Further, there is no evidence in the record that the cracks have prevented [plaintiff]

from using his boat. Accordingly, there is no genuine issue as whether [defendant] breached its implied warranty of merchantability.

What is the flaw in this analysis?

4. To be effective under subsection (3) of section 2–316, must the disclaimer be conspicuous?

5. What language is effective under section 2–316(3) to disclaim implied warranties? Should "as is" suffice? According to several surveys commissioned by the FTC in the 1970s, approximately 25–50% of consumers do not understand the legal effect of "as is." Many consumers believe the phrase applies to apparent or disclosed defects (e.g., dents) but not to latent defects. FTC Staff Report, Sale of Used Motor Vehicles 262–65 (1978).

Which of the following expressions should be effective under section 2–316(3):

a) "No warranties, express or implied, have been made by the Seller unless endorsed hereon in writing."

b) "This car is sold as it stands."

c) "This car is sold in its present condition."

d) "There is no guarantee on the car in connection with this agreement. The purchaser has no guarantee whatsoever unless a separate written agreement is obtained at the time of sale."

e) "The foregoing express warranty is in lieu of all other warranties, express or implied."

f) Of what relevance, if any, is section 1–201(b)(3)?

6. In determining the effectiveness of language of disclaimer under section 2–316(3), of what relevance is the seller's conduct? Specifically, do "circumstances indicate otherwise" when the seller of a car makes deceptive statements about its quality?

In Murray v. D & J Motor Company, Inc., 958 P.2d 823 (Okla.Civ.App. 1998), plaintiff told defendant's salesman that she needed a reliable van so that she could transport her ailing, disabled daughter. When plaintiff noticed a rattling noise during a test drive, the salesman told her that the engine had been replaced, that it had been inspected by a mechanic, and that there was nothing wrong with it. Plaintiff purchased the van, pursuant to documents that stated the vehicle was sold "as is." Within a day of the purchase, the engine broke down. The court stated:

[A]mong the circumstances that could render a purported "as is" or "with all faults" disclaimer unreasonable and ineffective are fraudulent representations or misrepresentations concerning the condition, value, quality, characteristics or fitness of the goods sold that are relied upon by the Buyer to the Buyer's detriment. Therefore if the disclaimer . . . [is] tainted with, or by, such misrepresentations or false representations, that then is a "circumstance" that will preclude an effective disclaimer. To hold otherwise would allow a seller to profit from his fraud and to be effectively granted a license to mislead or conceal facts.

Id. at 830 (reversing the action of the trial court in upholding defendant's demurrer to the evidence).

7. If it is appropriate for the law to impose quality standards even in the absence of an express undertaking by the seller or the manufacturer, why should the seller or manufacturer be able to modify that standard?

8. Another limitation on warranty disclaimers appears in UCC section 2–302, empowering a court to refuse enforcement of any contract or clause that it finds to be unconscionable. Chapter 9 explores the content of the unconscionability doctrine.

––––––

As an alternative to disclaiming warranties, the seller may permit them to arise, but attempt to limit the relief available to the consumer for any breach. Thus manufacturers and sellers typically provide that in the event of a defect, the manufacturer (or seller) will repair or replace the defective part but will not be liable for any damages. If enforced, this contractual provision forecloses the remedies that otherwise would be available under the UCC: return of the purchase price and recovery of damages for loss of the bargain and for consequential loss (§§ 2–608, 2–711, 2–714, 2–715). To a limited extent, the UCC gives the seller the right to repair or replace defective parts even if the contract is silent on that matter (§ 2–508). But the Code also expressly validates contractual limitations of remedy that extend the seller's right to cure beyond what section 2–508 permits. Please read section 2–719. The following case concerns the enforceability of a provision limiting the consumer's remedy and the consequences of holding that the limitation is not valid.

Murray v. Holiday Rambler, Inc.

Supreme Court of Wisconsin, 1978.
83 Wis.2d 406, 265 N.W.2d 513.

CONNOR T. HANSEN, J.

On January 23, 1974, the plaintiffs purchased a 22–foot 1973 Avenger motorhome for a total sales price, including sales tax, license fees and trade-in allowance on another motorhome owned by the plaintiffs, of $11,007.15. . . .

The plaintiffs had problems with the motorhome from the day they took possession. It was returned repeatedly to KOA Trailer Sales, Inc. (hereinafter KOA) as an authorized dealer for the manufacturer, Holiday Rambler, Inc., (hereinafter Holiday Rambler), and various repairs and adjustments were performed at the expense of Holiday Rambler. Mr. Murray estimated that by July 1974, the motorhome had been returned to KOA nine or ten times.

In July 1974, the plaintiffs traveled to Colorado in the motor home. On the trip they experienced difficulty with the operation of it in a number of respects. We describe the various problems with the vehicle in greater detail in discussing the issue of whether the limited warranty had failed its essential purpose.

On returning to Wisconsin in mid-July, the Murrays took the motor-home to KOA, and were assured that it would be repaired, either by KOA or by Holiday Rambler, apparently without expense to the Murrays. There was testimony that the Murrays agreed to this.

Arrangements were then made to have the vehicle taken to the Holiday Rambler factory in Wakarusa, Indiana, for any necessary adjustments. Holiday Rambler informed the Murrays, however, that they would be required to pick up the vehicle at the Indiana factory themselves.

Mr. Murray decided not to have the repairs made. Instead, he picked up the motorhome at KOA, drove it home and hired a lawyer. By letter dated August 15, 1974, the Murrays informed KOA that they were revoking acceptance of the motorhome and that they demanded payment of $11,900. In September 1974, KOA apparently offered to reimburse the Murrays for the expense of traveling to the Holiday Rambler factory, but the Murrays rejected this offer, and this action was commenced.

[The trial court gave judgment for plaintiffs for $14,923.03. Defendants appealed.]

The issues presented are as follows:

1. Does Holiday Rambler's limited warranty, together with its disclaimer of all other warranties, preclude revocation of acceptance of the motorhome?

2. Were the plaintiffs entitled to revoke acceptance of the motor-home?

3. Were the plaintiffs entitled to recover damages for loss of use of the motorhome?

LIMITED WARRANTY AND WARRANTY DISCLAIMER

Holiday Rambler and KOA contend on this appeal that the limited express warranty given by Holiday Rambler prevents the plaintiffs from revoking acceptance of the motorhome.

Under the Uniform Commercial Code, (hereinafter UCC) a seller of goods may limit his contractual liability in two ways. He may disclaim or limit his warranties, pursuant to sec. 402.316, Stats., or he may limit the buyer's remedies for a breach of warranty, pursuant to sec. 402.719. These methods are closely related, and in many cases their effect may be substantially identical. Conceptually, however, they are distinct. A disclaimer of warranties limits the seller's liability by reducing the number of circumstances in which the seller will be in breach of the contract; it precludes the existence of a cause of action. A limitation of remedies, on the other hand, restricts the remedies available to the buyer once a breach is established.

In the present case we believe the "PRE–DELIVERY INSPECTION & ACCEPTANCE DECLARATION" is an attempt to both disclaim warranties and limit the remedies available to the buyer upon breach.

Sec. 402.316, Stats. permits a seller to limit or exclude both implied and express warranties. Language limiting implied warranties must be conspicuous and otherwise consistent with the provisions of sec. 402.316 and must not be unconscionable in light of the circumstances at the time the contract was made. Sec. 402.302.

The document signed by Mr. Murray purported to exclude all warranties, express or implied, and stated in part, above his signature:

WARNING: THE PURCHASER IS EXPECTED TO READ THIS DOCUMENT BEFORE IT IS SIGNED

. . . THE PURCHASER SHOULD NOT SIGN THIS STATEMENT UNTIL ALL OF THE ITEMS INDICATED ABOVE HAVE EITHER BEEN PERFORMED OR EXPLAINED TO HIS SATISFACTION. . . .

The undersigned parties attest to the fact that the above representations are, to the best of their knowledge, true and that the purchaser has received a copy of this Pre–Delivery Inspection and Acceptance Declaration and read thoroughly the MANUFACTURER'S UNDERTAKING AVENGER CORPORATION on the reverse side.

The reverse side of this document stated:

MANUFACTURER'S UNDERTAKING—

AVENGER CORPORATION[3]

THERE ARE NO WARRANTIES EXPRESSED OR IMPLIED AND PARTICULARLY THERE ARE NO WARRANTIES OF MERCHANTABILITY OR FITNESS FOR A PARTICULAR PURPOSE MADE BY AVENGER CORPORATION FOR ITS PRODUCTS.

AVENGER CORPORATION, as the manufacturer, in lieu thereof *undertakes and agrees that the product identified on the Pre–Delivery and Acceptance Declaration (reverse side) was free of defects in material and workmanship at the time of its delivery to the dealer and the initial user and owner;* and

If the attached Pre–Delivery and Acceptance Declaration is properly filled out and returned to Avenger Corporation at Nappanee, Indiana, within five days of delivery of this trailer to the original user; and

If such Avenger product or its component parts (other than tires) shall fail within one year from the date of delivery to the original user

---

3. The Avenger Corporation, now dissolved, was a wholly-owned subsidiary of Holiday Rambler.

because the product or component part was defective when installed; and

If the owner-user will return the trailer to a service facility authorized by Avenger Corporation within fifty-two (52) weeks after initial delivery, *Avenger Corporation will in the method it determines to be necessary replace, or repair, at its sole option any such defective product or component at its own cost and expense.*

THERE ARE NO *OTHER* WARRANTIES OF ANY KIND, EXPRESS OR IMPLIED, AND NO *OTHER* OBLIGATIONS, EITHER EXPRESS OR IMPLIED, INCLUDING SPECIFICALLY ANY OBLIGATION FOR INCIDENTAL EXPENSES OF ANY NATURE UNDERTAKEN BY AVENGER CORPORATION AS THE MANUFACTURER. (Emphasis added.)

The language used in the document constitutes a warranty ". . . that the product . . . was free of defects in material and workmanship at the time of its delivery. . . ." Because this express warranty conflicts with the preceding disclaimer of all warranties, the language of express warranty must control. . . .

. . .

The damages which would otherwise be available upon a breach of contract may be altered or limited by the parties pursuant to sec. 402.719. This section gives the parties substantial latitude to fashion their own remedies for breach of the contract. However, the UCC disfavors limitations on remedies and provides for their deletion where they would effectively deprive a party of reasonable protection against breach.

The drafters of the UCC recognized that:

". . . it is of the very essence of a sales contract that at least minimum adequate remedies be available. If the parties intend to conclude a contract for sale within this Article they must accept the legal consequence that there be at least a fair quantum of remedy for breach of the obligations or duties outlined in the contract. . . ." Official Comment 1, sec. 2–719, UCC.

Accordingly, any clause purporting to limit remedies in an unconscionable manner will be deleted, making the ordinary UCC remedies available as though the stricken clause had never existed. Official Comment 1.

In addition, sec. 402.719(2) provides:

(2) Where circumstances cause an exclusive or limited remedy to fail of its essential purpose, remedy may be had as provided in this code.

This provision dictates that:

". . . [W]here an apparently fair and reasonable clause because of circumstances fails in its purpose or operates to deprive either party of the substantial value of the bargain, it must give way to the general remedy provisions of this Article." Official Comment 1.

The warranty in the present case, like most motor vehicle warranties, limited the buyer's remedies to repair or replacement of defective parts. . . . Such a limitation is not, on its face, unconscionable. Sec. 402.719(2) specifically recognizes the possibility of such a limitation.

However, where the limited remedy fails of its essential purpose, the limitation will be disregarded and ordinary UCC remedies will be available. Sec. 402.719(2). The purpose of an exclusive remedy of repair or replacement, from the buyer's standpoint, is to give him goods which conform to the contract—in this case, a motorhome substantially free of defects—within a reasonable time after a defect is discovered. Conte v. Dwan Lincoln–Mercury, supra; Beal v. General Motors Corp. (D.C.Del.1973), 354 Fed.Supp. 423; Moore v. Howard Pontiac–American, Inc., (Tenn.App.1972), 492 S.W.2d 227.

> ". . . [E]very buyer has the right to assume his new car, with the exception of minor adjustments, will be 'mechanically new and factory furnished, operate perfectly, and be free of substantial defects'. . . .

> "After the purchase of an automobile, the same should be put in good running condition; that is the seller does not have an unlimited time for the performance of the obligation to replace and repair parts. The buyer of an automobile is not bound to permit the seller to tinker with the article indefinitely in the hope that it may ultimately be made to comply with the warranty. 46 Am.Jur. Sales § 732; 77 C.J.S. Sales § 340. At some point in time, if major problems continue to plague the automobile, it must become obvious to all people that a particular vehicle simply cannot be repaired or parts replaced so that the same is made free of defect. . . ." Orange Motors of Coral Gables v. Dade Co. Dairies, 258 So.2d 319, 320, 321 (Fla.App.1972), quoting Zabriskie Chevrolet, Inc. v. Smith, 99 N.J.Super. 441, 240 Atl.2d 195 (1968).

Although individual nonconformities may not be substantial in and of themselves, the obligation to repair or replace parts may fail of its essential purpose where the cumulative effect of all the nonconformities substantially impairs the value of the goods to the buyer. Zoss v. Royal Chevrolet, Inc., 11 U.C.C. Rep. 527, 532 (Ind.Super.1972).

Where the seller is given reasonable opportunity to correct the defect or defects, and the vehicle nevertheless fails to operate as should a new vehicle free of defects, the limited remedy fails of its essential purpose. The buyer may then invoke any of the remedies available under the UCC, including the right to revoke acceptance of the goods, under sec. 2–608 of the UCC.

In the present case the jury determined that the plaintiffs had cause to revoke the acceptance of the motorhome. The verdict of a jury will not be disturbed by this court if, viewing the evidence in the light most favorable to the verdict, any credible evidence fairly admits of an inference supporting the verdict. Here there was ample credible evidence to support the jury's implicit finding that the defendants had failed to provide the plaintiffs with a motorhome substantially free of material defects within a reasonable time.

The testimony favorable to the verdict showed the following: Mr. Murray experienced problems with the lights and battery of the vehicle on the day he took possession and, although repairs were attempted, the lights continued to dim, the electrical system went dead on several occasions, and the generator did not charge the battery properly. The wiring of an outdoor light short-circuited where it passed through a sharp-edged metal wall. There were problems with the clock. There was an exposed, allegedly non-energized, 120–volt wire coming from the main electrical panel. Plaintiffs' expert witness testified that the wiring in the 12–volt electrical system was of an insufficient gauge for the type of fuses used by the manufacturer, that this wiring was not in conformity with the applicable electrical code, and that there was a danger of overheating in the electrical system.

The original gas tank and an auxiliary gas tank, installed by KOA at the Murrays' request prior to delivery, were both apparently improperly vented. As a result, it was extremely difficult to fill the tanks; gasoline would spew out of the tanks when the caps were removed; and gasoline fumes came up into the passenger compartment. Mr. Murray testified that on one occasion, service station attendants were able to put only twenty cents' worth of gasoline into both tanks. Apparently as a result of problems with the carburetor, the vehicle would stall. Dirt and soldering flux were found in the fuel filter, which was replaced, as was the fuel pump.

There were problems with the air suspension system. There was testimony that this resulted in uneven distribution of weight on the tandem set of wheels in the rear of the vehicle, putting insufficient weight on the front wheels and causing steering problems. Repairs were made to the suspension system, but the steering problems persisted. Mr. Murray complained that the front brakes were not operating properly, and despite adjustments, had difficulty with the front wheels.

KOA apparently remedied various problems with the furnace and refrigerator, with an oil filter, and with a rattling engine cowling. KOA corrected the LP fuel tank gauge, which, as installed at the factory, indicated "full" when the tank was empty, and vice versa; KOA also supplied a missing handle for the tank and drained water which was inside the tank when it left the factory.

Unusual pressure caused a water line to come uncoupled. Mr. Murray advised KOA about this problem but repaired it himself.

There was also testimony regarding problems with folding seats, the furnace fan, the exhaust fan above the stove, a splash board which came unfastened, and the oven door, which fell off. Although there was conflicting testimony as to whether these parts were defective, the testimony of the Murrays with regard to these problems was not inherently incredible.

It is the position of the defendants that KOA successfully repaired every defect complained of by the Murrays, and that the Murrays were satisfied with the repair service. The evidence on this point was conflicting, and the jury could reasonably have believed Mr. Murray's testimony that he had never told KOA he was satisfied with the vehicle and that, on the contrary, he had repeatedly sought to return the troublesome Avenger and to recover his purchase price and the motorhome he had traded in.

Although the Murrays agreed that KOA had never refused to attempt a requested repair, this testimony does not affect their right to revoke acceptance. The limited remedy of repair or replacement of defective parts fails of its essential purpose whenever, despite reasonable opportunity for repair, the goods are not restored to a nondefective condition within a reasonable time, whether or not the failure to do so is willful.

In July 1974, the Murrays traveled to Colorado in the motorhome. They experienced continued problems filling the gasoline tanks. At one point they were forced to leave the vehicle to avoid gasoline fumes which filled the interior. Gasoline spewed from the tanks when the tank caps were removed, and they were asked to leave one service station after the attendant was thus doused with gasoline.

Mr. Murray testified that the vehicle stalled while ascending one mountain and that the rear brakes malfunctioned while descending another.

On the return trip, the electrical system malfunctioned while the Murrays were inside a South Dakota restaurant. Lights came on; smoke filled the vehicle, and wiring was burned. Defendants' expert agreed that this fire may have been caused by a short circuit where a wire passed through the sharp-edged metal wall of the vehicle.

After this incident, the electrical system did not charge properly, and the plaintiffs were unable to use the air-conditioner. The plaintiffs opened the windows, and several screens blew out. The electrical system went out completely in Ellsworth, Wisconsin, and the plaintiffs traveled the rest of the way to their home near Menomonie, Wisconsin, by automobile.

This evidence amply supports the conclusion that, despite reasonable opportunity for repair, the defendants had failed to provide the Murrays with goods conforming to the contract—that is, with a safe and substantially non-defective motorhome—within a reasonable time after purchase. The limited remedy therefore failed of its essential purpose, and the remedy of revocation became available. . . .

REVOCATION OF ACCEPTANCE

Pursuant to sec. 402.608, acceptance may be revoked where nonconformities substantially impair the value of the goods to the buyer and where acceptance is revoked within a reasonable time and before any substantial change in the condition of the goods.

The jury found that the various nonconformities substantially impaired the value of the motorhome to the plaintiffs, and the defendants do not challenge this finding directly. KOA does so indirectly, however, when it states that the defects could have been repaired for approximately $200 and that this figure was minor in relation to the purchase price.

However, the $200 figure, offered by the defendants' witnesses, did not reflect approximately $150 expended in previous efforts at repair by KOA and approximately $50 expended by the plaintiffs for various repairs. Nor did it include any incidental or consequential damages incurred by the plaintiffs. Moreover, this estimate included only the cost of replacing damaged wiring and adjusting the seats in the vehicle; it did not include any allowance for correction of the reported problems with the gas tanks, suspension system, brakes or various minor items. On this record, and considering the nature of the reported problems with gasoline fumes, electrical short circuits and brake malfunctions, the jury could reasonably have concluded that the nonconformities substantially impaired the value of the vehicle to the plaintiffs.

KOA next contends that the plaintiffs did not revoke acceptance within a reasonable time or before a substantial change in the condition of the motorhome. These are questions of fact for the jury. By the time of trial, the plaintiffs had driven the motorhome approximately 3,650 miles, including approximately 2,200 miles on the Colorado trip. However, Mr. Murray testified that he had repeatedly asked KOA to accept return of the motorhome and to give him back his purchase price. These requests were refused. In view of Mr. Murray's testimony that he had no use of the motorhome from the time he took possession on January 30, 1974, until the time he first sought to revoke acceptance on March 10, 1974, the jury could reasonably have found that there had been no substantial change in the condition of the motorhome.

Moreover, the formal revocation of August 15, 1974, followed months of nearly continuous efforts at repair. It is the policy of the Uniform Commercial Code to encourage parties to minimize losses resulting from defective performance by working out their differences. The defendants had a right, under the limited warranty, to attempt to cure the nonconformities within a reasonable time, and the plaintiffs justifiably awaited the results of these efforts. . . .

[Therefore], the jury in the instant case could reasonably have determined that the plaintiffs were entitled to revoke acceptance of the motorhome.

DAMAGES FOR LOSS OF USE

The jury awarded the plaintiffs $2,500 for loss of use of the motorhome from the date of revocation of acceptance, August 15, 1974, to the date of the verdict. KOA argues that the plaintiffs were precluded by the terms of the limited warranty from recovering any incidental or consequential damages, including any damages for loss of use of the vehicle.

Where the exclusive limited remedy of the contract fails of its essential purpose, however, the buyer is entitled to invoke any of the remedies available under the UCC. Sec. 402.719(2). This includes the right to recover consequential damages under sec. 402.715.

Consequential damages include any loss caused by general or particular needs of the buyer of which the seller had reason to know at the time of contracting and which could not reasonably be prevented by cover or otherwise. Sec. 402.715(1). Consequential damages have specifically been held to include damages for loss of use of an inoperable motor vehicle. Bob Anderson Pontiac, Inc. v. Davidson (Ind.App.1973), 293 N.E.2d 232; Williams v. College Dodge, Inc., 11 UCC Rep. 958 (Mich.Dist.Ct.1972).

A buyer . . . may not recover damages which he could reasonably have prevented. Sec. 402.715(2)(a). For this reason, loss-of-use damages may not be recovered for an indefinite period. However, such damages are properly available for periods during which a buyer, relying in good faith on the seller's assurances that defects will be cured, is unable to use the vehicle which he has purchased. See Jerry Alderman Ford Sales, Inc. v. Bailey (Ind.App.1972), 291 N.E.2d 92, 105.

The defendant, KOA, relies upon Russo v. Hilltop Lincoln–Mercury, Inc.(Mo.App.1972), 479 S.W.2d 211. There, defective wiring had caused an automobile to be totally burned. The Missouri Court of Appeals held that, because the car could not be repaired, the limited warranty remedy of repair or replacement of defective parts was inapplicable. Accordingly, the buyer was allowed to recover, not merely the replacement cost of the defective wiring, but rather the full value of the car.

Implicit in this holding was a determination that the limited warranty remedy had failed of its essential purpose. Nevertheless, when the Missouri court turned to the buyer's claim for damages for the rental cost of a replacement car, the court held that such damages were excluded by the terms of the warranty and that this exclusion had not failed of its essential purpose.

This result is inconsistent with the many decisions which have held that consequential damages may be recovered where a limited contractual remedy excluding such damages has failed.

Moreover, the result of the *Russo* case, supra, which permitted the buyer to recover some UCC damages but not others, is inconsistent with the apparent intention of the drafters. Sec. 402.719(2) provides that once a limited remedy fails of its essential purpose "remedy may be had as provided in this code." In such a case the exclusive contractual remedy ". . . must give way to the general remedy provisions of this Article." Official Comment 1.

Thus, although an express warranty excludes consequential damages, when the exclusive contractual remedy fails, the buyer may recover consequential damages under sec. 402.715 as though the limitation had never existed. The instant plaintiffs were therefore entitled to recover any consequential damages which they could prove, including reasonable damages incurred as a result of loss of use of the motorhome.

However, we are of the opinion that the plaintiffs have not sustained their burden of proof with regard to loss of use damages in the amount of $2,500. . . .

Here, there was evidence with regard to the period of time during which the motorhome was unusable, and with regard to the approximate rental cost of a replacement motorhome, but there was no evidence of the extent to which the motorhome would have been used by the plaintiffs if it had not been defective. . . .

Damages for loss of use of a recreational vehicle should be founded upon credible evidence of the use which would have been made of the vehicle if not for the defects, or upon evidence of expenses actually incurred as a result of the vehicle's inoperability. Such losses should not be calculated simply by reference to the number of days the vehicle sits idle, absent evidence that the vehicle would have been in use for the entire period.

The only definite testimony concerning lost use of the motorhome was to the effect that the Colorado trip was cut short by one week. Apart from this testimony, there was no basis from which the jury could determine the amount of any damages suffered by the plaintiffs due to the loss of use of the motorhome. With the exception of damages for this one-week period, the $2,500 damages awarded by the jury were speculative.

. . .

By the Court. Judgment affirmed in part; modified in part; reversed in part and cause remanded for further proceedings not inconsistent with this opinion. On appeal, costs are awarded to the respondent.

QUESTIONS AND NOTES

1. For a disclaimer of warranties to be effective, it must meet the standard of section 2–316. For a limitation of remedies to be effective, it must meet the standard of section 2–719. Therefore, to determine whether a contract term is enforceable, the first step is to determine whether it is a disclaimer of warranties or a limitation of remedies. See UCC section 2–316(4), Official Comment 2.

Was the clause in question in Murray a disclaimer of implied warranties or a limitation of remedies? Did the court apply the proper test to determine its enforceability?

Which section would determine the effectiveness of a clause providing, "Buyer may not recover damages for defects in this product"?

2. Is there a requirement of conspicuousness for clauses limiting the consumer's remedies in the event of a breach of warranty?

3. Problem. Consumer purchases a non-stick fry pan. Accompanying the pan is a statement:

> GlideFree Cookware is warranted to free from defects in material and workmanship under normal household use for a period of 10 years. This pan will continue to release food for a full 10 years when our care and use instructions are followed. We will repair or replace (at our option) any defective part or item during the guarantee period. Should

you have a problem with your pan, please return it to us at 136 Woodlawn Rd., Waterloo, IA.

This warranty does not cover damage caused by overheating, accident, misuse, or abuse. Incidental or consequential damages are expressly excluded by this warranty.

After three years food no longer glides out of the pan without sticking. May Consumer recover damages for this breach of warranty?

4. In Ford Motor Co. v. Reid, 465 S.W.2d 80 (Ark.1971), the manufacturer gave several express warranties that various parts of a car were free of defects. The warranty document also provided:

All the warranties shall be fulfilled by the Selling Dealer (or if the owner is traveling or has become a resident of a different locality, by any authorized Ford or Lincoln–Mercury dealer) replacing with a genuine new Ford or Ford Authorized Reconditioned part, or repairing at his place of business, free of charge including related labor, any such defective part.

The warranties herein are expressly IN LIEU OF any other express or implied warranty, including any implied WARRANTY of MERCHANTABILITY or FITNESS, and of any other obligation on the part of the Company or the Selling Dealer.

Are the buyers limited to having defects repaired, or may they assert other remedies?

When we read the second paragraph of the general warranty provisions under the guidelines of Ark.Stat.Ann. § 85–2–316(1) that words "tending to negate or limit warranty" are to be construed whenever reasonable as consistent with each other but if the clauses are inconsistent then the words of disclaimer of express warranties must give way to the words creating the express warranty, we reach the conclusion that the mandatory language "all the warranties shall be fulfilled by the selling dealer * * * "is an instruction to the dealer and not a limitation on other remedies of the buyer. This construction is supported by Ark.Stat.Ann. § 85–2–719(1)(b) which provides that "resort to a remedy as provided is optional unless the remedy is expressly agreed to be exclusive, in which case it is the sole remedy."

There is no language anywhere in the warranty form "expressly" stating that the remedy of repair or replacement of defective parts is to be the exclusive remedy. The language in the third paragraph of the "General Warranty Provisions" goes only to "obligations" and "warranties," not to remedies. As Section 85–2–301 (Add.1961), General Obligations of Parties, shows "The obligation of the seller is to transfer and deliver * * * in accordance with the contract." Remedies are not "obligations," they are the rights arising from failure to perform obligations. This is further made clear by the provisions of Section 85–2–316(4) cross referencing to contractual remedy section of the Code as governing those phases of the agreement. If the Ford Motor Company intended the repair remedy to be exclusive, as it now contends, it should have stated that intention in express language.

465 S.W.2d at 84–85. Compare Clark v. International Harvester Co., 581 P.2d 784, 796–97 (Idaho 1978) ("We are not inclined to torture the plain meaning of the language in such a clause in order to reach an interpretation different from that clearly expressed").

5. Under section 2–719(2) an exclusive, limited remedy is binding on the buyer unless the limited remedy fails of its essential purpose. What is the essential purpose of a limited remedy, e.g., repair or replacement of defective parts? See the last sentence of Official Comment 1. Is that how the court in *Murray* defines the essential purpose of a repair-or-replace remedy? Compare Beal v. General Motors Corp., 354 F.Supp. 423, 426 (D.Del.1973):

> The purpose of an exclusive remedy of replacement or repair of defective parts, whose presence constitutes a breach of an express warranty, is to give the seller an opportunity to make the goods conforming while limiting the risks to which he is subject by excluding direct and consequential damages that might otherwise arise. From the point of view of the buyer the purpose of the exclusive remedy is to give him goods that conform to the contract within a reasonable time after a defective part is discovered.

6. When does a repair-or-replace remedy fail of its essential purpose? In Lankford v. Rogers Ford Sales, 478 S.W.2d 248 (Tex.Civ.App.1972), plaintiff's car had many defects, ranging from trivial to hazardous. Defendant repaired the defects, though for some it took as many as five tries. In eighteen months the car was in the shop for repairs for a total of forty-five days for fifty different defects. An exasperated plaintiff sued for damages, arguing that the limited remedy had failed of its essential purpose. The court responded:

> Plaintiff admits that on each and every occasion that a defect has occurred, the same has been repaired by a Ford dealer. Thus, there is no allegation of any repudiation of the limited warranty, nor any allegation of any wilful failure or refusal to make the repairs needed nor any allegation of dilatory, careless or negligent compliance with the terms of the limited warranty. In the absence of such circumstances, we must conclude, as a matter of law, that the limited warranty has not failed in its essential purpose.

Id. at 251. How does this differ from the position of the court in *Murray*?

7. If the limited remedy fails of its essential purpose, then the buyer may seek any applicable remedy provided by the UCC. If the buyer wishes to retain the product notwithstanding its defects, section 2–714(2) permits recovery of the shortfall between the value of the product and the value that the product would have had if it had not been defective. Alternatively, the buyer may recover the repair costs, even if, according to some courts, they exceed the amount determined by using the difference-in-value measure. Jones v. Abriani, 350 N.E.2d 635 (Ind.App.1976).

On the other hand, if the buyer wishes to be rid of the product, that remedy may be available, too. Under section 2–608(1), if the defects substantially impair the value of the product to the buyer, the buyer may revoke his or her acceptance (if one of the conditions in subsections (a) and (b) is satisfied, which is almost always the case for new products and is usually the case for used products). Note that the UCC does not refer to this as rescission, but rather as revocation of acceptance. See Ramirez v. Autosport, 440 A.2d 1345, 1350 (N.J.1982). Some courts have borrowed from non-UCC rescission cases the requirement that the buyer must surrender, or at least tender, any benefits received (viz., the product). Other courts permit revocation of acceptance even if the buyer has not made a formal tender. This is not to say, however, that the buyer may continue to use the product after making a revocation of acceptance.

Most courts, as *Murray*, seem fairly liberal in permitting revocation of acceptance a relatively long time after the purchase, at least if the reason for the delay is the seller's assurances and attempts at repair. A more troublesome aspect of section 2–608(2) is the requirement that revocation occur before any substantial change in the condition of the product that is not caused by its own defects. If a car is driven for a year, even if the buyer has waited that long because of the seller's assurances and repair efforts, has not the condition of the car substantially changed? Note how the court in *Murray* finessed this problem.

Revocation of acceptance under section 2–608 is available only if the defects in the product substantially impair the value of the product to the buyer. But even if revocation of acceptance is not available because of lack of substantial impairment, the buyer may still be able to escape from the transaction. In Jones v. Abriani, 350 N.E.2d 635 (Ind.App.1976), it was obvious on delivery that the buyers' mobile home was defective. When the buyers said they did not want the home in that condition, the seller informed them she would not return their $1,000 downpayment. The buyers took the home, along with the seller's obligation to repair. The court held this did not amount to "acceptance" of the goods under section 2–606, and the buyers' rejection of the mobile home over a year later was timely. Hence, they were entitled to cancel the transaction and recover their downpayment (§ 2–711(1)).

If the defects are not obvious when the buyer takes delivery of the product, use of it may amount to acceptance. Once the buyer has accepted the goods, it is too late to reject them, and the buyer will have to rely on revocation of acceptance. Testo v. Russ Dunmire Oldsmobile, Inc., 554 P.2d 349 (Wash.App.1976). But taking delivery of the goods is not the same thing as acceptance. Therefore, if the buyer discovers the defects very soon after delivery, rejection may still be possible. See section 2–606(1)(b) (buyer has reasonable opportunity to inspect); Zabriskie Chevrolet, Inc. v. Smith, 240 A.2d 195 (N.J.Super.1968) (car broke down as the buyer was driving it home from the showroom).

8. Problem. *Consumer* buys a car from *Dealer*. *Manufacturer* warrants the car to be free of defects but limits the remedy to repair and replacement.

The car is defective, and for several months *Dealer* attempts repairs. For reasons unrelated to this transaction, *Dealer* goes out of business. *Consumer* takes the car to another dealer, who attempts repairs pursuant to *Manufacturer's* warranty and limited remedy. Eventually, the remedy fails of its essential purpose, and the value of the car to *Consumer* is substantially impaired. *Consumer* sues *Manufacturer*. What relief is available?

9.   Each of the sections of the UCC that provides a measure of damages in the event of the seller's breach permits the buyer to recover consequential damages. As defined in section 2–715 and applied to a defective automobile, consequential damages might include such things as rental cost of a replacement vehicle, food and lodging (if the breakdown occurs away from home), lost wages, finance charges allocable to the period of time after the buyer revokes acceptance and ceases using the car, and any increase in operating expenses (e.g., for gas, oil, or tires) resulting from the defects. The UCC, however, permits the seller to exclude consequential damages (§ 2–719(3)). Any time the parties provide for a limited, exclusive remedy under section 2–719(1)(b), they are in effect excluding consequential damages. But frequently, the contract contains a separate provision expressly excluding consequential damages.

Why does the court in *Murray* permit the consumer to recover consequential damages? Under section 2–719(2), when the limited remedy fails of its essential purpose, "remedy may be had as provided in this Act." But "this Act" includes section 2–719(3). Under subsection 3, what test governs the enforceability of a provision excluding consequential damages? Is the court correct in asserting that whenever the limited remedy fails of its essential purpose, the buyer should be able to recover consequential damages? Should it make any difference whether the exclusion is separately and expressly stated or is implicit in the exclusive remedy? In Razor v. Hyundai Motor America, 854 N.E.2d 607, 615–22 (Ill.2006), the court addressed this issue:

> There are two main schools of thought on the issue. Some courts and commentators conclude that a limited remedy failing of its essential purpose operates to destroy any limitation or exclusion of consequential damages in the same contract. This approach is known as the "dependent" approach, because the enforceability of the consequential damages exclusion depends on the survival of the limitation remedy.
>
>   . . .
>
> Plaintiff suggests that the dependent approach is followed by a majority of jurisdictions to consider the issue. While this may have been true 15 to 20 years ago, it is no longer the case. Rather, the majority of jurisdictions now follow the other of the two main approaches, the "independent" approach. . . . This school of thought holds that a limitation of consequential damages must be judged on its own merits and enforced unless unconscionable, regardless of whether the contract also contains a limitation of remedy which has failed of its essential purpose.

. . .

When a contract contains a limitation of remedy but that remedy fails of its essential purpose, it is as if that limitation of remedy does not exist for purposes of the damages to which a plaintiff is entitled for breach of warranty ("remedy may be had as provided in this Act"). When a contract contains a consequential damages exclusion but no limitation of remedy, it is incontrovertible that the exclusion is to be enforced unless unconscionable. Why, then, would a limitation of remedy failing of its essential purpose destroy a consequential damages exclusion in the same contract? We see no valid reason to so hold.

. . .

The two provisions—limitation of remedy and exclusion of consequential damages—can be visualized as two concentric layers of protection for a seller. What a seller would most prefer, if something goes wrong with a product, is simply to repair or replace it, nothing more. This "repair or replacement" remedy is an outer wall, a first defense. If that wall is breached, because the limited remedy has failed of its essential purpose, the seller still would prefer at least not to be liable for potentially unlimited consequential damages, and so he builds a second inner rampart as a fallback position. That inner wall is higher, and more difficult to scale—it falls only if unconscionable.

. . .

[The dependent approach] seems to ignore the plain language of the contract in a fundamental way—for if the buyer does not intend to renounce consequential damages when the limited remedy as failed, in what context *could* the disclaimer of consequential damages operate? . . . [W]e believe this is a fundamental defect in the dependent approach, that it renders the disclaimer of consequential damages an utter nullity. If a limited remedy has *not* failed of its essential purpose, that is of course the buyer's only remedy, by definition—this is what it means to have a limited remedy. So in this circumstance a disclaimer of limited damages would be of no effect because it would be redundant. If . . . the disclaimer of limited damages ought not to be enforced when the limited remedy *has* failed of its essential purpose, the language would never have any effect. Moreover, to the extent that the independent approach encourages parties to pay attention in the drafting process, we see this as point in favor of the independent approach, rather than the contrary.

. . .

A seller's deliberate or negligent failure to supply a limited remedy can be taken into consideration in determining whether enforcement of a consequential damages waiver is unconscionable. The unconscionability determination is not restricted to the facts and circumstances in existence at the time the contract was entered into. . . . Accordingly, we believe that a plaintiff must be allowed to point to a defendant's conduct, or any other circumstance which he believes would make enforcement of a consequential damages exclusion unconscionable. But the plain language of the UCC indicates that this step, of evaluating whether the exclusion is unconscionable, must be taken before a contractual consequential damages exclusion may be done away with.

In *Murray* the court holds that plaintiffs revoked acceptance on March 10. Assuming there were no finding of unconscionability, the court in *Razor* would not permit plaintiffs to recover damages for loss of use with respect to either the period before March 10 or the period after March 10. Can you develop an argument for treating these two periods differently?

10. Problem. *Consumer* buys a new car and receives an express warranty that the car is not defective. *Manufacturer* limits the remedy for breach of warranty to repair or replacement of any defective parts. A four-dollar part in the steering mechanism is defective and breaks while *Consumer* is lawfully traveling at 45 mph. *Consumer* loses control of the car and crashes. She escapes without personal injuries, but the crash damages the car (repairs cost $5,800) and destroys the new $600 TV she was just bringing home from the store. *Manufacturer* offers to replace the four-dollar part, but refuses to repair the car unless *Consumer* pays for the repairs. What are *Consumer's* rights under section 2–719?

11. Problem. *Consumer* buys a car from *Dealer* for $23,000. The car develops numerous problems, requiring repeated repairs. *Dealer* makes some repairs, unsuccessfully attempts others, and fails even to attempt to correct some of the defects. After several months (and 3,000 miles), *Consumer* gives up on *Dealer* (and the car) and sends a letter demanding return of her purchase price. *Dealer* refuses to take the car back. *Consumer* files a law suit, which comes to trial two years later. Meanwhile, she has continued to use the car, which now has 25,000 miles on it. Assuming that the repair-or-replace remedy has failed of its essential purpose, may *Consumer* revoke acceptance? If so, how much of the $23,000 price should she get? See UCC §§ 2–711(1), 2–608(3), 2–606(1)(c), 2–602(2)(a).

12. Section 2–719(3) provides that a limitation of consequential damages for personal injuries caused by a breach of warranty is prima facie unconscionable. But section 2–316 permits the seller to disclaim implied warranties altogether. Can a seller escape warranty liability for personal injuries simply by disclaiming all implied warranties? Is Official Comment 3 to section 2–719 dispositive?

13. The EU. In 1999 the European Union adopted a rule on warranties in consumer transactions. Directive 1999/44/EC of May 25, 1999, on certain aspects of the sale of consumer goods and associated guarantees, 1999 O.J. L171/12. This Directive compels the Member States to adopt legislation that meets the standards of the Directive. Article 2 of the Directive establishes quality standards for consumer goods. Article 3 imposes liability on the retailer. Excerpts follow:

Article 2.   Conformity with the contract.

1.   The seller must deliver goods to the consumer which are in conformity with the contract of sale.

2. Consumer goods are presumed to be in conformity with the contract if they:

> (a) comply with the description given by the seller and possess the qualities of the goods which the seller has held out to the consumer as a sample or model;

> (b) are fit for any particular purpose for which the consumer requires them and which he made known to the seller at the time of conclusion of the contract and which the seller has accepted;

> (c) are fit for the purposes for which goods of the same type are normally used;

> (d) show the quality and performance which are normal in goods of the same type and which the consumer can reasonably expect, given the nature of the goods and taking into account any public statements on the specific characteristics of the goods made about them by the seller, the producer or his representative, particularly in advertising or on labelling.

3. There shall be deemed not to be a lack of conformity for the purposes of this Article if, at the time the contract was concluded, the consumer was aware, or could not reasonably be unaware of, the lack of conformity, or if the lack of conformity has its origin in materials supplied by the consumer.

4. The seller shall not be bound by public statements, as referred to in paragraph 2(d) if he:

> —shows that he was not, and could not reasonably have been, aware of the statement in question;

> —shows that by the time of conclusion of the contract the statement had been corrected, or

> —shows that the decision to buy the consumer goods could not have been influenced by the statement.

5. Any lack of conformity resulting from incorrect installation of the consumer goods shall be deemed to be equivalent to lack of conformity of the goods if installation forms part of the contract of sale of the goods and the goods were installed by the seller or under his responsibility. This shall apply equally if the product, intended to be installed by the consumer, is installed by the consumer and the incorrect installation is due to a shortcoming in the installation instructions.

Article 3.   Rights of the consumer.

1. The seller shall be liable to the consumer for any lack of conformity which exists at the time the goods were delivered.

2. In the case of a lack of conformity, the consumer shall be entitled to have the goods brought into conformity free of charge by repair or replacement, in accordance with paragraph 3, or to have an appropriate reduction made in the price or the contract rescinded with regard to those goods, in accordance with paragraphs 5 and 6.

3.   In the first place, the consumer may require the seller to repair the goods or he may require the seller to replace them, in either case free of charge, unless this is impossible or disproportionate.

A remedy shall be deemed to be disproportionate if it imposes costs on the seller which, in comparison with the alternative remedy, are unreasonable, taking into account:

—the value the goods would have if there were no lack of conformity,

—the significance of the lack of conformity, and

—whether the alternative remedy could be completed without significant inconvenience to the consumer.

Any repair or replacement shall be completed within a reasonable time and without any significant inconvenience to the consumer, taking account of the nature of the goods and purpose for which the consumer required the goods.

4.   The terms 'free of charge' in paragraphs 2 and 3 refer to the necessary costs incurred to bring the goods into conformity, particularly the cost of postage, labour and materials.

5.   The consumer may require an appropriate reduction of the price or have the contract rescinded:

—if the consumer is entitled to neither repair nor replacement, or

—if the seller has not completed the remedy within a reasonable time, or

—if the seller has not completed the remedy without significant inconvenience to the consumer.

6.   The consumer is not entitled to have the contract rescinded if the lack of conformity is minor.

. . .

Article 7.   Binding nature.

1.   Any contractual terms or agreements concluded with the seller before the lack of conformity is brought to the seller's attention which directly or indirectly waive or restrict the rights resulting from this Directive shall, as provided for by national law, not be binding on the consumer.

Member States may provide that, in the case of second-hand goods, the seller and consumer may agree [to] contractual terms or agreement which have a shorter time period for the liability of the seller than that set down in Article 5(1). Such period may not be less than one year.

2.   Member States shall take the necessary measures to ensure that consumers are not deprived of the protection afforded by this Directive as a result of opting for the law of a non-member State as the law applicable to the contract where the contract has a close connection with the territory of the Member States.

a.   Note the similarity between Article 2, Paragraph 2 with UCC sections 2–313, 2–314, and 2–315. Does Paragraph 2(d) have a counterpart in the UCC?

b.   Subject to the holdings in *Berg* and *Knipp*, UCC section 2–316 permits a seller to disclaim implied warranties. To what extent does the Directive permit a seller to disclaim its implied warranties? Is there a rationale for the difference?

c.   If a product fails to conform to the contract, what is the consumer's remedy under the Directive? How does this differ from the consumer's remedy under the UCC?

d.   If after several attempts the seller is unable to effect repairs, UCC section 2–719(2) permits the consumer to recover damages. Under the EU's Directive, if the consumer asks for repair of a nonconforming product, what are the consumer's rights if the seller's several attempts at repair are unsuccessful?

e.   How would Problem 10 (page 354 supra) be resolved under the Directive?

D.   BEYOND THE UCC

Warranty protection for consumers has moved beyond the UCC. One set of additional rules applies to motor vehicles and tries to make the UCC rules more effective. Another set of rules applies to all goods and changes the UCC rules.

(1) LEMON LAWS

Since 1982 every state has enacted a so-called "lemon law" to deal with new cars that are so defective that the seller or manufacturer cannot remedy the defects. The statutes vary considerably in detail from state to state, but they share several major features. For a stated period of time (commonly twelve months or twelve thousand miles, whichever occurs first), a new car must conform to the warranty given by the manufacturer. If, within a reasonable number of attempts, the dealer or manufacturer is unable to remedy a defect that substantially impairs the value of the car, the manufacturer must either replace the car or refund the purchase price. The statutes define what constitutes a reasonable number of attempts at repair as either a) a specified number of attempts (typically four) to repair any given defect or b) the car's being out of service for a specified number of days (typically thirty) during the statutory warranty period. If the defect is safety related, some statutes reduce the reasonable number of attempts (typically to two).

One objective of the laws is to eliminate the automobile manufacturers' traditional position of refusing to recognize a consumer's revocation of acceptance, no matter how many times the consumer has brought a car in for repairs. (See Note 6, page 350.) Another objective is to provide a precise standard for when the repair-or-replace remedy fails of its essential purpose under UCC section 2–719(2). A third objective is the encouragement of nonjudicial methods to resolve disputes concerning defective automobiles. The lemon laws achieve this objective by requiring consumers to use certain arbitration programs, if the manufacturers have chosen to establish them.

The Statutory Supplement contains the lemon laws of New York and Missouri. Please read McKinney's N.Y.Gen.Bus.Law section 198–a and answer the following questions.

1.   How would the New York statute affect the dispute in Murray v. Holiday Rambler, Inc.?

2.   If the plaintiffs in *Murray* opted for and were entitled to a refund of the price, how much of an offset would defendant be entitled to under section 198–a(c)?

3.   If a car is a lemon, who decides whether the manufacturer provides a replacement rather than a refund?

Now please read the Missouri statute, Vernon's Ann.Mo.Stat. sections 407.560–407.579, and answer the following questions.

1.   How would the Missouri statute affect the dispute in Murray v. Holiday Rambler, Inc.?

2.   If a car is a lemon, who decides whether the manufacturer provides a replacement rather than a refund?

3.   If the problem with a car is that a particular defect persists, notwithstanding repeated attempts to repair it, how many attempts must the consumer permit before being entitled to return the car?

4.   If the plaintiffs in *Murray* opted for and were entitled to a refund of the price, how much of an offset would defendant be entitled to under section 407.567?

The statutes in some states contain a specific formula for determining the amount of the offset. Section 198–a(a)(4) of the New York statute is an example. For another formula, see Tenn.Code Ann. § 55–24–203 (one half of the amount allowed per mile by the Internal Revenue Service for use of a personal vehicle for business purposes)

5.   If plaintiffs in *Murray* were not entitled to relief under the Missouri lemon law, could they seek relief under UCC sections 2–719(2) and 2–608?

6.   Does the New York or Missouri statute apply when the consumer acquires an automobile by lease rather than by purchase? Some states have special provisions applicable to leases. See section 198–a(c)(2) of the New York statute (and the definition in section 198–a(a)(6)). For another approach, see the Minnesota lemon law:

> A consumer who leases a new motor vehicle has the same rights against the manufacturer under this section as a consumer who purchases a new motor vehicle, except that, if it is determined that the manufacturer must accept return of the consumer's leased vehicle

pursuant to subdivision 3, then the consumer lessee is not entitled to a replacement vehicle, but is entitled only to a refund as provided in this subdivision. In such a case, the consumer's leased vehicle shall be returned to the manufacturer and the consumer's written lease with the motor vehicle lessor must be terminated. The manufacturer shall then provide the consumer with a full refund of the amount actually paid by the consumer on the written lease, including all additional charges set forth in subdivision 3, if actually paid by the consumer, less a reasonable allowance for use by the consumer as set forth in subdivision 3. The manufacturer shall provide the motor vehicle lessor with a full refund of the vehicle's original purchase price plus any early termination costs, not to exceed 15 percent of the vehicle's original purchase price, less the amount actually paid by the consumer on the written lease.

Minn.Stat.Ann. § 325F.665(4).

7. When a manufacturer is required to repurchase a car from a consumer, what do you suppose the manufacturer does with it? To deal with this likelihood, the New York lemon law provides:

Upon the sale or transfer of title by a manufacturer, its agent or any dealer of any second-hand motor vehicle, previously returned to a manufacturer or dealer for nonconformity to its warranty or after final determination, adjudication or settlement pursuant to section one hundred ninety-eight-a or one hundred ninety-eight-b of the general business law, the manufacturer or dealer shall execute and deliver to the buyer an instrument in writing in a form prescribed by the commissioner setting forth the following information in ten point, all capital type: "IMPORTANT: THIS VEHICLE WAS RETURNED TO THE MANUFACTURER OR DEALER BECAUSE IT DID NOT CON-FORM TO ITS WARRANTY AND THE DEFECT OR CONDITION WAS NOT FIXED WITHIN A REASONABLE TIME AS PROVIDED BY NEW YORK LAW." Such notice that a vehicle was returned to the manufacturer or dealer because it did not conform to its warranty shall also be conspicuously printed on the motor vehicle's certificate of title.

McKinney's N.Y.Veh. & Traffic L. § 417–a(2).

The Minnesota statute goes a step further:

(a) If a motor vehicle has been returned under the provisions of subdivision 3 or a similar statute of another state, whether as the result of a legal action or as the result of an informal dispute settlement proceeding, it may not be resold or re-leased in this state unless:

(1) the manufacturer provides the same express warranty it provided to the original purchaser, except that the term of the warranty need only last for 12,000 miles or 12 months after the date of resale, whichever is earlier; and

(2) the manufacturer provides the consumer with a written statement on a separate piece of paper, in 10–point all capital type, in substantially the following form: "IMPORTANT: THIS VEHICLE

WAS RETURNED TO THE MANUFACTURER BECAUSE IT DID NOT CONFORM TO THE MANUFACTURER'S EXPRESS WARRANTY AND THE NONCONFORMITY WAS NOT CURED WITHIN A REASONABLE TIME AS PROVIDED BY MINNESOTA LAW."

The provisions of this section apply to the resold or released motor vehicle for [the] full term of the warranty required under this subdivision.

(b) Notwithstanding the provisions of paragraph (a), if a new motor vehicle has been returned under the provisions of subdivision 3 or a similar statute of another state because of a nonconformity resulting in a complete failure of the braking or steering system of the motor vehicle likely to cause death or serious bodily injury if the vehicle was driven, the motor vehicle may not be resold in this state.

Minn.Stat.Ann. § 325F.665(5). What is the manufacturer's likely response to subsection (b)?

A number of states require that the vehicle's title certificate bear a legend branding the vehicle a lemon. Three facts tend to undermine the effectiveness of this requirement:

1) If the manufacturer anticipates that a court will conclude that a vehicle is a lemon, the manufacturer may offer to repurchase it outside the formal lemon law procedure. This may avoid the need to brand the title. But see Cal.Civ.Code § 1793.23(d) (the title-branding requirement applies when a manufacturer reacquires a motor vehicle in response to a request by the buyer because the vehicle did not conform to the manufacturer's warranty).

2) Most vehicle purchases are financed, and in some states the department of motor vehicles (DMV) sends the new title directly to the financer. If so, the purchaser of a car with a branded title does not see the title until he or she completes the payments several years after the purchase. Even in states in which the DMV sends the title certificate to the consumer, the consumer may not receive the certificate until weeks after the transaction is consummated.

3) Through a series of sham sales, a used car dealer can launder the title (see "Double Dealers," page 99 supra).

Other remedies, of course, may exist for these practices. See, e.g., Morris v. Mack's Used Cars, 824 S.W.2d 538 (Tenn.1992) (seller liable under the little-FTC act for failing to disclose that the vehicle had been wrecked and reconstructed even though the title certificate disclosed this fact and the sales contract contained an "as is" clause); Harris, Woman Wins Suit over Sale of Bad Car, Akron Beacon Journal, Aug. 6, 1999, at 1 (verdict for $270,000 when the manufacturer disclosed only that the car was repurchased from a prior owner "to promote customer goodwill"). Lemon laundering remains a serious problem. See *www.safetyforum.com*.

8. The Missouri statute refers to informal dispute settlement procedures that comply with 16 C.F.R. Part 703. The reference is to a regulation the

Federal Trade Commission promulgated pursuant to section 110(a) of the Magnuson–Moss Warranty Act. Section 110(a) was a Congressional attempt to encourage arbitration of disputes concerning defective products. From its enactment in 1975 to 1982, however, auto manufacturers did not establish programs that complied with the federal standards. It was not until the widespread enactment of state lemon laws incorporating the federal standards into state law that some of the major auto manufacturers sought to establish complying programs. But the determination whether a program actually complies with the standards is a matter for each state to decide, and the states have reached differing conclusions. E.g., see Motor Vehicle Mfrs. Ass'n of United States v. O'Neill, 523 A.2d 486, 491 (Conn.1987) (none complies). For good analyses of lemon laws, see Basanta, The Illinois New Car Buyer Protection Act—An Analysis and Evaluation of the Illinois Lemon Law, 84 So.Ill.U.L.J. 1 (1984); Note, Lemon Laws: Putting the Squeeze on Automobile Manufacturers, 61 Wash.U.L.Q. 1125 (1984). For a description of the lemon laws in all 50 states, see Nowicki, State Lemon Law Coverage Terms: Dissecting the Differences, 11 Loyola Consumer L.Rev. 39 (1998).

Consumer dissatisfaction with manufacturer-sponsored alternative dispute resolution runs high. See, e.g., Morrow, Bitter Lemons, Smart Money, p. 107, January 1995; The Sour Truth About Lemon Laws, Consumer Reports, p. 40, January 1993 ("the road to satisfaction for lemon owners has turned out to be badly potholed. Weak laws, including many that allow auto manufacturers to run the arbitration process; poor oversight by the states; and miles of red tape have stymied consumers at every turn"). Within a few years after enacting their lemon laws, a dozen states amended them to create state-run arbitration programs and to require that manufacturers participate in them to resolve warranty disputes. Courts have rejected constitutional and preemption challenges to mandatory arbitration programs in Texas, Minnesota, and New York.

(2) MAGNUSON–MOSS WARRANTY ACT

The Magnuson–Moss Warranty Act does not require the seller to give a warranty. Chapter 4 (pages 222–23 supra) reveals, however, that if a "written warranty" is given, the warrantor must disclose certain information concerning that warranty. To that extent the Magnuson–Moss Act is not a quality control statute but rather a disclosure statute. Even section 104, which appears to set minimum standards, is literally only a disclosure provision. There are, however, several aspects of the Act that are relevant to quality standards.

To start with, the disclosure requirements are themselves an indirect attempt to set quality standards: the statute sets standards for the so-called "full" warranty and requires suppliers to label their warranties as "full" or "limited." The legislative history reveals a belief, or at least a hope, that suppliers would choose to offer full warranties because of competitive pressures and because of negative consumer reaction to suppliers who thought so little of their own products that they were willing to offer only a "limited" warranty. Three years after enactment, however, there was little change in the amount of protection offered by manufacturers' warranties. Comment, An Empirical Study of the Magnuson–Moss Warranty Act, 31 Stanford L.Rev. 1117 (1979). Even today, relatively few manufacturers give "full" warranties.

Perhaps the most far-reaching aspect of Magnuson–Moss is its response to the phenomenon of the seller's giving something with one hand (an express warranty) and taking away twice as much with the other (via limitation of remedies and disclaimer of implied warranties). Section 108 invalidates disclaimers of implied warranties, not only by persons giving full warranties, but by persons giving limited warranties, too.

In Ventura v. Ford Motor Corp., 433 A.2d 801 (N.J.Super.App.Div.1981), plaintiffs purchased a new car that turned out to be defective. When repairs proved ineffective, plaintiffs sued the dealer (Marino Auto Sales) and the manufacturer, seeking to revoke their acceptance of the car and recover the price. The manufacturer warranted that the dealer would "repair or replace free any parts found . . . to be defective . . . within the earlier of 12 months or 12,000 miles." The contract between plaintiffs and the dealer contained a disclaimer of "all warranties" and a provision that "[t]he selling dealer . . . agrees to promptly perform and fulfill all terms and conditions of the [manufacturer's warranty]." The court granted rescission:

> We will first consider the application of this act to the dealer, Marino Auto. As quoted above, paragraph 7 of the purchase order contract provides that there are no warranties, express or implied, made by the selling dealer or manufacturer except, in the case of a new motor vehicle, "the warranty expressly given to the purchaser upon delivery of such motor vehicle. . . ." This section also provides: "The selling dealer also agrees to promptly perform and fulfill all terms and conditions of the owner service policy." . . . The provision in paragraph 7 in these circumstances is a "written warranty" within the meaning of § 101(6)(B) since it constitutes an undertaking in connection with the sale to take "remedial action with respect to such product in the event that such product fails to meet the specifications set forth in the undertaking. . . ." In our view the specifications of the undertaking include, at the least, the provisions of the limited warranty furnished by Ford. . . .
>
>   . . . Accordingly, having furnished a written warranty to the consumer, the dealer as a supplier may not "disclaim or modify [except to limit in duration] any implied warranty to a consumer. . . ." The result of this analysis is to invalidate the attempted disclaimer by the dealer of the implied warranties of merchantability and fitness. Being bound by those implied warranties arising under state law, N.J.S.A. 12A:2–314 and 315, Marino Auto was liable to plaintiff for the breach thereof as found by the trial judge, and plaintiff could timely revoke his acceptance of the automobile and claim a refund of his purchase price. N.J.S.A. 12A:2–608 and N.J.S.A. 12A:2–711. . . .

Plaintiff also could have recovered damages against Ford for Ford's breach of its written limited warranty. Marino Auto was Ford's representative for the purpose of making repairs to plaintiff's vehicle under the warranty. . . .

One question posed by this case is whether recovery of the purchase price from the manufacturer was available to plaintiff for breach of the manufacturer's warranty. If the warranty were a full warranty plaintiff would have been entitled to a refund of the purchase price under the Magnuson–Moss Warranty Act. Since Ford's warranty was a limited warranty we must look to state law to determine plaintiff's right to damages or other legal and equitable relief § 110(d)(1). Once privity is removed as an obstacle to relief we see no reason why a purchaser cannot also elect the equitable remedy of returning the goods to the manufacturer who is a warrantor and claiming a refund of the purchase price less an allowance for use of the product. See Seely v. White Motor Co.

QUESTIONS

1.   What is left of UCC section 2–316? Or to put it another way, was the time spent on Section C of this chapter wasted?

2.   Since the prohibition of disclaimers applies only when the supplier gives a written warranty, it is essential to understand the meaning of that term. Note that the excerpt from Ventura v. Ford Motor Corp. states that the selling dealer gave a written warranty when its purchase order stated, "The selling dealer also agrees to promptly perform and fulfill all terms and conditions of the [manufacturer's express warranty]." Would the result be the same if the manufacturer's warranty stated, "The selling dealer will make any repairs or replacements necessary to correct defects in material or workmanship"?

3.   In the last paragraph of the excerpt from Ventura, the court suggests that section 110(d)(1) eliminates any requirement of privity. Not all courts agree:

> Ford argues that State privity laws are preserved under the Act and must be considered by the Court before a plaintiff may assert an implied warranty claim under Magnuson–Moss. Ford bases its privity argument on the express provisions of the Act. It notes that although the Act provides for a Federal cause of action for breach of implied warranty, the Act defines implied warranty as "an implied warranty arising under State law (as modified by sections 108 and 104(a) of this act) in connection with the sale by a supplier of a consumer product." Section 101(7), 15 U.S.C. § 2301(7). . . .
>
> In response plaintiffs have argued that State law privity doctrines do not apply under Magnuson–Moss because the Act creates a new Federal private cause of action for breach of implied warranty. Therefore, plaintiffs assert, the requirement that vertical privity exist be-

tween the purchaser and Ford is eliminated under the Act and cannot serve as a barrier for pursuing implied warranty claims. Specifically, plaintiffs cite to the Act's definition of "consumer," "supplier," and "warrantor" as a basis for arguing that state privity law has been superseded. When reading those definitions into section 110(d)(1), plaintiffs argue, the Court must conclude that any person to whom the vehicle is transferred during the life of the implied warranty is entitled to enforce that warranty by bringing suit.

Certainly, it is axiomatic that where the meaning of the statute is plain on its face, this Court need not take further inquiry into its purpose. See Consumer Product Safety Commission v. GTE Sylvania, Inc., 447 U.S. 102, 108, 100 S.Ct. 2051, 2056, 64 L.Ed.2d 766 (1980). Here, Congress has specifically provided that implied warranties "arise" under State law. Section 101(7), 15 U.S.C. 2301(7). If, in this action, there are to be any implied warranty claims at all under Magnuson–Moss, they must "originate" from or "come into being" from state law.[4] Therefore, if a State does not provide for a cause of action for breach of implied warranty where vertical privity is lacking, there cannot be a Federal cause of action for such a breach.

The statutory history in this matter is also clear. In a Senate report from the Committee on Commerce, the committee stated that:

> It is not the intent of the Committee to alter in any way the manner in which implied warranties are created under the Uniform Commercial Code. For instance, an implied warranty of fitness for a particular purpose which might be created by an installing supplier is not, in many instances, enforceable by the consumer against the manufacturing supplier. *The Committee does not intend to alter currently existing state law on these subjects.*

Senate Comm. on Commerce, S.Rep. No. 151, 93d Cong., 1st Sess. 21 (1973) (emphasis added). Other portions of the Act's statutory history support the conclusion that state implied warranties, including privity requirements, are not to be changed by the enactment of Magnuson–Moss. See, e.g., Hearings on Consumer Warranty Protection before the Subcomm. on Commerce & Finance of the House Comm. on Interstate and Foreign Commerce, 93d Cong., 1st Sess. 91, 94 (March 20, 1973).

. . .

Plaintiffs, however, argue that the definitions "consumer," "supplier," and "warrantor" in section 101 abolish any state law privity requirements. They assert that by transposing these definitions into the subsection that provides for civil actions by consumers for breach of warranty, the Court is compelled to conclude that State privity requirements are abolished. When transposing these definitions of section 101, section 110(d)(1) provides:

---

4. The Random House Dictionary of the English Language (Random House, N.Y. 1969) defines arise as "1. to come into being, action, or notice; originate; appear; spring up."

. . . a consumer [including "a buyer (other than for purposes of resale) of any consumer product, any person to whom such product is transferred"] who is damaged by the failure of a supplier ["any person engaged in the business of making a consumer product directly or indirectly available to consumers"] [or] warrantor ["any supplier or other person who . . . is or may be obligated under an implied warranty"] ["arising under State law"] . . . to comply with . . . an implied warranty ["arising under State law"] . . . may bring suit. . . .

In adding these definitions to section 110(d)(1), it is still evident to this Court that an action under Magnuson–Moss may be brought by a "consumer who is damaged by the failure of a supplier to comply with any obligation under [the act] . . . includ[ing] implied warranties arising under State law." H.R.Rep. No. 93–1107, 93d Cong., 2d Sess., reprinted in 1974 U.S.Code Cong. & Ad.News 7702, 7723. The definitions do not alter the requirement that an implied warranty, if it is to arise at all, must arise under State law and "[i]f state law requires vertical privity to enforce an implied warranty and there is none, then, like the yeastless souffle, the warranty does not 'arise.'" Feinstein v. Firestone Tire & Rubber Co., 535 F.Supp. at 605 n. 13.

Walsh v. Ford Motor Co., 588 F.Supp. 1513, 1524–26 (D.D.C.1984), vacated on other grounds and remanded, 807 F.2d 1000 (D.C.Cir.1986). Which court is correct?

Compare the view of the Supreme Court of Illinois:

Focusing on that part of the definition stating the term means "an implied warranty arising under State law," some authors maintain that if the law of the State holds that privity is essential to implied warranty, then an action such as is involved in our case cannot be maintained. However, the definition also states that the term means an implied warranty arising under State law *"(as modified by sections 108 and 104(a) of this title)."* (Emphasis added.) Section 108(a) raises the question as to whether it modifies implied-warranty State-law provisions to the extent that any written warranty given by a manufacturer to a remote purchaser creates an implied warranty by virtue of Magnuson–Moss. At the very least we must acknowledge that the provisions of section 108 clearly demonstrate the policy of Magnuson–Moss to sustain the protection afforded to consumers by implied warranties.

The Act broadly defines "consumer" in section 101(3) as "a buyer (other than for purposes of resale) of any consumer product, any person to whom such product is transferred during the duration of an implied or written warranty * * * and any other person who is entitled by the terms of such warranty * * * or under applicable State law to enforce against the warrantor * * * the obligations of the warranty." It has been suggested that this broad definition of "consumer" and the provisions of section 110(d)(1), which section authorizes a "consumer" to maintain a civil action for damages for failure of a "supplier" or "warrantor" to comply with any obligation of a written or implied warranty, effectively abolish vertical privity. We do not think we can focus on any one section of Magnuson–Moss but should read the sections referred to together to accomplish the purpose of Magnuson–Moss of furnishing broad protection to the consumer.

In resolving this murky situation we find helpful, and accept, Professor Schroeder's analysis and suggestion as a reasonable solution. In cases where no Magnuson–Moss written warranty has been given, Magnuson–Moss has no effect upon State-law privity requirements because, by virtue of section 101(7), which defines implied warranty, implied warranty arises only if it does so under State law. However, if a Magnuson–Moss written warranty (either "full" or "limited") is given, by reason of the policy against disclaimers of implied warranty expressed in Magnuson–Moss and the provisions authorizing a consumer to sue a warrantor, the nonprivity "consumer" should be permitted to maintain an action on an implied warranty against the "warrantor." (Schroeder, *Privity Actions Under the Magnuson–Moss Warranty Act*, 66 Calif.L.Rev. 1, 16 (1978).) The rationale of this conclusion, though not specifically articulated by Professor Schroeder in the article, would hold that under Magnuson–Moss a warrantor, by extending a written warranty to the consumer, establishes privity between the warrantor and the consumer which, though limited in nature, is sufficient to support an implied warranty under sections 2–314 and 2–315 of the UCC. The implied warranty thus recognized, by virtue of the definition in section 101(7) of Magnuson–Moss, must be one arising under the law of this State.

Szajna v. General Motors Corp., 503 N.E.2d 760, 768–69 (Ill.1986).

4. Section 108 invalidates disclaimers not only when a supplier makes a written warranty, but also when a supplier enters into a service contract with the consumer. Please read section 108(a)(2). Section 101(8) defines "service contract" as "a contract in writing to perform, over a fixed period of time or for a specified duration, services relating to the maintenance or repair (or both) of a consumer product." Although manufacturers typically make written warranties—and therefore cannot disclaim implied warranties (§ 108(a)(1))—retailers often do not make any written warranty. Indeed, they typically disclaim implied warranties. If, however, a retailer agrees in writing that, for an additional $400, it will repair anything that goes wrong with the product during the first two years after the manufacturer's warranty expires, section 108 prohibits the dealer from disclaiming implied warranties.

Problem. In connection with selling *Consumer* a used car, *Dealer* sells her a contract in which a third party, *GoldStar Warranty*, promises to effect repairs: can *Dealer* disclaim the implied warranty of merchantability? Should it matter that *Dealer* retains 75% of the $400 and forwards only 25% to *GoldStar*?

5. Problem. *Manufacturer* sells cars with a limited warranty for 12 months or 12,000 miles, whichever comes first. In addition, *Manufacturer* provides a limited warranty on the engine and transmission for 24 months or 24,000 miles, whichever comes first. If *Manufacturer* limits the duration of implied warranties to 12 months or 12,000 miles, has it violated section 108(b)? If so, what remedies are available?

6. Could *Manufacturer* in the preceding problem accomplish its objective by using a service contract instead of a written warranty?

7. Section 108(b) is one of the most troublesome aspects of the Magnuson–Moss Act, but for an entirely different reason than suggested by the preceding questions. According to UCC section 2–725(2), if a product is defective, the breach of the implied warranty of merchantability occurs when the product is delivered. What then does it mean to say, as Magnuson–Moss Act section 108(b) does, that the seller may limit the duration of implied warranties?

Does it refer to the time within which the consumer must sue? the time within which the defect must become apparent? the time by which the consumer must notify the seller of a breach of warranty? the time by which the consumer must present the product for repairs? In connection with this question, consider UCC sections 2–725(1) and 2–607(3).

8. Section 108(b) sets four limitations on the supplier's ability to limit the duration of implied warranties: (a) the duration of the written warranty must be reasonable; the limitation on the duration of implied warranties (b) must be set forth in clear and unmistakable language, (c) must be prominently displayed on the face of the warranty, and (d) must be conscionable.

If the duration of the written warranty is reasonable, is it ever possible for the limitation on the duration of implied warranties to be unconscionable? In Carlson v. General Motors Corp., 883 F.2d 287 (4th Cir.1989), the court stated that the reasonableness of the duration of the written warranty is a function of "how long, given past experience, consumers legitimately can expect to enjoy the use of a product 'worry-free.' Courts should focus, in other words, on whether purchasers should 'reasonably' expect that, after a certain period, the product might well need repair." Id. at 295. But, the court added, the conscionability of the limitation on the duration of implied warranties requires a court to consider, among other things, the manufacturer's knowledge that the product is likely to break down long before consumers would reasonably expect it to.

9. May a seller limit the remedies available to the consumer in the event of breach of warranty, i.e. is UCC section 2–719(1) still effective in consumer transactions?

May a seller exclude consequential damages, i.e. is section 2–719(3) still effective?

10. Another substantive regulation of the content of warranties appears in section 102(c), which prohibits the warrantor from making a warranty conditional on the consumer's use of a second product. This prohibition applies to limited, as well as full, warranties. What rationale might there be for this prohibition?

Can a manufacturer of bedding offer the consumer a choice of a 5–year limited warranty on a mattress if purchased alone and a 10–year limited warranty on the mattress if the consumer also purchases the matching box springs?

11. Does the Magnuson–Moss Warranty Act confer any rights on consumers who lease cars? See sections 101(3), (6), (7). After noting that the Act does not create warranties, but rather takes as its starting point whatever warranties exist under the UCC, one court stated:

> Because the protections of the Magnuson–Moss Warranty Act are so intertwined with and dependent upon the warranty provisions of the Uniform Commercial Code, the Magnuson–Moss Warranty Act should be construed to reach the same consumer transactions that are covered by the code. A broader construction would make no sense because the Magnuson–Moss Warranty Act provides virtually no protections in transactions beyond the scope of the Uniform Commercial Code. A narrower construction would be inconsistent with the purposes of the legislation of providing more meaningful protections to consumers entitled to the warranty protections of the Uniform Commercial Code. Consequently, we will extend the Magnuson–Moss Warranty Act to those "leasehold" transactions that are generally recognized to be within the coverage of the code.

Henderson v. Benson–Hartman Motors, Inc., 33 Pa.D. & C.3d 6, 23 (Ct. Com.Pl.1983). Under this view, the applicability of the Magnuson–Moss Warranty Act to consumer leases depends on whether state law recognizes warranties in consumer lease transactions. What is the flaw in this approach? Is it fatal?

In DiCintio v. DaimlerChrysler Corp., 768 N.E.2d 1121 (N.Y.2002), the court properly looked at the definition of "consumer" in Magnuson–Moss section 101 and concluded that the plaintiff was not a consumer because he was not a buyer of the car. What is the flaw in this conclusion?

(3) USED CARS

Section 109(b) of the Magnuson–Moss Warranty Act directs the FTC to initiate a rulemaking proceeding "dealing with warranties and warranty practices in connection with the sale of used motor vehicles." Pursuant to this command, the FTC studied the matter and concluded that deception was widespread. Its initial proposal required the seller of used cars to perform an inspection of specified parts of the cars and disclose the condition of each part on a form to be affixed to a window of the car. The Commission subsequently dropped the inspection requirement, but continued to propose that the seller be required to disclose the condition of various parts of the car. Diluting the proposal still further, the Commission then promulgated a regulation that would have required the seller to use a window sticker to disclose any express warranties and any major defects known to the seller. 46 Fed.Reg. 41,358 (August 14, 1981). Congress was unwilling to allow the FTC to place this burden on used car dealers and exercised its power under section 21a(a)(2) of the FTC Act (15 U.S.C. § 57a–1(a)(2)) to veto the regulation.

The Supreme Court held that the legislative veto under section 21a(a)(2) was unconstitutional. United States House of Representatives v. Federal Trade Commission, 463 U.S. 1216 (1983), affirming 691 F.2d 575 (D.C.Cir.1982). See also Immigration and Naturalization Service v. Chadha, 462 U.S. 919 (1983). Meanwhile, the validity of the regulation was challenged under the FTC Act. In response to this suit, the FTC reconsidered the regulation and scrapped the provision requiring the seller to disclose the existence of defects of which he or she is aware. The Commission ultimately promulgated the Used Motor Vehicle Trade Regulation Rule (16 C.F.R. Part 455), which appears in the Statutory Supplement.

Perhaps because the FTC Rule is so diluted, several states have enacted lemon laws regulating the sale of used cars. E.g., Mass.Gen.Laws ch.90, § 7N1/4 (seller of a used car must provide an express warranty covering the full cost of repairs of defects that impair safety or use, for up to 90 days after the purchase).

QUESTIONS AND NOTES

1. The New York statute appears in the Statutory Supplement. Please read McKinney's N.Y.Gen.Bus.Law section 198–b and answer the following questions.

   a.   How would the New York statute apply on the facts of Knipp v. Weinbaum (page 334 supra)?

   b.   Can sellers of used cars in New York disclaim implied warranties? See Magnuson–Moss Warranty Act section 108(b).

2. A Maine statute (Me.Rev.Stat.Ann. tit. 10, § 1474) provides that in connection with the sale of a used car the car dealer "warrants that the motor vehicle . . . has been inspected in accordance with [the state law requiring annual safety inspections]" and "[t]hat the motor vehicle is in the condition and meets the standards required by that law. . . ." The dealer must furnish the buyer with a written statement containing this warranty. Can sellers of used cars in Maine disclaim implied warranties?

3. Can sellers of used cars who affix to the window the notice required by the FTC Rule (16 C.F.R. § 455.2) disclaim implied warranties?

4. Most states have not enacted lemon laws for used cars. But the new-car lemon law may provide some protection for purchasers of used cars. If a consumer purchases a used vehicle that still is within the period of the manufacturer's express warranty, the lemon law applicable to new cars may still apply to that vehicle. Hence, if before the manufacturer's warranty expires, the car has irremediable nonconformities that substantially impair its value, the consumer may have the remedies specified in the lemon law. Subaru of America, Inc. v. Peters, 500 S.E.2d 803 (Va.1998). Contra, Schey v. Chrysler Corp., 597 N.W.2d 457 (Wis.App.), rev. denied, 602 N.W.2d 760 (Wis.1999).

5. California has gone even further. Dealers there must permit the consumer to purchase a two-day right of cancellation. The consumer who purchases this option may cancel the contract and return the car even if there is nothing wrong with it. The cost of this option may not exceed $75–400, depending on the cash price of the car. If the consumer exercises the right of cancellation and returns the car, the dealer may charge a restocking fee of up to $175–$500, again depending on the price of the car. Any amount paid for the option must be credited toward the restocking fee. Cal. Veh. Code § 11713.21.

(4) THE NEXT STEP

Although the Magnuson–Moss Warranty Act prohibits sellers who give written warranties from disclaiming implied warranties, it does not prohibit disclaimers by sellers who do not give written warranties. Nor does it prohibit the exclusion of consequential damages. Several states have taken one or both of these additional steps, usually by way of amendment of UCC section 2–316. Perhaps the most far reaching of these statutes is W.Va. Code, section 46A–6–107:

> Notwithstanding any other provision of law to the contrary with respect to goods which are the subject of or are intended to become the subject of a consumer transaction, no merchant shall:
>
>> (1) Exclude, modify or otherwise attempt to limit any warranty, express or implied, including the warranties of merchantability and fitness for a particular purpose; or
>>
>> (2) Exclude, modify or attempt to limit any remedy provided by law, including the measure of damages available, for a breach of warranty, express or implied.

Any such exclusion, modification or attempted limitation shall be void.

In some states the modification of section 2–316 is not so radical, as illustrated by the Minnesota statutes:

§ 325G.18   Implied warranties

Subdivision 1. Unless disclaimed in the manner prescribed in subdivision 2, every consumer sale in this state shall be accompanied by an implied warranty that the goods are merchantable, and, in a consumer sale where the seller has reason to know that the goods are required for a particular purpose and that the buyer is relying on the seller's skill or judgment to select or furnish suitable goods, an implied warranty of fitness. A seller may, however, limit damages or remedies for breach of implied warranties as provided in [the U.C.C.].

Subdivision 2. Disclaimer. No consumer sale on an "as is" or "with all faults" basis shall be effective to disclaim the implied warranty of merchantability, or where applicable, the implied warranty of fitness, unless a conspicuous writing clearly informs the buyer, prior to the sale, in simple and concise language each of the following:

(1) The goods are being sold on an ''as is'' or ''with all faults'' basis; and

(2) The entire risk as to the quality and performance of the goods is with the buyer.

. . .

§ 325G.19 Express warranties

Subdivision 1.   Disclaimers. No express warranty arising out of a consumer sale of new goods shall disclaim implied warranties of merchantability, or, where applicable, of fitness.

Subdivision 2.   Honoring of express warranties. The maker of an express warranty arising out of a consumer sale in this state shall honor the terms of the express warranty. In a consumer sale, the manufacturer shall honor an express warranty made by the manufacturer; the distributor shall honor an express warranty made by the distributor; and the retail seller shall honor an express warranty made by the retail seller.

Subdivision 3.   Liability of manufacturer to retailer. Every manufacturer who makes an express warranty pursuant to a consumer sale, who authorizes a retail seller within this state to perform services or repairs under the terms of the express warranty shall be liable to the retail seller in an amount equal to that which is charged by the retail seller for like service or repairs rendered to retail consumers who are not entitled to warranty protection.

Minn.Stat.Ann. §§ 325G.18–325G.19. Altogether, more than a dozen states have totally or partially restricted the seller's ability to disclaim implied warranties and to limit remedies. See generally Clifford, Non–UCC Statutory Provisions Affecting Warranty Disclaimers and Remedies in Sales of Goods, 71 N.C.L.Rev. 1011 (1993).

Other kinds of statutes may also afford remedies to consumers who encounter products of poor quality. For example, little-FTC acts proscribing unfair or deceptive acts and practices may apply to the seller's conduct. Thus, courts have held that the repeated failure to perform warranty repairs is a violation. State ex rel. Webster v. Milbourn, 759 S.W.2d 862 (Mo.App.1988) (failure to perform on numerous contracts); Jacobs v. Yamaha Motor Corp., 649 N.E.2d 758 (Mass.1995) (repeated failure to perform on one contract); Valley Vista Condominium Owners Ass'n v. Gates Eng'r Co., 56 Antitrust & Trade Reg. Rep. (BNA) 256 (D.D.C.1989) (same).

Even if the seller attempts to make the promised repairs, its conduct may violate the statute. For example, in Ford Motor Co. v. Mayes, 575 S.W.2d 480 (Ky.App.1978), plaintiffs' new pickup truck was defective. The dealer tried several times to remedy the problem but was unable to do so. Plaintiffs revoked their acceptance, returned the truck to the dealer, and sued the manufacturer. The contract contained the auto industry's standard limitation of remedies, but the court held that the limited exclusive remedy failed of its essential purpose under UCC section 2–719(2). The court then held that the manufacturer's continued insistence on the limited remedy, even after that remedy had failed of its essential purpose, constituted an unfair act or practice.

Another court held that it violates the little-FTC act to represent that defects have been corrected. Milt Ferguson Motor Co. v. Zeretzke, 827 S.W.2d 349 (Tex.App.1991). And nondisclosure that a used car has been reconstructed following an accident may violate a little-FTC act even if the vehicle is sold "as is." Morris v. Mack's Used Cars, 824 S.W.2d 538 (Tenn.1992). Accord, Hinds v. Paul's Auto Werkstatt, Inc., 810 P.2d 874 (Or.App.1991).

Still another case exemplifying the usefulness of the little-FTC acts is Latino v. Ford Motor Co., 526 N.E.2d 1282 (Mass.1988). The Supreme Judicial Court of Massachusetts held that when an arbitration panel orders a manufacturer to refund the purchase price of an automobile, the manufacturer's failure to make the refund within the time specified by the lemon law is a violation of the little-FTC act. (The Massachusetts little-FTC act provides for treble damages.)

In some states, including Pennsylvania and Texas, the legislature has taken the initiative by making breach of warranty a violation of that state's little-FTC act. 73 Pa. Stat. Ann. § 201–2(4)(xiv); Vernon's Tex. Code Ann., Bus. & Com.Code § 17.50(a)(2).

Finally, the FTC Act also applies to some problems concerning defective products. One example is the International Harvester case, page 62 supra and page 511 infra, in which the FTC held that a manufacturer's failure to disclose a defect was an unfair act or practice. Another example is In re Saab–Scania of America, Inc., 3 Trade Regulation Reporter (CCH) ¶ 22,314 (F.T.C.1985) (consent decree), in which the FTC took the position that an auto importer's failure to disclose a paint defect in its new cars violated section 5.

QUESTIONS

1. Consider the position of a seller in one of the states that invalidates warranty disclaimers. If the seller gives a limited warranty for twelve months after the date of purchase, can the seller limit the duration of implied warranties to this same twelve-month period?

2. Does the Minnesota statute (pages 370–71 supra) go any further than the Magnuson–Moss Act? Does it even go as far?

3. Compare the Massachusetts statute, Mass.Gen. Law Ann. ch. 106, section 2–316A, which provides:

> (1) The provisions of section 2–316 shall not apply to the extent provided in this section.
>
> (2) Any language, oral or written, used by a seller or manufacturer of consumer goods and services, which attempts to exclude or modify any implied warranties of merchantability and fitness for a particular

purpose or to exclude or modify the consumer's remedies for breach of those warranties, shall be unenforceable.

(3) Any language, oral or written, used by a manufacturer of consumer goods, which attempts to limit or modify a consumer's remedies for breach of such manufacturer's express warranties, shall be unenforceable, unless such manufacturer maintains facilities within the commonwealth sufficient to provide reasonable and expeditious performance of the warranty obligations.

. . .

(5) The provisions of this section may not be disclaimed or waived by agreement.

What is the purpose of this statute?

4. Assume you have a client who has purchased a new car that turns out to be a lemon, and assume further that the seller and manufacturer thus far have been unable to remedy all the defects. In seeking relief, what are the relative advantages and disadvantages of the UCC, the lemon law, the Magnuson–Moss Act, and the little-FTC act?

5. The move toward strict tort liability for defective products began decades ago, received decisive judicial acceptance in 1962 (Greenman v. Yuba, page 311 supra), and swept the country thereafter. But since the beginning of this movement, indeed even since 1962, several other changes have occurred, including the following:

a) the barrier of privity continues to crumble, even for economic loss (Morrow v. New Moon Homes, Nobility Homes v. Shivers, page 324 supra);

b) Magnuson–Moss Act section 108 and statutes in several states invalidate disclaimers of implied warranties, as may the common law doctrines of assent and unconscionability (Berg v. Stromme, page 327 supra; Henningsen v. Bloomfield Motors, Inc., 161 A.2d 69 (N.J.1960));

c) the UCC relaxes the requirement that a consumer give the seller notice of breach of warranty (§ 2–607, Official Comment 4; revised § 2–607(3)(a));

d) long-arm statutes make distant manufacturers amenable to litigation in the consumer's home jurisdiction; and

e) courts adopting comparative negligence tend to apply that doctrine to strict liability cases (cf. UCC section 2–314, Official Comment 13).

Query, if these lines of development continue, is there any need for strict liability in tort? See Swartz v. General Motors Corp., 378 N.E.2d 61 (Mass.1978); Shanker, Strict Tort Theory of Products Liability and the Uniform Commercial Code: A Commentary on Jurisprudential Eclipses, Pigeonholes and Communications Barriers, 17 W.Res.L.Rev. 5 (1965).

6. What are the economic implications of invalidating disclaimers of implied warranties and limitations of remedies? In A Theory of the Consumer Product Warranty, 90 Yale L.J. 1297 (1981), Professor Priest identifies two theories to explain the scope and content of express warranties. He describes the first and older theory as "the exploitation theory." This theory emphasizes the adhesion nature of consumer contracts and posits the manufacturer's ability to dictate the terms of any warranty. Professor Priest describes the second theory as "the signal theory." This theory recognizes that at the time of purchase the consumer finds it difficult or impossible to evaluate the quality of a product accurately. Hence the consumer looks to the warranty as a signal of the product's quality: the better the quality of the product, the less expensive it is for the manufacturer to warrant it and therefore the better the warranty. Therefore, a generous warranty signals to the consumer that the product is of relatively high quality. The disclosure provisions of the Magnuson–Moss Act exemplify this theory. As an alternative to these two theories of product warranties, Professor Priest proposes a third theory, which he calls "the investment theory." Under this theory, a "warranty is viewed as a contract that optimizes the productive services of goods by allocating responsibility between a manufacturer and consumer for investments to prolong the useful life of a product and to insure against product losses. According to the theory, the terms of warranty contracts are determined solely by the relative costs to the parties of these investments." Id. at 1298. Some excerpts* follow:

> In the common view, a warranty serves as both an insurance policy and a repair contract. As an insurance policy, a warranty provides that if, within a certain period, the product or some part of the product becomes defective, the manufacturer will compensate the buyer for the loss by repair, replacement, or refund of the purchase price. As a repair contract, a warranty fixes an obligation upon the manufacturer for some period of time to provide, without charge, services necessary to repair a defect in order to prolong the useful capacity of the product.
>
> A warranty operates as an insurance policy to the extent that the occurrence of a product defect is probabilistic. To insure for a loss is to redistribute wealth from periods in which no losses are suffered to the period in which the loss occurs. A manufacturer can redistribute wealth in this manner by collecting a premium in the sale price from a broad set of consumers for whom the prospects of loss during any single period are unrelated. The market insurance premium reflects both the expected loss for the period and some share of the costs to the insurer of aggregating these unrelated contingencies, called loading costs. A consumer may prefer, however, some personal form of temporal wealth redistribution in the face of a loss. A consumer self-insures

* 90 Yale L.J. 1297, 1308–19, 1346–51 (1981). Reprinted by permission of The Yale Law Journal Company and Fred B. Rothman & Company from The Yale Law Journal, Vol. 90, pp. 1297, 1308–19, 1346–51.

for product losses by accumulating savings for the replacement of defective products, by reserving future time for product repair, or, more simply, by expecting to tolerate a defect once it occurs. These methods of self-insurance, of course, also involve costs of transaction. As a general proposition, therefore, we may expect to observe market insurance in a warranty only where the sum of the expected loss and loading costs of market insurance is less than the sum of the expected loss and transaction costs of self-insurance.

As a repair contract, a warranty reflects the respective costs to the consumer and the manufacturer of repair services. Repair by the consumer and manufacturer are substitutes, and the consumer can be expected to purchase repair services as part of the warranty wherever the manufacturer's price is less than the consumer's cost of providing the repair himself Obviously, a consumer can (and frequently does) provide many repair services more cheaply than a manufacturer. It is plausible, for example, that where shelves fall in a refrigerator, repair by the consumer is cheaper. Of course, since the consumer and manufacturer are always free after the purchase of the good to negotiate for the provision of services of this kind, the warranty itself is valuable only if it reduces transaction costs for future agreements. Thus, a warranty may be expected to allocate responsibility to the manufacturer for those types of repairs that most frequently are difficult or burdensome for consumers to provide themselves.

Although the above example, as well as most uses of the word "repair," refers to investments designed to return a product to a condition it enjoyed at some previous period of time, it is worthwhile to consider "repair service" to a product more broadly as any investment designed to optimize the performance of the product over time. Viewed in this light, for example, restraining young children from swinging on a refrigerator door represents an investment in a form of "repair" that may well be less costly than hiring a serviceman at a later date to install new hinges. Similarly, a manufacturer may anticipate future repair services by technological investments in the design of the product that make its operation less susceptible to interruption—designing brackets to hold refrigerator shelves more securely, for example—or by investments to control a consistent quality of production.

With respect to repair investments of this nature, however, a warranty serves a role beyond that of reducing transaction costs. The warranty promise establishes and enforces the obligation of the manufacturer to make investments in the design of the good or in quality control. Such an agreement between the parties subsequent to the sale could not achieve the same result as easily, so that there are advantages to "tying" the warranty to the sale of the product. The warranty in this regard operates as a performance bond of the manufacturer. The value of the bond is equal to the costs to the manufacturer of defective product claims. As long as the manufacturer makes appropriate investments, the bond will not be forfeited. The decision to allocate repair investments of this nature between the manufacturer and consumer, however, is identical to the decision of who should bear typical repair costs. As before, we would expect the parties to allocate between themselves, according to relative costs, all investments in "repair," whether in the form of direct reconditioning services, of product design, or of a consumer's care for or maintenance of the product so as to extend its useful life.

It is evident that the various activities described as repair are substitutes for insurance. Repair, like insurance, is a means of reducing the magnitude of a loss from an unexpected event such as a defect. It is important now, however, to depart from the common view of the warranty and to distinguish more clearly between repair as a redistribution of wealth over time, like insurance, and repair as an allocative investment which alters the productive capacity of the good. The first example of repair—the reinstallation of the refrigerator shelves by the consumer—is a form of self-insurance for the loss. The owner bears the full cost of time and energy necessary to replace the shelves after the event occurs, which, in this case, appears to be cheaper than buying market insurance requiring the manufacturer to replace the shelves. But neither repair by the consumer nor by the manufacturer directly alters the probability of the loss occurring and, thus, is like insurance. The second example—restraining the child from swinging on the refrigerator door—is an allocative investment by a consumer that extends the useful life of the product by reducing the probability of a future loss. Certainly, the burdens of a parent increase as the discipline of children becomes more strict or specific. But, again, it may well be cheaper for a consumer to restrain his child than either to buy market insurance for repair of the door or to pay the manufacturer to design a refrigerator with hinges as sturdy as playground equipment.

Thus, in this terminology, a consumer's decision to accommodate himself to a scratch in the surface of an appliance is an example of self-insurance of the defect. The consumer's earlier efforts to reduce the likelihood of the scratch, for example, by increasing the level of his care or by isolating the appliance, is an allocative investment by the consumer. The manufacturer's promise in a warranty to repair the scratch after it occurs is market insurance. And the manufacturer's production decision to make the surface more resistant to abrasion is an example of an allocative investment by the manufacturer.

Self-insurance, market insurance, and allocative investments by consumers and manufacturers, therefore, are each substitute methods of reducing losses in order to optimize productive services. A consumer selects among these methods according to the relative prices and marginal productivities of each with respect to expected elements of product loss. As the price of market insurance rises, other things equal, the quantity of it demanded will decline, and the demand for self-insurance and for manufacturer or consumer allocative investments will increase. Similarly, as the cost of an allocative investment by the consumer rises—say, in our second example, by the addition of a child to the consumer's family, which makes it more difficult to reduce the probability of loss—the relative attractiveness of market insurance, self-insurance, or an allocative investment by the manufacturer is enhanced. These various ways of reducing product losses, however, may not be perfect substitutes, An individual is likely to select some combination of these four methods to optimize expected utility. For example, as the value of a consumer product or of the consumer's life increases—and, as a result, the potential risk from a defect increases— the consumer may increase consumption of each of the four.

. . .

[T]wo forms of investment by consumers will affect the likelihood of defects in any consumer product. The first is the consumer's selection of a product suitable for his expected needs. Warranty claims are likely to be more frequent, for example, where a washing machine is undersized or a vacuum cleaner underpowered, or where there occurs some unexpected increase in the demands that the consumer makes on the product. If the consumer accurately anticipates his uses, and if he selects a product designed most appropriately for those uses, the productive capacity of the good is more likely to be preserved. The second form of investment is the consumer's decision about the extent to which he will use the product. A consumer who operates an appliance infrequently may be said to be preserving the life of the product by choosing to store rather than to use it.

Initially, this conception may seem foreign because it is common to infer from personal experience some "normal" use of a product. Indeed, the law requires judges and juries to make inferences of "normal" use by implying in product sales a warranty of merchantability that a product is "of fair average quality" and is "fit for the ordinary purposes for which such goods are used." If it were possible to infer some "normal" use of a good, then the decision of an individual consumer to use or not to use the good would be analytically irrelevant.

But preferences regarding the frequency of use of a product differ among consumers. The preferences of the particular set of consumers for whom the product has been designed in order to optimize sales cannot be determined by inference. Where the dominant set of purchasers operates the good infrequently and, thus, where the "normal" use of the good is storage, the level of the consumers' allocative investments in preservation of the product is high. As a consequence, the level of the manufacturer's allocative investment in product design or in insurance that optimizes productive services may be very low. In such a case, the design or manner of production of the product may be optimal even though the product appears grossly defective when operated with greater frequency, which is to say, when operated with lower allocative investments in care by consumers.

A warranty in this view is the instrument that expresses consumer preferences for allocative or insurance investments. It is a contract that divides responsibility for allocative investments and insurance between the consumer and the manufacturer. The content of the contract is determined by the respective costs to the two parties of allocative investments or insurance. According to this approach, a manufacturer makes investments to prolong product life up to the point at which the marginal cost of such investments equals the marginal benefit. A manufacturer, then, offers market insurance for those losses or items of service for which market insurance is less costly than insurance or allocative investments by the consumer himself.

To the extent that a manufacturer disclaims liability or excludes or limits warranty coverage, however, it shifts to the consumer the obligation to make allocative investments to preserve the product or to self-insure for its loss. A disclaimer or an exclusion of coverage is the functional equivalent of provisions, common in other contracts, that explicitly require one of the parties to take certain actions to prevent breach or to insure for losses from uncertain events. The theory predicts that disclaimers of liability and exclusions of coverage will be observed in consumer product warranties for those specific allocative or insurance investments that the consumer can provide more cheaply than the manufacturer. In this view, disclaimers and exclusions can be said to be demanded by consumers because of the relative cheapness of consumer allocative investments or of self-insurance. . . .

. . .

C.   Defining Standardized Contracts: Reducing Differences in Risks

The task of defining optimal warranty provisions resembles the task of defining optimal rate classes in insurance contracts. In all insurance contexts, it is advantageous for an insurer to segregate applicants according to the level of risks added to the insurance pool. If the risk of loss of an individual can be predicted, then the insurance premium can be tailored to reflect the likelihood of future payouts. In particular, insurance coverage can be offered at a lower premium to an individual for whom the risk of loss is relatively low.

For most types of insurance, of course, it is prohibitively costly either to predict exactly the risk that an individual brings to a pool or to charge individual premiums. As a consequence, an insurer is forced to lump individuals into separate classes or, sometimes, into a single class. The premium charged each member of the class must reflect the average level of risk of the class. Thus, the premium undercharges relatively high-risk individuals and overcharges relatively low-risk individuals. . . .

It is common for life, medical, accident, and home insurers to obtain information about applicants prior to making contracts in order to place applicants in appropriate insurance classes. Insurers routinely solicit information about age, sex, property location and value, as well as medical records and driving histories in order to construct rate classes. Some insurers make it possible for individuals with characteristics that tend to be correlated with low levels of risk, such as abstemious smoking and drinking habits, to identify themselves in order to qualify for lower premiums. Analogues to these methods of discrimination, however, are not immediately apparent in the context of consumer product insurance. Typically, insurance policies for consumer product losses are tied to the sale of the product itself, so that the insurance pool invariably consists of all consumers who have purchased the product.

Consumers may differ in two general ways with respect to risk under a product warranty. First, the amount of use of a product during the period of warranty coverage may vary considerably between consumers. Compare, for example, the expected service costs to a washing machine manufacturer from a family with many children and from a family with only a single child. The costs of service to the large family will almost certainly be greater. If the manufacturer could define warranty coverage in terms of number of washloads, however, as an automobile manufacturer defines coverage in terms of mileage, then the expected costs from the two families to the manufacturer might be similar. But for washing machines, as well as for most other consumer appliances, the least costly measure of use appears to be duration of ownership. As a consequence, no matter what the period of coverage, the amount of use of the machine by the two families is likely to differ greatly. The insurance premium must be set to cover all expected costs of service. Thus, smaller families at the margin may find warranty protection to be worth less than its cost.

Second, the risk of loss may differ between consumers with respect to what I will call the "intensity" of product use. Compare now for the large and small families, the expected service costs to a television manufacturer. The amount of use of the television that is, the number of viewing hours, might be identical for the two families. Nonetheless, the probability of a warranty claim is likely to be higher for the larger family, because of the greater number of individuals operating the set, because of the greater frequency of channel changes, and because of the greater risk in a large family that the set will be jostled, that the antenna will be struck, or that the machine will otherwise be treated roughly.

I define "intensity" of use as inversely related to the marginal cost to the consumer of "care" for the machine, that is, the cost of allocative investments to reduce the probability of a loss. The cost of monitoring the activities of children is likely to increase as the number of children increases. Thus, the family with many children is more likely than the family with a single child to substitute recovery under a warranty for allocative investments in care of the machine. As a consequence, the cost to the manufacturer of warranty coverage will be greater for the machine sold to the larger family. Again, at the margin, consumers with smaller families may find it advantageous to shift their purchases to machines sold without, or with less, warranty coverage.

Although product insurers do not directly acquire information about consumers prior to sale, a variety of subtle methods can enable them to segregate consumers. For example, a manufacturer can develop models of a product that differ with respect to characteristics related to differences in intensities or amounts of consumer use. A manufacturer of washing machines may produce models that differ in motor size or washbasket volume that are differentially convenient to families of different sizes. If these product characteristics segregate consumers according to the extent or intensity of use, then the manufacturer can offer, for each individual model, different allocative investments and levels of warranty coverage determined by the expected warranty claims for each model.

This technique, however, may achieve only partial success. The advantage to a manufacturer of culling out higher intensity or higher volume consumers from a particular insurance pool is to enable it to offer warranty coverage at a relatively lower premium, or greater coverage at the same premium, of models designed for lower volume or intensity uses. A lower premium or more extended coverage, however, makes those machines relatively more attractive to all consumers, including those who expect to use the machine with greater intensity or in higher volume. At the margin, some of these consumers can be expected to purchase machines undersized for their needs. Such purchases substitute the extended warranty coverage of the lower volume machine for the mechanical superiority of the higher volume machine. This adverse selection by higher volume or intensity consumers will force manufacturers to reduce the extended coverage of the lower volume machine or to charge a higher premium for it. Either reaction will reduce the attractiveness of the lower volume machine to the lower risk members of the pool.

A separate but closely related method of segregating consumers is to offer warranty contracts with different terms at different premiums in conjunction with the sale of a given product. Recently, the domestic automobile manufacturers have introduced insurance policies for separate fees extending coverage for periods beyond the basic twelve-month warranty. The optional service contract of many appliances is similar. . . .

Finally, a manufacturer may segregate consumers by means of explicit contractual provisions in the warranty. A manufacturer, for example, may exclude warranty coverage for a particular use of a product or specific class of consumers for which the volume or intensity of use is relatively high. The common provision that excludes coverage of commercial use is an obvious example. This provision narrows the class of those insured to domestic users of the product and may be incorporated to enforce a manufacturer's segregation of domestic and commercial purchasers by model design.

Some elements of product loss, however, may be excluded from coverage in the warranties of all product models. A common example is the exclusion of liability for consequential damages. The unavailability of any coverage of some loss, nonetheless, may be related to the reduction of differences in risk between members of the insurance pool. Where consumers differ substantially in the incidence or magnitude of a loss, such as consequential damages, there may be no single premium attractive to a sufficient number to justify offering coverage. Put another way, the increase in the premium required for coverage of such losses may be greater than the benefit of coverage to large numbers of consumers. If so, the sale of product insurance may be optimized by excluding coverage altogether.

Warranty exclusions are a form of product standardization. An exclusion of some element of loss is indistinguishable analytically from the exclusion of, say, magenta and aquamarine as product colors. If the number of consumers willing to purchase machines of unusual colors is very small, it may not be worth the cost for the manufacturer to introduce the colors into the product line. Similarly, if the incidence or magnitude of an element of loss differs greatly between consumers of a product, the market for insurance may not be sufficiently large to justify offering insurance. Such a warranty exclusion enables the manufacturer to offer, for losses not excluded, either more extensive or less costly warranty coverage than if no exclusion were made, just as the production of appliances in a limited range of colors lowers price by reducing the costs of production and distribution. In this respect, consumers of the product may be said to have demanded the exclusions.

The segregation of consumers by explicit contractual provisions, however, is effective only to the extent that the manufacturer can identify prior to sale those consumers, product uses, or elements of loss for which differences in risk across the set of potential consumers are great. All those not identified and segregated must be lumped into a common pool, high-risk and low-risk alike. The terms of the standard warranty, then, establish the minimum level of coverage that is demanded uniformly by each member of the large class of purchasers; that is, a base level that can be supplemented in the variety of ways suggested above by those consumers desiring more extensive protection. The standard level of coverage comprises the minimum performance bond necessary to encourage appropriate investments by manufacturers in the design or mechanical qualities of the product and the minimum insurance coverage demanded by the lowest risk members of the consumer pool.

III. An Empirical Examination of the Theories

[In this part Professor Priest reports on his study of sixty-two actual warranties, given by a variety of manufacturers for a variety of products. He notes that the warranties are by no means identical and concludes that his "investment theory" explains both the similarities and the differences better than the other two theories do.]

It is a common belief that warranty content has little influence on consumer purchase decisions because a consumer only learns warranty terms after purchase or after discovery of a defect. This belief has been closely connected with the exploitation theory; it explains how a manufacturer is able to impose one-sided warranty terms. The signal theory also accepts the proposition in large part: although consumers may possess some general warranty information prior to purchase, they remain totally ignorant of large numbers of significant provisions. Thus, according to both the exploitation and signal theories, there is little relationship between consumer preferences and warranty terms.

The actual influence of consumer preferences, of course, is an empirical question. Neither exploitation nor signal theorists have compiled direct empirical support for the absence of influence. The strongest direct evidence, perhaps, derives from introspection. Most of us can recall occasions as consumers in which we have been uninformed about warranty content at the time of purchase. If the large majority of consumers behave similarly, how is it possible, even in competitive product markets, for consumer preferences to influence the way manufacturers draft warranties?

Competition with respect to warranty content may take two forms. First, manufacturers compete, not over the entire set of consumers, but over the set of marginal consumers. If a small group of consumers reads warranties and selects among products according to warranty content, manufacturers may be forced to draft warranties responsive to the group's preferences, even though the large majority of consumers generally neglect warranty terms. Second, warranty content may affect the repeat purchase rather than the initial purchase decision. A consumer may select among competing brands according to his experience with a specific product and with its warranty. If so, manufacturers may be forced to draft warranties responsive to consumer preferences in order to assure a continued custom.

. . .

IV. Implications of the Investment Theory

. . .

A. *Optimal Prevention and Insurance*

Courts have accepted the view that manufacturers employ standardized warranties to exploit consumers, and they have responded to exploitative behavior in two ways. Courts have interpreted sales transactions to provide more extensive warranty protection to consumers than the manufacturers themselves have offered voluntarily. The implication of warranties of merchantability and fitness—as well as the prohibition on disclaiming these warranties—and the expansion of the set of beneficiaries of warranties by the elimination of the privity of contract requirement are examples. In addition, courts have refused to give effect to manufacturer attempts to segregate consumers by the level of risk they bring to the warranty pool. Courts have refused to enforce warranty provisions that limit remedies and that exclude consequential damages, in particular, personal injury damages for which manufacturers are now strictly liable.

The implications of the investment theory with respect to these developments are clear: the warranty coverage required by courts is suboptimal and increases the likelihood of product defects. It is well-established that if, in a competitive market, consumers have different accident probabilities, sales of contracts to insure—or to invest to reduce the probability of loss—are optimized where the seller segregates consumers according to levels of risk and sells each class of consumers a separate contract at a separate premium reflecting the accident probability of the class. If sellers are prevented from segregating consumers according to risk levels, however, both manufacturers and consumers are worse off. First, there may be no single insurance-allocative investment contract that satisfies the preferences of both low-and high-risk consumers. Put another way, at a common premium, losses may be so disparate as to be uninsurable. Second, even if a manufacturer can devise some single insurance-allocative investment package that is attractive to some high-and low-risk consumers, such a contract is likely to satisfy the preferences of these consumers less fully than would separate contracts. . . .

A third implication of the investment theory is more striking and suggests another method of testing the theory. The investment theory regards consumer investments to prolong the life of a product as a substitute for manufacturer investments to prolong product life. The warranty allocates responsibilities between the parties according to the relative costs of these investments; that is, the warranty allocates responsibilities to (places liability on) consumers where the marginal cost of consumer investments is lower than the marginal cost of manufacturer investments. Judicial decisions expanding the manufacturer's warranty liability lead, however, to the substitution of manufacturer investments for consumer investments. It follows that judicial decisions lead to the substitution of more costly investments in place of less costly investments and, thus, increase the marginal cost of investments to prolong product life. As the price of prolonging product life (or any commodity) increases, the quantity of it demanded declines. Therefore, judicial decisions expanding the warranty liability of manufacturers will lead, at the margin, to fewer investments that serve to prolong product life and to prevent defects than before. As a consequence, product life will diminish and fewer defects will be prevented. Although seemingly ironic, the investment theory implies that the judicial expansion of manufacturer warranty liability diminishes product life and increases the rate of product defects.

B. *The Investment Theory, Personal Injury Loss, and Strict Liability*

The most dramatic development in product warranty law in the last two decades is the abandonment of principles of warranty interpretation and the adoption of a strict liability standard in cases involving personal injury from a defective product. Crucial to the adoption of the strict liability standard is the empirical assumption that consumers can take no action to prevent personal injury loss. Given the assumption, it is difficult to justify warranty provisions excluding recovery for personal injury damages.

Consumers, however, may prefer the exclusion of personal injury losses from warranty coverage for various reasons. If personal injury losses, like other forms of product loss, differ substantially among consumers of a product, those consumers for whom the risk is relatively low may be better off if no personal injury coverage whatsoever is offered. First, contrary to the empirical assumption of the policy of strict liability, consumers may differ with respect to the precautions that they take or the care with which they use the product. Again, actions "preventing" (reducing the probability of) personal injury loss may take subtle forms. Consumers who take care, say, not to use machine products in the presence of bystanders or who use such products only infrequently may subject the warranty pool to a substantially lower level of risk than more intensive users. This class of consumers may demand the exclusion of personal injury losses from warranty coverage, and if the class is sufficiently large, manufacturers might find that competition requires incorporation of the exclusion.

The exclusion of personal injury losses can optimize investments to reduce the probability of product losses and to insure in a second way. Product insurers are seldom able to obtain information about individual consumers that health, home, and automobile insurers commonly employ to define optimal risk classes. In general, product insurers must treat all consumers as equals and charge each a warranty premium reflecting the average risk level of the pool. The individual information collected in other insurance contexts, however, may be effective in segregating optimal classes for product insurance. If so, it would optimize insurance sales to offer product liability coverage as an aspect of health, home, or automobile insurance, rather than as a separate policy tied to the sale of each product. An insurer could charge a lower than average premium to a consumer for whom the risk of loss or the magnitude of expected damage is relatively low, such as a consumer who is employed as a manual laborer, earns a wage rather than a salary, makes lower than average earnings, or has a small family or relatively less valuable possessions. Again, it is the consumer who subjects the pool to relatively low levels of risk—whether the low level of risk derives from relative carefulness or from a lower expected dollar loss from a disabling accident—who is most harmed by lumping consumers into a single product insurance pool. Thus the adoption of a strict liability standard has a regressive redistributional effect. Consumers who are more careless or earn higher than average incomes are those for whom the warranty premium is less than the level of risk that they introduce into the pool and are therefore the beneficiaries of the strict liability standard.

QUESTIONS

1. If Professor Priest's analysis is sound, should courts and legislatures refuse to enforce a manufacturer's exclusion of consequential damages and limitation of remedy? Is the analysis sound?

2. If there are few manufacturers of a given product such as automobiles, what incentive is there for a manufacturer to give a generous warranty?

(5) THE STANDARD OF QUALITY: HOW HIGH AND HOW PRECISE?

The final step to be taken, after creating implied warranties and prohibiting disclaimers and limitations, is the creation of quality standards that are more detailed and perhaps more rigorous than "merchantability." An Illinois statute makes the seller of a new or used car liable for a stated percentage of the cost of repairs to the power train for thirty days after delivery. Ill. Consol. Stat. Ann. ch. 815, § 505/2L. The statute is silent on the question of how good the power train must be, but it may be read as creating a standard of perfection. The statute, however, permits the seller to disclaim this obligation, so the standard might more accurately be described as "perfection unless the seller decides otherwise."

Health and safety are the areas in which mandatory standards, at least at the federal level, are most developed. Thus, the long-standing federal regulation of food, drugs, cosmetics, and flammable fabrics has been joined by regulation of automobiles (Highway Safety Act of 1966) and consumer products generally (Consumer Product Safety Act (1972)). The Consumer Product Safety Act, 15 U.S.C. § 2051 et seq., applies to all consumer products except those specifically excluded (generally products regulated by other federal agencies) and empowers the Consumer Product Safety Commission (CPSC) to promulgate "consumer product safety standards" to "prevent or reduce an unreasonable risk of [personal] injury." In addition, the Commission may ban products that it concludes present an unreasonable risk of injury and cannot be dealt with by means of a safety standard. And if an already distributed product poses a substantial risk of injury, the Commission may compel the supplier to repair, modify, or replace the product or refund the purchase price. Violators of the Act are subject to civil and criminal penalties, administrative sanction, and civil liability to consumers, who may recover compensation for injuries caused by a knowing violation of a safety standard or other Commission rule.[1]

---

1. The National Highway Traffic Safety Administration (NHTSA) has similar powers with respect to automobiles and tires. The NHTSA has ordered recalls of millions of cars for correction of defects and millions of tires for replacement.

If the CPSC promulgates a safety standard to prevent or reduce the risk of injury, should a manufacturer whose product complies with the standard be liable to a consumer who is injured by the product? See Raymond v. Riegel Textile Corp., 484 F.2d 1025 (1st Cir.1973); Gryc v. Dayton–Hudson Corp., 297 N.W.2d 727 (Minn.1980); Consumer Product Safety Act § 25(a), 15 U.S.C. § 2074(a).

The power of both the CPSC and the NHTSA is confined to risks of personal injury. Should their powers be expanded to enable them to deal with products that are shoddy but do not necessarily pose a risk of personal injury?

E. SERVICES

The preceding materials have examined legal standards concerning the quality of goods in consumer transactions. This section examines the quality standards applicable to services. As the division of labor has become more pronounced and as the complexity of consumer products has increased, consumers increasingly rely on others for desired services. Unfortunately, too often these services are defective. For example, in 1974 the FTC tested the performance of television repairers in three cities by seeking the repair of TV's that were in good condition except for one bad tube. In two of the cities, half the sets came back with more than the one tube repaired. The Department of Transportation commissioned a similar but more sophisticated test for automobile repairers. This 1979 study revealed that more than one fourth of auto repairs were unnecessary and that of the money charged for all repairs, more than half was for these unnecessary repairs. For decades auto repairs have ranked near the top in surveys of consumer complaints.

For a person injured by a defective product, the doctrines of the Uniform Commercial Code and the Restatement (Second) of Torts provide relief. But the UCC in its terms applies only to "transactions in *goods*" (§ 2–102), and the Restatements (Second) and (Third) apply only to one who sells a "*product*." Where does that leave the consumer who is injured by defective services? Traditionally, the answer almost always has been, the consumer recovers only upon proof of negligence. That is still the usual answer today. This section explores whether the answer should be changed.

Newmark v. Gimbel's, Inc.

Supreme Court of New Jersey, 1969.
54 N.J. 585, 258 A.2d 697.

FRANCIS, J.

[Defendant operated several beauty parlors, and plaintiff was a regular patron of one of them. On the day in question, plaintiff sustained severe hair and scalp injury as a result of the application of a permanent wave solution selected for her and applied by one of defendant's employees.

Plaintiff sued, charging negligence and breach of implied warranty. The trial court dismissed the warranty count because warranty liability arises only in connection with the sale of goods, whereas this transaction was the rendition of services. On the negligence count, the jury found for defendant, and the trial court rendered judgment for defendant. Plaintiff appealed, and the intermediate appellate court reversed the trial court on the issue of the existence of an implied warranty of fitness of the permanent wave solution. Defendant appealed to the Supreme Court of New Jersey.]

In dismissing the cause of action based on warranty, the trial court expressed the view that the transaction with Mrs. Newmark was not a sale within the contemplation of the Uniform Commercial Code, N.J.S.A. 12A:2–106(1), but rather an agreement for the rendition of services. Therefore, it was not accompanied by any warranty of fitness of products used in rendering the services, and the liability of the beauty parlor was limited to the claim of negligence. Having in mind the nature of a permanent wave operation, we find that the distinction between a sale and the rendition of services is a highly artificial one. If the permanent wave lotion were sold to Mrs. Newmark by defendants for home consumption or application or to enable her to give herself the permanent wave, unquestionably an implied warranty of fitness for that purpose would have been an integral incident of the sale. Basically defendants argue that if, in addition to recommending the use of a lotion or other product and supplying it for use, they applied it, such fact (the application) would have the effect of lessening their liability to the patron by eliminating warranty and by limiting their responsibility to the issue of negligence. There is no just reason why it should. On the contrary by taking on the administration of the product in addition to recommending and supplying it, they might increase the scope of their liability, if the method of administration were improper (a result not suggested on this appeal because the jury found no negligence).

The transaction, in our judgment, is a hybrid partaking of incidents of a sale and a service. It is really partly the rendering of service, and partly the supplying of goods for a consideration. Accordingly, we agree with the Appellate Division that an implied warranty of fitness of the products used in giving the permanent wave exists with no less force than it would have in the case of a simple sale. Obviously in permanent wave operations the product is taken into consideration in fixing the price of the service. The no-separate-charge argument puts excessive emphasis on form and downgrades the overall substance of the transaction. If the beauty parlor operator bought and applied the permanent wave solution to her own hair and suffered injury thereby, her action in warranty or strict liability in tort (Santor v. A. & M. Karagheusian) against the manufacturer-seller of the product clearly would be maintainable because the basic transaction would have arisen from a conventional type of sale. It does not accord with logic to deny a similar right to a patron against the beauty parlor operator or the manufacturer when the purchase and sale were made in anticipation of and for the purpose of use of the product on the patron who would be charged for its use. Common sense demands that such patron be deemed a consumer as to both manufacturer and beauty parlor operator.

A beauty parlor operator in soliciting patronage assures the public that he or she possesses adequate knowledge and skill to do the things and to apply the solution necessary to produce the permanent wave in the hair of the customer. When a patron responds to the solicitation she does so confident that any product used in the shop has come from a reliable origin and can be trusted not to injure her. She places herself in the hands of the operator relying upon his or her expertise both in the selection of the products to be used on her and in the method of using them. The ministrations and the products employed on her are under the control and selection of the operator; the patron is a mere passive recipient.

The oft-quoted statement that in the modern commercial world the liability of a manufacturer or a retail seller of a product should not be made to depend strictly upon the intricacies of the law of sales is most pertinent here. Santor v. A. & M. Karagheusian; Henningsen v. Bloomfield Motors, Inc.. . . .

. . . It seems to us that the policy reasons for imposing warranty liability in the case of ordinary sales are equally applicable to a commercial transaction such as that existing in this case between a beauty parlor operator and a patron. Although the policy reasons which generate the responsibility are essentially the same, practical administration suggests that the principle of liability be expressed in terms of strict liability in tort thus enabling it to be applied in practice unconfined by the narrow conceptualism associated with the technical niceties of sales and implied warranties. (This seems to be the overall import of the Appellate Division statement that the "core" question is whether "warranty principles" permit a recovery in this kind of case.) One, who in the regular course of a business sells or applies a product (in the sense of the sales-service hybrid transaction involved in the present case) which is in such a dangerously defective condition as to cause physical harm to the consumer-patron, is liable for the harm. Consumption in this connection includes all ultimate uses for which the product is intended. Restatement (2d) Torts § 402A, comment *l* adopts this view. Obviously the ultimate use of the Helene Curtis permanent wave solution intended by both manufacturer and beauty parlor operator was its application to the hair of a patron. And as Comment *l* to the Restatement section says, "the customer in a beauty shop to whose hair a permanent wave solution is applied by the shop is a consumer."

. . .

In arguing against strict liability in tort or liability under the Uniform Commercial Code for breach of implied warranty, defendants point out further that the permanent wave solution is bought from the manufacturer and applied to their patrons from the original package. Thus they say they have no greater opportunity to discover any injurious or defective quality than does the patron. But they occupy the status of retailers, and lack of opportunity to inspect the goods they supply to the publicly solicited customer does not relieve them of liability. Restatement § 402A, comment *f*. It has long been settled that retailers and those whose relationship with their patrons or consumers place them in that classification, are subject to a heavy burden of liability. The liability has been predicated upon breach of implied warranty of fitness or more recently in terms of strict liability in tort. Henningsen v. Bloomfield Motors. . . .

Accordingly, in light of all of the above, and particularly the testimony of the plaintiffs' dermatologist attributing the hair and scalp injury to the permanent wave solution, in our judgment a factual issue was presented at trial for jury determination as to (1) whether the permanent wave solution was defective, and (2) whether it was the proximate cause of the dermatitis. An affirmative answer by the jury would warrant a verdict for the plaintiffs.

The judgment of the Appellate Division is affirmed for the reasons stated, and the cause is remanded for a new trial.

QUESTIONS AND NOTES

1. The language of the UCC sections on warranties refers only to the sales of goods. But see section 2–313, Official Comment 2:

> Although this section is limited in its scope and direct purpose to warranties made by the seller to the buyer as part of a contract for sale, the warranty sections of this Article are not designed in any way to disturb those lines of case law growth which have recognized that warranties need not be confined . . . to sales contracts. . . . [T]he matter is left to the case law with the intention that the policies of this Act may offer useful guidance in dealing with further cases as they arise.

And consider section 2–314(1), which provides, in part, that "the serving for value of food or drink to be consumed either on the premises or elsewhere is a sale."

2. After Newmark, what standard governs the liability of persons who sell services? In what sense is it strict tort liability?

3. Five years after deciding Newmark, the New Jersey Supreme Court decided Realmuto v. Straub Motors, Inc., 322 A.2d 440 (N.J.1974). A used car malfunctioned while plaintiff was test driving it. Defendant's salesman said the problem was in the carburetor and would be fixed. Defendant installed a rebuilt carburetor, and plaintiff bought the car. Within a week after delivery, the accelerator stuck and the car crashed. The trial court held that the evidence was not sufficient to establish that the repairs caused the accident. The Supreme Court disagreed and then went on to consider the applicability of strict liability to the case. The court reserved the question whether strict liability applies to sellers of used products generally, but stated "we are of the view that a used car dealer ought to be subject to strict liability in tort with respect to a mishap resulting from any defective work, repairs or replacements he has done or made on the vehicle before the sale. . . ." Id. at 444.

a) In what way does *Realmuto* go beyond *Newmark*?

b) Does *Realmuto* stand for the proposition that persons rendering services are strictly liable for injuries caused by defects in those services?

4. What basis is there for having standards of liability for the sale of services that are different from the standards for the sale of goods?

a) Recall the policy bases underlying strict tort liability for defective products. Do these reasons apply to defective services, too? What policies underlie the creation of implied warranties by the UCC? Do they apply to service transactions? Are there other reasons to extend strict liability to defective services?

b) There is very little disagreement with the court's conclusion in Greenman v. Yuba Power Products (page 311 supra) that the manufacturer of the defective product should be liable. The consumer, you will recall, was injured because the power tool had "inadequate set screws." But why did the tool have inadequate set screws? The defect must have resulted either from the conduct of someone who designed the product or from the conduct of someone who assembled the product. *Greenman* is not unique in this respect: most product defects result from defective design or defective production. But design and production are essentially services, so even in products cases, liability ultimately is for defective services. Note that the Restatement (Third) establishes different rules for design defects than for manufacturing defects. Is this appropriate? Should strict liability in tort extend to services rendered by auto repairers, construction contractors, hair stylists, architects, lawyers, and doctors?

c) To pursue these questions further, see Hoven v. Kelble, 256 N.W.2d 379 (Wis.1977); Greenfield, Consumer Protection in Service Transactions—Implied Warranties and Strict Liability in Tort, 1974 Utah L.Rev. 661.

5. An alternative to tort and contract law as a means of protecting consumers against inadequate quality in service transactions is statutory regulation of the persons who provide services. This regulation occurs on a trade by trade (or profession by profession) basis. It may take the form of requiring demonstration of competence before engaging in a business, as it commonly does for the granting of licenses to practice medicine, law, and other professions. But it is not limited to regulation of the professions. Kansas City, Missouri, for example, adopted a similar scheme for television repairers. See McClellan v. Kansas City, 379 S.W.2d 500 (Mo.1964).

Regulation may also take the form of requiring registration by persons wishing to engage in the regulated activity. The legislation may set low standards for registration, but provide for loss of registration by anyone who fails to meet a level of performance specified by the legislation itself or by administrative regulation. California, for example, requires television and appliance repairers to obtain registration, which may be revoked for "incompetence or negligence" or "any willful departure from or disregard of accepted trade standards for good and workmanlike installation or repair. . . ." West's Ann.Cal.Bus. & Prof. Code, §§ 9830, 9841(a)(4), (6).

A third form of regulation is by certifying the competence of those who meet established standards. Since persons not certified are still permitted to engage in the activity, this is the mildest form of regulation and depends on the operation of the market to shift business away from those who are not certified and toward those who are.

For a detailed examination of these kinds of regulation (and others), see M. Carrow, The Licensing Power of New York City (1968).

CHAPTER 8

LIMITS ON THE PRICE OF CREDIT

A. SALE CREDIT AND LOAN CREDIT

A consumer who wishes to purchase an item and defer payment typically has a choice of several ways of financing the purchase. One alternative is to enter an installment sales contract with the seller and pay the price of the item in installments. Another is to borrow money from a lending institution, use the proceeds to pay the seller the full price all at once, and repay the lender in installments. And a third alternative is to use a credit card issued either by the seller or by a bank, repaying the credit card issuer in installments.

The first option, known as sale credit, was not commonly singled out for express statutory treatment until the 1950s. Now, however, almost every state has a retail installment sales act (RISA) governing various aspects of credit sales. The statutes vary with respect to the kinds of goods covered (automobiles, all goods except automobiles, or all goods) and with respect to the terms that the parties must or must not include in the contract. Like the federal Truth-in-Lending Act, the RISAs typically require disclosure of the credit terms of the contract. Unlike the federal statute, some of them also regulate the cost of credit.

The second method of financing a purchase, borrowing from a lending institution, is known as loan credit. Loan credit has been regulated for centuries, indeed millennia, by the usury laws. During most of the nineteenth and twentieth centuries, the maximum rates were set so low (typically six percent) that loaning money to consumers in small amounts did not provide a large enough return to induce persons with money to loan it to consumers. Thus consumers who needed money were forced to look to lenders who charged more than the law allowed. Perhaps to compensate for the risk of getting caught, or perhaps just because they had the borrower over a barrel, loan sharks charged very high rates. For example, one basis on which loan sharks have done business is six for five, that is, for a loan of five dollars for one week, the borrower repays six dollars. This is a rate of twenty percent per week, or over one thousand percent per year.

The unavailability of loans at lawful rates induced the states to adopt legislation raising the interest rates that lenders may charge consumers. This legislation has taken several forms. The earliest response, in the 1920s, was the enactment of so-called small loan acts. These statutes authorize rates much higher than the rates permitted by the usury statutes, in some states as high as 36% or more per year. In exchange for the high rate, the lender must obtain a license and submit to a high degree of supervision and investigation. The enactment of small loan acts was followed by the enactment of other kinds of statutes, e.g., pawnbroker, credit union, and installment loan acts. In addition to relaxing the rate limits, these statutes typically require disclosure of terms and regulate the other terms of the contract. For an excellent description of the development and content of statutes regulating sales credit and statutes regulating loan credit, see B. Curran, Trends in Consumer Credit Legislation, ch. III–IV (1965). For a history of consumer credit, see L. Calder, Financing the American Dream (1999). See generally S. Homer & R. Sylla, A History of Interest Rates (4th ed.2005). The Statutory Supplement contains a sample retail installment sales act and a sample small loan act. Carper v. Kanawha Banking & Trust Co., the next principal case, contains a typical usury statute at page 397 infra.

The pattern of regulation in each state is quite complex: there are different kinds of credit (e.g., installment sales credit, motor vehicle credit, installment loans, small loans); and there are different kinds of creditors (e.g., banks, finance companies, small loan companies, pawnbrokers, rent-to-own merchants, payday loan companies). A different statute may apply to each kind of loan and each kind of creditor, so in deciding whether a creditor has violated a rate regulation statute, the first problem is deciding which statute applies to the particular transaction. Federal statutes complicate the matter. The National Bank Act of 1864 empowers a federally chartered bank to charge interest at the rates allowed by the state in which it is located. 12 U.S.C. § 85. This has been interpreted to mean that national banks may charge whatever rate is allowed under state law for the particular kind of loan in question. 12 C.F.R. § 7.4001. Thus if a national bank makes a "small" loan, it may charge the high rates authorized by the small loan act even though the bank does not possess the license that state law requires for lenders who want to charge those high rates.[1] In 1980 Congress extended this most-favored lender status to federally insured depository institutions, such as state banks and state or federal credit unions. 12 U.S.C. §§ 1785(g), 1831d(a). To eliminate any advantage that federally insured institutions might have over state-chartered, non-insured institutions, many state legislatures have enacted parity statutes. These statutes empower state-chartered institutions to extend credit at whatever rates their federal counterparts may charge. The Supreme Court has held that the permissive limits of section 85 of the National Bank Act apply even when the lender makes loans to a resident of another state. Marquette National Bank v. First of Omaha Service Corp., 439 U.S. 299 (1978); Greenwood Trust Co. v. Massachusetts, 971 F.2d 818 (1st Cir.1992), cert. denied 506 U.S. 1052 (1993). Hence, when a bank in Delaware or South Dakota (states that have no interest rate limits on certain loans) issues credit cards or makes other loans to consumers residing in states that do have interest rate limits, the bank need not comply with the law of the consumer's residence. See also Smiley v. Citibank, 517 U.S. 735 (1996).

---

1. Alternatively, the bank may charge interest at one percent in excess of the regional federal reserve bank's discount rate on ninety-day commercial paper.

Since these states are the homes of the credit-card operations of the issuers of the vast majority of credit cards, there is no statutory limit on the finance charge and other fees that most consumers may have to pay.

This preemption of the law of the consumer's residence does not apply to nondepository lending institutions, such as payday lenders, or to persons extending sales credit, such as sellers and sales finance companies. Their rates remain subject to the law of the state in which the consumer resides.

This interplay of federal and state law has given rise to numerous, complex issues of statutory analysis. The materials in this chapter, however, do not address these issues. Rather, they explore some of the more fundamental concepts necessary for understanding any system of rate regulation.

B.   WAYS OF PRESENTING THE COST OF CREDIT

A creditor may present the cost of credit in several ways, including the total dollar cost, the amount of each monthly installment, and the rate of charge. As the problem on page 184 supra reveals, the rate may be expressed as an add-on, discount, or actuarial rate. The Truth-in-Lending Act adopts the actuarial method and requires creditors to disclose the cost of credit as an annual percentage rate. Usury statutes also typically contemplate the actuarial method. But retail installment sales acts, small loan acts, and other special-interest loan statutes vary considerably, many authorizing the computation of charges by either the add-on or the discount method. Therefore, a creditor subject to one of these statutes must use one method (e.g., add-on) to determine the maximum charge that it may impose, and another method (viz., actuarial) to determine how it must disclose that charge to the consumer. Who do you suppose would want the rate to be stated in terms of the add-on or discount method? Why?

C.   JUDICIAL INTERPRETATION OF RATE REGULATION STATUTES

(1) LOAN OR FORBEARANCE

Carper v. Kanawha Banking & Trust Co.

Supreme Court of West Virginia, 1974.
157 W.Va. 477, 207 S.E.2d 897.

HADEN, JUSTICE:

This is an appeal by Fairmont Mobile Homes, Inc., a corporation and Kanawha Banking & Trust Company, a corporation, from a jury verdict and an adverse judgment. . . .

Factually, this transaction began in the summer of 1968. Roy Gene Carper, in anticipation of marriage and establishing a separate home for himself and his affianced, shopped several places for a mobile home. On July 22, 1968, Roy Gene Carper, accompanied by his fiancé, apparently settled on a mobile home offered for sale by the defendant, Fairmont. . . . [O]n this date, Carper paid Fairmont a $1,000.00 down payment and ordered a mobile home which he understood was to cost him $6,000.00 plus $180.00 consumer sales tax. Thereafter, Fairmont . . . ordered the mobile home from the basic manufacturer with a delivery date six weeks to two months hence. . . .

It appears from uncontradicted testimony that the Bank first became involved in the transaction on August 2 or 3, 1968, and, on August 14, 1968, it agreed conditionally to finance the credit transaction. The contract, payable in installments at the "Kanawha Banking and Trust Co.," was completed and fully executed on September 28, 1968, and then assigned to the Bank under date of October 9, 1968.

According to Fairmont and the Bank, Carper, not having other sources of credit available to him, was offered the mobile home at a cash price of $6,180.00, including tax, or at a credit price of $9,144.00, payable in equal monthly installments of $95.25 for eight years. Fairmont alleges these figures were communicated to Carper upon the partial completion of the papers on July 22, 1968. The appellants say that Carper accepted the terms of the credit sale and agreed that Fairmont should arrange the financing with Kanawha Banking & Trust Company, a lending organization which liked to help young people. The evidence showed that the Bank was one of several institutions with whom Fairmont had previously conducted similar business. According to Fairmont's agent Ball, all the papers signed by Carper were completed on July 22, 1968, with the notable exception that the effective date of the conditional sales contract was not added until September 28, 1968, three days before the delivery of the subject mobile home. This was done, according to Ball, so that Carper would not be liable for payments on the loan until he had accepted delivery of the mobile home which he had ordered. Further, as demonstrated by other instruments, Fairmont used the time period to secure a credit report on Carper and to obtain the Bank's agreement to finance the transaction.

According to Carper's version, he made a bargain to buy the mobile home for $6,180.00, including tax, on the basis of paying $1,000.00 cash at the time the bargain was made, and with a further agreement with Fairmont to finance the balance due of $5,180.00 on a contract, the terms of which would result in ninety-six equal payments of $95.25 per month for a period of eight years. Upon inquiry as to the interest rate, Carper was told by Ball who filled out the papers that the interest rate would be six and one-half percent, and that it would be computed upon the balance due of $5,180.00, plus a figure of $835.60 for property and credit life insurance premiums which aggregated a total of $6,015.60 to be paid by Carper. The conditional sales contract explicitly carries on its face a total amount due of $9,144.00, a figure which Carper and his wife Barbara deny was communicated to them. Carper's factual contention was that he had not agreed to pay more than six and one-half percent interest on the amount to be financed.

The conditional sales contract reflects that the difference between the remaining cash balance due of $6,015.60 and the $9,144.00, characterized as "the total time balance due," was a figure of $3,128.40, characterized by the contract as "finance charge." From the testimony of Fairmont and the Bank, the finance charge was computed by applying six and one-half percent "add-on interest" to the balance of $6,015.60. . . . Actual computation reveals an effective simple interest rate of eleven and twenty-three hundredths percent (11.23%).

. . .

After the final execution of the conditional sales contract . . . which reflected a first payment due on November 10, 1968, and . . . installments payable to Kanawha Banking & Trust Company, Charleston, West Virginia, the mobile home was delivered to Carper and accepted by him on October 1, 1968.

Sometime before the November payment was due, the Bank sent a loan passbook to Roy Gene Carper stating the amount of the debt due being $9,144.00 and reciting the terms of payment and length of loan. In addition, the loan passbook or accompanying paper apportioned the finance charge of $3,128.40 and identified $2,406.24 as being interest prospectively due to the Bank, and $722.16 as being interest prospectively due to Fairmont. Subsequent testimony elicited from the Bank demonstrated that the Bank's share of the add-on figure was five percent and Fairmont's share was to be one and one-half percent. Testimony of the Bank's officer Craig was that the finance charge calculated at the six and one-half add-on rate, was, if considered to be interest, in excess of the interest rate permitted by law.

Other papers admitted into evidence demonstrate that a credit life insurance policy insuring Carper's life was purchased in the stated amount of $5,445.00 and a physical damage insurance policy covering the actual cash value of the mobile home on September 28, 1968 was purchased from a separate company in the value of $6,200.00.

Carper made timely payments of the monthly amounts required by the conditional sales contract to the Bank up to and including the time this civil action was instituted on May 26, 1969. The testimony indicates that during the period from November of 1968 to the latter part of May 1969, Carper had had difficulty with the quality of the mobile home and, in that it was not repaired to his satisfaction, consulted counsel to obtain satisfaction of his complaints against Fairmont and the Bank which culminated in the institution of this civil action.

Carper's complaint alleged that the conditional sales contract was "for the forbearance of money" and called for "a greater rate of interest than is permitted by law," alleging both parties to have notice of that infirmity. . . .

All parties agree that the basic issue to be resolved is whether the questioned commercial transaction and the conditional sales contract sued upon containing finance charges which, if interest, exceeded the lawful rate allowable by law in West Virginia, were subject to the usury laws of the State of West Virginia. Fairmont and the Bank strongly assert that the transaction in question was exempt *as a matter of law* from the usury statutes of the State of West Virginia as being a *bona fide* sale of personal property on a time-price sale basis.

. . .

Usury is the exaction of a greater sum for the use of money than the highest rate of interest allowed by law. It was not prohibited at common law and rests entirely upon statutory prohibition or regulation. The first usury statutes of England, which were remarkably similar to their modern counterparts, were enacted at a time when that nation began its rise as a mercantile empire. Such acts were a parliamentary response to the distaste for excessive exactions of interest, which itself had been contractually enforceable only for a little over a century.

Similar statutes were enacted in our Mother State of Virginia early in the Commonwealth's history. Likewise, prohibitions against usury have been an integral part of the public policy and statutory law of this State since its proclamation.

[At the time of the transaction in this case,] the governing statute provided:

> All contracts and assurances made directly or indirectly for the loan or forbearance of money or other thing at a greater rate of interest than six per cent, except where such greater rate is specially allowed by law, shall be void as to any excess of interest agreed to be paid above that rate, and no further except where otherwise specially provided by law. . . .

In both historical and contemporary usury statutes, one of the essential elements which must appear from a transaction said to be usurious is a loan or forbearance of money. The generally accepted technical definitions, which distinguish between a loan and a forbearance, are to be found in 45 Am.Jur.2d, Interest and Usury § 117 (1969):

> A "loan" is an advancement of money or other personal property under a contract or stipulation, express or implied, whereby the person to whom the advancement is made binds himself to repay it at some future time, together with such other sum as may be agreed upon for the use of the money or thing advanced.

Forbearance, on the other hand, "signifies a contractual obligation of a lender or creditor to refrain during a given period of time from requiring a borrower or debtor to pay a loan or debt that is due and payable." Id. The definitions are meant to highlight the distinction between a loan and a forbearance; being that a loan is a contemporaneous transaction evidencing the creation of a debt to be repaid, while a forbearance is a subsequent agreement entered into between a debtor and creditor to secure the repayment of a debt previously created and matured.

It is asserted by Fairmont and the Bank that inasmuch as the instant transaction involves a *sale of property*, and since a sale of property is not a loan or forbearance of money, it is not within and subject to the strictures of the usury laws. This legal argument is well asserted, at least on an historical basis. Its genesis is a judicially created rule, characterized by most as the "time-price doctrine," which has been traditionally called upon to justify the exemption of property sales from the requirements of usury laws. The doctrine seems to have had its origin as to sales of personal property in the 1774 case of Floyer v. Edwards, I Cowp. 112 (K.B.1774). There the court distinguishing between interest charges on loans and higher prices for deferred payment of sales of gold and silver wire, held that a seller may offer such articles at two different prices, a cash price and a credit or time price. The rule came to be recognized that it was immaterial if the time price exceeded the cash price by more than the statutory allowance for interest on a loan for the same duration.

The foremost American statement of the rule came from the United States Supreme Court and is to be found in the case of Hogg v. Ruffner, 66 U.S. (1 Black) 115, 119 (1861). This case adopted the time-price doctrine in respect to credit sales of real property.

In this jurisdiction three early cases passed upon the same question and recognized and applied the doctrine to sales of real property. . . . The case of Swayne v. Riddle, 16 S.E. 512 (W.Va.1892), paraphrased the rule as follows:

> To constitute usury there must be a borrowing and lending, with intent to exact more interest than is allowed by law, or a forbearance in consideration of such interest being paid. But if what is called "interest," or what is aimed at on the basis of a certain rate of interest, is in fact a part of the purchase-money or price of a tract of land sold, and not a mere cover for a loan or for the forbearance of money, it is not usurious, but is as really a part of the purchase-price for the land as is the principal sum.

Three years later, the case of Crim v. Post, 23 S.E. 613 (W.Va.1895) recognized the foregoing rules but there determined a transaction to be patently usurious where it was obvious that a lender had negotiated with the borrower new loans at usurious rates, including a bonus to the lender, to replace old notes at previous usurious rates. This transaction presumably involved both a usurious loan and a usurious forbearance. In that case the Court appended a significant *caveat* limiting the applicability of the time-price doctrine as previously enunciated . . . and said in Syllabus Point 3:

> But the statute contemplates that a search for usury shall not stop at the mere form of the bargains and contracts relative to such loan, but that all shifts and devices intended to cover a usurious loan or

forbearance shall be pushed aside, and the transaction be dealt with as usury if it be such in fact.

Of utmost importance is that in both the *Crim* and *Swayne* cases, the Court recognized that whether a questioned transaction was usurious—or a *bona fide* sale of personal property saved by the time-price doctrine, was a determination "in fact."

All parties to this appeal, including the West Virginia Bankers Association and the West Virginia Retailers Association, *amicii*, recognize that, since the *Crim* case, the time-price doctrine has not been questioned or construed by this Court until the present case. Our problem then is to reassess and evaluate the validity and applicability of the time-price doctrine *vis-à-vis* the usury statute to a modern commercial transaction exemplified by the conditional sales contract binding Carper, Fairmont and the Bank to the financing arrangement involved in the sale of a mobile home. Squarely, we must determine whether the time-price doctrine is a viable exception to the usury laws in a modern retail installment sales transaction involving consumer credit.

From the [foregoing] cases there is derived a general rule for the credit sale of property. If the negotiation between the seller and the buyer involves a *bona fide* quotation of both a cash price and a credit price, the transaction does not involve usury, even though the quoted credit price is such as to exceed the cash price plus lawful interest thereon. This rule is generally recognized throughout the country. It is also generally recognized that this rule may apply where the credit instrument, the sales contract, is assigned by the vendor to a lending institution and also where a note is given for the balance of the price. Lundstrom v. Radio Corporation of America, 405 P.2d 339 (Utah 1965); Annot. supra 1065, 1091, § 7 and many cases cited therein. Fairmont and the Bank would have us stop there. They say that if a commercial transaction is couched in form within the requirements of the general rule, that is, if there appears on the face of the sales contract both a sales and a time price, the transaction is *presumed in law* to be excepted from the application of the usury laws. . . .

But, *quare*: Is every quotation by its mere recitation *ipso facto* to be accorded *bona fides*? For two reasons appearing in the law of the cases previously cited, we reject the contention that the time-price doctrine is a rule of law commanding the courts to ignore the usury statutes in the context of a credit sale of property. In each statement of the general rule, reference is made to the word *"bona fide"* and also to the words "in fact." Therein lies the germ for thought which results in the modern judicial resolution of commercial transactions claimed to be usurious. That this approach also has traditional and historical prestige is apparent from the language of the *Crim* case which holds that no shift or device nor mere form within the contract shall turn away a court or jury from closely scrutinizing aspects of the contract which may be usurious. If a transaction is actually a device to evade usury laws, it is not saved by any attempted differential between a claimed "cash price" and a claimed "credit price." Thus, if the sale of personal property is really made on a cash estimate, and time is given to pay the price, and an amount is assumed to be paid greater than the cash price with legal interest, the transaction may be, in fact, usurious.

In other words, within the contemplation of the parties contracting, if they deem or intend a sale of personal property to be based upon a cash price coupled with contemporaneous or subsequent arrangements to finance the balance of the sale, the terms of which provide for a total amount due greater than the cash price with legal interest, then the factual issue arises.

Consequently, we hold that whether a sale of personal property is *bona fide* and thus without the protections of the usury statute or part of a plan or device to evade the application of the usury law is a question of fact for the jury.

When considering cases where usury is a factual question *vis-à-vis* the time-price doctrine, courts have come to recognize certain indicia to test for the presence or absence of usury in the context of the questioned commercial transaction.

First, on the rationale that a buyer must be presented with a realistic opportunity to choose between a cash and a credit price before becoming bound to a contract, the question of whether both prices were adequately and seasonably disclosed is a consideration for the trier of fact.

Second, where the financing transaction is tripartite, the jury may examine the closeness of the relationship between the seller and the lender which may be demonstrated by the presence or absence of any of the following: (a) Seller's agreement with the buyer to finance the balance or arrange a loan; (b) Additional profit to a seller through dealer reserves; (c) Splitting of profit between the seller and lender from insurance premiums or other charges required of the buyer-borrower; and (d) Papers signed by buyer-borrower in blank. . . .

Third, when credit terms expressed to the buyer-borrower are couched and calculated in terms of "interest or percentage," a further indicia arises.

. . .

In the case below, the parties negotiated a bargain on July 22, 1968, in which Fairmont agreed to sell and Carper agreed to purchase a customized mobile home for a cash price of $6,000.00, upon the further understanding that Carper only had $1,000.00 down payment and that the balance would have to be financed. Fairmont agreed to finance the transaction by finding a bank which would lend the money to cover the balance. Fairmont suggested that Kanawha Banking & Trust Company would be the lending institution to handle the transaction and that the Bank would finance the balance at six and one-half percent interest. From the testimony offered by the Bank, its officer Craig agreed to finance the transaction in accordance with the terms communicated to it by Fairmont on or about August 14, 1968. The parties concluded their agreement by the execution of a conditional sales contract effective September 28, 1968. In that Carper was told by Fairmont's agent Ball that he only had to pay six and one-half percent interest on the balance due while also being dissuaded from reading the partially completed papers and becoming aware of the total-amounts due under the conditional sales contract by Ball telling him it wasn't necessary to read the papers and that Fairmont needed them only to order the mobile home, it therefore follows that a time-price was not communicated to Carper. Rather, it appears, and the jury must have so found, that the sale was conducted on a cash estimate basis. Additionally, as the parties spoke of the financing arrangement in the terms of *interest* and a *loan*, it is evident they treated the transaction as a sale of property coupled with a loan or forbearance to pay a debt to another debtor. Further, considering the negotiation intervals in the transaction from July 22 to September 14, to September 28 when the conditional sales contract was completed and the parties became bound, it is also apparent that the seller arranged the financing and, in the manner of doing so, acted as agent for the lending bank. This conclusion is further bolstered by the fact that the contract provided for the sharing of profits on the transaction in various forms between Fairmont and the Bank and that all these profits were "costs" to the buyer-borrower Carper which were additional charges and part of the cumulative total of the loan or forbearance transaction represented by the conditional sales contract.

Depending upon one's perspective of the entire transaction it may appear in one light either as a sale coupled with a loan, or as a sale coupled with a forbearance. The answer is that the historical distinction between loan and forbearance is obliterated in the tripartite financing arrangement employed in this case and commonly employed in the installment sales industry to finance consumer items.

From Carper's standpoint, he was obligated to pay the difference between his down payment and the cash price of the mobile home, plus tax, to Fairmont when the mobile home was delivered. Having communicated his inability to pay the difference in cash, he agreed to finance or borrow the difference from the banking source provided him by Fairmont, on the consideration of paying an additional $835.00 for insurance premiums and an additional six and one-half percent simple interest on the balance due.

Based upon Carper's obligation under the contract to pay a financed total of $9,144.00 for a $6,000.00 item of property, the Bank agreed to lend Fairmont $6,015.60 cash. Using this form of commercial transaction, the Bank: lessened its risk of lending money by sharing it with Fairmont; obtained security and insurance on the security and the loan; and realized more profit from the loan than the highest rates permitted by law.

From Fairmont's perspective, the financing arrangement which expanded the sales bargain from $6,000.00 plus tax to $10,144.00 total receipts, represented aspects of both a loan and a forbearance. The forbearance was to Carper; the loan arose in its dealings with the Bank. Fairmont, by agreeing to provide money to Carper to finance the balance, and by borrowing from the Bank on Carper's credit, received enough cash to pay the manufacturer, the freight, the tax commissioner, and still obtain an immediate profit of $721.86. Because of its further agreement with the Bank, it stood to gain twice its cash-price profit on the sale, share its risk of extending a forbearance to Carper and also gain additional profit from insurance premiums charged Carper to insure his life and the mobile home.

. . .

From the foregoing it is quite obvious that Fairmont realizes far more in a sale of the mobile home coupled with a "financing" than it does on a straight cash sale. We conclude that something more than a mobile home was sold to Carper. He also bought insurance policies and the ability to extend his matured obligation to Fairmont over an eight-year period. Fairmont, under this arrangement, receives the best of both worlds. It has sold a mobile home, has gained an additional profit by acting as agent in the financing arrangement, and has obtained the immediate access to its normal cash sale profit.

From the Bank's standpoint it has obtained one additional loan, which is the life blood and essence of its business and, as recourse is a condition of the contract, it shares the risk of loss with its partner in the financing venture. Additionally, the Bank and Fairmont, by characterizing interest as "finance charges," would have realized 11.23 percent annual interest rate on money loaned and financed when the usury law applicable to the transaction permitted only an 8 percent charge.

The jury found this particular transaction to have been in violation of the usury law. . . . [W]e find no error in the jury determination and we agree with the trial court that the verdict finding of usury was amply supported by the evidence.

. . .

If there is quarrel with the public policy involved in the usury statute *vis-à-vis* the realistic cost of money in today's market and the availability of high-risk consumer credit, these are questions which should be answered in legislative halls. The capacity of the judicial branch to appreciate the magnitude of these problems is not matched with the ability to enact remedial laws.

The judgment of the Circuit Court of Raleigh County is affirmed.

Affirmed.

SPROUSE, JUSTICE (concurring):

I concur with the majority opinion. There are assuredly areas in which a lender should be able to charge higher interest rates than would be desirable or permissible for a well-secured conventional loan. Flexible interest rates for the sale of goods would not only stimulate the economy, but would compensate the lender for higher risk and costlier loan administration. There are undoubtedly some circumstances involving real estate sales where higher interest rates for a loan or forbearance would be in the public interest. There are also other commercial transactions in which a permissible range of interest rates rather than one fixed maximum rate would better serve the public policy of this State.

The "time-price" doctrine, however, in my opinion is a fiction created to serve this public policy. It is fallacious for the State to permit only an 8 percent interest charge when the borrower or buyer desires to repay the loan proceeds over a period of time, but to allow a higher interest rate when the lender utilizes the magic words indicating a present cash price, but a higher price if payment is to be made at a later date. Aside from the basic fiction, the weakness of the doctrine is that it permits each lender to determine the public policy questions of what additional charge a borrower should pay for various risks, loan administration difficulties, or other commercial problems. While lenders should have flexible interest rates for different type loans or forbearances, the welfare of lender, borrower and the public would be better served if the "time-price" doctrine were completely repudiated and permissible limits established by the legislature.

QUESTIONS AND NOTES

1. In Hogg v. Ruffner, 66 U.S. (1 Black) 115, 118–19 (1861), the leading American case on the time-price doctrine, the Supreme Court said:

> But it is manifest that if A propose to sell to B a tract of land for $10,000 in cash, or for $20,000 payable in ten annual installments, and if B prefers to pay the larger sum to gain time, the contract cannot be called usurious. A vendor may prefer $100 in hand to double the sum in expectancy, and a purchaser may prefer the greater price with the longer credit, and one who will not distinguish between things that differ may say, with apparent truth, that B pays a hundred per cent for forbearance, and may assert that such a contract is usurious but whatever truth there may be in the premises, the conclusion is manifestly erroneous. Such a contract has none of the characteristics of usury; it is not for the loan of money, or forbearance of a debt.

In Schauman v. Solmica Midwest, Inc., 168 N.W.2d 667, 670 (Minn.1969), the court stated that

> the power to determine the extent of the increase of the credit price over the cash selling price is incident to the owner's right to fix the latter and is a matter of contract between the parties. Courts have observed that in calculating the addition to the cash price the owner may consider all factors which influence vendors, such as profit, return on investment, overhead, handling charges, risks involved, insurance, sale discount of contract for deferred payments, and perhaps other items. Thus, other considerations than interest are properly involved in the credit price, such as risk incident to financing the contract, expenses connected therewith, etc.

Does this explain why the courts created and continue to recognize the time-price doctrine? Does it justify the doctrine?

Seventeen months elapsed between the oral argument and the rendition of judgment in the appeal in *Carper*. Why do you suppose it took so long?

2.   Problem. *Consumer*, who wants to buy a new car, says to *Dealer*, "I want a Civic, and I have $400 per month to spend." *Dealer* looks at her book of charts and replies, "OK, at $400 per month, it will take you forty-eight months to pay for this car." They sign a contract for $400 per month for forty-eight months. If the increase over the cash price is greater than the charge permitted by the usury statute, does *Consumer* have a good claim?

3.   At the beginning of its opinion, the court in *Carper* recites the parties' respective versions of the facts of the case. Precisely what differences are there between the two versions? Why doesn't the time-price doctrine apply?

4.   Carper sued both Fairmont and the bank for violating the usury statute. If the court had concluded that the transaction between Carper and Fairmont was a credit sale within the time-price doctrine, would that have disposed of Carper's claim against the bank? Would the bank have made a loan or forbearance? Would it matter if the bank had kept all of the so-called 6½ percent, rather than splitting it with Fairmont?

5.   In National Bank of Commerce v. Thomsen, 495 P.2d 332 (Wash.1972), Carter Motors, a new car dealer, and National Bank had a contract that called for Carter to sell conditional sale contracts to the bank and to guarantee payment by the consumers who signed the contracts. The bank provided Carter with charts for determining the amount of time-price differential to charge. The bank also supplied the contract documents that Carter was to use. These documents provided that the consumer was to make his payments directly to the bank. Defendant Thomsen purchased a car from Carter, signing a conditional sale contract that Carter promptly transferred to the bank. When Thomsen stopped making payments, the bank sued; he counterclaimed, alleging usury. The court stated:

> The plaintiff attaches much significance to the fact that there was no direct contact between it and the defendant prior to the signing of the contract. We do not find this fact controlling. Even if the plaintiff had not authorized the dealer to represent to purchasers that it would finance their purchases of new cars, the representation was made and it was ratified by the plaintiff when it accepted the contract, which showed on its face that all payments were to be made to the plaintiff.
>
> Ratification is the affirmance by a person of a prior act which did not bind him but which was done or professedly done on his account, whereby the act, as to some or all persons, is given effect as if originally authorized by him. Restatement (Second) of Agency § 82 (1958). As stated in section 83 of this chapter, affirmance is either (a) a manifestation of an election by one on whose account an unauthorized act has been done to treat the act as authorized, or (b) conduct by him justifiable only if there were such an election.

· The conduct of the plaintiff in this instance falls within these principles. The true nature of the transaction was that plaintiff placed in the hands of the dealer indicia of authority to represent that it would finance new car purchases, that the representation was in fact made to the defendant, and that the purchase was in fact financed by the plaintiff. Thus, at the moment the contract was signed, the defendant became indebted, not to the dealer, but, in accordance with terms of the contract, to the plaintiff. The plaintiff loaned him the money with which to purchase the car. The fact that the dealer guaranteed the loan does not change the nature of the basic transaction.

. . .

It is correct that one who sells goods or services on credit is not a lender of money. But a third party who pays the seller on behalf of the purchaser is, insofar as his relations with the purchaser are concerned, a lender of money. In a case such as this, where the purchase is financed from the beginning, there is never a true *conditional* sale. The sale is complete as far as the vendor is concerned. He does not extend credit to the purchaser; rather, he is paid in full at the time of purchase. The "conditional sale contract" is then but a security device to protect the party who finances the purchase.

. . .

. . . [I]n this case . . . a cash sale was effected and the conditional sale was used as a security device to protect the institution which loaned the defendant the money to purchase the automobile.

We bear in mind that usury must exist, if it exists at all, at the inception of the contract. Here, it was never contemplated that the dealer would extend credit to the defendant. Rather, the agreement was that the full purchase price would be paid, and that a portion of the purchase price which the defendant was not prepared to pay would be loaned to him by a financing institution. It was represented to him that the plaintiff would make the loan, and the plaintiff did so.

Since the transaction, as between the plaintiff and the defendant, was a loan of money, the time price differential represented interest, and the interest charged was greater than that permitted under RCW 19.52.020.

495 P.2d at 337–39.

In what ways is the court's rationale different from the rationale of the court in *Carper*?

6. After the date of the transaction in *Thomsen*, the Washington legislature amended its retail installment sales act to limit the amount sellers may charge for the privilege of deferring payment. Washington abolished the limit in 1992, but RISAs in some other states still limit the charge. These statutes, however, do not necessarily render decisions like *Thomsen* obsolete. Do you see why?

7. Problem. *Health Spa* sells annual memberships for $360. Purchasers may pay the $360 at the outset or may, if they wish, pay it in twelve installments of $30. On February 1 *Consumer* purchases a one-year membership, signing an installment sales contract in which he promises to pay the $360 in twelve installments. Later that same day *Health Spa* assigns the contract to *Bank* for $300. Is there a violation of the usury statute if the statute permits a maximum of $27 on a loan of $300 to be repaid in twelve monthly installments?

8. Problem. *Consumer* wants to purchase a television that costs $540, but she wants to defer payment. She signs an installment sales contract with *Seller* in which she agrees to pay twelve monthly installments of $50. For a loan of $540, the applicable statute authorizes a charge of $60. Is there a violation of the statute? Would it matter if *Seller* immediately assigns the contract to *Bank* for $525?

9. Problem. *Consumer* wants a new car but cannot pay cash. He responds to *Dealer's* advertisement of cars for lease. After selecting the car of his dreams, he completes an application form that asks for information concerning his financial condition. *Dealer* sends the application form to *Leasing Company*, which approves the application. *Leasing Company* pays *Dealer* $22,500, the retail value of the car and obtains title to it. *Leasing Company* and *Consumer* then sign an open-end lease agreement in which *Consumer* agrees to make monthly payments for four years. The agreement provides that at the end of four years *Consumer* will be liable to the extent the actual value of the car is less than $12,500, which is the value that *Leasing Company* predicts the car will have in four years. In addition, *Consumer* has the option, at any time, to acquire title to the car upon payment of $12,500 plus all scheduled monthly payments not already paid.

Is there a loan or forbearance?

10. Problem. *RTO* leases a TV to *Consumer*. The contract provides that *Consumer* may terminate at any time but that if she pays the $15 weekly rental fee for 78 consecutive weeks (a total of $1,170) she will become the owner of the TV. If the retail value of the TV is $500, can *Consumer* challenge the transaction under the usury laws?

11. Problem. *Consumer* owns a house worth $135,000, on which the mortgage balance is $48,000. She has missed several of her $375 monthly mortgage payments, and *Bank* has commenced foreclosure proceedings. *FS* sends *Consumer* a letter:

> I am sorry to learn that your home is in foreclosure. We can help. We are Foreclosure Specialists and can help you stay in your home. Please make an appointment to see us.

Consumer goes to the office of *FS*, which asks her a few questions and then tells her that with the help of *FS* she will get to stay in her home and will only have to increase her monthly payments to $410. She is very pleased and returns the next day to sign the papers.

Consumer sends *FS* $410 each month for twelve months, at the end of which time *FS* sends her a letter asking whether she wants to exercise the repurchase option. *Consumer* is quite confused and brings the contract documents to you. You read the documents and learn that the contract provides that *Consumer* will convey her house to *FS*, which in turn agrees to pay the $2,250 arrearage owed *Bank* and to lease the house back to her for one year at $410 per month. The contract also gives her the option to repurchase the house at the end of one year upon payment of $2,250. *Consumer* is shocked to learn this since she never intended to sell her house to *FS*—or anyone else, for that matter—and she does not have $2,250. Can you help her? Is the transaction a loan or forbearance and therefore subject to the usury laws?

Can you think of any other basis for helping her?

(2) Principal Amount and Duration of the Loan

Problem. To finance the purchase of a car, *Consumer* wants to borrow $5,000 from *Bank*. *Bank* is willing to loan money only to its depositors and tells *Consumer* that if she wants the loan, she will have to open and maintain a non-interest-bearing checking account with a minimum balance of $1,000. Under the applicable usury statute, the maximum that may be charged for a loan of $5,000 for one year is $400. They form a contract in which *Bank* loans *Consumer* $5,000, to be repaid, along with $400 interest, one year later. Is the transaction usurious?

Would it matter if instead of the checking account, *Bank* required *Consumer* to maintain an interest-bearing savings account?

Tri–County Federal Savings & Loan Association v. Lyle

Court of Appeals of Maryland, 1977.
280 Md. 69, 371 A.2d 424.

Singley, Judge.

[In April 1974 Deveroe and Florence Lyle borrowed $60,000 from Tri–County for the purpose of constructing a home. The Lyles signed a note for $60,000 plus 8% interest. In addition, they paid $60 for an appraisal fee, $10 for a credit report, and $90 for nine inspections that were to occur during the course of construction. Tri–County gave the Lyles $60,000, of which $15,000 went to the seller of the lot on which the house was to be built and $45,000 was deposited by Tri–County in its general checking account at a bank. The $45,000 was to be paid out in nine installments to the contractor who was building the house. It was Tri–County's practice to deposit funds from various sources into this checking account and to make payments from it for various purposes (e.g., employees' salaries). Tri–County maintained a ledger showing the status of each construction loan and always had on deposit in this (and other) checking accounts enough funds to cover all its construction loan obligations.

In September, for reasons not disclosed in the report, the Lyles abandoned their construction plans. They repaid Tri–County the $15,000 that had been paid to the seller of the lot, and Tri–County credited them with the $45,000 it still had in the checking account. Tri–County also repaid them the $90 for inspections that were never conducted. Pursuant to the loan contract, during the five months that the loan had been outstanding, the Lyles had made monthly payments of interest on the $60,000. These payments totaled $2,173.29.]

The Lyles brought suit in the Circuit Court for Charles County, alleging that the $60.00 appraisal fee and the $10.00 fee for a credit report, neither of which was returned to the Lyles, and the eight per cent interest charged from 11 April 1974 to 24 September 1974 on the $45,000.00, an amount never subject to the Lyles' control and never utilized by them, rendered the loan usurious and entitled them to recover from Tri–County, by virtue of the provisions of Maryland Code (1957, 1972 Repl.Vol.) Art. 49, § 8, the greater of three times the charges and interest at a rate in excess of eight per cent or $500.00 and claimed $5,631.54.

The trial judge found the fees "not [to be] a payment of interest over and above the eight per cent allowed by law." He noted that the $45,000 "was deposited in the bank, admittedly deposited with other funds," and that the testimony of the president of Tri–County "was that there is a general ledger which controls, which they use to control the funds that are put in the bank and that they retain sufficient funds in several banks to cover all outstanding construction loans which are in progress . . . at any given time." He concluded:

> So the Court, gentlemen, feels that the commitment was made, the testimony shows that the funds were available for the benefit of Mr. and Mrs. Lyle, in accordance with their agreement. They agreed that the funds were to be retained by the lending institution in accordance with their agreement and there is nothing that I can find in any statute in the State of Maryland, which prevents the individual from entering into this agreement authorizing the lending institution to make such disbursal of funds as, for which they had signed the deed of trust.

> The Court, for that reason, will grant the motion [of Tri–County to dismiss] and will enter a verdict, enter a judgment nisi in favor of the defendant.

The Court of Special Appeals concluded that the credit appraisal and inspection fees played no role in the alleged usury and we agree. The $90.00 inspection fee was returned to the Lyles when they determined not to proceed with construction. The appraisal fee and the fee for the credit report were paid by Tri–County to others, and under the rule of B.F. Saul Co. v. West End Park, 246 A.2d 591 (Md.1968), a fee or charge collected by the lender and paid to others is to be excluded from the computation of interest by virtue of Code (1957, 1972 Repl.Vol.) Art. 49, § 1(b)(6)(C).

The interest charged on the $45,000.00 of the loan proceeds retained by Tri–County is an entirely different matter, however. At no time was this under the Lyles' control, or under their partial control, as it might have been had it been held in escrow by others for their account, even though subject to restrictions. It was deposited in Tri–County's general account, and remained there from the day the Lyles signed the note until repayment was made. The cases relied on by Tri–County, are clearly inapposite. In both cases, the sums borrowed were credited to the mortgagors, to be released on certain conditions.

See also 45 Am.Jur.2d, Interest and Usury § 113 at 100 (1969), relied on in part by Tri–County:

> If as a condition of making a loan the borrower is required to leave part of the money on deposit with the lender, the transaction is usurious if the interest paid for the loan amounts to more than legal interest on the sum actually available for the use of the borrower. If, however, the agreement for a loan contemplates that the entire amount shall be available to the borrower at once, the mere fact that he leaves a part thereof with the lender for a time, or that a brief delay in paying it over to him occurs, does not make the transaction usurious in the absence of a corrupt intent to evade the law against usury.

> .   .   .

> When Code (1957, 1972 Repl.Vol.) Art. 49 was amended by Chapter 453 of the Laws of 1968, Section 3 provided in part that:

> Interest may be charged not in excess of the rate of six per cent (6%) per annum simple interest *on the unpaid balance*, except that interest may be charged at the rate not in excess of eight per cent (8%) per annum simple interest *on the unpaid balance* under an agreement in writing between the lender and the borrower. (emphasis added)

Section 6 of the same Article provided that "Usury is the collection by a lender of either interest or other charges in amounts greater than allowed by this article" and Section 8 permitted the recovery of the greater of $500.00 or three times the excessive interest.

We are entirely in accord with the concept adopted by the Court of Special Appeals, that whether a loan is usurious depends on the collection of interest on the unpaid balance at a rate greater than that permitted by statute, and that the balance clearly means that which is owed by a borrower to a lender. Webster's New International Dictionary of the English Language 206 (2d ed. 1949) defines balance as "An equality between the sums total of the two sides of an account," or alternatively as "The excess on either side, or the difference between the two sides, of an account."

The concept of the collection of interest on an unpaid balance of a loan makes this case distinguishable from those involving the imposition of a commitment fee for an undertaking to lend money at some future date, see Goldman v. Connecticut General Life Insurance Company, 248 A.2d 154 (Md.1968) and Ehlen v. Selden, 59 A. 120 (Md.1904), holding that there can be no recovery of a commitment fee when the contemplated borrowing is never consummated.

Here the "unpaid balance" referred to by Art. 49, § 3 was the $15,000.00 owed by the Lyles to Tri–County: the $45,000.00 was a balance beyond their control, to which they had no access until they commenced the construction of their house. So long as it remained in the sole control of Tri–County, and was not utilized by the Lyles, the imposition of the interest charged was usurious, because the $45,000.00 was not and could not be a part of the unpaid balance of the loan to the Lyles.

JUDGMENT OF THE COURT OF SPECIAL APPEALS AF-FIRMED. . . .

QUESTIONS

1. Would it have mattered if Tri–County had set up an escrow account for the $45,000 balance of the loan? Why or why not?

2. Would it have mattered if the house had been built as planned and Tri–County periodically had disbursed funds to the contractor: would the transaction still be usurious? Why or why not?

3. Problem. *Seller*, who operates a department store, comes to you for advice. A graduate student working for *Seller* over the summer has suggested an alternative to the store's current charge account system. Under the plan *Seller* would create coupon books. Each book would contain coupons of varying denominations, with a total value of $60 per book. Consumers could use the coupons as cash in *Seller's* store. To obtain a coupon book, a consumer would enter an installment sales contract with *Seller*, obligating the consumer to repay $60 plus a finance charge of $3 (the maximum permitted) in six monthly installments of $10.50. The first payment would be due thirty days after the consumer first uses a coupon from the book. What legal advice would you offer?

4. Compare *Tri-County*, the hypothetical preceding *Tri-County*, and the hypotheticals in Questions 2–3 supra. In each, what is the essence of the creditor's attempt to avoid the limit set by the usury statute? How are all four of the situations essentially similar?

5. Problem. *Borrower* is an independent trucker who wishes to buy a new $80,000 rig. *Lender* is willing to make a loan to *Borrower*, but only if *Borrower* agrees to borrow a larger sum, $101,000. (A state statute provides that the usury law does not apply to loans in excess of $100,000 made exclusively for business or commercial purposes.) *Borrower* takes the loan, at a rate in excess of that permitted by the usury statute. *Lender* sends a check for $80,000 to the seller of the rig and gives a check for $21,000 to *Borrower*, who uses it in connection with her trucking activity. What argument can you make on behalf of the proposition that *Lender* has violated the usury statute?

6. Problem. *Seller* wishes to sell his car, on which he still owes *Bank* $5,000 on the loan *Bank* made when *Seller* acquired the car two years ago. This loan carries an interest rate of 10%. *Seller* agrees to sell the car to *Buyer* for $7,500 on these terms: *Buyer* is to pay $500 down and make monthly payments to *Seller* on the remaining balance of the price ($7,000) at an interest rate of 12%; *Seller* is to continue making the payments to *Bank* on the original loan. Does *Seller* violate the usury statute if the maximum permitted by the statute is 12%?

Should it matter whether *Bank* is contractually obligated to permit *Buyer* to assume the loan it had made to *Seller*?

7. In Petersen v. Philco Finance Corp., 428 P.2d 961 (Idaho 1967), plaintiffs purchased dry-cleaning equipment. The cash price of the equipment was $23,750, of which plaintiffs paid $2,247 down, leaving a balance of $21,503. A finance charge of $5,161 was added, making a "total time balance" of $26,664, which plaintiffs were to pay in 48 monthly installments of $555.50. The seller immediately assigned the contract to defendant finance company. Plaintiffs paid for thirteen months, reducing the contract balance to $19,443, and then defaulted. Several months later, plaintiffs and defendant finance company entered an extension agreement under which the parties agreed to stretch out the period of repayment an additional 25 months beyond the date of the last payment called for by the original contract. Plaintiffs agreed to pay an additional $2,430, making the total remaining balance $21,873, to be paid in 58 monthly installments of $377.12. After several months plaintiffs again defaulted. Plaintiffs sued the seller and the finance company, alleging that both the conditional sales contract and the extension agreement violated the usury statute. Defendants counterclaimed for breach of the two contracts. The trial court held that the conditional sales contract was not usurious because of the time-price doctrine, but that the extension agreement was. Plaintiffs and defendant finance company both appealed.

The Supreme Court of Idaho affirmed, refusing to abrogate the time-price doctrine because "this question is more properly for the legislature." Hence the original transaction was not usurious. As to the extension agreement, defendant conceded that the transaction was not within the time-price doctrine and that the usury statute did apply. The dispute concerned the period of forbearance.

> [T]he parties originally contracted for a deferred payment period extending over 48 months. Thirteen months had elapsed, and while the contract was admittedly in default, and by its terms due and payable, respondent, as holder of the contract, agreed to forbear collecting the amount due for an additional 25 months of time. The sum of $7,221.50 had been paid under the contract which left an unpaid balance of $19,442.50 at the time of the extension agreement on August 1, 1963. The amount charged for the time extension was $2,430.31, which added to the unpaid balance of $19,442.50, made a total balance of $21,872.81, payable thereafter in 58 consecutive monthly installments. The sum of $2,430.31 was *add-on* interest, computed at six percent (6%) per annum on the unpaid balance.

> This interest figure would net respondent an annual simple interest rate in excess of that permitted by I.C. § 27–1905, if the forbearance extended for 25 months, but not if it extended for 58 months. The

question, consequently, dispositive of the issue of whether the extension agreement was usurious, is whether by virtue of the extension agreement, the forbearance allowed by the holder of the contract for a period of 25 months, was actually for an additional 25 months, or for a 58–month total period. The district court concluded the appellants obtained a forbearance from the holder of the conditional sale contract or respondent for a period of 25 months only.

Under the terms of the original contract, each unpaid installment would have drawn interest at the highest legal rate. However, the district court determined that respondent in effect waived this remedy in choosing not to cancel the original contract and declare the entire balance immediately due and payable by reason of the default. Under this interpretation, the extension agreement was a modification of the original contract and provided for the forbearance of the amount due under the contract for 25 months. Respondent contends this is an unfair interpretation for the very reason that it could have declared the unpaid balance immediately due and payable; and, presumably, then have turned around and loaned to appellants the sum of $19,442.50 to pay off the contract balance, legally drawing even a higher rate of interest for the term of 58 months than was in fact charged. That reasoning is fallacious; and appellants, having defaulted on the contract, had become the necessitous debtor, for whose protection the usury statute was enacted. The extension agreement was properly ruled usurious.

428 P.2d at 969. Do you agree with plaintiffs that since the finance company's assignor originally had agreed to forbear for a period that still had 33 months to run, the forbearance contemplated by the extension agreement was only the additional 25 months? or with the finance company, that in the extension agreement defendant was agreeing to wait 58 months for full payment? Why is defendant's argument "fallacious"?

Reconsider your answer to Question 4 supra.

Refinancing an existing obligation is a common occurrence. Sometimes it happens because the market rate of interest has dropped and the consumer can lower his or her payments by refinancing, i.e. paying off the existing loan. Other times it happens because the consumer is about to, or has, defaulted, and by lengthening the period of repayment can lower the monthly payments. This is *Peterson*. More materials on refinancing appear in Section (4) of this chapter and in Section A of the next chapter.

(3) Cost of the Loan

Except for the problems considered in the preceding section, if the lender imposes only one charge on the borrower and labels it "interest," it is relatively easy to determine whether the lender has charged more than the statute permits. If, however, the lender imposes several charges and gives them different labels, it may not be so easy to determine whether the cost of the loan exceeds the amount that the statute permits.

PROBLEMS

1. *Buyers* have contracted to buy a house from *Sellers* for $150,000. *Buyers* want to finance this purchase by borrowing $130,000, and *Mortgage Company* is willing to loan them this amount at 12%, which is the maximum permitted by the usury statute. *Mortgage Company*, however, requires *Buyers* to pay five points, i.e. 5% of the principal amount of the loan, at the closing. Does *Mortgage Company* violate the usury statute?

If *Mortgage Company* requires *Sellers*, rather than *Buyers*, to pay the five points, is the transaction usurious?

In the second case, if you had a choice of plaintiffs in a suit to recover for violation of the usury statute, would you choose to represent *Buyers* or *Sellers*?

2. *Consumer* is planning his vacation and wants to borrow $800, to be repaid in twelve monthly installments. The applicable statute permits the lender to charge $96. *Lender* is willing to make the loan but requires *Consumer* to buy a road atlas for $25. The regular retail price of the atlas is $15. Does *Lender* violate the statute?

Would it matter if the regular price of the atlas were $25? Cf. People v. Coleman, 59 N.W.2d 276 (Mich.1953).

Equitable Life Assurance Society v. Scali

Court of Appeals of Illinois, 1966.
75 Ill.App.2d 255, 220 N.E.2d 893, reversed 38 Ill.2d 544, 232 N.E.2d 712 (1967).

THOMAS J. MORAN, PRESIDING JUSTICE.

This is an appeal from a mortgage foreclosure decree entered in favor of the plaintiff mortgagee, Equitable Life Assurance Society. The defendant mortgagors, Mauro L. Scali and his wife, Joanna, defended the action on the ground, among others, that the mortgage loan was usurious. Their appeal from the adverse ruling of the lower court presents a case of first impression in this State.

In 1957 the defendants purchased a home in Deerfield, Illinois, for $34,000.00 and obtained $25,000.00 of the purchase money by borrowing that amount from the plaintiff. The loan was secured by a twenty-five year mortgage at five per cent interest. At the time of the loan, plaintiff had appraised the market value of the property at $38,500.00. The amount of the loan was, therefore, roughly two-thirds the market value of the property.

As a condition of the loan, the plaintiff also required Scali to take out an Equitable life insurance policy in the amount of $25,000.00, and to assign the policy to Equitable as collateral security for the loan. At the time of the loan, Scali already had life insurance policies in force with the Northwestern Mutual Life Insurance Company in the face amount of $58,500.00. It appears that the "family income" provisions of these Northwestern Mutual policies brought their total value to approximately

$75,000.00. These Northwestern Mutual policies were permanent insurance and not term insurance.

Scali testified that he inquired of the Equitable agent as to whether he could assign his Northwestern policies to Equitable as collateral security for the loan, in lieu of purchasing an additional life insurance policy from Equitable. He was informed that this could not be done, and that Equitable would accept only a new or already existing Equitable policy. This testimony was not contradicted by the plaintiff, and the record is clear that, at the time of the loan in question, every mortgage loan made by Equitable had to be secured by one of its own insurance policies on the life of the borrower, regardless of what other life insurance the borrower might already have had or have been willing to acquire in lieu of an Equitable policy. . . . Moreover, the Equitable policy had to be one of ordinary life insurance, and not term insurance, which would have been less costly to the insured.

The defendants were required to make monthly payments of $195.73. Of this amount, $146.25 was for the principal and interest on the mortgage loan, and $49.48 was for the life insurance premium. The payments on the mortgage and the insurance policy were inseparable, and it was provided that any default in payment on the insurance premiums would be considered a default on the mortgage, and the entire loan would become due.

Beginning in the latter part of 1958, Scali encountered problems with his employment and the monthly payments to Equitable were often delinquent. This situation continued for several years, and finally this foreclosure action was filed by Equitable in 1964.

In their answer to the complaint, the Scalis raised the affirmative defense of usury, pleading that the insurance premium was an additional charge exacted for the loan, and that when the insurance premium was added to the stipulated five per cent interest, the total charge for the loan exceeded the seven per cent maximum permitted by statute. It was their theory that, because of the usurious nature of the transaction, all interest on the loan was forfeited and, pursuant to Ill.Rev.Stat. Ch. 74, sec. 6, defendants were entitled to a set-off against the remaining amount due on the principal, of all interest and insurance premiums paid, together with reasonable attorneys' fees and court costs.

It was stipulated that the monthly payment on a $25,000.00 loan for twenty-five years at seven per cent interest—the legal maximum—was $176.70. As previously noted, the combined payment of the Scalis was $195.73.

One normally thinks of "usury" as the simple practice of charging a greater amount of "interest," clearly labeled as such, than the law allows. Since the "interest" in this case was only five percent, whereas the law allows seven per cent, it is apparent at the outset that we are not dealing with the typical usury case, and, as we have indicated, there is no reported decision in this State which deals with the question presented.

We start with the fact that, by the terms of the statute itself, "usury" is by no means limited to the charging of excessive "interest." Sec. 5 of Ch. 74, Ill.Rev.Stat., provides that:

> No person or corporation shall directly or indirectly accept or receive, in money, goods, discounts or thing in action, or *in any other way*, any greater sum *or greater value* for the loan, forbearance or discount of any money, goods or thing in action, than is expressly authorized by this Act or other laws of this State. * * * (Emphasis added.)

The basic law concerning usury seems relatively uniform throughout the country, and it is clear that under certain circumstances the requirement of insurance in connection with a loan can, in some instances, render the entire transaction usurious. The cases from other jurisdictions are collected in a comprehensive annotation at 91 A.L.R.2d 1344, entitled "Usury: requiring borrower to pay for insurance as condition of loan."

The general rule in other jurisdictions is that " * * * the requirement by a lender, whether an insurance company or otherwise, that the borrower should as a condition for obtaining the loan take out, and pay premiums on, a policy of insurance, and assign it to the lender as additional security for the loan, * * * does not, though making the cost of the loan exceed the highest legal interest, *necessarily* constitute usury where there is no showing that the requirement is intended to be, or is exacted as, *a mere shift or device to cover usury*," 91 A.L.R.2d at 1348. We have added the emphasis in the foregoing quotation to demonstrate how any statement of the general rule—and the quoted statement puts it about as well as any we have seen—simply begs the question. The cases have been decided on their particular facts, and this is the only way they can be decided. In some factual situations, there has been no difficulty in detecting the usury involved, since the insurance requirement has been a mere sham. For instance, there are cases where the borrower has been charged for insurance the lender was supposed to obtain for him, but no insurance was obtained. The "premium" simply went into the lender's pocket, where, commingled with the "interest" he was already getting, it caused all contents of the pocket to be regarded as usurious. There are other cases where the insurance was actually obtained, but the premium charged was patently in excess of the actual cost of the insurance. Here again, the courts have concluded that this kind of transaction is usurious. There is another class of cases which has a more direct bearing on the matter before us. These are the cases which hold that a transaction can be rendered usurious by a requirement that the borrower take out insurance which is excessive in amount or is otherwise unnecessary. In Strickler v. State Auto Finance Co., 249 S.W.2d 307 (Ark.1952), it was held to be usurious to charge the borrower premiums on life and health insurance, in addition to the full legal interest rate, since it appeared that the loan was adequately secured by a mortgage on the borrower's household furniture, which could have been insured for a small premium, and that the borrower did not want the life and health insurance policies. In Moore v. Union Mut. Life Insurance Co., Fed. Case

No. 9777 (CC Neb. 1876), it was held to be usurious under Nebraska law to require an $80,000.00 life insurance policy in connection with a loan of $20,000.00. In Miller v. Life Insurance Co., 24 S.E. 484 (N.C.1896), the court held that it was usurious for the life insurance company lender to require the borrower to take out a life insurance policy with it in the full amount of the loan when the company was already charging the maximum legal rate of interest on the loan and the loan was secured by a trust deed on real estate worth approximately twice the amount of the loan.

From the foregoing cases, and our own reflection on the matter, we deduce a principle with we think is applicable to the present case. In determining whether the insurance requirement is usurious or not, the test is whether the insurance is reasonably necessary to secure the loan. This would not be the only test, of course, but it is the one which is relevant to the instant case. In a case where the lender is not also the insurer, or is not in any way benefiting from the insurance premiums, then the lender would not be "accepting" or "receiving" any additional value by reason of the premiums, and probably could not be charged with usury. However, where the lender requiring the insurance is itself the insurer, or agent for the insurer, there is no doubt that the lender is receiving something of value for the loan—namely, the profit involved in the insurance transaction—in addition to the interest charged. Where the insurance is not reasonably necessary to secure the loan, and the total of interest and the insurance premium exceeds the legal rate of interest, usury is what we have.

The plaintiff cites many cases in support of the general rule that an insurance requirement does not necessarily render a loan transaction usurious. The cases it cites, however, did not involve situations where the borrower was required to take out insurance which was not in fact necessary to secure the loan.

The plaintiff also argues that the insurance premiums were not payments made for the loan, but were, rather, payments made for $25,000.00 worth of life insurance, and that there was, therefore, adequate consideration for the premiums quite aside from the mortgage loan. The memorandum opinion of the trial court is based largely upon his acceptance of this argument. However, the fallacy of this argument is that, once you accept it, there is no limit to its persuasiveness, or the amount of insurance compared to the amount of the loan as found in the *Moore* case, supra. If the premium were a reasonable and customary one for that amount of insurance, then the borrower would be receiving what he pays for in the way of insurance. Would this make the transaction proper? If plaintiff's argument is correct, apparently it would. However, we think that no court would have any difficulty in finding that such a scheme was a transparent device to make life insurance profits in addition to the legal interest rate. We think there is some merit to plaintiff's argument, but it relates to a different point altogether. If the question is not whether the insurance is necessary, but whether the premium is excessive, then it is important to know whether the borrower paid for more insurance than he received. But where the contention is made that the insurance simply was not necessary to secure the loan, no matter what the premium, it is no answer to say that the borrower got the insurance he paid for.

The defendants in the instant case do, in fact, claim that they were paying an excessive premium, primarily because they were required to take out ordinary life insurance rather than the cheaper term insurance. They also complain that certain conditions of the policy were unduly onerous, such as the requirement that cash reserves be applied only to payment of the mortgage indebtedness. We think these matters are debatable at best, and, if defendants' argument were limited to these, we would not be inclined to reverse the determination of the trial court.

Defendants also raise questions as to whether this tie-in between the mortgage loan and the insurance violates the federal anti-trust laws, but we need not determine such question in order to decide this case. Instead, we believe the crux of the case is the relatively clear-cut question of whether this life insurance policy was reasonably necessary to secure the mortgage loan. This was a loan of $25,000.00. It was secured, first of all, by real estate which, according to plaintiff's own appraisal, was worth $38,500.00 at the time of the loan. We do not by any means think that this is dispositive of the question of whether life insurance is proper as additional security. Real estate values have a way of fluctuating; property can depreciate; foreclosure proceedings are expensive and time consuming. The weight of authority is to the effect that, in a proper case, insurance on the life of the borrower can properly be required in addition to the security provided by the real estate, and we are not inclined to depart from that view in this case. However, this does not mean to say that the security afforded by the real estate is to be disregarded, either. It has relevance in connection with the additional fact that Scali already had life insurance policies with another company in the face value of about $58,500.00 which he was prepared to assign to Equitable as additional security for the loan. Try as we may, we cannot see why real estate valued at $38,500.00, together with life insurance policies with a value of at least $58,500.00, for a total value of $97,000.00, should not be sufficient security for a loan of $25,000.00. Put another way, we do not think that in order properly to secure this loan, it was reasonably necessary for Equitable to sell Scali another insurance policy in any amount, let alone one in the amount of $25,000.00. We conclude from the evidence that Equitable was at least as interested in selling life insurance as it was in making this mortgage loan, and that the purpose of requiring Scali to buy the policy was not to provide necessary security for the loan but was, rather, to make a profit on the life insurance in addition to the interest on the loan.

. . .

We believe that the defendants have proved their defense of usury, and that they are entitled to relief. . . . The case is reversed and remanded for further proceedings consistent with these views. . . .

On appeal to the Supreme Court of Illinois, the court reversed. It stated, in part:

It is the province of usury laws to limit the amount which a lender may charge for the use of money, the basic purpose of which is to protect a borrower from the exaction of excessive interest. Obviously, all charges are not interest, and it is only those exacted as additional cost for the use of money that renders usurious an otherwise legal interest rate. To hold that premiums for life insurance required by a lender are a charge for the use of money not only prohibits a practice generally recognized as useful but overlooks completely the value of the coverage to the borrower. In the event of death his loan would be paid from the insurance proceeds and his family or other devisee takes title free and clear of the mortgage indebtedness. On the other hand, if he survived long enough to repay his loan, the face amount of the policy together with accumulations would be paid to his beneficiary.

We think it would be illogical and contrary to sound public policy to hold the requirement of life insurance as a prerequisite to securing a loan to thereby render the loan usurious. Nor does it make any difference whether the requirement is that the insurance be secured from the lender (assuming that the terms are the same as those of other companies) or from other carriers. Since premiums cannot be classified as additional charges by the lender for the use of money when the insurance is procured from outside sources, they likewise are not an added charge for use of money when the insurance is procured from the lender. It is not within the province of the courts to decide whether or how much insurance is reasonably necessary to secure a loan. Circumstances vary so widely that the question would have to be determined on an *ad hoc* basis. This approach taken by the Appellate Court, apparently influenced by the fact of existing insurance, would result in chaos. Application of usury laws by the courts under these circumstances could be construed as a device to regulate loan and insurance practices and should be avoided. Lenders, not the courts, should have the right to determine what constitutes adequate security for their loans under proper regulatory and supervisory bodies.

We are of the opinion that the requirement that a borrower acquire and assign life insurance of the lender up to the amount of his loan as additional security for the loan does not render the interest usurious, absent a showing from an examination of the entire transaction that the insurance requirement was a mere device to collect usurious interest.

There is nothing in this record to justify a holding that the intent and purpose of plaintiff was to collect usurious interest. The premiums and policy terms were identical with policies sold to nonborrowing assureds, and the rates charged were competitive with other companies. The judgment of the Appellate Court, Second District, is therefore reversed, and the decree of the circuit court is affirmed.

232 N.E.2d 712, 715–16 (1967).

Martorano v. Capital Finance Corp.

Court of Appeals of New York, 1942.
289 N.Y. 21, 43 N.E.2d 705.

Lehman, Ch. J.

On December 28, 1940, the plaintiff borrowed from the defendant the sum of $300, giving to the defendant a promissory note for that amount with interest from date "payable monthly, at the rate of 3% per month on any part of the unpaid principal balance of this loan not in excess of $150.00 and 2 1/2% per month on any remainder of the unpaid principal balance of this loan until said loan with interest as aforesaid is fully paid." As security for the loan the plaintiffs executed a wage assignment and chattel mortgage upon their household goods and upon an Oldsmobile motor car.

"In order to obtain said loan, Salvatore Martorano, the plaintiff, was required at the time of the making of said loan and before its completion, to apply for insurance" on the automobile and "said insurance was obtained and the premium paid out of the proceeds of said loan" by means of a check dated December 28, 1940, in the amount of six dollars, which was payable to Salvatore Martorano and delivered to the plaintiff as part of such proceeds at the time the loan was consummated. The plaintiffs claim that by reason of these conceded facts the contract of loan violates section 352 of article IX of the Banking Law, chapter 524 of the Laws of 1941 as thereafter amended. The controversy was submitted to the Appellate Division upon a statement of agreed facts. By a divided court the Appellate Division directed judgment in favor of the plaintiffs.

Section 352 of the Banking Law (Cons. Laws, ch. 2), provides in part:

In addition to the maximum rate or amount of interest, consideration, or charges above specified, no further or other charge or amount whatsoever for any examination, service, brokerage, commission, expense, fee, or bonus or other thing or otherwise shall be directly or indirectly charged, contracted for, or received, except the lawful fees, if any, actually and necessarily paid out by the licensee to any public officer for filing, recording, or releasing in any public office any instrument securing the loan, which fees may be collected when the loan is made or at any time thereafter. If any interest, consideration or charges in excess of those permitted by this act are charged, contracted for, or received the contract of loan shall be void and the licensee shall have no right to collect or receive any principal, interest, or charges whatsoever.

Without insurance a chattel mortgage upon an automobile provides, it is plain, less security for the repayment of a loan than a chattel mortgage upon an automobile which is insured. Certainly mortgagees of real or personal property not infrequently recognize that; and as a condition of granting a loan they stipulate that an insurance policy upon the mortgaged property payable to the mortgagee as interest may appear, must be obtained. The cost of the insurance which the mortgagor must purchase is an expense which the mortgagor must bear in order to meet the conditions upon which the lender is willing to make the loan. The cost of repairing the mortgaged property would also be an expense to the mortgagor if the lender refused to make a loan upon property in need of repair, but neither is an "expense" which is "directly or indirectly charged, contracted for or received" by the lender within the meaning of the statute.

As the prevailing opinion of the Appellate Division (263 App.Div. 79, 80) states: "It seems plain that the intention of the statute was that the interest fixed therein should completely compensate the lender for all charges and expenses of every character attached to the loan with the exception of those specifically set forth in the statute. To hold otherwise would open the door to the imposition of charges and alleged expenses which would add to the burden of the borrower and confer upon the lender compensation in excess of that contemplated by the statute." The test, then, is whether the lender has placed upon the borrower the burden of an additional charge in order to give to the lender "compensation in excess of that contemplated by the statute." That is in accord with the test formulated by the court under an earlier statute in London Realty Co. v. Riordan (207 N.Y. 264, 268).

Here the cost of the insurance gives to the lender the indirect benefit of better security for the repayment of the loan. It can give to the lender no other benefit. Under no circumstances can the lender receive more than the principal amount of the loan and the compensation expressly permitted by the statute. Out of that compensation the lender pays for every service connected with the making of the loan and every other expense to which the lender might be put in connection with the loan, and the lender has not stipulated for reimbursement for such expenses. The statute does not forbid the lender from demanding, as a condition of making the loan, that the borrower shall provide the form of security for repayment of the loan which the lender deems adequate, even though the borrower may be put to some expense in order to furnish the stipulated security. The lender may, of course, not impose such condition as a cover for obtaining greater compensation than the law permits, and here there is no claim that the lender could or did obtain additional compensation in any form. That the borrowers for their own convenience chose to pay the cost of insurance out of the proceeds of the loan, of course, does not render illegal what would otherwise be legal.

. . .

The judgment of the Appellate Division should be reversed and judgment directed in favor of the defendant, without costs.

LEWIS, J. (dissenting).

I cannot agree with the decision about to be made which involves an interpretation of the following portion of section 352 of the Banking Law: [quoted in majority opinion]

The quoted portion of the statute gives us evidence of a studied effort by the Legislature to enact a law which will accomplish the elimination of the "loan shark" evil. To that end there were inserted in section 352 prohibitions which are broad in scope—broad enough, as I believe, to prohibit a licensed lender under article IX of the Banking Law from *requiring,* as a prerequisite to a loan, that the borrower shall furnish prepaid fire and theft insurance covering the mortgaged chattel. It may well be that as a matter of practical dealing between business men, such a requirement is a matter of common practice and certainly is good judgment. But we are concerned here with limitations upon those rights given to a licensed lender by a statute designed to protect the borrowers of small sums against excessive charges in connection with that method of financing—charges which have been the subject of grave abuse. If the Legislature had intended to permit the practice which is to be approved by a majority of the court, it would have enacted a law which would specifically permit such a practice, as has been done in the States of California, Florida, Colorado and Oregon.

In London Realty Co. v. Riordan (207 N.Y. 264), this court was called upon to determine whether the exaction from a borrower of a payment of ten dollars to a licensed lender's attorney, for services in examining the title to mortgaged property, had the effect of making the loan void. That decision was in 1913 when the statutory prohibitions were not as broad in scope as they are today. In the course of the opinion Chief Judge Cullen stated for the court: (p. 268) "I think that the case fell directly within the terms of the statute, not necessarily as a device for excessive interest, *but as a charge which, under the statute, the lender is forbidden to exact either in its own favor or in favor of any one else.*" At that time the court made clear its intention not to extend the charges which a licensed lender might require of the borrower as a condition of the loan.

In the present case I attach importance to that paragraph of the agreed statement of facts which states—"That *in order to obtain said loan * * ** the plaintiff was *required* at the time of the making of said loan and *before its completion*, to apply for insurance. * * * "(Emphasis mine.) The appellant-lender asserts that the requirement which is made, that insurance upon the mortgaged chattel be furnished by the borrowers, was merely preliminary to the loan. We are told that there was no contractual relationship with respect to insurance between the borrowers and lender. I do not so interpret the agreed facts. The requirement by the lender that the borrowers should furnish fire and theft insurance upon the chattel with premium prepaid—which insurance we may assume would have to be kept in force until the loan is paid—cannot be said to be merely a preliminary requirement but is a part of the contract of loan. The agreed facts inform us that " * * * the plaintiff was *required* at the time of the making of said loan and before its completion, to apply for insurance on said 1936 Oldsmobile and that said insurance was obtained and the premium paid out of the proceeds of said loan * * * ." Furthermore, I think it significant that the fire and theft insurance coverage which the borrowers furnished was a participation in a master policy issued by an insurance company to the lender with loss, if any, payable to the lender and borrowers as their interests may appear.

I am not left in doubt that by such an arrangement—*"required"* of the borrowers as a prerequisite to the loan—the lender receives a benefit at the expense of the borrowers who must pay a premium for a stated term before the "completion" of the loan. That benefit is something of value received by the lender in connection with the loan. Indeed, it is the view of a majority of the court, as expressed by the opinion herein, that "Here, the cost of the insurance gives to the lender the indirect benefit of better security for the repayment of the loan." I believe that such benefit, concededly received by the lender, is—within the language of section 352— "in addition to the maximum rate or amount of interest, consideration, or charges" which the statute permits. . . .

I believe the rule of London Realty Co. v. Riordan (supra) is decisive in the case at bar. There, as we have seen, the lender required the borrower to pay for the services of attorneys to examine the title of the mortgaged property; and there the lender received no part of the attorneys' fees. So, in the case before us, the lender required the borrower to pay for fire and theft insurance upon the mortgaged chattel and received no part of the premium. In the *Riordan* case the benefit to the lender was assurance of good title; in the present case the benefit to the lender is assurance against loss of the chattel by fire or theft.

My conclusion is that the expense item of six dollars which was *"required"* of the borrowers by the lender "at the time of making of said loan and before its completion" is, in the circumstances disclosed by the agreed facts, a substantial item. I do not regard it in this instance as a device to cover an excessive interest charge. However, as a benefit to the lender incidental to the loan, I believe the requirement of prepaid insurance upon the mortgaged chattel bears such a reasonable relation to the amount charged by the lender for the loan as to violate the prohibitions contained in section 352 of the Banking Law.

Accordingly, I dissent and vote for affirmance.

LOUGHRAN, FINCH and RIPPEY, JJ., concur with LEHMAN, CH. J.; LEWIS, J., dissents in opinion in which CONWAY and DESMOND JJ., concur.

Judgment accordingly.

QUESTIONS AND NOTES

1. As exemplified by *Scali* and *Martorano*, it is common in consumer credit transactions for the creditor to require or recommend the purchase of insurance. In *Scali* the insurance was ordinary life insurance, available to consumers entirely independently of a credit transaction. It is much more common for the creditor to sell "credit insurance," so named because it is sold only as an incident to the extension of credit.

There are three principal kinds of credit insurance: life, health and accident, and casualty. The first two protect against risks to the borrower's body; the third protects against risks to the property that serves as collateral for the extension of credit. As to credit life insurance and credit health and accident insurance, there are two kinds of policies. One is a master policy for group insurance. It is issued to the creditor and covers the life and/or health of the persons who enter credit contracts with the creditor. The other kind is an individual policy issued to each debtor. Under each kind of policy, the consumer pays a premium.

Under the master policy approach, if the actual loss experience of the creditor is less than the loss experience on which the insurance rates are set, the creditor receives a refund from the insurance company. If the creditor does not pass on to the consumer a pro rata share of this refund, does the creditor violate the usury statute?

Under the individual policy approach, the creditor acts as an agent for the insurance company and receives a commission in connection with the sale of each policy to a consumer. Is this commission relevant to determining whether there is a violation of the usury statute?

Regulation of credit insurance is the subject of Chapter 10 infra.

2. The cases in this chapter preceding *Martorano* all arose under usury statutes, but *Martorano* arose under a small loan act. The enactment of small loan acts in the 1920s and 1930s was a response to the unavailability of loans to consumers at the rates permitted by the usury statutes. It represented recognition that if consumer loans were to be available, lenders needed permission to charge more than the six-to-eight percent permitted by the usury statutes. Hence the statutes raised the limits for small loan companies; but they did not abolish the limits altogether. And to make sure there was no misunderstanding about that, they typically contained language like that of the New York statute quoted in Martorano (page 419 supra): "In addition to the maximum rate . . . no further or other charge or amount whatsoever for any . . . expense, fee, . . . or other thing or otherwise shall be directly or indirectly charged, contracted for, or received, except [official filing fees]."

Is *Martorano* properly decided under this statute? Is it distinguishable from London Realty Co. v. Riordan, on which the dissent relies?

3. The risk of nonpayment is not the same for all consumers. If the lender cannot lawfully charge a rate of interest that provides sufficient compensation for the risk incident to a loan to a particular consumer, the lender is likely to refuse to make the loan. The following hypothetical, however, suggests an alternative:

Consumer wants to buy a camper from *Seller* for $14,000. To finance this, she seeks a $10,000 loan from *Bank*. *Bank* agrees to loan $10,000 at 15%, the maximum permitted by the applicable statute, if *Consumer's* father will guarantee repayment. Has *Bank* violated the statute?

Many high-risk consumers are not able to turn to their fathers for assistance. But they may be able to turn to a loan broker. The loan broker serves two functions. First, the broker locates a lender who might be willing to loan money to the consumer. In this respect the broker is similar to a real estate agent or an employment agency. Secondly, the loan broker guarantees the consumer's performance, i.e. guarantees that the consumer will repay the loan. In this respect the broker is like the father in the problem above. With the additional inducement of the broker's guarantee, the lender may be willing to make the loan to the consumer. As you might expect, the loan broker's motivation is not love or altruism. Rather, the broker charges the consumer a fee for this service.

4. Problem. *Consumer* wants to borrow $500. He goes to *Broker,* who arranges a loan by *Lender* to *Consumer.* Under the usury statute, the maximum charge for this loan is $45. *Consumer* agrees to pay *Lender* $545 and to pay *Broker* $35 as a brokerage fee. Is there a violation of the usury statute? If so, by whom?

Would it make any difference if instead of agreeing to pay $545 to *Lender* and $35 to *Broker, Consumer* agrees to pay $580 to *Broker,* who in turn agrees to forward the $545 to *Lender*?

Consider O'Connor v. Lamb, 593 S.W.2d 385 (Tex.Civ.App.1979), in which O'Connor sought Lamb's assistance in obtaining a loan.

> The principal amount of the loan Lamb made to O'Connor was $2,500. In order to make the loan, Lamb borrowed the $2,500 from his own bank on his own credit. Lamb then delivered the $2,500 in cash to O'Connor. In exchange, Lamb required O'Connor to execute a promissory note in the amount of $3,000, payable in 90 days. At the expiration of 90 days, O'Connor was unable to pay and Lamb brought suit on the note for $3,000. O'Connor answered and filed a counterclaim alleging that the $500 difference between the amount of the loan and the amount of the note constituted "interest". . . . The trial court rendered judgment for Lamb on the note for $3,000 plus attorney's fees and ordered that O'Connor take nothing on her counterclaim. It is from this judgment that O'Connor has appealed.

> Lamb contends that the judgment is correct because he rendered "services" in addition to making the loan, i.e., he had earlier cashed a check for O'Connor after banking hours and, in this loan transaction, he had borrowed the money from a bank and had delivered the loan proceeds to O'Connor's office. The "service" rendered by Lamb in cashing the check antedated the loan transaction. Furthermore, there is no testimony in the record of an agreement to pay for such service at the time rendered, which later could be deemed to justify all or any part of the $500 Lamb added to the loan transaction. The "service" rendered by Lamb borrowing the money from a bank and in the delivery of the loan proceeds to O'Connor's offices was a part of the loan transaction itself as Lamb testified the money was exchanged for O'Connor's note at that time. Lamb did not testify that there was any knowledge of or an agreement by O'Connor to pay for this asserted service.

> Neither can the $500 charge be justified as a fee for negotiating a loan with the bank. In determining whether a loan transaction is usurious, it is substance, rather than form, that is investigated. An agent or a broker may lawfully charge a commission or a fee for his

services in negotiating a loan with a third party, and the fee or commission will not be taken into consideration in determining whether or not the loan was usurious. A fee or commission, however, may not be charged by a party who merely lends his own money. Consequently, if Lamb acted as a broker or agent in the sense that he negotiated a loan between O'Connor and the bank, then his "fee" for obtaining the loan, i.e., the $500, is not interest but rather a valid charge for services rendered. If, on the other hand, Lamb is himself the lender, then the $500 differential is compensation for the use, forbearance or detention of money and does constitute interest.

The undisputed facts of this case show that Lamb was the lender rather than a broker. Lamb did not endorse a loan from the bank to O'Connor, nor did he act as a surety or guarantor on a bank loan. Rather, the loan was made directly from Lamb to O'Connor. No third party was involved. Borrowing money on his own credit in order to obtain the cash to make a loan to O'Connor did not authorize Lamb to charge a fee or commission. Consequently, the $500 included in the note in excess of the money actually advanced must be considered interest.

593 S.W.2d at 386–87.

In what way(s) is this transaction different from the preceding hypotheticals? The court states that "it is substance, rather than form, that is investigated." The maximum permissible charge for the loan in *O'Connor* was $62.50. If the bank had loaned $2,500 directly to O'Connor and Lamb had guaranteed payment, it evidently would have been permissible for the bank to charge O'Connor $62.50 and for Lamb to charge O'Connor $437.50. If so, is the court looking at substance or at form?

5. Problem. *Twist* is a semi-professional hockey player who wants to borrow $3,000. He is an avid motorcyclist, and his contract with *Team* provides that if he is injured off the ice and cannot play, then he does not get paid. *Lender* knows that *Twist* makes $2,000 per week and is willing to loan money in reliance on these wages. Because of the provision in the employment contract, however, *Lender* will make the loan only if *Twist* agrees not to ride a motorcycle so long as the loan remains unpaid. If *Lender* charges the maximum amount permitted by the usury statute plus this promise not to ride a motorcycle, is the loan usurious?

6. In recent years another kind of loan broker has assumed a significant position in the consumer credit marketplace. Many consumers now use the services of brokers to obtain home mortgages. Indeed, in recent years brokers have originated more than half of all mortgage loans. These mortgage brokers typically do not guarantee the performance of the consumer; rather, their role is limited to serving as an intermediary between the consumer and the source of funds for the loan. One of the primary benefits to the lender is that it may operate on a nationwide basis without incurring the expense and aggravation of having to maintain an office in each community in which it may want to make loans. By attracting more lenders to the home mortgage market, this development has had the effect of increasing the quantity of funds available for mortgage loans.

Further increasing the quantity of funds is the phenomenon of securitization. Lenders (or their intermediaries) bundle a large quantity of loans into a package and sell that package to an underwriter that issues securities to investors, who pay for the securities in the expectation that they will receive dividends as consumers repay their loans. Although the securitization process has vastly increased the money available for home mortgage loans, it has played a central role in the financial crisis that began in 2007. Much of that is beyond the scope of this book, but Chapter 14 considers the impact on the consumer of the fact that his or her loan has been transferred one or more times and ultimately is held by a trustee for the investors whose funds made the loan available. For a description of the securitization process, see Peterson, Predatory Structured Finance, 28 Cardozo L. Rev. 2185, 2208–13 (2007).

Mortgage brokers play a critical role in the securitization process. As the only person in communication with the consumer, the mortgage broker determines what loan products will come to the consumer's attention. Some brokers present a wide range of options, and some present a single offer. To be sure, the loans for which a consumer qualifies depend in large part on the consumer's creditworthiness. But the range of offers presented by the broker also depends on the income, social, and—notwithstanding the Equal Credit Opportunity Act—racial and ethnic class of the consumer. In addition, it depends on the incentives of the mortgage broker. If the mortgage broker receives more compensation for generating a sub-prime (i.e. high-interest) loan than for a prime loan, there is a temptation to encourage consumers to enter sub-prime loan contracts even though they qualify for loans at rates available to prime borrowers. Many brokers have given in to this temptation. Thus in recent years mortgage brokers have formed loan contracts that have one or more of the following characteristics:

- the consumer is not required to provide proof of his or her income, called no-doc (for no-documentation) loans, also called "liar's loans"

- the consumer is not required to make any down payment (compared to the traditional requirement of 20% or the more recent requirement of 10%)

- adjustable-rate loans, known as adjustable-rate mortgages (ARMs), in which the interest rate is set very low for two or three years, then quickly increases to a level much higher than the rate for a 30–year fixed-rate loan

- loans to consumers whom the mortgage broker knows can afford to make the initial monthly payments but cannot afford to pay the taxes and insurance on the house, and cannot afford to make the monthly payments that will be due in two-to-three years when an ARM resets to a higher interest rate and a higher monthly payment

Many consumers who enter loan transactions with these characteristics are not fully aware of other loans that might be available to them because their mortgage broker has presented them with a single opportunity. Many of these consumers wind up defaulting on their loans and losing their homes. Can you think of a way to deal with this problem? An outright ban on loans with the features listed above may not be the answer, because most of the features may be appropriate under certain circumstances. For example, an ARM may be perfectly appropriate for a consumer who has a job in which the compensation rises rapidly on a consistently predictable basis or a consumer who knows he or she will be moving out of town in two-to-three years and prepaying the loan at that time. Can you think of any other ways to deal with the problem?

7. Mortgage brokers establish business relationships with one or more remote lenders. The lender distributes (typically at least once a day) to one or more mortgage brokers a term sheet describing the terms on which it will make loans to consumers, including the creditworthiness standards that the consumer must meet. When a consumer contacts a broker, the broker gathers information about the consumer, examines the consumer's creditworthiness, and selects one of its lenders as the source for that particular loan. The broker submits the completed application to the lender for approval and, if the lender approves, prepares the loan documents for the consumer to sign. The loan documents may show the remote lender as the lender in the transaction, but more commonly they show the broker as the lender. The broker, however, does not actually supply the funds. Rather, the funds come from the remote party, and the arrangement calls for the broker immediately to assign the loan (i.e. the right to receive payments) to that party. In the mortgage loan industry, this is known as a table-funded loan. Since the documents show the broker as the lender, if the broker does not accurately describe the process, the consumer may not know that the real lender is the remote party.

For its services the broker typically charges the consumer a fee, perhaps a flat dollar amount but more often stated as a percentage of the amount of the loan. Should this fee be viewed as interest?

In addition, the broker may receive compensation from the lender. Why, after all, should the broker place its business with Lender A rather than Lender B? To the extent the broker performs services for the lender, compensation is appropriate and permitted. To the extent the payment is a pure referral fee (or, pejoratively, a kickback), it is not. A federal statute, the Real Estate Settlement Procedures Act (RESPA) explicitly deals with this matter. Although it is predominantly a disclosure statute, RESPA also provides in section 8 (12 U.S.C. § 2607):

> (a) No person shall give and no person shall accept any fee, kickback, or thing of value pursuant to any agreement or understanding, oral or otherwise, that business incident to or a part of a real estate settlement service involving a federally related mortgage loan shall be referred to any person.

(b) No person shall give and no person shall accept any portion, split, or percentage of any charge made or received for the rendering of a real estate settlement service in connection with a transaction involving a federally related mortgage loan other than for services actually performed.

(c) Nothing in this section shall be construed as prohibiting

(1) . . .

(2) the payment to any person of a bona fide salary or compensation or other payment for goods or facilities actually furnished or for services actually performed, . . .

(d)(1) Any person or persons who violate the provisions of this section shall be fined not more than $10,000 or imprisoned for not more than one year, or both.

(2) Any person or persons who violate the prohibitions or limitations of this section shall be jointly and severally liable to the person or persons charged for the settlement service involved in the violation in an amount equal to three times the amount of any charge paid for such settlement service.

. . .

The Department of Housing and Urban Development (HUD) has elaborated that to fall with the protection of subsection (c), the amount paid must bear a "reasonable relationship to the market value of the goods or services provided." Regulation X, 24 C.F.R. § 3500.14(g)(2). This law, as it applies to lenders and brokers, is designed to limit the ability of a lender to pay brokers for placing their mortgage business with the lender. Hence, the lender cannot pay a referral fee; and although the lender may pay the broker for its services in completing the paperwork and the credit investigation, it may not pay an amount greatly in excess of the reasonable market value of those services. This much is clear.

But there is more. The term sheet describing the terms on which the lender is willing to make loans states the minimum interest rate that the lender will accept. It does not prohibit the broker from forming a loan contract with the consumer at a higher rate, which of course will produce increased revenues. These increased revenues are known as "yield spread premium." The arrangement between the broker and the lender may call for the lender to pay the broker all of the yield spread premium, or it may call for them to split the premium. Does payment of all or part of the yield spread premium violate RESPA?

8. In a case challenging yield spread premium as a violation of RESPA, a District Court wrote:

. . . Inland Mortgage Corporation is a mortgage lender and servicer based in Indianapolis, Indiana. Premiere Mortgage Company is a Birmingham, Alabama mortgage broker. By an agreement dated March 15, 1994, Premiere and Inland agreed that, from time to time, Inland would purchase loans originated by Premiere. Premiere, however, would not furnish the capital for these loans; instead, Premiere would "register" loans with Inland, and Inland would supply the loan proceeds to Premiere. After the loan was consummated, Premiere would then be obligated to deliver the loan "package" to Inland, including the promissory note, mortgage, evidence of insurance, and assignments of all rights Premiere held. The contract further provided that Inland would compensate Premiere for these loan purchases in accordance with Inland's "Pricing Policy and Procedures." Inland's "Pricing Policy and Procedures" recited that Inland would distribute "established daily prices" each day at 11:00 a.m. Eastern time, and that it would continue to honor those prices until 9:30 a.m. the following day.

In keeping with its contracts with Premiere and other mortgage brokers, Inland released daily price sheets showing the "prices" it was willing to pay for various loans. The "price" was expressed as a percentage of the loan amount, and was influenced by factors such as the type of loan, the "lock-in" period, and the interest rate on the loan. For a loan of "par value," Inland paid nothing to the broker; for "below par" loans, Inland required the broker to pay "discount points" to Inland; and for "above par" loans, Inland paid the broker a "yield spread premium." The undisputed evidence in the record indicates that Inland's prices were set by market forces, such as the cost of capital, competitors' prices, and other economic factors.

The Culpeppers contacted Premiere on October 30, 1995, to inquire about the possibility of obtaining a mortgage loan through Premiere. The Culpeppers went through the loan application process, and later found a home to purchase.* On December 7, 1995, the Culpeppers chose to "lock in" the 7.5% interest rate that Premiere was offering at that time.[4] On that same day, Premiere "registered" the Culpeppers' loan with Inland. The loan closed on December 15, 1995, and Premiere acted as the lender during closing. Shortly after the loan closing, Premiere, in accordance with its contract with Inland, executed assignments of the Culpeppers' note and mortgage to Inland.

The HUD-1 statement given to the Culpeppers at the closing showed that the Culpeppers paid Premiere a 1% origination fee ($760.50) for Premiere's services. In addition, Premiere received a $1263.61 "yield spread premium" from Inland, which was also disclosed on the HUD-1 form. The amount of the yield spread premium was calculated as follows: consulting Inland's price sheet for December 7, 1995 (the Culpeppers' "lock-in" date), under the category "Government Products–30 year fixed," the Culpeppers' loan was a 7.5% loan with a 15–day "lock-in" period, yielding a figure of −1.375. An additional .25 was subtracted, due to the fact that the amount of the

---

* In connection with this purchase, they needed to borrow $76,050.—Ed.

4. The Blankensopp Affidavit establishes as undisputed fact that the 7.5% rate obtained by the Culpeppers was a competitive market rate for a loan like the Culpeppers' in the Birmingham area market on December 7, 1995.

Culpeppers' loan exceeded $50,000. Adding these figures yielded
– 1.625, which was the percentage yield spread premium Inland paid to
Premiere.[5]

. . .

Here, the Culpeppers' claim is that the yield spread premium paid
by Inland to Premiere was a "referral fee" proscribed by § 2607(a). In
other words, the Culpeppers argue that Inland paid Premiere the yield
spread premium in exchange for Premiere "referring" the Culpeppers'
loan to Inland, so that Inland could provide the "settlement service" of
funding the loan.

Inland argues, by contrast, that the yield spread premium was
simply the market-driven payment to Premiere for an asset—the loan
itself. Inland relies on an exception to § 2607(a), which reads as
follows:

> Nothing in this section shall be construed as prohibiting . . . (2)
> the payment to any person of a bona fide salary or compensation
> or other payment for goods or facilities actually furnished or for
> services actually performed.

12 U.S.C. § 2607(c). Inland characterizes the yield spread premium as
"payment for goods," that is, the purchase price of the Culpeppers'
loan.

Culpepper v. Inland Mortgage Corp., 953 F.Supp. 367 (N.D.Ala.1997).

The District Court held that payment of a yield spread premium does
not violate RESPA. The Eleventh Circuit reversed and remanded. Culpepper v. Inland Mortgage Corp., 132 F.3d 692 (11th Cir.1998).

9. In 1999, in response to the Eleventh Circuit's decision in Culpepper,
HUD issued a policy statement interpreting section 8. RESPA Statement of
Policy 1999–1, 64 Fed.Reg. 10080 (Mar. 1, 1999). It indicated disapproval of
the decision and articulated a two-part test for determining whether a
lender's payment to a mortgage broker is legal:

1) were services actually performed for the compensation paid?

2) were the payments reasonably related to the value of those services?

If the answer to either question is, no, then the payment violates section 8.

In 2001 the *Culpepper* case was back before the Eleventh Circuit.
Applying the two-part test of the Policy Statement, the court held that for
the first test to be satisfied, the compensation must have been paid in
exchange for the services performed, and not (even partially) in exchange
for a referral. The court emphasized that the amount of the yield spread
premium depended entirely on the interest rate of the loan, regardless of
the nature or quantity of services the broker provided the lender. Therefore, a jury could find that the payment was not entirely for the broker's

---

5. The Culpeppers' loan amount was
$77,761.00. Multiplying that figure by 1.625%
produced a yield spread premium of
$1,263.61.

services but was at least in part a referral fee. Culpepper v. Irwin Mortgage Corp., 253 F.3d 1324 (11th Cir.2001).

This prompted HUD to issue a clarification of its 1999 Policy Statement. RESPA Statement of Policy 2001–1, 66 Fed. Reg. 53052 (Oct. 18, 2001). Some excerpts:

> One of the primary barriers to homeownership and homeowners' ability to refinance and lower their housing costs is the up front cash needed to obtain a mortgage. The closing costs and origination fees associated with a mortgage loan are a significant component of these up front cash requirements. Borrowers may choose to pay these fees out of pocket, or to pay the origination fees, and possibly all the closing fees, by financing them; i.e., adding the amount of such fees to the principal balance of their mortgage loan. The latter approach, however, is not available to those whose loan-to-value ratio has already reached the maximum permitted by the lender. For those without the available cash, who are at the maximum loan-to-value ratio, or who simply choose to do so, there is a third option. This third option is a yield spread premium.

> Yield spread premiums permit homebuyers to pay some or all of the up front settlement costs over the life of the mortgage through a higher interest rate. Because the mortgage carries a higher interest rate, the lender is able to sell it to an investor at a higher price. In turn, the lender pays the broker an amount reflective of this price difference. The payment allows the broker to recoup the up front costs incurred on the borrower's behalf in originating the loan. Payments from lenders to brokers based on the rates of borrowers' loans are characterized as "indirect" fees and are referred to as yield spread premiums.[1]

> A yield spread premium is calculated based upon the difference between the interest rate at which the broker originates the loan and the par, or market, rate offered by a lender. The Department believes, and industry and consumers agree, that a yield spread premium can be a useful means to pay some or all of a borrower's settlement costs. In these cases, lender payments reduce the up front cash requirements to borrowers. In some cases, borrowers are able to obtain loans without paying any up front cash for the services required in connection with the origination of the loan. Instead, the fees for these services are financed through a higher interest rate on the loan. The yield spread premium thus can be a legitimate tool to assist the borrower. The availability of this option fosters homeownership.

> .   .   .

> HUD also recognizes, however, that in some cases less scrupulous brokers and lenders take advantage of the complexity of the settlement

---

1. Indirect fees from lenders are also known as "back funded payments," "overag- es," or "servicing release premiums."

transaction and use yield spread premiums as a way to enhance the profitability of mortgage transactions without offering the borrower lower up front fees. In these cases, yield spread premiums serve to increase the borrower's interest rate and the broker's overall compensation, without lowering up front cash requirements for the borrower. . . .

. . . In determining whether a payment from a lender to a mortgage broker is permissible under Section 8 of RESPA, the first question is whether goods or facilities were actually furnished or services were actually performed for the compensation paid. The fact that goods or facilities have been actually furnished or that services have been actually performed by the mortgage broker does not by itself make the payment legal. The second question is whether the payments are reasonably related to the value of the goods or facilities that were actually furnished or services that were actually performed.

In applying this test, HUD believes that total compensation should be scrutinized to assure that it is reasonably related to goods, facilities, or services furnished or performed to determine whether it is legal under RESPA. Total compensation to a broker includes direct origination and other fees paid by the borrower, indirect fees, including those that are derived from the interest rate paid by the borrower, or a combination of some or all. The Department considers that higher interest rates alone cannot justify higher total fees to mortgage brokers. All fees will be scrutinized as part of total compensation to determine that total compensation is reasonably related to the goods or facilities actually furnished or services actually performed. HUD believes that total compensation should be carefully considered in relation to price structures and practices in similar transactions and in similar markets.

. . .

Under the first part of HUD's test, the total compensation to a mortgage broker, of which a yield spread premium may be a component or the entire amount, must be for goods or facilities provided or services performed. HUD's position is that in order to discern whether a yield spread premium was for goods, facilities or services under the first part of the HUD test, it is necessary to look at each transaction individually, including examining all of the goods or facilities provided or services performed by the broker in the transaction, whether the goods, facilities or services are paid for by the borrower, the lender, or partly by both.

It is HUD's position that neither Section 8(a) of RESPA nor the 1999 Statement of Policy supports the conclusion that a yield spread premium can be presumed to be a referral fee based solely upon the fact that the lender pays the broker a yield spread premium that is based upon a rate sheet, or because the lender does not have specific knowledge of what services the broker has performed. HUD considers the latter situation to be rare. The common industry practice is that lenders follow underwriting standards that demand a review of originations and that therefore lenders typically know that brokers have performed the services required to meet those standards.

Yield spread premiums are by definition derived from the interest rate. HUD believes that a rate sheet is merely a mechanism for displaying the yield spread premium, and does not indicate whether a particular yield spread premium is a payment for goods and facilities actually furnished or services actually performed under the HUD test. Whether or not a yield spread premium is legal or illegal cannot be determined by the use of a rate sheet, but by how HUD's test applies to the transaction involved.

The second part of HUD's test requires that total compensation to the mortgage broker be reasonably related to the total set of goods or facilities actually furnished or services performed.

The 1999 Statement of Policy said in part:

The Department considers that higher interest rates alone cannot justify higher total fees to mortgage brokers. All fees will be scrutinized as part of total compensation to determine that total compensation is reasonably related to the goods or facilities actually furnished or services actually performed.

Accordingly, the Department believes that the second part of the test is applied by determining whether a mortgage broker's total compensation is reasonable. Total compensation includes fees paid by a borrower and any yield spread premium paid by a lender, not simply the yield spread premium alone. Yield spread premiums serve to allow the borrower a lower up front cash payment in return for a higher interest rate, while allowing the broker to recoup the total costs of originating the loan. Total compensation to the broker must be reasonably related to the total value of goods or facilities provided or services performed by the broker. Simply delivering a loan with a higher interest rate is not a compensable service. . . .

The 1999 Statement of Policy also stated:

The level of services mortgage brokers provide in particular transactions depends on the level of difficulty involved in qualifying applicants for particular loan programs. For example, applicants have differences in credit ratings, employment status, levels of debt, or experience that will translate into various degrees of effort required for processing a loan. Also, the mortgage broker may be required to perform various levels of services under different servicing or processing arrangements with wholesale lenders.

In evaluating mortgage broker fees for enforcement purposes, HUD will consider these factors as relevant in assessing the reasonableness of mortgage broker compensation, as well as comparing total compensation for loans of similar size and similar characteristics within similar geographic markets.

66 Fed. Reg. at 53053–56.

10.   In *Culpepper* the consumers needed to borrow $76,050. With fees, they wound up borrowing $77,761. The yield spread premium was calculated as a percentage (1.625%) of this amount. The HUD Policy Statement asserts that the yield spread premium is a kickback only if it (coupled with anything the borrower has paid directly to the broker) exceeds the reasonable compensation for all the services provided by the broker. In *Culpepper* the broker received $2,024.11 ($760.50 from the Culpeppers and $1,263.61 from the lender). Plaintiffs failed to show that this sum was not reasonably related to the services they received, and they lost the litigation. Culpepper v. Irwin Mortgage Corp., 491 F.3d 1260 (11th Cir.2007) (yes, this litigation, which commenced in 1996, was not finally resolved until 2007). If the Culpeppers had borrowed $10,000 more than they actually did, the yield spread premium would have been $162.50 higher, but the broker would not have provided any more services that it did in the actual case. Is this relevant to the analysis articulated in HUD's Policy Statement?

The rationale for yield spread premium is the desire of the borrower to roll the closing costs into the cost of the loan, in the form of a higher interest rate. This suggests that if the closing costs are $1,000, the broker might select the interest rate that enables the lender to pay it $1,000. But what if the broker selects a higher rate because that higher rate is the market rate, or because the broker knows that the borrower (who lacks sophistication or who trusts the broker to get the lowest rate) will accept a higher rate: to establish a violation of RESPA, what should the borrower have to prove?

11.   In Schuetz v. Banc One Mortgage Corp., 292 F.3d 1004, 1014–16 (9th Cir.2002), the court rejected a borrower's claim that a yield spread premium violated section 8. But consider the views of the judge who dissented from the court's holding:

> The problem with treating the "yield spread premium" as payment for services rendered to the borrower, to be evaluated for reasonableness in each individual case, is that the relationship between the amount of the premium and the value of the services is entirely fortuitous. Because the yield spread premium is calculated purely by the extent to which the borrower's interest rate is above par, sometimes it will be what the broker's services are worth, but only by chance. It's like a stopped clock that shows the right time twice a day, but the clock doesn't measure the time, and the yield spread premium doesn't measure the value of services. Indeed, the higher the interest rate the broker's client pays, the bigger the yield spread premium the broker gets. This makes the premium tend to be inversely proportional to the value of the services to the borrower. Whether the amount approximates the value of services for Schuetz or not, she should have been allowed to go forward with her class action, because it is precisely the fortuitousness that makes the yield spread premium violate RESPA.

RESPA prohibits "kickbacks" by lenders to mortgage brokers. I see the phrase "yield spread premium" as an obfuscatory way of avoiding calling a kickback a kickback. A kickback is "a usually secret rebate of part of a purchase price . . . to the one who directed or influenced the purchaser to buy from such seller." It is a payment by a third party to an agent to act on behalf of the third party rather than the principal. The home buyer hires a mortgage broker to shop for a good loan for her, but the broker takes $500 from a lender to steer the buyer to the lender, if the buyer can be persuaded to sign a loan with interest above par. This is how the "yield spread premium" is calculated. The measure has nothing to do with how much work the broker does. Instead, it is based on one thing: how far above par the interest rate is.

Conceivably, the yield spread premium could be good policy to promote home ownership, as HUD and the majority suggest. The theory would be that some home buyers might not be able to get their loans if they have to pay the broker's reasonable fee up front for doing all the work of putting them together with a lender, and the "yield spread premium" lets them roll the fee into the financing and pay it over the term of their mortgage, perhaps twenty or thirty years. But Congress is no more bound by the "law and economics" school than by "Mr. Herbert Spencer's Social Statics."

There are several problems with vindicating the yield spread premium on this theory that the yield spread premium is a means of, in practical economic effect, financing closing costs. One is that Congress didn't enact it. It prohibited kick-backs whether they work out as good economics or not. The second is that the record doesn't support it. No evidence has been shown to us that the yield spread premium offsets foregone closing costs. Schuetz was charged closing costs anyway, and it was not demonstrated that they should have been higher to compensate the broker, or that the yield spread premium capitalized the value of any inadequacy of the closing costs she paid compared to the value of the broker's services.

Third, Congress may have been right to reject kickbacks as a matter of economics. The yield spread premium doesn't necessarily roll over the amount of the broker's reasonable fee into the loan and capitalize that portion of the fee as the yield spread premium fee paid by the lender to the broker. The HUD test merely requires that the resulting closing costs be "reasonably related to the value of the goods or facilities that were actually furnished or services that were actually performed," but this does not require that the yield spread premium be subtracted from the closing costs, so the borrower may not actually benefit from the increase in her interest rate. Few but the most alert and aggressive borrowers are likely to spot the obscure "yield spread premium" charge on their closing statement, obtain and comprehend an accurate and coherent explanation from the broker's employee of what it means, and leave in a huff if they don't want to pay the extra interest. Both its obscurity of meaning and its relative size, perhaps a few hundred dollars, of closing costs in the thousands, on a five or six figure loan, may give Congress a reason to protect buyers from it.

It is tempting to defer to HUD anyway because of its expertise, but I do not think we can properly defer to HUD's interpretation. First, the yield spread premium is a kickback, and kickbacks are expressly prohibited by the statute, which says that "[n]o person shall give and no person shall accept any . . . kickback." That express language cannot be interpreted away. RESPA does create several exceptions to its expansive reach, including the most arguably applicable: an exception for "(1) the payment of a fee . . . (c) by a lender to its duly appointed agent for services actually performed in the making of a loan." As discussed above, the yield spread premium has no relation to the services actually performed by the mortgage broker. The yield spread premium is not within RESPA's explicit exceptions.

12.   In any given case would it be relevant to know whether the broker offered the consumer a choice of paying a larger broker's fee and a lower interest rate?

13.   Mortgage brokers may perform valuable services for lenders. Many are reputable companies, in the business for the long haul, and desire to maintain a good reputation with lenders, and with borrowers. They handle the application process, including a review of the consumer's financial situation, and search for a lender that will extend credit to a consumer in that situation. There are certain incentives, however, that tend to induce the broker to disregard the interests of the consumer (and the lender). Depending on the terms of the loan, it is very unlikely the consumer will default during the first two or three years of the loan. Since the broker receives its full compensation at the time of closing, the broker's incentives to close as many loans as possible may exceed its incentives to help the lender maintain sound underwriting practices and to serve the best interests of the borrower. Thus there are numerous instances of a broker's falsifying the borrower's income, failing to disclose to the borrower that the interest rate will reset in a very short time to a level that exceeds the borrower's ability to pay, or other practices that mislead the lender or the consumer. Several states have enacted legislation addressing the practices of mortgage brokers, and many observers have called for federal regulation.

14.   The phenomenon of yield spread premiums, also known as "overages" and "upcharges," exists in the auto financing industry, too. E.g., *Carper*, page 394 supra; Perino v. Mercury Finance, 912 F.Supp. 313 (N.D.Ill.1995); Bramlett v. Adamson Ford, page 42 supra. RESPA does not apply to these transactions, so neither the disclosure requirement nor the prohibition on kickbacks applies. Does any other disclosure requirement apply? What other laws, if any, bear on the permissibility of overages in motor vehicle financing?

(4) PREPAYMENT AND REFINANCING

Occasionally, the consumer may be in a position to pay off a loan or an installment sales contract before its scheduled due date. This may occur because of a windfall, an accumulation of savings, or an opportunity to replace the obligation with a loan at a lower rate of interest. Should the consumer have the right to terminate the contract prematurely, and if so, is the creditor entitled to collect finance charges allocable to the period between the date of prepayment and the scheduled due date?

Davis v. Hinton

Supreme Court of Tennessee, 1975.
519 S.W.2d 776.

FONES, CHIEF JUSTICE.

Appellant executed a note in the principal sum of $4,750.00, payable to appellee with interest from date at 8% per annum. The note, dated on an unspecified day in September, 1972, was given for the balance of the purchase price of certain real property. It called for the payment of $750.00, plus accrued interest, on January 15, 1973, and $1,000.00 per year, plus accrued interest, on January 15 in the years 1974 through 1977. The note did not contain any provision concerning prepayment.

On January 15, 1973, the appellant paid to the appellee the first payment of $750.00 plus accrued interest. On May 9, 1973, the appellant tendered to the appellee the entire principal amount of $4,000.00, then owing under the note, plus the sum of $114.78, which represented the accrued interest at 8% on the $4,000.00 principal, from January 15, 1973 to May 9, 1973. The appellee refused to accept the $114.78, and insisted upon the full amount of interest that would have been due over the entire term of the note, i.e., $800.00. Appellant paid the $800.00 by check, noting thereon that it was paid under protest.

Subsequently, appellant instituted suit in the General Sessions Court of Hardin County, claiming that he had overpaid interest in the amount of $685.22. The General Sessions Court entered judgment for the appellant for $644.35 and costs. The appellee appealed to the Circuit Court of Hardin County, where the case was heard on a stipulation of fact, and a decree entered in favor of the appellee. Appellant then appealed directly to this Court, in accordance with T.C.A. § 16–408.

The sole issue presented for our determination is whether the maker of an installment note bearing interest from date, can terminate interest, by paying prior to the due dates the full principal amount plus accrued interest, when the note does not contain any provision for prepayment. We hold that the maker cannot do so, without the consent of the payee.

Our research has revealed only one case in Tennessee that has directed itself to this issue. In Crowley v. Kolsky, 57 S.W. 386 (Tenn.Ch.App.1900), it was held that in the absence of any agreement, the payee of a note had a legal right to collect interest for the full term of the note, notwithstanding the fact that the payor, of his own accord, paid the note in full before maturity. The voluntary prepayment did not entitle the payor to free himself from the terms of the note, nor permit him to refuse to pay the interest accruing between the date of payment of the note and its maturity. While the facts in *Crowley,* supra, differ slightly from those present in the case at bar, the variance is not material.

The result reached is supported by fundamental principles of contract law. Generally, a creditor can no more be compelled to accept payments on a contract before they are due than a debtor can be compelled to make such payments before they are due. . . .

For this reason, prepayment privileges contained in the terms of a contract or note were developed for the benefit of the debtor. Under such a privilege, the debtor obtains the right to discharge the debt before maturity. Usually he will give up something in return for this privilege.

The courts of the vast majority of jurisdictions, including Tennessee, have held that when such a privilege is given the debtor by contract, it is not usurious to condition the exercise of the privilege upon the payment of interest to the date of payment plus a bonus in addition. Silver Homes, Inc. v. Marx & Bensdorf, Inc., 206 Tenn. 361, 333 S.W.2d 810 (1960). The bonus may be interest to the stipulated maturity date. Even where the loan contract did not contain provisions for prepayment, and the loan was voluntarily repaid before maturity, the courts have held that the lender may receive or retain interest to the maturity date without being guilty of usury.

Appellant has made no claim of usury in the present case. However, we think that the usury cases lend indirect support to the view we presently espouse. In Reichwein v. Kirshenbaum, 98 R.I. 340, 201 A.2d 918 (1964), the Rhode Island Supreme Court considered a claim of usury based on the voluntary prepayment of a loan, that had not provided for the prepayment privilege in the loan contract. They rejected the claim by saying that the debtor had sought and been granted a privilege, not otherwise his. The interest from the date of prepayment until maturity was not to be treated as interest, but rather as a charge for a new and separate agreement to terminate his indebtedness.

For us to allow the appellant to terminate his indebtedness prior to maturity in this case, while only paying the interest accrued, is to allow him to alter the terms of the note, and make a new and separate agreement binding upon the creditor, without any charge or consideration given by the debtor in return. We decline to do so.

QUESTIONS AND NOTES

1.   The court states that plaintiff did not assert a claim of usury. Should he have asserted that claim: given the actual duration of the loan, didn't the lender receive more than eight percent interest?

2.   If plaintiff wasn't arguing a violation of the usury statute, what *was* he arguing? What "fundamental principles of contract law" support the result the court reaches?

For a history of the law concerning prepayment of loans, see Alexander, Mortgage Prepayment: The Trial of Common Sense, 72 Cornell L.Rev. 288 (1987).

3.   Unlike the contract in Davis v. Hinton, most consumer credit contracts expressly provide that the consumer may prepay at any time. Indeed, statutes frequently require them to do so, at least for certain kinds of transactions. E.g., New Jersey Retail Installment Sales Act, N.J.Stat.Ann. § 17:16–43 (reproduced in the Statutory Supplement). If the consumer prepays, not all of the finance charge will have accrued at the time of prepayment. Most contracts recognize this by stipulating the method for determining the amount that the consumer must pay. The most commonly used method is known as the sum-of-the-digits method. Under this method the consumer must pay the entire unpaid balance of the obligation less a credit, or rebate. The amount of the credit is determined in the following way: assign a number to each month in which a payment is due, starting with the last month in which payment is due and increasing by one digit until reaching the first month in which a payment was due. For a one-year contract, the last month would be assigned 1, and the first month would be assigned 12. (For a three-year contract, the last month would be assigned 1, and the first, 36.) The consumer's rebate equals the total finance charge multiplied by a fraction. The denominator of this fraction is the sum of the digits representing all the months of the contract. The numerator is the sum of the digits representing the months that have not yet arrived at the time of prepayment. An example may help. If the consumer wishes to prepay a twelve-month loan after only three months, the fraction to be applied to the finance charge would be:

$$\frac{9 + 8 + 7 + 6 + 5 + 4 + 3 + 2 + 1}{12 + 11 + 10 + 9 + 8 + 7 + 6 + 5 + 4 + 3 + 2 + 1} = \frac{45}{78} = .574$$

Note that although 75% of the twelve-month period still remains, the credit is considerably less than 75% of the finance charge.[1] The reason for this is that the amount of credit is greatest at the beginning of the loan and declines steadily thereafter. Since the finance charge allocable to each month depends on the amount of credit outstanding that month, the largest monthly finance charge is also allocable to the first month, and it, too, declines steadily thereafter.

The sum-of-the-digits method is known also as the Rule of 78s, because the denominator on a twelve-month obligation is 78. Most states have codified the consumer's right to prepay a loan or installment sale obligation

---

1.   If the consumer were to prepay a 36–month loan after three months, the fraction would be:

$$\frac{33 + 32 + 31 + \ldots 3 + 2 + 1}{36 + 35 + 34 + \ldots 3 + 2 + 1} = \frac{561}{666} = .842$$

Thus although 91.7% of the 36–month term remains, the credit would be only 84.2% of the finance charge.

and have stipulated or authorized use of the Rule of 78s to compute the amount of the rebate. E.g., N.J.Stat.Ann. § 17:16C–43; UCCC §§ 2.509, 2.510(4). The Rule of 78s, however, is not the only way to compute the credit due in the event of prepayment. The actuarial method, which must be used for purposes of *disclosing* the finance charge, may be used as well for purposes of *computing* the finance charge and also any rebate of the finance charge. Indeed, it is a more accurate way of determining what portion of the finance charge has been earned at any given point in time. The Rule of 78s always produces lower rebates than the actuarial method. For relatively small, short-term obligations with low rates of finance charge, the difference is less than a dollar. For larger, longer-term obligations, however, the difference is significant. E.g., see Dechow v. Sko–Fed Credit, 536 N.E.2d 1382 (Ill.App.1989) (difference between actuarial and Rule of 78s calculations was $6,000). An excellent description and analysis of the rule is Hunt, The Rule of 78: Hidden Penalty for Prepayment in Consumer Credit Transactions, 55 B.U.L.Rev. 331 (1975). A growing appreciation of the extent to which the Rule varies from the actuarial method of calculating rebates has led some courts and legislatures to prohibit its use altogether or to limit its use to shorter term transactions. E.g., Denley v. Peoples Bank, 553 So.2d 494 (Miss.1989); UCCC § 2.510(4)–(5) (48 months). As a result of legislation in 1992, federal law now confers the right to prepay, mandates a credit for unearned interest, and, in any precomputed consumer credit transaction longer than 61 months, prohibits the use of the Rule of 78s. 15 U.S.C. § 1615(b) (codified in the Truth-in-Lending Act).

To the extent of the difference between the actuarial method and the Rule of 78s, the consumer incurs a penalty for prepaying the obligation. In many cases, however, there is more. The applicable statutes may authorize the creditor to compute the credit for unaccrued finance charge not on the *total* finance charge, as above, but rather on the finance charge less a so-called "acquisition charge." E.g., N.J.S.A. § 17:16C–43. In addition, some contracts, especially those for home loans, provide that in the event of prepayment the consumer must pay a penalty consisting of a stated percentage of the original principal or of the principal that is being prepaid. A variation is to call for this penalty if the consumer prepays the obligation within five years of the inception of the contract, but not if the prepayment occurs thereafter. The matter typically is governed by state statute. Is there any justification for permitting an acquisition charge that applies only to prepayment relatively early in the transaction? for permitting a penalty?

4. There is another context in which the consumer's obligation is satisfied before its originally scheduled date. A large percentage of consumer credit contracts are refinanced before the consumer completes performance. Probably the most common explanation for this is the consumer's inability to pay the amount called for on a regular basis. If the monthly payment is too large for the consumer to handle, the parties may agree to an *extension*, in which they reduce the amount of each monthly payment but increase the period of time over which payments are to be made. See Petersen v. Philco Finance, page 411 supra. Since the consumer has the use of the credit for a longer period of time than originally contemplated, the new contract will call for additional finance charge.

Another common reason for refinancing is the consumer's desire to obtain additional credit from the creditor while the initial credit is still partially outstanding. When the consumer borrows additional money (or buys other goods) from the creditor, the obligations from the two transactions may be *consolidated* into one agreement, which supersedes the original contract. The transaction typically takes the form of a new loan in an amount that enables the consumer to pay off the first loan as well as obtain additional cash. Since the consumer receives an additional amount of credit, again the new contract will call for additional finance charge. The next case examines a problem in connection with refinancing.

In re Branch

Referee in Bankruptcy of the United States District Court for the Eastern District of Tennessee, 1966.
Printed in Hearings before the Subcommittee on Consumer Affairs of the House Committee on Banking and Currency, 90th Cong., 1st Sess., p. 962.

BARE, REFEREE.

. . .

William Sylvester Branch . . . filed an original petition under Chapter XIII on February 21, 1966. The debtor is 46 years old, married, and employed as a porter at the East Tennessee Tuberculosis Hospital, earning $200.00 per month. With his petition, he submitted his wage earner plan providing for payment out of his future earnings and wages the sum of $20.00 each week. The plan further provided that Merit Finance Company (Merit), a secured creditor, receive fixed monthly payments of $60.00. Merit, on March 9, 1966, filed its proof of claim in the amount of $2,870.00, accepting the debtor's plan.

Merit is an industrial loan and thrift company operating under the provisions of Tennessee Code Annotated. Secs. 45–2001–45–2017. Merit asserts that it holds a note secured by a second mortgage on the debtor's home, and a security interest in the debtor's household goods and an automobile, all executed November 19, 1965, at Knoxville, Tennessee. Merit's claim is based upon the following transactions.

(1) On December 22, 1964 the debtor negotiated a loan with Merit. He executed a note in the sum of $72.00 payable in 12 monthly installments of $6.00 each. Merit's ledger card indicates the $72.00 note was made up of the following items and charges:

Cash received by debtor $59.04
Interest 4.32
Investigation charge 2.88

Life insurance premium 1.44
Accident and health premium 4.32
    Total of note 72.00

(2) On January 23, 1965, the first loan was renewed or "flipped."[2] The debtor executed a new note in the amount of $378.00 payable in 18 monthly payments of $21.00 each. Merit's ledger card indicates the following items and charges:

Payment to Merit on unpaid balance old loan (credit given for
    insurance premium rebate, $4.94) . . . . $ 68.06
Paid Franklin Finance Company for borrower 108.00
Cash to borrower 95.11
Property insurance 15.00
Interest 34.02
Investigation charge 15.12
Life insurance premium 11.34
Accident and health premium 28.35
Recording fee (security agreement, household furniture) 3.00
    Total of note 378.00

Repayments by debtor: $21.00—February 22, 1965; $84.00—March 6, 1965.

(3) On March 6, 1965, the second loan was renewed or "flipped." Merit's ledger card indicates a new note in the amount of $552.00 was executed, payable in 24 monthly installments of $23.00 each. The ledger card indicates the following items and charges:

Payment to Merit on unpaid balance old loan (rebate insurance
    premium, $45.58) $227.42
Cash to borrower 149.70
Interest 66.24
Investigation charge 22.08
Life insurance premium 22.08
Accident and health premium 41.40
Property insurance premium 22.08
Recording fee 1.00
    Total of note 552.00

Repayment by debtor: $21.85—April 24, 1965 (late fee charged $1.15); $23.00—July 1, 1965.

(4) On August 10, 1965, the third loan was renewed or "flipped" and a new note executed in the amount of $672.00, repayable in 24 monthly installments of $28.00 each. Merit's ledger card indicates the following items and charges:

2. "Industrial loan and thrift companies . . . freely engage in the practice of 'flipping,' whereby a borrower who has repaid a portion of a loan is allowed to make or is enticed to make another loan whereupon the new loan is set up combining the new amount with the old balance on which all allowable charges have already been made, and the full amount of allowable charges is again imposed on the new balance." *Final Report of the Legislative Council of the 80th General Assembly, State of Tennessee (1968).*

Payment to Merit on unpaid balance old loan (rebate insurance
    premium, $56.72) $450.43
Cash to debtor 9.89
Interest 80.64
Investigation fee 26.88
Life insurance premium 26.88
Accident and health premium 50.40
Property insurance premium 26.88
Total of note 672.00

Repayments on the above loan appears as follows: $28.00—September 9, 1965; $28.00—October 9, 1965.

(5) On November 19, 1965, the fourth loan was renewed or "flipped" and this time a note executed in the sum of $2952.00, payable in 36 monthly payments of $82.00 each. Merit's ledger indicates the following items and charges:

Payment to Merit on unpaid balance old loan (rebate insur-
    ance premium, $79.90) . . . . $ 536.10
Paid City Finance Company 1,044.00
Paid Consolidated Credit Company 72.00
Cash received by debtor 10.28
Interest 531.36
Investigation charge 118.08
Life insurance premium 177.12
Accident and health premium 280.44
Property insurance premium 177.12
Recording fee 5.50
Total of note 2,952.00

Repayment of debtor on this loan: $82.00—1966.

A resume of the debtor's five loans with Merit, from December 22, 1964, to November 19, 1965, indicates the following:

Received by debtor or paid to others for his benefit $1,548.02
Interest charges 716.58
Investigation charges 185.04
Insurance premiums (net after rebate) 678.41
Recording charges 9.50

Repayments by the debtor total $287.85. As indicated heretofore Merit says the debtor owes it $2870.00 at this time.

The question before the court is whether Merit's claim is free from usury. . . . In my opinion Merit's claim is not free from usury and such usurious charges must be disallowed.

. . . . The legal rate of interest in this state is fixed by Tennessee Code Annotated 47–14–104 at the rate of six dollars ($6.00) for the use of one hundred dollars ($100) for one (1) year. ". . . and every excess over that rate is usury."

Tennessee Code Annotated 45–2007(f) authorizes industrial loan and thrift companies ". . . to deduct interest in advance on the face amount of the loan for the full term thereof."

. . .

As pointed out heretofore the first loan was "flipped" four times within a period of eleven months; total benefits received by the debtor amounted to some $1548.02; interest totaling $716.58 was charged. In no instance was interest rebated when the loan was "flipped."

It will also be observed from the notes filed in this proceeding that in every instance interest has been charged on interest, e.g., consider the fifth loan made by the debtor. The debtor executed a note in the amount of $2952.00 which includes interest amounting to $531.36. The interest figure was arrived at by charging interest on the face amount of the note, to which the interest had already been added, thus interest is charged on interest.

Did the "flipping" of the loans by Merit in the transactions under consideration enable it to obtain an excess over the legal rate of interest?

When the first loan was made, the debtor executed a note in the amount of $72.00. This amount includes $4.32 interest for twelve months. One month later the loan was "flipped." The face amount of the new note includes $68.06 payment to Merit on the first loan (rebate given for insurance premiums). Although the debtor had already been charged with interest on $72.00 for twelve months, the $68.06 balance is added into the face amount of the second note ($378.00) and interest is again charged— this time for eighteen months. In the third loan interest is again charged on $227.42 remaining unpaid on the second loan, again for eighteen months. In the fourth loan interest is again charged on $450.43 balance on the third loan, this time for a thirty-six month period. In the fifth loan interest is again charged on $536.10 balance on the fourth loan, again for a thirty-six month period. These transactions indicate interest on interest on interest on interest on interest. Yet the statute says the legal rate of interest in this State is $6.00 for the use of $100.00 for one year "and every excess over that rate is usury."

When the first loan was made the debtor was entitled to the use of $72.00 for one year. He was charged $4.32 interest. When the loan was "flipped" at the end of one month, however, he was again charged interest on $68.06 of the original $72.00. Six per cent interest on $72.00 for one month (deducted in advance) is $0.36. Yet the debtor was given no rebate for interest when the loan was "flipped."

A period of one and one-half months intervened between the "flipping" of the second and third loans. The second note is for $378.00, interest charged is $34.02 for an eighteen-month period. Interest on $378.00 for one and one-half months is $2.84. Again the debtor was given no rebate when the loan was "flipped."

The third note is for $552.00, interest charged is $66.24. A period of approximately five months intervened between the third and fourth loan. Interest on $552.00 for five months is $13.80. Again the debtor was given no rebate for interest when the loan was "flipped."

The fourth note is for $672.00, interest charged is $80.64. A period of approximately three and one-half months intervened between the fourth and fifth loans. Interest on $672.00 for three and one-half months is $11.76. Again the debtor was given no rebate when the loan was "flipped."

The fifth note is for $2952.00, interest charged is $531.36. Although the fourth loan had some 21 months yet to run and interest had been charged for that period, the debtor was given no rebate for interest.

Had new loans been made instead of "flipping" the prior loans Merit could not have charged interest on the old loan, e.g., the second loan would have been for $203.11 plus legal charges, which total considerably less than the $378.00 note executed by the debtor. The same is true of the other loans. When the third loan was "flipped" the debtor received only $9.89; the face amount of the note was increased however from $552.00 to $672.00 even though the debtor had repaid $44.85 on the third loan. The reason for "flipping" the loans is obvious.

It is my conclusion that Merit "flipped" the loans so that it could again collect interest (and investigation charges) on the old balances even though interest (and investigation charges) had already been imposed. Does such practice constitute usury under the Tennessee statute and decisions?

If the transaction is intended as a device to evade the statute, it constitutes usury.

When the facts are made to appear, no scheme or device to avoid application of usury statutes, regardless of how ingenious or intricate [the] scheme or device may be, will permit anyone guilty of participating in a usurious transaction to escape its consequences, and consent or cooperation of one paying the usurious interest is immaterial.

In determining whether or not a given transaction is usurious, the court will disregard form and look to substance.

. . .

It is my conclusion that the "flipping" of loans in the transactions under consideration was a plan or scheme to enable Merit to obtain an excess over the legal rate of interest. The consent or cooperation of the debtor is immaterial. The transaction is a continued one; although new advances were made and new instruments were executed, each note refers to the previous one.

. . .

[Judge Bare allowed Merit's claim in the amount of $1,511, which represented $324 paid to Branch, $1,224 paid on his behalf to other creditors, $7 permissible investigation and filing fees, and $244 interest, less payments of $288 that Branch had made to Merit.]

QUESTIONS AND NOTES

1. Is *Branch* consistent with Davis v. Hinton?

2. In *Branch* there are two entirely distinct ways in which interest is charged on interest. What are they?

3. For many lenders the majority of their business consists of refinancing existing loans. In re Branch reveals some of the reasons for this. Initially it appears that Branch desired additional credit (to pay off Franklin Finance and obtain cash—first $95, then $149). By the third flip, however, Branch was in default and probably agreed to the refinancing as a way to avoid loss of the car and furniture that he had pledged as collateral. From the lender's perspective, not only did it stand to be paid unearned interest, it also charged an "investigation" fee even though it had "investigated" Branch only a month earlier. Moreover, although it refunded part of the insurance premiums, it refunded much less than a pro rata part: in the January transaction, the lender kept 14% of the premium even though the refinancing occurred at the end of the first month of the 12–month loan. In several of the transactions, the lender imposed a charge for recording fees. The changing amount of these fees suggests that it retained some or all of the fees rather than paying the stated amount to the recording office. To the extent the lender need not rebate any of these charges, it has a strong incentive to encourage refinancing.

A former finance company employee who had been a salesman and branch manager at three different major finance companies, testified at a Senate hearing that his job depended on his flipping loans and packing them with credit insurance and other add-ons. He testified that employees were encouraged to call customers every three months to encourage them to refinance into larger loans. " 'You're under tremendous pressure to meet a quota,' he said. 'If your numbers [aren't] where upper management wants them, you're fired.' " Timmons and Prakash, "Predatory" Subprime Tactics Denounced in Senate, Am. Banker, March 17, 1998, at 1. See Marsh, The Hard Sell in Consumer Credit: How the Folks in Marketing Can Put You in Court, 52 Consumer Fin. L.Q. Rep. 295 (1998) (describing training materials and financial incentives lenders use to encourage their loan officers to induce consumers to refinance existing loans).

The judge in *Branch* used usury as the basis for denying the recovery sought by the lender. Other relevant bases include fraud (e.g., Emery v. American General Finance, Inc., 71 F.3d 1343 (7th Cir.1995)), unconscionability (Besta v. Beneficial Loan Co., 855 F.2d 532 (8th Cir.1988)), and deceptive practices statutes (In re Milbourne, 108 B.R. 522, 535–39 (Bankr. E.D.Pa.1989)). See Golann, Beyond Truth in Lending: The Duty of Affirmative Disclosure, 46 Bus. Law. 1307 (1991).

Federal law now requires creditors to make an adjustment in the event of a prepayment or refinancing. 15 U.S.C. § 1615. But it requires the adjustment only for the "interest charge," not for other charges. And it does not prohibit use of the Rule of 78s for transactions of five years or less. Hence, the incentives to flip still exist.

4. See UCCC sections 2.504–2.505, 3.304. Flipping is considered again in the next chapter (page 475).

5. In recent years loan flipping has occurred in a new form. Consumers who find themselves short of cash near the end of a pay period may obtain needed funds by resort to a so-called payday lender. This entity will loan money for a short period of time, typically less than two weeks, to tide the consumer over until the next payday. To obtain the funds, say, $100, the consumer gives the lender a post-dated check in the amount of the loan and a fee, often 15% of the amount borrowed, in this example, $15. (As an alternative to giving a post-dated check, the consumer may authorize the lender to debit his or her checking account at the end of the term.) At the end of the loan term, the consumer either directs the lender to deposit the check or repays the $100 (and gets the check back from the lender). If the consumer is not able to repay the $100, the consumer may renew, or roll over, the loan for another two weeks, upon payment of an additional $15. And so on, and so on.

Payday loans have been defended as the last resort for consumers who need to borrow but do not have such other alternatives as credit cards or loans from family or friends. They have been criticized as a form of oppression of necessitous consumers who are desperate and therefore are willing to agree to anything, unaware that they will be caught in an ever-worsening debt trap.

Empirical studies have revealed that the vast majority of borrowers do not repay their loans after the initial period. Indeed, a report by the North Carolina Banking Commission in 2000 revealed that fewer than 16% of borrowers paid off their loans after the initial term. More than half engaged in six or more rollovers. A California study of transactions in 2006 found that only 27% of borrowers borrowed only one time. More than 95% of the loans in 2006 were to repeat borrowers, mostly in the form of consecutive loans. A loan that starts out as very short term thus morphs into a loan in which the interest payments exceed the principal amount of the loan. (At $15 per transaction, it only takes six renewals (plus the initial fee) before the finance charge exceeds the $100 principal.) The North Carolina study revealed that almost 85% of the industry's revenue came from consumers who engaged in six or more transactions per year. Hence, although the public solicitation of payday lenders focuses on the consumer who needs help making it to the next payday, it appears that the business model of the payday lender relies on loans to consumers who cannot repay at the end of the initial period.

In a number of states, the courts have held that payday loans are subject to one or another of the state's small loan laws, which have maximum rates lower than the going rate for payday loans. Lenders have attempted several evasionary devices. Some have sold internet access (via terminals in their stores), alleging that the consumer pays for the internet access as well as for the loan. Others have developed buying clubs, alleging that the fee covers club membership as well as the loan. Courts have seen through these, and other, subterfuges, just as the court did in People v. Coleman (Problem 2, page 413).

Many states have enacted statutes specifically regulating payday loans, sometimes at the urging of payday lenders (in those states that have subjected payday loans to the small loan laws), sometimes at the urging of consumer groups (in those states that have not). These statutes tend to limit the maximum charge for a loan and limit the number of renewals or rollovers. They also address other aspects of the transaction, such as the lender's use of criminal bad-check laws to coerce repayment or civil bad-check laws to obtain the penalties those statutes authorize (e.g., three times the amount of the bad check). The effectiveness of the reforms varies widely.

Payday loan stores are concentrated around military bases and in neighborhoods in which the population consists largely of African–American, Hispanic, or low-income consumers. See Peterson & Graves, Predatory Lending and the Military: The Law and Geography of 'Payday' Loans in Military Towns, 66 Ohio St. L.J. 653 (2005). When military officials observed that excessive high-interest-rate indebtedness of members of the armed forces threatened the nation's military preparedness, Congress responded by enacting legislation that caps interest on loans to members of the armed forces at 36%. 10 U.S.C. § 987. The statute adopts several other limitations on loan transactions that might serve as a model for credit transactions with consumers generally.

(5) REMEDIES

The sanctions for violating rate regulation statutes vary considerably. Under some statutes the sanction is simply loss of so much of the interest as is in excess of the lawful amount (e.g., the West Virginia statute in *Carper*, page 394 supra). Under others, the lender may recover and keep the lawful interest but suffers a penalty of a multiple of the excessive portion (e.g., the Maryland statute in *Tri-County*, page 407 supra). Still other statutes take this a step further and in addition to the penalty also deny the lender the right to the lawful interest (e.g., the Washington statute in *Thomsen*, page 404 supra). Most severe are those statutes that require forfeiture not only of all interest, but also of all principal (e.g., Conn.Gen.Stat.Ann. § 37–8).

What is the sanction under the following usury statute, Nev.Rev.Stat. § 99.050:

> (1) Parties may agree for the payment of any rate of interest on money due or to become due on any contract which does not exceed the rate of 12 percent per annum. . . .

> (3) Any agreement for a greater rate of interest than specified in this section is null and void and of no effect as to such excessive rate of interest.

Is the lender who contracts for more than twelve percent entitled to collect any interest? See Pease v. Taylor, 496 P.2d 757 (Nev.1972).

In addition to the remedies under state law for violating state usury statutes, there is a federal remedy for some violations of state usury statutes. The Racketeer Influenced and Corrupt Organizations Act (RICO), 18 U.S.C. §§ 1961(6), 1962, makes unlawful the "collection of unlawful debt," which is defined as a debt in which the interest rate is at least twice the maximum permitted by the applicable state or federal law. Section 1964(c) provides for recovery of treble damages and costs, including attorney's fees.

(6) OPEN-END CREDIT

A few courts have held that open-end sales credit entails a loan or forbearance and therefore is subject to the usury statute. E.g., State v. J.C. Penney Co., 179 N.W.2d 641 (Wis.1970). More courts, however, have reached the opposite conclusion, holding that open-end plans contemplate credit sales that are within the time-price doctrine. E.g., Dennis v. Sears, Roebuck & Co., 446 S.W.2d 260 (Tenn.1969).

Most states now have statutes that specifically regulate the terms of open-end credit contracts. Predictably, however, the legislation has not foreclosed dispute over what is permitted or required. For example, the finance charge is a function of the amount of credit outstanding each month. But, it turns out, there are several ways to determine that amount. In Haas v. Pittsburgh National Bank, 526 F.2d 1083 (3d Cir.1975), plaintiff alleged that the Pennsylvania Goods and Services Installment Sales Act prohibited the method of determining the monthly balance that defendant banks used. The Court stated:

> A person desiring to establish a Master Charge or BankAmericard revolving charge account completes a credit application form containing the terms of the account agreement. This application then is reviewed by the bank to which it is submitted. If the application is approved, a Master Charge or BankAmericard card is issued. Under the account agreements in use at the defendant banks, the cardholder may present this card to purchase merchandise from merchants who have agreed to honor the credit card. The merchant imprints a sales draft describing the merchandise with the cardholder's number and gives the cardholder a copy. The merchant then submits the sales draft to the bank which issued the credit card, and the bank in turn pays the merchant the face amount of the sales draft, less an agreed discount. The cardholder's purchase is posted to his revolving charge account.

> The balance in the cardholder's account is computed on the basis of monthly billing cycles. On the last day of the billing cycle, the "billing date," the bank's computer reviews all transactions posted to the cardholder's account during the billing cycle. The computer then calculates the service charge, if any, and prints out a monthly statement which is mailed to the cardholder. This statement shows, *inter alia,* the balance owing at the beginning of the billing cycle, all purchases and payments made during the billing cycle, the service charge, and the balance owing at the end of the cycle. . . .

III.   Previous Balance Method

Plaintiffs contend that the previous balance method of determining the balance on which a service charge is imposed is contrary to the provisions of the Sales Act. When the Sales Act was adopted in 1966, the previous balance method was the method most commonly used by both large and small retail merchants in Pennsylvania. Defendants Mellon Bank and Pittsburgh National Bank used this method until February and November of 1972, respectively. Defendant Equibank discontinued use of the previous balance method on May 31, 1971. The previous balance method still is employed by many retailers, including a major department store in Pittsburgh. We must determine whether the Pennsylvania legislature, in enacting the Sales Act, intended to proscribe continued use of the previous balance method.

A.   Operation of the Previous Balance Method

Under the previous balance method, the balance on which the service charge is computed is the balance outstanding on the first day of the billing cycle. This balance is the same as that outstanding on the last day of the previous billing cycle. Purchases, payments, and credits occurring during the billing cycle are not taken into account unless the entire balance outstanding at the close of the previous billing cycle is discharged. If the previous balance is fully offset by payments and credits posted during the billing cycle, no service charge is imposed for that billing cycle.

The manner in which the previous balance method operates is most effectively described by example. Assume that a cardholder's billing date is the thirtieth of each month and that on March 30 the balance in the cardholder's account is zero. If the cardholder purchases $100 worth of merchandise on April 25, that purchase will appear on the cardholder's April 30 statement but will not be included in the balance on which the service charge for the month of April is calculated. The April service charge will be one and one-quarter percent of zero, or zero. The five days' use of the $100 is called the "free ride" since no service charge is imposed. If the purchase had been made on April 5, the "free ride" would have been for 25 days.

In the example, the balance outstanding on April 30 is $100. This balance is also the balance on the first day of the May billing cycle and, therefore, is the balance on which the May service charge will be imposed unless the balance is fully discharged before the end of the May billing cycle. Thus, if the cardholder pays $75 on account on May 5 and no other transactions occur during May, the service charge for the May billing cycle will be one and one quarter percent of $100, the previous balance, or $1.25. The service charge for May is computed in this manner even though $100 was outstanding during only five days and the cardholder had the use of only $25 during the rest of the May billing cycle. The actual rate of service charge for May thus is much higher than the nominal rate of one and one-quarter percent specified in the Sales Act. Of course, if the cardholder had discharged his entire previous balance during May, no service charge at all would have been imposed in connection with the April 25 purchase.

B. Other Methods

At least three methods other than the previous balance method may be available to banks and merchants in computing the monthly service charge. All three of the defendant banks now use a variant of the average daily balance method. Under the "true" average daily balance method, the sum of all actual daily balances in the cardholder's account during the billing cycle is divided by the number of days in the cycle. The resulting quotient is the average daily balance upon which the service charge is imposed. The variant presently utilized by defendants is known as the "hybrid" average daily balance method. The "hybrid" method differs from the "true" method only in that purchases during the current billing cycle are not included in the daily balances. The cardholder, as under the previous balance method, gets a "free ride" until the first day of the new billing cycle, at which time the previous month's purchases are added into the balance. Use of both the "true" and "hybrid" methods may be impractical for smaller merchants who are unable to afford computer time.

A third method of accounting is the adjusted balance method, which is no more difficult to employ than the previous balance method and is the method most favorable to the cardholder. Under the adjusted balance method, all payments and other credits posted to the cardholder's accounts during the billing cycle are subtracted from the balance outstanding at the beginning of the cycle. Purchases during the current billing cycle are not taken into account. The resulting figure is the balance upon which the service charge is computed. Purchases then are added in to arrive at the beginning balance for the next billing cycle.

Another possibility is the ending balance method. This method takes into account payments and other credits as well as purchases in calculating the balance upon which the service charge is imposed. Thus, if purchases exceed credits during the billing cycle, the cardholder is charged a full month's service charge on the difference which may be outstanding for only a few days.

The court ultimately concluded that the statute prohibited use of the previous balance method.

QUESTIONS AND NOTES

1. See UCCC section 2.202(2).

2. Credit card plans of banks (e.g., MasterCard, Visa) are similar in most respects to credit card plans of sellers (e.g., Sears). There is, however, one important difference: in addition to the contract with the consumer, the bank also has a contract with the seller. Under this contract the seller sends the sales slip from each credit sale to the bank, the bank pays the seller the face amount of the sales slip, and the seller pays the bank a fee (usually in the range of 2–4% of the face amount of the sales slip). The bank then collects the face amount of the sales slip (plus any appropriate finance charge) from the consumer. The seller is willing to take less than 100% of the cash price for two reasons: (1) the bank's participation relieves the seller of the costs of maintaining a separate credit plan (determining customers' creditworthiness, bookkeeping, collection, and bad debt loss), and (2) the seller's competitors may be offering this form of credit to their customers.

Is the existence and amount of this charge by the bank to the seller relevant to determining whether the bank has violated a statute limiting the amount the bank may charge the consumer?

What is to prevent the seller from offering to give cash customers a discount equal to the amount the bank deducts in connection with customers' use of the bank's credit card? Would this practice have any implications for determining compliance with disclosure requirements? disclosure by whom? Would it have any implications for determining compliance with rate regulation statutes? See Truth-in-Lending Act sections 167(b), 171(c).

3. Since the era of *Haas*, credit card issuers have developed still other methods of determining the balance on which the finance charge will be assessed. An increasingly popular one is known as the "two-cycle average daily balance method." Under this approach the issuer calculates the average daily balance for the current month and the average daily balance for the preceding month if in that preceding month the consumer incurred no finance charge because he or she paid the balance in full. The issuer applies the periodic rate to the sum of these two figures. The effect of this method is to retroactively eliminate the free-ride period for the month in which the consumer paid the balance in full. As with the average daily balance method described in the excerpt from *Haas*, the two-cycle method may include or exclude current purchases from the calculation of the average daily balance. Several states restrict the methods that an issuer may use. E.g., Mass. Ann. Laws ch. 140D, § 20 (adjusted balance or average daily balance); UCCC § 2.202(2). These restrictions are largely ineffective, however, because limitations on interest rates and the methods of calculating them are governed by the law of the state in which the bank is located, not the state in which consumer resides. See page 393 supra. And the states in which the major credit-card issuing banks are located allow them free rein in determining the balance on which to impose a finance charge.

4. In some states the rate regulation statutes permit a higher charge for open-end credit than for closed-end credit. Sellers and creditors in these states therefore have an incentive to structure their transactions as open-end credit. If a consumer approaches a lender for a loan to remodel his or her kitchen, can the lender charge the higher rate permitted for open-end credit? Compare the similar problem under the Truth-in-Lending Act (page 197 supra).

D.   THE BROADER QUESTION

Usury originally meant charging interest in any amount; today it means charging more than is permitted by law. But why does the law impose any restraints on what lenders may charge? Except in the case of monopolies, the United States generally relies on the market to determine the price of goods and services. Why have we not relied on the market to determine the price of credit? The answer begins with ancient religious views concerning the immorality of loaning or borrowing money. Modern advocates of controlling the price of credit also point to the typically unequal positions of borrower and lender: the borrower perceives his or her need to borrow money to be much greater than the lender's need to loan money; the borrower may be unsophisticated and undereducated; the borrower may not appreciate just how high the risk of default is. Proponents of regulation also argue that competition does not operate satisfactorily in the consumer credit market and that lenders typically set their rates at the maximum figure permitted by law.

A case from the Fifth Circuit illustrates how charged with emotion the issue is. In Williams v. Public Finance Corp., 598 F.2d 349 (5th Cir.1979), the court held that the lenders had violated the Georgia rate regulation statute and also had violated the Truth-in-Lending Act. Thus the lenders were subject not only to the sanction provided by the rate regulation statute—forfeiture of all principal and interest—but also to the sanction of the Truth-in-Lending Act—twice the (uncollectible) finance charge. Responding to the lenders' argument that cumulating these sanctions was unduly harsh, the court stated,

> Moreover, we eschew an analysis of these statutory cases limited by the common law doctrines of compensation for breach of contract. These cases involve penal statutes, and we are compelled to enforce their clear and direct commands whether or not they seem to be overcompensating in a contract or tort analysis. There is nothing inherently wrong, excessive, or immoral in a borrower receiving two bounties for catching a lending beast who has wronged him twice—first, by sneaking up on him from behind, and then by biting him too hard. The private attorney general who exposes and opposes these credit wolves is not deemed unduly enriched when his valor is richly rewarded and his vendor harshly rebuked. Nor does the state's punishment for the usurious bite interfere with Congress's punishment for the wearing of sheep's clothing.

> We have come, or gone, a long way from Shakespeare's ancient caution, "Neither a borrower, nor a lender be." In today's world borrowing and lending are daily facts of life. But that a fact becomes diurnal does not mean it has been cleansed of its dire potential. We still heed the Bard's advice, but in our own modern way—by strict regulation of the strong and careful protection of the weak and

unwary. While the well-intended efforts of our many sovereigns may at times sound more like discordant and competing solos than mellifluous duets, we, as judges, must restrain our impulse to stray from the score.

Id. at 359–60. Judge Clark disagreed:

> Finally, though I join in the result reached by the court on the Truth-in-Lending Act issues presented in these cases, I cannot join in the language employed by the court or the spirit it appears to express. The court characterizes the lender involved in these cases as "credit wolves" dressed in "sheep's clothing," and the borrowers as persons of "valor" to be "richly rewarded" for "catching a lending beast." These pejoratives obscure the economic realities and legal issues that ought to govern these cases. . . . The violations found are based on judicial precedent that is not internally consistent, and, in any event, are extremely technical. Such a factually arcane and logically dubious "violation" is certainly not the stuff of which credit "wolves" ought to be made.

> There is no magic in the small loan business. It operates on the same economic principles that govern any other industry in a free society. Government regulation of consumer loans increases the cost of borrowing money or decreases its availability. As stiff penalties are more and more frequently imposed by courts for even the most technical violations of state and federal law, loan companies inevitably must offset such losses or go out of business. Either the cost of loans must increase or lenders must limit their availability to better credit risks. It is naive to believe that strict enforcement of technicalities will benefit the necessitous borrower. The consumer loan business thrives at maximum rates set by law because the market will bear their high cost. State and federal legislatures have chosen to regulate the consumer loan business, and it is the duty of courts to enforce those regulations ungrudgingly. But the interpretation of state and federal consumer credit laws cannot be distilled into terms so simple as the wolves and the sheep. Courts are not assigned the task of heaping coals on the heads of lenders. Indeed, the facts of life demonstrate that unreasonably severe application of technicalities to lenders only increases the cost of borrowing to those who can least afford it.

Id. at 361–62.

Judge Clark emphasizes the economic consequences of stringent interpretation of rate regulation statutes. Others have examined the economic consequences of the statutes themselves. Contrary to the assertion of advocates of statutory ceilings, the interest rate does not always rise to the ceiling. Prominent examples of this are home mortgage loans and automobile loans. Therefore, there is nothing inherent in the consumer credit market that suggests that competition can not work to set the price just as it does in other markets. Granted, if there are no limits on the rates that lenders may charge, some ignorant or unsophisticated consumers will be victimized. The question remains whether imposing ceilings is the best way to deal with this problem. Even if the imposition of ceilings is effective to deal with the problem, what other consequences flow from fixing ceilings? Do those other consequences outweigh the benefits of statutory limits?

Both theoretical analysis and empirical studies lead to the conclusion that the effect of a rate ceiling is to exclude certain consumers from the credit market.[3] In the absence of a ceiling, the market would set the interest rate; that rate would be determined in large part by the lender's costs of obtaining funds to loan, the lender's other costs of doing business, and a return on the lender's investment. When the statutory ceiling is too low to permit the lender to cover these items, the lender must either conduct its business at a loss, go out of the consumer loan business, or reduce its costs sufficiently to permit it to continue generating a profit. The likeliest alternative is the third, and the likeliest way to reduce costs is to eliminate loans to those persons who present the highest risk of nonpayment.[4] This means that the high-risk consumer is excluded from the consumer credit market and must either do without credit or obtain credit from a loan shark. Note the irony: one justification for usury laws is to protect the necessitous borrower against the overreaching lender. Yet the very imposition of rate ceilings propels the necessitous borrower into the hands of the overreaching lender.

These and similar arguments have led to near unanimity among economists and legal scholars employing economic analysis. They conclude that legislatures ought to abolish rate ceilings altogether or at least ought to raise them high enough that they will not interfere with the operation of the market. The following excerpts reveal, however, that not all observers agree with the economic analysis or believe that economic analysis should dictate the answer to the question whether there should be a ceiling on rates for consumer credit.

Wallace, The Uses of Usury: Low Rate Ceilings Reexamined

56 B.U.L.Rev. 451, 452–62, 468, 474–81, 488–89, 495–97 (1976).

The main argument made by the critics [of low rate ceilings] is that low ceilings, if effective, reduce the availability of consumer credit to those with low incomes. Reduced availability interferes with the freedom of those denied credit to buy what they want with discretionary income. Rate

---

3. For a fuller explication of the economic analysis, see, e.g., NCCF, Consumer Credit in the United States ch. 6–7 (1972); Baxter, Section 85 of the National Bank Act and Consumer Welfare, 1995 Utah L.Rev. 1009; Boyes & Roberts, Economic Effects of Usury Laws in Arizona, 1981 Ariz.St.L.J. 35; Durkin, An Economic Perspective on Interest Rate Limitations, 9 Ga. State L.Rev. 821 (1993); Study, An Empirical Study of the Arkansas Usury Law: "With Friends Like That . . ." 1968 U.Ill.L.F. 544.

4. A similar phenomenon exists with respect to the regulation of rates for sales credit. If a statute holds rates below the rates that would be established by the market, sellers will tend to eliminate credit to highest-risk consumers or include part of the cost of the credit in the cash price, or both. See, e.g., Lynch, Consumer Credit at Ten Per Cent Simple: The Arkansas Case, 1968 U.Ill. L.F. 592, 599–608.

ceilings have also been charged with being ineffective, reducing competition and efficiency, and discouraging economic growth in the state that harbors them.

Although there have been a few rumblings in response, the critics' charges to date remain basically uncontested. My aim is to suggest that the critics' position, stripped of its free choice and efficiency verbiage, is extraordinarily narrow. Low rate ceilings, if properly used, are potentially effective and beneficial regulatory tools. Of course, like most regulatory tools, they also have their costs. But the critics—apparently influenced by the conviction that, as a normative matter, the theoretical free market shows the best way to structure debtor creditor relationships—have focused only on the costs. This article attempts to readjust the uneven balance. Although those who ultimately set the guidelines for credit policy in a state or the nation must determine by their own values whether the costs outweigh the benefits, they cannot do so wisely when the relevant factors have been only halfway explored.

. . . [C]eilings raise resource allocation issues. It has been urged, for example, that high or no ceilings will encourage competition, efficiency and economic growth. There has been, to be sure, some dissent from this view, mostly on the ground that the proof of negative effect is inconclusive. I doubt, however, that the telling argument for low ceilings is made by denying their adverse effect on competitive efficiency. A potentially more fruitful focus is their distributive effect. As a society, we have recognized that many distributive programs interfere to some extent with resource allocation and that we must frequently trade off losses in competitive efficiency to obtain improved distribution. An important question thus becomes whether low ceilings offer an improvement in distribution significant enough to offset some loss in competitive efficiency. Because the issue is evidently one of values, and therefore ultimately of ethics, it must be resolved at least in part by reference to alternative distributive policies and their attendant costs, including any cost in worsened resource allocation. It should be clear that I am not here referring to distributive policy in any narrow sense limited to dollar transfers, but rather viewing it broadly as encompassing the way society allocates benefits and burdens among its members. Who enjoys the opportunity to use credit and who is given protection from hazard are in this sense distributive questions.

In this vein, the critics of low ceilings may be fairly taken to argue that unrestrictive ceilings will improve the just distribution of opportunity to use the marketplace while low ceilings will do the opposite. They have urged, for example, that low income people should have the opportunity to decide to use high cost credit if they desire to do so. High ceilings will make available more credit to low income people, and with credit they can choose the degree to which they want to buy or borrow. On the other hand, the concerns advanced below to justify low ceilings take their distributive effect in a different light. For example, I urge that low ceilings may provide a significant measure of protection to high risk borrowers by keeping them out of a potentially hazardous situation. If I am correct, rate ceilings can be distributively justified as improving the treatment of the less advantaged because high risk credit users tend to be drawn from their ranks. In any event, the difference between the critics and proponents of low ceilings appears to turn on divergent views of whether low ceilings will improve distribution and whether any improvement they may achieve is worth the cost in reduced efficiency of resource allocation.

.   .   .

II.   THE UTILITY OF RATE CEILINGS IN A MODERN ECONOMY

A position championing free choice and efficiency in a society dominated by a utilitarian ethic, as is ours, has great initial persuasiveness. There are four countervailing considerations, however, that deserve careful attention before the society rejects use of low rate ceilings.

A.   *Low Ceilings as Protection*

One purpose of low rate ceilings is to protect consumers from the hardship associated with default on high risk credit. The traditional argument of the critics has been that lowered ceilings will only *apparently* lower prices charged individuals and will in many cases actually result in the denial of credit to the highest risk borrowers. The argument is probably true in most instances. However, low ceilings that have this effect may nonetheless be justifiable. Elsewhere in the consumer market we have restricted the availability of certain products because it is thought that the only effective protection for the consumer is to ban the product completely. Credit—particularly high price, high risk credit—might be similarly viewed. Default represents for many a failure to meet basic middle class norms of behavior. It also usually results in collection techniques that explicitly recognize that the most effective means of inducing the debtor to pay is to impose psychological pressure. Since credit always carries with it some risk of default, and high price credit a substantial risk, the debtor and his family constantly risk experiencing considerable disruption and psychic pain.

Any attempt to support low rate ceilings on these grounds must establish that there are serious enough risks associated with credit default to justify restricting the availability of high risk credit. Restricting the availability of credit creates at least an apparent limitation on freedom of choice which may be viewed as undesirable. Even if the risks are judged to be serious, the question remains whether equivalent protection could be achieved by some alternative regulatory approach that is not extremely expensive to establish and operate and that interferes less than a low ceiling with highly valued objectives like providing freedom of opportunity to use credit. For example, the traditional approach to consumer credit problems has been to propose banning certain collection techniques like wage garnishment that seem to carry a high risk of psychic harm to the debtor and his family. But the possibility exists that low ceilings may more effectively reduce the risk associated with credit to acceptable proportions or that they may be less costly in direct expense and interference with important values.

B.   *Low Ceilings to Improve Economic Development*

A second advantage of low ceilings that counterbalances the appeal to free choice and efficiency is the possibility of using low ceilings to alter the allocation of credit within a state or the nation for developmental purposes. Consumer credit seems to have a significant short term impact on the purchase of consumer durables; it has been said that it also affects long-term durable demand. If a state or perhaps the national government determined that developmental concerns demanded a shift in the capital resources of the society from consumer durables to some other sector to accomplish better wealth distribution—for example, by producing more jobs in the short run or increasing the supply of low income housing—low ceilings would be an available tool that might be useful as one aspect of a plan to accomplish this objective. Attractive alternative investment opportunities would have to be permitted, and probably encouraged, to avoid the flight of capital that might otherwise occur.

.   .   .

C.   *Low Ceilings to Discourage Overreaching and Deception*

Limiting unwanted pricing practices is a third advantage of low ceilings. The undesirable pricing practices share in common a creditor decision to charge certain operating costs to one class of customers rather than to another. Some of the practices can be objected to as unfairly discriminatory, as when the creditor chooses to give some customers free credit and charge the costs to others. Other practices seem more to involve deception, as when the creditor offers credit for a particular period at a stated price, knowing that before the loan is repaid the customer will almost certainly have to pay substantial additional charges of which he is now only dimly aware. If these practices are thought objectionable, pricing controls can restrict them.

.   .   .

D.   *Control of Credit Pricing to Further a Reformed Credit System That Excuses All but Negligent Default*

Using restrictions on post-default charges to assist reform of the basic liability rules in consumer credit is a final advantage of price control. Some recent consumer credit reform proposals seem to reflect dissatisfaction with holding the defaulting debtor strictly accountable to the creditor for the amount of the debt. This dissatisfaction can ultimately lead to advocating a system in which the debtor would be excused from certain types of default. Such a system, although apparently a novel suggestion, would be no more than the extension of a no-fault insurance model to consumer credit.

.   .   .

[After articulating these four possible objectives of setting low ceilings, Professor Wallace turns to a detailed examination of the first of the objectives: protecting high-risk consumers against the economic and psychic injury of default.]

III.   EVALUATING LOW RATE CEILINGS AS PROTECTION AGAINST EXCESSIVELY RISKY CREDIT

. . .

The controversy whether protection justifies restrictions on borrowing ability and freedom of action caused by low rate ceilings revolves around a classic ethical question. To what extent is it proper to limit an individual's freedom of action in order to protect that individual? A universally acceptable resolution has never emerged, and I do not suggest that I have found one. Nonetheless, an examination of the precise effect lowered ceilings would have on freedom of action will reveal a degree of infringement to which only the most extreme libertarians could object. I will first describe the distributive benefit provided by lowered ceilings and then turn to the objection that lowered ceilings interfere with freedom of choice.

1.   The Purpose of Low Ceilings Reexamined and Refined

I have already urged that a lowered ceiling can be used to improve a society's overall distribution of benefits and burdens among its members. At this point, it is necessary to specify the distributive improvement that might be achieved. The protection from a high risk of default afforded by a lowered ceiling is not expected to transfer wealth in the same direct way as a welfare payment. A lowered ceiling, by protecting the debtor family from a threat to stability and psychic harm, should, however, help maintain a minimum standard of existence sufficient to preserve the dignity of the individual. Proposals for various minimum standards are usually justified as a means to promote equality and to satisfy the basic conditions for assuring the citizen the ability to exercise and enjoy freedom. The low ceiling system hypothesized can therefore be viewed as an attempt to equalize in part the distribution of such important social goods as family stability and the ability to enjoy and exercise freedom. Of course, the contribution a low ceiling system would make toward securing these goods is only a partial one, but it may nonetheless be an important complement to other programs with the same objectives.

2.   The Apparent Infringement on Freedom I: Who Is Hurt by Low Ceilings?

Lowered ceilings would limit credit to three identifiable classes of borrowers, and only the third class could rationally complain that its freedom of action was being impaired. The first class consists of those who would not use high risk credit if they fully understood the extent and seriousness of the risk involved. The evidence indicates that consumers understand little about the terms and conditions of the credit they purchase. On the other hand, they probably do understand that if they fail to repay, serious consequences will follow. But a large group of high risk debtors may well fail to comprehend their own degree of risk. No one tells them, as they might, "Eight out of fifty of your class will have serious trouble repaying; two or three out of one hundred of your class will default and be subjected to repossession." [A study of the National Commission on Consumer Finance] provides some evidence that the size of this group of unaware borrowers may be substantial and that the members of this group may not object to the elimination of high risk credit. Of those who were denied high risk credit by a legislative change in Maine's small loan laws, thirty-six percent indicated that they were pleased to be rid of the "burden" of the finance company, and another twenty-seven percent "felt about the same" without credit as with it.*

A second class of those who would be affected by lowered ceilings is composed of those people who are simply not competent to run their own affairs. Although I suspect this class to be rather small, few would object to protecting those who fall within its bounds. Those who have advocated high rate ceilings have usually argued that the creditor has a strong self-interest in identifying members of this class of borrowers and refusing to extend them credit. Outside of certain peculiar submarkets, this incentive no doubt exists and is quite strong. But the problem is that a creditor's ability to distinguish members of this class is limited by the cost of obtaining the necessary information and by the difficulty of ever knowing fully the subjective motivations, intelligence and fortune of another person. In fact, there may be more than a few members of this class who are not filtered out by creditors. They might be protected by a lowered ceiling.

The disadvantage of the lowered ceiling is to the third class: those who are intelligent enough to handle their own affairs and willing after intelligent consideration to run the risk of high cost, high default credit, but who cannot in fact obtain credit from an alternative low risk source. To this class of borrowers the interference with the ability to arrange their own lives is not so insignificant as to be fairly ignored. Use of credit to purchase durable goods may sometimes produce a net savings to the consumer. Moreover, consumption behavior is a frequently practiced form of individual expression in this society. By purchasing certain goods on credit, an individual may hope to enjoy a more satisfying mixture of amenities and necessities than he could otherwise acquire.

The critics have always denounced low ceilings because of the kind of interference with freedom which would fall on the third class. As the critics have framed the problem, low ceilings are undesirable because they obstruct personal liberty (in choice of lifestyle) for an improper purpose, paternalistic intervention. This argument focuses on the interests of the third class rather than of the first and second classes, and it has therefore misstated the issue. In fact, the ethical question is whether, despite the protection provided the first two classes at no real loss in liberty, the

---

* See Littwin, Testing the Substitution Hypothesis: Would Credit Card Regulation Force Low–Income Borrowers into Less Desirable Lending Alternatives? Available at www.papers.ssrn.com.—Ed.

infringement of the personal liberty of the third class is so unacceptable as to require that lowered ceilings not be used as a tool of social policy.

The argument in response may begin from an ethical premise quite similar to the one underlying the critics' position. Although the state ought not to limit personal liberty solely for a paternalistic purpose, it properly may infringe on it in order to help and protect others. This statement of the relation of the individual to the state is a familiar feature of utilitarian philosophy, and lowered ceilings are consistent with it. Their use for protection would not be for a paternalistic purpose. They are designed to protect the first and second classes whose liberty is not decreased by the protection, although at the expense of the third class.

Alternatively, one may begin from the premise that some infringement on personal liberty by the state is acceptable when the infringement is slight, affects economic rather than political rights, and improves the distribution of benefits in the society. If we accept this position, as many others have, the question becomes whether the infringement caused by lowered ceilings can fairly be called minor. There are several reasons why it can be. First, although low ceilings limit somewhat the ability to buy major durable goods on credit, the alternative ways of spending the money involved might be thought adequate to compensate for the loss. The payments that would have gone to repay the debt with interest could be spent on lower priced items or saved. Although some advantageous opportunities—for example, the possibility that a washing machine bought on credit would result in net savings to a large family—will no doubt be lost, the alternatives will be adequate in most cases, such as when use of public transportation would be cheaper than driving a private car purchased on credit. Second, lowered ceilings do not interfere with the restricted individual's ability to express himself through a wide range of purchase behavior on a cash basis. Third, if credit were not available, equally valued new outlets for expression other than purchase behavior might emerge as substitutes. And, finally, the shape our consumption desires take appears to be influenced to some degree by social pressures, and particularly by the cumulative effect of massive advertising. The resulting purchase behavior is therefore an amalgam of individual preference and social conformism. As a result, restrictions on purchase behavior are not wholly restrictions on individual freedom of choice.

The foregoing analysis demonstrates that the interference with individual liberty occasioned by lowered ceilings will not be nearly as burdensome as some have thought. In addition, it is clear that our society already tolerates numerous forms of protective legislation that interfere significantly with an individual's ability to spend wealth in precisely the way he wants. The Consumer Product Safety Commission, for example, has the power to ban unsafe products from the market, even though some who realize they are unsafe may want to buy them. Thus, I am not persuaded that low ceilings must be rejected out of hand simply because they would somewhat compromise the value of individual liberty. The conclusion does not directly follow, however, that such ceilings are justifiable. At most, low ceilings for the protective purposes I am advocating would be set so as to restrict borrowing by only a small portion of the population. The dominant society would still be able to use credit freely. The exclusion of the poorest members of society from the dominant culture might therefore be exacerbated. For the third class of borrowers, those who want to use risky credit, the restriction on freedom to borrow caused by low ceilings is actually a decrease in the ability to participate in the dominant culture. Although the lack of empirical evidence prevents accurately assessing how serious this widening of the gulf between rich and poor would be, the potential for harm is great enough to demand that the widening be seriously examined.

3.   The Apparent Infringement on Freedom II: Inequality

The unavoidable conclusion from what has gone before is that any infringement on freedom of action caused by low ceilings involves a question more of unequal economic treatment for the disadvantaged than of a significant infringement on liberty. Insofar as the critics have based their attack on the argument that low ceilings interfere with freedom, they may be fairly charged with mislabeling the basic issue. Low ceilings can be justified as an attempt to promote equality by preserving the basic dignity of the debtor and the debtor family. Conversely, high ceilings arguably permit high risk debtors to share in some degree the consumption opportunities of the more fortunate although, of course, at higher interest costs. Two mutually exclusive schemes of social organization, the low and the high ceiling systems hypothesized, both seek to justify themselves as methods for promoting equality. The type of equality that each seeks to promote, however, is different. Low ceilings promote equality by seeking to avoid catastrophes that would destroy stability, self-esteem and family life. The focus is on conserving the little property and security held by high risk debtors, most of whom presumably fall in the lower ranks of wealth. High ceilings promote equality by expanding the opportunities of the same group, at the attendant cost of increasing the risks, and potentially the rewards, of that group. The basic issue in the controversy over low ceilings, then, is the ethical problem of determining which type of equality should be given priority.

4.   The Priority of Protection

A strict utilitarian would resolve the priority problem just posed in favor of the alternative that produced the greatest good for the greatest number. So analyzed, the decision might be thought best resolved by a surrogate for majority vote of the borrowers involved. The relevant empirical question would then be whether the first and second classes described above were greater in number, or perhaps in intensity of opinion, than those in the third class, the group most disadvantaged by low ceilings.

There is a pragmatic objection, however, that may be raised to basing resolution of this problem on strict utilitarian grounds. The utilitarian test for priority raises difficult, and possibly unresolvable, questions. How can we determine the greatest good in a conflict of this nature when the answer immediately turns empirical and fades into interpersonal comparisons of utility, as it must? How can we decide satisfactorily whether the first and second classes are numerically larger than the third; whether the feelings on the question held by the first and second classes are stronger than those of the third? The only satisfactory answer may be that we cannot avoid such questions. But if the manifest defects of the market as a device for resolving such questions lead us to reject its verdict, as I have argued we must, then informed intuition and belief seem to be the substitute with which we must be content. As I argue below, the lowered ceiling position has, on the present state of the evidence, as much intuitive appeal in utilitarian terms as does that of its critics.

Another approach to wealth distribution questions . . . suggests that some of these difficulties with utilitarianism can be avoided. If the criterion of choice between conflicting policies should be . . . to select whichever program favors the least advantaged group of society, the controlling question is apparently narrower than that involved in a strict utilitarian judgment. Arguably, the least advantaged groups affected by low ceilings are the first and second classes, while the third class is by comparison the most advantaged. The first class, composed of those who now use high risk credit but would not if they understood the degree of risk they run, seems easily viewed as less competent and less secure than the members of the third class, composed of those who would willingly take on the risk of default in light of the potential rewards. The few studies made of the relation between personality and attitude toward risk-taking support this view. The fact that the second class seems clearly more disadvantaged than the third adds additional support to this justification for low rate ceilings.

. . .

Despite these difficulties, the principle that society should generally favor the least advantaged in making a wealth distribution choice has strong appeal. The choice between a low ceiling and a high one is a choice between hurting the first and second classes on the one hand or the third class on the other. The first two classes seem the most deserving, unless either they are very small in comparison to the third or the protection from psychic harm provided by lowered ceilings is insignificant.

. . .

D. . . . Will Low Ceilings Interfere Excessively with the Competitive Structure of the Industry?

The National Commission on Consumer Finance staff has offered evidence to suggest that in the long run low ceilings will tend to reduce the competitiveness of the credit industry. Presumably, a decrease in competitiveness would have the same effect on the credit industry as that experienced in many other industries—reduced efficiency, increased profits and, of course, increased price of credit. Willingness to innovate may also decrease. Advocates of low ceilings must therefore justify them against the important charge that, regardless of the protection afforded, their anticompetitive effects make them ultimately against the interests of consumers. . . .

The anticompetitive effects of the types of lowered ceilings hypothesized here should not be overestimated. A twenty percent APR mean rate ceiling will only affect competition in the market for a relatively small proportion of consumer credit. Although that market may have a tendency toward concentration, reduced innovation, inefficiency and excess profit taking, in the main the industry should remain controlled by competitive forces. Thus, there is little reason to fear that, for example, the whole industry would fail to adapt to technological advances, since the competitive sector should pull the noncompetitive sector along. Of course, the usual effects of concentration, higher prices and somewhat restricted availability would have to be expected.

In view of the limited anticompetitive effects to be expected, it is necessary to examine more closely the nature of their impact to determine whether these effects will substantially offset the improvement in distribution anticipated from lowered ceilings. If lowered ceilings do decrease competition, the most apparent effect on consumers would be to burden with slightly higher prices all credit users who qualify for borrowing. The adverse effects on the group of low risk, presumably better off individuals would be the price of protecting the high risk group denied credit. Thus, the burden of the anticompetitive effects will fall most heavily on the more advantaged groups, producing a minimum of interference with any distributive improvement that is accomplished. The ethical justification for a distributive program that favors the least fortunate at the expense of the more fortunate should be clear.

. . .

IV. CONCLUSION

Recently, there has been much criticism and little defense of low consumer credit rate ceilings. The result has been an unbalanced view of the issues involved. An overview of the potential of lowered ceilings suggests several uses that appear to deserve thorough consideration before a state or the nation elects a high ceiling policy. Furthermore, close examination of one use—protecting high risk debtors from the psychic harm associated with default—suggests that a moderately low ceiling applied to all forms of consumer credit provides a significant improvement in the distribution of benefits within society. There will, of course, be those who disagree. When considerations of social policy turn on the degree of psychic harm which one or another class must bear, empirical evidence can only help uncover the right decision, it cannot identify it with certainty. A conclusion in favor of a particular alternative must instead turn on the exercise of careful judgment, informed by the available evidence and shaped by the relevant ethical considerations. My purpose has been to show those who set rate ceiling policy that a reasonable judgment can be made to use lowered ceilings for protective purposes. A fair evaluation of the empirical evidence and relevant ethical considerations supports, on balance, lowered ceilings instead of the high ceiling alternative generally proposed. Of course, those who assess differently the real world—the workings of the credit industry, the motivations of credit users and the effectiveness of government regulation—will dispute this conclusion. The available empirical evidence certainly does not preclude differences on this basis, and I would prefer more evidence correlating default harm with high risk credit before advocating wide adoption of lowered ceilings. But in my judgment the most reasonable conclusion is that the psychic harm caused by default will have great impact on high risk debtors if they do borrow and default, while losing the benefits of credit and suffering pain and embarrassment when it is denied will have a relatively slight effect.

Differing interpretations of the evidence should not be exaggerated, however. The disagreement over rate ceiling policy arises from a basic difference as to the ethical considerations which should be brought to bear on the decision. In this respect, the argument for lowered ceilings appears to rest on stronger grounds than that advanced by its critics. The ethical justification for lowered ceilings begins from the premise that any program designed to improve the distribution of benefits and burdens in the society must at a minimum favor those who are the least advantaged. Lowered ceilings appear to satisfy this criterion. They will protect two classes of debtors, both of which now use high risk credit but are unaware of the risks they run when they do so, at the expense of a third class which seems likely to be better off than the others. In contrast, the ethical position of those who oppose lowered ceilings remains obscure. On the surface the critics argue that low ceilings will intolerably impair individual liberty and must therefore be rejected. Yet close analysis demonstrates little, if any, impairment of the liberty of the two classes of debtors who are to be protected. Although the freedom of the third class to use credit is in fact impaired, any program to improve distribution will probably encroach somewhat on the freedom of others to do what they want. Few will disagree that some limited encroachment on freedom is acceptable if a significant improvement in distribution results.

Some critics have also premised their position on a version of utilitarianism. They argue that high ceilings will maximize the sum of social satisfaction, but they fail to inquire whether those less well off at the start are those who end with the greatest improvement. A high ceiling program would favor the third class of debtors—those who are aware of the risks of high risk credit and want to use it—at the expense of the first two classes. It is difficult to see how social conditions are improved when the effect of a program is to worsen the lot of the least advantaged classes affected. If the critics have an ethical justification for high ceilings which rests on a different foundation, they have failed to explain it.

Reformers have tended to decide questions of social organization involving the marketplace by an easy reliance upon the standard wisdom that an unregulated market, on balance, will produce the best result. Thus, they first suggest solving a social problem in the marketplace by increasing the conformance of the real market to the intellectual model of the unregulated market. Yet defining the best social organization is an ethical question, and the ethical underpinnings of the results of the unregulated market seem increasingly out of tune with the ethical views of the dominant culture. When the market exposes individuals to risk of severe physical or psychic harm, ethical concerns will likely reject reliance on the unregulated market. The Consumer Product Safety Commission's authority to ban unsafe products is one demonstration of this rejection. Therefore, it is no surprise that a close examination of the consumer credit system leads in a similar direction. Rate ceilings will be, in effect, a ban on unsafe credit. What should surprise is the failure to notice the similarity between banning unsafe products and banning unsafe credit. But the model of the unregulated market seems to hold an almost magic fascination; unfortunately, the magic tends to bewitch rather than clarify. Although economic analysis helps identify a reform program's cost and benefits, it also tends to obscure the relevant ethical questions. The only antidote is to inquire continually whether the market will reach an ethically justifiable result. When that question is asked about consumer credit, the answer suggests lowered rate ceilings, inconsistent though they may be with the very essence of an unregulated market.

QUESTIONS

1. Professor Wallace admits that statutory ceilings on the price of consumer credit reduce the efficiency of the market. Why does he nevertheless favor rate regulation?

2. Does it make sense to view high-priced credit as "unsafe?" See Pottow, Private Liability for Reckless Consumer Lending, 2007 U.Ill.L.Rev. 405.

3. In examining how low ceilings will help consumers, Professor Wallace asserts that low ceilings will result in denial of credit to three groups of consumers: those who would not use high-cost credit if they fully understood the risk; those who are not competent to manage their own affairs; and those who are competent and fully understand the risk, yet still want high-cost credit. He views two of these classes as better off and one as worse off, under a low-ceiling system. Are low ceilings justifiable merely because two classes are better off and only one class is worse off? Who determines, and by what criteria, whether persons in the three classes are "better off" or "worse off"?

4. For another defense of rate regulation, see Morris, Consumer Debt and Usury: A New Rationale for Usury, 15 Pepperdine L.Rev. 151, 158 (1988):

> To the extent that usury prescribes the rate of interest lenders may charge borrowers, usury paternalistically substitutes government judgment for that of the parties to the transaction, displacing the market dialogue by eliminating bargaining at least on that term. Viewed on a larger scale, however, usury has another important market effect: its effect on the supply of credit. Usury is a mechanism for controlling the amount of credit in society. By controlling lender incentive to lend by limiting profits from lending, usury laws counter-

balance forces increasing the supply of credit. As such, it is a proxy for society's interest in controlling the amount of credit more than society's interest in controlling lender profit.

See also Brown, An Argument Evaluating Price Controls on Bank Credit Cards in Light of Certain Reemerging Common Law Doctrines, 9 Ga. State L.Rev. 797 (1993); Rougeau, Rediscovering Usury: An Argument for Legal Controls on Credit Card Interest Rates, 67 U.Colo.L.Rev. 1 (1996); McCall, Unprofitable Lending: Modern Credit Regulation and the Lost Theory of Usury, available at www.papers.ssrn.com.

5. The dramatic rise in free market interest rates between 1978 and 1982 was followed by a dramatic drop in rates. During the period in which rates were rising, the rates charged on bank credit cards increased to the statutory maximums of 18–22%. Between 1982 and 1992 the banks' cost of funds fell substantially, but the rates on bank credit cards did not. See Note, Credit Card Interest Rates and Their Immunity to Market Fluctuations, 7 Ann.Rev. Banking Law 463 (1988). Does this belie the claim that we should rely on competitive forces in the marketplace to regulate interest rates?

In addition to the phenomenon of bank card rates, consider the following information concerning bank loans and finance company loans. Historically, the rates charged by banks have been significantly lower than the rates charged by finance companies. An obvious explanation for this is that finance company customers present a higher risk of default than bank customers and therefore do not meet the creditworthiness standards of banks. But a statistical survey of consumers revealed that customers of finance companies and customers of banks have very similar levels of income and outstanding debt. Avery et al., Survey of Consumer Finances, 1983: A Second Report, 70 Fed.Res.Bull. 857, 867 (1984) (Table 11: less than 6% difference in median income and median debt). This analysis suggests that the obvious explanation may not be the real explanation. What else might explain the difference in interest rates between banks and finance companies? What might explain why consumers borrow from finance companies even though they could qualify for less expensive credit from banks? And what implications do these explanations have for the proposition that we should rely on competition to regulate the price of credit?

6. The record-high interest rates in the late 1970s made the debate more urgent: rates rose so high that under most rate regulation statutes even low-risk borrowers were unable to obtain credit. This made it even clearer than it had been that "high" and "low" were relative terms, and the pressure for raising the ceiling on consumer credit costs became irresistible. Indeed, the slowness of some states to act led to federal intervention. After taking some temporary steps in the 1970s, Congress enacted the Depository Institutions Deregulation and Monetary Control Act of 1980. Pub.L. 96–221, 94 Stat. 151. For qualifying lenders, this Act preempts state regulation of home mortgage loans.

The Act also preempts state regulation of interest rates on mobile homes. To qualify for this preemption, however, the lender must comply with federal regulations that require the lender to give the consumer a 30–day opportunity to cure defaults before the creditor repossesses, forecloses, or accelerates. 12 U.S.C. § 1735f–7a(c); 12 C.F.R. § 590.4.[5] If the creditor's contract fails to comply with the regulations, then state law continues to govern the finance charge. In Quiller v. Barclays American/Credit, Inc., 727 F.2d 1067, 1071–72 (11th Cir.1984), reinstated on rehearing en banc, 764 F.2d 1400 (11th Cir.1985), cert. denied 476 U.S. 1124 (1986), the contract provided:

> If Customer defaults on any obligation under this contract, or if Holder shall consider the indebtedness or the Collateral insecure, the full balance may, upon election of Holder, without notice, subject to any notice of right to cure, become due and payable, less the required rebate of the Finance Charge. . . . Customer agrees in any such case to pay said amount or, at Holder's election, to deliver the Collateral to Holder, and Holder may, without notice or demand for performance or legal process, peaceably enter any premises, but not into any dwelling, where the Collateral may be found, peaceably take possession of it and custody of anything found in it.

The court stated:

> In determining whether the terms and conditions of this agreement comply with the Board's consumer protection regulations, we should keep in mind that Congress included manufactured home financing in its preemption scheme only on the condition that consumer-debtors would be guaranteed certain safeguards. See H.Conf.Rep. No. 96–842, 96th Cong., 2d Sess. 79, *reprinted in* 1980 U.S.Code Cong. & Ad.News 298, 309. Because purchasers of mobile homes frequently are unaware of complicated rules of contract construction, we should examine the contract through the eyes of the typical consumer and determine whether the lender could use the terms of the contract to impose illegal burdens on a debtor with no knowledge of his statutory rights. It would be unrealistic to assume that every illegal act will be corrected through litigation. See General Finance Corp. of Georgia v. Sprouse, 577 F.2d 989 (5th Cir.1978) (when interpreting contracts in light of consumer legislation, court should consider actual operation of contract in commercial world, effect upon consumer not familiar with legal rights, and risk that contract might allow lender to employ ambiguous provisions to his advantage). The rule of construction that ambiguities and inconsistencies should be resolved against the drafter, is particularly appropriate in the areas protected by consumer legislation.

> . . .

5. The regulations also limit late charges and balloon payments.

The agreement includes language that, on its face, is contrary to the requirements of the statute and regulations. It permits the creditor (1) to foreclose on the loan "without notice;" (2) to repossess "without notice or demand for performance or legal process;" and (3) to demand payment of the full balance upon the debtor's default or the creditor's insecurity "without notice." These provisions are inaccurate statements of the creditor's rights under federal law. The only language that might apprise the debtor of his statutory right to notice is the vague qualification that the creditor's express, contractual powers to immediately foreclose, repossess and accelerate are "subject to any notice of right to cure." Unless the debtor has acquired knowledge of his statutory right to cure from some outside source, however, this language will not accurately notify him of his contractual rights. The qualification would, at most, inform the debtor that he *may* have a right to cure, but the law guarantees him an *absolute* right to cure. This inconsistent language goes further than simply remaining silent on the debtor's right to notice upon default; by declaring the creditor's unauthorized power to foreclose immediately, the consumer is given an affirmative misrepresentation as to his statutory guarantees.

The court held that since the contract did not conform to the federal regulations, the preemption provision did not apply, and the contract was governed by state usury law.

7.   Except for conferring most-favored lender status on federally insured depository institutions, federal preemption of state usury laws has been confined to housing-related loans. Consequently, state legislatures also confronted the problem of record-high interest rates in the late 1970s, and they responded by raising their ceilings on consumer loans. Several even abolished the ceilings altogether, at least for some kinds of loans. For many forms of consumer credit, most states continue to regulate the maximum rate of charge. The principles addressed in this chapter, therefore, remain relevant.

CHAPTER 9

OTHER LIMITS ON THE TERMS OF THE DEAL

The preceding two chapters have examined limitations on the quality and price terms of consumer contracts. This chapter continues the theme by exploring several related doctrines that limit these and other contractual terms. The doctrines explored here also pose limits on the formation and enforcement of consumer contracts, but the focus of this chapter continues to be the substance of the deal. The first case concerns a doctrine with which you are already familiar; the case itself may be an old friend.

A. BROADLY PHRASED STANDARDS

(1) UNCONSCIONABILITY

Williams v. Walker–Thomas Furniture Co.

United States Court of Appeals, District of Columbia Circuit, 1965.
350 F.2d 445.

J. SKELLY WRIGHT, CIRCUIT JUDGE:

Appellee, Walker–Thomas Furniture Company, operates a retail furniture store in the District of Columbia. During the period from 1957 to 1962 each appellant in these cases purchased a number of household items from Walker–Thomas, for which payment was to be made in installments. The terms of each purchase were contained in a printed form contract which set forth the value of the purchased item and purported to lease the item to appellant for a stipulated monthly rent payment. The contract then provided, in substance, that title would remain in Walker–Thomas until the total of all the monthly payments made equaled the stated value of the item, at which time appellants could take title. In the event of a default in the payment of any monthly installment, Walker–Thomas could repossess the item.

The contract further provided that "the amount of each periodical installment payment to be made by [purchaser] to the Company under this present lease shall be inclusive of and not in addition to the amount of each installment payment to be made by [purchaser] under such prior leases, bills or accounts; *and all payments now and hereafter made by [purchaser] shall be credited pro rata on all outstanding leases, bills and accounts due*

470

the Company by [purchaser] at the time each such payment is made." (Emphasis added.) The effect of this rather obscure provision was to keep a balance due on every item purchased until the balance due on all items, whenever purchased, was liquidated. As a result, the debt incurred at the time of purchase of each item was secured by the right to repossess all the items previously purchased by the same purchaser, and each new item purchased automatically became subject to a security interest arising out of the previous dealings.

On May 12, 1962, appellant Thorne purchased an item described as a Daveno, three tables, and two lamps, having total stated value of $391.10. Shortly thereafter, he defaulted on his monthly payments and appellee sought to replevy all the items purchased since the first transaction in 1958. Similarly, on April 17, 1962, appellant Williams bought a stereo set of stated value of $514.95.[1] She too defaulted shortly thereafter, and appellee sought to replevy all the items purchased since December, 1957. The Court of General Sessions granted judgment for appellee. The District of Columbia Court of Appeals affirmed, and we granted appellants' motion for leave to appeal to this court.

Appellants' principal contention, rejected by both the trial and the appellate courts below, is that these contracts, or at least some of them, are unconscionable and, hence, not enforceable. In its opinion in Williams v. Walker–Thomas Furniture Company, 198 A.2d 914, 916 (1964), the District of Columbia Court of Appeals explained its rejection of this contention as follows:

> Appellant's second argument presents a more serious question. The record reveals that prior to the last purchase appellant had reduced the balance in her account to $164. The last purchase, a stereo set, raised the balance due to $678. Significantly, at the time of this and the preceding purchases, appellee was aware of appellant's financial position. The reverse side of the stereo contract listed the name of appellant's social worker and her $218 monthly stipend from the government. Nevertheless, with full knowledge that appellant had to feed, clothe and support both herself and seven children on this amount, appellee sold her a $514 stereo set.
>
> We cannot condemn too strongly appellee's conduct. It raises serious questions of sharp practice and irresponsible business dealings. A review of the legislation in the District of Columbia affecting retail sales and the pertinent decisions of the highest court in this jurisdiction disclose, however, no ground upon which this court can declare the contracts in question contrary to public policy. We note that were the Maryland Retail Installment Sales Act, Art. 83 §§ 128–153, or its equivalent, in force in the District of Columbia, we could grant appellant appropriate relief. We think Congress should consider corrective

---

1. At the time of this purchase her account showed a balance of $164 still owing from her prior purchases. The total of all the purchases made over the years in question came to $1,800. The total payments amounted to $1,400.

legislation to protect the public from such exploitive contracts as were utilized in the case at bar.

We do not agree that the court lacked the power to refuse enforcement to contracts found to be unconscionable. In other jurisdictions, it has been held as a matter of common law that unconscionable contracts are not enforceable. While no decision of this court so holding has been found, the notion that an unconscionable bargain should not be given full enforcement is by no means novel. In Scott v. United States, 79 U.S. (12 Wall.) 443, 445, 20 L.Ed. 438 (1870), the Supreme Court stated:

> * * * If a contract be unreasonable and unconscionable, but not void for fraud, a court of law will give to the party who sues for its breach damages, not according to its letter, but only such as he is equitably entitled to. * * *

Since we have never adopted or rejected such a rule, the question here presented is actually one of first impression.

Congress has recently enacted the Uniform Commercial Code, which specifically provides that the court may refuse to enforce a contract which it finds to be unconscionable at the time it was made. The enactment of this section, which occurred subsequent to the contracts here in suit, does not mean that the common law of the District of Columbia was otherwise at the time of enactment, nor does it preclude the court from adopting a similar rule in the exercise of its powers to develop the common law for the District of Columbia. In fact, in view of the absence of prior authority on the point, we consider the congressional adoption of § 2–302 persuasive authority for following the rationale of the cases from which the section is explicitly derived. Accordingly, we hold that where the element of unconscionability is present at the time a contract is made, the contract should not be enforced.

Unconscionability has generally been recognized to include an absence of meaningful choice on the part of one of the parties together with contract terms which are unreasonably favorable to the other party. Whether a meaningful choice is present in a particular case can only be determined by consideration of all the circumstances surrounding the transaction. In many cases the meaningfulness of the choice is negated by a gross inequality of bargaining power. The manner in which the contract was entered is also relevant to this consideration. Did each party to the contract, considering his obvious education or lack of it, have a reasonable opportunity to understand the terms of the contract, or were the important terms hidden in a maze of fine print and minimized by deceptive sales practices? Ordinarily, one who signs an agreement without full knowledge of its terms might be held to assume the risk that he has entered a one-sided bargain. But when a party of little bargaining power, and hence little real choice, signs a commercially unreasonable contract with little or no knowledge of its terms, it is hardly likely that his consent, or even an objective manifestation of his consent, was ever given to all the terms. In such a case the usual rule that the terms of the agreement are not to be questioned should be abandoned and the court should consider whether the terms of the contract are so unfair that enforcement should be withheld.

In determining reasonableness or fairness, the primary concern must be with the terms of the contract considered in light of the circumstances existing when the contract was made. The test is not simple, nor can it be mechanically applied. The terms are to be considered "in the light of the general commercial background and the commercial needs of the particular trade or case." Corbin suggests the test as being whether the terms are "so extreme as to appear unconscionable according to the mores and business practices of the time and place." We think this formulation correctly states the test to be applied in those cases where no meaningful choice was exercised upon entering the contract.

Reasonableness/unfair

Because the trial court and the appellate court did not feel that enforcement could be refused, no findings were made on the possible unconscionability of the contracts in these cases. Since the record is not sufficient for our deciding the issue as a matter of law, the cases must be remanded to the trial court for further proceedings.

So ordered.

DANAHER, CIRCUIT JUDGE (dissenting):

The District of Columbia Court of Appeals obviously was as unhappy about the situation here presented as any of us can possibly be. Its opinion in the *Williams* case, quoted in the majority text, concludes: "We think Congress should consider corrective legislation to protect the public from such exploitive contracts as were utilized in the case at bar."

My view is thus summed up by an able court which made no finding that there had actually been sharp practice. Rather the appellant seems to have known precisely where she stood.

There are many aspects of public policy here involved. What is a luxury to some may seem an outright necessity to others. Is public oversight to be required of the expenditures of relief funds? A washing machine, e.g., in the hands of a relief client might become a fruitful source of income. Many relief clients may well need credit, and certain business establishments will take long chances on the sale of items, expecting their pricing policies will afford a degree of protection commensurate with the risk. Perhaps a remedy when necessary will be found within the provisions of the "Loan Shark" law, D.C.Code §§ 26–601 et seq. (1961).

I mention such matters only to emphasize the desirability of a cautious approach to any such problem, particularly since the law for so long has allowed parties such great latitude in making their own contracts. I dare say there must annually be thousands upon thousands of installment credit transactions in this jurisdiction, and one can only speculate as to the effect the decision in these cases will have.

I join the District of Columbia Court of Appeals in its disposition of the issues.

QUESTIONS AND NOTES

1. Does *Williams* stand for the proposition that it is unconscionable to sell luxury items to a person on welfare?

2. The security device used by Walker–Thomas is known as a cross-collateral clause. Does *Williams* stand for the proposition that a cross-collateral clause is unconscionable?

3. The court in *Williams* develops a two-part test for unconscionability. What are the two parts of the test? Are both parts essential to a finding of unconscionability? Should they be?

In A & M Produce Co. v. FMC Corp., 186 Cal.Rptr. 114, 121–22 (Cal.App.1982), the court stated:

> The Uniform Commercial Code does not attempt to precisely define what is or is not "unconscionable." . . . [U]nconscionability has both a "procedural" and a "substantive" element. . . .
>
> Of course the mere fact that a contract term is not read or understood by the non-drafting party or that the drafting party occupies a superior bargaining position will not authorize a court to refuse to enforce the contract. Although an argument can be made that contract terms not actively negotiated between the parties fall outside the "circle of assent" which constitutes the actual agreement, commercial practicalities dictate that unbargained-for terms only be denied enforcement where they are also *substantively* unreasonable. No precise definition of substantive unconscionability can be proffered. Cases have talked in terms of "overly-harsh" or "one-sided" results. . . . The most detailed and specific commentaries observe that a contract is largely an allocation of risks between the parties, and therefore that a contractual term is substantively suspect if it reallocates the risks of the bargain in an objectively unreasonable or unexpected manner. But not all unreasonable risk allocations are unconscionable; rather, enforceability of the clause is tied to the procedural aspects of unconscionability such that the greater the unfair surprise or inequality of bargaining power, the less unreasonable the risk reallocation which will be tolerated.

Is the court suggesting that it may suffice if there is *either* procedural *or* substantive unconscionability?

4. What should it take to satisfy the procedural element, absence of meaningful choice? One court has suggested that it suffices that the consumers with whom the merchant does business "did not have free access to credit." Brown v. C.I.L., Inc., 1996 WL 164294, *8 (N.D.Ill.1996) (denying lender's motion for summary judgment). Is the court correct?

In Stirlen v. Supercuts, Inc., 60 Cal.Rptr.2d 138 (Cal.App.1997), the court held that in a contract of adhesion the procedural element of unconscionability is satisfied. Should other states follow California's lead?

5. Since the deregulation of home mortgage interest rates in the early 1980s, there has been an explosion in the availability of credit to consumers whose credit records are blemished, known as subprime borrowers. The positive side of this is that the availability of home ownership has increased immensely. Unfortunately, there also is a negative side. The high interest rates have attracted home improvement contractors, loan brokers, and lenders that seem to be interested in maximizing their returns without regard to the impact their activity has on their customers. Too often the lender uses deception to ensnare consumers in loans with high closing costs, often concealed; high interest rates; and onerous terms. Often it is apparent from the outset that the consumer's income is not sufficient to cover the monthly payments and other obligations imposed by the loan. When the consumer defaults, the lender induces the consumer to refinance time and again, causing the pyramiding of charges and the increasing of the debt, as in *Branch* (page 441 supra), until the loan principal approximates the consumer's equity in the home. Since the home secures the debt, the end result often is the loss of the home altogether.

In 1994 Congress enacted the Home Owners Equity Protection Act (HOEPA), amending the Truth-in-Lending Act, to address some of these problems. (TIL § 129, Regulation Z § 226.31, –.32, –.34). As revised, it applies to closed-end credit transactions that are secured by the consumer's residence, but not if the credit is used for the purchase or construction of the residence. In addition, the loan must have one of two triggers: 1) the annual percentage rate must be at least ten percent more than the Treasury rate for loans of comparable duration (unless the lender has a first lien mortgage, in which event it need only be eight percent more than the Treasury rate); or 2) the loan fees must exceed the larger of $561 (as of 2008, to be adjusted annually for changes in the consumer price index) or eight percent of the principal amount of the loan. If a loan is covered by HOEPA, the creditor must make disclosures in addition to those required by the rest of the Truth-in-Lending Act (Regulation § 226.31, –.32). In addition, HOEPA imposes several substantive restraints on the creditor (Regulation Z § 226.34).

The next principal case arose before the enactment of HOEPA. Even today, of course, HOEPA applies only if the loan contains one of the triggers. As you might imagine, a lender that does not want to comply with HOEPA can avoid its constraints by keeping the annual percentage rate and fees just below the triggers. Hence it is necessary to consider other potential limits on the conduct of creditors in loan transactions. The foregoing materials in this chapter have considered unconscionability as a limit on conduct in *sales* transactions. The next case examines whether unconscionability imposes limits on loan transactions as well.

Cheshire Mortgage Service, Inc. v. Montes

Supreme Court of Connecticut, 1992.
223 Conn. 80, 612 A.2d 1130.

BORDEN, J.

. . .

The relevant facts are as follows. The defendants were a married couple from Puerto Rico who had been living on the mainland of the United

States for more than twenty years. In February 1984 the defendants purchased a home in New Haven for $25,000.[6] They financed the purchase with a down payment of $3000 and a $23,700 mortgage loan from People's Bank, with monthly mortgage payments of $407. In July 1987 Tech Energy, a Connecticut home repair and improvement company, contacted Dalila Montes and offered to provide vinyl siding for the defendants' home at a cost of approximately $10,000. The defendants agreed to purchase the siding, and thereafter Tech Energy submitted a loan application of the defendants to the Tolland Bank in order to finance the cost of the siding. The loan application stated that the defendants had a monthly income of $1195. Tolland Bank denied the application.

Tech Energy then submitted the same Tolland Bank loan application to the plaintiff in order to obtain a second mortgage loan. The plaintiff approved the loan based upon the following factors, in addition to the information contained in the loan application. The plaintiff had obtained a credit report indicating that the defendants had been regularly paying their first mortgage loan to People's Bank. The plaintiff also took into consideration the fact that there was "good loan equity in this case" and that the funds were going to be used to improve the property and, thus, the security for the loan. Furthermore, Dalila Montes stated to the plaintiff's president that, in addition to the income listed on the application form, Luis Montes "had some additional income" from work in "some sort of trade." Neither the plaintiff nor the defendants documented the amount of this additional income or its specific source. On the basis of the foregoing information, the plaintiff approved the loan and placed the defendants in a "no-income verification loan program." Under the "no-income verification loan program" the plaintiff did not require the defendants to verify the amount of Luis A. Montes' additional income.

The loan closing was held on November 16, 1987. The defendants were required to grant to the plaintiff a second mortgage on their residence in order to secure the loan. In order for the plaintiff to obtain a second mortgage position, however, it was necessary to pay off three prior liens on the defendants' residence—a lien held by the state for child support in the amount of $8950, a lien held by the city of New Haven welfare department in the amount of $1290.31 and a judgment lien for a medical bill in the amount of $2431. These prior liens on the residence totaled $12,671.31. Therefore, the principal amount of the loan, as stated in the note and the loan closing statement, was $26,500, which included the payment of the prior liens, $9902 for the cost of the siding,[8] $1300 in closing costs,[9] a $2500

---

6. On October 10, 1990, the property was appraised at $90,000.

8. The cost of the siding was apparently $9902. The plaintiff's disclosure statement noted that one half of that amount, or $4951, was to be paid to Tech Energy, and the same amount was to be paid to Peter K. Motti, the plaintiff's closing attorney, as trustee. Appar-

ently, Tech Energy had been paid one half its fee in advance, and the other one half was to be disbursed by Motti as the work progressed.

9. The plaintiff's disclosure statement disclosed the following closing costs to the defendants for the November 16, 1987 loan:

prepaid finance charge and $126.69 paid directly to the defendants. The annual interest rate was 18 percent. The promissory note provided that the defendants were to make thirty-five monthly payments of $399.38, and a final "balloon" payment of $26,810.61.

Approximately seven months later, after they had made seven timely mortgage payments, the defendants sought another loan for approximately $9000 from the plaintiff to be used for additional improvements to their home in order for them to sell it within one year. On the basis of a new credit report indicating that the defendants had continued to pay their first mortgage and had made every payment on the plaintiff's second mortgage, the plaintiff approved the new loan. The loan closing was held on May 26, 1988.[10] The principal amount of the new loan, as stated in the note and the loan closing statement, was $43,500, which included $27,070.05 to pay off the November, 1987 loan, $2451.33 in closing costs,[12] a $4350 prepaid finance charge and $9628.62 paid directly to the defendants. The annual interest rate was 19 percent. The promissory note provided that the defendants were to make thirty-five monthly payments of $691.17, and a final "balloon" payment of $44,075.03. The defendants made no payments on this mortgage loan.[13]

The plaintiff thereafter filed this foreclosure action. The defendants proffered special defenses, alleging [among other things, that it was] an unconscionable contract. . . . The trial court rejected the defendants' special defenses and counterclaims and rendered a judgment of strict foreclosure. The defendants appealed. . . .

I

The defendants' first claim is that the trial court improperly concluded that the terms of the two second mortgage loan transactions were not unconscionable and thus were enforceable. The defendants argue that the loan transactions were procedurally unconscionable, due to the defendants' "lack of knowledge and lack of voluntariness," and that the transactions were substantively unconscionable due to the "oppressive character of the

Title fee	$ 200
Attorney's fee	$ 750
Document preparation fee	$ 200
Recording fee	$ 50
Credit investigation fee	$ 100
	$1300

10. The defendants note that the closing for this loan took place in a restaurant parking lot. The closing attorney, Peter K. Motti, testified that the defendants had gotten lost on the way to his office. Motti testified that he had decided that it would be quicker to meet the defendants at the restaurant to close the loan rather than bringing "them through the center of town, because it can be confusing to get to the office."

12. The plaintiff's disclosure statement disclosed the following closing costs to the defendants for the May 26, 1988 loan:

Appraisal fee	$ 200.00
Title fee	$ 250.00
Attorney's fee	$ 700.00
Credit life insurance	$1,251.33
Recording fee	$ 50.00
	$2,451.33

13. Almost none of the $9628.62 paid to the defendants was used to improve the house. The defendants' marriage was subsequently dissolved, and some of the loan proceeds were used to pay Dalila Montes' attorney in the dissolution proceeding.

contract terms." We conclude, however, from the facts as found by the trial court and as supported by sufficient evidence in the record, that the mortgage transactions in question were not unconscionable.

We first consider our standard of review of a claim of unconscionability. "The question of unconscionability is a matter of law to be decided by the court based on all the facts and circumstances of the case. Thus, our review on appeal is unlimited by the clearly erroneous standard." This means that the ultimate determination of whether a transaction is unconscionable is a question of law, not a question of fact, and that the trial court's determination on that issue is subject to a plenary review on appeal. It also means, however, that the factual findings of the trial court that underlie that determination are entitled to the same deference on appeal that other factual findings command. Thus, those findings must stand unless they are clearly erroneous. This is particularly apt in a case such as this, where the factual claims involve the extent of the defendants' lack of commercial acumen, their unfamiliarity with the English language resulting in their inability to comprehend the terms of the mortgage that they signed, and their unfamiliarity with the ordinary incidents of mortgage loans. The trial court is in a unique position to assess such factual questions.

. . .

The defendants argue that the mortgage loan transactions were procedurally unconscionable due to their "lack of knowledge" about the terms of the loans and their "lack of voluntariness" in entering into the loans. The defendants argue that because of their illiteracy in English and their lack of business acumen, the terms of the mortgages unfairly surprised them and that, therefore, there was a "lack of voluntariness" in the transactions. The defendants bolster this claim by the fact that they were unrepresented by counsel in both loan transactions. They contend, moreover, that they did not know that they would have to pay off the prior liens on their home in order to obtain the November 1987 mortgage loan. Were the defendants' arguments based upon favorable factual findings, they might well have prevailed on appeal. Their assertions, however, are contrary to the facts found by the trial court.

The trial court found, on the basis of its observation of both defendants, who testified without the aid of a Spanish interpreter, that neither defendant had any difficulty with the English language, in understanding any questions put to them by counsel or the court, or in understanding the judicial proceedings. The court also found that the defendants had entered into a prior mortgage transaction, namely, their first mortgage with People's Bank. The court further found that the defendants were "intelligent and energetic" persons, and that, having lived in the mainland United States for more than twenty years, they understood its judicial, "legal and financial systems." Finally, the court found that the defendants defaulted on the mortgage, not because they did not understand their obligations thereunder or because their income while living together was insufficient to support the mortgage payments, but because the breakdown of their marriage subsequent to the mortgage closing impaired their financial situation. These findings are adequately supported by the evidence in the record.

Both defendants testified that the attorney closing the loan fully explained the documents to them. Luis Montes testified that he had no questions and Dalila Montes testified that she fully understood the terms of the loan. The attorney for the plaintiff testified that he had spent approximately one-half hour fully explaining each document to them. Furthermore, Dalila Montes testified that although the plaintiff's lending officer spoke both English and Spanish, Dalila Montes spoke to her only in English. Regarding the defendants' lack of business acumen, the defendants had been through a loan closing once before when they had purchased their home and, therefore, the trial court was entitled to infer that they had had some experience with loan transactions. Moreover, although the defendants had a right to be represented by their own counsel, which was fully explained to them by the plaintiff's attorney, the defendants signed a form waiving that right. Also, the plaintiff's president testified that "[e]very customer we work on is told right up front [that] we would have to secure a second position on the security." The trial court could infer from this statement that the defendants were so informed. Further, it is clearly stated on the forms, which were fully explained to the defendants, that the prior liens on their home were being paid. There was evidence, moreover, that the defendants' financial situation had deteriorated after they had separated, and that Dalila Montes had used some of the mortgage proceeds to pay her legal fees resulting from their marital dissolution. Finally, although Dalila Montes testified that she could not read or write in any language and although Luis Montes testified that he speaks English only a "little bit," the trial court was not required to, and did not, credit that testimony.

Thus, the trial court's findings, adverse to the defendants' claims of procedural unconscionability, are supported by the record and are not clearly erroneous. On the basis of those findings and the record, we cannot conclude that this transaction was procedurally unconscionable as a matter of law.

The defendants next argue that the mortgage loan transactions were substantively unconscionable due to the oppressive "mathematics" of the loan transaction. This claim is based on the defendants' contention that they had only the $1195 in monthly income listed on the loan application form with which to pay the $1098 monthly mortgage payments due for the first and second mortgages. Thus, the defendants argue, they were left with only $97 per month for living expenses after the mortgage payments. On the basis of these figures, they claim "it is obvious that [the plaintiff did not] believe the defendants would make the payments," and that the plaintiff intended only to foreclose on the loan in order to reap the equity in their home. This argument, however, like the defendants' earlier arguments regarding procedural unconscionability, founders on the absence of a factual foundation. First, the trial court did not find either that the plaintiff believed that the defendants would fail to make their mortgage payments, or that the plaintiff intended simply to reap the defendants' equity in the home by making a loan to them that the plaintiff knew they could not repay. Nor is such a finding compelled by this record, because there was evidence to support a contrary finding, namely, that the defendants were able, and considered themselves able, to make the payments.

The plaintiff's president testified that Dalila Montes had told the plaintiff that her husband had additional income. Therefore, the plaintiff could reasonably have believed that the defendants had more monthly income than was reported on the loan application form. Such a belief was somewhat bolstered by the fact that the defendants had made every mortgage payment on their first mortgage and had made all seven payments on the initial, November, 1987 loan.[16] Moreover, the defendants represented to the plaintiff that they intended to use the loan proceeds to improve their home so that they could sell it within one year. Since the defendants had made the previous seven loan payments, there was evidence to support a finding that the plaintiff could have reasonably believed that the defendants would continue to do so until they sold the property within the year. Moreover, the trial court specifically found that the defendants' separation and marital dissolution caused their default. Thus, although in a case where the court has found an intentional reaping of equity a mortgagor might prevail on a claim of unconscionability, this record does not compel such an inference.

The defendants next argue that it was unconscionable for the plaintiff to charge a 10 percent prepaid finance charge on the November 1987 loan transaction and then charge another 10 percent prepaid finance charge again, within six months, on the May 1988 loan transaction. We disagree.

General Statutes § 36–224*l* permits a person engaged in the secondary mortgage loan business, such as the plaintiff, to charge prepaid finance charges in an amount not greater than 10 percent of the principal amount of the loan. The November 1987 transaction was unrelated to the May 1988 transaction. The defendants sought the loan in November 1987 in order to finance vinyl siding for their home. In May 1988 the defendants sought a loan for additional home improvements, with the intention to sell the property within one year.

Had the defendants obtained the May 1988 loan from a second mortgage company other than the plaintiff, that company certainly could have required payment of the November 1987 loan in order to secure a second mortgage position and could have charged 10 percent in prepaid finance charges pursuant to § 36–224*l*. Thus, the fact that the plaintiff charged the

---

16. After the November, 1987 loan, the defendants were burdened with $806 in monthly mortgage payments, consisting of $407 to People's Bank and $399 to the plaintiff. That sum represented 67 percent of their $1195 monthly income listed on the loan application. Thus, a substantial portion of the defendants' stated income was devoted to shelter. The fact that the defendants nonetheless had been successfully meeting the prior mortgage payments arguably supports an inference that their total actual income exceeded $1195 per month.

same amount for undertaking a new and increased risk does not ipso facto make this transaction unconscionable. Moreover, there was no evidence that the interest rates or points charged on either loan, or on the two loans taken together, were beyond the ordinary charges then prevailing in the secondary loan market. Indeed, the only evidence regarding that issue was that those charges were "in the middle of the market on the private sector loan." We cannot conclude, therefore, that, solely because the plaintiff charged a total of twenty points on two separate, albeit closely related in time, loan transactions, that the second loan transaction was unconscionable.

In sum, while the defendants may have been imprudent in entering into the May 1988 transaction, we cannot conclude, on the basis of the record in this case, that the defendants were oppressed or unfairly surprised, or that the terms of the transactions were so one-sided as to be unconscionable as a matter of law.

. . .

BERDON, J., dissenting in part and concurring in part.

We sit as a court of equity in reviewing this appeal from the granting of foreclosure of the defendants' property. A long standing equitable principle requires that "[e]quity will not afford its aid to one who by his conduct or neglect has put the other party in a situation in which it would be inequitable to place him [or her]." Glotzer v. Keyes, 125 Conn. 227, 231–32, 5 A.2d 1 (1939). . . . Since I believe that the cumulative effect of the two loans made by the plaintiff and secured by the mortgages (second mortgage I and II) is unconscionable under established principles of equity, I would not enforce the terms of the note secured by second mortgage II according to its tenor.

Instead, the majority allows the equitable powers of this court to be used to the advantage of the plaintiff mortgagee, Cheshire Mortgage Service, Inc., a sophisticated money lender, in the foreclosure of a mortgage on the property of the defendant mortgagors, Luis Montes and Dalila Montes. The defendants are uneducated Hispanic persons who are far from fluent in the English language,[1] and who were not represented by counsel. Compounding these problems, the closing attorney for the plaintiff chose to conduct the closing for second mortgage II out of his vehicle at the parking lot of a restaurant in Branford.

[After quoting extensively from *Williams v. Walker–Thomas*, the dissenting opinion continues:]

In the present case, the loan transactions began with a contractor's attempt to finance the sale of vinyl siding to the defendants for their home through the Tolland Bank and now ends in this foreclosure action in which they may lose their home. Unable to obtain conventional financing at the bank for the siding, the contractor took the defendants' application that was originally completed for the Tolland Bank "down the line" into the

---

1. One defendant could not read any English and the other a "little bit."

hands of the plaintiff. The defendants then completed the two loan transactions with the plaintiff.

At the time of entering into the loans, the defendant Luis Montes, who had previously suffered a heart attack, was afflicted with a kidney disease that necessitated dialysis treatment, which left him permanently disabled and unable to work. The defendants had a total monthly income of $1195, including Luis Montes' social security disability benefits. The trial referee found that the defendants "were not neophytes in the financial world," but this finding is not supported by the evidence. The trial referee predicated his finding on the fact that when the defendants originally purchased their home for $25,000, it was financed by a first mortgage of $23,700 from People's Bank that provided for monthly payments of $407, including property taxes. The defendants' participation in one legitimate transaction with People's Bank, however, does not support the trial referee's conclusion that they had the sophistication to understand fully the present transactions and the financial implications.

Under the terms of second mortgage II, plus the seven monthly payments previously made under second mortgage I, the defendants would have been required to pay principal, bonus points,[2] interest, attorney's fees, and other associated costs totaling $70,486.61 for less than four years of financing. In return, they only received benefits in cash, payment to other creditors and the vinyl siding, totaling $32,328.62.[4] The result is a net cost of $38,157.99 to the defendants for approximately forty-two months of financing. Equalizing these costs of $38,157.99 over that period (seven months under second mortgage I and thirty-five months under second mortgage II), the cost of the net actual economic benefits of $32,328.62 was $908.52 per month. This amounts to a shocking 33.7 percent per annum costs for the financing, which the plaintiff conceded was fully secured. Furthermore, when second mortgage II was entered into the defendants received an additional benefit of only $10,897.95 (cash of $9628.62 and credit life insurance of $1251.33), for which they not only had to pay interest but also bonus points of $4350 which, put in percentage terms, was a bonus of approximately 40 percent. Although the exorbitant rates on a fully secured loan, under the circumstances of this case, do not shock the conscience of the majority, they do mine.[6]

The defendants' case, however, does not stop there. Equally problematic is that the defendants could never repay either one of the loans that had been secured by the mortgages. Second mortgage I required monthly payments of $806.38 ($407 for the first mortgage and taxes and $399.38 for

---

2. Bonus points are referred to in the majority opinion as the "prepaid finance charge."

4. The actual cash and economic benefits derived from the two loan transactions under second mortgage I and II are as follows:

Vinyl siding	$ 9,902.00
Prior debts paid	12,671.31
Cash from second mortgage I	26.69
Cash from second mortgage II	9,628.62
	$32,328.62

6. A question of unconscionability is a matter of law; and, as the majority points outs, it "is subject to a plenary review on appeal."

second mortgage I) from the defendants' monthly income of $1195, which amounts to 67 percent of their total income. How could they be expected to live on the balance of $388.62, that is, pay for utilities, heat, food, clothing and other necessities, plus any payroll deductions?

Second mortgage II called for outrageous payments of $1098.17 per month ($407 for the first mortgage and taxes and $691.17 for second mortgage II) or a whopping 92 percent of the defendants' gross monthly income. The majority speculates that the defendants had additional income because they were able to live and pay second mortgage I for seven months. When this speculation is applied to second mortgage II, it is obvious that the monthly payments were outrageous because the defendants were unable to make a single payment.

Furthermore, the defendants could never be expected to pay the balloon payments—the lump sum payment due at the end of the term of the loan—on second mortgage I in the amount of $26,810.61 and on second mortgage II in the amount of $44,075.03, both of which were in excess of the original principal amounts of the notes secured by the mortgages.[7] As the court in Campbell Soup Co. v. Wentz, 172 F.2d 80, 84 (3d Cir.1948), stated, the "sum total of its provisions drives too hard a bargain for a court of conscience to assist."

To justify its finding that the loans were not unconscionable, the trial referee and the majority rely on the plaintiff's claim that it was told that the defendant Luis Montes had some additional income, not shown on the application. There is no evidence to support such a finding. The plaintiff's president, Richard Coppola, was unable to testify as to the dollar amount of this additional income, there was no documentary evidence to support this claim and there was not even a note in the corporation's records to verify that he was so advised. "It does not seem too much to say that one who voluntarily extends credit by disregarding a known risk, or risks which could be discovered by a reasonable effort, should bear the loss when loss occurs. If such a standard imposes some brake on the credit boom, it would be a brake wisely applied in the interests of both the consumers and the extenders of credit." V. Countryman, "Improvident Credit Extension: A New Legal Concept Aborning?" 27 N.Mex. L. Rev. 1, 23 (1975).

It is clear to me that the defendants could neither pay the monthly payments nor pay the balloon payment at the end of the term of the loan. Indeed, the loan secured by second mortgage II was made solely on the basis of the equity that the defendants had in the house. "Many financial experts refer to such mortgage companies as 'equity skimmers' because the loans are based not on a person's ability to repay them, but on the amount of equity in their home. They charge that the companies make these loans with the intention of foreclosing upon the homeowner and reaping a profit through the equity in the home." J. Morris, "Borrowers Beware," Man-

---

7. The note secured by second mortgage I was $26,500, and the note secured by second mortgage II was $43,500. This reminds me of the days of the "company store" that extended credit on a basis that never allowed the employee customer to become debt free.

chester, New Hampshire, Sunday News, Feb. 4, 1990, p. A–7. The evidence indicated that at the time of the foreclosure the house had a value of $90,000. The possible practice of equity skimming under the circumstances of this case is unconscionable and this court should hold as much.

The defendants concede that they are not entirely without blame; any credit extension that is improvident on the part of the creditors is also improvident on the part of the debtor. Nevertheless, "typically the creditor is better equipped—by education, experience, resources, and the nature of his role—to avoid and distribute the risk of improvidence. Hence, as between the two blameworthy participants in the improvident credit extension, it seems . . . that in most cases the burden of loss should be placed on the improvident creditor by means of a remedy conferred on the improvident debtor." V. Countryman, supra, 17. Surely, taking into consideration the circumstances of the defendants, this is such a case. "[P]rotection must be given to those who do not have the economic sophistication or the awareness possessed by others who may be less concerned about credit; the [Connecticut Unfair Trade Practices Act (CUTPA)] must be applied to protect the unthinking, the unsuspecting and the credulous . . . ." Exposition Press, Inc. v. Federal Trade Commission, 295 F.2d 869, 872 (2d Cir. [1961]), cert. denied, 370 U.S. 917. Murphy v. McNamara, 36 Conn. Sup. 183, 190, 416 A.2d 170 (1979).

The majority treats this case just as it would a transaction between commercial parties. It relies on [cases between parties in business.]

Instead of reviewing this case through the lens of commercially savvy parties, we must determine whether the loans were unconscionable on the basis of a transaction between a professional mortgage lender and unsophisticated credit consumers who had a total monthly income below the poverty level. Paraphrasing the language of the United States Supreme Court in Hume v. United States, 132 U.S. 406, 411, 10 S. Ct. 134, 33 L. Ed. 393 (1889), unconscionability is defined as a transaction that no person in his or her senses and not under delusion would make on the one hand and no honest and fair person would accept on the other. . . . Applying this standard, I conclude that the cumulative effect of both loan transactions was unconscionable.

Accordingly, I would reverse on this issue. . . .

QUESTIONS AND NOTES

1. If unconscionability is a question of law for the court to decide, why does the Connecticut Supreme Court feel bound by the conclusion of the trial court? In what way does the view of the dissenting judge differ on this matter? Is the majority's position consistent with the position of the federal court in *Williams v. Walker–Thomas*?

2. Did Dalila Montes tell Cheshire Mortgage that her husband had income in addition to the income listed in the credit application form? If so, how much?

3. With respect to the first loan, the principal amount of the loan was stated as $26,500. The terms of the loan called for defendants to pay almost $400 per month for three years, at the end of which time they would make a payment of $26,800, or more than the original principal of the loan. If at the time of making the loan they did not have enough cash to pay for the $9,900 siding job, how do you suppose they thought they would have almost three times that amount just three years later? How do you suppose Cheshire Mortgage thought they would pay off the loan?

4. Note the disagreement between the majority and the dissent with respect to the substantive element of unconscionability. What is the rationale for the prepaid finance charge on the first loan (in the amount of $2,500) and on the second loan (in the amount of $4,350)?

5. On similar facts, other courts have invoked unconscionability to limit the enforceability of loan contracts. E.g., Besta v. Beneficial Loan Co., 855 F.2d 532 (8th Cir.1988); Beneficial Mortgage Co. v. Leach, 2002 WL 926759 (Ohio App.2002). Cf. Fidelity Financial Services v. Hicks, 574 N.E.2d 15 (Ill.App.1991) (UDAP violation); In re Milbourne, 108 B.R. 522 (Bankr. E.D.Pa.1989) (same). And the FTC has invoked deception and unfairness under section 5 of the FTC Act, proceeding against dozens of lenders just since 1998. This action by the FTC has produced notable settlements, including one with First Alliance Mortgage Co. for $60 million.

6. Would the transaction(s) in *Cheshire Mortgage* violate HOEPA?

7. For more extensive treatment of predatory lending, see Peterson, Predatory Structured Finance, 28 Cardozo L.Rev. 2185 (2007); Engel & McCoy, A Tale of Three Markets: The Law and Economics of Predatory Lending, 80 Tex.L.Rev. 1255 (2002); Mansfield, The Road to Subprime 'HEL' Was Paved with Good Congressional Intentions: Usury Deregulation and the Subprime Home Equity Market, 51 S.C.L.Rev. 473 (2000); Drysdale & Keest, The Two–Tiered Consumer Financial Services Marketplace: The Fringe Banking System and Its Challenge to Current Thinking About the Role of Usury Laws in Today's Society, 51 S.C.L.Rev. 589 (2000); Joint U.S. Dep't of Housing and Urban Dev.–U.S. Dep't of the Treasury Task Force on Predatory Lending, Curbing Predatory Home Mortgage Lending (June 2000), available at *www.huduser.Publications/pdf/treasrpt.pdf.*

8. Consider the following excerpt from "Practitioner's View of Contract Unconscionability," 8 U.C.C.L.J. 237 (1976), a speech by Richard W. Duesenberg, who left his position as Professor of Law at New York University to become Assistant General Counsel at Monsanto Corp.*

> Long ago, in 1750, an English court observed that an unconscionable contract is one no man in his senses would enter. Perhaps this was and remains the highwater mark of the doctrine of unconscionability. Its codification in the Uniform Commercial Code and its unwholesome

intrusion in the realm of the serious law of contracts cannot but be looked upon with disfavor. . . .

As with several other sections of the Code, the volume of literature and commentary on Section 2–302 has far outstripped what the section itself has been allowed to do. Not all of it has been complimentary. One writer summed up the product of its drafting with this: "It is easy to say nothing with words."[1]

Others, however, have stumbled over each other showering bouquets on their new-won love—more, one surmises, because she is perceived as a means for satisfying their desires without enduring the hard job of discovering good reasons, than for any intrinsic advance in contract law. . . .

Others see the section as being put in the Code for the consumer. This overlooks that its origins go back long before the current epidemic of hyperinfracaniphilia.[3] The word "consumer" is not used once, either in the section or in its Official Comments. When it is stated that Section 2–302 "marks the birth of a new doctrine fashioned out of old policies and a new concern for the basic rights of the consumer,"[4] it may be asked: Where is the evidence? . . .

To all such observations, ranging from those which say the section says nothing to those reading it as a new birthright for an allegedly forgotten class, the thoughtful lawyer will respond contemptuously. The practitioner, after all, is no longer in school playing with serious hypotheticals, the answers to which, whether right or wrong or neither, will cause not even a ripple. He is protecting the rights of clients—live people with valuable rights challenged in the contexts of vigorous competing claims. He has a right to know what a statute like this is intended to mean.

Unfortunately, neither a review of the Code itself nor a study of the Official Comments to the section will satisfy a lawyer's urge that the skeleton be adorned with flesh to see if it's worth embracing. Section 2–302, while it empowers a court to strike or rewrite unconscionable bargains or terms, stands naked of any effort at all to tell us what it is that should fall victim to this new-found convention. As to the Official Comments, they indulge in a classic tautology by decreeing that the basic test of unconscionability is "whether, in the light of the general commercial background and the commercial needs of the particular trade or case, the clauses involved are so one-sided as to be unconscionable under the circumstances existing at the time of the making of the contract." This is hardly better than writing, "That is unconscionable which is unconscionable." Busy lawyers have little time for that kind of help.

1. Leff, "Unconscionability and the Code—The Emperor's New Clause," 115 U.Pa.L.Rev. 485, 559 (1967).

3. "Excessive love for the underdog."

4. Terry & Fauvre, "The Unconscionable Offense," 4 Ga.L.Rev. 469 (1970).

Even the ten pre-Code decisions set out as examples of what the section was intended to permit are no more instructive. The only thread running through these pearls is the use of a form contract, and it is perfectly absurd to conclude that the use of the form is either necessary for or indicative of an unconscionable bargain. Preprinting serves a commercially useful function, in both merchant-to-merchant, and merchant-to-consumer transactions. Oh yes, they all but one involve either a warranty disclaimer or remedy limitation. But in each, the court got around these clauses on other pretexts. Why, then, the need for enabling legislation? A fair question.

The drafters' attempted answer is a classic "bootstraplifting" apologia. It is, they say, to allow the courts to do overtly what they have learned to do covertly. Now, part of the genius of the common law has been that it has accommodated change as changing times and circumstances demanded. The process is step by step, oftentimes laborious; but a rationale is never wanting. Certainly, there have been imperfections, as always there are in the course of human action. But is to manipulate the rules of offer and acceptance, or to construe away harsh terms as against the dominant [purpose] of a contract, any worse than to condemn a clause or a whole contract for no given reason at all? A poor reason is at least a reason. . . .

Perhaps the most foreboding reach of Section 2–302's proscription has been against allegedly excessive prices. This is particularly noteworthy, in light of the traditional "hands-off" attitude of the common law toward the price set for a voluntary relinquishment of ownership. If alleged excessive price becomes subsumed within its meaning, as is threatened, the opportunity is opened for a challenge of many unhappy deals. While no case yet has said that, in the total absence of other highly individualistic factors which were independently adequate to the results reached, price alone is the basis of unconscionability, several have come close. One is American Home Improvement, Inc. v. Mac-Iver,[8] which aptly illustrates the danger lurking in a statute standing in the wings for a judge to call on stage at will. Without any basis, it simply decreed that a time-price yielding an annual interest of about 18 percent was unconscionable. In one fell swoop, the whole small loan industry was hanging by a judge's gastric pathos. . . .

However, there is a better reason than the good work of lawyers for the feeble mark Section 2–302 has made on our jurisprudence. While many jurists may articulate it only crudely or even not at all, they nonetheless accept that contract is an important principle of order for free men. Not an end in itself, freedom of contract is a means toward self-expression. In a very real sense, it is both an instrument of change and an instrument of order. Of change, in the sense that through it individuals are able to find a meeting place of promise and obligation for the achievement of individual objectives. Of order, in the

8.   105 N.H. 435, 201 A.2d 886 (1964).

sense that such agreements are a matter of private legislation between parties for the prescribing of their conduct one to the other. They are not directed to act by custom, tradition, or the commands of the realm. They decide their relations as a matter of their own volition. It is, therefore, an institution of freedom, deeply rooted in the moral sentiments supportive of individualism and repugnant to collective authoritarianism.

Emanating from this orientation is the principle that it is not the function of government—of the courts—to make contracts for individuals, but to construe and enforce them. Obviously, this is not to say that nothing beyond the words used is relevant. The doctrines of fraud, duress, misrepresentation, mistake, rules relating to fiduciaries, and those affording special favor to idiots and incompetents are only a smattering of the potpourri of examples where the law gives status and declines equal treatment to unequals. But all of these and others like them have specific reasons assigned for their being, and not solely the arrogance of one who sits with power to say: "It is my conscience which decides whether you shall have the right to your bargain."[12] History has had enough of the omniscient sitting in seats of authority. As Cardozo reminded us long ago, judges are not "knights-errant, roaming at will in pursuit of their own ideals of beauty or of goodness."

The pervasiveness of these thoughts in American law diminishes dramatically the burden which the word "unconscionable" must bear when in the hands of judicial decision-makers. Rather than becoming a shiny sword for Cardozo's knight-errant to substitute his will for that of the parties, Section 2–302 has done little more than require a hearing and additional pages in lawyers' briefs. Its own vacuousness, ironically to those who saw this as its chief asset, has accommodated this development. Unavailing in the merchant context, its use in consumer transactions has been largely confirmatory of what had otherwise been achieved or nearly achieved through common law development. Strict liability and public policy arguments have effectively, without the section, paralyzed warranty disclaimers and remedy limitations in consumer deals, and every single case where unconscionability has figured . . . in a successful challenge of an allegedly excessive price, individual facts sufficient to carry the burden of showing fraud or duress were involved. . . .

A different view has been expressed by Irving Younger, who left *his* position as Professor of Law at New York University to become Judge of the Civil Court of the City of New York. Younger, A Judge's View of Unconscionability, 5 U.C.C.L.J. 348, 351–52 (1973):*

---

12. See Younger, "A Judge's View of Unconscionability," 5 U.C.C.L.J. 348, 352 (1973).

* Reprinted by permission from the Uniform Commercial Code Law Journal, Volume 5, Number 4, Spring 1973, Copyright 8 1973, Warren, Gorham & Lamont Inc., 210 South Street, Boston, Mass. All Rights Reserved.

Many of us are accustomed to, and indeed enamored of, the elaborate logical machinery which in other areas of the law makes things work. I would cite, for example, taxation, perpetuities, negotiable instruments. In the area of unconscionability, there is no such machinery. Unconscionability is the sole test, a test that can be defined only in terms of itself. My effort to explain how I decide a case of unconscionability may add up to the proposition that the judge's conscience is his ultimate guide. So be it. In a complex society which includes large numbers of people helpless to protect themselves from the rapacity of others and folly of their own, is it not well that somewhere in the system sits a man or woman empowered by the system to say, "It is not right that you have your bargain of your brother, and so you shall not"?

For a similar, more recent view, see Discover Bank v. Owens, 822 N.E.2d 869, 872–75 (Cleveland Mun.Ct.2004):

Over the next six years Owens continued to make payments on her account, but because of finance charges and fees her balance was never again to be under her credit limit of $1,900. Despite never using her credit card again, Owens was charged a monthly over-limit fee ranging from $20 to $29 per month. From May 1997 to May 2003, Owens was assessed a total of $1,518 in over-limit fees from the time her balance went above $1,900 because of accrued finance charges in May 1997.

During this time period, despite the growing record of payment difficulties, Discover also continued to debit Owens's account for its CreditSafe Plus product [providing insurance against disability and unemployment]. From May 1997 to May 1999, Owens was charged a total of $369.52 for a product which, despite her being on Social Security Disability, evidently did not apply to her credit predicament.

During this six-year period, Owens continued to attempt to meet her obligation and did make numerous payments. From May 1997 to May 2003 Owens paid Discover a total of $3,492. Since many of the payments were below the minimum monthly payment required and because other monthly payments were in fact not timely made, Owens further was assessed numerous late-payment fees, which over the six-year period totaled $1,160.

In short, despite never using the credit card again and having paid $3,492 on a $1,900 debt, with all the fees and accrued finance charges, Owens was nevertheless faced with a $5,564.28 balance still owing on the account.

How does something like this happen? Had Owens simply stopped paying on her account in May 1997, as perhaps some unscrupulous person might have considered, her account would have been closed and charged off at approximately $2,000, an amount that Discover would have sought to collect at the court seven years ago. . . .

But because Owens was not unscrupulous and evidently did her absolute best despite being on Social Security Disability, she found herself in debt so deeply that she ultimately came to the sad conclusion that it was a debt out from under which she could never climb. The court does not have before it the records prior to January 1996 to know just what Owens may have purchased for a few hundred dollars using her Discover card. Whatever it was it certainly cannot have been worth the thousands of dollars she actually paid and most certainly was not worth the additional thousands of dollars still expected today by Discover.

No doubt some of the responsibility for this situation rests with Owens. It might have been unfair for a creditor to extend easy credit at stiff terms to someone who clearly was in a difficult financial predicament in the first place, but no one forced Owens to open the account and accept the card in the first place, and certainly no one forced her to use it, despite its allure for easy access to money in difficult financial times. Owens might have sought financial or legal counsel several years ago to work out some suitable arrangement with Discover, yet her instincts were always that she wanted to plug away at meeting her financial obligations. While clearly placing her on the moral high road, that same highway unfortunately was her road to financial ruin.

How is it that the person who wants to do right ends up so worse off? It is plain to the court that the creditor also bears some responsibility. Discover kept Owens's account open and active long after it was painfully obvious that she was never going to be able to make payments at the expected level. . . . Even if plaintiff was technically within its rights in its handling of defendant's account, it was unreasonable and unjust for it to allow defendant's debt to continue to accumulate well after it had become clear that defendant would be unable to pay it. . . .

After reviewing the cardmember agreement that plaintiff contends was applicable in this case, it is clear that the operation of its terms as it applied to Owens was unconscionable. This was not a case where Owens recklessly used her credit card to purchase items beyond the agreed-upon credit limit. After the fees and finance charges put her balance over the $1900 credit limit, Owens never used the credit card again. Sixty months later, however, Discover continued to charge Owens a $29 monthly fee despite the fact that she had made payments nearly twice the $1,900 she owed in the first place. The court further questions the CreditSafe fees consistently charged to Owens's account. At what point in the life of an unemployed, disabled, impoverished person was such a product ever designed to be used?

. . . This court is all too aware of the widespread financial exploitation of the urban poor by overbearing credit-card companies. Defendant has clearly been the victim of plaintiff's unreasonable, unconscionable and unjust business practices. Equity suffers no wrong to be without a remedy. This court has broad legal and equitable powers, and now brings them to bear for the debtor in this case. The appropriate remedy is clear: Judgment for defendant.

9. In Jones v. Star Credit Corp., 298 N.Y.S.2d 264 (Nassau County S.Ct.1969), the court wrote:

On August 31, 1965, the plaintiffs, who are welfare recipients, agreed to purchase a home freezer unit for $900 as the result of a visit from a salesman representing Your Shop At Home Service, Inc. With the addition of the time credit charges, credit life insurance, credit property insurance, and sales tax, the purchase price totaled $1,234.80. Thus far the plaintiffs have paid $619.88 toward their purchase. The defendant claims that with various added credit charges paid for an extension of time there is a balance of $819.81 still due from the plaintiffs. The uncontroverted proof at the trial established that the freezer unit, when purchased, had a maximum retail value of approximately $300. The question is whether this transaction and the resulting contract could be considered unconscionable within the meaning of Section 2–302 of the Uniform Commercial Code. . . .

There was a time when the shield of "caveat emptor" would protect the most unscrupulous in the marketplace—a time when the law, in granting parties unbridled latitude to make their own contracts, allowed exploitive and callous practices which shocked the conscience of both legislative bodies and the courts.

The effort to eliminate these practices has continued to pose a difficult problem. On the one hand it is necessary to recognize the importance of preserving the integrity of agreements and the fundamental right of parties to deal, trade, bargain, and contract. On the other hand there is the concern for the uneducated and often illiterate individual who is the victim of gross inequality of bargaining power, usually the poorest members of the community.

. . .

Fraud, in the instant case, is not present; nor is it necessary under the statute. The question which presents itself is whether or not, under the circumstances of this case, the sale of a freezer unit having a retail value of $300 for $900 ($1,439.69 including credit charges and $18 sales tax) is unconscionable as a matter of law. The court believes it is.

Concededly, deciding the issue is substantially easier than explaining it. No doubt, the mathematical disparity between $300, which presumably includes a reasonable profit margin, and $900, which is exorbitant on its face, carries the greatest weight. Credit charges alone exceed by more than $100 the retail value of the freezer. These alone, may be sufficient to sustain the decision. Yet, a caveat is warranted lest we reduce the import of Section 2–302 solely to a mathematical ratio formula. It may, at times, be that; yet it may also be much more. The very limited financial resources of the purchaser, known to the sellers at the time of the sale, is entitled to weight in the balance. Indeed, the value disparity itself leads inevitably to the felt conclusion that knowing advantage was taken of the plaintiffs. In addition, the meaningfulness of choice essential to the making of a contract, can be negated by a gross inequality of bargaining power. (Williams v. Walker–Thomas Furniture Co.)

a.   Is Jones v. Star Credit Corp. an appropriate instance for invoking Judge Younger's "It is not right that you have your bargain of your brother, and so you shall not"? Is Mr. Duesenberg's criticism of the judicial use of unconscionability applicable to *Jones?*

b.   In an omitted passage, the court says "there is no reason to doubt [that section 2–302] is intended to encompass the price term of an agreement." If the principle of the section is "the prevention of . . . unfair surprise" (UCC § 2–302 Official Comment), isn't there in fact some reason to doubt whether unconscionability encompasses price?

c.   Problem. *Consumer* can purchase a complete set of the Best Encyclopedia in New York City for $250. He can also purchase it at his home in one of the remote regions of Ecuador from one of Best's travelling salespersons, for $1,200. Would the latter transaction be unconscionable?

How is this far-fetched hypothetical relevant to Jones v. Star Credit?

d.   In the late 1960s the FTC studied the credit practices of 96 appliance and furniture retailers in the District of Columbia. FTC, Economic Report on Installment Credit and Retail Sales Practices of District of Columbia Retailers (1968). The study revealed significant differences between retailers whose customers were of relatively low income and retailers whose customers represented a broader segment of the general population.

> The survey disclosed that without exception low-income market retailers had high average markups and prices. On the average, goods purchased for $100 at wholesale sold for $255 in the low-income market stores, compared with $159 in general market stores.
>
> .   .   .
>
> Despite their substantially higher prices, net profit on sales for low-income market retailers was only slightly higher and net profit return on net worth was considerably lower when compared to general market retailers. It appears that salaries and commissions, bad-debt losses, and other expenses are substantially higher for low-income market retailers. Profit and expense comparisons are, of course, affected by differences in type of operation and accounting procedures. However, a detailed analysis was made for retailers of comparable size and merchandise mix to minimize such differences.
>
> Low-income market retailers reported the highest return after taxes on net sales, 4.7 percent. Among the general market retailers, department stores had the highest return on net sales, 4.6 percent. Furniture and home furnishings stores earned a net profit after taxes of 3.9 percent; and appliance, radio, and television retailers were the least profitable with a net profit of only 2.1 percent on sales.

Id. at x–xi. Was the price in Jones v. Star Credit Corp. unconscionable?

Perdue v. Crocker National Bank

Supreme Court of California, 1985.
38 Cal.3d 913, 216 Cal.Rptr. 345, 702 P.2d 503.

BROUSSARD, JUSTICE.

[Plaintiff filed a class action against defendant bank, challenging the validity of fees imposed by defendant on customers who write checks on accounts containing insufficient funds to cover the checks (referred to in the opinion as NSF checks). At the time of opening a checking account, defendant requires the customer to sign a card that defendant thereafter uses to verify the customer's signature. In "extremely small type," this card states that the customer agrees that "this account and all deposits therein shall be . . . subject to all applicable laws, to the Bank's present and future rules, regulations, practices and charges, and to its right of setoff . . . ."

[Defendant demurred to plaintiff's complaint. The trial court sustained the demurrer, and plaintiff appealed. The intermediate appellate court affirmed, and plaintiff appealed to the Supreme Court of California.]

> I.   Plaintiffs first cause of action: whether the signature
>   card is a contract authorizing NSF charges.

. . .

The cases unanimously agree that a signature card such as the Crocker Bank card at issue here is a contract. "The bank is authorized to honor withdrawals from an account on the signatures authorized by the signature card, which serves as a contract between the depositor and the bank for the handling of the account." (Blackmon v. Hale (1970) 1 Cal.3d 548, 556, 83 Cal.Rptr. 194, 463 P.2d 418.)

Plaintiff does not seriously dispute this proposition. His complaint alleges that the depositors "agreed to pay [the bank's] maintenance charge . . . ." in return for checking privileges, and one could infer that they agreed to do so by affixing their signatures to the card.

Plaintiff argues, however, that even if a signature card is a contract to establish a checking account, it is not a contract authorizing NSF charges. He contends that the contract is illusory because it permits the bank to set and change the NSF charges at its discretion, and without assent from the customer except such as may be inferred from the fact that the customer does not cancel his account after the bank posts notice of its rates.

Plaintiff relies on the rule that "[a]n agreement that provides that the price to be paid, or other performance to be rendered, shall be left to the will and discretion of one of the parties is not enforceable." (Automatic Vending Co. v. Wisdom (1960) 182 Cal.App.2d 354, 357, 6 Cal.Rptr. 31.) That rule, however, applies only if the total discretion granted one party renders the contract lacking in consideration. If there are reciprocal promises, as in the present case, the fact that the contract permits one party to set or change the price charged for goods or services does not render the contract illusory. Thus in Cal. Lettuce Growers v. Union Sugar Co. (1955) 45 Cal.2d 474, 289 P.2d 785, the court upheld a contract permitting the buyer of sugar beets to set the price to be paid. The buyer did not have arbitrary power, the court explained, because "where a contract confers on one party a discretionary power affecting the rights of the other, a duty is imposed to exercise that discretion in good faith and in accordance with fair dealing." (P. 484, 289 P.2d 785 . . . .)

. . .

II. Plaintiff's second cause of action: whether the bank's NSF charges are oppressive, unreasonable, or unconscionable.

Plaintiff's second cause of action alleges that the signature card is drafted by defendant bank which enjoys a superior bargaining position by reason of its greater economic power, knowledge, experience and resources. Depositors have no alternative but to acquiesce in the relationship as offered by defendant or to accept a similar arrangement with another bank. The complaint asserts that "The disparity between the actual cost to defendants and the amount charged by defendants for processing an NSF check unreasonably and oppressively imposes excessive and unfair liability upon plaintiffs." Plaintiff seeks a declaratory judgment to determine the rights and duties of the parties.

Plaintiff's allegations point to the conclusion that the signature card, if it is a contract, is one of adhesion. The term contract of adhesion "signifies a standardized contract, which, imposed and drafted by the party of superior bargaining strength, relegates to the subscribing party only the opportunity to adhere to the contract or reject it." (Graham v. Scissor–Tail Inc. (1981) 28 Cal.3d 807, 817, 171 Cal. Rptr. 604, 623 P.2d 165.) The signature card, drafted by the bank and offered to the customer without negotiation, is a classic example of a contract of adhesion; the bank concedes as much.

In Graham v. Scissor–Tail, Inc., supra, we observed that "To describe a contract as adhesive in character is not to indicate its legal effect . . . . [A] contract of adhesion is fully enforceable according to its terms [citations] unless certain other factors are present which, under established legal rules—legislative or judicial—operate to render it otherwise." (Pp. 819–820, fn. omitted.) "Generally speaking," we explained, "there are two judicially imposed limitations on the enforcement of adhesion contracts or provisions thereof. The first is that such a contract or provision which does not fall within the reasonable expectations of the weaker or 'adhering' party will not be enforced against him. [Citations.] The second—a principle of equity applicable to all contracts generally—is that a contract or provision, even if consistent with the reasonable expectations of the parties, will be denied enforcement if, considered in its context, it is unduly oppressive or 'unconscionable.' " (P. 820, fns. omitted.)[9]

9. The Court of Appeal decision in A & M Produce Co. v. FMC Corp. (1982) 135 Cal.App.3d 473, 186 Cal.Rptr. 114, offers an alternative analytical framework. It treats

In 1979, the Legislature enacted Civil Code section 1670.5, which codified the established doctrine that a court can refuse to enforce an unconscionable provision in a contract.[10] Section 1670.5 [is identical to UCC § 2–302.]

In construing this section, we cannot go so far as plaintiff, who contends that even a conclusory allegation of unconscionability requires an evidentiary hearing. We do view the section, however, as legislative recognition that a claim of unconscionability often cannot be determined merely by examining the face of the contract, but will require inquiry into its setting, purpose, and effect.

Plaintiff bases his claim of unconscionability on the alleged 2,000 percent differential between the NSF charge of $6 and the alleged cost to the bank of $0.30.[11] The parties have cited numerous cases on whether the price of an item can be so excessive as to be unconscionable. The cited cases are from other jurisdictions, often from trial courts or intermediate appellate courts, and none is truly authoritative on the issue. Taken together, however, they provide a useful guide to analysis of the claim that a price is so excessive as to be unconscionable.

To begin with, it is clear that the price term, like any other term in a contract, may be unconscionable. Allegations that the price exceeds cost or fair value, standing alone, do not state a cause of action. Instead, plaintiff's case will turn upon further allegations and proof setting forth the circumstances of the transaction.

The courts look to the basis and justification for the price including "the price actually being paid by . . . other similarly situated consumers in a similar transaction." (Bennett v. Behring Corp. (S.D.Fla.1979) 466 F.Supp. 689, 697, italics omitted.) The cases, however, do not support defendant's contention that a price equal to the market price cannot be

---

"unconscionability" as the only basis for refusing to enforce a provision. (Graham v. Scissor–Tail, Inc., supra, 28 Cal.3d 807, 171 Cal.Rptr. 604, 623 P.2d 165, spoke of "frustration of reasonable expectations" and "unconscionability" as alternative bases for refusing enforcement.) A & M Produce then divided the analysis of unconscionability into two elements—procedural and substantive. The procedural element included "oppression" arising from unequal bargaining power and "surprise" arising from the assertion of hidden and unexpected provisions. The substantive element involved consideration of whether the provision was one-sided, unreasonable, and lacked justification. (See 135 Cal.App. 3d at pp. 485–487, 186 Cal.Rptr. 114.)

Graham v. Scissor–Tail, Inc. comports somewhat more closely to the California precedent; A & M Produce conforms more closely to the Uniform Commercial Code and the cases decided under that code. Both pathways should lead to the same result.

10. Section 1670.5 is based upon Uniform Commercial Code section 2–302, but [applies to all contracts, not just those within the scope of Article 2 of the UCC.] . . .

11. The bank's briefs claim the alleged $0.30 cost is too low and plaintiffs briefs admit that a higher figure, but still $1 or less, might be more accurate. We do not, however, find in plaintiff's briefs a sufficiently clear concession to enable us to depart from the general principle that, in reviewing a judgment after the sustaining of a general demurrer without leave to amend, we must assume the truth of all material factual allegations in the complaint. (Alcorn v. Anbro Engineering, Inc., supra, 2 Cal.3d 493, 496, 86 Cal.Rptr. 88, 468 P.2d 216.)

held unconscionable. While it is unlikely that a court would find a price set by a freely competitive market to be unconscionable, the market price set by an oligopoly should not be immune from scrutiny. Thus courts consider not only the market price, but also the cost of the goods or services to the seller, the inconvenience imposed on the seller, and the true value of the product or service.

In addition to the price justification, decisions examine what Justice Weiner in *A & M Produce* called the "procedural aspects" of unconscionability. Cases may turn on the absence of meaningful choice, the lack of sophistication of the buyer, and the presence of deceptive practices by the seller.

Applying this analysis to our review of the complaint at hand, we cannot endorse defendant's argument that the $6 charge is so obviously reasonable that no inquiry into its basis or justification is necessary.[12] In 1978 $6 for processing NSF checks may not seem exorbitant,[13] but price alone is not a reliable guide. Small charges applied to a large volume of transactions may yield a sizable sum. The complaint asserts that the cost of processing NSF checks is only $0.30 per check, which means that a $6 charge would produce a 2,000 percent profit; even at the higher cost estimate of $1 a check mentioned in plaintiff's petition for hearing, the profit is 600 percent.[14] Such profit percentages may not be automatically unconscionable, but they indicate the need for further inquiry.[15]

12.   In Jacobs v. Citibank, N.A. (1984) 61 N.Y.2d 869, 474 N.Y.S.2d 464, 462 N.E.2d 1182, the New York Court of Appeals upheld a summary judgment for defendant bank in a suit attacking NSF check charges. In rejecting the claim that such charges were unconscionable, the court said that "[p]laintiffs have failed to show that they were deprived of a meaningful choice of banks with which they could do business and that the terms of these agreements with defendant were unreasonably favorable to the bank." (P. 872, 474 N.Y.S.2d 464, 462 N.E.2d 1182.)

While the New York court ruled on a motion for summary judgment, we rule upon a demurrer, and look only to plaintiff's allegations, not to the proof he had advanced to support those allegations. Plaintiff here has alleged that the charges imposed by defendant bank were excessive, and that similar arrangements would be imposed by other banks. Such allegations, which we must assume to be true, distinguish the New York decision.

13.   Defendant cites Merrel v. Research & Data, Inc. (1979) 3 Kan.App.2d 48, 589 P.2d 120, which held a $5 fee imposed by

merchants for NSF checks was a "modest" amount (p. 123) and not unconscionable. NSF checks pose a substantial inconvenience to a seller, who has been deceived into an involuntary extension of credit to a customer whose credit standing may not be very good. A bank, however, is not deceived. It checks the balance of the account, and may reject any overdraft. A fee reasonable to compensate the merchant for the cost, inconvenience, and risk of an NSF check may be excessive if exacted by a bank.

14.   The complaint does not state the market price for the service of processing NSF checks, although one might infer it is similar to defendant's price since plaintiff alleges that if he did not contract with defendant, he would be "forced to accept a similar arrangement with other banks." The complaint does not set a figure for the "fair" or "true" value or worth of the service.

15.   We observe that the bank charges the same fee whether it honors or rejects an NSF check. The fee, consequently, cannot be intended as compensation for the credit risk arising from paying such a check, or for the interest on the amount loaned.

Other aspects of the transaction confirm plaintiff's right to a factual hearing. Defendant presents the depositor with a document which serves at least in part as a handwriting exemplar, and whose contractual character is not obvious. The contractual language appears in print so small that many could not read it. State law may impose obligations on the bank (e.g., the duty to honor a check when the account has sufficient funds (Allen v. Bank of America, supra, 58 Cal.App.2d 124, 127, 136 P.2d 345)), but so far as the signature card drafted by the bank is concerned, the bank has all the rights and the depositor all the duties. The signature card provides that the depositor will be bound by the bank's rules, regulations, practices and charges, but the bank does not furnish the depositor with a copy of the relevant documents. The bank reserves the power to change its practices and fees at any time, subject only to the notice requirements of state law.

In short, the bank structured a totally one-sided transaction. The absence of equality of bargaining power, open negotiation, full disclosure, and a contract which fairly sets out the rights and duties of each party demonstrates that the transaction lacks those checks and balances which would inhibit the charging of unconscionable fees. In such a setting, plaintiff's charge that the bank's NSF fee is exorbitant, yielding a profit far in excess of cost, cannot be dismissed on demurrer. Under Civil Code section 1670.5, the parties should be afforded a reasonable opportunity to present evidence as to the commercial setting, purpose, and effect of the signature card and the NSF charge in order to determine whether that charge is unconscionable.

. . .

VI.   Conclusion.

. . . We conclude that the trial court erred in sustaining defendant's demurrer without leave to amend and in entering judgment for defendant.

The judgment is reversed, and the cause remanded to the superior court for further proceedings consistent with this opinion.

QUESTIONS

1.   The court holds that even if one party has the unilateral power to fix the contract price, the contract is not illusory. Might it nevertheless be unconscionable for the bank to provide that the price of various bank services will be determined unilaterally by the bank from time to time? If so, why? If not, are there any limits on the price fixed by the bank? Is Uniform Commercial Code section 2–305 relevant?

2.   Is the $6 charge for NSF checks unconscionable? What remains to be decided upon remand?

3.   In footnote 12, the court cites a decision by the New York Court of Appeals. Exactly why is that case distinguishable from *Perdue*?

4.   Problem. *Consumer* pays *Seller* with a check that is returned to *Seller* because *Consumer* has insufficient funds in his account. Pursuant to her standing policy, *Seller* assesses a fee of $50, which *Consumer* pays. *Consumer* now sues *Seller*, alleging unconscionability. If the trial court determines that the charge is unconscionable, should it grant *Consumer's* request for damages of $50?

In addition to section 2–302, please consider revised section 1–305(b).

5. It is clear that unconscionability is a vague concept. Should the legislatures attempt to define it? If so, what should be the elements of the definition? If not, how can sellers and creditors intelligently plan their transactions?

See UCSPA § 4(a), (c)(2); UCCC § 5.108(1), (4)(c).

6. Problem. *Discount Store* advertises 13–inch color televisions for $129. The TV's are house brands, i.e. their labels bear *Store's* name and do not disclose the identity of the manufacturer. *Department Store* sells Magnavox 13–inch color TV's for $289. Is *Department Store's* conduct unconscionable? Is it unconscionable for *Appliance Store* to sell *its* house brand 13–inch color TV for $289?

7. In Laswell v. Chrysler Corp., 351 S.E.2d 675 (Ga.App.1986), plaintiff purchased a new car, and in connection with that purchase, plaintiff also purchased the manufacturer's "added coverage Protection Plan." She paid the dealer $699, of which the dealer forwarded $89 to the manufacturer and pocketed the remainder ($610). Can plaintiff claim unconscionability?

8. Unconscionability has been a popular topic in the law reviews. Among the most thought-provoking analyses are Leff, Unconscionability and the Code—The Emperor's New Clause, 115 U.Pa.L.Rev. 485 (1967); Murray, Unconscionability: Unconscionability, 31 U.Pitt.L.Rev. 1 (1969); Hillman, Debunking Some Myths About Unconscionability: A New Framework for U.C.C. Section 2–302, 67 Corn.L.Rev. 1 (1981); Rakoff, Contracts of Adhesion: An Essay in Reconstruction, 96 Harv. L.Rev. 1174 (1983). Recent works have incorporated the learning of cognitive psychology. E.g., Korobkin, Bounded Rationality, Standard Form Contracts, and Unconscionability, 70 U.Chi.L.Rev. 1203 (2003); Marrow, Crafting a Remedy for the Naughtiness of Procedural Unconscionability, 34 Cumb.L.Rev. 11 (2003).

9. In *Perdue v. Crocker* (at page 493) the court states that unconscionability is one limitation on the enforceability of contracts of adhesion. The other, according to the court, is the doctrine of reasonable expectations: "[an adhesion] contract provision which does not fall within the reasonable expectations of the weaker or 'adhering' party will not be enforced against him." The Restatement (Second) of Contracts Section 211 puts it this way:

> (3) Where the other party has reason to believe that the party manifesting such assent would not do so if he knew that the writing contained a particular term, the term is not part of the agreement.

Comment *f* elaborates:

> . . . Although customers typically adhere to standardized agreements and are bound by them without even appearing to know the standard terms in detail, they are not bound to unknown terms which are

beyond the range of reasonable expectation. A debtor who delivers a check to his creditor with the amount blank does not authorize the insertion of an infinite figure. Similarly, a party who adheres to the other party's standard terms does not assent to a term if the other party has reason to believe that the adhering party would not have accepted the agreement if he had known that the agreement contained the particular term. Such a belief or assumption may be shown by the prior negotiations or inferred from the circumstances. Reason to believe may be inferred from the fact that the term is bizarre or oppressive, from the fact that it eviscerates the non-standard terms explicitly agreed to, or from the fact that it eliminates the dominant purpose of the transaction. The inference is reinforced if the adhering party never had an opportunity to read the term, or if it is illegible or otherwise hidden from view. This rule is closely related to the policy against unconscionable terms and the rule of interpretation against the draftsman. . . .

There is a significant difference between the sentence quoted from *Perdue* and the articulation of the Restatement. Can you identify it? Which version is preferable?

In Bell v. Congress Mortgage Company, Inc., 30 Cal.Rptr.2d 205 (Cal.App.1994), the court applied the principle of *Perdue* to deny enforcement of a clause in a loan contract that required "all disputes as to this agreement and accompanying loan documents" to be resolved by arbitration. The court stated:

> In the instant case, the trial court applied [the] two-pronged limitation on the enforcement of adhesion contracts in reaching its decision. The court found that although this arbitration clause was not oppressive or unconscionable, it did not fall within the reasonable expectations of the borrowers.
>
> Appellants articulate the issue for appeal in terms of whether the provisions pertaining to arbitration were "sufficiently conspicuous" to be within the reasonable expectation of the borrowers. We decline the invitation to limit our inquiry to the four corners of the Consent and Compliance Agreement. [Instead], we consider the borrowers' level of sophistication and experience, and the circumstances attendant to the signing of the agreement as well as whether the provision was sufficiently conspicuous.
>
> Thus, extrinsic evidence pertaining to the relative bargaining strengths of the parties, the nature and the extent of the negotiations, and a myriad of other circumstances providing a commercial context for the execution of the contract are relevant to this inquiry.
>
> The trial court record is replete with evidence that appellants engaged in practices which were both unlawful and designed to deceive unsophisticated and inexperienced borrowers as to their essential contractual rights. We recognize that the allegations are not yet proven in the crucible of trial, but they establish a nexus of facts consistent with

the trial court's finding of unenforceability. The trial court is "the ultimate authority on contested facts" and as a reviewing court, we must accept as true those evidentiary declarations in the record which support its determinations. A sampling of those declarations reveals allegations that borrowers were required to sign promissory notes and deeds of trusts in blank which would later be filled out by appellants; that appellants made no mention of the arbitration provisions; that loan documents were modified after their execution; that arbitration provisions were not read by the borrowers; and that no neutral party such as an escrow officer was present.

Moreover, the borrowers are generally elderly, unsophisticated and financially distressed individuals who relied upon the good graces of skilled sales persons from a substantial corporate lender. The declarations submitted by respondents provide an abundance of evidence from which to conclude that inclusion of the arbitration provision in the Consent and Compliance Agreement was beyond the reasonable expectations of these borrowers.

We consider also the placement of the provision in the context of the entire packet of documents executed. We look, therefore, to the volume of documents,[4] the context in which the challenged provision is placed, the technical nature of the text, the existence of a check off or other method of highlighting the provision, the verbal instructions provided, and the nature of any rights surrendered. Here, the compelled arbitration clause was placed in a paragraph in the middle of one of the documents. It was in no way highlighted or otherwise set apart. More importantly, it was contained in a document whose every other significant provision was a recitation of rights guaranteed the borrower. In that context, the potential for misapprehension is substantial.

. . .

The circumstances attendant to the execution of the Congress Mortgage agreements provide a compelling basis for upholding the decision of the trial court. . . .

30 Cal.Rptr.2d at 208–10.

———

(2) Unfairness

Without a doubt, unconscionability is difficult to define and apply. Another limit on the terms of consumer contracts is unfairness, which presents similar difficulties.

---

4. As noted by the court in A & M Produce, Co., supra, ". . . the length, complexity and obtuseness of most form contracts may be due at least in part to the seller's preference that the buyer will be dissuaded from reading that to which he is supposedly agreeing [which] almost inevitably results in a one-sided 'contract.' "

Commonwealth v. DeCotis

Supreme Judicial Court of Massachusetts, 1974.
366 Mass. 234, 316 N.E.2d 748.

WILKINS, J.

. . . The defendants are engaged in the business of renting lots in Pine Grove on which mobile homes are placed by their owners. Since 1970 the defendants have also been in the business of selling mobile homes. A mobile home owner who becomes a tenant of the defendants is subjected to the terms of a rental agreement. The first form of rental agreement used by the defendants made no reference to any obligation of the tenant to pay a fee to the defendants on the sale of his mobile home. From September 1969, to about May 1970, the defendants used a form of rental agreement which stated that mobile homes must be removed on resale although "exceptions might be made if a mobile home is sold to respectable adults with no children or pets." The agreement stated further that "[t]he management must interview the new tenant before accepting a deposit" and added "[f]or this concession and service rendered there will be a $250 service charge to the seller." A third form of agreement, adopted about May 1970, changed the service charge to ten per cent of the selling price. It is clear that some tenants did not receive rental agreements prior to committing themselves to the installation of their mobile homes in Pine Grove and that some tenants did not learn of the practice of imposing a resale fee until long after they had moved into Pine Grove.

The Attorney General asserts that the imposition and collection of the so called "service charge" or resale fee is an unfair and deceptive trade practice under G. L. c. 93A. Although the final decree directs the repayment of any resale fee paid since 1965, the first resale fee was collected by the defendants in October of 1968. Eighteen people paid a resale fee of $250, and twenty-one paid a resale fee of ten per cent of the sale price, an amount which was generally larger than $250. One fee was $1,200. In these instances no services were rendered by the defendants in connection with the sale, although the prospective purchaser was interviewed and approved as a new tenant by the defendants or their representative. The judge found that the fee, unrelated to services rendered or the length of tenancy, was arbitrary.

Many of the prospective tenants are retired or near retirement age, living on fixed incomes. Once a mobile home has lost a substantial portion of its mobility by its placement on a foundation with utility connections and associated landscaping, the expense of moving the home for the purposes of sale are substantial in relation to its market value. The market value of such a home in place is significantly greater than its market value as a mobile home to be moved. Finding a nearby location acceptable under local zoning regulations presents significant problems to a person seeking to move a mobile home from Pine Grove. Few mobile homes have been moved from Pine Grove.

. . .

The defendants . . . contend that they engaged in no deception or unfair act or practice. In light of the facts found by the judge and by us, such an argument can succeed only if as matter of law their conduct was not an unfair or deceptive act or practice within the meaning of those words in G. L. c. 93A, § 2(a).

The defendants argue that their actions were not deceptive or unfair because resale charges were uniformly collected by mobile home park operators in the Commonwealth. Such a fact was not proved and, even if it had been, the existence of an industry-wide practice would not constitute a defense to unlawful conduct.

The defendants contend that the Legislature has indorsed the reasonableness and fairness of their resale fee practices by a 1973 amendment to G. L. c. 140, § 32L. That amendment provides (in part) that a mobile home park licensee may "upon the proposed sale of such a home, contract with the mobile home owner to sell the home for a fee not to exceed ten per cent of the sale price of such home." Otherwise no such licensee may "impose by any rule or condition of occupancy any fee, charge, or commission for the sale of a mobile home located in a mobile home park." This fee authorized by statute for selling a mobile home relates to services in selling the mobile home, not unlike those of a real estate agent. The defendants' practice of collecting a fee for no services at all clearly is not indorsed by the 1973 amendment.[5]

The closest question presented by the defendants' conduct arises in those circumstances where, before a mobile home owner committed himself in any respect, he knew that the defendants were asserting a right to resale charge. In such a situation, assuming the disclosure was full and fair, the defendants may well not have been engaged in any deceptive act or practice.[6] Although deception may not have been involved where the disclosure by the defendants to the prospective tenant was timely and complete, we believe that the practice of charging a fee for no service whatsoever was an unfair act or practice within the intent of § 2(a) of G.L. c. 93A and that it was therefore unlawful.

Chapter 93A furnishes no definition of what constitutes an unfair act or practice made unlawful by § 2(a). We are directed by § 2(b) to consider interpretations of unfair acts and practices under the Federal Trade Commission Act as construed by the Commission and the Federal courts.

---

5. Arguments that no mobile home owner who sold a mobile home in Pine Grove ever received less on resale than the cost of the home to him or her, even if proved, would not prevent the defendants' conduct from being unfair. Similarly, the fact that the defendants as sellers of new mobile homes may have lost revenue from sales of new homes when used homes were sold in their park does not justify their practices as lawful.

6. In other situations, however, the acts of the defendants certainly had an element of deception, arising from nondisclosure. Adequate disclosure was lacking where no information concerning resale fees was furnished before the tenant assumed an obligation to lease, such as (a) where the rental agreement was silent on the subject and (b) where a rental agreement disclosing the resale fee practice was not furnished until after the tenant had made a commitment to occupy a lot at Pine Grove.

Unfairness under the Federal act has not been limited to practices forbidden at common law or by criminal statute. In fact the Federal act was passed in 1914 to overcome the narrow approach of what the common law regarded as unfair competition, and in effect to permit, by the gradual process of judicial inclusion and exclusion, a new definition of what is unfair. The present language of § 5 of the Federal Trade Commission Act concerning unfair or deceptive acts or practices was added in 1938. It also contains flexible proscriptions. Judge Learned Hand stated that the duty of the Federal Trade Commission "in part at any rate, is to discover and make explicit those unexpressed standards of fair dealing which the conscience of the community may progressively develop." Federal Trade Commn. v. Standard Educ. Soc., 86 F.2d 692, 696 (2d Cir.1936), revd. in part 302 U.S. 112 (1937).

The existence of unfair acts and practices must be determined from the circumstances of each case. We do not now undertake to establish general rules which may be applied in other situations. The nature of the statute and the development of the law under the comparable Federal statute indicate that such an attempt would be undesirable.

What we can determine is that the collection of resale charges by the defendants was an unfair act or practice. That provision of the Uniform Commercial Code which permits a court to refuse to enforce a contract or a contract provision which is unconscionable provides a reasonable analogy here. Such a comparison was made by the Supreme Court of New Jersey in Kugler v. Romain, 58 N.J. 522, 545–547 (1971), where the New Jersey Consumer Fraud Act was interpreted to permit the invalidation of consumer sales because of unconscionable prices. In the *Kugler* case, sales contracts were held to be invalid in part because, although the purchasers received something of value, the value received was unconscionably disproportionate to the price paid. In our case the defendants furnished no goods or services in connection with the resale of mobile homes in Pine Grove. They undertook to impose an arbitrary provision on persons of limited means and limited choice for residences. The defendants were able to collect the resale fees solely because their tenants were in a position in which they had no reasonable alternative but to pay and to agree to pay. It was financially preferable to sell a mobile home on site in Pine Grove for ninety per cent of its fair market value (or for $250 less than its fair market value) than to sell that home for relocation. The willingness of tenants to pay resale fees, and even to contract knowingly to pay those fees, does not make the collection of such a fee fair. It merely demonstrates the extent to which the defendants had their tenants at their mercy.[7] The extraction of a resale fee for no services rendered in these circumstances was an unfair act or practice under G. L. c. 93A, § 2(a).

---

7. The defendants' claim that other mobile home park operators in Massachusetts were engaged in the same practice merely accentuates the ineffective bargaining position of a person who wished to place a mobile home on leased premises in a mobile home park in this State. It is not surprising that substantial regulatory legislation respecting the operation of mobile homes was recently enacted.

QUESTIONS AND NOTES

1. The court says that "[t]he existence of unfair acts and practices must be determined from the circumstances of each case. We do not now undertake to establish general rules which may be applied in other situations." What does the court mean by this? Is the definition of unfairness idiosyncratic to each judge? How can a seller or creditor determine in advance whether to include a given provision in the contract? Aren't some standards necessary?

Can you extract from the court's opinion any standards for determining unfairness? What factors does the court cite? Do they look familiar?

2. Immediately preceding the passage quoted in Question 1, the court quotes Judge Learned Hand: "The duty of the Federal Trade Commission, 'in part at any rate, is to discover and make explicit those unexpressed standards of fair dealing which the conscience of the community may progressively develop.'" Even if this states an appropriate standard for a statute to be administered by an agency like the FTC, which can conduct investigations to ascertain the "conscience of the community," is it an appropriate standard for a statute that is administered by the courts?

3. If consumers knew of the resale fee at the time they signed the contracts in *DeCotis*, how can the fee be unfair? Why should a consumer be able to enter a contract with full awareness of a given term and then escape enforcement of it? Is this fair to the merchant?

4. In 1973 the Massachusetts legislature enacted a statute to regulate mobile home parks. Among other things, it prohibited operators of mobile home parks from adopting regulations that were "unreasonable, unfair, or unconscionable." The statute provided that violations of that prohibition were violations of the little-FTC act involved in *DeCotis*. The state attorney general sought to enforce this prohibition against the operator of a park who had adopted a rule prohibiting "for sale" signs. The trial court held that the park's rule did not violate the statute because "for sale" signs may be unsightly and because they may create the impression that the park is an undesirable place to live. In Commonwealth v. Gustafsson, 346 N.E.2d 706 (Mass.1976), the Massachusetts Supreme Judicial Court disagreed:

> Although "For Sale" signs can be unattractive, this consideration must be weighed against the importance of the tenant's right under the mobile home statute to sell his home on the lot. Despite a growing demand for mobile homes, there is a shortage of available land. In view of the scarcity of land, a mobile home owner may find it difficult, as well as expensive, to move his home to a new lot. In addition, the market value of the mobile home will be, to a considerable extent, dependent on the availability of a lot space, and, thus, if a tenant is unable to sell his home on the lot, his investment may be rendered almost worthless. For these reasons, a tenant's right to sell his home on his lot is of substantial importance, and the statute may properly forbid a park owner from restricting this right unnecessarily.

> Admittedly, Gustafsson could ensure the attractiveness of his park by enacting reasonable rules regulating the type and size of signs and the areas in which they may be displayed. However, we believe that a total prohibition of "For Sale" signs constitutes an unreasonable restriction on a tenant's right to sell his home on the lot, for it unnecessarily restricts a seller's options in dealing with the public, and is contrary to the intent of *DeCotis*, which enjoined the park owner from "limiting . . . the resale of mobile homes" by park tenants.

Id. at 713.

What standard is the court adopting for determining whether the rule is "unreasonable, unfair, or unconscionable"? Does it appear to be the same standard the court used in *DeCotis*?

5.   May the entire transaction itself, rather than just one or more terms of the deal, be unfair? The enforcing authority in Wisconsin thought so, as it issued a cease and desist order preventing the sale of term papers and take-home exams to college students. The entire business was "inimical to the best interest of the student, the college or university he attends, and the public" and was therefore unfair. In re Inksetter, No. 997 (Wis. Dept. of Ag.), cited in Jeffries, Protection for Consumers Against Unfair and Deceptive Business, 57 Marq.L.Rev. 559, 576 (1974).

6.   The Illinois little-FTC statute directs the courts to consider interpretations of section 5 of the FTC Act. 815 Ill. Consol. Stat. 505/2. In Fitzgerald v. Chicago Title & Trust Co., 361 N.E.2d 94 (Ill.App.1977), affirmed 380 N.E.2d 790 (Ill.1978), plaintiffs challenged as unfair a title company's practice of kicking back ten percent of its revenue to the banks that channeled business to it. If the product had been a tangible good, rather than intangible services, the title company's practice would have violated the Clayton Act, 15 U.S.C. § 12 et seq., and therefore would automatically have been a violation of FTC Act section 5. But since the product was services, there was no violation of the Clayton Act. Unlike the Clayton Act, however, the Illinois statute expressly applied to sales of services and intangible property. Thus the court held that "[u]nder the applicable federal interpretations [of the FTC Act], we conclude that plaintiffs' allegations that the payments by [the title company] constituted an unfair method of competition and an unfair trade practice, state a cause of action under . . . the Illinois [little-FTC] Act." Id. at 97.

Since conduct that violates section 5 of the FTC Act may automatically violate a state's little-FTC act, it may be useful to examine the standards of unfairness under the federal statute.

Letter From FTC to Consumer Subcommittee of Senate Committee on Commerce, Science, and Transportation

December 17, 1980.

Dear Senators Ford and Danforth:

. . .

In response to your inquiry we have . . . undertaken a review of the decided cases and rules and have synthesized from them the most important principles of general applicability. Rather than merely reciting the law, we have attempted to provide the Committee with a concrete indication of the manner in which the Commission has enforced, and will continue to enforce, its unfairness mandate. In so doing we intend to address the concerns that have been raised about the meaning of consumer unfairness, and thereby attempt to provide a greater sense of certainty about what the Commission would regard as an unfair act or practice under Section 5.

.   .   .

Commission Statement of Policy on the Scope of the Consumer Unfairness Jurisdiction

.   .   .

The present understanding of the unfairness standard is the result of an evolutionary process. The statute was deliberately framed in general terms since Congress recognized the impossibility of drafting a complete list of unfair trade practices that would not quickly become outdated or leave loopholes for easy evasion. The task of identifying unfair trade practices was therefore assigned to the Commission, subject to judicial review, in the expectation that the underlying criteria would evolve and develop over time. As the Supreme Court observed as early as 1931, the ban on unfairness "belongs to that class of phrases which do not admit of precise definition, but the meaning and application of which must be arrived at by what this court elsewhere has called 'the gradual process of judicial inclusion and exclusion.' "

By 1964 enough cases had been decided to enable the Commission to identify three factors that it considered when applying the prohibition against consumer unfairness. These were: (1) whether the practice injures consumers; (2) whether it violates established public policy; (3) whether it is unethical or unscrupulous.[8] These factors were later quoted with apparent approval by the Supreme Court in the 1972 case of *Sperry & Hutchinson*.[9] Since then the Commission has continued to refine the standard of unfairness in its cases and rules, and it has now reached a more detailed sense of both the definition and the limits of these criteria.

Consumer injury

Unjustified consumer injury is the primary focus of the FTC Act, and the most important of the three *S & H* criteria. By itself it can be sufficient to warrant a finding of unfairness. The Commission's ability to rely on an independent criterion of consumer injury is consistent with the intent of

---

8.   .   .   .   Statement of Basis and Purpose, Unfair or Deceptive Advertising and Labeling of Cigarettes in Relation to the Health Hazards of Smoking, 29 Fed.Reg. 8324, 8355 (1964).

9.   FTC v. Sperry & Hutchinson Co., 405 U.S. 233, 244–45 n. 5 (1972).   .   .   .

the statute, which was to "[make] the consumer who may be injured by an unfair trade practice of equal concern before the law with the merchant injured by the unfair methods of a dishonest competitor."

The independent nature of the consumer injury criterion does not mean that every consumer injury is legally "unfair," however. To justify a finding of unfairness the injury must satisfy three tests. It must be substantial; it must not be outweighed by any countervailing benefits to consumers or competition that the practice produces; and it must be an injury that consumers themselves could not reasonably have avoided.

First of all, the injury must be substantial. The Commission is not concerned with trivial or merely speculative harms. In most cases a substantial injury involves monetary harm, as when sellers coerce consumers into purchasing unwanted goods or services or when consumers buy defective goods or services on credit but are unable to assert against the creditor claims or defenses arising from the transaction. Unwarranted health and safety risks may also support a finding of unfairness. Emotional impact and other more subjective types of harm, on the other hand, will not ordinarily make a practice unfair. Thus, for example, the Commission will not seek to ban an advertisement merely because it offends the tastes or social beliefs of some viewers, as has been suggested in some of the comments.

Second, the injury must not be outweighed by any offsetting consumer or competitive benefits that the sales practice also produces. Most business practices entail a mixture of economic and other costs and benefits for purchasers. A seller's failure to present complex technical data on his product may lessen a consumer's ability to choose, for example, but may also reduce the initial price he must pay for the article. The Commission is aware of these tradeoffs and will not find that a practice unfairly injures consumers unless it is injurious in its net effects. The Commission also takes account of the various costs that a remedy would entail. These include not only the costs to the parties directly before the agency, but also the burdens on society in general in the form of increased paperwork, increased regulatory burdens on the flow of information, reduced incentives to innovation and capital formation, and similar matters.

Finally, the injury must be one which consumers could not reasonably have avoided. Normally we expect the marketplace to be self-correcting, and we rely on consumer choice—the ability of individual consumers to make their own private purchasing decisions without regulatory intervention—to govern the market. We anticipate that consumers will survey the available alternatives, choose those that are most desirable, and avoid those that are inadequate or unsatisfactory. However, it has long been recognized that certain types of sales techniques may prevent consumers from effectively making their own decisions, and that corrective action may then become necessary. Most of the Commission's unfairness matters are brought under these circumstances. They are brought, not to second-guess the wisdom of particular consumer decisions, but rather to halt some form of seller behavior that unreasonably creates or takes advantage of an obstacle to the free exercise of consumer decisionmaking.

Sellers may adopt a number of practices that unjustifiably hinder such free market decisions. Some may withhold or fail to generate critical price or performance data, for example, leaving buyers with insufficient information for informed comparisons. Some may engage in overt coercion, as by dismantling a home appliance for "inspection" and refusing to reassemble it until a service contract is signed. And some may exercise undue influence over highly susceptible classes of purchasers, as by promoting fraudulent "cures" to seriously ill cancer patients. Each of these practices undermines an essential precondition to a free and informed consumer transaction, and, in turn, to a well-functioning market. Each of them is therefore properly banned as an unfair practice under the FTC Act.

Violation of public policy

The second *S & H* standard asks whether the conduct violates public policy as it has been established by statute, common law, industry practice, or otherwise. This criterion may be applied in two different ways. It may be used to test the validity and strength of the evidence of consumer injury, or, less often, it may be cited for a dispositive legislative or judicial determination that such injury is present.

Although public policy was listed by the *S & H* Court as a separate consideration, it is used most frequently by the Commission as a means of providing additional evidence on the degree of consumer injury caused by specific practices. To be sure, most Commission actions are brought to redress relatively clear-cut injuries, and those determinations are based, in large part, on objective economic analysis. As we have indicated before, the Commission believes that considerable attention should be devoted to the analysis of whether substantial net harm has occurred, not only because that is part of the unfairness test, but also because the focus on injury is the best way to ensure that the Commission acts responsibly and uses its resources wisely. Nonetheless, the Commission wishes to emphasize the importance of examining outside statutory policies and established judicial principles for assistance in helping the agency ascertain whether a particular form of conduct does in fact tend to harm consumers. Thus the agency has referred to First Amendment decisions upholding consumers' rights to receive information, for example, to confirm that restrictions on advertising tend unfairly to hinder the informed exercise of consumer choice.

Conversely, statutes or other sources of public policy may affirmatively allow for a practice that the Commission tentatively views as unfair. The existence of such policies will then give the agency reason to reconsider its assessment of whether the practice is actually injurious in its net effects. In other situations there may be no clearly established public policies, or the policies may even be in conflict. While that does not necessarily preclude the Commission from taking action if there is strong evidence of net consumer injury, it does underscore the desirability of carefully examining public policies in all instances.[27] In any event, whenever objective evidence of consumer injury is difficult to obtain, the need to identify and assess all relevant public policies assumes increased importance.

Sometimes public policy will independently support a Commission action. This occurs when the policy is so clear that it will entirely determine the question of consumer injury, so there is little need for separate analysis by the Commission. In these cases the legislature or court, in announcing the policy, has already determined that such injury does exist and thus it need not be expressly proved in each instance. An example of this approach arose in a case involving a mail-order firm.[28] There the Commission was persuaded by an analogy to the due-process clause that it was unfair for the firm to bring collection suits in a forum that was unreasonably difficult for the defendants to reach. In a similar case the Commission applied the statutory policies of the Uniform Commercial Code to require that various automobile manufacturers and their distributors refund to their customers any surplus money that was realized after they repossessed and resold their customers' cars.[29] The Commission acts on such a basis only where the public policy is suitable for administrative enforcement by this agency, however. Thus it turned down a petition for a rule to require fuller disclosure of aerosol propellants, reasoning that the subject of fluorocarbon safety was currently under study by other scientific and legislative bodies with more appropriate expertise or jurisdiction over the subject.[30]

27. The analysis of external public policies is extremely valuable but not always definitive. The legislative history of Section 5 recognizes that new forms of unfair business practices may arise which, at the time of the Commission's involvement, have not yet been generally proscribed. See [page 506] supra. Thus a review of public policies established independently of Commission action may not be conclusive in determining whether the challenged practices should be prohibited or otherwise restricted. At the same time, however, we emphasize the importance of examining public policies, since a thorough analysis can serve as an important check on the overall reasonableness of the Commission's actions.

28. Spiegel, Inc. v. FTC, 540 F.2d 287 (7th Cir.1976). In this case the Commission did inquire into the extent of the resulting consumer injury, but under the rationale involved it presumably need not have done so. See also FTC v. R. F. Keppel & Bro., 291 U.S. 304 (1934) (firm had gained a marketing advantage by selling goods through a lottery technique that violated state gambling policies). . . . Since these public-policy cases are based on legislative determinations, rather than on a judgment within the Commis-

sion's area of special economic expertise, it is appropriate that they can reach a relatively wider range of consumer injuries than just those associated with impaired consumer choice.

29. A surplus occurs when a repossessed car is resold for more than the amount owed by the debtor plus the expenses of repossession and resale. The law of 49 states requires that creditors refund surpluses when they occur, but if creditors systematically refuse to honor this obligation, consumers have no practical way to discover that they have been deprived of money to which they are entitled. See Ford Motor Co., 94 F.T.C. 564, 618 (1979) appeal pending, Nos. 79–7649 and 79–7654 (9th Cir.); Ford Motor Co., 93 F.T.C. 402 (1979) (consent decree); General Motors Corp., D. 9074 (Feb. 1980) (consent decree). By these latter two consent agreements the Commission, because of its unfairness jurisdiction, has been able to secure more than $2 million for consumers allegedly deprived of surpluses to which they were entitled.

30. See Letter from John F. Dugan, Acting Secretary, to Action on Smoking and Health (January 13, 1977). See also Letter

To the extent that the Commission relies heavily on public policy to support a finding of unfairness, the policy should be clear and well-established. In other words, the policy should be declared or embodied in formal sources such as statutes, judicial decisions, or the Constitution as interpreted by the courts, rather than being ascertained from a general sense of national values. The policy should likewise be one that is widely shared, and not the isolated decision of a single state or a single court. If these two tests are not met the policy cannot be considered as an "established" public policy for purposes of the *S & H* criterion. The Commission would then act only on the basis of convincing independent evidence that the practice was distorting the operation of the market and thereby causing unjustified consumer injury.

Unethical or unscrupulous conduct

Finally, the third *S & H* standard asks whether the conduct was immoral, unethical, oppressive, or unscrupulous. This test was presumably included in order to be sure of reaching all the purposes of the underlying statute, which forbids "unfair" acts or practices. It would therefore allow the Commission to reach conduct that violates generally recognized standards of business ethics. This test has proven, however, to be largely duplicative. Conduct that is truly unethical or unscrupulous will almost always injure consumers or violate public policy as well. The Commission has therefore never relied on the third element of *S & H* as an independent basis for a finding of unfairness, and it will act in the future only on the basis of the first two.

. . .

QUESTIONS AND NOTES

1. According to the letter, unfairness may consist of unjustified consumer injury. What criteria must the injury meet in order to be unjustified?

Has the FTC furthered the clarity and rigor of section 5? In American Financial Services v. Federal Trade Commission, 767 F.2d 957 (D.C.Cir. 1985), the court stated, "While the Commission's three-part unfairness standard sets forth an abstract definition of unfairness focusing on 'unjustified consumer injury,' it does little towards delineating the specific 'kinds' of practices or consumer injuries which it encompasses. . . . [D]espite the Policy Statement's purpose of providing greater certainty in application of the unfairness doctrine, it falls short of providing any concrete guidance to the court. . . ." Id. at 971–72. Nevertheless, the court accepted the 1980 Policy Statement as articulating appropriate standards for determining unfairness. The FTC had applied those standards in the course of promulgating a regulation that prohibited the use of certain contractual

from Charles A. Tobin, Secretary, to Prof. Page and Mr. Young (September 17, 1973) (denying petition to exercise § 6(b) subpoena powers to obtain consumer complaint information from cosmetic firms and then to transmit the data to FDA for that agency's enforcement purposes).

terms. The court rejected a challenge to the regulation, holding that the Commission had the authority to promulgate the regulation and that the Commission properly applied the Policy Statement criteria.

2.   Would the practices of the mobile home park operator in *DeCotis* be unfair under the FTC's interpretation of the standard?

3.   Compare the standard of unfairness as articulated by the FTC to the standard of unconscionability as articulated by *Williams v. Walker–Thomas* and *Perdue v. Crocker*. In what ways, if any, are the standards different? In what respects is one better than the other?

4.   In 1994 Congress amended the FTC Act to incorporate the FTC's 1980 Policy Statement into the statute. It added a new subsection to section 5:

(n) Standard of Proof; Public Policy Considerations

The Commission shall have no authority under this section or section 18 [15 U.S.C. § 57a] to declare unlawful an act or practice on the grounds that such act or practice is unfair unless the act or practice causes or is likely to cause substantial injury to consumers which is not reasonably avoidable by consumers themselves and not outweighed by countervailing benefits to consumers or to competition. In determining whether an act or practice is unfair, the Commission may consider established public policies as evidence to be considered with all other evidence. Such public policy considerations may not serve as a primary basis for such determination.

In re International Harvester Co.

Federal Trade Commission, 1984.
104 F.T.C. 949.

[The facts and procedure of the case appear at page 62 supra. After describing the law of deception under the Federal Trade Commission Act, the Commission turned to a description of the law of unfairness under the FTC Act.]

II.   APPLICABLE LEGAL STANDARDS

. . .

Unfairness

The Commission's unfairness jurisdiction provides a more general basis for action against acts or practices which cause significant consumer injury. This part of our jurisdiction is broader than that involving deception, and the standards for its exercise are correspondingly more stringent. It requires the complete analysis of a practice which may be harmful to consumers. To put the point another way, unfairness is the set of general principles of which deception is a particularly well-established and streamlined subset.

Over the past four years the Commission has devoted considerable attention to clarifying these general principles. In 1980 we prepared a formal policy statement describing our jurisdiction over unfair practices. The statement took as its point of departure the familiar language of the *Sperry & Hutchinson* case. It declared that most unfairness cases would be brought under the consumer injury theory identified in that decision. It also systematized the essential elements of that theory. An actionable consumer injury must be: (1) substantial; (2) not outweighed by any offsetting consumer or competitive benefits that the practice produces; and (3) one which consumers could not reasonably have avoided.

The first element to this analysis is that the injury must be substantial. Unlike deception, which focuses on "likely" injury, unfairness cases usually involve actual and completed harms. While in most cases the harm involved is monetary, the policy statement expressly noted that "unwarranted health and safety risks may also support a finding of unfairness."

The second element is that the conduct must be harmful in its net effects. This is simply a recognition of the fact that most conduct creates a mixture of both beneficial and adverse consequences. In analyzing an omission this part of the unfairness analysis requires us to balance against the risks of injury the costs of notification and the costs of determining what the prevailing consumer misconceptions actually are. This inquiry must be made in a level of detail that deception analysis does not contemplate.

Finally, the third element is that the injury be one that consumers could not reasonably have avoided through the exercise of consumer choice. This restriction is necessary in order to keep the FTC Act focused on the economic issues that are its proper concern. The Commission does not ordinarily seek to mandate specific conduct or specific social outcomes, but rather seeks to ensure simply that markets operate freely, so that consumers can make their own decisions.[47]

To accomplish these goals the Commission may require that consumers be given the information that is critical to an informed choice.[48] There is also a need for principled limits on this concept, of course, since virtually any piece of information may be useful to some consumers. While this balance must ultimately be struck in the context of the individual case, the

---

47. Some commentators have interpreted our policy statement as involving essentially a general balancing of interests, with all the imprecision of that course, rather than a definable economic rule. In fact, however, the principal focus of our unfairness policy is on the maintenance of consumer choice or consumer sovereignty, an economic concept that permits relatively specific identification of conduct harmful to that objective. See Averitt, The Meaning of "Unfair Acts or Practices" in Section 5 of the Federal Trade Commission Act, 70 Geo.L.J. 225 (1981).

48. Ordinarily information disclosure is handled by market forces, of course. Sometimes, however, a market failure occurs, as when the balance between the risk of tort losses and the risk of lost sales produces significant disincentives to disclosure, or when the costs of non-disclosure become hard to quantify, as in certain safety issues. Corrective FTC action would then be appropriate.

Commission has decided on certain general principles. In most cases it is appropriate to limit mandatory disclosure to those core aspects of a transaction that virtually all consumers would consider essential to an informed decision. These are the same basic characteristics discussed above in connection with common-law merchantability: (1) information bearing on fitness for intended use, and (2) information bearing on significant hidden safety hazards.

These characteristics are applied here in a slightly different way, however. In an assessment of deceptive omissions we are applying a relatively streamlined set of principles and so we must be careful not to go too far and infer warranties too freely about relatively improbable safety hazards. We therefore take a relatively cautious view of the information that must be disclosed under that theory. In an assessment of unfairness, on the other hand, we conduct a full cost-benefit analysis, in which we weigh the consumer benefits of disclosure against their likely costs, and so there is less risk of an overbroad result. We can therefore take a more inclusive view of the information that must be disclosed under this approach.

In short, an omission may be found unfair even though it is not deceptive. To do so, however, requires a more thorough analysis than is used in deception cases.

III. ANALYSIS OF THE CASE

In this section we will apply our general legal theory to the specific facts of the case. . . .

Unfairness

. . . The unfairness theory, it will be recalled, is the Commission's general law of consumer protection, for which deception is one specific but particularly important application. Unfairness calls for a somewhat more detailed analysis of a challenged practice. This focuses on three criteria: (1) whether the practice creates a serious consumer injury; (2) whether this injury exceeds any offsetting consumer benefits; and (3) whether the injury was one that consumers could not reasonably have avoided. We find that all three criteria are satisfied in the present case.

There clearly has been serious consumer injury. At least one person has been killed and eleven others burned. Many of the burn injuries have been major ones, moreover, resulting in mobility limitations, lasting psychological harm, and severe disfigurement. These injuries are of a kind that satisfies the first unfairness test. It is true that they involve physical rather than economic injury, but the Unfairness Statement reaches such matters. It is also true that they involve only limited numbers of people, but the Statement provides that conduct causing a very severe harm to a small number will be covered as well. A number of previous Commission cases have in fact been brought to correct injuries less numerous and less severe than those involved here.

The second criterion states the consumer injury must not be out-weighed by any countervailing benefits to consumers or to competition that the practice also brings about. This inquiry is particularly important in the case of pure omissions. Since the range of such omissions is potentially infinite, the range of cost-benefit ratios from actions to force disclosure is infinite as well, raising the possibility that a particular action may be ill-advised. We believe that this criterion is also satisfied in the present case, however. The consuming public has realized no benefit from Harvester's non-disclosure that is at all sufficient to offset the human injuries in-volved.[57]

The principal tradeoff to be considered in this analysis is that involving compliance costs. More information may generally be helpful to consumers, but all such information can be produced only by incurring costs that are ultimately born as higher prices by those same consumers.[58] One must determine the level of preexisting customer knowledge, ascertain the actual facts on a particular issue, and communicate those facts effectively to the affected customers. Such activities are not always cheap. Harvester's Fuel Fire Prevention Program, for example, which finally led to an effective warning, involved both media advertisements and a direct mailing to 630,000 tractor operators, and cost the company approximately $2.8 million. The costs of monitoring and experimentation undertaken in previous years undoubtedly raise the final figure even higher than this. The Commission should not impose costs of such magnitude without first comparing them with the benefits to be expected.

Here, however, we have no doubt that such a calculation favors disclosure. Harvester's expenses were not large in relation to the injuries that could have been avoided. Nor do we mean to rule out the possibility that some other, less expensive form of notification—such as a clearly worded warning in the operating manual—would also have been suffi-cient.[59] We therefore conclude that the costs and benefits in this case satisfy the second unfairness criterion.

Finally, the third unfairness criterion states that the injury must be one that consumers could not reasonably have avoided. Here tractor operators could in fact have avoided their injuries by following a few relatively simple safety rules. If they had refrained from removing the cap from a hot or running tractor—something that both the owner's manuals

---

57. Whenever an omission results in serious bodily injury it is, of course, especially likely that a cost-benefit analysis will favor disclosure.

58. Other, non-monetary costs may also be incurred. For example, if the Commission requires disclosure of one fact, a seller may be less inclined to volunteer other facts, re-sulting in a net diminution of information.

59. In making these calculations we do not strive for an unrealistic degree of preci-sion, valuing an injury or a life at precisely x

many dollars. We assess the matter in a more general way, giving consumers the benefit of the doubt in close issues. This course follows from the Commission's long tradition of giv-ing especial care to issues involving physical safety. See, e.g., Firestone Tire & Rubber Co., 81 F.T.C. 398, 451, 456 (1972). What is im-portant, however, is that we retain an overall sense of the relationship between costs and benefits. We would not want to impose com-pliance costs of millions of dollars in order to prevent a bruised elbow.

and common knowledge suggested was a dangerous practice—fuel geysering would have been completely precluded. Harvester therefore argues that one necessary element of unfairness is not present.

Upon full consideration, however, we believe that this element is satisfied as well. The issue here is whether the safety rules for these tractors were adequately disclosed. Whether some consequence is "reasonably avoidable" depends, not just on whether people know the physical steps to take in order to prevent it, but also on whether they understand the necessity of actually taking those steps. We do not believe that this need was fully appreciated here. Farmers may have known that loosening the fuel cap was generally a poor practice, but they did not know from the limited disclosures made, nor could they be expected to know from prior experience, the full consequences that might follow from it. This is therefore not a situation in which the farmers themselves are primarily responsible for their own accidents.

3rd element of unfairness satisfied

The record contains much testimony suggesting that the victims of the phenomenon did not realize that a fuel geyser was possible. One farmer stated that he had removed gas caps "many, many" times in order to check on fuel level, without having had gas spew out of the filler neck. Another states that: "Not in my wildest imagination had I thought that could happen." Still another explained that he regularly loosened the cap to relieve pressure-related hissing noises:

* facts

> It [the hissing] happened a few times a day, two or three or four times a day. It just kind of—it is something you didn't feel like you wanted to keep driving. That noise kind of hissing at you. So you just leaned ahead and loosened the gas cap a little bit. The air would come out and that would be all there would be to it. There would be a puff of air and it would quit.

In short, loosening the fuel cap was something that farmers did on many occasions, without consciousness of any particular risk, beyond the presumably obvious requirement of having to keep open flame away from the filler neck, which they felt quite able to do.

Since fuel geysering was a risk that they were not aware of, they could not reasonably have avoided it. This is so even though they had been informed of measures to prevent it. Such information was not the same thing as an effective warning:

> [I]mplicit in the duty to warn is the duty to warn with a degree of intensity that would cause a reasonable man to exercise for his own safety the caution commensurate with the potential danger.[64]

Such a warning was not provided in this case. We therefore find that the three elements of unfair conduct are present, and that Harvester's nondisclosures violated Section 5 of the FTC Act.

holding

. . .

64. Tampa Drug Co. v. Wait, 103 So.2d 603, 609 (Fla.1958).

V.   REMEDY

Finally, we have the issue of remedy. Having found that Harvester was engaged in unfair practices, we must now determine what corrective measures the public interest will require. This inquiry can be framed as a series of three questions. Should we issue a general order requiring disclosure of safety hazards in all of Harvester's agricultural equipment? Should we issue an order focused more narrowly on the facts of this particular case and requiring disclosure of just the fuel geysering hazard? Or should we conclude that Harvester has already taken adequate corrective measures and therefore enter no order at all?

.   .   .

Under the particular circumstances of this case, however, we will select [the] third option. That is to issue no order at all. Our reasons for doing so are twofold. First, Harvester's voluntary notification program has already provided all the relief that could be expected from a Commission order. Second, the changing technology of the tractor industry has obviated any concern that Harvester might return to its earlier violation. The industry has moved massively from gasoline to diesel power, thus eliminating concerns over issues relating to gasoline safety. Harvester has not made a gasoline tractor since 1978, and, as the ALJ found, "does not appear likely to do so again in the future." We therefore conclude that no order is necessary in the present case.

VI.   CONCLUSION

This case is in most respects a routine dispute over the proper contours of consumer information disclosure. We have resolved that dispute by holding that disclosure was necessary here.

En route to that holding we also had to identify the proper legal framework to use when assessing pure omissions. We have decided that such omissions should be judged as cases of possible unfairness rather than of possible deception. Since pure omissions do not most probably reflect deliberate acts on the part of the sellers, we cannot be confident, without a cost-benefit analysis, that a Commission action would do more good than harm. Yet a cost-benefit analysis is required only under an unfairness and not under a deception approach. We will therefore treat these matters in unfairness terms in order to ensure that such an analysis is made. In so deciding we hope to have added something further to the clarity and rigor of our statute, so that decisions on the merits may henceforth be made and predicted with greater precision.

QUESTIONS AND NOTES

1.   One of the elements of unfairness is substantial injury. In support of its conclusion that severe harm to a small number of consumers amounts to the requisite substantial injury, the Commission states, "A number of previous Commission cases have in fact been brought to correct injuries less numerous and less severe than those involved here.'' This reliance on precedent stands in stark contrast to the FTC's treatment (in the deception portion of its opinion) of the previous Commission cases concerning deceptive omissions (page 67).

2.   Was there substantial injury in *International Harvester*? Granted, personal injuries are among the kinds of injury contemplated by the FTC's standard, and granted further that deaths or severe burns are substantial injury, why isn't the incidence of injury relevant to whether International Harvester's practices caused substantial injury to consumers? The injury rate, over a forty-year period, was one thousandth of one percent. If the ''substantial injury'' component of the FTC's test is satisfied in *International Harvester*, won't it be satisfied in *every* case in which a seller's product or conduct causes personal injury?

3.   Are you persuaded that the injury was not reasonably avoidable? What is the relevance of the fact that the owner's manuals specifically stated that one should not remove the fuel cap when the tractor engine was running or was hot?

4.   Hardly a week goes by without the announcement that a merchant or financial institution has compromised the privacy of its customer's financial data, whether by theft of a lap-top or by a hacker's intrusion into a data base. The FTC believes that unfairness may be a tool for dealing with this problem. In 2005 and 2006 it entered consent decrees with BJ's Wholesale Club, DSW, and CardSystems Solutions to resolve complaints that the three companies engaged in unfair acts or practices by failing to have adequate procedures to safeguard the security of their customers' credit card and debit card information. For a view critical of this use of the unfairness doctrine, see Scott, The FTC, the Unfairness Doctrine, and Data Security Breach Litigation: Has the Commission Gone Too Far? 60 Admin.L.Rev. 127 (2008).

5.   Between 1966 and 1975 Orkin Exterminating Co. offered termite treatment pursuant to a contract that provided for ''lifetime'' protection against termite infestation. The contract stated that Orkin would provide initial treatment at a specified cost. It also stated that for an annual fee of a stated amount, payable on each anniversary of the contract, Orkin would reinspect the premises and retreat them if any new infestation had occurred. If the premises were structurally modified, the agreement would terminate unless the parties agreed to additional treatment and/or an adjustment of the annual fee. (For contracts formed after 1975, the contracts provided that Orkin could increase the annual renewal fee, but the pre–1975 contracts had no such provision.) By 1980 Orkin's expense of reinspection and retreatment exceeded the annual fees fixed in the pre–1975 contracts. Consequently, Orkin unilaterally increased the annual fee on more than 200,000 contracts. Between 1980 and 1984, this increase produced more than $7,500,000 in increased revenues. Of the 200,000 customers affected, 40,000 did not renew, and 6,000 who complained were granted rollbacks to the renewal fee specified in their respective contracts. In 1984 the FTC challenged Orkin's unilateral increase as an unfair act or practice. In re Orkin Exterminating Co., 108 F.T.C. 263 (1986), affirmed 849 F.2d 1354 (11th Cir.1988), cert. denied 488 U.S. 1041 (1989). The Commission held that the unilateral increase was unfair and ordered Orkin to cease and desist from charging or collecting a renewal fee higher than the amount specified in the contract. En route to this order, the Commission stated:

> Plainly, a breach of contract or a systematic program to breach numerous contracts constitutes an "act or practice" under Section 5. The remaining question is whether such an act or practice is unfair.[66]
> . . .

Orkin suggests that the Commission's interpretation of its unfairness jurisdiction should be guided by court decisions construing breach of contract under state "little FTC Acts," which, like Section 5, prohibit unfair acts or practices. The courts have read these state laws not to reach simple breach of contract. The Commission is not bound to follow judicial interpretations of state "little FTC Acts" in construing Section 5. It can restrain unfair business practices in interstate commerce "even if the activities or industries have been the subject of legislation by a state or even if the intrastate conduct is authorized by state law."[67] Although the state cases are not controlling, we would consider their reasoning if those cases more closely paralleled the case before us. They do not.

The state court decisions Orkin cites stand for the proposition that private controversies arising out of simple breaches of contract under certain state statutes do not violate those statutes. This case is not a dispute between private parties. The requirement under Section 5 that the Commission determine that an enforcement action is in the public interest provides an essential feature missing in private actions brought under state laws. The Commission has made that determination here. Unlike the conduct in Orkin's state law cases, the conduct at issue in this proceeding is not the breach of a single contract but is rather a widespread, systematic program Orkin implemented to effect a unilateral modification of its own standard contract terms agreed to by many thousands of consumers. Under the state statutes construed in the cases Orkin cites, the relief also differs fundamentally from that permitted under Section 5. The state laws, unlike the federal statute, at least in some instances, provide for imposition of treble damages in

---

66. The Commission has previously found liability under Section 5 on an unfairness theory for conduct inconsistent with the contractual obligations of various respondents. *See, e.g., Jay Norris Corp.,* 91 F.T.C. 751, 848 (1978), aff'd, 598 F.2d 1244 (2d Cir.), *cert. denied,* 444 U.S. 980, 100 S.Ct. 481, 62 L.Ed.2d 406 (1979) (retention of customer payments without performing the bargained for prompt delivery of merchandise); *Skylark Originals, Inc.,* 80 F.T.C. 337, 350–

51 (1972), aff'd, 475 F.2d 1396 (3d Cir.1973) (failure promptly to honor money-back guarantee as represented in advertisements and catalogs).

67. *Peerless Products v. FTC,* 284 F.2d 825, 827 (7th Cir.), *cert. denied,* 365 U.S. 844, 81 S.Ct. 804, 5 L.Ed.2d 809 (1961). *Accord, Spiegel, Inc. v. FTC,* 540 F.2d 287, 292–93 (7th Cir.1976).

private actions where violations are found. Neither Section 5 generally nor the complaint in this proceeding seeks monetary damages.

We need not and do not find that every breach of contract subjects the breaching party to liability under Section 5. We simply conclude that the conduct at issue here falls within the scope of the Commission's authority under that statute.

. . .

A finding of substantial unjustified consumer injury is essential to a conclusion that a business act or practice is unfair under Section 5. In considering whether conduct is unlawful as an unfair act or practice, the Commission will consider whether the consumer injury is: (1) substantial; (2) not outweighed by an offsetting consumer or competitive benefits that the practice produces; and (3) one that consumers could not reasonably have avoided.

The Commission finds that Orkin's failure to honor some 207,000 pre–1975 contracts caused actual and substantial harm to consumers. The harm resulting from Orkin's conduct consists of increased costs for services previously bargained for and includes the intangible loss of the certainty of the fixed price term in the contract. The breach also injured the market more generally by undermining consumers' ability to rely on the terms of fully integrated, standard form contracts used by businesses to simplify and facilitate routine transactions.

Although the financial injury to each individual customer is relatively small if measured on a yearly basis, Orkin's fee increase was not for just one year. Repeated payment of the higher yearly fee imposes a continuing and cumulative monetary burden on the consumer over the period of the contract. As Orkin's figures show, the fee increases affected some 207,000 customers. We are not concerned with trivial or merely speculative harms, but an injury may be substantial if it does a small harm to a large number of people. Over $7.5 million in increased renewal revenue in an approximately four year period, at the unjustified expense of consumers, is not insubstantial . . . .

We turn now to whether this substantial consumer injury is "harmful in its net effects." As the Commission explained in *International Harvester,* conduct can create a mixture of both beneficial and adverse consequences. Our task is to balance these consequences. Orkin did not purport to offer its customers anything new when it raised the annual renewal fees. The increase in the fee was not accompanied by an increase in the level of service provided or an enhancement of its quality. The action apparently was intended to enable the company to compensate for its rising costs, costs that Orkin claims it had not anticipated at the time it entered into the pre–1975 contracts. By raising the fees, Orkin unilaterally shifted the risk of inflation that it had assumed under the pre–1975 contracts to its pre–1975 customers who lost the benefit of a fixed annual renewal fee. As [Administrative Law] Judge Barnes concluded, "[a]ll that customers have received from the increase in annual renewal fees is the additional burden of paying more for Orkin's services than they had originally agreed upon.''

Nor did raising the annual renewal fee for these consumers result in benefits to competition. Information concerning the availability, nature and prices of products and services plays an indispensable role in the allocation of resources in a free enterprise system. In a competitive market, one may assume that consumers will choose the seller who offers the lowest price for a given level of quality. Normally, in such a market, the seller with the lowest price has the lowest cost per unit and is the most efficient. The market rewards the efficient seller to the ultimate benefit of consumers.

The market forces that reward efficient competitors would be impaired if a seller is allowed to gain a competitive edge by unilaterally changing the bargains it has made. Orkin's refusal to perform as promised under its contracts threatens the integrity of contracts and reduces the reliability of price information available to consumers in making their purchase decisions.

. . . Orkin argues that competition will suffer if the renewal fees on the pre–1975 contracts are returned to their initial level, because lower fees would discourage or prevent customers holding those contracts from transferring their business to the respondent's competitors. We fail to see why [this] argument is relevant to whether Orkin's fee increase violates Section 5. . . . Indeed, the argument implicitly concedes that the pre–1975 customers do in fact know and appreciate the benefit of their bargain with Orkin. A fee roll-back would simply reestablish the original bargain. That competitors might thrive if a respondent is permitted to flout accepted standards of commerce is not a benefit to competition cognizable in an analysis of unfairness under Section 5. We conclude that the injury to consumers and to competition resulting from Orkin's increase of the annual renewal fees on its pre–1975 contracts is not outweighed by countervailing benefits.

The next question is whether Orkin's pre–1975 customers reasonably could have avoided the injury they suffered from the increase of their annual renewal fees ''through the exercise of consumer choice.'' Consumers may act to avoid injury before it occurs if they have reason to anticipate the impending harm and the means to avoid it, or they may seek to mitigate the damage afterward if they are aware of potential avenues toward that end. . . .

It cannot be argued seriously that consumers reasonably could have avoided the injury resulting from Orkin's renewal fee increase before it became effective. The pre–1975 contracts provided consumers no notice nor even a reason to suspect that the company might raise the annual renewal fee at will. . . .

Nor, generally, could consumers effectively have mitigated the damage they sustained from Orkin's action after the fact. Orkin did not notify its pre–1975 customers that it would consider exceptions to the fee increase. . . . Indeed, it would have been pointless for Orkin to effectuate the fee increase and, simultaneously, to notify its customers that if they preferred not to pay the higher mount, they need not do so.

Orkin asserts that customers with pre–1975 contracts could have refused to pay the increased renewal fee and transferred their business to one of Orkin's competitors that would have assumed the obligations contained in the Orkin pre–1975 contracts for the original renewal fee price or "for less than the levels to which Orkin raised these fees in 1980." . . . Even viewed in the light most favorable to Orkin, the evidence does not show that Orkin's competitors assumed or would have assumed the obligations of Orkin's pre–1975 contracts without imposing conditions that would have resulted in additional costs to Orkin's customers, nor does it show that they would not subsequently have increased their annual fees. . . .

Even if customers could transfer their contract to another firm, that might not be satisfactory. Orkin represents that it is the "world's largest termite and pest control company" and that customers "generally contacted Orkin because of its reputation, stature in the industry, and length of time in business." These claims are borne out by several of the consumer affidavits presented by Orkin. The assertion that customers could have mitigated the injury they sustained from the respondent's fee increase by switching to a competing firm does not account for the harm inherent in compelling those customers to deal with a smaller company of lesser stature and repute than Orkin. Nor does it account for the transaction costs to customers faced with the need to search for a reliable or reputable firm willing to provide the same services on the same terms as those in Orkin's pre–1975 contracts and to complete a new agreement with that firm. . . .

The Commission finds that the respondent's pre–1975 customers could not reasonably have avoided or mitigated the injury that they sustained as a result of Orkin's increase of their annual renewal fee, and it concludes that the respondent's increase of the annual renewal fee on its pre–1975 contracts constituted an unfair act or practice in violation of Section 5.

6. If Orkin has to roll back its renewal fee on pre–1975 contracts, isn't it likely to increase the renewal fees on its post–1975 contracts and to increase its prices charged to new customers to make up the lost revenue?

7. At the beginning of the excerpt, the FTC rejects the idea that every breach of contract is an unfair act or practice. Numerous state courts have expressed a similar reaction to this idea in the context of little-FTC acts. This reaction is similar to their conclusion that mere breach of contract is not necessarily a deceptive act or practice. See page 155 supra. Why does the FTC think that *Orkin* involves more than simply a breach of contract?

FTC Chairman Daniel Oliver concurred in the decision of the Commission. His concurring opinion stated:

I have no difficulty agreeing with Orkin's proposition that a breach of contract, without more, does not violate Section 5. It is normally not our role to become involved in breaches of contract because private enforcement of private agreements is generally more efficient than governmental intervention. The appropriate question, however, is whether other circumstances apart from simple breach of contract bring this case within the Commission's unfairness jurisdiction. In other words, is there a market failure present in this case?

The only market failure that I perceive on the record presented here is the fact that private actions for damages were not likely to be effective. The Unfairness Statement itself recognizes that in those circumstances injury may not be reasonably avoidable by consumers. "In some senses any injury can be avoided—for example, by hiring independent experts to test all products in advance, or by private legal actions for damages—but these courses may be too expensive to be practicable for individual consumers to pursue." Unfairness Statement, n. 19. In this case some, perhaps many, Orkin customers were unable or unwilling to avail themselves of their private remedies because the individual losses are so small. When that is the case the normal incentives provided by the common law of contracts do not operate in the same fashion that they would in most instances.

The common law provides a framework within which parties can structure private agreements. Contracts are entered against the background of the existing rules that define obligations and remedies. The common law generally does not require that parties perform under their agreements. To cite Judge Posner: "it is not the policy of the law to compel adherence to contracts but only to require each party to choose between performing in accordance with the contract and compensating the other party for any injury resulting from a failure to perform." R. Posner, *Economic Analysis of Law* 88 (2d ed. 1977). The knowledge that the alternative to performance is compensation provides an incentive not to breach except in situations when the party breaching a contract is better off after paying damages to the other party.

If compensation for breach can be avoided, however, there is a breakdown in the normal incentive systems created by the common law of contracts. This not only encourages inefficient breaches, but also alters the underlying agreement by shifting costs or risks from the party who voluntarily assumed them to the other, nonbreaching party. As explained more fully below, then, an unfairness analysis of this record reveals a situation different from the "mere breach of contract" that Orkin posits.

. . . It is efficient for parties to be able to plan for future events and contingencies by entering contracts for performance at a subsequent time. Such agreements are only practical, of course, when they can be enforced. The enforcement mechanism for breach of contract has been developed through the common law. The rules developed through the judicial system provide a framework for private agreements, and in most cases provide the appropriate incentives for parties to either perform or breach and pay damages.[14]

With a large number of small contracts, however, the cost of litigating an individual loss may be greater than the expected individual recovery. In such situations the market may not provide an adequate disincentive for contract breach. Thus, the question for purposes of this element of the unfairness test is whether actions for contract damages are an economically feasible method of damage avoidance.

This type of market failure underlies many of the Commission's enforcement initiatives. In deception cases common law rights of action are frequently available to consumers, but the individual damages are normally too small to justify the necessary litigation. . . .

When these principles are applied to the instant case it becomes readily apparent that this is more than a simple breach of contract, and that Orkin's actions in unilaterally raising the annual renewal fees in these contracts is an unfair act within the meaning of Section 5. Individual private actions for damages would not have been effective in this case, given the small dollar amount of the increase in the annual renewal fee charged to each consumer.[16] Moreover, class actions are often not effective vehicles for obtaining relief. In addition, of course, it is unlikely that Orkin customers realized that they were being deprived of a legally enforceable right.

I therefore conclude that the respondent's pre–1975 customers could not reasonably have avoided or mitigated the injury that they sustained as a result of Orkin's increase of their annual renewal fee. I conclude that the respondent's increase of the annual renewal fees on its pre–1975 contracts constituted an unfair act or practice in violation of Section 5, and I concur in entry of the order proposed by the majority.

8. What standards emerge from the majority and concurring opinions for deciding whether any particular breach of contract amounts to an unfair act or practice? For example, could a consumer who formed a contract with Orkin between 1966 and 1975 recover under a state deceptive practices statute that tracks the language of the FTC Act? Would it be relevant that the state statute provides for treble damages? for recovery of attorney's fees?

---

14. It is not necessary that parties always perform. In fact, it is sometimes more efficient for parties to breach if it costs less to compensate the other party than it does to perform.

16. Even where private actions are brought under state Little FTC Acts for breaches of contract like the present one, this market failure may still be involved. Consumers in situations like the current one might well contend that the problem was that the company breached the contracts in circumstances where they knew or should have known that individual breach of contract actions were not likely.

9. *Orkin* stands for the proposition that systematic breach of contract may be unfair. In New York, where the little-FTC act proscribes deception but not unfairness, an appellate court has held that systematic breach of contract may be deceptive. State v. Wilco Energy, 728 N.Y.S.2d 471 (S.Ct.App.Div.2001) (a company that supplied home heating oil increased the price to customers who had entered two-year fixed-price contracts).

10. The foregoing materials on unfairness have focused on unjustified consumer injury as the test. Recall, however, that the FTC (and Congress) have also specified contrary-to-public-policy as an alternative test (see pages 508–10 supra). So has the Connecticut Supreme Court, and it had occasion to apply both tests in *Cheshire Mortgage v. Montes* (page 475 supra). In passages reproduced above the court held that the loan transactions were not unconscionable. In omitted portions of the opinion, however, the court held that 1) Cheshire had violated the Truth-in-Lending Act by improperly including a $55 fee in the "amount financed" rather than in the "finance charge"; and 2) Cheshire had violated a state usury statute by imposing a prepaid finance charge $490 larger than the statute permitted. The court then considered whether Cheshire had engaged in unfair acts or practices in violation of Connecticut's little-FTC act. Using the approach specified in the FTC's letter to Congress, the court held that Cheshire's conduct violated public policy, as found in federal and state statutes. The federal statute embodies a policy of disclosure, and the state statute embodies a policy of protecting consumers against excessive prices. Conduct in violation of these two statutes also violates the little-FTC act as conduct contrary to public policy.

11. In Leardi v. Brown, 474 N.E.2d 1094 (Mass.1985), a lease provided: "THERE IS NO IMPLIED WARRANTY THE PREMISES ARE FIT FOR HUMAN OCCUPATION (HABITABILITY) except so far as governmental regulation, legislation or judicial enactment otherwise requires." Plaintiffs sued, claiming that the lease violated the state's little-FTC act. The court agreed:

> . . . By itself, the bold face provision is contrary to our decision in Boston Hous. Auth. v. Hemingway, 363 Mass. 184, 199, 293 N.E.2d 831 (1973), where we held that "in a rental of any premises for dwelling purposes . . . there is an implied warranty that the premises are fit for human occupation. . . . This warranty . . . cannot be waived by any provision in the lease or rental agreement."
>
> The defendants contend that this provision is rendered perfectly lawful by the inclusion, in small print, of words to the effect that the implied warranty is disclaimed "except so far as governmental regulation, legislation or judicial enactment otherwise requires." We disagree. General Laws c. 93A, § 2(b), expressly incorporates judicial interpretations of the Federal Trade Commission Act, 15 U.S.C. § 45(a)(1) (1982). Under that statute, an act or practice is deceptive if it possesses "a tendency to deceive." Trans World Accounts, Inc. v. F.T.C., 594 F.2d 212, 214 (9th Cir.1979). In determining whether an act or practice is deceptive, "regard must be had, not to fine spun

Rule

distinctions and arguments that may be made in excuse, but to the effect which it might reasonably be expected to have upon the general public." P. Lorillard Co. v. F.T.C., 186 F.2d 52, 58 (4th Cir.1950).

Taken as a whole, paragraph eight clearly tends to deceive tenants with respect to the "landlord's obligation to deliver and maintain the premises in habitable condition." Boston Hous. Auth. v. Hemingway, supra 363 Mass. at 198, 293 N.E.2d 831. Paragraph eight suggests, as the judge found, that the implied warranty of habitability is "the exception and not the rule, if it exists at all." Indeed, the average tenant, presumably not well acquainted with our decision in Boston Hous. Auth. v. Hemingway, supra, is likely to interpret the provision as an absolute disclaimer of the implied warranty of habitability. The conjunction of bold face and small print suggests, as the judge recognized, "a clear and calculated effort to further mislead tenants." It suggests to tenants that their signatures on the lease constitute a waiver of their right to habitable housing.

Paragraph five of the standard apartment lease, which the judge below characterized as "an unabashed attempt to annul or render less meaningful" rights guaranteed by the State sanitary code, seems drafted with the same impermissible purpose which evidently motivated paragraph eight. It provides that "[u]nless Tenant shall notify Landlord to the contrary within two (2) days after taking possession of the premises, the same and the equipment located therein shall be *conclusively presumed* to be in good, tenantable order and condition in all respects, except as any aforesaid notice shall set forth" (emphasis added). So even if tenants are sufficiently sophisticated to understand that paragraph eight is not an absolute disclaimer of the right to habitable housing, paragraph five unlawfully suggests that this right is waived unless notification is made within two days after the tenant moves in. Consequently, we conclude that there was no error in the judge's conclusion that paragraphs five and eight were deceptive and unconscionable, particularly when those provisions are viewed in the context of the fundamental nature of the implied warranty of habitability.

Holding

474 N.E.2d at 1099–1100.

Little–FTC acts that contain a laundry list of deceptive practices often make it unlawful to represent that an agreement confers rights, remedies, or obligations that it does not confer or that are prohibited by law. E.g., West's Cal.Civ.Code § 1770(a)(14); Vernon's Tex.Codes Ann., Bus. & C. § 17.46(b)(12). They also typically prohibit conduct that creates a likelihood of misunderstanding. See Orlando v. Finance One, Inc., 369 S.E.2d 882 (W.Va.1988) (waiver of exemption rights "to the extent permitted by law" violates the little-FTC act because another statute makes any waiver of those rights void and unenforceable). Contra, Credit Union One v. Stamm, 867 P.2d 285 (Kan.1994). See generally Kuklin, On the Knowing Inclusion of Unenforceable Contract and Lease Terms, 56 U.Cinci.L.Rev. 845 (1988).

Little–FTC acts typically authorize the state's attorney general to promulgate regulations that have the force of law. Pursuant to this authority, the Attorney General of Massachusetts adopted a regulation making it a violation of the act for an entity to "fail to comply with existing statutes, rules, regulations or laws, meant for the protection of the public's health, safety, or welfare promulgated by the Commonwealth or any political subdivision thereof intended to provide the consumers of this Commonwealth with protection." 940 Code Mass.Regs. § 3.16(3). To similar effect is 15 Mo. Code State Regs. § 60–8.090.

12. The limits posed by the doctrine of unfairness are not confined to the substantive terms of consumer transactions. Unfairness also sets standards for the formation of contracts, see Advertising of Ophthalmic Goods and Services, 16 C.F.R. Part 456; the performance of contractual obligations, as in *Orkin*; and the enforcement of contractual rights, as in Ford Motor Co. v. Mayes, page 371 supra.

(3) GOOD FAITH

Unconscionability and unfairness present definitional problems of sufficient magnitude to occupy judges and theorists (and students) for many an hour. But there is still more. A third vague doctrine also limits the conduct of the merchant (and the consumer).

Best v. United States National Bank

Supreme Court of Oregon, 1987.
303 Or. 557, 739 P.2d 554.

LENT, J.

[Plaintiffs brought a class action against defendant bank, challenging the validity of fees imposed by defendant on customers who wrote checks on accounts containing insufficient funds to cover the checks (NSF checks). In addition to challenging the fees as unconscionable, as in *Perdue*, page 493 supra, plaintiffs also alleged that defendant breached an obligation to use good faith in setting the fees. The trial court granted defendant's motion for summary judgment on both claims. The intermediate appellate court affirmed the summary judgment on the unconscionability claim but reversed the summary judgment on the good faith claim. Plaintiffs and defendant both appealed.]

The depositors claim that the Bank's NSF fees were unconscionable because the fees were greatly in excess of the Bank's costs for processing NSF checks. The doctrine of unconscionability, however, is largely inapplicable to this case, and, to the extent that it may apply, we conclude that the fee set by the Bank was not unconscionable.

Unconscionability is a legal issue that must be assessed as of the time of contract formation. Thus the doctrine applies to contract terms rather than to contract performance. The only contract term relevant to NSF fees was a statement in the preprinted "account agreement" signed by the depositors when they opened their accounts: "This account is subject to Bank service charges existing at any time." The parties agree that "service charges" included NSF fees. The specific fee charged, then, was not part of the depositors' agreement with the Bank; rather, the fee was set by the Bank as part of its performance of the account agreement. The unconscionability doctrine is inapplicable to the amount of the fee.

If the depositors were or should have been aware of the fee amounts and tacitly agreed to the amounts . . . , they could challenge the agreements as unconscionable. Summary judgment on their unconscionability claim, however, would still be appropriate.

Although the depositors assert that the Bank's NSF fees were two or three times the Bank's NSF processing costs, the fees were relatively small and were similar to NSF fees charged by other banks. Moreover, apart from the adhesive nature of the account agreement, the record reflects few indicia of one-sided bargaining. The depositors could close their accounts at any time and for any reason. There is no evidence that the depositors were not of ordinary intelligence and experience. There is also no evidence that the Bank obtained any agreement from the depositors through deception or any other improper means. The circuit court's grant of summary judgment on the depositors' unconscionability claim was proper.

II.

The depositors claim that the Bank had an obligation to set its NSF fees in good faith and that it breached this obligation by setting its fees at amounts greatly in excess of the costs incurred by it in processing NSF checks.

Nothing in the depositors' account agreement with the Bank expressly limited the Bank's authority to set NSF fees. This court has long stated, however, that there is an obligation of good faith in the performance and enforcement of every contract. This obligation limited the Bank's apparently unlimited authority to set NSF fees, and the depositors can recover for the breach of this obligation just as they could for the breach of any other contractual obligation.

The Bank and *amicus curiae* First Interstate Bank of Oregon argue that the doctrine of good faith is inapplicable because the depositors agreed to the NSF fees by maintaining their accounts, which they could close at any time. Whether the depositors agreed to the specific fees charged, however, is a question of fact that cannot be decided on a motion for summary judgment. The argument of the Bank and *amicus* assumes that the depositors knew or should have known the amount of the fees when they wrote their NSF checks. This assumption does not necessarily follow from the evidence. The practice of Bank employees who opened accounts was not to inform depositors of the amount or even of the existence of NSF fees unless the depositor inquired. The Bank also did not notify depositors when it increased its NSF fees. In the absence of inquiry, a depositor would ordinarily know the amount of the fee only if the depositor had been charged a fee, in which case the amount would appear on the depositor's monthly statement of account. Moreover, even if the depositor discovered the current amount of the NSF fee, the depositor could never be certain of the fee that would be charged because the Bank could increase or decrease the fee at any time without notice. It would be improper under this evidence to conclude on a motion for summary judgment that the depositors agreed to the charges through failing to close their accounts.

Assuming that there was no agreement, the question before us is whether there is a genuine issue of material fact whether the Bank set its NSF fees in good faith.

The purpose of the good faith doctrine is to prohibit improper behavior in the performance and enforcement of contracts. Because the doctrine must be applied to the entire range of contracts, definitions of good faith tend to be either too abstract or applicable only to specific contexts. For this reason, Professor Summers has argued that good faith should be conceptualized as an "excluder," by which he means that good faith should be defined only by identifying various forms of bad faith. Summers, *The General Duty of Good Faith—Its Recognition and Conceptualization,* 67 Cornell L.Rev. 810 (1982); *see also* Summers, *"Good Faith" in General Contract Law and the Sales Provisions of the Uniform Commercial Code,* 54 Va. L.Rev. 195, 199–207 (1968). This is also the approach adopted by the Restatement (Second) of Contracts § 205 (1979):[a]

> "The phrase 'good faith' is used in a variety of contexts, and its meaning varies somewhat with the context. Good faith performance or enforcement of a contract emphasizes faithfulness to an agreed common purpose and consistency with the justified expectations of the other party; it excludes a variety of types of conduct characterized as involving 'bad faith' because they violate community standards of decency, fairness or reasonableness."

Restatement (Second) of Contracts § 205, *comment a* (1979).

> "Subterfuges and evasions violate the obligation of good faith in performance even though the actor believes his conduct to be justified. But the obligation goes further; bad faith may be overt or may consist of inaction, and fair dealing may require more than honesty. A complete catalogue of types of bad faith is impossible, but the following types are among those which have been recognized in judicial decisions: evasion of the spirit of the bargain, lack of diligence and slacking off, willful rendering of imperfect performance, abuse of power to specify terms, and interference with or failure to cooperate in the other party's performance."

Restatement (Second) of Contracts § 205, *comment d* (1979).

This does not mean that decisions as to what constitutes bad faith must be *ad hoc* and standardless. Without attempting to give positive

a. "Every contract imposes upon each party a duty of good faith and fair dealing in its performance and its enforcement."—Ed.

content to the phrase "good faith," it is possible to set forth operational standards by which good faith can be distinguished from bad faith within a particular context. Professors Summers and Burton, although in substantial disagreement with each other, have proposed such standards. *See* Summers, *supra*, 67 Cornell L.Rev. at 823–24; Burton, *Breach of Contract and the Common Law Duty to Perform in Good Faith,* 94 Harv.L.Rev. 369 (1980).

This court also has not attempted to set forth a comprehensive definition of good faith. But in line with the Restatement and traditional principles of contract law, the court has sought through the good faith doctrine to effectuate the reasonable contractual expectations of the parties. When one party to a contract is given discretion in the performance of some aspect of the contract, the parties ordinarily contemplate that that discretion will be exercised for particular purposes. If the discretion is exercised for purposes not contemplated by the parties, the party exercising discretion has performed in bad faith.

To illustrate, . . . the parties to an employment contract generally contemplate that an employer may use its discretion to fire an at-will employee if the employer is dissatisfied with the employee's performance or if the employee's services are no longer required. The parties do not ordinarily contemplate, however, that the employer may fire the employee in order to deprive the employee of benefits to which the employee would otherwise have become entitled if the employment had continued. An employer who does the latter breaches its obligation to perform in good faith.

In this case, the Bank had the contractual discretion to set its NSF fees. . . . That discretion had to be exercised within the confines of the reasonable expectations of the depositors. It is therefore not necessarily sufficient, as the Bank contends, that the Bank acted honestly in setting its NSF fees or that its fees were similar to those of other banks. Undoubtedly, parties to a contract always expect that the other party will perform the contract honestly and, where the performance of a commercial enterprise is at issue, ordinarily expect that it will do so in a commercially reasonable manner. But the reasonable expectations of the parties need not be so limited.

So far as we can discern from the record, the depositors did not explicitly argue before the circuit court that the Bank's setting of its NSF fees was not in accord with their contractual expectations. Their complaint alleged only that the Bank's NSF fees were greatly in excess of its reasonable costs. In their argument on the Bank's motion for summary judgment, they treated the good faith and unconscionability doctrines as substantively equivalent, arguing that the Bank's NSF fees were set in bad faith because they were set at amounts that were unconscionable. Before the Court of Appeals, however, the depositors argued that the fees were set in bad faith not only because the fees were unconscionable but because the depositors reasonably expected the Bank to exercise its discretion to set NSF fees for the purpose of permitting it to recover its costs of processing

NSF checks. Although this argument was not explicitly made before the circuit court, we will address both arguments on review because the nature of the good faith obligation has been somewhat unclear.

When a party has the contractual right to specify a price term, the term specified may be so high or low that the party will be deemed to have acted in bad faith regardless of the reasonable expectations of the other party. In this respect the good faith and unconscionability doctrines tend to run together. In general, however, whether a specified price violates the obligation of good faith should be decided by the reasonable contractual expectations of the parties. In this instance we conclude that the Bank's NSF fees were not so high as to be evidence of bad faith for that reason alone.

Nevertheless, we believe that there is a genuine issue of material fact whether the Bank set its NSF fees in accordance with the reasonable expectations of the parties. The record shows that when the depositors opened their accounts, the only account fees that would ordinarily be discussed would be the Bank's monthly and per check charges, if any. The sole reference to NSF fees was contained in the account agreement signed by the depositors, which obligated them to pay the Bank's "service charges in effect at any time." Because NSF fees were incidental to the Bank's principal checking account fees and were denominated "service charges," a trier of fact could infer that the depositors reasonably expected that NSF fees would be special fees to cover the costs of extraordinary services. This inference could reasonably lead to the further inference that the depositors reasonably expected that the Bank's NSF fees would be priced similarly to those checking account fees of which the depositors were aware—the Bank's monthly checking account service fees and per check fees, if any. By "priced similarly," we mean priced to cover the Bank's NSF check processing costs plus an allowance for overhead costs plus the Bank's ordinary profit margin on checking account services.

Finally, assuming that the Bank's obligation of good faith required the Bank to set its NSF fees in accordance with its costs and ordinary profit margin, there was evidence that the Bank breached the obligation. The Bank's own cost studies show that its NSF fees were set at amounts greatly in excess of its costs and ordinary profit margin. Internal memoranda and depositions of Bank employees permit the inference that the Bank's NSF fees were set at these high levels in order to reap the large profits to be made from the apparently inelastic "demand" for the processing of NSF checks and in order to discourage its depositors from carelessly writing NSF checks. A trier of fact could find that both of these purposes were contrary to the reasonable expectations of the depositors when they agreed to pay whatever NSF fee was set by the Bank.

Because there are genuine issues of material fact with respect to the depositors' breach of good faith claim, the trial court erred in granting the Bank summary judgment on this claim.

. . .

QUESTIONS AND NOTES

1. The court asserts that unconscionability is "a legal issue that must be assessed as of the time of formation." What basis is there for this assertion?

Might not it be unconscionable for a bank to provide that the price of various bank services will be determined unilaterally by the bank from time to time?

2. The court does not cite *Perdue*, decided two years earlier by the California Supreme Court. How do you suppose the Oregon court would have decided *Perdue* if it had arisen in Oregon?

3. A statutory source of the obligation of good faith is UCC revised section 1–304, which provides, "Every contract or duty within [the UCC] imposes an obligation of good faith in its performance or enforcement."[1] Unlike its failure to define or articulate standards for unconscionability, the UCC does define "good faith." Section 1–201(b)(20) states that " 'Good faith' . . . means honesty in fact and the observance of reasonable commercial standards of fair dealing."[2] Does the definition of good faith make the application of section 1–304 easier than the application of section 2–302 or section 5 of the FTC Act and analogous state statutes?

4. The court in *Best* does not articulate a "comprehensive definition" of good faith. It does, however, address the content of the good faith standard in the context of a contract that leaves the details of performance to the discretion of one of the parties. What does the standard of good faith require of the party with that discretion? How does that standard differ from the requirements of UCC section 2–103(1)(b): did the bank fail to observe reasonable commercial standards of fair dealing?

5. Short of lowering its NSF fees, could the bank do anything to comply with its obligation to perform in good faith?

6. The court states that the bank never notified its new customers of the amount of the NSF fee, nor did it notify existing customers when it raised the fee. What if these facts did not exist, i.e. what if the bank gave new customers a schedule of its current fees and mailed notice of increases in the fees to its existing customers? By increasing the fee, would the bank breach its obligation to act in good faith? These were the facts before the Oregon Supreme Court in Tolbert v. First National Bank of Oregon, 823 P.2d 965 (Ore.1991). The court reversed the lower appellate court and granted summary judgment for the bank:

> The contract in this case is not unusual in that it explicitly granted one party the right to exercise its discretion regarding one aspect of the performance and enforcement of the contract. In chang-

---

1. Formerly UCC § 1–203 (1978).

2. Formerly UCC § 1–201(19)(1978), which provided, " 'Good faith' means honesty in fact in the conduct or transaction concerned." Section 2–103(1)(b), however, con-

tains a definition of "good faith" applicable to merchants. That definition is virtually identical to the definition that now appears in Article 1. Which definition applies in *Best*?

ing the amount of the NSF fees, Bank enforced a right specifically granted to it under the contract. Because the exercise of that right was pursuant to Bank's unilateral discretion, the good faith obligation discussed in *Best* applies. Whether any changes in the NSF fees were determined in good faith, therefore, "should be decided by the reasonable contractual expectations of the parties." Best v. U.S. National Bank.

We emphasize that it is only the objectively reasonable expectations of parties that will be examined in determining whether the obligation of good faith has been met. In the context of this case— when (1) the parties agree to (and their contract provides for) a unilateral exercise of discretion regarding changes in one of the contract terms, and (2) the discretion is exercised after prior notice—we hold as a matter of law that the parties' reasonable expectations have been met.

. . .

Unlike the situation in *Best*, where the depositors were aware of the pricing mechanism for some service charges, and were entitled reasonably to expect that similar charges would be priced accordingly, in this case there is no evidence that depositors were aware of any particular pricing formula. Accordingly, it would be unreasonable for depositors to have any expectation that changes in NSF fees would be pursuant to any particular formula.

823 P.2d at 970–71.

What pricing formula did the depositors in *Best* reasonably expect the bank to use, and what was the basis for that expectation? What other pricing mechanism could the depositors in *Tolbert* reasonably expect their bank to use?

Under the court's approach in *Tolbert*, does good faith impose any limit on the bank's exercise of its contractual power to set the NSF fee?

What is the relevance of the fact that the customer is free at all times to close his or her account?

7.   Besides unconscionability (*Perdue*) and good faith (*Best*), what other bases are there for challenging the enforceability of NSF fees?

8.   The UCC and the Restatement both impose an "obligation of good faith *and fair dealing*" (emphasis added). What is the difference between good faith and fair dealing, or are the two terms simply different ways of saying the same thing? If they denote different standards, should a party be liable if he or she satisfies one but not the other?

9.   The best articles examining the meaning of good faith include Burton, Good Faith Performance of a Contract Within Article 2 of the Uniform Commercial Code, 67 Iowa L.Rev. 1 (1981); Burton, Breach of Contract and the Common Law Duty To Perform in Good Faith, 94 Harv.L.Rev. 369 (1980); Gillette, Limitations on the Obligation of Good Faith, 1981 Duke

L.J. 619; Summers, The General Duty of Good Faith—Its Recognition and Conceptualization, 67 Cornell L.Rev. 810 (1982).

REVIEW QUESTION

Manufacturer sells electric drills, along with a special attachment for buffing automobile finishes. *Manufacturer* warrants the product to be free of defects for one year from the date of purchase. The warranty conspicuously provides that in the event of a defect *Manufacturer* will repair or replace the defective drill or part but that *Manufacturer* will under no circumstances pay for any consequential damages of any kind. Consumer purchases a drill, with a buffing attachment. While *Consumer* is polishing her car, the attachment flies off, severely cutting her arm and denting and scratching her car. When *Consumer* notifies *Manufacturer*, the latter points to the language in the warranty and offers to repair the product. *Consumer* reluctantly consents and, after *Manufacturer* makes the repairs, signs an agreement stating that *Manufacturer* has fulfilled its responsibility to her.

Consumer has second thoughts and comes to your office to see if she can get compensation for the injury to her arm and her car. What would you advise?

a) Which, if any, of the three doctrines in this section could *Consumer* use to justify recovery of damages if she were to sue?

b) Can anything be done to prevent *Manufacturer* from including the language concerning consequential damages in its warranty?

(4) EUROPEAN APPROACHES

In 1993 the EU adopted Directive 93/13/EEC of April 5, 1993, on unfair terms in consumer contracts, 1993 O.J. L95/29. It provides, in part:

Article 3

1. A contractual term which has not been individually negotiated shall be regarded as unfair if, contrary to the requirement of good faith, it causes a significant imbalance in the parties' rights and obligations arising under the contract, to the detriment of the consumer.

2. A term shall always be regarded as not individually negotiated where it has been drafted in advance and the consumer has therefore not been able to influence the substance of the term, particularly in the context of a pre-formulated standard contract.

The fact that certain aspects of a term or one specific term have been individually negotiated shall not exclude the application of this Article to the rest of a contract if an overall assessment of the contract indicates that it is nevertheless a pre-formulated standard contract.

Where any seller or supplier claims that a standard term has been individually negotiated, the burden of proof in this respect shall be incumbent on him.

3.   The Annex shall contain an indicative and non-exhaustive list of the terms which may be regarded as unfair.

Article 4

1.   Without prejudice to Article 7, the unfairness of a contractual term shall be assessed, taking into account the nature of the goods or services for which the contract was concluded and by referring, at the time of conclusion of the contract, to all the circumstances attending the conclusion of the contract and to all the other terms of the contract or of another contract on which it is dependent.

2.   Assessment of the unfair nature of the terms shall relate neither to the definition of the main subject matter of the contract nor to the adequacy of the price and remuneration, on the one hand, as against the services or goods supplies in exchange, on the other, in so far as these terms are in plain intelligible language.

Article 5

In the case of contracts where all or certain terms offered to the consumer are in writing, these terms must always be drafted in plain, intelligible language. Where there is doubt about the meaning of a term, the interpretation most favourable to the consumer shall prevail. This rule on interpretation shall not apply in the context of the procedures laid down in Article 7(2).

Article 6

1.   Member States shall lay down that unfair terms used in a contract concluded with a consumer by a seller or supplier shall, as provided for under their national law, not be binding on the consumer and that the contract shall continue to bind the parties upon those terms if it is capable of continuing in existence without the unfair terms.

. . .

Article 7

1.   Member States shall ensure that, in the interests of consumers and of competitors, adequate and effective means exist to prevent the continued use of unfair terms in contracts concluded with consumers by sellers or suppliers.

2.   The means referred to in paragraph 1 shall include provisions whereby persons or organizations, having a legitimate interest under national law in protecting consumers, may take action according to the national law concerned before the courts or before competent administrative bodies for a decision as to whether contractual terms drawn up for general use are unfair, so that they can apply appropriate and effective means to prevent the continued use of such terms.

3.   With due regard for national laws, the legal remedies referred to in paragraph 2 may be directed separately or jointly against a number of sellers or suppliers from the same economic sector or their associations which use or recommend the use of the same general contractual terms or similar terms.

.   .   .

ANNEX

TERMS REFERRED TO IN ARTICLE 3(3)

1.   Terms which have the object or effect of:

(a) excluding or limiting the legal liability of a seller or supplier in the event of the death of a consumer or personal injury to the latter resulting from an act or omission of that seller or supplier;

(b) inappropriately excluding or limiting the legal rights of the consumer vis-à-vis the seller or supplier or another party in the event of total or partial non-performance or inadequate performance by the seller or supplier of any of the contractual obligations, including the option of offsetting a debt owed to the seller or supplier against any claim which the consumer may have against him;

(c) making an agreement binding on the consumer whereas provision of services by the seller or supplier is subject to a condition whose realization depends on his own will alone;

(d) permitting the seller or supplier to retain sums paid by the consumer where the latter decides not to conclude or perform the contract, without providing for the consumer to receive compensation of an equivalent amount from the seller or supplier where the latter is the party cancelling the contract;

(e) requiring any consumer who fails to fulfil his obligation to pay a disproportionately high sum in compensation;

(f) authorizing the seller or supplier to dissolve the contract on a discretionary basis where the same facility is not granted to the consumer, or permitting the seller or supplier to retain the sums paid for services not yet supplied by him where it is the seller or supplier himself who dissolves the contract;

(g) enabling the seller or supplier to terminate a contract of indeterminate duration without reasonable notice except where there are serious grounds for doing so;

(h) automatically extending a contract of fixed duration where the consumer does not indicate otherwise, when the deadline fixed for the consumer to express this desire not to extend the contract is unreasonably early;

(i) irrevocably binding the consumer to terms with which he had no real opportunity of becoming acquainted before the conclusion of the contract;

(j) enabling the seller or supplier to alter the terms of the contract unilaterally without a valid reason which is specified in the contract;

(k) enabling the seller or supplier to alter unilaterally without a valid reason any characteristics of the product or service to be provided;

(*l*) providing for the price of goods to be determined at the time of delivery or allowing a seller of goods or supplier of services to increase their price without in both cases giving the consumer the corresponding right to cancel the contract if the final price is too high in relation to the price agreed when the contract was concluded;

(m) giving the seller or supplier the right to determine whether the goods or services supplied are in conformity with the contract, or giving him the exclusive right to interpret any term of the contract;

(n) limiting the seller's or supplier's obligation to respect commitments undertaken by his agents or making his commitments subject to compliance with a particular formality;

(o) obliging the consumer to fulfil all his obligations where the seller or supplier does not perform his;

(p) giving the seller or supplier the possibility of transferring his rights and obligations under the contract, where this may serve to reduce the guarantees for the consumer, without the latter's agreement;

(q) excluding or hindering the consumer's right to take legal action or exercise any other legal remedy, particularly by requiring the consumer to take disputes exclusively to arbitration not covered by legal provisions, unduly restricting the evidence available to him or imposing on him a burden of proof which, according to the applicable law, should lie with another party to the contract.

2.   Scope of subparagraphs (g), (j) and (*l*)

(a) Subparagraph (g) is without hindrance to terms by which a supplier of financial services reserves the right to terminate unilaterally a contract of indeterminate duration without notice where there is a valid reason, provided that the supplier is required to inform the other contracting party or parties thereof immediately.

(b) Subparagraph (j) is without hindrance to terms under which a supplier of financial services reserves the right to alter the rate of interest payable by the consumer or due to the latter, or the amount of other charges for financial services without notice where there is a valid reason, provided that the supplier is required to inform the other contracting party or parties thereof at the earliest opportunity and that the latter are free to dissolve the contract immediately.

Subparagraph (j) is also without hindrance to terms under which a seller or supplier reserves the right to alter unilaterally the conditions of a contract of indeterminate duration, provided that he is required to inform the consumer with reasonable notice and that the consumer is free to dissolve the contract.

(c) Subparagraphs (g), (j) and (*l*) do not apply to:

transactions in transferable securities, financial instruments and other products or services where the price is linked to fluctuations in a stock exchange quotation or index or a financial market rate that the seller or supplier does not control;

contracts for the purchase or sale of foreign currency, traveller's cheques or international money orders denominated in foreign currency;

(d) Subparagraph (*l*) is without hindrance to price-indexation clauses, where lawful, provided that the method by which prices vary is explicitly described.

QUESTIONS

1. What is the consequence of a merchant's inclusion of an unfair term?

2. The general standard of unfairness appears in Article 3. How would it apply to the facts of *Orkin* (Question 4, page 517 supra)?

How does it differ from the standard under the FTC Act?

3. The Annex to the Directive contains a laundry list of terms that are declared to be unfair. American law renders many of these terms unenforceable, but not necessarily because they have been determined to contravene a standard of unfairness. Consider & 1(a) (public policy), (c) and (f) (lack of consideration), (e) (failure to meet standards for liquidated damages). But American courts would be likely to enforce several of the provisions that the Europeans find objectionable, e.g., & 1(*i*), (n), (*o*).

4. To see how France and Germany have implemented the Directive, see French Consumer Code Article L132, available at 195.83.177.9/ upl/pdf/code_29.pdf; German Civil Code §§ 307–310, available at bundesrecht.juris.de/englisch_bgb/german_civil_code.pdf. See also Winn & Webber, The Impact of EU Unfair Contract Terms Law on U.S. Business-to-Consumer Internet Merchants, 62 Bus. Lawyer 209 (2006).

5. In 2005 the EU adopted Directive 2005/29/EC of 11 May 2005, on Unfair Commercial Practices. Applicable to business-to-consumer transactions, this Directive prohibits ''unfair commercial practices,'' which it defines as materially distorting the economic behavior of the average consumer. Its focus is on acts and practices that are misleading or coercive, thereby impairing the consumer's freedom of choice.

For a description of the Directive and its impact on the law of the United Kingdom, see Twigg–Flesner et al., An Analysis of the Application and Scope of the Unfair Commercial Practices Directive (2005), available at www.dti.gov.uk/ccp/consultpdf/final_report180505.pdf.

B.   TOPICAL STATUTES

(1)   PROHIBITION OF OBJECTIONABLE TERMS

In addition to relying on vague standards like unconscionability, unfairness, and good faith, legislatures have banned or regulated specific contractual terms or transactions that are abusive to consumers. For example, *Williams v. Walker–Thomas* concerns a cross-collateral clause. The court cited a section of the Maryland Retail Installment Sales Act (Md.Code 1957, art. 83, § 137) that required the creditor to allocate payments and permitted the consumer to redeem repossessed goods. The effect of this statute was to prohibit the kind of term that Walker–Thomas used. (The statute was superseded in 1975 by Md.Code Comm.L. § 12–618(c)-(e), but the substance remains unchanged.) (Similar protection appears in the New Jersey Retail Installment Sales Act. N.J.Stat.Ann. 17:16C–28, 17:16C–29.)

Section 12–607 of the current Maryland statute contains the following list of prohibited contractual terms:[3]

(a) Provisions prohibited. A holder may not take or receive any instrument from a buyer or a surety for a buyer, which contains:

(1) Except as provided in subsection (b) of this section, any blank space to be filled in after the instrument is signed by a party to it;

(2) A confession of judgment or any power of attorney to appear for the buyer or for a surety for the buyer to confess judgment;

(3) A schedule of payments under which any installment, except the down payment, is more than double the average of all other installments, excluding the down payment, or under which the interval between any consecutive installments is less than one-half the average of all other intervals, unless the buyer is given an absolute right, on default in any of the excess or irregular installments, to have the schedule of unpaid installments, including that in default, revised to conform in both amounts and intervals to the average of all preceding installments and intervals;

(4) A provision for repossession of the goods or for the acceleration of the time when any part or all of the time balance becomes payable, if the condition of the repossession or acceleration is that the holder considers himself insecure;

---

3. For analogous provisions in the New Jersey statute, see N.J.S.A. §§ 17:16C–22, 17:16C–26, 17:16C–35 to–39.

(5) A provision by which the buyer waives or purports to waive a tort claim or by which the seller has the right to enter unlawfully upon any premises;

(6) A provision by which a person acting on behalf of a holder in connection with the formation or execution of an agreement is treated as an agent of the buyer; or

(7) An assignment or order for payment of wages, whether earned or to be earned.

Subsection 3 prohibits what is known as a balloon payment (recall *Cheshire Mortgage*, page 475 supra), a device that may mislead a consumer into believing that a transaction is affordable when in fact it is not. The monthly payments may be within the consumer's means, but the final payment may be larger than all the preceding payments put together. This device has enjoyed a revival in the residential financing field, even for prime borrowers, where fluctuating interest rates make lenders hesitant to commit themselves to a fixed interest rate for twenty to thirty years. As an alternative they may loan money pursuant to a contract that calls for payments computed on the assumption that the loan will be repaid over twenty-five years, but provides that at the end of five or seven years the entire remaining balance is due. The expectation is that at the end of specified period, the lender will refinance the loan at the then current interest rate. Does this explain the result in *Cheshire Mortgage*? (N.B. The Maryland statute, like the New Jersey statute, is part of the retail installment sales act and would not apply to real estate loans.)

The other subsections of the Maryland statute quoted above deal with terms concerning the seller's enforcement of the contract if the consumer defaults. These kinds of problems are the subject of Part III of this book.

(2) REGULATION OF TROUBLESOME TRANSACTIONS

Sometimes abusive practices result in a comprehensive statute designed to permit the transaction-type but eliminate the abusive practices. Retail installment sales acts are an example of this. So are home solicitation sales, also known as door-to-door sales.

Home solicitation sales offer the consumer the convenience and comfort of the home while the seller presents information about a product. With respect to some products, such as vacuum cleaners, home solicitation sales also permit the consumer to see the product demonstrated under actual working conditions. On the other hand, home solicitation sales may entail deception and abuse. The salesperson may gain entry to the home by misrepresenting that the purpose of the visit is to conduct a survey or present the consumer with a gift or sample. The home setting may result in lowered sales resistance, especially if the consumer does not initially understand the purpose of the seller's visit. Unlike solicitations made in the seller's store, the consumer who becomes disenchanted with the product or with the seller is not free to walk away. And since the seller occupies the status of a quasi-guest whom the consumer has invited into the home, the consumer may be reluctant to ask the seller to leave. The consumer may even feel that a request to leave will create a risk of physical abuse. These factors combine to produce a situation in which the seller is able to use high pressure tactics, lasting for hours, to induce the consumer to enter into a soon-to-be-regretted transaction. The problem is compounded by the size of the salesperson's commission (in one reported case it was half the total sales price) and the consumer's inability to compare the seller's price to the price charged by other sellers. It is also compounded by the absence from the scene of the salesperson's supervisor, thereby making it very difficult for the seller to supervise the conduct of the sales personnel. For examples of high-pressure, home solicitation sales, see King v. Towns, page 12 supra, Williams v. Walker–Thomas Furniture Co., page 470 supra, and Jones v. Star Credit Corp., page 491 supra. For detailed treatment of the problem, see Sher, The "Cooling–Off" Period in Door-to-Door Sales, 15 U.C.L.A.L.Rev. 717 (1968); Project, The Direct Selling Industry: An Empirical Study, 16 U.C.L.A.L.Rev. 883 (1969).

One solution to the problem is to prohibit door-to-door sales altogether. The Green River ordinances (so named because of litigation concerning an ordinance adopted by Green River, Wyoming) take this approach by making unrequested solicitation at a private residence punishable as a nuisance. But complete prohibition may not be the best answer. While some products sold door-to-door are of low quality and some sellers engage in the conduct described above, not all door-to-door sellers and their products are so abusive of consumers. On the contrary, some enjoy excellent reputations, such as World Book (encyclopedias); Electrolux (vacuum cleaners); and Tupperware, Avon, Fuller Brush, Amway, and Mary Kay Cosmetics (household products). So some solution other than outright prohibition seems appropriate.

An effective way to deal with deception concerning the purpose of the seller's visit is to require the salesperson to identify himself or herself and the purpose of the visit before saying anything else to the consumer or entering the home. The FTC has taken this approach in several proceedings against door-to-door sellers.[4] But this remedy fails to address the problem of excessive sales pressure.

Another approach is to require door-to-door sellers to register or obtain licenses, for which they would have to post a bond and/or meet minimum standards concerning character and solvency. This remedy, however, is fairly difficult to enforce and depends on the efforts of public officials.

The most popular solution, therefore, is to give the consumer a chance to back out of the deal after the salesperson has left the home. Over forty states have adopted some form of rescission right in connection with home solicitation sales (e.g., UCCC §§ 3.501–3.505), though there are numerous variations among the states. In 1972 the FTC adopted a rule of nationwide application giving consumers a right of rescission. Cooling–Off Period for

---

4. E.g., Encyclopedia Britannica, Inc. v. FTC, 605 F.2d 964 (7th Cir.1979).

Door–To–Door Sales, 16 C.F.R. Part 429. Read the provisions of the UCCC and the FTC rule, and answer the following questions.

PROBLEMS

1.   At a street fair, *Consumer* purchases a necklace from a crafts person and pays for it with a check. Under the FTC regulation, must *Consumer* be given the right to rescind? Under the UCCC?

2.   Under the FTC regulation, what are the consequences of the seller's failure to give the consumer notice of the right to rescind? Under UCCC section 3.502?

3.   A representative of *Furnace Company* knocks on *Consumer's* door and asks if he may examine the furnace. *Consumer* agrees, and *Salesman* looks at the furnace. *Salesman* informs *Consumer* that his furnace is cracked and is leaking noxious vapors, and that *Consumer* and his family will be lucky if they wake up the next morning. When the dust settles, *Consumer* has contracted to purchase a new furnace. Must *Consumer* be given the right to rescind?

4.   A representative of *Furnace Company* places calling cards on the front doors of the houses in *Consumer's* neighborhood. A few days later *Consumer's* furnace breaks down, and she calls *Furnace Company* to repair it. Must she be given the right to rescind?

5.   As a matter of customer relations, many businesses already permit consumers to back out of contracts by returning the goods in unused condition. Examples include grocery stores, department stores, sporting goods stores, clothing and shoe stores, and many others. It is true also of many businesses that sell services. Should this be required of all sellers? Is it already? See UCC sections 1–303(c),[5] 2–202(a).

6.   Home solicitation sales have been troublesome in Europe, too, and the EU has responded. Directive 85/577/EEC of December 20, 1985, to protect the consumer in respect of contracts negotiated away from business premises, 1985 O.J. L372/31.

---

5.   Formerly UCC § 1–205(2) (1978).

CHAPTER 10

Credit Insurance

Several risks confront the person who extends credit to consumers. These risks, which affect the consumer's ability or willingness to pay, include:

- termination of the debtor's employment

- death of the debtor

- prolonged illness or disability of the debtor

- destruction or theft of the subject matter of the transaction, e.g., a car

- destruction or theft of the collateral that secures the consumer's obligation

- assertion by a third party of a prior claim to the collateral

Each of these risks reduces the likelihood that the creditor will be paid, but insurance is available to protect against each of them. This chapter addresses the issues that arise in connection with insurance against these risks, especially the risk of the death or disability of the debtor.

A. Introduction

If a debtor dies, his or her estate remains liable for satisfaction of the debt. But the creditor and the debtor probably contemplated that the source of funds for payment of the debt would be the debtor's wages, which of course have ceased. The assets in the debtor's estate may be insufficient to pay the debt. Even if the assets are sufficient, use of them to pay the creditor may create a financial strain for the debtor's family. Similarly, if the debtor suffers prolonged illness or disability, the interruption of income may make payment of the debt more difficult than originally contemplated. Hence, it is common for creditors to procure credit life insurance and/or credit health and accident insurance on the consumers to whom they extend credit. Credit life insurance provides for payment of the unpaid balance of the debt in the event of the debtor's death. Credit health and accident insurance (also known as credit disability insurance) provides for payment of the monthly installments as they accrue in the event of the debtor's disability. Credit insurance thus removes a burden from the debtor or the debtor's estate. It also enables the creditor to avoid bad debt losses in those cases in which payment could not or would not be made; and it enables the creditor to avoid the loss of good will incidental to pressing a bereaved family or a disabled debtor for payment of a debt.

Credit life insurance originated in 1917, and credit health and accident insurance originated a few years later. Neither form was widespread before 1950. Since then, however, the growth of credit insurance has been phenomenal, paralleling the tremendous growth of consumer credit. By 1979 credit life insurance companies wrote over $99 billion of insurance, for which consumers paid over $2.5 billion. The numbers have continued to rise. Today consumers pay six billion dollars per year for the various types of credit insurance.

Along with the spectacular growth of credit insurance have come numerous problems. To deal with these problems, the National Association of Insurance Commissioners (NAIC), an organization of state insurance regulators, promulgated the NAIC Model Bill To Provide for the Regulation of Credit Life Insurance and Credit Accident and Health Insurance. The latest version of this model appears in the Statutory Supplement. Approximately forty states have adopted the model bill or substantially similar legislation. The UCCC contains additional provisions on credit insurance, to supplement other laws on the subject. UCCC Article 4.

Credit insurance is available in the form of either individual or group policies. To sell individual policies, the insurance company appoints one (or more) of the creditor's employees to be its agent for the purpose of selling insurance. The consumer owns the policy, but the creditor is the primary beneficiary of the insurance.

Group insurance, on the other hand, is sold by the insurance company to the creditor, who is both the owner and the beneficiary. The policy either covers all the credit customers of the creditor or just those customers who desire to have their obligations to the creditor covered by credit insurance and elect to participate in the group policy.[1] The creditor pays a premium based on the size and duration of the debts of consumers whose lives or health are insured. Creditors who insure all their customers pass the costs of the insurance on to the customers as part of the finance charge. Creditors who obtain insurance only on those customers who desire the coverage typically pass on the cost of the insurance in the form of a separate, identifiable charge for credit insurance. Group credit insurance is much less expensive than individual credit insurance, and the vast majority of credit insurance is group insurance.

In connection with both individual and group insurance, the insurance company compensates the creditor for the creditor's expenses in handling the insurance and for bringing business to the insurance company. This compensation usually takes the form of a commission, but it may consist also of a refund of premiums that reflects the claims experience of the insurer with respect to the customers of the creditor.

---

1. The policy may exclude certain categories of the creditor's customers, e.g., persons over 65 years of age.

B.   EXCESSIVE COVERAGE

Credit insurance is more expensive than ordinary insurance. Consequently, it generally is not in the consumer's best interest to purchase any more credit insurance than is necessary to pay off the particular debt. If the consumer desires a substantially larger amount of insurance, ordinary insurance is a better buy. (Indeed, ordinary insurance may be preferable even for covering the debt, but it is not available in the small amounts and short durations of most consumer credit transactions.) On the other hand, since the creditor receives compensation from the sale of insurance, it is in the creditor's interest to sell as much credit insurance as possible. Hence, the creditor may sell the consumer more insurance than is necessary to pay off the debt in the event of the consumer's death or disability. Or the creditor may sell insurance for a longer term than the duration of the indebtedness. Or the creditor may sell level term insurance, i.e. in an amount that remains the same throughout the period of indebtedness even though the debt continuously is being reduced by payments. See NAIC Model Bill sections 4(A)(1), 4(B), 5; UCCC section 4.106(1).

The creditor's pecuniary benefit from the sale of credit insurance causes another problem of excessive coverage. Even if the consumer already has ample life insurance coverage and can provide the protection desired by the creditor simply by making the creditor a beneficiary under an existing life insurance policy, the creditor may persuade the consumer to purchase credit life insurance. (Compare Equitable Life Assurance Society v. Scali, page 413 supra.) Section 11 of the NAIC Model Bill addresses this problem.

Another problem of excessive coverage is known as pyramiding. If the consumer refinances the debt, the creditor may sell insurance to cover the new obligation. Instead of canceling the original insurance and passing on the refund from the insurance company, however, the creditor may cancel the insurance and retain the refund. (Cf. In re Branch, page 441, supra.) See NAIC Model Bill sections 5, 8(B); UCCC section 4.110.

There is still another problem of excessive coverage. Even in the absence of credit insurance, if a debtor dies before repaying a debt, the debtor's family or estate typically pays off the creditor. One expert estimated that in eighty percent of the cases in which the debtor dies before the debt is fully paid, the creditor would receive payment even if there were no credit insurance.[2] If the creditor knows there is an eighty percent chance that the debtor's estate will pay the debt out of non-insurance sources, the creditor may be tempted to let the estate, rather than the insurance

---

2.   Subcomm. on Financial Institutions of the Sen. Comm. on Banking and Currency, Hearings on Consumer Credit Insurance Act of 1969, 91st Cong., 1st Sess. 186 (Testimony of Ronald Roberts, American National Insurance Co.) (hereinafter cited as 1969 Hearings).

company, pay the debt.[3] When this happens, the debtor's estate does not receive the benefit that the debtor contracted for. Even worse, a dishonest creditor might submit a claim on behalf of the consumer's estate but continue to collect installments from the debtor's family, thereby receiving double payment. The NAIC Model Bill seeks to deal with these abuses by requiring sufficient disclosure to make debtors and their families aware of the existence and term of insurance coverage. See sections 6(A)–(D); UCCC section 4.105(1).

To explore the effectiveness of the NAIC Model Bill to deal with problems of excessive coverage, please consider the following questions.

QUESTIONS

1. May a creditor sell level term insurance? Should a creditor be able to sell level term insurance? If the debt originally is $2,000 and is $1,000 when the debtor dies, what amount does the insurer pay and to whom?

The Georgia small loan act permits lenders to accept "reasonable insurance" as security, provided that the "insurance shall be reasonably related . . . to the amount and term of the loan and . . . shall not exceed the amount of the loan." Does this statute permit level term insurance? See Mason v. Service Loan & Finance Co., 198 S.E.2d 391 (Ga.App.1973). Cf. UCCC § 4.202(1)(a).

2. If a creditor loans $6,000 to be prepaid in 36 equal monthly installments and imposes a finance charge of $1,200, what amount of insurance is necessary to protect the creditor?

In Winkle v. Grand National Bank, 601 S.W.2d 559 (Ark.1980), the debtors borrowed $25,000 for their business, agreeing to repay $39,596 (which included a finance charge of $11,600 and a premium of almost $3,000 for credit life insurance in the amount of $39,596).

The chancellor found that Ark.Stat.Ann. § 66–3806(1) was violated because "the maximum amount which could have ever been paid under the policy would be something in the neighborhood of $25,000." That statement does not demonstrate a violation of the statute which provides: "The amount of credit life insurance shall not exceed the original amount of indebtedness." The original amount of indebtedness was the face amount of the policy and the note—$39,596.40. If the word "indebtedness" had not been defined in the same act of which § 66–3806(1) is a part, it might be argued persuasively, but not conclusively, that the chancellor applied the statute properly. The word "indebtedness," as defined by Ark.Stat.Ann. § 66–3804(5), however, includes "the total amount payable by a debtor to a creditor in connection with a loan or other credit transaction." The total amount payable by the Winkles on the effective date of the policy to the bank

3. The creditor's compensation from the insurance company varies inversely with the amount that the insurance company has to pay in claims: hence, the lower the claims, the higher the creditor's experience refund.

on this credit transaction, if the note had been paid according to its terms, was $39,596.40. By the terms of the note, the Winkles promised "to pay to the order of Grand National Bank (herein called Bank), at its office in Hot Springs, Arkansas, the sum of Thirty-four Thousand Eight Hundred Eighty–Eight and 80/100 Dollars, in 120 installment[s] of $329.97 beginning December 20, 1975, and on the same date each month thereafter until paid in full . . . ."

Id. at 571.

Do you agree? What is the "original amount of indebtedness"?

What rationale, if any, is there for permitting the sale of credit life insurance in an amount larger than the amount necessary to satisfy the debt?

Should the creditor be able to sell insurance in an amount large enough to pay the insurance premium?

Should the creditor be able to collect finance charge on the amount of the insurance premium?

C. Coercion

One of the most controversial aspects of credit insurance is the voluntariness of consumers in acquiring it. Creditors maintain that they do not require consumers to buy life or disability insurance, but rather that consumers perceive the benefits of the insurance and want it. In a survey conducted around 1970, over ninety percent of persons who had purchased either life or disability insurance, or both, said they would do so again in connection with future loans. C. Hubbard, ed., Consumer Credit Life and Disability Insurance 80, 81 (1972). Yet the same study found that more than twenty-three percent of consumers who had purchased credit life insurance, and more than eighteen percent of those who had purchased credit disability insurance, believed they were required to do so. Id. at 75. Later surveys have produced similar results.

The percentage of consumers who buy credit life insurance is very high—for many creditors the penetration rate approaches one hundred percent. A possible explanation of this is that consumers believe it is valuable and want to buy it. Another possible explanation is the psychological position of the consumer. The consumer is likely to perceive himself or herself as more dependent on the proposed transaction than the creditor is. So when the creditor says, "It's a good idea to have life insurance. Do you want it?" the consumer may perceive that the creditor is more likely to extend credit if insurance is part of the deal. And the creditor may enhance the likelihood of the insurance sale by assuming that the consumer will purchase it rather than asking whether the consumer wants it, as in, "Sign here for credit insurance; it's included." On the other hand, the penetration rate for disability insurance is substantially lower than for life insurance. Does that not, as some have suggested, show that consumers are able to distinguish between life insurance and disability insurance and do indeed decide for themselves whether they really want to buy credit insurance?

Statutes in some states prohibit the creditor from requiring the consumer to purchase credit insurance. Of course, if the prohibition appears in the small loan laws, it has no effect on creditors who are regulated by other laws, e.g., banks and retailers. The NAIC Model Bill does not forbid the creditor from requiring insurance, but it mandates that the creditor allow the consumer to procure the insurance from another source (§ 11). As a practical matter, however, this provision is ineffective. Do you see why?

The materials in Chapter 8 raise the question whether the cost of insurance should be included in "interest" for purposes of statutes limiting the amount that creditors may charge for credit. A similar problem arises under the Truth-in-Lending Act: should the cost of insurance be included in "finance charge" for purposes of disclosure? While some proponents of truth-in-lending argued for including insurance premiums in the finance charge, the statute as enacted does not take that approach. Rather, the key criterion is voluntariness:

§ 106.   Determination of finance charge

. . .

(b) Charges or premiums for credit life, accident, or health insurance written in connection with any consumer credit transaction shall be included in the finance charge unless

(1) the coverage of the debtor by the insurance is not a factor in the approval by the creditor of the extension of credit, and this fact is clearly disclosed in writing to the person applying for or obtaining the extension of credit; and

(2) in order to obtain the insurance in connection with the extension of credit, the person to whom the credit is extended must give specific affirmative written indication of his desire to do so after written disclosure to him of the cost thereof.

See also Regulation Z, which at the time of the decisions to be considered below, was as follows:

SECTION 226.4—DETERMINATION OF FINANCE CHARGE

(a) General rule. Except as otherwise provided in this section, the amount of the finance charge in connection with any transaction shall be determined as the sum of all charges, payable directly or indirectly by the customer, and imposed directly or indirectly by the creditor as an incident to or as a condition of the extension of credit, whether paid or payable by the customer, the seller, or any other person on behalf of the customer to the creditor or to a third party, including any of the following types of charges:

. . .

(5) Charges or premiums for credit life, accident, health, or loss of income insurance, written in connection with any credit transaction unless

(i) the insurance coverage is not required by the creditor and this fact is clearly and conspicuously disclosed in writing to the customer; and

(ii) any customer desiring such insurance coverage gives specifically dated and separately signed affirmative written indication of such desire after receiving written disclosure to him of the cost of such insurance.[4]

Compare the current version, Regulation Z section 226.4(d). What is the rationale of a rule that ties disclosure to voluntariness?

In Anthony v. Community Loan & Investment Corp., 559 F.2d 1363 (5th Cir.1977), plaintiff challenged the sufficiency of defendant's disclosure statement on several grounds, including the failure to include the insurance premiums in the finance charge. The trial court gave summary judgment for defendant, and the Fifth Circuit affirmed:

The security agreement provided:

CREDIT LIFE AND DISABILITY INSURANCE is not required to obtain this loan. Such insurance will only be procured for the term of the loan if Customer(s) request(s) Creditor to obtain such insurance by signing below:

I desire Credit Life and Disability Insurance at the cost of *$137.39*.

9/4/73   /s/Lena Mae Anthony
Date   Signature

. . .

The regulations authorize the exclusion of an insurance premium from the finance charge if the fact that insurance is not required is clearly disclosed to the customer in writing and the customer desiring such insurance coverage signs a specific dated and affirmed written indication of such desire after receiving written disclosure of the cost of the insurance. All of these requirements were met in this case.

Although plaintiff asserts that she never requested or desired insurance coverage, but merely signed the documents when told to do so, this assertion is insufficient to vary the terms of the contract or to negate the creditor's full compliance with the disclosure requirements of Regulation Z. The defendant correctly contends that, absent a claim of illiteracy, fraud or duress, no extraneous oral evidence can be presented by the plaintiff to prove that the defendant gave her the

---

4. The Act takes a similar approach for casualty insurance. See section 106(c); Regu- lation Z section 226.4(d)(2).

impression that the insurance was required. An FTC informal staff opinion has said:

> A written disclosure statement given to the consumer as required by the Truth–In–Lending Act, before consummation of the transaction, is a protection against oral misrepresentations that induce a loan. Consumers must learn to inspect disclosure statements before signing a contract, otherwise the purpose of the Act and Regulation Z will be frustrated.

FTC Informal Staff Opinion of Dec. 9, 1969, CCH CONS. CRED. GUIDE ¶ 30,309. Consumers should not be encouraged to avoid reading or to ignore the information the Act requires to be provided. In addition, the Court can apply the parol evidence rule in this situation to further, not derogate, the purposes of the Act. In this situation therefore Georgia's parol evidence rule is not in conflict with the purposes of the Federal statute.

Finally, summary judgment was appropriate on this issue because there was no issue as to any material fact. Anthony's affidavit reads in material part:

> That I never requested or desired any insurance coverage in connection with the loan transaction. That all of the documents I signed were filled out by the loan company and I merely signed the documents when told to do so.

Thus, the affidavit does not place in question whether the defendant "required" purchase of credit life insurance coverage.

Id. at 1369–1370.

See Stanley v. R. S. Evans Motors of Jacksonville, Inc., 394 F.Supp. 859, 861 (M.D.Fla.1975):

> Here, however, all the legal requirements of TILA disclosure were met by defendant. Defendant's president testified that neither it nor Atlantic Discount at any time required credit life insurance as a condition to the sale of an automobile on credit, and that neither required such insurance of this particular plaintiff. The Contract contains the NOTICE TO BUYER and lists every disclosure required by law, the acknowledgment of which is dated and signed separately by plaintiff. Although plaintiff may not have fully understood the terms of the Contract, this cannot be attributed to defendant's failure to comply. Plaintiff has charged defendant with violating the requirements of a statute and regulation; there is, however, nothing that the law requires which defendant did not do. Under these circumstances, liability does not attach.

Exactly why does the court in *Anthony* say that plaintiff may not offer testimony supporting her claim that defendant gave her no choice concerning insurance? And what are the flaws in the court's reasoning? See Marine Midland Bank v. Burley, 425 N.Y.S.2d 429 (N.Y.App.Div.1980).

In another case the court was equally inhospitable to a consumer's claim of compulsion:

In this case, the insurance authorization disclosed:

The purchase of [credit insurance] is not required by lender in order for borrower to obtain this loan. Such insurance may be obtained by the borrower at his option. . . .

I (or we), borrower herein, having first examined the premium cost for [credit insurance] do hereby elect to purchase the insurance as checked with a mark in the above boxes if any.

. . .

This authorization was dated and signed by plaintiff.

Plaintiff contends that the recitals as to insurance are not true. As proof that insurance was required, she submits her affidavit that she applied for a loan, returned the next day, and was presented with the entire contract, including the insurance authorization, filled out. Plaintiff further states in her affidavit that before she signed she noticed the insurance purchase, did not want insurance, but said nothing about it since she figured that it was required.

If what plaintiff says is true, she has not proved that credit insurance is required. She cannot prove that unless she asks whether the insurance is required and is told that it is. Her assumption that it is required is not enough. It is natural for anyone, no matter how sophisticated, who wants to borrow money to be unwilling to displease the lender over a small matter. This tendency helps a lender put on a hard sell such as plaintiff described. The importance of these insurance sales to consumer lenders and their effectiveness in procuring them is well known. But selling insurance in the manner described by plaintiff does not amount to requiring insurance.

The Truth in Lending Act requires written disclosures to facilitate credit shopping. Here, plaintiff did not use the disclosures. Plaintiff is not entitled to oral disclosure that credit insurance is not required.

The courts have all held that the debtor is estopped from contending that insurance was required if the insurance authorization recites that it was not. This court has held that the debtor is estopped unless she can show fraud or other duress.

A better statement of the rule is that plaintiff must prove that the creditor specifically and unequivocally informed her that insurance is required in order to contradict the recital to the contrary. Thus, if plaintiff proves that she told the creditor that she did not want the insurance and the creditor told her that no loan would be made without insurance, plaintiff has met her burden.

Mims v. Dixie Finance Corp., 426 F.Supp. 627, 631 (N.D.Ga.1976). How does this court's rationale differ from the rationale of *Anthony*? Is it any sounder?

Contrary to the court's statement, some courts do believe that the insurance authorization form is not conclusive on the question of voluntariness. In addition to *Burley*, supra, see In re Dickson, 432 F.Supp. 752, 759 (W.D.N.C.1977); In re USLIFE Credit Corp., infra.

In re USLIFE Credit Corp.

Federal Trade Commission, 1978.
91 F.T.C. 984, modified 92 F.T.C. 353, reversed sub nom. USLIFE Credit Corp. v. Federal Trade Commission, 599 F.2d 1387 (5th Cir.1979).

CLANTON, COMMISSIONER:

I.   BACKGROUND

On September 26, 1975, the Commission issued a complaint against respondents USLIFE Corporation and its subsidiary, USLIFE Credit Corporation, alleging violations of the Truth in Lending Act, Regulation Z, and the Federal Trade Commission Act. The issues at stake here concern the sale by USLIFE Credit of credit life and credit disability insurance in connection with its consumer loan business.

The complaint alleges that respondents violated Section 226.4(a)(5) of Regulation Z by engaging in acts and practices which operated "to defeat the elective language of the insurance authorization disclosures by obscuring from consumers knowledge about the [insurance] option." More specifically, the following practices were cited as illustrative of those which defeated the optional selection of insurance:

(1) oral quotation of monthly repayment figures that include insurance charges;

(2) automatic inclusion of insurance charges in loan agreement papers;

(3) placement of an "X" at the appropriate signature line on the insurance authorization form prior to obtaining the customer's selection of insurance;

(4) failure to inform consumers as to the purposes of their signatures; and

(5) inclusion of charges for insurance in the "records of disbursements" section of the loan agreement without adjusting the finance charge and the annual percentage rate.

The administrative law judge (ALJ) issued his decision dismissing the complaint on January 27, 1977. Having found that respondents' official policy was not to require insurance, the ALJ concluded that the practices utilized by respondents did not run afoul of the credit statute or its implementing regulations. In particular, the law judge found that respondents' employees were instructed to explain loan terms to customers and to avoid oral quotations which included insurance. He determined further that insurance was not automatically included in loan forms prior to customer authorization, borrowers were not pressured into signing the forms, and respondents did not otherwise thwart consumers' opportunity to read over the relevant forms. Finally, the judge found that use of "Xs" and other similar marks on the signature lines served as a convenience to customers in finalizing the loan agreement, rather than creating the impression that insurance was obligatory. In sum, the ALJ found no basis for concluding that respondents' acts or practices were responsible for any impression prospective borrowers may have had that insurance was required.

. . .

II. THE REQUIREMENTS OF THE TRUTH IN LENDING ACT

. . .

Respondents contend that since the general purpose of the Act and Regulation Z is to insure uniform disclosures, and not to serve as an "antifraud" statute, no violation will lie if the creditor's policy is to make insurance coverage optional and the policy is disclosed in writing to customers. We reject such a restrictive interpretation of the statute. The issue here relates not to respondents' official policy, or the adequacy of their written disclosures, but to whether certain practices utilized by respondents effectively prevented consumers from exercising a free and knowing choice as to their insurance option. That is, despite respondents' official policy, have they engaged in practices that serve to obscure or defeat this policy, including the written disclosures contained in their loan agreements?

Legislative and judicial authorities alike convince us that, notwithstanding a creditor's official policy to the contrary, a further examination of the creditor's practices is in order to establish whether the insurance election has been undermined and the statute violated. The significance of the written disclosure of insurance costs is emphasized in the regulations and elaborated upon in the following excerpt from the Conference Report on the Truth in Lending Act:

> Under the conference substitute, such [insurance] charges may not be excluded [from the finance charge] unless the coverage of the debtor by the insurance is not a factor in the approval by the creditor of extension of credit, *and this is clearly disclosed to the debtor. The creditor must also disclose to the prospective debtor the cost of such insurance, and may not include it in the financing package unless the debtor gives specific affirmative written indication of his desire to have it.* If . . . insurance is written in connection with any consumer credit transaction, without complying with all of the foregoing requirements, then its cost must be included in the finance charge. . . . (emphasis supplied)

As the underscored language indicates, more than pro forma compliance with the statute is called for. Both the optional nature and cost of the insurance must be clearly disclosed and, *before* including insurance in the loan agreement, the creditor must obtain the consumer's written authorization. During debate in the House on the Conference Report, the floor manager of the bill, Congresswoman Lenore Sullivan, reinforced the importance of preserving consumer choice in deciding whether to purchase credit insurance:

> In the final bill, credit life insurance is included in the finance charge if the consumer does not have a free opportunity to decide whether he wants the coverage, or if the insurance is a factor in the extension of credit.

Thus, even if insurance is not a factor in the creditor's decision to extend credit, insurance costs will be included in the finance charge provided the consumer does not have a "free opportunity" to exercise his or her choice. The result is the same whether the creditor officially requires insurance coverage or informally does so through practices which undermine the would-be borrower's voluntary election. Surely, a determination as to whether the choice was truly "free" contemplates an inquiry into the facts and circumstances surrounding the credit transaction.

The cases also support this view. In F.T.C. v. Jorgensen, 4 Cons. Cred.Guide (CCH) ¶ 98,594 (D.D.C.1975), the court dismissed out of hand a creditor's claim that a Commission inquiry into the practices surrounding the use of an insurance authorization form would amount to an ad hoc amendment to Regulation Z. The court held that "Regulation Z would be meaningless indeed if its requirements could be met in form and ignored or overridden in practice. An inquiry into actual practice is therefore appropriate." Likewise, in Fisher v. Beneficial Finance Co. of Hoxsie, 383 F.Supp. 895 (D.R.I.1974), the court observed that while a consumer's mere allegation that insurance was mandatory was insufficient to support a motion for summary judgment in her favor, she was free to introduce evidence at trial "that the defendant by its conduct did actually require . . . insurance to be purchased as a condition of [the] loan."

Finally, we take note of the Federal Reserve Board's own interpretations of Section 226.4(a)(5). In addressing specific requests for advice on proper application of this provision, the Board's staff has advised, for example, that even where insurance is officially labeled "optional," the practice of including insurance costs in the loan papers prior to obtaining the consumer's approval would have "the practical effect of precluding the customer's free exercise of choice as to whether he wishes the insurance. Without that choice Congress specified that the premiums would have to appear in the finance charge."[9] In fact, evidence of such a practice alone

---

9. FRB Letter No. 398 (August 26, 1970), [19691974 Transfer Binder] Cons. Cred.Guide (CCH) ¶ 30,576. See also FRB Letter No. 408 (September 14, 1970), [19691974 Transfer Binder] Cons.Cred.Guide (CCH) ¶ 30,586.

There is some hint in the court's decision in Fisher v. Beneficial Finance, supra, at 900,

that FRB Letter No. 408 supersedes the interpretation in FRB Letter No. 398. In fact, a close reading of the two letters shows them to be perfectly consistent. In Letter No. 398, the staff expressed its view that a "separate disclosure" of the cost of insurance prior to the consumer's election was the best method for insuring that the election was knowingly

might be sufficient to establish liability. Clearly, other practices surrounding a credit transaction, in addition to those cited by the Federal Reserve Board, are also integral to a proper assessment of the voluntary nature of the insurance option and should be examined.[10]

Even if our interpretation were not so clearly expressed in the language and legislative history of the specific provision at issue here, the broader purpose of the Truth in Lending Act supports the proposition that a consumer's insurance choice must be freely and knowingly exercised before the costs can be excluded from the finance charge and the annual percentage rate. . . . In striving to promote uniformity and simplicity, Congress relied heavily upon the annual percentage rate. As Senator Proxmire, the bill's principal sponsor in the Senate, stated:

> [T]he bill would require that in most forms of credit the creditor would disclose the annual percentage rate. This is the universal common denominator by which the cost of money is measured. It permits a consumer to readily compare the cost of credit among different lenders regardless of the length of the contract or the amount of the downpayment. In effect, the annual percentage rate is a price tag for the use of money.

Moreover, Congress realized that the utility of this "price tag" indicator would be severely eroded if creditors were free to eliminate from the costs of extending credit a variety of charges and fees that were actually conditions and terms upon which the credit would be extended—a practice Congress found to have occurred with some frequency. Accordingly, the Act specified the types of additional and extraordinary fees and charges, including insurance, that must be included in the finance charge and reflected in the annual percentage rate.

The scheme established by Congress, with its reliance on the annual percentage rate, demands careful adherence to the principle that insurance costs must be reflected in the annual percentage rate unless such costs are made wholly optional. Where insurance is required, it must be treated as a cost of the credit since it automatically becomes part of the credit transaction. Where it is optional, it can be eliminated from the cost of credit but only because the consumer has been informed of its separate cost and has had full opportunity to accept or reject it. Were creditors free to manipulate their insurance costs, Congress' goal of preserving the comparability of

---

made. It was further noted that his "separate disclosure" should appear on the insurance authorization form itself.

Letter No. 408 reiterated this view but counseled the requester that the staff did not intend to imply that disclosure on the authorization form itself was the only method by which compliance could be achieved. The staff advised that if the creditor could prove that the disclosure was actually made before the consumer's election, § 226.4(a)(5) would be satisfied. Significantly, though, the staff

did not back away from its advice in Letter No. 398 and suggest that incorporation of the insurance charges within the terms of the loan agreement would be a permissible method of disclosure.

10.   To the extent that Stanley v. Evans Motors, 394 F.Supp. 859 (M.D.Fla.1975), and Mims v. Dixie Finance, 426 F.Supp. 627 (N.D.Ga.1976), two cases cited by respondents, indicate the contrary, we respectfully decline to follow them.

credit offerings would be readily defeated. Given the sensitive nature of the annual percentage rate as a cost-of-credit barometer, it strikes us that the Congressional purpose can be achieved only if Section 226.4(a) is construed to require the inclusion of insurance costs in the finance charge whenever insurance is not truly voluntary.

. . .

III. RESPONDENTS' PRACTICES

A. *Insurance Election*

There is no dispute that USLIFE Credit's official policy provides that insurance is optional and that this policy was appropriately embodied in each credit contract by inclusion of a written notice disclosing the optional nature of the insurance.

Indeed, by operation of law in 19 of the 20 states in which USLIFE Credit does business, the company is prohibited from requiring insurance. As we have previously noted, however, such a policy alone does not suffice to absolve respondents from liability under TILA. A further examination of respondents' practices, therefore, is in order to determine respondents' compliance with the statute.

In the typical loan transaction, the consumer would contact USLIFE Credit, either by phone or in person, to inquire about the possibility of obtaining a loan. Respondent's personnel would ascertain the purpose, amount needed, and other data necessary to determine credit worthiness. After appropriate credit checks, the loan office would call back to confirm whether the loan would be granted and, if so, to obtain further information for processing the required documents. Once approved, the consumer was invited to come into the appropriate USLIFE credit office to finalize the transaction. At this final visit the loan papers, including insurance authorization forms, were signed.

The complaint charges that respondents engaged in a variety of practices which had the effect of defeating the voluntary insurance election. Among others, these include: (1) quoting monthly repayment figures to consumers which include insurance, (2) automatically including insurance charges on the loan agreement and disclosure papers presented to consumers for signature, (3) marking an "X" by the signature line reserved for authorization of insurance without permission of the borrower, and (4) presenting pre-typed loan agreements to consumers for signing without disclosing the purpose of the signatures.

Respondents do not dispute that repayment terms are quoted which include insurance, or that loan documents containing insurance charges are prepared in advance of presentation to borrowers for signature and before they have received written disclosure of the insurance option.

Rather, they contend that such actions are not taken without first informing customers that insurance is voluntary and obtaining their consent. Similarly, respondents argue, and the ALJ agreed, that showing customers where to sign by 'X's or otherwise is merely a convenience to assist them in signing on the proper line after exercising their option to purchase insurance. Respondents also assert that the terms of loans, including insurance charges, were explained to customers before signing.

. . .

In connection with the advance preparation of loan documents which include insurance, we are unable to agree with respondents and the ALJ that this practice was wholly innocuous. Although such action may at times have been preceded by oral disclosures that insurance was optional there is considerable evidence that in many instances the disclosures were inadequate or non-existent.

For example, Mr. Dionne, former manager of respondents' Houston office, testified that he did not present insurance as an option on renewal loans. In elaborating on his response for the ALJ, Mr. Dionne stated:

> Did I present [insurance] as an option, no sir, I did not, that's the thing . . . nor did any other individual who may have been closing a loan when the information would be taken over the phone or whatever
> . . . .

. . .

Further, witnesses Stricklen and George, who were both supervised by the same regional manager, testified that they were under standing orders not to make loans without insurance. Mr. George stated that if a customer refused insurance, he would have to call his supervisor and get approval. To avoid telling customers that insurance was required, other tactics were used, such as advising them that "the company's policy was we like to have insurance on every loan. . . ." Those efforts were apparently quite successful since Mr. George acknowledged that he could not recall any instance where insurance was not sold.

Consumer testimony provides further corroboration that borrowers were not fully informed about their right to decline insurance before it was inserted in the loan agreement. . . . For example, . . . Mr. Richardson indicated that insurance was never discussed until closing when the loan officer went over the terms of the loan and read off that "the payment was so much and the insurance would be so much. . . ."

. . .

This evidence, we believe, thoroughly substantiates the complaint's allegation that insurance was included in many loan documents prior to closing without the consumer's knowledge. At other times, insurance may have been discussed but borrowers were not aware that it was voluntary. In our view, such action is inherently inconsistent with the statutory scheme, which contemplates *written* disclosure of the insurance option and its cost *before* consumers make their choice. Even if consumers are informed at the outset that insurance is not required, oral disclosures are inherently unreliable, particularly where the lender, as here, has an economic stake in the sale of insurance. While there is obviously nothing improper in respondents engaging in the sale of credit insurance, such an interest only underscores the importance of assuring that the written disclosures are not undermined.

Respondents nevertheless contend that the practice involved here is merely a convenience to consumers who have already made their insurance selection orally during the first communication with respondents and that any potential for misunderstanding is cured by respondents' practice of "going over" the loan forms with the customer. . . . [U]nlike the ALJ we believe that "going over" already completed loan papers (which include insurance) is not an obvious benefit to consumers from the point of view of insuring full understanding of their insurance options. The mere reiteration of the amount of the insurance costs may serve to reinforce the notion in consumers' minds that insurance is part of the deal.

. . . That is not to say that all customers were misled by respondents' practices into believing that insurance was required. The record is clear that respondents were not able to sell insurance on every loan. Some customers obviously understood that insurance was voluntary and managed to resist respondents' inducement to purchase it. Nevertheless, in confronting completed loan papers which show that insurance coverage is included in the terms of the agreement, we believe it is not unreasonable for consumers to conclude that insurance is simply part of the transaction. In addition, as the record indicates, pointing out the insurance charges at closing may well strengthen that belief.

. . .

In addition to the charge that insurance is included in loan documents before written notice is provided to customers, the complaint further alleges that respondents used marks ("X"s) to indicate where consumers were to sign for insurance. A related allegation is that customers were asked to sign the insurance authorization portion of the loan agreement without disclosing the purpose of the signature. As the ALJ found, these practices occurred and respondents admit that marks were used, though they contend that such action merely served to assure that customers signed on the proper line after voluntarily deciding to purchase insurance.

While it is certainly appropriate, indeed desirable, for respondents to explain the loan documents to customers, it is quite another thing for respondents to suggest by marks or otherwise that the signature authorizing insurance is needed to complete the loan transaction. The record reveals that the practice of placing an "X" by the signature line or asking customers to "sign here" contributed to the belief of borrowers that insurance was a necessary part of the loan package. This practice, coupled with the prior preparation of loan papers containing insurance, prevented consumers from making a fully informed choice as to their insurance options.

. . .

In sum, we believe there is ample evidence to conclude that respondents' conduct falls short of the requirements of the Truth in Lending Act and Regulation Z. Such a finding is warranted solely from respondents' inclusion of insurance in loan documents prior to giving consumers proper written disclosure of their options. Other practices, such as telling customers about credit insurance charges without disclosing that insurance is voluntary and asking customers to sign for insurance (through check marks or otherwise) before they have elected to purchase such coverage, contributed to borrower confusion about the voluntary nature of the insurance. These practices, independently and collectively, served to obscure and undermine the statutorily required disclosures. As a result, respondents' failure to include the cost of insurance in the calculation of the finance charge and annual percentage rate constitutes a violation of the credit statute and Section 5 of the FTC Act.

Obviously, by our holding here we do not imply that respondents must guarantee that consumers fully understand the import of the written disclosures concerning their insurance options. Further, even with adequate disclosures, it is certainly possible that the vast majority of consumers, as respondents suggest, will still elect to purchase insurance. What we do emphasize is that respondents must scrupulously avoid actions which undercut the importance of the written disclosures and render them meaningless. Where insurance charges are included in the loan papers prepared for closing, the likelihood that consumers will receive the full benefit of the subsequent written disclosures is greatly reduced. That is particularly true given respondents' desire to sell insurance and the reluctance by all parties to incur the delay associated with the preparation of new papers (or a check reimbursing the premium). In our view, both the express language and policy of the Truth in Lending Act require more.

. . .

ORDER GRANTING IN PART, AND DENYING IN PART, RESPONDENTS'
PETITION FOR RECONSIDERATION

By CLANTON, COMMISSIONER:

Respondents have petitioned for reconsideration of our recent opinion and order . . . .

. . . . [R]espondents rely upon new authorities to support their contention that their compliance with the TILA may be measured only by the adequacy of the written disclosure form . . . .

Respondents cite Anthony v. Community Loan & Investment Corp., and a recent FRB Official Staff Interpretation, FC–0119 (Oct. 20, 1977) [1974–1977 Transfer Binder] Cons.Cred.Guide (CCH) ¶ 31,705 in support of the first contention. Neither of these authorities, however, compels us to alter our decision.

In the *Anthony* case, a private suit for damages under TILA, the Fifth Circuit held that a credit customer's assertion that she had neither requested nor desired insurance, but had simply signed the loan documents which included an insurance election, was insufficient to vary the terms of her contract or to negate the executed insurance authorization. In reaching this result, the court applied the Georgia parol evidence rule to exclude plaintiff's proffered oral evidence that defendant had given her the impression that insurance was required.

Notwithstanding that the findings of fact in the instant case are bottomed, in part, upon the type of consumer testimony which was excluded by the Fifth Circuit in *Anthony*, we do not view that decision as necessarily inconsistent with our own. Sound reasons of judicial administration may argue for not entertaining such oral testimony in the context of private damage litigation, where doing so might weaken the principles underlying the parol evidence doctrine or open the gates of the courthouse to frivolous litigation. But these factors are not present here.

It is clear that the Commission, as a law enforcement agency, empowered by Congress with a mandate to prevent unfair and deceptive practices and to enforce the TILA and Regulation Z, may hear all such evidence as is necessary to establish whether violations of law have occurred. Frequently, the existence of a pattern of deception can be proved only by resort to oral testimony, including so-called "parol evidence." The evidentiary standard on which the *Anthony* decision is based is simply not applicable to an FTC administrative enforcement proceeding. A recent case regarding the admissibility of parol evidence in administrative proceedings is on point. In Western Union Telegraph Co. v. FCC, 541 F.2d 346, 353 (3d Cir.1976), cert. den., 429 U.S. 1092 (1977), the Third Circuit held that "as a matter of administrative law, . . . the Commission was not bound to apply the parol evidence rule."

Accordingly, we do not believe that *Anthony* is inconsistent with our earlier determination in this matter, to which we adhere. Nothing in the Commission's Rules of Practice, including Section 3.43(b), requires or suggests a different result.

Next, review of FRB Official Staff Interpretation FC–0119 demonstrates that respondents have misunderstood the thrust of that letter. FRB staff there address only the sufficiency of the wording of the disclosure in the correspondent's form. No intimation that an inquiry may not properly be carried beyond the form itself may be drawn from that letter. Indeed, two subsequent FRB Staff Opinion Letters reveal that the FRB staff interprets Regulation Z in a manner squarely in accordance with our recent decision in this case.

In FRB Letter No. 1270 (December 20, 1977), 5 Cons.Cred.Guide (CCH) ¶ 31,756, the author of FC–0119 wrote:

> FC–0119 was intended by staff to deal only with the method by which a customer might indicate, in writing, his or her desire for credit life, accident, health, or loss of income insurance in order to comply with § 226.4(a)(5)(ii) of Regulation Z. Staff did not and does not mean to suggest that, because a customer gives a proper 'specifically dated and separately signed affirmative written indication' of his or her

desire for such insurance, there may be no further inquiry as to whether the customer's election to obtain the insurance was truly voluntary and not required by the creditor. Whether a customer desired such insurance is a question of fact, which can only be answered by reference to all the circumstances of a particular transaction. Inquiry into these circumstances is, of course, not foreclosed by the presence of a customer's signature on an insurance authorization.

And in FRB Letter No. 1286 (March 21, 1978), 5 Cons.Cred.Guide (CCH) ¶ 31,777, FRB staff noted:

> While the customer's signature on a document would be some evidence of voluntariness, of course, it would not conclusively establish that the insurance was not required. Any number of collateral acts or practices by a creditor could negate the apparently affirmative nature of the customer's election to purchase insurance.
>
>   * * *
>
> Routine inclusion of the insurance premium in the preparation of the credit documents . . . might be evidence that the creditor had created the impression that the insurance was a condition of the extension of credit.

Since we are in accord with these FRB Staff Opinions and since, as respondents acknowledge, such opinion letters are entitled to great weight with respect to the proper interpretation of Regulation Z, we decline to modify our decision.

USLIFE Credit Corp. v. Federal Trade Commission

United States Court of Appeals, Fifth Circuit, 1979.
599 F.2d 1387.

VANCE, CIRCUIT JUDGE.

. . .

The Commission concedes that USLIFE Credit has complied technically with [Reg. Z 226.4(a)]. In other words, (a) USLIFE Credit does not require insurance coverage, (b) that fact is clearly and conspicuously disclosed on USLIFE Credit's forms, and (c) insurance coverage is sold only on the basis of a specific dated and separately signed order following written disclosure of its cost. In addition the Commission made no allegation or finding of customer illiteracy, fraud or duress.

The Commission's May 23, 1978, decision took no note of this court's decision in Anthony v. Community Loan & Investment Corp. *Anthony* was relied on by the lender in its petition for reconsideration. The Commission responded in a second final opinion dated September 14, 1978, by characterizing *Anthony* as nothing more than an application of Georgia's parol evidence rule. It concluded that the rule which this court applied in private damage litigation would not apply in administrative enforcement proceedings.

We do not read *Anthony* so narrowly. *Anthony* involved a "closed-end, non-sale credit transaction." There, as here, the credit corporation complied technically with Regulation Z. Ms. Anthony contended that she neither requested nor desired insurance coverage, but merely signed the documents where told to do so. She was not allowed to testify that defendant gave her the impression that insurance was required. The Commission did not distinguish the controlling facts in *Anthony* from those in the present case, and we perceive no basis for distinguishing them.

In *Anthony* we quoted an FTC informal staff opinion as follows:

A written disclosure statement given to the consumer as required by the Truth–In–Lending Act, before consummation of the transaction, is a protection against oral misrepresentations that induce a loan. Consumers must learn to inspect disclosure statements before signing a contract, otherwise the purpose of the Act and Regulation Z will be frustrated.

. . . Disagreeing with the thrust of this opinion, the Commission points out that it is not the agency entrusted with the authority to promulgate implementing regulations under the Truth in Lending Act, that it is only one of several agencies that have enforcement responsibilities under the Act and that its informal staff opinion is not entitled to any special deference. The point is well taken and applies equally to the interpretations of law and regulation incorporated into the decision under review. In its prior decision this court found the FTC informal opinion to be persuasive, however, and that decision is binding on this panel.

In endorsing the FTC staff statement the *Anthony* court stated,

Consumers should not be encouraged to avoid reading or to ignore the information the Act requires to be provided. In addition, the Court can apply the parol evidence rule in this situation to further, not derogate, the purposes of the Act. *In this situation therefore Georgia's parol evidence rule is not in conflict with the purposes of the federal statute.*

The Commission simply missed the point of the decision in connection with the parol evidence rule. The rule was not in conflict with the statute because the testimony it barred was not testimony of a material fact.

We recognized in *Anthony* that there may be exceptions in the case of illiteracy, fraud or duress. Under the facts which are before us, however, literal, technical compliance with the regulation is all that is required.

The Commission argues in brief that we must afford consumers a "free and knowing choice as to their insurance option." With respect to the particular question under consideration, both the statute and the regulation are clear and understandable. To the extent that the Commission's position would impose additional requirements or conditions, it is addressed to the wrong forum. The idea that disclosure requirements should be broadened to provide more meaningful information to borrowers than is now required is a matter for the consideration of Congress.

We conclude that the Commission's decision is contrary to law. Its order must be vacated and set aside.

QUESTIONS

1. In *Anthony* and in *USLIFE*, the Fifth Circuit relies on a 1969 letter written by a member of the FTC staff. The FTC, of course, is one of the agencies charged with enforcing the Truth-in-Lending Act (§ 108(c)). It is the Federal Reserve Board, however, that is empowered to issue regulations (§ 105) and to issue official interpretations having the force of law (§ 130(f)). The Act gives the FTC neither of these powers. In light of this and in light of Ford Motor Credit Co. v. Milhollin (pages 186–88 supra), how appropriate is it for the Fifth Circuit to rely on the 1969 FTC letter while completely ignoring the FRB unofficial staff opinion letters cited in the FTC's second opinion (pages 558–60 supra)?

2. If the creditor asks the consumer whether he or she wants to buy credit life insurance, and the consumer says "no," does the creditor violate the Truth-in-Lending Act by responding, "Then I won't extend credit"? According to Gary v. W. T. Grant, [1974–1980 Transfer Binder] Consumer Credit Guide (CCH) ¶ 98,550 (N.D. Ga.1975), the answer is "no." How can that be?

3. Problem. *Department Store* includes in its monthly billing statement the following notice:

> For your protection we have arranged with Apple Insurance Company to make inexpensive group life insurance available to all our credit customers. If you die, this insurance will pay off any debt that you owe us, thereby relieving your family of the burden of paying this debt. The cost of this insurance has been added to your monthly bill and varies in amount depending on the amount you owe us. If you desire this protection, simply pay the total bill or the minimum payment amount. If for some reason you do not want this insurance, which we have already purchased for you, simply send us a letter to that effect.

Consumer receives this notice and calls you on the phone. He does not want the insurance and asks you what to do. What should he do? Has *Store* violated the Truth-in-Lending Act? Has *Store* violated any other law?

Store includes in its monthly billing statement a flyer describing a set of carving knives, for $39.95. The flyer states: "We are sure you'll agree this is an outstanding value. If you want to buy the set, you need not do anything. We will send it to you and add the cost to your next month's bill. If you do not want to purchase the carving set, simply place an 'x' in the box for that purpose on the billing statement." Is there anything objectionable about *Store's* conduct? Is there anything unlawful about it?

Is the latter hypothetical relevant to the credit insurance problem that precedes it?

4. *Anthony* and *USLIFE Credit* examine whether the creditor has complied with the disclosure provisions of the Truth-in-Lending Act. What other sources of law that you have already studied might be relevant to determining the legality of the creditors' conduct in these cases?

D. EXCESSIVE PRICE

The foregoing problems of voluntariness and excessive coverage are real and continuing. The most vigorously debated aspect of credit insurance, however, is its cost. While group credit insurance is much less expensive than individual credit insurance, group credit insurance is still much more expensive than other group life insurance. Two questions immediately come to mind: why is it more expensive and why don't debtors buy the cheaper regular group life insurance instead of credit insurance?

To answer the latter question first, assume that a consumer borrows $3,000 or buys a video system for $3,000. Assume also that the consumer is to repay the debt in twelve equal monthly installments. For several reasons, the consumer who wants insurance is likely to buy it from the creditor. First, the reason for the consumer's presence in the creditor's place of business is the loan or the video equipment. The insurance is merely incidental to the other, primary transaction. Secondly, the cost of the insurance is rather small, both absolutely and also in comparison either to the amount of credit being extended or to the finance charge. Insurance rates are expressed in terms of dollars of premium per hundred dollars of insurance per year, e.g., $.60/$100/ year. At this rate, the cost of credit life insurance on the consumer in this hypothetical would be $.60 x 30 (100's) x 1 (year), or $18. (Rates for group credit life range from approximately $.30/$100 to over $1/$100.) At an annual percentage rate of 18%, the finance charge would be approximately $300. For most consumers, it is not worth the effort to search for a better price on the insurance. Thirdly, the consumer is unlikely to know that the going rate for regular group life insurance is much less than $.60/$100. And finally, one cannot buy regular group life insurance in the amount of $3,000. It is available only in larger amounts. Hence, even though credit life insurance is more expensive than regular life insurance, consumers desiring insurance in connection with credit transactions inevitably buy it from or through the creditor.[5]

As for the other question, why credit life insurance costs more than regular life insurance, the answer is twofold. The main differences between ordinary group insurance and group credit insurance are that for credit insurance the duration is shorter (coextensive with the extension of credit) and the amount of insurance on each person is smaller. The credit insurance company must charge a higher rate in order to recoup its fixed costs. Moreover, group life insurance is commonly found in the employment

---

5. For larger credit transactions, creditors do not have such a stranglehold on the market. Thus, consumers who borrow money to finance a house and who also desire life insurance commonly purchase insurance from someone other than the creditor.

context, in which the employer pays all or a part of the premiums for insurance on the lives of the employees. The employer also typically absorbs part of the costs of administering the insurance, thereby relieving the insurance company of costs that otherwise would be reflected in the premium.

By far the main reason for the greater expense of credit insurance, however, is the phenomenon of reverse competition. Two aspects of the transaction are primarily responsible for this phenomenon: the purchaser and owner of the group policy is the creditor, not the consumer; and it is not feasible for consumers to shop around for the insurance. Hence, the insurer competes for the business of the creditor, not the consumer, and the creditor may not care how much the insurance costs because the creditor will pass the cost directly on to the consumer. Indeed, the more the insurer charges for the insurance, the more the insurer may pay the creditor for finding people whose lives the insurer may insure. The upshot is that the insurer most likely to get the creditor's business is the one with the *highest* price.

Compensation of the creditor by the insurer occurs in several ways. The insurance company may pay a commission to the creditor, an experience refund based on the amount the insurance company pays out in claims, or both. Compensation also may occur by use of reinsurance.

Reinsurance is designed to distribute the risk of a particular loss over a broader base than just one insurer has. If an insurer does not want to bear the entire risk of a calamity, it may invite another company to share that risk (and the premiums). In the credit insurance area, however, the primary purpose of reinsurance is to put a share of the premiums in the hands of the creditor. The creditor purchases from an independent insurance company a group policy covering the lives of the creditor's customers. The creditor passes the cost on to the customers and sends the premiums to the insurer. The creditor, however, also forms its own insurance company. Instead of operating as a full-fledged insurance company, however, the subsidiary operates as a reinsurer.[6] The independent insurance company enters a contract with the creditor's subsidiary insurance company. Under this contract the independent company agrees to reinsure with the creditor's subsidiary a stated percentage of the insurance that the independent insurer has on the customers of the creditor. Supposedly in exchange for transferring the risk of loss to the creditor's subsidiary, the independent insurance company agrees to pay the creditor's subsidiary a stated percentage, usually about ninety percent, of the premiums it receives from the

---

6. To sell insurance, a company must be licensed in every state in which it does business, and it must conduct its business in compliance with the statutes and regulations of each of those states. These requirements make the business quite complex. A company engaged solely in reinsurance, however, can avoid much of the complexity.

Many creditors have subsidiary or sister corporations in the insurance industry. The automobile manufacturers, for example, long have had both credit and credit insurance subsidiaries. With the ongoing consolidation in the financial services industries, it is even more common than before for a lender and a credit insurance company to be under the same corporate umbrella.

creditor. The independent company retains approximately ten percent of the total premiums as compensation for its administrative, actuarial, and other expenses; the creditor's subsidiary pays the claims out of its ninety percent. If, as has been typical, claims take half of this, the creditor's subsidiary insurance company enjoys a net gain of almost fifty percent of the premiums paid by the creditor's customers.

In addition to these three forms of direct compensation of the creditor, insurance companies may offer indirect forms as well. For example, the insurer may permit the creditor with a group policy to pay the premium on a monthly basis. Since the creditor charges the consumer at the outset for the premium for the entire term of the loan, the creditor has the use of the entire premium until, month by month, it is paid to the insurer.[7]

The amount of compensation to the creditor under any one of these systems may be the same as under the others. The form it takes in a particular case is determined by state law or the historical practices of the parties.

To summarize, then, the benefits to the creditor from credit insurance include a reduction of bad debt loss, payments from the insurer, and in some cases the free use of someone else's money. Receipt of these benefits, of course, does not necessarily mean that the price of credit insurance is too high. But other facts suggest that the price is, indeed, higher than the benefit to the consumer warrants. The cost of credit life insurance is higher than the cost of other group life insurance. And the ratio of the total benefits received by consumers to the total premiums paid by consumers is very different for credit life than for other life insurance. While most regular group life insurance plans return eighty percent or more of premiums in the form of payments on claims, many credit insurers return less than forty percent.[8] More than thirty years ago the NAIC called for a minimum loss ratio of fifty percent, that is, insurers should be required to return half their premium income in the form of insurance benefits. In 1979 the NAIC recommended an increase in the minimum loss ratio to sixty percent. Others think that an even higher loss ratio is appropriate. According to them, the overcharge to consumers exceeds one billion dollars per year.[9] The following materials explore several ways to deal with this problem of excessive prices for credit insurance.

---

7. There are other forms of indirect benefit as well. For example, the insurer may deposit a large sum of money in a non-interest-bearing checking account at a bank that buys insurance from it.

8. For the credit insurance industry as a whole, in 1977 premiums were $1,450,000,000, and death benefits were $508,000,000 for a loss ratio of just over one third. American Council of Life Insurance, Life Insurance Fact Book 41, 57 (1978). See 1979 Hearings at 13 (Statement of James H. Hunt, Massachusetts Division of Insurance) (after properly adjusting for an increase in

reserves, the ratio is 38%). By 1993 the loss ratio had risen to 45%, but since then it has been declining.

9. 1979 Hearings at 13 (Statement of James H. Hunt) (estimate for 1980: $947 million). Senator Metzenbaum, who chaired the subcommittee conducting the hearings, estimated the annual overcharge at $900 million. Id. at 3. In 2001 a study by the Consumer Federation of American and the Center for Economic Justice estimated the overcharge as $2.5 billion. Credit Insurance Overcharges Hit $2.5 Billion Annually, available at www.consumerfed.org/pdfs/credins/pdf.

Robinson v. Rebsamen Ford, Inc.

Supreme Court of Arkansas, 1975.
258 Ark. 935, 530 S.W.2d 660.

FOGELMAN, JUSTICE.

After having repossessed and sold an automobile Robinson had purchased from it on an installment sales contract, Rebsamen Ford, Inc., sued Willie Robinson to recover a deficiency judgment of $901.18. Robinson pleaded usury as an affirmative defense. He alleged that Rebsamen Ford had procured credit life insurance for him for a premium of $36.76, without disclosing to him that comparable insurance could have been purchased at a much cheaper price under Ford Life Insurance Group Policy No. 2200 and that he would have selected this policy if given an opportunity to do so. He also alleged that Rebsamen Ford was paid 35% of the premium charged to him on the insurance procured but no commission would have been paid to it on the Ford Life Insurance group policy. He alleged that the compensation derived by Rebsamen Ford, when added to the interest otherwise charged, produced a rate of return to Rebsamen Ford of more than 10% per annum and made the contract void for usury. This appeal comes from a summary judgment granted on the motion of Rebsamen Ford. Since we agree with Robinson that there was a material fact issue, we reverse.

Most of the critical facts were admitted. Rebsamen Ford could have procured coverage for Robinson under Ford Life Insurance Group Policy No. 2200 at a cost of 44 cents per $100 of credit per annum, while the insurance obtained came at a premium of 75 cents per $100 of credit per annum, or $36.76, from which Rebsamen Ford was paid a commission of $12.87. Of this commission, $6.56 was refunded by Rebsamen Ford when Robinson defaulted on the installment sales contract.

.   .   .

In his response to the motion for summary judgment, Robinson incorporated the affidavit of Keith Sloan, the life and health actuary of the Arkansas Insurance Department, who stated that his duties included approval of forms and rates and processing of statistics relating to credit life insurance. He deposed that benefits identical to those obtained by Robinson in the policy issued were offered at a cheaper price by eight insurance companies. He also stated that the principal difference in the cost of the policy Robinson was issued and Ford Life Group Policy No. 2200 was attributable to the compensation allowed to the agent and that the differences in eligibility for coverage and risks covered by the two policies were considered minor by the industry and the Insurance Department.

Robinson's own affidavit was to the effect that he was not informed by Rebsamen Ford that he could have obtained a less expensive policy which provided the same benefits as the one by which he was covered. Otherwise, Robinson voluntarily elected to take the insurance issued. It was admitted that several of appellee's employees, including members of its sales and clerical staffs possessed some information concerning costs and benefits of credit life insurance. The installment sales contract recites that the finance charge, calculated on the unpaid portion of the purchase price and the insurance issued, was calculated on the basis of 10% per annum.

Appellee's and the circuit court's reliance upon Poole v. Bates–Pearson Auto Sales, 257 Ark. 764, 520 S.W.2d 273, is misplaced because of the difference in the factual situations. There we held that an automobile sales contract was not rendered usurious by the mere fact that the automobile dealer received compensation from the insurance carrier for issuance of credit life insurance voluntarily taken by its purchaser, where there was no contention that the insurance charge was excessive. We carefully pointed out in *Poole* that there was no difference in purchasing the insurance from the dealer and in purchasing it from some other company in that there was no showing that the premium would have been less if purchased elsewhere. We emphasized that in such a situation no unlawful profit was involved.

. . .

The affidavits of Sloan and Robinson are clearly sufficient to show the existence of a material issue of fact. They are not controverted and must be taken as true. If, indeed, Robinson was not informed by Rebsamen Ford that he was eligible for and could elect a cheaper policy affording substantially the same benefits as that he took, the fact that the seller of the automobile also received a commission as an insurance agent on the policy taken but would not have received anything for obtaining the cheaper policy and the difference in cost was largely attributable to the commission to the seller would constitute substantial evidence from which the fact finder might find that the collateral transaction was a cloak for usury. We have recognized that an insurance agreement can be a cloak or device for the evasion of the usury laws. Our result in this case is influenced to some degree but not controlled by the public policy statements contained in Ark.Stat.Ann. § 66–3029. Under that section, it is declared that it is the public policy of the state that life insurance agents and solicitors are charged with the responsibility of exercising discretion and good faith in a sales presentation or transaction.

. . .

The judgment is reversed and the cause remanded for further proceedings consistent with this opinion.

QUESTIONS

1. The court purports to reconcile its conclusion here with its earlier conclusion in Poole v. Bates–Pearson Auto Sales that the receipt by a creditor of compensation from a credit insurance company does not render a loan usurious. What is the critical difference between the two cases?

2. In light of *Robinson* and *Poole*, what would you advise your creditor clients to do to avoid usury? If you represented a consumer who had paid

$.75/$100 for credit life insurance, what would you try to prove when the creditor sued your client for defaulting on a loan?

3. In In re Dickson, 432 F.Supp. 752 (W.D.N.C.1977), plaintiffs and their trustee in bankruptcy sued a lender for violation of the Truth-in-Lending Act and the North Carolina little-FTC act. With respect to the latter, the court stated:

> 1. Defendant is a subsidiary of a bank holding company. As a result, it is subject to the Bank Holding Company Act, 12 U.S.C. § 1841 et seq., and Regulation Y, 12 C.F.R. § 225.1 et seq. Section 225.4(a)(9) gives bank holding companies, themselves or through their subsidiaries, the authority to sell credit life insurance. In amending Regulation Y to extend this authority, the Federal Reserve Board expressed the expectation that any bank holding company or subsidiary that extends credit insurance pursuant to this authority will exercise a fiduciary responsibility to the purchaser. 36 Fed. Register 15526 (8/17/71). Thus, defendant may fairly be considered a fiduciary of plaintiff for the purposes of the sale of credit life insurance in question.

> The evidence discloses that defendant charged the Dicksons a premium roughly twice as high as a premium considered adequate by the North Carolina Insurance Commissioner, and received a 25% rebate as a commission.

> North Carolina General Statutes § 53–180(g) prohibits unfair and deceptive trade practices in the conduct of defendant's business. The court concludes that selling credit insurance at inflated premiums, receiving a 25% commission, and failing to disclose these facts, while in a fiduciary relationship with the borrower, constitutes an unfair and deceptive trade practice within the meaning of the statute.

Id. at 760–61. This passage suggests another basis for attacking the sale of insurance at great profit to the creditor. What basis does the court cite for holding the creditor to be a fiduciary with respect to its customers? Is the principle limited to bank holding companies? Is the court's holding limited to situations in which the creditor sells insurance at a cost in excess of the sanctioned rate?

Browder v. Hanley Dawson Cadillac Co.

Court of Appeals of Illinois, 1978.
62 Ill.App.3d 623, 20 Ill.Dec. 138, 379 N.E.2d 1206.

LORENZ, JUSTICE, delivered the opinion of the court as modified on denial of the petition for rehearing:

Plaintiffs brought separate actions on their own behalf and on behalf of all others similarly situated seeking injunctive relief, damages, and attorneys fees. The two complaints, which are substantially the same, alleged that defendants had acted improperly in selling plaintiffs credit life and disability insurance. . . . Because of the identity of issues on appeal we have consolidated these cases. On appeal, plaintiffs in both cases contend that the trial court erred in granting defendants' motions to dismiss, arguing that the two complaints state valid causes of action.

. . . Tyrone and Lucille Browder alleged that they purchased a used 1970 Cadillac from Hanley Dawson on April 8, 1974, for $2,661. They entered into a retail installment contract whereby they paid $800 cash and financed the balance with General Motors Acceptance Corporation (GMAC) over 24 months. As part of the financing agreement they purchased credit life insurance through Hanley Dawson at a cost of $43.53 and credit disability insurance at a cost of $93.72. GMAC assessed them $732.05 as finance charges, a 24.99% annual rate.

. . .

The premium charged for the life insurance in all three instances was based on a rate of $0.65 per $100 of initial insurance per annum. Of the total premiums charged plaintiffs, the car dealers retained 40%.

The crux of both complaints is that Hanley Dawson and C. James as General Motors dealers failed to inform plaintiffs that a cheaper but comparable Prudential policy ($0.375 per $100) was available through them. . . .

In Count II of both complaints plaintiffs alleged that C. James and Hanley Dawson violated their common law fiduciary duty as insurance brokers and the Consumer Fraud and Deceptive Business Practices Act [815 Ill. Consol. Stat. § 505/1 et seq.] when they failed to disclose the availability of and offer the cheaper, but comparable, Prudential life insurance policy. They request as damages all charges for insurance in excess of that which would have been imposed for Prudential insurance.

Determination of the common law portion of Count II requires an analysis of whether C. James and Hanley Dawson are insurance brokers, and if so, whether they were acting as agents for plaintiffs.

As purveyors of insurance defendants are either insurance agents or insurance brokers. An insurance broker has been defined as:

> * * * one who procures insurance and acts as middleman between the insured and the insurer, and solicits insurance business from the public under no employment from any special company, but, having secured an order, places the insurance with the company selected by the insured, or, in the absence of any selection by him, with the company selected by such broker. 22 ILP Insurance § 71, at 102.

An insurance broker is distinguished from an insurance agent in that he is not permanently employed by any principal, but holds himself out to employment by the public. His employment in each case is that of a special agent for a single object.

Whether a person is an insurance agent or an insurance broker is determined by his acts and is dependent upon who called him into action, who controls his movement, who pays him and whose interests he represents.

If it is determined that Hanley Dawson and C. James are insurance brokers rather than insurance agents, it will be necessary to determine whether they were acting as agents for the insureds. The term "agent" here is to be distinguished from "insurance agent." Although there is support for the proposition that an insurance broker is by definition an agent of the insured, whether a broker is an agent for the insured, the insurer or both is actually a question of fact. While a broker usually represents the insured, he may become the agent of the insurer or even of both parties. Accordingly, the court must closely examine the facts in each case to determine whether a seller of insurance is an agent or broker and to whom he may owe a duty.

. . . From this analysis it is obvious that whether C. James and Hanley Dawson were brokers acting as agents on plaintiffs' behalf is not a question of law to be determined solely from the pleadings. Rather, this determination can only be made after a full hearing. Accordingly, we must remand the common law allegations of Count II for further proceedings.

Should the facts prove C. James and Hanley Dawson to be agents of the insureds, they would be governed by the principles of agency law in which the relationship between principal and agent is fiduciary in character. In all transactions affecting the subject of the agency the law dictates that an agent must act in utmost good faith and must make known to his principal all material facts within his knowledge which may in any way affect the transaction and the subject matter of his agency. Certainly price must be considered a material fact. In Janes v. First Federal Savings and Loan Association of Berwyn (1974), 57 Ill.2d 398, 312 N.E.2d 605, the Supreme Court held that defendant's failure to disclose to plaintiff borrower, in an accounting of loan proceeds, that it had obtained a 10% rebate on funds disbursed to the title insurance company was a violation of fiduciary duty.

Similarly here, if C. James and Hanley Dawson are shown to be agents of plaintiffs, then failure to disclose the availability of comparable lower cost insurance would be a breach of fiduciary duty.

C. James and Hanley Dawson contend, however, that it is legally impossible for a used car dealer to be a fiduciary. They argue that as a fiduciary a car dealer would be required to disclose the profit made on the sale of the car, on the sale of any trade-in, on the financing of the purchase price and on the sale of any insurance. However, more is involved here than a mere buyer-seller relationship which might not of itself give rise to a fiduciary duty. Merely because defendants here operate two businesses under one roof does not mean that the standards of selling cars must apply to selling insurance. When defendant car dealers sell insurance the common law duties of either insurance brokers or insurance agents apply. Thus, it is possible defendant car dealers might owe a fiduciary duty to customers who buy insurance.

Defendant car dealers also argue that because a fiduciary cannot accept a commission from third parties (Janes v. First Federal) but an insurance broker must receive his commission from the insurance company (except in very limited circumstances not applicable here) (Ill. Rev.Stat.1973, ch. 73, par. 1065.40), an insurance broker cannot, as a matter of law, be a fiduciary of the insured. We disagree. Although the above section of the Insurance Code requires a broker to deduct his commission from the premiums, it does not otherwise relieve a broker of his common law obligations as agent of the insured.

In the statutory portion of Count II, plaintiffs allege that C. James and Hanley Dawson violated the Consumer Fraud and Deceptive Business Practices Act. Section 2 of the Act prohibits:

> * * * the use * * * of any * * * misrepresentation or the concealment, suppression or omission of any material fact, with the intent that others rely upon the concealment, suppression or omission of such material fact, * * *.

Plaintiffs argue that C. James and Hanley Dawson were concealing, suppressing or omitting a material fact in failing to disclose the cheaper insurance.

Because of the relatively recent passage of section 2 of Consumer Fraud [Act], there is little Illinois case law interpreting this section. However, we note that Matter of Dickson (W.D.N.C.1977), 432 F.Supp. 752, considered the issue raised here in reference to a North Carolina statute (N.C.G.S. 53–180(g)) which prohibits unfair or deceptive trade practices in making loans to borrowers. There the court concluded that:

> "[S]elling credit insurance at inflated premiums, receiving a 25% commission, and failing to disclose these facts, while in a fiduciary relationship with the borrower constitutes an unfair and deceptive trade practice within the meaning of the statute." Matter of Dickson, at 761.

We agree and therefore hold that the statutory allegation in Count II states a cause of action.

Defendant car dealers argue that the *Dickson* decision was the result of the totality of circumstances in that case. However, the circumstances were: (1) the failure to disclose to the borrower that he could procure credit insurance from other sources, (2) the failure to disclose to him that defendant made a commission on the sale of the insurance, and (3) charging an excessive premium for insurance. All these factors are alleged in the instant case.

. . .

For the foregoing reasons the judgment of the circuit court dismissing . . . Counts II . . . in both complaints is reversed and . . . remanded for further proceedings not inconsistent with the opinions expressed herein.

QUESTIONS

1. What facts would be relevant to determining whether the creditor is a broker or an insurance agent? Indeed, even if the creditor is a broker, does it necessarily follow that the creditor is the agent of the consumer? If not, what facts would be relevant to determining whether the creditor-broker is an agent of the consumer or an agent of the insurer?

2.   The court in *Browder* implies that the North Carolina court's interpretation of the North Carolina statute in *Dickson* supports the result in the case at hand. Does it?

What if the creditor has a contract with only one insurer: would the imposition of fiduciary status on the creditor mean that the creditor's failure to disclose that other insurance companies write credit life insurance at lower rates is a violation of the Illinois statute? Compare carefully the language of the two statutes.

3.   The imposition of a fiduciary obligation on the creditor may also occur in contexts other than the sale of credit insurance. For example, mortgage lenders typically require the borrower to buy title insurance. The lender, however, selects the title company and pays the bill, later collecting reimbursement from the borrower by deducting the amount paid as part of the closing costs of the loan. What if the title company pays the lender a commission for producing a customer or offers the lender a "prompt payment" discount? In Janes v. First Federal Savings and Loan Association, 312 N.E.2d 605 (Ill.1974), the court held that the lender was a fiduciary of the borrower. The court stated:

> The loan statement furnished to the plaintiffs by Berwyn [the lender] recited the total amount of the loan that had been made to them and the purpose and amount of each of the disbursements which they authorized Berwyn to make from that fund. It contained the following statement to be signed by the plaintiffs and by Berwyn: "The undersigned acknowledge the receipt and correctness of this Loan Statement and authorize and ratify the disbursement of the funds as shown above."
>
>   .   .   .
>
> The appellate court considered the possibility of the existence and breach of a trust, but rejected any right to recover on such a theory on the ground that "the relationship of mortgagor and mortgagee does not of itself show the existence of a confidential or fiduciary relationship." More is involved here, however, than a relationship of mortgagor and mortgagee "of itself," and in our opinion count I of the complaint alleges a fiduciary relationship. The loan statement attached to the complaint is an accounting by Berwyn for its disposition of the money which the plaintiffs had borrowed from it. The statement recites the amount borrowed by the plaintiffs, and it contains their authorization to Berwyn to make specific dispositions of that sum of money. Any disposition of those funds for a purpose other than as authorized by the plaintiffs was improper and a violation by Berwyn of the duty which it owed to the plaintiffs. With respect to the sum designated as title charges, the plaintiffs authorized Berwyn to pay . . . Chicago Title. They did not authorize Berwyn to retain any portion of either

amount for itself, whether by way of discount or rebate. . . . Restatement of Restitution, Section 197, states:

Sec. 197.   Bonus or Commission Received by Fiduciary

Where a fiduciary in violation of his duty to the beneficiary receives or retains a bonus or commission or other profit, he holds what he receives upon a constructive trust for the beneficiary.

Comment:

a.   *Bribes and commissions.* The rule stated in this Section is applicable not only where the fiduciary receives something in the nature of a bribe given him by a third person in order to induce him to violate his duty as fiduciary, but also where something is given to him and received by him in good faith, if it was received for an act done by him in connection with the performance of his duties as fiduciary. Thus, if a trustee, or corporate officer, or an agent entrusted with the management of property insures the property in a company of which he is an agent, and he receives from the company a commission for placing the insurance, he is accountable for the commission so received and holds it upon a constructive trust for his beneficiary.

* * *

c.   *Where no harm to beneficiary.* The rule stated in this Section is applicable although the profit received by the fiduciary is not at the expense of the beneficiary. Thus, where an agent to purchase property for his principal acts properly in making the purchase but subsequently receives a bonus from the seller, he holds the money received upon a constructive trust for his principal. The rule stated in this Section, like those stated in the other Sections in this Chapter, is not based on harm done to the beneficiary in the particular case, but rests upon a broad principle of preventing a conflict of opposing interests in the minds of fiduciaries, whose duty it is to act solely for the benefit of their beneficiaries.

And the Restatement (Second) of Agency, section 388 states:

Sec. 388.   Duty to Account for Profits Arising out of Employment.

Unless otherwise agreed, an agent who makes a profit in connection with transactions conducted by him on behalf of the principal is under a duty to give such profit to the principal.

Comment:

a.   Ordinarily, the agent's primary function is to make profits for the principal, and his duty to account includes accounting for any unexpected and incidental accretions whether or not received in violation of duty.

. . .

Illustrations:

. . .

3. A, acting for P, takes out insurance on P's premises, advancing the amount of the premium and having the insurance taken in his own name to secure his advances. The insurance company declares a rebate or dividend upon the premiums paid. A is under a duty to credit this to P in spite of a contrary usage among insurance agents, not known to P.

We hold that count I stated a cause of action for breach of fiduciary duty with respect to the title insurance Berwyn procured in behalf of the plaintiffs.

Id. at 609–11.[10]

4. Is it really appropriate to view the creditor as a fiduciary? Does the creditor occupy a position of trust and confidence? Sellers generally do not occupy a fiduciary relationship with their customers. Is the court in *Browder* correct in asserting that the standards that apply to selling cars do not necessarily apply to defendant's sale of credit insurance?

The National Commission on Consumer Finance recognized the possibility of viewing the creditor as a fiduciary. See NCCF, Consumer Credit in the United States 287 n.23 (1972):

An interesting approach to regulating insurance rates is making the creditor a "fiduciary" of the debtor. The Commission considered this approach but decided against adopting it. Basically, the idea would require a creditor offering credit insurance to act as a fiduciary *vis-à-vis* the debtor as regards the insurance. This would call for his obtaining the "best buy" in insurance for the debtor and for his accounting to the debtor for any profits beyond a reasonable fiduciary fee. Apart from administrative problems that seem obvious, the Commission believes that this approach would be impractical. In a sales credit transaction, for example, the creditor is not considered a fiduciary concerning the price or quality of the goods, nor is he considered a fiduciary concerning the finance charge. Since the credit insurance charge is always the smallest dollar item of a typical sales credit transaction, it would not be feasible to create a new legal obligation for that item alone.

Obviously, the Illinois court does not agree. Who is correct?

5. Problem. *Consumer* wishes to finance the purchase of her house by borrowing $60,000 from *Bank*. During the negotiations, the loan officer

---

10. On the other hand, in La Throp v. Bell Federal Savings and Loan Association, 370 N.E.2d 188 (Ill.1977), the same court held in a 4–3 decision that where a borrower contracts to pay a lender monthly installments that the lender is to aggregate and use to pay taxes and insurance premiums, the lender is not a fiduciary. Therefore, the lender has no obligation to account to the debtor for any earnings of the lender on the escrowed amounts. Contra, Carpenter v. Suffolk Franklin Savings Bank, 291 N.E.2d 609 (Mass.1973); Buchanan v. Brentwood Federal Savings and Loan Association, 320 A.2d 117 (Pa.1974).

asks whether *Consumer* wants credit life insurance, and she says yes. In preparing the loan documents, however, the loan officer fails to check off the box signifying that *Consumer* wants the insurance, and the payment terms are calculated without including any insurance premium. *Consumer* pays regularly for several years, then dies. If *Bank* never procured insurance and never charged *Consumer* for it, is *Bank* liable to *Consumer's* estate for breach of fiduciary duty?

Now assume that during the negotiations, neither *Consumer* nor the loan officer mentions credit life insurance. At the closing, *Consumer* signs loan documents that contain spaces for indicating the cost of credit life insurance and whether or not the borrower wants to purchase it, but these spaces are entirely blank. *Consumer* pays regularly for several years, then dies. Is *Bank* liable to *Consumer's* estate for breach of fiduciary duty?

For a good discussion of the role and responsibility of lenders in connection with credit life insurance, see Budnitz, The Sale of Credit Life Insurance: The Bank as Fiduciary, 62 N.C.L.Rev. 295 (1984).

6. The consumer may be able to recover even without establishing a fiduciary relationship. In Fitzgerald v. Chicago Title & Trust Co., 380 N.E.2d 790 (Ill.1978), plaintiffs invoked the little-FTC act to challenge the title company's payment to the creditor. The court stated:

> The complaint alleges that by the payment of commissions, discounts, allowances or credits "to savings and loan associations, banks, real estate brokers, attorneys and other persons, firms or corporations acting as agents, representatives or intermediaries for and on behalf of plaintiffs and members of plaintiffs' class" and the intentional, deliberate and deceptive concealment and failure to disclose that such payments were made, defendant had engaged in an "unfair method of competition and unfair and deceptive trade practice." The complaint alleges further that invoices submitted by defendant enumerated "customary buyers' charges" and "customary sellers' charges" and that plaintiffs, who did not know that defendant had made the rebates, discounts or allowances, paid the amounts shown in the invoices, and were not reimbursed; that plaintiffs were required to pay unreasonable and unnecessary charges for defendant's services and as the result suffered damages. Under the facts alleged, if defendant's actions were taken with the intent that others rely upon the invoices which did not disclose the fact that a rebate was being paid, and plaintiffs paid charges which they may have been entitled to recoup from their respective agents (see Janes v. First Federal Savings & Loan), the complaint states a cause of action under section 2 of the Consumer Fraud and Deceptive Business Practices Act.

Id. at 794–95. But see Perrin v. Pioneer National Title Insurance Co., 404 N.E.2d 508 (Ill.App.1980) (title insurer does not violate the Act by failing to disclose that it charges lower prices to developers than to consumers).

7. The court in *Janes* (Question 3 supra) refers to agency principles as well as fiduciary principles. In Lucas v. Continental Casualty Co., 170

S.E.2d 856 (Ga.App.1969), plaintiff bought a car from Smith Motors. In discussing credit insurance, plaintiff told the salesman about his heart condition. According to plaintiff, the salesman assured him that he would nevertheless be covered by health and accident insurance that Smith Motors offered its customers. When plaintiff suffered a heart attack, the insurer refused to pay, alleging that the policy expressly excluded disability resulting from pre-existing conditions. Plaintiff sued, but the trial court rendered summary judgment for the insurer. The appellate court reversed and remanded, holding that plaintiff could recover upon proving that the salesman who sold him the car and the insurance was an agent of the insurer and that the salesman had waived the exclusionary provision. Accord, Union Security Life Ins. Co. v. Crocker, 667 So.2d 688 (Ala.1995), modified, 709 So.2d 1118 (Ala.1997). Cf. South Branch Valley National Bank v. Williams, 155 S.E.2d 845 (W.Va.1967) (bank's employee is not the agent of the insurer, so the insurer is not liable under a policy issued to an ineligible debtor).

Statutory and Administrative Price Controls

As recommended by the NAIC, several states require credit life insurers to adopt premium rates that produce a loss ratio of at least fifty or sixty percent. Most of these states also have adopted a so-called "prima facie" rate, which insurers may use until they have generated enough claims experience in the state to permit a determination of the actual rate necessary to produce the required loss ratio. Other states have simply set a maximum rate, without any reference to loss ratio.

These approaches—setting maximum rates and setting minimum loss ratios—have both practical and theoretical problems. Because of reverse competition, any maximum rate soon becomes the standard rate, with few insurers having lower rates. Thus, when a state promulgated a maximum rate that was higher than the rate that a particular creditor and its insurer had been charging, the creditor insisted that the insurer increase the rate, so that the insurer could increase its payments to the creditor.[11]

A second problem with establishing maximum rates is that it is impossible to determine the "proper" rate. Insurance companies may have differing claims costs and differing degrees of efficiency. A rate appropriate for an efficient company with average claims experience may be too low for a less efficient company with higher-than-average claims. Low rates may result in a concentration of the credit insurance business into a relatively small number of companies. On the other hand, if rates are set high enough for the survival of less efficient companies, the more efficient insurers can charge more than is necessary to induce them to write credit life insurance.

---

11. Hearings on Credit Insurance Before the Subcomm. on Antitrust and Monopoly of the Sen. Comm. on the Judiciary, 90th Cong., 1st Sess. 2427–28 (testimony of Lawrence M. Cathles, Jr., Aetna Life Insurance Co.) (hereinafter cited as 1967 Hearings).

The rates for credit life insurance set by state legislatures or by state insurance commissioners vary from less than $.40/$100 of initial indebtedness (e.g., California and New York)[12] to $1/$100 of initial indebtedness (e.g., Alabama and Louisiana). The maximum rate in most states is in the $.60–.75 range. Some large companies do very little business in the high-rate states because they are unwilling to charge at or near the maximum rate and creditors are unwilling to do business with them at lower rates.

The minimum-loss-ratio method of price control has its difficulties, too. On the practical side is the problem of inadequate enforcement resources. For the loss ratio method to be effective, there must be periodic inspection and review of the experience of each credit insurance company doing business in the state. This review has not occurred. Consequently, of ten loss-ratio states surveyed in the mid-to-late 1970s, only one had an overall loss ratio over fifty percent (and that state had a mechanism for automatically lowering rates when a company's loss ratio with a particular creditor fell below fifty percent.)[13]

Another difficulty with the loss-ratio approach is selecting the appropriate ratio for the standard. And that difficulty leads to the heart of the problem. Mortality statistics reveal that benefits pursuant to credit life insurance run approximately $.25 per $100 of initial indebtedness.[14] At a loss ratio of fifty percent, the maximum premium rate would be $.50/$100,[15] leaving $.25/$100 for the insurance company's other expenses and its profit. At a loss ratio of sixty percent, the maximum rate would be approximately $.42, leaving $.17 for the insurer. And at a loss ratio of eighty percent, which is the prevailing rate in Canada, the maximum rate would be approximately $.31, leaving $.06 for the insurer. Cost data for insurance companies, as well as the Canadian experience, suggest that insurance companies will write the insurance even if they are receiving only $.06–.15/$100 to cover their non-mortality expenses and their profits. As the premium approaches the $.25 mortality figure, however, there is less and less available for the insurance company to pay to the creditor for the creditor's role in the sale of the insurance. Thus the issue is, to what extent should the creditor be permitted to receive compensation for its role in the sale of insurance?

12. In an effort to account for differing levels of costs and efficiency, several states, including California and New York, have "decremental" rates—the actual rate depends on the total volume of the insurer or on the size of the group policy written. So the maximum charge for insuring the customers of a large bank or auto dealer is lower than the maximum charge for insuring the customers of a small appliance store or a small finance company.

13. 1979 Hearings at 49, 50–51 (Statement of Robert A. Sable, National Consumer Law Center). In forty states the maximum rates were too high to produce a loss ratio of fifty percent. This was still true in 2000, according to a study co-sponsored by the Consumer Federation of America (cited in footnote 9, page 565 supra).

14. Id. at 49.

15. Actually, the proper rate would be slightly less than $.50/$100 because, inter alia, the premiums are paid in full in advance. See 1979 Hearings at 13 (Statement of James H. Hunt, Massachusetts Division of Insurance).

The answers range from one extreme to the other. Creditors and insurers have argued that creditors are in business to make a profit. The creditor performs a valuable marketing function for the insurer and, just like an ordinary insurance agent, is entitled to be paid for that service. The creditor also performs numerous administrative services.[16] And, they argue, since the insurance is separate and distinct from the credit, one who sells it is entitled to profit from the sale of it.[17] One proponent of this view

16. One insurance company executive described the tasks of the creditor as follows:

The creditor is trained to explain the coverage to the debtor and if the debtor desires the coverage, the creditor must prepare and complete a single premium policy or group certificate which must reflect the name of the debtor—the amount of insurance—the effective date of coverage—the scheduled term of the coverage—the scheduled termination date of the coverage—the amount of the premium or identifiable insurance charge separately for credit life and credit disability insurance—the amount of monthly disability indemnity and the name of the second beneficiary, if any. In the event of a refund, the creditor is required to calculate the refund and pay or credit same to the debtor or his account and we require that a signed request and acknowledgment of refund be secured by the creditor from the debtor. The creditor is also required, on a weekly, semimonthly or monthly basis, depending on the size of the account, to compute the total premium due and forward same along with all the above information relating to the individual coverages to American National. In the event of a claim, the creditor is required to furnish the necessary claim forms and secure all the necessary information and forward same to us for the payment, settlement or adjustment thereof. The creditor is also required to get all the necessary supplemental information which we may require in connection with a claim and forward same to us with necessary correspondence in answer to our questions in connection therewith. The creditor is also required to pay for any special rate and refund charts in order to help reduce the number of errors in the improper calculation thereof. In the event the insurance proceeds exceed the amount of unpaid indebtedness, we prepare a sepa-

rate check for the named second beneficiary or estate and forward same to the creditor for delivery to the proper party. The creditor is further required to secure and forward proof of continuing disability each month for disabled debtors in connection with their credit disability coverage. In addition, the creditor is required to handle the necessary correspondence and make all the necessary adjustments resulting from the hundreds of errors we find each month as outlined above.

1969 Hearings at 192–93 (Statement of Ronald Roberts, American National Insurance Co.). See also 1967 Hearings at 2550–51 (Statement of Oscar A. Lundin, General Motors Acceptance Corp.); In re Local Finance Corp., 48 T.C. 773, 797 (dissenting opinion) (1967).

17. According to an executive of the Iowa Automobile Dealers Association,

any agency selling credit or other insurance, whether it be a dealership or other, is entitled to a sales commission for the services performed.

There is a common saying that a successful meatpacker must profitably utilize all of the parts of a pig except the squeal. In the highly competitive field of automotive retailing in Iowa, the same analogy applies. Therefore, the board and staff of the Iowa Automobile Dealers Association . . . are continuously urged by the membership to explore every merchandising avenue reasonably related to the retail sale and servicing of motor vehicles that will assist all members in improving their profits and, at the same time, offer better services and more convenience to their customers.

1967 Hearings at 2596 (Statement of Alfred W. Kahl).

Indeed, a representative of one creditor who agreed that a fifty percent loss ratio was

analogized the creditor to an automobile dealer whom all agree is entitled to a profit on the radios, air conditioning, and other options and accessories sold in connection with new cars.[18] Finally, insurers are concerned about the adverse impact on their business if creditors do not receive any compensation. They fear creditors would no longer sell as much credit insurance as they have been.[19] A decrease in sales would of course decrease the insurer's income, but the decrease might be magnified by the phenomenon of adverse selection—creditors would tend to focus their efforts to sell insurance on those customers whom they believed were most likely to die or become disabled. Since the insurer would be insuring primarily the poorest risks, insurance rates would have to increase, perhaps to a level even higher than current rates.

On the other hand, there is a case to be made against compensation of creditors by insurers. When credit insurance first became available, creditors insured their customers without passing on any separate, identifiable charge. Some banks and credit unions still do this. These consumers have no choice about the insurance, but the cost of it is reflected in the finance charge, which they may compare with the finance charge of competing creditors. Opponents of creditor compensation emphasize the benefits to the creditor of having insurance on the lives and health of consumers. An executive of a credit insurance company estimated that credit life insurance enables creditors to collect approximately $100 million per year of otherwise uncollectible debts.[20] This suggests that it is in the interest of creditors to make insurance available to their customers even if they do not receive any compensation from the insurer.[21]

Another argument for opposing creditor compensation focuses on the relationship between creditor and consumer with respect to insurance. As a practical matter, the consumer cannot shop around elsewhere for insurance, so the creditor has a captive market. Notwithstanding the Truth-in-

appropriate also argued that a lower ratio was also acceptable: "The prima facie rate in effect is the retail selling price that has been given the blessing of the insurance department. Being in the profit business under a free enterprise system, we see nothing wrong in selling at this rate." Id. at 2446 (Testimony of Elliott Taylor, Pacific Finance Corp.).

18. E.g., 1967 Hearings at 2588 (Testimony of Robert S. Olson, Ford Motor Credit Company).

19. Id. at 2156 (Testimony of Ronald Roberts, American National Life Insurance Co.).

20. 1969 Hearings at 186 (Statement of Ronald Roberts, American National Insurance Co.).

21. Credit insurance may be analogous to group life insurance sold to employers on their employees. Employers perceive this as a benefit for their employees and provide it as a fringe benefit. Employers do not insist on any compensation from the insurance companies, and they do not pass the cost on to their employees. Consequently, the rates are much lower than the rates for credit insurance. Creditors and insurers attack this analogy. They point out that for credit insurance the average amount of insurance is much less, the average duration of insurance is much shorter, and the administrative and other burdens of the owner of the policy (viz., the creditor) much greater. E.g., see 1969 Hearings at 120–21 (Statement of Robert N. Tyler, Old Republic Life Insurance Co.). In emphasizing that employers absorb the expense of insurance on their employees because it helps attract and keep good employees, these proponents evidently ignore the benefit to creditors in obtaining insurance on the lives of their customers.

Lending Act disclosures, the consumer may be unaware that insurance is part of the deal[22] or may believe that the prospects for obtaining credit will be enhanced by agreeing to purchase insurance. These are the facts that led to the notion, not yet widely accepted by the courts, that the creditor is a fiduciary of the consumer. They also support the proposition that the creditor ought not receive compensation from the insurer.[23]

If the decision is to regulate the compensation that the insurer pays the creditor for the creditor's role in the sale of credit insurance, there are several ways to do it. Two methods already have been described: set the maximum premium for credit insurance at a low enough figure (e.g., $.35–.40) or mandate a high enough loss ratio (e.g., 80–85%)[24] to preclude the insurer from paying much, if anything, to the creditor. Cf. UCCC § 4.203(2). But there are other possible approaches as well.

One of these other approaches is to limit directly the amount of compensation that the insurer may pay the creditor. As of 1979, half the states had done this.[25] But of these, half set the limit at forty percent of the premium paid by the consumer, and several set it at fifty percent. In only one state was the limit as low as twenty-five percent. Another approach, focusing on issuers of group policies, is to prohibit the insurer from paying experience refunds to the creditor. The creditor, however, can evade this prohibition by forming its own insurance company and using a program of reinsurance.[26] Alternatively, states could prohibit creditors from making any identifiable charge to consumers for insurance premiums. Then whatever part of the cost that the creditor wanted to pass on to the consumer

---

22. More than a third of consumers may misperceive the existence of credit insurance. Huber, Consumer Perception of Credit Insurance on Retail Purchases, Monograph No. 13, Credit Research Center, Purdue University (1978) (of two retailers' credit cardholders, 25% erroneously believed they had purchased insurance); Coapstick & Geistfeld, Retail Credit Users' Awareness of Their Credit Insurance Coverage, 13 J.Cons.Aff. 311 (1979) (37% were unaware that they had purchased insurance). More recent surveys are consistent with these.

23. The Michigan Motor Vehicle Sales Finance Act prohibits the payment to or receipt by a car dealer of any portion of any insurance premium. Mich. Comp. L. § 492.131(c). To evade this prohibition, some dealers or their family members established insurance agencies for the purpose of selling a group policy—issued by a bona fide credit insurance company—to the dealership. Credit insurance companies arranged to set up the separate dealer-related insurance agency. Each agency sold only one policy, viz., to the dealer who controlled it. The insurance company paid commissions to the dealer-related

insurance agency. Acknowledging that an insurance agency may be truly independent of a car dealer, even if owned by a family member, the Michigan Attorney General opined that if the dealer controls or manages the insurance agency, there is a violation of the statute. Op. Mich. Atty. Gen. No. 6630 (1990).

24. These examples contemplate credit life insurance. For credit disability insurance, the maximum premium would be higher and the minimum loss ratio would be lower.

25. See 1979 Hearings at 134. The Supreme Court of Oklahoma has held, however, that consumers have no private remedy under the UCCC or the insurance laws against an insurance company that exceeds the commission limit. Jennings v. Globe Life & Acc. Ins. Co., 922 P.2d 622 (Okla.1996) (UCCC §§ 4.104, 5.202, 6.113 only permit recovery from a creditor for overcharges by the creditor).

26. For other approaches, see 1967 Hearings at 2434–35 (Statement of L.M. Cathles, Jr., Aetna Life Insurance Co.).

would have to be included within the overall finance charge. Some small loan acts have taken this approach by providing that beyond the finance charge permitted by the statute, there may be no additional charges whatsoever.[27]

QUESTIONS

1. The Executive Director of the National Consumer Law Center has stated,

> It's fashionable to say that there are no simple solutions. In credit life insurance, I don't think that is true. By prohibiting a separate charge for credit insurance as is already done with credit unions nearly every problem in credit life insurance would disappear.
>
> If a creditor believed that credit insurance should be offered because of its benefits to the creditor, its customer or both, the creditor could offer it. The cost would be another business expense. Instead of seeking the most expensive insurance the creditor would have the normal incentives to seek the cheapest insurance. Obviously, the incentive to provide excess insurance would also disappear.
>
> To the extent that the cost of the insurance raised creditor costs significantly the creditor could increase the cost of its product by raising interest rates just as it might if its salaries or other insurance costs increased. But this rise in costs, which would be reflected in the creditor's annual percentage rate disclosed in its Truth in Lending statement, would be visible to consumers, not hidden in the fine print.

1979 Hearings at 57 (Statement of Robert A. Sable). This solution contemplates the enactment or revision of federal statutes. Is such a "simple solution" available to each of the states? Specifically, what interrelationship would there be between the state law prohibiting a separate, identifiable charge and the Truth-in-Lending Act?

2. If creditors could not impose a separate charge for insurance, what would be the effect on competition? Could a creditor provide insurance if any competing lender did not provide it? Noting that credit unions and banks are increasingly entering the lending field once reserved for finance companies, the authors of an extensive study of credit insurance stated, "if consumers do have choices among credit packages, then it would be a serious defect of economic choice not to charge a separate fair rate for an optional service such as credit insurance." C. Hubbard, ed., Consumer Credit Life and Disability Insurance 276 (1972).[28] Do you agree?

3. Referring to the "no separate, identifiable charge" approach, a vice president of Aetna Life Insurance Company stated,

---

27. Other small loan acts expressly permit the creditor to pass on the cost of credit insurance. See In re Branch, page 441 supra.

28. This study was financed by the credit and credit insurance industries.

> Although some of us might believe that credit insurance would continue to be offered by the banks, there is no certainty of this and we must face the possibility that if creditors were faced with the necessity of paying the entire cost, they just would not provide credit insurance. . . .

1967 Hearings at 2420 (Testimony of Lawrence M. Cathles).

If the effect of insurance is to reduce bad debt loss, why would creditors *not* provide it?

4. The study referred to in Question 2 supra, also stated,

> [F]ocusing attention on the creditor as beneficiary actually is misleading because creditors are only points of value transfer. Although the creditor receives payment from the insurance company if a loss occurs, at the same time he must reduce indebtedness of the insured by a related amount. The insured receives the proceeds of the insurance as a positive amount of money which he no longer owes. Thus, it is easy to destroy the creditor-as-beneficiary argument, but there is no doubt that creditors receive benefits from credit insurance policies other than premium retention. In the event of a loss the creditor is not put in the position of attempting to collect from a bereaved or stricken family which is likely to be in straightened circumstances. Relief from such difficult collection situations improves the public image of the creditor and reduces his collection costs.
>
> Economic theory would allocate whatever costs are saved by the creditor, including the cost of bad will, to premium reduction for the debtor. Unfortunately the amounts of such costs, which are highly subjective in character, are unknown. A convincing case could be advanced that creditor retention might well be eliminated. Reduction of both collection costs and bad will could serve to compensate the creditor for acting as quasi-agent for credit life and disability insurance. Such a proposal has not been given sufficient exposure to the industry to justify its adoption for recommended premium rate tables.

Hubbard at 277.

5. If the high cost of credit insurance is attributable to the phenomenon of reverse competition, in which the insurance companies compete for the business of the creditor by offering high commissions, one way to achieve lower rates is to restructure the market so that the insurance companies will compete by offering low premiums. The Massachusetts banking department promulgated a regulation requiring banks to seek at least three bids from credit insurance companies and to accept the lowest qualified bid. The effects of adopting this regulation were immediate and dramatic: rates dropped by forty percent.

E. CLAIMS ABUSE

Even if the consumer has purchased credit insurance, perhaps paying too much for it and perhaps buying more of it than is necessary to protect either the consumer or the creditor, the possible abusive practices have not ended. It is still possible for the insurer or the creditor to deprive the consumer of the insurance benefits even though death or disability has occurred. For the insurance contract typically excludes various risks and limits the eligibility of the consumer.

The most common examples of exclusions from coverage relate to death or illness caused by conditions or ailments existing before the effective date of the insurance coverage. The rationale for this exclusion is clear and strong: the insurance company does not want persons who know they are disabled or terminally ill to enter credit transactions with the intention of having the insurer pay their obligations. And since it is difficult to prove that a consumer knew of the impending tragedy, the clauses are not limited to ailments that the consumer actually knew of. Hence, a consumer who is ignorant of a pre-existing or latent ailment may purchase insurance, only to be denied benefits when the ailment becomes manifest. See Southards v. Central Plains Insurance Co., 441 P.2d 808 (Kan.1968) (consumer not covered because of pre-existing kidney condition, even though he was ignorant of its existence). For extreme cases, see Lucas v. Continental Casualty Co., pages 554–55 supra; Union Security Life Ins. Co. v. Crocker, 667 So.2d 688 (Ala.1995), modified, 709 So.2d 1118 (Ala. 1997) ($1 million punitive damages).

The most common limitation on eligibility is that the consumer must not be beyond a certain age, e.g., sixty-five. Should an insurance company be able to deny benefits to an elderly consumer to whom the creditor has sold credit insurance? Cf. Watkins v. Valley Fidelity Bank & Trust Co., 474 S.W.2d 915 (Tenn.App.1971).

Another claims abuse is delaying payment. The insurer may entrust the creditor with some of the administrative tasks in claims settlements. If the creditor's arrangement with the insurer also calls for an experience refund, the creditor has an incentive to impede the consumer's assertion of a claim and seek payment from the consumer rather than the insurer. Hence, the creditor may require the claimant under a disability policy to provide monthly statements of disability, accompanied by a physician's statement. Or the creditor may seek to induce payment by the consumer notwithstanding the entitlement to insurance benefits. See Bank One Milwaukee, N.A. v. Harris, 563 N.W.2d 543 (Wis.App.1997) (unconscionable practice in violation of the Wisconsin Consumer Act for creditor to treat as in default a consumer who it knows to be entitled to disability insurance benefits); Corbin v. Regions Bank, 574 S.E.2d 616 (Ga.App.2002) (repossession is wrongful if creditor fails to submit claim for disability insurance benefits). Compare Newsome v. Prudential Insurance Co., 166 S.E.2d 487 (N.C.App.1969) (When the insurer, for reasons unspecified in the report, refused to pay, the creditor repossessed the collateral. The court held that once the debt was satisfied by repossession, the right to enforce the policy passed to the debtor's estate.) Accord, Vogelsang v. Credit Life Insurance Co., 255 N.E.2d 479 (Ill.App.1970).

F.   REFINANCING

Problems may occur also in connection with refinancing a consumer debt. Since some kinds of transactions, e.g., small loans, have a very high incidence of refinancing, these problems may be quite serious. Sometimes the problems do not result from intentional manipulation by the creditor. For example, assume that a policy excludes coverage of death by suicide within six months of the formation of the contract. Eighteen months after borrowing money, the consumer refinances the loan. A month later he commits suicide. Is he covered? See Founders Life Assurance Co. v. Poe, 251 S.E.2d 247 (Ga.1978) (yes). In other cases, however, creditor manipulation may be present. In United Companies Mortgage and Investment of Hammond, Inc. v. Estate of McGee, 372 So.2d 622 (La.App.1979), the debtor became terminally ill while he had three loans from plaintiff outstanding. Plaintiff's employees went to the debtor's home to persuade him to refinance the loans. Less than two weeks after refinancing the debt, he died. The insurer cited a pre-existing condition clause and refused to pay. When plaintiff sued the debtor's estate, the court held that plaintiff occupied a fiduciary position and should have explained to the debtor that the consequences of refinancing would be the exclusion of coverage for this ailment, which did not exist at the time of the original loans. Accord, Suburban State Bank v. Squires, 427 N.W.2d 393 (Wis.App.1988) (creditor should have told consumer that refinancing would entail loss of coverage under disability insurance policy).

Another problem in connection with refinancing, mentioned at page 441 supra, is pyramiding—selling insurance to cover the new loan without cancelling the insurance on the original loan. The UCCC (§ 4.110) prohibits this practice.

Even if the creditor cancels the insurance, problems may exist. In MIC Life Insurance Co. v. Hicks, 825 So.2d 616 (Miss.2002), a consumer purchased a car (and credit life insurance) from a dealer. The dealer sold the contract to GMAC. A year later the consumer paid off the loan, and GMAC sent him a notice, attached to another document, which stated, "we suggest that you contact the dealer or the insurance company regarding a possible rebate of the credit life" premium. Since the insurance contract required the insurer to refund any unearned premium within 30 days of a prepayment, without any requirement that the consumer request a refund, the court held the insurer liable for the amount of the refund that should have been made. The court also held that if the insurer and GMAC had agreed that GMAC would send a rebate notice instead of causing the insurer to send a rebate on its own, GMAC could be liable for conspiring to retain unearned premiums, thereby breaching its obligations of good faith and fair dealing.

G. PROPERTY INSURANCE

The foregoing materials have focused primarily on life insurance and secondarily on health and accident insurance. Creditors also often sell property insurance. Most closed-end consumer credit is secured credit, that is, the creditor takes a security interest in specified assets of the consumer. Typically the creditor's standard form contract includes a provision that obligates the consumer to maintain casualty insurance on the collateral, to protect against the risks that the collateral is stolen, damaged, or destroyed.

Property insurance is also a source of substantial income for creditors. The loss ratios may be as low as 7–25%, and the commissions to creditors as high as 60%.[29] Over a ten-year period from 1957–66, GMAC's income from the sale of casualty insurance on collateral averaged over four million dollars per year. This was almost six times GMAC's income from credit life and disability insurance.[30]

The Truth-in-Lending Act, following the lead of state small loan acts, provides that if the creditor sells casualty insurance to the consumer, the premium for the insurance must be included in the finance charge unless the creditor discloses that the consumer may acquire the insurance from an insurer of the consumer's choice. Notwithstanding this disclosure, in transactions in which the creditor takes a security interest in the consumer's household goods,[31] most consumers wind up purchasing casualty insurance from the creditor. If the consumer already has homeowner's insurance, this insurance may be entirely duplicative of the existing coverage. One common abuse in connection with this kind of insurance is for the creditor to sell it in the amount of the debt even though the benefits cannot exceed the value of the collateral. Another is for the creditor to sell insurance that covers all the consumer's household goods even though the creditor has a security interest in only some of them. These practices may violate substantive law (see UCCC § 4.301(1)(a)) and trigger inclusion of at least part of the insurance premium in the finance charge for disclosure purposes (see Regulation Z § 226.4(d)(2)).

With respect to credit secured by the consumer's automobile, there is more. In addition to requiring the consumer to maintain casualty insurance on the vehicle, the contract typically empowers (but does not require) the creditor to obtain casualty insurance if the consumer fails to obtain and maintain it. Given the risks to which the collateral is subject, this seems reasonable. Insurance purchased by the creditor under these circumstances

---

29. 1979 Hearings at 42–43 (Testimony of Robert S. Sable, National Consumer Law Center).

30. 1967 Hearings at 2557 (Letter to the Subcommittee from O.A. Lundin. President of GMAC).

31. An FTC regulation limits the extent to which a creditor may do this. 16 C.F.R. Part 444. This subject is considered in Chapter 12.

is known variously as collateral-protection insurance, creditor-placed insurance, or force-placed insurance.

When the creditor acts on this authorization, it usually obtains single-interest insurance that protects only the creditor's interest in the vehicle, not the consumer's. This means that if the vehicle is worth more than the amount of the debt at the time the vehicle is destroyed or stolen, the insurance pays off the debt but does not pay any excess to the consumer. In addition, the insurance may not provide any benefits unless the vehicle is stolen or repossessed. For these reasons, the insurance provides under-coverage. Simultaneously, however, the insurance may provide over-coverage. Many creditors purchase insurance that covers more than the risk of casualty to the vehicle. Additional coverages include the expenses of repossession and post-repossession storage, amounts necessary to discharge mechanics' liens, payment of the debt if the value of the collateral is not large enough to satisfy it, payment of the insurance premium if the consumer fails to pay it, and more. For an excellent description and analysis, see Sheldon, Force–Placed Automobile Insurance: Consumer Protection Problems and Potential Solutions (1996) (publication of AARP's Public Policy Institute). To the extent the creditor charges the consumer with the expense of these additional coverages, the creditor is in breach of the contract provision that authorizes it to obtain insurance comparable to the insurance that the contract requires the consumer to maintain. Logsdon v. Fifth Third Bank, 654 N.E.2d 115 (Ohio App.1994).

As with other forms of credit insurance, excessive cost is an issue. The premiums for collateral protection insurance may be calculated as a percentage of the loan balance (including unaccrued finance charge). They typically are several times the cost of insurance obtainable by the consumer (and do not include liability coverage). Upon purchasing the insurance, the creditor may revise the monthly payment of the consumer to cover the cost of the insurance (and the finance charge on the premium). Alternatively, the creditor may finance the premium for the balance of the term of the loan with no payments due until the end of the term. In one highly publicized case, the initial indebtedness was $9,000 (plus finance charge), but when the consumers made their last payment, the creditor presented them with a bill for collateral-protection insurance (and accrued finance charge on the insurance premium) of $9,500. Brannigan, Country Justice, Wall St. J., April 12, 1995, at A1 (jury awarded $38 million in punitive damages). In another case a lender placed a five-year policy at a premium of $6,800, accrued finance charges of $7,400 on that premium, and when the consumer made the last payment on the loan presented him with a bill for more than $14,000. Since 1990 there have been numerous individual and class actions challenging the legality of various aspects of collateral protection insurance.

With respect to household goods, still another form of property insurance has been common in recent years. Non-filing insurance protects not against the risk of casualty but against the risk that the creditor's security interest in the collateral will be determined to be inferior to the security interest of another party. This could happen, for example, if the consumer borrows from another lender and gives a security interest in the same goods, or if a person with a judgment against the consumer seizes the goods pursuant to a writ of execution. A creditor may protect against these risks by filing a financing statement with the appropriate state official. And some creditors, viz., those who are financing the consumer's acquisition of the collateral, are protected against these third parties even without any filing. (See UCC § 9–309(1) (purchase money security interests in consumer goods are perfected without filing).) Nevertheless, instead of filing a financing statement (the expense of which they may disclose as part of the amount financed, see Regulation Z § 226.4(e)(1)), some creditors choose to obtain and charge the consumer for non-filing insurance.

As with collateral protection insurance, this insurance often covers risks in addition to the stated risk. In many instances, so-called non-filing insurance actually is default insurance, because it protects against the risk of the consumer's failure to pay the debt, as well as the risk that the creditor's security interest might be defeated. Indeed, the contract between the creditor and the insurer may limit the insurer's liability to 90% of the "premiums" paid to the insurer. To the extent the money paid to the insurance company amounts to a reserve for bad debts and the creditor's access is limited to a percentage of the amounts it has paid, it is questionable whether there really is any insurance. To the extent that the cost of the bad debt reserve (or default insurance) is imposed on the consumer, it actually is within the definition of finance charge for disclosure purposes and the definition of interest for rate regulation purposes. This practice also has been heavily litigated in recent years. E.g., Edwards v. Your Credit Inc., 148 F.3d 427 (5th Cir.1998); Warehouse Home Furnishing Distributors v. Whitson, 709 So.2d 1144 (Ala.1997); W.S. Badcock Corp. v. Myers, 696 So.2d 776 (Fla.App.1996).

H. UNEMPLOYMENT INSURANCE

The most rapidly growing form of credit insurance is unemployment insurance. The premiums consumers paid for this insurance almost doubled between 1995 and 2000, growing from $600 million to $1.1 billion. Unemployment insurance protects against the risk that the consumer will become involuntarily unemployed. In the event of unemployment, the insurance benefit in connection with closed-end credit transactions equals the monthly payment. In open-end transactions, the benefit equals the minimum monthly payment, even if the consumer had been paying a larger amount before losing his or her job. Other common features of this insurance are a waiting period before any benefits are payable and a limit on the number of payments, so that the benefits may run out before the debt is satisfied. According to a study in 2001, while the premiums paid by consumers have been increasing, the claims paid by insurers have been decreasing: the loss ratios for unemployment insurance have been less than ten percent.

*

PART III

ENFORCEMENT BY THE CREDITOR

Parts I and II have examined the formation and the substance of consumer contracts. The next two Parts examine the enforcement of rights incident to those contracts. Part IV addresses enforcement by the consumer, while Part III considers enforcement by the creditor. It examines the procedural and contractual devices (including security interests) that the creditor may use to facilitate enforcement of the contract. It also examines nonjudicial enforcement of the consumer's promise to pay.

CHAPTER 11

COERCIVE COLLECTION TACTICS

Most consumers pay their debts. Indeed, statistics reveal that only about two-to-three percent of the amount of credit extended to consumers becomes delinquent. Still, since the vast majority of consumers in this country are indebted, and since the aggregate amount of consumer credit (even excluding home loans) exceeds $2.5 trillion, even two percent is a lot of money. Thus it is not surprising that creditors devote considerable energy to inducing consumers to pay delinquent debts. This chapter explores the limits on how creditors may expend this considerable energy.

To start with, a description of traditional tactics is in order. Collection efforts usually begin with a letter, sent anywhere from seven to sixty days after the debtor first becomes delinquent. The initial letter may be informative and conciliatory, in case the debtor merely has forgotten to pay. If the debtor does not respond, this first letter is followed by letters that become less and less conciliatory, threatening "drastic action," legal action, communication with the consumer's employer or other persons, and destruction of the consumer's credit rating. The tone of the letters may become abusive, even vulgar. The letter-writing campaign usually is computerized and automatic, so that the only event that will stop the letters is payment. If letters fail to produce payment, the creditor may try telephone calls and personal visits to the consumer. As with the letters, these contacts may start off reasonably, but soon increase in frequency and abusiveness. The creditor may also communicate with third parties, such as the consumer's employer, relatives, neighbors, friends, and co-workers. The purpose of these contacts is to induce the person to pay the consumer's debt or at least pressure the consumer to pay it off.

The level of ingenuity of collectors is extremely high. Unfortunately, the same cannot always be said about their ethics. To ascertain information concerning the consumer's employment or assets, the collector may lie about the purpose of the call. Thus, one collector falsely represented that the debtor's children had been in a serious automobile accident. Other offensive tactics abound. For example, a collector boarded up the doors and windows of the debtor's house—while the debtor was inside. Another, a hospital, refused to release a new-born baby from the hospital because of the parents' failure to pay a disputed portion of the bill. Still another swiped the debtor's artificial leg while he was taking a shower. And, finally, a magazine publisher collected debts owed to it by delinquent advertisers by employing a human stench bomb named Andy. "Dressed in a 22–year-old raincoat that he has impregnated with the most horrible substances available, Andy plunks himself down in the reception room or office of the debtor and refuses to move until a payment is made. Andy and his raincoat generate such vile smells . . . that secretaries and customers gasp and flee the room. In practically all cases, they return with a payment." Swift, Keeping Up With Youth, Parade Magazine, p. 15, December 2, 1979. Said Andy, "My raincoat drives people wild, but I can't smell a thing. I've got permanently blocked sinuses."

Andy may have permanently blocked sensibilities, but this is not true of the persons he and other debt collectors contact. The injuries inflicted by various campaigns of coercion include diminished job performance, loss of employment, embarrassment, assorted physical and emotional injuries, marital difficulties, even suicide.

Your reaction to the propriety of placing a lot of pressure on a consumer may depend on your perception of the reason for the consumer's failure to pay the debt. What do you think explains the failure of most delinquent debtors to pay? A leading study of the matter found that loss of income was the principal reason given by debtors and was *a* factor in half the cases. More than 25% of the delinquent debtors suffered at least temporary job loss, and another 20% suffered illness of one or more wage earners in the family. Overextension of credit was a factor for about 25% of the debtors, but of these, half also experienced a loss of income. So overextension accounted for only 10–15% of the delinquencies. Almost 20% failed to pay because of some perceived misconduct by the seller, such as misrepresentation or breach of warranty. Of all the delinquencies, only about one percent were deadbeats, refusing to pay debts for which they claimed no defense. D. Caplovits, Consumers in Trouble: A Study of Debtors in Default (1974). A later study reveals a similar picture. E. Warren & A. Tyagi, The Two–Income Trap 81 (2003) (87% of the sample cited job loss, divorce, or medical expenses as reasons for resorting to bankruptcy).

With respect to each of the above categories of delinquent debtors, why would the creditor employ highly coercive tactics? What interests of the consumer does the creditor invade by using the tactics described above? Do the interests of the creditor (or others) justify the invasion of the consumer's interests?

A.   COMMON LAW LIMITS

Public Finance Corp. v. Davis

Supreme Court of Illinois, 1976.
66 Ill.2d 85, 4 Ill.Dec. 652, 360 N.E.2d 765.

RYAN, JUSTICE.

. . .

From the pleadings it appears that Davis was indebted to Public Finance on a promissory note executed by her and secured by a security interest in her household goods. She made regular payments on the obligation until August 1, 1974. On February 24, 1975, Davis then being in default, Public Finance filed a complaint seeking judgment against her for the balance due on the note. Davis counterclaimed and, following the allowance of a motion to dismiss the counterclaim, filed an amended counterclaim which is in two counts, both counts seeking recovery on the theory of intentional infliction of severe emotional distress. [The trial court dismissed the amended counterclaim for failure to state a claim and rendered judgment for Public Finance. The intermediate appellate court affirmed, and Davis appealed.] The sole question to be decided is whether the amended counterclaim stated a cause of action. We find that it did not.

In Knierim v. Izzo (1961), 22 Ill.2d 73, 174 N.E.2d 157, this court recognized the intentional causing of severe emotional distress as a separate and additional tort which one author has been prompted to call a "new tort." (Prosser, Intentional Infliction of Mental Suffering: A New Tort, 37 Mich.L.Rev. 874 (1939).) . . . We . . . will test the two counts of the amended counterclaim by the requirements of the cause of action as stated in section 46 of the second Restatement, the decisions of other jurisdictions recognizing the cause of action and by the authors on the subject. See Magruder, Mental and Emotional Disturbance in the Law of Torts, 49 Harv.L.Rev. 1033, 1059 (1936); Prosser, Law of Torts, sec. 12 (4th ed. 1971).

The extensive comments and illustrations to section 46 are helpful in delineating the conduct which gives rise to this cause of action. First, the conduct must be extreme and outrageous. The liability clearly does not extend to mere insults, indignities, threats, annoyances, petty oppressions or trivialities. "It has not been enough that the defendant has acted with an intent which is tortious or even criminal, or that he has intended to inflict emotional distress, or even that his conduct has been characterized by 'malice,' or a degree of aggravation which would entitle the plaintiff to punitive damages for another tort. Liability has been found only where the conduct has been so outrageous in character, and so extreme in degree, as to go beyond all possible bounds of decency * * *." Restatement (Second) of Torts sec. 46, comment *d* (1965).

Second, infliction of emotional distress alone is not sufficient to give rise to a cause of action. The emotional distress must be *severe*. Although fright, horror, grief, shame, humiliation, worry, etc. may fall within the ambit of the term "emotional distress," these mental conditions alone are not actionable. "The law intervenes only where the distress inflicted is so severe that no reasonable man could be expected to endure it. The intensity and the duration of the distress are factors to be considered in determining its severity." Comment *j*. See, also Prosser, Law of Torts sec. 12, at 54 (4th ed. 1971).

Third, reckless conduct which will support a cause of action under the rules stated is conduct from which the actor knows severe emotional distress is certain or substantially certain to result. (Comment *i*.) Liability extends to situations in which there is a high degree of probability that severe emotional distress will follow and the actor goes ahead in conscious disregard of it. Prosser, Law of Torts 60 (4th ed. 1971).

Fourth, as is stated in comment *e*, the extreme and outrageous character of the conduct may arise from an abuse of a position or a relation with another which gives the actor actual or apparent authority over the other or power to affect his interests. This interpretation of the rule is applicable to collecting creditors and would apply to a creditor in its attempt to collect a lawful obligation.

Count I of the amended counterclaim alleges the conduct of Public Finance which Davis claims entitles her to recover. Stripped of the conclusions, it is charged that on or about September 1, 1974, Davis informed Public Finance she was no longer employed, was on public aid and did not have enough money to make regular payments on her obligations; that in order to collect the account Public Finance from September 1, 1974, to April 4, 1975, called Davis several times weekly, frequently more than once a day; that in order to collect the account agents of Public Finance went to Davis' home one or more times a week; that on October 15, 1974, when Davis' daughter was in the hospital, an agent of Public Finance, in order to collect the account, called the defendant at the hospital; that on that day Davis informed the agent of the severity of her daughter's condition, that she, herself, was sick and nervous and asked that Public Finance refrain from calling her at the hospital; that on the same day an agent of Public Finance again called Davis at the hospital; that after an employee of Public Finance induced Davis to write a check and promised that the check would not be processed, Public Finance phoned an acquaintance of Davis and informed her that Davis was writing bad checks; that in November 1974 an employee of Public Finance called at Davis' home and after being told that Davis had no money with which to make a payment, with Davis' permission, used her phone to call Public Finance and to describe and report the items of Davis' household goods; that on that day the employee "failed or refused" to leave Davis' home until her son entered the room.

Count II realleges the conduct of Public Finance alleged in count I and further alleges that Davis suffered from hypertension and a nervous condition; that she was particularly susceptible to emotional distress; that she had frequently informed agents of Public Finance of her condition and that Public Finance had notice that Davis was particularly susceptible to emotional distress.

The conduct alleged is not of such an extreme and outrageous nature as to constitute a basis for recovery under the theory alleged. Davis was legally obligated to Public Finance and was in default in making the payments. As stated in Restatement (Second) of Torts, section 46, comment *g*, in such a case the actor is not liable "where he has done no more than to insist upon his legal rights in a permissible way, even though he is well aware that such insistence is certain to cause emotional distress." A creditor must be given some latitude to pursue reasonable methods of collecting debts even though such methods may result in some inconvenience, embarrassment or annoyance to the debtor. The debtor is protected only from oppressive or outrageous conduct.

In cases wherein courts have permitted the action to be brought or have sustained recovery for severe emotional distress, the collecting tactics of the creditor have involved the use of abusive and vituperative language, shouting and railing at the debtor, repeated threats of arrest and ruination of credit, threats to appeal to the debtor's employer to endanger his employment and accusations of dishonesty. "[L]iability usually has rested on a prolonged course of hounding by a variety of extreme methods." Prosser, Law of Torts 57 (4th ed. 1971).

Returning to the allegations in count I we note that Davis alleges that the course of conduct pursued was in order to collect the account. This Public Finance had a right to do, as long as the methods employed were not outrageous. As to the numerous telephone calls, there is no allegation as to what was said by the person making the calls. The same is true of the allegations of the several visits to Davis' home and of the calls to Davis at the hospital. Davis has not alleged that the agents of Public Finance used abusive, threatening or profane language or that they conducted themselves other than in a permissible manner. There is no allegation concerning these calls or the visits to the house that can serve to characterize Public Finance's conduct as extreme or outrageous. The mere fact that a second call was made to Davis at the hospital after she had requested that they not call her there cannot be so considered, since there is no allegation as to what was said or even that the second call was for the purpose of collecting the past due obligation.

As to the visit of an employee of Public Finance to Davis' home and using her phone to call Public Finance and to inventory and describe her household goods, again we must consider that her obligation was past due and that it was secured by the household goods. Also the allegation that the employee of Public Finance "failed or refused" to leave until Davis' son entered the room contains only an innuendo and not an allegation of any threatening or coercive conduct which could be called outrageous.

We consider the most serious allegation to be the charge that Public Finance induced Davis to write a check for the amount owed with the assurance that the check would not be presented for payment and then subsequently phoned Davis' acquaintance and informed her that Davis was writing bad checks. This conduct was wrong and no doubt caused Davis considerable embarrassment and distress. However, this appears to be a single isolated act. In Lewis v. Physicians and Dentists Credit Bureau, Inc. (1947), 27 Wash.2d 267, 273, 177 P.2d 896, 899, the court stated that persons "who do not pay their bills cannot object to some publicity in connection with attempts to collect them; their tender sensibilities are protected only from 'undue or oppressive publicity.'" Also, in comment *j* to section 46 it is stated that the intensity and duration of the distress are factors to be considered in determining the severity of the emotional distress. We do not consider that the specific allegation of this single impermissible act constitutes extreme and outrageous conduct calculated to cause severe emotional distress.

There can be no doubt that the conduct of the employees of Public Finance disturbed Davis and possibly caused her emotional distress. The allegations demonstrate that the employees were persistent in their efforts to collect the past due obligation and possibly were persistent to the point of being annoying; however, with the possible exception noted, count I contains no allegation of extreme or excessive conduct. We must therefore hold that count I does not state a cause of action for severe emotional distress.

Even assuming, as we must under the allegations of count II, that Public Finance knew that Davis suffered from hypertension and was nervous the conduct alleged is not actionable. Knowledge that another is peculiarly susceptible to emotional distress may make a person's conduct actionable when it otherwise would not be. "The conduct may become heartless, flagrant, and outrageous when the actor proceeds in the face of such knowledge, where it would not be so if he did not know." (Restatement (Second) of Torts sec. 46, comment *f*.) However, comment *f* emphasizes that major outrage, even under such circumstances, is still essential to the tort. As stated above, the complaint contains no allegations of abusive or threatening language or conduct coercive in nature. Public Finance was attempting to collect a legal obligation from Davis in a permissible though persistent and possibly annoying manner.

For the reasons stated we hold that counts I and II of the amended counterclaim do not state a cause of action for either intentional or reckless infliction of severe emotional distress. The judgment of the appellate court is affirmed.

Judgment affirmed.

. . .

DOOLEY, JUSTICE, with whom CLARK, JUSTICE joins, dissenting:

. . .

We agree with the majority that in measuring this intentional conduct it must be "extreme and outrageous" except that a lesser grade of conduct will support a cause of action where the actor has knowledge of the fact that emotional distress is substantially certain to result. The emotional distress, we further agree, must be severe. However, neither is a problem here since the amended counterclaim also alleged the finance company engaged in an outrageous course of conduct with the intention of causing severe emotional distress and as a proximate result counter-plaintiff sustained severe emotional distress.

This pleading, it must be remembered, was dismissed for failure to state a cause of action. "Outrageous," "intentional," and "severe" are words of common understanding. So long as they are requisite to the statement of a cause of action, they are proper in a pleading of this nature. The conduct described as such must be considered in the context of time, place, surrounding circumstances, and knowledge by the actor that it will reasonably cause emotional distress. Not to be overlooked is the person making the appraisal. Certainly the dowager would consider conduct "highly outrageous" which the youth would regard as prosaic. So long as reasonable men might differ in their evaluation of the character of the conduct, the judicial function is exhausted.

.   .   .

QUESTIONS AND NOTES

1.   The Restatement (Second) of Torts provides:*

§ 46.   Outrageous Conduct Causing Severe Emotional Distress

(1) One who by extreme and outrageous conduct intentionally or recklessly causes severe emotional distress to another is subject to liability for such emotional distress, and if bodily harm to the other results from it, for such bodily harm.

(2) Where such conduct is directed at a third person, the actor is subject to liability if he intentionally or recklessly causes severe emotional distress

(a) to a member of such person's immediate family who is present at the time, whether or not such distress results in bodily harm, or

(b) to any other person who is present at the time, if such distress results in bodily harm.

.   .   .

Comment:

.   .   .

b. As indicated in Chapter 47, emotional distress may be an element of damages in many cases where other interests have been invaded, and tort liability has arisen apart from the emotional distress. Because of the fear of fictitious or trivial claims, distrust of the proof offered, and the difficulty of setting up any satisfactory boundaries to liability, the law has been slow to afford independent protection to the interest in freedom from emotional distress standing alone. It is only within recent years that the rule stated in this Section has been fully recognized as a separate and distinct basis of tort liability, without the presence of the elements necessary to any other tort, such as assault, battery, false imprisonment, trespass to land, or the like. This Section may be regarded as an extension of the principle involved in the rules stated in §§ 21–34 as to the tort of assault.

. . .

d.   Extreme and outrageous conduct. The cases thus far decided have found liability only where the defendant's conduct has been extreme and outrageous. It has not been enough that the defendant has acted with an intent which is tortious or even criminal, or that he has intended to inflict emotional distress, or even that his conduct has been characterized by "malice," or a degree of aggravation which would entitle the plaintiff to punitive damages for another tort. Liability has been found only where the conduct has been so outrageous in character, and so extreme in degree, as to go beyond all possible bounds of decency, and to be regarded as atrocious, and utterly intolerable in a civilized community. Generally, the case is one in which the recitation of the facts to an average member of the community would arouse his resentment against the actor, and lead him to exclaim, "Outrageous!"

. . .

e.   The extreme and outrageous character of the conduct may arise from an abuse by the actor of a position, or a relation with the other, which gives him actual or apparent authority over the other, or power to affect his interests. Thus an attempt to extort money by a threat of arrest may make the actor liable even where the arrest, or the threat alone, would not do so. In particular police officers, school authorities, landlords, and collecting creditors have been held liable for extreme abuse of their position. Even in such cases, however, the actor has not been held liable for mere insults, indignities, or annoyances that are not extreme or outrageous.

Illustrations:

. . .

7.   A, a creditor, seeking to collect a debt from B, sends B a series of letters in lurid envelopes bearing a picture of lightning about to strike, in which A repeatedly threatens suit without bringing it, reviles B as a deadbeat, a dishonest man, and a criminal, and threatens to garnish his wages, to bother his employer so much that B will be discharged, and to "tie B up tight as a drum" if he does not pay. B suffers severe emotional distress. A is subject to liability to B.

8.   A, a creditor, seeking to collect a debt, calls on B and demands payment in a rude and insolent manner. When B says that he cannot pay, A calls B a deadbeat, and says that he will never trust B again. A's conduct, although insulting, is not so extreme or outrageous as to make A liable to B.

. . .

h. Court and jury. It is for the court to determine, in the first instance, whether the defendant's conduct may reasonably be regarded as so extreme and outrageous as to permit recovery, or whether it is necessarily so. Where reasonable men may differ, it is for the jury, subject to the control of the court, to determine whether, in the particular case, the conduct has been sufficiently extreme and outrageous to result in liability.

. . .

j. Severe emotional distress. The rule stated in this Section applies only where the emotional distress has in fact resulted, and where it is severe. Emotional distress passes under various names, such as mental suffering, mental anguish, mental or nervous shock, or the like. It includes all highly unpleasant mental reactions, such as fright, horror, grief, shame, humiliation, embarrassment, anger, chagrin, disappointment, worry, and nausea. It is only where it is extreme that the liability arises. Complete emotional tranquility is seldom attainable in this world, and some degree of transient and trivial emotional distress is a part of the price of living among people. The law intervenes only where the distress inflicted is so severe that no reasonable man could be expected to endure it. The intensity and the duration of the distress are factors to be considered in determining its severity. Severe distress must be proved; but in many cases the extreme and outrageous character of the defendant's conduct is in itself important evidence that the distress has existed. . . .

The distress must be reasonable and justified under the circumstances, and there is no liability where the plaintiff has suffered exaggerated and unreasonable emotional distress, unless it results from a peculiar susceptibility to such distress of which the actor has knowledge. . . .

It is for the court to determine whether on the evidence severe emotional distress can be found; it is for the jury to determine whether, on the evidence, it has in fact existed.

. . .

k. Bodily harm. Normally, severe emotional distress is accompanied or followed by shock, illness, or other bodily harm, which in itself affords evidence that the distress is genuine and severe. The rule stated is not, however, limited to cases where there has been bodily harm; and if the conduct is sufficiently extreme and outrageous there may be liability for the emotional distress alone, without such harm. In such cases the courts may perhaps tend to look for more in the way of outrage as a guarantee that the claim is genuine; but if the enormity of the outrage carries conviction that there has in fact been severe emotional distress, bodily harm is not required.

. . .

2. The court in *Davis* states three elements of the tort: the conduct is so outrageous as to be beyond all bounds of decency; the emotional distress is severe; and the defendant knows the emotional distress is substantially certain to occur. Why does the court think these elements were not present in Davis' complaint?

> a) With respect to the phone calls at the hospital, Davis' complaint stated that her "daughter was confined to a hospital with a brain tumor"; that she was awaiting word on her daughter's condition; that she told the caller "of the severity of her daughter's condition and . . . that she was herself sick and had nervous problems"; and that she asked the caller to "refrain from further calls to her at the hospital." Nevertheless, the caller phoned again. Why do you suppose he did that?

> b) With respect to the incident at Davis' home in November 1974, when the collector asked to use Davis' phone, why do you suppose she let him? Why do you suppose the collector wanted to use her phone rather than a public pay phone?

> c) With respect to this incident at Davis' home, the court states that the allegation that the collector refused to leave until Davis' son entered the room contains "only an innuendo." Evidently the court contemplates a hint of "threatening or coercive conduct." How threatening or coercive must the conduct be? Look again at the precise conduct alleged: could it be described as outrageous?

> d) Davis' complaint also stated that after being informed that she had no funds in her checking account, the collector induced her to write a check anyway, "to demonstrate 'good faith,'" promising her that the check "would not be processed." Do you believe him, i.e. why would he want her to give him a check if she had no funds in the account?

> e) What is the standard for determining whether a petition states a cause of action?

3. Consider also Restatement (Second) of Torts section 312:*

> § 312. Emotional Distress Intended

> If the actor intentionally and unreasonably subjects another to emotional distress which he should recognize as likely to result in illness or other bodily harm, he is subject to liability to the other for an illness or other bodily harm of which the distress is a legal cause,

> > (a) although the actor has no intention of inflicting such harm, and

> > (b) irrespective of whether the act is directed against the other or a third person.

Comment:

. . .

b.   There is a considerable degree of duplication between the rule stated in this Section and that stated in § 46, which deals with the intentional or reckless infliction of emotional distress by extreme and outrageous conduct. In most of the cases in which the intentional infliction of emotional distress results in foreseeable bodily harm, the known risk of such bodily harm is sufficient in itself to make the act one of extreme outrage, and to bring the case within § 46. This is true, for example, where the actor screams threats and violent abuse at a person whom he knows to be at death's door with a weak heart. The action may be maintained, and the damage for the bodily harm may be recovered, on the basis of the intentional tort. (See § 46, Comment *j.*) This Section permits the alternative of a negligence action in such a case. The rule stated here extends, however, somewhat further than the rule of § 46. It permits the negligence action in any case where it may be found that the conduct, although intended to inflict emotional distress, amounts to something less than extreme outrage, but nevertheless involves an unreasonable risk, which the actor should recognize, that bodily harm will result. As stated in § 313, there may be a similar liability where the emotional disturbance is not inflicted intentionally, but negligently.

. . .

c.   In order that the actor be liable under the rule stated in this Section, it is necessary that he act unreasonably. There are many situations in which it is reasonable, indeed inevitable, to subject another to a distress which is recognizably likely to have serious physical consequences. Thus, it may be necessary to inform even an ill woman of the death of a dearly loved relative.

. . .

4.   In MacDermid v. Discover Financial Services, 488 F.3d 721 (6th Cir. 2007), a consumer who suffered bipolar disease defaulted on a credit card debt. The creditor threatened to have her arrested and prosecuted for fraud in connection with opening the account. The creditor continued making this threat even after the consumer's husband informed it of her fragile mental condition. Allegedly in response to the creditor's pressure, the consumer committed suicide. Her husband sued to recover for intentional infliction of emotional distress, and the trial court dismissed the claim. The Sixth Circuit reversed, holding that, under the allegations of the complaint, the creditor's threat of criminal prosecution in an attempt to enforce a civil claim could be actionable. On remand the creditor moved for summary judgment, which the court denied. 2008 WL 918489 (M.D.Tenn.2008).

5.   Inducing the debtor to write a check even though the check will not clear is a common tactic. The creditor may assert that it is sought as a sign of good faith, as in *Davis;* or the creditor may assure the consumer that it will not be cashed until there are sufficient funds in the account. Whatever the asserted reason, the real reason is usually the leverage the creditor obtains: if the creditor deposits the check, it will be returned because the debtor has no account at all or because the funds in the account are not sufficient to pay the check. The creditor is then in a position to take the check to the prosecuting attorney and claim a violation of a bad-check statute, e.g., Mass.Gen.L.Ann. ch. 266, § 37:

> Whoever, with intent to defraud, makes, draws, utters or delivers any check, draft or order for the payment of money upon any bank or other depository, with knowledge that the maker or drawer has not sufficient funds or credit at such bank or other depository for the payment of such instrument, although no express representation is made in reference thereto, shall be guilty of attempted larceny, and if money or property or services are obtained thereby shall be guilty of larceny. As against the maker or drawer thereof, the making, drawing, uttering or delivery of such a check, draft or order, payment of which is refused by the drawee, shall be prima facie evidence of intent to defraud and of knowledge of insufficient funds in, or credit with, such bank or other depository, unless the maker or drawer shall have paid the holder thereof the amount due thereon, together with all costs and protest fees, within two days after receiving notice that such check, draft or order has not been paid by the drawee. The word "credit," as used herein, shall be construed to mean an arrangement or understanding with the bank or depository for the payment of such check, draft or order.

At every step of the way, however, the creditor offers the debtor the opportunity to abort the criminal proceedings, simply by paying the debt (or at least the amount of the check). This conduct of the creditor may be tortious, as an abuse of legal process or as malicious prosecution. On the whole, however, debtors have not been very successful in using these theories to gain redress for excessive collection tactics.

The creditor may hire an attorney to assist in nonjudicial enforcement. Before participating in collection efforts that invoke the criminal law, however, the attorney should consider the following:

Rule 4.4 Respect for Rights of Third Persons

In representing a client, a lawyer shall not use means that have no substantial purpose other than to embarrass, delay, or burden a third person. . . .[1]

---

1. ABA, Model Rules of Professional Conduct (1983). Cf. ABA, Code of Professional Responsibility DR 7–105 (1978):

(A) A lawyer shall not present, participate in presenting, or threaten to present criminal charges solely to obtain an advantage in a civil matter.

This provision of the Code has no counterpart in the Model Rules, but several states have interpreted the prohibition to be implicit. E.g., Fla.Comm. on Professional Ethics, Op. 89–3 (1989); N.J. Advisory Comm. on Professional Ethics. Op. 595 (1986).

Voneye v. Turner

Court of Appeals of Kentucky, 1951.
240 S.W.2d 588.

SIMS, JUSTICE.

For convenience we will refer to the parties as they appear in the trial court. A general demurrer was sustained to the petition, which was dismissed when plaintiff declined to further plead, and the sole question presented on this appeal is, did the petition state a cause of action.

The petition averred plaintiff is now and was at all times mentioned therein an employee of the United States Government in the Louisville Medical Depot, and that John M. Turner at all times complained of was an officer, agent and employee of the Aetna Finance Company, a corporation; that on Aug. 10, 1948, James E. Tinsley borrowed from the company $300 evidenced by a note due in monthly installments which plaintiff signed as his surety; that Turner as agent of the company talked over the telephone to the personnel director of plaintiff's employer relative to the delinquency of Tinsley on the note on which plaintiff was surety, and on April 27, 1949, through the United States mail sent to the personnel director this letter:

Personnel Director

Louisville Medical Depot,

Louisville, Ky.

Dear Sir:

Am writing you as per our telephone conversation of April 26th in regard to your employee, Charles Voneye. Mr. Voneye signed a note here on Aug. 10, 1948, in the amount of $300 for his cousin, Mr. James E. Tinsley. At the time of this writing the balance is $281.84. The account is now five (5) full payments in arrears. As I told you on the phone, I contacted Mr. Voneye a number of times and he informed me that he definitely was not going to pay. Mr. Tinsley is not working and he has not worked since Jan. 24th. When he does work he is an automobile salesman, and he has had trouble finding a job due to the current used car market.

Enclosed you will find a self-addressed stamped envelope. Anything you can do for us in this matter will certainly be appreciated.

The petition further averred that the writing and delivery of this letter to plaintiff's employer was for the purpose of coercing payment of the note by plaintiff and of exposing him to public contempt, ridicule, aversion or disgrace, which was an invasion of his right of privacy and caused him to suffer great mental pain, humiliation and mortification for which he should recover $10,000 compensatory and $5,000 punitive damages.

It appears that the doctrine of right of privacy emanated from Judge Cooley's statement (Cooley on Torts, 2nd Ed. p. 29), "Of The Right To Be Let Alone." In 1890 Samuel D. Warren and Louis D. Brandeis wrote an article in 4 Harvard Law Review 193, expanding Cooley's "Right To Be Let

Alone," where evidently Judge Cooley was speaking of the right of freedom from assault, into the right to be free from mental as well as physical attack.

Redress for the invasion of the right of privacy has been recognized so generally in recent years that it no longer may be questioned. Brents v. Morgan, 221 Ky. 765, 299 S.W. 967, 55 A.L.R. 964; Thompson v. Adelberg & Berman, 181 Ky. 487, 205 S.W. 558, 3 A.L.R. 1594; LaSalle Extension University v. Fogarty, 126 Neb. 457, 253 N.W. 424, 91 A.L.R. 1491.

Many of the invasions of the right of privacy for which recovery has been sought are the result of unwarranted and humiliating methods put in motion by creditors to collect debts. When the method employed is such as to constitute an actionable invasion of one's right of privacy, the truthfulness of the matter disclosed is no defense to the action. To this extent the right to recover for invasion of privacy differs from a right based on libel. . . .

But the right of privacy is not absolute. As was written in one of the several excellent amici curiae briefs filed on the rehearing of this cause: "No individual can live in an ivory tower and at the same time participate in society and expect complete non-interference from other members of the public."

In our leading case on the subject, Brents v. Morgan, Judge Logan defined the right of privacy: "It is generally recognized as the right to be let alone, that is, the right of a person to be free from *unwarranted* publicity, or the right to live without *unwarranted* interference by the public about matters with which the public is not necessarily concerned." (Our italics.) The texts bear out this statement of the rule. In Restatement of the Law of Torts, § 867, p. 398, the actionable invasion is referred to as one which "unreasonably and seriously interferes with another's interest in not having his affairs known * * * to the public."

Let us apply the letter written in this case to the above rule so clearly enunciated in Brents v. Morgan and determine whether or not plaintiff's right of privacy was invaded. The letter informed plaintiff's employer that plaintiff, as surety for his cousin, James E. Tinsley, had signed a $300 note on Aug. 10, 1948; that at the time the letter was written five full payments on the note were in arrears and Tinsley was not employed and plaintiff had informed defendant he was not going to pay the obligation. It ended by enclosing a self-addressed and stamped envelope and saying, "Anything you can do for us in this matter will certainly be appreciated."

The letter did not contain a threat or a coercive word, nor one word of contempt, ridicule, aversion or disgrace. Ordinarily, an employer is interested in the ability and reputation of his employees as to payment of debts, which makes for efficiency in work and saves the employer the annoyance and expense of answering garnishments. So with reason it cannot be said this letter was directed to one who had no interest in or was not concerned with plaintiff's payment of his just and legal obligation. A debtor when he creates an obligation must know that his creditor expects to collect it, and the ordinary man realizes that most employers expect their employees to meet their obligations and that when they fall behind in so doing the employer may be asked to take the matter up with them. Indeed, most debtors would prefer to have their delinquencies referred to their employers in a courteous and inconspicuous manner rather than to have a suit filed against them and their wages garnisheed.

The instant case is strikingly like Patton v. Jacobs, 118 Ind.App. 358, 78 N.E.2d 789, . . . [in which] the Court of Appeals of Indiana remarked that an employer has a natural and proper interest in his employee paying her debts, as it saves the employer the annoyance of garnishment proceedings. The court further remarked that the employer has a right to hire only people who pay their debts and may take a reasonable pride in the reputation of employees in this respect, and the employer is not in the category of the general public which can have no legitimate interest in a purely private matter between creditor and debtor.

In Lewis v. Physicians & Dentists Credit Bureau, 27 Wash.2d 267, 177 P.2d 896, 899, [t]he opinion contains this language: "People who do not pay their bills cannot object to some publicity in connection with attempts to collect them; their tender sensibilities are protected only from 'undue or oppressive publicity.'"

The case at bar is distinguished from our cases of Brents v. Morgan and Thompson v. Adelberg & Berman. In the Brents case the creditor, a garage owner, caused a notice 5 feet by 8 feet to be placed on his show window reading:

Notice

Dr. W. R. Morgan owes an account here of $49.67. And if promises would pay an account, this account would have been settled long ago. This account will be advertised as long as it remains unpaid.

It needs no argument to convince anyone that this was a flagrant violation of Dr. Morgan's right of privacy.

In the Thompson case the creditor had numerous yellow placards stuck up on plaintiff's premises reading: " 'Our Collector,' * * * 'was here for payment.' 'We would save you the annoyance of his further calls, if you will pay at the store.'" Then in large capital letters on the placards appeared " 'The Union Clothing Store.'" This placarding of Mrs. Thompson's home with such notices was as much a violation of her right of privacy as the posting of the notice in the garage show window in the Brents case.

Likewise, the instant case is readily distinguished from the foreign cases relied upon by plaintiff. . . .

In LaSalle Extension University v. Fogarty, the University knew Fogarty denied the debt, yet it wrote him 37 letters and one to his employer and two to his neighbors. Some of these letters were in lurid envelopes and in one, both the letterhead and the envelope bore the facsimile of lightning about to strike someone. One read: "Honest men pay their debts. Dishonest men do not pay their debts. You owe us $140. Classify yourself." Another letter contained a pseudo garnishment notice. It is manifest such tactics were a gross invasion of Fogarty's right of privacy.

. . .

The judgment is affirmed.

CAMMACK, C.J., and MILLIKEN and MOREMEN, JJ., dissenting.

QUESTIONS AND NOTES

1. The theory of action in *Davis* is intentional infliction of emotional distress. In *Voneye* the debtor tries invasion of the right of privacy. This theory has been described as consisting actually of four separate torts, two of which may be invoked to redress excessively coercive collection tactics: intrusion into the debtor's solitude and publication of private facts. Which of these two is involved in *Voneye?*

2. What interests of the creditor are served by permitting communication with the debtor's employer? What, if any, interests of the employer are served by these communications? What interests of the debtor are invaded? After evaluating the weight of each of these interests, do you think a creditor should be permitted to enlist the aid of the debtor's employer? Consider the following:

> [W]e are referred to certain cases in which it is said that the employer may properly be told of such debts because he has a legitimate interest in the matter, since a debt-free employee is a more efficient employee. The argument proves too much. A lovesick employee, also, is far from efficient. Should we call upon the boss to scotch the romance? What we are looking at, in essence, is simply a matter of human dignity, the right to live our own lives without the meddlesome interference of others, the simple right to be let alone. We can be sued for our debts. In event of default, that we may expect. Wages may be garnisheed. We can be made subject to the execution of legal process and our property seized. The creditor's arsenal is both ample and effective as respects this type of small debtor. We will not add to these weapons the right to "have the heat put on" in the front office, in short (to revert to legal phraseology) the right to invade privacy.

Hawley v. Professional Credit Bureau, Inc., 76 N.W.2d 835, 843 (Mich. 1956) (dissenting opinion). Are you persuaded? (A majority of the Michigan Supreme Court was not.)

3. In Fennell v. G.A.C. Finance Corp., 218 A.2d 492, 495 (Md.1966), the creditor wrote the debtor's corporate employer as follows, in part:

> All our attempts to have Mr. Fennell pay this moral and legal obligation have been in vain.
>
> We realize that [you] cannot act as a collection agency, however, we feel quite sure [you] do not condone this type of behavior; in as much as this man is directly or indirectly handling your funds and is acting as a representative of your company.

It is our contention that when a man is having financial difficulties, the greater the pressure is exerted the more likely the tendency is to infringe and tip the till.

We feel quite certain that if your office would discuss this matter with Mr. Fennell and his immediate supervisor, Mr. Herbert C. Brown, and direct the subject to contact us, we could enter into a mutually satisfactory arrangement for the liquidation of this account.

Thank you for your cooperation in this matter.

Should this publication be actionable? As for the effects on the debtor of these communications, see Holt v. Boyle Brothers, Inc., 217 F.2d 16, 16–17 (D.C.Cir.1954):

The personnel officer informed Holt in a memorandum that the Laboratory had been asked to help collect a debt and that "failure to honor your just debts may reflect adversely on your suitability for continued employment with the Navy. Each of the communications received from your creditors is filed in your personal folder and inevitably serves as part of the total record considered when personnel actions of vital importance to you are taken. * * * If as a result of failure to meet your obligations, evidence is accumulated reflecting upon your suitability for continued employment, your removal may be effected.* * * "

4. As *Voneye* makes clear, not every publication of private facts is actionable. Typically, the courts say the invasion must be *unreasonable*. In the words of Gouldman–Taber Pontiac, Inc. v. Zerbst, 100 S.E.2d 881, 883 (Ga.1957):

The right of privacy is not absolute but is qualified by the rights of others. "No individual can live in an ivory tower and at the same time participate in society and expect complete non-interference from other members of the public." Voneye v. Turner, supra. A recluse who completely extricated himself from society might well expect no interference whatever from the outside world. But one who, like the plaintiff, is employed by a large corporation, who is an active participant in the business world, who has an automobile and drives it upon the highways, has it serviced and repaired, and obtains credit for goods and services used in repairing her car, may expect reasonable conduct on the part of those with whom she does business and from whom she gets credit. Where she seeks and obtains credit from one such as the defendant, she may expect the creditor to investigate her and her reputation, particularly for paying her bills, to ascertain for whom she works, and to communicate with her employer for information about her. She may expect her employer to want her to pay her bill, and may further expect her creditor to use reasonable means to persuade her to do so, and on failure to persuade to force her to do so through the courts. When she accepts the credit, she impliedly consents for her creditor to take all reasonable and necessary action to collect the bill. Writing to her employer, as this creditor did, was in our opinion a reasonable exercise of his rights and constituted no unwarranted or unreasonable interference with her right of privacy.

The words are innocuous enough; the difficulty lies in determining whether particular conduct is reasonable. Surely it is reasonable for a potential creditor to investigate the creditworthiness of an applicant for credit. And having extended credit and being unable to locate the debtor, the creditor ought to be able to make some effort to locate the debtor. But this does not necessarily include communicating with the employer for the purpose of procuring an additional source of coercion on the debtor. To what extent does the court in *Voneye* consider the debtor's perspective?

5. The branch of invasion of the right of privacy consisting of intrusion into one's solitude has been invoked in many cases, often successfully. The cases in which courts hold the creditors to have gone too far tend to be cases involving numerous phone calls (often at inconvenient times), personal visits, and abusive language. Illustrative are Biederman's of Springfield, Inc. v. Wright, 322 S.W.2d 892 (Mo.1959) (numerous visits to the debtor's place of employment; loud, abusive, and insulting language); and Housh v. Peth, 133 N.E.2d 340 (Ohio 1956) (numerous phone calls, including three within fifteen minutes at the debtor's place of employment, causing her employer to threaten discharge). Plaintiff's attorney in Public Finance Corp. v. Davis might have fared better had she relied on invasion of the right of privacy.

6. In the intentional infliction cases, courts require the collector's conduct to be "outrageous." In the privacy cases, on the other hand, courts speak of "unreasonableness." Notwithstanding this difference in terminology, *Voneye* and other cases, which conclude that *as a matter of law* communication with a debtor's employer is not actionable, make it "reasonably" clear that the standard in the privacy cases approaches the standard in the intentional infliction cases.

As to both theories, why should the standard be "outrageous"? Why should a debt collector be able to act in an "unreasonable" manner?

7. Sometimes the creditor demands payment even though the debtor actually is not indebted. This situation may occur because of, inter alia, failure to credit a payment, mistaken identity, breach of warranty (or other claim) causing a greater loss to the debtor than the amount still owed the creditor, or the statute of limitations. Should these facts be relevant to setting the limits on the creditor's conduct? Compare Beneficial Finance Co. v. Lamos, 179 N.W.2d 573, 583–84 (Iowa 1970),

> [T]he character of the obligation, whether it is undisputed or not, does reflect and taint the reasonableness of practices used to collect it. If there is an undisputed amount owed and the debtor refuses to pay, tactics used to collect might well be more drastic than those permissible where no debt is owed or its existence is disputed.
>
> Of course, reasonableness of the dispute would have some bearing on the issue.

and Story v. J.M. Fields, Inc., 343 So.2d 675, 677 (Fla.App.1977),

> [Determining whether a collector's phone calls amount to "harassment" can be done only by] considering not only the frequency of the calls, but also the legitimacy of the creditor's claim, the plausibility of the debtor's excuse, the sensitivity or abrasiveness of the personalities and all other circumstances that color the transaction.

with Timperley v. Chase Collection Service, 77 Cal.Rptr. 782, 784 (Cal.App. 1969),

> The fact that the debt was disputed and the fact that respondents knew the likelihood of appellant's being pressured by his employer to pay it do not in themselves, as we have indicated, serve to remove the communication from the scope of [the collector's right to communicate with the employer].

B.   STATUTORY INTERVENTION

(1) COLLECTION PRACTICES

Although several tort theories place limits on collection tactics, none of these theories developed specifically to deal with collection conduct. And none of them, it turns out, is capable of giving consideration to all the interests that may be present. Consequently, objectionable conduct may not be actionable. Moreover, conducting litigation to establish outrageousness is expensive, especially for a consumer who cannot afford to pay the underlying debt.

One solution to the problem of the harassed debtor is the creation of a separate collection tort, and this appears to be what Texas, Louisiana, and perhaps South Dakota have done. Even with a special collection tort, of course, the costs of litigation remain high. Other states, and the federal government, have adopted statutory solutions. The statutes fall into two categories, though some states (and the federal government) have adopted statutes in both categories. One of these categories consists of the broadly phrased FTC and little-FTC acts.

The FTC has successfully challenged deception in the context of skip-tracing, i.e. ascertaining the consumer's current address, employer, or bank. Thus, the FTC has stopped skip-tracers from telling debtors that an important package would be sent to them upon receipt of the specified information. Rothschild v. FTC, 200 F.2d 39 (7th Cir.1952) (the packages contained three pen points). More recently the FTC has focused on direct collection attempts. It has ordered an end to a collection agency's practice of threatening legal action when none was imminent. Trans World Accounts, Inc. v. FTC, 594 F.2d 212 (9th Cir.1979). It has, by consent decree, ordered another collection agency not to communicate (or threaten to communicate) with the debtor's employer or with any other person not liable for the debt (except for the debtor's spouse or attorney). In re Nosoma Systems, Inc., 88 F.T.C. 458 (1976). And it has, again by consent decree, ordered a creditor not to misrepresent that an attorney is involved in the matter or that legal action is about to occur or will occur in the future. In re American Family Publishers, 116 F.T.C. 66 (1993).

Little–FTC acts also may protect the consumer against overzealous collection efforts. The Supreme Court of Kansas has held that the statute prohibiting deceptive acts and practices in connection with consumer transactions applies to debt collection. State v. Midwest Service Bureau of Topeka, Inc., 623 P.2d 1343 (Kan.1981); accord, Liggins v. The May Co., 337 N.E.2d 816 (Ohio Ct.Com.Pl.1975). On the other hand, the North Carolina Supreme Court held that debt collection practices are not within the phrase "trade or commerce" as used in that state's little-FTC act (even though "commerce" as used in the FTC Act includes the collection of debts). State v. J.C. Penney Co., Inc., 233 S.E.2d 895 (N.C.1977). The North Carolina legislature promptly amended the statute. N.C.Gen.Stat. § 75–1.1(a).

Notwithstanding the foregoing, the most notable development in connection with debt collection has been the enactment of statutes designed specifically to regulate that conduct. The first stage was the enactment, in over half the states, of statutes regulating collection *agencies*. These statutes typically require the debt collector to obtain a license, for which the applicant must demonstrate integrity, good reputation, and financial responsibility, and must, in some states, pass a written examination. The statutes contain a list of prohibited practices, such as using or threatening violence, communicating in the name of a lawyer, using forms that simulate legal process or names that simulate the names of government entities, and publishing deadbeat lists. The lists vary considerably in the specific practices they single out.

Violation of the statute subjects the agency to criminal sanctions and suspension or revocation of its license. The sanctions, however, do not include civil liability to the debtor. Enforcement of the statute therefore depends on the efforts of the criminal prosecutor and the administrative agency that supervises collection agencies. Prosecutors typically do not assign high priority to debt collection abuse, and the effectiveness of the administrative agency is perhaps best revealed by the fact that the legislation frequently requires that a majority of the commissioners be in the business of debt collection. Licensing statutes are therefore of questionable effectiveness, and, in any event, they do not provide any remedy for the consumer who is injured by a violation.

The absence of any private remedy and also the restriction of coverage to collection agencies led several states in the 1970s to enact legislation to correct these shortcomings. These statutes apply to all persons collecting debts, not just collection agencies, and they provide a remedy for individual consumers. Like their predecessors, they contain lists of prohibited practices though, again, the specific practices on the lists vary from state to state. The Wisconsin statute is illustrative:

427.104   Prohibited practices

(1) In attempting to collect an alleged debt arising from a consumer credit transaction or other consumer transaction where there is an agreement to defer payment, a debt collector shall not

(a) Use or threaten force or violence to cause physical harm to the customer, or the customer's dependents or property;

(b) Threaten criminal prosecution;

(c) Disclose or threaten to disclose information adversely affecting the customer's reputation for credit worthiness with knowledge or reason to know that the information is false;

(d) Initiate or threaten to initiate communication with the customer's employer prior to obtaining final judgment against the customer, . . . but this paragraph does not prohibit a debt collector from communicating with the customer's employer solely to verify employment status or earnings or where an employer has an established debt counseling service or procedure;

(e) Disclose or threaten to disclose to a person other than the customer or the customer's spouse information affecting the customer's reputation, whether or not for credit worthiness, with knowledge or reason to know that the other person does not have a legitimate business need for the information, but this paragraph does not prohibit the disclosure to another person of information permitted to be disclosed to that person by statute;

(f) Disclose or threaten to disclose information concerning the existence of a debt known to be reasonably disputed by the customer without disclosing the fact that the customer disputes the debt;

(g) Communicate with the customer or a person related to the customer with such frequency or at such unusual hours or in such a manner as can reasonably be expected to threaten or harass the customer;

(h) Engage in other conduct which can reasonably be expected to threaten or harass the customer or a person related to the customer;

(*i*) Use obscene or threatening language in communicating with the customer or a person related to the customer;

(j) Claim, or attempt or threaten to enforce a right with knowledge or reason to know that the right does not exist;

(k) Use a communication which simulates legal or judicial process or which gives the appearance of being authorized, issued or approved by a government, governmental agency or attorney-at-law when it is not;

(*l*) Threaten action against the customer unless like action is taken in regular course or is intended with respect to the particular debt; or

(m) Engage in conduct in violation of a rule adopted by the administrator after like conduct has been restrained or enjoined by a court in a civil action by the administrator against any person pursuant to the provisions on injunctions against false, misleading, deceptive or unconscionable agreements or conduct.

. . .

427.105   Remedies

(1) A person injured by violation of this chapter may recover actual damages and the penalty provided in s. 425.304; but notwithstanding any other law actual damages shall include damages caused by emotional distress or mental anguish with or without accompanying physical injury proximately caused by a violation of this chapter.

. . .

425.304   Remedy and penalty for certain violations

A person who commits a violation to which this section applies is liable to the customer in an amount equal to the greater of:

(1) Twice the amount of the finance charge in connection with the transaction, except that the liability under this subsection shall not be less than $100 nor greater than $1,000; or

(2) The actual damages, including any incidental and consequential damages, sustained by the customer by reason of the violation.

Wis.Stat.Ann. §§ 425.304, 427.104–.105.

In addition to the list of specifically prohibited practices, some states have a catch-all provision, such as the Massachusetts prohibition against debt collection "in an unfair, deceptive or unreasonable manner." Mass. Gen.Laws Ann. ch. 93, § 49.

This movement among the states toward consumer-enforced debt collection statutes affected the drafting of the UCCC. In the original (1968) version of the UCCC, section 6.111(1)(c) empowered the Administrator to prevent "fraudulent or unconscionable conduct in the collection of debts," but provided no remedy to consumers who were injured by that fraudulent or unconscionable conduct. The 1974 version, however, recognizes a private right of action. Section 5.108(2).

Despite the trend toward consumer-oriented statutes, by the mid–1970s more than a quarter of the states still had no statutory regulation of debt collection and another quarter had only ineffectual regulation. Meanwhile, the abuses continued.[2] So, effective in 1978, Congress added the Fair Debt Collection Practices Act (FDCPA) as Title VIII of the Consumer Credit Protection Act (reproduced in the Statutory Supplement).

---

2. See Hearings on H.R. 11969 Before the Subcommittee on Consumer Affairs of H. Comm. on Banking, Currency and Housing, 94th Cong., 2d Sess. (1976).

The FDCPA imposes both procedural and substantive limits on debt collectors. Within five days of an initial communication with the consumer, the debt collector must send written notice informing the consumer of the amount of the debt, the name of the creditor, and the consumer's right to obtain verification of the debt (section 809). If the consumer disputes the debt, or any portion of it, the collector must cease nonjudicial collection efforts until the collector obtains verification of the debt and sends that verification to the consumer. Substantively, the Act limits the debt collector's ability to communicate with persons other than the consumer (§§ 804, 805), and it prohibits the use of harassment (section 806), deception (§ 807), and unfair practices (§ 808). The Act provides for enforcement by means of private remedies (§ 813) and administrative proceedings (§ 814).

For the Act to apply, however, the collector must meet the statutory definition of "debt collector." Please read section 803(6).

Problem. *Communications, Inc.*, makes the following solicitation to lenders and debt collectors: "Can't track down your customers' phone numbers because they have unlisted numbers? No problem. We will mail them a notification, informing them that they have received a phone-a-gram and requesting them to call us so that we can deliver it. When they do, we will capture their phone number, even if it is unlisted and even if they have caller-ID blocking!"

This conduct violates section 807(10), but section 807 only prohibits "debt collectors" from engaging in deception. Is *Communications, Inc.*, a "debt collector"?

Problem. *Card Issuer* issues a Visa card to *Consumer*, who becomes seriously delinquent. In attempting to collect this debt, *Card Issuer's* employees repeatedly phone *Consumer* before she leaves for work at 7:30 am and after she arrives home at 6:00 pm. Has *Card Issuer* violated the Act (see section 805(a))?

QUESTIONS

1. In what respects, if any, would the parties in Public Finance Corp. v. Davis and Voneye v. Turner violate the Wisconsin statute quoted above?

2. In what respects, if any, would they violate the Fair Debt Collection Practices Act? See sections 805–08.

3. Problem. *Consumer* receives a memo from her employer: "I have just been contacted about the debt you owe *Seller*. Take care of this matter immediately. I do not wish to be bothered about my employees' debts." As *Consumer's* attorney, would you elect to proceed under a common law tort theory, the Wisconsin statute, the UCCC, or the FDCPA?

4. Problem. *Consumer* receives a letter from Medical Account Collections, Inc.: "Dr. Hart has referred your overdue bill ($210) to us for collection. We expect to receive your check within a month. In the meantime, perhaps you would like to see our latest catalog of concrete boots. Pay up before it is too late." As *Consumer's* attorney, would you elect to proceed under the UCCC or the FDCPA?

Upon investigation, you discover that Dr. Hart's clinic transfers all its accounts to Medical Account Collections sixty days after the date of treatment, whether or not the patients' insurance companies have completed processing the patients' claims. Does this affect your answer? See section 803(6)(F).

5. Problem. *Consumer* borrowed $800 and has been unable to repay it. He comes to you with a fistful of letters (50 in all) that he has received in the last two months from *Collection Agency*. He tells you also of several phone calls he and his wife have received in the last month. What are *Consumer's* rights under the federal act? What would you advise him to do?

6. Problem. *Consumer's* employer receives the following letter:

Dear *Employer*,

I understand that *Consumer* is in your employ. It is very important to *Consumer* that I get in touch with her right away. Could you please check your records and let me know her address, phone number, and current salary? If you don't object, perhaps I'll stop by and talk to her one afternoon next week.

Is there a violation of the FDCPA?

7. Would it violate section 807 of the FDCPA for a debt collector to write or state the following:

a) "If you don't pay this debt, and *Creditor* gets judgment against you, you may lose your car, your TV, even your home."

b) "If you don't pay this debt, we will have to sue you."

c) "Do you know what happens to people who don't pay their bills? They can be sued, suffer judgment, and lose all their property."

d) "It is our policy to attempt to settle these matters out of court before making any decision to refer them to an attorney for collection. Unless we receive your check, we will proceed with collection procedures."

8. What would you advise a creditor to do when she receives a letter from her collection agency stating that pursuant to section 805(c) the debtor has directed it to cease communicating?

9. In Lewis v. ACB Business Services, Inc., 135 F.3d 389 (6th Cir.1998), the consumer sent the debt collector (ACB) a letter directing it to cease communications. Thereafter, ACB sent him a letter, stating in part:

Your account has been transferred to my office for final review. In a percentage of cases, I find that payment arrangements may not have been offered by our affiliated office. In order to provide you with an opportunity to pay this debt, please select one of the following payment arrangements and enclose payment, or provide me with a number where I can contact you to discuss terms.

[1]   . . .

[2]   . . .

[3]   . . .

If you have any questions regarding the payment plans, give me a call or provide me with a number where I can contact you. For your convenience, I can arrange for you to pay your account using Visa and/or MasterCard.

Contact : M. Hall

Payment Supervisor

(800) 767–5971

This is an attempt to collect a debt. Any information obtained will be used for that purpose.

Has ACB violated section 805(c)? At the time of the facts in *Lewis*, section 807(11) made it a violation of the Act for a debt collector to fail to disclose, "in all communications made to collect a debt . . . that the debt collector is attempting to collect a debt and that any information obtained will be used for that purpose." Does this bear on the legality of ACB's letter? In 1996 Congress amended section 807(11) to require this disclosure only in the *initial* communication. If ACB sent the letter today, but dropped the last sentence, would it violate section 805?

10.   Section 814 provides that a violation of the FDCPA is a violation of section 5 of the FTC Act. Does this mean that a violation of the FDCPA is also a violation of a state's little-FTC act?

11.   In Rutyna v. Collection Accounts Terminal, Inc., 478 F.Supp. 980 (N.D.Ill.1979), plaintiff was a retired, 60–year-old widow, suffering from high blood pressure and epilepsy. In connection with a doctor's bill that she disputed, defendant collection agency sent her a letter:

You have shown that you are unwilling to work out a friendly settlement with us to clear the above debt.

Our field investigator has now been instructed to make an investigation in your neighborhood and to personally call on your employer.

The immediate payment of the full amount, or a personal visit to this office, will spare you this embarrassment.

Alleging that this letter caused her to become "very nervous, upset, and worried," specifically that defendant would cause her embarrassment by informing her neighbors of the debt and about her medical problems, plaintiff sued under the FDCPA and moved for summary judgment. The court stated:

(1) Harassment or abuse (§ 806). The first sentence of § 806 provides: "A debt collector may not engage in any conduct the natural consequence of which is to harass, oppress, or abuse any person in connection with the collection of a debt." This section then lists six specifically prohibited types of conduct, without limiting the general

application of the foregoing sentence. The legislative history makes clear that this generality was intended:

> In addition to these specific prohibitions, this bill prohibits in general terms any harassing, unfair or deceptive collection practice. This will enable the courts, where appropriate, to proscribe other improper conduct which is not specifically addressed. 1977 U.S. Code Cong. & Admin. News at p. 1698.

Plaintiff does not allege conduct which falls within one of the specific prohibitions contained in § 806, but we find that defendant's letter to plaintiff does violate this general standard.

Without doubt defendant's letter has the natural (and intended) consequence of harassing, oppressing, and abusing the recipient. The tone of the letter is one of intimidation, and was intended as such in order to effect a collection. The threat of an investigation and resulting embarrassment to the alleged debtor is clear and the actual effect on the recipient is irrelevant. The egregiousness of the violation is a factor to be considered in awarding statutory damages (§ 813). Defendant's violation of § 806 is clear.

(2) Deception and improper threats (§ 807). § 807 bars a debt collector from using any "false, deceptive, or misleading representation or means in connection with the collection of any debt." Sixteen specific practices are listed in this provision, without limiting the application of this general standard. § 807(5) bars a threat "to take any action that cannot legally be taken or that is not intended to be taken." Defendant also violated this provision.

Defendant's letter threatened embarrassing contacts with plaintiff's employer and neighbors. This constitutes a false representation of the actions that defendant could legally take. § 805(b) prohibits communication by the debt collector with third parties (with certain limited exceptions not here relevant). Plaintiff's neighbors and employer could not legally be contacted by defendant in connection with this debt. The letter falsely represents, or deceives the recipient, to the contrary. This is a deceptive means employed by defendant in connection with its debt collection. Defendant violated § 807(5) in its threat to take such illegal action.

(3) Unfair practice/return address (§ 808(8)). The envelope received by plaintiff bore a return address, which began "COLLECTION ACCOUNTS TERMINAL, INC." § 808 bars unfair or unconscionable means to collect or attempt to collect any debt. § 808 specifically bars:

> (8) Using any language or symbol, other than the debt collector's address, on any envelope when communicating with a consumer by use of the mails or by telegram, except that a debt collector may use his business name if such name does not indicate that he is in the debt collection business.

Defendant's return address violated this provision, because its business name does indicate that it is in the debt collection business. The purpose of this specific provision is apparently to prevent embarrassment resulting from a conspicuous name on the envelope, indicating that the contents pertain to debt collection.

The court granted summary judgment for plaintiff on the issue of liability and subsequently awarded plaintiff $750 for actual damages and $500 as additional damages under section 813(a)(2)(A). 13 Clearinghouse Rev. 968 (1980).

What standard does the court use to determine whether the debt collector's conduct harassed, oppressed, or abused? What standard does the court use to determine whether the debt collector's conduct was false, deceptive, or misleading?

Jeter v. Credit Bureau, Inc.

United States Court of Appeals, Eleventh Circuit, 1985.
760 F.2d 1168.

R.   Lanier Anderson, III, Circuit Judge.

.   .   .

I.   FACTS AND PROCEDURAL BACKGROUND

Credit Bureau operates a debt collection agency subject to the FDCPA. Credit Bureau attempts to collect money on behalf of creditors who refer accounts (i.e. alleged debts) to Credit Bureau for collection. One of Credit Bureau's clients during the time period preceding this lawsuit was Associated Consumers Club ("Associated Consumers"). Sometime prior to October 25, 1983, Jeter incurred what Associated Consumers believed was a valid legal debt with Associated Consumers. On October 25, 1983, Jeter's account was referred by Associated Consumers to Credit Bureau for collection. On March 4, 1983, Credit Bureau sent Jeter a letter which reads as follows:

Take notice that the above creditor claims you are indebted to him as shown.

Although duly demanded, the same has not been paid. You have ignored our previous contacts.

Therefore, you are hereby notified that unless satisfactory arrangements are made within five (5) days from this date, we will recommend to our client, suit and subsequent action (judgment, garnishment, levy, and/or attachment proceedings) may be instigated against you by their attorneys.

Respond now and avoid the necessity of further action. An envelope has been enclosed for your convenience.

After March 4, and prior to April 7, 1983, neither Credit Bureau nor Associated Consumers took any further action with regard to Jeter's account. Jeter did not respond to the letter during this time period. On

April 7, 1983, Credit Bureau sent Jeter another letter which reads as follows:

> This is our final notice to you before recommending that our client give the account to their attorney for legal action.
>
> Although it may cause you embarrassment, inconvenience and further expense, we will do so if the entire balance is not in this office within the next five days.
>
> To insure proper credit, please return this notice with your payment in the envelope enclosed.
>
> Attend to it now—This is a final notice.

Neither Credit Bureau nor Associated Consumers took any action with regard to Jeter's account subsequent to the April 7, 1983, letter.

Sometime prior to May 11, 1983, Jeter hired a lawyer, Elizabeth Leonard. On May 11, 1983, Ms. Leonard sent a letter on Jeter's behalf to Credit Bureau stating Jeter's position that she owed no money to Associated Consumers. A copy of the letter was sent to Associated Consumers. Thereafter, Credit Bureau determined that the collection of Jeter's account was impractical, closed its files, and made no further contact with Jeter.

On June 16, 1983, Jeter sued Credit Bureau in the federal district court for the Northern District of Georgia claiming violations of the FDCPA. First, Jeter claimed that as a consequence of Credit Bureau's letters and its subsequent inaction, Credit Bureau had violated § 807(5) for "threatening to take any action that cannot legally be taken or that is not intended to be taken" and § 807(10) for using "any false representation or deceptive means to collect or attempt to collect any debt . . . ." Second, Jeter claimed that Credit Bureau had "engage[d] in . . . conduct the natural consequence of which [was] to harass, oppress, or abuse any person in connection with the collection of a debt" in violation of § 806.

After limited discovery, the district court, responding to Credit Bureau's motion for summary judgment and Jeter's motion for partial summary judgment, granted summary judgment to Credit Bureau on all issues. This appeal ensued.

. . .

II. APPLICABLE LEGAL STANDARD

The district court held that in determining whether the FDCPA has been violated the court was obligated to "decide whether a 'reasonable consumer' would be deceived, mislead [sic], or harassed by the letters at issue in this case." Relevant administrative adjudications and case law under the Federal Trade Commission Act ("FTC Act"), 15 U.S.C. § 41, et seq., upon which we rely by analogy, and persuasive authority under the FDCPA lead us to the conclusion that the district court applied an improper standard.

Section 5 of the FTC Act declares unlawful all "unfair or deceptive acts or practices in commerce." 15 U.S.C. § 45(a)(1). An act or practice is deceptive or unfair under § 5 if it has the tendency or capacity to deceive. The FTC Act was enacted to protect unsophisticated consumers, not only "reasonable consumers" who could otherwise protect themselves in the market place. The leading case of Charles of the Ritz Distributors Corp. v. FTC, 143 F.2d 676 (2d Cir.1944), is instructive. In *Charles of the Ritz*, the petitioner was charged by the FTC with falsely advertising its cosmetic preparation "Charles of the Ritz Rejuvenescence Cream" because the name "rejuvenescence" and the accompanying advertisement "represented, directly or by inference, that [the] cosmetic preparation [would] rejuvenate the skin of the user thereof or restore youth or the appearance of youth to the skin of the user." Id. at 678. In affirming the FTC's finding of deception, the Second Circuit defined "capacity to deceive" as follows:

> There is no merit to petitioner's argument that, since no straight-thinking person could believe that its cream would actually rejuvenate, there could be no deception. Such a view results from a grave misconception of the purposes of the Federal Trade Commission Act. That law was not "made for the protection of experts, but for the public—that vast multitude which includes the ignorant, the unthinking, and the credulous," Florence Mfg. Co. v. J.C. Dowd & Co., 2 Cir., 178 F. 73, 75 [(1910)]; and the "fact that a false statement may be obviously false to those who are trained and experienced does not change its character, nor take away its power to deceive others less experienced." Federal Trade Commission v. Standard Education Soc., 302 U.S. 112, 116 (1937) . . . .

Id. at 679. The standard enunciated by *Charles of the Ritz,* supra, has been followed in an enormous number of federal court and FTC decisions, and controlling precedent in this circuit is in accord. . . . Unfair and deceptive debt practices have been the frequent subject of FTC enforcement action. See State v. O'Neill Investigations, Inc., 609 P.2d 520, 529 n. 29 (Alaska 1980) (citing numerous cases). The FTC and the federal courts have consistently held that it is a deceptive practice to falsely represent that unpaid debts would be referred to a lawyer for immediate legal action. E.g., Trans World Accounts v. FTC, 594 F.2d 212, 215 (9th Cir.1979); Wilson Chemical Co., 64 FTC 168, 185 (1964). In these cases, consistent with the legal standard in other actions under § 5, the FTC has looked not to the "reasonable consumer," but to a less sophisticated consumer and whether the debt collection practice has a tendency or capacity to deceive. See e.g., Wilson Chemical Co., supra, 64 FTC at 185.

The above discussion indicates that, prior to the passage of the FDCPA, the FTC had protected unsophisticated consumers from debt collection practices which have a tendency or capacity to deceive. Credit Bureau argues that the FTC jurisprudence under § 5 is irrelevant to litigation under the FDCPA. Our review of the authorities leads us to precisely the opposite conclusion. In its "findings and declaration of purpose" incorporated in the FDCPA, Congress found that despite prior FTC enforcement in the area "[t]here is abundant evidence of abusive, deceptive and unfair debt collection practices by many debt collectors. . . . Existing laws and procedures for redressing these injuries are inadequate to protect consumers." § 802(a), (b). The legislative history echoes these purposes and concerns. S.Rep. No. 95–382, 95th Cong., 1st Sess., *reprinted in* 1977 U.S.Code Cong. & Ad.News 1695, 1697 ("The committee believes that the serious and widespread abuses in this area and the inadequacy of existing State and Federal laws make this legislation necessary and appropriate"). It would be anomalous for the Congress, in light of its belief that existing state and federal law was inadequate to protect consumers, to have intended that the legal standard under the FDCPA be *less* protective of consumers than under the existing "inadequate" legislation. . . .

In light of the purposes of the FDCPA, the general FTC jurisprudence under § 5, and the prior FTC enforcement in the debt collection area, we conclude that the district court erred in judging Credit Bureau's actions by reference to the "reasonable consumer." Our position is supported by a majority of the federal courts to address this question. . . .

Because we believe that Congress intended the standard under the FDCPA to be the same as that enunciated in the relevant FTC cases, and because we believe that "[t]he FDCPA's purpose of protecting [consumers] . . . is best served by a definition of 'deceive' that looks to the tendency of language to mislead the least sophisticated recipients of a debt collector's letters and telephone calls," Wright v. Credit Bureau of Georgia, Inc., 548 F.Supp. 591, 599 (N.D.Ga.1982), we adopt the . . . standard of "least sophisticated consumer". . . .

III.   FALSE OR MISLEADING REPRESENTATIONS?

Jeter claims that the letter sent by Credit Bureau violated §§ 807(5) and (10). These subsections provide:

> A debt collector may not use any false, deceptive, or misleading representation or means in connection with the collection of any debt. Without limiting the general application of the foregoing, the following conduct is a violation of this section:
>
> . . .
>
> (5) The threat to take any action that cannot legally be taken or that is not intended to be taken.
>
> . . .
>
> (10) The use of any false representation or deceptive means to collect or attempt to collect any debt or to obtain information concerning a consumer.

Jeter has presented two theories for relief under subsection (5). First, Jeter claims that Credit Bureau's letters indicate that it would recommend legal action upon the expiration of the five-day period referred to in the letters or shortly thereafter and, as such, amounted to threats to take actions which were not intended to be taken. Second, Jeter claims that Credit Bureau *never* intended to recommend legal action. Jeter also maintains that the letters, individually and/or collectively, were deceptive within the meaning of subsection (10). We will discuss in turn Jeter's two theories for relief under subsection (5), and then her claim under subsection (10).

A. Claim Under Subsection (5)

Subsection (5) of § 807 does not require application of the legal standard developed in Part II, supra. The subsection (5) issue is simply whether or not Credit Bureau *intended* to take the action threatened. Thus, subsection (5) requires proof of a fact which amounts to a *per se* violation of § 807. The sophistication, or lack thereof, of the consumer is irrelevant to whether Credit Bureau "threatened to take any action . . . that [was] not intended to be taken."

First, we consider Jeter's claim that Credit Bureau falsely threatened to take legal action in the immediate or near future. It is undisputed in the record that Credit Bureau did not recommend legal action immediately upon the expiration of the five-day period after it sent the letters to Jeter or shortly thereafter. The district court's reliance on the fact that "[a]n officer of the defendant has stated that the defendant did, in fact, intend to recommend legal action," is not by any means dispositive with regard to whether Credit Bureau intended to recommend legal action upon the expiration of the five-day period. The party seeking summary judgment bears the burden of demonstrating that there is no genuine dispute as to any material fact, and all evidence and all reasonable factual inferences therefrom must be viewed in a light most favorable to the party opposing the motion. Clemons v. Dougherty County, 684 F.2d 1365, 1368 (11th Cir.1982). Although the parties agree on the basic facts in this case, they disagree upon the proper inferences to be drawn from the letters sent by Credit Bureau to Jeter. Such a disagreement, if reasonable, is one for resolution by the trier of fact, not by the court in a summary judgment context. See Lighting Fixture and Electric Supply Co. v. Continental Ins. Co., 420 F.2d 1211, 1213 (5th Cir.1969). If one reads the letters literally, the alleged debtor is simply required to make payment to Credit Bureau within five days, and if the alleged debt is not paid, Credit Bureau will recommend suit sometime thereafter. However, a reasonable jury could read the letter as a threat to recommend legal action immediately upon the expiration of the five-day period or shortly thereafter. For instance, the first letter says that Credit Bureau would recommend legal action "unless satisfactory arrangements are made within five (5) days." The letter goes on to tell the alleged debtor to "[r]espond now and avoid the necessity of further action." A jury could have interpreted this language as indicative of a threat to recommend legal action immediately upon expiration of the five-day period, if Jeter had not paid the alleged debt. Similarly, Credit Bureau's second letter to Jeter states that Credit Bureau will recommend legal action "if the entire balance is not in this office within the next five days." The letter goes on to tell Jeter to "[a]ttend to it now. . . ." In short, the jury could reasonably have found that Credit Bureau's reference to a five-day period preceding the recommendation of a lawsuit against Jeter was indicative of a threat to recommend legal action immediately upon the expiration of the five-day period or shortly thereafter if the alleged debt was not paid.

Thus, the jury has two tasks. First, it must ascertain the meaning of Credit Bureau's letters to determine just what was threatened. As indicated above, a reasonable jury may find that the letters evidence a threat to recommend legal action immediately upon expiration of the five-day period or shortly thereafter. If the jury so finds, it must then decide whether Credit Bureau intended to take such threatened action in this case. . . .

B.   Claim Under Subsection (10)

We turn now to Jeter's subsection (10) claim. Here, the legal consequences of Credit Bureau's failure to recommend legal action within five days does require the application of the legal standard enunciated in Part II, supra.

We conclude that the district court erred in granting summary judgment to Credit Bureau. As we have indicated in Part III.A., supra, a reasonable jury could well have interpreted Credit Bureau's letters as threatening to take legal action immediately upon expiration of the five-day periods or shortly thereafter, if the debtor had not yet paid the alleged debt. Under subsection (10), we must consider whether the "least sophisticated consumer" would be deceived by Credit Bureau's letters, i.e. whether the letters were a "deceptive means" to collect alleged debts, valid or invalid, by the use of false or deliberately ambiguous threats to recommend legal action. It may be, although we doubt it, that a "reasonable consumer" would have taken Credit Bureau's letters as empty threats to recommend legal action at some undisclosed time in the distant future; however, the fact that Jeter hired a lawyer and responded to the second letter seems to support the opposite view.[11] In any event, we are confident that whether the "least sophisticated consumer" would construe Credit Bureau's letter as deceptive is a question for the jury. On remand, the jury should be instructed on the standard enunciated in Part II, supra, and allowed to determine whether, operating under that standard, Credit Bureau's letters were deceptive.

IV.   HARASSMENT OR ABUSE?

Jeter argues that the district court erred in granting summary judgment in favor of Credit Bureau on her claim under § 806. Section 806 reads as follows:

---

11. The district court opinion stressed the fact that Jeter was not deceived because she hired a lawyer and successfully warded off the Credit Bureau. First, we reiterate that the question is not whether Jeter was deceived, but whether the "least sophisticated consumer" would have been deceived. Of course, the extent of Jeter's deception is relevant to damages under the FDCPA. See §§ 813(a)(1), (2)(A). Second, on remand the evidence may well indicate that Jeter was deceived, her hiring of an attorney being a direct result of that deception. It is true that Jeter might have been injured worse. Upon receiving one or both of the letters, she could have immediately paid the debt, thinking she was about to be sued. This case, therefore, may well illustrate one of the purposes behind §§ 807(5) and (10). Congress apparently was aware that a false threat to sue in the near future might well be used to induce premature payment of an alleged debt with respect to which the consumer has a legitimate defense.

A debt collector may not engage in any conduct the natural consequence of which is to harass, oppress, or abuse any person in connection with the collection of a debt. Without limiting the general application of the foregoing, the following conduct is a violation of this section:

. . .

Subsections (1)–(6) do not proscribe Credit Bureau's conduct or the content of the two letters sent to Jeter.

. . .

However, § 806 is explicitly not limited to the conduct proscribed by subsections (1)–(6). . . . The district court decided, however, that it was inappropriate to characterize Credit Bureau's conduct as violative of § 806:

> The defendant in the present case merely threatened to institute legal action against the plaintiff. The sentence that the plaintiff objects to is the one that stated that the institution of such proceedings could possibly cause her "embarrassment, inconvenience, and further expense." The Court feels that this language would not oppress or harass a reasonable consumer. . . . [T]he defendant in the case at bar merely pointed out to the plaintiff the potential problems she might face if a lawsuit was brought against her. These problems could possibly arise in the defense of any lawsuit.

. . .

We note that the district court applied a "reasonable consumer" standard to Jeter's claim under § 806, a standard which we have rejected with respect to claims of misrepresentation and deception under § 807. However, we cannot simply apply a "least sophisticated consumer" standard. Whether a consumer is more or less likely to be harassed, oppressed, or abused by certain debt collection practices does not relate solely to the consumer's relative sophistication; rather, such susceptibility might be affected by other circumstances of the consumer or by the relationship between the consumer and the debt collection agency. For example, a very intelligent and sophisticated consumer might well be susceptible to harassment, oppression, or abuse because he is poor (i.e. has limited access to the legal system), is on probation, or is otherwise at the mercy of a power relationship. Although the standard enunciated in Part II, supra, is not precisely applicable here, we believe that the consumer protective purposes of the FDCPA require us to adopt an analogous standard for violations of § 806. Thus, we hold that claims under § 806 should be viewed from the perspective of a consumer whose circumstances make him relatively more susceptible to harassment, oppression, or abuse.

That a lawsuit might cause a consumer "embarrassment, inconvenience, and further expense" is a true statement. Such consequences of a debt collection (or any other) lawsuit are so commonplace that even a consumer susceptible to harassment, oppression, or abuse would not have been harassed, oppressed, or abused by the statement *in and of itself*. A simple warning of "embarrassment, inconvenience, and further expense" does not create a "tone . . . of intimidation . . . ." Rutyna v. Collection Accounts Terminal, Inc., 478 F.Supp. 980, 982 (N.D.Ill.1979). Of course, Credit Bureau's statement was part and parcel of general representations which a reasonable jury could find to be violative of §§ 807(5) and (10), i.e. potentially deceptive or false use of threats to recommend legal action. See supra Part III. Deception or falsehood alone, however, is wholly different from the conduct condemned in subsections (1) through (6) of § 806. Thus, we believe that Congress did not contemplate the prohibition of deceptive conduct per se within the confines of § 806.

Ordinarily, whether conduct harasses, oppresses, or abuses will be a question for the jury. Nevertheless, Congress had indicated its desire for the courts to structure the confines of § 806. S.Rep. No. 95–832, 95th Cong., 1st Sess., *reprinted in* 1977 U.S.Code Cong. & Ad.News 1695, 1698 (courts will proscribe "other improper conduct which is not specifically addressed"). The above discussion and a review of the case law . . . lead us to the conclusion that, even when judged by the consumer protective standard we adopt today, § 806 does not as a matter of law proscribe Credit Bureau's conduct in this case.[12] Thus, the district court's grant of summary judgment in favor of Credit Bureau on this issue is affirmed.

CONCLUSION

For the foregoing reasons, we affirm in part, reverse in part, and remand to the district court for proceedings not inconsistent with this opinion.

AFFIRMED in part, REVERSED in part, and REMANDED.

QUESTIONS

1. Note that the court in *Jeter* did not refer to the standards for determining deception that the FTC articulated in its 1983 Policy Statement (referred to in *International Harvester*, page 62 supra). Was it appropriate for the court to rely on *Charles of the Ritz*?

2. According to the court, if the jury on remand concludes that the language in the letters amounts to a threat to recommend legal action, the jury would have to decide whether defendant lacked the intention to recommend legal action. If you were representing the plaintiff on remand,

---

12. Jeter cites the case of Rutyna v. Collection Accounts Terminal, Inc., 478 F.Supp. 980 (N.D.Ill.1979), in support of her claim under § 806. In *Rutyna*, the plaintiff received a letter from the debt collector which stated that the debt collector's "field investigator has now been instructed to make an investigation in your neighborhood and to personally call on your employer." Id. at 981. The plaintiff quite reasonably became upset and worried that the debt collector's agent would begin informing her neighbors of her debt and related medical problems. *Rutyna* represents the type of coercion and delving into the personal lives of debtors that the FDCPA in general, and § 806 in particular, was designed to address. . . . The facts here do not remotely resemble those in *Rutyna*.

what evidence would you seek to uncover and introduce on the question of defendant's intention?

3. The court differentiates between subsection (5) and subsection (10) of section 807. What is the basis for applying the least-sophisticated-consumer standard to subsection (10) but not to subsection (5)?

4. The "least sophisticated consumer" appears to be a very low standard of deceptiveness. The courts have tempered *Jeter's* articulation:

> To serve the purposes of the consumer-protection laws, courts have attempted to articulate a standard for evaluating deceptiveness that does not rely on assumptions about the "average" or "normal" consumer. This effort is grounded, quite sensibly, in the assumption that consumers of below-average sophistication or intelligence are especially vulnerable to fraudulent schemes. The least-sophisticated-consumer standard protects these consumers in a variety of ways . . . .
>
> It should be emphasized that in crafting a norm that protects the naive and the credulous the courts have carefully preserved the concept of reasonableness. Indeed, courts have consistently applied the least-sophisticated-consumer standard in a manner that protects debt collectors against liability for unreasonable misinterpretations of collection notices. . . . [C]ourts have held that even the "least sophisticated consumer" can be presumed to possess a rudimentary amount of information about the world and a willingness to read a collection notice with some care.
>
> . . . [T]he existence of this substantial body of law demonstrates that the least-sophisticated-consumer standard effectively serves its dual purpose: it (1) ensures the protection of all consumers, even the naive and the trusting, against deceptive debt collection practices, and (2) protects debt collectors against liability for bizarre or idiosyncratic interpretations of collection notices.

Clomon v. Jackson, 988 F.2d 1314, 1319–20 (2d Cir.1993). Nevertheless, the Court of Appeals for the Seventh Circuit was moved to add:

> We agree with much of the analysis set forth by the Second Circuit in *Clomon*; however, we believe that a modification of the least sophisticated consumer standard as articulated in cases such as *Clomon* would relieve the incongruity between what the standard would entail if read literally, and the way courts have interpreted the standard.
>
> It strikes us virtually impossible to analyze a debt collection letter based on the reasonable interpretations of the least sophisticated consumer. Literally, the least sophisticated consumer is not merely "below average," he is the very last rung on the sophistication ladder. Stated another way, he is the single most unsophisticated consumer who exists. Even assuming that he would be willing to do so, such a consumer would likely not be able to read a collection notice with care (or at all), let alone interpret it in a reasonable fashion. . . .

In maintaining the principles behind the enactment of the FDCPA, we believe a simpler and less confusing formulation of a standard designed to protect those consumers of below-average sophistication or intelligence should be adopted. Thus, we will use the term, "unsophisticated," instead of the phrase, "least sophisticated," to describe the hypothetical consumer whose reasonable perceptions will be used to determine if collection messages are deceptive or misleading. We reiterate that an unsophisticated consumer standard protects the consumer who is uninformed, naive, or trusting, yet it admits an objective element of reasonableness. The reasonableness element in turn shields complying debt collectors from liability for unrealistic or peculiar interpretations of collection letters.

Gammon v. GC Services Limited Partnership, 27 F.3d 1254, 1257 (7th Cir.1994). Courts outside the Seventh Circuit have continued to articulate the test in terms of the least sophisticated consumer.

5. Problem. *Consumer* borrows $5,000 to finance the purchase of a car. He agrees to repay the loan in forty-eight monthly installments of $133, totaling $6,384. After paying six installments totaling $798, *Consumer* defaults. Ultimately, the lender turns the account over to *Collection Agency*, which sends a letter demanding immediate payment of the balance, $5,586, as well as a collection fee of two percent of the balance, or $111.72. Has *Collection Agency* violated section 807 or 808 of the FDCPA?

If *Consumer* denies owing the debt, or disputes the amount of the debt, or claims an inability to pay the debt, would it violate section 806 for the debt collector to call him a liar?

6. Problem. *Debt Collector* sends the following letter. Has he violated section 807?

48 HOUR NOTICE

TAKE NOTICE . . . That your creditor alleges that you are justly indebted in the amount listed with us for collection. Further we have been authorized to proceed with any necessary lawful action to effect such collection. Therefore, you have *48 Hours* in which to pay the amount indicated above.

TIME IS OF THE ESSENCE!

IF YOU REMIT WITHIN *48 HOURS* NO ACTION WILL BE TAKEN

7. Problem. *Debt Collector* sends the following letter.

Your account has been referred to my desk for processing. In a percentage of cases referred to us, we find it necessary to resort to legal proceedings through attorneys and the civil courts.

If this account is referred to counsel, and she determines that suit should be filed against you, it may result in the recovery of a judgment which may pursuant to law, include not only the amount of your indebtedness, but in addition, the amount of any statutory costs, legal interest, and where applicable, reasonable attorney's fees.

If the judgment is not thereon satisfied, it may be collected by attachment of and execution upon your real and personal property. Garnishment is also an available remedy to satisfy an unsatisfied judgment.

We, therefore, suggest two alternatives:

1.   Bring or send this balance personally by return mail.

2.   Come to this office personally to see me and make arrangements for the satisfaction of this account.

We are not representing either directly or by implication that legal action has been or is being taken against you at this time.

We would appreciate hearing from you or your attorney within the next forty-eight (48) hours.

Has *Debt Collector* violated section 807? Would it violate section 807 if the penultimate paragraph were changed to:

We do not mean to represent directly or indirectly that legal action has been, is being, or will be taken against you. We would, however, prefer that the money which is due be paid without necessity of further processing by us.

8.   Do the letters in Problems 6 and 7 violate section 809(a)? See especially subsections (3)-(4).

9.   Problem. *Debt Collector* sends the following:

We are sending this letter in an attempt to clear your long overdue account in the amount of $3,200. Effective immediately, and only during the next 30 days, our client will settle your outstanding balance due with a 30% discount off your balance. The settlement must be in one payment of $2,240 and must be received in our office no later than October 1.

Does this letter violate section 807(10)? Is there additional information you would like to have?

10.   Problem. *Consumer* received a discharge in bankruptcy, which eliminated her personal liability on a debt owed Sears, Roebuck. *DC*, a debt collector hired by Sears, writes a letter to the attorney who represented *Consumer* in the bankruptcy proceeding, stating that Sears is going to replevy several articles in which it holds a security interest, unless *Consumer* pays $350, which *DC* asserts to be the reasonable value of those articles. *DC* does not give the notices required by section 809, and the reasonable value of the collateral is $150. Is *DC* liable for violating sections 809 and 807(10), i.e. does the Act apply to a debt collector's communications with a consumer's attorney? The Ninth Circuit thinks not:

We . . . hold that communications directed solely to a debtor's attorney are not actionable under the Act. . . .

A consumer and his attorney are not one and the same for purposes of the Act. They are legally distinct entities, and the Act consequently treats them as such. For example, a debt collector who knows that a consumer has retained counsel regarding the subject debt may contact counsel, but may not generally contact the consumer directly, unless the attorney gives his consent. *See* [§ 805(a)(2)]. Subject to certain exceptions, a debt collector may not communicate in connection with a debt with "any person other than *the consumer, his attorney*, a consumer reporting agency . . . , the creditor, the attorney of the creditor, or the attorney of the debt collector." [§ 805(b)] (emphasis added). And "consumer" is defined broadly in [§ 805(d)] to include "the consumer's spouse, parent (if the consumer is a minor), guardian, executor, or administrator." Notably absent from this list of relatives and fiduciaries sharing in common the identity of "consumer" is a consumer's attorney.

The statute as a whole thus suggests a congressional understanding that, when it comes to debt collection matters, lawyers and their debtor clients will be treated differently. See U.S. Nat'l Bank of Or. v. Indep. Ins. Agents of Am., Inc., 508 U.S. 439, 455, 113 S.Ct. 2173, 124 L.Ed.2d 402 (1993) ("In expounding a statute, we must not be guided by a single sentence or member of a sentence, but look to the provisions of the whole law, and to its object and policy"). Specifically, it appears that Congress viewed attorneys as intermediaries able to bear the brunt of overreaching debt collection practices from which debtors and their loved ones should be protected. Section [805], for instance, covers "[c]ommunications in connection with debt collection." In regulating the ability of debt collectors to commence such communications, the Act is plainly concerned with harassment, deception, and other abuse. Accordingly, Congress sought to protect not just debtors themselves from illegal communications, but also others who would be vulnerable to the more sinister practices employed in the debt collection industry. Section [805(d)], as explained above, thus defines "consumer" broadly to include a range of the debtor's relatives and fiduciaries. The conspicuous absence of the debtor's attorney from that otherwise extensive list is telling. It suggests that in approaching the debt collection problem, Congress did not view attorneys as susceptible to the abuses that spurred the need for the legislation to begin with, and that Congress built that differentiation into the statute itself.

. . .

The purpose of the FDCPA is to protect vulnerable and unsophisticated debtors from abuse, harassment, and deceptive collection practices.

The Act's purposes are not served by applying its strictures to communications sent only to a debtor's attorney, particularly in the context of settlement negotiations. Congress was concerned with disruptive, threatening, and dishonest tactics. The Senate Report accompanying the Act cites practices such as "threats of violence, telephone calls at unreasonable hours [and] misrepresentation of a consumer's legal rights." S. Rep. 95–389, at 2. In other words, Congress seems to have contemplated the type of actions that would intimidate unsophisticated individuals and which, in the words of the Seventh Circuit, "would likely disrupt a debtor's life." *Pettit v. Retrieval Masters Creditor Bureau, Inc.*, 211 F.3d 1057, 1059 (7th Cir. 2000).

When an individual is represented by counsel who fields all communications relevant to the debt collection, these concerns quickly evaporate. Attorneys possess exactly the degree of sophistication and legal wherewithal that individual debtors do not. *See Kropelnicki v. Siegel*, [290 F.3d 118, 127–28 (2d Cir. 2002)] (when "an attorney is interposed as an intermediary between a debt collector and a consumer, we assume the attorney, rather than the FDCPA, will protect the consumer from a debt collector's fraudulent or harassing behavior").

Guerrero v. RJM Acquisitions LLC, 499 F.3d 926, 935, 938–39 (9th Cir. 2007).

Compare the view of the Seventh Circuit:

It would be passing odd if the fact that a consumer was represented excused the debt collector from having to convey to the consumer the information to which the statute entitles him. For example, sections [809(a)(1) and (2)] provide that the required notice must state the amount of the debt and the name of the creditor. Is it to be believed that by retaining a lawyer the debtor disentitles himself to the information? Or that the debt collector, though knowing that the debtor is represented, can communicate directly with him in defiance of the principle that once a party to a legal dispute is represented, the other party must deal with him through his lawyer, and not directly? We conclude that any written notice sent to the lawyer must contain the information that would be required by the Act if the notice were sent to the consumer directly.

The next question is whether debt collectors can, without liability, threaten, make false representations to, or commit other abusive, deceptive, or unconscionable acts against a consumer's lawyer, in violation of sections [806, 807, or 808]. These sections do not designate any class of persons, such as lawyers, who can be abused, misled, etc., by debt collectors with impunity. Section [806] forbids 'any conduct the natural consequence of which is to harass, oppress, or abuse *any person* in connection with the collection of a debt' (emphasis added). Section [807] forbids a debt collector to 'use any false, deceptive, or misleading representation or means in connection with the collection of any debt.' And section [808] forbids a debt collector to 'use any unfair or unconscionable means to collect or attempt to collect any debt.'

It is true that a lawyer is less likely to be deceived, intimidated, harassed, and so forth (for simplicity, we shall assume that only deception is alleged) than a consumer. But that is an argument not for immunizing practices forbidden by the statute when they are directed against a consumer's lawyer, but rather for recognizing that the standard for determining whether particular conduct violates the statute is different when the conduct is aimed at a lawyer than when it is aimed at a consumer.

The courts have ruled that the statute is intended for the protection of unsophisticated consumers (sophisticated consumers presumably do not need its protection), so that in deciding whether for example a representation made in a dunning letter is misleading the court asks whether a person of modest education and limited commercial savvy would be likely to be deceived. . . .

By the same token, the 'unsophisticated consumer' standpoint is inappropriate for judging communications with lawyers, just as it is inappropriate to fix a physician's standard of care at the level of that of a medical orderly. W. Page Keeton *et al.*, *Prosser & Keeton on the Law of Torts* § 32, p. 185 (5th ed. 1984). But what should the standard be? Most lawyers who represent consumers in debt collection cases are familiar with debt collection law and therefore unlikely to be deceived. But sometimes a lawyer will find himself handling a debt collection case not because he's a specialist but because a friend or relative has asked him to handle it. His sophistication in collection matters would be less than that of the specialist practitioner but much greater than that of the average unsophisticated consumer. He would not have to be an expert on the Fair Debt Collection Practices Act to be able to look it up and discover what information sections [809(a)(3)-(5)] require be disclosed to the consumer, and then compare the requirements with the content of the communication that he has received on his client's behalf. Since, therefore, most lawyers who represent consumers in debt-collection cases are knowledgeable about the law and practices of debt collection, since those who are not should be able to inform themselves sufficiently to be able to represent their consumer clients competently, and since the debt collector cannot be expected to know how knowledgeable a particular consumer's lawyer is, we conclude that a representation by a debt collector that would be unlikely to deceive a competent lawyer, even if he is not a specialist in consumer debt law, should not be actionable.

We have assumed for the sake of simplicity that the communication to the lawyer is alleged to be *deceptive*; what if instead it is alleged to be false or misleading, terms also found in section [807]? 'Misleading' is similar to 'deceptive,' except that it can be innocent; one intends to deceive, but one can mislead through inadvertence. A sophisticated person is less likely to be either deceived or misled than an unsophisticated one. That is less true if a statement is false. A false claim of fact in a dunning letter may be as difficult for a lawyer to see through as a consumer. Suppose the letter misrepresents the unpaid balance of the consumer's debt. The lawyer might be unable to discover the falsity of the representation without an investigation that he might be unable, depending on his client's resources, to undertake. Such a misrepresentation would be actionable whether made to the consumer directly, or indirectly through his lawyer.

. . .

. . . If you glance back at section [809(a)] you will see that it says that the written notice is required to be sent 'five days after the initial communication with a consumer.' The argument is that if there is no letter sent first ('initial communication') directly to the consumer, but instead the initial communication is to the consumer's lawyer, the condition for requiring the subsequent written notice containing specified information is not satisfied and therefore such a notice need never be sent either to the lawyer or to the consumer. All that this argument shows is how unsound it would be to suppose that a communication to a person's lawyer is not a communication to the person. It would make a consumer who had a lawyer worse off than one who did not, because neither he nor his lawyer would have a right to any of the information that the statute requires be disclosed to the consumer.

Evory v. RJM Acquisitions Funding L.L.C., 505 F.3d 769, 773–75, 777 (7th Cir.2007).

Which court is correct? Can the views be reconciled?

11. In at least six states, the statutes regulating debt collectors require them to make certain disclosures in addition to the disclosures required by the FDCPA. In response, collectors often include on the back side of their collection letters a series of paragraphs applicable to the residents of those states. The Colorado statute, for example, requires debt collectors to disclose that the consumer has a right to direct the collector to cease communication. The FDCPA confers this right on consumers but does not require the collector to disclose its existence to the consumer.

Problem. *Debt Collector* sends a collection letter to *Consumer*. On the back side it states, "The following notices apply to persons residing in the following states." In the third of six paragraphs, it states:

COLORADO: If you notify us in writing that you wish us to cease communication with you, then we will not communicate further with you.

If *Consumer* lives in a state other than Colorado, has *Debt Collector* violated the FDCPA?

12. Problem. *CheckMate*, a check guarantee service (see Questions 1–2, pages 232–33 supra) provides signs for *Merchant* to post at its checkout registers: "If you write a check that is dishonored, you authorize us to issue a draft on your account for the amount of the check plus a collection fee." *Consumer* writes a check for $110 that the bank dishonors. *CheckMate* issues a draft on *Consumer's* account in the amount of $135. Has *Check-Mate* violated the FDCPA?

13. As initially enacted the FDCPA exempted attorneys from its requirements, but Congress removed the exemption in 1986. Consequently, attorneys must comply with the Act, including sections 807(11) and 809. The

Supreme Court has held that this obligation exists even in connection with litigation. Heintz v. Jenkins, 514 U.S. 291 (1995). In 1996 Congress amended section 807(11) to accommodate formal court pleadings.

Attorneys who engage in debt collection must comply with all the provisions that apply to debt collection agencies, including the ban on deception. This imposes greater restraint on attorneys than on non-attorney debt collectors.

> A lawyer who merely rents his letterhead to a collection agency violates the Act [§ 812(a)], for in such a case the lawyer is allowing the collection agency to impersonate him. The significance of such impersonation is that a debtor who receives a dunning letter signed by a lawyer will think that a lawyer reviewed the claim and determined that it had at least colorable merit; so if no lawyer did review the claim, the debtor will have been deceived and the purpose of the Act therefore thwarted. Similarly, a lawyer who, like [defendant], is a debt collector violates section [807(3)] (and also section [807(10)] . . .) if he sends a dunning letter that he has not reviewed, since his lawyer's letterhead then falsely implies that he has reviewed the creditor's claim.

Boyd v. Wexler, 275 F.3d 642, 644 (7th Cir.2001). The court analyzed the number of collection letters sent by the firm (e.g., 23,342 in one particularly busy week) and considered the likelihood that an attorney reviewed each alleged debt. It reversed the trial court's grant of summary judgment for the attorney:

> . . . A reasonable jury could infer from the evidence . . . that the defendant violated the Fair Debt Collection Practices Act by rubber stamping his clients' demands for payment, thus misrepresenting to the recipients of his dunning letters that a lawyer had made a minimally responsible determination that there was probable cause to believe that the recipient actually owed the amount claimed by the creditor. A reasonable jury informed of the size of the firm and the duties of the three lawyers, which leave them little time for review of collection files, informed also of the circumstances from which an estimate can be made of the time that it takes a lawyer to review such a file with sufficient care to be able to make a responsible professional judgment that a legally collectible debt is owing, and informed finally of the enormous mass of mailings . . . in relation to the number and available time of [defendant's] tiny legal staff, could rationally conclude that [defendant's] claim to have reviewed these plaintiffs' files was false, that he had not reviewed them (nor had any other lawyer), and therefore that he had violated the Act.

Id. at 647.

14.   Problem. *Merchant* sends *Consumer* a bill stating that *Consumer* owes $850 and has made no payments in the last 90 days on his revolving charge account. *Consumer* sends *Merchant* a letter stating that he had paid the entire balance in a timely fashion, enclosing a copy of a cancelled check showing payment of $781.43 two months earlier. *Merchant* continues to report *Consumer* as delinquent on *Merchant's* monthly transmission of information to *Credit Bureau* and turns the debt over to *DC*, a collection agency. *DC* sends *Consumer* a letter demanding immediate payment. This letter complies with section 809. *Consumer* sends *DC* a letter explaining that he paid the debt, again enclosing a copy of the cancelled check. *DC* continues sending letters and, in addition, reports *Consumer's* delinquency to *Credit Bureau*.

Consumer comes to you for assistance. Does he have a claim against *Merchant*? *DC*? *Credit Bureau*? See FDCPA § 807; FCRA § 623(a)(1), (3), § 623(b), § 624(b)(1)(F); little-FTC act.

15. If a debt collector phones a consumer who is not at home, what message may the debt collector leave on the consumer's answering machine? See sections 804, 805(b), 806(6), 807(11).

16. To assist in the administration of the Act, the FTC staff has issued Staff Commentary on the Fair Debt Collection Practices Act, 53 Fed.Reg. 50,097 (1988). Since section 814(d) expressly denies rulemaking authority to the FTC, this Commentary does not have the insulating effect that some other agency staff commentaries do. Cf. Truth-in-Lending Act § 130(f), 15 U.S.C. § 1640(f); Equal Credit Opportunity Act § 706(e), 15 U.S.C. § 1691e(e). Nevertheless, the Commentary represents the considered judgment of those primarily responsible for administrative enforcement of the FDCPA.

17. The FDCPA provides for both administrative enforcement (§ 814) and private enforcement (§ 813). The private remedies include actual damages and "such additional damages as the court may allow, but not exceeding $1,000." In determining the amount of the additional damages, the court is to consider "the frequency and persistence of noncompliance by the debt collector, the nature of such noncompliance, and the extent to which such noncompliance was intentional" (§ 813(b)(1)). May the consumer who establishes multiple violations recover $1,000 for each violation, or does the $1,000 limit apply to the entire lawsuit? In Wright v. Finance Service of Norwalk, Inc., 22 F.3d 647 (6th Cir.1994), the panel initially hearing the case held that the limit applied separately for each violation. Upon rehearing en banc, however, the court held that the consumer was limited to $1,000 per lawsuit. Which decision is correct? Compare section 814(a) (violation of the FDCPA is a violation of the FTC Act, which calls for a civil penalty of up to $10,000 per violation). In United States v. National Financial Services, Inc., 98 F.3d 131 (4th Cir.1996), the court enforced a civil penalty of $500,000.

18. The FTC reports annually to Congress concerning its experience under the FDCPA. Every year the Commission receives thousands of complaints from consumers about violations of the Act, outnumbering all other kinds of complaints. Every year the FTC's report notes that the consumers' complaints include allegations that debt collectors continue to use profane or obscene language and racial and ethnic slurs. They also allege that debt collectors phone them at work even when the collector knows that the employer prohibits those calls. Some collectors made repeated phone calls, hanging up and recalling, all within a brief period of time. And some called early in the morning or late at night. All this conduct, of course, violates the Act.

For egregious conduct, $1,000, in addition to actual damages, is not much of a deterrent, especially if the limit is $1,000 per lawsuit rather than per violation. Hence, a role remains for the common law remedies covered in at the beginning of this chapter. E.g., Miele v. Sid Bailey, Inc., 192 B.R. 611 (S.D.N.Y.1996) ($12,000 actual and $60,000 punitive damages for repeated attempts to collect a debt that had been discharged in bankruptcy 15 years earlier). But the case that takes the cake is Household Credit Services, Inc. v. Driscol, 989 S.W.2d 72 (Tex.App.1998). To collect a $2,000 debt, the debt collector called innumerable times, including 26 calls in a two-hour period and 36 calls in one hour to the consumer's place of employment. The calls included profanity, a bomb threat, and a death threat. A jury awarded $2 million actual and $9 million punitive damages. On appeal the court reduced the award to approximately $300,000 actual and $1.25 million punitive damages. Another Texas court upheld a judgment of $5 million compensatory damages. GreenPoint Credit Corp. v. Perez, 75 S.W.3d 40 (Tex.App.2002).

19. In addition to the FDCPA and analogous state statutes, debt collectors may be subject to other statutes as well. For example, the federal Credit Repair Organizations Act, 15 U.S.C. §§ 1679–1679j (page 271 supra), targets entities that purport to help consumers clean up their tarnished credit records. But the Act may also apply to debt collectors. Section 403(a)(3) defines "credit repair organization" is "any person who . . . represent[s] that such person . . . will sell, provide, or perform any service, in return for the payment of money . . . for the express or implied purpose of . . . improving any consumer's credit record, credit history, or credit rating. . . ." Letters sent by debt collectors often refer to the impact that failure to pay will have on the consumer's credit report and often suggest that paying the debt will preserve or improve the consumer's credit record. In addition to its substantive limits on the behavior of credit repair organizations, the Act (§ 405) imposes disclosure requirements. For violation of the Act, section 409(a) provides that the consumer is entitled to recover all amounts paid to the credit repair organization, as well as actual and punitive damages.

Another control on collection conduct is the Communications Act of 1934, 47 U.S.C. § 201 et seq. Section 223(a)(1) makes it a crime, subject to fine, imprisonment, and civil penalty, for anyone

- to use a telephone to make any communication that is obscene or indecent with intent to abuse, threaten, or harass another person, or

- to cause a telephone to ring repeatedly with intent to harass.

Though there is no private remedy for violation of this statute, engaging in the criminalized conduct should be a violation of a state little-FTC act.

(2) FAIR CREDIT BILLING ACT

Under section 809(b) of the FDCPA, the consumer has a right to have the debt collector verify the debt before engaging in any further collection efforts. The forerunner of this provision appears in the Fair Credit Billing Act (FCBA), which Congress added to the Truth-in-Lending Act in 1975. Under section 161 of the FCBA, the consumer with an open-end credit account is given similar rights with respect to the *creditor*. If the consumer believes the creditor made a "billing error" (which is defined in section 161(b) and Regulation Z section 226.13(a)), the creditor must investigate and within ninety days must either correct the bill or explain why the creditor believes the bill to be correct.[3] Until so acting, the creditor may not take any action to collect the disputed debt (§ 161(a)(B)) and may not threaten to report the alleged delinquency to a credit bureau (§ 162). If the creditor investigates the matter and concludes that the bill is correct, the creditor is free to resume collection efforts, even though the consumer may continue to believe the bill is in error. See generally Regulation Z section 226.13. The consumer, of course, may still refuse to pay, and the materials in the preceding portions of this chapter govern the rights of the parties.

Section 127(a)(7) (Regulation Z §§ 226.6(d) and 226.9(a)) requires the creditor at the inception of the account, and annually thereafter, to send the consumer a notice of his or her billing rights. The creditor who fails to comply with section 161 or 162 is precluded from recovering the disputed amount, up to $50, even if the billing dispute is ultimately resolved in the creditor's favor (FCBA § 161(e)). In addition, the creditor is liable under section 130(a) for actual damages and twice the finance charge (subject to the $100–1000 collar in section 130(a)(2)). For an example of noncompliance with sections 161–62, see Bell v. The May Department Store Co., 6 S.W.3d 871 (Mo.1999). The creditor who fails to send the notices required by section 127 also is liable for damages under section 130(a).

In addition to its provisions on billing disputes, the FCBA imposes several other obligations on open-end creditors. The creditor must mail the bill at least fourteen days before the last day by which the consumer must pay in order to avoid additional finance charges on the amount stated in the bill (§ 163). The creditor must credit the consumer's account on the day a payment is received (§ 164) (an important requirement if the creditor computes the finance charge on the average daily balance or uses late payment as a reason to impose a fee or increase the annual percentage rate). And the creditor must refund any overpayments (§ 165).

QUESTIONS AND NOTES

1. Section 161(a)(B) prohibits the creditor from taking any action to collect a disputed debt until the creditor responds with a corrected bill or an explanation of why the original bill is correct.

---

3. To trigger this investigation, the request must be written. Many banks, however, follow the FCBA procedures even when the consumer makes an oral request.

a) Does this mean that the creditor cannot attempt to collect the portion of the bill that is not disputed?

b) May the creditor send subsequent bills that include the disputed amount? Is this "any action" to collect the disputed debt?

2. Problem. *Consumer* purchases a used washing machine from *Seller*, paying for it with his Visa card. Within a week after delivery, the machine breaks down, and *Seller*, pointing to an "as is" clause in the sales contract, refuses to do anything about it. Two weeks later, *Consumer* receives a bill from *Bank* for his Visa purchases. The bill includes an entry for the washing machine purchase from *Seller*. May *Consumer* invoke the above-described dispute resolution procedures of the FCBA?

CHAPTER 12

ENFORCEMENT OF THE SECURITY INTEREST

If efforts of the kind described in Chapter 11 do not produce payment, several alternatives remain. The creditor may simply give up and treat the unpaid obligation as a bad debt loss; or the creditor may sue the consumer and seek to enforce the resulting judgment; or the creditor may simply take enough of the consumer's assets to liquidate the debt. As stated, of course, taking the consumer's assets amounts to the tort of conversion and the crime of theft. But if the creditor has a security interest in those assets, taking them may be neither a tort nor a crime. This alternative, known as repossession, is the subject of this chapter.

The primary sources of regulation of security interests are Article 9 of the UCC and retail installment sales acts. This chapter focuses primarily on the UCC. Article 9 was extensively revised in 1999 and, as revised, has been enacted in every state. Most of the cases in this chapter were decided under the former version, the provisions of which appear at relevant places in the footnotes to the cases and the questions following them. The Statutory Supplement contains the current version.

Under section 9–201 of the UCC the consumer may give a security interest in personal property. The function of a security interest is, as its name suggests, to provide security for a debt owed by the consumer to the creditor. If the consumer fails to pay the debt, the creditor can look to the collateral, i.e. the property in which the creditor has a security interest, for satisfaction of the debt. Since the creditor's first and second alternatives above are so unpalatable, the creditor usually obtains a security interest in some of the consumer's property. This is true, at least, for closed-end credit; it is less true for open-end credit transactions. In considering the materials in this chapter, it is important to remember that the right of repossession belongs only to the creditor who has a security interest in property of the consumer.

PROBLEM

Pat purchased a late model used car from Honest Abe's Used Cars. The price, after deducting the value of the trade-in as a downpayment, was $7,000. To pay for the car, Pat promised to pay $252.80 for thirty-six months, for a total of $9,100.80. The contract contained the following clause, among others:

6.   Default. Time is of the essence of this contract. In the event Buyer defaults in any payment, or fails to obtain or maintain the insurance required hereunder, or fails to pay taxes on the property, or moves the property to a new location without Seller's consent, or fails to comply with any other provision hereof, or dies or becomes mentally incompetent, or a proceeding in bankruptcy, receivership or insolvency shall be instituted by or against Buyer or his property, or Seller deems the property in danger of misuse or confiscation, or Seller otherwise deems the indebtedness or the property insecure, Seller shall have the right to declare all amounts due or to become due hereunder to be immediately due and payable and Seller shall have all the rights and remedies of a secured party under the Uniform Commercial Code, including the right to repossess the property wherever the same may be found with free right to entry, and to recondition and sell the same at public or private sale. Upon request, Buyer shall deliver the property to Seller at a place designated by Seller. Seller shall have the right to retain all payments made prior to repossession and Buyer shall remain liable for any deficiency. Any personalty in or attached to the property when repossessed may be held by Seller without liability and Buyer shall be deemed to have waived any claim thereto unless written demand by certified mail is made upon Seller within 24 hours after repossession. Buyer agrees to pay reasonable attorney's fees (15 per cent if permitted by law) and other expenses incurred by Seller in effecting collection, repossession or resale hereunder. Seller's remedies hereunder are in addition to any given by law and may be enforced successively or concurrently. Waiver by Seller of any default shall not be deemed a waiver of any other default.[1]

Honest Abe's assigned the contract to State Bank, and Pat made the monthly payments to the bank. Many of the payments, however, were late, some recent ones by as much as three weeks. By February 1, Pat had made thirty payments, totaling $7,584, and was then current. On that day Pat's employer announced that adverse economic conditions were forcing a lay-off of half the employees. Since this employer is the largest one in the city, the news made the front page of the local paper and came to the attention of State Bank's collection manager, Lynn. When Pat failed to pay the next installment on February 4, its due date, Lynn became concerned that Pat would not be able to make any more payments and might even leave town. Consequently, Lynn decided to accelerate the unpaid balance of the loan and repossess the car. Lynn directed one of the bank's "repo men," Carrie, to bring the car in.

On February fifth, Carrie proceeded to Pat's residence and started to pick the lock on the front door of the car. Pat happened to notice someone tampering with the car and ran out, vituperatively demanding to know just what Carrie thought she was doing. When she explained, Pat informed her exactly what would happen to her if she didn't leave at once. Carrie left. At 2:30 that night, however, she returned in a tow truck, hooked it to Pat's

1. See Helfinstine v. Martin, 561 P.2d 951 (Okl.1977).

car, and drove to the bank's storage lot. Then she phoned the police to let them know what she had done.

In the morning Lynn sent Pat a letter stating that the bank would sell the car on February 15 and would hold Pat liable to the extent that the proceeds fell short of the unpaid balance ($1,516.80) plus the expenses of repossession and sale plus attorney's fees. Before receiving this letter, Pat (who had called the police to report the theft of the car) appeared at the bank with $252.80 (plus $15 for the delinquency charge stipulated by the contract). Lynn refused to release the car, stating that the bank had accelerated the debt and that Pat would have to pay the entire balance of $1,516.80 to get the car back. Pat protested, but to no avail.

On February sixteenth State Bank sold the car to Honest Abe's Used Cars for $900. According to the regional guidebook, cars of the same model were worth $1,200 in the wholesale market and $1,650 in the retail market. The bank sent Pat a letter stating that it had sold the car for $900, which amount it had credited against Pat's obligation, leaving a balance of $1,009.32. The bank had determined the amount still due in the following way:

Unpaid balance	$1516.80
Tow truck	265.00
Special compensation for after-hours work	35.00
Storage	50.00
Attorney's fees (15%)	272.52
TOTAL	$2,139.32
Credit upon resale	900.00
BALANCE	$1,239.32

Pat refused to pay, and State Bank sued for $1,239.32.

Before considering any of the succeeding materials in this chapter, please consider these questions:

1.   What is your impression of this transaction? Does the overall conduct of either party strike you as outrageous? unreasonable?

2.   Turning now to specifics, did State Bank have a security interest in Pat's car? Why do you suppose the bank included in the contract the lengthy clause quoted in the problem? What precise purpose(s) does it serve? Exactly what rights does it (attempt to) give the bank?

3.   If the consumer fails to make a payment on its due date, should the creditor be able to accelerate the entire unpaid balance and repossess the collateral?

4.   In a situation in which repossession should be permitted, should the creditor be able to repossess without first informing the consumer that repossession is imminent?

5.   In effecting repossession of the car, should a creditor be able to pick a lock to gain entry? break a window? Should repossession in the

dead of night be permitted? What if Carrie had stood her ground when Pat ordered her to leave: who should be liable for the resulting violence, if any?

6. Once the creditor has properly repossessed the collateral, should the consumer be able to regain it by paying merely the overdue installment?

7. Is there anything objectionable about the bank's disposition of Pat's car?

8. Assuming the creditor is entitled to repossess and sell the collateral when the debtor defaults, should the creditor be able to hold the debtor accountable for the balance of the debt? According to a study of consumers who had been sued for deficiency judgments after repossession, more than half believed that the repossession had relieved them of any further obligation to their creditors. Should this expectation be protected?

9. Assuming the consumer should be liable for the unpaid balance of the debt, should the consumer be liable also for the expenses of repossession and sale? In the problem, should Pat be liable for the listed expenses?

The succeeding materials explore these (and other) questions that arise when a creditor enforces a security interest in property of a consumer.

A. ACCELERATION AND THE DEFINITION OF DEFAULT

Fontaine v. Industrial National Bank

Supreme Court of Rhode Island, 1973.
111 R.I. 6, 298 A.2d 521.

POWERS, J. [Plaintiff purchased a new car from Shore City Lincoln–Mercury, Inc., pursuant to a retail installment contract calling for payments totalling $8800. Shore City assigned this contract to defendant bank.]

Under the contract, plaintiff promised to repay the loan in 36 monthly installments of $244.46 beginning March 26, 1970,

> * * * with a 'late charge' of five cents (5 per dollar of each installment hereof which is not paid in full within fifteen (15) days after the due date of such installment or the sum of Five Dollars ($5.00), whichever is less * * *.

The plaintiff made a total of eight such payments. The payments due for the months of March through July were made within 15 days from the 26th of the previous month. The payment which became due as of August 26, 1970, however, was made by a check which was three times dishonored and not finally credited to plaintiff until October 6, 1970. Meanwhile, another payment had become due as of September 26, 1970, and this was not made until October 23, 1970. The payment due as of October 26, 1970, was made on November 10, 1970.

Thereafter, on December 3, 1970, at which time plaintiff had not made the payment due as of November 26, 1970, an installment loan collector of defendant bank, received an anonymous telephone call. The caller informed the loan officer that plaintiff was preparing to leave for Florida. Coincidentally, on the same day, said loan officer learned from another agent of the bank that the car was being serviced at a garage near plaintiff's home. The agent giving this information had been previously assigned to contact plaintiff in connection with the aforementioned August and September defaults. Seeing the car at the garage in question on December 3, he called the collection officer to ascertain plaintiff's status.

Thus learning of the car's location on the day that he received the anonymous call, and having in mind plaintiff's record of erratic payments on the loan, he concluded that the security was in jeopardy and caused the car to be repossessed. In consequence, plaintiff commenced the instant action.

The plaintiff, in his complaint, predicated his cause of action on wrongful repossession. Answering, the bank defended on the ground that plaintiff was in default at the time the car was repossessed.[2]

In giving decision for plaintiff, the trial justice found in effect, that plaintiff was in default of the payment due on November 26, 1970. He noted, however, that such default was, in his words, "not too serious," in that, as he viewed it, the "total default was eight days." Moreover, in the judgment of the trial justice, defendant bank acted in bad faith when it repossessed without giving plaintiff notice of its intention.

In urging before us that the trial justice's decision is clearly wrong, defendant bank rests its appeal on the proposition that the trial justice erred in holding that, notwithstanding plaintiff being in default, defendant bank was precluded from exercising its right to repossess.

This is so, it primarily argues, because the fact of default gave defendant bank a contractual and statutory right to repossess regardless of what the trial justice may have considered to be circumstances mitigating the default. But even if this were not so, it further argues, the decision is clearly erroneous in that the trial justice's view of what he concluded were mitigating circumstances, is based on a misconception and overlooking of material evidence.

In view of what we consider to be the controlling issue, neither contention requires discussion.

From what has heretofore been narrated, it is obvious that the trial justice considered plaintiff in default because the payment due as of November 26, 1970, had not been made at the time the car was repos-

---

2. It is not disputed that by the terms of both the sale agreement and the Uniform Commercial Code . . . defendant as assignee of the seller had the right to repossess in the event of a default by plaintiff.

sessed. This consideration, however, completely overlooks the right of plaintiff, as provided by the sales agreement, to make payment within 15 days of the date that each payment became due.

The defendant bank does not dispute plaintiff's right to make a payment that would be timely if made within 15 days of the date that each payment became due. What it does argue is, that by the terms of the sales agreement, acceptance of payments made after plaintiff was in default would not constitute a waiver of such rights as inured to the seller or its assignee upon default.

Specifically, it points to the uncontradicted fact that the payment due as of August 26, 1970, was not made until 40 days thereafter, namely, on October 5, 1970. Continuing, the payment due as of September 26, 1970, was not made until October 23, 1970, 27 days after the date as of which it was due.

The provision of the sales agreement on which defendant bank relies provides in pertinent part:

> If Buyer shall default in the payment of any installment * * * all installments remaining unpaid shall, at the election of Seller, and without notice to Buyer, become immediately due and payable. The payment and acceptance of any sum on account shall not be considered a waiver of such right of election.

Relying on the foregoing, defendant bank takes the position that its acceptance of the October 5, October 23 and November 10 payments did not deprive it of the right that it clearly had on the 16th day after August 26th. Consequently, it is defendant bank's position that plaintiff's payment of the obligation due as of October 26, 1970, within the 15–day grace period, is without legal significance. Assuming for the sake of argument that such position is sound, we nevertheless cannot agree that the trial justice erred in giving decision for plaintiff. We are so persuaded because we believe that just as defendant bank had the right to demand payment in full or repossess at its election once plaintiff defaulted, the latter had the right to have the demand for payment made before repossession was proper. This court reached the same conclusion in Mosby v. Goff, 21 R.I. 494, 44 A. 930 (1899). There, defendant vendor to a conditional sales agreement of a piano which was to be paid for by weekly installments of one dollar accepted late payments but subsequently, after the time for other payments had passed, entered plaintiff's premises and repossessed the piano. This court held, in substance, that having accepted late payments the defendant vendor placed itself in the position of giving plaintiff vendee the right to have the full sum due demanded before the defendant vendor could repossess.

In adhering to the rationale of Mosby v. Goff, supra, we are not unmindful that there does not appear to have been a provision in the sales agreement of the cited case as there is here that the right of election to full payment or in lieu thereof repossession inures without notice. We think it to be so unconscionable as to be against public policy to give judicial sanction to an arrangement whereby a conditional sales vendee, once in default, is in constant peril of having the chattel summarily repossessed even though said vendee has been in faithful compliance with periodic payments for months or even years after the original default.

Here for example, although the period of time between default and repossession was a little less than three months, defendant bank, on its theory, could repossess in December 1972, two years later than when it did, even though in the intervening years, plaintiff had met every monthly obligation on time.

The defendant's appeal is denied and dismissed and the judgment appealed from is affirmed.

QUESTIONS AND NOTES

1. What basis is there for the court's assertion of the "right of plaintiff, as provided by the sales agreement, to make payment within 15 days of the date that each payment became due"?

2. In the last several paragraphs of its opinion, the court addresses two distinct problems: whether a creditor may accelerate an obligation because of a late payment that occurred long ago if the debtor has paid subsequent installments in a timely fashion as they have accrued; and whether a creditor may accelerate an obligation on account of a failure to pay promptly when the creditor has accepted late payments in the past. Which of these problems does *Fontaine* present? Which problem was present in Mosby v. Goff?

3. In Nevada National Bank v. Huff, 582 P.2d 364 (Nev.1978), the contract empowered the creditor (NNB) to accelerate the balance if the consumer (Huff) defaulted in any payment. The court stated:

> However, it is clear that even though no outright waiver of a secured party's right to rely upon such a clause occurs through a course of dealing involving the acceptance of late payments, a secured party who has not insisted upon strict compliance in the past, who has accepted late payments as a matter of course, *must*, before he may validly rely upon such a clause to declare a default and effect repossession, *give notice* to the debtor (lessee) that strict compliance with the terms of the contract will be demanded henceforth if repossession is to be avoided. Fontaine v. Industrial Bank of Rhode Island.

> . . . [T]he only ground upon which the Bank could have declared a default under the contract was Huff's one and one-half month arrearage in his payments: on October 21, Huff had paid only through September 1, instead of through November 1 as required under the contract. This delinquency clearly would constitute valid grounds for the declaration of a default under the contract.

> However, analysis of the course of dealing between Huff and NNB, both with respect to the specific transaction in question and with respect to the two similar transactions during the same time period,

reveals that it was a common occurrence for Huff to be behind in his monthly payments. In fact, Huff had been late with every single payment under the truck lease. Further, he had been two payments behind on two occasions, and three payments behind on one occasion. In spite of these delinquencies, NNB had never declared a default or invoked its right to repossess. . . . Rather, written and oral demands for payment had always been made upon him, and payment had always quickly followed.

This course of conduct established between Huff and NNB imposed upon NNB the duty, before it could properly rely upon the default and repossession clauses in the lease agreement, to give notice to Huff that strict compliance with the terms of the long-ignored contract would henceforth be required in order to avert repossession of the vehicle. Upon NNB's failure to give such notice, the jury could properly have concluded that NNB's repossession of the truck was wrongful.

Id. at 370.

Note that the court cites the principal case. Does *Fontaine* support the proposition for which the court cites it?

Why should a creditor's good-natured indulgence of a habitually tardy consumer adversely affect the creditor's rights? In Speigle v. Chrysler Credit Corp., 323 So.2d 360, 365 (Ala.App.1975), the court stated:

Granted, the evidence shows that there had been some late payments made by plaintiff prior to the default in question. But the default now in question was almost a month old, the plaintiff was out of work, had no money, and another payment was due in three or four days. A reasonable assessment of these facts would be that plaintiff was in default on one payment, was in imminent danger of being in default of a second payment and had no reliable prospects for making any future payments. These developments certainly presented defendants with new grounds of insecurity as to the likelihood of collecting payments legitimately owed them. Defendants' declaration of default is not inequitable or unjust in such a situation; consequently, the trial court was not in error in so holding.

In *Speigle* the creditor had acquiesced in "some" late payments. In Hale v. Ford Motor Credit Co., 374 So.2d 849, 853 (Ala.1979), the creditor had acquiesced in "repeated" late payments. Nevertheless, the court gave literal effect to a provision that a waiver of any default would not operate as a waiver of any other default:

A security agreement is effective according to its terms. 9–201.[a] The inadvertence of the debtor here cannot raise an estoppel against the contractual interest of the creditor under the express terms of the security agreement. There having been no modification of the express agreement, the secured party, upon default, had the right to take

---

a. The current version is substantively identical to its predecessor.—Ed.

possession of the collateral. Notice of the statutory right to take possession is not required.

4. What is the relevance, if any, of UCC sections 2–208 and 2–209?

5. In the cases described in Question 3, the consumer made payments after expiration of the so-called grace period. In Pizarro v. Credit Acceptance Corp., 2001 WL 1263682 (Ohio App.2001), plaintiff made the first 18 payments before expiration of the grace period, though most were made after the due date. With respect to each payment made late, she phoned the creditor in advance to inform it when the payment would be coming.

> Appellant testified at her deposition that somewhere around September 21 or 22, 1999, she called Credit and explained to a customer service representative that she would not be able to make her September 1999 payment on time due to the death of her mother and that she would send it in two weeks. Appellant claims the customer service representative responded "no problem" or "that's fine." Credit's records do not indicate a call from appellant until September 28, at which time appellant told Credit she would make the September payment on October 8. Appellant stated she called Credit again approximately two weeks later and told their customer service department that she would make the September payment with the October payment and the customer service representative again said "no problem." Credit had no record of such call. However, Credit did have a record of a conversation with appellant on September 30, at which time appellant promised payment "101199 100899 MON 348.05."

> Appellant testified that on October 21, 1999, she wrote two checks to Credit—one for $348.05 (including a $3 late fee, as required under the agreement), and the other for $345.05—and that both checks cleared Credit's bank on October 27, 1999. Credit's records indicate that a representative spoke to appellant on October 22, 1999, and appellant told the representative she sent the checks that day. Credit's log indicates that within a few minutes of appellant's call on October 22, a repossession recommendation was made because the account was about to be thirty days past due. The repossession recommendation was approved on October 25, 1999, [and the vehicle was repossessed on October 27].

What did the creditor say to plaintiff? What did the creditor mean by these words? What did plaintiff understand the creditor to mean? Which of these latter two questions is relevant?

The court stated:

> In the present case, appellant's claim for estoppel is actually based on two distinct grounds: (1) she was "lulled" into a false sense of security by the statements of Credit's customer service representative that her late payment for September 1999 was "no problem"; and (2) she was "lulled" into a false sense of security by Credit's history of accepting late payments without repossession. With regard to the former, we find appellant did not raise a genuine issue of material fact

with regard to any of the factors necessary to establish estoppel. Appellant failed to establish Credit made a factual representation that it would not enforce any of the provisions of the agreement with regard to the September 1999 payment. When appellant called Credit's customer service department on several occasions in September and October 1999, the representatives merely acknowledged appellant's promise to pay at a future date. There was no evidence she ever discussed with the representatives the right of repossession or waiver of any agreement provisions. Indeed, appellant testified there was no discussion or promise made by Credit regarding repossession. Appellant stated her only purpose for calling Credit was to inform them her payment would be late, and she did not request that they not repossess her car or waive any terms of the agreement. We also note that appellant, without any direction from Credit, added the three dollar late fee to her September 1999 payment, thereby indicating she knew Credit's alleged statement "no problem" did not constitute a blanket waiver of all late payment provisions, rights, and remedies. Accordingly, there was no factual representation made by Credit that it would not enforce the repossession provision upon which appellant could have reasonably relied.

Appellant also claims Credit had a past history of allowing her to make "late" payments without repercussions, and, thus, these past representations "lulled" her into believing that it would not enforce the agreement provisions if she made a "late" payment. However, technically, because the agreement contained a grace period, a payment was only considered "late" if it was received more than ten days beyond the due date. Appellant admitted in her deposition that her previous "late" payments prior to September 1999 had all been made within the ten-day grace period; thus, such payments were not actually "late." Appellant acknowledges that the only actual "late" payment she made was the September 1999 payment. Therefore, Credit could not have made any previous representations to appellant that it would not enforce its rights of repossession if appellant made a payment outside the ten-day grace period, given that none of appellant's previous overdue payments were ever made beyond the grace period. Thus, appellant could not have been reasonably "lulled" into a false sense of security based on any prior misleading representations.

6. It is standard drafting practice for the contract to provide that the creditor may accelerate in the event the creditor becomes insecure as to either the debt or the collateral. Presumably, the contract in *Fontaine* contained such a provision. Why didn't the bank rely on it?

The UCC permits the use of "insecurity" clauses, but recognizes their one-sidedness and limits the creditor's exercise of rights under them. Section 1–309[2] provides that under such a clause the creditor may accelerate "only if that party in good faith believes that the prospect of payment

---

2.   Formerly UCC § 1–208 (1978).

or performance is impaired. The burden of establishing lack of good faith is on the other party." The Code also defines "good faith," in section 1–201(b)(20)[3] as "honesty in fact and the observance of reasonable commercial standards of fair dealing." Hence, an insecurity clause hardly provides carte blanche to accelerate a consumer's obligation. Even under original Article 1, which contained a purely subjective definition of "good faith" (see footnote 3), the courts limited a creditor's use of an insecurity clause. Thus, in Universal C.I.T. Credit Corp. v. Shepler, 329 N.E.2d 620, 625–626 (Ind.App.1975), a concurring judge wrote:

> The insecurity clause gave to C.I.T. an option to repossess if it deemed either the debt or the collateral insecure.

> Such insecurity clauses are authorized by the Uniform Commercial Code, 1–208. Their precise meaning in Indiana has not been established, and debate continues among the several jurisdictions as to whether such provisions are purely subjective, requiring merely a "pure heart and empty head," or whether some objective standard of reasonableness is inherent in the requirement of good faith.

> It is clear that the drafters of the UCC intended to promote commercial dealing and credit financing by permitting creditors to realize upon their security in doubtful situations without the necessity of a specific default.

> It is, however, equally clear that a purely subjective test is subject to arbitrary abuse. It would allow a creditor to be unreasonable and place the debtor in an unjust position since the creditor might at any time call the entire debt and require the debtor to prove the nonexistent state of mind of the creditor. Thus, under this interpretation, the code would permit a creditor to destroy a viable contractual relationship without requiring him to justify his actions.

> Accordingly, the better decisions have injected some objectivity into the standard. . . .

> Professor Gilmore, quoted with approval by the court in Sheppard Fed'l Credit Union v. Palmer (5th Cir.1969), 408 F.2d 1369, 1371, n. 2, interprets § 208 to mean in substance that:

> ". . . [T]he creditor has the right to accelerate if, under the circumstances, a reasonable man, motivated by good faith, would have done so."

> I accept this as the better statement of the law.

> Thus, once the security agreement was admitted or proved in evidence, Shepler had the burden of establishing lack of good faith. This he might do by establishing:

---

3. Formerly UCC § 1–201(19) (1978) ("honesty in fact in the conduct or transaction concerned"). Approximately a third of the states that have adopted revised Article 1 have retained this definition of "good faith" in section 1–201(b)(20).

1.   That the reason for the creditor's action was not because of a feeling that the debt or security was insecure, i.e., the insecurity clause does not constitute a bootstrap defense where a creditor has repossessed relying on other grounds; or

2.   That upon a consideration of all the circumstances known to the creditor, a reasonable man motivated by good faith would not have taken the action; or

3.   That upon a consideration of all the circumstances, a reasonable man motivated by good faith would not have taken the action upon the circumstances known to the creditor without further preliminary action, such as inquiry directed to the debtor or other persons.

7.   Problem. *Consumer* purchases on credit a one-year-old color TV from *Seller*, who gives a 30–day warranty on all parts and labor. The contract gives *Seller* a security interest and provides that in the event of the buyer's default *Seller* may accelerate all unpaid installments. The set develops trouble on the 29th day, and three days later *Consumer* phones to report the breakdown. *Seller* denies liability under the warranty, pointing to the 30–day provision. *Consumer* insists that the breakdown occurred within the warranty period, but *Seller* offers only to repair it at the usual rates. *Consumer* refuses and informs *Seller* that he will make no further payments until *Seller* repairs the set under the warranty. May *Seller* accelerate the balance of the installments?

8.   The UCC does not define "default"; rather it permits the parties to define the term. See sections 1–201, 2–103(1)–(2), and 9–102. Does the answer to the preceding problem depend on whether they have done so?

Problem. *Consumers* (husband and wife) purchase a used car from *Dealer*, pursuant to a retail installment sales contract that gives *Dealer* the right to accelerate in the event of default and defines default as including "any failure to pay an installment." As part of the financing, *Dealer* sells *Consumers* credit life insurance and credit disability insurance, both insuring the husband. Two years later the husband is in a serious car accident and is no longer able to work. *Consumers* miss three consecutive monthly payments, and *Dealer* accelerates the debt and repossesses the car. Does *Dealer* have a right to do this?

Several states have enacted statutes to fill in this definitional gap in the UCC. The principal objective of these statutes is to eliminate the creditor's power to include "insecurity" within the definition of default. The New Jersey RISA focuses narrowly on this objective:

No retail installment contract or retail charge account . . . shall contain any acceleration clause under which any part or all of the balance, not yet matured, may be declared immediately due and payable because the retail seller or holder deems himself to be insecure and any such provision shall be void and unenforceable.

N.J.S.A. § 17:16C–35. Compare the following Minnesota statute, which prohibits provisions by which

> [i]n the absence of consumer's default, the holder may arbitrarily and without reasonable cause, accelerate the maturity of any part or all of the amount owing thereunder. . . .

Minn.Stat.Ann. § 325G.16(2)(b). How would Problem 7 be resolved in Minnesota?

The Massachusetts statutes, on the other hand, prohibit clauses that permit acceleration in the absence of the buyer's default and provide that a clause defining default is enforceable "only to the extent that the default is material and consists of [1] the buyer's failure to make one or more installments . . . or [2] occurrence of an event which substantially impairs the value of the collateral." Mass.Gen. Laws Ann. ch. 255B, §§ 20(3), 20A(a); ch. 255D, §§ 10, 21(a). This is similar to the approach of the UCCC. See section 5.109. How would Problem 7 be resolved under the UCCC?

9. Should the creditor be able to accelerate a debt and/or repossess collateral if the consumer's payment does not arrive on the due date? What if the payment arrives soon after the creditor has accelerated or repossessed?

The UCC permits repossession upon the occurrence of any default (§ 9–609). And it gives the consumer the right to regain the collateral, by a process known as redemption. To redeem, however, the consumer must pay the entire accelerated balance of the debt plus the creditor's expenses of repossession and perhaps also the creditor's attorney's fees (§ 9–623). Consequently, consumers rarely assert this right of redemption.

Another section of the UCC may give the consumer a right of redemption more favorable than the one provided by section 9–623. In Urdang v. Muse, 276 A.2d 397 (N.J.Super.1971), a consumer defaulted, and the creditor repossessed the collateral. The consumer tendered payment of three times the amount in default and asked the creditor to return the collateral. The creditor refused to do so unless the consumer paid the entire accelerated balance, as contemplated by the predecessor of section 9–623 (§ 9–506). The court held that the creditor's refusal to accept the consumer's offer was a breach of the obligation of good faith in the performance or enforcement of the contract. See UCC section 1–304. See generally Anderson, Good Faith in the Enforcement of Contracts, 73 Iowa L.Rev. 299 (1988).

Several states have modified the UCC's answers to the questions posed at the beginning of this chapter. A common approach is to establish a grace period, of 10–30 days, during which the creditor may neither accelerate nor repossess. The statute may establish a grace period either by prohibiting those acts during the specified period (e.g., UCCC § 5.111) or by defining default as the failure to make a required payment within the specified number of days after its due date (Iowa Code Ann. § 537.5109). Establishing a grace period recognizes and protects a tendency by consumers to be late (negligent?) in paying their bills. Should this tendency be protected, or should the rights of the parties perhaps be structured so as to encourage greater diligence by consumers?

Most reform legislation goes even further than providing a grace period. Typically, it also allows the consumer to cure a default by paying just the overdue installments (plus any default or delinquency charges that have accrued). Some of the statutes require the creditor to inform the consumer of the right to cure, prohibit repossession during a specified period after this notice, and cut off the right to cure once the creditor has repossessed. See, e.g., UCCC section 5.111. (The right of redemption under UCC section 9–623, such as it is, continues to exist.) In a few states the statutes give the consumer the right to cure *after* the creditor has repossessed the collateral. And most of the reform statutes limit the number of times a consumer may exercise the right to cure. The limits range from one time per contract (UCCC) to one or two times per year (Iowa, Wisconsin) to three times per contract (Massachusetts, West Virginia). Finally, in two states, the consumer who wishes to cure a default must provide a bond or a cash deposit to secure performance in the future (Ohio, Wisconsin).

In connection with mobile-home credit, a federal statute preempts state usury laws. To qualify for the benefits of preemption, however, the lender's contract must comply with several consumer protection provisions. 12 U.S.C. § 1735f–7. One of these protections is that the lender give the consumer thirty days advance notice and opportunity to cure defaults before the creditor repossesses the collateral, forecloses the mortgage, or accelerates the debt.[4] In Quiller v. Barclays American/Credit, Inc., 764 F.2d 1400 (11th Cir.1985) (en banc), cert. denied 476 U.S. 1124 (1986), the court held that even if the creditor's actual practice is to comply with this regulation, the creditor loses the benefit of preemption if the contract document provides for rights that are inconsistent with the regulation. See also Grant v. General Electric Credit Corp., 764 F.2d 1404 (11th Cir.1985) (en banc), cert. denied, 476 U.S. 1124 (1986).

10. If the contract permits acceleration of the *entire* balance in the event of default, the creditor may be in violation of other consumer credit statutes. For example, the contract may contravene a small loan act or retail installment sales act provision that requires a refund of unearned finance charge. See Aetna Finance Co. v. Brown, 323 S.E.2d 720 (Ga.App. 1984). Or the contract may be usurious. See Jim Walter Homes, Inc. v. Schuenemann, 668 S.W.2d 324 (Tex.1984); Brookshire v. Longhorn Chevrolet Co., 788 S.W.2d 209 (Tex.App.1990).

B.   REPOSSESSION

The focus of the preceding section is whether and when a creditor may repossess the collateral to enforce a security interest. The focus of this section is *how* the creditor may repossess. The UCC authorizes the secured creditor to obtain possession by means of judicial action (§ 9–609). It also authorizes the creditor to obtain possession by means of self-help. Since it

---

4. Other protections include the right to prepay, with a refund of unearned finance charge, and limitations on late charges and balloon payments. 12 C.F.R. § 590.4.

is simpler, faster, and cheaper than judicial proceedings, one would expect creditors always to repossess by self-help. And, indeed, it is the standard method for repossessing automobiles. But notwithstanding the advantages of self-help, creditors commonly use judicial proceedings to repossess most other kinds of collateral. What do you suppose explains this difference?

Deavers v. Standridge

Court of Appeals of Georgia, 1978.
144 Ga.App. 673, 242 S.E.2d 331.

Banke, Judge.

The appellants, Billy Deavers, Frank Deavers, and Walker Motor Co., appeal a jury verdict awarding the appellee, Mark A. Standridge, actual and punitive damages for the wrongful repossession of his automobile as being contrary to the evidence. They also appeal the overruling of several motions for directed verdict.

The appellants sold the appellee, pursuant to a conditional sales contract, a 1965 Chevrolet automobile. The balance due after trade-in allowance was $282.50 and was to be paid in 12 weekly installments due on the Friday of each week. The appellee testified that he was unable to make the second payment and that appellant Billy Deavers agreed orally that he could make two payments the following Friday (August 1). Billy Deavers testified that appellee never paid any money on the contract and denied making any agreement postponing the due date for the second payment. At trial the appellee was unable to produce the receipt allegedly given him upon payment of the first note.

The appellee testified that he was prevented from making the double payment on Friday, August 1, because he had to work an 11–hour shift, but that he had intended to make the payments the following day on his lunch hour. Instead, Ronnie Deavers, brother of the appellants, came by the appellee's place of employment that morning to repossess his car. Rather than consenting to the repossession, appellee testified that he drove the car to the appellant's place of business and tendered the overdue payments but that appellants refused the tender and demanded that he pay the entire unpaid balance. Appellee could not do so, so appellants repossessed the car. Appellee further testified that the appellants caused his car to be "blocked-in" by another and told him that he could just "walk his ass home." Appellee's witness confirmed that he tried to pay the past-due amount and that appellee's car was blocked in. The appellants deny either of these acts or that the appellee tendered all past-due monies. Appellee then filed this action seeking damages for the wrongful repossession of his car.

1.   Unless otherwise agreed in the contract between the parties, "a secured party has on default the right to take possession of the collateral . . . without judicial process . . ." so long as ". . . this can be done without breach of the peace . . ." Code Ann. § 109A–9–503.[a] Here the

---

a.   Former § 9–503 (now § 9–609):
Unless otherwise agreed a secured party has on default the right to take possession of the collateral. In taking possession a secured party may proceed without judicial process if this can be done without breach of the peace or may proceed by action. . . .

conditional sales contract clearly provided for repossession upon default of any payments; and even if we adopt appellee's version of the testimony regarding the oral agreement, he was still in default since he did not attempt to make the double payment until Saturday. Thus, the primary issue before this court on appeal is whether the appellants breached the peace in repossessing appellee's car such that they are now liable for damages.

Under our criminal law, abusive and insulting language constitutes a breach of the peace if there is an accompanying incitement to immediate violence. See Faulkner v. State, 166 Ga. 645(3), 144 S.E. 193 (1928). See also Code Ann. § 26–2610(a) (use of opprobrious or abusive words in presence of another which "naturally tend to provoke violent resentment," i.e., fighting words, is a misdemeanor).

The term "breach of the peace" used in Code Ann. § 109A–9–503 is not defined by the Uniform Commercial Code. However, decisions from other jurisdictions have indicated that the term has a much broader meaning as used in the Uniform Commercial Code than that usually attributed to it under the criminal law. See J. White and R. Summers, Uniform Commercial Code, 1972, pp. 972–975 (and cases cited therein) (1972). As White and Summers concluded, most courts find a breach of peace by any creditor who repossesses over the *unequivocal oral protest* of the defaulting debtor; and some courts even require that the debtor, if present, must affirmatively consent for the repossession to be lawful. Neither party in this case has argued that Georgia has (or has not) adopted a broad interpretation, and we issue no opinion on that subject at this time.

The trial judge, here, charged that "the term breach of the peace is a general term and includes all violations of the public peace or order or decorum." While the evidence offered by the appellee for proving a breach of the peace was not strong, we cannot say that the jury was unauthorized to find, in accordance with the appellee's testimony (as confirmed in part by his eyewitness), that the appellants' combined acts of blocking-in the appellee's auto and speaking to him in offensive, insulting language were sufficiently provocative of violence to constitute a breach of the peace.

. . .

3. The appellants contend that there was no evidence to support a finding of punitive damages and that the trial judge erred in overruling their motion for directed verdict. In their next enumeration of error, they allege that the jury's award of $1,000 in punitive damages was excessive.

It was not error to overrule appellants' motion for a directed verdict. Punitive damages are authorized whenever there is evidence of "wilful misconduct, malice, fraud, wantonness, or oppression, or that entire want of care which would raise the presumption of a conscious indifference to consequences." Southern R. Co. v. O'Bryan, 119 Ga. 147(1), 45 S.E. 1000 (1903). It was a jury question whether the appellants' physical act and statement amounted to wilful misconduct such that the imposition of punitive damages was justified.

. . .

Judgment affirmed.

QUESTIONS AND NOTES

1. As the court observes, the UCC does not define "breach of the peace." Certainly assault and battery amount to breach of the peace. But short of physical contact or the threat of it, what conduct should be prohibited?

a. Should a creditor be permitted to break into a debtor's home to repossess a TV? Should it matter whether a door (or window) is unlocked? Should it matter whether anyone is in the debtor's home at the time of the repossession?

b. Should a creditor be permitted to break into a debtor's garage to repossess a car? Should it matter whether the door is unlocked? wide open?

c. Should a creditor be permitted to repossess a car from a debtor's driveway? from the street in front of the dwelling?

d. Should the answers to the preceding questions be different if the contract provides that in the event of default the creditor "shall have . . . the right to repossess the property wherever the same may be found with free right of entry"?

2. In *Deavers* what is the court's standard for determining breach of the peace?

3. Problem. *Consumer* purchases a new car on credit from *Seller*, agreeing to pay for it in forty-eight monthly installments and giving *Seller* a security interest in it. She performs for ten months, at which time the car begins to rust. *Seller* refuses to remedy the problem, claiming that the warranty does not cover rust. *Consumer* has a body shop take care of it, deducts the repair bill from her payments to *Seller*, and informs *Seller* of the reason for the deduction. On a sunny Saturday afternoon, *Seller* attempts to repossess the car, but *Consumer* runs out of her house brandishing a gun and threatening to shoot. The repossessor wisely beats a hasty retreat, but returns a few days later at 3:00 a.m. and takes the car, while *Consumer* is peacefully asleep inside the house. Has *Seller* complied with section 9–609(b)(2)?

4. Consider the following excerpt from Ford Motor Credit Co. v. Byrd, 351 So.2d 557 (Ala.1977):

> On 22 October 1969 Byrd purchased from Bassett Ford, Inc., of Citronelle, Alabama, a 1970 Ford Torino under a retail installment contract which was assigned to FMCC. The payment schedule provided that Byrd would pay 36 monthly installments commencing on 6 December 1969. On 13 September 1972 the automobile was repossessed.

The circumstances surrounding the repossession are conflicting, but both parties concede Byrd was contacted by Sandy Craig, a confessed "repo man," at Byrd's home to discuss whether payments on the automobile were in arrears. Craig contending they were; Byrd contending to the contrary. As a result of this conversation, and at Craig's request, Byrd went to Bassett Ford, parked his automobile in front of that place and went inside to review his receipts against records of his account. While he was occupied in disputing that he was in default, the automobile was removed from where he parked it and locked up in a storage area behind Bassett's building. The evidence about these events clearly supports the jury's right to conclude that Byrd was lured to Bassett Ford so that possession of his auto might be obtained without his knowledge and consent, through stealth and trickery. . . .

The claims stated in Byrd's amended complaint are based on the theory that his auto was converted by FMCC after possession of it was obtained wrongfully through trickery and fraud after leading Byrd to believe he was being asked to drive it to Bassett Ford, where it was repossessed, so that there a good faith discussion of whether his account was in arrears would be continued.

FMCC says there can be no wrongful taking and conversion of Byrd's auto because it turns out he was in default and there was no breach of the peace in the taking. . . . Numerous cases of this court are cited in support of FMCC's contention; also decisions of the Court of Appeals, the Fifth Circuit, and one of a United States District Court. Some of these decisions involved cases where their right to recover was grounded on theories of trespass to chattels or on realty; others of them based on various other theories. A careful examination of them, however, reveals one salient distinction from this case. *At the very moment of repossession* of the chattel in the cited cases, there was not a contemporaneous bona fide dispute being made by the debtor regarding his or her default. FMCC argues that the evidence in this case established Byrd was at least one payment in default at the time the automobile was repossessed, therefore he cannot maintain an action for conversion, since by being in default, Byrd had no legal title to the automobile and no immediate right to possession; both essential elements of his claim.

What about § 9–503? Is self-help repossession permitted under all circumstances unless there is a concurrent breach of the peace? It is not. We cannot interpret § 9–503 to permit obtaining possession through trick, without knowledge upon the part of the debtor. To interpret § 9–503 to allow repossession in these circumstances would encourage practices abhorrent to society: fraud, trickery, chicanery, and subterfuge, as alternatives to employment of judicial processes that foster the concept of ours being a government of laws and not of men. If self-help erodes that concept then self-help must be limited as we will limit it here. Condoning FMCC's conduct under the circumstances presented here would defeat the desirable and fundamental policy of discouraging extrajudicial acts by citizens when those acts are fraught with the likelihood of resulting violence.

Public policy favors the resolution of disputes by resort to the courts and the judicial process. Unilateral action by FMCC, that might well have resulted in a breach of the peace and involvement of the criminal statutes, could easily have been avoided by suit to recover the automobile aided by pre-judgment seizure as provided in Rule 64(b), ARCP. Although speaking of an action for trespass in the repossession of an automobile, our court of appeals said of the rightful owner of a chattel: " * * * If he cannot regain possession of his property peaceably, he must appeal to the courts of the country. * * * " Singer Sewing Machine Co. v. Hayes, 22 Ala.App. 250, 114 So. 420 (1927). In citing that case with approval, as correctly enunciating the rule, the Supreme Court of Mississippi had this to say:

> " * * * The majority of people are honest and yield peaceable obedience to their contractual obligations. When they do not so yield, it is, in most cases, because there is some reason worthy of impartial examination or consideration why they do not. To allow the holder of such a contract to be his own judge, and to execute his judgment in any violent or forcible way he might choose, would be contrary to good order, would be provocative of retaliatory violence and breaches of the peace; wherefore, as a matter of public policy, no such right can exist." Commercial Credit Co. v. Spence, 185 Miss. 293, 184 So. 439 (1938).

Neither can the holder of a contract be his own judge and execute his judgment by artifice or trickery.

> " * * * Therefore, when appellant, as appears, by artifice or trickery obtained possession of the mortgaged property for one purpose, and asserted the right to retain such possession for another purpose, there was a conversion by it of appellee's property, and the action must be treated as one for conversion * * * " Cable Co. v. Greenfield, 196 Ky. 314, 244 S.W. 692 (1922).

The law cannot permit its subversion by devices such as here employed by FMCC in a self-help repossession. Possession of a chattel obtained through fraud, artifice, stealth, or trickery without consent of the owner, implied or expressed, is wrongful and will support an action for the conversion of the chattel. . . .

a.   Since Byrd was in default, FMCC was entitled to possession of the car. How can FMCC be liable for conversion if Byrd had no right to possession? Do the cases cited by the court support its decision?

b.   Is the court imposing a limitation on the creditor's repossession rights that is not present in section 9–609 (or former § 9–503)?

c.   What limits are there to this decision? Would a creditor be liable for deceiving an apartment-dwelling debtor into parking a car on the street instead of in the building's underground garage?

d. In most states the courts have not yet held that stealth or trickery violates section 9–609. If a court is unwilling to conclude that stealth or trickery amounts to a breach of the peace, is there any other basis for holding that the creditor's conduct violates the rights of the consumer?

5. With the arrival of the electronic age, new techniques for enforcing security interests have arisen. A dealer that sells a car on credit can equip the car with a device that prevents the car from starting unless the consumer enters a code that the dealer provides each month when the consumer makes the scheduled payment. If the consumer fails to pay on time, the dealer may refuse to supply the code, and the car will be inoperable.

Other devices use a global positioning system that is capable of tracking a car's location at all times and alerting the dealer when the car leaves a pre-programmed geographic area. These devices also may monitor the car's speed and provide the dealer with remote control over the ignition starter or the door locks. These features enable the creditor to prevent the consumer from leaving the state or the country, to locate the car in event of default, and to immobilize the car until the creditor comes to pick it up.

Problem. *Dealer* sells used cars on credit to consumers whose credit record is less than impeccable. She operates what is known as a Buy–Here, Pay–Here lot, and her customers return every month to make their payments. She has heard a sales presentation by a company that sells one of the devices described above, and she is convinced that this is a way to cut down on her defaults and to facilitate recovery of the cars when her customers actually do default. Before buying the devices, however, she consults you to determine the legal risks if she employs the system. What pitfalls, if any, do you see? What would you advise her to do?

6. Consumers frequently carry various items of personal property in their cars. This other property may be in the car when the creditor repossesses it. What is the creditor's liability with respect to the other property? If the creditor does not have a security interest in the other property, the creditor has no right to keep it, as section 9–609 gives the creditor rights only as to the collateral. Thus, in Varela v. Wells Fargo Bank, 93 Cal.Rptr. 428, 433 (Cal.App.1971), the court stated:

> Defendant contends that there was no conversion of the rings because it did not know of their presence in the auto nor did it intend to take ownership of them. However, "[t]he intent required [to constitute conversion] is not necessarily a matter of conscious wrongdoing. It is rather an intent to exercise a dominion or control over the goods which is in fact inconsistent with the plaintiff's rights." (Prosser, Law of Torts (3d ed. 1964) § 15, p. 83.) Necessarily, where an auto is repossessed, unless the repossessor empties the glove compartment and the trunk, it intends to possess at least temporarily its contents and to deprive the owner thereof. Here, having taken possession of the car with the rings in it, to the possession of which rings it had no right even temporarily, it was the bank's duty to protect the rings. Having

taken them without right and having failed to return them on demand, defendant is guilty of conversion.

As said in Poggi v. Scott (1914) 167 Cal. 372, 375 [139 P. 815]: "The foundation for the action of conversion rests neither in the knowledge nor the intent of the defendant. It rests upon the unwarranted interference by defendant with the dominion over the property of the plaintiff from which injury to the latter results. Therefore, neither good nor bad faith, neither care nor negligence, neither knowledge nor ignorance, are of the gist of the action." Thus, so far as the rings are concerned, defendant would be liable for their conversion even if it had had the right to repossess the vehicle. It took them from plaintiff's control and possession without right and has never returned them.

Therefore, creditors often attempt to protect themselves against a claim of conversion of property located in the collateral at the time of repossession. In Jones v. General Motors Acceptance Corp., 565 P.2d 9 (Okl.1977), the contract provided that "Seller may take possession of any other property in the hereinabove described motor vehicle at any time of repossession, wherever such property may be therein, and hold same for buyer at buyer's risk without liability on the part of seller." When the creditor refused to return the other property until the consumer paid the unpaid balance, the consumer sued and recovered:

> Neither appellee had any security interest in appellant's personal belongings which were in the repossessed automobile. Appellees were only privileged under the terms of the security agreement to detain appellant's personal property so long as was necessary to secure possession of the car. Once proper demand was made for return of the personalty taken with the automobile, the items should have been returned. Appellees' present willingness to redeliver possession to appellant of the allegedly wrongfully detained personalty does not remove the essentially tortious nature of the original unauthorized exercise of dominion.

Id. at 12.

Another clause creditors have used to attempt to forestall liability for conversion is "Any personalty in or attached to the property when repossessed may be held by Seller without liability and Buyer shall be deemed to have waived any claim thereto unless written demand by certified mail is made upon Seller within 24 hours after repossession." Should this provision be enforced against a consumer who orally requests the return of the other property?

Should a repossession company be able to impose a fee for storage and other services in connection with this other property? If so, should it be able to refuse to return the items until the consumer pays the fee?

7. In 1969 the United States Supreme Court held that it violates the Due Process Clause of the Constitution for a statute to permit a creditor to garnish a debtor's wages without prior notice and an opportunity for a hearing. Sniadach v. Family Finance Corp., 395 U.S. 337 (1969). In 1972 the Court extended this holding to the repossession context, striking down the replevin statutes of Florida and Pennsylvania. Fuentes v. Shevin, 407 U.S. 67 (1972).[5] In each of these cases, the creditor sought to use the judicial process. Section 9–503 of the UCC (as well as its successor, section 9–609), however, authorizes repossession by means of self help, with no judicial involvement at all. And so the issue arose, does self-help repossession violate the due process requirements of the Constitution? While some lower courts in the early 1970s found a constitutional violation, higher courts quickly came to the nearly unanimous view that self-help repossession, even though authorized by a statute, does not entail the state action necessary for the application of the Due Process Clause. The Supreme Court of the United States has consistently declined the opportunity to review these decisions.[6]

Even if the Constitution does not prohibit self-help repossession, a statute may. E.g., Wis.Stat.Ann. 425.206(1). See Whitford & Laufer, Impact of Denying Self–Help Repossession, 1975 Wis.L.Rev. 607.

C.   RIGHT TO A DEFICIENCY JUDGMENT

Repossession of the collateral is not necessarily the end of the matter. After repossession the creditor has two alternatives. The first is to retain the collateral in full satisfaction of the debt (§ 9–620) (sometimes known as "strict foreclosure"). The creditor's right to retain the collateral in satisfaction of the debt is subject to an important qualification: the consumer must assent. If the consumer has paid as much as sixty percent of the original obligation, the assent must be given expressly and in writing (§§ 9–620(e), 9–624(b)); if the consumer has paid less than sixty percent, the creditor must give the consumer an opportunity to object (i.e. negate assent) (§ 9–620(c)(2)).

The second alternative is to "dispose of" the collateral and hold the consumer liable for any remaining deficiency (§§ 9–610(a), 9–615(d)(2)). If the creditor disposes of the collateral, the disposition must comply with section 9–610(b) and sections 9–611 to 9–614, and the proceeds are distributed in accordance with section 9–615(a). The following materials deal with

---

5. A subsequent decision, however, permitted a creditor in Louisiana to seize collateral before giving notice to the consumer. Mitchell v. W. T. Grant Co., 416 U.S. 600 (1974). The Court believed the Louisiana statute provided sufficient procedural safeguards to comply with the requirements of due process. See also North Georgia Finishing, Inc. v. Di–Chem, Inc., 419 U.S. 601 (1975); Lugar v. Edmondson Oil Co., Inc., 457 U.S. 922 (1982).

6. Moreover, the Court has held that sale of property subject to a warehouse lien, as authorized by UCC section 7–210, does not entail state action. Flagg Brothers, Inc. v. Brooks, 436 U.S. 149 (1978). But see Svendsen v. Smith's Moving & Trucking Co., 429 N.E.2d 411 (N.Y.1981), cert. denied, 455 U.S. 927 (1982) (section 7–210 violates the state constitution).

the creditor's disposition of the collateral and the consumer's liability for any remaining deficiency.

First Fidelity Acceptance v. Hutchins

New Jersey Superior Court, 1998.
315 N.J.Super. 201, 717 A.2d 437.

Mark A. Sullivan, Jr., J.S.C.

Plaintiff First Fidelity Acceptance sues for the deficiency between the balance due on a retail installment contract for the sale of a motor vehicle after deduction of the proceeds of the sale of the repossessed vehicle.

On October 17, 1994 defendant Steve Hutchins purchased a 1988 Chevrolet Corsica for $7,480.36. The purchase was financed by plaintiff, First Fidelity Acceptance. Defendant defaulted in payment under the loan and the vehicle was repossessed on September 30, 1997. Plaintiff's suit is for the balance due after the repossessed vehicle was sold.

Defendant did not answer, and plaintiff seeks default judgment. The accounting submitted by the plaintiff is as follows:

Balance at Repossession	$6,492.65
Repossession and Storage Fees	510.00
Collection and Investigation Fees	50.00
Transportation and Sale Fees	510.00
Repair and Reconditioning Fees	635.33
	$8,197.98
Less physical damage loss payment	1,209.80
	$6,988.18
Less proceeds of sale	500.00
BALANCE DUE	$6,488.18

In addition, plaintiff seeks prejudgment interest of $171.92 and an attorney's fee of $698.81.

Of concern to the court is the fact that three items that would not have been necessary but for the repossession, i.e. the repossession and storage fees, the transportation and sale fees and the repair and reconditioning fees total $1,655.33, while the resale was only $500.00. It thus appears that, instead of reducing the balance, the repossession actually increased the balance by $1,155.33.

[The court cited the version of Article 9 that was in effect at the relevant time:

(1) A secured party after default may sell, lease or otherwise dispose of any or all of the collateral in its then condition or following any commercially reasonable preparation or processing. . . . The proceeds of disposition shall be applied in the order following to

  (a) The reasonable expenses of retaking, holding, preparing for sale, or lease, selling, leasing and the like and, to the extent provided for in the agreement and not prohibited by law, the reasonable attorneys' fees and legal expenses incurred by the secured party;

(b) The satisfaction of indebtedness secured by the security interest under which the disposition is made . . . .

(2) . . . [T]he secured party must account to the debtor for any surplus, and . . . the debtor is liable for any deficiency. . . .

(3) Disposition of the collateral may be by public or private proceedings . . . at any time and place and on any terms but every aspect of the disposition including the method, manner, time, place and terms must be commercially reasonable.][a]

It is well settled law [in New Jersey] that, if a creditor fails to dispose of the collateral in a commercially reasonable manner, a presumption arises that the collateral was worth the amount of the debt.

On a default a plaintiff need make only a prima facie showing to recover. Here the prima facie showing appears to be to the contrary, that plaintiff is not entitled to a deficiency. This court interprets the phrase "every aspect of the disposition" to include not just the sale of the collateral but also the decision to repossess it. It is not "commercially reasonable" to spend $1,655.33 repossessing and preparing for sale a car that is likely to sell for only $500.00.

Of further significance is that [the statute] provides that the expenses of retaking, holding, preparing for sale and reasonable attorney's fees are to be deducted from the proceeds of the disposition. Nowhere does the statute permit these expenses to exceed the amount of those proceeds. To so permit would cause the repossession of a chattel to increase rather than decrease the balance due. Such a result would not only be absurd but would run contrary to the whole purpose of secured transactions, whereby collateral is intended to guarantee the satisfaction of a claim, in whole or in part, not to do exactly the opposite.

Plaintiff will be given forty-five days from the date of this opinion to submit prima facie proof that "every aspect of the disposition" was commercially reasonable. Should it fail to do, the complaint will be dismissed pursuant to the presumption that the value of the collateral equaled the loan. Should plaintiff succeed in making such a showing, recovery will be allowed for the balance due on the loan. However, the expenses of retaking, holding, preparing for sale and reasonable attorney's fees will be limited to the $500.00 proceeds of the sale, any written agreement to the contrary being void as contrary to the statute.

QUESTIONS AND NOTES

1. Why do you suppose the balance due at the time of repossession, 35 months after the purchase, was only $988 less than the initial purchase price?

---

a. Former section 9–504. The analogous provisions now appear in sections 9–610 and 9–615.—Ed.

2.   When defendant defaulted, what was plaintiff supposed to do?

3.   Another example of a creditor's failure to make a commercially reasonable disposition is Franklin State Bank v. Parker, 346 A.2d 632, 634–35 (N.J.Dist.Ct.1975), where the creditor repossessed an automobile:

> [W]hen the automobile was offered for sale on June 29, 1974, it was not mechanically operational because defendant and his son were giving the automobile a tune-up, and the spark plugs, points and condenser had been removed preparatory to installation of new ones. The air filter also had been removed and placed on the floor of the garage near the automobile. This was the condition of the automobile when it was towed from defendant's garage.
>
> At no time before or after the repossession did plaintiff make any attempts to determine, by inspection or otherwise, why the automobile was not mechanically operational. The most routine observation under the hood of the automobile by one slightly familiar with the trade would have detected the missing parts.
>
> . . .
>
> The court finds that plaintiff failed to satisfy the "good faith" and "commercially reasonable" standards [which] required the plaintiff to at least make a casual inspection of the automobile to determine why the motor would not mechanically operate. If it had done so, it would have been obvious that the spark plugs, points, condenser and carburetor air filter were missing. The court takes judicial notice under Evid. R. 9(1) that eight spark plugs and a set of points can be purchased for less than $15. There would also be a labor charge to install these items. To dispose of the automobile for $50 because it was not operational when only minor repairs would have made the automobile mechanically operational is tantamount to conducting a sale in a manner that was not commercially reasonable.

4.   After a creditor repossesses collateral and before disposing of it, section 9–611 requires the creditor to notify the consumer of its intention. Section 9–612 addresses the timing of this notice, and sections 9–613 and 9–614 govern the content of the notice. Please read these sections.

The purpose of requiring notice of disposition is to enable the debtor to protect his or her interests, by redeeming the collateral, by attending and monitoring the disposition, or by finding someone to purchase the collateral from the creditor. Section 611(b) states, "a secured party that disposes of collateral under Section 9–610 shall send . . . a reasonable authenticated notification of disposition." The burden of proof with respect to notification and with respect to conducting a proper disposition is on the creditor. What if the consumer claims he or she never received any notice of disposition? See section 9–102(a)(74) and consider the following excerpt from Auto Credit of Nashville v. Wimmer, 231 S.W.3d 896, 901–03 (Tenn.2007):

> In the provisions of the statute that discuss providing reasonable notification to the debtor of the sale of the collateral, there is no

requirement for or mention of *receipt* of that notification. In fact, as used by the legislature in the general, introductory provisions of the UCC, "notifies" "is the word used when the *essential fact is the proper dispatch* of the notice, not its receipt. . . . *When the essential fact is the other party's receipt of the notice, that is stated.*" § 1–201, cmt. 26 (2001) (emphasis added). Because section 9–611(b) expressly says "send" and makes no references to "receive" or "receipt" in its notification requirement, it follows that the creditor is only required to ensure that the notification is properly sent and is not required to ensure its receipt.

There are four possible scenarios with regard to notification that can arise when a creditor takes possession of collateral and proceeds to sell that collateral. First, the creditor could send no notification, yet proceed with the sale. This would be in clear violation of the notification statute. Second, if the creditor sent the notification in compliance with the statute and knows for certain that the debtor received that notification, then the creditor could proceed with the sale without fear of adverse consequences.

Third is the situation where a creditor *knows* that the debtor has not received the notification, yet proceeds with the sale without making another attempt to notify the debtor. In Mallicoat v. Volunteer Fin. & Loan Corp., 415 S.W.2d 347, 350 (Tenn. Ct. App. 1966), the Court of Appeals held that it was not reasonable to proceed with the sale without making an additional attempt to contact the debtor when the creditor knew that the debtor had not received the notification of the proposed sale.

In *Mallicoat*, the creditor sent a notification of sale to the debtor by certified mail, but the notification was returned undelivered. Despite receiving the returned notification, the creditor proceeded to conduct a sale of the collateral and sued the debtor for a deficiency judgment. In holding the notification in that case insufficient under the predecessor statute to section 9–611, the Court of Appeals stated:

> In view of the undisputed proof in this case that the debtor did not receive the notice *and that the secured creditor was aware that he had not received it*, it is our opinion the creditor not only failed to show a compliance with the Act but that the record affirmatively shows a lack of compliance and a conscious disregard of the debtor's right to notice. The property was not perishable. The debtor lived in Knoxville where the creditor had its place of business and sold the property. In addition, the creditor had information as to where the debtor was employed and where his parents lived. Yet, the sale was allowed to proceed without any further effort to comply with the notice requirement.

Id. at 350 (emphasis added). The intermediate court's ruling in *Mallicoat* is consistent with the official comments to the revised Article 9, which were adopted in 2001. Those comments state that it is left to "judicial resolution, based on the facts of each case, . . . whether the requirement of 'reasonable notification' requires a 'second try,' i.e., whether a secured party who sends notification and learns that the debtor did not receive it must attempt to locate the debtor and send another notification." Section 9–611, cmt. 6.

Lastly, is the situation we are faced with in this case—where the creditor has sent proper notification in compliance with the statute, but does not know if that notification has been received. This is an issue of first impression in this Court, . . . and [we]hold that so long as the notification is "sent" within the meaning of Article 9, the creditor does not need to take additional steps to determine whether or not that notification has been received. . . .

To require every creditor to verify receipt of notification in every situation would place an unreasonable burden on them, making secured transactions in this state unduly cumbersome. It is quite conceivable that many debtors, when faced with the notification sent by certified mail, may refuse delivery, thus prolonging the time the creditor must wait to sell the collateral, causing additional costs to accrue to the creditor. Even without such affirmative acts by the debtor, any number of situations may arise which prevent actual receipt of written notification: debtors move, mail gets lost, or someone other than the debtor may receive the letter then misplace it.

In sum, we hold that the notification requirement in section 9–611 only requires the creditor to send proper notification and does not require the creditor to verify receipt. . . .

5. To be reasonable, when must the notification be given? In the case on page 676 infra, the consumer argued that notification is not reasonable if it is received only five business days before the date of sale. Is the argument sound? The version of Article 9 in effect at the time of that case did not elaborate on timing. The current version does. See section 9–612. How would plaintiff's argument—that the notice was defective because he received it only five days before the sale date—fare under current law?

For cases decided under the former version, see DeLay First National Bank & Trust Co. v. Jacobson Appliance Co., 243 N.W.2d 745 (Neb.1976) (notice must be received at least three days before the disposition); Franklin State Bank v. Parker, 346 A.2d 632 (N.J.Dist.Ct.1975) (three days is not enough). Applying the current version, another court has held that 11 days is not enough. Coxall v. Clover Commercial Corp., 781 N.Y.S.2d 567, 673–74 (N.Y. City Civ.Ct.2004). Is this a tenable conclusion?

6. The disposition of the collateral may be by public or private proceedings (§ 9–610(b)), but section 9–613(a)(1)(E) stipulates slightly different content for the notification depending on whether the creditor selects public or private disposition. In the problem at the beginning of this chapter, did the creditor give notice of public sale or private sale? Did the notice otherwise comply with section 9–614? For an attempt to determine whether the creditor's disposition was public or private, see *DeLay v. Jacobson*, Question 5 supra.

7. Problem. Following *Consumer's* default and *Seller's* repossession, *Seller* sends *Consumer* a letter accurately stating the accelerated balance of the debt. The letter also states, "We have received a bid of $3,500 for the car. Unless we hear from you at once, we intend to accept this bid." Is this notice adequate?

8. Problem. Following *Consumer's* default and *Seller's* repossession, *Seller* sends *Consumer* a letter accurately stating $2,240 as the accelerated balance of the debt. The letter also states, "You have the right to recover possession of the car by paying us the total balance ($2,240) plus our expenses in repossessing it ($175), or a total of $2,415. You may redeem the car by paying the sum of $2,415 within fifteen days from the date of this notice. If you do not redeem as aforesaid, the car will thereafter be sold at a private sale and you will be liable for any deficiency between the amount you owe us and the amount we receive at that sale." Is this notice adequate? (See also section 9–623.)

————

The next case concerns a claim by a creditor against a consumer who filed a petition in bankruptcy, so some understanding of the bankruptcy process is helpful. The description that follows is quite abbreviated and oversimplified, but it should suffice for present purposes.

Under the Bankruptcy Code a consumer may initiate the proceedings by filing a petition, and each of the consumer's creditors has an opportunity to submit a proof of claim that the consumer is indebted to it. The claim may be secured or unsecured, depending on whether the consumer has given a security interest in any of his or her property. If the debt owed the creditor (say, $10,000) is larger than the value of the collateral at the time of the bankruptcy proceedings (say, $7,000), the creditor is partially secured, in which event the creditor has both a secured claim (to the extent of the value of the collateral ($7,000)) and an unsecured claim (to the extent the claim exceeds the value of the collateral ($3,000)).

In bankruptcy each creditor who has a secured claim receives either the property in which it has a security interest or the value of that property. (The consumer gets to choose whether to surrender the collateral or pay its value.) In addition, the creditor may receive payment of part of its unsecured claim, on the same basis as the other creditors who have unsecured claims. In liquidation proceedings (Chapter 7 of the Bankruptcy Code), these distributions occur on a one-time basis, and the consumer is discharged from the balance of the debts. In so-called wage-earner plans (Chapter 13), the payments occur on a monthly basis out of money transferred every month from the consumer to the trustee in bankruptcy.

In the next case the creditor asserted a claim against the consumer and some of her property. It sought to enforce this claim in state court in an action to recover possession of that property. She responded by filing a petition seeking relief under Chapter 13. Under the Bankruptcy Code this filing operated as an automatic stay against all efforts by creditors, including secured creditors, to recover property of the consumer or to enforce claims against her.

In re Schwalb

United States Bankruptcy Court, District of Nevada, 2006.
347 B.R. 726.

HON. BRUCE A. MARKELL, UNITED STATES BANKRUPTCY JUDGE.

I. INTRODUCTION

"Then the bird does not belong to any of you?" Spade asked, "but to a General Kemidov?"

"Belong?" the fat man said jovially, "Well, sir, you might say it belonged to the King of Spain, but I don't see how you can honestly grant anybody else clear title to it—except by right of possession." He clucked. "An article of that value that has passed from hand to hand by such means is clearly the property of whoever can get hold of it."[1]

Possession is the central theme in this case. Pioneer Loan & Jewelry, a pawnbroker, possesses two certificates of title that list it as the owner of two motor vehicles. Michelle Schwalb, the debtor, possesses those vehicles. Pioneer claims exclusive ownership, and that Ms. Schwalb has no legal or equitable interest in the vehicles beyond mere possession. Schwalb counters that Pioneer has no interest in the vehicles because she never transferred title or granted any other interest in them to Pioneer.

. . .

II. RELEVANT FACTS

Michelle Schwalb is not a typical chapter 13 debtor. She holds no job, because she can't hold one. Seven years ago she had a brain tumor removed, leaving her unsteady and unable to concentrate for extended periods of time. Social Security disability payments are her only regular income. She is 34 years old, diabetic, has a non-working pituitary gland, and has initial symptoms of Grave's disease. She must take steroids to live. Ms. Schwalb lives with a man who fathered her only child, and they have been together as a family for thirteen or fourteen years. He works outside the home, and pays most of the household expenses.

. . .

Ms. Schwalb's father gave her the two vehicles at issue, a 1997 Infiniti QX4 Sport Utility Vehicle and a 2002 Cadillac Escalade. Before dealing with Pioneer, Ms. Schwalb had clean title to both vehicles. Then, sometime during 2004, the debtor, her father, and her partner decided they needed to

---

1. Dashiell Hammett, *The Maltese Falcon, reprinted in* THE NOVELS OF DASHIELL HAMMETT 397 (1965).

contribute funds to a business that Ms. Schwalb's partner ran. They went to Pioneer and obtained two loans totaling $20,000.

The business, however, failed. Ms. Schwalb had no way to repay Pioneer. At this point, Pioneer began to take action to obtain the vehicles. To understand the actions Pioneer took, however, it is necessary to review the transactions by which Ms. Schwalb obtained the $20,000.

Ms. Schwalb and her father initially approached Pioneer in June of 2004. Mr. Schwalb had done business with Pioneer and, at that time, enjoyed some goodwill with it. Ms. Schwalb's Infiniti QX4 Sport Utility Vehicle was offered as collateral, and Pioneer advanced $4,000 against possession of the certificate of title for the vehicle. The parties testified that Ms. Schwalb gave Pioneer her certificate of title after she signed it as seller. The buyer's name was left blank.

When she received the $4,000 in loan proceeds, Ms. Schwalb signed a document referred to by the parties as a pawn ticket. The pawn ticket is a preprinted form used by Pioneer in its pawnbroker business. It is a simple 5-inch-by-8-inch form, with text front and back. Among other things, the front has blanks for describing the property pawned, for the amount of the loan and for the repayment date.

On Ms. Schwalb's pawn ticket, the parties designated the property pawned as an Infiniti QX4 Sport Utility Vehicle, and included its Vehicle Identification Number (VIN). The ticket also contained the loan terms. Ms. Schwalb was to repay the $4,000 in 120 days, plus $1,605 interest. The disclosed annual interest rate was 122.04%. If Ms. Schwalb did not "redeem" the pawn and pay the loan within the 120 days, the pawn ticket indicated that "you shall . . . forfeit all right and interest in the pawned property to the pawnbroker who shall hereby acquire an absolute title to the same." Just before the blank on the pawn ticket in which the parties inserted the description of the Infiniti and its VIN, the pawn ticket indicated, in very small five-point type,[3] "You are giving a security interest in the following property: ." Pioneer did not retain possession of the vehicle. Ms. Schwalb drove off in it with her $4,000. Pioneer put the signed certificate of title in a safe on its premises.

The transaction with the Cadillac was essentially the same, except Pioneer advanced $16,000 against possession of the signed certificate of title, and the interest rate was 121.76%. This transaction occurred on August 19, 2004. In each case, Pioneer's representative testified that the amount Pioneer lent against the certificates of title was within Pioneer's general practice of lending no more than 30% to 40% of the retail value of the vehicle offered as collateral.

Approximately $1,605 in interest on the Infiniti loan was paid on or around November 6, 2004, thus extending the redemption period to March

3. In printing, a "point" is 1/72 of an inch. At five points, the statement was thus 5/72, or approximately .07 of an inch, tall. For comparison, most computer word processors tend to default to 12 points, or .167 of an inch, which is almost two and one-half times the size of the print Pioneer used. This is an example of a sentence in five-point type.

6, 2005. No interest was ever paid on the Cadillac loan. The final 120–day term expired on the Infiniti loan on March 6, 2005, and on December 17, 2004, for the Cadillac loan.

When Ms. Schwalb did not repay either loan, Pioneer took both certificates of title to the Nevada Department of Motor Vehicles ("DMV") where, sometime in April 2005, Pioneer requested that the DMV reissue the certificates showing Ms. Schwalb as the owner and Pioneer as the "lienholder." The DMV complied. After Pioneer's initial efforts to obtain the vehicles were unsuccessful, Pioneer then presented the newly reissued certificates of title to the DMV, this time requesting that the DMV reissue the certificates of title without any mention of Ms Schwalb, and listing Pioneer as the sole owner. Again the DMV complied. Pioneer then filed a state court lawsuit apparently alleging conversion and seeking recovery of both vehicles. There was testimony that Pioneer consulted with the local police regarding the necessity of changing the certificates of title to facilitate its legal action seeking recovery of the vehicles.

Ms. Schwalb filed her chapter 13 case on August 9, 2005. Pioneer elected not to file a proof of claim, instead opting to claim ownership of the vehicles. Pioneer attempted to obtain relief from stay so that it could obtain the vehicles, but withdrew that motion for procedural reasons.

Ms. Schwalb's plan, filed with her chapter 13 petition, proposes to pay her creditors over 36 months. Her monthly payment is $555 for the first 12 months of her plan, and $709 per month for the remaining 24 months of her plan.

Initially, Ms. Schwalb contends that Pioneer is not a secured creditor, and is barred from participating in her case as an unsecured creditor.[a] Her initial proposal is thus to pay Pioneer nothing under her plan. If Pioneer is found to be a secured creditor despite her objection, she proposes to value the collateral for the secured claims at $16,000 for the Cadillac loan and $4,000 for the Infiniti loan. The plan would then pay these two secured claims full over the life of the plan, together with 10% simple interest.

III.   PIONEER'S PROPERTY INTERESTS

The parties have focused on the nature of Pioneer's property interest, if any, in the two vehicles. . . . Pioneer contends that it owns both vehicles, and that Ms. Schwalb has no legal or equitable interest in them. Ms. Schwalb counters that Pioneer is not a pawnbroker with respect to the vehicles since it did not retain possession of them after making the loans. Ms Schwalb further argues that the language of the pawn ticket is insufficient to create an Article 9 security interest under Nevada's version of the Uniform Commercial Code (UCC).

Pioneer, if forced to yield on its ownership claims, contends that the language in the pawn ticket is sufficient under Nevada's version of Article 9 to create a security interest, and that it has not violated any of Article 9's requirements or restrictions. Ms. Schwalb, however, contends that Pioneer

---

a.   Because it failed to file a claim.—Ed.

did not comply with significant and mandatory provisions of Article 9. . . .

A. Pawnbrokers and the Pawning of Goods Generally

> All around the cobbler's bench
> The monkey chased the weasel
> The monkey thought that all was fun
> Pop! Goes the weasel!
>
> A penny for a spool of thread
> A penny for a needle
> That's the way the money goes
> Pop! Goes the weasel![6]

Under Nevada law, a pawnbroker is a "person engaged, in whole or in part, in the business of loaning money on the security of pledges, deposits or other secured transactions in personal property." NEV. REV. STAT. § 646.010. The parties agree that Pioneer is a licensed pawnbroker under this law. They disagree, however, on the significance of Pioneer's status, and to resolve those differences the court must investigate the history and current status of pawnbrokers, and the impact of pawnbroker status with respect to a nonpossessory vehicle loan.

1. Short History of Pawnbroking

Pawnbrokers engage in transactions in which a debtor pawns[7] goods in return for a short-term loan. Pawnbroking has a significant and positive place in the history of lending. Italian Banks and Pawnbroking: In Hock, THE ECONOMIST, May 27, 2006, at 73 (reporting that pawnbroking is a 500–year old business and stating that the bank claiming to be the world's oldest bank, the Monte dei Paschi di Siena, began in the pawn business). According to some accounts, Queen Isabella of Spain pawned her jewels to finance Columbus' trip of discovery. Jarret C. Oeltjen, Florida Pawnbroking: An Industry in Transition, 23 FLA. ST. U.L. REV. 995, 996 (1996).[8] At various times in our history, pawning one's clothes and other possessions was an ordinary and common occurrence.[9]

---

6. Nursery rhyme it may be, but its origins are in pawnbroking. In English slang (and the English version of the rhyme is printed above), to "pop" something is to pawn it; and a "weasel" was slang for a hatter's tool. WILLIAM MORRIS & MARY MORRIS, MORRIS DICTIONARY OF WORD AND PHRASE ORIGINS 457–58 (1977); BREWER'S DICTIONARY OF PHRASE AND FABLE 929 (16th ed., Adrian Room, rev. 1999).

7. The word "pawn" in this sense comes from Old French *pan* meaning skirt of a gown, which in turn is from Latin *pannum*, meaning cloth or something made out of cloth. JOSEPH P. SHIPLEY, DICTIONARY OF WORD ORIGINS 263 (1945); *see also* THE OXFORD DICTIONARY OF ENGLISH ETYMOLOGY 659 (C.T. Onions, ed., 1966). Until recently, most items pawned were clothing items. JOHN P. CASKEY, FRINGE-BANKING, CHECK-CASHING OUTLETS, PAWNSHOPS AND THE POOR 17 (1994).

8. This story is apparently apocryphal. CASKEY, *supra* note 7, at 15.

9. *See* CASKEY, *supra* note 7, at 17 (noting that, around 1828, more than half of the items pawned in New York City were clothing items).

Pawning one's goods differs from lending against them; in a typical pawn, a debtor deposits goods with the pawnbroker, and receives money in return. If the customer does not "redeem" his pawn within a specified time, tradition has it that the power to sell the goods deposited automatically passes to the pawnbroker. If the pawnbroker's subsequent sale of the goods does not cover the loan, the pawnbroker takes the loss; conversely, if the pawnbroker sells the goods for more than the money lent, custom allows the pawnbroker to keep the surplus. CASKEY, supra note 7, at 1. . . .

2. Recent History, and the Advent of "Title Pawns"

Despite its venerable history, pawnbroking has lately experienced something of a public relations crisis. Pawnbrokers are regulated in a manner designed to deter personal property theft, and often are found in low-income neighborhoods on the fringe of respectability. Despite efforts to improve this image, "the negative portrait lingers; pawnshops continue to be cast as 'nuisance businesses,' in the company of tattoo shops and massage parlors, and somewhere in rank between liquor stores and houses of prostitution." Oeltjen, supra, at 1001.

This negative perception has not been helped by the type of loans present here. As noted in a recent report sponsored in part by the Consumer Federation of America, "car title loans are marketed as small emergency loans, but in reality these loans trap borrowers in a cycle of debt. Car title loans put at high risk an asset that is essential to the well-being of working families—their vehicle." AMANDA QUESTER & JEAN ANN FOX, CAR TITLE LENDING: DRIVING BORROWERS TO FINANCIAL RUIN 2 (2005). As noted by Quester and Fox, some states have passed laws favorable to the title loan industry, while others have specifically prohibited pawnbrokers from engaging in "title pawn" transactions. . . .

3. Nevada's Regulation of Pawnbrokers and Title Pawn Transactions

[Pawnbrokers are regulated by both Nevada statutes and Las Vegas city ordinances, but this legislation focuses on traditional pawnbroking, not title lending.] . . .

B. Application of Article 9

Neither the state nor the local regulation specifically refers to the applicability of the primary statute related to personal property collateral—Article 9 of the UCC. Conversely, Nevada has not explicitly excluded pawnbroking from the scope of Article 9. The initial question is thus easily stated: Does Article 9 apply to Pioneer's two transactions with Ms. Schwalb?

1. Does Article 9 Apply to Traditional Pawnbroking Activities?

Pioneer contends . . . that pawnbroking is excluded from Article 9. That contention is false as a matter of statutory construction. Article 9 is intended to be the primary statute regarding the consensual personal property security. It is a marvel of drafting that consolidates and resolves many issues into one single statute. And it is intentionally broad; as noted in the comments, "all consensual security interests in personal property and fixtures are covered by this Article. . . . When a security interest is created, this Article applies regardless of the form of the transaction or the name that parties have given to it." Cmt. 2 to UCC § 9–109.

To achieve this breadth of coverage, Article 9 looks to substance over form. This is confirmed by its text: Article 9 states that it applies to any "transaction, *regardless of its form*, that creates a security interest in personal property or fixtures by contract." UCC § 9–109(a)(1) (emphasis supplied).

Given this broad scope, some states have altered the breadth of Article 9 . . . .

In the area of pawnbroking, however, Nevada has not adopted other states' practice of excluding some or all of pawnbroking's practices from Article 9. See, e.g., CAL. COMM. CODE § 9201(b) (2006) (exempting California's Pawnbroker Law from Article 9); 810 ILL. COMP. STAT. § 5/9–201(b)(5) (2006) (exempting Illinois' Pawnbroker Regulation Act); N.C. GEN. STAT. § 25–9–201(b) (2006) (exempting North Carolina's Pawnbrokers Modernization Act of 1989).

Given this lack of express exclusion, the court believes that Nevada would join the other states and commentators who have examined the issue, and concluded that pawnbroking is an activity governed by Article 9 of the UCC that neither the parties' contrary language nor an industry's contrary practice can alter.

2.   Pioneer's Transactions Are Not Traditional Pawn Transactions

Even if the court held that pawnbroking's practices are impliedly exempt from Article 9, Pioneer would not prevail for the simple reason that the transactions at issue are not those of a traditional pawnbroker. Pawnbrokers are bailees of personal property held as collateral for loans. If the loan is not paid—or, in the argot of pawnbroking, if the pawn is not redeemed—then the pawnbroker sells the goods held, and keeps the proceeds; the debtor is not liable for any deficiency, and the pawnbroker is not accountable for any surplus.

As a result, a true pawn requires a pledge, and a pledge requires delivery of the collateral to the pawnbroker.

Here, of course, Pioneer did not possess the vehicles (although state law permitted it to do so); at best, it was a bailee of the certificates of title, for whatever good holding on to pieces of officially issued paper did it. As such, the issue as to the exempt status of traditional pawnbroking activities is not directly raised by this case.

Pioneer argues that actual possession was not necessary. Since it had possession of the certificates of title, it has "constructive" possession of the vehicles, and that this constructive possession was sufficient to bring it under the protective reach of pawnbroking status. Nothing in the Nevada statutory scheme authorizes this view, and pre-UCC cases rejected it.

C. Applicability of Article 9 to Pioneer's Loans

As indicated above, Section 9–109 makes Pioneer's transactions with Ms. Schwalb subject to Nevada's version of Article 9. This was not unexpected. Pioneer's form of pawnbroking ticket expressly states that Ms. Schwalb was "giving a security interest" in the two vehicles to Pioneer. . . . As a result, the transactions here were covered by Article 9 of the UCC. This conclusion has serious repercussions for the parties.

[A lengthy description of the attachment and perfection of security interests is omitted. The court concludes that a security interest attached and that it was perfected. Furthermore, the security interest is enforceable in bankruptcy proceedings, even though Pioneer never filed a claim.]

3. Enforcement [of the Security Interest]

Perhaps the key difference that attends the application of Article 9 to the transactions at issue lies in how Pioneer may enforce its security interest. Its contract, the pawn ticket, is explicit. It states that:

> In the event of failure to pay the loan with 120 days from date hereof, you shall thereby forfeit all right and title unto such pawned property to the pawnbroker who shall thereby acquire an absolute title to the same.

Before Ms. Schwalb filed her case, Pioneer sought to enforce this clause by first applying to be listed as the owner on the certificates of title, and then by filing a state court action seeking possession of the vehicles.

a. Unenforceable Forfeiture Clause

Pioneer continues to seek enforcement of this forfeiture clause as written. It asserts that both vehicles belong, in all senses of that word, to it and to it alone. This assertion is misguided. Article 9 prohibits the waiver by debtors of certain provisions. In particular, Section 9–602 contains a long list of provisions that "the debtor . . . may not waive or vary." These include the provisions regarding: the obligation to proceed in a commercially reasonable manner, § 9–602(7), strict foreclosure, § 9–602(10), and the debtor's right to redeem the collateral, § 9–602(11).[27]

If the parties sign a security agreement containing prohibited waivers, and then seek to enforce them, courts most often remedy violations of Section 9–602 by simply reading the relevant documents as if the offending clause had never been included. They then assess the parties' conduct under the remaining provisions and the default standards set forth in Article 9.

These provisions are of special concern in consumer transactions. As noted in the official comments to Section 9–602:

> our legal system traditionally has looked with suspicion on agreements that limit the debtor's rights and free the secured party of its

---

27. The statute also prohibits a secured party's attempt to extract waivers of these antiwaiver provisions, § 9–602(12), and any attempt to disclaim liability for violations of Article 9's provisions. § 9–602(13).

duties. . . . The context of default offers great opportunity for over-reaching. The suspicious attitudes of the courts have been grounded in common sense. This section . . . codifies this long-standing and deeply rooted attitude. The specified rights of the debtor and duties of the secured party may not be waived or varied except as stated.

Cmt. 2, UCC § 9–602.

This wariness has been, for the most part, reflected in academic commentary on this subject. See, e.g., Barkley Clark, Default, Repossession, Foreclosure and Deficiency: A Journey to the Underworld and a Proposed Salvation, 51 Ore. L. Rev. 302, 303 (1972) (noting that a consumer "is as likely to read (let alone understand) [a security agreement] as he is to run windsprints in Red Square"); Michael M. Greenfield, The Role of Assent in Article 2 and Article 9, 75 Wash. U. L.Q. 289, 300 (1997) (arguing that a consumer's waiver of a statutory right at the time of contract formation "is highly suspect" and that the "small-print boilerplate" language of the waiver makes a consumer's assent "a fiction").[28]

b. Violations of Part 6 of Nevada's Article 9

If enforced as written, the pawn ticket forfeiture provisions would not only have waived and varied, but they would have effectively obliterated, Ms. Schwalb's right to prohibit Pioneer's strict foreclosure of her interest in the vehicles, as well as her right to redeem the vehicles after default and repossession. UCC §§ 9–602(10)–(11). But under Section 9–602, these rights may not be waived or varied by private agreement. The result of this clash is that, in accordance with the prevailing law under Article 9 cited above, the pawn tickets will have to be enforced without reference to their forfeiture provisions.

What effect does that erasure have? Initially, it makes Article 9's default standards, rather than the pawn tickets' forfeiture provisions, applicable to Pioneer's action in attempting to dispose of the vehicles. . . . Pioneer was obligated to proceed as to the vehicles in the manner required by Part 6 of Article 9. This it did not do. Because violations of Part 6 take on a significant role later in this opinion, it is appropriate to catalog the more egregious of Pioneer's violations.

The cornerstone duty placed on every secured party is the obligation to proceed in a commercially reasonable manner. Article 9 expresses this by requiring that "[e]very aspect of a disposition of collateral, including the method, manner, time, place and other terms, must be commercially reasonable." UCC § 9–610(b).

---

28. Some disagree. See Edward J. Heiser, Jr. & Robert J. Flemma, Jr., *Consumer Issues in the Article 9 Revision Project: The Perspective of Consumer Lenders*, 48 Consumer Fin. L.Q. Rep. 488, 493 (1994) (arguing that "[t]he idea that a consumer debtor is unsophisticated and completely at the mercy of secured parties ignores reality"); James J. White, *Work and Play in Revising Article 9*, 80 Va. L. Rev. 2089, 2095 (1994) (urging the drafting committee to "purge the idea of the noble consumer who borrows in ignorance, who is surprised by repossession and deficiency judgment, and who claims incredible promises by his creditor" because "the consumer class overflows with liars and cheats").

Although proceeding by judicial action may be commercially reasonable in some case, the manner in which Pioneer proceeded here was not. It sought judicial vindication as the sole owner of the vehicles, a status it claimed through operation of the forfeiture clause in its pawn ticket. Such forfeitures are authorized in some circumstances, and are referred to as "strict foreclosures." See UCC § 9–620.

But a secured party's ability to engage in a strict foreclosure with respect to a consumer is heavily circumscribed. In particular, a secured creditor may not strictly foreclose on consumer goods without the consumer's consent, UCC § 9–620(a)(1), and may not strictly foreclose on any collateral that it does not possess, id. § 9–620(a)(3). Neither of these conditions is present here, thus making Pioneer's attempts to strictly foreclose on the vehicles violations of Part 6 of Nevada's Article 9.

In addition, when Pioneer proceeded in state court as if the vehicles were its sole property, Pioneer violated its duty to give Ms. Schwalb the option to force a public disposition, and deprived her of the opportunity to redeem. UCC §§ 9–602(10)–(11). Proceeding in this contrary-to-law manner was perforce not commercially reasonable.

There were other violations. Article 9 is explicit that a secured party must notify a debtor before any disposition, UCC § 9–611(b), and is explicit on what that notice must contain. Id. § 9–613(a).[30] But Pioneer could not produce any notice that it sent to Ms. Schwalb, and she could not locate any notice she received from Pioneer. The parties, however, stipulated that Pioneer generally sends a notice to its borrowers on a standard form, and that they had no reason to believe that Pioneer did not send a notice on this standard form to Ms. Schwalb. Pioneer then produced an exemplar of that standard form. While the form appears to contain many of the required disclosures, it does not contain all of the required provisions. In particular, the notice violates UCC § 9–613(1)(d), which requires that any notice contain a statement that "the debtor is entitled to an accounting of the unpaid indebtedness and states the charge, if any, for an accounting."

Pioneer omitted this required disclosure, of course, because of Pioneer's belief in the validity of its forfeiture provisions, which did not mention any accounting. Pioneer's erroneous belief, even if in good faith, does not save it; there is no good faith defense to the failure to provide sufficient notice of a proposed disposition. See, e.g., Kruse v. Voyager Ins. Cos., 72 Ohio St. 3d 192, 196–97, 1995 Ohio 120, 648 N.E.2d 814, 817 (Ohio 1995) (failure to send notice to debtor was a violation of Article 9's notice

---

30. UCC § 9–613, which applies to all transactions except consumer-goods transactions, applies here rather than § 9–614, which applies to consumer-goods transactions. The difference, obviously, turns on whether the creation of the security interest occurred in a "consumer-goods transaction." [To be a "consumer-goods transaction," the obligation must be incurred primarily for personal, family, or household purposes.] UCC § 9–102(a)(24). While the vehicles are consumer goods as used by Ms. Schwalb, the loan was not incurred for personal, family or household purposes; it was instead incurred to obtain funds to invest in a business. Borrowing to invest or contribute to a business is not borrowing for "personal, family or household" purposes.

provisions); Wilmington Trust Co. v. Conner, 415 A.2d 773, 776 (Del. 1980) (failure to give credit for finance charges paid but unearned in notice of disposition was violation of Article 9's notice provisions).

. . .

D. Summary

Pioneer entered into two transactions with Ms. Schwalb that were and are subject to Article 9 of the UCC. Pioneer believed that each transaction was a pawn of the vehicle, and thus thought that Article 9 did not apply. Both of these beliefs were mistaken. First, the transaction was not a traditional pawn of the vehicles. Throughout her case and this litigation, Ms. Schwalb has retained possession of the vehicles. Thus, the traditional basis of pawnbroking—possession of the collateral by the pawnbroker—is absent.

This absence also has significant consequences for Pioneer with respect to the applicability of Article 9. Although the court expresses no opinion on the applicability of Article 9 to traditional possessory pawns, the nonpossessory financing in this case does come within Article 9. Although Pioneer did not believe that Article 9 applies, the "substance over form" rules of Article 9 render that belief irrelevant.

Applying Article 9 to the parties' agreement—the pawn ticket—shows that some of its key provisions are unenforceable, and that Pioneer violated Article 9 in the manner in which it has proceeded in this matter. The impact of those violations will be explored later, but first the nature and amount of Pioneer's claim in bankruptcy must be established.

IV. PIONEER'S CLAIMS IN BANKRUPTCY

. . .

Since the court has determined that the pawn ticket's forfeiture provisions are unenforceable, that means that Ms. Schwalb is the owner of the vehicles and that, at best, Pioneer is a secured creditor. But to determine the extent of its secured claim, the court must determine the amount of the claim and the value of the collateral.

1. Allowed Amount of Claim

The initial principal amounts of the loans are easy to calculate. Pioneer lent $4,000 on the Infiniti, and $16,000 on the Cadillac. From that point, as Nevada has no generally applicable usury limits, prepetition interest ran at the rate of 120% on each loan until the filing date. As a consequence, as of filing, Pioneer's accrued interest claim on the Infiniti loan was $3,629.59, and its accrued interest claim on the Cadillac loan was $18,673.98. When added to the original principal amounts, Pioneer's total claim outside of bankruptcy, as of the petition date, was $42,303.57—$7,629.59 on the Infiniti loan, and $34,673.98 on the Cadillac loan. . . .

2. Effect of Pioneer's Violation of Article 9 on Its Allowed Claim

. . . Pioneer's violations of Article 9 work significant reductions in its claim.

a.   Statutory Recovery Under UCC § 9–625

Under Article 9, there are significant consequences for failure to follow Article 9's provisions. Section 9–625(b) provides that "a person is liable for damages in the amount of any loss caused by a failure to comply with this article." Ms. Schwalb offered to prove damages under this section, but did not introduce any evidence on this point.

Notwithstanding this failure of proof, Ms. Schwalb may still have a remedy for Pioneer's failure to comply with the enforcement provisions of Article 9. The record firmly establishes numerous instances of Pioneer's noncompliance with Part 6 of Article 9. When such noncompliance exists, Section 9–625(c)(2) provides as follows:

> If the collateral is consumer goods, a person that was a debtor . . . at the time a secured party failed to comply with this part may recover for that failure in any event an amount not less than the credit service charge plus 10 percent of the principal amount of the obligation . . .

As characterized by Barkley and Barbara Clark, leading commentators on Article 9:

> This sanction has been characterized as both a minimum civil penalty and a liquidated damages provision. Its appeal is that it requires no showing of actual loss. . . . This minimum civil penalty, quietly tucked away in a corner of the statute, is probably the most glittering nugget of consumer protection found in all of Article 9.

CLARK & CLARK, supra, at ¶ 4.12[4], at pp. 4–335 to 4–336; see also 10 ANDERSON, supra, at § 9–507:166 ("Even if the consumer debtor cannot prove the actual damages sustained by the noncomplying sale of the collateral, the consumer debtor may recover the statutory minimum damages.").

Does Section 9–625 apply in this case? Initially, it requires the collateral to be consumer goods. Article 9 defines these as goods held or used for "personal, family or household purposes." UCC § 9–201(a)(23). Ms. Schwalb testified that she used the vehicles to go to doctors, to run errands and to transport her daughter, and that her partner used them to go to work. This use qualifies as family, if not personal, use.

There is also no doubt that Pioneer, as a secured party, failed to comply with Part 6 of Article 9. See Part III.C.3.b supra. This noncompliance can form the basis of an award under Section 9–625. Cf. Kruse v. Voyager Ins. Cos., 72 Ohio St. 3d 192, 1995 Ohio 120, 648 N.E.2d 814 (1995) (even if disposition of collateral is commercially reasonable, when collateral is consumer goods, debtor may recover under predecessor of Section 9–625 if secured party fails to provide debtor with reasonable notice of sale of collateral as required by UCC).

Thus, the statutory minimum penalty of UCC § 9–625(c) is applicable. That means that the "credit service charge[s]"—essentially all the paid and accrued interest here—are damages to which Ms. Schwalb is entitled. See, e.g., 4 WHITE & SUMMERS, supra, at § 34–14(c) ("We interpret that sentence to grant damages equal to the total interest charge (irrespective of the amount that has been paid) in addition to 10% of the original principal amount of the debt, irrespective of how much of the principal has been repaid").

For the two loans, there is $22,303.56 of "credit service charge[s]." These charges consist of accrued but unpaid interest on both loans as of the filing, and $1,600 in interest actually paid on the Infiniti loan. In addition, the statutory damages include 10% of the principal amount of each loan. These amounts would be $400 for the Infiniti and $1,600 for the Cadillac. When added together, the interest and principal components of the statutory damages equals $25,903.56.

. . .

When these damages are recouped against Pioneer's claim, that leaves Pioneer with a claim of $2,000 on the Infiniti loan, and a claim of $14,600 on the Cadillac loan.

. . .

VI.   CONCLUSION

[Ms. Schwalb's Chapter 13 plan must include payments to satisfy Pioneer's secured claims of $2,000 and $14,600, and she is entitled to retain possession of the vehicles.]

QUESTIONS

1.   Section 9–609 states that after default, a secured party may repossess collateral and in doing so may proceed by self-help or by judicial process. Would it have been permissible for Pioneer to repossess the two vehicles by self-help? If so, then precisely why was it not commercially reasonable for Pioneer—before the filing of any bankruptcy proceedings—to use the state judicial process to obtain possession?

2.   The court relies on 9–602, which invalidates attempts by a creditor to get a consumer to waive several protections of Article 9. Section 9–603, however, provides that the parties may determine by agreement the standards for determining whether the creditor has complied with those protections, so long as those standards are not manifestly unreasonable. The contract cannot dispense with the requirement of section 9–611 that the creditor give reasonable notification of a disposition of collateral. It s common, therefore, for the contract to state that in the event of repossession, the creditor will give notice a specified number of days in advance of a disposition. Would a contractual provision that five days' notice shall suffice be enforceable? ten days? Is section 9–612(b) relevant?

In Coxall v. Clover Commercial Credit, Question 5, page 662 supra, the court stated that 11 days' notice was not "reasonable notification." Would it matter if the contract stated that ten days' notice would suffice?

3. The court holds that Pioneer's method of obtaining Schwalb's cars was inconsistent with Article 9's provisions on strict foreclosure (§ 9–620), which permit a creditor to obtain and keep collateral in satisfaction of a debt. Compare Moran v. Holman, 514 P.2d 817, 820–21 (Alaska 1973), in which a delinquent debtor surrendered possession of the collateral (a truck) to the creditor. After retaining the truck and using it for four months, the creditor sued to recover the unpaid balance of the debt. The court held that when a creditor "retains collateral which depreciates in value, such as a motor vehicle, for an unduly long period of time and uses the vehicle as his own, . . . the debtor may validly claim that his obligation has been satisfied. To rule otherwise would permit overreaching and inequitable abuses by some secured parties." What overreaching and inequitable abuses might occur? Is it essential to the court's holding that the creditor used the collateral as his own?

In *Moran*, decided under the original version of Article 9, the court in effect held that the creditor had opted for strict foreclosure, whether or not it had intended to. Courts often refer to this as constructive strict foreclosure. Article 9 now addresses this subject in section 9–620. Please read subsection (b), which apparently precludes the court's result in cases like *Moran*. If so, what is to prevent the creditor from simply repossessing collateral, using it, and suing the consumer for nonpayment?

4. If a creditor fails to comply with the requirements of Article 9, section 9–625 provides that the consumer is entitled to recover actual damages (subsection (b)) but in no event less than an amount equal to the sum of the credit service charge and ten percent of the principal amount of the obligation. In *Schwalb* this amounted to almost $26,000. Creditors thus have a powerful incentive to comply with the requirements of Article 9.

Wilmington Trust Co. v. Conner

Supreme Court of Delaware, 1980.
415 A.2d 773.

HERMANN, CHIEF JUSTICE:

. . .

I.

On December 6, Daniel B. Conner, the defendant, entered into a conditional sales contract for the purchase of an automobile. The contract was assigned by the automobile dealer to the Wilmington Trust Company, the plaintiff. After failing to make four consecutive monthly installment payments, the defendant defaulted on the contract. Despite efforts to dispose of the vehicle, including advertising in a local newspaper, the defendant was unable to sell the vehicle or meet his obligations. Consequently, on August 22, the defendant voluntarily surrendered the vehicle to the plaintiff.

On August 24, the plaintiff sent to the defendant, by registered mail, written notice stating that the "present balance" of the defendant's account with the plaintiff was $4,013.09, and that unless payment was "made by September 4, * * * this unit [would] be sold in accordance with applicable law." This notice was received by the defendant on August 28.

The automobile was placed on the plaintiff's lot after repossession and was not sold until about 18 months later. The sale was private and the car was bought for $1,000.00.

The plaintiff brought suit in the Court of Common Pleas claiming that a deficiency was due and owing in the amount of $2,587.69. This amount was later reduced to $2,262.19. The defendant's answer alleged that the notice of resale was defective, that the sale was not commercially reasonable and, therefore, that the plaintiff was barred from collecting a deficiency judgment. The defendant also counterclaimed for statutory damages under § 9–507(1).[a] Upon motion by the defendant, the Court of Common Pleas granted summary judgment in favor of the defendant. The Court held that a debtor was entitled to a statement in the notice of resale of the balance due on an installment sales contract. Since the figure in the notice did not reflect a refund credit of $654.61 for unearned finance charges and insurance premiums, as required by 5 Del.C. § 2908 and 5 Del.C. § 2906(g), the Court of Common Pleas concluded that the notice was defective under 6 Del.C. § 9–504(3).[b] That Court further held that, pursuant to the line of Delaware authority represented by Commercial Credit Corporation v. Swiderski, Del.Super., 195 A.2d 546 (1963), the plaintiff was precluded from obtaining any deficiency judgment against the defendant due to the notice defect. In addition, the Court awarded the defendant $1,445.32 in statutory damages under § 9–507(1).

On appeal, the Superior Court reversed the judgment of the Court of Common Pleas. Although it accepted the latter Court's finding that the stated balance in the notice was unduly inflated because of the plaintiff's failure to credit the account with the unearned finance charges and

---

a.   UCC § 9–507(1) (1978):

. . . If the collateral is consumer goods, the debtor has a right to recover in any event an amount not less than the credit service charge plus ten per cent of the principal amount of the debt or the time price differential plus 10 per cent of the cash price.

The current version of this provision appears at section 9–625(a)–(c).—Ed.

b.   UCC § 9–504(3) (1978):

Disposition of the collateral may be by public or private proceedings and may be made by way of one or more contracts. Sale or other disposition may be as a unit or in parcels and at any time and place and on any terms but every aspect of the disposition including the method, manner, time, place and terms must be commercially reasonable. Unless collateral is perishable or threatens to decline speedily in value or is of a type customarily sold on a recognized market, reasonable notification of the time and place of any public sale or reasonable notification of the time after which any private sale or other intended disposition is to be made shall be sent by the secured party to the debtor, if he has not signed after default a statement renouncing or modifying his right to notification of sale. . . .

The current version is much more elaborate and appears at sections 9–610 through 9–614.—Ed.

insurance premiums, the Superior Court concluded that such figure is not required under § 9B504(3). Moreover, since the defendant could not show that he had been misled or frustrated in his attempts to redeem the vehicle by this alleged defect, the Superior Court held that the inaccurate balance was not a defect under § 9–504(3) for the purposes of the motion for summary judgment. The Superior Court did agree with the Court of Common Pleas, however, that the notice was defective, since the plaintiff failed to indicate in the notice whether the subsequent sale was to be public or private.

Nevertheless, the Superior Court found that under the line of contrary authority represented by Associates Financial Services Co., Inc. v. DiMarco, Del.Super., 383 A.2d 296 (1978), if the creditor-plaintiff could overcome the presumption that the value of the collateral equals the value of the debt it could collect a deficiency judgment. It also concluded that the award of statutory damages was invalid since the defendant had not shown that the collateral was a "consumer good" as required by § 9–507(1).

. . .

II.

The defendant contends here that the notice provided him was defective for the following reasons: (1) the balance of the loan was overstated by $654.64; (2) the notice was received only five business days prior to the date after which a sale was to be made; (3) the plaintiff did not intend to sell the collateral quickly and thus, in retrospect, the notice period was unreasonable; and (4) the notice failed to explicitly specify whether the sale was to be public or private. Because of the conclusion we reach on the first of these arguments we need not decide any of the defendant's subsequent contentions.

Under the Uniform Commercial Code "reasonable notification" of the disposition must be given to the debtor. § 9–504(3). The Uniform Code, however, relegates the exact definition of "reasonable notification" to the individual states and, ultimately as a general rule, to their courts. The purpose of the requirement of "reasonable notification" is threefold: (1) it gives the debtor the opportunity to exercise his redemption rights under § 9–506 [now §§ 9–623, 9–624]; (2) it affords the debtor an opportunity to seek out buyers for the collateral; and (3) it allows the debtor to oversee every aspect of the disposition, thus maximizing the probability that a fair sale price will be obtained. Any aspect of the notice that is contrary to these purposes necessarily prevents it from being "reasonable notification."

The Court of Common Pleas held that the plaintiff's failure to account in the notice for the rebate of unearned finance charges and insurance premiums constituted a defect in the notice. We agree. Certainly the insertion of an unduly inflated figure in the notice discourages and perhaps frustrates the attempts of the debtor to find another buyer or to exercise his redemption rights.

The plaintiff contends that § 9–504(3) does not require that the balance due be stated in the notice for a private sale since it only demands "reasonable notification of the time after which any private sale . . . is to be made." Therefore, it is argued, an error in the balance stated cannot be a defect in the notice under § 9–504(3). We cannot accept this conclusion. The adoption of this rationale would lead to the absurd conclusion that the notice of resale may contain misleading information of any kind so long as certain statutory catch words or phrases are also included. Moreover, whether § 9–504(3) requires that the balance due be placed in the notice of resale is tangential to the issue in question. The key issue is whether "reasonable notification" was given. We hold that this notice, which contained a stated balance that was inflated $654.61 above the amount actually owed, was not "reasonable notification."

The plaintiff argues that it was impossible to give the defendant a net balance, since the finance charges and insurance premiums were constantly accruing, and the plaintiff was unable to predict when the collateral would be sold. This argument is unavailing. Had the plaintiff provided the defendant, for example, with a figure as of September 4 with an addendum reasonably and accurately stating a method by which debtor could compute the accruing interest and insurance premiums, this issue might have been decided otherwise. But, in the light of the plaintiff's statutory duty to rebate unearned finance charges and insurance premiums, a blatant assertion in the notice that the total amount under the contract was due, without reference to such possible rebates, was manifestly unreasonable.

We conclude, therefore, that the notice of resale sent by the plaintiff to the defendant was defective under § 9–504(3).

III.

Having concluded that the notice of resale was defective, we turn to the effect this conclusion has on the plaintiff's ability to collect a deficiency judgment under the Uniform Commercial Code. A quick resumé of the governing statutory provisions, set forth at length, supra, is in order: The creditor's initial right to collect a deficiency judgment is established by § 9–504(2): "If the security agreement secures an indebtedness, the secured party must account to the debtor for any surplus, and unless otherwise agreed, the debtor is liable for any deficiency." Under § 9–504(3), in order for the creditor to dispose of the collateral, he must send to the debtor "reasonable notification of the time and place of any public sale or reasonable notification of the time after which any private sale or other disposition is to be made." If it is shown that the creditor has not disposed of the collateral in accordance with the Code provisions, § 9–507(1)[c] gives "the debtor . . . a right to recover from the secured party any loss caused by a failure to comply with the provisions of this Part"; and if the collateral is consumer goods, statutory minimum damages are provided for.

---

c.   Revised § 9–625(b)–(c).—Ed.

The issue presented here is one of first impression in this Court. Under the predecessor to the Code, the Uniform Conditional Sales Act, the format of which was similar to that of the Code, strict compliance with the notice provisions was viewed as a condition precedent to the collection of a deficiency judgment. . . . With the enactment of the Uniform Commercial Code in Delaware in 1967, however, the applicability of such prior case law has come into question.

Currently, there is wide contrariety of judicial opinion regarding the creditor's right to a deficiency under the Uniform Commercial Code when the notice of resale is defective.

The apparent majority rule under the Code, the "absolute bar" theory, remains as it was under the Uniform Conditional Sales Act: failure to comply strictly with the notice provisions of the Code acts as an absolute bar to recovery of a deficiency judgment by the creditor.

A second theory, the "shift" theory, espouses the view that once the notice has been established as being defective, the creditor may recover a deficiency, but only to the extent that he can overcome the presumption that the value of the collateral equals the value of the debt.

A third view, the "set-off" theory, concludes that the creditor's right to a deficiency judgment is complete, subject only to set-off for the debtor's losses under § 9–507(1).

The plaintiff contends that the "shift" or "set-off" theories are the views most consistent with the language and spirit of the Code. Generally, it is argued that the language of § 9–504(2)[d] suggests that a creditor should not be prevented from collecting a deficiency judgment.

The plaintiff first contends that the "set-off" theory is the most correct and should be adopted by this Court. It argues that the letter and spirit of Article 9 of the Code mandate that § 9–507(1) be construed as the exclusive remedy for the injured debtor. This conclusion is deduced by the plaintiff from the two following propositions: (1) recovery of a deficiency is not specifically denied by the Code; and (2) because § 9–507(1) is the only section of Article 9 to treat damages arising from failure to comply with the Code, and there is silence as to any additional remedy for the debtor, the drafters must have intended § 9–507(1) to be the debtor's exclusive remedy.

In the alternative, the plaintiff argues that if § 9–507(1) is not seen as the exclusive remedy, the "shift" theory should be adopted. The plaintiff, like other proponents of the "shift" theory, contend that the "absolute bar" theory is punitive in nature and contrary to the theme of commercial reasonableness that pervades the Code. Moreover, they argue that the "shift" theory is inherently more fair. Finally, they contend that § 9–507(1) provides an adequate remedy for the debtor's losses; and that the

---

d. ". . . [T]he secured party must account to the debtor for any surplus, and, unless otherwise agreed, the debtor is liable for any deficiency." The current version appears in section 9–615(d).—Ed.

contrary results obtained under the Uniform Conditional Sales Act were attributable to the precise notice requirements, which are lacking in the Code.

We are unpersuaded by the plaintiff's arguments and conclude that Delaware should adhere to the "absolute bar" rule which was well settled in this jurisdiction under the Uniform Conditional Sales Act by Commercial Credit Corporation v. Swiderski, supra, and its progeny.

First, we are unable to accept the arguments that § 9–504(2) grants the creditor an undeniable right to a deficiency and that § 9–507(1) is the debtor's exclusive remedy. We note first that the Uniform Conditional Sales Act contained a provision strikingly similar to § 9–507(1). Former 6 Del.C. § 925 provided:

> If the seller fails to comply with the provisions of sections 918–921, and 923 of this title after retaking the goods, the buyer may recover from the seller his actual damages, if any, and in no event less than one-fourth of the sum of all payments which have been made under the contract, with interest.

This was not considered to be the exclusive remedy under the Uniform Conditional Sales Act. Moreover, we are unable to find any evidence that its counterpart in the Uniform Commercial Code was intended to be construed differently.

Neither § 9–504(2) nor § 9–507(1) expressly or impliedly deny the applicability of the *Swiderski* rule to cases under the Code. The failure of the drafters or the Legislature to include a provision barring creditors from collecting a deficiency, as relied on by the plaintiff, in no way indicates an intent to deny this remedy to debtors. Indeed, the Code specifically provides that other rules of law may control unless explicitly displaced by provisions of the Code. § 1–103.[e] Furthermore, the Code recognizes the applicability of other remedies as well. Section 1–106(1) provides:

> The remedies provided by this subtitle shall be liberally administered to the end that the aggrieved party may be put in as good a position as if the other party had fully performed but neither consequential or special nor penal damages may be had except as specifically provided in this subtitle *or by other rule of law*. (Emphasis added)[f]

In the light of these provisions the drafters' failure to provide a section denying a creditor the right to obtain a deficiency cannot be seen as an endorsement of the plaintiff's theory that § 9–507(1) was intended to be the debtor's exclusive remedy.

> [T]he more reasonable conclusion is that precisely because of their learning, skill and experience, the drafters of the Uniform Commercial Code, had they truly intended the remedy to be exclusive, would have been scrupulously careful to state it. Their omission of language in

---

e. Now section 1–103(b).—Ed.

f. Without substantive change, this provision appears as section 1–305 in Revised Article 1.—Ed.

§ 9–507(1) expressly indicating exclusivity of the remedy thus speaks volumes against the correctness of plaintiff's position.

Camden National Bank v. St. Clair, 309 A.2d at 332.

Finally, the case law under the Uniform Conditional Sales Act was settled by the time of the drafting and adoption of the Code and it is presumed, of course, that the General Assembly was aware of existing law. The failure of the drafters to expressly change the prevailing rule is persuasive evidence of the non-exclusivity of § 9–507(1) and the continued viability of the rule of *Swiderski*.

We must also reject the plaintiff's argument that the "shift" theory provides the more appropriate remedy. Contrary to plaintiff's protestations, we are unable to find any punitive aspects in barring the creditor from obtaining a deficiency judgment when it has provided the debtor with a defective notice. Under the rule of *Swiderski*, the creditor's strict compliance with the notice provisions is a condition precedent to the attainment of a deficiency judgment. Thus, the creditor's ability to collect a deficiency is pre-conditioned on compliance with a statutory remedy in derogation of common law. Failure to adhere to the relevant statute results not in punishment, but merely in the inability to invoke the operation of the remedial statutory provisions.

Plaintiff's arguments that principles of fairness or the remedy provided by § 9–507(1) militate in favor of accepting the "shift" theory are similarly unacceptable. The burdens placed on the creditor under the Code are minimal, while the results of his noncompliance may be very onerous to the debtor. This unequal relationship has been recognized by numerous cases. We are unable to see any unfairness in protecting the debtor's rights to the exclusion of those of the creditor when the creditor has been placed in such a high degree of control of the relationship and carries such a small burden in order to gain the advantages of the Statute.

Likewise, the adequacy of § 9–507(1) does not require the adoption of the "shift" rule. Indeed, it may be that the inadequacy of § 9–507(1) to protect the debtor's rights has led courts to seek additional deterrents.

Finally, we are unable to agree with the plaintiff's argument that the more liberal notice provisions of the Code require divergence from the pre-Code case law represented by *Swiderski*. The liberalization of the notice provisions of the Code, without more, does not necessarily mean that the concomitant remedies for failure to comply also have undergone similar changes. Indeed, as we noted previously there is very little difference between § 9–507(1) and its predecessor, former 6 Del.C. § 925. Moreover, while minor deficiencies in the notice provisions may no longer compel the finding that insufficient notice has been given, the mandate still exists to protect debtors from "unreasonable" notice. In the absence of clear contrary legislative intent, this continued need to protect the debtor's interests militates against any lessening of corrective measures.

Therefore, in view of the lack of contrary legislative intent or evidence in the Uniform Commercial Code suggesting the necessity for change, we adhere to the "absolute bar" rule which was approved in *Swiderski* and has so long prevailed in this jurisdiction, and reject the reasoning of Associates Financial Services Co., Inc. v. DiMarco, supra. The "absolute bar" rule has the advantage of certainty in a situation in which the lender enjoys a position of domination and control and the consumer-debtor is in a subordinate position in need of the protection the "absolute bar" rule affords.

Accordingly, in the instant case, we hold that the plaintiff is barred from obtaining a deficiency judgment against this defendant.

IV.

Turning now to the defendant's appeal from the dismissal of his counterclaim for statutory damages under § 9–507(1): In order to be eligible for such an award of statutory damages, a debtor must show that the creditor violated its duty under § 9–504(3) and that the collateral is a "consumer good" under § 9–507(1). Since it has already been established that the plaintiff's notice of resale was defective, the only remaining issue is whether the automobile constituted a "consumer good" under the Statute.

The Superior Court found that no evidence had been presented by the defendant to show that the collateral was, in fact, a "consumer good." The defendant argues that the ruling of the Superior Court was improper, since this was not raised in the Court of Common Pleas regarding an ordinary passenger automobile. The plaintiff contends that the decision was proper and that the issue was raised in oral argument.

Appeals from the Court of Common Pleas to the Superior Court are to be determined from the record below and are not to be tried de novo. On the record before us in this case, we are unable to find that the "consumer good" issue was raised in the Court of Common Pleas.

We must therefore conclude that the Superior Court erred in reversing the judgment of the Court of Common Pleas granting statutory damages to the defendant.

This opinion shall have prospective application only, except for this case and all other cases pending on appeal in this Court on the date hereof.

Reversed and remanded for further proceedings in accordance herewith.

QUESTIONS AND NOTES

1. Former section 9–504(3) did not expressly require notification of the unpaid balance of the debt. Why did the court hold that defendant's notice did not comply with the statute?

The notification requirements now appear in sections 9–611(b) and 9–614. Must the creditor notify the consumer of the unpaid balance? Would it violate those sections for a creditor to notify a consumer of the unpaid balance without adjusting that figure to reflect unearned finance charge?

2.   The primary issue in *Conner* concerns the consequences of the creditor's failure to provide reasonable notification of the disposition. The courts are sharply split on the proper resolution of this issue. Why does the court in *Conner* conclude that failure to comply with the notification provision bars the creditor from obtaining a deficiency judgment?

Perhaps the main reason of the court is the similarity of former section 9–507(1) to section 25 of the Uniform Conditional Sales Act (UCSA), which the UCC superseded. In cases arising under the UCSA, courts denied deficiency judgments even though that sanction was not expressed in section 25. However, according to Nickles, Rethinking Some U.C.C. Article 9 Problems, 34 Ark.L.Rev. 1, 162–66 (1980), the UCSA cases were not decided under that section, but rather under a different section that has no counterpart in the UCC.[7] Decisions applying the UCSA thus may not be persuasive.

Are the court's other reasons persuasive? Should the creditor who fails to comply with sections 9–611 through 9–614 automatically be denied a deficiency judgment? Section 9–626(a)(3)–(4) adopts the rebuttable presumption rule for commercial transactions, but subsection (b) leaves to the court the choice of remedies in consumer transactions.

3.   When a car dealer sells a car on credit and assigns (i.e. sells) the credit contract to a financial institution, the assignment may be recourse or non-recourse. If it is non-recourse, the assignment is final, and that formally ends the relationship between the dealer and the assignee with respect to that consumer's contract. If it is recourse, on the other hand, the assignment provides that if the consumer defaults, the assignee (financial institution) has the right to transfer the contract back to the dealer. This transfer to the dealer may occur as soon as the consumer defaults, or it may occur later than that, after the creditor has repossessed the vehicle, in which event the creditor may also transfer possession of the car to the dealer. This transfer ordinarily is not a section 9–610 disposition. See section 9–618: a dealer in a recourse financing is a "secondary obligor" under subsection (a), and the transfer of the collateral is not an Article 9 disposition, per subsection (b). The burden of complying with Article 9 (giving the proper notices and conducting a proper disposition) then falls to the dealer.

This does not mean that every transfer of collateral from the assignee to the dealer relieves the assignee of its Article 9 obligations and imposes those obligations on the dealer. For it to have this effect, the transfer must satisfy the requirements of section 9–618(a), and so it is possible for the assignee to remain obligated to comply with Article 9. See section 9–618, Official Comments 2–3. This possibility creates a potential for abuse, for a dealer and its assignee (who have an on-going relationship) have an

---

7.   The UCSA provided that if there was no resale by the creditor, the consumer's obligation was discharged. The courts thus treated the creditor's failure to conduct a proper resale as tantamount to a failure to sell altogether.

incentive to manipulate the details to maximize the economic benefit to them at the expense of the consumer.

An example of this is Coxall v. Clover Commercial Corp., 781 N.Y.S.2d 567, 570, 574–76 (N.Y. City Civ.Ct.2004):

> On October 21, 2002, Jason Coxall and Utho Coxall purchased a 1991 model Lexus automobile [from Jafas Auto Sales], executing a Security Agreement/Retail Installment Contract. The "cash price" on the contract was $8,100, against which the Coxalls made a "cash down payment" of $3,798.25 and financed the balance of $4,970. Apparently simultaneously with the sale, the contract was assigned to Clover Commercial Corp., whose name was printed on the top and at other places. . . .

> The Coxalls were required by the contract to make monthly payments of $333.68 each, beginning November 21, 2002. No payments were made, however, because Jason Coxall experienced mechanical difficulties with the vehicle soon after purchase. On February 19, 2003, Clover Commercial took possession of the vehicle, and on the next day mailed two letters to Jason Coxall; in one, Clover told Mr. Coxall that he could redeem the vehicle with a payment of $5,969.28, exclusive of storage charges and a redemption fee; in the other, Clover gave Mr. Coxall notice that the vehicle would be offered for private sale after 12:00 noon on March 3, 2003.

> On March 3, 2003, the Lexus was sold back to Jafas Auto Sales for $1,500. On April 22, 2003, Clover Commercial wrote to Jason Coxall demanding that he pay a "remaining balance" of $4,998.09.

> . . .

> "Every aspect of a disposition of collateral, including the method, manner, time, place, and other terms, must be commercially reasonable." (UCC 9–610(b)) Private dispositions, as compared to public auction, are encouraged "on the assumption that they frequently will result in higher realization on collateral for the benefit of all concerned." (UCC 9–610, Comment 2.) "A disposition of collateral is made in a commercially reasonable manner if the disposition is made . . . in conformity with reasonable commercial practices among dealers in the type of property that was the subject of the disposition." (UCC 9–627(b)(3))

> New York courts have determined commercial reasonableness by whether the secured party "acted in good faith and to the parties' mutual best advantage." When a secured party is seeking a deficiency from the debtor, the secured party bears the burden of proving the sale was commercially reasonable. (*See* UCC 9–626(a)(2)) "Whether a sale was commercially reasonable is, like other questions about 'reasonableness', a fact-intensive inquiry; no magic set of procedures will immunize a sale from scrutiny." (*Matter of Excello Press, Inc.*, 890 F.2d 896, 905 (7th Cir. 1989))

Here, Clover Commercial sold Mr. Coxall's Lexus in a private sale to the dealer from whom Mr. Coxall had purchased it. Clover Commercial provided no evidence on its procedure for the sale, its identification of prospective buyers, or any other details of the sale, except for the price. There was no showing that dealers sell their trade-ins in the same manner or that dealers or secured parties sell repossessed automobiles in the same manner. On the other hand, one court has noted that "the sale of [a] repossessed vehicle by private auto auction is in conformity with the reasonable commercial practices of lenders disposing of motor vehicles." This case is different, however, in that the vehicle was sold back to the dealer who sold it to the debtor. (*See* UCC 9–615(f), UCC 9–615, Comment 6)

All we have, therefore, as evidence of commercial reasonableness is the price. Clover Commercial received $1,500 on the sale of a Lexus that had been purchased by the Coxalls approximately four months earlier for $8,100; that is a sales price of 18.5% of the purchase price.

"The fact that a greater amount could have been obtained by a . . . disposition . . . at a different time or in a different method from that selected by the secured party is not of itself sufficient to preclude the secured party from establishing that the . . . disposition . . . was made in a commercially reasonable manner." (UCC 9–627(a)) But "[w]hile not itself sufficient to establish a violation of [code requirements], a low price suggests that a court should scrutinize carefully all aspects of a disposition to ensure that each aspect was commercially reasonable." (UCC 9–627, Comment 2.)

New York courts have, indeed, scrutinized "low price" sales.

"[M]arked discrepancies between the disposal and sale prices signal a need for closer scrutiny, especially where, as here, the possibilities for self-dealing are substantial . . . . Under these circumstances, we require some affirmative showing that the terms of the disposition were, in fact, commercially reasonable and hold that, in the absence of such a showing, we will be compelled to deny recovery in a suit for a deficiency judgment." (*Central Budget Corp. v. Garrett*, 48 A.D.2d 825, at 825–826 (1975))

A low price, of course, "might simply reflect a greatly depreciated piece of collateral." But, here, Clover Commercial acknowledged that Mr. Coxall's Lexus had not sustained any physical damage while in his possession. Clover's suggestion that the low price may have been due to the mechanical difficulties experienced by Mr. Coxall was contradicted by its own testimony that the car was running fine when repossessed, and would, in any event, be specious.

As previously indicated, Clover Commercial provided no evidence as to the commercial reasonableness of the sale; it provided no evidence that any prospective buyer was contacted, other than the original seller; and provided no evidence of the fair market value of the Lexus on the date of sale, or any other evidence that would justify a sale price of $1,500. In short, Clover Commercial failed to sustain its burden of showing that the sale of Mr. Coxall's Lexus was commercially reasonable.

Clover's failure to comply with Article 9 led the court to deny recovery of any deficiency and to impose liability on Clover for the statutory damages provided by section 9–625(c). See also Consumer Finance Corp. v. Reams, 158 S.W.3d 792, 797–98 (Mo.App.2005):

> . . . Here the only evidence adduced at trial regarding the reasonableness of the post-repossession sale was the admission of the bill of sale, which revealed that the collateral was sold at auction as well as the sale price of the vehicle.
>
> This evidence, standing alone, was not sufficient to meet its burden of proof that the sale of the collateral was conducted in a commercially reasonable manner. For example, there was no evidence in the record regarding whether Consumer Finance or other lenders utilized this method of sale and that particular auction venue with regard to other repossessed vehicles in the ordinary course of business. No evidence was admitted regarding what efforts, if any, were needed or made to prepare the collateral for sale. Nor was there any indication in the record that the price received for the collateral at auction was within the expected range for that type of vehicle in terms of its model, age, and condition.

The court denied the deficiency judgment. What is the relevance of whether "Consumer Finance or other lenders utilized this method of sale and that particular auction venue with regard to other repossessed vehicles in the ordinary course of business"?

4. Problem. To pay for a used car, *Consumer* borrows $7,000 from *Bank*, giving *Bank* a security interest in the car and agreeing to pay *Bank* $250 per month for 36 months. After performing for several months, *Consumer* defaults and *Bank* repossesses. Without sending any notice, *Bank* sells the car and sues for an alleged deficiency. *Consumer* counterclaims for damages under section 9–625(c)(2). If the case arises in a jurisdiction in which failure to send notice bars a deficiency judgment, should *Consumer* prevail on the counterclaim? If so, what should the damages be?

5. In addition to the denial of a deficiency judgment and/or liability for the minimum damages of section 9–625(c)(2), a creditor who fails to comply with the requirements of the UCC may be liable for punitive damages. E.g. Truck Center of Tulsa v. Autrey, 836 S.W.2d 359 (Ark.1992) ($7,000 for maliciously establishing a deficiency by disposing of the collateral to a purchaser who immediately sold it back to the secured party); Mitchell v. Ford Motor Credit Co., 688 P.2d 42 (Okl.1984) ($60,000 for wrongful repossession); Big Three Motors, Inc. v. Rutherford, 432 So.2d 483 (Ala. 1983) ($20,000, same); Deavers v. Standridge, page 650 supra.

6. After repossessing and selling the collateral, if the creditor seeks to recover a deficiency judgment against the consumer, the creditor must comply with section 9–616. That section requires the creditor to explain how it arrived at the amount it claims as a deficiency (§ 9–616(c)). This disclosure may facilitate the efforts of the consumer (or the consumer's attorney) to ascertain whether the creditor has properly credited unaccrued interest, unearned insurance premiums or benefits, or other credits. It also may trigger an inquiry into the propriety of the charges claimed in connection with the repossession and sale of the collateral.

What if the explanation lists a cost of $450 for "repossession expense," but the creditor actually paid the repossession company $350? Does the consumer have a remedy? See section 9–625(e)(5)–(6).

7. Empirical studies reveal that the retail value of repossessed automobiles typically is sufficient to discharge all of the unpaid balance of the consumer's obligation. E.g., Shuchman, Profit on Default: An Archival Study of Automobile Repossession and Resale, 22 Stan.L.Rev. 20 (1969). Yet the actual use of Article 9 procedures usually results in a substantial deficiency judgment against the consumer. The explanation for this phenomenon lies in the fact that the creditor makes the disposition under section 9–610 in the wholesale market, not the retail market. What justification is there for permitting wholesale dispositions? Should it matter whether the creditor is a bank or an auto dealer? Of what relevance is section 9–615(a)(1)? section 2–708(2)?

Several states have adopted legislation to change the rules for consumer transactions. In Pennsylvania, for example, the statute governing installment sales of motor vehicles requires the creditor to credit the buyer with the "reasonable value of the motor vehicle at the time of resale, . . . the resale price being prima facie, but not conclusive evidence, of such reasonable value . . . ." 69 Purdon's Penn.Cons.Stat.Ann. § 627. In what way(s) is this an improvement over the UCC?

Consider also the approach in Massachusetts:

> (e)(1) If the unpaid balance of the consumer credit transaction at the time of default was two thousand dollars or more the creditor shall be entitled to recover from the debtor the deficiency, if any, resulting from deducting the fair market value of the collateral from the unpaid balance due and shall also be entitled to any reasonable repossession and storage costs, provided he has complied with all provisions of this section.

> (2) In a proceeding for a deficiency the fair market value of the collateral shall be a question for the court to determine. Periodically published trade estimates of the retail value of goods shall, to the extent they are recognized in the particular trade or business, be presumed to be the fair market value of the collateral.

Mass. Gen. Laws Ann. ch. 255B, § 20B(e).

8. In an appendix to its opinion holding an automobile dealer in violation of FTC Act section 5, the Federal Trade Commission concluded that the UCC requires use of the retail value of repossessed automobiles:

Respondent has presented expert testimony in support of its view that an automobile dealer should be able to include an allowance for general overhead and dealership profit as part of the allowable expenses incident to the resale at retail of repossessed collateral. Alternatively, respondent suggests that the "proceeds" from a repossession should be measured simply by some estimate of the wholesale value of repossessed collateral at the time of repossession, even though no resale of the collateral may be undertaken except at retail.

Respondent's position is that the true value of repossessed collateral is most fairly measured by its wholesale value at the time of repossession. If the repurchase automobile dealer resells the collateral at retail, that dealer incurs both direct costs, such as out-of-pocket expenses of reconditioning and repair (for which the dealer can charge under the UCC), and indirect costs, such as a prorated share of general dealership expenses, advertising, lot rental, and the like. These indirect costs, just as much as the direct ones, contribute to the increase in value realized upon a car when it is sold at retail as compared to what it might fetch if sold at wholesale immediately after repossession. Accordingly, respondent argues, the dealer should be allowed to deduct an allowance for such indirect costs prior to crediting the consumer with any surplus. As for profit on the resale, respondent argues that the sale of a repossessed car imposes an opportunity cost upon the dealership, because sale of a repossessed vehicle takes the place of sale of another used car on which the dealer could realize a profit. Accordingly, argues respondent, the dealer should be entitled to realize a profit when it resells repossessed collateral.

Complaint counsel respond to this that the resale of repossessed collateral is nothing more than a debt collection activity. When a car is sold for the first time, the sales price includes a profit for the dealer, and this profit includes within it some allowance for the possibility that the debtor may default. When default occurs, resale of the repossessed collateral allows the dealer to realize his original profit, through recovery of the entire contract balance. Since the dealer's profit on each sale should already include an allowance for all costs incident to the sale (including debt collection costs) it would be unfair to permit the dealer to recover an additional profit, or share of the overhead, upon the repossession sale. No one, in complaint counsel's view, would suggest that when a finance company sues to collect an unpaid debt, or when an automobile dealer sues to collect an unpaid debt, the plaintiffs are entitled to charge the debtor for a ratable share of company overhead attributable to the time required by company employees to prepare for the lawsuit. Nor would it be suggested that the finance company or car dealer should be entitled to make a *profit* upon a suit for an unpaid debt, above and beyond the profit already included within the sales price or finance charge. The confusion in the case of the repossession transaction, in complaint counsel's view, results because the debt collection activity (i.e. the repossession sale) takes the same form as the principal line of business of the secured party (i.e.

selling cars) and this induces people to analyze the repossession transaction as being simply another sales transaction by the dealer, rather than one means of collecting a debt.

Deciding between these two positions depends very much upon one's view of what the goals of secured transactions law should be, the relative importance to be attributed to each of these goals, and how these goals can best be achieved.

Among the principal goals that have been suggested in this proceeding are the following:

> (1) Establishment of a clear, readily administered mechanism for preserving the debtor's equity in repossessed collateral; and

> (2) Deterring defaults.

Preservation of the debtor's equity in repossessed collateral is clearly a goal of Article 9. The law seeks to achieve this by requiring the secured party to act as a fiduciary for the debtor, to seek to obtain the best possible price for the collateral at a commercially reasonable sale, and to account to the debtor for any surplus.

Respondent argues that in pursuing this goal the law has gone too far, because when disposition occurs at retail, the debtor receives a windfall. This occurs because the value of his automobile is augmented by being resold by a dealer, but the amount of this augmentation cannot be entirely recovered. While the law does allow all recovery of out-of-pocket expenses, as well as direct sales commissions, it does not allow for recovery of such overhead items as general firm advertising, plant maintenance, and the like, all of which go into establishing a dealer's image and reputation and determine the price that it can charge for its cars. Giving the defaulting consumer a windfall, argues respondent, does more than is necessary to preserve his equity, and at the same time, deserves the goal of discouraging defaults, by creating an *incentive* for the debtor to default, rather than resell the car himself, if he desires or is forced to be rid of it.

This argument is certainly correct up to a point. That is, it seems quite plausible that in many cases, taking a given car, in a given state of repair, Francis Ford will be able to realize a higher price on that car than could the individual owner if he sought to sell it for himself, even allowing for the salesman's commission. The higher price may result in part from Francis Ford's reputation and good will, which an individual consumer would not have.

This observation, however, does not end the argument, for in any individual case it may be true that a car's value is not augmented by dealership good will, and, even where it is so augmented, the amount of the augmentation must be measurable, in fairness to the debtor. The position of respondent's experts appears to be that *any* increase in value of collateral beyond its "wholesale value" should be attributed to the dealer's efforts, and so should be recoverable by the dealer. *By definition* this position would eliminate the possibility of any surplus resulting from a retail resale, in obvious mockery of both the law and the facts.

For these reasons then, the rule disallowing recovery by the creditor of general overhead may be the most *practical* way to assure preservation of the debtor's equity. Though it may under some circumstances overstate that equity, it also ensures that that equity will be preserved against the encroachments that would result if essentially non-measurable costs could be charged against the debtor.

Without necessarily questioning that this view has some validity, respondent suggests that it results in a gross anomaly, because debtors whose cars are repossessed by a finance company not party to a recourse financing agreement receive only the benefits of a wholesale disposition of the collateral, while customers of Francis Ford and other dealers that engage in recourse financing receive the benefits of retail disposition. Francis then points to testimony of witnesses to the effect that the surpluses on wholesaled collateral appear with the frequency of Halley's Comet to show the incongruity.

The comparison with wholesale disposition may, however, be more a reflection upon the insufficiency of that method of resale than it is upon the excessive generosity of retail disposal of repossessed collateral. One study, for example, found that wholesale dispositions of repossessed cars yielded on average prices that were only 51% of retail *Redbook* value, and only 71% of *wholesale Redbook* value (compared to 93% of wholesale *Redbook* value obtained on a different group of unrepossessed used cars sold at wholesale auctions). Shuchman, Profit on Default: An Archival Study of Automobile Repossession and Resale, 22 Stan.L. Rev. 20, 31 (1969).

In the case before us, the Kelley Bluebook *wholesale* value of a number of the cars repossessed by Francis Ford's lenders exceeded the amount of the payoff. Presumably, Francis Ford, which claims to have determined repossessions by comparing wholesale price with payoff, did not pay surpluses on any of these cars because its used car manager concluded that they were in sufficiently poor condition so as not to be worth guide book values. This, indeed, reflects the view of some witnesses in this proceeding, to the effect that repossessed vehicles are generally in poorer condition than other used cars, and any car owner who surrenders his car does so because he knows that he could not resell it himself for the contract balance.

In any event, while there is no doubt that the law creates certain disparities among debtors, because some receive the benefit of wholesale and some of retail dispositions of their cars, it does not follow that this disparity results in a windfall for the beneficiaries of retail disposition. It may rather be that such debtors receive roughly what they should, while beneficiaries of wholesale disposition are regularly deprived of equity because of imperfections in the wholesale market, or in the types of wholesale disposition regularly employed.

Finally, we may return to the goal of default deterrence, which should underlie any scheme for regulating relations of debtors and creditors. We have observed that a strong argument for disallowing generalized overhead expenses is that it provides a precise way of measuring debtor's equity, and avoids its unfair extinguishment by means of unjustified allocations of overhead. Does this, however, encourage defaults, or fail to discourage defaults, by sparing debtors certain costs associated with the failure to pay?

One cardinal rule of cost allocation is that costs should be borne by the parties best able to avoid them. In the credit context, however, the application of this formula is unclear, because a great many defaults cannot be prevented by the defaulters. Some debtors are deadbeats, or become voluntarily and unjustifiably overextended, leading to default. Many others, however, default for reasons essentially beyond their control, in particular, illness, divorce, or loss of employment. Bending over backwards to ensure that these debtors bear every conceivable cost associated with their defaults is, therefore, unlikely to contribute substantially to deterring them.

The foregoing is not to say that debtors should not be made to pay the readily measurable costs associated with default, and indeed, this is the precise effect of the law, which allows the creditor to recover all out-of-pocket expenses, including towing, reconditioning costs, and the like. This alone is likely to act as a substantial deterrent to default (to the extent it is deterrable) because as soon as the car is repossessed the debtor's equity in it is immediately reduced by all costs directly related to the repossession (such as towing) which could have been avoided if default had not occurred. The question is simply how certain unmeasurable costs (i.e. overhead) should be divided. Should the law bend over backwards to ensure that no windfall is given to the debtor, so as to discourage defaults, even at the risk that the debtor may be deprived of his equity in the collateral? Or should the law bend over backwards to ensure that no extinction of the debtor's equity occurs, so as not to further penalize the debtor for an occurrence that in many cases he is powerless to prevent, even though this may mean that the debtor is given a slight windfall?

The allocation made by the Uniform Commercial Code is certainly one eminently reasonable way of striking a balance between two important policy goals. Defaults must be deterred, but debtors who do default should not be deprived of the built-up value of the collateral. No formula can do this perfectly in the real world, but the one recited in the text of this opinion, and required by the Uniform Commercial Code, does so in a sound, if not unchallengeable, fashion.

In re Ford Motor Co., 94 F.T.C. 607, 630–34 (1979), vacated sub nom. Ford Motor Co. v. Federal Trade Commission, 673 F.2d 1008 (9th Cir.1981). See generally Shuchman, Condition and Value of Repossessed Automobiles, 21 Wm. & Mary L.Rev. 15 (1979).

9. The approach of Article 9, which in section 9–615(d)(2) permits the creditor to repossess and sell the collateral and then sue the consumer for any deficiency, is not the only possible approach. Before enactment of the UCC, the law in some states was distinctly otherwise: the creditor had to choose between looking to the debtor and looking to the collateral. If the creditor repossessed the collateral, suit against the debtor for any deficiency was barred (again, known as strict foreclosure). The UCCC reverts to this pre-UCC approach, and more than twenty states have adopted some form of election of remedies for at least some consumer transactions. See UCCC section 5.103(2)–(4). Section 9–201(b)–(c) preserves this other law and subordinates Article 9 to it.

Problem. *Consumer* wants to purchase a 1998 Honda, which *Seller* is offering for $8,200. *Consumer* makes a downpayment of $800 and agrees to pay $8,280 in 24 monthly installments of $345. *Seller* immediately assigns the contract and security interest to *Bank*. After paying *Bank* $4,830, *Consumer* loses his job and makes no further payments. *Bank* asks you what it should do.

    a.   Assume the UCCC is in effect in your jurisdiction.

    b.   Assume Massachusetts law applies:

> The creditor may after gaining possession sell or otherwise dispose of the collateral. Unless displaced by the provisions of this section and section twenty A the rights and obligations of the parties, including the redemption and disposition of the collateral shall be governed by the provisions of Part 6 of Article 9 of [the Uniform Commercial Code]. Notwithstanding the provisions of Part 6 of Article 9 of [the UCC], if, in connection with a consumer credit transaction which involves an unpaid balance of two thousand dollars or less and which is at the time of default secured by a non-possessory security interest in consumer goods, the creditor takes possession of or accepts surrender of the collateral, the debtor shall not be liable for any deficiency. . . . For the purposes of this section the unpaid balance of a consumer credit transaction shall be that amount which the debtor would have been required to pay upon prepayment.

Mass. Gen. Laws Ann. ch. 255B, § 20B(d).

    c.   Assume Illinois law applies:

> Unless otherwise limited by this Act, the parties shall have the rights and remedies provided in Article 9 of the Uniform Commercial Code with respect to default, disposition, and redemption of collateral.

> If the buyer has paid an amount equal to 60% or more of the deferred payment price at the time of his default under the contract and if the buyer, at the request of the holder and without legal proceedings, surrenders the goods to the holder in ordinary condition and free from malicious damage, the holder must, within a period of 5 days from the date of receipt of the goods at his place of business, elect either (a) to retain the goods and release the buyer from further obligation under the contract, or (b) to return the goods to the buyer at

the holder's expense and be limited to an action to recover the balance of the indebtedness. . . .

815 Ill. Consol. Stat. § 375/20.

    d. Assume Ohio law applies:

    (B) Disposition of the collateral shall be by public sale only. Such sale may be as a unit or in parcels and the method, manner, time, place, and terms thereof shall be commercially reasonable. At least ten days prior to sale the secured party shall send notification of the time and place of such sale and of the minimum price for which such collateral will be sold, together with a statement that the debtor may be held liable for any deficiency resulting from such sale, by certified mail, return receipt requested, to the debtor at his last address known to the secured party, and to any persons known by the secured party to have an interest in the collateral. In addition, the secured party shall cause to be published, at least ten days prior to the sale, a notice of such sale listing the items to be sold, in a newspaper of general circulation in the county where the sale is to be held.

Ohio Rev. Code § 1317.16.

    e. Which of these statutes, including UCC sections 9–609 through 9–616, represents the best approach to the problem of default?

10. Problem. *Consumer* purchases on credit a new car from *Dealer* for $18,000. Three-and-a-half years later *Consumer* defaults, and *Dealer* accelerates and repossesses. After deducting unearned finance charge and adding expenses of repossession and sale, the balance due is $6,000. *Dealer* gives proper notice under sections 9–611 through 9–614 and attempts to resell the car at her used-car lot. She negotiates a sale to *Buyer*, in which *Buyer* trades in his car and pays $5,000. *Dealer* sues *Consumer* for a deficiency judgment of $1,000. Should she win?

Should it matter whether the trade-in allowance for *Buyer's* car is $500 or $2,500?

Assume that the contract with *Buyer* specifies a price of $7,500 and a trade-in allowance of $2,500. Is *Dealer* entitled to a deficiency judgment? What if *Dealer* alleges that the actual value of the trade-in is $500 and that she increased the price of the car from $5,500 to $7,500 so that she could offer *Buyer* an attractive trade-in allowance of $2,500?

Now assume that the contract with *Buyer* specifies a price of $5,500 and a trade-in allowance of $500. Is *Dealer* entitled to a deficiency judgment? What if *Consumer* alleges that the actual value of his car is $7,500, that the actual value of *Buyer's* trade-in is $2,500, and that *Dealer* reduced the price of the car and reduced the trade-in allowance, all in order to produce a deficiency?

11. The creditor's right to a deficiency judgment is but one side of the coin. If the creditor sells the collateral for more than the amount the consumer still owes, section 9–615(d)(1) requires the creditor to pay the surplus to the consumer. But how does the consumer discover that there is a surplus after the disposition of his or her vehicle? In other words, as a practical matter, what is to prevent the creditor from simply keeping the surplus? See section 9–616(b). Is this effective? See Official Comment 2.

12.   The materials in this chapter deal with restrictions on creditors in the repossession and sale of goods in which they have security interests. Do these restrictions apply also to persons who purport to lease goods to consumers on a week-to-week basis (see pages 212–14 supra)? Superficially, at least, the merchant simply leases the goods for one week, the consumer pays in advance for each week, and the merchant never extends credit. But consider the economic reality of the transaction, and consider UCC sections 1–203 and 9–109(a)(1) (Article 9 applies "to a transaction, regardless of its form, that is intended to create a security interest in personal property or fixtures . . .").

D.   RESTRICTIONS ON THE USE OF SECURITY INTERESTS

The final aspect of security interests to be examined in this chapter is the kind and amount of property in which the creditor may acquire a security interest. Presumably, no one would object to a seller's taking a security interest in the very goods the consumer is buying, nor would one object to a lender's taking a security interest in the goods that the consumer acquires with the proceeds of the loan. These are purchase money security interests. (See UCC section 9–103) But the creditor may seek to acquire a security interest in other property. A prime example has been the practice of some small loan companies to acquire security interests in all the household goods of their borrowers. See Public Finance Co. v. Davis, page 591 supra. Household goods, however, have notoriously little resale value. Consequently, resort to the collateral typically would satisfy only a small portion of the outstanding debt. Yet the loss of this kind of collateral is especially disruptive to the life of the consumer.

Another example of a non-purchase money security interest is the creation of a second lien on the consumer's home. The problem here is that the consumer may not fully appreciate the risks and consequences of default.

In response to these practices, many states prohibit non-purchase money security interests in household goods and in land. Frequently, the prohibitions appear in the statutes authorizing small loan companies and therefore apply only to those lenders. The UCCC, however, speaks more broadly. Section 3.301 specifies the property in which a seller may take a security interest, and sections 3.302–.303 address cross-collateral clauses, the abuse in Williams v. Walker–Thomas Furniture Co. (page 470 supra).

In 1985 the Federal Trade Commission promulgated a regulation restricting the use of security interests. See Trade Regulation Rule Concerning Credit Practices, 16 C.F.R. Part 444, reproduced in the Statutory Supplement. Section 444.2(a)(4) makes it an unfair act or practice for a creditor to take a non-possessory, non-purchase money security interest in household goods. Section 444.1(i) defines "household goods."

In which of the following items may a creditor take a security interest:

sewing machine	lawn mower
barbecue grill	freezer
hot tub	patio set
air conditioner	bicycle
stereo system	luggage
telephone answering machine	area rugs
golf clubs	camera
personal computer	piano
automobile	fur coat

E. Unfairness and Unconscionability

The foregoing materials on security interests have focused on the UCC and on legislation designed specifically to modify the UCC in consumer transactions. Other legislation may be relevant, too. For example, the broadly focused statutes examined in preceding chapters also apply to the enforcement of security interests. In addition to invoking the obligation of good faith in connection with the redemption of collateral (see Question 9, page 648 supra), courts have invoked unconscionability and unfairness. In Robinson v. Jefferson Credit Corp., 4 U.C.C. Rep. 15 (N.Y.Sup.Ct.1967), a creditor repossessed a consumer's car. The consumer tendered the overdue installments and also late charges and a repossession fee. The creditor accepted these sums but refused to return the car (later basing this refusal on a feeling of insecurity). The court held the creditor's conduct to be unconscionable. Is this a proper use of section 2–302? In Moore v. Goodyear Tire & Rubber Co., 364 So.2d 630 (La.App.1978), the court held that a repossession of a TV and a sewing machine that violated Louisiana law applicable to the enforcement of security interests was also a violation of Louisiana's little-FTC act. Therefore, the creditor was liable for the consumer's attorney's fees as well as his actual damages. And in California, where the sanction for failing to give proper notice of a repossession sale is denial of the right to a deficiency judgment, the Court of Appeals has held that a creditor who failed to a give proper notice violated the little-FTC act by suing for a deficiency judgment. Bank of America v. Lallana, 64 Cal.Rptr.2d 168 (Cal.App.1997). See also Jefferson Loan Co. v. Session, 938 A.2d 169 (N.J.Super.2008).

F. Leases

Leasing has become an increasingly popular method of acquiring consumer products—especially automobiles. Under a true lease the consumer uses the automobile for the specified period and then returns it to the lessor. The lease may give the consumer the option to purchase the vehicle for its market value at the expiration of the lease or for a fixed sum that represents the parties' estimate of that value. During the period of the lease, the lessor retains ownership of the car. Hence, the consumer does not give a security interest in it, and if the consumer defaults, there is no security interest to enforce. Therefore, the lease contract typically specifies what is to happen in the event of the consumer's default. Consider the following:

> If the Lessee fails to make any payment under this Lease when it is due, or if the Lessee fails to keep any other agreement in this Lease, the Lessor may terminate this Lease and take back the Vehicle. The Lessor may go on the Lessee's property to retake the Vehicle. Even if the Lessor retakes the Vehicle, the Lessee must still pay at once the monthly payments for the rest of the lease term and any other amounts that the Lessee owes under this Lease. The Lessor will subtract from the amount owed sums received from the sale of the Vehicle in excess of what the Lessor would have had invested in the Vehicle at the end of the lease term. The Lessee must also pay all expenses paid by the Lessor to enforce the Lessor's rights under this Lease, including reasonable attorney's fees as permitted by law, and any damages caused to the Lessor because of the Lessee's default. The Lessor may sell the Vehicle at public or private sale with or without notice to the Lessee.

QUESTIONS AND NOTES

1. Problem. *Consumer* leases a new automobile from *Lessor* for four years, pursuant to the following terms. *Consumer* gives a security deposit of $200 and agrees to make 48 monthly payments of $200, at the end of which *Consumer* has the option of purchasing the car for $4,200. After making 18 payments *Consumer* loses her job and defaults. *Lessor* repossesses the car and sells it at a wholesale auction for $3,600. Now *Lessor* sues for $3,872.12, derived as follows:

Gross balance due as of date of repossession	$6600.00
Security deposit rebate	− 200.00
Late charges	+ 47.12
Repossession and resale expenses	+ 125.00
Past due payments	+ 400.00
Resale proceeds	− 3600.00
Attorney's fees	+ 500.00
	3872.12

a.   Does the default clause in the lease authorize recovery of $3,872.12?

b.   The "gross balance due" of $6,600 represents the 30 remaining lease payments (totaling $6,000) plus the $600 difference between the estimated residual value ($4,200) and the price at which *Lessor* sold the repossessed vehicle ($3,600).

(1) Does the default clause authorize recovery of the $6,000?

(2) Does the default clause authorize recovery of the $600?

(3) If the answer to questions (a) or (b) is yes, does any statute or common law principle make the default clause unenforceable?

2. The leasing provisions of the Truth-in-Lending Act require the lessor to disclose the conditions under which the lessor may terminate the lease and the method of determining the amount of any penalty or other charge for early termination by the lessor. Truth-in-Lending Act § 182, Regulation M § 213.4(g)(12). Section 183(b) provides that penalties or other charges for early termination may be "only at an amount which is reasonable in the light of the anticipated or actual harm caused by the . . . early termination, the difficulties of proof of loss, and the inconvenience or nonfeasibility of otherwise obtaining an adequate remedy." This amounts to a substantive limit on the contract terms, viz., that any charge in the event of early termination must be reasonable. Does the default clause in this problem violate section 183(b)? If so, see section 130(a)(2)(A)(ii).

3. In 1987 the drafters of the UCC added Article 2A to govern lease transactions. Section 2A–504 permits the parties to stipulate damages for breach, but provides that the formula must be "reasonable in light of the then anticipated harm caused by the default." Does the formula in this problem pass that test? If not, then see section 2A–528.

4. In Miller v. Nissan Motor Acceptance Corp., 362 F.3d 209 (3d Cir. 2004), plaintiff returned his leased car one month before the scheduled end of his lease (in connection with his lease of a new car). The early-termination formula required him to pay the remaining monthly payments plus the residual value of the car, minus the amount for which the car was sold when it was returned to the lessee. When applied to plaintiff's case, the formula produced a figure of more than $5,000. That is, had he retained possession for one more month, he would have made the regular monthly payment of $267 and would have had no further liability. By surrendering possession when he did, however, he was liable for almost 20 times that amount.

Is this charge for early termination "reasonable in the light of the anticipated or actual harm caused by the . . . early termination, the difficulties of proof of loss, and the inconvenience or infeasibility of otherwise obtaining an adequate remedy" (§ 183(b))?

CHAPTER 13

OTHER CONTRACTUAL AND PROCEDURAL DEVICES TO FACILITATE COLLECTION

The use of a security interest is the creditor's principal method of enhancing the prospects for payment. But there are others, as well, and this chapter examines several of them.

A. WAGE ASSIGNMENTS

On its face, a wage assignment is an assignment by the consumer to the creditor of the consumer's right to receive wages, e.g.,

> Upon service of any demand hereunder, I authorize and direct my employer to pay 15% of my gross salary, wages, and other compensation for services to [creditor] on each payday until the total amount due under this contract is paid. I herewith release and discharge my employer from all liability to me for or on account of any and all monies paid in accordance herewith.

As long as the consumer makes the payments required by the contract, the wage assignment stays in the creditor's filing cabinet. If the consumer defaults, however, the creditor may serve it on the consumer's employer. Under the common law of contracts, the employer is thereafter obligated to give the creditor the wages earned by the consumer.

A wage assignment is tantamount to a security interest. It gives the creditor an interest in one of the consumer's assets, and the creditor may assert this interest nonjudicially to obtain payment directly from the encumbered asset. For the consumer who has few tangible assets of value, the ability to give a security interest in wages may be the difference between obtaining credit and being rejected. Nevertheless, by 1985 approximately half the states prohibited wage assignments in all consumer transactions, and several others permitted them only in connection with small loan transactions. The FTC Trade Regulation Rule Concerning Credit Practices, adopted in 1985 and reproduced in the Statutory Supplement, makes it unlawful for creditors to include a wage assignment clause in their contracts with consumers. 16 C.F.R. § 444.2(a)(3).

699

QUESTIONS

1.   What justification is there for prohibiting wage assignments? What is the rationale for an exception for small loans? Should the FTC have preserved this exception?

2.   One readily apparent effect of a wage assignment is the consumer's loss of income, since the wages are being diverted to the creditor. For a consumer with no accumulated savings, this could be disastrous. In 1968 Congress recognized the tremendous injury caused by a loss of wages and enacted sections 301–303 of the Consumer Credit Protection Act (reproduced in the Statutory Supplement). In view of the restrictions in section 303, is there still a need for state laws restricting wage assignments?

3.   It is a denial of due process for a state to permit a creditor to garnish a consumer's wages before the consumer has an opportunity to defend against the taking. Sniadach v. Family Finance Corp., 395 U.S. 337 (1969). Is the taking of wages by means of a wage assignment also unconstitutional? See Question 7, page 656 supra; Bond v. Dentzer, 494 F.2d 302 (2d Cir.1974).

B.   AGREEMENTS AND STATUTES CONCERNING PROCEDURE

The preceding section on wage assignments and the two preceding chapters (on debt collection and security interests) present nonjudicial techniques creditors use to enforce claims. Typically these techniques are less expensive than litigation and for that reason are more attractive to creditors. They are not always effective, however, and litigation is still necessary. Hence, there are several techniques that the creditor may use to minimize litigation costs.

(1) CONFESSION OF JUDGMENT

The first technique to be considered is the use of a contractual provision authorizing the creditor or an attorney selected by the creditor to appear on behalf of the consumer and confess judgment against the consumer. The provision is known as a confession of judgment clause. (If the provision appears in a promissory note, it may be called a *cognovit*.) If the consumer defaults, the creditor need only present this authorization to the court clerk, who either enters judgment against the consumer or passes it on to the judge, who perfunctorily renders judgment against the consumer. In this way the creditor avoids the delay and expense of a trial, but can enforce the claim (which is now a judgment) against the assets of the consumer.

Judicial and legislative reaction to creditors' use of the confession of judgment clause has been hostile. For example, in refusing to enforce a confession of judgment clause buried in fine print on the back side of a contract, the Supreme Court of Pennsylvania stated:

A warrant of attorney authorizing judgment is perhaps the most powerful and drastic document known to civil law. The signer deprives himself of every defense and every delay of execution, he waives exemption of personal property from levy and sale under the exemption laws, he places his cause in the hands of a hostile defender. The signing of a warrant of attorney is equivalent to a warrior of old entering a combat by discarding his shield and breaking his sword.

Cutler Corp. v. Latshaw, 97 A.2d 234, 236 (Pa.1953).

Confession of judgment clauses raise a constitutional issue: do they meet the standard for waiver of the Fifth and Fourteenth Amendment right to due process? In the context of a commercial contract whose terms were individually negotiated, the Supreme Court has held yes. D.H. Overmyer Co. v. Frick Co., 405 U.S. 174 (1972). Anticipating the consumer context, however, the Court added this caution:

Some concluding comments are in order:

1. Our holding necessarily means that a cognovit clause is not, *per* se, violative of Fourteenth Amendment due process. Overmyer could prevail here only if the clause were constitutionally invalid. The facts of this case, as we observed above, are important, and those facts amply demonstrate that a cognovit provision may well serve a proper and useful purpose in the commercial world and at the same time not be vulnerable to constitutional attack.

2. Our holding, of course, is not controlling precedent for other facts of other cases. For example, where the contract is one of adhesion, where there is great disparity in bargaining power, and where the debtor receives nothing for the cognovit provision, other legal consequences may ensue.

3. . . .

Id. at 187–88. See Swarb v. Lennox, 405 U.S. 191 (1972) (companion case to *Overmyer*). Subsequently, a three-judge court held that a Delaware statute authorizing confession of judgment clauses was unconstitutional:

. . . In *Overmyer* and *Swarb*, the Supreme Court was confronted with *per se* challenges to confession of judgment statutes. The issue before the Court was whether such statutes are unconstitutional on their face. . . . Rejecting the *per se* claim, the Supreme Court held that the constitutional right to a notice and a hearing on the merits prior to an entry of judgment are subject to waiver. The opinion stressed that waiver is an issue to be determined on the facts of each case. However, contrary to the defendant's contention, the Court did not decide the question of the timing of this factual determination.

. . .

Reiterating what the Supreme Court has frequently held, both *Overmyer* and *Swarb* support the position that procedural due process requires that an individual be afforded notice and a hearing on the merits before entry of judgment against him. At the hearing, the alleged debtor has the right to raise whatever defenses he may have against the validity of the underlying obligation. Since a signed cognovit note does not constitute proof of an effective waiver, a hearing and judicial determination are necessary, and an understanding and voluntary waiver must be shown prior to entry of judgment. Unless a hearing is conducted on the waiver question before the judgment is entered, an alleged debtor will be deprived of his due process rights on every occasion when an effective waiver had not occurred upon initial execution of the note. The only procedure guaranteeing that such deprivation will not take place is to require hearings on the waiver issue before permitting judgments to be entered. Therefore, [we hold] that the original 10 Del.C. § 2306 is unconstitutional insofar as it permitted the entry of judgments on cognovit notes prior to a hearing on the issue of whether the debtor had effectively waived his due process rights by executing the note. . . .

Osmond v. Spence, 359 F.Supp. 124, 126–27 (D.Del.1972).

As of the early 1980s, almost every state prohibited the use of confession of judgment clauses in at least some consumer transactions. E.g., UCCC § 3.306. The FTC's Credit Practices Rule extended the ban to all states and all transactions within the scope of the Rule. 16 C.F.R. § 444.2(a)(1).

(2) Default Judgments

(a) Sewer Service

Since confession of judgment clauses are unenforceable, the consumer must be given notice and an opportunity for a hearing before the creditor obtains a judgment. Most litigation against consumers, however, ends in judgment by default when the consumer fails to appear. What possible explanations are there for this phenomenon? One explanation, of course, is that the consumer knows that the creditor's claim is valid and for that reason does not contest liability. But this is only a partial explanation. Many consumers dispute their liability and are perfectly willing to litigate. Their ability to litigate, however, may be impaired by sewer service or forum abuse.

Due process requires an opportunity for a hearing, and the court may ensure that the consumer has that opportunity merely by scheduling a hearing. But the opportunity is of no value if the consumer does not know of it. Of course, when the creditor initiates suit, statutes and rules of procedure require service of process on the defendant. They also require the process server to file an affidavit affirming that service was made. Process servers, however, have been known to discard the summons but still complete the affidavit of service. Because of the presumed resting spot for the summons, this phenomenon is known as sewer service.

There are at least three possible reasons why the process server might discard the summons and knowingly submit a false affidavit to the court. First, after making several unsuccessful attempts at service, the server may simply tire of trying to locate the defendant. The server who is a deputy sheriff may feel that there are more important jobs to do. Second, the server may perceive a risk of physical injury in attempting to serve a particular defendant or in entering a particular neighborhood for the purpose of serving process. Third, the server's compensation may depend on the number of summonses served. In some states (e.g., New York) service of process is entrusted to nongovernmental entities that pay their employees on a piecework basis. Even in states where service is handled by the sheriff's office, the deputy may receive a small flat salary that is supplemented by compensation based on the number of services made. If the process server's compensation depends on the number of summonses served, there is a disincentive to make repeated attempts to effect service and file the affidavit only when service actually is made. Or, to put it another way, there is an incentive to lie.

Sewer service received a lot of attention in the late 1960s. Several empirical and anecdotal studies established the existence and the extent of the practice in several cities, including New York, Los Angeles, Chicago, Detroit, Boston, and Washington, D. C. One creditor, for example, obtained judgment by default in over ninety percent of the actions it brought. Could anything other than sewer service explain this failure of consumers to assert defenses when they were sued? One authority estimated that in actions against consumers to enforce consumer credit contracts, no more than half the defendants actually were served. By 1972 several proceedings had been commenced against process servers and attorneys who had engaged in sewer service. These proceedings had varying objectives, from imposition of criminal sanctions,[1] to vacating all the judgments obtained by a particular creditor[2] to recovery by a consumer of damages for denial of constitutional rights and for the tort of abuse of process.[3] Since 1972, however, sewer service has received scant attention outside New York. A possible explanation for this is that sewer service no longer occurs. Since most litigation against consumers still ends in judgment by default, however, this explanation is unlikely. A 1986 study of the problem in New York City revealed that 98% of the process servers covered by the study engaged in sewer service. In almost 40% of the cases examined, the process servers claimed to be in two (or more) places at the same time.[4] If sewer service is a continuing practice, what can and should be done to end it?

1. The crime was denial of constitutional rights under color of state law, 18 U.S.C. § 242. United States v. Wiseman, 445 F.2d 792 (2d Cir.1971); United States v. Barr, 295 F.Supp. 889 (S.D.N.Y.1969).

2. United States v. Brand Jewelers, Inc., 318 F.Supp. 1293 (S.D.N.Y.1970).

3. Judo, Inc. v. Peet, 326 N.Y.S.2d 441 (N.Y.City Civ.Ct.1971) (invoking 42 U.S.C. § 1983).

4. See Goldstein, Process Server's License Revoked by Consumer Agency for Fraud, N.Y.L.J., Feb. 7, 1996, at 1 (process server testified that he personally hand-delivered a summons to a consumer who proceeded to establish that she had been on vacation abroad at the time of the alleged service).

QUESTIONS

1. Is it really necessary that anything be done? When the creditor seeks to enforce the judgment, the consumer may move to set aside the judgment on the ground that he or she was not served with process. Is this a sufficient remedy?

2. New York City adopted a licensing system for nongovernmental process servers. The ordinance requires servers to keep detailed records of both successful and unsuccessful attempts to make service. These records make it easier to determine whether the server has made false affidavits of service, in which event the server's license may be revoked. Is this licensing approach likely to deal effectively with the problem of sewer service?

3. One way to alter undesirable conduct is to prohibit the conduct and attach some sanction for disregarding the prohibition. Licensing (and the criminal law) are examples. But another way to alter conduct is to restructure the situation to remove the incentives for that conduct and/or provide incentives for other, more desirable conduct. How might the legislature alter the setting so that process servers would no longer engage in sewer service?

(b) Forum Abuse

The second practice that impairs the consumer's constitutional right to a hearing is the selection of a forum that is inconvenient for the consumer. If the creditor has stores or offices in many states, the contract may contain a provision by which the parties consent to jurisdiction in the state where the creditor's main office is located. Then if the creditor later sues to enforce the consumer's obligation, the suit will be in that state, which may be hundreds or thousands of miles away from where the consumer lives and where the parties formed the contract. The creditor's purpose for including this provision may be to consolidate all litigation in one place, where its attorneys can handle it efficiently. Regardless of the purpose, however, the provision has another, frequently dispositive effect: to defend the case, the consumer must bear the expense and inconvenience of long-distance travel.

Forum abuse may exist with respect to venue, as well as jurisdiction. Venue statutes typically permit the plaintiff to bring the action either where the defendant resides, where the plaintiff resides, or where the parties are to perform their obligations.[5] Bringing an action in a distant city, even though it is in the same state in which the consumer resides, subjects the consumer who disputes the creditor's claim to substantial inconvenience and expense. As with jurisdiction abuse, the frequent result is judgment for the creditor by default.

---

5. In some states the venue statute omits the plaintiff's residence as a proper place for suit. Since venue is proper where the parties are to perform, however, the cred- itor may achieve the same result simply by including in the contract a provision calling for payment to be made in the city where the creditor wants to litigate.

Does the increased efficiency for the creditor resulting from consolidating legal proceedings in one location justify the use of a forum that is inconvenient to the creditor's customers? The FTC thought not, and alleging that the practice was unfair, it ordered several large national retailers, a small loan company, and a collection agency to cease and desist from suing at a place other than where the consumer resides or where the consumer signed the contract. All but one of the creditors consented to the entry of the order. The other creditor (Spiegel) contested the matter, lost, and appealed. The Court of Appeals for the Seventh Circuit affirmed the order:

> Spiegel is a Delaware corporation with its office and principal place of business in Chicago, Illinois. It is a catalog retailer engaged in the advertising, offering for sale, and distribution of clothes, household goods, appliances, tools, tires, and various other articles of merchandise. In the course of its mail order business, it receives orders in Illinois from purchasers in various states and ships products to them in their home states. It regularly extends credit to consumers in order to facilitate purchase of the products.
>
> Previously, in the course of its collection of retail credit accounts, Spiegel regularly used Illinois courts to sue allegedly defaulting retail mail order purchasers who resided outside of Illinois. The practice of filing suits in Illinois was terminated in February 1973 because this collection method proved unsatisfactory to Speigel.[3] In filing these collection suits Spiegel used the Illinois long-arm statute to establish jurisdiction. Spiegel voluntarily dismissed those actions where the defendant raised an objection to the inconvenience of the forum. Of course, in order to object the consumer had to travel to the Illinois court or obtain local counsel, an act which was often impractical considering the amount in dispute in most cases.
>
> Many of the customers sued by Spiegel live outside the State of Illinois. They received Spiegel's catalogs and advertising material in their homes and executed the contract to purchase in their home states. Almost all of them have no pertinent contact within the State of Illinois other than their dealings with Spiegel.
>
> The administrative law judge determined that the distance, cost and inconvenience of defending such suits in Illinois placed a virtually insurmountable burden on the out-of-state defendants to appear, answer and defend. Subsequently the Commission concluded that Spiegel's collection practices through the use of the Illinois courts was offensive to clearly articulated public policy and oppressive and injurious to consumers.

> . . .

---

3. According to Spiegel's brief this was due to the fact that judgments in Illinois, as in many other states, are not self-executing and require supplementary proceedings in other jurisdictions in order to collect the judgment. . . .

[After observing that conduct that conforms to state law may still be unfair within FTC Act Section 5, the court continued:]

In determining whether Spiegel's challenged practices are unfair under Section 5 of the Act, the Commission remained faithful to its previously announced criteria. A practice is unfair when it offends established public policy and when the practice is immoral, unethical, oppressive, unscrupulous or substantially injurious to consumers.

In this case, since the facts are not in dispute, the Commission only had to determine whether Spiegel's policy of using state long-arm statutes against distant mail order customers violated public policy and was injurious to consumers. In making that determination the Commission concluded:

> [S]piegel's practice of suing its out-of-state mail order customers in Illinois courts is patently offensive to clearly articulated public policy, intended to guarantee all citizens a meaningful opportunity to defend themselves in court.
>
> . . . [R]espondent's use of the Cook County forum, . . . forces the consumer who wishes to defend to appear in a courtroom hundreds or thousands of miles from home, at a cost in travel alone which may exceed the amount in controversy. The option of hiring a lawyer who would be able to file a motion contesting jurisdiction is likely to be equally unviable. Nor do we think it lessens the damage done to argue that judgments unfairly obtained by Spiegel would be rejected if it attempted to collect on them. Affirmative efforts to defend a collection suit can also impose costly and unaccustomed burdens on the consumer, and in any event there are many injurious uses which can be made of improper judgments, short of execution, such as sullying credit records. . . .

The Commission's observations concerning the difficulties and costs which stand in the way of consumers who wish to defend against suits in a distant forum are matters of common knowledge. Where suits involve relatively small debts, the choice of retaining counsel is not a practical alternative, even in one's home town, and, since travel costs alone may exceed the amount in controversy, a *pro se* appearance in an out-of-state forum is virtually foreclosed by economic considerations.

Spiegel, Inc. v. FTC, 540 F.2d 287, 290–94 (7th Cir.1976).

From the consumer's perspective, the decision in *Spiegel* appears to be a solid victory. But if Spiegel (and others) stop bringing litigation in distant forums, what will be the impact, if any, on *non*-defaulting customers? And since the FTC is unlikely to be able to pursue every creditor who systematically uses a forum inconvenient to its customers, how does *Spiegel* help the consumer who is subjected to the abuse?

Vargas v. Allied Finance Co.

Court of Civil Appeals of Texas. 1976.
545 S.W.2d 231.

MOORE, JUSTICE.

[Vargas, a resident of Starr County, purchased a television from Miller TV & Appliance, whose store was located in an adjoining county (Hidalgo). The contract and note provided that performance was to occur in Dallas County, approximately five hundred miles away. Miller TV assigned the contract and note to Allied Finance. When Vargas defaulted, Allied Finance sued him in Justice Court in Dallas County. Vargas sought a change of venue but failed to comply with the procedural requirements of the change-of-venue statute.

[Vargas then brought this action against Allied Finance in Dallas County, alleging a violation of the Deceptive Trade Practices–Consumer Protection Act, Vernon's Tex. Codes Ann. Bus. & C. § 17.46. Subsection (a) declares false, misleading, or deceptive acts or practices to be unlawful. Subsection (b) provides that "the term 'false, misleading, or deceptive acts or practices' includes, but is not limited to" a long list of specific acts. Vargas sought injunctive relief, but the trial court granted Allied Finance's motion for summary judgment.] As we view the record, the injunctive relief sought by plaintiff was properly denied.

Section 17.46 of the Act lists twenty deceptive acts or trade practices which are declared to be unlawful. Plaintiff concedes that no provision of the Act specifically declares the filing of suits against consumers in a distant forum to be an unfair trade practice. He contends, however, that because Sec. 17.46(c) of the Act directs the Texas courts when interpreting the Act to be guided to the extent possible by the interpretations given by the Federal Trade Commission to Section 5(a)(1) of The Federal Trade Commission Act, the courts of this State, are bound by the rulings of the Federal Trade Commission. Therefore, he takes the position that since the Federal Trade Commission, in a case styled In the Matter of Spiegel, Inc., has held that the filing of distant forum collection suits violates traditional notions of due process and amounts to an unfair trade practice, the activities of the defendant in the present suit must be held to amount to a violation of the Texas Deceptive Trade Practices Act. Based on this premise he contends that he is entitled to injunctive relief as provided for in the act in order to prevent the defendant from filing future suits against him in a distant forum.

We do not believe that the Federal Trade Commission's ruling in *Spiegel* is applicable here because that ruling dealt with interstate transactions where no state venue statute was involved. Even if the ruling were incorporated as a part of the Act in Texas, we do not believe the Act would be controlling because the proper forum for all litigation in this State is regulated by venue statutes.

Venue in the Justice Courts is regulated by Tex.Rev.Civ.Stat.Ann., Article 2390. The pertinent parts of the statute relating to the type of suit involved here reads as follows:

> Every suit in the justice court shall be commenced in the county and precinct in which the defendant . . . resides, except . . . :

> 4.   Suits upon a contract in writing promising performance at any particular place, may be brought in the county or precinct in which such contract was to be performed . . . .

While Article 2390 clearly authorizes suits to be filed and maintained against a defendant in a distant forum, its constitutionality is not challenged by this lawsuit. Plaintiff's sole ground for injunctive relief is based on the notion that the Deceptive Trade Practices Act of this state prohibits the filing of suits against consumers in a distant forum. To hold that the legislature in passing the deceptive Trade Practices Act intended to grant consumers a right to injunctive relief prohibiting the filing of suits in a distant forum would be to hold that the legislature intended by implication to repeal the above quoted venue provision of Article 2390, even though the Act contains no repealing clause.

As we construe the two statutes, the Deceptive Trade Practices Act is in the nature of a general statute while Article 2390 is a special statute enacted for the sole purpose of regulating venue in the justice courts. In 53 Tex.Jur.2d Statutes section 110, the following rule is stated:

> The enactment of a general law does not ordinarily operate as a repeal of a particular or special law, by implication, though both relate to the same subject matter. On the contrary, both statutes are permitted to stand, and the general law is applicable to all cases not embraced by the specific act. In other words, the particular act is construed as constituting an exception to the general law. This is a settled rule of construction, based on the presumption that a specific statute evidences the intention of the legislature more clearly than a general one, and therefore should control.

In view of the fact that Section 4 of the venue statute for Justice Courts expressly authorized the plaintiff to institute suit against the defendant in a distant forum in Dallas County, the venue statute must be construed as constituting an exception to the general law found in the Deceptive Trade Practices Act. For this reason, the plaintiff is not entitled to injunctive relief under the Act.

. . .

The problems confronting consumers in contesting distant forum suits is ably discussed by Professor Sampson in his article, Distant Forum Abuse in Consumer Transactions: A Proposed Solution, 51 Texas L.Rev. 269 (1973). The question of whether the venue statutes should be revised, as suggested therein, is a matter for the legislature and not the courts.

The judgment is affirmed.

QUESTIONS

1. The court rejects *Spiegel* for two reasons: it is distinguishable; and even if it is not distinguishable, the state deceptive practices statute does not repeal the venue statute.

a) Is *Spiegel* really distinguishable?

b) Does the court properly invoke the principle of statutory construction that the specific takes precedence over the general? Does the court properly apply it?

2. In 1977 the Texas legislature amended the statute specifically to include forum abuse in the list of prohibited practices. Under the amended statute, a creditor may sue only in the county where the contract was signed or the county where the consumer resides when the suit is commenced. Vernon's Tex. Codes Ann., Bus. & C. § 17.46(b)(22). The legislature also amended the statute governing venue in the Justice Court to restrict the creditor to the county and precinct where the contract was signed or where the consumer resides. Vernon's Ann. Tex.Civ.Prac. & Rem.Code § 15.092(c).

Schubach v. Household Finance Corp.

Supreme Judicial Court of Massachusetts, 1978.
375 Mass. 133, 376 N.E.2d 140.

WILKINS, JUSTICE.

[Plaintiffs, who lived in Holyoke, borrowed money from defendant at its Holyoke office. When they defaulted, defendant sued in Boston, approximately one hundred miles away. Plaintiffs filed this action, alleging violation of the Massachusetts little-FTC act. They sought dismissal of defendant's collection suit, payment of their extra expenses caused by defendant's bringing its suit in Boston, and payment of their costs and attorney's fees in this action.]

The only issue presented, and apparently the only argument advanced below by HFC in support of its motion to dismiss, is whether a practice which is permitted under State law nevertheless can be unfair under G.L. c. 93A. In construing the meaning of "unfair or deceptive acts or practices" in G.L. c. 93A, § 2(a), we are "guided by the interpretations given by the Federal Trade Commission and the Federal Courts to section 5(a)(1) of the Federal Trade Commission Act."

It is clear that the Federal Trade Commission (commission) regards the commencement of consumer collection suits in courts far from the consumers' homes as an unfair practice. The plaintiffs cite several complaints filed before the commission which have resulted in orders generally directing the respondents to cease and desist from instituting collection suits in any county other than that of the defendant's residence or that in which the defendant executed the contract sued on. The commission issued these orders, some of which applied to companies engaged in nationwide activities, without concern for whether a State statute might authorize the commencement of an action elsewhere.

In Spiegel, Inc. v. F.T.C., the Seventh Circuit Court of Appeals enforced the commission's order enjoining a practice substantially similar to that which HFC used in this case. . . . The court assumed that Spiegel's practice was lawful under Illinois law and recognized that, as to some defendants, Spiegel perhaps could obtain personal jurisdiction. Id. at 291. Nevertheless, the court held that the commission had the power to enjoin Spiegel from bringing such suits.

. . .

The fact that the *Spiegel* case involved suits against out-of-State consumers rather than in-State consumers makes no absolute difference in deciding whether the practice of a creditor is unfair. In the *Spiegel* case, the court limited its enforcement of the commission's order to out-of-State consumers because they alone were the subject of the complaint. The court, however, acknowledged the commission's argument that a limitation of enforcement of the order to out-of-State residents might mean that "Spiegel could sue a Cook County resident in Cairo, Illinois, hundreds of miles away from his residence," but added that "[i]n this extreme example, such conduct by Spiegel would amount to a violation of Section 5."[5]

We reject the argument that an act or practice which is authorized by statute can never be an unfair or deceptive act or practice under § 2(a) of G.L. c. 93A. The circumstances of each case must be analyzed, and unfairness is to be measured not simply by determining whether particular conduct is lawful apart from G.L. c. 93A but also by analyzing the effect of the conduct on the public. Commonwealth v. DeCotis, 366 Mass. 234, 316 N.E.2d 748 (1974). Chapter 93A "created new substantive rights by making conduct unlawful which was not unlawful under the common law or any prior statute." The fact that particular conduct is permitted by statute or by common law principles should be considered, but it is not conclusive on the question of unfairness. Because HFC supports its motion to dismiss on a ground which is not conclusive on the issue of unfairness, the judge's interlocutory order denying the motion to dismiss was correct. We do not express a view whether, on all the circumstances which may be disclosed at trial, HFC's commencing its collection action against the plaintiffs in Suffolk County, rather than in Hampden County, constituted an unfair act or practice under G.L. c. 93A, § 2(a).

Interlocutory order denying the motion to dismiss affirmed.

QUESTIONS AND NOTES

1. What does the court think of the reason that the *Vargas* court gave for distinguishing *Spiegel*? Does the Massachusetts court believe that the decision in *Vargas* was wrong? Do you agree?

---

5. Courts elsewhere have dealt with the question of "distant forum abuse." . . . Vargas v. Allied Fin. Co., 545 S.W.2d 231 (Tex.Civ.App.1976). The Texas statute under which the plaintiff proceeded dealt, however, with deceptive acts and not unfair practices. . . .

2. In *Spiegel, Vargas*, and *Schubach,* the jurisdiction and venue statutes authorized the conduct of the creditors. If the creditor selects a forum that the state statute does *not* authorize for initiation of the suit, the litigation may be terminated. The court clerk or the trial judge may spot the improper filing and act accordingly. And if neither of them does, the defendant may raise the matter. In Barquis v. Merchants Collection Association of Oakland, Inc., 496 P.2d 817 (Cal.1972), consumers filed a class action against a collection agency to enjoin its practice of suing in an improper county and using form complaints that violated the statute and disguised the fact that venue was improper. The court held that defendant's alleged practice was an abuse of process and also a violation of a statute prohibiting unfair competition, which was defined to include unfair business practices. The court held that plaintiffs stated a good claim for injunctive relief.

3. *Schubach* and the excerpt from *Spiegel* examine statutory limits on the creditor's ability to select the forum. The Constitution also may pose limits. In *Spiegel* the creditor relied on the Illinois long-arm statute, which provides that a person who transacts any business in the state is subject to Illinois jurisdiction. As applied to nonresident consumers who purchase goods from Spiegel by mail order, is the long-arm statute constitutional? The FTC thought not, but the Seventh Circuit held that the issue need not be determined. Nevertheless, the court did speak to the issue:

> Modern day long-arm jurisdiction stems from a landmark decision by the Supreme Court in International Shoe Co. v. Washington, 326 U.S. 310, 66 S.Ct. 154, 90 L.Ed. 95 (1945). Therein, Chief Justice Stone summarized the development of the concept of *in personam* jurisdiction in the following oft-quoted passage:
>
> > [D]ue process requires only that in order to subject a defendant to a judgment in personam, if he be not present within the territory of the forum, he have certain [minimal] contacts with it such that the maintenance of the suit does not offend "traditional notions of fair play and substantial justice."
>
> The "minimal contacts" standards of *International Shoe*, however, did not provide for a simple, mechanical test. Instead the courts have adopted a case-by-case approach in evaluating the contact of the defendants with the forum. The Sixth Circuit recently attempted a review of the major decisions since *International Shoe* in In–Flight Devices Corp. v. Van Dusen Air, Inc., 466 F.2d 220 (6th Cir.1972). The Court set out a three-part test to determine whether jurisdiction was proper:
>
> > 1.   the defendant must purposely avail himself of the privilege of acting in the forum state or causing a consequence in the forum state;
> >
> > 2.   the cause of action must arise from the defendant's activities in the forum state; and

3. the acts of the defendant or consequences caused by the defendant must have a substantial enough connection with the forum to make the exercise of jurisdiction over the defendant reasonable.

In applying this triple test, however, the Court warned at p. 226:

> It is imperative that it be understood that the flexibility, and therein the virtue, of the *International Shoe* test is retained in the third condition and no mechanical consideration of the first two elements of the test can eliminate the need for an appraisal of the overall circumstances of each case if jurisdiction is to be found.
>
> . . .
>
> As a consequence of these decisions it is impossible to make an abstract determination that an Illinois court would have proper jurisdiction over a suit against a defaulting mail order purchaser. In some decisions, where the case-by-case method has been employed, there are rulings which might favor jurisdiction in situations similar to the instant problem.[5] On the other hand, there is some language in In–Flight Services v. Van Dusen Air, Inc., supra,[6] and other cases[7] which state that it would be unfair to find jurisdiction in a foreign forum over a suit based simply on a mail order contract.

540 F.2d at 291–92. The court stated that the statute was not per se unconstitutional and that the issue of constitutionality would have to be decided on a case-by-case basis. Id. at 294.

On the other hand, the Supreme Court of Alaska actually held that forum abuse is unconstitutional. In Aguchak v. Montgomery Ward Co., Inc., 520 P.2d 1352 (Alaska 1974), consumers challenged the state venue statute. The consumers, who lived in a small, remote Eskimo village accessible only by air, purchased goods in Anchorage from Montgomery Ward. When they defaulted, Ward brought suit in Anchorage, five hundred miles from the consumers' residence. They did not appear, and Ward obtained judgment

---

5. See O'Hare International Bank v. Hampton, 437 F.2d 1173 (7th Cir.1971) (a single telephone call based on a contract to be performed in Illinois); Ziegler v. Houghton–Mifflin Co., 80 Ill.App.2d 210, 224 N.E.2d 12 (2d Dist.1967) (a single mailing and telephone communication); Travelers Health Ass'n v. Virginia, 339 U.S. 643, 70 S.Ct. 927, 94 L.Ed. 1154 (1950) (defendant's primary contacts with the forum state were by mail); McGee v. International Life Insurance Co., 355 U.S. 220, 78 S.Ct. 199, 2 L.Ed.2d 223 (1957) (solicitation of a single life insurance contract by mail). In each of these cases jurisdiction was upheld based upon a finding of sufficient contact with the forum state.

6. The Court stated at p. 227, footnote 13:

[I]t would certainly be unfair to hold consumers answerable in a foreign forum for unpaid bills simply on the basis of a "mail order contract."

7. In Geneva Industries, Inc. v. Copeland Construction Corp., 312 F.Supp. 186, 188 (N.D.Ill.1970), Judge Will stated in dicta:

The notion that any customer of an Illinois based mail order house such as Sears Roebuck or Montgomery Ward would be subject to the jurisdiction of Illinois courts is obviously violative of the most minimal standard of minimum contacts and the fundamental structure of the federal system.

by default. After their wages were taken in partial satisfaction of this judgment, they moved for relief from the judgment, alleging that the court lacked jurisdiction over them and that the proceedings denied them due process. The trial court denied this motion, and they appealed, ultimately to the Alaska Supreme Court:

Small claims, like other actions in the district courts, are subject to change of venue when the defendant cannot, without unnecessary expense and inconvenience, defend the action in the plaintiff's chosen forum. In addition, under the rules of procedure followed in small claims cases, a party may file a written statement showing the nature of any defense he may have.[16] A pleading seeking change of venue could have been filed in the instant action, and, given the prohibitive expense of defending the claim in the plaintiff's forum, one would expect venue would have been transferred if there had been a reasonable likelihood that the defendants intended to present any defense requiring the introduction of evidence at a hearing.

Ordinarily defects in venue are waived by the failure of the defendant to make a timely motion for a change of venue, and no inquiry into the reasons for failure to make such a motion is normally entertained. However, in this appeal the Aguchaks are not challenging venue *per se*. Instead, they are contending that a summons form which fails to inform indigent bush defendants of the option of filing written pleadings in a small claims action filed in a distant forum fails to convey the constitutionally required information to afford them an opportunity for a hearing of their defenses.

We hold that the summons served upon the Aguchaks was defective when tested against the clause of the Alaska Constitution which provides that "No person shall be deprived of life, liberty, or property, without due process of law." We reach this conclusion by applying the clause to the unique relation between bush and metropolitan areas in Alaska, and by looking to the manner in which the similar federal due process provision has been interpreted.

We concur with the California Supreme Court's understanding in discussing somewhat different problems of distant venue debt collection, that the bulk of collection suit defendants, due to indigency, "cannot afford to engage counsel to advise them of their 'venue' rights."[24] The difficulties of locating counsel in the outlying areas of Alaska exacerbate the already substantial impediments to defense of the collection suit. Although the analogy is not perfect, we find persuasive the holding of the United States Supreme Court that notice effected in a valid, statutorily authorized manner was constitutionally

---

16. Dist.Ct.Civ.R. 9(b) provides:

A party defending against a claim may follow the same procedure—by either filing a written instrument which shows the nature and extent of his defense, or by filing a short and plain statement in writing showing the nature of his defense.

24. Barquis v. Merchants Collection Ass'n of Oakland, 7 Cal.3d 94, 101 Cal.Rptr. 745, 753, 496 P.2d 817, 825 (1972).

defective where the recipient was known to be an unprotected incompetent. In that case the Court held that the failure to appoint a guardian before foreclosure of property tax liens violated due process of law. Here, of course, the defendants are neither incompetent nor in need of guardians; but the proper tailoring of notice "to the capacities and circumstances" of indigent bush defendants requires the communication of substantially more information regarding the methods by which such defendants can respond to a distant lawsuit than is presently imparted.[27] A notice that fails to inform the indigent bush defendant of the right to file a written pleading is not "reasonably calculated . . . to . . . afford him an opportunity . . . ."[29] "to be heard 'at a meaningful time and in a meaningful manner.' "[30]

. . .

We therefore hold that the summons served upon the Aguchaks in this action was constitutionally defective because it did not adequately convey the information necessary to their defense against Ward's claim. The district court's assumption of personal jurisdiction over the Aguchaks based on such a summons therefore violated the due process rights which inure to the Aguchaks under art. I, § 7 of the Alaska Constitution. . . .

Reversed and remanded.

Id. at 1355–1358.

The court carefully rests its decision on the *state* constitution. The court also refers to "the unique relation between bush and metropolitan areas in Alaska." ("[W]e use the term 'bush' to refer to those sparsely inhabited, minimally accessible areas of the state which participate only marginally in the urban money economy." Id. at 1353.) Is the principle of *Aguchak* limited to Alaska? Should it apply to a suit by a creditor in Dallas against a consumer in El Paso (600 miles away)?

4.   Contrast Williams v. The Illinois State Scholarship Comm., 563 N.E.2d 465 (Ill.1990), in which the court held that it violated the Due Process Clause of the United States Constitution for a lender—in this case a state agency—to sue in Cook County consumers who had defaulted on student loans but who did not live in Cook County and had not gone to school there. The court reached the same conclusion with respect to a subsequently enacted statute that *required* the creditor to bring collection actions *only* in Cook County.

5.   The preceding materials have considered limitations on the creditor's advantageous use of the state's long-arm and venue statutes. Can the creditor evade these limitations by including in the credit contract a provision by which the consumer consents to jurisdiction or venue?

---

27. By contrast, the form summon used by the Fourth Judicial District Fairbanks informs the small claims defendant of the right to file a written answer.

29. Mullane v. Central Hanover Bank and Trust Co., 339 U.S. at 314.

30. Bush v. Reid, 516 P.2d at 1219, citing Boddie v. Connecticut, 401 U.S. at 378.

In *Williams*, Question 5 supra, the court refused to enforce contractual provisions by which the consumers acquiesced in the creditor's selection of Cook County as the venue for actions to enforce their obligations. Similarly, a California court held that a contractual provision specifying venue conflicted with the venue statute and therefore was contrary to public policy and unenforceable. Alexander v. Superior Court, 8 Cal.Rptr.3d 111, 117 (Cal.App.2003).

Notwithstanding these decisions, it is very common for consumer contracts to provide that all litigation must take place in a specified jurisdiction. In many instances the purpose is not to facilitate litigation by the merchant against the consumer. Rather, it is to impede or prevent litigation by the consumer against the merchant. If enforceable, the effect of these contract provisions is that if a consumer has a complaint against a creditor or a merchant, the consumer must litigate in the merchant's home state. In 1991 the United States Supreme Court validated this practice when it upheld a provision in a cruise line contract that called for litigation of all disputes between the parties to be brought in the state of Florida. Carnival Cruise Lines, Inc. v. Shute, 499 U.S. 585 (1991). The plaintiff, who resided in Washington and purchased a ticket for a cruise that began and ended in California, thus had to assert her claims in Florida.

Does the decision in *Carnival Cruise* affect the continued vitality of the decisions in *Spiegel* and *Schubach*? in *Aguchak*? in *Williams*? In *Carnival Cruise* the Court stated that forum selection clauses remain "subject to scrutiny for fundamental fairness." Id. At 595. Applying this standard, the lower courts have enforced some clauses, e.g., Schlessinger v. Holland America, N.V., 16 Cal.Rptr.3d 5 (Cal.App.2004), and invalidated others, e.g., America Online, Inc. v. Superior Court, 108 Cal.Rptr.2d 699 (Cal.App. 2001); Scarcella v. America Online, Inc., 811 N.Y.S.2d 858 (N.Y. App. Term 2005).

6. Another avenue may exist for dealing with forum abuse (and sewer service, too). See Rule 5015 of McKinney's N.Y. CPLR:

Rule 5015. Relief from judgment or order

(a) On motion. The court which rendered a judgment or order may relieve a party from it upon such terms as may be just, on motion of any interested person with such notice as the court may direct, upon the ground of:

. . .

3. fraud, misrepresentation, or other misconduct of an adverse party; . . . .

(c) On application of an administrative judge. An administrative judge, upon a showing that default judgments were obtained by fraud, misrepresentation, illegality, unconscionability, lack of due service, violations of law, or other illegalities or where such default judgments were obtained in cases in which those defendants would be uniformly entitled to interpose a defense predicated upon but not limited to the foregoing defenses, and where such default judgments have been obtained in a number deemed sufficient by him to justify such action as set forth herein, and upon appropriate notice to counsel for the respective parties, or to the parties themselves, may bring a proceeding to relieve a party or parties from them upon such terms as may be just. The disposition of any proceeding so instituted shall be determined by a judge other than the administrative judge. . . .

See also UCCC §§ 1.201(8) and 5.113 and Fair Debt Collection Practices Act § 811(a). The UCCC provisions have not been enacted everywhere, but the FDCPA is effective in all states. Does it make all the preceding material on forum abuse moot?

C. ATTORNEY'S FEES

If the creditor cannot obtain payment without first getting judgment against the consumer, and if the creditor cannot get that judgment by default, then the next best thing from the creditor's perspective is for the consumer to pay the creditor's litigation expenses. Typically, of course, the court does make an award of "costs" to the prevailing litigant. But these costs generally include only amounts that the prevailing party has paid the court to initiate and continue the judicial process, e.g., fees for filing, service of process, and jurors. They do not include attorney's fees, typically the largest by far of all litigation expenses. The general rule in the United States is that unless authorized by statute, a successful litigant may not recover attorney's fees from the other party. Section 9–615(a)(1) of the UCC, which permits the parties to agree for the payment of attorney's fees, is such a statute. So are retail installment sales acts and most other consumer credit acts. Consequently, virtually every contract within the scope of these statutes contains a provision that the consumer will pay any attorney's fees the creditor incurs in the event of default by the consumer. The amount of the fees may be determined by a standard of "reasonableness" or it may be stipulated as a percentage (usually in the 10–20% range) of the unpaid balance at the time of default.

Peoples Finance & Thrift Co. v. Blomquist

Supreme Court of Utah, 1964.
16 Utah 2d 157, 397 P.2d 293.

CROCKETT, JUSTICE:

Plaintiff, an industrial loan corporation, sued defendant for $1,245 balance due on a promissory note; to foreclose a chattel mortgage on defendant's automobile; and for attorney's fees as a necessary expense of collection as provided in the note. After suit was filed defendant tendered full payment with interest and costs but refused to pay attorney's fees.

The parties entered into an agreement whereby the plaintiff took the money tendered and released defendant's car, but reserved for determination this issue: whether the covenant to pay the costs of collection in case of default, including a reasonable attorney's fee, in addition to the maximum interest allowed by law, makes the contract usurious. The trial court ruled that it did not and awarded the plaintiff's attorney's fee. Defendant appeals.

The maximum interest of one per cent per month, plus an investigation fee, permitted under the Industrial Loan Act, Section 7–8–3, U.C.A. 1953, as amended, is the amount the law entitles the lender to charge for the loan of his money. If the payments are made as agreed, the transaction is complete, and there is nothing usurious about it. Only if the borrower fails to make his payments does it become necessary to enforce collection and incur attorney's fees. It could hardly be considered equitable to permit a borrower to take advantage of his own default and turn an otherwise lawful contract into a usurious one unenforceable against him. In the event the borrower does not abide by his commitment, a contingency arises which brings into operation what might be regarded as a supplemental agreement by which he had undertaken to pay the expenses of enforcing the contract. Exacting a covenant to take care of such a contingency and to protect the lender against such costs in order to insure that he will get the interest and charges the law allows him as provided in the contract, is not properly characterized as demanding additional interest.

The context of our statutes relating to interest charges corroborates the foregoing conclusion. The general statute Section 15–1–2, U.C.A.1953 provides for a maximum interest of 10 per cent per annum. In a separate subsection (b) it states that the loan "may provide for reasonable collection costs and for a reasonable attorney's fee in the event of default or delinquency." This seems to indicate plainly that the provision for attorney's fee in case of default is something separate and in addition to the interest provided for. Similar reasoning applies to the provisions in regard to industrial loans. In the same section, 15–1–2, subsection (f) provides: "That industrial loan corporations may contract for and receive interest and charges at the rates * * * [provided for] in chapter 8, Title 7 Utah Code Annotated 1953." The matter of the interest rate permitted being covered in one subdivision of the statute, and the provision authorizing reasonable collection costs and attorney's fees in the other (subsection (b)), it seems only reasonable to suppose that the interest and charges were to be allowed when the loan was paid as agreed; whereas, the collection of the money in case of default would be something else, for which the reasonable costs of collection, including attorney's fees, could be charged. The trial court correctly so ruled.

Affirmed. . . .

New Finance, Ltd. v. Ellis

Supreme Court of Alabama, 1969.
284 Ala. 374, 225 So.2d 784.

HARWOOD, JUSTICE.

The sole question presented on this review is:

[Does] the Alabama Small Loan Act, prohibit a licensee under such Act from incorporating in a note evidencing a loan, a provision that the borrower will pay "all expenses of collecting this note, with or without suit, including a reasonable attorney's fee, paid to the lender's attorney."

We judicially know that prior to the Alabama Small Loan Act in 1959, the small loan operator went unrestrained by an effective statutory regulation. Those whose chief motivation was greed preyed upon the ignorant, the uninformed, and the necessitous.

For decades concerned citizens and organizations made strenuous but futile efforts to have enacted legislation looking toward elimination of this evil. For some years, it was one of the main projects of the Junior Bar Section of the Alabama Bar. The efforts of all of these interested combinations eventually came to fruition in the passage of the Small Loan Law.

The amounts of the loans made by the small loan operator is often small, $10.00, $20.00, $50.00, etc. An interest rate of 8% per annum would not be economically feasible when considered in the light of office expenses, bookkeeping, and collection costs, plus the fact that many of those seeking small loans are poor credit risks.

The thinking of those experts in the field of small loans has been that the interest rate on such loans should be sufficiently high to enable a lender to have a fair return on his operations, and at the same time effectively limit the charges permitted to be imposed by the lender. The increase in the permissible rate of interest should be sufficiently high to take care of the costs of the lender's operations, including the credit risks involved. For this quid, a quo of higher charges in the form of full protection should be thrown around the borrower. See Euel Screws, Report of Committee on Small Loans Studies, Junior Bar Section, 20 Alabama Lawyer. It was the almost unanimous conclusion of virtually all of the studies made in this field through the years that the two factors above (interest rate, and borrower protection) could best be obtained by a realistic interest rate on small loans, and a strict and fixed limitation on all permissible charges additional to such higher interest.

. . .

Section 290(1) and (2) [of Ala. Code of 1940] provides that the maximum rate of interest that may be contracted for by a duly licensed small loan operator is 3% per month on the unpaid balance not in excess of $200.00, and an interest rate of 2% per month on the unpaid balance in excess of $200.00.

On loans of $75.00 or less, a licensee is permitted, in lieu of the charges above mentioned, to make charges according to a formula set forth in the Act.

By Section 292, a licensee may accept as additional security on loans of $100.00 or more, insurance on the life of the borrower, the premium for which cannot exceed 75¢ per annum for each $100.00 of life insurance.

By Section 290(7), a licensee may also collect from the borrower the actual fees for recording or releasing any instrument securing the loan.

Thus, in addition to the interest charges permitted, the charges for insurance, and for recording fees, are the only additional charges we have found permitted in the Act.

The Court of Appeals based its opinion upon the pertinent portions of Section 290(8) of the Small Loan Act, set forth in the opinion of the Court of Appeals as follows:

> No further or other charges shall be directly or indirectly contracted for or received by any licensee, including insurance premiums of any kind, except those specifically authorized by this Act * * *. If any amount in excess of the charges permitted by this Act is charged, contracted for, or received, except as the result of an accidental and bona fide error or computation, the contract of loan shall be void and the licensee shall have no right to collect or receive any cash advanced, charges or recompense whatsoever; * * *. Any borrower may recover the full amount of principal and charges paid by him on any contract made in violation of this section, together with a reasonable attorney fee, * * *.

In brief on certiorari counsel for appellant insists that the opinion of the Court of Appeals is erroneous in that, (1) the Small Loan Law is penal in nature and should be strictly construed, and (2) to hold impermissible a provision for the payment of collection costs, including a reasonable attorney's fee to be paid to the lender's attorney, is contrary to the public policy of this State.

As to the first contention, it is true that some courts have termed penal small loan acts similar to ours.

On the other hand, the Supreme Court of Maryland has observed that:

> "The whole trend of modern thought is that the reasonable adequate protection of the borrower can only be afforded by regulation. * * * It was to mitigate rather than eradicate the evils incident to the business (small loan) and to afford to the borrower the greatest practicable measure of protection that the act (Small Loan Act) was passed. It is therefore remedial in its nature, and should be construed liberally so as to effect its purpose." (Par. ours.) Liberty Finance Co. v. Catterton, 161 Md. 650, 158 A. 16.

Counsel for complainant complains that the opinion of the Court of Appeals "does not even purport to analyze the Act."

The Court of Appeals did set forth the pertinent provisions of the Act on which it based its conclusions. The language of these provisions is clear and unambiguous. It limits the charges that may be imposed by the licensee in language clearly expressing the intention of the Legislature to do just that. The clearly expressed intention of the Legislature must be given effect, and there is no room for construction. We cannot see therefore that it matters whether the Act be considered penal, or remedial.

As to the effect of public policy on the construction of the Act, it is certainly clear that it has been the policy of this State through its history to permit the costs of collection, including reasonable attorney's fees, to be contracted for, and such stipulation does not render the loan contract usurious. . . .

But the above rule relates to loan transactions within the influence of our regular usury laws permitting interest charges of 8 per cent.

By the Small Loan Act, our Legislature has provided that licensees qualifying under the Act may legally charge the much higher interest rates and fixed charges provided for in the Act. At the same time it clearly expressed its intent that loans made within the purview of the Small Loan Act could not be burdened directly or indirectly with any additional charges other than for insurance costs and record fees. If such additional charges were received, charged, *or contracted for,* the loan contract was void, and the borrower would be entitled to recover full amount of the principal and charges paid by him, together with a reasonable attorney's fee.

Thus as to loans made under the provisions of the Small Loan Act, the intent of the Legislature is also clear. Public policy as to this type of loan must be considered as fixed by the intent of the Legislature.

It is apparent to us that the Legislature in fixing the interest rates in the Small Loan Act intended that out of the abundance of the higher interest rate, the lender should pay collection costs just as other litigants are ordinarily required to do.

The language of the Act discloses a studied intent to make it strictly inclusive as to permissible charges to be assessed against the borrower. If the purposes of the Act are to be fulfilled, it should not be eroded by indirection.

As noted by the Court of Appeals, the courts of our sister States are not in accord as to whether a provision for the payment of an attorney's fee vitiates the loan contract under the Small Loan Act of the particular State, in which some of the Acts contain language similar to the Alabama Acts.

Probably the numerical weight of authority, and in our opinion the sounder conclusion, rests with the view of those courts holding that the clear and unambiguous language of the Act in reference to additional permissible charges, necessarily dictates the conclusion that the inclusion of a provision for payment of attorney's fees in case of default is prohibited by the explicit terms of the Act. We so hold in reference to the Alabama Small Loan Act.

Writ denied.

QUESTIONS AND NOTES

1. By what process does the court in *Peoples Finance* reach its decision? in *New Finance*?

2. In *Peoples Finance* the court states that amounts payable as attorney's fees are not properly characterized as interest because they merely insure that the lender "will get the interest and charges the law allows him." What is the flaw in this reasoning?

3. Unlike the Alabama statute, the small loan acts in some states specifically authorize the recovery of attorney's fees. E.g., West's Fla.Stat.Ann. § 516.031(3)(a)(7).

Most other legislation regulating consumer credit expressly authorizes agreements concerning attorney's fees, but the statutes take a variety of positions with respect to the details. In Arizona, for example, the court may award attorney's fees even if the contract makes no provision for them. Ariz.Rev.Stat. § 12–341.01(A). Illinois has a similar provision, but applicable only to retail installment sales. 815 Ill.Consol.Stat. § 405/12. New York specifically invalidates attorney's fees provisions in retail installment sales contracts, but at the same time enforces them in motor vehicle installment sales contracts and in revolving charge account agreements. McKinney's N.Y.Pers.Prop.L. §§ 302(7), 402(6–a), 413(5). Wisconsin, on the other hand, goes to the opposite end of the spectrum, prohibiting attorney's fees provisions in most consumer credit contracts. Wis.Stat.Ann. § 422.411(1). The drafters of the UCCC waffled on the question, leaving each state free to elect either a prohibition of attorney's fees provisions altogether or a prohibition only in connection with high-interest small loans (UCCC § 2.507 (Alts. A & B)).

4. Should the consumer be liable for the attorney's fees the creditor incurs in enforcing a claim? Persons advocating the creditor's position have argued that since the expense is occasioned by the conduct of a specific consumer, it is appropriate to place the burden of that expense on that consumer, rather than treating it as a business cost ultimately borne by all customers of the creditor. They also have argued that liability for this expense provides the consumer with an incentive to pay rather than default. Are these arguments persuasive?

>   a.   What percentage of consumers default? What is the relevance of this to the issue of liability for attorney's fees?

>   b.   Why do consumers default? What is the relevance of this?

Consumer advocates, on the other hand, have argued that liability for attorney's fees deters consumers from asserting defenses and encourages creditors to litigate. Do you agree?

5. If contractual provisions making the consumer liable for the creditor's attorney's fees are enforceable, how should the amount of that liability be determined? The problem is greatest in connection with default judgments: a 15% attorney's fee provision in connection with a debt of $4,000 produces a liability of $600. But most collection work is done by attorneys who each handle enough cases to have streamlined the office procedures: the routine work of filling in blanks on form complaints and filing them with the court is all done by non-lawyer office personnel. Because of mass production techniques, the attorney's actual costs are but a few dollars. Should a consumer who suffers a default judgment have to pay $600 as so-called attorney's fees?

In New York, where statutes permit the creditor to recover up to a stated percentage of the debt as attorney's fees, the courts have concluded that the stated percentage is an upper limit and the creditor is not automatically entitled to that amount. Rather, the creditor must affirmatively establish the amount of reasonable attorney's fees, which in no event may exceed the stated percentage. Broadstreets Inc. v. Parlin, 348 N.Y.S.2d 724 (N.Y.City Civ.Ct.1973). See also First National Bank v. Brower, 368 N.E.2d 1240 (N.Y.1977) (enforcing a local court rule that attorney's fees awards in default judgment cases be based on the court's determination of the reasonable value of the attorney's services). There is similar authority for the proposition that the court may fix the amount of a reasonable attorney's fee when the contract stipulates it to be a fixed percentage of the debt. City Bank & Trust Co. v. Hardage Corp., 449 So.2d 1181 (La.App. 1984).

Besides requiring a judicial determination of the amount of the attorney's fee award, can you think of any other solution to the problem of excessive liability in default judgment cases?

The New York statutes, and also UCCC section 2.507 (Alternative B), authorize an award of attorney's fees only if the attorney is not a salaried employee of the creditor. What is the rationale for this limitation?

D.   WAIVER OF EXEMPTIONS

Even if a creditor has a judgment for the unpaid balance of the debt and for the expenses of obtaining that judgment, the creditor still may not receive the money: the consumer may not pay the judgment. When this happens, the creditor must resort to post-judgment collection procedures. These procedures are beyond the scope of this book, but one aspect of the subject deserves mention. A creditor with a judgment (known as a judgment creditor) may enforce that judgment by directing the sheriff to seize and sell the consumer's property. Generally speaking, all of the consumer's property is subject to seizure and sale, except for assets that the legislature has declared to be exempt. Exemptions vary dramatically from state to state but generally include a homestead (real property on which the consumer resides), a portion of the consumer's wages, clothing, and household furnishings. Subject to two possible exceptions, exempt assets may not be seized to satisfy the judgment.

The first exception is for security interests. If the consumer gives a creditor a security interest in a particular asset, that creditor may direct its seizure even if the asset is exempt.[7] The second exception is for waivers of

---

7. But see pages 695–96 supra: state and federal law prohibits non-purchase money security interests in certain property. One rationale for this is to preserve the consumer's exemption rights. A similar invalidation

exemption. A creditor may include in the contract a provision in which the consumer waives the right to claim property as exempt. If this provision is enforced, then the judgment creditor will be able to enforce the judgment against all the assets of the consumer. A waiver of exemptions thus enhances the likelihood of payment by maximizing the amount of property available for satisfaction of any judgment (and costs). At least, this is the theory. A waiver of exemptions does enhance the prospects of payment, but it does not ensure payment. Do you see why?

Because waivers of exemption frustrate the policy underlying the exemption statutes, many legislatures and courts have declared them to be unenforceable. E.g., Va. Code 1950, § 34–22; Iowa Mutual Insurance Co. v. Parr, 370 P.2d 400, 404 (Kan.1962). And the FTC's Credit Practices Rule prohibits their use. 16 C.F.R. § 444.2(a)(2).[8] For a discussion of the security interest and waiver exceptions to the protection afforded by exemption laws, see Vukowich, Debtors' Exemption Rights, 62 Geo.L.J. 779, 848–52 (1974); Haines, Security Interests in Exempt Personalty: Toward Safeguarding Basic Exempt Necessities, 57 Notre Dame Law. 215 (1981).

E.   COSIGNERS

Another way for the creditor to increase the amount of property available if the consumer defaults is to find a person to cosign the contract with the consumer. Then if the consumer defaults, the creditor can look to the assets of the cosigner as well as the assets of the consumer. From the consumer's perspective, the usefulness of having a cosigner is that it may enable the consumer—especially one who is young or poor or has a questionable credit record—to obtain credit from a creditor who otherwise would decline to extend it. There are, however, several problems.

The idea of getting one person to guarantee the performance of another is neither new nor unique to consumer transactions. The law of suretyship has been around for a long time, and so has the practice by commercial entities of requiring performance bonds by the persons with whom they deal. The consumer cosigner, however, is not merely a surety. The contract typically provides that the cosigner "shall remain liable as principal until the obligation has been paid." Therefore, if the consumer defaults, the creditor may immediately pursue the cosigner even though the consumer is readily available.[9]

As you might suspect, many persons are reluctant to incur potential liability just to enable another person to obtain goods or services. Hence there is an incentive for the creditor to deceive the prospective cosigner

appears in the federal Bankruptcy Act, 11 U.S.C. § 522(f).

8. The Bankruptcy Code also invalidates waivers of exemptions. 11 U.S.C. § 522(e).

9. Another problem is that frequently the cosigner does not receive a copy of the contract. So until the creditor sues, the cosigner cannot determine whether he or she is really liable.

into believing he or she is signing the document merely as a reference for the consumer or as a witness to the contract between the creditor and the consumer. Not all persons, of course, are deceived; some are aware of the significance of cosigning. Therefore, the creditor may structure the negotiations to make the prospective cosigner feel that a refusal to cosign the contract is a statement that he or she lacks faith in the consumer.

Finally, the existence of a cosigner may give the creditor a powerful collection tactic with respect to the consumer. The consumer may be embarrassed about having had to seek the assistance of the cosigner in the first place and may wish to shield the cosigner from any further involvement with the creditor. Therefore, if a dispute develops between the creditor and the consumer, the consumer may forego assertion of valid claims or defenses in order to prevent the creditor from dunning or suing the cosigner.

QUESTIONS AND NOTES

1. The drafters of the UCCC responded to these problems in section 3.208. Does this section deal with the problems adequately? Compare the FTC Credit Practices Rule, section 444.3. Is this provision more or less protective of consumers than UCCC section 3.208?

2. Compare the Illinois Retail Installment Sales Act, 815 Ill.Consol.Stat. § 405/19:

> Each person, other than a seller or holder, who signs a retail installment contract, retail charge agreement, or any other agreement or instrument in a retail installment transaction may be held liable only to the extent that he actually receives the goods sold or services furnished in the retail installment transaction, except that a parent or spouse who co-signs such contract, agreement or instrument may be held liable to the full extent of the deferred payment price notwithstanding such parent or spouse has not actually received the goods sold or services furnished under such retail installment transaction and except to the extent such person other than a seller or holder, signs in the capacity of a guarantor of collection.
>
> The obligation of such guarantor is secondary, and not primary. The obligation arises only after the seller or holder has reduced his claim against the primary obligor and execution has been returned unsatisfied, or after the primary obligor has become insolvent or it is otherwise apparent that it is useless to proceed against him.
>
> No provision in a retail installment contract obligating such guarantor is valid unless:
>
>> (1) there appears below the signature space provided for such guarantor the following:
>>
>>> "I, hereby guarantee the collection of the above described amount upon failure of the seller named herein to collect said amount from the buyer named here."; and

(2) unless the guarantor, in addition to signing the retail installment contract, signs a separate instrument in the following form:

EXPLANATION OF GUARANTOR'S OBLIGATION

You _____ (name of guarantor) by signing the retail installment contract and this document are agreeing that you will pay $_____ (total deferred payment price) for the purchase of _____ (description of goods or services) purchased by _____ (name of buyer) from _____ (name of seller).

Your obligation arises only after the seller or holder has attempted through the use of the court system to collect this amount from the buyer.

If the seller cannot collect this amount from the buyer, you will be obligated to pay even though you are not entitled to any of the goods or services furnished. The seller is entitled to sue you in court for the payment of the amount due.

The instrument must be printed, typed or otherwise reproduced in a size and style equal to at least 8 point bold type, and may contain no other matter (except a union printing label) than above set forth and must bear the signature of the co-signer and no other person. The seller shall give the co-signer a copy of the retail installment contract and a copy of the co-signer statement.

A person actually receives the goods sold or services furnished in a retail installment transaction when he or she physically possesses the goods or benefits from the goods or services or when someone authorized by the person physically possesses the goods or benefits from the goods or services. A person's separately signed written authorization is conclusive proof of that person actually receiving the goods sold or services furnished in any action by or against an assignee of the contract. Notwithstanding the provisions of this paragraph, a person signing a retail installment contract as a guarantor is liable only pursuant to the provisions in this Act relating to guarantors.

Is this an improvement over the UCCC? the FTC Rule? Is it adequate? Why are spouses and parents singled out for exclusion from the protection of the statute?

3. Can you think of any way to deal with the problem of psychological coercion in procuring the cosigner's signature?

4. Problem. Does the FTC cosigner rule, section 444.3, require *Seller* to supply the cosigner notice in the following situations:

a. *Consumer* and *Friend* share an apartment. They want to acquire a sound system, and they sign an installment purchase contract with *Seller*.

b. *Consumer* lives with her parents. In connection with selling her a piano, *Seller* requires her parents to sign the contract.

c.   *Consumer* applies for credit in connection with the purchase of a car. *Seller* states that because of blemishes on *Consumer's* credit record, he needs a cosigner. *Consumer's* uncle agrees to help, and *Seller* lists *Consumer* and his uncle as co-buyers, and both their names appear on the title issued by the Department of Motor Vehicles.

d.   *Consumer* and his parents jointly own the house in which *Consumer* lives. The parents live elsewhere. *Consumer* wants to build an in-ground hot tub. *Seller* is willing to extend credit to *Consumer*, but only if his parents also sign the contract, which they do.

Would it matter if the subject matter of the contract were a swimming pool?

e.   *Consumer* lives with his parents. In connection with selling him a piano, *Seller* requires his parents to give a security interest in their automobile.

PART IV

ENFORCEMENT BY THE CONSUMER

The final Part of this book examines problems in connection with the enforcement of the consumer's contractual and statutory rights. Chapter 14 addresses the question of whom the consumer may sue, and Chapter 15 considers some practical barriers to litigation by the consumer.

CHAPTER 14

AGAINST WHOM?

The answer to the question posed by the title of this chapter seems obvious: the aggrieved consumer should look to the seller or lender for redress. Occasionally, however, the conduct of the seller or lender is not the cause of the injury; and occasionally the seller or lender is not amenable to suit (because it has gone out of business or is otherwise judgment proof). This chapter explores the vicarious liability of one person, with whom the consumer may not have dealt, for injuries caused by another person. The materials in Chapter 7 provide one example of vicarious liability: a consumer may recover from a retailer for personal injuries caused by a defective product that was manufactured by someone else. This chapter examines several other situations in which there may be vicarious liability. The underlying question is, when is it appropriate to make one person liable for the misconduct of another person?

A. LIABILITY OF A FRANCHISOR FOR THE MISCONDUCT OF ITS FRANCHISEE

The law of agency recognizes that a person may act not only directly but also indirectly through others. If a principal directs his or her agent to act in a certain way, the law does not hesitate to hold the principal responsible just as if the principal had acted personally. If the principal does not direct the specific act that results in injury, the causal connection is less clear but the principal still may be legally responsible. For example, an automobile dealer who authorizes an employee to form contracts with consumers on behalf of the dealer will be bound to a contract so formed by the employee even if the price or other term is not as favorable as the dealer would like. This is one reason why the sales contract typically contains an integration clause limiting the authority of the salesperson and informing the consumer of that limit.

A business that has many retail outlets may operate in two different ways. One way is to hire employees to run the stores. Under agency principles, the business that operates this way is liable for injuries caused by the conduct of the persons working at the retail stores. The second way for a business to operate, known as franchising, is to license other persons to use its name and sell its product. The two methods are not mutually exclusive: a business may operate in both ways simultaneously, i.e. run its own retail outlets and also license others to sell products in its name.

It would be possible for franchisors to make the franchisees their agents, but in fact they do not do this. Instead, the franchise agreement characterizes the relationship as a license and specifically *denies* the existence of agency. If the franchisee is not the franchisor's agent, to what extent should the franchisor be liable for the conduct of the franchisee? If the franchisor directs the franchisee to engage in unlawful conduct, the franchisor is liable. E.g., Maryland v. Cottman Transmissions Systems, Inc., 587 A.2d 1190 (Md.App.1991). Similarly, if the franchisee sells a defective product manufactured or distributed by the franchisor, the franchisor is liable to the consumer. Even if the franchisor merely approves the design of a product that the franchisee procures elsewhere, the franchisor may be liable. See Kosters v. Seven–Up Co., 595 F.2d 347 (6th Cir.1979), holding a franchisor liable for injuries caused by a soft drink carton whose defective design it had approved. But what if the franchisor's connection with the injury-producing conduct is more remote?

Drexel v. Union Prescription Centers, Inc.

United States Court of Appeals, Third Circuit, 1978.
582 F.2d 781.

BIGGS, CIRCUIT JUDGE.

[Plaintiff alleged that her husband went to Union Prescription Center, a drug store, to have a prescription filled. Six weeks later he returned to have the prescription refilled. Instead of furnishing the drug called for, however, the store negligently provided a different drug. Plaintiff's husband took the drug and died. Plaintiff sued Union Prescription Centers, Inc., a corporation that sold a Union Prescription Center franchise to Joseph Todisco, who operated the store that supplied the fatal drug. Defendant franchisor moved for summary judgment, and the trial court granted the motion.]

II.   VICARIOUS LIABILITY

Appellant contended in the district court and asserts on appeal that UPC is vicariously liable for Todisco's alleged negligence either because UPC retained sufficient control over the operation of the Reading drugstore to establish a master-servant relationship or because UPC "held itself out" to the public as the owner or operator of the Reading store. We shall examine these theories in turn. In so doing, we heed the well-established principles that the moving party in a motion for summary judgment must show that there is no genuine issue as to any material fact and that the moving party is entitled to judgment as a matter of law, and that the evidence and the inferences drawn therefrom must be considered in a light most favorable to the party opposing the summary judgment motion.

A.   *Appellant's Master–Servant Theory*

We first consider appellant's contention that summary judgment was erroneous because factual questions exist requiring jury resolution with respect to the precise nature of the relationship between UPC and its franchisee. Under Pennsylvania law, when an injury is done by an "independent contractor," the person employing him is generally not responsible to the person injured. However, when the relationship between the parties is that of "master-servant" or "employer-employee," as distinguished from "independent contractor-contractee," the master or employer is vicariously liable for the servant's or employee's negligent acts committed within the scope of his employment. While Pennsylvania courts have set forth numerous criteria to determine whether a given person is an employee-servant or an independent contractor, "the basic inquiry is whether such person is subject to the alleged employer's control or right to control with respect to his physical conduct in the performance of the services for which he was engaged. . . . The hallmark of an employee-employer relationship is that the employer not only controls the result of the work but has the right to direct the manner in which the work shall be accomplished; the hallmark of an independent contractee-contractor relationship is that the person engaged in the work has the exclusive control of the manner of performing it, being responsible only for the result." Green v. Independent Oil Co., 414 Pa. 477, 483–84, 201 A.2d 207, 210 (1964). Actual control of the manner of work is not essential; rather, it is the right to control which is determinative.

Difficulties arise, of course, in the application of these familiar principles to the facts of a given case. Each case must be decided on its own facts. The difficulties are perhaps especially evident where, as here, the alleged master and servant also occupy the status of franchisor and franchisee. Some degree of control by the franchisor over the franchisee would appear to be inherent in the franchise relationship, see generally Brown, Franchising—A Fiduciary Relationship, 49 Texas L.Rev. 650 (1971), and may even be mandated by federal law.[1] However, as several courts have discerned, the mere existence of a franchise relationship does not necessarily trigger a master-servant relationship, nor does it automatically insulate the parties from such a relationship. Whether the control retained by the franchisor is also sufficient to establish a master-servant relationship depends in each case upon the nature and extent of such control as defined in the franchise agreement or by the actual practice of parties. The fact that the franchise agreement expressly denies the existence of an agency relationship is not in itself determinative of the matter.

In the present case there is no evidence that UPC exercised actual control over the manner in which Todisco operated the Reading store. Instead, both parties rely upon various provisions of the Franchise Agree-

---

1. Under the provisions of the Lanham Act, 15 U.S.C. §§ 1051 et seq., the owner of a trade mark may license his mark to a "related company," "provided such mark is not used in such manner as to deceive the public." Id. § 1055. A "related company" is defined as "any person who . . . is *controlled* by" the trade mark owner, and the owner may lose his mark by "abandonment" if its use is discontinued or if the manner of its use "causes the mark to lose its significance as an indication of origin." Id. § 1127 (emphasis added). We note that neither party herein has discussed the applicability or relevance of the Lanham Act to the facts of the present case.

ment as supporting their respective contentions regarding UPC's right to control Todisco's performance. While acknowledging that a franchise agreement may disguise what is essentially a master-servant relationship, appellee argues that the present Agreement at most creates only an independent contractor relationship. Under the terms of the Agreement, appellee observes, Todisco is merely the recipient of a license granted by UPC to operate a Union Prescription Center under that name and to use UPC's service mark and logo in conjunction therewith, in return for which Todisco pays to UPC a four and one-half percent monthly royalty out of the store's gross receipts. In fact, stresses appellee, the Agreement specifically provides that the franchisee pays all business expenses and taxes, bears the risk of litigation arising out of the store's operation, has some say in choosing the inventory, and is required to identify himself as owner of the store on all signs and printed matter bearing the UPC mark.

Appellant contends, conversely, that the Franchise Agreement, considered as a whole, provides sufficient indicia of control to raise a factual question respecting the nature of the relationship between UPC and its franchisee. Appellant relies upon numerous contractual provisions which allegedly accord UPC the right to control specific details of the store's operation and which restrict Todisco's exercise of personal managerial discretion. Thus, under the terms of the Agreement: the franchisee "acknowledges that the public image and good name of the Union Prescription Centers requires the perpetuation of quality standards . . . and further requires the management and marketing advice of UPC in order to avoid improper or degrading techniques"; the franchisee may operate only under the UPC name and logo; UPC approves the location of the store and has the right to inspect the premises during normal business hours; the franchisee must maintain the exterior and interior of the store premises in a "clean, orderly and attractive condition and shall maintain all structures, furnishings, fixtures, equipment and decorations in such a manner as to insure an attractive appearance of the Prescription Center"; the franchisee must adhere to UPC's interior and exterior standard colors, lighting, design, equipment, and fixtures, and any new construction, facilities, or equipment must conform to such "national standards"; the franchisee must maintain a "neat, orderly arrangement of displayed merchandise and a high degree of cleanliness"; the store must be operated "as part of a national organization securing its strength through adherence to UPC's uniformly high standards of service, appearance, quality of equipment and proved methods of operation," and the franchisee agrees to "conform strictly" to "all such national standards" and to the provisions of the Franchise Agreement; UPC has the "unqualified right" both to review the store's operations and consult with the franchisee on operating problems and to inspect the store "so as to assure maintenance of the high standards of the Union Prescription Center program, the goodwill of the public, and compliance with the provisions of this Agreement and with various licensing laws."

The Agreement further provides that the franchisee must exercise best efforts to secure union members for all construction and repair work and to have all invoices, statements, letterheads, prescription blanks, and other printed materials printed in union shops; UPC designates the nature and minimum inventory requirements for the store subject to the franchisee's approval and, at franchisee's request, will make available pharmaceutical items bearing the UPC label; the franchisee may not supplement his inventory with items not directly related to the prescription, convalescent, or medical field without UPC's written consent; the franchisee must deliver and maintain inventory control data, delivery receipts, and records as prescribed by law and such other inventory records as required by UPC; UPC uniformly designates the equipment and fixtures for each store, to be paid for by the franchisee, and the franchisee authorizes UPC to order on his behalf equipment and fixtures necessary, in the sole judgment of UPC, to commence the store's operation; the franchisee must keep the store open for business a minimum of 46 hours per week; the franchisee must use UPC's standard forms in operating the store, including prescription labels and files, rental contracts, letterheads, business cards, and accounting and inventory records; the franchisee must use UPC's uniform accounting system and make monthly financial reports to UPC; the franchisee must schedule specified inventory dates and mail a copy of the results to UPC on forms acceptable to the Internal Revenue Service.

The Franchise Agreement states that the franchisee must preserve complete records of all sales and purchases in a manner and form prescribed by UPC; UPC may examine and audit the franchisee's books and records at any reasonable time; the franchisee must purchase and maintain various types of insurance policies prescribed by UPC and must name UPC as an insured, and if the franchisee fails to do so, UPC may purchase such insurance on his behalf and at his cost; the franchisee must use and pay for all advertising and promotional materials developed by UPC, and must submit any other materials to UPC for written approval prior to the distribution thereof; the franchisee must utilize insignia, equipment, decals, personnel uniforms, truck signs and colors required by UPC; the franchisee must conduct his business "in a manner that will reflect favorably at all times upon UPC . . . and the good name, goodwill and reputation thereof"; UPC may terminate the license and Agreement if, *inter alia,* the franchisee breaches any provision of the Agreement, in which case the franchisee must, at UPC's option, completely transfer to UPC a list of all employees, files, prescription lists, customers, and facilities, thereby effecting "a complete and effective transfer of the business" to UPC; the franchisee is subject to a restrictive covenant and UPC has a right of first refusal with regard to transfer of the business; the franchisee indemnifies UPC against all liabilities of any kind arising out of the operation of the business.

In determining that no master-servant relationship existed between UPC and Todisco, the learned district judge reasoned that the provisions of the Franchise Agreement cited by plaintiff

> only give defendant-franchisor the tools with which to protect the proprietary interest in its name and goodwill. Nowhere in the agree-

ment is there any provision giving defendant the right to control the manner in which Todisco was to perform the daily chores of the business. The restrictions in the agreement concerning the type of advertising, logos, and inventory do not give defendant the right to dictate the manner in which Todisco was to fill prescriptions; nor does the right retained by defendant-franchisor to inspect the premises and to terminate the agreement constitute such control over Todisco's manner of performance as to create vicarious liability. . . . Defendant was not concerned with the "means" by which Todisco conducted his pharmacy business; it was concerned only with the "results" of his work.

428 F.Supp. at 666 (citations omitted).

While bearing in mind that we must not strain to discover issues of fact where none exist, we nevertheless conclude that the agreement, considered as a whole, is not free of ambiguity or the possibility of inferences contrary to the district judge's construction and interpretation of that document. When read in its entirety and in a light most favorable to appellant, the Agreement appears so broadly drawn as to render uncertain the precise nature and scope of UPC's rights vis-à-vis its franchisee. Thus, in the absence of further evidence of what the subscribing parties to the Franchise Agreement meant and understood by its terms, it cannot be determined as a matter of law on the present record that UPC did not have the right to control the manner of Todisco's performance or that UPC was not the "master" of Todisco.

Many of the provisions cited by appellant indicate that UPC reserved the right to control numerous specific facets of the franchisee's business operation, ranging from the appearance and contents of the store, its advertising and promotional programs, and its accounting, inventory, and record-keeping systems, to the minimum number of weekly operating hours, the type of prescription labels and files, personnel uniforms, and the color of delivery trucks. However, even assuming, as the district judge observed, that these more specific manifestations of control only evidence UPC's concern with the "result" of the store's operation rather than the "means" by which it was operated, other provisions of the Agreement are so nebulously and generally phrased as to suggest that UPC retained a broad discretionary power to impose upon the franchisee virtually any control, restriction, or regulation it deemed appropriate or warranted. When a franchisee is required, *inter alia*, to perpetuate "quality standards," to submit to UPC's management and marketing advice "to avoid improper or degrading techniques," to maintain the premises and equipment in an "attractive condition," to ensure "a high degree of cleanliness" and a "neat, orderly arrangement" of merchandise, to conform all equipment and facilities to UPC's "national standards," to adhere strictly to UPC's "uniformly high standards of service, appearance, quality of equipment and proved methods of operation," and to conduct his business "in a manner that will reflect favorably at all times upon UPC," and when the franchisor has the "unqualified right" to review the store's operations and

to inspect the store "to assure maintenance of [UPC's] high standards
. . . , the goodwill of the public, and compliance with the provisions of
this Agreement and with various licensing laws," as well as the right to
terminate the relationship for breach of any provision of the Agreement,
including those here cited, we believe that reasonable minds could differ as
to whether or not UPC had the right to control Todisco's physical conduct
and the manner in which he operated the store, including the prescription-
filling activity. . . .

We therefore conclude that on the present record genuine issues of
material fact exist regarding the nature of the relationship between appellee and its franchisee which preclude the entry of summary judgment.

B.   *Appellant's Holding Out or Apparent Agency Theory*

As an alternative theory upon which to impose liability on UPC,
appellant argues that . . . UPC led the public, including the decedent, to
believe that it was dealing not with a local independent pharmacist, but
rather with UPC, a nationally established and uniformly controlled establishment. . . .

Appellant relies, *inter alia,* upon § 267 of the Restatement (Second) of
Agency (1958), which provides as follows:

> One who represents that another is his servant or other agent and
> thereby causes a third person justifiably to rely upon the care or skill
> of such apparent agent is subject to liability to the third person for
> harm caused by the lack of care or skill of the one appearing to be a
> servant or other agent as if he were such.

Insofar as we are aware, no Pennsylvania court has discussed the applicability of § 267 to that state's agency law or otherwise squarely considered
the liability of an ostensible principal for the negligence of an ostensible
agent. It is thus our function in this diversity action to "predict" whether
the Pennsylvania courts would apply a "holding out" or "apparent agency"
theory, such as that formulated in § 267, on the facts presented in this
case. . . .

We agree . . . that the Supreme Court of Pennsylvania would adopt
§ 267 or some similar principle of "apparent agency." . . .

Contending that no affirmative holding out ever occurred, and, indeed,
that it took substantial steps to ensure that the public was accurately
apprised of Todisco's status, appellee relies upon the following provision of
the Franchise Agreement: "The Owner [franchisee] shall show his name
(corporate, partnership or individual) in connection with the use of such
licensed mark following 'Union Prescription Center' in conjunction with
the word 'license' or otherwise identify himself as the owner of the Union
Prescription Center under a license from UPC, on all invoices, statements,
letterheads, prescription blanks and other printed matter, as well as on all
signs posted on the Union Prescription Center premises. Applications for
local licenses or other entries in public records will be made in the Owner's
name." In addition, stresses appellee, Todisco, when deposed, stated that a

nameplate reading "Joseph J. Todisco, Jr., Registered Pharmacist" was displayed on the counter in front of him in the store; that he had registered in the fictitious names index for Berks County under the fictitious name "Union Prescription Center"; and that he had registered with the state Board of Pharmacy under the name "Union Prescription Center" as well as under his own name.

Appellant, however, relies upon evidence tending to demonstrate that in fact customers of the Reading store were led to believe that they were dealing with the corporate defendant, UPC, and that they were given no notice that the store was an entity independently owned and operated by Todisco. When deposed by plaintiff, Todisco stated that there was no place in the store where customers could note that he was a "franchisee." The bags, prescription labels, and cash register receipts used by the Reading store (appended as exhibits to the deposition transcript) all bear the name "Union Prescription Centers" or "Union Prescription Center," the bags also bearing a logo, and fail to identify Todisco as the owner or operator of the store. Similarly, Todisco testified that the store's local advertising, through media such as ball point pens, local newspapers, and nail files, all say "Union Prescription Center" and omit any mention of Todisco's name. Todisco further stated that the store is listed in the Reading phone directory as "Union Prescription Center" and that the telephone is answered "Union Prescription Center."

According to appellant, such indicia of apparent agency are directly attributable to UPC, the ostensible principal, because UPC, through the regulatory provisions of the Franchise Agreement, controlled the manner in which the Reading store was perceived by the public. Appellant points to the following provisions of the Agreement: The franchisee [owner] may promote and advertise only with the logo, service mark, or insignia prepared and submitted by UPC to the owner; UPC has established interior and exterior standard colors, lighting, design, equipment and fixtures designed to provide national identification; . . . Owner is required to utilize insignia, equipment, decals, personnel uniforms, truck signs and colors, indoor signs and posters, and such other advertising and promotional materials as may be required by UPC to maintain uniformity of appearance, national recognition, point of purchase impact and full penetration of promotional opportunities; Owner must submit to UPC for written approval prior to dissemination any advertising or promotional material that has not been developed by UPC; Owner is required to use the standard Union Prescription Center sign or signs as specified by UPC; UPC specifies that owner shall use standard forms in the operation of the Prescription Center, including prescription labels, letterheads, and business cards.

. . .

Appellee's assertion that no representations of agency or authority were ever made is contradicted by appellant's evidence suggesting that in fact UPC, by strictly controlling the manner in which the franchisee was perceived by the public, created an appearance of ownership and control purposefully designed to attract the patronage of the public. . . . While appellee, emphasizing that the Franchise Agreement required the franchisee to identify himself as owner of the store in conjunction with his use of UPC's mark and logo, asserts that it cannot be held accountable for Todisco's failure in this regard and that it had no notice of it, a review of all the evidence reveals that several representatives of UPC actually visited Todisco's store on numerous occasions and that UPC had an unqualified right to inspect the Reading store. Thus, a potential question is presented as to whether UPC had actual or constructive knowledge of Todisco's failure to appraise the public of his status and acquiesced therein. . . . The issue, we note, is not what agreements were entered into between UPC and Todisco to establish a relationship other than agency, but rather what representations were actually made to the customers of the Reading store. Moreover, the sign identifying Todisco as "Registered Pharmacist" could reasonably be viewed as merely a statement of professional qualification rather than, as appellee insists, a clear indication Todisco independently owned and operated the store. So, too, while it is urged that Todisco manifested ownership in registering with both the county and the state pharmacy board, there is no evidence that decedent was or should have been aware of such facts. These are all factors to be weighed and considered by the finder of fact in determining whether the elements of apparent agency have been established.

We stress that our decision here expresses no view whatsoever as to the ultimate outcome or disposition of this case. In order to recover on a theory of apparent agency, plaintiff must establish not only the element of representations but also that of justifiable reliance on those representations. . . .

The judgment will be reversed and the cause remanded for proceedings consistent with this opinion.

QUESTIONS AND NOTES

1. The franchise agreement in *Drexel* stated that the franchisor and the franchisee "are not and shall not be considered joint venturers, partners *or the agents of each other*" (emphasis added). In light of this language, how can the court conclude that the existence of an actual agency relationship is a question of fact?

2. In footnote 5 the court alludes to the franchisor's dilemma. The franchisor's most important asset may be the trade name that identifies its product or service. To preserve its rights to that name, the franchisor must exercise sufficient control over the franchisee to ensure that the product or service being sold by the franchisee is the same as the product or service being sold by the franchisor. Hence, to protect its trademark and trade name, the franchisor *must* exercise some control over the franchisee. But if the franchisor exercises "too much" control, it may be held to be in an agency relationship with the franchisee. In Nichols v. Arthur Murray, Inc., 56 Cal.Rptr. 728, 732 (Cal.App.1967), the court held that the franchisee was the agent of the franchisor, who therefore was liable for the amount plaintiff had paid the franchisee for dance lessons. The court stated:

> The subject agreement, in substance, conferred upon defendant the right to control the employment of all employees of the franchise holder whether or not their duties related to teaching or supervising dancing instruction; to fix the minimum tuition rates to be charged; to select the financial institution handling, financing or discounting all pupil installment contracts; to designate the location of the studio, its layout and decoration; to make refunds to pupils and charge the amounts paid to the franchise holder; to settle and pay all claims against defendant arising out of the operation of the contemplated enterprise; to reimburse itself for the payment of any such refunds or claims, and the expense of any litigation in connection therewith, from a fund consisting of weekly payments by the franchise holder to defendant in an amount equal to 5% of the gross receipts; to invest the proceeds of this fund and pay the franchise holder only such portion of the income therefrom as defendant "shall determine should be properly allocated"; to control all advertising by the franchise holder, which was required to be submitted to defendant for approval prior to use; and to exercise a broad control over the operation of the enterprise under a provision requiring the franchise holder "to conduct the studio, to be maintained and managed by Licensee, in accordance with the general policies of the Licensor as established from time to time," and directing that failure to maintain such policies shall be sufficient cause for immediate cancellation of the agreement.

> Other provisions evidencing the nature of the control vested in defendant were those requiring the franchise holder to honor unused lessons purchased by a pupil from another franchise holder at the rate of $2.50 per hour, and to pay that amount for unused lessons purchased from the former when furnished by the latter; also requiring the franchise holder to maintain records, and submit copies thereof weekly to defendant, setting forth the names and addresses of pupils enrolled during the week, the amounts paid by all pupils, number of lessons taken by each pupil, and the names of all pupils taking lessons; and further requiring the franchise holder to furnish defendant with duplicates of all social security and unemployment insurance reports, and all federal and state tax returns.

The court in Chevron Oil Co. v. Sutton, 515 P.2d 1283, 1286 (N.M.1973), reached a similar conclusion:

> In the present case, there is a substantial dispute as to a material fact, and this should foreclose summary judgment. The fact in dispute is whether or not Chevron exercised such control over Sharp as to bring the doctrine of respondeat superior into play. Independent stations of the appellant were required to: (1) diligently promote the sale of Chevron's brand products; (2) remain open for certain hours and days and "meet the operating hours of competitors"; (3) keep the premises, restrooms and equipment in a "clean and orderly condition";

(4) present a "good appearance"; and (5) promote Chevron's image to the motoring public. In addition, Sharp also (6) sold Chevron products and dispensed gasoline and oil provided by the Chevron organization; (7) received the benefit of Chevron advertising; (8) wore uniforms containing the Chevron emblem; (9) used calling cards which billed the station as "Lee Sharp Chevron and Four Wheel Drive Equipment" (apparently with Chevron's consent); and (10) the customers of the Sharp station were permitted to charge purchases of both products and repairs on Chevron credit cards. No one of these factors is controlling, but all are useful in determining whether or not control was present. By using all of these factors, there is a sufficient factual question as to whether or not there was an actual master-servant relationship.

Accord, Singleton v. International Dairy Queen, Inc., 332 A.2d 160 (Del.Super.1975). But not all courts agree. Consider Coe v. Esau, 377 P.2d 815, 817–18 (Okl.1963):

> . . . It is indeed a matter of common knowledge and practice that distinctive colors and trade mark signs are displayed at gasoline stations by independent dealers of petroleum product suppliers. These signs and emblems represent no more than notice to the motorist that a given company's products are being marketed at the station.
>
> . . .
>
> The facts and circumstances adduced by plaintiff's evidence are insufficient to raise the necessary inference that [Conoco] either had the right to control or exercised the right to control the conduct of Esau in the operation of his station. Esau was free to, and did, handle tires and automotive accessories of other suppliers; he procured his own personnel, determined the daily business hours and the methods of doing business. The petroleum products supplied by [Conoco] were sold to Esau on a cash basis.

More recently, the Supreme Court of Wisconsin signaled deeper disagreement with the imposition of vicarious liability on franchisors. In Kerl v. Dennis Rasmussen, Inc., 682 N.W.2d 328, 331–32, 342 (Wis.2004), plaintiff sued for tortious injury inflicted by an employee of an Arby's franchisee. She sued Arby's as well as the franchisee, DRI. The trial court granted summary judgment to Arby's, and the Wisconsin Supreme Court affirmed:

> The rationale for vicarious liability becomes somewhat attenuated when applied to the franchise relationship, and vicarious liability premised upon the existence of a master/servant relationship is conceptually difficult to adapt to the franchising context. If the operational standards included in the typical franchise agreement for the protection of the franchisor's trademark were broadly construed as capable of meeting the "control or right to control" test that is generally used to determine respondeat superior liability, then franchisors would almost always be exposed to vicarious liability for the torts of their franchisees. We see no justification for such a broad rule of franchisor

vicarious liability. If vicarious liability is to be imposed against franchisors, a more precisely focused test is required.

We conclude that the marketing, quality, and operational standards commonly found in franchise agreements are insufficient to establish the close supervisory control or right of control necessary to demonstrate the existence of a master/servant relationship for all purposes or as a general matter. We hold, therefore, that a franchisor may be held vicariously liable for the tortious conduct of its franchisee only if the franchisor has control or a right of control over the daily operation of the specific aspect of the franchisee's business that is alleged to have caused the harm.

Here, although the license agreement between Arby's and DRI imposed many quality and operational standards on the franchise, Arby's did not have control or the right to control DRI's supervision of its employees. . . . [Granted, the franchise agreement provided, "LICENSEE shall hire, train, maintain and properly supervise sufficient, qualified and courteous personnel for the efficient operations of the Licensed Business," and it gave the franchisor the right to terminate the franchise if the franchisee violated the terms of the franchise agreement. But] DRI has sole control over the hiring and supervision of its employees. Arby's could not step in and take over the management of DRI's employees. Arby's right to terminate because of an uncured violation of the agreement is not the equivalent of a right to control the daily operation of the restaurant or actively manage DRI's workforce. Accordingly, we agree with the court of appeals and the circuit court that there is no genuine issue of material fact as to whether DRI is Arby's servant for purposes of the plaintiffs' respondeat superior claim against Arby's: clearly it is not. Arby's cannot be held vicariously liable for DRI's alleged negligent supervision of [DRI's employee].

3.   For examples of franchise agreements and the control they give the franchisor over the franchisee, see *Drexel*, 582 F.2d at 797–810 (franchise agreement reproduced in full); J.M. v. Shell Oil Co., 922 S.W.2d 759, 761–63 (Mo. banc 1996) (oil company franchise agreement); Note, Liability of a Franchisor for Acts of the Franchisee, 41 S.Cal.L.Rev. 143, 145–46 n.12 (summary of provisions in an Arthur Murray franchise agreement).

4.   Agency is not limited to the franchise context. Rather, it may exist whenever one person exercises or has control over the way in which another conducts business. Thus, in England v. MG Investments, Inc., 93 F.Supp.2d 718 (S.D.W.Va.2000), the court held that a mortgage broker might be an agent of a lender, so that the lender would be liable for the injury caused by fraudulent conduct of the broker.

5.   The foregoing notes have addressed actual agency. The court in *Drexel* also concludes there is a question of fact concerning apparent agency. What must a consumer establish to invoke apparent agency? Closely related to apparent agency are the concepts of apparent authority and agency by estoppel. See Restatement (Third) of Agency §§ 2.03, 2.05, 3.03 (2006).

If the rationale is that Todisco appeared to the public to be acting for UPC, why does the court emphasize the provisions of the contract between Todisco and UPC rather than the perceptions of the public?

Problem. Adams opens an auto repair shop. Unknown to Midas International, Inc., Adams calls his business "Midas." Adams negligently repairs *Consumer's* brakes, causing *Consumer's* car to crash. May *Consumer* assert apparent agency to recover against Midas International, Inc.?

6. What representations of authority are sufficient to justify a conclusion of apparent agency? For example, should the presence of numerous trade name signs at a gas station suffice? One court stated that on these facts the argument of apparent agency

> has no support in reason or authority. As well argue that, because the word "Chevrolet" or "Buick" is displayed in front of a place of business, General Motors would be estopped to claim that it was not the owner of the business. It is a matter of common knowledge that these trademark signs are displayed throughout the country by independent dealers.

Reynolds v. Skelly Oil Co., 287 N.W. 823, 827 (Iowa 1939). Accord, Mobil Oil Corp. v. Bransford, 648 So.2d 119, 120 (Fla.1995) ("In today's world, it is well understood that the mere use of franchise logos and related advertisements does not necessarily indicate that the franchisor has actual or apparent control over any substantial aspect of the franchisee's business or employment decisions").

On the other hand, in Gizzi v. Texaco, Inc., 437 F.2d 308 (3d Cir.1971), the court held that it was a question of fact whether Texaco's signs, advertising, and motto ("Trust your car to the man who wears the star") represented a franchisee's authority to act on behalf of Texaco. See Emerson, Franchisors' Liability When Franchisees Are Apparent Agents: An Empirical and Policy Analysis of "Common Knowledge" About Franchising, 20 Hofstra L. Rev. 609, 651–56 (1992) (overwhelming percentages of survey respondents erroneously believed that various nationally known retailers were owned by the franchisors). Consider also Cullen v. BMW of North America, Inc., 490 F.Supp. 249, 253–54 (E.D.N.Y.1980), where plaintiff sued the importer-distributor to recover the $18,000 he had paid the dealership (Bavarian Auto Sales), which went out of business before delivering his car:

> [P]laintiff claims BMW/NA permitted Bavarian to display prominently the BMW logo on its premises, in advertising and promotional campaigns, and on Bavarian's stationery and sales invoices in accordance with "reasonable suggestions set forth by BMW/NA." Dealer Standard Provisions § 4(c). The record reveals that Bavarian's sale slips clearly read "Bavarian Auto Sales and Service, Inc." and these words were flanked on either side by the BMW logo. The Bavarian stationery contained, moreover, the words "authorized sales and service" beneath the BMW logo. Plaintiff asserts that under these circum-

stances a man of reasonable prudence could conclude that Bavarian was BMW/NA's agent.

. . . BMW stands for Bayerische Motoren Worke or Bavarian Motor Works. Unlike the situation in *Oberlin* and *Stalzer,* in which the entities were clearly separate and distinct, Bavarian Motor Works and Bavarian Auto Sales and Service, Inc., are sufficiently alike—taken together with other indicia of agency—as to make summary judgment on plaintiff's contention that an agency by estoppel arose inappropriate at this time. Although the claim might be difficult to establish at trial, plaintiff should have the opportunity to present the issue to a trier of fact. Nothing in the court's comments, of course, should be construed as an opinion on the merits of this or any other claim.

7. An essential element of apparent agency is reasonable reliance, that is, the plaintiff must reasonably have relied on the defendant's manifestations that the person with whom the plaintiff dealt was the agent of the defendant. Reliance and reasonableness of the reliance obviously are questions of fact, but the jury (or other fact finder) may not consider these questions unless the consumer introduces sufficient evidence to support the claim. What level of proof must the consumer make?

In Gizzi v. Texaco, Inc., Question 6 supra, the trial court directed a verdict for Texaco but the Third Circuit reversed because plaintiff testified that Texaco's extensive advertising, which was designed to convey the impression that Texaco dealers were skilled in automotive servicing, had instilled in him a sense of confidence in Texaco and its products. On the other hand, in Crittendon v. State Oil Co., 222 N.E.2d 561 (Ill.App.1966), plaintiff sued State Oil for damage to his car that occurred while it was in the possession of one Mendenhall, with whom plaintiff had left it for repairs. The service station displayed two signs containing the word "State," and tools and repair facilities were plainly visible. There were no other signs, but Mendenhall was not actually the agent of State. Plaintiff recovered judgment against State on the theory of agency by estoppel. The Illinois Court of Appeals reversed:

In the case at bar, we do not believe that the evidence proved that the plaintiff relied on the signs as evidencing that Mendenhall was the agent of State. It is true that the plaintiff testified that he believed he was leaving his car with a representative of State, but he did not testify that this conclusion was based upon the inference he drew from the signs. There is no evidence that he had otherwise dealt with State or relied upon the reputation of State. Plaintiff had purchased products from the station only within the previous period of two months—the same period of time that Mendenhall had operated the station—and he conversed with Mendenhall concerning his experience in the repair of Chevrolets. No inquiry was made concerning Mendenhall's business relationship with State.

The evidence is consistent with the conclusion that the plaintiff was relying upon his dealings with Mendenhall and the latter's representations relative to his qualifications to repair Chevrolet automobiles, rather than any holding out by State that the repair work to be done on his car would be done by an agent of State. We do not believe that the evidence justifies the conclusion that the plaintiff had the repair work done, or dealt with the station in question, in reliance upon a holding out that he was dealing with State's agent. Thus, even if the presence of the two signs and the visibility of a grease rack, tools, and a place on the premises where cars could be repaired, could be said to be a holding out sufficient to give rise to an agency by estoppel— which we do not believe to be the case—the record before us does not support the conclusion that the plaintiff acted in reliance thereon.

Id. at 565. What additional evidence would have been necessary for the court to have affirmed the judgment of the trial court? How does plaintiff's evidence differ from the evidence of the plaintiff in *Gizzi*?

In B.P. Oil Corp. v. Mabe, 370 A.2d 554 (Md.1977), plaintiff's car overheated, and he went to a BP station operated by Faison. Instead of adding water to the radiator, the service station employee added gasoline, causing an explosion and a fire. Plaintiff's brother, a passenger in the car, testified that there was an Exxon station across the street from the BP station. Instead of pulling into the Exxon station, however, plaintiff waited until traffic cleared and turned into the BP station. Plaintiff testified that for over a year he had regularly done business with a BP station near his home. The jury returned a verdict for plaintiff, but the trial court granted judgment n.o.v. for defendant. The intermediate appellate court reversed and rendered judgment on the verdict. The Maryland Court of Appeals reversed:

> In this instance Mabe is an adult. [He testified that] he was attracted to Faison's station by "[n]othing except for the [fact that it was a] BP station, [and it] had BP signs, BP gas, BP pumps." This, added to the statement of Mabe that his reason for choosing the station in question was that he "always buy[s] BP gasoline, always deal[s] with BP," is but little different from a statement that one always buys a particular make of shoes, wears clothes with a certain label, drives an automobile produced by a certain manufacturer, eats a certain brand of breakfast cereal, or smokes a certain kind of cigarette. In short, the record lacks any evidence of reliance upon the part of Mabe. There has been comment in some of the cases and in the brief of Mabe relative to advertising which may have enticed prospective customers into places of business. The record in this instance is completely silent as to any advertising on the part of BP.

Id. 563–64. One judge dissented:

> What Mabe observed were the indications by signs and advertising that the station was a BP station; nothing attracted him "except for the BP station, . . . BP signs, BP gas, BP pumps." The attendant "had a BP uniform" which was "[g]reen with the yellow BP," "had a BP hat and just a regular BP service man." . . .

Moreover, in my view, a jury could find that BP's manifestations, reasonably interpreted, caused Mabe to believe that BP consented to have Faison service his car. According to the majority's position, it is common knowledge that a substantial portion of gas stations are independently owned and that the signs mean merely that a customer may purchase BP products. The short answer is that many stations are company owned, and BP, as a principal, is responsible for the information which came to Mabe's attention. In this instance, although Mabe saw all these indicia of BP control, he saw no sign—and there was none—which stated that Faison was the sole owner of the business. In my view, Mabe reasonably assimilated the information available to him and concluded that Faison was a BP agent. . . .

I believe also that the evidence was sufficient to permit a jury to conclude that Faison's apparent authority caused Mabe justifiably to rely on Faison's skill. . . . Mabe testified that in addition to the BP station, there were two other stations within sight when he noticed that his engine was overheating. He chose to enter the BP station because "I always buy BP gasoline, *always deal with BP*." (Emphasis added.) That he had patronized a BP station near his home for about a year prior to the accident provided support for this testimony. Mabe's statement, although perhaps not explicit, clearly permitted the jury to infer that he trusted the skill of those whom he thought were BP's agents, as well as the quality of BP's products.

The majority, on the other hand, emphasizes that Mabe presented no evidence to show that BP's media advertising encouraged reliance on the skill of BP's agents, and therefore concludes that it was unreasonable for Mabe to rely on Faison's *skill*. Rather, in the majority's view, reliance only on Faison's *products* was justified.

The logic of the majority's opinion completely escapes me. BP's media advertising is irrelevant to the determination of reliance because Mabe has presented a compelling case of justification for his reliance, superior to any which he might have presented had he relied solely on advertising. Mabe relied not on impersonal media commercials, but rather on his substantial and continuous personal experience with BP over a period of more than a year. In short, Mabe's patronage of a BP station, although not Faison's BP, more effectively established Mabe's trust in BP's skill and products than any advertising could have hoped to accomplish.

Id. at 564–65. Why do you suppose the majority thinks that evidence that a consumer always selects a particular product is not evidence of reliance on the producer of that product? See Cullen v. BMW of North America, Inc., 531 F.Supp. 555, 560 (E.D.N.Y.1982), a continuation of the litigation referred to in Question 6 above:

Although plaintiff offered into evidence various public manifestations of a relationship between Bavarian and BMW/NA, he failed to prove his reliance on Bavarian's *authority to act* for BMW/NA. Similarly, there is no evidence of Cullen's belief that the transaction was entered into by or for BMW/NA. On the contrary, plaintiff's own testimony shows there was an absence of reliance on advertisements, on the similarity between the corporate names of Bavarian and BMW/NA (Bavarian Motor Works), or on the BMW logo appearing on the sales slip.

Plaintiff did testify as to his reliance on the BMW logo appearing on the outside of Bavarian's premises, but the question remains to what his reliance was directed. The testimony shows not a belief that Bavarian had authority to act for BMW/NA, but that the BMW logo represented a particular quality of cars sold at Bavarian. Since this testimony indicates, at most, Cullen's reliance on Bavarian's authority to sell BMW automobiles, plaintiff failed to carry its burden of proving the belief essential to agency by estoppel.

Similarly, in O'Banner v. McDonald's Corp., 670 N.E.2d 632, 635 (Ill.1996), when a consumer sued to recover for injuries sustained when he slipped and fell in a bathroom in a McDonald's restaurant, the court stated,

. . . [T]he record before us is devoid of anything remotely suggesting that the necessary reliance was present here. The pleadings and affidavit . . . state only that [plaintiff] slipped and fell in the restroom of a McDonald's restaurant. They give no indication as to why he went to the restaurant in the first place. The fact that this was a McDonald's may have been completely irrelevant to his decision. For all we know, [plaintiff] went there simply because it provided the closest bathroom when he needed one or because some friend asked to meet him there.

8. If the consumer succeeds in establishing an agency relationship between the franchisor and the franchisee, the franchisor is liable for the franchisee's conduct. Should the franchisor be liable for all of the franchisee's conduct? If not, what criteria should determine which conduct of the franchisee should be attributed to the franchisor?

Should the franchisor be liable for the franchisee's negligence in connection with performing the obligations of the contract with the consumer? See *Drexel* and Chevron Oil Co. v. Sutton, quoted in Question 2 supra.

Should the franchisor be liable for the franchisee's simple failure to perform the obligations of the contract with the consumer? See Nichols v. Arthur Murray, Inc., discussed in Question 2 supra, and Wood v. Holiday Inns, Inc., 508 F.2d 167 (5th Cir.1975).

Should the franchisor be liable for the franchisee's fraud? See Kuchta v. Allied Builders Corp., 98 Cal.Rptr. 588 (Cal.App.1971) (yes); Hollingsworth v. American Finance Corp., 271 N.W.2d 872 (Wis.1978) (yes, even though the conduct was fraudulent also against the principal).

Should the franchisor's liability depend on whether the consumer's theory is apparent agency rather than actual agency?

9.   If a debt collection agency violates the Fair Debt Collection Practices Act, can the consumer recover from the creditor whose debt the agency is attempting to collect?

Would it be relevant that the debt collector was to receive as compensation one half of whatever it collected from the consumer? that the debt collector was empowered to settle the claim on whatever terms it believed desirable?

Assume that an independent repossession company is hired by a creditor to repossess a consumer's car. If the repossession company commits a breach of the peace in violation of UCC section 9–609, is the creditor liable?

10.   Agency is not the only theory under which the franchisor is liable for the acts of the franchisee. Negligence may also be available. For example, in *Cullen v. BMW*, Question 7 supra page 741, at 743, the distributor (BMW/NA) knew that the financial condition of the dealer (Bavarian) was precarious and that the dealer had in the past failed to deliver cars to consumers who had made deposits on them. The court held that the distributor owed a duty to plaintiff

> to prevent the risk of harm to BMW customers which results when dealers, whose financial instability and unscrupulous business practices are known to BMW/NA, are permitted to maintain the appearance of a responsible authorized BMW dealer subsequent to termination of the dealer agreement. . . . Not only did there exist a significant relationship between BMW/NA and Bavarian, defendant had ample opportunity to prevent Bavarian from wrongfully obtaining plaintiff's money while holding itself out as an authorized dealer.
>
> As the facts indicate, upon expiration of the dealer agreement, three weeks prior to the sales contract with plaintiff, defendant could have caused Bavarian to remove all BMW signs, refrain from using BMW trademarks and printed materials, and cease operating as an authorized BMW dealer. Thus . . . defendant acquiesced to circumstances which it should have reasonably known presented a substantial risk of harm to plaintiff. Most importantly, defendant had both opportunity and capability to decrease or foreclose the risk of harm. Therefore, a duty of care arose to avoid subjecting BMW customers to the unreasonable exposure to financial injury.

531 F.Supp. at 563–64. The court proceeded to hold that BMW/NA breached that duty and was liable for the $18,000 that plaintiff had paid Bavarian. On appeal, a divided Second Circuit reversed the trial court's judgment, holding that it was not foreseeable to defendant that the dealer would engage in the criminal act of absconding with plaintiff's money. 691 F.2d 1097 (2d Cir.1982).

11.   Problem. *Consumer* purchases a heat pump system for her house from *Dealer*. The system is made by *Manufacturer*, who has appointed *Dealer* to be its authorized dealer. *Dealer* also sells the heating and air conditioning equipment of other manufacturers. *Dealer* improperly installs the system, causing it to malfunction and need repairs costing $2,000. In addition, *Consumer* incurs temporary heating costs of $200. Can *Consumer* recover from *Manufacturer*?

B.   Liability of the Financer for the Misconduct of the Seller

(1)   Background

Few sellers of consumer goods actually wait for the consumer's monthly payments. Instead, they typically have the consumer sign an installment contract and/or a promissory note, which they promptly transfer to a financial institution. Or they may encourage the consumer to procure the credit elsewhere, either by borrowing money from a lender or by using a bank credit card to charge the purchase. Common to each of these forms of credit is that ultimately the consumer's obligation is to make installment payments to the financer. Also common to each form is a potential problem: what should the consumer do if the product is defective, or if the transaction is unconscionable, or if the seller has procured the transaction by misrepresentation? Of course, the consumer has a claim against the seller. But may the consumer, while pursuing this claim against the seller, suspend the monthly payments to the financer? And if the financer sues, may the consumer counterclaim against the financer for the injury caused by the seller?

It is commonly said that the assignee of a contract stands in the shoes of the assignor. This means that the assignee's right to enforce the contract is subject to performance of the contract by the assignor. It suggests an affirmative answer to the questions above: if the seller has breached a warranty, the financer's right to payment is subject to the consumer's right to relief for the seller's breach. Historically, however, the answer has been "no," because sellers and financers developed techniques for making the consumer's obligation to pay independent of the seller's obligations to perform its promises and comply with applicable legal requirements.

One technique entails the use of a promissory note. The original version of Article 3 of the UCC divides promissory notes into two categories—negotiable and not negotiable. To be a negotiable instrument, the note must meet the requirements of sections 3–104 to 3–112. A person who acquires a negotiable instrument in good faith, for value, and without notice of any defense to it is a holder in due course.[1] And a holder in due course takes the note free of most claims and defenses that arise in consumer transactions.[2] Hence, these provisions require the consumer who signs a promissory note to pay the financer even though the seller has failed to perform. The following excerpt from the report of the National

---

1. See Sections 3–302(1), 3–303, 3–304, 1–201(19), (25).

2. Section 3–305.

Commission on Consumer Finance explains why the law developed this way:

> In 1758, in the case of Miller v. Race, the King's Bench of England held that a Bank of England promissory bearer note was "treated as money; as cash" by business men dealing "in the ordinary course and transaction of business." The court decided that when such a note was stolen and thereafter sold to a person who paid fair value and had no notice of the theft (a bona fide purchaser), that bona fide purchaser would prevail over all persons claiming the note, even the original owner. The rationale for this decision was based on the fear that the growth and soundness of commerce would have been impeded or destroyed if a contrary decision were reached. This fear was probably well-founded because promissory notes of the Bank of England were not "legal tender," but were nevertheless "passed from hand to hand, serving many of the purposes of paper money, which did not exist in England at the time." To allow persons other than bona fide purchasers to claim ownership to the note would indeed have had an adverse affect on commerce.
>
> With the development of paper money, the emphasis on affording a good faith purchaser of notes and contracts freedom from claims to the instrument gradually shifted to permit the good faith purchaser to cut off defenses which the obligor may have against paying the note.

NCCF, Consumer Credit in the United States 34 (1972). For a fuller treatment, see Eggert, Held Up in Due Course: Codification and the Victory of Form Over Intent in Negotiable Instrument Law, 35 Creighton L. Rev. 363 (2002).

The holder in due course doctrine applies to promissory notes, but not to installment contracts (because they do not meet the definition of negotiable instruments in section 3–104). Hence creditors developed another technique for making the consumer's obligation independent of the seller's obligation. It consists of a contractual provision by which the consumer promises not to assert against any assignee of the contract any defense he or she might have against the seller. If this promise is enforceable, the assignee can enforce the consumer's obligation to pay even though the seller has failed to perform. This contractual provision is known as a waiver of defenses clause and is expressly validated by section 9–403 of the UCC. Consequently, whether the seller uses a promissory note, an installment sales contract, or both, the UCC permits the cut-off of claims and defenses.

But that is not all. If for some reason neither the holder in due course doctrine nor a waiver of defenses clause is available, there is still another technique for insulating the financer from the consumer's claims and defenses. The only basis asserted thus far for subjecting the financer to the claims and defenses the consumer has against the seller is that the seller has transferred to the financer the right to receive the consumer's payments. If there is no transfer from the seller to the financer, then that basis is gone. Hence, instead of selling on credit and assigning the contract to the financer, the seller may steer the consumer to a particular lender whom the seller knows will loan the money that the consumer needs for the purchase. Since the consumer obtains the financing directly from the lender, and since the loan is nominally an independent transaction, the lender's right to payment is not subject to the seller's performance of the separate sales contract. This technique is known as direct-loan financing. Sometimes a seller transports or accompanies the consumer to the lender, a practice known as "dragging the body."

Courts have been troubled by the unfairness implicit in making the consumer pay even though the seller has failed to perform. The more the financer controls or participates in the seller's business, the greater the unfairness. Therefore, the courts developed the "close-connectedness" doctrine, under which they deny holder in due course status to financers whose connection with the seller is sufficiently close. The theory is similar to the theory underlying the courts' conclusion that a sale of goods on credit, coupled with an immediate transfer to a financer, is really a loan subject to the usury laws (see pages 394–407 supra). Thus, depending on the particular facts, courts have viewed the seller as the agent of the lender, have viewed the seller and lender as one intertwined entity, and have concluded that the lender lacked the good faith necessary for holder in due course status. They have applied the close-connectedness doctrine not only to preclude the holder of a negotiable instrument from being a holder in due course, but also to preclude the financer from enforcing a waiver of defenses clause.

The leading case is Unico v. Owen, 232 A.2d 405, 410, 412–13 (N.J. 1967), in which the court stated:

> In the field of negotiable instruments, good faith is a broad concept. The basic philosophy of the holder in due course status is to encourage free negotiability of commercial paper by removing certain anxieties of one who takes the paper as an innocent purchaser knowing no reason why the paper is not as sound as its face would indicate. It would seem to follow, therefore, that the more the holder knows about the underlying transaction, and particularly the more he controls or participates or becomes involved in it, the less he fits the role of a good faith purchaser for value; the closer his relationship to the underlying agreement which is the source of the note, the less need there is for giving him the tension-free rights considered necessary in a fast-moving, credit-extending commercial world.
>
>   . . .
>
> Unico is a partnership formed expressly for the purpose of financing Universal Stereo Corporation, and Universal agreed to pay all costs up to a fixed amount in connection with Unico's formation. The elaborate contract between them, dated August 24, 1962, recited that Universal was engaged in the merchandising of records and stereophonic sets, and that it desired to borrow money from time to time from Unico, "secured by the assignment of accounts receivable, prom-

issory notes, trade acceptances, conditional sales contracts, chattel mortgages, leases, installment contracts, or other forms of agreement evidencing liens." Subject to conditions set out in the agreement, Unico agreed to lend Universal up to 35% of the total amount of the balances of customers' contracts assigned to Unico subject to a limit of $50,000, in return for which Universal submitted to a substantial degree of control of its entire business operation by the lender. As collateral security for the loans, Universal agreed to negotiate "to the lender" all customers' notes listed in a monthly schedule of new sales contracts, and to assign all conditional sale contracts connected with the notes, as well as the right to any monies due from customers.

Specific credit qualifications for Universal's record album customers were imposed by Unico; requirements for the making of the notes and their endorsement were established, and the sale contracts had to be recorded in the county recording office. All such contracts were required to meet the standards of the agreement between lender and borrower, among them being that the customer's installment payment term would not exceed 36 months and "every term" of the Unico–Universal agreement was to "be deemed incorporated into all assignments" of record sales contracts delivered as security for the loans. It was further agreed that Unico should have all the rights of Universal under the contracts as if it were the seller, including the right to enforce them in its name, and Unico was given an irrevocable power to enforce such rights.

In the event of Universal's default on payment of its loans, Unico was authorized to deal directly with the record buyers with respect to payment of their notes and to settle with and discharge such customers. Unico was empowered to place its representatives on Universal's premises with full authority to take possession of the books and records; or otherwise, it could inspect the records at any time; and it was given a "special property interest" in such records. Financial statements were required to be submitted by Universal "at least semi-annually"; and two partners of Unico were to be paid one-quarter of one per cent. interest on the loans as a management service charge, in addition to the interest to be paid Unico. Significant also in connection with the right to oversee Universal's business is a warranty included in the contract. It warrants that Universal owns free and clear "all merchandise referred to and described in [the sales] contracts, * * * at the time of making the sale creating such contracts." Obviously this was not the fact, otherwise Universal would not have discontinued shipping records to its customers, such as Owen. If Universal did not have such a store of records, as warranted, Unico might well have had reason to suspect its borrower's financial stability.

This general outline of the Universal–Unico financing agreement serves as evidence that Unico not only had a thorough knowledge of the nature and method of operation of Universal's business, but also exercised extensive control over it. Moreover, obviously it had a large, if not decisive, hand in the fashioning and supplying of the form of contract and note used by Universal, and particularly in setting the terms of the record album sales agreement, which were designed to put the buyer-consumer in an unfair and burdensome legal strait jacket and to bar any escape no matter what the default of the seller, while permitting the note-holder, contract-assignee to force payment from him by enveloping itself in the formal status of holder in due course. To say the relationship between Unico and the business operations of Universal was close, and that Unico was involved therein, is to put it mildly.

To the extent the courts insist on the existence of substantial involvement by the financer in the seller's business, relief for consumers is incomplete. For example, in Block v. Ford Motor Credit Co., 286 A.2d 228 (D.C.App.1972), the consumer (Block) bought a car that proved to be defective. When the seller failed to make repairs, the consumer unilaterally reduced the amount of his installment payments. The assignee-financer sued, relying on a waiver of defenses clause. The trial court gave judgment for the financer, and the appellate court affirmed:

> According to Block "good faith" is lacking here because there is a close connection between the seller, an authorized Ford dealer, and the assignee, FMCC, a wholly-owned subsidiary of the Ford Motor Company.
>
> . . .
>
> We are unable to say that the trial court's conclusion based upon the undisputed evidence was clearly erroneous. While Maryland recognizes the "close connectedness doctrine," there is no showing on this record that FMCC had a substantial voice in, or control of, or a vested interest in the underlying transaction. See Unico v. Owen, 50 N.J. 101, 232 A.2d 405 (1967). The following facts—(1) that FMCC prepared and supplied sales contract forms to the seller; (2) that it permitted its name to be displayed for advertising purposes in seller's place of business; (3) that it was aware of some complaints about the seller; and (4) that it acquired about 2,500 such contracts from the seller in each of the last three years—are not sufficient alone to demonstrate that FMCC had a substantial voice in, or control of, or a vested interest in the underlying sales transaction.

Id. at 232–33. See also Sullivan v. United Dealers Corp., 486 S.W.2d 699 (Ky.1972) (fact that the financer and the seller had done a large amount of business over a twelve-year period is not enough to preclude holder in due course status). On the other hand, see Union Mortgage Co. v. Barlow, 595 So.2d 1335 (Ala.1992) (financing arrangements between a home improvement contractor and a lender make the contractor an agent of the lender, which is responsible for misconduct of the contractor); Bramlett v. Adamson Ford, page 42 supra.

Legislatures also have grappled with the problem of the holder in due course doctrine in consumer transactions. By the early 1970s over forty states had enacted at least some restriction on the creditor's ability to cut off the consumer's claims and defenses. In some states the restrictions apply to all consumer transactions; in most, however, they apply to only some kinds of consumer transactions. And only a few statutes enable the consumer to assert seller-related claims and defenses against a direct lender. The restrictions tend to fall into two categories. Compare the approach in Wisconsin:

> (1) In a consumer credit sale or lease transaction, no seller or lessor shall take a negotiable instrument (§ 403.104), other than a check, as evidence of the obligation of the customer.

> (2) In a consumer loan transaction which constitutes an interlocking loan (§ 422.408), no creditor shall take a negotiable instrument (§ 403.104), other than a check, as evidence of the obligation of the customer.

> (3) The holder to whom an instrument issued in violation of this section is negotiated, notwithstanding that the holder may otherwise be a holder in due course of such instrument, is subject to all claims and defenses of the customer against the payee, subject to sub. (4).[3]

with the approach in Missouri:

> The rights of a holder or assignee of an instrument, account, contract, right, chattel paper or other writing other than a check or draft, which evidences the obligation of a natural person as buyer, lessee, or borrower in connection with the purchase or lease of consumer goods or services, are subject to all defenses and setoffs of the debtor arising from or out of such sale or lease, notwithstanding any agreement to the contrary, only as to amounts then owing and as a matter of defense to or setoff against a claim by the holder or assignee; provided, however, with respect to goods only, the rights of the debtor under this section may be asserted to the seller at the address at which he did business at the time of the sale and must be so asserted within ninety days after receipt of the goods.[4]

See also UCCC sections 3.307, 3.404(1). What is the critical shortcoming in the approach of the Missouri statute?

(2) THE FTC RULE

Because the case law and statutory approach at the state level was so spotty, in 1975 the FTC promulgated a trade regulation rule entitled Preservation of Consumers' Claims and Defenses, but commonly known as the Holder Rule, 16 C.F.R. Part 433 (reproduced in the Statutory Supplement). Please read it carefully. Note that the Rule applies not only to notes and contracts used by a seller, but also to direct loans from a lender to a consumer if the consumer uses the proceeds to buy goods or services from a

---

3. Wis.Stat.Ann. § 422.406.   **4.** Vernon's Ann.Mo.Stat. § 408.405.

seller who has the specified relationship with the lender. The Rule thus goes further than the law had gone in all but a few states.

(a) Transactions Covered

The heart of the Rule is the notice that must be included in the note or contract. The general intent of the notice is to make the consumer's obligation dependent on the seller's performance. Before examining in detail the effect of the notice, however, it is necessary to understand when the creditor must include the notice.

QUESTIONS

1. Which of the following transactions are within the scope of the Rule:

(a) the sale of aluminum siding to a homeowner.

(b) the construction of a garage to be attached to an existing house.

(c) the sale of a tractor to a farmer for $15,000.

(d) the sale of a $30,000 mobile home to a consumer whose adult child will live in it. (Note the reference in section 433.1(e) to the Truth-in-Lending Act and Regulation Z; see Regulation Z section 226.3(b).)

(e) the issuance of a credit card by Sears Roebuck & Co.

(f) the lease of a TV for an indefinite period for $30 per month, terminable by the lessee at any time after the first month.

2. The Rule applies not only to persons who sell on credit, but also to persons who sell for cash, if the source of the consumer's cash is a lender with a referral or affiliation relationship with the seller. The UCCC, in section 3.405, also subjects the lender to the consumer's claims and defenses against a closely connected seller. The UCCC spells out six specific situations in which the consumer may assert rights against the lender. The FTC rule, on the other hand, is much less detailed (§ 433.1(d)(1)-(2)). Which of the following are within section 433.1(d):

(a) When *Consumer* indicates a desire for credit, *Seller* directs her to *Lender* as a likely source.

(b) *Seller* regularly supplies customers with a printed list of the six lenders whose offices are closest to *Seller's* store.

(c) When *Consumer* indicates a desire for credit, *Seller* suggests three lenders and asks *Consumer* to pick one. She does. *Seller* then calls the one she has selected, passes on pertinent information, and asks whether the lender would be willing to make the loan. (Is this transaction within UCCC section 3.405?)

3. Problem. *Seller* sells *Consumers* a mobile home for $30,000, using a contract document supplied by *Financer*. This document contains the FTC Notice. Four years later interest rates decline and *Consumers* want to

refinance this transaction to take advantage of the lower rates. *Bank* agrees to make this loan. Must *Bank* include the Notice in its contract?

4. Problem. Assume *Lender* is affiliated with *Seller*. If *Lender* loans *Consumer* $3,000 and *Consumer* uses the proceeds to buy a used car from *Seller* for $2,500 and to pay off a MasterCard debt of $500, is the transaction a "purchase money loan"?

If *Seller* not only sells the car but also loans the $500 is the transaction within the Rule?

5. Problem. *Seller* and *Bank* have an agreement that *Seller* will refer its credit customers to *Bank* and *Bank* will give those applicants preferential treatment.

Consumer has a checking account at *Bank*. Under the terms of this account, if *Consumer* does not have sufficient funds in the account to cover a particular check, *Bank* will automatically loan *Consumer* the amount necessary to cover the check. The finance charge and other terms of this potential loan are spelled out in the agreement establishing the checking account.

Consumer sees an ad by *Seller* and decides to purchase a refrigerator from *Seller*. *Consumer* pays for the item by writing a check for $900 even though he knows he only has $500 in his checking account.

Is this a "purchase money loan"?

(b) Consequences of Noncompliance

The Rule requires the inclusion of a legend in the contract or note that the consumer signs. And the contracts and notes in most consumer transactions comply with the Rule and contain the legend. But what if a seller or lender erroneously takes the position that the Rule does not apply to its transactions? For example, for a number of years proprietary vocational schools and their financers erroneously took the position that the FTC Rule did not apply to them. Other sellers and lenders may erroneously believe that they do not have the relationship necessary for the existence of a "purchase money loan." Or they may simply disregard the law. In these situations several questions arise:

(1) What remedy does the consumer have against the seller or lender who omits the language?

(2) If the consumer has a complaint about the seller's conduct or performance, may the consumer assert the complaint against the holder of the contract? For example, assume that a used car dealer fails to include the required language on an installment contract, which the dealer then assigns to a bank. If the car is not merchantable, does the consumer still have to pay the bank? Compare UCCC sections 3.307, 3.404(1).

(3) What is the relationship between state law and the FTC Rule? If a creditor in St. Louis omits the required statement, does the Missouri statute apply? If the creditor includes the required statement,

does the Missouri statute apply? If a creditor in Milwaukee includes the required statement, does the Wisconsin statute apply?

Iron & Glass Bank v. Franz

Pennsylvania Court of Common Pleas, 1978.
9 D. & C.3d 419.

WETTICK, J.

These are actions by Iron and Glass Bank (Iron and Glass) to recover money allegedly owing on two loan agreements. . . . [D]efendants aver that they are excused from making payments on the loan agreements because the proceeds from the loans were used to purchase goods and services from First Lady Spa, Inc. (Spa), which breached its agreements with defendants. In their new matter, defendants further aver that the promissory notes upon which plaintiff sued were executed to purchase these goods and services; that the promissory notes were prepared by, at the direction of and in the offices of Spa; and that Iron and Glass and Spa had a long course of dealings in which all loan documents dealing with the purchase of memberships in Spa were prepared by employees of Spa in the name of Iron and Glass in an effort to defraud buyers by cutting off rights and defenses.

Iron and Glass has filed motions for judgments on the pleadings. The issue raised by these motions is whether Iron and Glass, as the holder of these promissory notes, is subject to the claims and defenses which defendants may have against Spa.

I.

Iron and Glass contends that it entered into a simple cash loan agreement with defendants, governed by the Consumer Discount Company Act, and consequently the default by a third party from whom defendants purchased goods and services with the funds which they borrowed from Iron and Glass has nothing to do with the transactions between Iron and Glass and defendants. In support of this contention, Iron and Glass relies upon the documents governing the transactions which on their face are personal loan agreements between Iron and Glass and defendants.

Defendants, on the other hand, contend that these transactions are governed by the Goods and Services Installment Sales Act, which protects claims of buyers from being cut off through assignment (see § 1401(a) of the act).[a] The Goods and Services Installment Sales Act governs retail installment contracts which include any contracts for a retail installment sale between a buyer and a seller of goods and services purchased for other than a commercial or business use. . . . Thus the critical issue is wheth-

---

a. No contract, obligation or agreement shall contain any provision by which:

(a) The buyer agrees not to assert against a seller a claim or defense arising

out of the sale or agrees not to assert against an assignee such a claim or defense. . . .

Pa. Cons. Stat. Ann. tit. 69, § 1401(a).—ed.

er we view the Spa/Iron and Glass/defendants' dealings as a single transaction for the purchase of goods and services for a time sale price payable in installments or as a cash transaction between Spa and defendants for the purchase of goods and services with proceeds obtained from a separate loan transaction between Iron and Glass and defendants. And for the reasons set forth below, we believe that Spa/Iron and Glass/defendants dealings should be treated as a single transaction.

According to the allegations in defendants' pleadings, defendants approached Spa to purchase goods and services on credit; it was the decision of Spa to provide the credit through Iron and Glass's papers; Iron and Glass was selected by Spa—and not defendants; and the proceeds from the loan could be used only to purchase goods and services from Spa.

Under these facts the transaction although purportedly cast as two events—a loan and sale of goods and services—is actually one transaction for the purchase of goods and services on credit because the purchase is part and parcel of the loan agreement. And because the legislature, through the Goods and Services Installment Sales Act, provides protections to consumers who purchase goods and services on credit, such protections should extend to all credit transactions in which the seller supplies, provides or arranges for the extension of credit in order to effect the purposes of the legislation. Unless we look at substance—and not form—to determine when the Goods and Services Installment Sales Act applies, we permit the act to be avoided at the will of the very persons whom the act is intended to regulate. Clearly, this could not have been the intention of our legislature.

In almost every consumer credit transaction, financing is ultimately provided by a lending institution. Typically, the purchaser enters into an installment sales agreement with the seller and the seller immediately assigns this agreement to a lending institution which has already reviewed the purchaser's credit rating and agreed to accept the assignment. The seller, however, accomplishes the same result by using the documents of the lending institution to which the installment sales agreement would have been assigned. Thus if we permit the seller who secures credit in this fashion to avoid the Goods and Services Installment Sales Act, we render ineffective the regulatory scheme.

. . .

II.

The Federal Trade Commission recently adopted a trade regulation rule . . . .

If the allegations in defendants' answer and new matter are correct, Spa violated this trade regulation rule by referring defendants to Iron and Glass and accepting, as payment for its goods and services, the proceeds from a loan agreement between Iron and Glass and defendants which did not contain a provision subjecting the holder of the agreement to any claims and defenses which defendants could assert against Spa. However, these allegations set forth no violation of the Federal trade regulation rule on the part of Iron and Glass because the rule . . . places a duty only on the seller to insure that the preservation of defenses provision is included within the loan agreement. Thus as a matter of Federal law, defendants' answer and new matter do not set forth a defense to plaintiff's action arising out of this Federal trade regulation rule.

However, where a creditor knows that a seller of goods or services is acting in an illegal manner as a matter of state law, the creditor shall not be insulated from the seller's wrongdoings. Although the Motor Vehicle Sales Finance Act makes it unlawful only for the seller to require the execution of a note by the buyer which, when separately negotiated, will cut off rights or defenses which the buyer may have against the original seller (69 P.S. § 615(G)),[b] our appellate courts have held that the assignee of a negotiable note executed in violation of this act, who knows or should have known of the violation, takes the note subject to any rights or defenses which the buyer may have against the original seller. . . .

In addition, we rule that Iron and Glass's knowing participation in a transaction which violated the FTC "preservation of defenses" trade regulation rule constitutes an unfair or deceptive act or practice within the meaning of section 2(4)(xvii) of the Pennsylvania Unfair Trade Practices and Consumer Protection Law, which defines an unfair or deceptive act or practice to include "engaging in any other fraudulent conduct which creates a likelihood of confusion or of misunderstanding." Thus defendants are entitled to the protections of section 3 of the act which declares unlawful any unfair or deceptive act or practice, as defined in section 2 of this act. . . .

The FTC regulation preserving defenses serves to eliminate confusion and misunderstanding created through an artificial bifurcation of a transaction by an installment seller in an effort to insulate the duty to pay from the duty to perform. The FTC is a Federal regulatory body created by Congress to, inter alia, develop commercial standards which bar practices that are overreaching and unfair. Consequently, where the FTC has defined conduct which creates a likelihood of confusion or mistake as an unfair trade practice, we construe our Unfair Trade Practices and Consumer Protection Law to incorporate this standard.

This construction of section 2(4)(xvii) of this act is supported by Com. v. Monumental Properties, Inc., 459 Pa. 450, 329 A.2d 812 (1974). According to the court's decision in the Monumental Properties case, the Pennsyl-

b. Section 615 provides, in part:

F. No installment sale contract shall contain any provision relieving the holder, or other assignee, from liability for any legal remedies which the buyer may have had against the seller under the contract or under any separate instrument executed in connection therewith.

G. No installment sale contract shall require or entail the execution of any note or series of notes by the buyer, which when separately negotiated, will cut off as to third parties any right of action or defense which the buyer may have against the original seller.—Ed.

vania Unfair Trade Practices and Consumer Protection Law is remedial legislation which shall be liberally construed to effect the purpose of preventing fraud. The legislature, according to our Supreme Court, chose not to delineate precisely the types of unfair and deceptive practices outlawed but rather chose a more flexible standard because of the recognition of the legislature that "no sooner is one fraud specifically defined and outlawed then another variant of it appears." And thus this section was designed to cover "generally all unfair and deceptive acts or practices in the conduct of trade or commerce."

According to the Monumental Properties decision, our Consumer Protection Law is based upon the Federal Trade Commission Act, and we should look to decisions under these acts for guidance and interpretation.

The FTC trade regulation rule barring the cut-off of defenses by assignment was promulgated pursuant to the provisions of the Federal Trade Commission Act which declare unlawful "unfair methods of competition" and "unfair or deceptive acts or practices." Thus by enforcing this trade regulation rule through the Pennsylvania Unfair Trade Practices and Consumer Protection Law which also outlaws "unfair methods of competition" and "unfair or deceptive acts or practices," we are using Federal models of the state consumer protection law "for guidance and interpretation."

Because the allegations within defendants' answer and new matter that Spa arranged the Iron and Glass/defendants loan, that defendants used the funds from this loan to purchase goods and services from Spa, and that Spa breached its agreement with defendants entitle defendants to assert against Iron and Glass any claims and defenses which defendants could assert against Spa, we deny Iron and Glass's motions for judgment on the pleadings.

QUESTIONS

1. Exactly why does the court conclude that the transaction is subject to the retail installment sales act rather than the small loan act?

2. Why doesn't the court rest its decision on the FTC Rule? Did the seller and the lender not violate the Rule?

3. In the latter part of its opinion, the court concludes that the lender violated the little-FTC act. What is the effect of this violation:

(a) Does it enable defendants to assert the seller's breach of contract?

(b) Does it enable defendants to recover damages for the lender's violation? Pennsylvania's little-FTC act provides:

Any person who purchases or leases goods or services primarily for personal, family or household purposes and thereby suffers any ascertainable loss of money or property, real or personal, as a result of the use or employment by any person of a method, act or practice declared unlawful by section 3 of this act, may bring a private action, to recover actual damages or one hundred dollars ($100), whichever is greater. The court may, in its discretion, award up to three times the actual damages sustained, but not less than one hundred dollars ($100), and may provide such additional relief as it deems necessary or proper. . . .

73 Penn.Stat. § 201–9.2(a).

4. With respect to the consumer's ability to assert claims when the required language is missing, compare the approach of the FTC Rule with the approach of sections 3.307 and 3.404(1) of the UCCC.

(c) Effectiveness of the Rule

The Rule is designed to enable the consumer to assert seller-related claims and defenses against the financer. Assuming the seller complies, to what extent does the Rule achieve this objective?

If the seller includes the required language on a promissory note and then negotiates the note to a financer, the financer probably is not a holder in due course under original section 3–302 of the UCC. This is so because the required language so qualifies the consumer's promise to pay that it is not "an unconditional promise or order to pay a sum certain." Therefore, the note is not a negotiable instrument, and the holder is not a holder in due course. In any event, the required language becomes part of the instrument and overrides the UCC's holder in due course doctrine.

In 1990 Article 3 was extensively revised, including several changes in recognition of the FTC Rule. Revised section 3–106(d) provides in effect that a note containing the language required by the FTC Rule may be a negotiable instrument but that a holder of that instrument is not a holder in due course. Stripped of holder in due course status, the holder is subject to the consumer's claims and defenses, within the parameters of the FTC-mandated language.

QUESTIONS

1. Assume that the seller includes the notice and assigns the contract. If the product is defective, may the consumer sue the financer, or may the consumer raise the claim only if the financer sues? Compare the Missouri statute, page 751 supra.

2. Problem. *Consumer* buys a small riding lawn mower from *Seller* pursuant to an installment sales contract that states a cash price of $1,600, a downpayment of $240, and twelve installment payments of $130, totaling $1,800. The contract complies with the FTC Rule. After *Consumer* has paid one installment of $130, *Seller* assigns the contract to *Bank*, and *Consumer* makes additional payments to *Bank* totaling $390. Then, while mowing her lawn one day, *Consumer* carefully sets the brake and gets off to remove a small branch in the path of the mower. A defect in the brake allows the mower to roll forward, severely injuring *Consumer's* right foot. She incurs medical expenses of $8,000 and pain and suffering that she values at $12,000. When *Consumer* fails to make any further payments, *Bank* sues. May *Consumer* counterclaim for her loss?

Would the result be different under UCCC section 3.404?

3. Problem. *Seller* includes in her contracts the notice required by the FTC Rule, and also the following provision:

> Buyer agrees not to assert against any subsequent holder as assignee of this contract any claim or defense that Buyer may have against the manufacturer or any intermediate supplier of the goods purchased hereunder.

Why would *Seller* include this provision? Is it consistent with the FTC Rule?

4. Problem. *Consumers* hire *Contractor* to remodel their kitchen. To pay for the work, they borrow $5,200 from *Bank*, which is affiliated with *Contractor*. As a result of the affiliation relationship, *Bank* includes the Holder Rule language in the loan contract. The loan contract also states, "*Bank* does not guarantee the material or workmanship nor does *Bank* inspect the work performed in exchange for the proceeds of this loan." *Contractor's* performance is grossly defective. What are *Consumers'* rights?

5. Please reread Question 3, page 753. Assume *Bank* includes the Holder Rule notice in its contract, and assume further that the home has defects. When *Consumers* stop paying, *Bank* sues. Can *Consumers* successfully assert their seller-related claims and defenses against *Bank*?

Ford Motor Credit Company v. Morgan

Supreme Judicial Court of Massachusetts, 1989.
404 Mass. 537, 536 N.E.2d 587.

O'CONNOR, JUSTICE.

[Defendants purchased a new Mercury from a dealer who assigned the retail installment contract to plaintiff. The contract, which contained the legend required by the FTC Rule, called for 36 monthly payments of $137. Defendants made the payments for 15 months, during which time "they experienced several problems with the automobile, such as water leaking into the trunk, a faulty head gasket, rust, hood misalignment, and loss of shine. Their greatest complaint was that, when left unattended, the transmission would shift from 'park' to 'reverse,' and would have to be shifted back to 'park' before the vehicle could be started." They encountered financial difficulty and made no further payment. Plaintiff repossessed the car, but before plaintiff could sell the car, it was extensively damaged by vandals. Plaintiff sued to recover the unpaid balance of the contract. Defendants counterclaimed alleging, *inter alia*, that the dealer had committed fraud. The jury found for defendants, and the trial court held that they had a valid defense in plaintiff's action to recover the unpaid installments.

But the court also held that defendants could not recover damages on any of their counterclaims. They appealed.]

The Morgans' first contention is that the explicit language of the notice provision contained in the contract, which subjects holders to all "claims and defenses which the debtor could assert against the seller" permits them to recover affirmatively from Ford Credit for the dealer's wrongdoing. As the Morgans acknowledge, that notice provision is mandated by a Federal Trade Commission (FTC) rule which provides that it is an unfair or deceptive act or practice to take or receive a consumer credit contract which fails to include that provision. 16 C.F.R. § 433.2 (1978). Therefore, we look to the FTC's purpose in enacting the rule as a guide to our interpretation of the contract provision.

The rule was designed to preserve the consumer's claims and defenses by cutting off the creditor's rights as a holder in due course. Federal Trade Commission, Preservation of Consumers' Claims and Defenses, Final Regulation, Proposed Amendment and Statement of Basis and Purpose, 40 Fed. Reg. 53505, 53524 (Nov. 18, 1975). Under the holder in due course principle, which would apply were it not for the contract provision mandated by the FTC rule, the creditor could "assert his right to be paid by the consumer despite misrepresentation, breach of warranty or contract, or even fraud on the part of the seller, and despite the fact that the consumer's debt was generated by the sale." 40 Fed. Reg. at 53507. Thus, "[being] prevented from asserting the seller's breach of warranty or failure to perform against the assignee of the consumer's instrument, the consumer [would lose] his most effective weapon—nonpayment." Id. at 53509. Eliminating holder in due course status prevents the assignee from demanding further payment when there has been assignor wrongdoing, and rearms the consumer with the "weapon" of nonpayment.

The FTC anticipated that in addition to nonpayment, affirmative recovery, that is, a judgment for damages against the assignee-creditor, would be available in limited circumstances. Thus, in its statement of policy and purpose, the FTC spelled out the avenues of relief under the rule as follows: "[A] consumer can (1) defend a creditor suit for payment of an obligation by raising a valid claim against a seller as a set-off, and (2) maintain an affirmative action against a creditor who has received payments for a return of monies paid on account. [T]he latter alternative will only be available where a seller's breach is so substantial that a court is persuaded that rescission and restitution are justified. The most typical example of such a case would involve non-delivery, where delivery was scheduled after the date payments to a creditor commenced." 40 Fed. Reg. at 53524. The FTC re-emphasized this point in stating, "[c]onsumers will not be in a position to obtain an affirmative recovery from a creditor, unless they have actually commenced payments and received little or nothing of value from the seller. In a case of non-delivery, total failure of performance, or the like, we believe the consumer is entitled to a refund of monies paid on account." Id. at 53527. Finally, the FTC anticipated that the rule would enable the courts to weigh the equities in the underlying sale, and "remain the final arbiters of equities between a seller and a consumer." Id. at 53524. Thus, the function of the rule is to allow consumers to stop payments, and, in limited circumstances, not present here, where equity requires, to provide for a return of monies paid. The FTC did not intend that the rule would, as a matter of course, entitle a consumer to a full refund of monies paid on account. It follows, of course, that there is no merit to the Morgans' assertions that the contractual language allows them affirmative recovery even beyond the amount they paid in. To expose a creditor to further affirmative liability would not only contravene the intention of the FTC, but would "place the creditor in the position of an absolute insurer or guarantor of the seller's performance." Home Sav. Ass'n v. Guerra, 733 S.W.2d 134, 136 (Tex.1987). This we decline to do.

The Morgans do not quarrel with the judge's conclusion that, in the circumstances, they had no right to rescind the sale. Further, they do not argue that they received little or nothing of value from the dealer. We do not imply that such an argument would have been appropriate. However, absent such a showing, and absent any support for the argument that the language in the contract should receive any interpretation other than the one the FTC intended it to have, the Morgans' contention that the language mandated by 16 C.F.R. § 433.2 (1978), affords them a right to affirmative recovery is without merit.[5] . . .

QUESTIONS

1. Please reread the legend required by the FTC Rule. The court's decision seems inconsistent with each sentence. Why does the court nevertheless conclude that defendants cannot assert their claims affirmatively in this case?

2. In an omitted portion of the opinion, the court states that defendants had paid plaintiff $2,056. The court holds that defendants do not have to pay the remaining $2,879, but they cannot get back any portion of the $2,056. What if defendants had only paid one installment instead of 15, i.e. what if they had only paid $137 and still owed $4,799. If plaintiff sued to recover the balance, how much could it recover? How much of the $137 could defendants get back by way of compensation for the dealer's fraud?

Compare the economic position of the parties after the litigation in *Morgan* with the position of the parties in this hypothetical variation. On what basis is the difference justified?

5. We do not hold that a consumer may only assert his rights defensively in response to a claim initiated by an assignee for balance due on the contract. This would be in clear contravention of the FTC's intention. 40 Fed. Reg. at 53526. Eachen v. Scott Hous. Sys., Inc., 630 F. Supp. 162, 164–165 (M.D.Ala. 1986). "Under such circumstances the financ- er may elect not to sue, in the hopes that the threat of an unfavorable credit report may move the consumer to pay." 40 Fed. Reg. at 53527. Therefore, it is clear that the account debtor may initiate suit to enforce his right, however limited it may be, to discontinue credit payments.

3. Under the approach of the court in *Morgan*, under what circumstances would a consumer be able to obtain affirmative recovery? In other words, when can it be said that "a seller's breach is so substantial that a court is persuaded that rescission and restitution are justified"? The FTC's Statement of Basis and Purpose refers to nondelivery and total failure of performance. Are these the only instances?

4.   The court quotes a passage from the Statement of Basis and Purpose that the court interprets as restricting the consumer's ability to assert claims affirmatively to cases in which rescission is appropriate. This passage refers only to a seller's breach of contract. Does the court think that the Rule permits the consumer to assert claims and defenses that are not based in contract? If so, and the consumer may assert claims based in tort, does the restriction on affirmative recovery apply to those claims, too? to claims based on statutory violations, e.g., the Equal Credit Opportunity Act?

If the court in Morgan believes that the restriction on affirmative claims applies to tort claims, recall that one of the remedies for fraud is rescission. See Halpert v. Rosenthal, page 26 supra. Why then does the court in *Morgan* hold that this case is not an appropriate one for affirmative recovery?

5.   Courts in several other jurisdictions agree with *Morgan* that the Rule permits affirmative recovery from the financer only if the seller's breach justifies rescission. Other courts, however, as well as the staff of the FTC, do not. In 1999 the head of the FTC's Division of Credit Practices wrote a letter rejecting the reasoning and conclusion of *Morgan*. And in Jaramillo v. Gonzales, 50 P.3d 554, 561 (N.M.App.2002), the court stated:

. . . [F]or three reasons we conclude that the Holder Rule does not limit affirmative claims to those instances where rescission would be appropriate.

First, the commentary [in the Statement of Basis and Purpose] is not a rule, but rather a lengthy explanation of the history and reasoning behind the rule. Second, the rule is unambiguous. It simply mandates the inclusion of specific language in consumer credit contracts. There is nothing in the rule that limits the types of claims or defenses that may be brought against the assignee. Because the rule is unambiguous, there is no basis for referring to commentary to understand the meaning of the language in the rule.

Third, even if we were to look to the commentary to determine the meaning of the rule, we note that the commentary is not limited to the narrow statement relied on by the Bank. Rather, the commentary discusses at length the rationale for the rule and concludes that the purpose of the rule is to reallocate the costs of seller misconduct in the consumer market, "compelling creditors to either absorb seller misconduct costs or return them to sellers." 40 Fed. Reg. at 53,523. In discussing the measures available to the assignee, it is clear the FTC contemplated that consumer claims could be for something less than total rescission and that it was for the assignee to determine which mechanisms for allocating costs of seller misconduct best served its purposes. Lozada v. Dale Baker Oldsmobile, Inc., 91 F.Supp.2d 1087, 1095 (W.D.Mich.2000). Thus, the whole purpose of the rule is to shift the liability for seller misconduct from the consumer to the seller and assignee. This purpose surely would not be promoted by limiting consumer claims to only those circumstances where rescission was appropriate. Viewing the commentary as a whole, we conclude there is no basis to limit the claims that a consumer may bring against the assignee.

Moreover, the FTC Guidelines for the Holder Rule state that the required notice under the rule "protects the consumer's right to assert against the creditor *any* legally sufficient claim or defense against the seller. The creditor stands in the shoes of the seller." Guidelines on Trade Regulation Rule Concerning Preservation of Consumers' Claims and Defenses, 41 Fed. Reg. 20,022, 20,023 (May 14, 1976) (emphasis added). These Guidelines make it clear that affirmative action for recovery, other than complete rescission, is contemplated in appropriate cases.

The language of the FTC Holder Rule is clear and unambiguous and contains no limitation on the kind of action or defense a consumer may raise against an assignee. Therefore, Plaintiffs were not required to show that the mobile home had little or no value when it was delivered to them before asserting their claim against the Bank.

See also Beemus v. Interstate National Dealer Services, 823 A.2d 979, 985 (Pa.Super.2003), in which the appellate court agreed with *Jaramillo* and wrote:

> To limit consumer claims to only those situations where rescission of the contract is appropriate would, in many instances, confound the FTC's goal of shifting liability for seller misconduct from the consumer to the seller or its assignee. While it may be true that, as a practical matter, a debtor entitled to an affirmative recovery of damages in excess of the amount due on an account will typically also be entitled to rescission, we conclude there is no basis for transforming that prediction into a legal limitation on affirmative consumer claims.

6. The European Union has issued a directive on credit agreements. Directive 87/102/EEC of Dec. 22, 1986, for the approximation of the laws, regulations and administrative provisions of the Member States concerning consumer credit, 1987 O.J. L42/48. It addresses several aspects of consumer credit contracts, including disclosure of the cost of credit (a la the Truth-in-Lending Act), prepayment of credit obligations, repossession, etc. Article 11 provides:

> 1. Member States shall ensure that the existence of a credit agreement shall not in any way affect the rights of the consumer against the supplier of goods or services purchased by means of such an agreement

in cases where the goods or services are not supplied or are otherwise not in conformity with the contract for their supply.

2. Where:

(a) in order to buy goods or obtain services the consumer enters into a credit agreement with a person other than the supplier of them; and

(b) the grantor of the credit and the supplier of the goods or services have a pre-existing agreement whereunder credit is made available exclusively by that grantor of credit to customers of that supplier for the acquisition of goods or services from that supplier; and

(c) the consumer referred to in subparagraph (a) obtains his credit pursuant to that pre-existing agreement; and

(d) the goods or services covered by the credit agreement are not supplied, or are supplied only in part, or are not in conformity with the contract for supply of them; and

(e) the consumer has pursued his remedies against the supplier but has failed to obtain the satisfaction to which he is entitled,

the consumer shall have the right to pursue remedies against the grantor of credit. Member States shall determine to what extent and under what conditions these remedies shall be exercisable.

3. Paragraph 2 shall not apply where the individual transaction in question is for an amount less than the equivalent of 200 ECU.

Unlike the FTC Holder Rule, the Directive does not rely for its effectiveness on the inclusion in the contract of mandated language preserving the consumer's claims and defenses. How does this affect its effectiveness? Which of the two approaches, implemented as they are, is more effective?

7. The FTC Rule does not impose liability on lenders. Should the FTC amend the Rule to make it a violation of section 5 of the FTC Act for an affiliated lender to take or receive a contract that fails to contain the required notice? an unaffiliated lender? With respect to either affiliated or unaffiliated lenders, are the policy considerations any different than they are for placing the burden of compliance on the seller?

In considering these questions, it is especially important to think beyond the perception that it is unfair for the seller and the creditor to structure the transaction in such a way that the consumer must continue paying even though the seller has failed to perform. There may be other relevant policies. Consider the following excerpts from Rohner, Holder in Due Course in Consumer Transactions: Requiem, Revival, or Reformation? 60 Cornell L.Rev. 503, 534–35, 538–44, 547, 549 (1975)*:

B. *What Effect Does the Abolition of Holder in Due Course Have on the Cost and Availability of Consumer Credit?*

A priori, the elimination of creditors' freedom from consumer claims and defenses means that those creditors will be unable to collect some obligations they might otherwise collect. Facing such a prospect, financers have several options. They might, for instance, calculate as best they can their prospective lost revenues, adjust their rates—upward—accordingly, and continue financing consumer transactions as before. Or they might decide that the increased risk makes it unprofitable to deal in consumer paper when there are safer profits to be made investing in, say, pork bellies or soy bean futures. Or they might attempt some combination of these: slightly higher rates with a more discriminating selection of participating dealers. Theoretically, too, they might insist on better quality control and improved sales practices to minimize the instances of consumer dissatisfaction, or larger dealer reserve accounts to shunt losses back to the retailers.

. . .

Whether the impact will be felt more in the cost of credit or in its availability will depend in large measure on whether the additional risks of nonrecovery can be distributed to all consumer debtors. It is often assumed that increased costs can always be "passed through" to consumers, but the assumption may be unfounded for many retail creditors or financers who find themselves bound by rate ceilings on one side and competitive pressures on the other. So, before presuming too much, one must be satisfied that consumer creditors can *fairly* be charged not only with the risk of increased losses but also with the resulting burden of distribution.

C. *Does Abolition of Holder in Due Course Produce a More Rational Allocation of Marketplace Risks?*

American jurisprudence has created a universe of legal responsibilities for sellers of goods or services, and the liabilities that flow from defaults in these responsibilities are intended by the law to rest on the seller as a cost of his business. Abnormal losses therefore occur when either the financer or the consumer is required to pay for defective goods or services. It is the risk of these abnormal losses that calls for attention, under first principles of risk allocation which dictate that they should be borne by the party best able to prevent and distribute them.

It is doubtless true that when holder in due course theory is used to visit the costs of defective merchandise on the consumer buyer, he has little if any power to distribute that loss. . . . Financers, on the other hand, have broader, though not unlimited, opportunities to spread the losses which would result from uncollectible paper.

Theoretically, the financer has several ways of distributing projected losses. For one, he may charge more for his credit directly to consumer borrowers or directly to the merchants whose paper he discounts. This is not always a free option, however, for his rates may already be at the legal ceiling. . . . Further, increasing his price puts the financer at a distinct competitive disadvantage. For example, direct bank loans for automobile purchases are generally cheaper than financing through third party finance companies. Abolition of holder in due course, if reflected in finance companies' rates. would only increase the disparity between them.

Alternatively, the financer can try to distribute losses by shunting them back to the dealer whose default caused the loss in the first place and who presumably can redistribute them through its price structure. The devices by which this may be accomplished vary, and for some creditors, under some circumstances, may just not be available at all. In typical transactions where the financer purchases consumer paper regularly from a dealer, incentive payments are made to the dealer in the form of a percentage of the finance charge. Many creditors maintain reserve accounts in which accumulate portions of the discounted prices of consumer obligations. These funds are released periodically to the dealers as the obligations are paid off, and thus represent a kind of contingency fund from which the creditor can withhold amounts equal to what it cannot collect from the consumer debtors. Either of these devices can be manipulated to increase the financer's return and lessen the dealer's, and the National Commission found it "logical to assume" that financers would protect themselves in this way. In addition, financers may purchase consumer paper on a pure recourse basis whereby the dealer is a virtual guarantor of uncollectible items. When negotiable notes are used, the dealer's indorsement leaves him liable to pay the holder on dishonor or liable to the holder for breach-of-warranty damages even if the dealer indorses "without recourse."

Thus, on paper there are ample devices through which the financer can throw losses back to the seller, who must then worry about redistribution. All of them, however, depend on the dealer's agreeing to them and such agreement may not be happily tendered. One would think that if recourse rights are so easy to incorporate into financing arrangements creditors would long ago have insisted on them as universal practice—for what financer would not want to supplement his primary, holder in due course reinforced rights against the consumer debtor with secondary rights against the dealer-assignor? Yet the landscape is strewn with creditors who had no usable recourse rights. Were these creditors foolhardy, or is it equally possible that the dealer was the dominant party whose wishes controlled? Moreover, even the clearest of contractual charge-back rights can avail the creditor nothing against the seller who has skipped the state or gone bankrupt.

The interlocking loan pattern presents unique obstacles to the lender who wishes to retain contractual recourse rights against the seller. Since no paper flows from seller to financer, traditional notions of indorser liability or warranty do not apply. Incentive payments and reserve funds are possible, but more difficult to structure. If the formally independent, but in fact related, lender is denied holder in due course status he may be able to negotiate indemnification agreements with his associated dealers. More useful to the lender may be efforts to develop a traditional legal recourse theory such as unjust enrichment or subrogation to the rights of the debtor. Perhaps the safest technique would be to include in all consumer loan agreements a contingent assignment by the consumer to the lender of his rights against the original seller.

. . .

To assess fairly the ability of various financers to distribute losses, therefore, one must recognize that there are some limiting forces at work in the marketplace: rate ceilings, possible restrictions on reserve funds, uncertain recourse by direct lenders, and competitive pressures. It is then appropriate to allocate the risks of defective products to financers rather than consumers only on the premise that creditors often, or usually, have opportunities to distribute losses—not on the premise that they always do. One can also view the pressure to abolish holder in due course across the board as a technique to put pressure on the rate-makers, and to influence creditors to insist on workable recourse arrangements with the sellers of goods they finance. In this light some proposed statutes may be chargeable with overkill in that they seem to disregard distributability as a criterion for denying holder in due course status. And where distributability is downplayed, the case for abolishing the doctrine must rest on the financer's greater ability to prevent bad merchant practices at the threshold.

. . .

How can a financer police his dealers? He can investigate a dealer's general reputation for honesty, integrity, and solvency. He can periodically renew that investigation. He can insert into his dealer agreements language like that in contracts between credit card issuers and participating merchants wherein the dealer promises to "establish a fair policy for the exchange or return of merchandise." In home improvements, the creditor might insist on completion certificates, or inspect, or otherwise verify completion of the work. But he can hardly run quality tests on all toasters in the dealer's inventory, nor can he easily eavesdrop on the automobile salesman's pitch. Transaction-by-transaction supervision of the dealer's goods and practices by employees of the creditor is impracticable to say the least. The financer's ability even to urge good practices or to influence the quality of goods or services sold is dependent on his relative indispensability to that merchant. Perhaps a large auto financer such as General Motors Acceptance Corporation can indirectly influence these matters through its and the dealer's corporate parent, but it is most doubtful whether local lenders could do the same with respect to area merchants, even where the revised Uniform Consumer Credit Code, for example, would treat them as interlocked.

What financers collectively can do to police the market, however, is withdraw, or threaten to withhold, their credit supply from merchants with bad track records. It is this power to cut off the dealer's essential commodity that is the tangible policing mechanism. In contrast to consumers who have at best the atomistic power to punish merchants who dissatisfy by refusing to trade with them in the future, financers who regularly support the credit operations of given dealers hold weighty economic billy clubs. To the extent, therefore, that abolishing holder in due course is justified on this ground, it carries the clear implication that financers should exercise that clout to freeze out misfeasant and malfeasant sellers even where it is not economically necessary for them to do so—i.e., even where the financer can charge back all disputed obligations. Risk allocation principles, in this context, are instruments of a positive social policy—the starving out of merchants whose products or sales techniques cannot sufficiently and regularly satisfy legal norms.

D.   *What Degrees of Independence from the Seller Will Justify Freedom from Defenses for Some Financers?*

The theoretical answer to this query flows easily from the discussion above: susceptibility to consumer product-related defenses ought not be thrust on a financer who genuinely cannot effect the twin goals of risk distribution and prevention. But how can one measure the varying capabilities of varying lenders in even more varying credit marketing patterns?

At one extreme is the closely related, perhaps even affiliated or jointly controlled, financer who regularly discounts consumer paper for the retail dealer. To the maximum extent any financer can bear, distribute, and prevent losses, he does. At the other extreme is, for example, the bank which makes an unsecured signature loan directly to a consumer for purposes unknown to the bank, and perhaps even unknown to the consumer beyond a general intention to refurnish his living room. The bank is probably lending at the highest permissible rate, and has absolutely no way to turn the uncollectible loan back onto the distant furniture supplier with whom the consumer ultimately deals.

Hardly anyone would dispute the propriety of abolishing holder in due course in the first pattern; even the most vigorous proponent of consumer protection likely would not argue for retaining defenses in the latter. But where between them is the proper divide? . . . Proper legislative policy, therefore, would seem to require, in any statute retaining consumer defenses against lenders, itemization of only those "interlocks" which clearly point to such a course of dealing between lender and seller that the lender could be expected to contract for recourse rights for its own self-protection. . . .

In short, one cannot reasonably subject to consumer claims and defenses any otherwise independent lender merely on the ground that he knows or has reason to know the purpose of the loan, without indulging a pure deep-pockets rationale on the consumer's behalf. The crucial and important question, instead, is whether the lender's relationship to the seller presents the lender with reasonable opportunity to charge back consumer obligations where there are proved or apparently meritorious defenses. Traditional credit patterns, where notes or contracts are taken by the seller in the first instance and then transferred on to a financer, clearly meet this test . . . . The growing concern for the "interlocking loan" ought not be allowed to produce an over-reaction that ignores marketplace reality and that may for that reason increase unnecessarily the marginal cost and unavailability of consumer credit.

8. For economics-oriented analyses of financer liability, see Schwartz, Optimality and the Cutoff of Defenses Against Financers of Consumer Sales, 15 B.C.Ind. & Com.L.Rev. 499 (1974); Geva, Optimality and Preservation of Consumer Defenses—A Model for Reform, 31 Case–W.Res.L.Rev. 51 (1980); Note, The FTC's Holder in Due Course Rule: An Ineffective Means of Achieving Optimality in the Consumer Credit Market, 25 U.C.L.A. L. Rev. 821 (1978); Note, Direct Loan Financing of Consumer Purchases, 85 Harv.L.Rev. 1409 (1972).

(3) CREDIT CARDS

At about the time the FTC was considering and adopting its Preservation of Consumers' Claims and Defenses Rule, Congress enacted the Fair Credit Billing Act (FCBA) (adding it to the Consumer Credit Protection Act). The principal focus of the FCBA is the resolution of disputes concerning the accuracy of monthly bills in connection with open-end credit. See pages 634–35 supra. Section 170 (and Regulation Z section 226.12(c)), however, provide that the credit card issuer is liable for the misconduct of the seller. Note the limitations on the creditor's liability, and compare them to the limits under the FTC rule.[5]

QUESTIONS AND NOTES

1. Why is section 170 limited to transactions in excess of $50? to transactions close to the consumer's home? Does the rationale of these limits apply to any greater or lesser degree in the situations addressed by the FTC Rule? Should the FTC Rule be amended to include these limits?

2. Problem. *Consumer* purchases a lawn mower from *Hardware Store* for $300, paying for it with her Visa card, issued by *Bank*. *Store* warrants that the mower will be free of defects for twelve months, but three months later

---

5. But note also that the FTC Rule does not apply to credit card issuers (§ 433.1(c)). Cf. UCCC section 3.403.

it breaks down. So far *Consumer* has received two billing statements from *Bank* and each time has sent *Bank* a check for $35, or a total of $70. She returns the mower to *Store,* which makes repairs. After the repairs the mower runs, but not as well as it should. *Consumer* uses it for two weeks, during which time *Bank* sends another bill and *Consumer* pays another $35. The mower then stops working altogether, and *Consumer* again returns it to *Store.* After attempting to repair it, *Store* concludes that the mower cannot be repaired. *Store* claims that *Consumer* misused the mower and refuses to have anything further to do with *Consumer* or her mower. *Consumer* makes one more payment of $35 to *Bank*, and then informs *Bank* she will not pay the $160[6] balance still due on her Visa account. *Bank* sues.

   (a) Under FCBA section 170 does Consumer have to pay the balance?

   (b) Can she successfully counterclaim for the $140 she has already paid *Bank*?

   (c) Would the answer to the preceding question be the same if the card issuer were *Hardware Store, Inc.*, and the seller were a franchisee doing business under the trade name *Hardware Store*?

   (d) Would the answers to the three preceding questions be different if UCCC section 3.403 applied instead of FCBA section 170?

3. When the FTC promulgated the Holder Rule in 1975, probably the majority of credit card transactions between a consumer and a distant seller occurred when the consumer was traveling away from home. Today, however, the majority of such transactions probably are internet, mail-order, or phone-order sales. Telemarketing has become a major activity—and a major concern—because sometimes the sellers engage in fraudulent or deceptive practices. This conduct may violate common law or statutory standards, but distance and expense make it impractical for the consumer to obtain relief. It is similarly difficult for a state's attorney general to enforce a little-FTC act against distant sellers, though the Telemarketing and Consumer Fraud and Abuse Prevention Act, at 15 U.S.C. § 6103(a), empowers the state attorney general to enforce the federal statute. (See pages 113–22 supra.) Still, the consumer is remediless. Should Congress drop the geographic limitations in section 170, thereby permitting the consumer to receive compensation from the card issuer?

   A little background information may be helpful because in the context of a bank credit card there actually are several parties in addition to the consumer and the seller. The credit card company, e.g., Visa or Master-Card, forms contracts with banks, empowering the banks in turn to form two kinds of contracts. One is a contract with a consumer, pursuant to which the bank issues a credit card to the consumer. The other is a contract with a seller, in which the bank authorizes the seller to honor credit cards bearing the trademark of the credit card company (i.e. Visa or

---

6. For purposes of this problem, ignore the inevitable fact that *Bank* assesses a finance charge on the unpaid balance of the Visa account.

MasterCard). This contract with the seller obligates the bank to accept the credit slips presented by the seller and to pay the seller the amount shown on them. In exchange, the seller pays the bank a fee, typically 1–4% of the face amount of the credit slips. Among the numerous other provisions of this contract is one that gives the bank the right to charge back to the seller's account amounts that a cardholder refuses to pay because of a dispute with the seller.

When the consumer uses a bank card to purchase goods or services, the seller in city A sends the information to the bank with whom it contracted. This bank sends the information to a central clearinghouse, which credits the bank's account and debits the account of the bank in city B that issued the card to the consumer, who may be in city B, but is just as likely to be in city C. The card-issuing bank then bills the consumer for the amount of the purchase. The following diagram illustrates the flow (start with Consumer in the lower left corner):

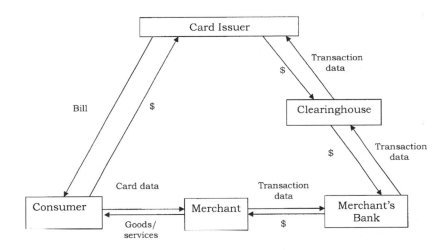

The primary rationale for abolition of the holder in due course and related doctrines is the financer's ability to influence the behavior of the seller. But in the situation described above, the consumer wants to assert the claim or defense against the bank that issued the card and is sending a bill for the amount of the purchase. That bank has no ability to control the activity or the financing of the distant seller. Should Congress nevertheless abolish the geographic limits in section 170?

The FCBA is not the only source of protection against the risk of misconduct by the seller. Visa USA, Inc. and MasterCard International have established charge-back operating procedures for card-issuing banks to follow. These procedures recognize dozens of reasons for charge-backs, in addition to the "claims and defenses" that a consumer may assert pursuant to FCBA section 170. Friedman and Giloley, Consumer Potholes on the Electronic Highway, Credit World, 14 at 15 (Sept./Oct. 1995). Unfortunately, these reasons are not publicized, and consumers may not be able to enforce the procedures against the participating banks.

(4) NATURE OF THE CLAIM OR DEFENSE

The preceding materials focus on the consumer's ability to assert breach of warranty as a defense or counterclaim against the financer. Breach of warranty, however, is not the only claim or defense that the consumer might have. Should the legal nature of the consumer's grievance be relevant to his or her ability to assert that grievance against the financer?

QUESTIONS

1. Please reread Question 2, page 758 supra. Under the FTC Rule, it does not matter whether *Consumer's* claim is breach of warranty or strict liability in tort. Does it matter under UCCC sections 3.404–.405? Would it matter under FCBA section (assuming *Consumer* used a credit card rather than an installment contract)? Is there any justification for drawing a distinction based on the type of claim?

2. Again with respect to Question 2, page 758 supra, if the seller has violated Truth-in-Lending Act section 128(a)(2), by miscomputing the amount financed, may *Consumer* hold *Bank* liable for twice the finance charge? See section 131.

If the president of *Bank* is the sole shareholder of *Seller* and if *Seller* and *Bank* have an arrangement under which *Seller* assigns all its installment contracts to *Bank*, is *Bank* liable for *Seller's* violation of section 128(a)(2)?

As originally enacted, the Truth-in-Lending Act was silent on the question of assignee liability, and the courts made the answer turn on the closeness of the connection between the seller and the assignee. In 1980 Congress added section 131(a), which subjects the assignee to liability "only if the violation . . . is apparent on the face of the disclosure statement . . . ." Hence, as a matter of Truth-in-Lending law, if the violation is apparent on the face of the disclosure statement, the assignee is liable for the seller's violation of the Truth-in-Lending Act, whether or not the document contains the language required by the FTC Rule. But what if the violation is *not* apparent on the face of the disclosure statement but the retail installment contract contains the FTC-mandated legend? Which prevails, the "only if" language of Truth-in-Lending Act section 131(a) or the "all claims and defenses" language on the contract?

3. If an auto dealer violates the federal odometer statute, which is completely silent on the question of assignee liability, is the bank to whom the dealer assigns the contract liable for the statutory penalty (treble damages or $1,500, whichever is more)?

Problem. *Dealer* intentionally misrepresents the history and condition of a used Jaguar, thereby inducing *Consumer* to purchase it for $35,000. The contract contains the requisite notice, and *Dealer* assigns it to *Financer*. After *Consumer* has paid a total of $12,000, she learns that the frame is twisted and that the car had been involved in a serious accident. Because of the twisted frame, the car was worth only $20,000 when she purchased it. May *Consumer* assert her fraud claim against *Financer*? May she recover punitive damages from *Financer*?

4. Little–FTC acts, state and federal odometer acts, and the Magnuson–Moss Warranty Act each confers on the successful consumer the right to attorney's fees. Are attorney's fees therefore recoverable from the financer if the consumer successfully asserts rights under these statutes against the financer rather than the seller?

5. May a state attorney general enforce a little-FTC act against an assignee-financer who did not know of or participate in the seller's unfair or deceptive conduct?

(5) MORTGAGE LENDING

The FTC Holder Rule applies to "any sale or lease of goods or services." It does not apply to loans made to acquire real estate or to refinance those loans. In this arena, therefore, the holder in due course doctrine continues to operate, impairing the ability of the consumer to assert common law claims (e.g., fraud and unconscionability) or statutory violations against the entity that holds the consumer's promissory note. This has been a significant problem in connection with subprime loans, though the close-connectedness doctrine may help. For examination of the close connection between the wrongdoer and the holder of subprime mortgage notes, see Connor, Wall Street and the Making of the Subprime Disaster (National Training & Information Center), available at www.ntis-us.org//documents/WallStreetandtheMakingoftheSubprimeDisaster.pdf. For thorough discussion of the matter, see Eggert, Held Up in Due Course: Predatory Lending, Securitization, and the Holder in Due Course Doctrine, 35 Creighton L.Rev. 503 (202); Peterson, Predatory Structured Finance, 28 Cardozo L.Rev. 2185 (2007).

Should a lender who loans money to a consumer to enable the consumer to buy a new home be vicariously liable for the misconduct of the developer that builds and markets the new home? The Holder Rule does not apply to the sale and financing of real estate, and the drafters of the UCCC intended to exclude loans in connection with the purchase of real estate from section 3.405. (See section 1.301(15)(b).) Hence, if a consumer buys a new house by means of either a loan from a bank or an installment contract that the builder transfers to a bank, the bank is not liable for the seller's misconduct. Should it be liable? Is real estate financing sufficiently similar to other consumer credit transactions that the financer should be vicariously liable for the seller's misconduct?

C.   MISCONDUCT OF THE FINANCER OR OTHER THIRD PARTIES

The focus of the preceding section is the vicarious liability of the financer for the misconduct of the seller. The financer is also liable, of course, for its own misconduct. For example, Chapter 4 (Truth-in-Lending Act) and Chapter 8 (rate regulation) present two examples of statutory regulation of financers. This final section of Chapter 14 considers the standards of conduct that the common law fixes for financers and other third parties.

(1) FINANCERS

The agency principles discussed in Section A of this chapter also apply to financers who have contractual relationships with the persons who deal with consumers. For example, the contract by which a lending institution empowers a mortgage broker to originate loans with consumers may give the lender sufficient control over the conduct of the broker to create an agency relationship. England v. MG Investments, Inc., 93 F.Supp.2d 718 (S.D.W.Va.2000). Other bases for liability exist as well.

If a financial institution knowingly participates in a seller's unlawful conduct, and perhaps even if it just knowingly accepts the benefits of that conduct, the financer may be liable for conspiracy or for aiding and abetting. In Williams v. Aetna Finance Co., 700 N.E.2d 859, 868–69 (Ohio 1998), a home improvement contractor, Blair, preyed on elderly African–American homeowners who were likely to have substantial equity in their homes. He had an arrangement with a branch of ITT Financial Services for expedited financing of his customers. After securing a contract with Williams and obtaining several thousand dollars from her, he abandoned the work at her home. She sued the lender and won. The lender appealed, and the Supreme Court of Ohio affirmed:

> The tort of civil conspiracy is "a malicious combination of two or more persons to injure another in person or property, in a way not competent for one alone, resulting in actual damages." Kenty v. Transamerica Premium Ins. Co. (1995), 72 Ohio St.3d 415, 419, 650 N.E.2d 863, 866. For a thorough analysis of the elements of civil conspiracy and an explanation of how the tort subtly differs from the related aiding and abetting theory of liability, see, generally, Halberstam v. Welch (C.A.D.C.1983), 227 U.S.App.D.C. 167, 705 F.2d 472.

> An underlying unlawful act is required before a civil conspiracy claim can succeed. . . .

> The court of appeals found that there was no testimony in the record that would justify a finding that any ITT representative misrepresented a fact material to the loan agreement to Williams . . . .

We disagree with this specific part of the court of appeals' analysis. If ITT and Blair did engage in a conspiracy to defraud Williams, as Williams alleged, then, as a consequence of the existence of the conspiracy, the finding could be upheld that ITT representatives engaged in fraud against Williams. In a conspiracy, the acts of coconspirators are attributable to each other. See Prosser & Keeton on Torts (5th ed.1984) 323, Section 46 ("All those who, in pursuance of a common plan or design to commit a tortious act, actively take part in it, or further it by cooperation or request, or who lend aid or encouragement to the wrongdoer, or ratify and adopt the wrongdoer's act done for their benefit, are equally liable.")

After a comprehensive review of the record, we determine that the jury reasonably determined on the sum total of the evidence presented that employees of ITT conspired with Blair to defraud Williams, with resulting damages to her. . . . ITT's role in the conspiracy was to allow Blair to have access to loan money that was necessary to further his fraudulent actions against customers such as Williams. Thus, ITT employees themselves affirmatively committed fraud by the very acts of making the loans to Williams and others.

See also In re First Alliance Mortgage Co., 471 F.3d 977 (9th Cir.2006) (holding a unit of Lehman Brothers liable for aiding and abetting a subprime mortgage lender); Armstrong v. Edelson, 718 F.Supp. 1372 (N.D.Ill.1989); Knight v. International Harvester Credit Corp., 627 S.W.2d 382 (Tex.1982). In these situations, the financer's liability is not limited by the language of the FTC Rule. See Peterson, Predatory Structural Finance, 28 Cardozo L.Rev. 2185, 2247–56 (2007) (discussing theories of aiding and abetting, conspiracy, and joint venture).

The standard of reasonable care is applicable to financers, though it may be difficult to determine whether consumers are within the group of persons to whom the financer owes the duty of reasonable care. In Connor v. Great Western Savings and Loan Association, 447 P.2d 609 (Cal.1968), a developer negligently constructed houses with inadequate foundations. The purchasers of the houses sued the developer and also the lender who provided both construction financing for the developer and long-term financing for the purchasers. The Supreme Court of California held that the financer owed a duty to the purchasers to exercise reasonable care to prevent the developer from constructing and selling seriously defective homes. Courts in California and elsewhere have limited *Connor* by emphasizing the ways in which the lender's involvement in the entire project went beyond the usual role of a lender who finances the construction and purchase of new housing. E.g., Bradler v. Craig, 79 Cal.Rptr. 401 (Cal.App. 1969); Snyder v. First Federal Savings & Loan Association, 241 N.W.2d 725 (S.D.1976). Nevertheless, the seed has been planted. Thus, in another case a consumer contracted to purchase a truck, which he financed by borrowing money from a credit union. The credit union issued its check directly to the seller, who went out of business before delivering the truck to the consumer. The credit union sued, and the consumer defended on the ground that the credit union was negligent in issuing its check to the seller before the seller had delivered the truck to the consumer. The trial court granted the credit union's motion for summary judgment, evidently reasoning that the credit union was a holder in due course and therefore was entitled to enforce the note free of the consumer's defenses against the seller.[7] The Supreme Court of Alaska affirmed, but noted:

> If facts were set forth in opposition to the motion for summary judgment which gave rise to a duty on the part of [the credit union] to make certain that there was clear title in the vehicle before [the seller] was paid, the fact that the credit union was a holder in due course of the note might not be a complete defense. However, the facts alleged here do not demonstrate such a duty.

Charmley v. Alaska Municipal Employees Federal Credit Union, 588 P.2d 1267, 1268 n. 5 (Alaska 1979). What facts would give rise to a duty on the part of the financer to see that the seller delivered the truck?

Another standard of conduct for the lender appears in Janes v. First Federal Savings & Loan Association, 312 N.E.2d 605 (Ill.1974). Plaintiffs borrowed money from defendant in connection with the purchase of their homes. Defendant required title reports and title insurance, which it procured on plaintiffs' behalf and at plaintiffs' expense. Thereafter the title company returned to defendant ten percent of the amounts paid by plaintiffs. The Illinois Supreme Court held that defendant was under a fiduciary obligation to pass this ten percent rebate on to plaintiffs. See also Fitzgerald v. Chicago Title & Trust Co., 380 N.E.2d 790 (Ill.1978) (title company's payment of rebates to lenders without disclosing to borrowers that payments would be made constitutes a violation *by the title company* of the little-FTC act). But see Perrin v. Pioneer National Title Insurance Co., 404 N.E.2d 508 (Ill.App.1980) (no violation of the little-FTC act merely because the title company's charges for its services are less for builder-developers than for consumer-buyers).

Persons other than financers may unwittingly find themselves in a fiduciary relationship with consumers. H & R Block offers so-called "refund anticipation loans" to customers for whom it prepares tax returns and who are entitled to refunds. These loans actually are extended by another entity, with which Block has an arrangement and which shares its fees with Block. Courts have held that Block may have a fiduciary duty to its customers, which it breaches if it fails to disclose the true nature of the loans or the financial benefit it receives from them. Green v. H & R Block, Inc., 735 A.2d 1039 (Md.1999) (agency); Basile v. H & R Block, Inc., 761 A.2d 1115 (Pa.2000) (no agency); Basile v. H & R Block, Inc., 777 A.2d 95 (Pa.Super.2001) (may be confidential relationship even if no agency relationship).

---

7. Section 3–302(2) of the UCC provides that the payee may be a holder in due course.

(2) REAL ESTATE BROKERS

Third parties other than lenders may play a role in consumer transactions. An example is real estate brokers. Chapter 1 addressed the question of liability to a home purchaser for misrepresentation and for failure to disclose material information. The focus there was on the liability of the seller (e.g., Halpert v. Rosenthal, page 26) and of the broker of the buyer (e.g., Pumphrey v. Quillen, page 30). How about the broker of the seller?

Problem. *Seller* wants to sell his house, which has experienced severe soil problems, caused by the builder's failure to properly compact the soil before constructing a house on the site. *Seller* has restored the appearance of the property but has done nothing to remedy the underlying problem. *Seller* lists his house with *Real Estate Agent A* but does not communicate any of this to *Agent A*.

Buyer contacts *Real Estate Agent B* for assistance in finding and buying a house. *Agent B* learns of *Seller's* house through the multiple listing service and shows it to *Buyer*. *Buyer* purchases the house for $150,000 and moves in. Several months later there is substantial earth movement, resulting in severe cracks in the driveway and in the walls of the house. Investigation reveals that it will cost $20,000 to remedy the subsoil problem and repair the house and driveway. Should *Seller* be liable for failing to disclose the subsoil problem?

Should *Agent A* be liable? Should it matter if he knew that the house was built on fill, which he knows must be properly compacted before being used for home sites?

Should it matter if he had seen that the floor in one of the rooms was not level, or that there was netting on a slope of the yard (placed there to repair the effects of a prior slide)?

In Easton v. Strassburger, 199 Cal.Rptr. 383 (Cal.App.1984), the court held that the seller's broker owes the buyer a duty of reasonable care. The broker must conduct a reasonable inspection of property he or she lists for sale and must disclose defects that a reasonable inspection would reveal.

Should the courts extend *Easton* to impose liability on a real estate agent who fails to exercise reasonable care to discover material facts that are not related to the quality of the structure? Consider these examples: the house was the scene of a mass murder ten years earlier (compare Question 3, page 42 supra); the neighbors frequently throw large and loud parties; there have been repeated burglaries in the neighborhood; a large apartment building is to be built across the street.

(3) ENDORSERS

Still other third parties may be liable for their conduct in connection with consumer transactions, even if they are not direct participants in the transaction. E.g., in Hanberry v. Hearst Corp., 81 Cal.Rptr. 519 (Cal.App. 1969), plaintiff sued defendant magazine publisher for injuries she sustained as a result of defectively designed shoes. Defendant had permitted the distributor of the shoes to use its "Good Housekeeping's Consumers' Guaranty Seal" in connection with the advertising and sale of the shoes. The court held that defendant's endorsement ("We have satisfied ourselves that the products . . . are good ones") imposed on defendant the duty to use reasonable care in issuing its seal. Accord, Alexander v. Certified Master Builder Corp., 1997 WL 756605 (D.Kan.1997). And in Blankenship v. Better Business Bureau, 782 S.W.2d 131 (Mo.App.1989), the court held that the BBB could be liable for failing to provide all the information it knew in response to the consumers' inquiry.

The liability of endorsers extends also to celebrities who promote consumer products. E.g., see In re Cooga Mooga, 92 F.T.C. 310 (1978), in which singer Pat Boone agreed to a consent decree holding him liable for deceptive claims for an acne medicine he advertised. Several years later actors Lloyd Bridges and George Hamilton confronted liability for negligently making deceptive claims in advertisements for an investment opportunity. See Ramson v. Layne, 668 F.Supp. 1162 (N.D.Ill.1987).

The kind of conduct necessary to constitute an endorsement is not entirely clear. In Emery v. Visa International Service Association, 116 Cal.Rptr.2d 25 (Cal.App.2002), the court held that Visa did not become an endorser merely by allowing a merchant to place the Visa logo on letters of solicitation that it sent to consumers. On the other hand, another court held that the publisher of a Yellow Pages telephone directory might be liable to a consumer who was injured during a liposuction procedure. The publisher had permitted the physician to place an ad stating "Board Certified" in a section devoted to "Surgery, Plastic and Reconstructive," even though it knew he actually was certified only in dermatology and dermatologic surgery. Knepper v. Brown, 50 P.3d 1209 (Ore.App.2002).

(4) CORPORATE OFFICERS AND DIRECTORS

One purpose of incorporating a business is to insulate the owners from personal liability. There are exceptions, however, to this insulation. For example, liability on behalf of the officers or directors of a corporation may arise if they directly participate in the unlawful conduct of the corporation. E.g., Rayner v. Reeves Custom Builders, Inc., 691 N.W.2d 705 (Wis.App. 2004), rev. denied, 697 N.W.2d 472 (Wis.2005); New York v. Thurcon Props., Ltd., 613 N.Y.S.2d 868 (App.Div.1994); Mother & Unborn Baby Care v. Texas, 749 S.W.2d 533 (Tex.App.1988); Pollice v. National Tax Funding L.P., 225 F.3d 379 (3d Cir.2000) (general partner liable for limited partnership's violation of FDCPA). Liability also may arise if the officers or directors have actual knowledge of the unlawful conduct and do nothing to prevent it or if the facts justify piercing the corporate veil. E.g., Nelson v. Schanzer, 788 S.W.2d 81 (Tex.App.1990).

(5) OTHERS

Professionals and others who provide services may be liable to the consumer even though they provided the services to someone else and had no contractual relationship or other contact with the consumer. E.g., Rocker v. KPMG LLP, 148 P.3d 703 (Nev.2006) (accountants to organization that provided automobile service contracts sold by dealers to consumers); Petrillo v. Bachenberg, 655 A.2d 1354 (N.J.1995) (attorney for seller of real estate held liable to buyer); Ensminger v. Terminix International Co., 102 F.3d 1571 (10th Cir.1996) (termite inspector hired by sellers held liable to buyers).

(6) FEDERAL TRADE COMMISSION ACT

Questions of vicarious liability may arise under the FTC Act. For example, may the officers or directors of a corporation be liable for violations by the corporation? If they participate in the offensive activity or if they have actual knowledge of it, the answer is, yes. E.g., Federal Trade Commission v. Amy Travel Service, 875 F.2d 564, 573 (7th Cir.1989); FTC v. First Alliance Mortgage Co., No. SACV 00–964 DOC (C.D.Cal. Mar. 21, 2002) (settlement) (CEO liable for $20 million). May a corporation whose subsidiary violates the FTC Act be subjected to cease and desist proceedings? To do so ignores the separateness of the two entities. To fail to do so enables the parent corporation to form another subsidiary to engage in the very conduct the first subsidiary was told to stop. See P.F. Collier & Son Corp. v. Federal Trade Commission, 427 F.2d 261 (6th Cir.1970) (parent liable). Compare Jenkins v. Union Corp., 999 F.Supp. 1120 (N.D.Ill.1998) (parent not liable for subsidiary's violation of FDCPA).

Another example is liability of a supplier for the deception of a retailer who is not a subsidiary of the supplier. Should it matter whether the retailer is, on the one hand, a department store or, on the other hand, a franchisee of the supplier? See In re Grolier, Inc., 91 F.T.C. 476 (1978); State v. Master Distributors, Inc., 615 P.2d 116 (Idaho 1980); Note, FTC Attempts To Abolish Vicarious Liability Defenses for Deceptive Sales Practices: Strict Liability for Manufacturers? 25 Hastings L.J. 1142 (1974).

Still another example is liability of one who facilitates the unlawful conduct by providing credit card processing services. E.g., In re Citicorp Credit Services, 116 F.T.C. 87 (1993) (consent decree in which processor agreed to investigate and/or terminate merchants who have a high chargeback rate). See Telemarketing Sales Rule, 16 C.F.R. § 310.3(c) (prohibiting credit card laundering). In In re U.S. Oil and Gas Corp., No. 812 3232 (Apr. 30, 1991), reported in Trade Reg. Rep. (CCH) ¶ 22,985, the FTC pursued an assortment of entities that facilitated a merchant's violation of section 5, including an insurance company, an insurance brokerage firm, a law firm, an accounting firm, banks, and the local and national Better Business Bureaus. The action resulted in a $47 million settlement. Saddler, FTC Penalizes Third Parties in Fraud Case, Wall St. J., May 1, 1991, at B1. And in United States v. Mercantile Mortgage Co., 2002 WL 32967001 (N.D.Ill. 2002), the FTC obtained a consent decree against a lender for the unfair and deceptive practices of an independent mortgage broker.

CHAPTER 15

REMEDIES

The principal remedies for breach of contract aim either to restore the status quo ante or to give the injured party the promised benefit. There are, however, other possible objectives, especially in the context of consumer transactions. They include termination of offensive conduct and punishment of persons who engage in that conduct. This chapter examines remedies that further each of these goals, but it concentrates on rescission and on solutions to the practical problems that consumers encounter when they seek to obtain what they have contracted for.

A. ESCAPE FROM THE DEAL

(1) TRANSACTIONS IN GOODS

Jones v. Abriani

Court of Appeals of Indiana, 1976.
169 Ind.App. 556, 350 N.E.2d 635.

LOWDERMILK, J.

[Plaintiffs ordered a mobile home from defendants, making a downpayment of $1,000. When it arrived, the home had several defects and failed in several respects to conform to the home plaintiffs had ordered. When plaintiffs objected to these defects and nonconformities, defendants informed them that they would lose their downpayment if they did not take the home. Plaintiffs therefore had defendants install the home on a lot that defendants owned and rented to plaintiffs. Additional defects manifested themselves within the next several months. The list of these defects occupies almost a full page of the court's opinion.

Plaintiffs sued to rescind the purchase. The trial court, however, rendered judgment not for rescission but rather for $5,000 expectancy-based compensatory damages and $3,000 punitive damages. Plaintiffs evidently were satisfied with this judgment, but defendants appealed. After determining that the evidence amply supported the trial court's finding of facts, the court continued:]

The appellants' only other claimed errors concern the amount of damages awarded by the trial court. They raise issues in regards to the method of determining the compensatory damages, the sufficiency of the proof as to the amount of compensatory damages, and the sufficiency of the proof as to the elements of fraud necessary to sustain the punitive damage award.

It is first necessary to determine the basis of liability. Inasmuch as the mobile home in question falls within the definition of "goods" as set out in 2–105 of the Uniform Commercial Code, this sale is governed by the rules set out in Article 2 of the Code.

We first point out that valid grounds for rejection of the mobile home existed in this case under 2–601, the Perfect Tender Rule, which provides that "if goods or the tender of delivery fail in any respect to conform to the contract, the buyer may (a) reject the whole . . . ." While tender does not necessarily have to be "perfect," see Whaley, Tender, Acceptance, Rejection and Revocation—The UCC's "TARR" Baby, 24 Drake L.Rev. 52 (1974) (hereinafter cited as Whaley) the mobile home in this case clearly failed to meet the contract requirements. The seller did have a right to cure minor defects after proper notice according to the terms of 2–508, but the evidence demonstrates that no such cure was ever forthcoming within the contemplated time of performance, or at any time.

Defendants contend that the Abrianis had no right to demand return of the down payment or reject the home as delivered because of the following liquidated damages provision that appears in the sales agreement:

> Upon failure or the refusal of the purchaser to complete said purchase for any reason (other than cancellation on account of increase in price) the cash deposit may have such portion of it retained as will reimburse the dealer for expenses and other losses occasioned by purchaser's failure to complete said purchase. . . .

The clause is applicable only if a perfect tender has been made. The defendants must first perform their part of the contract of sale before the buyers can be held liable for breach under a liquidated damages clause. Cf. Section 2–718. The Abrianis could not fail to complete the purchase until the defendants performed by tendering the goods to be purchased under the contract terms.

Sellers also contend that the goods were in substantial compliance with the contract, . . . [but] it is clear from the facts set out above that there were . . . substantial defects in the home and variances from the contract terms that would amount to imperfect tender.

We hold that the evidence was sufficient to sustain a finding that a valid rejection was made by the Abrianis, and that the sellers' threats to withhold the down payment were not justified under the law.

The Abrianis' complaint requested rescission of the contract, but it is not clear whether the theory relied on was rejection under 2–601, or revocation of acceptance under 2–608. Ordinarily, acceptance with knowledge of a defect is made on the reasonable assumption that the non-conformity would be cured. Failure to seasonably cure raises a right to revoke acceptance under 2–608(1)(a).

In the case at bar, revocation of acceptance would have been an acceptable remedy, but we believe that rejection would have been a more appropriate remedy. Here the Abrianis did not make an acceptance as contemplated by the Code, but rather agreed to take possession of the goods until such time as sellers had an opportunity to cure their defective tender. In fact, had it not been for sellers' threats, it appears that the Abrianis would not have voluntarily accepted the goods even if the seller had made assurances that they would repair the defects. The Abrianis were entitled to "try out" the goods to discover defects in the home for a reasonable period before acceptance occurs. 2–606(1). This is especially true where defects are apparent at the time of delivery, the buyer refuses delivery on that basis, the seller makes assurances that he will eventually perform the contract and repair the defects, and the buyer takes possession of the goods to try them out and further inspect the goods to determine if they will ever meet the contract terms. Clearly, that is the case here. Over and over again, the courts have stated that the seller's repeated assurances of cure extend the reasonable time for notice of rejection.

In regard to the buyers' use of goods after the notice of rejection, 2–602(2)(a) states that "after rejection any exercise of ownership by the buyer with respect to any commercial unit is wrongful as against the seller . . ." We note that there is no mention of the actual consequences of use of the goods after a valid rejection. Many courts have held that use of the goods converts a rejection into an acceptance, and while that is a reasonable outcome in most cases, we believe the unique facts in the case at bar merit a different conclusion. See Whaley, supra, 24 Drake L.Rev. at 65. The use of the goods by the Abrianis was a result of the oppressive conduct of the sellers at a time when the sellers knew that the Abrianis needed a home and knew that all of their money was invested in the mobile home. While the use of the home by the Abrianis was wrongful as against the seller, such use was the direct result of the oppressive conduct of the sellers in not allowing the buyers to reject, and we do not believe that it is necessary to conclude that use of the goods cancelled the rejection.

Under 2–711(3), the Abrianis had a security interest in the goods for the amount of purchase price paid. The official comments to that section note that price "paid" includes the signing of a negotiable note, as was the case here. The Abrianis had a right to possession of the goods under this section, until their note was returned to them, although they had no right to use the goods, unless it could be found that such use helped preserve the goods through continued care as was the case in Minsel v. El Rancho Mobile Home Center, Inc. (1971), 32 Mich. App. 10, 188 N.W.2d 9.

The sellers had the burden of showing their damages as the result of any wrongful use by the buyers. Where the decrease in the value of the goods is due to their own defects, rather than the use of the goods by the buyers, there would be little provable damage. Compare with 2–608(2).

As noted above, even were we to assume that the Abrianis accepted the home in question, they would still be entitled to revocation of acceptance under 2–608. Certainly it is clear that if any acceptance took place, it must have been made with the reasonable assumption that the defects would be cured, which is one of the specific grounds set out for revocation of acceptance in 2–608(1). There can be no doubt that the nonconformity in the goods substantially impaired the value of the home to the Abrianis. The Abrianis filed their lawsuit shortly after it finally became apparent that none of the promises made by the sellers would be kept. Finally, there has been no substantial change in the condition of the home other than those changes that resulted because of the home's own defects. Therefore, the conditions of 2–608 have been fulfilled, and revocation of acceptance would be proper. Use of the goods after revocation of acceptance was not final here for the same reasons set out above in regards to rejection. See 2–608(3) and 2–602(2)(a).

We also find that the Abrianis should be allowed to recover under theories of breach of express warranty and breach of implied warranty of merchantability.

Section 2–313(1)(c) provides that "any sample or model which is made part of the basis of the bargain creates an express warranty that the whole of the goods shall conform to the sample or model." Thus, the seller expressly warranted that the mobile home contracted for would conform with the model home that the Abrianis viewed at Jonesy's Mobile Home Sales. Additionally, 2–313(1)(a) provides that "any affirmation of fact or promise made by the seller to the buyer which relates to the goods and becomes part of the basis of the bargain creates an express warranty that the goods shall conform to the affirmation or promise." Thus, the promises made by the sellers to the Abrianis to induce them to accept the mobile home amount to express warranties. The promise that all defects would be repaired is a promise that amounts to an express warranty under 2–313(1)(a), the breach of which gives rise to an action for damages under the Code. Section 2–209(1) provides that "[a]n agreement modifying a contract within this article needs no consideration to be binding."

In addition, the sellers breached the implied warranty of merchantability under 2–314. . . .

The mobile home in question was clearly below average, of poor quality, and was not fit for its ordinary purpose, i.e., to serve as a modern, comfortable home where one can entertain guests without being embarrassed about bald carpets, crooked doors, and a leaky roof.

The contract did contain some language to the effect that "there are no warranties expressed or implied" made by the seller, but such language is clearly ineffective in this case. Under 2–316(2), a written exclusion or modification of the implied warranties must be conspicuous and mention the word "merchantability." Here, there was no mention of the word "merchantability."

Additionally, the disclaimer language must be conspicuous. Here, while the disclaimer was underlined (as was nearly half the page), we believe its placement on the reverse side of the form buried in a whole page of fine print, made such disclaimer inconspicuous, rather than conspicuous, and thus ineffective as a matter of law.

Further, the disclaimer of the express warranty was ineffective under 2–316(1). That section provides that if it is unreasonable or impossible to construe the language of an express warranty and the language of a disclaimer as consistent, the disclaimer becomes inoperative.

In summation, we find that grounds for relief were made out on at least four different theories: refusal to recognize a valid rejection; refusal to recognize a rightful revocation of acceptance; breach of express warranty; and breach of implied warranty of merchantability. It is not clear on what theory the trial court awarded relief of $5,000.00 compensatory damages. In regards to the first two theories, buyers were entitled to cancellation of the contract under 2–711, and any other damage they could show under that section or section 2–713. In the alternative, they were entitled to damages for breach of warranty under the second two theories, the measure of which is controlled by 2–714.

There was no request for, nor proof of, any incidental or consequential damages. In regard to defendants' breach of express and implied warranties, the measure of damages is clearly the difference between the value of the goods accepted, and the value the goods would have had, had they been as warranted. The sellers made express warranties that they would repair any defects in the home. In this case, one reasonable way of measuring the difference in the value of the goods between what was actually delivered (a defective mobile home) and what was warranted (a mobile home with the defects repaired) is the cost of repairing the defects. Thus, the evidence in the record that shows the cost of repairs to be $3,000 to $4,000 would be sufficient to uphold the trial court's verdict as to $4,000 compensatory damages. Also, section 2–714(2) states that the usual rule for breach of warranty (difference in value) will apply "unless special circumstances show proximate damages of a different amount." In Southern Concrete Products Company v. Martin (1972), 126 Ga.App. 534, 191 S.E.2d 314, the court upheld an award of damages for the cost of repair of the goods much higher than the original cost of goods, where the buyer used the goods only because the seller assured him that the seller would make good the cost of bringing the goods into conformity with the contract. The court found that the buyer's reliance on such assurances were "special circumstances" that showed proximate damages in a different amount. Under the circumstances of this case, both theories support our holding that cost of repair is a correct measure of damages.

While rejection or revocation of acceptance is available to the plaintiffs in this case, we cannot say that those are the only reasonable remedies for such a wrong. Where the plaintiffs have wrongfully used an item for a substantial length of time after a valid rejection or revocation of acceptance has taken place, (as in the case at bar,) it may be appropriate for the trial court to let the parties accept the goods and then receive damages for the cost of repairs, rather than rescinding the contract. Such relief is reasonable in the case at bar, and absent objection from plaintiffs, we will not disturb such a finding.

. . .

The Abrianis showed that they suffered substantial damages; however, they failed to properly quantify the cost of repairing each of the defective items, no doubt due to the fact that they were seeking rescission of the contract at the time of trial. Since no cross-appeal was taken, we must assume that they acquiesced in the trial court's award of damages in lieu of rescinding the contract. We have already noted that the only cost of repair proven at trial was that it would cost $3,000 to $4,000 to fix up all of the defects in the trailer. Thus, the proven damages amount to only $4,000. There was no estimate as to the cost of repairing or replacing the damaged furniture in the trailer, and thus any award of damages for this item is clearly speculative in nature and cannot be allowed.

. . .

We find it necessary to order remittitur in the amount of $1,000, or in the alternative, that a new trial be granted to the defendants.

. . .

QUESTIONS AND NOTES

1. Section 2–601 appears to retain the common law perfect tender rule, under which the buyer may refuse to perform unless the seller's performance is exactly as promised. An examination of other sections, however, reveals that the UCC actually departs from this principle. For example, if the buyer refuses to accept the seller's nonconforming performance, section 2–508 gives the seller the right to remedy the nonconformities. Subsection (1) restricts the seller's right to cure to the time preceding the deadline for delivery. Subsection (2) permits the seller to cure even after the delivery deadline has passed. See Bartus v. Riccardi, 284 N.Y.S.2d 222 (N.Y.City Ct.1967) (when the buyer rejected delivery of a new, improved version of the product for which he had contracted, the seller was entitled to additional time to deliver the older model).

The court in *Abriani* says that the seller had the "right to cure minor defects after proper notice according to the terms of 2–508." Does this mean that plaintiffs had to take the mobile home and let the seller remedy the defects?

2. If the consumer does not discover until some time after delivery that the product does not conform to the requirements of the contract, may the consumer still reject it? See sections 2–602, 2–606, 2–607(2).

3. Section 2–711 specifies the remedies of the buyer who rejects the goods. Here, too, the UCC varies from the common law. Since the objective of rescission is to cancel out the transaction and restore the plaintiff's pre-contract position, recovery at common law is limited to the value of any benefit the plaintiff has conferred on the defendant. Section 2–711(1), however, permits the buyer to recover not only the money already paid the seller but also damages for lost expectancy. See also section 2–721.

4. Even if the consumer's conduct amounts to acceptance, rescission still may be available: section 2–608 permits the buyer to "revoke acceptance" of the goods. Section 2–711(1) states the consequences of revocation of acceptance. Note that they are the same as the consequences of rejection in the first place. Therefore, does it matter whether the consumer rejects nonconforming goods under section 2–601 or relies on section 2–608(1)(a) and accepts the goods on the assumption that the seller will cure the nonconformity?

Assume that the consumer objects to the product as defective (as in *Abriani*) and the seller induces the consumer to take it by promising to repair the defects. What are the consumer's rights if the seller does not make the repairs? In Murray v. Holiday Rambler, page 339 supra, the court held that when the seller was unable to repair the defects, the limited remedy failed of its essential purpose (§ 2–719), thereby making all the UCC remedies available. One of the remedies so made available is revocation of acceptance. (Please reread note 7, page 350).

5. Problem. *Consumer* buys a new garden tractor from *Seller*. The contract contains the usual warranty and limitation of remedy. When it turns out that the tractor is a lemon and that, despite repeated attempts, *Seller* cannot repair all the defects, should *Consumer*

(a) sue and return the tractor to *Seller*,

(b) sue and leave the tractor in her shed until the court resolves the dispute, or

(c) sue and continue using the tractor?

(2) OTHER TRANSACTIONS

The preceding subsection considered rescission under the UCC. Other sources, both common law and statutory, also authorize rescission. For example, the common law remedies for misrepresentation include rescission and restoration of the status quo ante. And statutes (as well as the FTC regulation) governing home solicitation sales provide a cooling-off period during which the consumer may rescind the sale (pages 539–41 supra). A similar cooling-off period appears in the Truth-in-Lending Act, not in connection with door-to-door sales, but rather in connection with contracts in which the creditor obtains a security interest in the consumer's residence. Please read Truth-in-Lending Act section 125(a), (d), and (e) (and Regulation Z section 226.23(a), (c), (e), (f)).

QUESTIONS

1. Problem. *Consumer* buys a house from *Seller* for $80,000. She borrows $50,000 from *Bank*, which along with another $17,000 she pays to *Seller*. She promises to pay *Seller* the remaining $13,000 of the price in monthly installments. To secure this credit, she gives *Bank* a first mortgage in the property, and she gives *Seller* a second mortgage.

a) Does *Consumer* have a right to rescind the transaction with *Bank*?

b) Does *Consumer* have a right to rescind the transaction with *Seller*?

c) Several years later *Consumer* hires *Contractor* to convert her screened-in porch into an all-weather family room. As security for her payment, she gives *Contractor* a mortgage in her house. Does she have a right to rescind?

    1) Does it matter whether she still owes money to *Bank* and *Seller*?

    2) Does it matter whether she is to pay *Contractor* a lump sum upon completion or is to pay in twenty-four monthly installments?

    3) If she does not give *Contractor* a mortgage, would she have a right to rescind the contract with *Contractor*?

d) The following October *Consumer* contracts with *Heatco* for a new furnace, to be paid for in twelve monthly installments. Does she have a right to rescind? Does it matter whether *Heatco* installs the furnace the day after the parties form the contract?

e) On June 1 *Consumer* contracts with *Siding Company* for the installation of aluminum siding on her house. The price is $10,000, which *Siding Company* arranges for *Consumer* to borrow from *Finance Company*. On June 1 *Siding Company* gives *Consumer* a disclosure statement, which includes notice of her right to rescind by giving notice by June 4. *Siding Company* commences work on June 5 and completes the job July 1. On July 1 *Consumer* signs a completion certificate. *Siding Company* presents the certificate to *Finance Company*, which thereupon gives *Siding Company* $10,000. At the same time, *Consumer* signs a note for $10,000 (plus a finance charge), payable to *Finance Company*, which gives her a disclosure statement. On July 2 *Consumer* notifies *Finance Company* that she is rescinding the loan contract and notifies *Siding Company* that she is rescinding the siding contract. May she rescind either or both?

2. Section 125(d) authorizes the Federal Reserve Board to adopt regulations by which consumers may waive their right of rescission. The Board has done so, see Regulation Z sections 226.15(e), .23(e). The Board has also prohibited performance by the creditor before expiration of the rescission period, unless the consumer has waived the right of rescission. Sections 226.15(c), .23(c).

Problem. *Consumer* applies for a loan from *Lender*. *Lender* processes the application and notifies *Consumer* that she has approved the loan and requests him to come in to sign the papers. As he is about to sign, *Lender* informs him that the funds will not be available for three days. When *Consumer* protests, *Lender* explains that the only way she can advance the funds that day is if he writes out a statement explaining that he needs the money for a personal financial emergency. After thinking for a few moments, he writes, "I need the money immediately to meet a personal financial emergency. I need the funds to obtain immediate medical treatment for my daughter." *Lender* makes the funds available on the spot. In fact, *Consumer* doesn't even have a daughter.

Has *Lender* violated the Act? If so, what sanction is available for violating section 125 (or Regulation Z section 226.23)?

3. What is the sanction if the creditor violates section 226.23(c) and begins performance before expiration of the rescission period?

4. Problem. *Consumer* borrows money from *Lender*, giving a security interest in his home. *Lender* erroneously omits an $8 brokerage fee from its disclosure of the finance charge. *Lender* gives *Consumer* the following notice:

> You are entering into a transaction that will result in a security interest in your home. You have a legal right under federal law to cancel this transaction within three business days from the date of this transaction, *January 7, 2009.* If you cancel, the security interest in your home also is cancelled. Within twenty days of receiving your notice of cancellation, we will take the steps necessary to reflect that the security interest has been cancelled, and we will return to you any money or property you have given to us. Until we do these things, you may keep any money or property we have given you. After we have done these things, you must offer to return the money or property, or its reasonable value.

> If you wish to cancel this transaction, you may do so by sending us a letter to that effect or by completing and returning one of the attached notices.

May *Consumer* rescind on January 15?

5. Rescission under the Truth-in-Lending Act differs in several important respects from rescission at common law. The rescinding party at common law may not recover any damages other than the value of the benefit conferred on the other party. On the other hand, section 125(g) expressly permits the consumer both to rescind and also to recover damages under section 130. Indeed, even before section 125 expressly authorized both forms of relief, most courts reached that conclusion anyway. What is there about section 130 that removes the apparent inconsistency in permitting both rescission and recovery of damages?

Another important difference between common law rescission and section 125 rescission concerns the mechanics of the remedy. The common law rule is that the person desiring to rescind must, at the time of rescission, tender a return of any benefit already received. Without this tender, an attempted rescission is ineffectual. The procedures under section 125 are distinctly different. Please read section 125(b) and Regulation Z section 226.23(d).

Mayfield v. Vanguard Savings & Loan Association

United States District Court, E.D. Pennsylvania, 1989.
710 F.Supp. 143.

LOWELL A. REED, JR., DISTRICT JUDGE.

. . .

FACTS

The record shows that defendant made a loan to Anna Mayfield and her husband on August 4, 1986. The Mayfields received $4,716.23 in cash proceeds. Defendant also paid off a second mortgage on the Mayfields' home with a balance of $5,371.23, paid the Mayfields' water and sewer bill of $1,428.72 and paid $870.76 then due on the Mayfields' first mortgage. To this total was added $1,070 in points or loan fees to defendant, $300 in attorney's fees to defendant's lawyer, and about $500 in other closing costs. The total was then written as a loan of $14,000 at an interest rate of 20% with a resulting future liability of $44,258.40, to be paid in monthly installments of $245.88 over 15 years. Defendant took a mortgage on the Mayfields' home at 7000 Cedar Park Avenue, Philadelphia to secure the loan. The Mayfields were given a loan disclosure statement and notice of right to cancel on July 30, 1986.

The Mayfields made the first two scheduled payments of $245.88 each in October and November, 1986. They then contacted defendant to explain that they were having difficulty paying the loan payment and their first mortgage payment of $171 on their income of $634 per month from social security and veteran's pension benefits. Defendant offered to refinance the prior loan and their first mortgage with a new loan which was written on January 19, 1987. The only new advances from this loan were $6,265.43 to pay off the first mortgage on the Mayfields' home and $160 to pay a water and sewer bill. To that were added the prior balance to defendant, a new origination fee of $1,930 and about $1,500 in other closing costs. That total was written as a loan of $24,686.04 at an interest rate of 20% with a resulting future liability of $85,872.60, payable in monthly installments of $477.07. Defendant took another mortgage on the Mayfields' home to secure the loan. The only disclosure statement and notice of right to cancel given to the Mayfields concerning the new loan was received by them on December 2, 1986. According to Mrs. Mayfield's uncontested affidavit she made two payments of $911.00 each on this second loan transaction.

On October 28, 1987, counsel for the Mayfields wrote a letter to defendant and its attorney rescinding the loan under TILA, 15 U.S.C. § 1635(a), which letter was received on October 30, 1987. Defendant took no action within twenty days after the rescission letter to remove the mortgage from the Mayfields' home or to return the money already received from the Mayfields. Mrs. Mayfield filed this action on January 19, 1988, to enforce the rescission and to obtain actual and statutory damages under TILA.[1]

PLAINTIFF'S RIGHT TO RESCIND

It appears from the response of defendant to plaintiff's motion that it does not contest that plaintiff has a right to rescind the loans it made to her and her husband. Nor would defendant have a basis to do so. Whenever a consumer credit transaction results in a creditor acquiring a security

---

1. Mr. Mayfield died on March 23, 1988.

interest in an obligor's home, as is the case here, § 125(a) gives the obligor "the right to rescind the transaction until midnight of the third business day following the consummation of the transaction or the delivery of the disclosures required under this section and all other material disclosures required under this part, whichever is later . . ." § 125(a). . . .

Rule

The failure of defendant to correctly make all material disclosures required to be made under § 128 . . . entitled plaintiff to rescind the loan. Section 128 requires a creditor to disclose, inter alia, the extent of the collateral being taken for the loan. § 128(a)(9). The disclosure statements for the August 1986 and January 1987 loans indicated that the loans were secured by "the property being purchased" which was clearly an incorrect disclosure as these were not purchase money loans. Plaintiff and her husband purchased their home years before the present security interests in it were taken. The failure to accurately disclose a security interest taken is a material nondisclosure which also entitles a consumer to rescind a loan within the three year rescission period.

. . .

PLAINTIFF'S RIGHT TO DAMAGES

Section 130(a) of TILA provides for statutory penalties equal to twice the finance charge of the credit transaction up to a maximum of $1,000 for failing to comply with the disclosure requirements of the Act. Multiple disclosure violations made in connection with a single loan transaction entitles a person to only a single recovery. § 130(f). However, if a consumer rightfully exercises the right to rescind and the creditor fails to comply with its obligations under § 125 the consumer is entitled to an additional award of damages under § 130(a) for each transaction rescinded. The right to damages, however, is subject to a one year limitations period which starts running "from the date of the occurrence of the violation." § 130(e).

Plaintiff is entitled to $3,000 in statutory damages. First, the record indicates that the finance charge on both the transactions far exceeded $500 and therefore plaintiff is entitled to the maximum statutory award of $1,000 per violation. The record also establishes that defendant did not comply with the requirements of § 125 when plaintiff rightfully exercised her right to rescind the two loan transactions. Section 125 requires a creditor to return to the obligor any money or property received from the obligor and to take any action necessary to reflect the termination of any security interest created under the credit transaction within twenty days after receipt of a notice of rescission. § 125(b). It is undisputed that defendant did not do either after receiving plaintiff's valid rescission notice. Therefore, plaintiff is entitled to an award of $2,000 for defendant's failure to comply with § 125; that is $1,000 for each transaction.

Plaintiff is also entitled to an award of $1,000 for the failure of defendant to make all material disclosures with respect to the January 1987 loan transaction discussed previously. However, plaintiff is not entitled to, and for that reason has not requested, an award for the material nondisclosures with respect to the August 1986 loan transaction because this action was filed more than a year after the August 1986 loan transaction and thus is untimely with respect to an award of damages for the failure to disclose.

EFFECT OF RESCISSION

The TILA provides that when an obligor exercises his right to rescission, he or she is not liable for any finance or other charge and any security interest given by the obligor becomes void upon the rescission. § 125(b). In addition, as I noted previously, upon receipt of the rescission notice the creditor must return any down payment or other monies it received from the obligor and take the steps necessary to reflect the termination of the security interest. Thereafter, the obligor is to return to the creditor the property he or she received or its reasonable value. Id. If the creditor does not take possession of the property within twenty days after tender by the obligor, ownership of the property vests in the obligor without obligation on his part to pay for it.

Plaintiff argues that the failure of defendant to comply with her notice of rescission entitles her under § 125 to the return of the payments she already made on the loans to date and to a declaration that her remaining indebtedness is extinguished. As noted above, § 125 provides for forfeiture of the proceeds of the consumer transaction if the creditor does not take possession within 20 days after tender of the proceeds by the obligor. There is some precedent for the proposition that because § 125 requires the obligor to tender the proceeds only after the creditor appropriately reacts to the rescission by returning the property given and satisfying any security taken within twenty days, the recalcitrance of a creditor to accept a valid rescission obviates the obligor's requirement to tender and leaves the obligor with both a right to recover any payments made and a vesting of the proceeds of the transaction in himself without an obligation to repay it. See Gill v. Mid–Penn Consumer Discount Co., 671 F.Supp. 1021, 1026 (E.D.Pa.1987), aff'd mem., 853 F.2d 917 (3d Cir.1988). However, in the majority of prior cases the courts have either explicitly held that an obligor must tender or offer to tender the proceeds of the consumer transaction before finding a forfeiture, Bustamante v. First Fed. Sav. and Loan Ass'n, 619 F.2d 360, 365 (5th Cir.1980); or the particular circumstances of the case indicated that the consumer had tendered the proceeds in those cases where a forfeiture was found. Arnold v. W.D.L. Investments, Inc., 703 F.2d 848, 853 (5th Cir.1983). Although mindful that the statutory language contemplates a tender by the debtor after the creditor has performed his duties, several courts that have expressly addressed whether or not a tender by the consumer is required before finding a forfeiture of the proceeds of a transaction by the creditor, have found tender to be required to insure compliance with the congressional purpose of restoring the parties to the status quo. *Bustamante*; *Gerasta*. In this case, plaintiff does not allege, nor is there evidence of record that establishes, that plaintiff tendered the loan proceeds. Moreover, while I find from the uncontradicted evidence of record that defendant's conduct was questionable in that it was extremely careless in complying with the TILA statutory requirements and charged plaintiff, who was in a desperate credit situation, excessive settlement charges and an unconscionable interest rate far above the prevailing market rate thereby placing her home in jeopardy, there is no real evidence of record that defendant tried to deceive or cheat plaintiff. Evidence of deceit is a factor that may be considered in determining whether the equitable remedy of forfeiture is appropriate. In the absence of evidence of fraud or deceit by defendant and of a tender of the proceeds by plaintiff, I conclude that plaintiff has a continuing duty to return the proceeds of the loans. It remains to be decided, however, the amount of proceeds plaintiff must return and how such amount must be paid.

Plaintiff contends that if I find that defendant has not forfeited the loan proceeds, she is only required under the TILA to repay the amount of loan proceeds she actually received and not the amount that defendant advanced on her behalf to pay off the first and second mortgages on her home and the outstanding water bills or the amount advanced for closing costs on the present mortgage. I agree with plaintiff that she is not liable for the finance charge or any of the other charges related to the credit transactions such as, for example, the charges for title insurance, settlement and recording fees. The TILA provides that after rescission, the consumer "is not liable for any finance charge or other charge," § 125(b). The meaning of this provision is explained in the Official Staff Commentary of the Federal Reserve Board, which states that the consumer need not pay:

> finance charges already accrued, as well as other charges such as application or commitment fees or fees for the title search or appraisal, whether paid to the creditor, paid directly to a third party, or passed on from the creditor to the third party. It is irrelevant that these amounts may not represent profit to the creditor.

Federal Reserve Board, Official Staff Commentary § 226.23(d)(2)–1. Federal Reserve Board interpretations of the TILA are binding on courts unless they are "demonstrably irrational." Ford Motor Credit Co. v. Milhollin, 444 U.S. 555, 565, 100 S.Ct. 790, 797, 63 L.Ed.2d 22 (1980).

I disagree with plaintiff that she is not required to repay that amount that defendant advanced to pay off the first and second mortgages on plaintiff's home and her outstanding water and sewer bills. . . . The money advanced to discharge plaintiff's indebtedness on the two preexisting mortgages and for the water and sewer bills was as surely delivered to plaintiff as if defendant had delivered such amount payable to plaintiff and plaintiff, in turn, had endorsed it over to pay her bills. Thus, I find that plaintiff is liable to repay both the amount of proceeds which she actually received, $4,716.23, and the amounts advanced by defendant to pay off plaintiff's previous mortgage obligations, $12,507.43, and plaintiff's water and sewer bills, $1588.72, for a total of $18,812.38. Of course, the amount plaintiff has already paid defendant, $2,313.76, and the amount plaintiff paid at the closing on the August, 1986 loan, $385.00, shall be deducted from that amount. Thus, the total amount plaintiff must repay defendant is $16,113.62. However, in view of the Congressional purpose of restoring the parties to the status quo ante, I will order plaintiff to repay such amount to defendant at $171.00 per month, which was the amount of her monthly mortgage payments prior to the two loan transactions.

ATTORNEY'S FEES AND COSTS

Plaintiff requests and is entitled to, having succeeded in this action, an award of reasonable attorney's fees and costs under § 130(a)(3). Therefore I will order that plaintiff submit a petition for an award of attorney's fees and costs.

. . .

QUESTIONS AND NOTES

1. The second transaction occurred on January 19, 1987. Plaintiffs did not attempt to rescind until October 28, 1987, more than nine months later, and the court allowed it. Why did the right of rescission not expire on January 22?

2. Under section 125(b) when the consumer rescinds, the creditor must return amounts already received and must remove the security interest as an encumbrance on the land. After the creditor has done these two things, the consumer must return the property or its value to the creditor. What if the consumer wrongfully fails to return the property or its value? What may the creditor do?

3. Because the statutory scheme leaves the creditor in such a vulnerable position, the courts have tended to make the consumer's right to rescind conditional on the return of the principal of the loan (or value of the goods) to the creditor. In 1980 Congress added the last sentence of section 125(b) to authorize the courts to do this. Note that this sentence merely empowers the courts to vary the statutory procedures, it does not direct them to do so. Nevertheless, the court in *Mayfield* seems to believe that the courts should vary the procedures unless there is good reason not to. Under what circumstances would the court adhere to the statutory procedures?

4. At the time of the second transaction, plaintiffs had monthly payments of $171 on the first mortgage and $245 on the loan from defendant. They told defendant that on a monthly income of $634, they could not afford to make these payments. Defendant responded by offering to refinance their debt. At least two aspects of the refinancing are noteworthy. First, although this transaction was less than six months after the original one, defendant charged more than $3,000 in loan fees. (You may recall this phenomenon from In re Branch, page 441 supra, and Cheshire Mortgage Service v. Montes, page 475 supra.) Secondly, plaintiffs' new monthly obligation was $477, or $60 more than the amount defendant already knew they could not afford. In conditioning rescission on the consumer's return of benefits received, courts have emphasized their equity powers. E.g., Palmer v. Wilson, 502 F.2d 860 (9th Cir.1974). Should the court in *Mayfield* have exercised its equity power to require the consumer to repay the $16,000, or should it have adhered to the procedures and sanctions specified in section 125(b)?

5. If a court conditions rescission on the consumer's tender of any amounts already received, should the consumer also have to pay interest on the amounts to be returned? Is section 125(b) dispositive? See Rachbach v. Cogswell, 547 F.2d 502 (10th Cir.1976).

6. Problem. In 2007 *Consumers* borrowed $30,000 from *Lender*, giving *Lender* a second mortgage in their home. In 2008 *Consumers* borrowed $42,000 from *Lender*, using a portion of the proceeds to pay off the 2007 loan and using the balance to pay for renovations to their home. Six months later, identifying violations of the Truth-in-Lending Act in connection with the 2007 loan, they delivered to *Lender* a notice of rescission. Do *Consumers* have the right to rescind the 2007 loan?

If the 2008 refinancing of the 2007 loan were made by *Bank* instead of *Lender*, do *Consumers* have a right to rescind the 2007 loan?

7. Problem. *Consumer* buys a used car from *Dealer* for $5,000, giving a security interest in the car and in her house. *Dealer* fails to give proper notice of the three-day right to rescind. One year later, when she owes $4,000, *Consumer* encounters financial difficulties and defaults. She consults you, and on your advice, she sends *Dealer* a letter rescinding the transaction. *Dealer* repossesses and sells the car for $3,500. When *Dealer* sues for a deficiency judgment, you defend by pointing to the rescission and file a counterclaim for Truth-in-Lending Act damages of $1,000 (plus costs and attorney's fees). What should the court do?

Would the analysis or the result be any different if *Consumer* had financed the transaction by borrowing $5,000 from *Lender*, instead of purchasing on credit from *Seller?*

B. OBTAINING THE BENEFIT OF THE DEAL

An examination of remedies requires not only a determination of the remedy that will effectuate each of the consumer's rights, but also a consideration of the problem of litigation costs. The problem is especially significant in connection with consumer transactions because frequently the consumer's injury is relatively small in amount. If litigation costs exceed the amount of the injury, the consumer whose rights have been violated is financially better off not asserting those rights. And the consumer who does assert them might echo the words of Voltaire: "Only twice in my life have I felt utterly ruined: once when I lost a lawsuit and once when I won."[1] This section explores ways to deal with the high costs of enforcing the rights of consumers.

---

1. Quoted in Kosmin, The Small Claims Court Dilemma, 13 Houston L.Rev. 934, 935 (1976).

(1) INCREASING THE RECOVERY

(a) Attorney's Fees

The largest expense of litigation is the litigant's attorney's fee. Under the so-called American Rule, however, in the absence of a statutory or contractual provision to the contrary, courts generally deny this litigation expense to the victorious litigant.[2] Thus the Supreme Court stated:

> Almost a half century ago, the Massachusetts Judicial Council pleaded for reform, asking, "On what principle of justice can a plaintiff wrongfully run down on a public highway recover his doctor's bill but not his lawyer's bill?" We recognize that there is some force to the argument that a party who must bear the costs of his attorneys' fees out of his recovery is not made whole. But there are countervailing considerations as well. We have observed that "one should not be penalized for merely defending or prosecuting a lawsuit, and that the poor might be unjustly discouraged from instituting actions to vindicate their rights if the penalty for losing included the fees of their opponents' counsel." Fleischmann Distilling Corp. v. Maier Brewing Co., 386 U.S. 714, 718, 87 S.Ct. 1404, 1407, 18 L.Ed.2d 475 (1967). Moreover, "the time, expense, and difficulties of proof inherent in litigating the question of what constitutes reasonable attorney's fees," ibid., has given us pause, even though courts have regularly engaged in that endeavor in the many contexts where fee shifting is mandated by statute, policy, or contract. Finally, there is the possibility of a threat being posed to the principle of independent advocacy by having the earnings of the attorney flow from the pen of the judge before whom he argues.
>
> The American Rule has not served, however, as an absolute bar to the shifting of attorneys' fees even in the absence of statute or contract. The federal judiciary has recognized several exceptions to the general principle that each party should bear the costs of its own legal representation.

F. D. Rich Co. v. Industrial Lumber Co., 417 U.S. 116, 128–29 (1974).

The judicial exceptions include cases creating a "common fund," in which the court permits an award of fees out of a fund created by the litigation, and cases creating a "substantial benefit," in which the court "permits the award of fees when the litigant, proceeding in a representative capacity, obtains a decision resulting in the conferral of a 'substantial benefit' of a pecuniary or nonpecuniary nature." Serrano v. Priest, 569 P.2d 1303, 1309 (Cal.1977). Another exception exists when the plaintiff acts as a "private attorney general," in which the court permits an award of fees to a litigant who vindicates some important public policy. The Supreme Court has held that the "private attorney general" theory is not available in federal court (Alyeska Pipeline Co. v. Wilderness Society, 421 U.S. 240

---

2. See pages 716–22 supra for consideration of the enforceability of a contractual provision for the creditor's recovery of attorney's fees.

(1975)), but state courts are free to embrace it, and the California Supreme Court did so in *Serrano*.

Although the facts necessary for application of these exceptions to the American Rule rarely exist, attorney's fees often are available to consumers who prevail on their claims against merchants. This is because many statutes applicable to consumer transactions specifically provide for the recovery of attorney's fees. Most little-FTC acts require or authorize the courts to award attorney's fees to the successful consumer. Similar provisions appear in many state and federal topical statutes, including the Magnuson–Moss Warranty Act[3] the Truth-in-Lending Act[4] the Consumer Product Safety Act,[5] the Equal Credit Opportunity Act,[6] the Fair Debt Collection Practices Act,[7] and others. When the applicable statute requires an award of fees (e.g., Truth-in-Lending Act § 130(a)(3)), the trial court has discretion only in setting the amount of the fee award. When the statute merely authorizes the court to award attorney's fees (e.g., Magnuson–Moss Act § 110(d)), the court has discretion to make the award as well as determining the amount of any award. E.g., Scott v. Blue Springs Ford Sales, Inc., 215 S.W.3d 145 (Mo.App.2006) (when plaintiff recovered actual damages of $26,000 and punitive damages of $840,000 for defendant's violation of the Magnuson–Moss Warranty Act and the state little-FTC act, it was not an abuse of discretion for the trial court to deny an award of attorney's fees).

Postow v. Oriental Building Association

United States District Court, District of Columbia, 1978.
455 F.Supp. 781, affirmed in part 627 F.2d 1370 (D.C.Cir.1980).

WILLIAM B. JONES, DISTRICT JUDGE.

[Plaintiffs recovered $22,350 in a class action against defendant for its violations of the Truth-in-Lending Act. Plaintiffs now seek recovery of their attorney's fees, as provided by section 130(a)(3).]

Plaintiffs have petitioned for attorneys' fees calculated at $75.00 an hour for approximately 270 hours' work and for a matching bonus award to compensate them for the risks involved in litigation prosecuted for a fee contingent on success. Plaintiffs have also petitioned for attorneys' fees for the services of "law clerks" calculated at $30.00 an hour for approximately 40 hours. Finally, plaintiffs seek costs which were denied by the Clerk of the Court for a $1,414.20 fee charged by plaintiffs' expert witness and for $452.82 spent by the attorneys in out-of-pocket disbursements and in taking depositions.

I.

While the statute authorizes the Court to award reasonable fees, in determining what is reasonable the Court must consider the twelve factors

3.   § 110(d)(2).

4.   § 130(a)(3).

5.   § 23(a), 15 U.S.C. § 2072(a).

6.   § 706(d).

7.   § 813(a)(3).

delineated in Evans v. Sheraton Park Hotel, 164 U.S.App.D.C. 86, 503 F.2d 177 (1974). In structuring their memoranda to the Court on this determination, the parties have treated with those factors. Defendant has additionally asserted two threshold challenges to the award of any fees in this case: first, it attacks the constitutionality of the statutory provision for fees to prevailing plaintiffs and not to prevailing defendants as denial of due process to and equal protection for defendants in Truth in Lending litigation; second, it asserts that plaintiffs were not "successful" in this action as required by the express language of the provision.

Defendant's constitutional challenge raises what may either be phrased a due process or an equal protection issue by its contention that the unilateral award of attorneys' fees to successful plaintiffs impairs creditors' access to the courts to defend themselves against allegations of violating the Truth in Lending laws. Defendant states that this discrimination presents creditors with a no-win alternative in going to court: if they succeed in their defense, they are still out the cost of litigation which may exceed the penalty for the alleged violation; if they fail, they are then liable for the cost of the plaintiffs' prosecution in addition to their own litigation expenses and any damages that may be awarded.

The defendant cites Boddie v. Connecticut, 401 U.S. 371, 91 S.Ct. 780, 28 L.Ed.2d 113 (1971) as support for its constitutional position. There the Supreme Court held that it was a violation of due process for a state to deny access to indigents to the state's divorce courts because of a filing fee that such indigents were unable to pay. . . . *Boddie* was subsequently elaborated upon and clarified by the Court in United States v. Kras, 409 U.S. 434, 93 S.Ct. 631, 34 L.Ed.2d 626 (1973). In *Kras*, the Court noted that the *Boddie* case involved the absolute denial to the indigent-plaintiffs of the only legal avenue to adjust the marital relationship and the fundamental associational interests that surround the establishment, maintenance, and dissolution of that relationship. In *Kras*, the Court refused to extend this limited holding to the similar denial of access to federal bankruptcy courts to indigents unable to pay a filing fee. The Court dismissed due process concerns because it noted that the adjustment of the creditor-debtor relationship at issue in *Kras* was not in the exclusive control of the government, but that the parties had the option of private settlement "[h]owever unrealistic [that] remedy may be in a particular situation." Nor did the Court find in *Kras* that the creditor-debtor relationship and its adjustment through federal bankruptcy proceedings concerned a fundamental interest or that debtors were a suspect class such that the Court must scrutinize the filing fee requirement for a "compelling governmental interest" necessary to sustain its constitutionality under either due process or equal protection analysis. Rather, the Court found that this financial bar to the bankruptcy courts concerned matters of economics and social welfare for which the applicable standard in determining the propriety of Congress' action is that of "rational justification." . . .

In the present case the provision of attorneys' fees to successful plaintiffs and the denial of attorneys' fees to successful defendants does not bar the latter's access to the courts. It may encourage settlement, but it does not force it. Moreover, the very availability of settlement cuts against defendant's constitutional challenge because it removed the due process concern found in *Boddie* in the government's monopolization of the legal means to adjust a relationship. As in *Kras*, the creditor-debtor relationship present in the instant case involves no fundamental interest and the discrimination of plaintiffs over defendants effects no suspect classification that compels this Court to scrutinize the attorneys' fees provision for a compelling governmental interest.

The Court must therefore inquire only as to the existence of a rational justification for the discriminatory award of attorneys' fees provided by the Act. Such a justification is readily apparent: to provide for the supplementary enforcement of the Act by encouraging suits brought by injured consumers. Numerous courts have recognized that the Congress intended such supplementary enforcement by these so-called "private attorneys general." Alleged violations of the Act run into the thousands with over ten thousand law suits filed so far and more being filed each day at a rate of greater than two thousand suits a year. Most of these suits are for statutory rather than actual damages, because of difficulties in proving the latter or the purely technical nature of the violation. Statutory damages, however, have somewhat conservative maximum limits, making it not unusual for the costs of litigation to exceed the damages awarded.[6] Without fee awards, therefore, consumers would have little practical incentive and perhaps even less financial ability to bring suits under the Act.

It might be argued that discrimination could have been avoided by making fee awards available for both parties. . . . But to provide attorneys' fees to successful defendants against plaintiffs who have acted in good faith would obviously retard, if not totally frustrate, the encouragement of supplementary private enforcement of the Act.

In a different legal context, the Supreme Court has identified two equitable considerations which support a finding of a rational justification for the discriminatory award of attorneys' fees to successful plaintiffs: . . . (1) "the plaintiff is the chosen instrument of Congress to vindicate a policy that Congress considered of the highest priority" and (2) an award to a successful plaintiff is an award against "a violator of federal law."

These same equitable considerations are present in the attorneys' fees provision in the Truth in Lending Act and support a finding of a rational basis for the discriminatory effect of the provision. The express purpose of the Truth in Lending Act is "to assure the meaningful disclosure of credit

---

6. For example, Gillard v. Aetna Finance Co., Inc., 414 F.Supp. 737 (E.D.La. 1976) ($1,400 attorneys' fees for a legal aid lawyer; $635 statutory damages); Pedro v. Pacific Plan, 393 F.Supp. 315 (N.D.Cal.1975) ($3,000 attorneys' fees; $2,000 statutory damages); Burley v. Bastrop Loan Co., Inc., 407 F.Supp. 773 (W.D.La.1975) (statutory [damages] barred by statute of limitations, but attorneys' fees authorized); Starks v. Orleans Motors, Inc., 372 F.Supp. 928, 933 (E.D.La.), aff'd 500 F.2d 1182 (5th Cir.1974) ($644 statutory damages; attorneys' fees $2,000); Welmaker v. W. T. Grant Co., 365 F.Supp. 531 (N.D.Ga.1972) ($380 statutory damages; $17,500 attorneys' fees).

terms so that consumers . . . [can] avoid the uninformed use of credit. . . ." 15 U.S.C. section 1601. The obvious beneficiaries of the Act are the consumers. If the 2,000 plus suits filed each year represent even the majority of the alleged violations of the Act, the government has the option of creating a substantial bureaucracy to detect and prosecute these numerous alleged violations or to rely on the self interest of the injured consumer to perform these tasks.[8] The latter option is undoubtedly more cost efficient from the government's standpoint and is probably more efficient overall, assuming that consumers are in a better position to detect violations committed against them than some government agency would be. Because private litigation is as a supplement, rather than as an alternative to public enforcement of the Act, its encouragement through attorneys' fees and damages cannot help but effect a fuller compliance with the Act.

. . .

As the Supreme Court noted in *Alyeska,* "the circumstances under which attorneys' fees are to be awarded and the range of discretion of the courts in making those awards are matters for Congress to determine." . . . [T]he Supreme Court has implicitly recognized that the discriminatory provision of attorneys' fees to only successful plaintiffs is a legitimate legislative option for Congress to adopt, and, in fact, expressly cites . . . the instant provision of the Truth in Lending Act as an example of Congress' exercise of its discretion in this area.

In view of the foregoing, the Court finds that the encouragement of the private enforcement of the Truth in Lending Act by injured consumers against alleged violators of federal law provides a rational basis for the Act's discriminatory attorneys' fee provision to sustain its constitutionality as it has been challenged by the defendant in this case.

Defendant's second threshold challenge asserts that plaintiffs were not "successful" in this action as required by the Act's provision for attorneys' fees. Specifically, defendant refers to the language of the provision which permits attorneys' fees "in the case of any successful action to enforce the foregoing liability. . . ." Defendant's challenge has two bases: (1) that the Court dismissed the more significant claim of the two asserted in plaintiffs' complaint, and (2) that the Court, not the plaintiffs' attorneys, developed the legal analysis upon which the Court granted judgment to the plaintiffs.

As a practical matter, plaintiffs were as successful as they could be in this particular action. The Act allows only one recovery per consumer credit transaction regardless of the number of separate violations of the Act committed. 15 U.S.C. section 1640(g). Nothing in the provision or in the rest of the Act justifies an inference that "success" means something other than being awarded judgment on the merits. Even judgments based on technical violations are successes, for the Act itself is highly technical and

8. The Court notes that the provision of civil penalties in the Act is "to provide creditors with a meaningful incentive to comply with the law without relying on an extensive new bureaucracy." Sen.Rep.No. 93–278, p. 14.

Congress has provided for such technical successes by the provision of statutory damages. In any case, the success of plaintiffs in the present case has substantial merit, even if it does lack the element of actual damages, because it pinpoints the proper time for disclosure in a common commercial transaction and thereby effects the express purpose of the Act of providing useful, timely disclosure of consumer credit terms.

The second base of this threshold challenge, consideration of the Court's independent input and analysis into the final decision on the merit of plaintiffs' "successful" claim, is directed at the personal contribution of the plaintiffs' attorneys to the resolution of this case and to the addition of legal insight and guidance in this continually developing area of the law. Review of the Court's Memoranda and Orders filed in this case discloses that defendant's contention is not totally without merit. But the merit that it does have is not sufficient to justify the complete denial of fees. Instead the Court will defer this point for later consideration in the immediately following determination of the reasonable amount of attorneys' fees to award.

II.

In Evans v. Sheraton Park Hotel, 164 U.S.App.D.C. 86, 503 F.2d 177 (1974), our Court of Appeals adopted the Fifth Circuit's delineation of the various factors for courts to consider in determining the reasonableness of attorneys' fees:

1.   The time and labor required;

2.   The novelty and difficulty of the questions presented in the case;

3.   The skill required to perform the legal services properly;

4.   The preclusion of other employment by the attorneys due to the acceptance of the case;

5.   The customary fee;

6.   The type of fee charged: contingent or fixed;

7.   The time limitations imposed by the client or circumstances;

8.   The amount involved and the results obtained;

9.   The experience, reputation, and ability of the attorneys;

10.   The undesirability of the case;

11.   The nature and length of the professional relationship with the client;

12.   The awards in similar cases.

1.   The time and labor required.

Plaintiffs' attorneys spent approximately 270 hours on this case and employed "law clerks" for an additional 40 hours of work. The time spent by the attorneys has been adequately documented by affidavits which specify hours and dates of work on individual aspects of the case. Documentation for the time claimed for the law clerks was included in these same affidavits, but was of the most general nature, listing only hours worked each month with no indication of the type of work performed. Defendant asks the Court to reduce the hours claimed for the amount of time spent on the "unsuccessful" claim and to deny any fees for the law clerk time as unauthorized in a claim for *attorneys'* fees.

. . . In the present case, the two claims were briefed and considered in one motion. There was no independent litigation of either claim. It would be probably impractical to require the attorneys to identify how much time was spent on the unsuccessful claim. The Court notes that the attorneys were working in a constantly evolving area of the law. The prosecution of the unsuccessful claim was a reasonable effort even though hindsight now shows it to have lacked merit and, in light of the aforementioned single recovery rule, to have been unnecessary. Reduction of the attorneys' fees because of an unsuccessful claim brought in good faith would needlessly penalize the attorneys for being unable "to divine the exact parameters of the courts' willingness to grant relief" and be contrary to the Congressional policy of encouraging private enforcement of the Act.

The Court does find merit in defendant's opposition to an award of fees for the work performed by law clerks. Plaintiffs cite no authority for the proposition that attorneys' fees should be awarded for the work of persons who are not attorneys. The Court notes that the expenses of paralegal services are recoverable, either as fees or as costs, in successful antitrust actions. Such fees may be appropriate in complex antitrust cases where highly trained, specialized paralegals perform services that would otherwise be performed by young attorneys.

As noted before, however, the documentation submitted on the law clerks employed by plaintiffs' attorneys is incomplete. It does not indicate the qualifications of these law clerks or specify the work performed. The Court is therefore unable to discern whether the law clerks performed services that would have otherwise been performed by the attorneys or whether they performed administrative tasks or general legal research, either of which would be more properly included in the attorneys' hourly rates as part of their general overhead costs. Even if the Court were disposed to award fees for the work of these clerks, the incomplete documentation gives the Court no guidance in determining what would be reasonable rates to charge for their hours claimed. . . .

2.   *The novelty and difficulty of the issues.*

This case has been vigorously litigated over a four year period. Defendant's actions and omissions set the pace for the suit. Early in the case, before the certification of the class and before even the discovery regarding the class was completed, the defendant filed a motion to dismiss which presented two questions of first impression . . . .

The Court's decision on the motion resulted in a ruling on the merits in favor of the defendant as to the first claim and against it as to the second claim. Furthermore, the Court granted, over defendant's objections, plaintiffs' motion to maintain the action as a class action. Subsequently, the

Court granted the oral motion of the plaintiffs for summary judgment on the second claim. Having lost on the merits, defendant then challenged the Court's certification of the class . . . .

As this skeletal history of the case shows, it did involve several novel and somewhat complex issues. In light of these issues and the defendant's tenacious defense of its position on each, the Court finds that the 270 hours spent by plaintiffs' attorneys on the case to be reasonable and will not reduce those hours. On the other hand, the Court does not find that the issues and their treatment by plaintiffs' attorneys was such that an increase in the hours claimed or, more appropriately, an increase in the hourly rate assessed for the attorneys' services is warranted. The briefs and arguments of plaintiffs' counsel were helpful to the Court, but often they provided only a mere impetus to the Court's ultimate resolution of the issues. On some of the key issues, . . . the Court was required to rely on its own investigation and analysis of precedents and the Act's legislative history to reach its final decision. Thus, the Court notes that the attorneys' overall treatment of the issues was adequate, but not of such an unusually good quality to merit an increase in the fees awarded.

3.   *The skill requisite to perform the legal services properly.*

As was touched upon immediately above, plaintiffs' attorneys had the necessary skill to address the substantive issues adequately, and they also had the required skill to handle the procedural difficulties inherent in prosecuting a class action.

4.   *The preclusion of other employment.*

Plaintiffs' attorneys do not claim a specific, direct preclusion of other employment, but they assert that they have an "active practice" so that the 270 hours spent on this case forced them to turn down employment. It is difficult for the Court to accord any weight to this factor in light of this broad, unsupported statement. Furthermore, the Court finds some merit in defendant's contention that the publicity surrounding this case may well generate future offers of employment that will more than compensate the attorneys for their present, unspecified lost opportunities.

5.   *The customary fee.*

Plaintiffs state that the customary fee charged by both their attorneys and by attorneys of comparable skill is $75.00 an hour. The Court takes notice that such an hourly rate is reasonable for experienced lawyers in the Washington, D. C. area for the work that was performed in this case. As defendant points out, however, the younger of plaintiffs' two attorneys was but two years out of law school at the instigation of this suit. The affidavits filed by the attorneys also disclose an apparent partner-associate relationship between the attorneys with the younger attorney conferring with the senior attorney and preparing memoranda, motions, and briefs which were later reviewed by the senior attorney. The time spent in conferences and on drafts and reviews does not appear to be unduly repetitive or overlapping that a reduction of the hours claimed would be appropriate. But, when added to the consideration of the younger attorney's relative inexperience at the outset of the case, this apparent relationship provides a clear signal to the Court that a reduction of the rate charged for the younger attorney's services is in order. The Court will accordingly set the rate of compensation for the work of the younger attorney, whose hours, incidentally, represent approximately two thirds of the total hours claimed, at $60.00 an hour.

6.   *Whether the fee is fixed or contingent.*

Attorneys typically charge higher fees for work performed on a contingency fee basis to compensate the attorneys for the risk factor in such employment. Some courts have attempted to incorporate this consideration into their statutory award of attorneys' fees by adding "bonus" or "incentive" awards commensurate with the risk of loss undertaken. The risk of loss to the attorneys dissipated early in this action when the plaintiffs prevailed on the merits by the Court's March 1975 decision on the defendant's motion for summary judgment. With success on the merits, the attorneys were assured of receiving reasonable compensation for their efforts because of the Act's mandatory provision of attorneys' fees. At that time, the attorneys had logged approximately 30% of the total hours now claimed and still had the bulk of their work concerning the class action, such as discovery, notification of the class, and the determination of statutory damages before them.

A second reason given for bonus awards for contingency litigation is to attract more lawyers into accepting such cases where a public benefit might be conferred by their success. This consideration is especially appropriate in areas of litigation generally considered undesirable by the bar. This case does confer a public benefit, but it is difficult to quantify how great a benefit or how much of the benefit is the result of the work of the plaintiffs' attorneys. As noted above, the attorneys often provided merely the impetus for the Court's decision on the several issues raised in the case. Finally, the Court notes that consumer litigation is not an undesirable area of practice in this age of consumerism.

In light of the limited nature of attorneys' risk in litigating this case, their limited personal contribution to the aspects of the case conferring a benefit to the public as well as to their clients, and the general acceptability of Truth in Lending litigation, the Court finds that the base award it will make to the plaintiffs' attorneys will adequately compensate them for the risks they assumed in prosecuting this case on a contingency fee basis, sufficiently reward them for their contributions to the public's benefit, and encourage other attorneys to bring such meritorious litigation.

7.   *Time limitations imposed by the client or the circumstances.*

Plaintiffs assert that the short statute of limitations provided by the Act required their attorneys to research and prepare for the basic suit in a "relatively short period of time." . . . They stand in the same position as any other attorney who represents a client in a Truth in Lending suit and the Court is not inclined to rule that every such attorney should automatically have his attorneys' fees increased because Congress has decided that suits should be filed soon after the alleged violations occur.

8.   *The amount involved and the results obtained.*

This factor is not as determinative in Truth in Lending litigation as it might be in other types of cases because of the limits placed on the award of damages by the Act. As noted before, Truth in Lending cases do not usually result in awards of actual damages because of problems of proof or the purely technical nature of the violation. The statutory damages provided by the Act were limited to $1,000 for individual actions and $100,000 or 1% of the creditor's net worth in class actions. Section 130(a)(2) as amended in 1972.[10] The Act also requires the courts to consider in determining the amount of the award in a class action, among other relevant factors: the amount of actual damages, the frequency and persistency of the creditor's non-compliance, the creditor's resources, the number of persons affected, the extent to which the creditor's non-compliance was intentional. The limits on class damages are to prevent the catastrophic loss that could otherwise occur in class actions with many persons in the class. S.Rep.No. 93–278, pp. 14–15. The additional considerations direct the courts to individualize the damages to fit the nature of the violation and the ability of the violator to pay. No limit is placed on the awards of actual damages. The obvious concern in limiting statutory damages is to avoid unduly penalizing a creditor with an assessment of damages which are essentially a windfall to the successful plaintiffs. This concern does not apply to the awards of attorneys' fees for these fees represent actual expenses incurred by the plaintiffs or, in contingency cases such as this, compensation for their attorneys. The award of attorneys' fees is not a windfall to plaintiffs, and their reduction or denial would occasion a real loss to them. There is little reason to look to the limited award of statutory damages to determine the reasonableness of attorneys' fees which are generated by the unlimited costs of litigation.

Plaintiffs did not seek actual damages in this case. Because of the net worth of the defendant, damages were limited to $44,700.84. Upon examination of the aforementioned additional considerations for the Court to review in assessing damages, the Court further reduced the award to one half of the amount allowed. The attorneys' fees sought by plaintiffs exceeds this award, and the fees that the Court will eventually award will approximate it. Defendant objects that it is an "unreasonable judicial system which would permit the attorney to get an award larger than the client's." Defendant's contention ignores the purpose for limiting statutory damages and the fact that attorneys' fees do not confer any benefit on the plaintiffs or their attorneys other than to make them whole.

---

10.   Section 130 was amended a second time on March 23, 1976. That amendment provided that the ceiling for recovery in class actions would be the "lesser of $500,000 or 1 per centum of the net worth of the creditor." . . .

The Court also notes the litigation expenses incurred by the plaintiffs were largely generated in response to defendant's tenacious defense on every procedural and substantive issue in the case, up to and including the present motions. Defendant set the pace in this suit from filing a dispositive motion before the completion of discovery, to resisting discovery, to challenging the award of any damages and attorneys' fees. Defendant certainly has the right to assert all defenses, but it must bear the cost incurred by the necessary responses to its tactics.

Finally, as the Court noted heretofore, there is precedent for an award of attorneys' fees in Truth in Lending cases exceeding or approximating the award of damages. See note 6, supra.

9. *The experience, reputation, and ability of attorneys.*

Defendant does not challenge the qualifications of plaintiffs' attorneys except in noting the younger attorney's relative inexperience at the commencement of the suit. This factor has been discussed above.

10. *The undesirability of the suit.*

This factor is directed toward cases that may be unpopular in the community. A suit under the Truth in Lending Act is not such a case.

11. *The nature and length of the professional relationship with the client.*

The named plaintiff employed the class plaintiffs' attorney Kass as their counsel for the transaction which gave rise to the basic suit.

12. *Awards in similar cases.*

Courts have made numerous awards of attorneys' fees under the Act. As noted above, awards of attorneys' fees exceeding or approximating the award of damages are not uncommon. Defendant's opposition to the award of fees on this factor is limited to this point which was discussed above and dismissed.

. . .

The attorneys' fees that the Court will award plaintiffs' counsel are:

Mr. Kass: 85–3/4 hrs. at $75	$ 6,431.25
Mr. Skalet: 195.3 hrs. at $60	11,718.80[11]
	$18,150.05

III

Costs

The Clerk of the Court has taxed the defendant for costs of $189.03. . . .

---

11. Mr. Skalet's hours include the ten hours spent on the petition for attorneys' fees.

Plaintiffs' motion seeks to augment the costs awarded by the Clerk. Specifically, plaintiffs seek reimbursement for $1,414.20 spent for an expert witness, $180.66 for the costs of depositions, $136.23 for "postage and copying, taxis and out-of-pocket expenses."

Generally, costs for expert witnesses are limited to the statutory fee for witnesses rather than the actual fees charged by the witness, which is what plaintiffs seek by their motion. An exception is sometimes made when the proponent of the expert witness has secured the prior approval of the Court. Plaintiffs did not obtain the Court's approval, but they argue that they should still be awarded the actual fees because it was defendant's obstinate resistance to discovery regarding its net worth which required the employment of the expert. There is no question that the defendant would not stipulate to its net worth, an item of information necessary to the determination of the maximum statutory damages the Court could award. Plaintiffs' expert provided the Court with this information. The federal rules, however, provide less expensive ways to obtain this same information, such as requests for admissions and the service of interrogatories, and plaintiffs' failure to employ these available methods precludes them now from receiving the $1,414.20 they seek as expert witness fees.

Plaintiffs' request for an award to cover their counsel's unspecified out-of-pocket expenses must also be denied. Such expenses are not normally taxable as costs. . . .

QUESTIONS AND NOTES

1. For the consumer to be entitled to an award of attorney's fees, the consumer must be the "prevailing party." To be the "prevailing party" the consumer must obtain relief beyond a declaration that the defendant violated a statute. Nagle v. Experian Information Solutions, Inc., 297 F.3d 1305 (11th Cir.2002); Crabill v. Trans Union, L.L.C., 259 F.3d 662 (7th Cir.2001). See Buckhannon Board & Care Home, Inc. v. West Virginia Department of Health & Human Resources, 532 U.S. 598 (2001). But it suffices that the consumer recovers a nominal amount of statutory damages. E.g., Thornton v. Wolpoff & Abramson, L.L.P., 2008 WL 185517 (11th Cir.2008) (jury award of $1). And the court may award fees for work in unsuccessfully defending against a defendant's appeal if the overall result in the litigation is favorable to the consumer. Nigh v. Koons Buick Pontiac GMC, Inc., 478 F.3d 183, 188–89 (4th Cir.2007) (Supreme Court reduced consumer's recovery from $24,000 to $1,000).

Once the court determines that the plaintiff is entitled to attorney's fees, the problem becomes ascertaining the amount of the award. The statutes typically speak of "reasonable" attorney's fees. One approach would be to define reasonable as the same percentage of the consumer's recovery as appears in the contractual provision governing the creditor's right to attorney's fees. Why do you suppose this approach has not been adopted? Another approach would be to award the consumer whatever amount the consumer was actually obligated to pay his or her attorney. Why do you suppose this approach has not been adopted either?

Fixing the fee is within the discretion of the trial court and is reviewable only for abuse of that discretion. But even that limited review is impossible if the trial court does not articulate the basis for the award. Consequently, starting with Johnson v. Georgia Highway Express, Inc., 488 F.2d 714 (5th Cir.1974), most federal courts of appeal have directed the district courts to use factors like those in *Postow*. This corresponds roughly with the factors promulgated by the American Bar Association for setting fees:

> A lawyer shall not make an agreement for, charge, or collect an unreasonable fee. . . . The factors to be considered in determining the reasonableness of a fee include the following:
>
> (1) the time and labor required, the novelty and difficulty of the questions involved, and the skill requisite to perform the legal service properly;
>
> (2) the likelihood, if apparent to the client, that the acceptance of the particular employment will preclude other employment by the lawyer;
>
> (3) the fee customarily charged in the locality for similar legal services;
>
> (4) the amount involved and the results obtained;
>
> (5) the time limitations imposed by the client or by the circumstances;
>
> (6) the nature and length of the professional relationship with the client;
>
> (7) the experience, reputation, and ability of the lawyer or lawyers performing the services; and
>
> (8) whether the fee is fixed or contingent.

ABA, Model Rules of Professional Conduct, Rule 1.5(a).* ABA, Code of Professional Responsibility, DR 2–106(B) is substantially similar.

Numerous federal statutes provide that a successful plaintiff may recover an award of reasonable attorney's fees from the defendant. The Supreme Court has taken the position that the courts should determine the amount of the award by multiplying a reasonable hourly rate times the hours reasonably necessary to handle the matter. E.g., Blum v. Stenson, 465 U.S. 886 (1984) (lodestar approach). The Court has made it clear, however, that many of the factors cited in Johnson v. Georgia Highway Express are relevant to determining the reasonable amount of time involved and the reasonable hourly fee. "[M]any of the *Johnson* factors 'are subsumed within the initial calculation' of the lodestar . . . [T]he 'novelty

---

and complexity of the issues,' 'the special skill and experience of counsel,' the 'quality of representation,' and the 'results obtained' from the litigation are presumably fully reflected in the lodestar amount. . . ." Pennsylvania v. Delaware Valley Citizens' Council for Clean Air, 478 U.S. 546, 565 (1986). In Arbor Hill Concerned Citizens Neighborhood Association v. County of Albany, 522 F.3d 182 (2d Cir.2008), the Second Circuit purported to reconcile the *Johnson* approach with the "lodestar" approach, arriving at what it called the "presumptively reasonable fee."

2. In Duval v. Midwest Auto City, Inc., 578 F.2d 721, 726–27 (8th Cir.1978), plaintiffs sued for defendants' violation of the federal odometer statute. The trial court gave judgment for plaintiffs for $3,960. The court also awarded them attorney's fees in the amount of $14,205. Defendants challenged the attorney's fees award as unreasonable in relation to the amount of damages.

> To accomplish its remedial purposes the Act provides in § 409 [now codified at 49 U.S.C. § 32710(a)] for the recovery of treble damages or $1500, whichever is the greater. The same section makes recovery of reasonable attorney fees a mandatory feature of a defendant's liability upon proof of a violation. We agree with the district court's observation that these provisions are a response to legislative recognition that, as a practical matter, "in many situations, the amount of damage under the Act will be so small that few attorneys will pursue his client's case with diligence unless the amount of the fee be proportionate to the actual work required, rather than the amount involved."

> In rejecting defendants' argument, we do not minimize the significance of the amount of recovery as a factor in determining the reasonable value of an attorney's services. That factor, however, must be placed alongside the others, and all must be placed in the context of a concrete case. We hold that where, as here, a remedial statute requires the awarding of attorney fees as an element of recovery, a showing that the trial court's award exceeds the amount of damages does not, standing alone, amount to an abuse of discretion.

> The judgment of the district court is affirmed.

While concluding that the amount of recovery is not controlling, the court states that it is a factor to be considered. The amount of recovery is also on the ABA's list of factors to consider. In the context of the ABA rule, why is the amount of recovery relevant to fixing a reasonable fee? Is this reason equally relevant to determining the amount of a reasonable fee to be assessed against a defendant pursuant to a consumer protection statute? Is it relevant at all? See UCCC section 5.201(8).

Compare Earl v. Beaulieu, 620 F.2d 101 (5th Cir.1980), in which Earl purchased a car from Beaulieu. Earl defaulted and then sued for Beaulieu's violation of the Truth-in-Lending Act. The court stated:

> Defendant Beaulieu—who [is barely] literate—had failed to furnish Earl with a technically proper disclosure statement under the

Truth-in-Lending Act. Central Florida Legal Services, Inc. therefore descended upon him in the form of a five-page complaint alleging, among other things, such transgressions as are set out in the margin. As these allegations are, in main, technically correct, Mr. Beaulieu in due course was taught the concrete worth of good grammar, of carefully screening his clientele, and of a thorough working knowledge of such edicts as Regulation Z. In the district court their combined value came to $220.00 damages, $24.00 costs, and attorney's fees of $100.00— represented by a Federal Judgment in favor of his customer, Plaintiff Earl. Not content with its triumph below, Central Florida Legal Services, Inc., continues to pursue the public interest by this appeal in which the sole relief sought is, to quote the brief's concluding instructions to our court,

> The portion of the court's order of November 16, 1979, which awarded attorney's fees, must be vacated and the cause remanded with directions to award fees of $1,020.00 based upon the undersigned attorney's affidavit and the criteria set forth in *Johnson* without the three additional criteria considered by the lower court. Additional attorney's fees and costs must also be awarded for rehearing and appeal pursuant to Sosa v. Fite, 498 F.2d 114, 122 (5th Cir.1974).

Appellant having directed us to the *Johnson* criteria, we turn to them. Among them we find, numbered (8), "The amount involved and the results obtained." No moral issues, aggrieved classes, or pressing intangibles are involved here, only money damages, in a small—and foreseeably small—amount. In the course of the seventeen hours spent at the trial level in pursuing this tiny routine matter, plaintiff's attorneys prepared the following: a lengthy, multi-count, typed complaint meticulously detailing the deficiencies of Mr. Beaulieu's used car order when viewed as a T.I.L. disclosure statement; two sets of interrogatories to the foredoomed, pro se defendant; two sets of requests for admission; a motion and memorandum of law for summary judgment; a pretrial stipulation, and so on and on. On this appeal we are presented with a twenty-one page brief and a reply brief directed to defendant's five-page pro se attempt at an appellee's brief, plus the above-quoted request for a remand for more proceedings, a demand for attorney's fees for the appeal, and so forth. Somewhere along the line, a certain sense of proportion has been lost as the unfortunate Mr. Beaulieu, like the proverbial butterfly, is broken on the wheel by the monstrous engines wheeled into place by the Congress to bear upon Clayton's Garage.

> Concluding, we return to *Johnson*. In it we note its closing passage, emphasizing the great discretion that remains with the trial judge in these matters and the desirability of settlement where possible:[3]

---

3. The trial court found that plaintiff Earl rejected a reasonable settlement offer by Mr. Beaulieu and considered this as an additional factor to those of *Johnson* in fixing plaintiff's attorney's fees. This seems to us entirely appropriate.

We are mindful of the difficult job of the trial judge in cases of this kind, and that in all probability his decision will be totally satisfactory to no one. The cross-appeals taken in this case are witness to the usual view of parties litigant to such an award. The trial judge is necessarily called upon to question the time, expertise, and professional work of a lawyer which is always difficult and sometimes distasteful. But that is the task, and it must be kept in mind that the plaintiff has the burden of proving his entitlement to an award for attorney's fees just as he would bear the burden of proving a claim for any other money judgment.

In cases of this kind, we encourage counsel on both sides to utilize their best efforts to understandingly, sympathetically, and professionally arrive at a settlement as to attorney's fees. Although a settlement generally leaves every litigant partially dissatisfied, so does a judicial award for attorney's fees.

By this discussion we do not attempt to reduce the calculation of a reasonable fee to mathematical precision. Nor do we indicate that we should enter the discretionary area which the law consigns to the trial judge.

488 F.2d at 720.

We have written at such length on this matter only in deference to the legislative branch, which confided it to us in unmistakable terms. Bearing in mind Cromwell's suggestion to the Long Parliament, which we find apposite at this point[4] we determine to conclude it finally if that lies within our powers.[5] For the services of Central Florida Legal Services, Inc., at trial and on appeal, we allow legal fees in a total and composite amount equal to the entire and undisputed damages recovered in its case. That amount is $220.00. Each party shall bear his own costs of appeal. The judgment of the court below is to this extent modified and, as so modified, it is affirmed.

Finally, compare Mirabal v. General Motors Acceptance Corp., 576 F.2d 729 (7th Cir.1978), a Truth-in-Lending Act case in which the trial court rendered judgment for plaintiffs for $8,000. On an earlier appeal, the court reduced this to $2,000. The trial court allowed $2,000 as attorney's fees, and plaintiffs' attorney petitioned for review. The appellate court affirmed:

[P]etitioner alleged that he had expended 350 hours on the case, 120 at the trial level and 230 on the appeal. . . .

The instant case involves a car costing less than $5,000 and a loan of less than $2,500. Plaintiffs ultimately prevailed to the extent of

---

4. You have sat too long here for any good you have been doing. Let us have done with you. In the Name of God, go!

5. Certiorari, of course, remains a possibility.

$2,000 after getting somewhat over $8,000 at the original trial. Petitioner has thus received in attorney's fees an amount equal to that which his clients recovered in total.

Although the determination of hours necessary to effectively handle a case is not subject to exact determination, the amount which petitioner claims to have spent on the present case seems clearly out of proportion with the amount in controversy. Moreover, Congress has limited the liability of Truth in Lending Act violators to $1,000 per violation. To grant attorney's fees greatly in excess of a client's recovery requires strong support from the circumstances of the particular case. The instant case involved a one-time individual claim based mainly on a bona fide arithmetical error. As this court declared in Sprogis v. United Air Lines, Inc., 517 F.2d 387, 391 (7th Cir.1975), when it balked at the fee request presented there:

> First, this case does not represent the typical . . . claim envisioned by Congress and in the past sponsored by various public interest organizations. Second, the claim for attorneys' fees is not proportionate to the recovery of damages by plaintiff. Third, the precedential value of this decision is not controlling in light of [its reliance on an admitted arithmetical error].

Additionally, to grant large attorney's fee awards on the basis of relatively small injury would encourage suits which do not further the client's interest or the public's interest. The costs of these suits already forces many claims to settlement. See Landers, Some Reflections on Truth in Lending, 1977 Ill.L.F. 660, 680–81. Indeed, petitioner himself has inadvertently provided this court with an example of the questionable results in such suits. See Plaintiffs' Reply Memorandum and the letter attached to it. There petitioner made a settlement in a Truth in Lending case in which his client received $400 while petitioner was paid $12,000 as attorney's fees for the settlement. While such disproportionate sums may be exacted in settlement agreements, we should be loathe to automatically provide judicial approval for such results when these cases reach the courts.

Petitioner also claims that the attorneys for GMAC were paid over $30,000 and that this amount is indicative of what he should be paid. This contention was repeated at oral argument. This circuit has held that it is an abuse of discretion to determine attorney's fees solely on the basis of hours spent times billing rate. Petitioner wants us to go a step further and award him a fee based on what the *opposing side* spent in time and money. This ignores the fact that a given case may have greater precedential value for one side than the other. Also, a plaintiff's attorney, by pressing questionable claims and refusing to settle except on outrageous terms, could force a defendant to incur substantial fees which he later uses as a basis for his own fee claim. Moreover, the amount of fees which one side is paid by its client is a matter involving various motivations in an on-going attorney-client relationship and may, therefore, have little relevance to the value which petitioner has provided to his clients in a given case.

Therefore, for the reasons discussed above, we conclude that the district court properly acted within its discretion in setting the award of attorney's fees at $2,000.

576 F.2d at 730–31. Is the court saying that the amount the creditor pays its attorneys is irrelevant to setting a reasonable fee for the consumer's attorney? Is it irrelevant? How do you suppose the trial court arrived at the figure $2,000? Does the award in *Mirabal* further the purpose of Congress in including an attorney's fees provision in the Truth-in-Lending Act?

Should the court be influenced by the extent to which the judgment helps consumers other than the plaintiff?

Courts continue to address the propriety of granting awards of attorney's fees in amounts much larger than the amounts their clients recover. See Williams v. First Government Mortgage & Investors Corp., 225 F.3d 738 (D.C.Cir.2000), in which the client recovered $35,200 and the court awarded attorney's fees of $199,340; and Riter v. Moss & Bloomberg, Ltd., 2000 WL 1433867 (N.D.Ill.2000), in which the clients' maximum recovery was $2,000 and the court awarded attorney's fees of $173,000.

3. In addition to the factors listed in *Postow,* should the amount of the award also depend on whether the court is awarding attorney's fees because of a statutory provision that requires it, because of the creation of a common fund or a public benefit, because of the creditor's obdurate behavior, or because of the consumer's having acted as private attorney general?

Should the weight to be given the amount of damages awarded to the consumer (Question 2 supra) depend on the court's reason for awarding attorney's fees?

4. Consider the underlying issue: if a consumer succeeds in asserting rights protected by a statute, *should* the statute provide for an award of attorney's fees? What policy underlies the general rule denying attorney's fees to the successful litigant? Is this policy applicable to litigation under consumer protection statutes? If so, what reasons peculiar to the consumer context justify overriding it?

5. Some states refuse to enforce contractual provisions in which the consumer promises to pay the creditor's attorney's fees (see Note 3, page 721 supra). One of these is Wisconsin. Is it appropriate, then, for Wisconsin to provide that the creditor who violates the state's consumer protection act is liable for the consumer's attorney's fees? See Wis.Stat.Ann. § 425.308:

(1) If the customer prevails in an action arising from a consumer transaction, the customer shall recover the aggregate amount of costs and expenses determined by the court to have been reasonably incurred on the customer's behalf in connection with the prosecution or

defense of such action, together with a reasonable amount for attorney fees.

(2) The award of attorney fees shall be in an amount sufficient to compensate attorneys representing customers in actions arising from consumer transactions. In determining the amount of the fee, the court may consider:

(a) The time and labor required, the novelty and difficulty of the questions involved and the skill requisite properly to conduct the cause;

(b) The customary charges of the bar for similar services;

(c) The amount involved in the controversy and the benefits resulting to the client or clients from the services;

(d) The contingency or the certainty of the compensation;

(e) The character of the employment, whether casual or for an established and constant client; and

(f) The amount of the costs and expenses reasonably advanced by the attorney in the prosecution or defense of the action.

6. Problem. *Consumer* seeks your advice about a problem she is having with *Seller*. You agree to represent her on a contingent fee basis, taking as your fee whatever the court allows as attorney's fees. You file suit against *Seller*, asserting a violation of the state's little-FTC act. The trial court dismisses the action for failure to state a claim. You appeal, and the appellate court reverses and remands for trial. At that point, *Seller's* attorney proposes a settlement in which *Seller* would pay $350, which is the most *Consumer* would be entitled to under the statute. Would you advise her to accept the offer? Would you even inform her of the offer? How do you propose to pay your rent?

Freeman v. B & B Associates

United States Court of Appeals, D.C. Circuit, 1986.
790 F.2d 145.

WALD, CIRCUIT JUDGE.

[In 1981 plaintiffs borrowed money from defendant, giving a security interest in their home. Defendant improperly treated a discount fee, a finder's fee, and other charges as part of the "amount financed," instead of treating them as part of the "finance charge." As a result, the annual percentage rate was 62% instead of the 22% that defendant disclosed. In 1983 plaintiffs sent defendant a rescission notice and, when defendant threatened foreclosure, sued to prevent the foreclosure and to recover damages for defendant's violations of the Truth-in-Lending Act. Three months before the scheduled trial, defendant proposed a settlement, pursuant to Rule 68 of the Federal Rules of Civil Procedure. Under this proposal, defendant would permit plaintiffs to obtain judgment for rescission and plaintiffs would pay defendant $360, representing the excess of the actual "amount financed" over the amounts plaintiffs had paid on the loan. Defendant's proposal, however, stated that it "specifically excludes all liability for attorneys' fees." Plaintiffs accepted this settlement offer, then applied to the court for an award of attorney's fees under section 130 of the Truth-in-Lending Act. The court permitted plaintiff's attorney, Fox, to intervene as a party plaintiff. The court held that in the settlement plaintiffs had waived their claim for attorney's fees, but that Fox, their attorney, had an independent claim for attorney's fees. It awarded him $31,860 in fees. Defendant appealed.]

II.   An Attorney's Independent Right Under TILA

. . .

The District Court did not base its finding of an attorney's independent right of action on the explicit language of the statute but rather looked to the general objectives of TILA. According to the District Court, a refusal to find a separate attorney cause of action for fees would frustrate a "critical objective of the Truth-in-Lending Act, i.e. to assure the services of attorneys for persons pursuing claims under the Act." Memorandum on Defendants' Motion for Reconsideration at 8. The District Court's analysis borrowed heavily from the reasoning in James v. Home Construction Company, 689 F.2d 1357 (11th Cir.1982). In *James* the Eleventh Circuit found that a successful attorney in a TILA case had standing to seek fees after the settlement of the borrower's underlying claim. The settlement agreement, however, expressly left open the existence of the lawyer's fees. The Eleventh Circuit found that under these circumstances section 130(a)(3) created a "right of action" for attorneys to seek fee awards, reasoning that

> If settlement of a TILA case precluded the plaintiff's attorney from seeking a fee award, nothing would prevent indigent clients, who have no financial interest in statutory fee awards, from freely bargaining them away without personal detriment. Such a result would enable creditors who have violated the Act to escape liability for attorney's fees; such a practice would thwart both the statute's private enforcement scheme and its remedial objectives. . . . Congress could not have intended such a result.

James, 689 F.2d at 1359.

While we are sensitive to the concerns underlying the District Court's opinion and the Eleventh Circuit's holding in *James,* we do not think they support the creation of an attorney's independent right of action under TILA for fees. The District Court is correct that a major congressional goal behind TILA was the creation of a system of private enforcement. See Gram v. Bank of Louisiana, 691 F.2d 728, 729 (5th Cir.1982). The court's analysis, however, ignores the fact that Congress specified how this remedial purpose was to be effectuated. The words of the statute show that Congress chose to create its system of private enforcement by giving borrowers access to a source of funds with which to compensate an attorney.

The words of section 130 unambiguously vest the right to recover attorneys' fees in the client rather than in the attorney. Section 130 states that "any creditor who fails to comply with any [disclosure] requirement . . . with respect to *any person* is liable to *such person* in an amount equal to . . . the costs of the action, together with a reasonable attorneys' fee as determined by the court." (emphasis supplied). In other words, under the statute the creditor is liable for attorneys' fees to the person to whom the creditor failed to make the required TILA disclosures, i.e. to the *borrower*. We find nothing in the words of the statute suggesting any right to fees in an attorney which is independent and separate from the right of the borrower-client to collect attorneys' fees. See also Smith v. South Side Loan Company, 567 F.2d 306, 307 (5th Cir.1978) (award of attorneys' fees is right of party suing, not his attorney); cf. Evans v. Jeff D., 475 U.S. 717, 730 & n. 19, 106 S.Ct. 1531, 1539 & n. 19, 89 L.Ed.2d 747 (1986) (Congress bestowed statutory eligibility for attorneys' fees under 42 U.S.C. § 1988 on party, not attorney).

Because we find that section 130 clearly places the right of action for attorneys' fees in the borrower, we will not ignore the words of the statute in pursuit of some disembodied congressional purpose. While the language of TILA "should be construed liberally in light of its broadly remedial purpose," see Gram v. Bank of Louisiana, 691 F.2d at 729 (quoting Thomas v. Myers–Dickson Furniture Company, 479 F.2d 740, 748 (5th Cir.1973)), this does not mean that a court may interpret TILA to encompass any policy that increases the total number of TILA suits brought. A court looks to legislative purposes for guidance where the words of a statute permit alternate constructions or where an actual conflict between statutory provisions exists. In interpreting ambiguous provisions of TILA we agree that a court should strive to effectuate the congressional goal of encouraging private litigants to assert their rights under the statute. We do not, however, find in the words of section 130(a)(3) any indication that an attorney possesses a cause of action for attorneys' fees independent of his client's cause of action.

We also regard the District Court's reliance on James v. Home Construction Company as misplaced. *James* involved an attorney's standing to pursue his client's claim for attorneys' fees under TILA. *James* is silent on the question of an attorney's right of action where the client has expressly waived any claim to attorneys' fees. To the extent that language in *James* suggests a more general right of action under TILA by attorneys for their fees, we must disagree for the reasons already stated above. See also Evans v. Jeff D., 475 U.S. at 730 n. 19, 106 S.Ct. at 1539 n. 19 (suggesting disapproval of this aspect of *James*). In fact, however, we read the rationale in *James* as applicable solely to the issue of the attorney's standing to seek attorneys' fees. See Moore v. National Association of Securities Dealers, Inc., 762 F.2d 1093, 1099 n. 10 (D.C.Cir.1985) (opinion of MacKinnon, J.) (attorney's right to fees under Title VII is one of subrogation to his client's). But cf. Smith v. South Side Loan Company, 567 F.2d at 307–08 (suggesting TILA attorney may never have standing). This more limited reading of *James* accords with cases in which an attorney has been found in some circumstances to have standing to pursue *his client's* claim for attorneys' fees in civil rights cases. See, e.g., Lipscomb v. Wise, 643 F.2d 319 (5th Cir.1981) (although award of attorneys' fees is made to prevailing party, attorney is the only person aggrieved if fees are denied). In *Lipscomb*, the Fifth Circuit held that to permit an attorney to appeal a denial of attorneys' fees to his client furthers the congressional purpose of encouraging private enforcement of the civil rights laws. *Lipscomb* did not deduce from this congressional purpose any right of an attorney for fees independent of the right of his client, however. Instead, the court found merely that the attorney had standing to advance his client's right to fees.

Finally, we do not think that our refusal to find an independent attorney cause of action for fees in any sense does violence to the congressional purpose behind section 130(a)(3). We view the purpose of section 130(a)(3) more narrowly than does the District Court. "Section 130 is intended to allow aggrieved *consumers* to participate in policing the Act," Gram v. Bank of Louisiana, 691 F.2d at 729 (emphasis added); it is not intended to appoint attorneys themselves as private attorneys general. Congress sought to encourage injured borrowers to bring TILA suits by providing them with funds to pay an attorney. This narrower view of the congressional purpose is consistent with existing cases holding that an attorney's fee award is not subject to setoff, and once awarded becomes in effect an asset of the attorney rather than the client. See, e.g., Plant v. Blazer Financial Services, Inc., 598 F.2d 1357, 1366 (5th Cir.1979). These cases hold only that the congressional purpose behind section 130(a)(3) would be frustrated if the funds awarded for payment of attorneys' fees were used for some other purpose; they do not suggest any independent right of an attorney for fees. See also Evans v. Jeff D., 475 U.S. at 731, 106 S.Ct. at 1539 (party may assign his right to fees to his attorney).

III.   FAILURE TO CROSS-APPEAL THE VALIDITY OF THE WAIVER

Fox and the Freemans also attempt to argue on appeal that the Freemans' waiver of attorneys' fees through the accepted offer of judgment was invalid under an extension of Moore v. National Association of Securities Dealers, Inc., 762 F.2d 1093 (D.C.Cir.1985). While acknowledging that in *Moore* this court upheld a waiver of attorneys' fees as part of a settlement agreement, appellees read *Moore* to suggest several factors which will as a matter of law invalidate a fee waiver in situations different from that involved in *Moore*. According to the appellees, under the circumstances of this case B & B Associates' offer of judgment could not condition virtually full relief on the merits upon a waiver of statutorily provided attorneys' fees. B & B Associates' offer, they contend, pitted client against attorney and took undue advantage of an attorney's ethical duty to serve his client's interest. The waiver was therefore invalid since contrary to the public policies underlying the TILA fee provision.

We find that the validity of the Freemans' waiver of attorneys' fees is not properly before the court because Fox and the Freemans failed to take a cross-appeal from the judgment of the District Court. . . .

An appellate court . . . will freely consider any argument by an appellee that supports the judgment of the district court including arguments rejected by the district court and even arguments contradicting the logic of the district court. Only when an appellee attempts to overturn or modify a district court's judgment must the appellee file a cross-appeal. While a cross-appeal is not a jurisdictional requirement, it is the "proper procedure," and the failure to file a cross-appeal ordinarily precludes review where an appellee seeks to enlarge his rights or lessen those of an adversary. See, e.g., 15 C. Wright, A. Miller & E. Cooper, Federal Practice and Procedure § 3904, at 415 (1976). Courts will on occasion excuse the failure to file a cross-appeal but only in cases involving exceptional circumstances.

The issue for this court therefore is whether the argument appellees raise that their waiver of attorneys' fees was invalid is essentially an attempt to modify the relief granted by the District Court or merely asks us to affirm the District Court on other grounds. If Fox and the Freemans seek only to enforce the District Court's decree, we may consider their argument. "But if a finding for appellees on this claim would necessarily enlarge the relief, we may not and should not consider it." See Phillips v. Pennsylvania Higher Education Assistance Agency, 657 F.2d 554, 567 (3d Cir.1981), cert. denied, 455 U.S. 924, 102 S.Ct. 1284, 71 L.Ed.2d 466 (1982).

In the instant case, a finding for Fox and the Freemans on their waiver argument *would* necessarily modify the judgment of the District Court. We cannot conclude that appellees attack only the reasoning of the District Court. If the Freemans' waiver of attorneys' fees is invalid because the offer of judgment was unduly coercive and contrary to the congressional policy underlying TILA, this court must vacate the entire offer of judgment.

Appellees argue that the proper relief for an impermissibly coercive offer of judgment is for the court to award attorneys' fees while keeping the rest of the offer of judgment intact. We find this contention fatally flawed. In a recent challenge to a settlement agreement which granted injunctive relief conditional on plaintiffs' waiver of any claim for attorneys' fees under 42 U.S.C. § 1988, the Supreme Court held that a district court could not enforce such a settlement on the merits and also award attorneys' fees. See Evans v. Jeff D., 475 U.S. 717, 106 S.Ct. 1531, 89 L.Ed.2d 747 (1986). According to the Supreme Court, Rule 23(e) of the Federal Rules of Civil Procedure does not permit a court to materially modify a proposed settlement and order its acceptance over either party's objection. See also Moore v. National Association of Securities Dealers, Inc., 762 F.2d at 1110 n. 21 (opinion of MacKinnon, J.) (for a court to unilaterally modify a settlement which contemplated no payment of attorneys' fees would undermine the settlement process); id. at 1114 (Wald, J., concurring in the judgment) (court "should be reluctant to enforce the defendant's promise while depriving it of the agreed consideration") (footnote omitted).

The concerns expressed in Evans v. Jeff D. regarding a court's inability to materially modify proposed settlements under Rule 23(e), which *obligates* a court to assess the reasonableness of any settlement in a class action, are even more compelling in the context of an offer of judgment. A court's discretion to reject a waiver of attorneys' fees in an offer of judgment, to the extent it exists at all, appears to be far more circumscribed than its discretion to determine reasonableness under Rule 23(e).[5] Under an offer of judgment pursuant to Rule 68 of the Federal Rules of Civil Procedure, a defendant allows judgment to be taken against him. Cf. Marek v. Chesny, 473 U.S. 1, 105 S.Ct. 3012, 3015, 87 L.Ed.2d 1 (1985). The terms of the offer of judgment, if accepted by the plaintiff, are binding on the defendant because of the defendant's consent. Elimination of an express and integral term from an offer of judgment—such as the Freemans' waiver of attorney's fees—destroys the binding force of the offer on the defendant by vitiating the defendant's consent. The defendant submits to be bound by the offer of judgment as the defendant has formulated it. The express terms of this offer of judgment are material and thus not severable. The District Court could not know that B & B Associates would have submitted to a different offer of judgment. And absent the defendant's consent, a court has no power to enforce the offer of judgment. Cf. Evans v. Jeff D., 407 U.S. at 727, 106 S.Ct. at 1537 (court has no power under Fed.R.Civ.Pro. 23(e) to materially modify a settlement and order its acceptance over either party's objection).

If this court accepted appellees' argument that the Freemans' waiver was invalid, we would necessarily vacate rather than reform the offer of judgment. Because reversal of the District Court on the issue of the validity of the Freemans' waiver of attorneys' fees would substantially modify the original relief granted to the parties, Fox and the Freemans were obligated to file a cross-appeal. Although the District Court originally awarded attorneys' fees to Fox independently, the court did not alter in any way the original offer of judgment, which provided for rescission of the Freemans' loan agreement, the payment of costs by B & B Associates and the return of $360.57 to B & B Associates. The original offer of judgment also provided an explicit waiver of the Freemans' claim for attorneys' fees. To vacate the offer of judgment, therefore, would clearly modify the rights of B & B Associates under the original judgment of the District Court. In the

---

5. While opining that a district court ordinarily has no obligation to evaluate the reasonableness of a fee waiver outside the class action context, see 475 U.S. at 738 n. 30, 106 S.Ct. at 1543 n. 30, the Supreme Court in *Evans* explicitly reserved the question of whether a district court could (or must) refuse to approve a fee waiver outside the class action context in three specific situations. These situations included the existence of a "routine . . . policy designed to frustrate the objectives of the Fees Act," a "vindictive effort to deter attorneys from representing plaintiffs in civil rights suits," and a "situation [that] presents a grossly unfair choice to the plaintiff and his/her counsel, and [where] permitting such offers to be made would seriously undermine the purpose of fee shifting provisions." See *Evans*, 475 U.S. at 740 & n. 32, 106 S.Ct. at 1544 & n. 32.

absence of a cross-appeal we will not consider the validity of the Freemans' waiver of attorneys' fees which was involved in accepting the offer.

. . .

In their brief to this court, Fox and the Freemans state that they would oppose any vacation of the offer of judgment as that "would do violence to the purposes of Rule 68 and would unfairly burden the district court and the Freemans. The Freemans accepted the offer [of judgment] and will adhere to that decision even if their legal argument on this appeal fails." Brief of Appellees at 21 n. 6. Unfortunately, appellees cannot avoid the consequences of the argument they ask us to consider on appeal. To accept their argument that the offer of judgment was facially invalid . . . would require a modification of the judgment of the District Court. There is just no way for appellees to eschew that relief and still prevail on their plea that the Freemans should not have been able to waive attorneys' fees. Thus, appellees' waiver argument can avail them nothing absent a properly filed appeal to modify the judgment of the District Court.

IV.   CONCLUSION

We find that under TILA an attorney has no cause of action for fees separate from and independent of the underlying claim of his client. We therefore vacate the District Court's award of attorneys' fees to Fox. We also find that the failure of appellees to appeal the issue of the validity of the Freemans' waiver of their claim for attorneys' fees precludes our consideration of this point. Accordingly, the offer of judgment, as originally drafted by B & B Associates and accepted by the Freemans, remains binding on the parties.

So ordered.

QUESTIONS

1.   The court refuses to consider the validity of plaintiffs' waiver of their right to attorney's fees because they failed to appeal the trial court's holding that they had waived it. This suggests that the result might have been different if only plaintiffs had filed a cross-appeal. But the court states that the relief available on appeal, if plaintiffs had appealed and succeeded, would have been to overturn the entire settlement. And plaintiffs' brief expressly disavowed this relief. One would expect this posture to be typical: if the only relief available is scrapping the entire settlement, why would there ever be an appeal by a plaintiff who had agreed to a settlement offering substantially all the relief he or she had sought?

Consequently, the relief plaintiffs sought was enforcement of all the terms of the settlement except for the one offensive provision. Why does the court reject this relief? Can you think of any analogy that would justify a contrary conclusion?

2.   The court cites Evans v. Jeff D., 475 U.S. 717 (1986), decided just one month before the court announced its decision in *Freeman*. *Evans* was a class action civil rights case in which the plaintiffs sought injunctive relief. One week before trial, defendants proposed a settlement, offering virtually all the relief that the plaintiffs had sought, but conditioning the settlement on a waiver, subject to approval of the court, of plaintiffs' right to attorney's fees and costs. For settlement of a class action, Rule 23(e) of the Federal Rules of Civil Procedure requires judicial approval of the settlement. The trial court approved the settlement, including the waiver of attorney's fees. The Ninth Circuit, however, invalidated the waiver of attorney's fees and remanded for determination of a reasonable fee. The Supreme Court reversed the Ninth Circuit, holding that while the court must approve or disapprove settlements of class actions, it does not have the power to approve only some portions of a settlement (viz., the injunctive relief) and alter other portions (viz., the waiver of attorney's fees). The Court held that it is permissible for a party to waive the right to attorney's fees, and it upheld the trial court's approval of the settlement.

The statute in *Evans,* 42 U.S.C. § 1988, provides that "the court, in its discretion, may allow the prevailing party . . . a reasonable attorney's fee." Compare Truth-in-Lending Act section 130(a)(3), which makes the award of attorney's fees mandatory. Should that affect the applicability of Evans v. Jeff D?

3. If, as in *Freeman,* courts will enforce a plaintiff's waiver of rights to attorney's fees, would a defendant's attorney be guilty of malpractice if he or she failed to suggest a fee waiver as part of any settlement?

4. In Coleman v. Fiore Brothers, Inc., 552 A.2d 141 (N.J.1989), the court held that if plaintiffs, represented by a nonprofit, prepaid legal services corporation, agreed to a settlement with no mention of attorney's fees in the settlement agreement or during the settlement negotiation, they were precluded from recovering attorney's fees following performance of the settlement agreement. Hence, plaintiffs lost, and their attorneys received no compensation. The court also indicated, however, that henceforth it is not ethically permissible for a nonprofit public interest law firm to negotiate for attorney's fees at the same time it negotiates a settlement on the merits. Nor is it permissible for the defendant to attempt to negotiate the two matters simultaneously. The merits of the plaintiff's claim must be settled separately and first.

The court refused to extend this rule to the situation in which the plaintiff is represented by a private attorney. In that context the defendant may insist on simultaneous negotiation of the plaintiff's claim on the merits and the plaintiff's claim for attorney's fees. Is the court's distinction between public interest attorneys and private attorneys justified? With respect to the latter, how can the plaintiff's attorney ensure compensation for his or her services?

Some state and local bar opinions had taken the position that it is unethical for defendants to request fee waivers in connection with proposed settlements. E.g., Committee on Professional and Judicial Ethics of the Association of the Bar of the City of New York, Op. No. 82–80 (1985); Id., No. 80–94, reported in 36 Record of NYCBA 507 (1981); District of

Columbia Legal Ethics Committee, Op. No. 147, reprinted in 113 Daily Washington Law Reporter 389 (1985). In the wake of *Evans*, they have reversed this position. E.g., District of Columbia Legal Ethics Committee, Op. No. 289 (1999).

(b) Minimum Damages

Statutes designed to protect consumers frequently provide liability for the consumer's actual damages or a stated dollar amount, whichever is more. The statutes vary considerably, however, with respect to the amount of the minimum damages. For example, just among little-FTC acts the minimum damages vary from $25 (Massachusetts) to $1,000 (Hawai'i), with $200 being the most common amount. And some (e.g., North Carolina and Texas) provide for a multiple of actual damages. Other kinds of consumer protection statutes also provide for minimum damages. Examples include the Truth-in-Lending Act (twice the finance charge but in no event less than $100),[8] the Florida Collection Practices Act ($500),[9] the federal odometer statute (treble damages but not less than $1,500),[10] and even the UCC (the amount of the finance charge plus ten percent of the cash price or the loan).[11]

What is the rationale of these provisions? What purposes does a minimum damages provision serve? To achieve the objectives you have identified, should the amount of the minimum award be closer to Massachusetts' $25 or Hawai'i's $1,000? What drawbacks are there to the use of minimum damages?

Before reading the next principal case, please review Weigel v. Ron Tonkin Chevrolet Co., page 133 supra.

Scott v. Western International Surplus Sales, Inc.

Supreme Court of Oregon, 1973.
267 Or. 512, 517 P.2d 661.

DENECKE, JUSTICE.

. . .

The plaintiff's son was looking for a tent to take backpacking. He wanted a tent that would be suitable for use in the snow. For this reason he wanted a window with a closing flap that could be secured and eaves. Plaintiff and his son looked at a tent in defendant's store. The tent was in a sealed package with a card enclosed stating "Nylon Net Rear Window with ZIPPERED flap." A diagram on the card pictured the flap. The card also pictured a tent with eaves.

---

8. § 130(a)(2)(A).

9. West's Fla.Stat.Ann. § 559.77.

10. 49 U.S.C. § 32710(a).

11. § 9–625(c)(2) (for the creditor's failure to comply with the requirements governing repossession and sale of collateral).

Plaintiff bought the tent. The plaintiff and his son brought the tent home and took it out of its package. They found the tent did not have these two features. At the rear there was only a vent which could not be securely closed. Plaintiff immediately tried to return the merchandise. However, defendant would not give him a refund and plaintiff refused a credit for future purchases because the only item he wanted was a tent. The defendant did not have any tent which had the features plaintiff's son wanted.

Plaintiff brought this action pursuant to ORS 646.638, which provides:

(1) Any person who purchases * * * goods * * * and thereby suffers any ascertainable loss of money or property, real or personal, as a result of the wilful use or employment by another person of a method, act or practice declared unlawful by ORS 646.608, may bring an individual action in an appropriate court to recover actual damages or $200, whichever is greater. * * *.

ORS 646.608(g) declares the misrepresentation of goods to be unlawful.

Plaintiff alleged in essence the facts we have set forth and further alleged: "As a result of defendant's above mentioned conduct, plaintiff has suffered an ascertainable loss of money and is entitled to recover the sum of Two Hundred Dollars ($200.00)."

The defendant did not move against or demur to the complaint but now contends on appeal that the complaint does not state a cause of action. Defendant also contends that the trial court should have granted its nonsuit because plaintiff failed to prove an ascertainable loss.

We conclude the complaint states a cause of action. Under the statute there is no need to allege or prove the amount of the "ascertainable loss"; the plaintiff is only claiming the minimum of $200 which is recoverable if an ascertainable loss of any amount is proved. If the defendant was of the opinion that it was inadequately informed by this allegation, before answering, it should have moved to require the plaintiff to make the allegation more definite and certain.

The judgment of nonsuit was properly denied. "Ascertainable" can reasonably be interpreted to mean, capable of being discovered, observed or established. As we have already stated, the amount of the loss is immaterial if only $200 is sought.

There was evidence of an "ascertainable loss." The tent was purchased for $38.86. The inference is that the tent, as represented, had that value. The tent sold did not have some of those represented features. The inference can be drawn that because the tent did not have a window with a closing flap or eaves it had a value of less than $38.86. To repeat, the plaintiff did not have to prove in what amount the value of the tent was reduced because it was not as represented. He merely had to prove he suffered some loss.

Defendant also contends it was entitled to a nonsuit because the statute requires a "wilful" misrepresentation and there was no evidence of wilfulness. ORS 646.605(8) provides: "A wilful violation occurs when the person committing the violation knew or should have known that his conduct was a violation."

The evidence in this case may not be susceptible to the interpretation that the defendant knew of the misrepresentation; however, the evidence was certainly sufficient for the trial court to find the defendant should have known.

The defendant sold so many tents that it had one employee designated as tent manager. One of his duties was to familiarize himself with the various tents offered for sale. Defendant had sold a substantial number of tents of the model sold plaintiff. Defendant had a separate tent display area in which a tent of the kind purchased by plaintiff was set up for display. (This display area was not shown plaintiff nor was he told of its existence.) In the displayed tent defendant placed another tent of the same kind, wrapped in its plastic package.

From this evidence the trier of the facts could find the defendant should have known of the discrepancies between the representations made on the card and the actual product, as exhibited by the displayed tent.

Affirmed.

QUESTIONS

1.   Why does the statute limit recovery to cases in which there is "ascertainable loss"? The court says that "ascertainable" can reasonably mean capable of being established. Was the loss in this case "ascertainable"? What else might "ascertainable" mean? Which meaning ought to apply?

2.   The Connecticut Unfair Trade Practices Act (CUTPA) does not provide for minimum damages but it, too, limits relief to "any person who suffers any ascertainable loss of money or property, real or personal, as a result of the use or employment of a [prohibited] method, act or practice." Conn. Gen.Stat.Ann. § 42–110g(a). In Hinchliffe v. American Motors Corp., 440 A.2d 810, 814–817 (Conn.1981), the Connecticut Supreme Court held that the consumer need not prove a specific amount of actual damages:

>   [T]he inclusion of the word "ascertainable" to modify the word "loss" indicates that plaintiffs are not required to prove actual damages of a specific dollar amount. "Ascertainable" means "capable of being discovered, observed or established." Scott v. Western International Sales.

>   "Loss" has been held synonymous with deprivation, detriment and injury. It is a generic and relative term. "Damage," on the other hand, is only a species of loss. The term "loss" necessarily encompasses a broader meaning than the term "damage."

>   Whenever a consumer has received something other than what he bargained for, he has suffered a loss of money or property. That loss is ascertainable if it is measurable even though the precise amount of the loss is not known. CUTPA is not designed to afford a remedy for

trifles. In one sense the buyer has lost the purchase price of the item because he parted with his money reasonably expecting to receive a particular item or service. When the product fails to measure up, the consumer has been injured; he has suffered a loss. In another sense he has lost the benefits of the product which he was led to believe he had purchased. That the loss does not consist of a diminution in value is immaterial, although obviously such diminution would satisfy the statute. To the consumer who wishes to purchase an energy saving subcompact, for example, it is no answer to say that he should be satisfied with a more valuable gas guzzler.

.   .   .

Adoption of the defendants' view, that ascertainable loss is equivalent to actual damages, would eviscerate the private remedy provided by CUTPA. The ascertainable loss requirement is a threshold barrier which limits the class of persons who may bring a CUTPA action seeking either actual damages or equitable relief. Were we to construe that barrier as a requirement that all plaintiffs show actual damages, any person who bought an item which was deceptively advertised but was actually of a value equal to or greater than the item as advertised would not be able to obtain a rescission under CUTPA.

Such a construction impairs the efficacy of the equitable remedies provided by CUTPA, and prevents the statute from achieving the remedial effect which the legislature desired.   .   .   .

The plaintiff who establishes CUTPA liability has access to a remedy far more comprehensive than the simple damages recoverable under common law. The ability to recover both attorneys' fees; General Statutes § 42–110g(d); and punitive damages; General Statutes § 42–110g(a); enhances the private CUTPA remedy and serves to encourage private CUTPA litigation. The legislative history   .   .   . demonstrates that CUTPA seeks to create a climate in which private litigants help to enforce the ban on unfair or deceptive trade practices or acts. To interpret CUTPA narrowly, perhaps on the ground that a victimized consumer has other, less complete, remedies available to him, effectively negates this legislative intent.

.   .   . Subsection (d) of § 42–110g expressly contemplates plaintiffs' judgments which do not include an award of money damages. "In a class action where there is no monetary recovery, but other relief is granted on behalf of a class, the court may award, to the plaintiff, in addition to other relief provided in this section, costs and reasonable attorneys' fees." This demonstrates that CUTPA is not limited to providing redress only for consumers who can put a precise dollars and cents figure on their loss. To equate, as do the defendants, "ascertainable loss of money or property" with "actual damages in a particular amount" would render nugatory a significant portion of CUTPA. Because the plaintiffs in the present case sought both actual damages and equitable relief, any failure to prove a particular amount of pecuniary damages does not render their action subject to a judgment of dismissal for failure to make out a prima facie case.

Even if we restrict our analysis to an action seeking monetary damages only, the trial court was still incorrect in dismissing the action. Under the standard we articulate today the plaintiffs demonstrated that they suffered an ascertainable loss when they produced evidence fairly suggesting that, as a result of an unfair or deceptive trade practice, they received something different from that for which they had bargained. We need not be concerned at this stage of the proceedings with what actual damages, if any, they may ultimately recover. . . .

Closely analyzed, the plaintiffs' evidence also overcomes the higher threshold of showing diminution in value as a result of the allegedly deceptive representation that the vehicle had full-time four-wheel drive. Their testimony, if fully credited, indicated that what was advertised as Quadra–Trac four-wheel drive, was actually something less desirable than full-time four-wheel drive. The trier could infer that the presence of the advertised feature added some value to the vehicle because "Quadra–Trac" was listed on the price sticker as an accessory item included in the vehicle's total price. Because it was a "standard feature," however, no specific dollar value is assigned on the sticker.

The vote in *Hinchliffe* was 3–2. The dissenting judges stated:

"Ascertainable" means "capable of being ascertained." "Ascertain" is defined as "to make . . . certain, sure, or confident . . . to find out or learn for a certainty. . . ." The definition of "loss" includes "decrease in amount, magnitude, or degree." Webster, Third International Dictionary; see Black's Law Dictionary (5th Ed.). Employing these definitions, I would hold that a plaintiff meets the threshold requirement of "ascertainable loss" when he introduces evidence from which the trier of fact could find or infer that the consumer suffered an actual loss of money or property. The particular amount of loss, however, need not be shown.

When misrepresentation is the alleged unfair or deceptive act, practice or method of competition, the easiest way to demonstrate actual loss may be by offering evidence that the actual value of the product sold is less than what it would have been worth if it had been as represented (usually the selling price). The difference represents the actual loss suffered by the consumer.

. . . CUTPA's requirement of proof of at least a nominal actual loss of money or property functions to separate injured consumers from all others and to distinguish honest businessmen from unscrupulous ones. The act was not intended to subject honest businessmen to the risk of class actions and to a possible liability for attorneys' fees and punitive damages.

This interpretation of the phrase "ascertainable loss" does not mean that persons may misrepresent their products to the public with impunity under the law as long as a consumer is unable to prove some actual loss of money or property. CUTPA gives the commissioner of consumer protection tremendous powers to prevent such deception without any requirement of establishing ascertainable loss. Likewise, as noted in the majority opinion, a consumer may seek rescission under the common-law tort of deceit, even though there have been no actual damages.

The majority opinion sets out the following rule after analyzing the meaning of ascertainable loss: "Whenever a consumer has received something other than what he bargained for, he has suffered a loss of money or property . . . . That the loss does not consist of a diminution in value is immaterial . . . ." To allow a consumer to establish a prima facie case under CUTPA without demonstrating at least a nominal "diminution in value" ignores not only the letter of CUTPA, particularly the use of the word "loss," but also the spirit of the act. Under such an interpretation, if the defendants had represented that one of its vehicles would travel twenty-five miles per gallon of gasoline, they would be open to a lawsuit under CUTPA if the vehicle actually performed more economically. Such a result could not have been within the intention of the legislature. In their zeal to promote liability under CUTPA, the majority has disregarded both the legislature's intent and its use of the word "loss."

In the appeal before us, the plaintiffs never claimed, nor was there any evidence to support a claim, that the actual value of the vehicle purchased by them differed from its value as represented. . . .

Who is correct? Is the majority's distinction between "loss" and "damage" sound? (On remand the trial court held that plaintiff failed to establish that defendant's advertisement was unfair or deceptive. The Supreme Court of Connecticut affirmed. 470 A.2d 1216 (Conn.1984).)

3. The judgment affirmed by the Oregon Supreme Court in *Scott* was for the minimum damages of $200, plus punitive damages of $400, plus attorney's fees of $650, plus costs of $57.35, for a total of $1,307.35. Is an award of that magnitude appropriate for the kind of conduct described by the court?

4. Are minimum damages appropriate even if the defendant's violation of the statute is "innocent"? For example, in Pennington v. Singleton, 606 S.W.2d 682 (Tex.1980), plaintiff bought a boat from defendant, who represented that recent repairs made the boat as good as new. Although defendant believed this to be true, it was not true, since the repairs did not adequately cure the problem. Plaintiff sued, alleging a violation of the Texas little-FTC act, which provided for treble damages. Defendant contended that the statute was penal; that in failing to require knowledge of falsity it failed to define the prohibited conduct with sufficient certainty; and that it therefore violated due process to penalize him for an innocent misrepresentation. The court acknowledged that "deception is more reprehensible when done intentionally," but rejected the constitutional attack.

As a matter of legislative policy, should minimum damages be available only for knowing violations of a statute?

(c) Punitive Damages

Punitive damages present still another way to increase the amount of the consumer's recovery. Punitive damages are available if the defendant commits a tort and has a sufficiently bad state of mind. The torts most commonly inflicted on consumers are fraud (see Jones v. West Side Buick, page 7, and King v. Towns, page 12, supra); conversion (in the context of repossession, see Question 6, page 655 supra); and invasion of privacy and intentional infliction of emotional distress (in the context of nonjudicial collection of unsecured debts, see pages 591–608 supra).

Courts commonly state that punitive damages are not available for breach of contract. But they also say that it is not fatal to a claim for punitive damages that the consumer sues for breach of contract, so long as the defendant's conduct amounts to a tort as well as a breach of contract. Typically, however, conduct that amounts to a breach of contract does not amount to a tort, even if the defendant's state of mind is ill will, a desire to injure the consumer, or a complete lack of concern for the effect on the consumer. When this is the case, should the consumer be able to recover punitive damages?

In Morrow v. L.A. Goldschmidt Associates, Inc., 468 N.E.2d 414 (Ill.App.1984), defendants constructed and sold housing that did not comply with the contract or with the building code. Despite repeated requests, they failed to correct the defects. The Illinois Court of Appeals held that willful and wanton misconduct may constitute a tort and reversed the trial court's dismissal of the portions of plaintiffs' complaint requesting punitive damages. The Supreme Court reversed and reinstated the trial court's dismissal of the claims for punitive damages. 492 N.E.2d 181 (Ill.1986). On the other hand, the Supreme Court of Vermont has concluded that punitive damages may be awarded for willful and wanton breach of the implied warranty of habitability. Hilder v. St. Peter, 478 A.2d 202 (Vt.1984). And a Texas court has held that a creditor's "conscious indifference" to the consumer's rights under UCC Article 9 justifies punitive damages. Winkle Chevy–Olds–Pontiac, Inc. v. Condon, 830 S.W.2d 740 (Tex.App.1992).

The obvious purposes of imposing punitive damages are to punish the defendant and to deter the defendant and others from engaging in similar conduct in the future. Is it relevant that fraudulent activities may be criminal offenses? Does it violate the constitutional prohibition against double jeopardy for a state to subject a person to a fine (or imprisonment) in criminal proceedings and also to punitive damages in a civil proceeding? The Indiana Supreme Court thought so and long ago held that a court may not award punitive damages if the defendant's conduct is punishable as a crime. Koerner v. Oberly, 56 Ind. 284 (1877); Taber v. Hutson, 5 Ind. 322 (1854). In the other forty-five states in which a plaintiff may recover punitive damages, however, courts have answered the question in the negative and award punitive damages even though criminal proceedings are a possibility. A similar problem exists if the defendant is in a regulated trade, since the offensive conduct may trigger an administrative proceeding resulting in revocation of the defendant's license to do business.

Apart from the constitutional objection, is it fair to subject the defendant to two (or more) penalties for the same conduct? Indeed, is it even fair to award punitive damages without affording the defendant the procedural safeguards incident to criminal proceedings? In an action to recover for assault and battery, the Supreme Court of Wisconsin observed:

> Suffice it to say that whatever shortcomings the award of punitive damages may have, nevertheless, it must be remembered that it has the effect of bringing to punishment types of conduct that though oppressive and hurtful to the individual almost invariably go unpunished by the public prosecutor. Under the law of Wisconsin (sec. 59.47(2), Stats.), a district attorney is not obliged to prosecute an assault and battery and may leave the injured party to prosecute through his own attorney. Certainly, the criminal law seldom reaches an assault and battery case. By allowing punitive damages the self interest of the plaintiff will lead to prosecution of the claim, while the same self interest of the plaintiff would lead him to refrain from instituting a criminal action at his own expense. Punitive damages serve not only the aggrieved victim of an assault, but also society, for by this device, a quasi-criminal action is prosecuted, when ordinarily it would not be prosecuted at all. The multiple-damage suits countenanced by our statutes recognize the principle that certain types of violations will not be prosecuted unless the injured parties' judgment is fattened by the equivalent of punitive damages. These are civil actions (e.g., antitrust suits) where the public interest is served by the incentive given to private litigation. Certainly the consolidation of claims for compensation and punitive damages in one cause of action is in accord with modern principles of avoiding multiple trials.

Kink v. Combs, 135 N.W.2d 789, 798 (Wis.1965).

QUESTIONS AND NOTES

1. What objectives besides punishment and deterrence might punitive damages serve? (Recall Sections (a) and (b) supra and reread the passage from *Kink*.)

2. Is not an award of punitive damages likely to be counterproductive: aren't the damages merely another expense of doing business, ultimately to be reflected in the defendant's prices and paid for by subsequent customers?

3. The trial court's determination of the amount of punitive damages is subject to limited appellate review. Many appellate courts state that they will overturn an award only if it shocks the court's conscience or appears to be the product of passion and prejudice on the part of the jury. On the other hand, most courts require that the amount of punitive damages bear a reasonable relationship to the amount of actual or compensatory damages. The meaning of "reasonable relationship," however, is not clear. For example, one court held that punitive damages that were forty times compensatory damages were excessive as a matter of law, while another court affirmed an award that was fifty times compensatory damages. Egan v. Mutual of Omaha Insurance Co., 620 P.2d 141 (Cal.1979) ($5,000,-000:$125,000); Lou Leventhal Auto Co. v. Munns, 328 N.E.2d 734 (Ind.App. 1975) ($1,500:$30, after court stated it was a "close question" whether any punitive damages at all were appropriate).

If a seller induces a consumer to buy a set of pots and pans by falsely representing that her pots and pans cause cancer (see King v. Towns, page 12 supra), the consumer's actual damages may be quite small. Is an award of punitive damages that is "reasonably related" to the actual damages likely to be effective as either punishment or deterrent?

4. What factors should be considered in fixing the amount of a punitive damages award? For example, are the plaintiff's litigation expenses relevant? In Connecticut the award *may not* exceed the plaintiff's nontaxable expenses of litigation. Doroszka v. Lavine, 150 A. 692 (Conn.1930). In about ten other states, litigation expenses are one factor to be considered. In still others, they are not to be considered at all. Which of these three positions is the soundest?

5. In Jones v. Star Credit (Note 9, page 491 supra) the court held the seller's conduct to be unconscionable, and it therefore refused to hold the consumer liable for the contract price. Could the consumer have counterclaimed for punitive damages because of the seller's unconscionable conduct? In Star Credit Corp. v. Ingram, 347 N.Y.S.2d 651 (N.Y.City Civ.Ct. 1973), an action by the same creditor against another consumer, the court stated:

> After extended litigation in this Court, Judge Budd G. Goodman awarded punitive damages to the individual defendants herein on their counterclaim, in addition to actual damages, on the grounds that "plaintiff's conduct was a gross fraud upon the general public involving high moral culpability."
>
> This case was referred to me to assess the amount of punitive or exemplary damages to be awarded to the defendants, Mr. & Mrs. Dazell Ingram.
>
> In this case, the record discloses that plaintiff finance company under assorted names, guises and postures, has been responsible for creating and implementing a broad consumer fraud scheme, victimizing thousands of residents of ghetto areas, over a period of many years. Plaintiff devised a refrigerator-food plan sales scheme, permeated with fraudulent representations, grossly unconscionable profit, and a divestiture of meaningful legal redress to its customers by diversion of most of the consumers' payments to itself, to thereby render its puppet seller financially incapable of satisfying victimized purchasers.

The record discloses that this plaintiff and its principals have been engaged in this type of fraud for many years; that the nominal seller and plaintiff shared common office space; that customers were subjected to high pressure sales predicated upon false statements; compelled to pay five to ten times the legitimate cost of freezers, and many times the cost of food for an economical food plan which did not exist; that thousands of purchasers were victimized; that plaintiff continued its operation after its corporate predecessors and principals were the subject of an intensive investigation by the Attorney General of the State of New York, which resulted in a broad consent injunction against the predecessor corporation and its principals in an attempt to end the fraudulent scheme; that thousands of sales were thereafter made to new victims including this defendant; that plaintiff continued plying its fraudulent scheme in disregard of the injunction, being willing when compelled under rare circumstance to return money to persistent isolated victims of its malicious, wanton, willful and gross fraud upon the general public.

In the instant case, it is clear that all prior legal action, against this plaintiff, and its predecessors has been ineffective, to halt this widespread fraudulent scheme.

"[I]n the calculation of [its] expected profits, the [plaintiff] wrongdoer is likely to allow for a certain amount of money which will have to be returned to those victims who object too vigorously, . . . perfectly content to bear the additional cost of litigation as the price for continuing his illicit business. It stands to reason that the chances of deterring him are materially increased by subjecting him to the payment of punitive damages." (Walker v. Sheldon, 10 N.Y.2d 401, 406, 223 N.Y.S.2d 488, 492, 179 N.E.2d 497, 499) (1961).

There is however, no rigid mathematical formula for determining the amount of punitive damages that should be awarded. Consequently, "[T]he question of the amount of . . . punitive damages to be awarded [is] a matter for the [trier of fact]."

Some courts have found a way to limit discretion in awards of punitive damages by requiring some "reasonable relationship" between actual and exemplary damages. (cf. Leombruno v. Julian, Sup., 37 N.Y.S.2d 618, rev'd on other grounds, 264 App.Div. 981, 37 N.Y.S.2d 202 (1942)).

An exhaustive review of the authorities discloses no mandate requiring acceptance of the "reasonable relationship" theory. Most courts reject the idea that the "reasonable relationship" is a fixed mathematical ratio between the two awards. Some define "reasonable relation" in a slightly different manner, saying that there must be a proper relationship between the exemplary damages and the type of injury inflicted. However, a test of "reasonable relationship" fails to carry out the punitive function of exemplary damages, since it stresses the harm which actually results rather than the social undesirability of the defendant's behavior. Flexibility of admonition should not be vitiated by adhering to a "reasonable relation" test.

This court also rejects the "reasonable relationship" formula in this kind of case. If these damages are to be awarded to protect the public from continuation of a fraudulent consumer scheme, the damages must be taxed in an amount which will accomplish the purpose of providing a deterrent to improper behavior.

In this case defendants' counterclaim demands $15,000 for punitive damages. This court is restricted to that demand, and accordingly the exemplary damages are hereby assessed at $15,000. This court would have been willing to assess a greater sum in damage to provide a greater deterrent to the continuation by this plaintiff of its fraudulent scheme.

This court would be remiss if it did not acknowledge its gratitude and appreciation to John J. Witmeyer, III and his employer Mudge, Rose, Guthrie & Alexander for their heroic efforts pro bono publico in this case. Without their dedication and proficient legal assistance these defendants might remain remediless victims of this consumer fraud, and the public interest would not have been advanced in this instance.

6. The Supreme Court has declared that the Due Process Clause limits the ability of the courts to impose liability for punitive damages. In BMW of North America, Inc. v. Gore, 517 U.S. 559, 574 (1996), the Court invalidated a punitive damages award of $2 million for a manufacturer's nationwide practice that caused the plaintiff to suffer $4,000 actual damages. It stated, "Elementary notions of fairness enshrined in our constitutional jurisprudence dictate that a person receive fair notice not only of the conduct that will subject him to punishment but also of the severity of the penalty that a State may impose." It cited three "guideposts" to be considered: the degree of reprehensibility of the defendant's conduct; the relationship between the punitive damages and the actual or potential harm to the plaintiff; and the relationship between the punitive damages and any civil penalty authorized for comparable cases. Applying these criteria in a case in which a car dealer's violation of the little-FTC act caused actual damages of $11,500, the Supreme Court of Oregon upheld a jury's award of $1 million. Parrott v. Carr Chevrolet, Inc., 17 P.3d 473 (Ore.2001). A Missouri court upheld a jury's punitive damages award of $500,000 for a used car dealer's failure to disclose that the truck he sold plaintiff was a rebuilt wreck. Krysa v. Payne, 176 S.W.3d 150 (Mo.App.2005) ($18,000 compensatory damages). And the Fourth Circuit upheld a jury's punitive damages award of $80,000 in connection with a consumer's recovery of $1,000 in statutory damages for a creditor's violation of the Fair Credit Reporting Act. Saunders v. Branch Banking & Trust Co., 526 F.3d 142 (4th Cir.2008).

7. The focus thus far has been the availability of punitive damages in connection with enforcement of common law rights. Punitive damages may be available also in connection with enforcement of statutory rights.

Examples include the Truth-in-Lending Act (actual damages plus twice the finance charge),[12] the Fair Debt Collection Practices Act (actual damages plus "such additional damages as the court shall allow, but not exceeding $1,000"),[13] the Fair Credit Reporting Act (actual damages plus "such amount of punitive damages as the court may allow"),[14] the Equal Credit Opportunity Act (actual damages plus "punitive damages in an amount not greater than $10,000"),[15] the federal odometer statute (three times actual damages but not less than $1,500),[16] and some state little-FTC acts.[17] In addition to making punitive damages available, some of these statutes specify the factors to be considered in fixing the amount of the award.[18]

8. Problem. Shortly after purchasing a car from *Seller* for $5,700, *Consumer* discovers that the car has been driven many more than the 32,000 miles indicated by the odometer and is worth only $4,500. Investigation reveals that *Seller* is engaged in a scheme of buying high-mileage used cars in another state, transferring them several times with the intent and effect of producing disclosure certificates with low mileage figures, and rolling back the odometers. *Consumer* sues, alleging fraud and violation of the federal odometer statute. He seeks $1,200 actual damages and $50,000 punitive damages on the first count; $3,600 on the second count; and attorney's fees. If *Seller's* conduct amounts to both common law fraud and a violation of the statute, to what relief is *Consumer* entitled?

To pay for the car, *Consumer* had borrowed $3,000 from *Bank*. When he discovered *Seller's* fraud, he stopped making the installment payments to *Bank*, which repossessed the car. At the time of the repossession, *Consumer's* deer rifle and golf clubs were in the trunk of the car. *Bank* gave two weeks' notice of disposition and sold the car, rifle, and golf clubs at public auction for a total of $2,400. *Bank* now seeks a deficiency judgment. *Consumer* denies *Bank's* right to a deficiency judgment and counterclaims for damages under section 9–625(c) and for punitive damages. What should the court do?

9. For articles discussing punitive damages for breach of contract, see Dodge, The Case for Punitive Damages in Contracts, 48 Duke L.J. 629 (1999); Sebert, Punitive and Nonpecuniary Damages in Actions Based upon Contract: Toward Achieving the Objective of Full Compensation, 34 U.C.L.A.L.Rev. 1565 (1987); Sullivan, Punitive Damages in the Law of Contracts: The Reality and the Illusion of Legal Change, 61 Minn.L.Rev. 207 (1977).

---

12. § 130(a).

13. § 813(a)(2).

14. § 616(2).

15. § 706.

16. 49 U.S.C. § 32710(a).

17. E.g., Conn.Gen.Stat.Ann. § 42–110g(a) (punitive damages); Mass.Gen.Laws Ann. ch. 93A, § 9(3) (2–3 times actual damages).

18. E.g., TILA § 130(a); FDCPA § 813(b); ECOA § 706(b). If the statute does not specify the factors to be considered, the courts still require malice or willful and wanton conduct. E.g., Bruntaeger v. Zeller, 515 A.2d 123 (Vt.1986).

(2) Reducing the Costs

Awards of attorney's fees, minimum damages, and punitive damages address the problem of litigation costs by increasing the consumer's recovery beyond the actual damages suffered. Their common objective is to produce a net recovery that equals or exceeds the amount of the actual loss. This section examines the converse approach to the same objective: reducing the consumer's costs, so that the net recovery approximates the amount of the actual loss.

(a) Nonjudicial Mechanisms

Better Business Bureau. The primary expenses of enforcing the consumer's rights are attorney's fees and other litigation costs (investigation, expert witnesses, etc.). A system of dispute resolution that does not depend on lawyers and courts would therefore go a long way toward eliminating current barriers to enforcement. And several such systems exist. The most obvious, of course, is communicating the complaint directly to the seller or creditor. Hence the little-FTC acts in some states seek to encourage nonjudicial resolution of disputes by prohibiting litigation unless the consumer first makes a written demand for relief, to which the potential defendant may respond by offering a settlement. The consumer may refuse the offer and sue, but if the court determines that the offer was reasonable, the consumer may not recover more than the amount of the settlement offer and may not recover costs or attorney's fees. Mass.Gen.Laws Ann. ch. 93A, § 9(3); Vernon's Tex.Code Ann., Bus. & C.Code, § 17.505. Cf. Magnuson–Moss Warranty Act § 110(d). Even if there is no statutory encouragement to settle a dispute, most complaints are resolved to the satisfaction of the consumer as a result of informal communications. Of course, not all complaints are resolved by informal communications, so other mechanisms may be useful.

Perhaps the most widely known is the program of the Better Business Bureau (BBB). A consumer with a complaint may notify the local branch of the BBB, which communicates the complaint to the other party. The BBB follows this up by attempting to ascertain how the problem was resolved. The BBB maintains a file on each merchant about whom it has received a complaint. If a consumer inquires about a particular merchant, the BBB discloses whether other consumers have complained about that merchant and whether they were satisfied by its responses. This program resembles mediation, but the BBB does not attempt to persuade or to exert pressure on either side to accept any particular resolution. If a business acts unscrupulously or consistently fails to respond to consumer complaints, the BBB may terminate its membership. But studies have revealed that in larger cities as few as five-to-ten percent of the businesses are members of the BBB. Consequently, for the vast majority of businesses in the market place, the BBB does not have the clout of terminating the membership of repeated offenders. Some have questioned the reliability of the BBB in responding accurately and honestly to consumer inquiries. See Blankenship

v. Better Business Bureau, 782 S.W.2d 131 (Mo.App.1989) (cause of action exists against BBB for failing to disclose all the information it possessed).

Voluntary programs. In several industries manufacturers have banded together to establish systems for the resolution of disputes with consumers. Examples include the home construction industry (Home Owners' Warranty (HOW) Program), the major appliance industry (refrigerators, washing machines, etc.) (Major Appliance Consumer Action Panel (MACAP)), the auto industry (AUTOCAP), the carpet industry (Carpet and Rug Industry CAP), the furniture industry (Furniture Industry Consumer Advisory Panel), and the funeral industry (ThanaCAP). In other industries some manufacturers have their own individual systems for resolving disputes.

Under the CAP programs, the manufacturers establish a panel. The members of the panel, who are experts in home economics, engineering, and consumer rights, are independent of the industry. A consumer who is unable to resolve a dispute by communicating with the seller or the manufacturer may submit a complaint to the panel. The panel writes the manufacturer about the problem and waits for the manufacturer to act. If the manufacturer does not resolve the problem satisfactorily, the panel recommends a solution.

Several aspects of the CAP programs have drawn criticism. One concerns the impartiality of the panels. Although the panel members may feel completely independent of the industry, they are dependent on the industry for their funds and their staff. This dependence may undermine their impartiality or at least their appearance of impartiality. Another problem is procedural. Members of the panel may reside in different locations, so most complaints must be handled by correspondence. This may impede communication and the resolution of factual issues. Finally, decisions of the panel are not binding on the manufacturers. So the manufacturer is free to disregard the panel's recommendation, though it is unlikely that a manufacturer who supports the program will reject many decisions of the panel.

To encourage the creation of systems like the CAP's, Congress included subsection 110(a) in the remedies section of the Magnuson–Moss Warranty Act. Please read all of section 110(a). What incentives does a manufacturer have to set up an informal dispute settlement mechanism (IDSM)? What disincentives exist? The FTC has promulgated regulations pursuant to section 110(a)(2). Informal Dispute Settlement Procedures, 16 C.F.R. Part 703. Consider especially sections 703.3, 703.6(c)–(e), 703.7(c), 703.8. Do the regulations provide any additional incentives for a manufacturer to adopt an IDSM? Do they provide any additional disincentives?

Does section 110 or the FTC regulations prohibit the use of IDSM's that do not comply with the Act and the regulations? Only a few IDSM's have received the blessing of the FTC as being in compliance with the regulations. What changes in the statute or the regulations might induce other manufacturers to establish qualifying IDSM's?

Chapter 7 (at page 357 supra) describes the widespread enactment of lemon laws. A common feature of these statutes is a requirement that, before litigating, the consumer must resort to an informal dispute settlement mechanism if the manufacturer has established one that complies with the FTC regulations. Imposition of this requirement has encouraged the automobile manufacturers to try to bring their IDSM's into compliance. Despite the manufacturers' efforts, however, the attorneys general of several states have determined that the IDSM's do not yet comply. To the extent this is true, resort to them is not mandatory for consumers asserting rights under the lemon laws.

Several states have amended their lemon laws to promote the use of alternative dispute resolution. New York, for example, has established its own standards for IDSM's and has provided that if an automobile manufacturer has an IDSM, it must comply with those standards. N.Y.Gen.Bus.Law § 198–a(g). This scheme has survived a challenge that alleged that the Magnuson–Moss Warranty Act preempts a state's power to specify minimum standards for an IDSM. Motor Vehicle Manufacturers Ass'n of the United States v. Abrams, 899 F.2d 1315 (2d Cir.1990). Texas, on the other hand, has not left to the manufacturers the decision whether to establish an IDSM. Rather, aggrieved consumers may present their lemon law complaints to the state's Motor Vehicle Commission. Vernon's Ann.Tex–Civ.Stat., art. 4413(36) § 6.07, upheld in Chrysler Corp. v. Texas Motor Vehicle Com'n, 755 F.2d 1192 (5th Cir.1985). Consumers who are dissatisfied with the outcome of this informal proceeding may litigate if they so choose.

For a sense of the variety of nonjudicial systems for resolving disputes and a description of more than 100 of them, see ABA, Dispute Resolution Program Directory (1981). For discussion of alternative mechanisms, see A. Best, When Consumers Complain (1981); L. Nader, ed., No Access to Law (1980); Jones & Boyer, Improving the Quality of Justice in the Marketplace: The Need for Better Consumer Remedies, 40 Geo.Wash.L.Rev. 357 (1972).

Involuntary Programs (Mandatory Arbitration). For many decades arbitration has been very popular for resolving labor and commercial disputes. More recently, the BBB and others have provided arbitration systems for consumer disputes, too. Under these systems a business will agree with the provider that it will have its consumer disputes submitted to arbitration. When a dispute with a consumer arises and is not resolved by direct dealing between the parties, the consumer may opt for arbitration.

A major advantage of arbitration in the commercial context is the expertise of the arbitrator, who typically is a member of the same industry as the disputing parties. In the consumer context, however, this advantage may not exist: neither an industry member nor a consumer advocate is likely to be perceived as neutral enough for each party to accept as the arbitrator. Is there any way to obtain the benefit of having a knowledgeable arbitrator?

A system of arbitration depends on the willingness of the parties to agree to arbitrate. What incentives are there for the consumer to agree to resolve disputes by arbitration? Are there disadvantages to the consumer? From the merchant's perspective, what are the advantages and disadvantages of arbitration? If you were the owner of a business, would you agree to submit all disputes to arbitration?

Should arbitration be mandatory, i.e. should the legislature enact a statute requiring that all disputes concerning consumer transactions be resolved by arbitration rather than litigation?

Legislatures have not concluded that arbitration should be mandatory, but many merchants have. They include banks and other financers; sellers of cars, computers, mobile homes, and new houses; and providers of medical, cell phone, pest control, and other household services. The form contracts of merchants increasingly are likely to include a provision requiring that any claims of the consumer be resolved by arbitration. Under these contracts, then, the use of arbitration to resolve disputes is not optional with the consumer. The contracts may, however, be drafted to leave the merchant free to enforce the consumer's payment (or other) obligation by means of litigation. If enforceable, then, they enable the merchant to shunt into arbitration those disputes that it does not want to litigate.

Historically, English and American courts were hostile to arbitration, viewing it as a displacement of the judiciary and a usurpation of the judicial function. To change this attitude, Congress enacted the Federal Arbitration Act in 1925. 9 U.S.C. § 1 et seq. Section 2 of the Act provides:

> A written provision in . . . a contract evidencing a transaction involving commerce to settle by arbitration a controversy thereafter arising out of such contract or transaction . . . shall be valid, irrevocable, and enforceable, save upon such grounds as exist at law or in equity for revocation of any contract.

9 U.S.C. § 2. Subsequent sections direct the courts to stay litigation pending completion of the arbitration proceedings.

In a series of decisions over the last 35 years, the Supreme Court has made it clear that this federal statute applies even if the plaintiff wants to litigate in state court. The Court also has held that the federal statute preempts state statutes that establish different rules for arbitration agreements than for other agreements. Doctor's Associates, Inc. v. Casarotto, 517 U.S. 681 (1996) (§ 2 preempts a Montana statute requiring conspicuous notice that a contract contains an arbitration clause). In Allied–Bruce Terminix Cos. v. Dobson, 513 U.S. 265, 281 (1995), the Court stated:

> . . . § 2 gives States a method for protecting consumers against unfair pressure to agree to a contract with an unwanted arbitration provision. States may regulate contracts, including arbitration clauses, under general contract law principles and they may invalidate an arbitration clause "upon such grounds as exist at law or in equity for revocation of *any* contract." 9 U.S.C. § 2 (emphasis added). What States may not do is decide that a contract is fair enough to enforce all

its terms (price, service, credit), but not fair enough to enforce its arbitration clause. The Act makes any such state policy unlawful, for that kind of policy would place arbitration clauses on an unequal "footing," directly contrary to the Act's language and Congress' intent.

Under this line of cases, a consumer may mount a judicial challenge to the enforceability of an arbitration clause on grounds of fraud, mistake, duress, unconscionability, etc. If, however, the challenge goes to the enforceability of the entire contract rather than just the arbitration clause, then the arbitration clause kicks in and judicial relief is unavailable unless the arbitrator decides that the contract is unenforceable (in which event the arbitration clause within the contract is not enforceable either, and the consumer can enforce statutory rights and common law rights that arise outside the contract (e.g., tort)).

Simpson v. MSA of Myrtle Beach, Inc.

South Carolina Supreme Court, 2007.
373 S.C. 14, 644 S.E.2d 663, certiorari denied, 128 S.Ct. 493 (2007).

CHIEF JUSTICE TOAL. . . .

Appellant MSA of Myrtle Beach, Inc. d/b/a Addy's Harbor Dodge ("Addy"), a car dealership, and Respondent Sherry H. Simpson ("Simpson") entered into a contract whereby Simpson traded in her 2001 Toyota 4Runner for a new 2004 Dodge Caravan. Directly above the signature line on the first page of the contract, the signee was instructed in bold to "SEE ADDITIONAL TERMS AND CONDITIONS ON OPPOSITE PAGE." The additional terms and conditions contained an arbitration clause stating the following:

10. ARBITRATION Any and all disputes, claims or controversies between Dealer and Customer or between any officers, directors, agents, employees, or assignees of Dealer and Customer arising out of or relating to: (a) automobile warranty, workmanship, or repair; (b) the terms or enforceability of the sale, lease, or financing of any vehicle; (c) any claim of breach of contract, misrepresentation, conversion, fraud, or unfair and deceptive trade practices against Dealer or any officers, directors, agents, employees, or assignees of Dealer; (d) any and all claims under any consumer protection statute; and (e) the validity and scope of this contract, shall be settled by binding arbitration in accordance with the Commercial Arbitration Rules of the American Arbitration Association. The parties expressly waive all rights to trial by jury on such claims. Provided, however, that nothing in this contract shall require Dealer to submit to arbitration any claims by Dealer against customer for claim and delivery, repossession, injunctive relief, or monies owed by customer in connection with the purchase or lease of any vehicle and any claims by Dealer for these remedies shall not be stayed pending the outcome of arbitration. The filing fees for arbitration shall be paid by the party initiating arbitration. The arbitrator may allocate the other arbitration fees as he/she

deems appropriate. In addition to any discovery permitted by the Commercial Arbitration rules, any party may take one deposition of an opposing party. The parties agree to exchange all exhibits to be used in arbitration 7 days before arbitration. The arbitrator shall determine the controversy in accordance with the terms of this contract between the parties and shall not consider any parol evidence which purports to alter, modify, vary, add to, or contradict such contract. The arbitrator shall give effect to all applicable statutes of limitation. Any arbitration under this agreement shall take place in Horry County, South Carolina and Customer agrees that the courts of Horry County, South Carolina shall have exclusive jurisdiction over enforcement of this contract and any award made by any arbitrator pursuant to this contract. In no event shall the arbitrator be authorized to award punitive, exemplary, double, or treble damages (or any other damages which are punitive in nature or effect) against either party. Unless otherwise agreed in writing, no claims against Dealer shall be consolidated with other claims in the nature of a class action.

Six months later, Simpson filed a complaint in the Horry County court of common pleas alleging Addy violated the South Carolina Unfair Trade Practices Act and the South Carolina Manufacturers, Distributors, and Dealers Act by misrepresenting the trade-in value of the vehicle, artificially increasing the purchase price, and failing to provide all rebates promised. Simpson sought damages consistent with the maximum statutory remedies permitted for violations of these statutes.

Addy's answer denied Simpson's allegations and asserted that the contract between the parties contained an arbitration clause such that the matter should be stayed and that Simpson's only remedy was to file for arbitration. Addy contemporaneously filed a motion for protective order and/or to stay and compel arbitration. Thereafter, Simpson filed a memorandum in opposition to Addy's motion alleging that the arbitration clause was unconscionable and unenforceable.

At the motion hearing, the trial court ordered the parties to attempt mediation. After the parties notified the trial court that mediation failed, the trial court issued an order denying Addy's motion on the grounds that the arbitration clause was unconscionable. Addy filed this appeal.

. . .

II. Denial of Addy's motion for protective order and/or to stay and compel arbitration.

Addy argues that the trial court erred in denying Addy's motion for protective order and/or to stay and compel arbitration. We disagree.

There is a strong presumption in favor of the validity of arbitration agreements because both state and federal policy favor arbitration of disputes. The South Carolina Uniform Arbitration Act (UAA) provides that in any contract evidencing a transaction involving commerce, a written provision to settle by arbitration shall be valid, irrevocable, and enforceable. S.C. Code Ann. § 15–48–10(a) (2005). Unless a court can say with positive assurance that the arbitration clause is not susceptible to an interpretation that covers the dispute, arbitration should generally be ordered.

Despite these clear rules, arbitration is a matter of contract law and is available only when the parties involved contractually agreed to arbitrate. Accordingly, a party may seek revocation of the contract under "such grounds as exist at law or in equity," including fraud, duress, and unconscionability. S.C. Code Ann. § 15–48–10(a). Arbitration will be denied if a court determines no agreement to arbitrate existed. S.C. Code Ann. § 15–48–20(a).

General contract principles of state law apply in a court's evaluation of the enforceability of an arbitration clause. In South Carolina, unconscionability is defined as the absence of meaningful choice on the part of one party due to one-sided contract provisions, together with terms that are so oppressive that no reasonable person would make them and no fair and honest person would accept them. *Carolina Care Plan, Inc. v. United HealthCare Servs., Inc.*, 361 S.C. 544, 554, 606 S.E.2d 752, 757 (2004). If a court as a matter of law finds any clause of a contract to have been unconscionable at the time it was made, the court may refuse to enforce the unconscionable clause, or so limit its application so as to avoid any unconscionable result. S.C. Code Ann. § 36–2–302(1) (2003).

In analyzing claims of unconscionability in the context of arbitration agreements, the Fourth Circuit has instructed courts to focus generally on whether the arbitration clause is geared towards achieving an unbiased decision by a neutral decision-maker. *See Hooters of Am., Inc. v. Phillips*, 173 F.3d 933, 938 (4th Cir. 1999). It is under this general rubric that we determine whether a contract provision is unconscionable due to both an absence of meaningful choice and oppressive, one-sided terms.

A. Absence of meaningful choice

Addy argues that the facts do not show that Simpson had no meaningful choice in agreeing to arbitrate. We disagree.

Absence of meaningful choice on the part of one party generally speaks to the fundamental fairness of the bargaining process in the contract at issue. In determining whether a contract was "tainted by an absence of meaningful choice," courts should take into account the nature of the injuries suffered by the plaintiff; whether the plaintiff is a substantial business concern; the relative disparity in the parties' bargaining power; the parties' relative sophistication; whether there is an element of surprise in the inclusion of the challenged clause; and the conspicuousness of the clause.

There are many cases in this jurisdiction and others involving the enforceability of arbitration clauses in adhesion contracts between commercial entities and consumers. Each transaction is analyzed on its own particular facts in conjunction with the federal and/or state policies favoring arbitration. We begin our inquiry with a focus on the decisions of courts in Ohio, which have heard numerous cases in the very recent past specifically addressing issues of unconscionability of arbitration clauses embedded in adhesion contracts between automobile retailers and consumers [citing four cases].

The Ohio courts characterize automobiles as a "necessity" and factor this characterization into a determination of whether a consumer had a "meaningful choice" in negotiating the arbitration agreement. Under the Ohio courts' rationale, "the presumption in favor of arbitration clauses is substantially weaker when there are strong indications that the contract at issue is an adhesion contract, and the arbitration clause itself appears to be adhesive in nature. In this situation there arises considerable doubt that any true agreement ever existed to submit disputes to arbitration." *Williams v. Aetna Fin. Co.*, 700 N.E.2d 859, 866 (Ohio 1998).

Turning to the instant case, we first note that under general principles of state contract law, an adhesion contract is a standard form contract offered on a "take-it-or-leave-it" basis with terms that are not negotiable. *Muñoz v. Green Tree Fin. Corp.*, 343 S.C. 531, 541, 542 S.E.2d 360, 365 (2001). Neither party disputes that the contract entered into by Simpson and Addy was an adhesion contract as such contracts are standard in the automobile retail industry. Adhesion contracts, however, are not per se unconscionable. Therefore, finding an adhesion contract is merely the beginning point of the analysis. *Lackey v. Green Tree Fin. Corp.*, 330 S.C. 388, 395, 498 S.E.2d 898, 902 (Ct. App. 1998).

We agree with the rationale of the Ohio courts and proceed to analyze this contract between a consumer and automobile retailer with "considerable skepticism." Under this approach, we first observe that the contract between Simpson and Addy involved a vehicle intended for use as Simpson's primary transportation, which is critically important in modern day society. Applying the factors considered by the Fourth Circuit in analyzing arbitration clauses, we also acknowledge Simpson's claim that she did not possess the business judgment necessary to make her aware of the implications of the arbitration agreement, and that she did not have a lawyer present to provide any assistance in the matter.

Moreover, regardless of the general legal presumptions that a party to a contract has read and understood the contract's terms, we also find it necessary to consider the otherwise inconspicuous nature of the arbitration clause in light of its consequences. The loss of the right to a jury trial is an obvious result of arbitration. However, this particular arbitration clause also required Simpson to forego certain remedies that were otherwise required by statute.[3] While certain phrases within other provisions of the additional terms and conditions were printed in all capital letters,[4] the arbitration clause in its entirety was written in the standard small print,

---

3. Specifically, the arbitration clause prohibited an arbitrator from awarding double or treble damages.

4. This included phrases in the "Disclaimer of Warranties" provision and the "Used Vehicle Disclosure." We note that S.C. Code Ann. § 36–2–316 (2003) requires disclaimers of implied warranties to be "conspicuous."

and embedded in paragraph ten (10) of sixteen (16) total paragraphs included on the page. Although this Court acknowledges that parties are always free to contract away their rights, we cannot, under the circumstances, ignore the inconspicuous nature of a provision, which was drafted by the superior party, and which functioned to contract away certain significant rights and remedies otherwise available to Simpson by law. . . . .

Accordingly, we find that when considered as a whole and in the context of an adhesion contract for a vehicle trade-in, the circumstances reveal that Simpson had no meaningful choice in agreeing to arbitrate claims with Addy.

B. Oppressive and one-sided terms

1. Limitation on statutory remedies in an arbitration clause

Addy contends that the arbitration clause's limitation on statutory remedies was not oppressive and one-sided. We disagree.

The arbitration clause in Simpson's contract with Addy provides that "[i]n no event shall the arbitrator be authorized to award punitive, exemplary, double, or treble damages (or any other damages which are punitive in nature or effect) against either party." Simpson's underlying complaint filed in civil court alleged, among other things, that Addy violated the South Carolina Uniform Trade Practices Act (SCUTPA) and the South Carolina Regulation of Manufacturers, Distributors, and Dealers Act (Dealers Act). The SCUTPA requires a court to award treble damages for violations of the statute.[5] Similarly, the Dealers Act requires a court to award double damages for violations of the statute.[6]

. . .

The general rule is that courts will not enforce a contract which is violative of public policy, statutory law, or provisions of the Constitution. *Carolina Care Plan*, 361 S.C. at 555, 606 S.E.2d at 758. In our opinion, this rule has two applications in the present case. First, this arbitration clause violates statutory law because it prevents Simpson from receiving the mandatory statutory remedies to which she may be entitled in her underlying SCUTPA and Dealers Act claims. Second, unconditionally permitting the weaker party to waive these statutory remedies pursuant to an adhesion contract runs contrary to the underlying statutes' very purposes of punishing acts that adversely affect the public interest. Therefore, under the general rule, this provision in the arbitration clause is unenforceable.

Accordingly, we find the provision prohibiting double and treble damages to be oppressive, one-sided, and not geared toward achieving an unbiased decision by a neutral decision-maker. In conjunction with

---

5. *See* S.C. Code Ann. § 39–5–140(a) (1976) (providing that a "court *shall* award three times the actual damages sustained and may provide such other relief as it deems necessary or proper" [emphasis added]).

6. *See* S.C. Code Ann. § 56–15–110(1) (2006) (providing that an individual "*shall* recover double the actual damages by him sustained" [emphasis added]).

Simpson's lack of meaningful choice in agreeing to arbitrate, this provision is an unconscionable waiver of statutory rights, and therefore, unenforceable.

2.   *Dealer's remedies not stayed pending outcome of arbitration*

Addy argues that the arbitration clause's provision reserving certain judicial remedies to the dealer and authorizing the award of the dealer's remedies even if the consumer's arbitration proceedings have not concluded is not oppressive and one-sided. We disagree.

While stating that "all disputes, claims or controversies between Dealer and Customer" are to be settled in binding arbitration, the arbitration clause notes several exceptions. Specifically, the clause provides:

> Nothing in this contract shall require the Dealer to submit to arbitration any claims by Dealer against Customer for claim and delivery, repossession, injunctive relief, or monies owed by Consumer in connection with the purchase or lease of any vehicle and *any claims by Dealer for these remedies shall not be stayed pending the outcome of arbitration.* [emphasis added]

Our courts have held that lack of mutuality of remedy in an arbitration agreement, on its own, does not make the arbitration agreement unconscionable. *See Muñoz*, 343 S.C. at 542, 542 S.E.2d at 365 (holding that an arbitration agreement between a consumer and a lender was not unconscionable where it allowed the lender to seek foreclosure while requiring the consumer to arbitrate any counterclaim in the foreclosure action); *Lackey v. Green Tree Financial Corp.*, 330 S.C. at 402, 498 S.E.2d at 905 (same). The primary basis for this conclusion in *Muñoz* and *Lackey* was that requiring one party to seek a remedy through arbitration rather than the judicial system did not deprive that party of a remedy altogether. *See Muñoz*, 343 S.C. at 542, 542 S.E.2d at 365. The *Lackey* court additionally explained that the judicial remedies which the lender in that case had reserved for itself (*i.e.* replevin and foreclosure actions) provided specific procedures for protecting the collateral and the parties during the pendency of the arbitration proceedings. *Lackey*, 330 S.C. at 401, 498 S.E.2d at 905. Because these protections related to both parties and were facilitated by enforcement procedures specified by law, the court of appeals concluded that, regardless of the lack of mutuality of remedy, the arbitration clause bore "a reasonable relationship to the business risks" inherent in secured transactions. *Id.*

However, the essence of Simpson's unconscionability claim is not the general lack of mutuality of remedy, but rather the arbitration agreement's express stipulation that the dealer may bring a judicial proceeding that completely disregards any pending consumer claims that require arbitration. The clauses at issue in *Muñoz* and *Lackey* contained no such directives. To this effect, we can easily envision a scenario in which a dealer's claim and delivery action is initiated in court, completed, and the vehicle sold prior to an arbitrator's determination of the consumer's rights in the same vehicle. As the arbitration agreement between Simpson and Addy is written, the dealer collects on a judgment awarded in a judicial proceeding regardless of any protections for the collateral afforded by law.

Addy's suggestion that there are procedural motions[8] available to the consumer which offset any potentially inconsistent effects of this provision, in our opinion, shows an informal acknowledgement on the part of Addy that such a provision on its face is indeed one-sided. These procedural mechanisms only act to place an additional burden on the consumer to ensure that the vehicle in controversy is not disposed of in a court proceeding initiated by the dealer before the adjudication of the consumer's claims in arbitration.

We continue to abide by our previous holdings in *Muñoz* and *Lackey* that lack of mutuality of remedy will not invalidate an arbitration agreement. However, we find that the provision in the arbitration clause dictating that the dealer's judicial remedies supersede the consumer's arbitral remedies is one-sided and oppressive and does not promote a neutral and unbiased arbitral forum. Accordingly, in light of Simpson's lack of meaningful choice in agreeing to arbitrate, the provision is unconscionable and unenforceable.

3. Limitation on bringing warranty claims in a judicial forum

Addy argues that Simpson may not attack the arbitration clause on the grounds that it violates the Magnuson–Moss Warranty Act (MMWA), 15 U.S.C.A § 2301 *et seq.* (1997), because Simpson's underlying claims alleged no violation of the MMWA. We disagree.

The arbitration clause in the contract between Simpson and Addy states that it applies to "any and all disputes" including "automobile warranty" and "any consumer protection statute"—all of which implicate the MMWA. The provision further specifies that such matters are to be resolved only by "binding arbitration."

Rules promulgated by the Federal Trade Commission (FTC) state that informal dispute resolution procedures set forth in written warranties under the MMWA are not to be legally binding on any person. 16 C.F.R. § 703.5(j) (2006). *See also Richardson v. Palm Harbor Homes, Inc.*, 254 F.3d 1321 (11th Cir. 2001). Moreover, the MMWA has been interpreted to supersede the FAA with respect to consumer claims for breach of written warranty. *See Boyd v. Homes of Legend, Inc.*, 981 F. Supp. 1423, 1437–38 (M.D. Ala. 1997). Therefore, the federal government has made it clear that parties may not agree to arbitrate an MMWA claim as the arbitration clause between Simpson and Addy attempted to do here.

This Court will not enforce a contract which is violative of public policy, statutory law, or provisions of the Constitution. The fact that Simpson did not bring a claim under the MMWA is irrelevant to our conclusion that the inclusion of the MMWA in the scope of the arbitration

---

8. Specifically, Addy suggests that a motion for protective order or a motion to stay pending arbitration.

clause is unenforceable as a matter of public policy. Accordingly, we hold that this provision of the arbitration clause is an unconscionable and unenforceable violation of public policy.

C. Severability

In the alternative to its argument that the arbitration clause is not unconscionable, Addy suggests that any provision found by this Court to be unconscionable may be severed from the clause and arbitration allowed to otherwise proceed. In fact, it seems as though the "Additional Terms and Conditions" section of the contract anticipated just such a scenario. Paragraph fifteen (15) articulates a severability clause providing that:

> In the event any provision of this contract shall be held invalid, illegal, or unenforceable, the validity, legality, and enforceability of the remaining provisions shall not be affected or impaired thereby.

We disagree.

In consideration of the federal and state policies favoring arbitration agreements, severability clauses have been used to remove the unenforceable provisions in an arbitration clause while saving the parties' overall agreement to arbitrate. *See Healthcomp Evaluation Servs. Corp. v. O'Donnell*, 817 So.2d 1095, 1098 (Fla. Ct. App. 2d Dist. 2002) (holding that an arbitration clause was divisible and therefore a severability provision acted to remove the unenforceable provision from the arbitration clause without affecting the intent of the parties); *Primerica Fin. Servs. v. Wise*, 217 Ga.App. 36, 456 S.E.2d 631, 635 (Ga. Ct. App. 1995) (upholding the trial court's application of a severability clause to an arbitration agreement "in light of the liberal federal policy favoring arbitration agreements and the parties' intentions in entering into those agreements"). Additionally, legislation permits this Court to "refuse to enforce" any unconscionable clause in a contract or to "limit its application so as to avoid an unconscionable result." S.C. Code Ann. § 36–2–302(1) (2003).

At the same time, courts have acknowledged that severability is not always an appropriate remedy for an unconscionable provision in an arbitration clause. Although, "a critical consideration in assessing severability is giving effect to the intent of the contracting parties," the D.C. Circuit recently cautioned, "If illegality pervades the arbitration agreement such that only a disintegrated fragment would remain after hacking away the unenforceable parts, the judicial effort begins to look more like rewriting the contract than fulfilling the intent of the parties." *Booker v. Robert Half Intn'l Inc.*, 367 U.S. App. D.C. 77, 413 F.3d 77, 84–85 (D.C. Cir. 2005) (citations omitted). Similarly, the general principle in this State is that it is not the function of the court to rewrite contracts for parties. *Lewis v. Premium Inv. Corp.*, 351 S.C. 167, 171, 568 S.E.2d 361, 363 (2002).

In this case, we find the arbitration clause in the adhesion contract between Simpson and Addy wholly unconscionable and unenforceable based on the cumulative effect of a number of oppressive and one-sided provisions contained within the entire clause. While this Court does not ignore South Carolina's policy favoring arbitration, we hold that the intent of the parties is best achieved by severing the arbitration clause in its entirety rather than "rewriting" the contract by severing multiple unenforceable provisions.[9]

Additionally, we note that there is no specific set of factual circumstances establishing the line which must be crossed when evaluating an arbitration clause for unconscionability. Therefore, in holding today that the arbitration clause in the vehicle trade-in contract between Addy and Simpson is unconscionable due to a multitude of one-sided terms, we do not overrule our decision in *Muñoz* where we held that an adhesion contract between a consumer and a lender was not unconscionable because it lacked mutuality of remedy. Instead, we emphasize the importance of a case-by-case analysis in order to address the unique circumstances inherent in the various types of consumer transactions.

Accordingly, we affirm the trial court's denial of the motion to compel arbitration.

MOORE, WALLER, BURNETT AND PLEICONES, JJ., concur.

QUESTIONS AND NOTES

1. An often-mentioned advantage of arbitration in the context of commercial transactions is that the decision is entrusted to an expert who can resolve the dispute based on fairness in the particular commercial setting rather than based on the letter of the law. With respect to consumer transactions, which often are governed by precise or technical requirements, e.g., the Truth-in-Lending Act, to what extent is this advantage present?

9. We acknowledge that in light of the state and federal policies favoring arbitration, many courts view severing the offending provision and otherwise proceeding with arbitration to be the preferred remedy for an unconscionable provision in an arbitration clause. However, we find the present case is distinguishable from those cases prescribing severability such that the invalidation of the arbitration clause in its entirety is the more appropriate remedy.

First, the arbitration clause in the contract between Simpson and Addy contained a total of three unconscionable provisions while arbitration clauses examined by courts prescribing severability generally contained only one offending provision. . . . Second, two of the provisions in this case were found unconscionable because the provisions contravened state and federal consumer protection law. The sheer magnitude of unconscionability present in a provision that prevents a party from vindicating the party's statutory rights, along with the fact that such a grossly unconscionable provision occurred not once, but *twice*, requires that we give significant consideration to a remedy in this situation that best serves the interests of public policy. *See Graham Oil Co. v. ARCO Prods. Co.*, 43 F.3d 1244, 1249 (9th Cir. 1994) (noting that severance of illegal provisions is inappropriate when the entire arbitration clause represents an "integrated scheme to contravene public policy" (citations omitted)).

Accordingly, while this Court generally would encourage severability of an unconscionable provision, we do not view the arbitration agreement between Simpson and Addy to be a proper candidate for the application of this remedy. *See . . . In re Cotton Yarn Antitrust Litig.*, 406 F. Supp. 2d 585, 604 (M.D.N.C. 2005) ("[W]here, as here, multiple provisions of the arbitration clauses are inconsistent with Plaintiffs' ability to effectively vindicate their statutory rights . . . , the Court finds that the better course of action in this case is to excise the arbitration clauses altogether").

The parties to a consumer transaction do not have the power to agree that a particular law should not apply to their particular transaction. By adopting arbitration rules that do not require the arbitrator to apply the law, however, a merchant may escape the restrictions that the legislature has mandated for the merchant's transactions. Consequently, the Supreme Court has stated, "By agreeing to arbitrate a statutory claim, a party does not forgo the substantive rights afforded by [a] statute; it only submits to their resolution in an arbitral, rather than a judicial, forum." Mitsubishi Motors Corp. v. Soler Chrysler–Plymouth, Inc., 473 U.S. 614, 628 (1985). Arbitration clauses now commonly provide that the arbitrator will resolve disputes "according to applicable law."

2. Another often-mentioned advantage of arbitration is that it costs less than litigation. In fact, however, arbitration often is more expensive. The fee to initiate arbitration proceedings typically is higher than the cost of filing a law suit, and there are several other costs in connection with arbitration proceedings that simply do not exist in litigation. In addition to a filing fee (which may be based on the size of the consumer's claim and which may exceed $1,000), there may be an administrative fee (perhaps per diem), a fee for a hearing room (per diem), the arbitrator's fee (hourly), [19] and others. Some of these fees are based on the size of the consumer's claim. In Eagle v. Fred Martin Motor Co., 809 N.E.2d 1161, 1176 (Ohio. App.2004), the fees included the following:

> (1) $75 for a single subpoena request; (2) $150 for each discovery order; (3) $100 for a continuance request; (4) $2,500 for a document hearing, or $1,500 for an initial participatory hearing session; (5) at least $1,250 to submit a post-hearing brief; (6) a fee for an objection to the request equal to as much as the cost of the original request; and (7) between $1,000 and $1,250 for a written findings of facts, conclusions of law or reasons for an Award. Ms. Eagle asserts that a conservative estimation of the fees she would likely have to incur for an in-person arbitration with a written opinion would range between $4,200 and $6,000. We note that there are additional fees associated with the NAF arbitration, such as fees for a request for reopening or reconsideration, and other procedural fees that may be assessed by the NAF as well. Suffice it to say, that, for virtually every piece of documentation requested by a party, a corresponding fee exists.[20]

And in Olshan Foundation Repair Co. v. Ayala, 180 S.W.3d 212 (Tex.App. 2005), the consumers paid defendant $23,000 to stabilize the foundation of their home. When the system failed, they sued for breach of contract and violation of the little-FTC act. On defendant's motion, the court enforced

19. Ting v. AT&T, 182 F.Supp.2d 902, 934 (N.D.Cal.2002) (fees in San Francisco averaged $1,899 per day); Phillips v. Associates Home Equity Services, 179 F.Supp.2d 840, 846 (N.D.Ill.2001) (fees in Chicago averaged $1,800 per day).

20. NAF (National Arbitration Forum) is one of the three leading providers. The others are American Arbitration Association (AAA) and Judicial Arbitration and Mediation Service (JAMS). Their rules and some information concerning current fees are available at their web sites.

an arbitration clause in the contract and ordered arbitration. The consumers paid $4,130 to initiate arbitration proceedings, only to be sent an invoice for their share of the expenses of the proceeding in the amount of $33,150. (The court held the arbitration clause was unconscionable.)

3.   To the extent that the high cost of arbitration is an issue, should the relevant/controlling inquiry be whether the expense is too high relative to the cost of litigation or whether the expense is more than the consumer can afford to pay? Should the size of the consumer's claim be relevant?

4.   Although the Supreme Court has made it clear that enforcement of an arbitration clause is subject to *any* defense to the enforcement of a contract, the defense most commonly asserted is unconscionability. It would not be consistent with the section 2 of the Federal Arbitration Act, as interpreted by the Supreme Court, for a court to conclude that arbitration clauses are per se unconscionable in all consumer contracts. Consequently, as in *Simpson*, courts apply the same standards to arbitration clauses that they apply in determining whether other provisions are unconscionable. These standards typically are some variation on the criteria articulated in the landmark case, Williams v. Walker–Thomas Furniture Company (page 470 supra): absence of meaningful choice by the consumer (i.e. procedural unconscionability) together with terms that unreasonably favor the party that imposed the term in question (i.e. substantive unconscionability).

Some courts conclude that the procedural element is satisfied whenever the contract is a contract of adhesion, viz., that the merchant is not willing to negotiate over the arbitration provision. E.g., Flores v. Transamerica HomeFirst, Inc., 113 Cal.Rptr.2d 376, 382 (Cal.App.2001) ("A finding of a contract of adhesion is essentially a finding of procedural unconscionability"). Others require more of a showing. For example, in American General Finance, Inc. v. Branch, 793 So.2d 738 (Ala.2000), there were two plaintiffs who resisted enforcement of an arbitration clause. One of them established that when the contract was formed, seven of eight lenders who were surveyed included arbitration clauses in their standard forms. The other consumer, however, formed her contract two years earlier, when only three of the eight included arbitration clauses. The court held that one consumer had no meaningful choice, but that the other consumer did.

Some contracts entail an ongoing service, such as credit card or checking accounts and wireless or land-line telephone service. These contracts often provide for revision of the terms upon specified notice by the service provider. The contracts typically provide that the revision will become effective if the consumer continues using the service. In recent years many of these entities have attempted to revise their contracts to add an arbitration clause, by sending a change-of-terms notice (typically inserted in the envelope that transmits a monthly bill). The courts are badly split on the enforceability of arbitration clauses issued in this way. Many courts view contractual language such as, "We may amend or change any part of this agreement," as broad enough to encompass arbitration clauses. Many others, however, hold that the contractual language only encompasses changes in terms that are express terms of the original contract, such as finance charges, late payment fees, credit limits, etc., and do not authorize adoption of terms, such as dispute resolution systems, that are outside the scope of the original contract. E.g., Stone v. Golden Wexler & Sarnese, P.C., 341 F.Supp.2d 189 (E.D.N.Y.2004).

If a credit card issuer or cell phone service provider includes an arbitration clause in a bill stuffer, does the consumer have any meaningful choice whether to accept it?

5. To determine whether an arbitration clause is substantively unconscionable, courts must determine whether it unreasonably favors the merchant or whether it is oppressive to the consumer. They have considered numerous features of various arbitration programs. Three of them, covered in *Simpson* and the preceding questions, are excessive cost, lack of mutuality, and elimination of remedies that the consumer would have if the dispute were to be litigated rather than arbitrated. As *Simpson* reveals, a clause is suspect if it imposes limits on those remedies, including the consumer's right to recover compensatory damages, punitive damages, or damages for emotional distress. Also suspect are clauses that foreclose the ability of a consumer to obtain injunctive relief or attorney's fees under statutes that specifically authorize these remedies. So are bans on class actions, a subject addressed later in this chapter (Note 8, page 881).

6. Another factor courts have considered in determining the substantive unconscionability of an arbitration clause is bias. The integrity of the dispute resolution process, of course, depends on the neutrality of the decision maker. There are several ways in which this neutrality may be called into question in any given case. In commercial arbitration, when the disputing parties are members of the same industry, it is an advantage to both of them that the decision maker be a member of that industry. In consumer arbitration, however, the parties are not both members of an industry. So an arbitration clause that calls for the arbitrator to be a member of the merchant's industry creates doubts about the impartiality of the arbitrator. See Broemmer v. Abortion Services of Phoenix, 840 P.2d 1013 (Ariz.1992) (in a malpractice action against an obstetrician/gynecologist, the contract called for the arbitrator to be an obstetrician/gynecologist); Graham v. Scissor–Tail, Inc., 623 P.2d 165 (Cal.1981) (in a promoter's dispute with a recording artist, the arbitrator was to be an executive of the artist's union). Many arbitrators are attorneys, some retired, some still in active practice. Is it relevant that many of the arbitrators on the arbitration service's list did or still do represent competitors of the merchant about whom the consumer is complaining? Is it relevant that an individual arbitrator gets paid only if he or she is selected to conduct the arbitration? See Walker v. Ryan's Family Steak Houses, Inc., 400 F.3d 370 (6th Cir.2005).

7. Other notable features of arbitration include the lack of judicial review of an arbitrator's decision and the absence of published opinions. This means, among other things, that the results of arbitration proceedings are not a matter of public record. Sometimes this confidentiality is reinforced by the arbitration clause itself: "Any arbitration shall remain confidential. Neither you nor AT&T may disclose the existence, content or results of any arbitration or award, except as may be required by law or to confirm and enforce an award." Ting v. AT&T, 182 F.Supp.2d 902, 931 (N.D.Cal.2002).

The confidentiality and lack of review is attractive to merchants. It enables them to make a judgment of the precedential value of a case, litigate those it wishes, and shunt into arbitration those that it wishes not to publicize. Even if it loses the arbitration, other consumers will not learn about it and even if they do, the adverse result will not establish a precedent to be reckoned with in a later arbitration (or litigation). Referring to the clause quoted in the preceding paragraph, the court noted, "this confidentiality provision means that a contract that affects seven million Californians will be interpreted largely without public scrutiny. This puts AT&T in a vastly superior legal posture since as a party to every arbitration it will know every result and be able to guide itself and take legal positions accordingly, while each class member will have to operate in isolation and largely in the dark." Id. at 932.

8.   Still another feature of an arbitration clause is the consumer's surrender of the right to a jury trial, which is guaranteed by the Seventh Amendment:

> In Suits at common law, where the value in controversy shall exceed twenty dollars, the right of trial by jury shall be preserved, and no fact tried by a jury, shall be otherwise re-examined in any Court of the United States, than according to the rules of the common law.

A person may waive his or her constitutional rights, but the standard for waiving those rights is higher than the standard for assenting to a contract. This is entirely separate from an inquiry into unconscionability. Hence, it is necessary to examine whether a consumer has effectively waived the Seventh Amendment right. To be effective, a waiver of constitutional rights must be knowing and voluntary. See Walker v. Ryan's Family Steak Houses, Inc., 400 F.3d 370 (6th Cir.2005) (waiver ineffective). For contrasting views, see Sternlight, Mandatory Binding Arbitration and Demise of the Seventh Amendment Right to a Jury Trial, 16 Ohio St. J.Disp.Resol. 669 (2001); Ware, Arbitration Clauses, Jury–Waiver Clauses, and Other Contractual Waivers of Constitutional Rights, 67 Law & Contemp.Probs. 167 (2004).

9.   The Supremacy Clause of the Constitution (page 163 supra) forecloses the ability of the states to prohibit arbitration in all or some kinds of consumer transactions. It does not, however, preclude Congress from doing so (do you see why?). In the Magnuson–Moss Warranty Act, Congress encouraged manufacturers to establish dispute resolution procedures known as informal dispute settlement mechanisms, and it directed the FTC to establish rules for these mechanisms. See page 834 supra. If a manufacturer creates a mechanism that conforms to the FTC's regulations, then the manufacturer can require a consumer to resort to the mechanism before the consumer can assert rights under the Act. One of the regulations stipulates that the decision of the mechanism must be non-binding: if the consumer is dissatisfied with the outcome of the manufacturer's procedures, the consumer can sue. May a manufacturer decide not to establish an informal dispute settlement mechanism and instead provide that all disputes concerning its warranties must be resolved by arbitration? See section 110(a)(3)(c)(*i*). The court in *Simpson* thinks not, but the courts are split on this question. Another statute creating similar doubt about the enforceability of arbitration clauses is the Credit Repair Organizations Act (page 271 supra), which provides:

> Any waiver by any consumer or any protection provided by or any right of the consumer under this subchapter (1) shall be treated as void; and (2) may not be enforced by any Federal or State court or any other person.

15 U.S.C. § 1679f(a). *Compare* Reynolds v. Credit Solutions, Inc., 541 F.Supp.2d 1248 (N.D.Ala.2008) (arbitration clause not enforced) *with* Gay v. CreditInform, 511 F.3d 369 (3d Cir.2007) (arbitration clause enforced).

The effect of the Magnuson–Moss Warranty Act on the enforceability of arbitration clauses may be in doubt. But Congress has enacted another provision that undeniably makes an arbitration clause unenforceable. In 2002 Congress amended the Automobile Dealers' Day in Court Act, 15 U.S.C. § 1221, to add section 1226, which provides that any disputes between automobile manufacturers and their franchised dealers may be resolved by arbitration only if the parties agree to it after the dispute has arisen. The legislative history of this statute includes the following statement:

> It is difficult to imagine the adjudication of substantive rights without the right to appeal, but the FAA offers no effective appeal from the award of an arbitration panel.
>
> .   .   .
>
> It is our position that a sales and service contract between a manufacturer of a motor vehicle and its franchised dealers is not a proper one to be interpreted or enforced by arbitrators, unless the arbitration route has been chosen voluntarily by both parties after the controversy arises. This is so, because this contract is a classic example of a contract of adhesion. It is not negotiated. It is handed to a dealer who is expected to make, or already has made, a substantial investment, on a "take it or leave it" basis.[21]

Can you reconcile the position of the automobile dealers in promoting enactment of this legislation with their inclusion of mandatory arbitration provisions in the contracts they draft for use with consumers?

10.   Problem. You are a legislative assistant to a state senator. She asks you to advise her on the desirability of a proposed bill:

---

21. Testimony of Gene N. Fondren, in support of H.R. 534, 106th Cong., 2nd Sess. (2000), available at 2000 WL 763559. Mr. Fondren spoke on behalf of the National Automobile Dealers Association and the Texas Automobile Dealers Association.

Section 1.   Short Title. This Act shall be known as the Fair Bargain Act.

Section 2.   Legislative Findings. The legislature finds that

(a) standard form contracts, in whatever form recorded, do not necessarily express the voluntary and informed assent of both parties; and

(b) the party drafting such a form will often foresee legal disputes with one or more of the parties to whom it is submitted for acceptance, while the party accepting such a form will seldom foresee such a legal dispute or prudently evaluate the loss of procedural rights affecting its outcome; and

(c) the party drafting such a form can unless restrained by law exploit the inadvertence, imprudence, or limited literacy of the party to whom it is presented for acceptance by including provisions disabling that party's procedural rights necessary or useful to the enforcement of substantive rights otherwise purportedly conferred by the contracts in which the provisions appear or by state or federal law; and

(d) this use of standard form contracts is unconscionable.

Section 3.   Definitions.

As used in this act:

(a) "Standard form contract or lease" means one prepared by a party for whom its use is routine in business transactions with consumers, borrowers, tenants, franchisees, or employees;

(b) "Rights enforcement disabling provision" means a contract provision modifying or limiting otherwise available procedural rights necessary or useful to a consumer, borrower, tenant, franchisee, or employee in the enforcement of substantive rights against a party drafting a standard form contract or lease, including a clause requiring the consumer, tenant, borrower, franchisee, or employee to

(1) Assert any claim against the party who prepared the form in a forum that is less convenient, more costly, or more dilatory than a judicial forum established in this state for the resolution of the dispute;

(2) Assume a risk of liability for the legal fees of the party preparing the contract, unless those fees are authorized by statute, reasonable in amount, and incurred to enforce a promise to pay money;

(3) Forego access to evidence otherwise obtainable under the rules of procedure of a convenient judicial forum available to hear and decide a dispute between the parties;

(4) Present evidence to a purported neutral party who may reasonably be expected to regard the party preparing the contract as more likely to be a future employer of the neutral than is that party's adversary;

(5) Forego recourse to appeal from a decision not based on substantial evidence or disregarding his or her legal rights;

(6) Decline to participate in a class action; or

(7) Forego an award of attorney's fees, civil penalties, punitive damages, or of multiple damages otherwise available under the law.

Section 4.   Rights Enforcement Disabling Provision Revocable.

(a) A rights enforcement disabling provision that is included in a standard form contract or lease is revocable by the consumer, borrower, tenant, franchisee, or employee.

(b)(1) Revocation shall be in writing and communicated within a reasonable time after a dispute between the parties to the contract has arisen and the consumer of goods or services, borrower, tenant, or employee has had an opportunity to seek counsel on the effect of the provision.

(2) A party seeking to enforce a rights enforcement disabling provision after it has been revoked shall be liable for any resulting legal costs, including a reasonable attorney's fee.

Section 5. Covered Transactions.

This Act shall not apply to a provision in any contract:

(a) For the sale of property having a value in excess of two hundred thousand dollars ($200,000), or for a loan in excess of two hundred thousand dollars ($200,000) to purchase property;

(b) For the lease of property having a value in excess of two hundred thousand dollars ($200,000), or for a loan in excess of two hundred thousand dollars ($200,000) to lease property;

(c) For the delivery of services having a value in excess of two hundred thousand dollars ($200,000), or for a loan in excess of two hundred thousand dollars ($200,000) to purchase services;

(d) Of employment providing for compensation in excess of one hundred thousand dollars ($100,000) a year;

(e) That is an agreement to maintain a local business franchise having gross receipts in excess of a million dollars ($1,000,000) a year; or

(f) That is a commercial letter of credit.

Section 6.   Agreements to Arbitrate Future Disputes Preserved.

Nothing in this Act shall preclude parties from making a binding agreement to arbitrate a future dispute if the arbitration agreement does not impose on any consumer, borrower, tenant, franchisee, or employee any rights enforcement disabilities.

Section 7. Severability.

The provisions of this Act are severable; the invalidity of any application of any provision of this Act for any reason shall not affect other applications, nor shall the invalidity of any provision affect the validity of other provisions.

What would you advise? Is this legislation good policy?

The Supreme Court has stated, "[G]enerally applicable contract defenses, such as fraud, duress, or unconscionability, may be applied to invalidate arbitration agreements without contravening § 2 [of the FAA, quoted on page 836 supra]. Courts may not, however, invalidate arbitration agreements under state laws applicable only to arbitration provisions." Doctor's Associates, Inc. v. Casarotto, 517 U.S. 681, 687 (1996). Is this legislation preempted by Section 2 of the FAA, as a law applicable only to arbitration provisions?

11. Mandatory arbitration has been a popular topic in the law reviews. Among the better treatments are Budnitz, Arbitration of Disputes Between Consumers and Financial Institutions: A Serious Threat to Consumer Protection, 10 Ohio St.J. Dispute Resolution 267 (1995); Symposium, The Coming Crisis in Mandatory Arbitration: New Perspectives and Possibilities, 67 Law & Contemp.Probs. 1 (2004); Symposium, Paying the Price of Process: Judicial Regulation of Consumer Arbitration Agreements, 2001 J.Disp.Res. 89; Alderman, Pre–Dispute Mandatory Arbitration in Consumer Contracts: A Call for Reform, 38 Hous.L.Rev. 1237 (2001); Ware, Arbitration and Unconscionability After *Doctor's Associates, Inc. v. Casarotto,* 31 Wake Forest L.Rev. 1001 (1996).

(b) Enforcement by a Public Agency

Another way to reduce the consumer's cost of enforcing his or her rights is to have someone else enforce them. And most consumer protection legislation provides for enforcement by a government agency or official. Some of these statutes permit both public and private enforcement,[22] but others provide only for enforcement by the public agency.[23]

The most visible kind of enforcement by a public agency is litigation to prevent or redress injury to numerous consumers. But less visible efforts are also possible and undoubtedly far outnumber the instances of litigation. These efforts include negotiating consent decrees and assurances of voluntary compliance, and they also include negotiating on behalf of individual consumers. Some state agencies and probably most local agencies intervene on behalf of individual consumers whose rights have been violated.

When a statute provides simply for public enforcement, the question arises whether the silence as to private enforcement indicates a legislative

22. E.g., Truth-in-Lending Act §§ 108, 130; Fair Credit Reporting Act §§ 616–17, 621; Fair Debt Collection Practices Act §§ 813, 814; Illinois Consumer Fraud and Deceptive Business Practices Act, 815 Ill. Consol. Stat. §§ 505/7, 505/10a; UCCC §§ 5.201, 6.104.

23. E.g., FTC Act § 5(b); Consumer Credit Protection Act § 306 (federal restrictions on garnishment); Arizona Consumer Fraud Act, Ariz.Rev.Stat. § 44–1528.

intention that aggrieved individuals not have a private right of action. With respect to consumer fraud acts, for example, courts have held that there is a private right of action. Sellinger v. Freeway Mobile Home Sales, Inc., 521 P.2d 1119 (Ariz.1974); Rice v. Snarlin, Inc., 266 N.E.2d 183 (Ill.App.1970). With respect to federal statutes, the courts are less inclined to do so. Thus, it has long been the law that there is no private remedy for violation of section 5 of the FTC Act. E.g., Holloway v. Bristol–Myers Corp., 485 F.2d 986 (D.C.Cir.1973). At one time the Supreme Court recognized implied private remedies if doing so would further the Congressional purpose in enacting the statute. More recently, however, the Court has repudiated this standard and now recognizes a private right of action only if there is some basis for believing that Congress intended one to exist. If Congress has not expressly created a private right of action, however, courts are unlikely to conclude that Congress intended one to exist. See LeVick v. Skaggs Co., 701 F.2d 777 (9th Cir.1983) (overruling a prior case and holding that there is no private right of action for an employer's violation of a statute prohibiting discharge of employees whose wages have been garnished).

Many statutes, both state and federal, provide for both public and private enforcement. It is not uncommon for state statutes to provide that a final judgment in an action brought by the attorney general is prima facie evidence of the facts on which it is based in any subsequent suit by a consumer. E.g., Ohio Rev.Code § 1345.10(A). Compare West's Rev.Code Wash.Ann. § 19.86.130, which provides that a judgment in favor of the attorney general "shall be prima facie evidence against such defendant." Does this mean that a judgment in favor of the *seller* would *not* be prima facie evidence in a subsequent suit by a consumer?

The statutes also may require the court clerk to notify the attorney general of the filing of any suit alleging a violation of the little-FTC act. E.g., Mass.Gen.Laws Ann. ch. 93A, § 10; Ohio Rev.Code § 1345.09(E). (The Ohio statute requires notice only if the consumer's suit is for declaratory or injunctive relief or if it is a class action. The Massachusetts statute is not so limited.) Upon receiving notice of a consumer's suit, the attorney general may intervene. Should the statutes go further and permit the attorney general to assume control of the suit? Should they permit the attorney general to halt the proceedings if, e.g., the litigation would compromise a pending investigation?

––––––––

The preceding paragraphs consider the question, *who* may enforce consumer protection statutes? There remains for consideration the question, *how* are the consumer's rights to be enforced, i.e. what remedies are available? Statutes that authorize suits by consumers uniformly provide for monetary recovery, which may consist of actual damages, minimum damages, or punitive damages, usually along with attorney's fees and costs. Injunctive or declaratory relief also may be available. Statutes that authorize suits by a public agency or official uniformly provide for injunctive and declaratory relief, but some of them do not mention recovery of damages on behalf of consumers. When the statute is silent on the matter, the courts have split on the question whether the public agency may recover damages on behalf of consumers. For example, the Ninth Circuit Court of Appeals has held that the FTC Act does not empower the Commission to order a respondent to refund moneys paid by consumers. Heater v. FTC, 503 F.2d 321 (9th Cir.1974). This conclusion enables businesses to engage in unfair or deceptive practices until the FTC catches up with them and orders them to stop. Nevertheless, the court believed that section 5(b), which authorizes the FTC to order a business to cease and desist unlawful activity, does not empower the Commission to order redress for past injury. Compare *Warner-Lambert*, page 82 supra. The FTC disagreed with the Ninth Circuit's decision in *Heater* and announced its intention to appeal. In re Holiday Magic, Inc., 84 F.T.C. 748, 1028 (1974). The Commission never actually sought review, however, perhaps because of the contemporaneous enactment of amendments to the FTC Act. In 1975 Congress added section 19, authorizing the Commission to sue in federal court to obtain damages from persons who violate section 5. Note the distinction in sections 19(a) and (b) based on whether the Commission establishes the violation by rulemaking or by adjudication. What is the rationale for this distinction? Note also that section 19 does not authorize the FTC to award damages. Rather, the Commission must persuade a court to grant this relief. The possibility of damages, however, has enabled the Commission staff to negotiate restitution in numerous cases resolved by consent decree. For additional treatment of the FTC's remedies, see pages 81–99 supra.

Like the FTC Act, many state anti-deception and other consumer protection statutes that provide for public enforcement do not expressly authorize the public official to obtain restitution or other monetary relief for injured consumers. Thus there is a question similar to the one in *Heater*: does the statutory omission mean that the public official may not seek monetary relief for injured consumers?

Kugler v. Romain

Supreme Court of New Jersey, 1971.
58 N.J. 522, 279 A.2d 640.

FRANCIS, J.

[Defendant sold a package of books and materials that he described as "A Complete Ten Year Educational Program" for children. His targets were minority group consumers of limited education and low income, whom he induced to purchase the books by making numerous misrepresentations. Defendant's price for the package was 2–1/2 times its reasonable market price, and the package had little or no educational value for the children of the persons in the targeted group. The New Jersey Attorney General sued, alleging violation of section 2 of the New Jersey Consumer Fraud Act, which provides:

The act, use or employment by any person of any deception, fraud, false pretense, false promise, misrepresentation, or the knowing concealment, suppression, or omission of any material fact with intent that others rely upon such concealment, suppression or omission, in connection with the sale * * * of any merchandise, or with the subsequent performance of such person as aforesaid, whether or not any person has in fact been misled, deceived or damaged thereby, is declared to be an unlawful practice; * * *.

N.J.S.A. § 56:8–2. The authorization for this proceeding appears in section 8:

Whenever it shall appear to the Attorney General that a person has engaged in, is engaging in or is about to engage in any practice declared to be unlawful by this act he may seek and obtain in an action in the Superior Court an injunction prohibiting such person from continuing such practices or engaging therein or doing any acts in furtherance thereof * * *. The court may make such orders or judgments as may be necessary to prevent the use or employment by a person of any prohibited practices, or which may be necessary to restore to any person in interest any moneys or property, real or personal which may have been acquired by means of any practice herein declared to be unlawful.

Id. § 56:8–8. The attorney general sought a declaration that the price of the package violated section 2 either because it constituted fraud, which is expressly included in the statute, or because it was unconscionable under UCC section 2–302, which he argued was implicitly included in the statute. He also sought an injunction, civil penalties, and restitution for all persons who had entered contracts with defendant.

The trial court held that defendant's specific misrepresentations violate section 2 and granted the injunction. It also granted restitution and civil penalties, but only as to 24 customers who testified at the trial, since there was no evidence before the court that defendant made misrepresentations to any other customers. The court held that the "exorbitant" price was not a fraud per se under section 2 and that unconscionability within UCC section 2–302 is a matter of private concern that cannot be asserted by the attorney general under the Consumer Fraud Act. The attorney general appealed, challenging the trial court's limitation of relief to the 24 customers who testified.]

We find ourselves in agreement with the Attorney General's contention that his claims for broader affirmative relief should be recognized. Denial of such relief would be unfortunate not only in this case, but it would operate as a serious impairment to the deterrent effect of the sanctions which we believe underlies the Consumer Fraud Act.

I.

In resolving the problems presented, first attention must be given to the authority and status of the Attorney General to institute an action in consumer fraud cases seeking affirmative relief not only for the benefit of specifically named consumers but also for a large number of unnamed consumers similarly situated who wish to be represented and to benefit by the judgment entered therein. Obviously a just resolution can be reached only through a sensitive awareness of the climate of our time as it has been influenced by legislative and judicial measures affecting the buyer-seller relationship in the marketing of consumer goods. There can be no doubt that, in today's society, sale of consumer goods, especially on an installment credit basis, has become a matter of ever-increasing state and national anxiety. In recent years New Jersey lawmakers have become deeply concerned with suppression of commercial deception in consumer transactions. The Consumer Fraud Act invoked here is only one example of the concern. To it may be added the Retail Installment Sales Act and the Home Repair Financing Act.

. . .

The existing statutes in our State, and particularly the Consumer Fraud Act and section 2–302 of the UCC, reveal that the Legislature did not limit its consideration or treatment of the need for consumer protection to the creation of private remedies between the individual buyer and seller. Obviously it recognized that the deception, misrepresentation and unconscionable practices engaged in by professional sellers seeking mass distribution of many types of consumer goods frequently produce an adverse effect on large segments of disadvantaged and poorly educated people, who are wholly devoid of expertise and least able to understand or to cope with the "sales oriented," "extroverted" and unethical solicitors bent on capitalizing upon their weakness, and who therefore most need protection against predatory practices. As we see the statutes cited, as well as the act establishing the Office of Consumer Protection, it seems plain that the lawmakers accepted the premise that the market bargaining process does not protect ordinary consumers from serious damage in a large number of transactions. Obviously, giving the consumer rights and remedies which he must assert individually in the courts would provide little therapy for the overall public aspect of the problem. It has been said that "[o]ne cannot think of a more expensive and frustrating course than to seek to regulate goods or 'contract' quality through repeated lawsuits against inventive 'wrongdoers'." Leff, "Unconscionability and the Crowd—Consumers and The Common Law Tradition," 31 U.Pitt.L.Rev. 349, 356 (1970). As Professor Leff suggests, mass consumer transactions growing out of unequal bargaining power and unfair practices should not be handled on a case-by-case basis. The emphasis must be upon public rather than private remedies, and the natural remedial step is government intervention.

Accepting the need for a public as well as a private remedy, the Legislature clearly empowered the Attorney General to police consumer practices and contracts. Section 8 authorized him to obtain an injunction against a seller who in marketing his products uses deception, fraud, false pretense, misrepresentation or concealment of material facts in violation of [Section 2]. And this remedy is available even though no consumer has in fact been misled or damaged thereby. But more important for purposes of the present case, in such an injunction action, as the cited section says, the court "may make such orders or judgments as may be necessary to prevent the use or employment by a person of any prohibited practices, or which may be necessary to restore to any person in interest any moneys or property, real or personal which may have been acquired by means of any practice herein declared to be unlawful." . . .

The purpose to be gleaned from the statute specifically involved here, when read in light of the other pertinent legislation adverted to, is that while private rights and interests were to be served, public interests of substantial consumer groups were likewise to be protected. . . . Consequently there is a tremendous need to find a simple, inexpensive solution which will accomplish the greatest possible good for the greatest possible number of consumers who have common problems and complaints vis-à-vis the seller. If the only available route has been pursuit of a private remedy by individual victims of the unfair practices specified by [Section 2], such a rule would require an unrealistic expenditure of judicial energy and would be inconsistent with current trends in consumer protective legislation.

In our judgment the statutes referred to above in their total impact, when considered in connection with the Attorney General's general statutory and common law authority to act in matters affecting the public welfare, require the conclusion that he has authority to bring action in the public interest either on behalf of specifically named buyers who have been imposed upon contrary to Section 2 thereof, or in the nature of a class action on behalf of all similarly situated buyers. Although the procedural aspects of such a suit need not be passed upon at this time, guidance may be found in [the rules of procedure] which relate generally to class actions.

. . .

II.

Since we are satisfied that the public welfare would be sufficiently adversely affected by a consumer good seller's engagement in practices condemned by [Section 2] to justify a remedial action by the Attorney General in behalf of consumers who constitute an ascertainable class of victims with a sufficient community of interest, we turn to his right to the specific relief denied below. Quite obviously the Attorney General recognized that a class action is not maintainable if the right of each individual claimant to relief depended upon a separate set of facts applicable only to him. Although the proof adduced at the hearing showed that defendant's agents practiced certain patterns of sales conduct, each of which deceived and misled a group of consumers, no effort was made to obtain separate adjudication of illegality of the contracts of each group of the 24 persons who participated in the trial or the contracts of all others similarly situated who were victimized by the same pattern of conduct. And no such issue is before us.

The Attorney General's claim was that there was one illegal aspect of the sales contract which was common to every transaction, namely the fixed price. . . . [H]e urged that under the circumstances the price was unconscionable under Section 2–302 of the Uniform Commercial Code and, as such, was within the proscription of Section 2 of the Consumer Fraud Act. . . . If the contention is sound, then it should follow that every consumer who executed the form agreement for the educational package described above at the price fixed by defendant ought to be considered similarly situated, and the Attorney General would therefore be entitled to a judgment invalidating the contract for the entire class of such consumers.

. . .

Unconscionability is not defined in Section 2–302 of the Uniform Commercial Code, and we agree that it is not mentioned by name in Section 2 of the Consumer Fraud Act. It is an amorphous concept obviously designed to establish a broad business ethic. . . .

The standard of conduct contemplated by the unconscionability clause is good faith, honesty in fact and observance of fair dealing. The need for application of the standard is most acute when the professional seller is seeking the trade of those most subject to exploitation—the uneducated, the inexperienced and the people of low incomes. In such a context, a material departure from the standard puts a badge of fraud on the transaction and here the concept of fraud and unconscionability are interchangeable. Thus we believe that in consumer goods transactions such as those involved in this case, unconscionability must be equated with the concepts of deception, fraud, false pretense, misrepresentation, concealment and the like, which are stamped unlawful under [Section 2 of the Consumer Fraud Act]. We do not consider that absence of the word "unconscionable" from the statute detracts in any substantial degree from the force of this conclusion. That view is aided and strengthened by the plain inference that the Legislature intended to broaden the scope of responsibility for unfair business practices by stating in Section 2 that the use of any of the described practices is unlawful "whether or not any person [the consumer] has in fact been misled, deceived or damaged thereby."

We have no doubt that an exorbitant price ostensibly agreed to by a purchaser of the type involved in this case—but in reality unilaterally fixed by the seller and not open to negotiation—constitutes an unconscionable bargain from which such a purchaser should be relieved under Section 2. If, therefore, in this case the price charged for the educational package is so exorbitant as to be unconscionable, Section 2 makes it unnecessary to decide whether the Attorney General could maintain a class action for all similarly affected consumers based solely upon violation of Section 2–302, the unconscionability clause of the Uniform Commercial Code. Adequate and proper relief for all consumers victimized by an unconscionable price may be obtained by the Attorney General through Section 2 of the Consumer Fraud Act under which his action was brought here.

Sale at an exorbitant price especially in the market described by the evidence in this case raises a strong inference of imposition. Here the facts reveal that the seller's price was not only roughly two and one half times a reasonable market price, assuming functional adequacy of the book package for the represented purpose, but they indicate also that most of the package was actually practically worthless for that purpose. Such price-value clearly constitutes unconscionability and renders Section 2 available to the Attorney General in a class-type remedial action for the benefit of all similarly situated consumers. . . .

As set forth above, we are satisfied that the price for the book package was unconscionable in relation to defendant's cost and the value to the consumers and was therefore a fraud within the contemplation of [Section 2]. Further, for the reasons stated we are convinced that a view that such price unconscionability gives rise only to a private remedy is an unreasonable limitation on the aim and scope of the Consumer Fraud Act. The public purpose to be served thereby (and we see the legislative emphasis as being more on public than on private remedies) can be accomplished effectively only by recognizing the authority of the Attorney General to intervene in behalf of all consumers similarly affected by the broadly described fraudulent sales tactics of merchandise sellers.

More specifically here, since the price unconscionability rendered the sales contract invalid as to all consumers who executed it, the Attorney General was entitled to a judgment so holding as to the entire class of such persons. Accordingly, the trial court's order must be modified to the end that such a judgment may be entered. The mechanics of effectuating the judgment with respect to the individuals comprising the class and of accomplishing the necessary restorative relief are left to the trial court.

As modified the judgment is affirmed and the cause is remanded for further proceedings consistent with this opinion.

QUESTIONS AND NOTES

1.   Why didn't the court hold that defendant's misrepresentations were a "deception, fraud, . . . [or] misrepresentation," in violation of section 2, as to all customers of defendant?

2.   The court cites language in section 8 of the Consumer Fraud Act authorizing the court to "make such orders or judgments as may be necessary to prevent the use or employment . . . of any prohibited practices . . . ." Is this language indispensable to the conclusion of the court? If section 8 only authorized the attorney general to seek injunctions and was completely silent as to any other relief, would not the attorney general still be able to obtain restitution for injured consumers?

What then is the effect of the quoted language? Does it authorize the attorney general to seek invalidation of contracts that are unconscionable under the UCC?

3.   The Washington little-FTC act contains language similar to that of section 8 of the New Jersey statute. The Supreme Court of Washington agreed with *Romain* that the statute authorizes the attorney general to obtain restitution for injured consumers. The court also held that the use of the attorney general's resources to procure a refund for individual consumers does not violate a state constitutional prohibition against making a gift of state funds to private parties. State v. Ralph Williams' North West Chrysler Plymouth, Inc., 510 P.2d 233 (Wash.1973).

4. Problem. *Seller* sells televisions for $25 per week for 24 weeks, or a total of $600. The cash price of the TV's is $450. This violates the rate regulation statute and *Seller* also violates the Truth-in-Lending Act. Neither the Truth-in-Lending Act nor the usury statute says anything about enforcement by the attorney general. May the attorney general nevertheless sue under the New Jersey Consumer Fraud Act to obtain relief for *Seller's* customers, including refunds of excess interest and the statutory penalty that each of the statutes provides?

5. Problem. *Dealer* sells cars on credit. When its customers default, *Dealer* repossesses the cars and sells them, but fails to comply with Part 6 of Article 9 of the UCC. Under the New Jersey Consumer Fraud Act, may the attorney general sue to enjoin this practice and compel *Dealer* to send refunds to each customer whose car was worth more than the amount owed when the car was repossessed?

6. At the very end of its opinion, the court in Kugler v. Romain sidesteps the matter of the mechanics of administering a restitution order. In at least some circumstances, the mechanics may pose difficult questions. For example, how should the court determine the total amount to be returned to consumers? How can the consumers be notified? If injured consumers do not claim the entire amount, how should the remainder be disposed of? Ordinarily the party seeking restitution must surrender any benefits already received. How should this requirement operate when a public official obtains a restitution order?

7. In addition to injunctive and restitutionary relief, statutes may empower the attorney general (or other public authority) to seek punitive relief. Thus, section 5(m) of the FTC Act provides for civil penalties of up to $10,000 for each violation of a trade regulation rule or a cease and desist order. Similarly, the little-FTC acts in over thirty states subject violators to civil penalties. But in the absence of express statutory authority for punitive damages, the court cannot impose them. People v. Superior Court, 507 P.2d 1400 (Cal.1973).

8. For additional treatment of remedies under comprehensive state statutes, see pages 155–57, supra.

(c) Small Claims Courts

Small claims courts are another mechanism for reducing the costs of enforcing the consumer's rights. These courts were established to provide a vehicle for redressing the grievances of persons who could not afford attorneys. They arose in the United States in the early part of this century, though they existed in England and Canada in the nineteenth century and in Denmark and Norway even earlier. Characteristics common to American small claims courts are a relatively low ceiling on the maximum relief available, encouragement of plaintiffs to appear without attorneys, and relaxed rules of procedures and evidence. These cost-saving features, however, are attractive to creditors as well as consumers, and small claim courts quickly became collection courts for businesses. By 1970 it was typical for more than eighty percent of the filings in a small claims court to be made by businesses, which obtained judgments by default in some eighty percent of the cases. In addition, if the court sits only in one central location and only during the day, use of the system is infeasible for many working consumers. Thus a mechanism established for the purpose of facilitating recovery by consumers may actually be a mechanism that facilitates recovery *against* consumers.

Initially the jurisdictional limit of small claims courts was $150 or less, but in most states the limit now is $2,000 or more. Some courts have evening or weekend sessions, and some have locations in residential neighborhoods. The proceedings tend to be relatively informal, with the judge helping each party fully present his or her side of the story. During, or even before the hearing, the court may encourage or require the parties to attempt to resolve their dispute by agreement. In New York, for example, when the parties appear for the hearing, they are given the option of submitting the case to binding, non-appealable arbitration.

For a historical analysis, see Steele, The Historical Context of Small Claims Courts, 1981 A.B.A.Res.J. 293. For localized empirical analyses, see Eovaldi & Meyers, The Pro Se Small Claims Court in Chicago: Justice for the "Little Guy"? 72 Nw.U.L.Rev. 947 (1978); Project, The Iowa Small Claims Court: An Empirical Analysis, 75 Iowa L. Rev. 433 (1990).

QUESTIONS

1. So long as a small claims court is available to them, businesses probably will continue to use it heavily. Should they be allowed to? Several states have concluded that corporations and assignees of contract rights should be excluded. What is the rationale of excluding assignees? If you were indebted to a corporation or an assignee, would you prefer to be sued in a small claims court or a general court?

A few states limit the number of claims that any one plaintiff may file in the small claims court. Examples of these limits are five per year, six per thirty-day period, and two per week. What is the rationale of this approach?

2. A handful of states prohibit the appearance of attorneys in small claims courts. Is this prohibition desirable? Is it constitutional?

3. Should the states permit jury trial in small claims courts? Can they constitutionally deny it?

4. One of the biggest obstacles to the effectiveness of small claims courts as a mechanism for the redress of consumer grievances is the difficulty of enforcing the court's judgment. In almost every state the successful consumer plaintiff must resort to the state's general system of enforcing judgments. This system is foreign to most consumers and is complex and time consuming. Would you favor the adoption of any of these suggestions to supplement the general enforcement system:

(a) prohibit the filing of suits by persons who have outstanding judgments rendered against them by the small claims court;

(b) treble the damages of any defendant against whom the small claims court has rendered three judgments;

(c) pay the amount of the judgment from state funds and permit the state to enforce the judgment against the defendant;

(d) hold in contempt of court any defendant who fails, without cause, to satisfy a judgment within a stated period of time;

(e) withhold the imposition of liability for the costs of the action (e.g., filing fees) against a defendant who promptly satisfies the judgment.

(d) Class Actions

Another way to reduce the consumer's cost of enforcing his or her rights is to induce other consumers who have been injured by the same defendant to share the expenses of the action. The other consumers may join as plaintiffs, but it may be difficult for one consumer to locate others who have suffered similar injuries. Consequently, the consumer may bring a class action, in which one or more persons sue on behalf of all persons who have the same grievance. Originally a creature of equity, the statutes or court rules of almost every American jurisdiction now authorize class actions. Most of these state laws are modeled after Rule 23 of the Federal Rules of Civil Procedure, which provides:

(a) Prerequisites to a Class Action. One or more members of a class may sue or be sued as representative parties on behalf of all only if

(1) the class is so numerous that joinder of all members is impracticable;

(2) there are questions of law or fact common to the class;

(3) the claims or defenses of the representative parties are typical of the claims or defenses of the class; and

(4) the representative parties will fairly and adequately protect the interests of the class.

(b) Class Actions Maintainable. An action may be maintained as a class action if the prerequisites of subdivision (a) are satisfied, and in addition:

(1) the prosecution of separate actions by or against individual members of the class would create risk of

(A) inconsistent or varying adjudications with respect to individual members of the class which would establish incompatible standards of conduct for the party opposing the class, or

(B) adjudications with respect to individual members of the class which would as a practical matter be dispositive of the interests of the other members not parties to the adjudications or substantially impair or impede their ability to protect their interests; or

(2) the party opposing the class has acted or refused to act on grounds generally applicable to the class, thereby making appropriate final injunctive relief or corresponding declaratory relief with respect to the class as a whole; or

(3) the court finds that the questions of law or fact common to the members of the class predominate over any questions affecting only individual members, and that a class action is superior to other available methods for the fair and efficient adjudication of the controversy. The matters pertinent to the findings include:

(A) the interest of members of the class in individually controlling the prosecution or defense of separate actions;

(B) the extent and nature of any litigation concerning the controversy already commenced by or against members of the class;

(C) the desirability or undesirability of concentrating the litigation of the claims in the particular forum;

(D) the difficulties likely to be encountered in the management of a class action.

.   .   .

In federal courts and in jurisdictions adopting a rule like Rule 23, most consumer class actions are brought under the authority of subsection (b)(3). What is the objective of this provision? What goal(s) does it seek to promote? Are there other objectives that class action litigation might have?

The following materials explore several problems of special importance in consumer class action litigation. The first two cases arose in a state where there is no statute or court rule governing the availability of class actions. The third case concerns the federal rule. How do the requirements in the two jurisdictions differ from each other?

Edelman v. Lee Optical Co.

Court of Appeals of Illinois, 1974.
24 Ill.App.3d 216, 320 N.E.2d 517.

MR. JUSTICE DRUCKER delivered the opinion of the court:

Plaintiffs, individually and as class representatives, filed an amended complaint alleging essentially the use of misleading merchandising techniques by defendants. Defendants moved to strike and dismiss. The court below found that the suit was "not properly maintainable as a class action" and struck the amended complaint, granting leave "to the five named plaintiffs to file an amended complaint stating their individual claims for relief against defendants." This plaintiffs failed to do, electing to stand on their class claim, and the suit was dismissed.

. . .

The amended complaint alleged that the named plaintiffs purchased single-vision lenses and eyeglass frames from defendants for prices ranging from $15.90 to $32 during 1972. Defendants are engaged in the retail optical business in Illinois. Since 1967 defendants have been advertising that a purchaser could obtain single-vision glasses for one low price. Their newspaper advertisements appearing in 1972 stated:

> "OUR ONE LOW PRICE INCLUDES: single vision clear or tinted lenses; your choice of any frame in our entire selection of modern frame styles and colors: carrying case."

Similar representations appeared in their shop windows and showrooms. It was further alleged that advertising in this manner was part of defendants' *"modus operandi* for doing business with plaintiffs and the class they represent" and that plaintiffs relied upon defendants' published representations of "one low price" for single-vision glasses.

Plaintiffs brought this action on behalf of themselves and all those who bought or will buy single-vision glasses from defendants for prices in excess of $8.95 or one to be set by the court.* In seeking injunctive relief and refunds for the amounts charged by defendants over $8.95 or a court-determined price, plaintiffs alleged that defendants had employed false and deceptive advertising practices and misrepresented material facts with the intent that they and members of their class rely on such misrepresentations and that these activities constitute common-law fraud and violations of the fraudulent sales provisions of the Sales Act, the Consumer Fraud Act, and the Uniform Deceptive Trade Practices Act.

. . .

It is well established that an action may not be maintained as a class action if the claims of the individual members of the class are based on separate and distinct questions of fact. Rice v. Snarlin, Inc., 131 Ill.App.2d 434, 266 N.E.2d 183. Thus it is required "that the claims of the purported members of a class action arise from the same transaction and from transactions so similar that they are tantamount to the same transaction." *Highsmith,* at 617.

This principle was illustrated in *Rice* in which a complaint was filed by a model and her mother alleging a violation of the Consumer Fraud Act by defendant in that it misrepresented and omitted or concealed material facts in its contract to place the model's name, address and telephone number in a directory listing to be sent to 500 companies. The plaintiffs sought

---

* $8.95 was apparently the lowest price at which single-vision glasses could be purchased from defendants.

damages and injunctive relief on behalf of themselves and, as class representatives, all those who had contracted with the defendant. In affirming the dismissal of the class action we held that the claim of each member of the class was dependent upon the facts surrounding the solicitation and negotiation of her individual contract and, therefore, since the nature of the defendant's representations may well have varied, the "plaintiffs and the members of the class they seek to represent fail to share the requisite common question of fact." *Rice,* at 443.

In the instant case, as in *Rice,* plaintiffs and the members of the class they seek to represent failed to share a requisite common question of fact. Specifically, each count of their complaint is dependent upon proof of reliance by purchasers of single-vision glasses on defendants' alleged misrepresentations. The claim of each member of the class is dependent upon a demonstration that he had knowledge of defendants' advertisements and was led into believing he could purchase any style of single-vision glasses for one low price. Clearly, where plaintiffs' class claims are essentially predicated on an allegation of false and misleading advertising, reliance is an essential element of their case, yet the class they seek to represent includes persons who may not have relied upon, or even seen, defendants' advertisements. We believe that a determinative question of fact is not common to the class and therefore this action is not properly maintainable as a class action.

. . .

QUESTIONS AND NOTES

1. Would it be more or less difficult to maintain a class action if Lee Optical had made the misrepresentations orally in the course of trying to sell eyeglasses?

2. Should the defendant be permitted to argue, in effect, that even though it made the misrepresentations with the hope that consumers would rely on them, the need for each consumer to prove that reliance precludes the availability of a class action?

In Vasquez v. Superior Court, 484 P.2d 964 (Cal.1971), plaintiffs brought a class action to rescind contracts for the purchase of freezers and frozen food that the seller had procured by fraud. In the course of holding that plaintiffs could maintain a class action, the California Supreme Court stated:

> In California, we do not lack authority on the subject of the amenability of consumer claims to class action litigation. Section 382 of the Code of Civil Procedure provides, " * * * when the question is one of a common or general interest, of many persons, or when the parties are numerous, and it is impracticable to bring them all before the Court, one or more may sue or defend for the benefit of all." In the leading case of Daar v. Yellow Cab Co., supra, 67 Cal.2d 695, 63 Cal.Rptr. 724, 433 P.2d 732, we held that . . . two requirements must

be met to sustain a class action. The first is existence of an ascertainable class, and the second is a well-defined community of interest in the questions of law and fact involved.

. . .

We next ascertain whether there are issues common to the class as a whole sufficient in importance so that their adjudication on a class basis will benefit both the litigants and the court. In this evaluation the mere fact that the transaction between Bay Area and each plaintiff was separately consummated is not determinative so long as each class member will not be required to litigate numerous and substantial issues to establish his individual right to recover.

. . .

The next element which plaintiffs must prove in order to prevail is reliance upon the alleged misrepresentations. If they can establish without individual testimony that the representations were made to each plaintiff and that they were false, it should not be unduly complicated to sustain their burden of proving reliance thereon as a common element.

The rule in this state and elsewhere is that it is not necessary to show reliance upon false representations by direct evidence. "The fact of reliance upon alleged false representations may be inferred from the circumstances attending the transaction which oftentimes afford much stronger and more satisfactory evidence of the inducement which prompted the party defrauded to enter into the contract than his direct testimony to the same effect."

Williston speaks in terms of a presumption: "Where representations have been made in regard to a material matter and action has been taken, in the absence of evidence showing the contrary, it will be presumed that the representations were relied on." (12 Williston on Contracts (3d ed. 1970) 480.) This rule is in accord with the Restatement. (Rest., Contracts, § 479, illus. 1.) Whether an inference (as held in Hunter v. McKenzie, supra, 197 Cal. 176, 185, 239 P. 1090) or a presumption (as described by Williston and the Restatement) of reliance arises upon proof of a material false representation we need not determine in this case. It is sufficient for our present purposes to hold that if the trial court finds material misrepresentations were made to the class members, at least an inference of reliance would arise as to the entire class.[9] Defendants may, of course, introduce evidence in rebuttal.

If the Court that decided *Edelman* adopted the view expressed in *Vasquez,* would the result in *Edelman* be different?

---

9. The requirement that reliance must be justified in order to support recovery may also be shown on a class basis. If the court finds that a reasonable man would have relied upon the alleged misrepresentations, an inference of justifiable reliance by each class member would arise. . . .

3. The injury sustained by each member of the class in *Edelman* was somewhere between $7 and $23. If plaintiffs are not allowed to maintain a class action, is not the court as a practical matter sanctioning defendant's use of fraudulent sales practices?

Brooks v. Midas–International Corp.

Court of Appeals of Illinois, 1977.
47 Ill.App.3d 266, 5 Ill.Dec. 492, 361 N.E.2d 815.

Mr. Justice Linn delivered the opinion of the court:

Plaintiffs appeal from the dismissal of those counts of its amended complaint which alleged a class action. The sole issue on appeal is whether the amended complaint sets forth facts sufficient to maintain a class action suit.

Plaintiff Brooks' counts of the amended complaint alleged that, although defendant guarantees that a replacement muffler will be installed for only an installation charge, defendant actually charges for replacement of parts such as clamps, hangers and pipes associated with the muffler system.

On July 7, 1971, plaintiff Brooks drove his automobile to a Midas Muffler Shop to purchase a muffler installation. He was charged $136.38 upon completion of the work. Two years later, plaintiff returned to a Midas Muffler Shop to have the muffler replaced. In addition to the installation charge of $9.50, a charge of $48.10 was assessed for replacement parts other than the muffler itself. Plaintiff Brooks alleged this additional charge to be in violation of the Consumer Fraud Act and the Uniform Deceptive Trade Practices Act in that defendant misrepresented its guarantee for the purpose of creating the impression in consumers' minds that no charges would be assessed other than an installation charge. It was further claimed that defendant's purpose was to induce plaintiff Brooks and other class members to purchase from defendant instead of its competitors.

The amended complaint seeks damages for Brooks and all members of the class for the various amounts paid in excess of the installation charge, and that a receiver be appointed to collect and administer the funds awarded as damages. In addition, injunctive relief is sought to enjoin defendant from its advertising practice, and from assessing any charges for muffler replacements other than an installation charge.

. . .

The trial court granted defendant's motion to strike and dismiss the amended complaint, ruling that the cause could not be maintained as a class action. . . .

The advantages inherent in a class action are to vindicate the rights of numerous claimants in one action when individual actions might be impracticable. Class actions in Illinois are governed by case law. It has been held that the basic test to be applied is "the existence of a community of interest in the subject matter and a community of interest in the remedy," among all who make up the purported class. This requires that "all members of the class [must be] found to have a common interest in the questions involved and the results * * *." Among the factors to be considered in deciding whether the required community of interest exists are whether the class members share a common question of law and fact; whether the claims arise from the same transaction or transactions so similar that they are tantamount to the same transaction; whether the named party can adequately represent the rights of the class; and whether the number of class members renders separate litigation impossible or impractical. These factors, while not conclusive of the question, serve as an aid in determining whether a valid class exists.

Section 2 of the Consumer Fraud Act provides:

"The act, use or employment by any person of any deception, fraud, false pretense, false promise, misrepresentation, or the concealment, suppression, or omission of any material fact *with intent that others rely upon such concealment, suppression or omission,* in connection with the sale or advertisement of any merchandise, *whether or not any person has in fact been misled, deceived or damaged thereby,* is declared to be an unlawful practice; * * *." (Emphasis supplied.)[a]

. . .

The community of interest requisite to the proper maintenance of a class action is present since the common interest centers on defendant's conduct in advertising its muffler guarantee. This advertising was alleged to have misrepresented and concealed the fact that the term "muffler" as employed by defendant referred only to one portion of the muffler system, and that other parts would require additional charges, whereas it was defendant's purpose by its advertising to create the impression in the minds of consumers that its guarantee meant replacement for only an installation charge.

Defendant asserts that a class action may not be maintained since the element of reliance is a question which is individual to each class member and thus defeats class action status. Defendant's contention is based upon the argument that different customers would have individual reactions to defendant's advertising and that some may have relied on the advertising while others may not have seen it at all. Under the common law, reliance was an element which had to be alleged in order to constitute a valid cause of action for misrepresentation or deceit. However, the language employed in the Consumer Fraud Act clearly indicates that it is the intent of the defendant in his conduct, not the reliance or belief of the plaintiff, which is the pivotal point upon which an action arises. (Cf. Edelman v. Lee Optical Co.) Section 2 of the Act specifically provides that the question of whether a person has been misled, deceived or damaged is not an element of an action brought under the Act. If, after trial, it is found that defendant did engage

a. The current version appears at 815 Ill. Consol. Stat. § 505/2.—Ed.

in an unlawful practice in its advertising, then the question common to all class members has been established in favor of plaintiffs.

. . .

Next we consider whether the transactions are the same or similar and find that this factor is also satisfied. "Illinois requires that the claims of the purported members of a class action arise from the same transaction and from transactions so similar that they are tantamount to the same transaction." A class action can properly be prosecuted where a defendant is alleged to have acted wrongfully in the same basic manner as to an entire class. In such circumstances, the common class questions still dominate the case, and the class action is not defeated.

In the present case, plaintiff alleged that defendant's advertising was the operative fact, common to each class member, which gave rise to the action. As we have already stated, whether defendant's advertising constituted an unlawful practice is the dominant question in this case.

In determining whether the class is adequately represented, the Illinois courts have focused on the issue of whether the absentee class members "are so represented by others who are before the court that their interests will receive actual and efficient protection." Here, the interests of plaintiff Brooks are the same as the class members recovery of monies paid to defendant for a muffler replacement in excess of the installation charge. Therefore, representation by plaintiff will afford the protection to absent parties which is required by due process.

The final factor to be considered is the question of whether the number of class members renders separate litigation impossible or impractical. We believe that the number of class members is so great as to be impractical to join them all as parties. At the same time, the proposed class is not so unwieldy, or so unidentifiable as to defeat the cause of action. Furthermore, we note that at oral argument plaintiff stated that the proposed class is limited to those whose transactions occurred in Illinois, which will aid in the identification and representation of the class.

Therefore, having found that all factors have been fully satisfied, we hold that a valid class action for damages exists under the Consumer Fraud Act, and that portion of Brooks' amended complaint which sought damages was improperly dismissed.

Plaintiff Brooks also sought injunctive relief under the Uniform Deceptive Trade Practices Act. Under section 7 of the Consumer Fraud Act, the Attorney General was given sole powers to obtain an injunction against a person "engaged in, engaging in, or is about to engage in" an unlawful practice. The Uniform Deceptive Trade Practices Act is not limited in this manner. The latter Act is a codification of the common law of unfair competition. As such, it has generally been held to apply to situations where one competitor is harmed or may be harmed by the unfair trade practices of another.

Section 2 of the [Uniform Deceptive Trade Practices] Act proscribes 11 specifically defined deceptive trade practices. Subsection 9 provides that a person engages in a deceptive trade practice when he "advertises goods or services with intent not to sell them as advertised." Subsection 12 prohibits "any conduct which similarly creates a likelihood of confusion or of misunderstanding." . . . The sole remedy under the Act is set forth in section 3, which provides:

> A person likely to be damaged by a deceptive trade practice of another may be granted an injunction against it in * * * terms that the court considers reasonable. Proof of monetary damage, loss of profits or intent to deceive is not required. Relief granted for the copying of an article shall be limited to the prevention of confusion or misunderstanding as to source.
>
> * * *
>
> The relief provided in this Section is in addition to remedies otherwise available against the same conduct under the common law or other statutes of this State.[b]

Although the Act was intended to protect businessmen and provide them with a remedy for unethical competitive conduct, its provisions have also been found applicable to cases where a consumer brings suit. The problem inherent in such consumer actions is the inability to allege facts which would indicate that the plaintiff is "likely to be damaged." Ordinarily, the harm has already occurred, thus precluding a suit for injunctive relief.

Such is the predicament which confronts plaintiff Brooks. Although he asks that defendant be enjoined from advertising its mufflers in a deceptive manner, he has already made his purchase. Whatever harm plaintiff may suffer from the advertisements has already occurred. The trial court, therefore, was correct in ruling that such practices by defendant are not likely to damage plaintiff.

That portion of the complaint in which plaintiff sought to restrain defendant from assessing any charges other than an installation charge for replacement of parts which it sold was also properly dismissed. The complaint failed to contain an allegation that plaintiff was likely to again be damaged in such manner, or even that he still owned the automobile which was the subject of the guarantee. Consequently, plaintiff failed to allege facts sufficient to indicate that he could be assessed additional charges at some future time.

Since plaintiff Brooks cannot succeed in obtaining injunctive relief in his individual action, the injunctive relief sought by him in his representative capacity on behalf of all class members is likewise unavailable.

For the aforementioned reasons, the judgment of the trial court striking and dismissing those portions of plaintiffs' amended complaint seeking injunctive relief is affirmed. The trial court's order striking and

b. The current version appears at 815 Ill. Consol. Stat. § 510/3.—Ed.

dismissing those portions of plaintiff Brooks' amended complaint seeking damages under the Consumer Fraud Act for himself and all class members similarly situated is reversed and the cause is remanded for further proceedings.

Affirmed in part; reversed and remanded.

QUESTIONS

1. As in *Vasquez* (see Question 2, page 866 supra), defendant in *Brooks* argued that the need of each plaintiff to establish reliance precludes the availability of a class action. And as in *Vasquez,* the court in *Brooks* rejects the argument, but for a different reason. What is it?

2. Is *Brooks* consistent with *Edelman*? Is *Brooks* an appropriate case for the use of a class action to redress fraudulent advertising?

3. Problem. *Seller* advertises that its camera is designed to permit the user to take excellent color pictures in dim light without any flash attachment. *Consumer* purchases one of the cameras and is unable to take "excellent color pictures in dim light." *Consumer* sues *Seller* for breach of express warranty, breach of implied warranty of merchantability, and breach of implied warranty of fitness. May *Consumer* maintain this suit as a class action? See Metowski v. Traid Corp., 104 Cal.Rptr. 599 (Cal.App. 1972).

Parker v. George Thompson Ford, Inc.

United States District Court, Northern District of Georgia, 1979.
83 F.R.D. 378.

Moye, District Judge.

This is an action for damages brought under the Truth-in-Lending Act, 15 U.S.C. § 1601 et seq.; the Motor Vehicle Information and Cost Savings Act, 15 U.S.C. § 1901 et seq.;[a] the Georgia Motor Vehicles Sales Finance Act, Ga.Code Ann. § 96–1001 et seq.; and the Georgia common law of fraud. The action is brought on behalf of plaintiff Carol Sue Parker, individually, and allegedly as a representative of all those allegedly similarly situated, and arises out of the credit sales of automobiles by defendant George Thompson Ford, Inc. ("Thompson Ford") to plaintiff Parker and others pursuant to installment sales contracts. Some of these contracts including plaintiff's contract, were assigned to defendant General Finance Corporation ("GFC"). Presently pending before the Court are plaintiff Parker's motion to maintain class action and for certification of the class and plaintiff's motion to compel discovery.

Plaintiff contends that defendant Thompson Ford devised a fraudulent and deceitful scheme whereby defendant represented to class members that in order to purchase an automobile on credit, they must first establish their

---

   a. Now codified at 49 U.S.C. § 32701 et seq.—Ed.

credit with Thompson Ford. Each class member could allegedly do this by making a "good faith" payment on a Supplemental Rental Agreement and entering into a series of monthly rental agreements until the credit reputation of the class member was established with defendant Thompson Ford. All class members allegedly executed a written Supplemental Rental Agreement with defendant by which defendant agreed to apply a "good faith" payment toward the purchase price of the automobile when later purchased and also agreed to sell the automobile at its depreciated book value. Plaintiff maintains that defendant Thompson Ford verbally represented to each class member that a substantial part of the monthly rental payments would be applied toward the purchase price of the automobile.

Plaintiff Parker contends that the Retail Installment Sales Contracts used by defendant Thompson Ford in the credit sales of automobiles to the class members failed to disclose the true selling price of each automobile and the application of the rental payments toward the purchase price of each automobile in violation of the Truth-in-Lending Act. Plaintiff also alleges that defendant Thompson Ford, with intent to defraud, failed to provide an odometer statement to the class members as required by [49 U.S.C. § 32705]. Plaintiff Parker further alleges that defendant Thompson Ford charged each class member a "service fee" which in fact was an additional finance charge, thereby allegedly rendering the interest rate charged each class member usurious under Ga.Code Ann. § 96–1004. Finally, plaintiff asserts that defendant wrongfully repossessed and converted automobiles that it sold on credit to class members at a time when it was holding funds of these class members in excess of any amounts that they owed under the Retail Installment Sales Contracts.

Plaintiff Parker has moved to maintain a class action and for class certification on behalf of a "main class" and six "subclasses" pursuant to Fed.R.Civ.P. 23(a), (b)(3), and (c)(4)(B) and pursuant to Ga.Code Ann. § 81A–123. With regard to Fed.R.Civ.P. 23(a), plaintiff contends that although the precise identity of the individual members is not yet known, and can be known only through discovery, the "main class" is so numerous that a joinder of all members is impracticable. Plaintiff further contends that there are questions of law and fact common to the class, that her claims are typical of the claims of each member of the class, and that, as the representative party, she will fairly and adequately protect the interests of the class as required by Fed.R.Civ.P. 23(a). In addition, plaintiff Parker maintains that the prerequisites of Fed.R.Civ.P. 23(b)(3) are satisfied because questions of law and fact common to the class members predominate over questions affecting only individual members and because a class action is superior to other available methods for the fair and efficient adjudication of this controversy.

In order to maintain a class action, the burden is on the prospective class representative to establish that the requirements of Fed.R.Civ.P. 23 have been met. . . .

After careful consideration of plaintiff Parker's motion and defendants' responses thereto, the Court concludes that plaintiff Parker has failed to establish that the requirements of Fed.R.Civ.P. 23 have been met in this action. Although there does exist a group of customers who have contracted with defendants on terms similar to those of plaintiff, the Court does not believe that plaintiff's situation is typical of that of the purported members of the class. Plaintiff Parker is in the position of having had a car repossessed with no deficiency asserted. Most members of the purported class, however, either still have their cars and a continuing relationship with defendants or have had their cars repossessed and face counterclaims for deficiencies. Since plaintiff would not be subject to such counterclaims and would receive no benefit from defeating these claims, plaintiff would have no incentive to expend time and effort vigorously defending others against these numerous counterclaims.

In addition, the record does not convincingly show that plaintiff is willing and able to assume the costs and expenses associated with bringing a class action. Plaintiff's counsel has allegedly promised to bear responsibility for the costs of this suit, but this can be no more than a guarantee of payment.[1] It is not an adequate substitute for assurance that plaintiff understands her potential obligation of bearing the costs of a class action and is prepared to underwrite these costs. For both of the above reasons, the Court believes that plaintiff has failed to show that she has met the requirements of Fed.R.Civ.P. 23(a)(3) and (4).

Moreover, it is also apparent that plaintiff Parker cannot satisfy the requirements of Fed.R.Civ.P. 23(b)(3) because: (1) common questions of law or fact do not predominate over individual questions of liability and damages; and (2) maintenance of this case as a class action is not superior to other methods of handling the controversy. With respect to plaintiff's claims under the Truth-in-Lending Act, a finding of fact would be required for each alleged class member to decide if credit was extended "primarily" for personal use or "primarily" for business use. If the latter is found, the Act would be inapplicable and there could be no alleged violation under the Act. In the instant action, credit was used to purchase motor vehicles, including trucks, and at least some of these vehicles were evidently used primarily for business purposes. Because of the potential for individual trials on this matter, it is clear that individual issues would predominate over common issues in this action.

Individual questions of liability would similarly predominate over common questions with respect to plaintiff's claim under section 408 of the Motor Vehicle Information and Cost Savings Act [now codified at 49 U.S.C. § 32705]. In order to establish a violation of this statutory section, the plaintiff must show that there has been (1) a failure to give the required disclosure with (2) an intent to defraud. Both elements require a determination of liability on an individual basis, and, thus, there would be no common question susceptible of determination in a class action.

---

1. Plaintiff is ultimately responsible for costs in accordance with Canon 5, Ethical Consideration 5–8, and [Disciplinary] Rule 5– 103(B) of the American Bar Association Code of Professional Responsibility which apply in this Court. Local Rule 71.54.

Furthermore, defendants' counterclaims against alleged class members for defaults in payments or other contract breaches would be compulsory to claims raised by plaintiff. Since these counterclaims must be brought in order to avoid being barred in any subsequent suit by principles of res judicata, individual adjudications on these counterclaims will be required and individual questions will predominate over class ones. In addition to increasing the number of separate trials which may be required, the presence of counterclaims raises the possibility of many members of the class "opting out" under Fed.R.Civ.P. 23(c)(2) because of the potential exposure to net recoveries in favor of defendants. As the court stated in *Alpert,* supra, "[a]n action which forces a significant portion of the class to take active steps to exclude themselves is inappropriate."

Fed.R.Civ.P. 23(b)(3) also requires that the court find that "a class action is superior to other available methods for the fair and efficient adjudication of the controversy." The class action must be *superior to* other means of adjudication, not merely "as good as" other methods. It is clear that class action treatment of this case is not "superior" to individual actions.

As discussed above, a determination of liability on the truth-in-lending and odometer claims will involve questions which must be determined on an individual basis. More importantly, the members of the alleged class cannot possibly recover as much from defendants Thompson Ford and GFC if this class is certified as they could in individual actions. In a class action brought under the Truth-in-Lending Act, no minimum recovery is applicable, and the total recovery in the action may not exceed the lesser of $500,000 or one per centum of the net worth of the creditor. § 130(a)(2)(B). In an individual action, however, the claimant is entitled to twice the amount of any finance charge in connection with the transaction, and the creditor's liability to the claimant may not be less than $100. § 130(a)(2)(A).

In the case *sub judice,* defendant Thompson Ford's net worth is $180,000, and the *maximum* total recovery against it for the class is $1,800. Defendant GFC's net worth is $2,846,415.05, and the *maximum* total recovery against it for the applicable class members is approximately $28,464. Since the number of alleged class members with claims against each defendant is between 300 and 400, each class member would recover less than $100, which is the minimum sum that each member could recover in a successful individual action against the defendant who was liable to him. Because class certification in this action would result in a relatively small recovery for the individual class members while exposing defendants to large administrative costs and requiring substantial amounts of court time for supervision of the action, class certification would clearly not be a superior method of adjudication in terms of efficiency.

For all of the foregoing reasons, the Court must deny class certification with regard to the truth-in-lending and odometer claims. Because the Court is denying class certification for those federal claims, there is no subject matter jurisdiction to support a class action on plaintiff's state law claims—

regardless of whether plaintiff is allowed to pursue the claims in this Court under the doctrine of pendent jurisdiction. Even if the Court had subject matter jurisdiction of the state law claims, it would nevertheless deny class certification with regard to these claims because they involve allegations of fraud and usury raising questions that relate primarily to individuals only. Individual questions would therefore predominate over questions common to the class. Accordingly, plaintiff Parker's motion to maintain class action and for certification of the class is hereby DENIED.

QUESTIONS

1. The court concludes that the case fails to satisfy subsection (a)(3) of Rule 23 because the claim of the named plaintiff is not typical of the claims of the class. Why does the court reach this conclusion?

The court also concludes that plaintiff fails to meet the requirements of subsection (a)(4), that the named plaintiff fairly and adequately protect the interests of the class. Why?

In many Truth-in-Lending Act cases, the creditor has filed a counterclaim to recover the unpaid balance still owed by the consumer. In most of these cases, the courts have refused to consider the counterclaim. E.g., see Whigham v. Beneficial Finance Co., 599 F.2d 1322 (4th Cir.1979), in which the court stated:

> The sole issue in Beneficial's appeal is whether its claim for the balance due on the loan is a compulsory counterclaim in the borrowers' action for violations of the Truth-in-Lending Act. A federal court has ancillary jurisdiction over compulsory counterclaims, but it cannot entertain permissive counterclaims unless they independently satisfy federal jurisdictional requirements. . . . Beneficial alleged no independent jurisdictional basis for its counterclaim.

> Federal Rule of Civil Procedure 13(a) declares that a counterclaim is compulsory "if it arises out of the transaction or occurrence that is the subject matter of the opposing party's claim . . . ." In applying the rule to particular cases, courts have considered whether the issues of fact and law raised by the claim and counterclaim are largely the same, whether substantially the same evidence bears on both claims and whether any logical relationship exists between the two claims.

> We conclude that a lender's claim for debt against a borrower who sues for violation of the Truth-in-Lending Act has none of the characteristics associated with a compulsory counterclaim. First, the lender's counterclaim raises issues of fact and law significantly different from those presented by the borrower's claim. The only question in the borrower's suit is whether the lender made disclosures required by the federal statute and its implementing regulations. The lender's counterclaim, on the other hand, requires the court to determine the contractual rights of the parties in accordance with state law. . . .

Second, the evidence needed to support each claim differs. The borrower need produce only the loan documents for consideration in light of the federal requirements. The lender, however, must verify the obligation and prove a default on loan payments.

Third, the claim and the counterclaim are not logically related. The lender's counterclaim alleges simply that the borrower has defaulted on a private loan contract governed by state law. The borrower's federal claim involves the same loan, but it does not arise from the obligations created by the contractual transaction. Instead, the claim invokes a statutory penalty designed to enforce federal policy against inadequate disclosure by lenders. To let the lender use the federal proceedings as an opportunity to pursue private claims against the borrower would impede expeditious enforcement of the federal penalty and involve the district courts in debt collection matters having no federal significance.

Is this relevant to the court's reasoning in *Parker?*

The majority of decisions are in accord with *Whigham*, but a substantial minority disagree. E.g., Plant v. Blazer Financial Services, Inc., 598 F.2d 1357 (5th Cir.1979).

2. The court evidently doubts the ability of the named plaintiff to pay the costs of maintaining a class action. One of these costs is for giving notice to members of the class, which the United States Supreme Court has held must be borne by the named plaintiffs. Eisen v. Carlisle & Jacquelin, 417 U.S. 156 (1974). This decision, of course, is controlling only for class actions in federal court. State courts may require the defendant to pay the cost of notifying the members of the class. See Cartt v. Superior Court, 124 Cal.Rptr. 376 (Cal.App.1975).

3. As another reason for concluding that the case is not appropriate for class action treatment, the court in *Parker* states that common issues do not predominate over issues unique to individual members of the class. There is a similar problem in *Brooks,* supra. Should the court in *Brooks* have dismissed the class action for this reason? If not, is *Parker* consistent with *Brooks?*

4. As still another reason for its decision, the court in *Parker* concludes that a class action is not superior to other methods of adjudication. What other methods are there? Why does the court find a class action to be not superior to these other methods? In Ratner v. Chemical Bank New York Trust Co., 54 F.R.D. 412 (S.D.N.Y.1972), the named plaintiff sought to represent a class of 130,000 persons in a Truth-in-Lending Act case. At the minimum recovery provided by section 130, defendant would have been liable for thirteen million dollars. The court refused to allow the class action:

[D]efendant points out that (1) the incentive of class-action benefits is unnecessary in view of the Act's provisions for a $100 minimum recovery and payment of costs and a reasonable fee for counsel; and (2) the proposed recovery of $100 each for some 130,000 class members would be a horrendous, possibly annihilating punishment, unrelated to any damage to the purported class or to any benefit to defendant, for what is at most a technical and debatable violation of the Truth in Lending Act. These points are cogent and persuasive. They are summarized compendiously in the overall conclusion stated earlier: the allowance of this as a class action is essentially inconsistent with the specific remedy supplied by Congress and employed by plaintiff in this case. It is not fairly possible in the circumstances of this case to find the (b)(3) form of class action "superior to" this specifically "available [method] for the fair and efficient adjudication of the controversy."

Id. at 416. Most other courts deciding the question also concluded that a class action was not the superior method for enforcing the Truth-in-Lending Act. Consequently, in 1974 Congress amended section 130 to eliminate the $100 minimum recovery for each member of a class and impose an upper limit on the recovery of a class. In 1976 Congress amended the section again to set the maximum liability at the present figure of the lesser of $500,000 or 1% of the defendant's net worth. If Congress amends a statute to facilitate the use of class actions, is it appropriate for a court to use that very amendment as a reason for denying a class action? Is there any way in which it can be said that a class action is the superior method for the fair and efficient adjudication of the controversy? What is the practical consequence of the court's denying the use of a class action in *Parker?*

More recently, an objection similar to the one in *Ratner* has been raised in connection with litigation under the Fair Credit Reporting Act, which similarly has a provision calling for statutory damages of $100–$1,000 per plaintiff, with no 1%/$500,000 cap on overall liability. In Murray v. GMAC Mortgage Corp., 434 F.3d 948, 954 (7th Cir.2006), the court acknowledged that an award of damages might be challenged as unconstitutionally large, in violation of the Due Process Clause, but held that any constitutional limit should be applied after the class has been certified and liability determined. And in Bernal v. Keybank, N.A., 2007 WL 2050405 (E.D.Wis.2007), the court characterized the creditor's argument as "boil[ing] down to the dubious proposition that it should not be held accountable for its actions because it broke the law too many times against too many people."

5. In Mace v. Van Ru Credit Corp., 109 F.3d 338 (7th Cir.1997), plaintiff brought a class action on behalf of all consumers who resided in Wisconsin and who received collection letters from defendants during a specified time. The Seventh Circuit earlier had held defendants liable in a class action on behalf of consumers in Connecticut who challenged letters similar to but not identical to the letters in issue here. Avila v. Rubin, 84 F.3d 222 (7th Cir.1996). The trial court denied certification of the class in *Mace* on two grounds: (1) in order to implement the FDCPA's 1%/$500,000 limit, a class action must be on behalf of a nationwide class; (2) if successful, the members of a nationwide class would recover a de minimis amount (28¢), which would not justify the significant administrative costs of a class action. The Seventh Circuit reversed:

A.   Damage Caps in the Fair Debt Collection Practices Act . . .

The defendants . . . advance a policy argument, from which the district court constructed a requirement for a nation-wide class. The district court reasoned that, if the damage cap of $500,000 can be applied anew to a series of state-wide (or otherwise limited) class actions, the damage limitation would become meaningless. This contention may be correct as far as it goes, although there is, of course, no way of telling whether such repeated class actions are possible or likely, here or generally. The other side of the coin is that to require a nation-wide class as the district court did here brings with it other problems that will be discussed later. There are other possible problems with the district court's reasoning. The FDCPA has a short, one-year statute of limitations making multiple lawsuits more difficult. Further, if a debt collector is sued in one state, but continues to violate the statute in another, it ought to be possible to challenge such continuing violations. Given the uncertainty of those policy considerations, there is no compelling reason to ignore the plain words of the statute. In any event, the case before us does not now present multiple or serial class actions to recover for the same misconduct. Hence, it would be premature to require a nation-wide class at this juncture. If and when multiple serial class actions are presented, it will be time enough to rule on such a pattern. At this point, there is no persuasive reason to require a nation-wide class.

B.   De Minimis Recovery

After prematurely reading a nation-wide class requirement into the FDCPA, the district court calculated the possible recovery. Because the most recent financial statements of the defendants (provided to the court in *Avila*) suggest a net worth of approximately $11 million, the damage cap (of one percent) would limit the class's recovery to a little over $100,000. The Wisconsin class was estimated to comprise 8,340 members. Extrapolating from this number, the district court posited a nation-wide class as large as 400,000. Such a class would result in a recovery per class member of only 28 cents, Memo. Or. at 27, as opposed to the projected $12 for each Wisconsin-only class member. The district court held that where "the recovery per class member would be de minimis and . . . the administrative costs would be unduly burdensome . . . a class action is not superior to other possible methods of fair and efficient adjudication." Memo. Or. at 29.

Since we have not decided that the FDCPA requires a nation-wide class, the district court's concerns about a de minimis recovery are currently moot. But even if a nation-wide class were appropriate, we believe that a de minimis recovery (in monetary terms) should not automatically bar a class action. The policy at the very core of the class action mechanism is to overcome the problem that small recoveries do not provide the incentive for any individual to bring a solo action prosecuting his or her rights. A class action solves this problem by aggregating the relatively paltry potential recoveries into something worth someone's (usually an attorney's) labor.

True, the FDCPA allows for individual recoveries of up to $1000. But this assumes that the plaintiff will be aware of her rights, willing to subject herself to all the burdens of suing and able to find an attorney willing to take her case. These are considerations that cannot be dismissed lightly in assessing whether a class action or a series of individual lawsuits would be more appropriate for pursuing the FDCPA's objectives.

The attorney's fees provision of the FDCPA is another factor that must be considered in connection with a de minimis bar. An attorney would presumably not take a contingency fee case where the projected recovery was $3.00 (leaving the attorney with a $1.00 fee). This, of course, is why some statutes allow for attorney's fees even when the plaintiff's monetary award is nominal. The attorney's fee provision makes the class action more likely to proceed, thereby helping to deter future violations. When individual class members are offered the right and opportunity to opt out of the class action, the statutory language "without regard to a minimum individual recovery" generally controls. [FDCPA § 813(a)(2)(B),] 15 U.S.C. § 1692k(a)(2)(B). In the present posture of the case, the de minimis issue is not before us, but it might arise in some form on remand.

III.   Cy Pres

Mace offers the availability of cy pres recovery as an alternative ground for class certification. Given that we have already found that a state-wide class action is sustainable and that a de minimis recovery does not bar certification, the issue of cy pres availability is no longer of concern. Nevertheless, because it is important to stress that cy pres recovery should be reserved for unusual circumstances, we briefly address Mace's arguments.

Cy pres, or fluid, recovery is a procedural device that distributes money damages either through a market system (e.g., by reducing charges that were previously excessive), or through project funding (the project being designed to benefit the members of the class). Simer v. Rios, 661 F.2d 655, 675 (7th Cir.1981). Cy pres recovery "is used where the individuals injured are not likely to come forward and prove their claims or cannot be given notice of the case." Id. at 675. Cy pres recovery is thus ideal for circumstances in which it is difficult or impossible to identify the persons to whom damages should be assigned or distributed. Here, damages, though small, would not be either difficult to assign or difficult to distribute. Further, there is no reason, when the injured parties can be identified, to deny them even a small recovery in favor of disbursement through some other means.

6. Problem. *Consumer* comes to you complaining that his new vacuum cleaner has a defect that neither the seller nor the manufacturer will repair. In the course of this interview, you ascertain that the installment sales contract used by the seller violates the Truth-in-Lending Act. Would you be wiser to pursue the breach of warranty or the Truth-in-Lending Act claim? Could either be maintained as a class action? If you brought a class action, and assuming that the seller used the same form contract nationwide, would there be any advantage to limiting the class to customers of the store at which *Consumer* purchased the vacuum cleaner or to customers who made purchases at the seller's stores located in your state? Would there be disadvantages to limiting the class in this way?

If another of your clients informs you that she has just received notice of *Consumer's* class action, what would you advise her?

If *Consumer* brings a Truth-in-Lending Act class action against the seller, would it be advisable for the seller to tender payment of $100 to *Consumer*?

7. As with other kinds of litigation, most certified class actions result in settlement. Two aspects of class action settlements have received substantial attention in recent years. One of these is the extent to which the settlement results in any real benefit to members of the class. *Compare* Clement v. American Honda Finance Corp., 176 F.R.D. 15 (D.Conn.1997) (court refused to approve a settlement in which class members would receive a nontransferable coupon redeemable for $150 toward the lease or purchase of a Honda or Acura financed by defendant) *with* Wolf v. Toyota Motor Sales, USA, Inc., 1997 WL 602445 (N.D.Cal.1997) (court approved a settlement in which class members would receive a transferable coupon for $150 redeemable for the lease or purchase of a new or used Toyota).

The other noteworthy aspect is the size of the attorney's fees, which sometimes amount to millions of dollars. For discussion of both of these aspects of class actions—and others—see National Assn. of Consumer Advocates, Class Action Guidelines (rev.2006) (available at www.naca.net).

8. Arbitration clauses revisited: the intersection of class actions and arbitration. In Green Tree Financial Corp. v. Bazzle, 539 U.S. 444 (2003), the Supreme Court addressed the availability of a class action in the context of arbitration proceedings. It held that if not prohibited by the arbitration agreement, arbitration may occur on a class-wide basis. Since the main reason for adoption of arbitration clauses in the first place was to foreclose the possibility of class actions, *Bazzle* created quite a stir. Since then, arbitration clauses in standard form contracts have been revised to contain an explicit prohibition on class arbitration. If enforced, then, the typical arbitration clause prohibits litigation and prohibits arbitration on a class-wide basis. The only mechanism for resolution of disputes (after such informal approaches as negotiation and mediation) is arbitration on an individual basis. Is this generation of arbitration clauses enforceable?

Scott v. Cingular Wireless

Washington Supreme Court, 2007.
161 P.3d 1000.

¶ 1   CHAMBERS, J. . . . .

I

¶ 3   Plaintiffs . . . purchased cellular telephones and calling plans from Cingular. The contracts they all signed were standard preprinted agreements that included a clause requiring mandatory arbitration. That arbitration clause, in turn, contained a provision prohibiting consolidation of cases, class actions, and class arbitration. Cingular also retained the right to unilaterally revise the agreement and, in July 2003, did so. Customers were informed via a monthly "bill stuffer" titled in bold print, "IMPORTANT INFORMATION CONCERNING YOUR CONTRACT." The revised arbitration clause still prohibited class actions.[2] It also specified that arbitration would be conducted according to American Arbitration Association (AAA) rules; that Cingular would pay the filing, administrator, and arbitration fees unless the customer's claim was found to be frivolous; that Cingular would reimburse the customer for reasonable attorney fees and expenses incurred for the arbitration (provided that the customer recovered at least the demand amount); and that the arbitration would take place in the county of the customer's billing address. It also removed limitations on punitive damages.

¶ 4   The plaintiffs' underlying suit asserts that they were improperly billed for long distance and/or out-of-network "roaming" calls[3] and that as a result of these improper billing practices, individual customers were overcharged up to around $45 a month. Plaintiffs filed a class action suit to challenge the legality of these additional charges. While the plaintiffs admit no individual consumer suffered a significant loss, they claim that in the aggregate, Cingular unilaterally overcharged the public by very large sums of money.

¶ 5   Cingular moved to compel individual arbitration. Plaintiffs resisted, arguing that the class action waiver is substantively and procedurally unconscionable and thus unenforceable. Among other things, they assert that the agreement is overly one-sided because it is inconceivable that Cingular would bring a class action suit against its customers. They also argue that the class action waiver, at least when coupled with the attorney fee provision, will prevent meritorious claims from being heard. In support, the plaintiffs submitted a declaration from attorney Sally Gustafson Garratt, who had previously served as the division chief for consumer protec-

---

2. The modified arbitration clause provides in part:

> **You agree that, by entering into this Agreement, you and Cingular are waiving the right to a trial by jury.** . . . You and Cingular agree that YOU AND CINGULAR MAY BRING CLAIMS AGAINST THE OTHER ONLY IN YOUR OR ITS INDIVIDUAL CAPACITY, and not as a plaintiff or class member in any purported class or representative proceeding. Further, you agree that the arbitrator may not consolidate proceedings [on] more than one person's

claims, and may not otherwise preside over any form of a representative or class proceeding, and that . . . if this specific proviso is found to be unenforceable, then the entirety of this arbitration clause shall be null and void.

We do not consider whether the bill stuffer was an effective method to modify the contract.

3. "Roaming" occurs when a subscriber of one wireless service provider uses another provider's facilities.

tion in the Washington State attorney general's office. She declared that the attorney general's office did not have sufficient resources to respond to many individual cases and often "relied on . . . private class action to correct the deceptive or unfair industry practice and to reimburse consumers for their losses." The plaintiffs also submitted a declaration of Peter Maier, an attorney in private practice who specialized in consumer law. He explained that the claims against Cingular "are too small and too complex factually and legally" to be adjudicated separately. Maier declared that he would be unwilling to take on such cases and opined, "it is very unlikely that any other private practice attorney would be willing to do so."

¶ 6 The trial court granted Cingular's motion, concluding that although Cingular's contract is a contract of adhesion, it is not sufficiently complex, illegible, or misleading to be deemed procedurally unconscionable. The court also found no substantive unconscionability. . . .

¶ 8 Cingular and its supporting amici[a] argue, however, that the majority of courts (at least at the time they made the argument) addressing the question have found class action waivers enforceable [citing cases from three federal and two state courts of appeal]. Plaintiffs respond that an increasing number of courts have found class action waivers in arbitration clauses substantively unconscionable [citing one federal appellate court, four federal district courts, four state supreme courts, and five state appellate courts]. There is a clear split of authority.

II

A.   Standard of Review

. . .

¶ 10   This case is somewhat unusual in our experience because it is not the arbitration clause itself the plaintiffs challenge. Instead, it is the class action waiver embedded within it. We begin by considering whether that waiver itself is unconscionable and unenforceable under Washington law.

B.   Public Policy

I. Class Actions and the Washington CPA

¶ 11   An agreement that has a tendency " 'to be against the public good, or to be injurious to the public' " violates public policy. An agreement that violates public policy may be void and unenforceable. Restatement (Second) of Contracts § 178 (1981). Washington's CR 23 authorizes class actions and demonstrates a state policy favoring aggregation of small claims for purposes of efficiency, deterrence, and access to justice. As we have noted before, when consumer claims are small but numerous, a class-

---

a. Amazon.com, Inc.; Intel Corporation; Microsoft Corporation; RealNetworks, Inc.; Association of Washington Business; Chamber of Commerce of the United States of America; and CTIA–The Wireless Association. Amici supporting plaintiffs were AARP; National Association of Consumer Advocates; Washington State Trial Lawyers Association Foundation; and the Attorney General of Washington.—Ed.

based remedy is the only effective method to vindicate the public's rights. Class remedies not only resolve the claims of the individual class members but can also strongly deter future similar wrongful conduct, which benefits the community as a whole. . . . That said, class action waivers have been found permissible in some contexts.

¶ 12   We turn to whether this class action waiver is unconscionable because it undermines Washington's CPA to the extent that it is "injurious to the public." The CPA is designed to protect consumers from unfair and deceptive acts and practices in commerce. RCW 19.86.020. To achieve this purpose, the legislature requires that the CPA "be liberally construed that its beneficial purposes may be served." RCW 19.86.920.

¶ 13   Private enforcement of the CPA was not possible until 1971, when the legislature created the private right of action to encourage it. Private actions by private citizens are now an integral part of CPA enforcement. *See* RCW 19.86.090. Private citizens act as private attorneys general in protecting the public's interest against unfair and deceptive acts and practices in trade and commerce. Consumers bringing actions under the CPA do not merely vindicate their own rights; they represent the public interest and may seek injunctive relief even when the injunction would not directly affect their own private interests.

¶ 14   Courts have previously held that class actions are a critical piece of the enforcement of consumer protection law. The reason is clear. Without class actions, many meritorious claims would never be brought. Class actions are vital where the damage to any individual consumer is nominal, and that vital piece is exactly what the plaintiffs claim the class action waiver before us seeks to eviscerate.

¶ 15   Thus, we conclude that without class actions, consumers would have far less ability to vindicate the CPA. Again, the CPA contemplates that individual consumers will act as "private attorneys general," harnessing individual interests in order to promote the public good. But by mandating that claims be pursued only on an individual basis, the class arbitration waiver undermines the legislature's intent that individual consumers act as private attorneys general by dramatically decreasing the possibility that they will be able to bring meritorious suits.

¶ 16   Without class action suits, the public's ability to perform this function is drastically diminished. We . . . conclude the class action waiver clause before us is an unconscionable violation of this State's policy to "protect the public and foster fair and honest competition," RCW 19.86.920, because it drastically forestalls attempts to vindicate consumer rights. To the extent that this clause prevents CPA cases, it is substantively unconscionable.[4]

II. *Exculpation*

¶ 17   We turn now to whether this class action waiver is unconscionable for effectively exculpating its drafter from liability for a large class of

---

4. Because we find the class action waiver substantively unconscionable, we find it unnecessary to address plaintiffs' claims of procedural unconscionability.

wrongful conduct. Contract provisions that exculpate the author for wrong-doing, especially intentional wrongdoing, undermine the public good. As our sister court said, " '[a] company which wrongfully extracts a dollar from each of millions of customers will reap a handsome profit; the class action is often the only effective way to halt and redress such exploitation.' " *Discover Bank v. Superior Court*, 36 Cal. 4th 148, 156, 113 P.2d 1100, 30 Cal.Rptr.3d 76 (2005).

¶ 18   Of course, on its face, the class action waiver does not exculpate Cingular from anything; it merely channels dispute resolution into individual arbitration proceedings or small claims court. But in effect, this exculpates Cingular from legal liability for any wrong where the cost of pursuit outweighs the potential amount of recovery. As the ever inimitable Judge Posner has aptly noted, "[t]he *realistic* alternative to a class action is not 17 million individual suits, but zero individual suits, as only a lunatic or a fanatic sues for $30." *Carnegie v. Household Int'l, Inc.*, 376 F.3d 656, 661 (7th Cir.2004).

¶ 19   In such cases, the ability to proceed as a class transforms a merely theoretically possible remedy into a real one. It is often the only meaningful type of redress available for small but widespread injuries. Without it, many consumers may not even realize that they have a claim. The class action provides a mechanism to alert them to this fact. Second, again, claims as small as those in this case are impracticable to pursue on an individual basis even in small claims court, and particularly in arbitration. Shifting the cost of arbitration to Cingular does not seem likely to make it worth the time, energy, and stress to pursue such individually small claims. The plaintiffs also presented evidence that the prohibitive cost actually does prevent claims. In addition to the declarations discussed above, it appears that no claims from Washington customers have been brought to arbitration against Cingular in the past six years.

¶ 20   Cingular contends that it has cured any concerns about access to a remedy by promising to pay all AAA filing, administrative, and arbitrator fees unless the arbitrator finds the claim frivolous, and by promising to pay the attorneys fees under certain circumstances. While laudable, it appears to us that these provisions do not ensure that a remedy is practically available. First, the attorney fees are awarded only if the plaintiffs recover at least the full amount of their demand.[5] A plaintiff could recover 99 percent of a claim and still not be awarded any attorney fees. Cingular's lawyers are undoubtedly paid regardless of result. But, if the consumer loses or achieves an award of one dollar less than sought, there is no award of fees. Even if all of the contingencies are met and attorney fees are awarded, the arbitrator may consider the amount in controversy in awarding fees. While technically, the plaintiffs are not prevented from hiring an attorney, practically, attorneys are generally unwilling to take on individual arbitrations to recover trivial amounts of money. This is, of course, precise-

---

5. The provision reads: "[I]f the arbitrator grants relief to you that is equal to or greater than the value of your Demand, Cin-gular shall reimburse you for your reasonable attorneys' fees and expenses incurred for the arbitration."

ly why class actions were created in the first place. . . . We . . . conclude that since this clause bars any class action, in arbitration or without, it functions to exculpate the drafter from liability for a broad range of undefined wrongful conduct, including potentially intentional wrongful conduct, and that such exculpation clauses are substantively unconscionable. . . .

C.   Federal Preemption

¶ 22   Next, Cingular argues that the Federal Arbitration Act (FAA) governs the contracts at issue and requires that we enforce the class action waiver. Section 2 of the FAA states that written arbitration agreements "shall be valid, irrevocable, and enforceable, save upon such grounds as exist at law or in equity for the revocation of any contract." 9 U.S.C. § 2. "Section 2 is a congressional declaration of a liberal federal policy favoring arbitration agreements, notwithstanding any state substantive or procedural policies to the contrary." *Moses H. Cone Mem'l Hosp. v. Mercury Constr. Corp.*, 460 U.S. 1, 24, 103 S. Ct. 927, 74 L. Ed. 2d 765 (1983). Our State also favors arbitration of disputes.

¶ 23   But Congress simply requires us to put arbitration clauses on the *same* footing as other contracts, not make them the special favorites of the law. As we held above, contracts that effectively exculpate their drafter from liability under the CPA for broad categories of liability are not enforceable in Washington, even if they are embedded in an arbitration clause. The arbitration clause is irrelevant to the unconscionability.

¶ 24   Class action waivers have very little to do with arbitration. Clauses that eliminate causes of action, eliminate categories of damages, or otherwise strip away a party's right to vindicate a wrong do not change their character merely because they are found within a clause labeled "Arbitration." At least based on the briefing before us, we see no reason why the purposes of favoring individual arbitration would not equally favor class-wide arbitration.

¶ 25   The FAA favors arbitration, not exculpation. As the United States Supreme Court has noted, arbitration can be a perfectly appropriate place for individuals to vindicate legislative policy, "so long as the prospective litigant effectively may vindicate its statutory cause of action in the arbitral forum." But this clause prevents the use of arbitration to vindicate a broad range of statutory CPA rights. We join those courts that have found that striking a class action waiver in an arbitration clause does not violate the FAA.

¶ 26   By its terms, the class action waiver is not severable from the arbitration clause. Because no party argues for severability, we enforce the language of the agreement between the parties and conclude that the entirety of the arbitration clause is null and void.

III

¶ 27   We conclude that the class action waiver before us effectively denies plaintiffs a forum to vindicate the consumer protections guaranteed by Washington law and effectively exculpates its drafter from liability for a broad range of wrongful conduct. Where many customers of the same company have the same or similar complaint and each is damaged a small amount, class action litigation or arbitration is the only practical remedy available. Under such circumstances, the class action waiver is substantively unconscionable. . . . We reverse and remand to the trial court for further proceedings consistent with this opinion.[7]

Alexander, C.J., and C. Johnson, Sanders, Owens, and Fairhurst, JJ., concur.

¶ 28 MADSEN, J. (dissenting). . . .

¶ 32 The majority concludes that the class action waiver is unconscionable because it violates public policy by forestalling attempts to bring class suits vindicating consumer rights. The Consumer Protection Act (CPA), chapter 19.86 RCW, unquestionably embodies the legislature's statement of strong public policy favoring private actions to enforce the act in addition to actions brought by the attorney general. . . .

¶ 33 However, nothing in the CPA states the legislature's intent, or even hints, that class suits are so essential to enforcement of the CPA that a class action waiver can never appear in a consumer contract governing transactions involving small amounts of money. Absent any such statement of policy by our state legislature, which is, after all, the branch of government establishing the public policy embodied in the CPA, I cannot agree to the majority's sweeping statement of its own policy that class suits can never be waived in such a contract.

¶ 34 The majority rests on the faulty premise that the purposes of the CPA require invalidation of all class action waivers. . . .

¶ 35 . . . [C]onsumer rights can be vindicated through individual actions where small claims are involved. As Cingular points out, its revised arbitration provision specifies that Cingular will pay all American Arbitration Association filing, administrative, and arbitrator fees, unless the arbitrator finds the claim frivolous. Thus, under this arbitration clause, the costs of arbitration do not present an insurmountable barrier to seeking recovery, even in the event of small value claims. Moreover, the arbitration agreement does not foreclose actions in small claims courts, and the plaintiffs can vindicate their consumer rights through actions in small claims court, at nominal costs.

. . .

---

7. We respectfully disagree with our learned colleague in dissent that this opinion presumes the CPA invalidates all class action waivers. We mean to say only that class action waivers that *prevent* vindication of rights secured by the CPA are invalid. We agree with our dissenting colleague that whether any particular class action waiver is unenforceable will turn on the facts of the particular case. We can certainly conceive of situations where a class action waiver would not prevent a consumer from vindicating his or her substantive rights under the CPA and would thus be enforceable.

¶ 38   The majority also reasons that the class action waiver acts as an exculpatory clause. . . .

¶ 39   Numerous courts have rejected the argument that the small claims at issue effectively made recovery unattainable, as a practical matter, where the arbitration agreement included financial protection for the consumers [citing three cases]. . . .

¶ 40   In many of the cases the majority cites for the proposition that class action waivers in arbitration agreements are unconscionable, the contracts at issue did not provide that the defendant would pay costs of arbitration. Because they essentially precluded any recovery by consumers due to small claims making individual actions impracticable and effectively served to insulate the other party from any liability for its misconduct, the courts found these class action waivers substantively unconscionable [citing four cases].

¶ 41   But as stated, in these cases there were no provisions for costs to be borne by the defendants comparable to Cingular's contractual obligations [describing 11 cases].

¶ 42   The majority's analysis ultimately is based on the premise that plaintiffs will be unable to obtain adequate legal representation because the individual claims at issue are too small and complex for plaintiffs to find lawyers willing to represent them.

¶ 43   Many courts have rejected the argument that the plaintiffs in the particular case would be unable to obtain legal representation because of its cost in comparison to potential recovery. For example, in [one case] the plaintiffs submitted affidavits from several attorneys who stated that the amount and cost of attorney time would far exceed any potential individual recovery and that the only practical method for pursuing the plaintiff's claim was through a class action. The court rejected this argument, noting that the Fair Credit Billing Act, 15 U.S.C. §§ 1666–1666j, which applied to the claim, provides that if the plaintiff is successful, the creditor will be liable for costs of the action as well as reasonable attorney fees. The court determined that this was adequate incentive for parties and attorneys, adding that despite the fact that the plaintiff and her lawyers might be "unwilling" to litigate because they believe there is "not . . . enough financial incentive," the court still could not conclude the class action waiver in the parties' arbitration clause was unconscionable.

¶ 44   . . . [P]laintiffs may not feel that there is "enough financial incentive" to pursue their small value claims, but . . . the majority should find the incentive is sufficient, particularly when coupled with Cingular's promise to pay attorney fees and expenses and the costs of arbitration, as well as any relief that is available in a court, including, presumably, exemplary damages and statutory penalties.

¶ 45   The majority's conclusion that the arbitration clause is substantively unconscionable is, in the end, a claim that legal representation will be essentially impossible to obtain for pursuing small value claims in arbitration proceedings and therefore by default Cingular will always "win." This same argument would apply as well to claims brought in small claims court, where legal representation is not permitted. Yet, of a certainty this court would not hold small claims court proceedings substantively unconscionable because plaintiffs cannot be represented by attorneys.

¶ 46 Because other effective avenues of recourse exist in this case, class suits are simply not necessary to vindicate the CPA under the terms of the contracts these plaintiffs signed, nor does the class action waiver act as an exculpatory clause.

¶ 47 Fundamentally, the majority ignores the fact that the class action waiver appears in an arbitration agreement. Section 2 of the FAA "is a congressional declaration of a liberal federal policy favoring arbitration agreements, notwithstanding any state substantive or procedural policies to the contrary." Every presumption must be indulged in favor of arbitration. Like federal law, state law expresses a strong public policy favoring arbitration of disputes.

¶ 48 In accord with the importance of enforcing arbitration agreements according to their terms when possible, the majority should, like other courts, determine whether a class action waiver in an arbitration agreement is substantively unconscionable on a case-by-case basis, considering all the surrounding circumstances. Instead, the majority adopts a sweeping rule that without doubt invalidates thousands, if not millions, of arbitration agreements without regard to the specific terms of those agreements.

¶ 49 This court should, instead, focus on the importance of satisfying the purpose of the FAA to ensure that private agreements to arbitrate are enforced according to their terms. Other courts have done so when faced with arguments that class action waivers should be invalidated.

¶ 50 The majority should not ignore the importance of arbitration and the liberal federal policy favoring arbitration agreements; it is not free to disregard federal law because a different outcome is preferred. This arbitration agreement is as "consumer friendly" as an arbitration agreement can be. The majority's refusal to enforce this agreement as written is, without any doubt whatsoever, contrary to federal policy favoring arbitration. Given the circumstances, if the contractual class action waiver is to be disregarded, it should be done only at the express direction of our state legislature.

. . .

CONCLUSION

¶ 57 In essence, the majority creates a public policy that forbids a class action waiver in consumer actions because it believes that the assistance of an attorney is required to remedy consumer wrongs. It reasons that attorneys will not represent litigants if the amount at stake is too small. Therefore, it declares that class suits are necessary so that attorneys will be attracted by the prospect of sufficient remuneration to justify their representation.

¶ 58 I would reject the argument that plaintiffs will be unable to obtain legal representation and therefore the arbitration agreement's class action waiver is unconscionable. Instead, because Cingular has promised to pay the costs of arbitration plus attorneys' fees and costs if the plaintiffs are successful in obtaining the relief they seek, plaintiffs are able to pursue their small value claims and the class action waiver does not effectively act as an exculpatory clause relieving Cingular of liability. The plaintiffs' important goal of vindicating the public interest under the CPA can be accomplished on an individual basis. I would hold that the plaintiffs have failed to show that the class action waiver is substantively unconscionable because it is one-sided in effect, as they have not shown an undue burden to one side or unfair advantage or benefit to the other. I would affirm the superior court's order compelling arbitration.

BRIDGE AND J.M. JOHNSON, JJ., concur with MADSEN, J.

QUESTIONS AND NOTES

1. The majority has two reasons for concluding the class action waiver is unconscionable. What are they?

2. The arbitration clause preserves the consumer's right to seek redress in small claims court. In ¶ 19 the majority states that in cases like *Scott* it is impractical to do this. Given the low filing fee (recoverable if the consumer prevails), why is it impractical?

If the claim being asserted carries with it the right to an award of attorney's fees, why is it impractical to pursue the claim in small claims court?

3. The dissent asserts (¶ 47) that it is significant that the class action waiver appears in an arbitration clause, suggesting that this enhances the enforceability of the waiver. Why is placement in the arbitration clause relevant?

4. As the dissent observes (¶ 50) Cingular's arbitration clause is extremely "consumer friendly": Cingular pays the entire administrative expense of the proceeding, the proceeding is to occur in the consumer's community, Cingular pays attorney's fees of the consumer who prevails in the arbitration, all remedies available in court are available in arbitration, and the consumer retains the option of suing in small claims court. If this arbitration clause is unconscionable, can any arbitration clause withstand an unconscionability attack in Washington?

5. In footnote 7 at the end of its opinion, the majority suggests that some class action waivers would be enforceable. Can you think of any situations in the consumer setting in which the majority would enforce a class action waiver?

6. In Szetela v. Discover Bank, 118 Cal.Rptr.2d 862, 868 (Cal.App.2002), the court held unconscionable an arbitration clause that required arbitration and prohibited the parties from bringing claims on behalf of a class. The court stated:

. . . It is the *manner* of arbitration, specifically, prohibiting class or representative actions, we take exception to here. The clause is not only harsh and unfair to Discover customers who might be owed a relatively small sum of money, but it also serves as a disincentive for Discover to avoid the type of conduct that might lead to class action litigation in the first place. By imposing this clause on its customers, Discover has essentially granted itself a license to push the boundaries of good business practices to their furthest limits, fully aware that relatively few, if any, customers will seek legal remedies, and that any remedies obtained will only pertain to that single customer without collateral estoppel effect. The potential for millions of customers to be overcharged small amounts without an effective method of redress cannot be ignored. Therefore, the provision violates fundamental notions of fairness. . . . It provides the customer with no benefit whatsoever; to the contrary, it seriously jeopardizes customers' consumer rights by prohibiting any effective means of litigating Discover's business practices. This is not only substantively unconscionable, it violates public policy by granting Discover a "get out of jail free" card while compromising important consumer rights.

7.   Often the contract contains a provision stipulating that dispute resolution must occur in a specified state and is to be governed by the law of that state. See Chapter 13, pages 704–16 supra. What if the specified state (e.g., Virginia) does not permit class actions: is the clause enforceable? On the same day it decided *Scott*, the Supreme Court of Washington, this time in a unanimous decision, decided Dix v. ICT Group, Inc., 161 P.3d 1016, 1020–22 (Wash.2007):

¶ 15   Forum selection clauses are prima facie valid. *The Bremen v. Zapata Off–Shore Co.*, 407 U.S. 1, 10 (1972). In general, a forum selection clause may be enforced even if it is in a standard form consumer contract not subject to negotiation. *Carnival Cruise Lines, Inc. v. Shute*, 499 U.S. 585, 589–95 (1991). . . .

¶ 16   A number of courts rely on the analyses in *Bremen* and *Carnival Cruise Lines* for determining the enforceability of a forum selection clause. A typical synthesis of the *Bremen* and *Carnival Cruise Lines* analyses that has been set out by a number of courts is as follows:

(1) [A] forum-selection clause is presumptively valid and enforceable and the party resisting it has the burden of demonstrating that it is unreasonable, (2) a court may deny enforcement of such a clause upon a clear showing that, in the particular circumstance, enforcement would be unreasonable, and (3) the clause may be found to be unreasonable if (i) it was induced by fraud or overreaching, (ii) the contractually selected forum is so unfair and inconvenient as, for all practical purposes, to deprive the plaintiff of a remedy or of its day in court, or (iii) enforcement would contravene a strong public policy of the State where the action is filed.

Gilman v. Wheat, First Sec., Inc., 345 Md. 361, 378, 692 A.2d 454 (1997).

¶ 17   We agree with this analysis, which is generally in agreement with statements in this state's appellate decisions. . . .

¶ 24   The individual consumer action to enforce RCW 19.86.020 and vindicate the public interest is . . . a significant aspect of a dual enforcement scheme under the CPA, which provides for individual private actions in addition to enforcement actions brought by the attorney general. But in some circumstances, the costs and inconvenience of suit may be too great for individual actions, even in small claims court. We agree, therefore, that class suits are an important tool for carrying out the dual enforcement scheme of the CPA. Individual claims may be so small that it otherwise would be impracticable to bring them; a class action may be the only means that the public interest may be vindicated.

¶ 25   Given the importance of the private right of action to enforce the CPA for the protection of all the citizens of the state, we conclude that a forum selection clause that seriously impairs a plaintiff's ability to bring suit to enforce the CPA violates the public policy of this state. It follows, therefore, that a forum selection clause that seriously impairs the plaintiff's ability to go forward on a claim of small value by eliminating class suits in circumstances where there is no feasible alternative for seeking relief violates public policy and is unenforceable.

Accord, Fiser v. Dell Computer Corp., 188 P.3d 1215 (N.M.2008).

INDEX

References are to pages.

†